Comparative Income Taxation

Comparative Income Taxation

A Structural Analysis

Fifth Edition

Principal Authors

Hugh J. Ault
Brian J. Arnold
Graeme S. Cooper

Wolters Kluwer

Published by:
Kluwer Law International B.V.
PO Box 316
2400 AH Alphen aan den Rijn
The Netherlands
E-mail: lrs-sales@wolterskluwer.com
Website: www.wolterskluwer.com/en/solutions/kluwerlawinternational

Sold and distributed by:
Wolters Kluwer Legal & Regulatory U.S.
920 Links Avenue
Landisville, PA 17538
United States of America
E-mail: customer.service@wolterskluwer.com

ISBN 978-94-035-3768-9

e-Book: ISBN 978-94-035-3778-8
web-PDF: ISBN 978-94-035-3788-7

Dedicated to Professor Hugh J. Ault, Scholar, Teacher and Mentor

Principal Authors

Hugh J. Ault is Professor Emeritus at Boston College Law School and the original author of *Comparative Income Taxation: A Structural Analysis*. He was a senior adviser at the Organisation for Economic Co-operation and Development's (OECD's) Centre for Tax Policy and Administration for many years and more recently a consultant for the United Nations Capacity Development Unit. He is the author of several influential articles on U.S. and international taxation and has been a visiting professor at universities in Europe, Asia, and Australia. He is the recipient of two honorary degrees for his contributions to international and comparative tax law from the University of Stockholm and the Catholic University of Leuven, Belgium.

Brian J. Arnold is Senior Adviser, Canadian Tax Foundation, Toronto and Professor Emeritus, Faculty of Law, Western University. He practiced tax law part-time for many years with two major Toronto law firms. He has been a consultant to various governments, the OECD, and the United Nations. He was a visiting professor at Harvard Law School from 2005 to 2011 and at New York University School of Law in 2005 and 2012. He is the author of the *International Tax Primer*, 5th edition (Wolters Kluwer, 2023).

Graeme S. Cooper is Professor Emeritus at the University of Sydney. He has also taught Tax at Law Schools in the U.S., Canada, Belgium, and The Netherlands. He is the author of many articles and several books published in Australia and internationally. He worked for the OECD in the mid-1990s and as a consultant on projects for the International Monetary Fund, World Bank, United Nations, the Australian government, and several foreign countries. He works as a consultant to Herbert Smith Freehills.

Contributing Authors

Takeshi Fujitani is Professor of Law at the Institute of Social Science, the University of Tokyo, Japan. He also taught at Hokkaido University (2004-2012), the University of Chicago Law School (2009, 2011), and at Columbia Law School (2019). He holds an LLM and SJD from Harvard Law School and LLB from the University of Tokyo. He has published a number of articles in the fields of tax law and policy, charities and taxation, public finance (budget) law, and the globalization of law.

Peter Harris is Professor of Tax Law at the University of Cambridge, where he is also Director of the Centre for Tax Law. He is the author of five international tax books, the most recent being *International Commercial Tax* (CUP, 2nd ed.) and holds key editorial posts in the tax field. Since 1998, he has acted as Technical Assistance Advisor for the International Monetary Fund and assisted numerous countries in drafting tax legislation and developing tax treaty policies.

Jinyan Li is a professor, co-director of LLM Tax Programs, and former interim dean of Osgoode Hall Law School, York University. She has published widely in tax law and policy, comparative tax law, and international tax law. She is currently a member of the Advisory Board, World Tax Journal and Belt & Road Initiative Tax Administration Cooperation Mechanism. She has been writing about Chinese tax law and policy since the 1980s and acted as an expert consultant on Chinese tax reforms.

Geoffrey Loomer is Associate Professor and, until the end of 2024, the Associate Dean, Administration and Research, at the University of Victoria Faculty of Law. He was a member of the Schulich School of Law at Dalhousie University from 2009 to 2018. Geoff completed his BSc (Economics) at UVic, LLB at the University of British Columbia, and BCL and DPhil at Oxford, focusing on corporate and international tax law and policy. Prior to his graduate studies, he practiced in the tax group of McCarthy Tétrault LLP. His publications include articles and book chapters addressing Canadian corporate tax, international tax policy, and tax avoidance, as well as two coauthored textbooks.

Glen Loutzenhiser was Professor of Tax Law, Faculty of Law, University of Oxford and Tutorial Fellow in Law at St Hugh's College, University of Oxford. He taught undergraduate courses on EU Law and Taxation Law and taught a graduate course in Business Taxation in a Global Economy. He was also a director and teacher on the part-time MSc in Taxation degree. Glen was a member of the editorial board of the *British Tax Review* and the sole editor of the taxation volumes of *Halsbury's Laws of England and Wales* and *Tiley's Revenue Law.*

Peter Melz is Professor Emeritus of Fiscal Law at the Faculty of Law, Stockholm University. He has published books and articles in the fields of capital gains, corporate and foundation taxation, and value-added tax. Since 1989 he has participated in a number of government commissions, most recently about the reform of corporate taxation.

Jérôme Monsenego is Full Professor of International Tax Law at Stockholm University. He obtained his PhD summa cum laude and was awarded an honorable mention by the jury of the IFA Mitchell B. Carroll Prize. He is a representative of the European Association of Tax Law Professors on the European Commission's Platform for Tax Good Governance and former chairman of the Swedish IFA branch.

Minoru Nakazato is Professor Emeritus at the University of Tokyo, where he has taught Tax Law for 25 years. He served as Chairman of the Tax Commission, an advisory committee for the Prime Minister of Japan, from 2013 to 2023. He is now the Governor of the Nishimura Institute of Advanced Legal Studies in Tokyo. He graduated from the Faculty of Law of the University of Tokyo and holds the degree of Doctor of Laws.

Yasutaka Nishikori is a partner at Nishimura & Asahi, a leading law firm in Japan. He is a 1992 graduate of the University of Tokyo and received an LLM from Harvard Law School in 2001. He is a lecturer at Keio University Law School and was also a visiting associate professor at the University of Tokyo Graduate Schools for Law and Politics. He has authored several tax articles, including articles for international publishers.

Christine Osterloh-Konrad holds Chair in Private Law, Commercial Law, Corporate Law, Tax Law, and Legal Philosophy at Tübingen University. Prior to taking up this position, she was Senior Research Fellow at the Max Planck Institute for Tax Law and Public Finance, where she completed her postdoctoral studies in 2017 with a thesis on comparative and theoretical perspectives on tax avoidance. She was also Lecturer in Law at Ludwig-Maximilian-University Munich and worked for some time in practice, mainly in the field of succession law. She has advised German, Norwegian, and U.S. institutions on the design of various legal instruments counteracting tax avoidance strategies and on the taxation of pass-through entities.

Frank Pötgens is a partner/tax lawyer at De Brauw Blackstone Westbroek in Amsterdam with a focus on international and European tax law. He is also Professor of International and European Tax Law at the Free University Amsterdam (*Vrije Universiteit Amsterdam*) and Deputy Justice at the 's-Hertogenbosch Appellate Court for tax cases. He obtained a PhD from Erasmus University Rotterdam for his thesis on the tax aspects of cross-border employees and their remuneration (published in the IBFD Doctoral Series under the title *Income from International Private Employment*).

Kees van Raad is Chairman of the International Tax Center Leiden, Professor Emeritus of International Tax Law at the University of Leiden, and of counsel to Loyens & Loeff. He has been a member of IBFD's Board of Trustees and the steering group for the OECD's International Network for Tax Research. He is Chairman of the International Fiscal Association's Jury for the annual Mitchell B. Carroll Prize; past member (1986-2006) of its Permanent Scientific Committee, general reporter, and member/chair of various IFA congress panels; and since August 2016, an honorary member of IFA. He was a member (1999-2012) and chairman (2006-2012) of the Executive Board of the European Association of Tax Law Professors and a member (2003-2015) of the Supervisory Board of the Max Planck Institute for Tax Law and Public Finance in Munich, Germany.

Mark Ramseyer teaches at Harvard, where he is the Mitsubishi Professor of Japanese Legal Studies. He grew up (and attended public elementary school) in Japan and studied at Goshen College, the University of Michigan, and Harvard Law School. For two years, he practiced corporate tax law in Chicago.

James R. Repetti is Professor at Boston College Law School and the inaugural holder of the William J. Kenealy, S.J. Chair. He is coauthor of the texts *Partnership Income Taxation*, *Introduction to United States International Taxation*, *Federal Wealth Transfer Taxation*, *Problems in Federal Wealth Transfer Taxation*, and *Tax Aspects of Organizing and Operating a Business*. He has acted as a consultant to the U.S. Senate, Internal Revenue Service, and Justice Department and has appeared as a commentator in publications such as the *Washington Post*, *Wall Street Journal*, *Bloomberg*, *Marketplace*, *Boston Globe*, *Christian Science Monitor*, and *Forbes Magazine*.

Diane M. Ring is Professor and the Dr. Thomas F. Carney Distinguished Scholar at Boston College Law School. In 2019, Diane was appointed Professor in Residence at the International Bureau for Fiscal Documentation. She has been a visiting professor at Harvard Law School and Radzyer Law School, Israel and has written extensively on U.S. and international taxation, including three U.S. casebooks and two U.S. National Reports for the International Fiscal Association. She has also been a consultant for the United Nations on projects involving the administration of tax treaties and the protection of the tax base of developing countries.

Marilyne Sadowsky is Associate Professor and Co-director of the Masters in Tax Law at the Sorbonne Law School (University of Paris I—Panthéon-Sorbonne). She is involved in the comparative tax law program created as part of the Winter course program "European Universities Cooperating in Tax Matters." She is a member of the executive committee of the International Academy of Comparative Law and of the Academic Committee of the European Association of Tax Law Professors. She coordinated the white paper on taxation for the International Law Association's 150th anniversary. She has been a visiting professor at Boston University Law School and a Hugh Ault Fellow at the Max Planck Institute for Tax Law and Public Finance in Munich. Her PhD thesis on *WTO Law, EU Law and Direct Taxation* received an honorable mention by the jury for the Mitchell B. Carroll Prize (IFA).

Wolfgang Schön is Director of the Department of Business and Tax Law at the Max Planck Institute for Tax Law and Public Finance in Munich and Honorary Professor at Munich University. He is a member of the Board of Trustees of the IBFD and an international research fellow at the Oxford University Centre for Business Taxation. He was Chairman of the Board of the European Association of Tax Law Professors and the Vice-Chair of the Permanent Scientific Committee of IFA. Wolfgang Schön has been a visiting professor at Tilburg University, Vienna University of Business and Economics, New York University (NYU), Columbia University, University of Pennsylvania, University of British Columbia, the Universities of Antwerp and Liège, and Bocconi University (Milan).

D.P. Sengupta, formerly of the Indian Revenue Service, is an independent tax expert. He was Chief Commissioner of Income Tax (Central), New Delhi and also served as Competent Authority for India. Subsequently, for over a decade, he served as Principal Consultant to the National Institute of Public Finance and Policy. He is the author of several articles on taxation, focusing especially on international tax and tax treaties.

Richard Vann is Professor Emeritus at the University of Sydney and has taught Tax Law and Policy at Harvard, New York University, and the Universities of London and Oxford. Richard worked in the past at the International Monetary Fund and OECD and held many government consultancies in Australia and elsewhere. He has been a consultant in the private sector since 1985.

Summary of Contents

Table of Contents

Foreword

The purpose of this book is to compare the solutions adopted by eleven countries to common problems of income tax design. As in other legal domains, a comparative study of income taxation can provide fresh perspectives from which to examine a particular national system. Increasing economic globalization also makes understanding foreign tax systems relevant to a growing set of transnational business transactions.

A comparative study is, however, notoriously difficult. Full understanding of a foreign tax system may require mastery not only of a foreign language but also of foreign business and legal cultures. It would be the work of a lifetime for a single individual to achieve that level of understanding of the eleven income taxes compared in this book.

Suppose, however, that an international group of tax law professors, each expert in their own national system, were asked to describe how that system resolved specific problems of income tax design with respect to individuals, business organizations, and international transactions. Suppose further that the leaders of the group wove the resulting answers into a single continuous exposition, which was then reviewed and critiqued by a wider group of tax teachers. The resulting text would provide a convenient and comprehensive introduction to foreign approaches to income taxation for teachers, students, policy makers, and practitioners.

That is the path followed by Hugh J. Ault, Brian J. Arnold, Graeme S. Cooper, and their collaborators in the development of this fascinating book. Henceforth, a reader interested in how other countries resolve such structural issues as the taxation of fringe benefits, the effect of unrealized appreciation at death, the classification of business entities, expatriation to avoid taxes, and so on can turn to this book for an initial answer. I am delighted that the Harvard Law School Fund for Tax and Fiscal Research was able to provide financial support for this important project. The resulting book should greatly facilitate comparative analysis in teaching and writing about taxation in the U.S. and elsewhere.

Alvin C. Warren, Jr.
Ropes & Gray Professor of Law Emeritus
Harvard Law School

Preface

This 5th edition of *Comparative Income Taxation* began in the same manner as the 4th edition, with a series of conversations between Hugh Ault, Brian Arnold, and Graeme Cooper in mid-2023 in response to an inquiry from our publisher about the possibility of a new edition. Given the extensive changes in both the domestic and international tax rules of the eleven countries covered in the book, we agreed that a new edition was appropriate. However, from our previous experience, we knew that revising a book as large as *Comparative Income Taxation*, with 19 nineteen contributors, was not to be undertaken lightly. As a result, we decided to pursue another edition only if most of the contributors to the 4th edition would agree to participate in the new edition. We were pleasantly surprised to find that, with one exception, all of the contributors to the 4th edition were enthusiastic about participating in a new edition.

The one exception was Guy Gest, Professor Emeritus and the former Director of the Advanced Masters of Tax Law programs at Paris II Pantheon-Assas University, who decided that he could not contribute to a 5th edition. Guy contributed to all of the previous four editions and was a pleasure to work with for more than 20 years, for which we cannot thank him enough. Fortunately, we were able to recruit Marilyne Sadowsky, Professor and co-director of the Masters in Tax Law at the University of Paris I Pantheon-Sorbonne, to take over responsibility for the parts of the book dealing with the French tax system. We also recruited Geoffrey Loomer, Professor and Associate Dean at the Faculty of Law, University of Victoria, to help out with the Canadian aspects of the book.

As with all the previous editions of the book, we wish to acknowledge the continuing support of Professor Emeritus Alvin Warren of Harvard Law School and the Harvard Law School Fund for Tax and Fiscal Research. We also want to recognize the contributions of Carol Hargreaves. As she has done with the previous three editions, Carol has supervised all phases of the preparation of the manuscript—integrating the revisions of the contributors, editing, formatting, and proofreading the entire manuscript—with her typical efficiency and attention to detail.

We want to thank the contributing authors, both present and past, for their enormous efforts in making this book a success. They have been uniformly a pleasure to deal with, providing high-quality drafts with just the right level of detail for this type of book and responding patiently to our many questions and editorial suggestions. In particular, we want to acknowledge the excellent contributions of Professor Glen Loutzenhiser, who passed away in early February 2025. Glen was a prolific author on a wide range of tax issues and a gifted teacher, who will be missed.

This edition of *Comparative Income Taxation* is dedicated to Hugh Ault. It may seem strange to dedicate a book to one of its principal authors, but, in Hugh's case, it is entirely appropriate. As we wrote in the preface to the 4th edition:

> The simple truth is that this is Hugh's book. He conceived the original idea for a comparative income tax book, selected the original contributors, and wrote the original text—taking the pieces written by the contributors on their domestic law with respect to the topic, weaving them into a seamless description, and adding the comparative analysis that makes the book unique.

The 5th edition is no different in this regard. Although the content has been updated, Hugh's influence can still be seen on almost every page. Hugh has been a mentor, colleague, and friend to many of the contributors to this book and to many others in the worldwide tax community. The dedication of this 5th edition of the book to Hugh is a suitable way for us, the authors, to recognize Hugh's contributions to this book and to international and comparative tax generally through his insightful scholarship, teaching, and work as a consultant to the OECD and the United Nations.

The content of the book is up-to-date as of September 2024.

Brian Arnold
London, Canada
Graeme Cooper
Sydney, Australia
September 30, 2024

List of Abbreviations

Australia	
AAT	Administrative Appeals Tribunal
ABN	Australian Business Number
ART	Administrative Review Tribunal
ATO	Australian Taxation Office
BEPS	Base Erosion and Profit Shifting
CGT	Capital Gains Tax
FBT	Fringe Benefits Tax
GDP	Gross Domestic Product
GST	Goods and Services Tax
ITAA	Income Tax Assessment Act 1936
MLI	Multilateral Convention to Implement Tax Treaty Related Measures to Prevent Base Erosion and Profit Shifting
OECD	Organisation for Economic Co-operation and Development
OPC	Office of Parliamentary Counsel
TIEA	Tax Information Exchange Agreement
TTE	Taxable/Taxable/Exempt
UK	United Kingdom
Canada	
CRA	Canada Revenue Agency
GAAR	General Anti-avoidance Rule
GDP	Gross Domestic Product
GST	Goods and Services Tax
ITA	Income Tax Act

MLI	Multilateral Convention to Implement Tax Treaty Related Measures to Prevent Base Erosion and Profit Shifting
OECD	Organisation for Economic Co-operation and Development
PPT	Principal Purpose Test
TIEA	Tax Information Exchange Agreement
U.S.	United States
UK	United Kingdom
China	
BEPS	Base Erosion and Profit Shifting
BRICS	Brazil, Russia, India, China, and South Africa
CFC	Controlled Foreign Corporation
DEIT	Domestic Enterprise Income Tax
EIT	Enterprise Income Tax
EJVIT	Equity Joint Venture Income Tax
FIE Tax	Income Tax on Foreign Enterprises and Foreign-Invested Enterprises
GAAR	General Anti-avoidance Rule
GDP	Gross Domestic Product
IFRS	International Financial Reporting Standards
IIT	Individual Income Tax
MLI	Multilateral Convention to Implement Tax Treaty Related Measures to Prevent Base Erosion and Profit Shifting
MOF	Ministry of Finance
NPC	National People's Congress
OECD	Organisation for Economic Co-operation and Development
SAT	State Administration of Taxation
STA	State Taxation Administration
VAT	Value-Added Tax
France	
ATAD	Anti-tax Avoidance Directive
BEPS	Base Erosion and Profit Shifting
BOFIP	Public Finance Official Bulletin (*Bulletin officiel des Finances Publiques*)
CASA	*Contribution additionnelle de solidarité pour l'autonomie*
CE	Conseil d'État
CFC	Controlled Foreign Company
CGI	General Tax Code (*Code général des impôts*)

CJEU	Court of Justice of the European Union
CRDS	Social Debt Reimbursement Contribution (*Contribution au remboursement de la dette sociale*)
CSG	Generalized Social Contribution (*Contribution sociale généralisée*)
DGFIP	Public Finances Directorate General (Direction Générale des Finances Publiques)
ECHR	European Convention on Human Rights
EEA	European Economic Area
EU	European Union
GDP	Gross Domestic Product
IRVM	*Impôt sur le revenu des valeurs mobilières*
LPF	Book of Tax Procedures (*Livre des procédures fiscales*)
MAE	Ministry of Foreign Affairs
MLI	Multilateral Convention to Implement Tax Treaty Related Measures to Prevent Base Erosion and Profit Shifting
OECD	Organisation for Economic Co-operation and Development
PPT	Principal Purpose Test
QPC	Question Prioritaire de Constitutionnalité
VAT	Value-Added Tax

Germany

ATAD	Anti-tax Avoidance Directive
CFC	Controlled Foreign Corporation
CITA	Corporate Income Tax Act
CJEU	Court of Justice of the European Union
EBITDA	Earnings Before Interest, Taxes, Depreciation, and Amortization
EU	European Union
FATCA	Foreign Account Tax Compliance Act
GAAR	General Anti-avoidance Rule
GDP	Gross Domestic Product
GFC	General Fiscal Code
GG	*Grundgesetz*
ITA	Income Tax Act
ITR	Income Tax Regulation
LLC	Limited Liability Company
LLP	Limited Liability Partnership

MLI	Multilateral Convention to Implement Tax Treaty Related Measures to Prevent Base Erosion and Profit Shifting
OECD	Organisation for Economic Co-operation and Development
OFD	*Oberfinanzdirektion(en)*
RTA	Reorganization Tax Act
SAAR	Specific Anti-avoidance Rule
VAT	Value-Added Tax
India	
AAR	Authority for Advance Rulings
AMT	Alternate Minimum Tax
BAR	Board of Advance Ruling
CBDT	Central Board of Direct Taxes
CITA	Commissioner of Income Tax (Appeals)
CTT	Commodities Transaction Tax
DDT	Dividend Distribution Tax
DTC	Direct Taxes Code
GAAR	General Anti-avoidance Rule
GDP	Gross Domestic Product
GIFT	Gujarat International Financial Tec
GST	Goods and Services Tax
HUF	Hindu Undivided Family
ICDS	Income Computation and Disclosure Standards
IFSC	International Financial Services Centre
IRS	Indian Revenue Service
ITA	Income Tax Act
ITAT	Income Tax Appellate Tribunal
LOB	Limitation-on-Benefits
MAT	Minimum Alternate Tax
MFN	Most-Favored-Nation
MLI	Multilateral Convention to Implement Tax Treaty Related Measures to Prevent BEPS
NTR	New Tax Regime
OECD	Organisation for Economic Co-operation and Development
OTR	Old Tax Regime
POEM	Place of Effective Management
PPT	Principal Purpose Test
STT	Securities Transaction Tax
TAS	Tax Accounting Standards

TIEA	Tax Information Exchange Agreement
UK	United Kingdom
VAT	Value-Added Tax
Japan	
CTA	Corporate Tax Act
FY	Fiscal Year
GAAP	Generally Accepted Accounting Principles
ITA	Income Tax Act
MLI	Multilateral Convention to Implement Tax Treaty Related Measures to Prevent Base Erosion and Profit Shifting
NISA	Nippon (Japan) Individual Savings Account
NTA	National Tax Agency (*Kokuzei-cho*)
OECD	Organisation for Economic Co-operation and Development
PAYE	Pay-as-You-Earn
STMA	Special Taxation Measures Act
TIEA	Tax Information Exchange Agreements
U.S.	United States
VAT	Value-Added Tax
The Netherlands	
APA	Advance Pricing Agreement
APV	Private Wealth Fund (*Afgezonderd Particulier Vermogen)*
ATAD	Anti-tax Avoidance Directive
ATR	Advance Tax Ruling
BR	Belastbaar Rendement
CITA	Corporate Income Tax Act
CJEU	Court of Justice of the European Union
CTA	Company Tax Act 1969
DivTA	Dividend Tax Act
EU	European Union
GSB	Net capital (Grondslag Sparen En Beleggen)
IFRS	International Financial Reporting Standards
ITA	Income Tax Act 2001 (Individuals)
MLI	Multilateral Convention to Implement Tax Treaty Measures to Prevent Base Erosion and Profit Shifting
OECD	Organisation for Economic Co-operation and Development
RG	Taxable net capital (*Rendementsgrondslag*)
TFEU	Treaty on the Functioning of the European Union

VAT	Value-Added Tax
WOO	Act on Open Government (*Wet Open Overheid*)
WTA	Wages Tax Act 1964
Sweden	
BFN	Accounting Standards Board (*Bokföringsnämnden)*
ECHR	European Convention on Human Rights
EU	European Union
GDP	Gross Domestic Product
ITA	Income Tax Act (*Inkomstskattelagen)*
MLI	Multilateral Convention to Implement Tax Treaty Related Measures to Prevent Base Erosion and Profit Shifting
OECD	Organisation for Economic Co-operation and Development
SFS	Swedish Code of Statutes (*Svensk Forfattningssamling)*
SOU	*Swedish Government Official Report* (*Statens Offentliga Utredningar)*
VAT	Value-Added Tax
United Kingdom	
BEPS	Base Erosion and Profit Shifting
CGT	Capital Gains Tax
CTA	Corporation Tax Act
DOTAS	Disclosure of Tax Avoidance Schemes
DST	Digital Services Tax
EU	European Union
GAAP	Generally Accepted Accounting Principles
GAAR	General Anti-avoidance Rule
GDP	Gross Domestic Product
HICBC	High-Income Child Benefit Charge
HMRC	His Majesty's Revenue and Customs
IFA	Institute for Fiscal Studies
ITA	Income Tax Act 2007
ITEPA	Income Tax (Earnings and Pensions) Act 2003
ITTOIA	Income Tax (Trading and Other Income) Act 2005
MLI	Multilateral Convention to Implement Tax Treaty Related Measures to Prevent Base Erosion and Profit Shifting
NIC	National Insurance Contribution
OECD	Organisation for Economic Co-operation and Development
PAYE	Pay-As-You-Earn

TIOPA	Taxation of International and Other Provisions Act 2010
TLRC	Tax Law Review Committee
UK	United Kingdom
VAT	Value-Added Tax
United States	
AMT	Alternative Minimum Tax
CFC	Controlled Foreign Corporation
FATCA	Foreign Account Tax Compliance Act
GDP	Gross Domestic Product
GILTI	Global Intangible Low-Taxed Income
IGA	Intergovernmental Agreement
IRC	Internal Revenue Code
IRS	Internal Revenue Service
LOB	Limitation-on-Benefits
MLI	Multilateral Convention to Implement Tax Treaty Related Measures to Prevent Base Erosion and Profit Shifting
OECD	Organisation for Economic Co-operation and Development
TCJA	Tax Cuts and Jobs Act
TIEA	Tax Information Exchange Agreement
Treas. Reg.	Treasury Regulation
U.S.	United States
Part II	
ACRS	Accelerated Cost Recovery System
CAA	Capital Allowances Act
CBDT	Central Board of Direct Taxes
CEST	Checking Employment Status for Tax
CGI	General Tax Code (*Code général des impôts*)
CGT	Capital Gains Tax
CITA	Corporate Income Tax Act
CJEU	Court of Justice of the European Union
CPP	Canada Pension Plan
CTA	Corporate Tax Act
EBITDA	Earnings Before Interest, Taxes, Depreciation, and Amortization
EC	European Commission
EIT	Enterprise Income Tax
EPF	Employees' Provident Fund
EU	European Union

FBT	Fringe Benefits Tax
FBTAA	Fringe Benefits Tax Assessment Act
FICA	Federal Insurance Contribution Act
HRA	House Rent Allowance
HUF	Hindu Undivided Family
IIT	Individual Income Tax
IRC	Internal Revenue Code
ISA	Individual Savings Account
ITA	Income Tax Act
ITAA	Income Tax Assessment Act
ITEPA	Income Tax (Earnings and Pensions) Act 2003
ITR	Income Tax Regulation
ITTOIA	Income Tax (Trading and Other Income) Act 2005
NIC	National Insurance Contribution
NPS	New Pension Scheme
OEITA	Order for Enforcement of Income Tax Act
OID	Original Issue Discount
PAYE	Pay-As-You-Earn
RRIF	Registered Retirement Income Fund
RRSP	Registered Retirement Savings Plan
RTA	Reorganization Tax Act
STA	State Tax Administration
STMA	Special Taxation Measures Act
TCGA	Taxation of Chargeable Gains Act
TFSA	Tax-Free Savings Account
UK	United Kingdom
VAT	Value-Added Tax
WKR	Work-Related Expense Scheme (*Werkkostenregeling*)
WTA	Withholding Tax Act
Part III	
ATAD	Anti-tax Avoidance Directive
BEPS	Base Erosion and Profit Shifting
CCPC	Canadian-Controlled Private Corporation
CFC	Controlled Foreign Corporation
CGI	General Tax Code (*Code général des impôts*)
CGT	Capital Gains Tax
CITA	Corporate Income Tax Act
CJEU	Court of Justice of the European Union
CTA	Corporate Tax Act
DDT	Dividend Distribution Tax

DWTA	Dividend Withholding Tax Act
EBITDA	Earnings Before Interest, Taxes, Depreciation, and Amortization
EEA	European Economic Area
EIT	Enterprise Income Tax
EU	European Union
GAAR	General Anti-avoidance Rule
IIT	Individual Income Tax
IRC	Internal Revenue Code
ITA	Income Tax Act
ITAA	Income Tax Assessment Act
LLP	Limited Liability Partnership
RTA	Reorganization Tax Act
STA	State Tax Administration
STMA	Special Taxation Measures Act
Part IV	
AOA	Authorized OECD Approach
APA	Advance Pricing Agreement
APV	Private Wealth Fund (*Afgezonderd Particulier Vermoge)*
ATAD	Anti-tax Avoidance Directive
BEAT	Base Erosion and Anti-abuse Tax
BEPS	Base Erosion and Profit Shifting
CBDT	Central Board of Direct Taxes
CFC	Controlled Foreign Corporation
CGI	General Tax Code (*Code général des impôts*)
CIT	Corporate Income Tax
CITA	Corporate Income Tax Act
CIV	Collective Investment Vehicle
CJEU	Court of Justice of the European Union
CPM	Comparable Profits Method
CRA	Canada Revenue Agency
CTA	Corporate Tax Act
CUP	Comparable Uncontrolled Price
DADT	Decree on Avoidance of Double Taxation 2001
DDT	Dividend Distribution Tax
EBITDA	Earnings Before Interest, Taxes, Depreciation and Amortization
ECJ	European Court of Justice
EEA	European Economic Area
EIT	Enterprise Income Tax

EU	European Union
FAPI	Foreign Accrual Property Income
FDII	Foreign Derived Intangible Income
FHTP	Forum on Harmful Tax Practices
FIC	Foreign Investment Company
FIE	Foreign Investment Entity
FIF	Foreign Investment Fund
FIRPTA	Foreign Investment in Real Property Tax Act
FTC	Foreign Tax Credit
GAAR	General Anti-avoidance Rule
GAT	General Act on Taxation
GFC	General Fiscal Code
GFTE	Global Forum on Transparency and Exchange of Information
GILTI	Global Intangible Low-Taxed Income
IIT	Individual Income Tax
IRC	Internal Revenue Code
ITA	Income Tax Act
ITAA	Income Tax Assessment Act
LLC	Limited Liability Company
LPF	Book of Tax Procedures (*Livre Des Procédures Fiscales*)
MLI	Multilateral Convention to Implement Tax Treaty Related Measures to Prevent Base Erosion and Profit Shifting
MOF	Ministry of Finance
OECD	Organisation for Economic Co-operation and Development
PCG	Practical Compliance Guideline
PE	Permanent Establishment
PFIC	Passive Foreign Investment Company
PPT	Principal Purpose Test
STA	State Tax Administration
STMA	Special Taxation Measures Act
TCJA	Tax Cut and Jobs Act
TDS	Deduction of Tax at Source
TFEU	Treaty on the Functioning of the European Union
TNMM	Transactional Net Margin Method
U.S.	United States
UK	United Kingdom

Introduction

As Otto Kahn-Freund, a comparative law scholar, wrote: "Comparative law ... is not a topic, but a method ... and a method of looking at one's own law."[1] Kahn-Freund's view of comparative law in general is equally applicable to tax law. Typically, tax students, tax officials, and tax practitioners study only their own tax system and inevitably come to assume that the way their system deals with problems is the only way to solve those problems. Studying other countries' tax systems provides a different and broader perspective on the underlying premises of one's own tax system and alternative solutions to what are often common problems.

This book presents a comparative analysis of some of the most important structural and design issues which are involved in income tax systems. It is aimed primarily at professors and students of tax law, both in the United States and abroad, whose central concern lies naturally in working with the concepts and principles of their own domestic systems. For them, the material is intended both to provide information on what other systems actually do, which is interesting in itself, and to suggest other approaches which might represent alternative ways of dealing with corresponding issues in a domestic setting. By introducing a comparative dimension, the materials can be used both to enrich classroom discussion of domestic problems and to give a starting point for further research and study. Who has not wondered, when discussing an interesting question such as the childcare deduction or the taxation of imputed income, how the tax systems of other countries approach these issues? While the answers are out there, they are hard to find and harder to evaluate. This book attempts to make the approaches of selected other systems more accessible.

Comparative tax analysis does not consist simply of describing aspects of the tax laws of multiple countries, although such descriptive information is valuable and, even with the Internet, can be difficult to find. At its best, comparative tax analysis attempts to explain how countries' tax laws differ and why or how they are similar despite superficial differences. The differences between countries' tax systems may be explained by a wide variety of factors, including different governmental institutions,

1. Otto Kahn-Freund, "Comparative Law as an Academic Subject" 82 *Law Quarterly Review* 40-41 (1966).

different processes for the formulation of tax policy, different distributions of economic power, different ideas about taxation, and environmental factors such as history and geography. Comparative tax analysis also involves consideration of how countries' tax systems have influenced one another and how international organizations, such as the European Union (EU), the Organisation for Economic Co-operation and Development (OECD), the International Monetary Fund, the United Nations, and the World Bank, influence tax systems.

With respect to international tax, the OECD and the United Nations have had a dominant influence on bilateral tax treaties through their Model Tax Treaties. These Model Treaties provide a useful and convenient tool for analyzing the provisions of a country's tax treaties by identifying the extent to which those provisions deviate from those of the Model Treaties. However, international organizations also have a significant influence on the domestic tax laws of many countries, including the countries examined in this book. Perhaps the best example of an organization with such influence is the EU. As discussed below, members of the EU are prohibited from enacting laws which violate or infringe on the four fundamental freedoms enshrined in the EU Treaty and they must enact laws to comply with the Directives of the European Commission. Thus, the EU has a profound impact on the domestic laws and treaties of its member countries, including the five EU member countries—France, Germany, The Netherlands, Sweden, and the United Kingdom (at least until Brexit)—studied in this book. The influence of the EU on countries' domestic tax laws and treaties presents a challenge for the comparative analysis in this book, which provides a country-by-country analysis of particular issues—namely, where a particular issue is affected by EU law, discussing the EU law with respect to each country would be repetitive. Therefore, we have decided to include a brief general discussion of EU institutions and fundamental EU rules which have a significant impact on the tax laws of the member countries in a separate section in this introductory chapter.

Comparative tax analysis is notoriously difficult. It requires information about other countries' tax systems, which, as noted above, may be difficult to obtain because of language differences and different terminology. Once the necessary information has been gathered, it is crucial to understand how a particular rule or set of rules in another country's tax system functions in the context of that system. Some rules may not be explicit (such as the principle in UK-based systems that income must have a generic source) but may nevertheless play an important role in that system. Moreover, tax law is often applied to legal transactions and relationships as determined under a country's private law rules. Therefore, in many situations, comparative tax analysis also requires an understanding of a country's underlying private law as a prerequisite for understanding its tax law. If this is not sufficient evidence of the difficulty of comparative tax analysis, add the complexity and dynamic, rapidly changing nature of most countries' tax systems. For the purposes of this book, we have attempted to overcome these difficulties by gathering together a distinguished group of tax academics and tax professionals who have proven expertise in their own tax systems and, in many cases, other countries' systems as well.

There are dangers in attempting to relate legal rules or concepts in one system to a seemingly similar situation in another system. The institutional and cultural backgrounds may be different and the actual operation of each individual rule depends on the overall structure of both the tax system and the legal system in general. Doing meaningful comparative analysis is especially difficult in the tax area, where political pressure, chance, and historical accident have all had an important influence on the development of each country's tax system. However, with appropriate caveats and cautions, there is much to learn in the tax field from a comparative analysis of common problems. One need not believe in the existence of a Platonic Tax Form to find useful insights in the experience of others.

The countries selected for comparison in the first three editions of this book—Australia, Canada, France, Germany, Japan, The Netherlands, Sweden, the United Kingdom, and the United States—all have relatively mature and sophisticated tax systems. One would expect, a priori, that many similar issues and questions would emerge, and this intuition is confirmed by the materials. The responses to the issues, however, vary substantially in many cases.

Several of the systems which are considered in this 5th edition belong to one of two broad legal "families." The approaches of the Commonwealth countries —Australia, Canada, India, and the United Kingdom—all display some of the expected degree of similarity, given their common historical roots. The Continental systems of France, Germany, The Netherlands, and Sweden, likewise, although to a lesser extent, have similarities in structure and result. In contrast, the United States system has developed without much influence from other systems, and the Japanese system has both Continental (especially German) features, as well as displaying a strong influence from American ideas in its post-war development.

Thus, while the details differ, there are some recognizable "family resemblances" within both the Commonwealth and Continental groups, as well as marked differences between the two families. A good example of the differences between the Commonwealth and Continental families is their treatment of capital gains. The Commonwealth systems all have, to varying degrees, schedular features, i.e., where different classes or categories of income may be taxed in different ways and at different rates, with varying rules for inclusion and deduction. Trust notions of "income" and "corpus" (capital) have also played an important role in developing tax concepts. Partly due to the concept of trust corpus, the taxation of capital gains has been the subject of special legislation and is often structured as a separate tax regime. Continental systems, as well, have significant points of resemblance. In all these systems, financial accounting rules have often been important in the development of tax principles, especially for the computation of business income. As a result, and in stark contrast to the Commonwealth tradition, capital gains realized in a business setting have usually been subject to the normal tax rules dealing with business profits. Capital gains of individual investors, however, have at least initially escaped tax, although the traditional approaches have often been modified by extending taxation to certain limited classes of gains.

Beyond these broad features, each of the systems has evolved its own particular set of approaches and principles, which are outlined in some detail in the individual Country Descriptions contained in Part I. These individually authored pieces present the overall structure of each country's income tax system and provide some feel for the "tax culture" or climate and institutional framework in which the substantive rules operate. They can be read as "stand-alone" descriptions of the systems or referred to periodically in connection with the subsequent discussion of specific issues in Parts II, III, IV of the book for a better understanding of how a particular country's rules operate with respect to those issues. It is essential to keep in mind some of the basic features outlined in the Country Descriptions when dealing with the later substantive material. For example, in thinking about the structure of the rules on corporate liquidations, it is crucial to remember that in some countries private capital gains of an individual are not taxable while business gains are subject to full taxation. Similarly, in considering items included in the tax base, taxation may depend on the taxable category, schedule, or box into which an item fits. To facilitate the necessary cross-references, some of the more important features of each system are summarized in tabular form in Parts II, III, and IV.

Following the Country Descriptions in Part I, the remaining three Parts deal with Basic Income Taxation, Taxation of Business Organizations, and International Taxation, respectively. As will be apparent, the organization is traditional and follows in broad outline the issues and questions typically covered in an academic tax course on each particular topic. Within each Part, the various substantive Subparts and Sections begin by outlining some of the structural issues or problems which have arisen with respect to each topic. The responses of the countries to the problems are described briefly, together with an attempt to identify common patterns or approaches and highlight unique or interesting solutions. The descriptions of the substantive rules vary in completeness, and not every issue is discussed in connection with every country. The focus is on structural and design issues, although there is some consideration of extrafiscal measures where they are especially significant.

Although the fundamental approach of the book and the emphasis on the structural aspects of income tax systems has been maintained in the 5th edition, the content of this edition has been revised and in some cases expanded significantly. Two new countries—China and India—were added to the other nine developed countries in the 4th edition in order to address a shortcoming in previous editions of the book, namely, the absence of any consideration of the issues from the perspective of developing countries with emerging economies. China and India are two of the most important developing countries because of their large and growing economies. Their income tax systems provide insights into the general perspective of developing countries and the special problems that they face. In addition, China and India provide fascinating examples of the different stages of development of income tax systems. China's income tax system is relatively young and has not yet developed rules to deal with issues that other mature systems have enacted sophisticated rules to deal with. In contrast, as a result of its colonial past, India has had an income tax system for over 150 years and its tax system is characterized by complex tax legislation and extensive tax case law similar to that of developed countries.

The 5th edition updates the text of the book to reflect changes in the countries' domestic tax laws and treaties from the 4th edition in June 2019 to September 2024. These changes have been extensive, especially with respect to international tax, primarily as a result of the continuing implementation of the G20/OECD Base Erosion and Profit Shifting (BEPS) Project, the 2021 update to the United Nations Model Treaty, and the attempts by several countries and international organizations to deal with the challenges posed by the digitalization of the economy to the existing international consensus on the allocation of taxing rights between source and residence countries, especially the OECD/Inclusive Framework's Two Pillar solution. New sections have been added to Part IV, Subpart C to deal with both Pillar One (section 7) and Pillar Two (the global minimum tax) (section 9) and the country responses to the BEPS Action 2 Report on hybrid mismatch arrangements (section 8). In addition, section 4 of Subpart B dealing with limitations on base-eroding payments to non-residents has been expanded to deal with the country responses to the BEPS Action 4 Report on base erosion through interest and other financial payments, which recommended that countries adopt earnings-stripping rules. The G20/OECD BEPS Project and the EU Anti-Tax Avoidance Directives are discussed throughout Part IV of the book.

Although the book is not suitable as a source for detailed information, it can be used as an effective research tool. The footnotes provide legislative and judicial sources as an aid to begin research on particular topics; however, in general, footnotes have been used sparingly to avoid interrupting the flow of the text. In addition, the Sources of Law section in each of the Country Descriptions in Part I provides basic information on a country's tax legislation, court cases, administrative material, and secondary sources.

Having briefly covered what the 5th edition covers, it is also a good idea to mention what it does not cover. The book does not deal with certain tax ideas or proposals that have been widely discussed and have gained some acceptance in the academic community, and in some cases have even been seriously considered by governments. For example, the existing arm's-length transfer pricing rules have been subject to widespread criticism, and many academics and international organizations have advocated switching to a system of formulary apportionment, under which income of a multinational group would be allocated among the countries in which the group operates on the basis of a formula based on factors such as sales, payroll, and assets. Some of the profit-split methods used by countries and approved in the OECD Transfer Pricing Guidelines contain elements of formulary apportionment and are discussed in Part IV, Subpart C, section 2. Although the OECD/Inclusive Framework's Pillar One proposals use formulary apportionment to allocate residual profits of the largest and most profitable multinationals to market jurisdictions, the proposals remain controversial and have not been widely endorsed.

Similarly, various ideas for dealing with the fundamental problems associated with the corporate tax—the integration (or lack of integration) of tax imposed on a corporation's income and tax imposed on dividends received by the corporation's shareholders and the treatment of corporate debt and equity used to finance a corporation's business activities—have been thoroughly analyzed by academics and considered by tax policy officials in some countries. These proposals include cash-flow taxes, a comprehensive business income tax (CBIT), proposed by the US Treasury in

1992,[2] and an allowance for corporate equity (ACE) which some countries have adopted to equalize, or at least reduce, the discrepancy between the tax treatment of corporate debt and equity by granting a deduction with respect to a corporation's equity capital.[3] Further, the EU has attempted for many years to persuade the Member Countries to adopt a common consolidated corporate tax base (CCCTB), under which the income of corporations would be computed on a harmonized basis in all the member countries; this proposal is discussed below in the Introduction to European Tax Law. Again, none of these proposals have been acted on by governments.

2. *See* U.S. Department of the Treasury, Integration of the Individual and Corporate Tax Systems: Taxing Business Income Once (1992). *See also* Alvin C. Warren Jr., Integration of Individual and Corporate Income Taxes (American Law Institute 1993).
3. *See* Institute for Fiscal Studies, Equity for Companies: A Corporation Tax for the 1990s (April 1991, IFS Commentary No. 26).

An Introduction to European Tax Law[4]

As mentioned above, this introduction to European Union (EU) law is intended to provide a basic understanding of EU institutions and laws which affect the tax laws of EU Member States. Readers who are not familiar with EU tax law may find it worthwhile to read the introduction before reading the chapters in Part I dealing with the EU Member States or to refer to the introduction when they encounter issues in Parts II, III, or IV which raise aspects of EU law.

1 THE HISTORICAL AND INSTITUTIONAL BACKGROUND

In 1957, six Western European countries (Belgium, France, Germany, Italy, Luxembourg, and The Netherlands) entered into the European Economic Community Treaty to establish a common market for sales of goods and services and other commercial activities. In 1992, through the Maastricht Treaty, the EU was founded to deal with additional matters, including internal security, judicial cooperation, and a common foreign and security policy. At the same time, the European Monetary Union and a common currency were established, although not all Member States (e.g., the United Kingdom) adopted the new currency. In 2009, pursuant to the Treaty of Lisbon, the European Community was fully absorbed by the EU. Two fundamental treaties governing the EU remain in place, although the Treaty on the European Union (TEU) has been enlarged and the European Commission (EC) Treaty has become the Treaty on the Functioning of the European Union (TFEU).

Over the years, the EU expanded from the original six countries to twenty-eight countries and now includes 27 Member States since the United Kingdom left the EU on January 31, 2020 ("Brexit"). Some major European countries, such as Switzerland, do not belong to the EU but have special relationships with the EU. Norway, Iceland, and Liechtenstein entered into the European Economic Area (EEA) Treaty, which provides the same fundamental freedoms as the TEU but does not automatically incorporate all

4. Prepared by Prof. Dr. Wolfgang Schön.

the secondary provisions enacted under the TEU or TFEU into EEA law. For example, the tax directives of the EU are not applicable to the Member States of the EEA.

The fundamental goal of the EU Treaties is the establishment of an internal or common market for the free flow of resources (goods, services, persons, and capital) across borders between the Member States and to promote undistorted competition (Article 3, TEU). The TEU establishes institutions—the European Council (heads of state of the Member States), the Council of Ministers (consists of ministers and other representatives of Member States and approves EU legislation), the European Parliament (elected by citizens of the EU and must consent to certain EU legislation, but not taxation), and the EC (the executive branch of the EU responsible for initiating all EU legislation)—to carry out the goals of the EU. These EU Institutions have the authority to enact laws or take other actions only to the extent that such authority is expressly provided in the EU treaties. Other important EU institutions are the Court of Justice of the European Union (CJEU—often referred to by its former name, the European Court of Justice (ECJ)) and the European Central Bank.

Article 288 of the TFEU provides for the following EU legal instruments:

- Regulations have direct effect for the European Institutions as well as Member States and their citizens but are very rarely used in the tax area.
- Decisions are made with respect to individual cases and, in the tax area, are mainly found in the context of the application of state aid provisions under Articles 107 et seq. of the TFEU, as noted below.
- Directives must be implemented by the Member States and are the most important instruments for harmonization in the tax area (both indirect and direct taxation) under Articles 113-115 of the TFEU.
- Recommendations and Communications are not binding on the Member States but are often used by the Commission, including with respect to measures to combat aggressive tax behavior, when a binding consensus on an issue cannot be achieved.

Bilateral and multilateral treaties entered into by Member States to further the goals of the common market, including the elimination of double taxation, are not prohibited by the EU treaties. The Member States have sometimes resorted to conventions or intergovernmental agreements in order to avoid European Institutions and exclude the jurisdiction of the CJEU (e.g., the EU Arbitration Convention and the EU Code of Conduct).

The CJEU is composed of judges from all Member States. Official advisors to the CJEU, the Advocates General, deliver detailed opinions in advance on cases before the Court. Their analysis is helpful but not binding on the Court in its decisions.

The CJEU has exerted considerable influence on EU law from the outset, often driving integration and strengthening the power of the European Community and the EU. For example, it has held that EU law prevails whenever there is a conflict with domestic law and that to a large extent EU law, especially the fundamental freedoms (discussed below), has "direct effect," and can be invoked by citizens in domestic courts without the need for EU law to be incorporated into domestic law. For Directives which have been implemented by a Member State, national law must be interpreted in accordance with the language and purpose of the Directives. However, citizens can also rely on Directives which have not been implemented, or have been implemented incorrectly or incompletely, where they confer clear and unconditional entitlements. While domestic courts are permitted to refer questions of European law to the CJEU under Article 267 of the TFEU, domestic courts of final appeal are obliged to refer such issues to the CJEU. In addition, under Article 258 of the TFEU, the EC is empowered to take Member States to court when they do not comply with European law, e.g., if they do not implement Directives correctly and on a timely basis or if their domestic legislation is not consistent with the fundamental freedoms or other provisions of the European treaties.

Although the EU does not have the power to introduce new taxes, under Articles 113 and 115 of the TFEU, it has the power to harmonize Member States' domestic legislation with respect to indirect and direct taxes which affect the functioning of the internal market. These harmonization measures require unanimity of the Member States of the Council to issue Directives (but not Regulations) dealing with discrimination and restrictions on cross-border economic activities, as well as disparities between the different laws of the Member States which may have damaging effects on the internal market. The limits on this power are unclear; for example, it is assumed that a Directive could not be issued to require Member States to harmonize their corporate or individual income taxes completely. Moreover, the borderline between tax Directives and non-tax Directives can be blurred. For example, in November 2021, the EU enacted a Directive on public country-by-country-reporting of large enterprises.[5] Although the purpose of this Directive is to fight tax avoidance by multinationals, it was justified by the Commission and the Council under the power to harmonize company law (accounting law) laid down in Article 50(1) of the TFEU.

Under an "enhanced cooperation" procedure in Article 20 of the TFEU, a group of at least nine Member States can legislate with respect to the internal market in their jurisdictions. Over the years, a couple of proposals, e.g., for a Financial Transaction Tax (FTT) and a Common Consolidated Corporate Tax Base (CCCTB) (discussed below), were discussed on this track, but to date, none of the proposals has led to final legislation.

According to Article 6(1) of the TEU, the EU recognizes the basic rights laid down in the "Charter of Fundamental Rights of the European Union" (European Convention on Human Rights (ECHR)) (freedom of speech and religion, equal treatment, protection of property, procedural rights, etc.). Unlike the fundamental freedoms, these rights cannot be invoked against Member States where they exercise their own legislative and administrative competences. They are binding only for the European Institutions and Member States implementing EU law (Article 51(1) of the ECHR). In recent years, the CJEU delivered a number of decisions confirming the constraints established for EU legislation, e.g., in the area of cross-border exchange of information.

5. Directive (EU) 2021 & 2101 of the European Parliament and of the Council of November 24, 2021 amending Directive 2013/34/EU as regards disclosure of income tax information by certain undertakings and branches, O.J. L 429/1 of December 1, 2021.

Under Article 107(1) TFEU, so-called state aid—"any aid granted by a Member State or through State resources in any form whatsoever"—is prohibited. The CJEU and the Commission have held since the beginning of the European Community that the concept of state aid includes tax incentives which reduce the tax burden on business. Thus, tax incentives providing particular taxpayers with a lower tax level than the 'normal' level must comply with Articles 107 and 108 of the TFEU. To give one widely publicized example: In September 2024, the CJEU confirmed a decision by the Commission to declare unlawful tax benefits for Apple arising from a beneficial application of the arm's length standard by the Irish Government with respect to two Irish subsidiaries of Apple, requiring the Irish Government to charge Apple with an additional tax of about EUR 13 billion.[6]

2 THE FUNDAMENTAL FREEDOMS

The TFEU provides that the internal market is promoted through four fundamental freedoms: the free movement of goods (Article 34), services (Article 56), persons (freedom of establishment) (Articles 45 and 49), and capital/payments (Article 63). All fundamental freedoms can be relied on by citizens in domestic courts. The extensive case law of the CJEU has established a reasonably consistent jurisprudence with respect to the scope of the four freedoms so that, in most situations, it does not matter which of the four freedoms is actually infringed.

All fundamental freedoms represent protections for cross-border economic activity within the EU. Two other subsidiary provisions can also be invoked in domestic courts even where no economic activity is involved:

- the general principle of non-discrimination (Article 18 of the TFEU); and
- the general right of free movement of EU citizens (Article 21 of the TFEU).

These two provisions apply only where a case is not covered by the four freedoms.

The fundamental freedoms apply to any cross-border activity taking place in EU territory; transactions with third countries are not covered except for transactions in the EEA (which includes Iceland, Liechtenstein, and Norway) and the free movement of capital between Member States and third countries. Since only the free movement of capital involves third-country entitlements, the borderline between free movement of capital and other freedoms must be examined carefully in particular cases.

The first—and basic—principle of the internal market is non-discrimination against foreign nationals, foreign goods and foreign capital. Although the language used to articulate the freedoms is unclear, it is widely accepted that non-discrimination is the starting point for the application of all four fundamental freedoms. In certain circumstances, discrimination may be justified by explicit provisions in the TFEU or by an 'overriding public interest' as established by the case law of the CJEU, which includes the necessity of fiscal supervision and the balanced allocation of taxing rights,

6. Case C-465/20 P (*Commission v. Ireland and Others*), judgment of September 10, 2024.

as well as anti-abuse measures against "wholly artificial arrangements." In two judgments of 2019, the CJEU even went so far as to award the status of a "general principle of EU law" to the concept that taxpayers are not entitled to rely on EU law (both under primary law and under the Directives) for abusive or fraudulent ends.[7]

The case law of the CJEU with respect to the four freedoms has had pervasive influence on the national tax laws of the Member States, including with respect to the following:

- the treatment of outbound investment by residents through permanent establishments or subsidiaries;
- the treatment of nonresident investors deriving income through a permanent establishment;
- limiting the scope of controlled foreign corporation (CFC) rules to wholly artificial arrangements;
- the application of progressive tax rates to nonresidents;
- relief for foreign losses of permanent establishments and subsidiaries;
- loss relief for multinational groups;
- dividends received from foreign companies and dividends paid by resident companies to nonresident shareholders;
- withholding taxes;
- thin capitalization rules; and
- exit taxes.

3 DIRECTIVES

Under Article 115 of the TFEU, the EU is empowered to issue Directives to align national tax laws in order to improve the framework of the internal market. Although this provision does not give European institutions authority to fully harmonize domestic tax laws, it can be used to address problems where a lack of harmonization forms an obstacle to the full use of the fundamental freedoms. Since any action in this regard requires unanimity of the Member States in the Council of Ministers, in practice, Directives have not been used frequently. Three Directives concern the formation of cross-border company groups:

- the Merger Directive covers cross-border reorganizations of corporate entities (Council Directive 90/434/EEC of July 23, 1990) as amended by various Council Directives;
- the Parent-Subsidiary Directive covers cross-border dividend payments between affiliated companies (Council Directive 90/435/EEC of July 23, 1990) as amended by various Council Directives;

7. Joined Cases C-116/16 and C-117/16, February 26, 2019 (*T Danmark et al.*); Joined Cases C-115/16, C-118/16, C-119/16 and C-299/16, February 26, 2019 (*N Luxembourg 1 et al.*).

- the Interest and Royalty Directive covers cross-border payments of interest and royalties (Council Directive 2003/49/EC of June 3, 2003) as amended by various Council Directives.

Several other directives provide obligations for Member States to support each other with respect to exchanges of information and recovery of tax claims. The scope of these directives has been substantially expanded in the wake of the Base Erosion and Profit Shifting (BEPS) Project when EU legislation introduced a number of BEPS recommendations into binding law (e.g., disclosure of reportable cross-border arrangements, exchange of information on rulings, and country-by-country reporting).

All directives in the field of direct business taxation contain provisions which give a certain leeway to governments to introduce domestic provisions in order to fight abusive tax-avoidance arrangements. This leeway was transformed into an obligation when the CJEU introduced the concept of a general anti-abuse principle under EU law which would defeat both diverging secondary EU law and domestic law.

In 2016 and 2017, as a result of the BEPS Project, the EU adopted two important Anti-Tax Avoidance Directives (ATAD I and ATAD II), requiring Member States to adopt a variety of anti-avoidance measures, including rules dealing with hybrid mismatches, earnings-stripping rules to limit interest deductions, CFC rules, exit taxes, and a general anti-avoidance rule (Council Directive (EU) 2016/1164 of July 12, 2016; Council Directive (EU) 2017/952 of May 29, 2017). Following up on this legislation, in 2021, the Commission proposed another directive aimed at "letterbox companies" (Proposal for a Council Directive laying down rules to prevent the misuse of shell entities for tax purposes and amending Directive 2011/16/EU (COM(2021)565 final), known as the "Unshell Directive"). Under this Directive, which has not yet been agreed to by the Member States, companies lacking certain factors indicating economic substance would be subject to reporting requirements and exchange of information between Member States. Moreover, income derived by these companies would be attributed directly to the shareholders.

4 THE COMMON CONSOLIDATED CORPORATE TAX BASE PROJECT

In 2011, the EC presented an extensive Proposal for a Council Directive on a Common Consolidated Corporate Tax Base (CCCTB) (COM(2011)121/4). This Proposal was meant to provide an option for multinational businesses to employ a single set of consolidated accounts for tax purposes for all subsidiaries and branches throughout the EU and to apply formulary apportionment to allocate the overall income of the corporate group to the individual Member States.

In 2016, the EC published two new proposals on a common tax base for multinational companies in Europe which signaled a major shift in the ultimate goal of the legislation (Proposal for a Council Directive on a Common Corporate Tax Base COM(2016) 685 final and Proposal for a Council Directive on a Common Consolidated Corporate Tax Base (CCCTB) COM(2016) 683 final). While the original proposal was designed primarily to reduce compliance costs and deadweight losses for business, the new proposal also addresses the need for tax authorities to reduce options for arbitrage and tax planning. The new proposal provided that CCCTB treatment would be mandatory for companies (although de facto optionality would live on with respect to the thresholds for financial and economic integration and the ongoing existence of third countries outside the CCCTB area).

Since none of these proposals gained traction with the Member States, the Commission came forward in 2023 with a new approach, "Business in Europe: Framework for Income Taxation (BEFIT)" (COM(2023)532 final), which builds on the earlier proposals but leaves open important issues, including the design of the formula for profit allocation between the Member States of the EU. It remains unclear whether this project will be more successful than its predecessors, in particular as the conformity of this proposal with global projects (Pillars One and Two) is in doubt.

5 TAXATION OF THE DIGITAL ECONOMY

An ongoing project of the EC concerns taxation of the digital economy. In March 2018, the Commission released two proposals:

(1) a Proposal for a Council Directive on a common system of a digital services tax on revenues resulting from the provision of certain digital services (COM(2018)148 final); and
(2) a Proposal for a Council Directive laying down rules relating to the corporate taxation of a significant digital presence (COM(2018)147 final).

The first proposal is meant to provide a "short-term" solution for the taxation of cross-border activities of highly digitalized businesses. Its main feature is a tax on a narrowly defined number of digital services provided by social network services, search engines, internet platforms, and the like. The tax is to be levied on taxable revenues such as advertising fees but is not conceived as a direct tax. Thus, the EC proposal is based on Article 113 TFEU and does not conflict with the provisions of double taxation treaties. In late 2018, it became clear that this proposal would not be approved by all or even a clear majority of EU Member States, although it had been whittled down in the course of negotiations to a mere tax on advertising fees.

The second proposal is meant to provide a "long-term" solution for a reallocation of taxing rights in the area of international business taxation. The main feature is the introduction of the concept of a "significant digital presence," which is meant to parallel the permanent establishment concept in the digital world. The allocation of profits to a significant economic presence uses both traditional aspects of transfer pricing practice and a profit split in order to share revenue between production countries and "user" or market countries. This proposal is currently on hold given the ongoing work of the OECD/G20 Inclusive Framework for new rules dealing with digital activities; the work of the Inclusive Framework is discussed in Part IV.

It remains unclear to what extent the EC will resume work on these proposals, which will likely depend on the outcome of the global negotiations on Pillar One of the OECD/G20 project on taxation of the digital economy.

6 THE MINIMUM TAXATION DIRECTIVE

Probably the most substantial achievement of EU tax policy in recent years has been the enactment of the Minimum Tax Directive,[8] which is meant to incorporate the outcome of the Organisation for Economic Co-operation and Development (OECD) Inclusive Framework's work on Pillar Two into European law. This Directive has a major effect on the Member States' legislation, as the Model Rules designed and agreed by OECD are merely "soft law" providing a "common approach" for all participants but do not oblige any signatory state to actually introduce a minimum tax. For the EU, however, the Minimum Tax Directive requires all Member States to introduce the Pillar Two global minimum tax and to implement all provisions contained in the highly detailed Directive.

For the future, this means that no Member State of the European Union will be able to withdraw from Pillar Two on their own since any amendment or termination of this binding Directive would require a proposal by the Commission and unanimous consent in the Council of Ministers. Moreover, any change to the Model Rules cannot be implemented by the Member States on their own, as they would need to change the Directive first. This leads to the highly problematic situation that ongoing adaptations at the OECD Inclusive Framework level (e.g., by means of administrative guidance) can be applied in the EU only if it can be shown that they are in line with the Directive (whose wording is largely identical with the original version of the Model Rules). Moreover, all provisions contained in the Directive are subject to the jurisdiction of the CJEU, which might lead to court decisions on the interpretation of the Directive (and, as a result, on the interpretation of the Model Rules) which might clash with international tax practice in other parts of the world.

8. Council Directive (EU) 2022/2523 of December 15, 2022 on ensuring a global minimum level of taxation for multinational enterprise groups and large-scale domestic groups in the Union, O.J. L 328/1 of December 22, 2022.

Part I General Description

Australia

Richard Vann & Graeme S. Cooper

1 HISTORY OF THE INCOME TAX

The federal income tax was introduced in 1915 as a measure to finance the war effort. The first income tax in Australia had been introduced in South Australia in 1884, prior to federation in 1901, and by 1907, all states had an income tax. Interestingly, at both the state and federal levels, the income tax was usually introduced in conjunction with a land tax, reflecting the significant influence in Australia of Henry George's work *Progress and Poverty*. Concerns about the operation of the income tax systems led to a Royal Commission in the early 1920s and a new federal income tax statute in 1922. Harmonization of state and federal income taxes was not achieved in this exercise. A further Royal Commission in the early 1930s produced a new federal tax statute, the *Income Tax Assessment Act 1936* (ITAA), which is still the current legislation in part and was the model for all state income taxes—that is, harmonization was achieved on this occasion.

The harmonization was short-lived since, with the advent of World War II, the federal government decided to take over the state income taxes and levy a single federal income tax. A new emphasis on federalism in the 1970s saw the federal legislation amended in a way which permitted states to levy income taxes if they wished, but the necessary precondition for making this a reality—namely, a cut in federal income tax rates to create room for state taxes—did not occur. The more centralist Labor Government of the 1980s and early 1990s repealed the legislation permitting states to levy income taxes.

Although several other commissions of inquiry were instituted from the 1950s to the 1970s, they had little major immediate impact other than giving rise to legislative measures to counter various forms of tax avoidance. Since 1980, there have been two major overhauls of the tax system in general and the income tax in particular. First, in the mid-1980s, the Labor government introduced a capital gains tax (CGT), a fringe benefits tax (FBT) (i.e., a final tax imposed directly on the provider of certain employment-related benefits, which replaced income tax on the recipients), a full imputation system in relation to company dividends, and a complete overhaul of the taxation of foreign source income of residents. These measures generally followed the common 1980s tax reform strategy of base broadening and rate cutting (with maximum individual tax rates falling from 60% to less than 49%).

Second, in 1998, the Liberal National (conservative) government adopted a comprehensive tax reform agenda with four major elements:

(1) reform of individual and company tax rates, including tax cuts, a tax-mix change, and greater integration of the income tax with the social welfare system;
(2) introduction of a value-added tax (called the Goods and Services Tax (GST)) with the revenue going by grants to the states under a major reform of fiscal federalism;
(3) overhaul of the tax administration, including broader withholding arrangements, integration of several tax-collection mechanisms, and binding oral tax rulings for individuals with simple tax affairs; and
(4) substantial changes to the individual and business tax base (50% discount for capital gains made by individuals, uniform capital allowances which abolished accelerated depreciation, introduction of a special regime for small business, and anti-avoidance rules on alienation of personal services income and noncommercial losses) and taxation of entities (a simplification of the imputation system, redrawing the debt and equity borderline, rollovers for takeovers and demergers, a comprehensive value-shifting regime, new thin capitalization measures, and tax consolidation for 100% common-owned corporate groups).

Not to be outdone, the Labor government, re-elected in late 2007, announced in 2008 yet another "root and branch" tax reform, along with a review of the social welfare system and its interaction with the income tax. This review adopted a more long-term vision as its mission, seeking to outline the broad features of a desirable tax system to be in place in two decades rather than setting out a series of immediate changes.

While this was going on, the government also introduced some major reforms, such as measures to deal with financial instruments, foreign currency transactions, hedging, and a dedicated regime for foreign investors in the real estate and infrastructure sectors, and signed the *Multilateral Convention on Mutual Administrative Assistance in Tax Matters*. Recent Australian tax policy has been preoccupied with curbing international tax avoidance, including strong support for the Organisation for Economic Co-operation and Development's (OECD's) Base Erosion and Profit Shifting (BEPS) Project: Australia has enacted anti-hybrid measures, rewritten its transfer pricing rules to align them more explicitly with the OECD Transfer Pricing Guidelines, and signed the *Multilateral Convention to Implement Tax Treaty Related Measures to Prevent Base Erosion and Profit Shifting* (MLI) (including agreeing to binding arbitration); it has also enacted domestic anti-avoidance measures modelled on the twin elements of the United Kingdom's (UK's) Diverted Profits Tax (branch tax avoidance and shifting income offshore). Australia also enacted in 2024 the OECD "Pillar Two" global minimum tax (along with a similar domestic minimum tax) starting retrospectively from January 1, 2024.

In short, Australian tax policy making has always proved to be a mixture of grand visions, major projects, and constant minor tinkering.

2 CONSTITUTIONAL ISSUES

Australia has a federal constitution under which the central government is given power to levy income taxes along with the states. To meet the emergency created by World War II, the federal government effectively excluded the states from the income tax arena. The drastic legislative measures adopted for this purpose, including a forcible seizure of state income tax offices, were upheld in the High Court of Australia, relying in part on the defense power in a major constitutional challenge by the states. Since that time, no state income tax has been levied in Australia and the federal income tax is the sole tax. The federal government was able to maintain this dominance in peacetime, mainly through the grants power in the Constitution, which the High Court held permitted the federal government to make grants to the states conditional on the states not levying an income tax.

The federal government also has the exclusive constitutional power to levy customs and excise duties, a provision originally intended to produce a customs union within Australia. The High Court has interpreted this power widely to include the imposition of sales taxes so that the states are effectively excluded from the major modern tax bases. Australia does not have a history of levying social security taxes, which in any event would almost certainly be at the federal level under constitutional powers conferred on the federal government by referendum in 1946 with respect to the social security area. Instead, the federal government requires employers to contribute to private retirement funds for their employees, a policy enforced through a tax imposed in the event of a failure to contribute.

3 TAX RATES

The Table shows the federal income tax rates for resident individuals in 2023-24 and from 2024-25:

2023-24		*2024-25*	
AUD 0-18,200	0%	AUD 0-18,200	0%
AUD 18,201-45,000	19%	AUD 18,201-45,000	16%
AUD 45,001-120,000	32.5%	AUD 45,001-135,000	30%
AUD 120,001-180,000	37%	AUD 135,001-190,000	37%
AUD 180,001 and above	45%	AUD 190,001 and above	45%

There are various tax credits for low-income earners, which raise the zero bracket higher in many cases. In addition, all taxable income of individuals is subject to the 2% Medicare levy (which can increase to 3.5% for individuals who do not also carry private health insurance) which, as its name suggests, is designed to offset a (small) part of the cost of Australia's universal health-care system. This levy is collected as part of the income tax and is not treated as a social security tax by the OECD. There is a phase-in of the levy at lower levels of income so that it is not collected from the very poor, but the phase-in is recaptured by a surcharge so that, above moderate levels of income, it operates as a flat-rate charge. As a result, the maximum individual rate is usually treated as 47%; this rate is used in fact in most legislation, which is designed to levy tax at top rates on, for example, the undistributed income of trusts. The FBT rate is also 47%.

Australia uses a taxable/taxable/exempt (TTE) (or, more accurately (ttE), with *t* indicating a concessional rate of tax) method for its retirement-income system, imposing tax at the rate of 15% on contributions to resident pension funds in the hands of the fund (and a further 15% tax collected from members whose income exceeds AUD 250,000); tax at 15% on the earnings of funds (with a proposal to increase the rate to 30% for earnings on account balances greater than AUD 3 million); benefits received after the age of 60 are generally exempt.

The corporate tax rate is a flat 30% for most public and large private companies. Small companies (those with turnover under AUD 50 million and no more than 80% passive income) are currently taxed at 25%. There are a few isolated cases where different corporate tax rates are charged; for example, pooled development funds generally pay tax at 25% (these funds provide venture capital to small and medium-sized enterprises).

4 COMPOSITION OF THE FISCAL SYSTEM

It follows from the constitutional situation discussed above that the states in Australia are denied direct access to the major tax bases. The states are thus forced to rely on a miscellany of taxes (mainly payroll tax, stamp duties on a variety of transactions, and taxes on land and motor vehicles) for about half their revenues, the remaining half coming in the form of grants from the federal government. With the introduction of the GST on July 1, 2000, and the provision of this revenue by the federal government to the states in lieu of general-purpose grants which had previously been made, some (but not all) of the pressure has been taken off the imbalance in the revenue-raising capacities of the respective tiers of government. Including the GST as, in effect, a state tax means that the federal government raises 70% of total taxes and the states 30%. Special-purpose grants are still used to provide federal money to the states (e.g., for the financing of public hospitals and major infrastructure).

The major tax by far in Australia is the federal income tax (including the FBT). According to the most recent data in the OECD Global Revenue Statistics Database, taxes on personal income and corporate profits account for about 62% of total tax revenue collected in Australia. The predominance of the income tax in Australia has existed for many years. Since the OECD first began to collect statistics in 1965, it has been in excess of 50% of total taxation. Even when the federal income tax became the only income tax in Australia during World War II, the income tax represented 42% of total revenues. According to the OECD information, total taxes have consistently hovered around 30% of the Gross Domestic Product (GDP) since the 1980s. Thus, Australia can claim to have one of the lowest tax-to-GDP ratios in the OECD, but the comparison is somewhat misleading because Australia does not impose social security taxes and some instruments (such as the compulsory employer contributions to private pension funds, currently at 11.5% of an employee's wages) are not classified as taxes.

5 BASIC STRUCTURE OF THE INCOME TAX

Nominally, Australia has a global income tax system since the basic inclusion provision covers income according to ordinary concepts (what the courts have held to be income) without reference to categories or sources of income. There are many specific inclusion provisions dealing with particular kinds of income (called statutory income), although it is still the case that the vast majority of assessable income in Australia enters the tax base through the basic concept of ordinary income. Despite the apparently global nature of income, in fleshing out the concept, the Australian courts have adopted a fairly narrow approach to what income is. This outcome can be attributed to a number of influences.

First, although Australian judges have always recognized that the Australian system is structured quite differently from the explicit schedular nature of the UK system, nonetheless, UK case-law concepts have often been applied in determining whether specific items are income, and in this way, the UK schedules and concept of sources of income have influenced developments in Australia. This explains why, for example, gambling and lottery winnings are not included in the general concept of income.

Second, as in the UK, which has always had a category of "other income" in its schedular structure, there are deeper and more ancient sources at work. A major influential concept of income which existed in the law during the period when the income tax was introduced in the UK and Australia was the trust law concept of income. Trust law distinguishes between the capital and the income beneficiaries of the trust, with the capital beneficiaries being entitled to any increments in the value of the property of the trust which generates its income. The influence of trust law has been most apparent in the exclusion of capital gains from the basic concept of income in the UK and Australia.

Third, accounting concepts of profit have had an influence, but since Australia does not often use accounting concepts explicitly in the tax legislation in dealing with business income (in contrast to the UK), the influence has been muted in Australia.

The general valuation rule adopted in the income tax in Australia has also followed that used in the UK, being the amount of money into which a nonmonetary item can be converted. Historically, this was a significant limiting factor in the taxation of benefits in kind, although the lack of detailed valuation rules and administrative unwillingness to issue them were also important. Two doctrines which seem to be more peculiarly Australian have been the cause of limitations on the income concept. First, it is clearly established that there is no doctrine that the reimbursement of an expense which is deductible to a taxpayer amounts to income (although it may be income in certain cases, such as general business receipts). Second, the Australian courts have held that where an amount is received in a lump sum which has income and non-income elements, it is not possible to apportion out the income elements (unless there is a clear agreement between the parties to the payment on the breakdown of the amount) and the whole is treated as not being income.

In the tax reform of the 1980s, the introduction of a CGT and an FBT added significantly to the tax base and overcame most of these problems, although, curiously, there still has been no direct and general abolition of the basic valuation and apportionment rules which limit the amount brought into income.

Although the Australian system has thus adopted many of the limiting features of the UK schedular system, the nominal global nature of the system means that many of the features of the UK system are not applied. In particular, generally speaking, special rules have not been enacted for the detailed treatment of different categories of income, with the result that all items of income are included on a current-year basis and losses on one type of income generally can be offset against other income (the major exception here being capital losses). Australia has also not been as much influenced by the UK source concept as has, say, Canada, although from time to time there are hints of such a concept. For example, it is still unclear to what extent losses arising from a particular income-earning activity which has come to an end can be deducted.

On the deduction side, Australia has a general deduction provision covering most deductions incurred to earn income. This provision does not apply to capital items, so it is necessary to find specific provisions dealing with capital expenses. Over the years, these specific provisions have been constantly extended on a piecemeal basis to the point where they cover most categories of capital expenses. In 2001, the rules on wasting capital expenses were consolidated and extended in the uniform capital allowances regime, and in 2006, the range of recoverable capital items was further extended, although the coverage is still not complete.

Australia applies essentially the same calculation of taxable income to all taxpayers, including individuals and companies, under the same statutory provisions. There are some special rules which apply to companies, such as trafficking in company losses, value shifting, intercorporate dividends, the imputation system, and the controlled foreign company regime, and, in recent years, an increasing number of special rules for small businesses. In addition, there is a special 50% tax concession for capital gains earned by individuals.

6 TAX LEGISLATION

6.1 Legislative Process

The Constitution requires that tax bills originate in the House of Representatives (the popularly elected House of Parliament, as opposed to the Senate, which has the same number of senators from each state) and that they deal with only one subject of taxation. The latter requirement has led to some fragmentation of tax legislation, with the result that most tax measures consist of one law spelling out the tax base and another law (or several laws) actually imposing the tax.

Typically, a tax bill takes several months to complete passage through Parliament, partly because the Senate prefers to have a committee report on a bill, which means that two sittings of the Senate are necessary for the legislation to pass. It is not uncommon for tax bills to take considerably longer periods to pass if the matter is very controversial or an election intervenes, as all bills lapse when an election is called and must be reintroduced. Federal elections are held on a three-year cycle in Australia.

All important tax bills originate from the government (the party or parties which control the House of Representatives under the Westminster system of government used in Australia). Although the government of the day in Australia, apart from one recent brief period, has not controlled the Senate for many years and may have to negotiate with minor parties for important or controversial legislation to pass, generally, the government (or, more accurately, the civil service) rather than the legislature is the driving force for tax policy and legislation in Australia. Tax legislation is so complex that most members of Parliament do not understand it. Apart from major tax reforms, there is an ongoing tax legislation program arising from various policy announcements from the government. In a typical year, there are about ten bills dealing with taxation which add 500 pages, and sometimes much more, to existing tax legislation.

One highly undesirable feature of the legislative process is that tax legislation is routinely made retrospective to its announcement date, a practice which, unlike in some other countries, does not create any constitutional issues in Australia. Initially, this practice was confined to tax avoidance measures but now applies even where the legislation concerns systemic issues. The Senate has adopted procedural rules to curb the worst features of this practice—unless the legislation is introduced into Parliament within six months after announcement, the Senate will generally pass the legislation only on a prospective basis, although this procedure is not always honored. Legislation which may have been consistent with the announcement when introduced may then be subject to major changes in Parliament, resulting in considerable uncertainty for taxpayers.

6.2 Statutory Style

From the 1960s, Australian income tax legislation began to be drafted in a peculiarly turgid and convoluted style out of a desire by the drafter to anticipate all possible applications of the specific statutory rules and to prevent their abuse. This approach can be blamed partly on the literal, nit-picking approach to interpretation of tax legislation formerly used by judges. However, at least part of the responsibility or blame seems to rest with the unsatisfactory drafting arrangements which existed in Australia, where the Office of Parliamentary Counsel (OPC) had a monopoly on drafting; coordination between this Office, the policy makers in Treasury, and the technical and administrative people in the Australian Taxation Office (ATO) had not worked very well, judging by the results (although Australia is by no means alone in having incomprehensible tax legislation).

By the early 1990s, the ITAA 1936 could lay claim to the dubious twin titles of being the longest income tax statute in the world and the most unreadable. By that time, the basic income tax statute, the ITAA 1936, was approaching 6,000 pages in length and, together with ancillary legislation such as the FBT and the International Tax Agreements Act, occupied four volumes more than 20 centimeters thick, printed on wafer-thin pages in closely crowded type. To the original 126 pages of 1936, a total of 500 pages were added in the four decades to 1976, a total of 1,000 pages in the next decade to 1986, and more than double the existing amount of legislation in the decade to 1996 (this explosion in growth being attributable to the extensive tax reform starting in the mid-1980s as well as the ongoing battle with tax avoidance). Australia's income tax, FBT, GST, and related laws consumed almost 13,000 pages and more than 9.5 million words before a clean-out in 2006. The problem is compounded by including virtually all the rules in legislation and leaving little or nothing to regulations (unlike the United States (U.S.), which, with Code and Regulations combined, can still claim to be the world champion in terms of total verbiage).

Not surprisingly, the bulk and complexity of the legislation have attracted criticism, especially from tax professionals, and there have been several attempts to deal with the problem, none of them successful to date. First, in the period 1994-1998, the government invested substantial resources in the Tax Law Improvement Project, whose brief was to redraft the legislation in a plain-English, user-friendly form without, however, effecting any significant changes in policy or meaning. By 1998, about one-third of the 1936 Act had been rewritten and enacted in tranches into the ITAA 1997. With the use of diagrams, flow charts, signposts, lists, etc., this redraft was easier to follow and eliminated some of the bulk. The redraft adopted the unusual approach of addressing the taxpayer as "you" so that the basic charging provision now reads "[Y]ou must pay income tax for each year ending on 30 June."

When the Liberal National government embarked on its major tax reform program in 1998, it abandoned the Tax Law Improvement Project part-way through. The project had been widely criticized as cosmetic, and there were constant arguments over whether various redrafted provisions had changed the underlying law. The government proposed to address the underlying causes of complexity. An ambitious proposal to redraft the whole legislation in a different structure was, however, abandoned after some years' work, although a significant project to identify and eliminate inoperative provisions in tax legislation proceeded and got rid of a few thousand pages (including, as it turned out, some operative provisions!).

There were also considerable changes in the policy and legislative process within the bureaucracy. A non-statutory but independent advisory body, the Board of Taxation, was created in 2000 and regularly reviews major substantive tax policy issues for the government (such as international taxation and the taxation of collective investment vehicles). The Board also investigated tax policy and legislation drafting processes, and the government adopted its recommendations. Policy, administrative, and drafting issues were proposed to be approached in an iterative and interactive way rather than in the linear way which had previously applied (Treasury developed policy, passed the outcome to the ATO to develop drafting instructions, which passed them to OPC to draft the legislation). The main concrete consequences of the current process are much more consultation on tax measures and the movement of ATO staff to the Treasury. The drafting monopoly of OPC remains. The current fashion used by OPC in drafting tax provisions (so-called principles-based drafting) has seen a preference for using generic terms (e.g., "financial benefit" rather than "money or property") and drafting provisions which describe their intended targets and the desired outcomes with calculated imprecision. The new style has resulted in legislation which is just as prolix but with greater scope for uncertainty.

6.3 Statutory Interpretation

Until the early 1980s, Australian Courts adopted a very strict literal approach to the interpretation of tax legislation, excluding any reference to extrinsic materials or the purpose of the legislature except insofar as that purpose was ascertainable from the words used. The approach is typified in the following quote:

> It is for the Parliament to specify, and to do so, in my opinion as far as language will permit, with unambiguous clarity, the circumstances which will attract an obligation on the part of the citizen to pay tax. The function of the court is to interpret and apply the language in which the Parliament has specified those circumstances.
>
> The court is to do so by determining the meaning of the words employed by the Parliament which is discoverable from the language used by the Parliament. It is not for the court to mould or to attempt to mould the language of the statute so as to produce some result which it might be thought the Parliament may have intended to achieve, although not expressed in the actual language employed. ...
>
> Parliament having prescribed the circumstances which will attract tax, or provide occasion for its reduction or elimination, the citizen has every right to mold the transaction into which he is about to enter into a form which satisfies the requirements of the statute. It is nothing to the point that he might have attained the same or similar result as that achieved by the transaction into which he in fact entered by some other transaction, which, if he had entered into it, would or might have involved him in a liability to tax, or to more tax than that attracted by the transaction into which he in fact entered. Nor can it matter that his choice of transaction was influenced wholly or in part by its effect upon his obligation to pay tax. The freedom to choose the form of transaction into which he shall enter is basic to the maintenance of a free society.[1]

From this time, three related developments have substantially improved the interpretation process, although it still can hardly be described as ideal. First, judges began to take a more purposive approach to their interpretation of tax legislation and to permit themselves to look at extrinsic material on their own motion. Second, the Acts Interpretation Act 1901, which contains many rules for the interpretation of

1. Chief Justice Barwick in *Westraders Pty Ltd* [1980] HCA 24, 144 CLR 55, 60-61. The Barwick court (1965-1981) is widely regarded as having taken literal, indeed taxpayer-biased, interpretations to extremes.

statutes, was amended to require a purposive approach in interpretation and access to extrinsic material where the statute was ambiguous. This both confirmed and encouraged the change in judicial attitude which was already underway. Third, the approach to drafting legislation began to change, as already noted, and more detailed, organized, and helpful explanatory memoranda began to be produced (the explanatory memorandum is the official government explanation which is introduced into Parliament at the same time as the legislation). The Tax Law Improvement Project, mentioned above, was intended to be the culmination of this process, but, as we have seen, it was not, and the story is still unfolding. Despite these changes and apart from whether statutory complexity can be eradicated, it remains to be seen whether a coherent and sustainable system of interpretation involving the cooperation of the legislature, the courts, and the administration will emerge.

The following explanation of the interpretive process is representative of the current approach:[2]

> It is now clear, if it ever was in dispute, that the task of construction is not one simply of taking each word used in a statute and applying the dictionary meaning of that word to arrive at a conclusion. The task is not as mechanical as that. While it is clear that the construction of a statute will commence with the words used and that it is a good start to assume that the words mean what they say, that is only a start to the process ....

However, the English language is seldom so clear and unambiguous that only one construction is open. It is for that reason that in judicial decisions in recent times which have discussed the process of construction, great importance has been attached to "context." Perhaps the most famous and often-cited passage to this effect is to be found in the judgment of the High Court in *CIC Insurance Ltd v. Bankstown Football Club Limited*, where Brennan CJ, Dawson, Toohey, and Gummow JJ, in a joint judgment, wrote:

> It is well settled that at common law, apart from any reliance upon s 15AB of Acts Interpretation Act 1901 (Cth), the court may have regard to reports of law reform bodies to ascertain the mischief which a statute is intended to cure. Moreover, the modern approach to statutory interpretation (a) insists that the context be considered in the first instance, not merely at some later stage when ambiguity might be thought to arise, and (b) uses "context" in its widest sense to include such things as the existing state of the law and the mischief which, by legitimate means such as those just mentioned, one may discern the statute was intended to remedy. Instances of general words in a statute being so constrained by their context are numerous. In particular, ... if the apparently plain words of a provision are read in the light of the mischief which the statute was designed to overcome and of the objects of the legislation, they may wear a very different appearance. Further, inconvenience or improbability of result may assist the court in preferring to the literal meaning an alternative construction which, by the steps identified above, is reasonably open and more closely conforms to the legislative intent.

2. *MLC Limited* [2002] FCA 1491, 126 FCR 37 at paras. 31-32, Hill, J.

In practice, judicial interpretation of tax legislation is arrayed along a continuum between literal and purposive, although not so apparently aligned with the political and philosophical views of judges as in the U.S.

7 COURTS DEALING WITH TAX MATTERS

7.1 Appeal Processes

Australia does not have a specialized tax court, although there is a long history of administrative tribunals with expertise in tax matters. Apart from significant constitutional differences between courts and tribunals, the main practical difference is that tribunals are part of the executive and generally stand in the shoes of the administrator when making decisions; therefore, they can re-exercise discretions which the administrator has. On appeal to a court, the administrative exercise of discretions can be challenged only on grounds recognized in administrative law, such as a decision being ultra vires.

When the ATO makes a tax assessment on a taxpayer, the first step in the appeal process is an objection to the assessment. This leads to a reconsideration of the assessment by the ATO. If the assessment stands after reconsideration, the taxpayer may ask for the decision to be reviewed by the Administrative Review Tribunal (ART) or appeal to the Federal Court. Hearings before the ART are in private, can be relatively informal (with the taxpayer often appearing in person), involve smaller appeal fees, and do not lead to orders for costs (i.e., each party effectively bears its own costs of the appeal). The ART has conference procedures designed to settle matters before they come to a hearing. Court appeals are relatively formal matters, with parties represented by lawyers who make extensive oral and written submissions. Costs follow the event in the usual case (i.e., the loser pays the winner's legal costs). The ATO runs a test-case program under which it will fund the taxpayer's legal expenses if the ATO desires to test a matter of important principle in the courts.

In any appeal, the onus is on the taxpayer to prove that the assessment is incorrect. The onus does not have great practical significance except in cases where the ATO has assessed on the basis of unexplained assets held by taxpayers which do not accord with their income tax returns (i.e., where the ATO considers that the taxpayer is concealing income). Written reasons, often very lengthy, are provided for all decisions and set out the facts, the law, and the reasoning by which the decision was reached. Virtually all tax decisions are publicly available in electronic form and are produced by commercial publishers in hard copy. The commencement of an appeal does not suspend the obligation to pay the tax in dispute, but generally, the ATO will suspend recovery proceedings while an appeal is underway (often on condition of payment of a proportion of the tax in dispute).

If the taxpayer has sought a review by the AAT, any further appeal to the Federal Court (single judge) can be only on a matter of law. From the Federal Court, there is a right of appeal to the Full Federal Court (three judges) on matters of law; from there, appeal to the High Court of Australia (five to seven judges) is not automatic but requires the leave of that Court. In some tax administration and collection situations, cases can be heard in the state rather than federal courts. Decisions of higher courts are binding on lower courts and tribunals. At any level of appeal, it is usual, but not obligatory, to follow previous decisions at that level on the same legal issue.

The ATO receives about 42 million tax returns every year, of which 700,000 were adjusted after review by the ATO (2022-2023). Taxpayers objected to about 23,000 of these adjustments. Disputes which proceed to litigation, whether before the ART or a court, are extremely rare: only 388 cases were initiated in 2022-2023.

7.2 Judicial Expertise

Tax was probably the first area in Australia to have specialist administrative tribunals (originally called Boards of Review). The Boards of Review were comprised of three members—one from the ATO, one accountant, and one lawyer. Because of the influence of the ATO in the appointments, the Boards were often regarded as pro-tax administration. By a quirk of the federal constitution, tax appeals from the Boards went directly to the High Court of Australia, the highest court in the land. For a time, the system worked well since the best judges in Australia had a certain expertise in taxation and usually produced sensible decisions.

The High Court managed to dispense with its constitutional jurisdiction in tax matters, first to state courts and then to the newly created Federal Court of Australia in the latter part of the 1970s. When the Boards were replaced in the 1980s, a Tax Division (now in the ART) was created, but the membership of that Division includes many members who do not have previous experience in taxation. There are some judges on the Federal Court who were tax specialists prior to appointment, and several others are regularly involved in tax appeals. No Federal Court judge works full-time on tax matters.

In the period from 1965 to 1981, the High Court under Chief Justice Barwick was generally regarded as strongly pro-taxpayer. Since then, the courts are generally regarded as having moved to a position which favors the tax administration against the taxpayer.

8 TAX ADMINISTRATION

Administration of the income tax (and other federal taxes) in Australia is a huge enterprise, one of the biggest in the country. The ATO has about 19,000 staff or one staff member per 1,400 population, and an annual operating budget of about AUD 4.5 billion. The administration of the income tax has been through several major changes and upheavals over the last forty years. The changes started in 1984 and have continued relentlessly since. The Australian experience reflects that of several other countries, which can be attributed to increasing international administrative sharing of experience and cooperation through the OECD and other mechanisms.

One catalyst for change was the Australian Audit Office, which produced a number of highly critical efficiency audits of the ATO in the mid-1980s (and was followed by major reviews by the House of Representatives Standing Committee on Finance and Public Administration in the late 1980s and by the Parliamentary Joint Committee on Public Accounts in the early 1990s). Such audits and parliamentary scrutiny are ongoing, but nowadays the ATO usually accepts and often anticipates the recommendations and works much more cooperatively with its many oversight bodies, which also include the Inspector General of Taxation and Tax Ombudsman, who deals both with systemic tax administration issues and some individual cases in the ombudsman role.

Australia has long had a system of universal filing of tax returns by taxpayers. There were 42 million returns received in the 2022-2023 year, including 12 million individual returns (Australia has a population of about 26.8 million). Until the mid-1980s, all tax returns were manually processed by officers who issued assessments on the basis of the returns as lodged with virtually no scrutiny or follow-up audit activity. Where the officer did not agree with the return as filed, an assessment was issued with an adjustment sheet (handwritten with special purple pens), and the taxpayer could then object to the assessment, which initiated the appeal process. While many cases were settled at this stage, there was very little direct contact between tax officials and taxpayers, matters being dealt with by correspondence. Most of the non-assessment resources of the ATO were devoted to withholding, collection, and appeals.

In the mid-1980s, the ATO took the first tentative steps toward self-assessment for companies (which was finally completed in the early 1990s) and self-assessment now effectively applies to all taxpayers. Individuals still do not pay tax when filing a return and receive a computer-generated formal notice of assessment advising tax due, whereas companies calculate their income and tax payable themselves. The most obvious initial effect of this change was to move resources out of assessing into audit, and, for the first time, many taxpayers actually came face-to-face with tax officers. In particular, large corporate audits generated a lot of heat and were not assisted from a public relations point of view by well-publicized dawn raids on banks and professionals seeking copies of documents about suspected tax schemes.

In the early 1990s, client service became a focus of activities of the ATO, with audit activity being reduced from late-1980s levels (when coverage was still not great) and resources moved into service areas. A non-statutory Taxpayers' Charter was introduced by the ATO in this context. In the late 1990s and early 2000s, much of the ATO's resources were devoted to implementing the extensive tax reform announced in 1998, and audit activity more or less ceased. Tax shelter promoters took advantage of this opportunity so that audit and enforcement once again became an urgent priority when the ATO returned to business as usual. The current ATO approach is a mix of carrots (service) and sticks (audits and penalties) based on a fairly sophisticated risk-assessment process and compliance model, as well as so-called real-time tax administration, under which the ATO tries to monitor what is happening in the real world of tax on a current basis rather than finding out only when tax returns are lodged sometime later.

Individual taxpayers responded to the changes in tax administration and the increasing complexity of the tax system following various tax reforms by continuing to use the help of professional tax-return preparers called tax agents (over 65% now use tax agents, a figure which has remained fairly constant). During its client-service phase, the ATO in turn produced a variety of products designed to assist individuals in preparing their own tax returns. The ATO is trying to get this population to adopt electronic filing; currently, about 32% of individuals prepare their own tax returns and file them online. The ATO now electronically pre-fills tax returns using information already in the possession of the ATO. Redesigning the system to reduce the number of individuals who must engage with the income tax has not been pursued; instead, the emphasis has been on the ATO collecting ever more information from third parties, in real time, and then requiring taxpayers to review and validate those reports.

With respect to tax administration for business taxpayers, as noted earlier, the 1998 tax reform had significant impacts on tax collection. Withholding on employment income by business has existed for many years in Australia, along with tax installment systems for business income. In the late 1980s, the tax file number used for many years within the ATO for internal tracking of files was given a formal statutory basis and began to be used for reporting and backup withholding purposes in relation to investment income, with some significant improvements in detection and compliance. At the same time, the collection and information matching capabilities of the ATO were greatly improved through the use of technology. Annual federal budgets regularly contain quite significant forecasts of revenue increases arising from improvements in administration based around technology, largely affecting business and thus requiring large tax technology investments by business as well as by the ATO.

The introduction of the GST was used as an opportunity for extending the tax-collection system. An Australian Business Number (ABN) was introduced which is effectively compulsory for taxpayers registered for GST. Even if they are not registered for GST, taxpayers with business income are well advised to obtain an ABN since otherwise payments received by them from other businesses are subject to withholding at 47% (so-called no-ABN withholding). This system has flushed out many habitual non-filers of income tax returns, including a number of senior lawyers who have subsequently been struck off the rolls of practicing barristers. Current GST turnover also began to be used to make installment payments of tax more current. Effectively, an installment rate for business income is derived from the previous year's income tax return as a percentage of turnover; that rate is then applied to the current monthly or quarterly turnover, depending on whether installments are due monthly or quarterly.

To implement these changes, a two-page Business Activity Statement was introduced to replace virtually all the various forms which were used previously for withholding and installment payments of tax.

The inexorable trend in all these developments has been for the ATO to require more information, from more sources, delivered in real time, and sent to it electronically, permitting greater levels of data matching and the automated identification of suspicious transactions and errors.

Compliance costs in Australia (which a number of 1990s studies suggested were already the highest in the world) are generally thought to have risen following tax reform. The difficulties in the relationship between the ATO and large businesses which emerged with self-assessment have not gone away. The ATO has responded by implementing a system for the independent review of its decisions affecting some large corporate taxpayers prior to litigation as well as various forms of compliance agreements with large businesses.

For tax professionals, there have also been important changes over this period. Self-assessment was accompanied by an expectation from government that the ATO would issue extensive public and private rulings which would be legally binding on the ATO. An informal private ruling system had been in operation for many years, and nonbinding public rulings began to be issued in 1982 as part of the introduction of freedom of information legislation in Australia. In 1992, legislation was passed formalizing this process (as part of the final stages of self-assessment), which led to significant growth in the number of public and private rulings. Public income tax rulings were issued on matters of general principle, although the number of these rulings has declined in the last decade. Public income tax rulings were also issued for transactions affecting significant numbers of taxpayers (such as capital-management activities by large listed companies) or involving widely marketed investment products. As a result of the 1998 tax reform, individuals with simple tax affairs can now obtain binding oral rulings for which the ATO has an elaborate recording system. After some scandals with private tax rulings and some technical problems with the original legislation (such as contesting private rulings before the courts), a review of self-assessment in 2004 led to a rewrite of the binding rulings legislation without changing its basic principles. Although nominally available to taxpayers directly, the great bulk of important ruling requests are handled through tax professionals.

With the substantial role played by tax agents noted above, questions about their regulation and professional standards have been raised, as well as the responsibilities of tax professionals more broadly. Legislation on the regulation of tax agents was enacted in 2009 to try to regulate the profession and codify the professional responsibilities of agents. In 2006, civil penalties were introduced for promoters of tax exploitation schemes, which generally are schemes caught by the general anti-avoidance rule (discussed below). The definition of "promoter" is broad and could apply to tax professionals, although "merely" providing advice about a scheme is excluded.

Under the private rulings system, the ATO receives a lot of unsolicited information about current taxpayer practices spontaneously: taxpayers seek the certainty of a binding ruling but in the process have to divulge the precise details of their proposed transaction. In 2016, the government decided to add a stick to this carrot: it announced that it will adopt the recommendations arising from BEPS Action 12 and require advisers to notify the ATO about some of the activities of their clients. The relevant legislation has not yet appeared and so the ATO filled the void in the interim, requiring some taxpayers to disclose more detailed information about "reportable positions" in their income tax returns.

9 GENERAL PRINCIPLES

9.1 Relation of Tax and Financial Accounting

The Australian courts generally give tax legislation primacy over accounting principles. The legislation nominally uses the global system and does not adopt "profits" as the measure of business income. It is thus easy to interpret the legislation as setting out its own criteria for taxability completely independent of accounting rules. Given that at many crucial points the legislation does not provide specific guidance on computing income or timing rules, the courts have sometimes adopted accounting principles as the guide in such cases, but the attitude is very much take it or leave it, as suits the particular judge. So far as any trend can be discerned, the courts seem over time to be moving toward greater consistency with accounting principles.

However, there are a number of situations where, rather than rely on financial accounting concepts, the legislation specifies its own bespoke tax accounting rules for transactions, partly arising out of bad judicial decisions. Moreover, there are now an increasing number of specific instances (particularly involving large multinational enterprises) where the drafters have decided it is simpler to adopt for tax purposes the position taken in financial accounting. Examples can be seen in the rules regulating financial instruments and in the thin capitalization regime. The OECD inspired global minimum tax will formally tie the measures in this regime to financial accounting. Where these statutory rules adopt "generally accepted accounting concepts" or the position in the audited financial accounts, changes to the accounting standards and practices will flow through into the tax system.

During the tax reform commencing in 1998, there was a debate about whether it would be better to leave the determination of business income to accounting concepts, with differing views on the potential for simplification of the legislation. The Ralph Review of Business Taxation ultimately rejected a European-style approach of explicitly adopting accounting concepts into the tax law. However, it did propose that differences between tax and accounting be systematically identified and removed where there was no clear policy reason for the difference.

9.2 Respect for Legal Form

Unless a transaction can be characterized as a sham, in the sense of not having under general law the legal effect that it purports to have, the courts generally respect the form of the transaction adopted for income tax purposes. Thus, the transfer of a right to income which is effective under property law is generally regarded as carrying the income with it for tax purposes (although there is specific legislation directed at this result for shorter-term assignments). Similarly, the sale and leaseback of an asset are respected rather than recast as secured financing, and it has been held that an embezzler was not assessable on interest earned on embezzled funds because the interest was subject to a constructive trust in favor of the company embezzled.[3]

There is, however, no uniform practice on this matter. Courts have been prepared to look at substance in the area of services income (whether payments under restrictive covenants are for genuine restrictions or not), but in the area of deductions, some of the most problematic court decisions in fostering tax avoidance elevated form over substance (e.g., what was really purchase price became deductible if given the form of rent for the use of the property).

Relatedly, there has been debate in cases as to whether tax motivations for transactions can affect the tax outcome—the traditional answer, as found in the quote from Barwick, CJ in *Westraders* above, has been no. After acceptance in the lower courts, the High Court of Australia rejected the UK judicial doctrine of fiscal nullity on the basis that there is a statutory anti-avoidance regime, so that judicial activism is unnecessary. Nonetheless, in some cases, including High Court cases, deductions have been denied on the basis that the expenses were tax-motivated. For example, in a complex annuity scheme which featured large interest deductions early in the period of the annuity and most of the income toward the end, with a power to unwind the transaction before the income arose, the High Court said that where income exceeded deductions, generally there was no need to look at motivation.[4] However, if deductions exceeded income, then motivation was relevant and if, in this case, the parties intended to unwind the scheme before the income arose (as was ultimately found to be the case), then the interest deduction was reduced to the amount of income derived in each year. Similarly, a lower court found that a collapsing prepaid interest scheme did not work because the purpose of paying the interest was to obtain a tax deduction and not to earn income, so it failed the income-earning test of the statute.[5] Once again, however, it is difficult to find consistency of approach in the courts.

9.3 Tax Avoidance and Anti-avoidance Legislation

The former manual assessment system and the apparent taxpayer bias of the judiciary from the mid-1960s encouraged very aggressive tax-avoidance activities by taxpayers and their advisers, which still lingers today. There was little chance of getting caught and if they did, then as likely as not, the courts would uphold the scheme. As a result, a large-scale publicly marketed tax-avoidance industry flourished from about the mid-1970s which to some extent made the payment of tax optional. The government was initially slow to react to these developments and the early amendments were themselves full of loopholes, which suggested to some observers tacit acceptance of the industry by the government.

By the late 1970s, when lengthy, unreadable anti-avoidance legislation seemed to have closed off most of the abuses, advertisements still appeared in the financial press offering to purchase companies for the value of their pre-tax income (less a percentage,

3. *Zobory* [1995] FCA 1226, 64 FCR 86.
4. *Fletcher* [1991] HCA 42, 173 CLR 1.
5. *Gwynvill Properties Pty Ltd* [1986] FCA 273, 13 FCR 138.

being the purchaser's fee or commission). There was no shortage of sellers who did not stay to ask what was being done with the companies (the assumption being that they would be put into a tax scheme which wiped out their tax liability). It came to the surface in a royal commission, investigating a notorious labor union heavily involved in criminal activities, that the companies were simply being stripped of their assets by the purchasers, dummy directors with criminal backgrounds appointed, and the records of the companies destroyed (metaphorically consigned to the "bottom of the harbor" as the scandal came to be called—that is, Sydney Harbor—although the activities were by no means confined to Sydney).

The legislative reaction was very severe. It was made a specific criminal offense to render a company unable to pay its tax (although, arguably, the general criminal law already had this result), and more importantly, retrospective legislation was passed making the vendors of the shares in the companies liable for the company tax which was not paid, even where small listed companies were involved. A new general anti-avoidance rule was enacted which overcame the defects of the previous rule. A significant share of resources of the ATO was involved in the exercise well into the 1980s. This included attacking not only the "bottom of the harbor" cases but also many of the real avoidance schemes. There was considerable success in the courts as the judicial tide turned (one notorious 1974 High Court of Australia case, often considered to be the start of the real "rot," was ultimately reversed in 1989).[6]

One of the root causes of the problem in a policy sense was the combination of a classical corporate tax system with no CGT so that most share sales were tax-free. The policy remedy came with the tax reform of 1985, introducing an imputation system of company taxation and a CGT. At the same time, the tax administration was undergoing its own reform, as noted above, partly to ensure that the same debacle could never occur in the future. This development, combined with the not-surprising suspicion of the tax profession among tax administrators arising from the tax-avoidance era, has meant that relations between the profession and the tax administration remain somewhat strained despite expressions and intentions of goodwill and cooperation on both sides.

Tax planning went into a less aggressive mode in the 1980s—rather than seeking to wipe out all tax liability through paper-shuffling, circular transactions, tax reduction through exploiting the debt-equity borderline, tax shelters of various kinds, tax planning using retirement-income vehicles, and timing differences became the main focus of attention, although more aggressive planning on the international scene was also evident. In the mid-1990s, however, the tax-avoidance industry began to flourish once again, partly as a result of the diversion of tax administration resources produced by the tax reform beginning in 1998, as noted above. Many employees who had bought into the schemes and been refunded virtually all the tax withheld on their employment income found that no action was forthcoming from the ATO to audit or challenge the schemes because of the ATO preoccupation on other fronts. The schemes consequently mushroomed, particularly among employees in the mining sector who combined

6. *Curran* [1974] HCA 46, 131 CLR 409, reversed in *John* [1989] HCA 5, 166 CLR 417.

(relatively) high levels of disposable income with low tax literacy, with tens of thousands of ordinary taxpayers participating. Once the ATO began to pursue the taxpayers after the main part of the 1998 reforms affecting administration had commenced, the issue became highly political and the ATO was forced to make very generous settlement offers. The government also decided to challenge the supply of tax-avoidance products by targeting the promoters of these schemes. As work on the schemes proceeded, it became evident that they were prevalent in all segments of the taxpayer population, including among well-paid executives and small businesses, and the efforts to clean them up took several years.

As a result, the ATO began litigating in a very significant way the anti-avoidance provision which had been passed in 1981 to deal with the previous round of tax avoidance, with a significant degree of success. Against this background, Australia's anti-avoidance rules can now be considered. The original provision was section 260, which read as follows:

> Every contract, agreement, or arrangement made or entered into, orally or in writing, ... shall so far as it purports to have the purpose or effect of in any way, directly or indirectly:
>
> a. altering the incidence of any income tax;
> b. relieving any person from liability to pay any income tax or make any return;
> c. defeating, evading, or avoiding any duty or liability imposed on any person by this Act; or
> d. preventing the operation of this Act in any respect, be absolutely void, as against the Commissioner, or in regard to any proceeding under this Act, but without prejudice to such validity as it may have in any other respect or for any other purpose.

Although there were ups and downs in the history, a series of decisions prior to 1980 deprived the provision of virtually any meaning. The major problems were as follows:

(1) With regard to the general inclusion and deduction provisions of the Act, the courts held that they had their own built-in protection if they were interpreted properly (which the courts had demonstrably failed to do) and so did not need the assistance of the anti-avoidance provision.

(2) With regard to the specific provisions of the Act, the courts held that where the legislation offered the taxpayer a choice, then the anti-avoidance provision did not apply if the taxpayer exercised such a choice. This was taken to extremes. For example, the Act has different rules for private and public companies and much elaborate tax planning was directed to avoiding characterization as a private company, which the courts held was the exercise of a choice.

(3) To supply the counterfactual for the application of the provision (what would have happened in the absence of the contract, etc.), the courts tended to look only to what the taxpayer did so that it seemed necessary for the taxpayer to start down one direction with a transaction and then change course midway

for tax reasons. A well-executed tax plan carried out from the very beginning was thus immune (the false-start principle).

(4) If the section applied, its effect was simply destructive of the contract, etc. It did not allow the Commissioner to construct an alternative that would give rise to tax; the tax liability had to be found in the ruins of the contract, etc.

The legislature enacted the more elaborate Part IVA to take the place of section 260. Under this Part, three elements have to be found: a scheme, a tax benefit, and an objective conclusion (not having regard to the parties' actual intentions) that the dominant purpose of the scheme was to obtain a tax benefit. A scheme is defined so broadly as to cover virtually any transaction, although the courts have held that it must be something which can stand and make sense on its own. A tax benefit is obtained when an amount is not included in assessable income of a taxpayer in a year of income where it would have been included, or might reasonably be expected to have been included if the scheme had not been entered into; there is a specific exclusion for elections under the Act, such as valuing inventory on the basis of cost or market value or electing to take a reinvestment rollover. A similar tax-benefit rule applies in the case of deductions, capital losses, withholding tax, and foreign tax credits. In determining whether the purpose of the scheme was to obtain the tax benefit, eight listed criteria, such as the form and substance of the scheme, the timing of the scheme, the change in financial positions that result from the scheme, and the connection between the parties, are used. When these criteria are satisfied, the Commissioner is given the power to determine that Part IVA applies.

Just what follows next, however, proved to be problematic. It seems to have been accepted that, for constitutional reasons, the law could not simply permit the ATO to impose tax on a basis which the ATO considered reasonable in the circumstances. Consequently, the legislation as originally drafted prescribed a rule stating that the taxpayer would be taxed on what they would have done, or might be expected to have done, instead of what they did. A series of cases followed where taxpayers and the ATO differed about what would have happened if the actual transaction had not occurred. This second-guessing of taxpayers' actions proved too problematic, and Parliament amended the provision to prescribe that taxpayers are to be taxed on the basis of a reasonable commercial alternative to the transaction they undertook.

At the time Part IVA was introduced, it was stated that it applied to transactions which were "blatant, artificial or contrived arrangements" as compared to "normal commercial transactions by which taxpayers legitimately take advantage of opportunities available for the arrangement of their affairs." It was successful in closing down the round-robin collapsible-paper schemes and for many years acted *in terrorem* against aggressive tax planning in genuine transactions.

As noted above, however, more recently considerable litigation has occurred, and is still occurring, over the operation of the rules. The High Court established the very important point that it is not a defense to obtaining a tax benefit to show that the taxpayer was just pursuing a commercial objective—that is, the rules go further than was stated at their time of introduction. Further, it is possible to look to professional advisers in deciding what the dominant purpose of the transaction was (taxpayers cannot claim exemption from the rules because they are ignorant of the complexities of the tax law). Thus, it is possible to apply the provision where the after-tax return on a deposit is higher if funds were artificially moved offshore to take advantage of an international exemption. Similarly, interposing a company between an Australian-resident company and a foreign-resident company to obtain an interest deduction which otherwise would have been quarantined to foreign income was struck down under the provision.[7]

The lower courts, however, initially had some difficulty in working out how much commerciality is enough. It was held that an offshore captive insurance arrangement was not subject to the rules,[8] nor was a sale and leaseback which significantly increased tax depreciation without any offsetting income[9] (these arrangements having been heavily marketed by merchant bankers). When the lower courts held that the rules did not apply to a split-loan product marketed by a financial institution, which increased deductibility of interest on an investment property by capitalizing interest on that property and paying off the principal of the part of the loan on the taxpayer's residence (interest on the latter type of loan being nondeductible), the High Court intervened again and held that the rules applied.[10] Since then, the lower courts have generally followed suit for the various schemes which were the subject of the latest round of mass marketing described above. Further, there is an increasing tendency for the courts to hold that, in any event, tax schemes do not comply with the particular provisions which they are trying to exploit. The lower courts have struggled in part because the government and legislature have never resolved satisfactorily the inherent conflict with anti-avoidance rules arising from tax concessions which encourage certain forms of activity and transactions.

Currently, the anti-avoidance rules are a significant deterrent to tax schemes. However, some wealthy taxpayers' greed seems to know no bounds, and, in view of the history recounted above, it is no surprise that some of them have gone underground and resorted to tax-evasion schemes offshore. In one such scheme, one of the "advisers" involved was raided in a Melbourne hotel and his computer was found to contain a list of clients. A round of prosecutions and extraditions involving some high-profile individuals followed in a project known as "Project Wickenby." The government has also become increasingly focused on solving the problem of the underground economy, establishing a Black Economy Taskforce, which made a number of recommendations directed at dealing with tax evasion of various kinds. One special area of focus has been the problem of "phoenix companies"—denuding companies of assets and directors in order to deprive the ATO of unpaid company tax and people to prosecute, which echoes the bottom-of-the-harbor era of the 1970s. The courts have been busy in recent years with desperate procedural actions by the

7. *Consolidated Press Holdings Ltd* [2001] HCA 32, 207 CLR 235.
8. *WD & HO Wills (Australia) Pty Ltd* [1996] FCA 1284, 65 FCR 298.
9. *Metal Manufactures Ltd* [2001] FCA 365, 108 FCR 150, *Eastern Nitrogen Ltd* [2001] FCA 366, 108 FCR 27.
10. *Hart* [2004] HCA 26, 217 CLR 216.

taxpayers concerned, but to date, the ATO has been largely successful in applying criminal and civil sanctions.

10 TAX TREATIES

Compared to many countries, Australia has a relatively modest and stable suite of bilateral income tax treaties, negotiated mostly with major trading partners and countries from which emigrants have arrived. It has comprehensive treaties with forty-six countries and an agreement with Taiwan, China. The treaties with Australia's trading partners are reviewed regularly, but many other treaties are now quite old, and while there have been signs that the government is keen to update treaties and expand the treaty network, there has been little progress. Australia also has thirty-six Tax Information Exchange Agreements (TIEAs) with tax havens, signed between 2007 and 2013. Some of these TIEAs are accompanied by separate additional-benefits agreements containing a few substantive tax rules. The appetite for negotiating individual agreements appears to have ceased once Australia signed the *Convention on Mutual Administrative Assistance in Tax Matters* in 2011, and it seems unlikely that any more Agreements will be added.

Australia's tax treaties generally follow the OECD Model Treaty, although there are several important departures, some reflecting oddities of the Australian income tax system and others reflecting Australian tax policy positions (and because many of Australia's treaties are quite old, reflecting policy positions which are no longer current):

- Because of the way Australia taxes fringe benefits provided to employees, several modifications to the OECD Model have been made in a few recent treaties. The tax imposed on employers is included as a covered tax and a special article gives the right to tax fringe benefits to the country which has the sole or primary taxing right with respect to salaries, wages, and other remuneration, attempting to align the treatment of the tax on fringe benefits with the treatment of other kinds of employee income for treaty purposes.
- Australia used to depart from the OECD Model by including a "deemed source of income" rule. This article explicitly changed Australian domestic law by conferring an Australian source on any income which "may be taxed" by Australia under the treaty. This article means the treaty is acting "as a sword," potentially increasing Australia's tax claims. Two recent decisions have confirmed the operation of the article: amounts earned by a non-resident company which met the definition of "royalty" became Australian source income and amenable to Australian income tax on that basis.[11] The treaty rule has now been legislated in domestic law, reinstating the usual order that claims to tax must be asserted in domestic law.

11. *Tech Mahindra Ltd v. Commissioner of Taxation* [2016] FCAFC 130; *Satyam Computer Services Ltd v. Commissioner of Taxation* [2018] FCAFC 172.

- Australia insists on imposing tax on royalties paid to residents of the other contracting state.
- Australia expands its source taxing claims over natural resources by changes to the definition of a permanent establishment (including substantial equipment used in Australia, processing in Australia by a related entity, and services related to natural resources) and special rules in Articles 6 and 8.
- Until about 2003, Australia would not agree to a non-discrimination article in a treaty and no pre-2003 treaties (except the treaty with the U.S.) include such a provision. The scope and meaning of the provision are now being tested in Australian courts.
- The interaction between the CGT, introduced in Australia in 1985, and Australia's treaties has proved especially problematic. Under Australia's domestic law, CGT is imposed on a source basis in several instances where Article 7 or Article 13 allocated the taxing right exclusively to the residence country. For many years, the ATO insisted that the CGT was not a covered tax so that domestic law operated unaffected by the treaty. That position was rejected by the courts,[12] but in the meantime, some treaties (most important, the treaties with the UK and the U.S.) had been negotiated to entrench the ATO position: capital gains were to be dealt with only under Article 13 (not, for example, under Article 7) and Article 13 was drafted to provide that it did not affect the domestic-law claim. Australia has abandoned that position for its more recent treaties following changes to domestic law, and modern treaties follow the usual allocation in Article 13 of the OECD Model. Australian domestic law generally imposes an exit tax on residents who depart Australia with unrealized gains on assets but in several cases allows a deferral until realization. Australia's treaties usually accommodate this deferral and allow Australia to tax capital gains made by former residents for several years after they have departed.

Australia signed the MLI in 2017. Legislation to enact the MLI as domestic law was passed in August 2018 and the MLI entered into force for Australia on January 1, 2019. Australia's notification of ratification nominated almost all of its bilateral income tax treaties as covered tax agreements (Australia did not nominate its 2015 treaty with Germany because it already contained many of the MLI positions, nor the agreement with Taiwan, China). Australia agreed to all the provisions of the MLI (choosing the principal purpose test to handle treaty abuse), including mandatory arbitration of tax disputes, except for Article 5 (since Australia's treaties employ credit rather than exemption) and Articles 10 and 12 (which deal with permanent establishments).

12. *Virgin Holdings SA v. Commissioner of Taxation* [2008] FCA 1503; *Undershaft (No 1) Limited v. Commissioner of Taxation* [2009] FCA 41.

11 SOURCES OF TAX LAW

Tax is always in the headlines in Australia. It has been the topic or a main topic of many federal elections in the last forty years. As noted above, there have been many colorful incidents involving the tax system. For the social history of taxation in Australia, there is no better source than the newspapers, many of which are now archived online.

The tax law, cases, and rulings are also readily available through free online sources. As noted above, the income tax is spread over a number of statutes, but the most important parts are in the 1936 and 1997 ITAAs, which are available on the Federal Register of Legislation, an electronic database which now sets out the authoritative versions of all federal laws: https://www.legislation.gov.au/. Explanatory memoranda are produced for all legislation and are increasingly helpful in the tax area, even to the point where they seem almost to supplant the text of the law. They are available from the same website and from the ATO's legal database: https://www.ato.gov.au/single-page-applications/legaldatabase#Law. The ATO produces an enormous volume of material on the interpretation and application of the law, including rulings and various types of guides, which are available on the ATO website. Cases, which are important sources of law for both general rules and the interpretation of detailed provisions, can be found at www.austlii.edu.au, a website which also has a tax-related section including legislation, cases, treaties, and online tax journals. Details of current tax reform projects are found at the Treasury website: https://treasury.gov.au/consultation.

Books and journals on taxation matters abound. The preeminent text on the general principles of the tax system is Parsons, *Income Taxation in Australia* (1985), which is available free online: https://open.sydneyuniversitypress.com.au/classic-taxation.html. The main commercial publishers in taxation are Wolters Kluwer (formerly CCH Australia) and Thomson Reuters, which both produce an annual version of tax legislation and several online commentary services. The best account of current tax law in book form can be found in Woellner, Barkoczy, Murphy, Evans & Pinto, *Australian Taxation Law* (31st ed., 2021), and there are several student casebooks, such as *Income Taxation Commentary and Materials* (10th ed., 2023). The main professional organization is The Tax Institute, which publishes *Taxation in Australia* and *Australian Tax Forum*, as well as many conference papers and series (*see* www.taxinstitute.com.au), and there are several other specialist tax journals: *Australian Tax Review*, *Australian Journal of Taxation* (www.jausttax.com.au), *Revenue Law Journal* (https://www.austlii.edu.au/cgi-bin/viewdb/au/journals/RevenueLawJl/), and *e-journal of Tax Research* (https://www.austlii.edu.au/cgi-bin/viewdb/au/journals/eJlTaxR/) the last three available free online.

Canada

Brian J. Arnold & Geoffrey Loomer

1 HISTORY OF THE INCOME TAX ACT

Canadian federal income tax was first imposed in 1917 as a temporary measure to help finance World War I. Until then, the major sources of federal revenue were customs and excise taxes. Over the period from 1917 to the early 1960s, the income tax became an increasingly important source of government revenue as rates increased and the tax base expanded on a rather ad hoc basis. Dissatisfaction with the resulting "system" led to the establishment of the Royal Commission on Taxation (the Carter Commission) in 1962 to make a comprehensive study of the Canadian tax system. In 1966, the Carter Commission issued its famous report, which proposed the adoption of a comprehensive tax base. The report led to a major overhaul of the income tax in 1972; the revised system was much more sophisticated and the legislation much more complex. Another, less significant, tax reform occurred in 1986-1987 in conjunction with, and partly in response to, the worldwide tax reform phenomenon which took place during that period.

2 CONSTITUTIONAL ISSUES

Under the Canadian constitution, the federal government has unlimited powers of taxation. The provinces have the power to levy "direct taxation" within the province on income earned in the province and on the worldwide income of persons who are resident in the province. All ten provinces and three territories levy income tax on individuals and corporations. The federal individual tax rates are set taking into account the provincial rates; for example, the federal corporate income tax contains a 10% abatement to make room for the provincial corporate tax. Pursuant to a long-standing tax-collection agreement between the federal and provincial governments, the federal government collects both individual and corporate tax on behalf of most of the provinces. In consideration, the provinces must adopt the federal income tax base, although they apply their own rates and provide a wide range of tax credits. Quebec is the only province which collects its own individual income tax; currently, only Alberta and Quebec collect their own corporate taxes.

3 TAX RATES

The 2024 federal income tax rates for individuals are as follows:

Taxable Income (CAD)	*Tax Rate (%)*
0-55,867	15
55,868-111,733	20.5
111,734-173,205	26
173,206-246,752	29
246,753 and over	33

Since 2000, brackets have been fully indexed for inflation. Various personal credits are similarly indexed for inflation. There is, however, no comprehensive relief for inflation with respect to amounts included in computing income.

Although provincial individual income taxes are based on the tax base as defined for federal income tax purposes, the provincial tax rates and brackets vary considerably from province to province. Provincial income taxes are levied on a progressive basis with three to eight brackets. Most, but not all, provinces index their brackets for inflation. The rates vary from 4% on the lowest bracket in Nunavut to 25.75% on the highest bracket in Quebec. As of 2024, Ontario is the only province which levies a substantial surtax on individuals. The combined federal and provincial individual rates for the top bracket vary from 44.5% in Nunavut to 54% and 54.8% in Nova Scotia and Newfoundland and Labrador, respectively.

The basic federal tax rate for corporations was reduced gradually over several years from 28% to 15%, effective for 2012 and subsequent years. The federal rate is formally ten percentage points higher, but there is a 10% abatement for provincial corporate income taxes. The provincial corporate income taxes are levied on the tax base computed in accordance with the same rules used to compute the federal tax base. In 2024, the provincial corporate tax rates varied from 8% in Alberta to 16% in Prince Edward Island. The combined federal and provincial corporate rates for 2024 vary from 23% in Alberta to 31% in Prince Edward Island. Canadian-controlled private corporations qualify for a special reduced rate of 9% on the first CAD 500,000 of active business income. All the provinces also provide reduced tax rates—typically 1% to 3%—for the active business income of Canadian-controlled private corporations.

The federal government and some provinces levy capital taxes on corporations. The federal capital tax is imposed only on large financial institutions with capital in excess of CAD 1 billion, at a rate of 1.25%.

4 COMPOSITION OF THE FISCAL SYSTEM

For the year ended March 31, 2023, federal income taxes comprised about 70.3% of total federal government revenues. Of this amount, corporate income taxes accounted for about 21.0%, while personal income taxes and nonresident income taxes made up the remaining 46.4% and 2.9%, respectively. While total federal income tax revenues have increased substantially over the past five years, the reliance on personal income taxes has decreased slightly, from 49.0% for the year ended March 31, 2018, to 46.4% for 2023, and the reliance on corporate income taxes has increased, from 15.2% for 2018 to 21.0% for 2023. Other important sources of federal revenue include employment insurance contributions (6.0%) and indirect taxes—the goods and services tax (GST) (a form of value-added tax) (10.3%) and customs duties and excise taxes (4.1%). For 2023, personal and corporate income taxes generated approximately CAD 207.9 billion and CAD 93.9 billion, respectively, out of total revenues of CAD 447.8 billion. For the 2022-2023 year, total tax revenues constituted 16.1% of Gross Domestic Product (GDP), exactly the same ratio as in 2001-2002.

5 BASIC STRUCTURE OF THE INCOME TAX

In Canada, the basic structure of the rules for calculating income tax payable is the same for both individuals and corporations and is contained in the same statute (the Income Tax Act (the Act)). Income is calculated on a source basis. Income in the broad economic sense which does not have a source is not income in the legal sense. Amounts lacking a source are not characterized as income and are not taxable unless they are expressly included in income under the Act. Perhaps the best example of this fundamental principle is a windfall gain such as a lottery prize, which is not considered to have the quality of income. Capital gains are another example, although, since 1972, a portion of such gains has been expressly required to be included in income. The inclusion rate for capital gains has varied over time; generally, it has been 50% but, effective June 25, 2024, it was increased to 66.67% for capital gains of individuals in excess of CAD 250,000 annually and for all capital gains realized by corporations and trusts. Capital gains are considered to be derived from the disposition of a source of income rather than income from a source; or, to use the well-worn metaphor, a capital gain represents the realization of all or part of the tree (capital) rather than the fruit (income) from the tree.

The source concept of income finds statutory expression in section 3 of the Act, which defines a taxpayer's income as: "income for the year from a source inside or outside Canada, including … the taxpayer's income for the year from each office, employment, business, and property." Section 4 goes on to provide that a taxpayer's income or loss from any source must be calculated on the assumption that the taxpayer had no income or loss from any other source during the taxation year and that only amounts reasonably applicable to that source of income are deductible. Section 4 also contains a similar provision with respect to the computation of income from sources in a particular place (geographical sources). This provision is relevant for the purpose of determining both a nonresident's income earned in Canada and the credit for foreign taxes on income earned by Canadian residents outside Canada.

It is clear from section 4(1)(a) of the Act that amounts are deductible in computing income from a generic source only if they can reasonably be regarded as applicable to that source. Although it does not necessarily follow that a source of income must exist at the time an expense is incurred in order for the expense to be deductible, the courts have so held. In the absence of an express statutory provision, expenses incurred either before a source of income exists or after it ceases to exist are not deductible because they are not applicable to a source of income.

The source concept of income has its roots in the "schedular" basis used in early United Kingdom (UK) income tax statutes.[1] Under this approach, income tax is levied only in respect of amounts included in various schedules; if an amount is not specifically included in one of these schedules, it is not subject to tax. The schedules specify the types of income subject to tax, as well as the persons subject to tax on such amounts. Generally, income and losses from different schedules cannot be aggregated because each schedule has its own computation rules.

The Canadian income tax system has never followed the UK schedular approach completely. Since 1917, the Canadian Act has required the inclusion of items of income from all sources—a clear attempt to escape the narrow confines of a schedular approach. Generally, however, the courts have limited the definition of income in section 3, referred to above, to income from the specifically enumerated sources: office or employment, business, and property. In addition, the Canadian system has permitted the aggregation of income and losses from various sources since 1972.

In Canada, as in the United Kingdom, the judicial exclusion of amounts from income on the basis of the source concept has been largely reversed by statute. For example, as mentioned earlier, since 1972, a portion of capital gains has been included in income. In addition, subsection 6(3) of the Act ensures that amounts received before employment commences or after it ceases must be included in income where they constitute compensation for services rendered. The increased use of accrual accounting for income tax purposes in recent times has effectively eliminated the problem of including in income amounts received after the cessation of a source of income. The practice has been for the government to overturn by legislation most court cases holding that amounts are not income because they lack a generic source.[2] For example, the Federal Court of Appeal held that a payment received by a shareholder for entering into a noncompetition covenant on the sale of the shares of a corporation was tax-free.[3] According to the Court, the amount was not income from employment, a business, or property, nor was it a capital gain because the shareholder could not be considered to have disposed of any property.[4]

1. *See* Part II below for a comparison of the schedular and global systems.
2. However, a Supreme Court decision, *The Queen v. Fries*, [1990] 2 SCR 1322, holding, without any analysis, that strike pay was not taxable, has not been reversed by statute.
3. *Manrell v. The Queen*, 2003 FCA 128.
4. This result was reversed by a statutory amendment adding s. 56.4, effective for amounts received after October 7, 2003.

In summary, the Canadian tax base includes the most significant items of income, whether or not they have a source under the case law. Windfall gains are the most significant items of income which are currently excluded from the tax base because they lack a source.

Although the source concept has been overridden by specific statutory provisions with respect to income items, it has not often been overridden with respect to deductions. Where the Act provides for the inclusion in income of amounts lacking a source, the inclusion is generally net of any expenses incurred in connection with the amounts. For example, the amount of a capital gain is the proceeds of disposition less the cost of the property and any selling expenses. Generally, however, expenses are not deductible under the Act unless they relate to income from an existing source. Moreover, there are many instances in which expenses are incurred after a source of income has ceased to exist and there is no ongoing income against which these expenses can be offset. Since 1993, a specific provision allows interest to be deducted in certain circumstances after the source of income has ceased to exist.

In summary, there are five major sources of income: office or employment, business, property, capital gains, and miscellaneous items. Taxpayers must calculate income and loss from each source separately and allocate reasonable deductions to each respective source. The rules for calculating income from the various sources differ, although for income from business and property the differences are minor. The major difference between income from employment and income from business or property is that the deductions permitted in computing employment income are severely limited. Once income and losses from the various sources have been computed, they are aggregated to obtain the taxpayer's "income," referred to in Canadian practice as "net income."

The next stage is the determination of a taxpayer's taxable income. Taxable income is net income less a few specific amounts, such as loss carryovers and dividends received by a Canadian corporation from other corporations. The relevant tax rate is then applied to the taxable income to determine the tax payable before credits. The allowable tax credits are very extensive because all personal deductions and exemptions were converted into tax credits in the mid-1980s. In recent years, many additional personal tax credits, such as credits for adoption expenses, home renovations, and first-time home buyers, have been introduced for nonfiscal reasons; credits for public transit and children's arts and fitness programs were introduced and then repealed on a change of government. Tax credits also include credits for foreign taxes and tax expenditures such as the investment tax credit.

6 TAX LEGISLATION

6.1 Tax Legislative Process

Important tax legislation is usually introduced pursuant to the annual budget of the Minister of Finance, although in recent years, increasing use has been made of press releases to announce new tax measures. In addition, technical tax amendments are often issued in the form of draft legislation for public comment without any announcement in a budget. Like all legislative proposals, tax bills must be passed by both the House of Commons (elected) and the Senate (unelected) and receive Royal Assent from the head of state (the Governor-General of Canada acting on behalf of the King). All tax bills which involve the raising of revenue must originate in the House of Commons.

Most tax changes are subject to some public consultations. The Minister of Finance consults widely with other levels of government and interest groups as part of the annual budget process. Draft tax legislation is usually issued to the public for comment before being tabled in Parliament, and Department of Finance officials meet regularly with representative groups of tax practitioners.

It can take several years for tax changes to be enacted. Rarely is draft legislation available at the time that a change is announced in a budget or press release. The preparation of draft legislation can take several months; once it becomes available, it is usually issued for public comment and consultation with tax practitioners. It is then revised and introduced into Parliament, although in the case of controversial measures, the revised draft legislation may first be issued for another round of public consultations. The speed of passage of tax legislation through Parliament depends on several factors, such as how important and controversial the legislation is and what other matters occupy the legislative agenda.

The significant delay between the announcement of tax changes and their enactment causes problems in situations where the changes take effect on announcement. Such changes are not effective until the legislation is fully enacted but, once enacted, they are effective from the prior date of announcement. This situation puts the tax administration (the Canada Revenue Agency (the CRA)) and taxpayers in a dilemma. Taxpayers can refuse to pay any tax owing pursuant to pending legislation; however, if the legislation is ultimately enacted, they will owe the amount with interest. The CRA usually proceeds on the assumption that the legislation will ultimately be enacted; as a result, tax returns, forms, and taxpayer information are produced in advance on that assumption. If proposed changes are not enacted, any tax paid pursuant to the proposed changes should be refunded.

6.2 Statutory Style

Prior to tax reform in 1972, the general style of Canadian legislation tended to be broad, generally worded provisions. For example, an income tax was levied on the income of residents of Canada, but there was no definition of a resident of Canada for this purpose. Similarly, the Canadian transfer pricing rules consisted of two simple provisions which required the amount charged in any transactions between a resident and a related nonresident person to be reasonable in the circumstances.

With tax reform in 1972, there was a clear change in the style of statutory drafting. The Act expanded dramatically. The 2023 version of the Act and Regulations consists of over 2,000 pages, making it by far the largest Canadian statute. The 1972 Act and virtually all amendments since that time are characterized by a high degree of technical complexity, reflecting the government's increasing reliance on detailed technical rules to resolve tax policy issues. Inevitably, the rules require ongoing revision as the instances in which they operate inappropriately are discovered. For the courts, the complexity and frequent amendment of the tax rules often have the effect, if not the intention, of precluding them from playing any significant role in the development of tax law. For tax professionals, the complexity of the Act is a double-edged sword. On the one hand, they complain bitterly about the pace of legislative change and the length and technical complexity of the provisions; on the other hand, they demand that the tax rules be certain and predictable, which requires still more detailed technical statutory rules. Despite these modern developments, there are still some aspects of the Canadian income tax system which are short, simply worded holdovers from the pre-1972 Act.

The style of statutory drafting of tax legislation in Canada is peculiar in several respects. For example, the provisions of the Act are drafted by professionals in the Department of Finance, whereas all other federal legislation is drafted by the Department of Justice. The Act was the only federal statute omitted from the periodic consolidation of federal statutes, in which each statute and the amendments to it are consolidated and the provisions renumbered and reorganized. This exception was justified in part because of the cost to the government and commercial publishers of republishing forms, brochures, loose-leaf services, etc., to reflect revised section numbers. The statutory drafting convention in Canada is that each provision consists of only one sentence regardless of the length and complexity of the provision, resulting in single-sentence provisions that can go on for several pages. A recent development in the style of statutory drafting is the frequent use of algebraic formulae for calculations.

Like all Canadian federal legislation, tax legislation is bilingual; the English- and French-language versions of the Act are equally authoritative. Typically, the Department of Finance develops tax policy and legislation in English; the English version is then translated into French. For purposes of interpretation, both language versions must be taken into account and, if they conflict, the meaning which best accommodates both versions applies (the shared-meaning rule).

6.3 Statutory Interpretation

Until 1984, Canadian courts generally applied a strict or literal approach to the interpretation of taxing statutes. This approach was originally adopted from the UK judicial tradition and was deeply ingrained, despite being obviously inappropriate. Strict interpretation resulted in some shocking judicial decisions.

In 1984, the Supreme Court of Canada, in the *Stubart Investments* case,[5] abandoned strict interpretation in favor of a so-called modern approach:

> Today there is only one principle or approach, namely, the words of an Act are to be read in their entire context in their grammatical and ordinary sense harmoniously with the scheme of the Act, the object of the Act and the intention of Parliament.

5. *Stubart Investments Ltd. v. The Queen*, [1984] 1 SCR 536.

The Supreme Court's endorsement of the modern approach was widely accepted by lower courts, the tax authorities, and tax practitioners. However, in a series of cases from 1994 to the mid-2000s, the Supreme Court made several inconsistent statements about its approach to statutory interpretation. Although the Court consistently confirmed that the modern approach is the correct approach to statutory interpretation, it nevertheless applied strict interpretation, or what the Court referred to in several cases as a "plain meaning" approach.

In 2005, in the first cases dealing with the general anti-avoidance rule (GAAR),[6] the Supreme Court referred to the modern approach to statutory interpretation as the "textual, contextual and purposive approach." Although the Court emphasized that this approach applies to all statutes, including tax statutes, it went on to indicate that "because of the degree of precision and detail characteristic of many tax provisions, a greater emphasis has often been placed on textual interpretation where taxation statutes are concerned." As a result, the Court has reiterated on a number of occasions that where the words of a provision are clear and unambiguous, they must simply be applied; on the other hand, where the words can be reasonably interpreted in more than one way, greater emphasis must be given to the context and purpose of the Act. However, even where the words appear clear, the Supreme Court admits that context and purpose must always be considered in order to determine whether there are latent ambiguities. The Court does not appear to recognize the inherent contradiction in its approach to statutory interpretation: if context and purpose must be considered to reveal latent ambiguities, how is it possible simply to apply clear and unambiguous provisions?

The Supreme Court's approach to statutory interpretation has had important implications for its perception of the role of the judiciary in combating tax avoidance. The Supreme Court has consistently held that taxpayers are taxable in accordance with the legal form of their transactions (and therefore economic substance or economic realities are irrelevant) and that entering into transactions solely to obtain tax benefits is irrelevant to the determination of the tax consequences.[7] According to the Supreme Court, in the absence of a specific statutory rule and subject to the GAAR, taxpayers are free to arrange their affairs to avoid tax. Moreover, it is Parliament's responsibility, not the courts' responsibility, to combat tax avoidance. Some Supreme Court decisions after 2010 have re-emphasized the role of the GAAR in addressing tax avoidance, but the rule remains notoriously difficult to interpret and apply.[8]

7 COURTS DEALING WITH TAX MATTERS

Taxpayers who choose to dispute the tax, interest, or penalties levied by the Minister of National Revenue must file a notice of objection to their assessment. This notice

6. *Canada Trustco Mortgage Co. v. Canada*, [2005] 2 SCR 601 and *Mathew v. Canada*, [2005] 2 SCR 643.
7. *See*, e.g., *Canada v. Loblaw Financial Holdings Inc.*, 2021 SCC 51.
8. *Copthorne Holdings Ltd. v. Canada*, [2011] 3 SCR 721 and *Deans Knight Income Corp. v. Canada*, 2023 SCC 16.

triggers an internal appeal process within the CRA; if the assessment is confirmed, the taxpayer may appeal to the courts. Except for certain large corporations, which must pay one-half of the tax assessed even where they dispute the tax, the amount of tax in dispute does not have to be paid until the dispute is finally resolved.

All tax appeals are heard in the first instance by a single judge of the Tax Court of Canada, under either a general procedure or an informal procedure. The informal procedure is available, on an elective basis for taxpayers, for cases involving CAD 25,000 or less of federal tax and penalties or a loss of CAD 50,000 or less. Under the informal procedure, there are no formal rules of evidence and taxpayers need not be represented by counsel. There is a limited right of appeal from an informal procedure decision to the Federal Court of Appeal. Decisions in informal procedure cases are not intended to have any precedential value; however, the Tax Court has occasionally followed decisions in informal cases.

The general procedure before the Tax Court is a formal trial with both sides usually represented by legal counsel. Because tax assessments are presumed by statute to be valid, the initial onus of proof is always on the taxpayer to show that the Minister's assessment is invalid. As a practical matter, this initial burden of proof is not very important because during the trial the burden shifts back and forth with the presentation of evidence. An adverse judgment of the Tax Court may be appealed to the Federal Court of Appeal, either by the government or the taxpayer; a final appeal lies to the Supreme Court of Canada, whose jurisdiction is largely discretionary. Unlike the Tax Court, the Federal Court of Appeal and the Supreme Court hear many types of cases other than tax cases. An appeal to the Federal Court of Appeal or the Supreme Court is restricted to questions of law or mixed questions of fact and law.

The number of tax cases decided annually by the three levels of courts for the period from 2020-2021 to 2022-2023 is shown in the following table:

Year	*Tax Court of Canada*	*Federal Court of Appeal*	*Supreme Court of Canada*
2020-2021	273	103	1
2021-2022	166	92	2
2022-2023	713	88	2

The total number of tax cases heard by the courts over the past decade has increased significantly.

Case law is an important aspect of Canadian income tax law. One of its main functions is to elaborate the meaning of the provisions of the Act—despite the detailed technical nature of the statutory provisions, vagueness and ambiguity are frequent. A considerable amount of case law each year involves the distinction between capital gains and ordinary income, the deduction of business expenses, and the deduction of personal tax credits.

Judicial decisions are binding unless reversed on appeal. The government will sometimes reverse by statute a judicial precedent with which it disagrees. As income tax has become the preserve of specialists, it has become more difficult for generalist courts to handle tax issues properly.

Canadian courts are obligated to provide reasons, usually in writing, for their decisions. Typically, judicial decisions, which are referred to as reasons for judgment, recite the facts of the case, the positions and arguments of the parties, and the decisions of the lower courts before providing the reasons for the court's decision. Dissenting decisions are common with respect to appeals to the Federal Court of Appeal or Supreme Court, where an odd number of judges hear each case (three in the case of the Federal Court of Appeal and five, seven, or nine in the case of the Supreme Court). Judges often cite a wide variety of materials in their decisions, including other cases, books, and articles, prior and subsequent versions of the statute, and government reports. Decisions of higher courts are binding on lower courts. A court is not bound to follow its own prior decisions but usually does so as a practical matter.

8 TAX ADMINISTRATION

The Canadian administration of the income tax system is based on a system of "voluntary compliance" or self-assessment. All taxpayers are legally obligated to file an annual tax return reporting their income and expenses accurately, along with a calculation of the amount of tax owing or the refund due. For the 2021 taxation year, the CRA handled just over 30.9 million individual tax returns and 2.5 million corporate returns; of these, 91% of individual returns and over 90% of corporate returns were filed electronically. Once filed, tax returns are then checked by the CRA to ensure that the required information is correct and the computations are mathematically correct. A notice of assessment showing the amount of tax owing is then sent to the taxpayer. Since fewer than 1% of all individual tax returns are actually audited by the CRA, the income tax system depends largely on voluntary compliance by taxpayers.

However, the system is not exclusively voluntary. Payments of salary and wages and other amounts are subject to withholding at source. In addition, taxpayers are required to make periodic instalments on account of tax payable for income which is not subject to withholding, and they are also subject to broad information-reporting requirements.

The rationale for the self-assessment system is cost-effectiveness. Costs to the government include the cost of printing returns, providing information and assistance to taxpayers, processing returns, and auditing a minimal number of returns filed. No other system is nearly as economical.

The CRA was created in 1999 and is responsible for the administration of the income tax system and other federal taxes such as the GST. Prior to 1999, the CRA's responsibilities were carried out by Revenue Canada, an ordinary government department. The shift to agency status was justified on the basis that it would insulate officials from political interference and provide more flexibility in dealing with human resource issues. In substance, the creation of the CRA caused considerable dislocation and expense but did not result in any significant changes in the administration of the tax system.

The administrative style of the Canadian tax administration has varied considerably over the past forty years. In the late 1970s and early 1980s, the CRA was accused of using "Gestapo" tactics and being insensitive to taxpayers' legitimate concerns—indeed, its performance was an important issue in the 1984 federal election. When the Progressive Conservative Party was elected in that year, it set out to make significant reforms to the tax administration. The central thrust of these reforms was to convert the CRA from an enforcement agency to a service agency. This shift in attitude had many consequences, from the silly (the CRA began to refer to taxpayers as "clients") to the serious (the CRA started to take a rather benign attitude to tax-avoidance transactions which complied literally with the words of the Act).

The CRA's preoccupation with service continues today. In the early 1990s, a so-called fairness package was adopted, which gave the CRA statutory authority to waive interest and penalties, accept late-filed elections, and make refunds for statute-barred years. In 2016-2017, the CRA dealt with over 413,000 fairness requests to waive interest and penalties; it waived over CAD 671 million. Each CRA office has one or more Fairness Committees to consider fairness requests from taxpayers.

The CRA is also responsible for delivering a number of social welfare programs and other spending programs through the income tax system. In these respects, the CRA is a service rather than a tax-collection organization. More recently, however, the CRA has placed increased emphasis on enforcement; in 2005, it initiated a special program to address aggressive international tax planning. In 2016-2017, the CRA received additional funding of CAD 1 billion to bolster its efforts in combating international tax avoidance. The CRA received a further CAD 1.2 billion beginning in 2022-2023 in order to expand audits of larger entities and nonresidents engaged in aggressive tax planning. The CRA is also part of the Joint International Tax Shelter Information Center (along with Australia, Japan, the UK, the United States (U.S.), and other countries), which involves a collaborative effort to deal with international tax avoidance.

The CRA's administrative practices have important ramifications in many areas of the tax system. In some areas, the law consists of little more than a generally worded statutory provision and a series of well-known administrative practices. These administrative pronouncements are not binding on the courts, taxpayers, or the CRA, but the courts have given them considerable weight in appropriate circumstances. The CRA generally adheres to its published positions and changes them only prospectively, with notice to the public. In general, the CRA makes its administrative practices widely known to the public; its administrative positions are available in published form and through the CRA's website. This open access to the CRA's administrative positions was effectively forced on it after the introduction of access-to-information legislation. It is not unusual for the CRA to issue inconsistent positions on some issues; this inconsistency can become problematic for the government in the course of litigation.

There is very little administrative discretion expressly permitted by the provisions of the Act. Such administrative discretion is viewed with disfavor by both the government and tax practitioners. As a practical matter, of course, CRA officials have significant amounts of administrative discretion in administering the Act, although any exercise of such discretion is subject to judicial review through the normal objection and appeal process. It is also subject to review by the Office of the Taxpayers' Ombudsperson and by the Auditor General, who scrutinizes all aspects of the CRA's administration of the tax system on a continuing basis. The Auditor General's annual reports on the CRA have attracted considerable public interest and led to important changes in the CRA's practices and in some cases to changes to the income tax legislation itself.

The behavior of Canadian taxpayers is probably broadly similar to that of American taxpayers. The general public meets its tax obligations grudgingly, and there is probably a good deal of small-scale cheating. Large corporations and wealthy individuals are sensitive to tax issues, and most do not hesitate to engage in aggressive tax planning.

Corporate and individual tax-avoidance arrangements remain problematic despite the adoption of specific anti-avoidance legislation and a GAAR. There is a common perception that tax professionals became increasingly aggressive between the 1980s and the 2010s; this behavior may have moderated more recently due, in part, to a proliferation of specific anti-avoidance rules.

9 GENERAL PRINCIPLES

9.1 Relationship Between Tax and Financial Accounting

Section 9 of the Act provides that a taxpayer's income from a business or property for a year is the "profit" from the business or property for the year. The term "profit" is not defined in the Act. The courts have held that profit is the net amount of gross revenue in excess of expenses, computed in accordance with the ordinary principles of commercial accounting and business practice. Although accounting principles and practices are important in the computation of profit, in the *Canderel* case[9] in 1998, the Supreme Court reiterated that the computation of profit for tax purposes is a question of law and that accounting practice, although relevant, is not controlling. In many instances, the use of accounting principles or practices is expressly overridden by the provisions of the Act. For example, accounting depreciation is not allowed for tax purposes; instead, a separate system of capital cost allowance has been established for income tax purposes. In addition, accounting practice may be displaced by overriding principles of income tax law such as the realization principle.

The courts have indicated that there is no requirement of conformity between the treatment of an item for financial accounting purposes and income tax purposes. Taxpayers are free to adopt any method for computing business income as long as it is not inconsistent with the provisions of the Act, case law, or well-established commercial practices. These well-established practices include generally accepted accounting principles, but they are not rules of law; rather, according to the Supreme Court, they are interpretive aids. If a taxpayer uses a method for computing income which does not contravene the provisions of the Act, is consistent with the case law principles for

9. [1998] 2 CTC 35 (SCC).

measuring income, and gives an accurate picture of the profit of the business for the year, that method is acceptable unless the Minister can establish that another method gives a more accurate picture of the taxpayer's income.

9.2 Respect for Civil or Private Law Form

It is clearly recognized in Canada that the income tax law is generally applied to legal rights and obligations determined under the general law. The Act is replete with terms such as "employment," "corporation," "person," and "paid-up capital" which derive their meaning from the general law; the Supreme Court has decided that terms in the Act which have well-established legal meanings must be given those meanings rather than their ordinary meaning.

There are two difficult aspects regarding the issue of the relationship between the general law and income tax legislation. First, because Canada is a federal state, occasionally the legal meaning is different in different provinces. This is particularly the case with respect to the province of Quebec, which has a civil law legal system (in contrast to all the other provinces and territories, which have a common law system). Ordinarily, the drafters and the courts strive to achieve consistency in the application of the law to taxpayers in various parts of the country. The courts and the CRA generally adhere to the relevant provincial law, although they have sometimes been known to take very flexible positions in order to achieve consistency. Special statutory provisions have been adopted with respect to legal concepts used in the province of Quebec, such as usufruct, rights of habitation, and emphyteutic leases. This is part of a broad government initiative, called bijuralism, which is intended to ensure that federal laws apply in the same way in Quebec and in the common law provinces.

Second, the application of the provisions of the Act to the offshore activities of Canadian taxpayers involves applying the Act to foreign legal rights and obligations. In general, the legal rights and obligations are determined under the foreign law; the Canadian tax law is then applied to those findings, which are, in effect, treated as findings of fact rather than law. For example, whether a foreign entity is characterized as a corporation or partnership for Canadian tax purposes is based on the legal rights and obligations of the members under the foreign law. If those rights and obligations are similar to those of shareholders of Canadian corporations, then the entity will be characterized as a corporation.

9.3 Anti-avoidance Doctrines and Rules

There is considerable confusion in Canada concerning the doctrine of substance over form. Canadian law derives from the House of Lords decision in 1936 in the *Duke of Westminster* case.[10] In that case, the House of Lords clearly rejected any doctrine under which the legal form of a transaction could be disregarded in favor of its economic substance. However, the House of Lords did recognize that the legal substance of a

10. *Duke of Westminster v. CIR* [1936] AC 1, 19 TC 4990, 51 TLR 467 (HL).

transaction prevails over the nomenclature used by the taxpayer to describe the transaction.

The Supreme Court of Canada has reaffirmed on several occasions that the *Duke of Westminster* case is deeply entrenched in Canadian tax law. Nevertheless, on several occasions, Canadian courts, including the Supreme Court, have made references to the doctrine of economic substance over form or economic realities, which seems to suggest that economic substance will prevail over legal form in certain circumstances. For example, in the *Bronfman Trust* case[11] in 1987, the Supreme Court of Canada stated:

> The recent trend in tax cases [has] been towards attempting to ascertain the true commercial and practical nature of the taxpayer's transactions ... Assessment of taxpayers' transactions with an eye to commercial and economic realities, rather than juristic classification of form, may help to avoid the inequity of tax liability being dependent upon the taxpayer's sophistication at manipulating a sequence of events to achieve a patina of compliance with the apparent prerequisites for a tax deduction.

Unfortunately, the Supreme Court did not analyze the connection between this statement and the *Duke of Westminster* case. In another case, the Supreme Court stated, without any elaboration, that substance would apply over form where it was consistent with the wording and purpose of the particular provision.[12]

In the *Shell Canada* case[13] in 1999, the Court rejected its earlier dicta from the *Bronfman Trust* case:

> This Court has repeatedly held that courts must be sensitive to the economic realities of a particular transaction, rather than being bound to what first appears to be its legal form ... But there are at least two caveats to this rule. First, this Court has never held that the economic realities of a situation can be used to recharacterize a taxpayer's *bona fide* legal relationships. To the contrary, we have held that, absent a specific provision of the Act to the contrary or a finding that they are a sham, the taxpayer's legal relationships must be respected in tax cases. Recharacterization is only permissible if the label attached by the taxpayer to the particular transaction does not properly reflect its actual legal effect ...
>
> Second, it is well established in this Court's tax jurisprudence that a searching inquiry for either the "economic realities" of a particular transaction or the general object and spirit of the provision at issue can never supplant a court's duty to apply an unambiguous provision of the Act to a taxpayer's transaction. Where the provision at issue is clear and unambiguous, its terms must simply be applied ...
>
> [T]his Court has made it clear in more recent decisions that, absent a specific provision to the contrary, it is not the courts' role to prevent taxpayers from relying on the sophisticated structure of their transactions, arranged in such a way that the particular provisions of the Act are met, on the basis that it would be inequitable to those taxpayers who have not chosen to structure their transactions that way ... The courts' role is to interpret and apply the Act as it was adopted by Parliament. Obiter statements in earlier cases that might be said to support a broader and less

11. *Bronfman Trust v. The Queen,* [1987] 1 SCR 32.
12. *Québec (Communauté Urbaine) v. Corp. Notre-Dame de Bon-Secours,* [1994] 3 SCR 3.
13. *Shell Canada Ltd. v. Canada,* [1999] 3 SCR 616.

> certain interpretive principle have therefore been overtaken by our developing tax jurisprudence. Unless the Act provides otherwise, a taxpayer is entitled to be taxed based on what it actually did, not based on what it could have done, and certainly not based on what a less sophisticated taxpayer might have done.

The main anti-avoidance doctrines referred to by Canadian courts in tax-avoidance cases are:

- the sham transaction doctrine. Under this doctrine, a transaction which attempts to give the appearance of legal rights and obligations which are different from the actual legal rights and obligations created between the parties can be disregarded for tax purposes. The sham doctrine requires an element of deceit and is applied only rarely;
- substance over form. As discussed above, this doctrine is limited to legal substance over legal form. It is very similar to the sham doctrine and is rarely applied;
- step-transaction doctrine. The Supreme Court has held that a series of transactions cannot be considered in interpreting the provisions of the Act unless they refer explicitly to a series of transactions;
- the business purpose test under which transactions which lack a business purpose other than the avoidance of tax may be disregarded. This doctrine was explicitly rejected by the Supreme Court of Canada in 1984 in the *Stubart* case.

Although these judicial doctrines are quite limited in scope, the Tax Court and the Federal Court of Appeal have occasionally struck down avoidance schemes by applying the ordinary rules of statutory interpretation or specific anti-avoidance rules. However, in the 1990s the Supreme Court upheld almost every tax-avoidance arrangement which came before it, including some blatantly artificial schemes lacking any commercial reality.

In 1987, the government enacted section 245 of the Act, a GAAR. Under this rule, where a transaction is an "avoidance transaction," the tax consequences of the transaction may be determined so as to disallow any tax benefit arising from the transaction. An avoidance transaction is defined to be any transaction which, by itself or as part of a series of transactions, results in a "tax benefit," broadly defined as any reduction, avoidance, or deferral of tax, unless the primary purpose of the transaction is something other than obtaining a tax benefit. Even where a transaction is an avoidance transaction, however, there is an exception for transactions which do not involve a misuse of the provisions of the Act or an abuse of the provisions of the Act read as a whole.

The Supreme Court has decided six cases involving the GAAR—the first two cases in 2005 and the most recent in 2023.[14] These cases have established the basic approach to the interpretation and application of the GAAR but have struggled to

14. *Canada Trustco* and *Mathew, supra* note 6; *Lipson v. Canada*, [2009] SCR 1; *Copthorne Holdings, supra* note 8; *Canada v. Alta Energy Luxembourg SARL*, 2021 SCC 49; and *Deans Knight, supra* note 8. The government was successful in four of the cases and was unsuccessful in two: *Canada Trustco* and *Alta Energy*.

articulate a principled approach for determining whether an avoidance transaction is abusive. Throughout these decisions, the Court has emphasized that, although the GAAR is intended to limit abusive tax avoidance, Parliament also intended to preserve "certainty, predictability, and fairness" for taxpayers, including taxpayers engaged in aggressive tax avoidance schemes. The cases also confirm that the GAAR is a provision of last resort which can be applied only after all the other provisions of the Act.

With respect to the definition of an avoidance transaction, the cases held that the burden of proof is on the taxpayer to establish that the primary purpose of a transaction is something other than obtaining a tax benefit. The concept of a series of transaction, which is crucial for the effectiveness of the GAAR, is limited to situations where there is a binding commitment to carry out one or more transactions if other transactions are carried out. However, the cases have given a broad interpretation of subsection 248(10), which extends a series to include any related transactions carried out "in contemplation of" the series, to include any transactions carried out before or after a series because of or in relation to the series.

With respect to the exception for avoidance transactions which do not misuse or abuse the provisions of the Act (the crucial issue in most GAAR cases), the Supreme Court has adhered to a two-stage approach: first, the object, spirit, purpose, or underlying rationale of the provisions relied on by the taxpayer for the tax benefit must be determined; second, it must be determined whether the avoidance transaction or the series of which it is a part frustrates or defeats that purpose. According to the Supreme Court, the first stage is a question of law; the second stage is a question of fact, although it seems clear that the second stage is a mixed question of fact and law. The government has the burden of establishing the purpose of the relevant provisions of the Act, and that purpose must be clear. The Supreme Court has refused to accept the distinction, set out explicitly in the English-language version of the GAAR, between a misuse of the provisions of the Act and the abuse of the provisions of the Act read as a whole because it thought that the Act could not be abused without misuse of some provision of the Act. A better reason is that the distinction disappears in the French version because the French term *abus* means both misuse and abuse.

The Supreme Court has failed to provide any clear guidance with respect to whether a transaction is abusive. For example, the Court has not provided any objective criteria, such as the absence of any pretax profit or the circular flow of funds, to be used for this purpose. Moreover, the Court has minimized the role of economic substance, despite an explicit reference to economic substance in the explanatory notes to the GAAR, by holding that economic substance is relevant only where the statutory provision on which the taxpayer relies for the tax benefit refers to or contemplates economic substance; and even then, a lack of economic substance is not determinative, but only a factor to be taken into account in deciding whether a transaction is abusive. In response, the GAAR was amended effective 2024 to state explicitly that economic substance is relevant to the analysis of abuse. The legislation now stipulates that if an avoidance transaction "is significantly lacking in economic substance," this is an important factor that "tends to indicate" that the transaction involves a misuse or abuse and then gives a non-exhaustive list of factors that could demonstrate a lack of economic substance.

One important outstanding issue with respect to the GAAR is the relationship between the well-established "textual, contextual and purposive" approach to the interpretation of statutes, including tax statutes, and the interpretive approach for determining whether a transaction is abusive under the GAAR. As noted above, the first stage in the determination of whether a transaction or series is abusive is to determine the object, spirit, or purpose of the relevant provisions. However, this task should already have been performed as part of the basic textual, contextual, and purposive interpretation of the provisions. It is unclear how the determination of abuse under the GAAR is different from the basic interpretation of the provisions of the Act. Some commentators have suggested that more emphasis is placed on the text in an ordinary exercise of interpretation, whereas more emphasis is placed on the purpose under the GAAR. The Supreme Court itself has suggested that the purpose of the two interpretive exercises is different: the purpose of the basic interpretation of the provisions of the Act is to determine what the words mean, whereas the purpose of the first stage of the abuse analysis under the GAAR is to determine the purpose or underlying rationale of the relevant provisions.[15]

10 TAX TREATY NETWORK

Canada has comprehensive tax treaties with ninety-four countries, as well as over twenty-five Tax Information Exchange Agreements (TIEAs) with tax havens. Canada's tax treaty network includes treaties with all its major trading partners, virtually all countries in which Canadian corporations have significant investments, and several low-tax jurisdictions. The expansion of Canada's tax treaty network has been driven by the limitation of the exemption for dividends from foreign affiliates of Canadian companies to foreign affiliates resident in countries with which Canada has a tax treaty or TIEA. Canada's treaty with the U.S. is special in the sense that it contains many provisions which are not included in the Organisation for Economic Co-operation and Development (OECD) Model Convention but are necessary to deal with problems arising from the close integration of the economies of the two countries and their conflicting tax rules.

As a member of the OECD, most of Canada's tax treaties follow the general pattern of the OECD Model treaty, subject to several major exceptions:

- Canada insists on imposing tax on royalties paid to residents of the other contracting state, although with numerous exclusions.
- Following U.S. treaty practice, Canada includes a domestic tax benefit provision in its treaties, which states that the treaty does not deprive taxpayers of the benefit of any deduction, allowance, etc., available under domestic law.
- Canada does not accept the principle of national treatment of residents of the other state for purposes of the nondiscrimination article but instead agrees only to provide most-favored-nation treatment.

15. *See Copthorne Holdings, supra* note 8, and *Deans Knight, supra* note 8.

- Most Canadian tax treaties contain special provisions allowing Canada to apply its thin capitalization rules to restrict the deduction of interest by Canadian companies to substantial shareholders resident in the other contracting state.
- Canadian treaties generally allow Canada to tax capital gains of its former residents for a period of five to ten years after they cease to be resident in Canada.

Canada has ratified the *Multilateral Convention on Mutual Assistance in Tax Matters*. It has also ratified the *Multilateral Convention to Implement Tax Treaty Related Measures to Prevent Base Erosion and Profit Shifting* (MLI). Although Canada has not listed all of its treaties as covered tax agreements and originally agreed only to the minimum standards in the MLI (improvements to the mutual agreement procedure, the principal purpose test (PPT) to deal with treaty abuse, and mandatory arbitration), it has now largely adopted the MLI's provisions with respect to the tie-breaker rule for dual-resident entities, the 365-day holding period for direct dividends, and the 365-day testing period for capital gains on shares which derive their value principally from immovable property in Canada.

11 SOURCES OF TAX LAW

Virtually all federal tax legislation—individual income tax, capital gains, and corporation tax—are contained in the Act. That Act also contains some special taxes which are not based on income, such as the capital tax on large financial institutions. Since the early 1980s, all Canadian tax legislation has been accompanied by explanatory notes, which are sometimes referred to by the courts as an aid to interpretation. These notes sometimes provide useful explanations of the purpose and operation of the provisions; sometimes, however, they simply paraphrase the words of the statute. The Act is supplemented by Regulations, which are detailed rules adopted by the Cabinet (not passed by Parliament). The Regulations vary enormously, from rules which should probably be in the Act to tables prescribing the amounts for employers to withhold from salaries and wages. Current amendments to the Act and Regulations are available online at www.canada.ca/en/department-finance.html. However, most tax professionals use one of the consolidated annotated versions of the legislation produced by the commercial publishers (Thomson Reuters and CCH).

The CRA issues a wide range of administrative material concerning income taxes. Information circulars, income tax folios (which started to replace interpretation bulletins in March 2013), and technical interpretations are particularly useful to determine the CRA's position with respect to the interpretation and application of the provisions of the Act. Most information circulars are intended to provide explanations of areas of the tax system for the general public. Income tax folios and technical interpretations deal with narrower, more technical issues and are intended for tax specialists. The CRA is not legally bound by its administrative positions as expressed in these publications, although, as a practical matter, it departs from published positions very infrequently; courts generally expect the CRA to adhere to its positions because taxpayers rely on those positions. The CRA also provides binding advance rulings to specific taxpayers on proposed transactions. These advance rulings are used extensively by large accounting and law firms for complex corporate transactions. The CRA charges for its rulings service on a cost-recovery basis. All the CRA's published material is available on its website, www.canada.ca/en/revenue-agency.html. The text of Canada's tax treaties and the status of the tax treaty network are available at www.canada.ca/en/department-finance.html.

Secondary sources (books, articles, etc.) and government reports are important sources of information on the Canadian income tax system. Courts often refer to this material in their decisions. The leading textbooks on income tax are Vern Krishna, *Fundamentals of Canadian Income Tax*, vol. 1, 2nd edition (Thomson Reuters, 2019) and vol. 2 (Thomson Reuters, 2018) and Jinyan Li, Joanne Magee, and J. Scott Wilkie, *Principles of Canadian Income Tax Law*, 10th edition (Thomson Reuters, 2022). There are two comprehensive loose-leaf services (Thomson Reuters and CCH) and several electronic services. The leading professional organization is the Canadian Tax Foundation, which publishes the *Canadian Tax Journal* (quarterly), an annual conference report, and monographs dealing with tax issues. The Foundation's website is www.ctf.ca. The 1966 *Report of the Royal Commission on Taxation* (the Carter Report) is probably the most important government report. The 1997 *Report of the Technical Committee on Business Taxation* (the Mintz Report), which was appointed by the Minister of Finance, provided a detailed analysis of the taxation of business income and made several recommendations to improve the system, only a few of which were adopted by the government.

China

Jinyan Li

1 HISTORY OF THE INCOME TAX

The first income taxes in the People's Republic of China were enacted by the National People's Congress (NPC) on September 10, 1980: the Individual Income Tax (IIT) and the Income Tax on Chinese-Foreign Equity Joint Venture Income Tax (EJVIT). Since then, the scope of the IIT has expanded greatly. The EJVIT was transformed into a comprehensive tax on all forms of enterprises and renamed the "Enterprise Income Tax" (EIT) in 2008; the IIT and EIT are totally separate taxes.

The history of these two income taxes mirrors that of the Chinese economic transformation. Until the commencement of economic reforms in the late 1970s, China had a centrally controlled, socialist economy with minimal private ownership or exposure to market forces and did not need to rely on income taxation to raise revenue, redistribute income, or regulate economic activities. Income taxes became necessary only when foreign companies and individuals were allowed to invest or work in China and earn income. Initially, the IIT and EJVIT were "foreign-related" taxes as they applied only to foreign individuals and foreign companies. Since 1980, the scope of both taxes has expanded in tandem with the growth of the Chinese market economy and globalization. The evolution of the IIT and the EIT reflects international tax norms, Chinese characteristics, and features of an economy in transformation. China's accession to the World Trade Organization in 2001 had a significant influence on the consolidation of taxes for domestically owned and foreign-owned enterprises, resulting in more tax neutrality for all enterprises regardless of ownership. As a result, the tax system has become more "market-friendly."

1.1 Individual Income Tax

In theory, the IIT, introduced in 1980, applied to any individual who resided in China for over a year. In effect, it applied only to foreign individuals because the exemption threshold exceeded the amount of income that Chinese citizens could earn at the time. It used a schedular system and applied progressive rates only to income from wages and salaries (5% to 45%) and a flat rate (20%) to income from independent personal services, investment, and property. Taxes were collected through withholding at source on a monthly or payment basis.

In 1986-1987, Chinese citizens became subject to income taxes under two interim measures introduced by the State Council. The Income Tax on Individual Industrial and Commercial Households applied to the taxpayer's income at progressive rates ranging from 7% to 60% with a surtax of 10% to 40% on annual income exceeding CNY 50,000 (approximately USD 17,000 at the official rate of exchange). The Individual Income Adjustment Tax was similar to an "excessive income tax." It applied to income from employment, personal services, and rent exceeding three times the basic wage at progressive rates ranging from 20% to 60%. These two taxes merged into the IIT in 1993.

Since the 1990s, most of the changes in the tax system have involved increasing the basic monthly exemption threshold for employees (e.g., from CNY 800 in 1980 to CNY 5,000 in 2018) and introducing some policy-based deductions for children's education, senior care, major medical costs, and retirement savings. The schedular structure and nominal tax rates remain largely unchanged. The 2018 amendments adopted "residence" as an explicit basis for claiming tax jurisdiction.

1.2 Enterprise Income Tax

The EJVIT, enacted in 1980, was joined by the Foreign Enterprises Income Tax, enacted in 1981. These two taxes were consolidated in 1991 into the Income Tax on Foreign Enterprises and Foreign-Invested Enterprises ("FIE Tax"). Meanwhile, separate taxes were imposed on each type of domestically owned enterprise (i.e., state-owned enterprises, collective enterprises, and private enterprises) in accordance with administrative regulations (as opposed to legislation promulgated by the National People's Congress (NPC)). These measures helped facilitate the transition of these entities into profit-seeking enterprises. In 1994, they were consolidated into a Domestic Enterprise Income Tax (DEIT).

In 2007, the FIE Tax (1991) and DEIT merged into the current EIT. The EIT legislation is the most "sophisticated" taxing statute in Chinese history. For the first time, all enterprises, regardless of ownership, were subject to the same tax law, indicating the "maturity" of Chinese market conditions for free competition. The EIT retains the international tax rules in the FIE Tax. A residence-source paradigm is followed: resident enterprises are taxable on their worldwide income and nonresidents are taxable on their Chinese source income. Anti-avoidance rules were strengthened and expanded to include transfer pricing and controlled foreign corporation (CFC) rules, as well as a general anti-avoidance rule (GAAR).

Since 2007, the EIT system has further evolved through administrative lawmaking by the State Council and the State Taxation Administration (STA) (formerly known as "State Administration of Taxation" or "SAT") and Ministry of Finance (MOF). The most notable changes include the implementation of the measures recommended by the G20/OECD (Organisation for Economic Co-operation and Development) Base Erosion and Profiting Shifting (BEPS) Project in regard to transfer pricing.

2 CONSTITUTIONAL ISSUES

Under the Constitution, China is a unitary state: i.e., all subnational governments (provinces and municipalities) are under the control of the Central Government and have no separate taxing powers. Subnational governments may be permitted by the national tax legislation to levy local taxes at a rate set within a specified range, but they cannot introduce any new taxes without permission. Tax revenues are assigned to subnational governments and, in this sense, the IIT is a "local tax."

According to the Constitution, it is the duty of citizens to pay taxes. Tax legislation can take the form of "law" (promulgated by the NPC), "regulations" (introduced by the State Council), and "administrative rules" issued by the STA or MOF. The NPC has the power to interpret "laws" and the State Council and the STA/MOF have the power to interpret "regulations" and administrative rules, respectively. The Courts are "judicial organs" and the Supreme Court is "responsible to the National People's Congress."

3 TAX RATES

3.1 IIT Rates

The IIT is levied at progressive rates for "comprehensive income" and business income and at a 20% flat rate for other types of income. More specifically, the rates are as follows:

(a) 3%-45% for comprehensive income (wages and salaries, personal services income, and royalties):

Annual Taxable Income (CNY)	*Tax Rate (%)*
Less than 36,000	3
More than 36,000-144,000	10
More than 144,000-300,000	20
More than 300,000-420,000	25
More than 420,000-660,000	30
More than 660,000-960,000	35
More than 960,000	45

(b) 5%-35% for business income:

Annual Taxable Income (CNY)	*Tax Rate (%)*
Less than 30,000	5
More than 30,000-90,000	10
More than 90,000-300,000	20
More than 300,000-500,000	30
More than 500,000	35

(c) 20% for interest, dividends, bonus dividends, rent, capital gains, and incidental income.

3.2 EIT Rates

The EIT rates are separate from IIT rates since the EIT was not designed to be integrated with the IIT. The general EIT rate is set at 25% to promote international competitiveness. This rate is reduced to 20% for small enterprises and 15% for qualified "advanced and new technology enterprises," certain integrated circuit-production enterprises, and other businesses that the central government wants to encourage.

The statutory rate of withholding tax on a wide variety of payments to nonresidents is 20%, but a concessionary rate of 10% is currently applicable for payments of interest, rents, royalties, and other passive income.

4 COMPOSITION OF THE FISCAL SYSTEM

The ratio of tax revenue to Gross Domestic Product (GDP) grew from 10.5% in 1994 to over 20% in 2015. However, the ratio fell in recent years to 18.8% in 2017, 8.0% in 2021, and 12.3% in September 2023.[1] In 2022,[2] as shown in the table below, income taxes produced 34.9% of total tax revenues, with the IIT accounting for 8.9% and the EIT accounting for 26%. Value-added tax (VAT) and consumption tax accounted for 28%, and other taxes made up the rest:

Tax	*Amount (CNY in Billion)*	*% of Total Tax Revenue*
VAT (general)	4,871.7	29%
Consumption Tax (general)	1,669.9	10%
VAT and Consumption Tax on Imports	1,999.5	12%
EIT	4,369.0	26%

1. World Bank, https://data.worldbank.org.cn/indicator/GC.TAX.TOTL.GD.ZS (in Chinese).
2. The Central Government of the People's Republic of China, "Budget Revenue and Expenditures in 2022," at https://www.gov.cn/xinwen/2023-01/31/content_5739311.htm (original in Chinese).

Tax	Amount (CNY in Billion)	% of Total Tax Revenue
IIT	1,492.3	8.9%
Total tax revenue	16,661.4	100%

5 BASIC STRUCTURE OF THE INCOME TAX

5.1 Individuals

The IIT applies to both residents and nonresidents. Residents are taxed on their global income, while nonresidents are taxed only on their Chinese source income. Residence in China is based on an individual having a domicile or habitual abode due to household registration in China or family and economic ties, or by spending more than 183 days in China in a taxation year. Chinese source income includes income from rendering services in China, leasing or licensing property for use in China, receiving interest or dividends from Chinese residents or gains from transferring real property situated in China, and transferring other types of property in China. Individuals without a habitual abode in China are exempt from the IIT on their Chinese source income if their stay in China is less than ninety days in a taxation year, and are exempt from tax on foreign source income if their stay in China is of less than six years' duration.

The IIT is a schedular tax. Income falls into three categories: "comprehensive income" (wages, salaries, income from personal services, and authors' royalties); business income; and income from property (interest, dividends, rent), capital gains, and incidental income (such as gambling winnings). In computing the amount of taxable income, actual costs and expenses are deductible only with respect to business income. For comprehensive income and income from property, only deductions expressly provided by statute are allowed. For example, in computing comprehensive income, there is an annual deduction of CNY 6,000 plus certain policy-based deductions for education, health care, and retirement savings, and a higher basic deduction is available to nonresidents. In computing taxable income from personal services, royalties, and rent, 20% of the gross revenue can be deducted.

The IIT is collected primarily through withholding. However, a tax return must be filed by individuals who have earned comprehensive income, whose income has not been subject to withholding, or whose Chinese household registration has been revoked. Requiring emigrants to file a tax return helps ensure the collection of IIT on income, including capital gains, and, as such, functions as an exit tax.

5.2 Corporations

Under the EIT, each enterprise is a separate taxpayer and there is no consolidation of the income or losses of related enterprises. Resident enterprises are taxed on their worldwide income with a credit for foreign taxes on foreign income. Nonresidents are taxable on Chinese source income at the standard rate of 25% on business income or investment income effectively connected with a business carried on in China and at a rate of 20% (or a concessionary rate of 10%) on investment income and capital gains.

Taxable income includes all types of income, as well as capital gains, and is computed largely in accordance with financial accounting rules. Dividends received by Chinese corporations from resident corporations are exempt from tax; in contrast, dividends received from nonresident corporations are taxable, although the tax is reduced by direct and indirect foreign tax credits. Transactions between resident enterprises and nonresident related parties are subject to transfer pricing rules, which are now being more robustly enforced by the STA. Losses can be carried forward for five years but cannot be carried back. The EIT also contains CFC rules which, in certain circumstances, require Chinese-resident taxpayers to pay tax on the income of their CFCs.

6 TAX LEGISLATION

6.1 Legislative Process for Income Tax Matters

Chinese tax legislation takes three forms, in the following hierarchical order: (1) "law" passed by the NPC; (2) "regulations" passed by the State Council; and (3) "administrative rules" issued by the STA or MOF.

Generally speaking, income tax laws and regulations are drafted by the STA (and/or MOF) and then reviewed, debated, and approved in accordance with the relevant procedures governing the legislative work of the NPC or State Council.

Proposed tax legislation is subject to public consultation. For example, in the case of the amendment to the IIT law in 2018, the State Council submitted a draft amendment bill to the Legal Committee of the Standing Committee of the NPC for review. The Legal Committee held hearings, solicited public comments on the draft amendments, and made some changes to the draft bill before submitting it for approval by the Standing Committee of the NPC, which approved the amendments on August 31, 2018. The State Council then published a draft version of the IIT Regulations for public consultation and issued the final legislation on December 18, 2018. The amended IIT came into effect on January 1, 2019. The STA is required to go through a public consultation process before finalizing its administrative rules and sometimes provides detailed explanatory notes to accompany those rules.

Under Chinese law, tax treaties are negotiated and concluded by the State Council and approved or terminated by the Standing Committee of the NPC.

6.2 Statutory Style

The statutory style differs for "laws," "regulations," and "administrative rules." Tax laws are drafted in general language, providing the architecture of the tax. For example, the EIT Law sets out the charging rules, computation rules, tax rates, method of tax payment, and anti-avoidance rules. However, because administrative matters are covered by the Tax Administration Law, they are not dealt with in the IIT Law or EIT Law. The Tax Administration Law authorizes the State Council to introduce implementation regulations, which supplement the IIT Law and EIT Law with more detailed rules.

Regulations provide details for provisions in the governing law. For example, the IIT Law stipulates that individuals are taxable on the basis of Chinese residence and source of income; the IIT Regulations define the meaning of residence and source of income. Regulations are more lengthy than laws. For example, the IIT Law contains about 4,030 words and the IIT Regulations about 5,107; the EIT Law contains about 5,282 words and the EIT Regulations about 16,544 words.

In some cases, the Regulations specifically delegate rulemaking power to the STA or MOF. For example, Article 119 of the EIT Regulations provides that the detailed rules for determining whether an enterprise is thinly capitalized should be specified by the STA or MOF. In other cases, the STA and MOF issue administrative rules under their own rulemaking powers, including, sometimes, filling legislative gaps resulting from the rapid changes in the Chinese economy and new issues facing the tax administration. For example, in order to implement measures recommended in the G20/OECD BEPS Project, the STA has issued public notices (which are in the nature of administrative rules) with respect to country-by-country reporting, transfer pricing analysis, and the mutual agreement procedure. The STA has also issued rules on the application of the GAAR and extended the scope of the GAAR to include offshore indirect transfers.

In terms of the length of legislation, the EIT system can be seen as a pyramid: the most detailed provisions are found in administrative rules (bottom layer) and the most generally worded provisions are found in the law (top layer). A good example is the legislation related to transfer pricing. Articles 41-44 of the EIT Law contain 375 words, Articles 109-115 of the EIT Regulations contain 1,256, and STA public notices [2016] No. 42, [2016] No. 64, and [2017] No. 6 contain over 26,000 words. The length and structure of administrative regulations attest to the important role of the STA in lawmaking.

6.3 Statutory Interpretation

Statutory interpretation as it understood in Western countries has little relevance for China, for several reasons. First, the power of interpretation rests with the lawmaking body (NPC, State Council, or STA), and not the courts. In theory, the NPC could interpret tax laws, but it has rarely done so in practice. The law authorizes the State Council to introduce implementation regulations, which function as "interpretations" of the law; similarly, administrative rules function as "interpretations" of implementation regulations. Thus, the lower level of legislation functions as "interpretation" of the higher level(s) of legislation, so that, in effect, the STA functions as the "interpreter" of tax legislation.

Second, Chinese courts adjudicate tax disputes under administrative litigation procedures and generally defer to the tax administration's interpretation. Under these procedures, a taxpayer alleges that a specific administrative act (a reassessment notice or collection) is unlawful and identifies the tax office which committed the act (typically the tax authority at the district or municipal level) as the defendant. The case is then heard by local judges, who are also part of the government and who generally have a "lower rank" (and prestige) than the head of the defendant tax office. These judges routinely defer to the tax administration with respect to the meaning of tax legislation and, in particular, the meaning of administrative rules. As a result, taxpayers often argue on the basis of "jurisdictional" issues (such as whether a specific tax office has the jurisdiction to inspect or audit the taxpayer) rather than on the meaning of the law. Moreover, few tax decisions deal with whether the tax rules were correctly applied by the tax authorities—judges typically paraphrase the position taken by the tax authorities and then state that that position is correct. At the time of writing, there appears to be only one case (*Guangzhou Defa*)[3] in which the court offered some type of rationale and attempted to interpret a provision in the Tax Administration Law concerning penalties, before agreeing with the tax authority on the meaning of "a reasonable price."

Third, taxpayers in China simply do not go to court to settle their disputes with the tax authorities. Even though the number of tax cases is increasing, the publicly reported tax decisions by the Supreme People's Court can be counted with one's fingers.

In practice, on the one hand, Chinese courts could be said to take a literal approach to interpreting the tax administrative rules or the position of the tax administration. On the other hand, the STA takes a purposive approach to interpreting the provisions of tax laws and regulations, and, in particular, anti-avoidance rules. The STA has also taken a substance-over-form approach to characterizing taxpayers' transactions.

7 COURTS DEALING WITH TAX MATTERS

7.1 Structure of the Courts

The structure of Chinese courts parallels the structure of the government: the Supreme People's Court (in Beijing), the High Courts of the provinces, the Intermediate Courts (municipal), and the District Courts (district level of a municipality). Each level of court is administratively responsible to its corresponding level of government (e.g., the Supreme People's Court is responsible to the NPC), but all levels of courts are part of a centralized judicial system.

Tax cases are dealt with by the administrative branch of the courts. There are no specialized tax courts. In November 2023, however, a joint (civil, criminal and

3. *Retrial Decision Re Guangzhou Defa Real Estate Construction Ltd. v. No. 1 Tax Inspection Bureau of Guangzhou City Local Tax Bureau*, Guangdong Province (广州德发房产建设有限公司与广东省广州市地方税务局第一稽查局再审行政判决书), Supreme People's Court of the People's Republic of China, Administrative Judges (2015) Xingtizi No. 13, April 17, 2017. For further discussion of the administrative features of the Chinese tax system, *see* Wei Cui, *The Administrative Foundation of the Chinese Fiscal State* (Cambridge University Press, 2023).

administrative) tax panel was formed by a district level court in Xiamen City to hear tax cases, which may create a precedent for other courts.[4] For example, in the *Guangzhou Defa* case, the taxpayer brought a suit before the Tianhe District People's Court in the first instance, appealed to the Intermediate Court of Guangzhou City, then to the High People's Court of Guangdong Province, and then received special permission to apply for reconsideration by the Supreme People's Court. At each level of court (including the Supreme People's Court), a panel of three judges hears the case. The panel of judges hearing the case may consult with the chief judge of the court (who is not on the panel) about its decision. In some cases, a judicial committee consisting of representatives of the Chinese Communist Party may also express its views about the case.

7.2 Judicial Style

The Chinese judicial style has undergone many changes in the past four decades and, in general, now more closely resembles that of civil law countries. For example, taxpayers and the defendant tax office have legal representation; each party presents facts and arguments and the panel of judges makes a collective decision. Judges do not render separate decisions and dissenting decisions are unheard of.

Unlike the situation in both common law and civil law countries, fact-finding does not seem to be limited to the Court of First Instance (or trial court), perhaps because presenting new evidence can be a ground for appeal. As a result, each appeal can be a trial de novo. Even the Supreme People's Court may make new factual findings.

Judgments are typically short by international standards and devoted mainly to a statement of facts and a recitation of each party's position and the relevant laws and regulations. The decision itself is generally brief, with limited analysis.

There is no systematic reporting of court decisions, although many courts now publish decisions on their websites.

8 TAX ADMINISTRATION

The STA, a ministry of the State Council, is responsible for administering tax legislation in China. The STA has unified subnational state tax bureaus and local tax bureaus. Its staff members account for about 10% of the entire Chinese civil service.[5]

The structure of the tax administration reflects the general structure of the government and the courts: the head office of the STA is in Beijing, with tax bureaus at provincial, municipal and district, and local levels. There are close to thirty parallel provincial tax authorities, numerous parallel municipal tax authorities within each province, and parallel district/local tax authorities within a municipality. Officials at

4. Peng Fei, "China's First! Si Ming District Court Created Joint Tax Panel," November 29, 2023, at https://new.qq.com/rain/a/20231129A06NL600 (original in Chinese).
5. State Administration of Taxation Annual Report (2019) https://www.chinatax.gov.cn/chinatax//n810219/n810744/c101701/c5157352/5157352/files/80ba56fa5469410f81bda62811df4391.pdf (original in Chinese).

the district/local levels report only to the immediately higher-level tax authority (i.e., the relevant municipal bureau). Tax authorities at a particular level (e.g., provinces) may borrow the practices of other authorities at the same level, but they are not required to do so unless instructed to do so by the STA. Municipal and provincial tax authorities also have their own websites. Day-to-day dealings with taxpayers take place at the district/local level; provincial-level tax bureaus and the head office are not generally involved in taxpayer files.

As mentioned above, the STA combines "rule-making," "administrative policy-making," and "regulatory" functions, supervising and guiding the work of lower-level offices. Thus, the scope of the powers of the STA is much broader than that of tax authorities in Western countries. Because of the limited role of the courts in resolving tax disputes, particularly those involving statutory interpretation, the STA and its lower-level offices effectively have the power to make rules, interpret the rules, and resolve disputes.

The Tax Administration Law specifies the rights and obligations of taxpayers and the powers and duties of the tax authorities. Because of the lack of tax litigation and reporting of tax decisions, it is difficult to assess the extent to which this law actually influences the conduct of the tax authorities.

The line between tax avoidance and tax evasion in China is not clear. This is particularly true for individuals and domestic enterprises (especially those owned by private investors). Taxpayers often avoid the obligation to pay tax by hiding information from the tax authorities. Research suggests that state-owned enterprises are among the "worst offenders" with respect to tax evasion.[6]

Tax professionals in China are predominantly accountants and registered tax agents. Lawyers are increasingly becoming involved in tax, but they account for a small segment of the tax profession.

9 GENERAL PRINCIPLES

9.1 Relation of Tax and Financial Accounting

In principle, financial accounting is relevant for purposes of the computation of revenues and deductions from business or productive activities of individuals and enterprises. For purposes of the IIT, however, financial accounting is much less relevant because individuals and individual industrial and commercial households (i.e., sole proprietors) may not use accountants to help with their tax reporting; instead, their tax liability may be established on a presumptive basis where no proper accounts are kept, or where there is no evidence that income has been computed accurately. For purposes of the EIT, financial accounting is important as the basis for computing income and taxable income, although financial accounting rules have been replaced by tax rules in some areas.

6. Travis Chow, Bin Ke, Hongqi Yuan and Yao Zhang, "What Types of Publicly Listed Firms Evade Taxes? Evidence from China," https://papers.ssrn.com/sol3/papers.cfm?abstract_id=3160421 (May 2018).

Accounting and financial accounting rules in China have greatly evolved over the past four decades. Prior to 1980, accounting practices for enterprises followed Soviet-style fund accounting based on "fund applications = fund sources." Since the Accounting Law was enacted in 1985, enterprises have been required to keep accounting records and follow accounting standards in reporting. Accounting Standards for Business Enterprises were introduced in 1992; Regulations on Financial Accounting Reports of Enterprises were introduced in 2000 and amended for listed companies in 2004, 2006, and 2014 in response to the evolution of International Financial Reporting Standards (IFRS). Currently, Chinese financial accounting standards are, in principle, consistent with IFRS.

The major areas of divergence between financial accounting and tax accounting include the recognition of capital expenditures, the timing and scope of deductions, and tax incentives.

9.2 Respect for Legal Form

The legal form of transactions is respected, but not in all cases. The purposes of transactions and tax legislation are very important, especially in tax-avoidance cases. For example, because the STA has wide discretionary powers under the broadly worded anti-avoidance rules in the "law" and "regulations," the STA's administrative rules regard the use of a low-tax jurisdiction or a corporate form without much substance as abusive.

9.3 Tax Avoidance and Anti-avoidance Legislation

In both the IIT and the EIT legislation, the most significant anti-avoidance rules target foreign taxpayers and international income. Domestic taxpayers (in particular, individuals and small businesses) generally do not engage in tax planning in order to reduce tax, largely because they often have a multidimensional relationship with local tax authorities, which is often personal and ongoing: they see local tax officials as "teachers about tax," "tax advisers," "ruling officers," or "assessors of tax liability." This type of relationship makes it difficult for tax officials to subsequently reassess taxpayers, who are often unsophisticated about issues of accounting and law, for tax-planning activities which the taxpayer thought (perhaps incorrectly) had been approved by the tax authorities. Thus, for taxpayers without much mobility, following the "advice" of the tax authorities is the safe course of action.

To date, anti-avoidance rules, such as transfer pricing rules, CFC rules, and the GAAR, target transactions between foreign-based multinationals and their affiliates in China and Chinese individuals earning foreign income through entities in tax havens. The essence of these rules is to ignore the legal form and emphasize the substance of the transactions and the purpose of the tax legislation. The purpose of tax provisions is interpreted broadly by the STA. For example, Article 6 of the EIT Regulations defines the source of gains from the transfer of an equity interest in a company to be the country in which the company is resident. Where shares of a nonresident holding company which owned a Chinese-resident company were transferred, the STA invoked the GAAR to tax the gain as Chinese source income; the rationale was that the value of the transferred shares was attributable to the value of the Chinese company and China was thus the source country of the capital gains.

The Chinese system does not have any rules to prevent the use of private corporations to defer tax or split income with family members. Because capital gains are treated as ordinary income, no rules are necessary to prevent surplus stripping. There are also no formal rules to provide relief from the economic double taxation of income earned through corporations.

10 TAX TREATIES

China concluded its first double tax agreement with Japan in 1983, within three years of introducing income taxes. At the end of 2023, China had comprehensive tax treaties with over 110 countries and a double tax arrangement (similar to a double tax treaty) with Hong Kong, Macau, and Taiwan. China has also concluded Tax Information Exchange Agreements with countries such as the Bahamas, the British Virgin Islands, and the Cayman Islands. China has signed the *Multilateral Convention on Mutual Assistance in Tax Matters*, the *Multilateral Convention to Implement Tax Treaty Related Measures to Prevent Base Erosion and Profit Shifting* (MLI), and the *Multilateral Competent Authority Agreement on Automatic Exchange of Financial Information*.[7]

China's extensive tax treaty network includes treaties with all OECD member countries, other BRICS countries (Brazil, Russia, India, China and South Africa), and many developing countries on every continent. The expansion of the treaty network has been driven by the growth of inbound and outbound investments and the perceived importance of tax treaties in promoting trade and investment. Many treaties with OECD countries which were concluded in the 1980s and 1990s have recently been renegotiated to reflect the fact that China became a capital-exporting country around the turn of this century and amid growing concerns about treaty abuse. China's "belt and road initiative" involving China's export of capital, typically in the form of infrastructure projects, has contributed further to the expansion of the treaty network.

China's tax treaties follow the general pattern of the OECD Model treaty but also contain some provisions of the UN Model treaty. For example, following the UN Model, the threshold for a permanent establishment is generally low, and royalties are taxable in the source country; as a result, the scope of source taxation is broader than under the OECD Model treaty. Earlier treaties contain tax-sparing clauses, but many such clauses have been phased out. Recent treaties have incorporated additional anti-abuse rules, including those recommended by the G20/OECD BEPS Project.

When China signed the MLI, the first round of updates included forty-six of China's tax treaties with most of its major trading and investment partners, but not the United States, which has not signed the MLI. The most significant update is the insertion of a treaty general anti-abuse rule (principal purpose test) into each covered

7. *See* STA, "Tax Treaties," at https://www.chinatax.gov.cn/eng/c101276/c101732/index.html.

treaty, alongside a new "preamble" reinforcing the principle that tax treaties are not intended to facilitate tax avoidance. Other updates include the revision of the tie-breaker test for corporate tax residence in some treaties and modernization of the mutual agreement procedure and associated enterprise articles in certain older treaties. However, the updates do not include the new permanent establishment rules, arbitration, or transparent-entity rules.

11 SOURCES OF TAX LAW

Sources of tax law in China are limited to legislation in the form of law, regulations, and administrative rules. Court judgments are not a source of law. Tax treaties are a source of tax law, as discussed above in section 10.

Not all publications by the STA are in the nature of "administrative rules." For example, advance rulings and circulars with respect to specific issues or "replies" to inquiries from a lower-level tax authority are not considered to be such rules. Although these types of publications are not "legislation," tax authorities follow them in practice, and since Chinese courts tend to defer to the positions of the tax authorities, they have de facto legal influence.

France

Marilyne Sadowsky

1 HISTORY

1.1 1914: The Birth of the Income Tax

Income tax was introduced in France to finance the war effort during the First World War, although earlier proposals for some type of income tax were made in 1884 and 1900, based on Joseph Caillaux's (who later became Minister of Finance) analysis of various foreign systems, including those of Germany, Austria, the United States, Great Britain, the Netherlands, Prussia, and Sweden. The French system was largely inspired by the Prussian and English models. In the end, income tax was created by two laws of 1914 and 1917. The first law of July 15, 1914 introduced a progressive general tax on all income; a second law of July 31, 1917 introduced a system of proportional taxation by income category, i.e., a "schedular" (*cédulaire*) system, comprising 6 schedules at the time (industrial and commercial profits; agricultural profits; noncommercial profits; salaries, wages, and pensions; taxes on securities and property income). While this system placed natural persons and legal entities on an equal footing, the idea of establishing a separate tax for legal entities, based in particular on the German and American models, had been put forward as early as 1926 by Professor Henry Laufenberger in his doctoral thesis.

The relatively complex structure of an income tax based on a mixed system—schedular taxes levied on categories of income and a progressive unitary tax based on overall income—was called into question during the interwar period, due to growing inequality. Between 1918 and 1948, the marginal tax rate rose from 10% to 70%.

1.2 1945: The Birth of the Wealth Tax

The first modern tax on wealth, under the name National Solidarity tax (*Impôt de solidarité nationale*), appeared in 1945. It was created after World War II to compensate for the inequalities created by the war. Indeed, while some people suffered considerable losses, others were fortunate enough to be able to keep their assets. The original aim of this tax was therefore to compensate for the inequality that had arisen between those who had been able to keep their assets and those who had lost them, by requiring the fortunate to share in the national solidarity effort. The tax comprised two levies: a progressive wealth tax and a wartime enrichment tax on increases in wealth in France between January 1, 1940 and June 4, 1945. The confiscation of illicit profits also contributed to the idea of tax justice, with the establishment of confiscation committees responsible for the seizure of such profits.

After World War II, trade unionists took up the fight for a tax on capital, through various reform projects presented in 1947 and then in 1965, which launched the idea of a wealth tax. The idea was taken up again in the second half of the 1970s, this time proposing to tax accumulated wealth rather than wealth being accumulated, so as not to penalize economic initiative. It was against this backdrop that the tax on large fortunes (*impôt sur les grandes fortunes*) was introduced by the 1982 Finance Act in order to make the richest pay to reduce inequalities. A fortune was considered "large" if it exceeded FRS 3,000,000 (today's equivalent of EUR 460,000) and was taxed at a progressive rate. The overriding objectives of this tax were tax justice and the redistribution of wealth. However, concerns about capital flight led to the abolition of the tax in 1986 and in 1988, a Wealth Solidarity Tax (*impôt de solidarité sur la fortune*) was introduced. "Solidarity" is the important word here since the tax was used to finance a minimum solidarity income paid to the poorest (*Revenu minimum d'insertion*) which was created at the same time. Then, in 2011, a major reform was carried out with a reduction in the wealth tax to compensate for the abolition of the "tax shield" (introduced in 2007, under which a taxpayer could not be taxed on more than 50% of their income). To offset this relief, in 2012 an "exceptional contribution on high incomes" was enacted and is still included in the income tax. This contribution is interesting because it gave rise to a constitutional decision (n°2012-662), providing a method for determining when a tax is confiscatory on the grounds of the principle of contributive capacity.

Finally, the solidarity tax on wealth was abolished in 2018 and replaced with a tax on real estate wealth to finance the real economy (*impôt sur la fortune immobilière*). The threshold for application of this tax remains set at EUR 1,300,000, but once this amount is exceeded, the six-bracket progressive scale applies from EUR 800,000 upwards. The rate schedule is progressive, with a 0% bracket up to EUR 800,000 and a 1.50% marginal rate over EUR 10,000,000. The cumulative amount of both this tax and the income tax is capped at 75% of the taxpayer's annual income.

Wealth tax applies to individuals. In the past, the tax base covered all assets of all kinds held by the taxpayer. Since 2018, the policy has changed and only real estate assets are currently subject to taxation. To avoid holding housing assets through intermediaries, the law requires all holding structures to be analyzed to determine whether real estate held through companies can be taxed. Real estate used for the taxpayer's professional activity or for the operational activity of a company with an industrial or commercial activity is excluded from the scope of this tax. Although

France has opted to maintain this type of tax, some countries that had abolished it have decided to reintroduce it to offset the effects of current economic problems.

1.3 1948: The Birth of Corporate Income Tax

The 1948 tax reform was a structural reform, involving no fewer than eleven laws, one of which gave the government the power to carry out this reform by decree. The decree of December 9, 1948 introduced the corporate income tax in order to enact a specific proportional tax on companies, the basis of which was, and still is, fundamentally determined according to the rules applicable to the schedular category of industrial and commercial income.

On the one hand, the main idea of the 1948 reform was to create a real break with the old system, which was seen as too complex, with numerous taxes each with their own specific rules and rates, an overwhelming tax burden for taxpayers, particularly individuals, and an emerging distinction between income from work and income from capital. In this respect, the equality of tax treatment between individuals and legal entities was unsatisfactory: although both categories of persons were subject to schedular taxes, only individuals paid the progressive general tax. In the case of companies, profits were subject to industrial and commercial profits tax at a rate of 24%, the same as for individuals, and any distributions were then subject to a 30% withholding tax on income from securities (*Impôt sur le revenu des valeurs mobilières*—IRVM) payable by the shareholder. In reality, commercial companies benefited from tax advantages resulting from loopholes in tax legislation and tax planning techniques specific to each type of company, such as the exemption of undistributed profits. This situation explains the change: before 1948, taxation was based on the nature or origin of income; since 1948, it has taken into account the legal status of the taxpayer, whether an individual or a company. The creation of a sui generis tax was therefore intended to offset the economic advantage of not taxing retained earnings. As a result, corporate profits became taxable at the standard corporate tax rate (24%), while profits distributed to shareholders were also taxed at the income tax rate, resulting in economic double taxation.

On the other hand, the 1948 reform did not aim to abandon the old system entirely. It was necessary to improve the income tax system introduced by Caillaux in 1917, without jeopardizing budget revenues, by finding a compromise between tradition and modernity. For this reason, Article 221 of the General Tax Code (*Code général des impôts*—CGI) now states that "corporate income tax is established under the same conditions and subject to the same penalties as income tax (industrial and commercial profits, taxed according to actual profit or according to the simplified system)." Thus, the method of calculating taxable profit is always determined by reference to the rules applicable to industrial and commercial profits. The determination of taxable income for companies leads to the determination of a global income subject either to income tax or to corporate income tax, depending on the type of company concerned.

The 1948 reform also led to changes in the income tax system, in two parts. The first part was a proportional tax, replacing the old schedular taxes, which took very little account of the taxpayer's personality; the new tax addressed the concepts of income generation for its ordinary part, or income distribution for its special part relating to securities income. The second part was a progressive surtax, replacing the old general income tax, which continues, with a few exceptions, largely identical to the old surtax. This surtax took into account the taxpayer's personality, as well as the concept of income disposal. The 1948 reform therefore produced a mixed system, based on both the nature of the income and the taxable person. It applied to individuals and could also be applied to legal entities since they could be subject to the progressive surtax.

Legal entities were in all cases specifically taken into account for purposes of corporate income tax. This tax was in fact designed for capital companies, the main aim being to combat certain fraudulent practices of large corporations and to ensure a fair distribution of the burden between individuals and legal entities. It was formerly reserved for capital companies and public enterprises of a commercial or industrial nature but could be extended to partnerships by option. Shareholders paid tax on the portion of income distributed to them. In addition, the tax applied to all corporate income. This new model was therefore built on old elements, which explains why a distinction is still made today between companies subject to income tax and those subject to corporate income tax.

The law of December 29, 1959 unified the income tax system by abolishing the proportional tax and the progressive surtax so that all income, whatever its origin, is now taxed according to the same scale, under the slogan "equal income, equal tax." In 1971, the income tax was renamed "*impôt sur le revenu*," abandoning its former name of "*impôt annuel unique sur les revenus des personnes physiques*," and continues to exist alongside the corporate income tax.

1.4 1990s: The Birth of Social Security Contributions and Levies

Given the low yield of income tax, additional taxes have been created over the last thirty years to cover the deficits of certain social and pension schemes. The generalized social contribution (*Contribution sociale généralisée*, CSG) and the social debt reimbursement contribution (*Contribution au remboursement de la dette sociale*, CRDS) were introduced in 1991 and 1996, respectively, and now amount to 9.2% (GSG) and 0.5% (CRDS). Finally, the "Solidarity Levy" (*Prélèvement de solidarité*) has applied since 2019 at a rate of 7.5% on income from assets and investments, replacing three previous levies or contributions created between 1998 and 2009. Depending on the nature of the income, in most cases, these proportional taxes add a total additional burden of 17.2% on the taxpayer (CSG at 9.2% for earned income or capital income, CRDS at 0.5%, and 7.5% social levy on income from assets and investments).

2 CONSTITUTIONAL ISSUES

2.1 General Principles

Taxes have historically played a central role in French constitutional laws. The 1958 Constitution and the laws to which it refers having the same legal value (the 1789 Declaration of Human and Civil Rights, the 1946 Preamble to the Constitution, the 2004 Charter of the Environment, and a set of unwritten rules derived from the Constitutional Council) contain many constitutional principles which can serve as a basis for reviewing tax law.

The main principles are well known. First, the principle of legality is expressed in Article 34 of the Constitution, which states that the law sets the rules relating to "the base, rates and collection procedures for taxes of all kinds." This exclusive competence of the legislature, an expression of the consent to taxation enshrined in Article 14 of the 1789 Declaration of Rights, is linked to Article 37 of the Constitution, which states that "matters other than those falling within the domain of the law are of a regulatory nature." However, the exclusive legislative authority of the legislature does not prevent tax matters from being delegated to the government, on the basis of Article 38 of the Constitution (rarely used in practice) or prevent the tax authorities from issuing interpretative instructions (*see* section 8.2).

Second, the principle of equality has two components: equality before the law, enshrined in Article 6 of the 1789 Declaration of Rights, which states that the law "must be the same for all, whether it protects or punishes," and equality before public burdens, contained in Article 13 of the 1789 Declaration of Rights, which states that "the common contribution must be equally distributed among all citizens according to their faculties." An interesting body of case law has developed since 2012 to determine when a tax is considered confiscatory on the basis of Article 13 of the 1789 Declaration of Rights, in order to ensure that the tax rate set by the legislature does not impose a burden on taxpayers which would result in a clear breach of equality. As a result, taxes must be levied in accordance with each person's ability to pay, and in an egalitarian way.

Other principles are sanctioned by the Constitutional Council, such as the principle of the necessity of taxation, contained in Article 14 of the 1789 Declaration of Rights, which implies that taxation is necessary because it has a budgetary purpose and enables public expenditure to be financed. The same applies to the retroactivity of fiscal law when the legislature introduces more severe tax penalties, which is prohibited by the Constitutional Court on the basis of an extensive assessment of Article 8 of the 1789 Declaration of Rights. Tax penalties must not be retroactive. Similarly, on the basis of Article 16 of the 1789 Declaration of Rights, retroactive laws cannot prejudice a taxpayer's rights that have been recognized by a court decision having the force of res judicata.

2.2 Constitutionality Review

Since 1958, all annual Finance Acts may be subject to constitutional review before they come into force, in which case, the law is referred to the Constitutional council by the

President of the Republic, Prime Minister, President of the National Assembly or Senate, or by at least 60 deputies or 60 senators. Since March 1, 2010, constitutional review has also been carried out *a posteriori*, on referral from the highest courts (*Conseil d'Etat* (CE) or *(Cour de cassation)*, depending on the tax concerned), to determine that a tax provision which has already come into force does not infringe rights and freedoms guaranteed by the Constitution. In this case, it is the petitioner who raises the question during proceedings before a court. This is known as a priority question of constitutionality (*Question Prioritaire de Constitutionnalité*—QPC). This type of control is becoming increasingly common in practice, with statistics published by the Constitutional Council in 2020 showing that tax law is the area in which the most decisions have been handed down since 2010, ahead of criminal law.

2.3 International and European Laws

Article 55 of the Constitution enshrines the principle of primacy of international tax treaties. Thus, a treaty may, from the time of its ratification or approval and subject to reciprocity, set aside the application of domestic tax law. In addition, in the *Schneider Electric* case of 2002, the administrative judge (CE) recognized the principle of subsidiarity of international tax treaties, making it possible to depart from the principle of primacy. This principle applies in two steps. First, the administrative judge considers national tax law "to determine whether, in this respect, the disputed taxation has been validly established and, if so, on the basis of what classification." Second, it is up to the court, where appropriate, "by comparing this classification with the stipulations of the treaty, to determine whether or not the treaty is an obstacle to the application of tax law." In reality, this principle is an interpretive grid adopted by the administrative judge in order to apply a tax treaty. However, the Supreme Judicial Court (*Cour de cassation*) rejected this method in 2005, stating that it is necessary first to refer to the tax treaty, thus creating legal uncertainty for taxpayers, depending on whether the tax in question falls within the jurisdiction of the *Conseil d'Etat* or the *Cour de cassation*.

While France's European commitments also fall within the scope of Article 55 of the Constitution, they are given a specific constitutional status. Indeed, Article 88-1 of the Constitution lays down the constitutional foundations of France's participation in the European Union (EU), which enabled the Constitutional Council in 2004 to enshrine the existence of a Community legal order into domestic law which is distinct from the international legal order, forming the basis for the constitutional requirement to incorporate EU directives into French law. In addition, the national legislature's room to maneuver in tax matters is limited by the freedoms of the internal market and competition law, in the forefront of which is state aid.

Finally, the 1950 European Convention on Human Rights (ECHR), which contains fundamental principles and freedoms similar to those contained in the 1789 Declaration of Rights, also plays an important role. In 2013, for example, the ECHR was the basis for the protection of taxpayers' legitimate expectations, i.e., the legitimate expectation of obtaining property or a claim, based on Article 1 of the Additional Protocol to the ECHR on the right to respect for property. Thus, drawing on this international and European environment, the Constitutional Council recognized that "without sufficient grounds of general interest, the legislature may neither undermine legally acquired situations nor call into question the effects that may legitimately be expected of such situations" or "situations born under the empire of previous texts," whether or not they are acquired.

3 TAX RATES

3.1 Progressive Income Tax

The income tax scale is adjusted each year to take account of currency erosion and inflation. The income tax scale was adjusted by 4.8% by the Finance Act for 2024. The 2024 scale applies to 2023 income:

Taxable Income (EUR)	*Tax Rate (%)*
11,294 or less	0
11,295-28,797	11
28,798-82,341	30
82,342-177,106	41
177,106 and over	45

The general structure of the income tax scale has changed little. The number of brackets was reduced in 2006 from 7 to 5 and the marginal rate of the progressive scale was also reduced, from over 60% before the mid-1980s to 45% since 2013. The progressivity method involves breaking down total income into different fractions, according to the 5 brackets, then subjecting each of these fractions to the corresponding tax rate in order to sum up the result obtained in the different brackets. This scale is applied on the basis of the composition of the tax household and the application of a family quotient, which reduces the progressive nature of income tax in favor of large families (*see* section 5.1). In reality, the French system is not purely global since it distinguishes between categories of income which are not taken into account in the same way—in fact, some items are taxed completely separately at a proportional rate, with the possibility of opting for the progressive scale (*see* section 5). The difficulty is that not all income categories are treated in exactly the same way.

3.2 Flat-Rate Individual Income Taxes

Social security contributions are high and represent a heavy burden, mainly on labor costs. The current rates of the CSG and the CRDS on wages, business income, pensions, and unemployment benefits are respectively 9.2% (initially 1.1%) and 0.5%. Depending on the nature of the income, certain rates change and the cumulative contributions applicable may vary. For example, the CSG on capital income and gains is 9.2%, to which must be added the 0.5% CRDS and the 7.5% solidarity levy, amounting to an overall rate of 17.2% since 2018. In contrast, some specific rates of CSG are levied on pensions so that, depending on the household's reference tax income and number of units, the rate may be zero, reduced (3.8%), median (6.6%), or normal (8.3%). Finally, a new additional contribution, the additional solidarity contribution for autonomy (*Contribution additionnelle de solidarité pour l'autonomie*—CASA), was created in 2004 to finance the loss of autonomy of elderly and disabled people. It is deducted from the amount of certain old-age and disability benefits paid to people domiciled in France, at a rate of 0.3%.

When these taxes are added to the income tax, the marginal rates of tax on income of individuals are much higher than they appear to be in the income tax rate schedule, even allowing for certain differences in their respective bases and a partial deduction of the CSG from the basis of the income tax.

3.3 Corporate Income Tax

The corporate income tax rate gradually rose to 50% in 1958, then began to fall in 1986, reaching 33.33% in 1993. In order to bring France in line with the European weighted average corporate income tax rate, but also to boost business competitiveness and attract investment, a reduction in the normal corporate income tax rate was made in 2017, gradually reducing the corporate income tax rate from 33.33% to 25% in 2022. In addition, a 3.3% social surtax is levied on corporate income tax in excess of EUR 763,000.

In 1997, a reduced corporate tax rate of 15% was introduced to strengthen the capital base of small- and medium-sized businesses, which have less access to bank loans and capital markets. Consequently, small- and medium-sized companies (i.e., those whose turnover does not exceed EUR 10,000,000 and whose equity is at least 75%-owned by individuals) benefit from a reduced rate of 15% applicable to profits up to EUR 42,500 (EUR 38,120 before 2023). Above this threshold, profits are taxed at the normal 25% corporate income tax rate. It is interesting that this lower rate for small and medium-sized companies persists, especially since the normal corporate tax rate has been significantly reduced without any adjustment to the reduced rate.

In addition, the following types of income enjoy special treatment: non-profit organizations are subject to the specific rates of 24% for income from assets (e.g., property rentals, agricultural profits) and 10% for income from movable property (e.g., bonds); dividends received from shareholdings in subsidiaries and capital gains on equity holdings are fully tax exempt, except for the inclusion in income of 5% of the dividends (or 1% in certain cases for integrated groups) and 12% for gross capital gains to offset the deduction of expenses with respect to such dividends and gains; finally, capital gains on the sale of shares in real estate companies held for at least two years are taxed at 19%. These examples confirm the existence of some specific carve-outs for small- and medium-sized enterprises. Certain reduced rates exist for these enterprises and reflect a political will to encourage research, non-profit organizations, or the transfer of shares in listed real estate companies.

4 BASIC STRUCTURE OF THE FISCAL SYSTEM

One of the traditional basic features of the French tax system was said to be that income taxes represent a small proportion of tax revenues compared to the systems of other developed countries. The main reason for this difference was that the income tax, although highly progressive, contained many exemptions, allowances, and tax reductions of all kinds so that its burden was concentrated on the highest income categories, while almost 50% of households were exempt.

These characteristics of income taxation remain fundamentally unchanged today; for example, in 2022, only 44% of tax households were taxed. However, a clear trend toward income taxation contributing a greater part of tax revenues has become apparent. According to statistics from the Ministry of Economy and Finance, in 2023: Value-Added Tax (VAT) accounts for 37.5% of gross tax revenues; income tax for 24.1%, corporate income tax for 18.4%, and 20% for other gross tax revenues. As a percentage of Gross Domestic Product (GDP), income taxes doubled during the last twenty-five years of the twentieth century, with a dramatic increase at the end of the 1990s. According to the latest Organisation for Economic Co-operation and Development (OECD) statistics, since 2000 income taxes account for about 11% of GDP, i.e., as much as taxes on goods and services—although there was a slight increase for taxes on goods and services in 2022 compared to income taxation, which had for many years been by far the most substantial source of public revenues (excluding social security).

This increase is easily explained by the creation of the CSG, the CRDS, and the social solidarity levy to help finance welfare benefits, and by the subsequent marked rise in the rate of the CSG and the solidarity levy. As a matter of fact, these new-style income taxes, with wide bases and flat rates, have proved very productive in terms of raising revenue (about EUR 119 billion for the CSG in 2023 and the other flat-rate income taxes, compared to approximately EUR 90.7 billion for income tax, EUR 72.2 billion for corporate tax, and EUR 100.4 billion for VAT, based on 2024 estimates).

At the same time, and for the same reason, social security contributions (not to be mistaken for the abovementioned social levies, which are income taxes) correspondingly decreased from 18.5% of GDP in the years 1985-1995 to about 16%-17% since 2000. They must be added to income taxes, since they are also essentially levied on income, and especially on earned income.

Tax revenues as a percentage of GDP, after having been rather stable (about 44%) after 1996, have substantially increased in the past few years and reached a record level of 46.2% in 2017 (compared to a 34.2% average in other OECD countries). While a decline was anticipated after 2017 and reached a low of 44.9%, the year 2022 saw a further rise to around 46.1%.

5 BASIC STRUCTURE OF THE INCOME TAX

5.1 Income Taxes on Individuals

Today, income tax is a direct tax on the total income of individuals in a tax household and on certain types of companies, namely, single individual companies with no legal personality of their own, and partnerships with legal personality of their own and unlimited liability.

The concept of income is not defined by the CGI—only certain characteristics of income are prescribed. Income is annual, global, net, and disposable. There are in fact two versions of the concept of income. The first arose in 1914, when the income tax system was created, with income seen in reference to civil law as a permanent source of income which can be renewed. The second concept, based more on economics, developed gradually by doctrine and jurisprudence, considers income to be a set of real net gains realized over the course of a year, whatever their form or source, and encompassing both occasional profits and capital gains. In the absence of a choice, we use both concepts.

There are 8 categories of income, 6 of which are inherited from the schedular system of 1917 (remuneration paid to directors of certain companies and capital gains are the last two categories). Currently, for traditional progressive income tax, gross taxable income necessarily falls into one of the following eight categories, which can be grouped into income from work (1 to 5) and income from capital (6 to 8):

(1) salaries, wages, pensions and life annuities;
(2) remuneration paid to directors of certain companies;
(3) industrial and commercial profits;
(4) agricultural profits;
(5) noncommercial profits;
(6) securities income;
(7) property income; and
(8) capital gains.

In 2010, it was proposed to merge certain categories to create a single category of professional profits, covering at least industrial, commercial, and noncommercial profits. This project was abandoned in the face of strong protest from the liberal professions, which are traditionally taxed in the noncommercial profits category. In addition, it was proposed to eliminate category 2 (company directors), seen as meaningless, since these directors almost exclusively receive salaries and wages (category 1). In the absence of reform, these discrepancies raise the deeper question of how to tax income from labor versus income from capital. An initial rebalancing in the taxation of these two types of income took place as early as 1991, with the extension of social security deductions to income from assets and, in particular, the creation of the CSG, which is intended to apply to all types of income. While this rebalancing has favored labor income, the correct balance is elusive, and several changes in tax policy can be explained by this desire to rebalance.

Three major difficulties have resulted from the current structure of eight income categories.

First, each of the eight categories retains its own specific set of rules (and often several different sets of rules) used to calculate net income or loss. Exclusions from income and deductible expenses are normally taken into account at their actual amount. However, in certain cases, expenses (or certain categories of expenses) may be deducted from gross income or sales on a flat-rate basis at the taxpayer's option (e.g., in the case of property income, the possibility of deducting a flat-rate amount of 30% of declared gross annual income (less than or equal to EUR 15,000)). In addition, with respect to industrial and commercial profits, noncommercial profits or agricultural profits, certain sales thresholds allow taxpayers to opt for the micro, simplified real, or normal real regimes, each with different reporting and accounting obligations.

Second, great instability is caused by often contradictory tax policies affecting certain categories of income, especially capital gains and dividends. Until 2004, capital gains on noncommercial real estate held by private individuals were taxed at a progressive rate, with an adjustment to take account only of real enrichment in order to correct for the effects of inflation. From 2004, the system changed to a proportional rate, replacing the inflation adjustment with a system of deductions based on the period of ownership. In 2013, the situation became even more complicated, with the introduction of a tax on large capital gains (over EUR 50,000), with progressive taxation depending on the amount of the capital gain. A similar change in policy applied to income from movable property. Although interest and dividends were formerly subject to the progressive income tax scale, in 2018 a proportional rate was adopted in order to encourage investment in shares. As a result, for individuals, dividends are no longer subject to the heavy progressive scale applicable to earned income but are taxed under the flat rate of 12.8% plus 17.2% for social security contributions, for a total of 30%. However, the taxpayer may opt for the progressive income tax rate in order to benefit from a 40% deduction of the gross amount received.

Third, the distinction between different categories of persons (individuals and companies) means that some companies may be subject to the progressive scale of income tax (single individual companies and partnerships), while others (capital companies) are subject to corporate income tax (*see* section 5.2). Certain complications arise from this situation. First, although the distinction between income tax and corporation tax was created in 1948, certain rules sometimes apply differently to income tax and corporation tax. For example, the distinction between short-term capital gains (less than two years) and long-term capital gains (more than two years) was applied indiscriminately as early as 1965 to business capital gains subject to income tax and corporate income tax, until a 1997 law maintained this distinction only for income tax. Thus, all capital gains realized by companies subject to corporate income tax are taxed as ordinary income, although numerous exemptions for entrepreneurs exist, notably to encourage the transfer of businesses. Second, another complicating factor may be the need to take into account the form of the company or the nature of the business. This is the case where a structure has mixed characteristics borrowing from partnerships and capital companies, For example, a limited partnership (*société en commandite simple*) is subject to both income tax and corporation tax, depending on whether the partner has limited or unlimited liability. This is also the case where the nature of the activity calls for taxation under corporate income tax (e.g., civil companies due to their commercial purpose). Finally, this distinction between income tax and corporate income tax also applies to the territorial application of income tax, since the principle of territoriality applies to corporate income tax and the income of nonresident individuals, while the worldwide principle applies to resident individuals. For legal entities, the place of operation is of primary importance, whereas for individuals it is the place of residence.

The basis for progressive personal income tax is, in principle at least, the algebraic sum of net income and losses of all categories earned by the various members of the same tax household. Consequently, an overall net income must then be determined. It is this net overall income that is taxed on the progressive scale, except for the specific examples of proportional taxation mentioned above.

Some specific rules apply for the deduction of certain losses or expenses and for the application of special allowances. The taxpayer may have a global loss or global positive income taxable on the progressive scale, which can give rise to two different situations. On the one hand, losses in the various categories are normally deductible from overall income, and any overall loss can be carried forward in computing global income for six years. In this respect, losses in certain categories are not deductible from overall income and can be offset only against income of the same kind under certain conditions (agricultural deficits, property deficits exceeding EUR 10,700, and losses from non-professional noncommercial activities). On the other hand, in the case of positive net income, certain expenses can be deducted. Only expenses relating to compulsory or court-ordered alimony payments are deducted directly from overall income. There is a ceiling on the deductibility of alimony paid to adult children (EUR 6,368 in 2023). The cost of caring for people over 75 years of age in the taxpayer's household is also deductible up to a certain limit (EUR 3,786 in 2023). Special allowances may be applied to this net overall income by certain taxpayers meeting strictly defined conditions (allowance in favor of certain elderly or disabled people, and allowance for married dependent children). Finally, specific deduction and territoriality rules apply to social security contributions; for example, CSG is only partially deductible from the income tax base and nonresidents are not entitled to deduct it at all.

The calculation of global income is influenced by the concepts of household (*foyer*) and family share system (*quotient familial*), which leads to treating the household as a single economic unit of taxation. Thus, taxable income is divided into a certain number of shares based on the taxpayer's situation and family expenses. The household can be composed of a single person or married couple or, since 1999, two unmarried partners who have entered into a civil partnership (*pacte civil de solidarité*), and, subject to certain elections or exceptions, dependent persons, mainly children. According to the family share system (*quotient familial*) created in 1945, the household net income is divided by the number of shares (approximately) corresponding to the number of people in the family, before being subjected to the single progressive tax schedule. The figure so obtained is then multiplied by the relevant number of shares to determine the gross tax. This system was created at the end of World War II in order to boost the birth rate and, by including family expenses in the tax rate, it reduced the progressive tax rate in favor of large families. With respect to the assessment of income tax, one of the biggest changes relates to the introduction of the withholding tax (*prélèvement à la source*) since 2019.

5.2 Corporate Income Tax

Under Article 206 of the CGI, capital companies are subject to corporate income tax regardless of their form or purpose. These companies are considered to be fiscally opaque and are taxed in their own name. Profits distributed to shareholders, either natural or legal person, are taxed in their hands at the time of distribution. Partner liability is limited to the capital contributed. Only profits made by companies operating in France or attributable to France under a tax treaty are taken into account. In this context, it is essential to determine the place of operation (Article 209 CGI).

Taxable profits are calculated by reference to the rules applicable to industrial and commercial profits. The determination of taxable income leads to the determination of net profit for corporation tax purposes. This profit must reflect the existence of an enrichment. Two definitions of net profit coexist in Article 38 of the CGI. Paragraph 1 gives an analytical definition based on a global approach to the company's income, which compares the income and expenses recorded in the income statement. Paragraph 2 gives a synthetic definition, based on changes in net assets (a balance-sheet approach). Determining taxable profit requires linking accounting and tax results, as well as making certain adjustments.

Two situations may arise for a company. Where the profit is positive, it will be taxed at the normal or reduced proportional rate. Unlike the situation for companies subject to income tax, where the company has a loss, the loss cannot be deducted from the partner's personal overall income. In this case, there are two possibilities, reflecting Franco-German convergence. The loss may be carried forward indefinitely (Article 209 CGI), subject to an annual limit of EUR 1 million plus 50% of the profit in excess of EUR 1 million. The remaining loss can continue to be carried forward under the same conditions until it is completely used up. Alternatively, the loss can be carried back one year only (Article 220 quinquies CGI), up to a ceiling of EUR 1 million per year. As a result, the company benefits from a tax credit which it can use to reduce corporate income tax payable for the five years following the year in which the carryforward option is exercised. At the end of this five-year period, the company may request repayment of the unused amount. Shareholders are subject to income tax when dividends are distributed (flat tax of 30% for individuals) or to corporate income tax (25% for corporate shareholders). In addition, profits earned in France by a foreign company through a permanent establishment are deemed to be distributed to nonresident shareholders; they are subject to a branch tax payable on the total profits of the permanent establishment through a 25% withholding tax, barring exceptions (notably on the basis of European law or the existence of a tax treaty).

As a result of the 2004 Finance Act, France no longer has a system for eliminating economic double taxation. Prior to this date, a mechanism created in 1965 (*avoir fiscal*) made it possible to limit the tax burden on profit distributions in order to encourage equity investment. When profits were distributed, individual or corporate shareholders received their dividends from the company, as well as a tax credit equal to half the sums actually paid out by the company. This system was eliminated after its extension to nonresident shareholders, which proved too costly for the French State, and also because the *Verkooijen* case of the Court of Justice of the European Union (CJEU) recognized a difference in tax treatment between domestic and foreign dividends.

In the past, to mitigate the effects of the territoriality principle of corporate income tax, which does not allow foreign losses to be set off against income from France, certain exceptions containing worldwide elements existed. These have all been abolished: worldwide and consolidated profits (*bénéfice mondial et consolidé*) (1965-2011), provisions for foreign establishments (1972-2003), and provisions for foreign establishments for small- and medium-sized businesses (2009-2014). As a result, the only current exceptions to the rigor of corporate tax territoriality are the specific regimes applicable to groups of companies. These schemes are optional and can be cumulative, provided that each of the conditions is met. The participation-exemption regime (*mère-fille*—Articles 145 and 216 FTC), created in 1917, provides a dividend exemption to ensure tax neutrality within the group and a capital gains exemption to encourage restructuring, in both cases subject to the inclusion in income of 5 % of the dividends, or 1 % in certain cases for integrated groups and 12 % for gross capital gains (*see* section 3.3). The tax consolidation regime (*intégration fiscale*—Article 223 A and 223 B CGI), created in 1988, enables companies to consolidate their results at the level of a group head company and authorizes the offsetting of profits and losses, as well as neutralizing certain intragroup transactions. One of the difficulties in applying this system is that all integrated companies must be subject to corporate income tax in France. This situation led to the development of a significant body of European case law and led to changes in the French system by authorizing two types of integration: horizontal (*SCA Group Holding BV* in 2014) and vertical (*Papillon* in 2008). Finally, there are specific rules applicable to corporate restructuring, including operations which modify share capital through techniques such as changes of capital or mergers and other similar operations (partial contributions of assets and demergers).

In reality, without going as far as the worldwide and consolidated profit regime, and pending the introduction of a European group regime, these specific group regimes allow certain tax breaks. Although groups of companies do not have legal personality, these tax regimes make it possible to take account of their economic reality by recognizing the real links that unite these companies and giving them legal effect.

6 LEGISLATION

6.1 Legislative Process

Most tax measures are enacted in the form of initial or amending Finance Acts. The initial Finance Acts set the course for the year, while the Amending Finance Acts rectify it. Both acts are normally passed in the same terms by both houses of parliament (*Assemblée Nationale* and *Sénat*) as part of an accelerated legislative process in which the *Assemblée Nationale*, the only house elected by direct universal suffrage, may, if necessary, have the last word. Finance bills are necessarily government bills but deputies may, under strict conditions, table new provisions or amendments as long as they do not entail a reduction in the level of public revenues (Article 40 of the Constitution). Consequently, only parliamentary amendments accepted or inspired by the government stand a chance of being included in the law.

Tax provisions can also be included in non-tax laws, and major tax reforms have been carried out in this way. However, they are usually of government origin and deputies' right to amend is limited in the same way as for finance bills.

The legislative process is rapid, whether for ordinary bills or finance bills. Parliament has just seventy days in which to vote on finance bills (first reading in the *Assemblée Nationale*—40 days; first reading in the *Sénat*—20 days; and parliamentary shuttle (*navette parlementaire*) between both chambers to reach a common agreement—10 days). There are no formal public hearings or consultations, although interested professional organizations may be consulted informally. It is rare indeed to see tax provisions emanating from an ad hoc extra-parliamentary committee of experts, except for the reforms of 1986 and 1987, which improved taxpayers' rights and guarantees, and the 2009 reform, which strengthened legal certainty in tax matters. Most debate therefore takes place within Parliament, and mainly within the Finance Committees of both chambers.

The initial Finance Bill for a given year is passed before the end of December of the previous year, but the provisions relating to income tax and corporation tax apply retrospectively, unless expressly provided otherwise, to income and capital gains realized during the previous year. In addition, especially during the 1980s and early 1990s, Parliament enacted numerous special tax provisions of a retrospective nature, often at the request of the government and often with the sole aim of overturning case law which ran counter to administrative interpretations and practices and with which the tax authorities disagreed. While there is no constitutional provision prohibiting tax laws from having retroactive effects, the Constitutional Court has set certain limits (*see* section 2). The number of such measures has fallen sharply in recent years.

6.2 Statutory Drafting

The French tax code, even when considered with its annexes (government decrees and ministerial orders), is far less voluminous than the U.S. Internal Revenue Code. This is probably because, for a long time, the French Parliament did not seek to consider all particular situations and, rather than setting out precise, specific, and rigid rules or comprehensive definitions and enumerations, it often preferred to formulate concise principles and provisions in general terms, adaptable to diverse and/or new situations through appropriate interpretations. In this way, much has been left to administrative and judicial interpretation.

This reality is becoming less and less true, and the question of rewriting the French Tax Code is sometimes raised. Many old provisions remain in force, such as, the statutory rules on the taxation of companies in the international field, which date back to 1948 and are condensed into several lines in the tax code. The recodification process is still very much alive and has led to the enactment of a new Goods and Services Tax Code (*Code des impositions sur les biens et les services*) in 2022, which recodifies sector-specific tax provisions. The Code now includes provisions relating to VAT, excise duties (energy, alcohol, and tobacco) and other sector-specific taxes (mobility, industrial, and craft activities), and will soon include those related to VAT.

As in many other legal systems, the style of drafting laws has changed considerably over the last few decades, in the sense that statutes tend to be much more numerous, detailed, and complex than before. One of the reasons for this change is the influence on French tax law of other equally complex and detailed laws, as shown by the laws resulting from the transposition of EU directives. Statutory tax law is also currently characterized by frequent changes. This reflects the increasing complexity of the technical, economic, and social context of the law, as well as the use of taxation as a means of exerting influence in economic and social affairs—and, perhaps as well, the growing influence of lobby groups on the legislative decision-making process. Moreover, tax rulemaking also has an impact on tax justice and equality. From a comparative law perspective, the French system appears to be one of the most complex, and there is still room for simplification.

6.3 Statutory Interpretation

In principle, the clear meaning of the text of the law always takes precedence over the preparatory work and considerations of fiscal or economic equity, and it is the judge who decides whether the text is clear or not. However, even where a provision is clear, it may be incomplete, imprecise, or unsuited to the particular situation in question. Interpretative ambiguity may result from a divergence in legal qualification between two parties or from a failure of the rule. The legal qualification of income implies clearly determining the nature of that income in order to determine the applicable tax regime. To interpret is to explain, to give meaning to what is obscure or ambiguous in a text, whether domestic law or a tax treaty. Certain definitions do not allow an item of income to be qualified, as in the case of the legal qualification to be given to the concept of tax on digital services within the meaning of a tax treaty. The same applies to concepts used in common law, which can be difficult to interpret in countries with a civil law tradition, such as the concept of "beneficial owner," which ultimately refers to a notion of ownership which differs from one system to another, or the concept of "permanent establishment" used by non-OECD member countries which may lead to an interpretation which differs from the interpretation given in the OECD Commentaries. The current proliferation of anti-abuse rules (*see* section 9.3), with no case law and few administrative guidelines, is another example.

Interpreters may be judges, legislators, advisors, taxpayers, or the tax administration. In international matters, the Ministry of Foreign Affairs (MAE) had a monopoly on treaty interpretation until 1990, when administrative judges recognized that they were not obliged to refer back to the MAE a treaty provision whose meaning was unclear, or to bow to the Minister's interpretation. For their part, the tax authorities, through their interpretation of the law, create an "administrative doctrine," which is enforceable against taxpayers; however, taxpayers have the right to require the tax authorities to apply administrative doctrine consistently (*see* section 8.2).

The methods of interpretation are well known: literal interpretation allows the letter of the law to take precedence over its spirit, while teleological interpretation allows the spirit to take precedence over the letter. If the literal meaning of a text does not have a clear meaning, the legislature's intention must be considered. Certain documents, such as the preparatory documents of laws or the negotiations of tax treaties, may be considered to establish the historical context in order to better understand the legislature's intention. While teleological interpretation is the rule in EU law, it is also increasingly used in domestic law (e.g., in matters of abuse of rights) to ascertain the objectives of the law. The use of certain adages also makes it possible to arbitrate conflicts between norms having the same value, such as *generalia specialibus non derogant*, or to strictly respect the literal meaning of the text, such as *exceptio est strictissimae interpretationis*. In all cases, the judge uses with caution certain methods of reasoning, such as *a contrario* reasoning, as this can lead to a distraction from the intention of the authors of the text. The same approach applies to reasoning by analogy, which can lead to the assimilation of two different contexts for two different provisions. In addition, judges rarely refer to the preparatory work and more readily use the main general principles of tax law, such as the annual basis of taxation.

Tax jurisdiction is divided between administrative judges and other judges (*see* section 7). Administrative judges are more activist than other judges. In this respect, it can be said that administrative judges create law, using many theories: the freedom to allocate assets to the business assets of the trader (CE May 24, 1967), the abnormal act of management (CE March 6, 2006) or the principle of subsidiarity of international tax treaties (CE June 28, 2002). In contrast, the civil courts tend to adopt a more literal and stricter style of interpretation.

Finally, it should be pointed out that French judges may refer a preliminary question to the CJEU in the event of a difficulty in the interpretation of European law which needs to be resolved before a French court can give judgment.

7 COURTS DEALING WITH TAX MATTERS

7.1 Structure of the Courts

In France, there is no single tax judge, a situation dating back to the Revolution. At that time, the idea was to entrust litigation involving indirect taxes, which were highly unpopular under the *Ancien Régime*, to judges who would defend the property and freedom of citizens, i.e., civil judges in their capacity as guardians of property. This legal dualism is a reflection of the separation of administrative and judicial authorities proclaimed since 1790, and more broadly of the separation of powers which, in particular, separates the judge and the legislator. This division of tax jurisdiction between the judicial and administrative courts is currently set out in Article L 199 of the *livres des procédures fiscales* (Book of Tax Procedures (LPF)). Disputes relating to direct taxes fall within the jurisdiction of the administrative courts, while those relating to indirect taxes, as well as disputes relating to registration duties, the solidarity tax on wealth, land registration, and related taxes, fall within the jurisdiction of the civil courts. In reality, direct taxes and sales or similar taxes raise administrative and economic problems which administrative courts are better suited to resolving, while other taxes raise issues more related to civil law (such as registration duties, inheritance, or donations) or criminal law (indirect taxes and customs). This division between the jurisdiction of the courts is therefore the result of history and has not changed since the Revolution: administrative courts still hear disputes related to income tax, corporate income tax, VAT, and direct local taxes (these issues account for around 90% of the volume of tax litigation), whereas civil courts hear disputes related to registration, death, gift, and wealth taxes, as well as stamp or excise duties. Consequently, to determine the appropriate judge, it is necessary to determine the nature of the tax. In the event of a conflict of jurisdiction between the administrative authority and the judicial authority, the *Tribunal des conflicts* resolves the conflict.

Depending on the case, administrative litigation may be brought in front of the administrative court (*Tribunal administrative*—first instance), the administrative Court of Appeal (*Cour administrative d'appel*) and the Supreme Court (*Conseil d'Etat*). Judicial tax disputes can be brought before civil or criminal courts. Civil courts include judicial tribunals (*Tribunaux judificiaires* et *tribunaux de proximité*) which, since 2020, have replaced the *Tribunal de grande instance* and the *Tribunal d'instance*, the appeal courts (*Cour d'appel*) and the Supreme Court (*Cour de cassation*) and criminal courts, divided between the police court for minor offenses (*Tribunal de police*), the correctional court for misdemeanors (tax fraud is a misdemeanor) (*Tribunal correctional*), the departmental criminal court (*Cour criminelle départementale*), and the assize court for felonies (*Cour d'assises*).

7.2 Tax Law Cases

Many procedural rules are common to both courts. In both cases, the procedure is written and the case is heard by means of briefs served on the parties. The services of a lawyer are optional in the first instance, but compulsory in appeal and cassation cases. In reality, the essential feature of the procedure is what is known as the "preliminary administrative complaint" (*réclamation contentieuse préalable*), which acts as a filter for all taxes, whether the dispute concerns assessment or collection; in practice, it serves to reduce the number of disputes brought before the courts. As a result, challenges to decisions taken by the tax authorities are mainly of a non-jurisdictional nature, with the filter of the preliminary procedure allowing almost all cases to be settled (90%). Where this is not the case, the dispute may enter the jurisdictional phase. In practice, almost all these contentious claims concern taxes which fall within administrative jurisdiction, so that they are almost exclusively dealt with by administrative judges. Because tax law deals with public order, the tax judge (administrative or judicial) has a certain number of prerogatives or obligations during the proceedings.

In criminal tax matters, the tax authorities can request that criminal proceedings be initiated. Only the public prosecutor's office can initiate criminal proceedings and only if authorized to do so by specific procedural acts, such as filing a complaint with the assent of the tax offenses commission (*Commission des infractions fiscales*), an independent administrative authority. Following a 2018 reform (leading to a fourfold increase in the number of cases referred to the judicial authorities), the tax authorities have been obliged to refer cases to the public prosecutor where the tax evaded exceeds EUR 100,000. Only the public prosecutor can then initiate criminal proceedings for tax fraud. In France, criminal and tax penalties may be combined, subject to the principle of proportionality.

7.3 Judicial Style

Judgments are generally quite short (rarely more than three or four pages), despite the efforts currently being made by tax judges to provide more detailed reasons. After a reference to the applicable legal provisions and a brief summary of the proceedings and the arguments exchanged by the parties, the reasons are written in a concise (and sometimes even a somewhat laconic) style. The judges' opinions, whether concurring or dissenting, are not published. However, the opinion given on each case, before the court deliberates, by one of the members of the court (in administrative courts, the *Commissaire du Gouvernement*, or *Rapporteur public* as from 2009) is a valuable tool for understanding the decision, even if it does not always follow the path mapped out in the Rapporteur's opinion. Rapporteurs' opinions are often published in specialized reviews. The doctrine of binding precedent is not applied as such, but once the position of the highest court (administrative or civil) has been clearly established, lower courts tend to follow this example, at least for a certain period of time.

8 ADMINISTRATION

8.1 Tax Assessment, Collection, and Auditing

The major tax reform of 1948 organized the tax administration around a General Tax Directorate (*Direction Générale des impôts*), bringing together the four major financial authorities of the day (direct taxation, indirect taxation, registration duties, and customs duties). At the same time, an accounting department (*Direction Générale de la comptabilité publique*), which became autonomous in 1943, was responsible for public accounting and collection, and is often referred to as the public treasury (*Trésor Public*). In 2008, these two departments merged to form the Public Finances Directorate General (*Direction Générale des Finances Publiques* (DGFIP)) which is now responsible for tax assessment, control, settlement, and collection. The Directorate General of Customs and Indirect Duties, for its part, remains responsible for all these functions, including customs duties and certain indirect taxes. Taxpayers have access to public finance centers throughout France, which act as one-stop tax offices for all questions relating to tax assessment and collection. These centers also offer specialized services for individuals and businesses. Tax inspection services also exist at the national level (*Direction Nationale des enquêtes fiscales, Direction Nationale des vérifications de situations fiscales personnelles*, and *Direction des vérifications nationales et internationales*), regional level (*Direction de contrôle fiscal*), and departmental level (*Brigades de contrôle et de recherche*); the Customs Department has its own inspection services.

The tax authorities are also open to mediation. Since 2002, a tax ombudsman (*médiateur*) for the Ministry of the Economy, Finance and Industry, reporting to the Minister, has been available to deal with individual complaints concerning the operation of the Ministry's departments in their relations with taxpayers. There is also a tax conciliator in each department. The Mediator of the French Republic can also be called upon in cases of serious administrative malfunction. Last but not least, a number of commissions are open to taxpayers, with a view to enhancing their involvement in the taxation process. Their role varies according to the nature of the commission or committee. For example, the tax offenses commission (*Commission des infractions fiscales*) examines cases referred to it by the Minister responsible for the budget. The taxpayer is notified of the Commission's referral and invited to provide any information it deems necessary within thirty days. Its opinions are binding on the tax authorities. Another example is the Committee on abuse of rights (*Comité de l'abus de droit*), which can be called on by the tax authorities or the taxpayer to rule on the classification of transactions which may have enabled tax to be evaded as abusive. Before 2019, in the event of an opinion in favor of the administration, the burden of proof was shifted to the taxpayer. Since 2019, this onus on the taxpayer has been removed, and, regardless of the committee's opinion, whether in favor of the taxpayer or the administration, the burden of proof of the validity of the rectification lies with the administration. The Committee's opinions are of considerable practical interest since they are published quarterly and are the subject of an annual report which provides information on the risks involved in certain transactions.

Tax audits are carried out by the tax authorities, who verify the accuracy of the declarations and documents provided by the taxpayer. The taxpayer must respond to requests for information and failure to do so is tantamount to a refusal, which may be sanctioned by automatic taxation on a unilaterally assessed basis. The tax authorities, for their part, can exercise their right to information by requesting documents from third parties, and can also visit a company's head office to check its accounts or carry out an overall examination of the personal tax situation of private individuals in order to verify the consistency between their lifestyle and the income they declare. Since 1985, home visits and searches can also be carried out for direct taxes and sales taxes, in the event of clear-cut fraudulent maneuvers, and since 2008 a flagrant tax procedure (*flagrance fiscale*) has enabled the tax authorities to carry out an immediate inspection under conditions strictly defined by law (Article L 16-0 BA LPF).

At the end of an audit, the tax authorities can rectify any under-assessment of tax within a so-called recovery period (*délai de reprise*), which can range from one year (local direct taxes) or three years (income tax, corporate income tax, and VAT) to ten years (concealed activities or tax fraud). As part of the rectification process, the taxpayer may be charged interest on late payments (0.20% per month), as well as late payment penalties in the event of misconduct on the part of the taxpayer (tax increases ranging from 5% to 100% depending on the case). In terms of collection, late payment penalties may also be applied and the taxpayer may be given formal notice to pay.

Failure to respond to the formal notice may result in prosecution. The French State has a prior claim privilege (*privilège du préalable*), which means that it does not have to resort to the courts to collect its debts. Since 2019, special procedures such as third-party seizures (*saisie administrative à tiers détenteur*) have enabled the state to compel third parties (employers, banks, notaries or co-contractors) to immediately pay the Treasury the funds held to the extent of the taxpayer's debt.

Taxpayers have a number of rights against the prerogatives of the tax authorities. Audit procedures are subject to a certain amount of formality, requiring the tax authorities to inform the taxpayer of the nature of and reasons for the planned adjustments, before any audit is carried out, failing which the procedure will be null and void. In addition, the duration of the audit is limited, depending on the tax concerned. Finally, the taxpayer is protected by principles such as the theory of abnormal management acts and the principle of symmetrical balance-sheet adjustment. A charter of the rights and obligations of the audited taxpayer, enforceable against the tax authorities, ensures that taxpayers are aware of all their rights.

8.2 Administrative Interpretations

The government may adopt regulations to ensure the application of laws, on the basis of Articles 34 and 37 of the Constitution. In addition to this regulatory power, there are administrative sources consisting of instructions and circulars, which cannot be used as a basis for taxation; their purpose is to interpret the law. These interpretations are known as "tax doctrine." Administrative doctrine consists of all the comments that the administration makes on tax laws as well as the instructions provided to its agents concerning the interpretation and application of those laws. In 2012, this tax doctrine was consolidated and made available online on a dedicated website, *Bulletin officiel des Finances Publiques* (Public Finance Official Bulletin (BOFIP "bofip.impots.gouv.fr")). The main draft tax instructions are published on this site and are enforceable as soon as they are put online.

Tax doctrine is enforceable against the administration and taxpayers are protected against changes in doctrine on the basis of Article L80A and L80B of the LPF. Thus, in order to provide the taxpayer with a degree of legal certainty, the administration cannot retroactively call into question the interpretation of a text or the assessment of a factual situation that it has formally accepted. Tax doctrine also includes rulings (*rescrits*) by which the administration takes a position on questions of fact and ministerial replies to questions raised by members of Parliament to obtain an answer on a specific point. Unlike general administrative doctrine, individual interpretations, i.e., the interpretation of a tax text by a tax authority with regard to a specific taxpayer, are not subject to mandatory publication. However, since 2005, rulings which provide general interpretations based on specific requests have been published anonymously on the BOFIP website.

The place of administrative doctrine in the hierarchy of norms is open to question. While there is no doubt that an administrative interpretation cannot add to or run counter to the law it interprets, once it has been established and the guarantee of

Article L80 A LPF is applicable, nothing stands in the way. Its constitutionality is therefore debatable since the enforceability of administrative doctrine is not affected by any conflict with a law or treaty. In addition, there is uncertainty whether a taxpayer can rely on administrative doctrine which is incompatible with the objectives of an EU Directive due to conflicting case law.

9 GENERAL PRINCIPLES

9.1 Relationship Between Tax and Financial Accounting

There is a link of "compatibility" between accounting law and tax law. According to a 1984 decree (Article 38 quater of appendix III of the CGI): "Companies must comply with the definitions of the general chart of accounts, insofar as they are not incompatible with the rules applicable to the tax base." As a result, tax is based primarily on accounting law, unless tax law provides otherwise. In other words, accounting principles apply to the determination of taxable income in the absence of different tax rules. The connection between the two is explained by the way taxable profit is determined, which involves starting from the accounting result and arriving at the tax result, leading to certain adjustments when tax law deviates from accounting law.

In practice, the administrative Supreme Court (*Conseil d'Etat*) tends to align tax rules with the provisions of the general chart of accounts and the opinions of the accounting standard committee (*Comité des normes comptables*). In this way, tax law often follows accounting law. Under the impetus of international accounting standards, accounting concepts are evolving, and the basic principle of the connection between accounting and taxation is being questioned, all the more so as the economic realism of accounting increasingly permeates tax law concepts.

9.2 Respect for Civil or Private Law Form

It is interesting to note that the theory of the autonomy of tax law, according to which a tax qualification can exist independently of the qualifications for purposes of other branches of law, was developed in the 1920s by Louis Trotabas. At the time, income tax had not yet reached the "age of reason," and tax law was presented as independent of other branches of law. Let there be no mistake: tax law is a law of superimposition, which requires understanding and taking into account the rules of public or private law to which it applies. As a result, there is a natural tendency for the legislature, when devising a tax rule, and the judge, when interpreting that rule, to take civil law reasoning into consideration. Thus, with respect to the concept of income (*see* section 5.1), it was the concept of fruit in the civil law sense of the term that was applied in the beginning: income is a permanent source that produces fruit which can be renewed. The same approach applies to stock, where a distinction is made between interchangeable and non-interchangeable stock, and which in fact reverts to the civil law distinction between fungible and non-fungible goods. It also applies to the tax concept of abuse of rights (*see* section 9.3), the theoretical basis of which is the civil law concept of abuse of rights, or whenever it is necessary to verify the legal nature of a contract in order to apply registration duties or to analyze property rights in order to determine the owner of an asset.

Nevertheless, tax law is a pragmatic body of law which often needs to detach itself from civil law in order to take account of its own particular situation. This explains why tax law sometimes is treated as independent of civil law. Conversely, tax law can sometimes be at the forefront of civil law. As early as 1872, tax law made the transfer of a civil or commercial clientele subject to transfer duties, considering the clientele as an element of the patrimony, in order to take into account the change of owner for the application of registration duties; in contrast, civil law did not recognize the transfer of civil clientele as valid until more than a century later, in 2000. Similarly, civil law defines a sale in terms of the transfer of ownership, whereas tax law goes further with respect to capital gains and includes the concepts of contribution to a company, exchange, cessation of activity, division, donation, withdrawal of assets, or even expropriation. In this way, tax law makes it possible to consider a transfer as taking place independently of the transfer of ownership, which remains the characteristic criterion of a transfer under civil law. As a result, for a very long time, case law considered that the determination of sales giving rise to industrial and commercial profits had to be made by reference to the definition of sale contained in Article 1583 of the Civil Code. This civil law reasoning poses a problem in tax matters: if the criterion used to determine when a tax claim should be attached to a financial year is the time of agreement on the item and the price, it may be that payment actually takes place later. In this context, and to avoid cash-flow difficulties for companies, Article 38-2 bis of the CGI has allowed this civil law analysis to be set aside for services and sales of inventory, but it is retained for sales of fixed assets, where the same difficulties do not arise.

9.3 Anti-avoidance Doctrines and Rules

Originally, only a general anti-abuse concept applied, namely, the theory of abuse of rights in Article L64 of the LPF in 1941, enabling the tax authorities to requalify an abusive transaction carried out by a taxpayer with the sole aim of reducing or evading tax. This concept, which today applies to all taxes, defines an abusive transaction as a fictitious act with an exclusively fiscal purpose which does not respect the objectives of the authors of the law. The penalty is severe, involving interest for late payment and a surcharge of 80% of the taxes avoided, reduced to 40% where the taxpayer is not the main beneficiary of the scheme or did not take the main initiative with respect to the scheme. Alongside this general measure, specific anti-abuse rules have been introduced for groups of companies in order to exclude them from the favorable group tax regime, e.g., in the area of mergers. It was only in 2017 that the *Conseil d'Etat* recognized the notion of abuse of tax treaties, declaring that national rules can apply (Article L 64 of the LPF) only if the treaty does not provide for an explicit *fraus legis* rule. This issue will become less relevant as, with the Base Erosion and Profit Shifting (BEPS) reform, many tax treaties include specific anti-abuse rules enabling tax authorities to override the literal meaning of the treaty in the event of abuse.

The other general measure created by the courts is the theory of the abnormal act of management, which makes it possible to neutralize the tax effects of abnormal behavior aimed at obtaining a tax saving. Where a company decides to impoverish itself for purposes unrelated to its own interests, the tax authorities can refuse to allow a deduction for the expenses and tax the company behind the act and its beneficiary. With a view to better controlling the abnormality of taxable results, other tools have been developed which are more specific to cross-border transactions. In transfer pricing matters, for example, on the basis of Article 57 of the CGI, the tax authorities can recharacterize part of a transaction in order to adjust the tax treatment of the originator of the abnormal transfer and its beneficiary. Outside a group, certain rules also exist to penalize asset transfers made by a company to a person or organization located outside France. With regard to the rules governing controlled foreign companies (CFCs), France introduced a rule in the 1980s to combat the relocation of profits to low-tax countries. Under Article 209 B CGI, the profits of foreign companies subject to a preferential tax regime, more than 50 % of which are controlled by a French company subject to corporate income tax, are subject to corporate income tax in France, except where safeguard clauses apply. At the same time, France set up a system to combat "rent-a-star company" schemes.

The current international context and the implementation of the BEPS project have led to a proliferation of anti-abuse measures. The incorporation of the EU Anti-tax Avoidance Directive (ATAD I) has created a new general anti-abuse rule applicable specifically to corporate income tax, and the creation of a "mini abuse of rights" (*mini abus de droit*) applicable beyond corporate income tax. In each of these cases, and without any specific sanction, the concept of abuse of rights has been extended to include a primarily fiscal "motive" (Article L 64 A LPF for the mini abuse of rights) or to a principal "purpose" (Article 205 A CGI for the corporate income tax rule), similar to the Principal Purpose Test (PPT) clause in tax treaties. It is not yet clear how these rules fit with existing tools, particularly in terms of sanctions. Other anti-abuse directives, ATAD II and ATAD III, also help to perfect these measures.

It is interesting to note that the fight against fraud and evasion was the motivation behind the 1948 reform, when the French corporate income tax was created. The preparatory work at that time shows that public opinion saw fraud as a "necessary corrective" to the heavy tax burden of the time. This same issue is also at the heart of the current international tax reform, demonstrating that taxpayer acceptance of taxation is still a contemporary issue. Fraud is often seen as a phenomenon of tax resistance. Even today, this attitude is still visible, and can take the form of social movements, as has been the case in several countries with regard to environmental taxation, such as the Yellow Vests or Red Caps movements in France.

10 TAX TREATY NETWORK

France has one of the most extensive treaty networks in the world, with a total of 128 countries or territories (including French Polynesia) with which it has entered into agreements, including some countries with both an income tax treaty and an inheritance tax treaty. This brings the total number of agreements to just over 130, in addition to those due to come into force. While the double taxation agreement with Finland had been terminated, a new agreement was signed in April 2023 but has not yet entered into force. The same applies to two countries with which France did not yet have an agreement, namely Moldova (signed in June 2022) and Rwanda (signed in June 2023). In addition, the Covid-19 pandemic has led the development of eight amicable or provisional agreements on teleworking with several border countries (Belgium, Germany, Italy, Luxembourg, and Switzerland), one of which is purely interpretive.

Unlike some other countries, France has not chosen to publish a national model tax treaty, even if one does exist. In practice, France more often uses the OECD Model, even if it sometimes departs from it for various reasons:

- to reduce or eliminate withholding taxes in the source country;
- to allow France to tax income and gains subject to withholding taxes in the source country (where the source country does not agree, France negotiates to include a most-favored-nation provision so that if the source country agrees to lower withholding taxes in a treaty with another country, the same rates of withholding tax become applicable in the treaty with France);
- to allow France to tax income and gains from shares or interests in entities deriving their value principally from immovable property located in France;
- to prevent double exemptions;
- to specify that French partnerships must be considered to be residents of France;
- to replace the exemption-with-progression method for foreign source income, which is not subject to the ordinary credit method, by a special tax credit which is always equal to the amount of French tax attributable to such income (post-1988 conventions);
- to ensure that France can apply various domestic anti-avoidance provisions; and
- to apply Article 24(1) of the non-discrimination article of the OECD Model only to individuals, in view of French case law on the concepts of nationality and residence of companies.

France has always supported the G20/OECD BEPS project. It has ratified the *Multilateral Convention to Implement Tax Treaty Related Measures to Prevent BEPS* (MLI), which came into force on January 1, 2019, and to date has listed 71% of its tax treaties. In this regard, several bilateral treaties have been published online in a consolidated form that takes into account the changes made by the MLI (*see*, for example, the treaty with South Africa (https://www.impots.gouv.fr/les-conventions-internationales)). In addition, France has expressed a number of reservations due to the particularities of its tax law (such as transparent dual entities) because its tax treaties already contain similar provisions (application of methods for eliminating double taxation and the right of a state to tax its own residents), or because of the complexity and/or legal uncertainty of certain MLI provisions (permanent establishments in third jurisdictions and dual-resident entities).

11 SOURCES OF TAX LAW

11.1 The Sources

The primary source of tax law is the law. As the ultimate expression of the sovereignty of the people, the Constitution delimits the sphere of competence of the legislative power in relation to the regulatory power (Articles 34 and 37 of the Constitution). Since 1950, tax laws have been codified in a single code, the CGI. Since 1992, the vast majority of tax procedural rules have been grouped together in a separate book, the LPF, which, from a legal point of view, forms part of the CGI; in addition, a new Code has been effective since 2022 (the Goods and Services Tax Code—*Code des impositions sur les biens et les services*).

Regulatory and administrative powers play an essential role in implementing tax law. Government decrees (*décrets*) and ministerial orders (*arrêtés*) are codified in different schedules to the CGI (as narrowly defined above), in special parts of the LPF, or in the new Goods and Services Tax Code. New administrative interpretations of tax provisions and rulings of general interest (without revealing the identities of the taxpayers involved) are periodically published in the BOFIP and ministerial responses posted on the French government's official website.

As already mentioned, case law is also a source of lawmaking and administrative judges have created several theories (*see* section 6.3). A certain vigor in constitutional jurisprudence can also be observed since the introduction of *a posteriori* constitutionality review. The text of the French Constitution (in English, German, and Spanish) and the decisions of the *Conseil Constitutionnel*, some of which have been translated into those languages, can be found on the website of the *Conseil Constitutionnel*.

There is also the increasingly visible influence of international and European law on French tax law. On the one hand, the ECHR will play a more important role in the future, not least because of France's ratification of Protocol No. 16 in 2018, which provides that the highest courts of signatory States be able to request advisory opinions from the Court on questions of principle relating to the interpretation or application of the rights and freedoms defined by the Convention or its protocols. In addition, the agreement reached in 2023 on the EU's accession to the ECHR is bound to raise new questions. On the other hand, the EU occupies a central place in the sources of tax law, and the harmonization of tax law is progressing in Europe. In addition to the influence of international tax treaties on French domestic law, EU law is implementing international tax reform, the principles of which are based on soft law. In this way, European directives make it possible to transform soft law principles into hard law. This is illustrated by the adoption by France of the Directive of December 14, 2022 aimed at ensuring a minimum level of worldwide taxation for certain groups of companies (Pillar Two GloBE Model Rules) and its implementation by the Finance Act for 2024.

Some sources, including secondary sources, such as scholarly articles, are not normative in nature, but are sometimes used by the courts in tax cases. For example, they can be used to justify the renunciation of certain revenues by a professional without it being considered abnormal in the case of provisions for charges and losses or in the case of non-trading profits.

11.2 Materials

The French government's official website publishes legislative and regulatory texts and court rulings by French supreme and appellate courts (https://www.legifrance.gouv.fr/).

The Ministry of Finance website (www.impots.gouv.fr) offers taxpayers (individuals and professionals) a personalized space for information (publication of the taxpayer's charter, for example) and tax payments. The site also includes all the international agreements signed by France, as well as the latest economic and tax news. The preparatory work of laws (particularly Finance Acts) and the reports of parliamentary commissions and committees are available on the websites of both parliamentary chambers (www.assemblee-nationale.fr; www.senat.fr). The French tax authorities publish their entire administrative doctrine (bofip.impots.gouv.fr) as well as a yearly treatise, *Précis de fiscalité* (www.impots.gouv.fr).

Selected decisions handed down by the two courts of highest jurisdiction (www.conseil-etat.fr; www.courdecassation.fr) are published in official collections: *Recueil des décisions du Conseil d'Etat (Rec.)*, also called *Recueil Lebon*, and *Bulletin des arrêts de la Cour de cassation—Chambres civiles (Bull. Civ.)*. Decisions of the greatest interest, irrespective of the court, are traditionally to be found in the main tax reviews: *Revue de Jurisprudence Fiscale*, Les Editions Francis Lefebvre and *Revue de droit fiscal* (*Dr. fisc.*), LexisNexis (*see* below). All texts and case law of the Constitutional Council are available on the Conseil's website (www.conseil-constitutionnel.fr).

One of the most exhaustive privately edited tax publications is published by Les Editions Francis Lefebvre (www.efl.fr) and consists of general documentation (*Documentation fiscal*), a special edition of the CGI and LPF (*Code pratique*), a comprehensive treatise (*Mémento pratique fiscal*), and three reviews: *Feuillets rapides* (weekly), *Bulletin fiscal* (monthly), and *Revue de jurisprudence fiscal* (monthly, case law and selected opinions of the *Commissaires du Gouvernement/Rapporteurs publics* before the *Conseil d'Etat*). Systematic cross-references between the different elements of this material are of great help (the digital version is *Navis fiscal*).

LexisNexis (www.lexisnexis.fr) also publishes general documentation (*JurisClasseur fiscal* and *JurisClasseur fiscal international*), supplemented by a weekly review (*Revue de droit fiscal*).

Germany

Christine Osterloh-Konrad & Wolfgang Schön

1 HISTORY

Under the constitution of the German Reich, founded in 1871, only the individual states, and not the Reich itself, had the power to impose income taxes. The history of modern income taxation in Germany starts with the Prussian Income Tax Act (ITA) of 1891, which introduced a systematic "source-based" approach to income taxation. In order to deal with the heavy financial burden of World War I, this legislative power was shifted to the German Reich by the Weimar Constitution of 1919. In 1920, a modern ITA (strictly following the comprehensive economic concept of income) and the first German Corporate Income Tax Act (CITA) were enacted. The 1920 Act did not survive the hyperinflation of 1922/1923 and was replaced by the pragmatic ITAs of 1925 and 1934, which provided the basic framework for today's ITA. The CITA has undergone three major reforms: in 1977, the "classical" system was replaced by an imputation system, which itself gave way to a "shareholder-relief" system in 2000; the Business Tax Reform of 2007 adapted the "shareholder-relief system" or "half-income system" to the final withholding tax system, which applies to all capital income derived from financial assets that are held as private assets ("modified partial-income system").

2 CONSTITUTIONAL ISSUES AND THE INFLUENCE OF EUROPEAN UNION LAW

2.1 Legislative Powers

The German Federal Constitution (*Grundgesetz*, GG (Basic Law)) of 1949 was designed to strengthen the political power of the states (*Länder*) in fiscal matters. As a result, the Federation (*Bund*) is competent to enact tax laws only if it is at least partly entitled to the tax revenues (e.g., income tax) or if federal legislation is necessary to ensure equal living conditions or to maintain legal or economic coherence in Germany.[1] If the *Bund* exercises a particular taxing right, the *Länder* are no longer authorized to legislate in that area.

The constitutional powers of the federal legislature in tax matters have been widely used; a 2014 judgment of the Federal Constitutional Court (*Bundesverfassungsgericht*) on the federal inheritance and gift tax confirmed that the threshold for federal legislation in tax matters is quite low.[2] Contrary to the original political concept of the GG, federal legislation in tax matters is of overwhelming importance and state legislation has become almost meaningless. Some residual taxing rights lie with the municipalities (*Gemeinden*): they impose local consumption and excise taxes and set the tax rate for the trade tax (*Gewerbesteuer*), both being taxes from which the revenue flows entirely to them.

Nevertheless, the *Länder* play an important part in federal legislation through their membership in the Council of States (*Bundesrat*). Because this body has substantial powers, including the power to veto tax bills where the *Länder* or local municipalities receive a share of the revenue,[3] *Bund* and *Länder* are bound to cooperate in any major tax legislation (in particular, with respect to income tax, corporate income tax, and value-added tax (VAT)).

2.2 Sharing of Tax Revenue

Tax legislation is mainly a federal matter and tax administration mainly a state matter.[4] Revenue from most of the more important taxes is shared among the *Bund*, the *Länder*, and municipalities.[5] However, revenue from federal excise taxes goes to the *Bund*, while estate duties and real estate transfer tax revenues go to the *Länder*. The municipalities are entitled to all the revenue from the trade tax (*Gewerbesteuer*), an important tax on income from trade and business.

Revenue-sharing mandated by the federal constitution is one of the major inroads on the constitutional separation of federal and state budgets, along with horizontal payments between rich and poor states and vertical payments from the Federation to individual states (*horizontaler und vertikaler Finanzausgleich*).[6]

2.3 Impact of Basic Rights on Taxation

The provisions framing the "fiscal constitution" of Germany with respect to the allocation of powers to the different levels of government and the "fundamental rights" enshrined in the German federal constitution both played an important part in

1. Article 105 para. 2 with reference to Basic Law, Art. 72 para. 2.
2. Federal Constitutional Court (*Bundesverfassungsgericht*), December 17, 2014, 1 BvL 21/1289 Reports (BVerfGE) 138, p. 136.
3. Basic Law, Art. 105 para. 4.
4. Basic Law, Art. 108.
5. Basic Law, Art. 106.
6. Basic Law, Art. 107.

developing German tax law after World War II. Particularly during the 1990s, major changes in German tax law were forced on the government by the Federal Constitutional Court, which may be directly approached by taxpayers.

Among the provisions of the "Bill of Rights" contained in Articles 1 to 19 of the federal constitution (GG), the following have a special impact on tax matters:

- Article 2, paragraph 1 GG (Right to Liberty of Persons): the Federal Constitutional Court has concluded that the state is not allowed to tax income which is necessary to maintain a minimum living standard.[7] This constitutional requirement may also be derived from the Social Welfare State Principle (Article 20, paragraph 3 GG) and from the protection of human dignity enshrined in Article 1, paragraph 1 GG. The tax-free amount of income must include not only necessary costs for nutrition, clothing, and accommodation but also a certain level of social security contributions for medical services and care.[8] There is an ongoing debate about whether the Social Welfare State principle implies a constitutional requirement for wealth redistribution via taxes.
- Article 3, paragraph 1 GG (Equality): this provision requires that the tax burden be shared equally among citizens, which the Federal Constitutional Court essentially interprets as the need to comply with the "ability-to-pay" principle, in particular with respect to income tax matters. Consequently, for example, there has been a long debate about whether a dual income tax system would be in line with the principle of equality, and the final withholding tax regime for interest income and current minimum taxation limiting loss carryforwards are still subject to constitutional criticism. Another important area where the equality principle has far-reaching consequences is the valuation of assets for tax purposes; valuation principles which lead to far-reaching and unevenly distributed deviations from market value were declared unconstitutional with respect to wealth tax as well as to inheritance and gift tax and property tax.[9] Furthermore, the Court ruled that a taxing statute which leaves too much leeway for avoidance transactions may also infringe on tax equality.[10] Finally, equality must also be achieved with respect to the practical enforcement of tax liabilities; this became particularly relevant for the taxation of interest income.[11]

  In addition, the Court has derived from Article 3, paragraph 1 GG an obligation on the legislature to avoid inconsistent results. This requirement of consistency (*Folgerichtigkeitsgebot*) is of overwhelming importance for the constitutional framework of tax law. It binds the legislature closely to its own

7. Federal Constitutional Court (*Bundesverfassungsgericht*), September 25, 1992, 2 BvL 5, 8, 14/91 Reports (BVerfGE) 87, p. 153.
8. Judgment of February 13, 2008, 2 BvL 1/06.
9. Federal Constitutional Court, June 22, 1995, 2 BvL 37/91 Reports (BVerfGE) 93, 121 (wealth tax); November 7, 2006, 1 BvL 10/02 Reports (BVerfGE) 117, 1 (inheritance and gift tax); April 10, 2018, 1 BvL 11/14 et al. Reports (BVerfGE) 148, 147 (property tax).
10. Judgment of December 17, 2014, 1 BvL 21/12 Reports (BVerfGE) 138, 136.
11. Judgment of June 27, 1991, 2 BvR 1493/89 Reports (BVerfGE) 84, p. 239; March 9, 2004, 2 BvL 17/02 Reports (BVerfGE) 110, 94.

decisions: Parliament may decide relatively freely on what to tax and what behavior to incentivize via taxes, but it must spell out its fundamental decisions consistently in the tax code. For example, any specific anti-avoidance rule (SAAR) must be designed according to the typical avoidance case it targets; such a rule runs the risk of being declared unconstitutional if its wording is so broad that it does not reflect the original purpose.[12]

- Article 6, paragraph 1 (marriage and family are under the special protection of the state): the Constitutional Court has decided that the sole fact of marriage may not increase the total tax burden of the spouses; therefore, the joint assessment of husband and wife was declared null and void; subsequent legislation provided for income splitting.[13] Moreover, the income of minor children must be assessed separately.[14] Finally, tax legislation must grant "adequate" allowances for child tuition and education.[15] During the last two decades, the Court has forced the legislature to extend, bit by bit, the tax regime for married couples to same-sex civil unions; in 2017, this development was completed by the introduction of same-sex marriage.
- Article 14 GG (Protection of Property and Inheritances): in a controversial judgment dating from 1995, the Constitutional Court concluded that taxation of income may not exceed (roughly) 50% of income.[16] In 2006, the Court overruled this judgment by denying that an absolute maximum tax rate may be derived from Article 14.[17] Nowadays, it is clear that only a confiscatory tax burden would infringe upon Article 14 GG.
- Article 20, paragraph 3 (Rule of Law): the Constitutional Court has concluded that retroactive legislation is admissible only under very narrow conditions because it must pass a proportionality test.[18] Moreover, the legislature is not entitled to enforce "authentic" interpretation by passing retroactive legislation aimed at clarifying the original intent behind tax law provisions, since this constitutes an infringement on the constitutional role of the courts calling for the "separation of powers."[19]

2.4 European Union Law Influences

During the past few decades, German tax law has been hugely influenced by European Union (EU) law, which is binding for all public institutions, including the national legislature, forcing it—*inter alia*—to change the corporate tax regime completely in 2000.[20] On the one hand, VAT law is largely harmonized, its interpretation governed by

12. Judgment of December 17, 2014, 1 BvL 21/12 Reports (BVerfGE) 138, 136.
13. Judgment of January 17, 1957, 1 BvL 4/54 Reports (BVerfGE) 6, p. 55.
14. Judgment of June 30, 1964, 1 BvL 16/62 Reports (BVerfGE) 18, p. 97.
15. Judgment of November 10, 1998, 2 BvR 1057/91 et al. Reports (BVerfGE) 99, p. 216.
16. Judgment of June 22, 1995, 2 BvL 37/91 Reports (BVerfGE) 93, p. 121.
17. Judgment of January 18, 2006, 2 BvR 2194/99.
18. Judgment of December 3, 1997, 2 BvR 882/97 Reports (BVerfGE) 97, p. 67.
19. Judgment of December 17, 2013, 1 BvL 5/08 Reports (BVerfGE) 135, p. 1.
20. *See* the Introduction for a brief discussion of the European institutions and laws which influence the tax laws of the Member States.

an ever-growing body of Court of Justice of the European Union (CJEU) decisions. On the other hand, direct taxation is heavily influenced by EU primary law, in particular by the fundamental freedoms: national legislatures are prohibited from discriminating against cross-border cases and are thereby forced to remove tax obstacles to cross-border economic activity. Further, in areas of particular importance for the functioning of the Common Market, specific EU directives have been enacted, for example, regulating the treatment of cross-border dividends or the fight against aggressive tax planning. Finally, EU state-aid law has lately been used as a means to attack preferential tax regimes, leading to a considerable level of legal uncertainty because it is often unclear where the benchmark for determining selectivity lies.

3 TAX RATES

3.1 Individual Income Tax

The German personal income tax rate schedule is based on a formula approach.[21] Effective for 2024, individuals pay taxes at progressive rates between 14% and 45%. Since German income tax law is governed by the nominal-value principle, it does not provide for indexation, with the effect that the average tax rate on real income increases with the rate of inflation.

In 2024, the basic personal exemption is EUR 11,604 for a single person and EUR 23,208 for a married couple. The federal income tax rates (marginal tax rates) for individuals (for married couples, the total amounts must be doubled) are as follows:[22]

EUR 11,604 or less	0%
EUR 11,605 up to 66,760	14.0% up to 42.0%
EUR 66,761 up to 277,825	42.0%
EUR 227,826 and up	45.0%

Effective as of 1995, a solidarity surcharge (*Solidaritätszuschlag*), originally 7.5% (5.5% since 1998) of the income and corporate income tax liability was introduced to raise additional revenue to cope with the financial needs caused by German reunification.[23] As time passed, the solidarity surcharge came under political pressure. In 2021, it was partially abolished, but remains in force for the top 10% of income earners.

3.2 Corporate Income Tax

The corporate income tax rate has experienced a dramatic fall over the last four decades. When the imputation system was introduced in 1977, the tax rate for retained

21. Income Tax Act (ITA), s. 32a.
22. ITA, s. 32a para. 1.
23. *Solidaritätszuschlagsgesetz.*

profits was aligned with the top marginal income tax rate of that year, at 56%. Starting in the late 1980s, the corporate income tax rate was gradually reduced to 40% in 1999. During the same period, the tax rate for distributed profits was reduced from 36% to 30%. When the imputation system was abolished in 2000, the corporate tax rate was set at 25% for retained and distributed profits alike. Since 2008, a tax rate of 15% applies.[24] However, in order to assess the full tax burden on corporate profits, it is necessary to take into account the additional burden under the trade tax regime, which, depending on local tax rates and modifications to the tax base, hovers around 15%.[25]

4 COMPOSITION OF THE FISCAL SYSTEM

4.1 Revenue Share of Specific Taxes

Germany is a high-tax country which levies a variety of different taxes, many of which are transaction taxes generating only a small amount of revenue. In 2022, the total tax revenue of the *Bund*, the *Länder*, and the municipalities amounted to EUR 895.7 billion. In relation to the 2022 Gross Domestic Product (GDP) of 3,876.81 billion,[26] the total tax revenue is 23.1%. The tax-to-GDP ratio (not including social security contributions) has varied between 22% and 25% during the past twenty-five years. For 2022, the most important taxes are listed in the following chart.[27]

Total German Tax Collection 2017 (Excluding Social Security Contributions)	*In bn. (EUR)*	*% of Tax Revenue*
- Wage withholding tax (*Lohnsteuer*)	227.2	25.4
- Assessed income tax (*veranlagte Einkommensteuer*)	77.4	8.6
- Not assessed taxes on earnings (*nicht veranlagte Einkommensteuer*)	32.6	3.6
- Withholding tax on interest and capital gains (*Abgeltungsteuer auf Zins- und Veräußerungserträge*)	6.6	0.7
Subtotal	343.8	38.4
Solidarity surcharge (*Solidaritätszuschlag*)	12.0	1.3
Corporate income tax (*Körperschaftsteuer*)	46.3	5.2
Trade tax (*Gewerbesteuer*)	70.2	7.8
Value-added tax—including VAT on imports (*Umsatzsteuer*)	284.9	31.8
Real estate transfer tax (*Grunderwerbsteuer*)	17.1	1.9
Insurance tax (*Versicherungssteuer*)	15.7	1.8
Energy Tax (*Energiesteuer*)	33.7	3.8

24. Corporate Income Tax Act (CITA), s. 23 para. 1.
25. *See* below, section 5.3.
26. Source: https://de.statista.com/statistik/daten/studie/14397/umfrage/deutschland-bruttoinlandsprodukt-bip/.
27. Sources: Monthly Report of the Ministry of Finance, January 2023; Annual Customs Statistics; *Statistisches Bundesamt*, Press Release Nr. 332, August 21, 2023.

Total German Tax Collection 2017 (Excluding Social Security Contributions)	*In bn. (EUR)*	*% of Tax Revenue*
Electricity tax (*Stromsteuer*)	6.8	0.8
Tobacco tax (*Tabaksteuer*)	14.2	1.6
Alcohol tax (*Alkoholsteuer*)	2.2	0.2
Customs (*Zölle*)	6.8	0.8
Car tax (*Kraftfahrzeugsteuer*)	9.5	1.1
Real property tax (*Grundsteuer*)	15.3	1.7
Estate and gift tax (*Erbschaft-und Schenkungsteuer*)	9.2	1.0
Total of approx. 20 other taxes	8.0	0.9
Total tax revenue	**895.7**	**100.0**

The revenue from assessed income tax, corporation tax, net worth tax, and inheritance tax appears rather low by international standards.

Members of Catholic or Protestant churches, as well as some other recognized religious communities, pay an 8% or 9% surcharge on their income tax (church tax, *Kirchensteuer*), which qualifies as an itemized deduction. As of 2022, the total revenue for the Catholic and Protestant churches (which is not included in the chart above) amounts to EUR 13.1 billion.[28]

4.2 Recent Trends in the Tax System

Following German reunification in 1990, a variety of special tax provisions and subsidies were introduced to promote investment in East Germany and restructure the East German economy. Because of the unexpectedly high costs of unification and a shortfall of tax revenues as of 1993, the German government felt compelled to increase taxes, in particular VAT, mineral oil tax, and other indirect taxes, thereby effecting a shift from direct to indirect taxes. Between 1995 and 2008, there was a major decrease in the tax rates for personal and corporate income tax, while the tax base was broadened gradually. At the same time, VAT rates and special consumption tax rates increased. Since 2012, however, revenues from direct taxation have been rising. In relation to total tax revenue, the share of direct taxes (personal and corporate income tax, trade tax, interest withholding tax, net worth tax, and similar taxes) is as follows:[29]

28. Source: https://de.statista.com/statistik/daten/studie/12520/umfrage/kirchensteuer-einnahmen-in-deutschland/.
29. Sources: Federal Ministry of Finance, Monthly Report March 2017, https://www.bundesfinanzministerium.de/Monatsberichte/2017/03/Inhalte/Kapitel-6-Statistiken/6-1-10-steueraufkommen-nach-steuergruppen.html; Federal Ministry of Finance, Steuereinnahmen nach Steuergruppen 2018-2022, https://www.bundesfinanzministerium.de/Content/DE/Standardartikel/Themen/Steuern/Steuerschaetzungen_und_Steuereinnahmen/Steuereinnahmen/entwicklung-der-steuereinnahmen.html.

1970	53.6%	2000	52.1%
1975	58.8%	2005	48.4%
1980	58.5%	2010	48.2%
1985	59.0%	2015	52.6%
1990	56.7%	2018	55.1%
1995	53.8%	2022	55.5%

In addition, there has been a growing tendency for the legislature to introduce new taxes, thus adding to the complexity of the tax system and making it both more difficult to assess the total tax burden on particular economic activities and to put those tax burdens into context. Prominent examples of new taxes are the nuclear fuel tax, introduced in 2010, and the aviation tax, effective as of 2011. In 2017, the Federal Constitutional Court declared the nuclear fuel tax to be null and void because it did not fit within one of the categories of taxes the federal legislature is competent to enact under the constitution.[30] In this landmark judgment, the court limited the right of the legislature to "invent" new types of taxes.

Recent changes to the tax system include a comprehensive investment taxation reform with a move from transparent to nontransparent taxation of investment funds (2018) and various types of tax relief aimed at alleviating the burdens of the Covid-19 crisis (e.g., a significant temporary reduction in the VAT rate for restaurants, an extension of the loss carryback regime, optional deductions for degressive depreciation, and a home office allowance). Further, in the course of "greening" the economy, numerous tax advantages for environment-friendly behavior have been introduced (e.g., for environment-friendly mobility and solar energy). Recently, a global minimum tax regime for large multinational companies has been enacted.

As public spending keeps growing enormously to address current problems, tax policy debates often revolve around the distribution of the associated tax burdens. A frequent topic in those debates is the current preferential treatment of real estate, in particular the far-reaching exemption from capital gains taxation under the income tax and the special treatment under the inheritance and gift tax.

4.3 Social Security Contributions

German social security contributions currently amount to roughly 40.9%[31] of the wages, salaries, and other compensation paid to employees and are borne by both employers and employees.

30. Judgment of April 13, 2017 2 BvL 6/13 Reports (BVerfGE) 145, p. 171.
31. As of the beginning of 2024, the social security tax rates amount to 18.6% for pension insurance contributions (up to an amount of EUR 90,600 (Western Germany)/EUR 89,400 (Eastern Germany) of income per year), 16.3% for health insurance contributions (on average) (up to an amount of EUR 62,100 of income per year), 2.6% for unemployment insurance (up to an amount of EUR 90,600 (Western Germany)/EUR 89,400 (Eastern Germany) of income per year), and 3.4% for childcare insurance contributions (up to an amount of EUR 62,100 of income per year); the latter percentage is slightly higher for those without children and decreases with every additional child.

In contrast to taxes, the share of social security contributions as a percentage of GDP had been increasing dramatically before the turn of the millennium, due to an aging population, better and more expensive medical services (including dentistry), longer periods for study, and earlier retirement. Several German governments have tried, with limited success, to reduce this extra burden on earned income, and in the last few years the share of social security contributions as a percentage of GDP has at least remained relatively stable. However, the German government recently announced a dramatic gradual increase in pension insurance contributions from 14.6% in 2024 to 22.3% in 2035. This announcement has triggered new discussions about intergenerational equity.

5 BASIC STRUCTURE OF THE INCOME TAX

5.1 Individual Income Tax

5.1.1 Principles of the Tax Base

Over the past 100 years, the concept of income under German law has undergone important changes. The Prussian Income Tax Law of 1891 followed a strict "source" approach, regarding as taxable only periodic income flowing from a constant "source" and disregarding any increases or decreases in the value of the source itself. Under the influence of Georg von Schanz, the German Income Tax Law of 1920 introduced an accruals-based income system, which did not survive the hyperinflation of the early 1920s.

The current system, which was framed mainly in 1925 and 1934, follows a mixed (pragmatic) approach: income tax is levied on the basis of a "synthetic income" comprising revenue from different categories. The differences among the particular categories have increased over time so that, arguably, the system has changed from a "global" to a "schedular" system. The most important difference is the special treatment granted to capital income: since 2009, income derived from privately held financial assets is subject to a final withholding tax of 25%,[32] and only 60% of income derived from shares qualifying as business assets is subject to regular income tax rates.[33] From time to time, the different treatment of labor income and capital income is subject to controversial debates, in particular with respect to the preferential treatment of interest which, in contrast to dividends, is not subject to an additional layer of (corporate) taxation. However, the promise made in the 2018 coalition government agreement to abolish altogether the 25% final withholding tax on interest has not been fulfilled so far.

Another general aspect of German income taxation is its traditional "dualism" (which should not be confused with the concept of a dual income tax mentioned above). ITA section 2(2) makes one major distinction among the seven sources of income listed in ITA section 2(1), which concerns the method of determining income:

32. ITA, s. 32d para. 1.
33. ITA, s. 3 No. 40.

(1) "profit income" (*Gewinneinkünfte*), incorporating three subcategories:
- income from agriculture and forestry (sections 13-14a ITA);
- income from trade or business enterprises (sections 15-17 ITA); and
- income from professional and certain other independent personal services (section 18 ITA).

(2) "excess income" (*Überschusseinkünfte*), incorporating four subcategories:
- income from dependent personal services (wages and salaries, section 19, 19a ITA);
- income from (private) capital investment (e.g., interest and dividends, section 20 ITA);
- rental and royalty income (section 21, 21a ITA); and
- income from certain other sources specifically defined in the ITA, such as so-called speculative transactions (sections 22, 23 ITA).

For purposes of the first three subcategories, "income" is defined as "profit" (*Gewinn*), i.e., as the difference in value between the net business assets at the end of the tax year and the net business assets at the end of the preceding tax year, plus withdrawals and less capital contributions.[34] For the last four sources of income, "income" is defined as the excess of receipts over expenditures to acquire, secure, and/or maintain revenue[35]—i.e., the cash method applies, supplemented by a deduction for depreciation.[36]

The main difference between these categories concerns capital gains or losses from the disposition of assets. Originally, this difference was quite substantial; however, it has been partly reduced in recent decades.

Under the "profit income" rule, all gains and losses related to a trade or business (including farming and professional services) are, in general, fully included in the tax base and taxed at ordinary tax rates on realization. Under narrow conditions, business capital gains may be subject to rollover relief.

In contrast, until 1998, capital gains or losses from the disposition of private assets, e.g., privately held company shares, bonds, real estate, and works of art, were, in principle, not subject to income tax; they were included in the tax base only if they were derived from the sale of a substantial participation (more than 25%) in the shares of a company[37] or from so-called speculative transactions.[38] A transaction was presumed to be speculative if a private asset was sold within a short period after its acquisition, i.e., two years in the case of real property and six months in the case of securities and other assets.[39] In 1999 and 2000, the threshold of a "substantial

34. ITA, s. 2 para. 2 No. 1 with reference to s. 4 para. 1.
35. ITA, s. 2 para. 2 No. 2 with reference to ss. 8-9a.
36. ITA, s. 9 para. 1 No. 7 with reference to s. 7.
37. ITA, s. 17.
38. ITA, s. 23 para. 1.
39. ITA, s. 22 No. 2 with reference to s. 23. It should be noted that the Federal Tax Court has developed the concept of a so-called professional real estate trader and applies the "profit income" method to taxpayers who buy and sell real estate with a turnover of more than three sales within five years.

participation"[40] was reduced to 1 %, thus excluding only portfolio shareholders in large public companies. Further, the holding periods for "speculative transactions" were extended to one year in the case of securities and ten years in the case of real estate.[41] The Business Tax Reform 2007 introduced a final withholding tax of 25 % for all profits and capital gains from privately held financial assets irrespective of any holding period.[42] An amount of 60 % of the capital gain from shares qualifying as business assets or from a privately held participation exceeding the 1 % threshold is taxed at the individual tax rate.[43]

The original dualistic system has remained in place for other assets, in particular for real estate. However, as mentioned above, the resulting income tax exemption of most private capital gains from real estate is currently under substantial political pressure.

In the computation of taxable income from all seven categories, all costs incurred in earning income are fully deductible[44] (although deductibility is restricted where there is some personal element); the deduction of related expenditure is prohibited by statute only with respect to the "final withholding tax" on capital income.[45] However, private expenses are not relevant for tax matters, thus separating the accrual of income from the consumption of income—a principle expressly stated in section 12 of the ITA.

5.1.2 *Private Expenses*

Only some narrowly defined types of private expenses, i.e., "special costs" (*Sonderausgaben*) and "extraordinary burdens" (*aussergewöhnliche Belastungen*) as well as certain personal allowances, reduce the tax base.

"Special costs"[46] include a wide range of expenses such as certain alimony payments, certain annuities, and church tax. The most relevant of these are social security contributions to a public pension scheme, health insurance, and unemployment insurance. Section 10a ITA gives certain taxpayers an additional reduction for private pension contributions. Section 10b ITA allows the deduction of certain donations for scientific, charitable, and specific cultural purposes (up to a limit of 20% of taxable income).

"Extraordinary burdens"[47] are private expenses which are recognized if they are unavoidable and incurred for legal, factual, or moral reasons, and provided that they exceed similar expenses of most other taxpayers (so that general allowances or tax-rate reductions do not cover the situation). However, there is no clear policy with respect to the tax treatment of extraordinary burdens.

40. ITA, s. 17 para. 1.
41. ITA, s. 23.
42. ITA, s. 32d para. 1.
43. ITA, s. 3 No. 40, s. 20 para. 8.
44. ITA, s. 4 paras. 4 and 9 para. 1.
45. ITA, s. 20 para. 9 sentence 1.
46. ITA, s. 10.
47. ITA, s. 33, 33a.

With respect to taxpayers' expenses for their own subsistence and family maintenance, the Constitutional Court has, in a series of landmark decisions,[48] forced the government to substantially raise the tax-free threshold for personal minimum expenses (from approx. EUR 2,500 in 1990 to over EUR 11,000 in 2024)[49] and for family expenses (including large amounts for the tuition and education of children). In addition, a reduced deduction of childcare costs for single parents was ruled void.[50] The current system even accounts for the additional burden borne by single parents by providing an additional tax allowance of EUR 4,260 (in 2024) for the first child.

5.1.3 Nonresident Taxpayers

In the case of nonresident individuals, the same categories and concepts are applied as those described above. However, following the "territoriality" concept of "limited tax liability,"[51] income of nonresidents is subject to tax only where it is derived from German sources.[52] Consequently, nonresidents are denied certain tax advantages and personal allowances.[53] In this context, the treatment of nonresident taxpayers is heavily influenced by European law. For example, in order to avoid conflict with European nondiscrimination rules, the German legislature introduced a rule allowing nonresidents that receive 90% or more of their income from German sources to apply for "extended unlimited tax liability."[54] Similarly, the deductibility of private tax consulting fees was abolished for all taxpayers when the CJEU decided that denying this deduction to nonresident taxpayers in German tax law was an infringement of the right of free movement under the EC Treaty.[55]

5.2 Corporate Income Tax

5.2.1 Taxable Entities

Since 1920, juridical persons and several other legal entities have been subject to corporate income tax under the CITA (*Körperschaftsteuergesetz*). The most important entities subject to corporate income tax are corporations (stock corporations, limited partnerships with shares, limited companies, and European Companies).[56] The CITA also covers various other entities of minor importance, such as commercial cooperatives, mutual insurance associations, and other juridical persons under private law. Finally, nonincorporated state-held businesses are also subject to corporate income

48. Federal Constitutional Court (*Bundesverfassungsgericht*), September 25, 1992, 2 BvL 5, 8, 14/91 Reports (BVerfGE) 87, p. 153; December 9, 2008, 2 BvL 1/07 Reports (BVerfGE) 122, p. 210.
49. ITA, s. 32a para. 1.
50. Judgment of October 17, 1984 1 BvR 527/08 Reports (BVerfGE) 68, p. 143.
51. ITA, s. 1 para. 4.
52. ITA, s. 49.
53. ITA, s. 50, 50a.
54. ITA, s. 1 para. 3.
55. CJEU, July 6, 2006, C-346/04 (*Conijn*).
56. CITA, s. 1 para. 1.

tax, thus removing a competitive tax advantage for those businesses. Some hybrid legal forms recently created in other countries (limited liability partnerships (LLPs) and limited liability companies (LLCs)) have not yet been introduced into German company law. Nevertheless, foreign LLPs and LLCs active in Germany can qualify for corporate tax treatment under a comparability test.

Partnerships, including limited partnerships with a corporate general partner (*GmbH & Co. KG*, of which approximately 150,000 exist in Germany), are not generally subject to corporate income tax. The income of a partnership is assessed on the basis of a single tax return for the whole partnership.[57] It is then allocated to the partners for tax purposes regardless of the actual distribution of profits. The law thus follows a (limited) transparency concept.

Recently, the legislature has introduced the possibility of opting into the two-layered corporate taxation regime for business and liberal-profession partnerships as well as for other registered civil law partnerships.[58] If a partnership exercises the option, it is treated as a corporation for tax purposes. Due to some legal uncertainty, it is not yet clear whether the new regime will be an attractive alternative to transparent taxation; so far, only very few partnerships have taken advantage of the option.

5.2.2 Tax Base

All income earned by corporations is deemed to be income from a trade or business.[59] For other entities subject to corporate income tax (in particular, associations without legal personality, state-held institutions, certain foundations, and other asset conglomerations under private law), the general income categories listed in the ITA for individual taxpayers apply.[60]

A major feature of the corporate tax base is the treatment of "hidden distributions" or "constructive dividends." Since corporate tax law does not allow the deduction of distributions or constructive dividends to shareholders,[61] it provides that "hidden distributions" must be added to the corporate tax base. "Hidden distributions" include any expenditure or waived income of a company resulting from the relationship between the company and a shareholder (e.g., inadequate consideration for services delivered by a shareholder). The factual problems with respect to the identification of a "hidden distribution" are a major cause of lawsuits between companies and the tax authorities and provide a substantial risk of criminal tax liability.

57. ITA, s. 15, General Fiscal Code (GFC), s. 180 para. 1 No. 2.
58. CITA, s. 1a.
59. CITA, s. 8 para. 2.
60. CITA, s. 8 para. 1.
61. CITA, s. 8 para. 3 sentence 2.

5.2.3 *Tax System*

One of the most important factors in German tax policy is the relationship between corporate taxation and income taxation. The corporate tax structure, introduced in 1977, contained two fundamental aspects:

(1) The top rate of personal income tax and the top rate of corporate income tax on retained income were equal (56% at the time). Thus, there was neutrality as to the legal form of an enterprise (corporation, partnership, sole trader).
(2) In the case of distributions, the corporate tax rate was reduced (to 36% in 1977) and fully credited against the personal income tax of the shareholder, thus achieving neutrality as to the allocation of income (reinvestment or consumption). This reduction in the corporate rate was also aimed at strengthening the German capital market.

This corporate tax system worked well for many years but became subject to heavy pressure in the 1990s. On the one hand, strong tax competition emerged between the Member States of the European Community and other countries. Massive reductions of the tax rate in other industrialized states made it necessary for Germany to gradually reduce its top corporate tax rate, to 40% on retained profits by 1999. At the same time, it seemed—from a revenue perspective—impossible to grant similar tax reductions in the field of income tax. Thus, corporate tax rates and marginal income tax rates drifted further and further apart.

On the other hand, the "imputation system," which was "standard" in the 1970s in Europe, displayed discriminatory features that seemed no longer to be sustainable under the fundamental freedoms enshrined in the EC Treaty. The main problem with the imputation system was that it was not extended to foreign source dividend income and thus discriminated against investments in companies resident in other Member States. In addition, nonresidents holding shares in German companies were not granted imputation tax credits. Finally, German permanent establishments of companies from other Member States were effectively taxed at a higher rate than German subsidiaries, thus distorting the choice between permanent establishments and subsidiaries.

The 2000 Business Tax Reform was designed to modernize the German system. The "imputation system" was replaced by a "shareholder-relief" system, which combined a low corporate income tax rate with a substantial tax reduction at the shareholder level. On the one hand, the tax rate applying to both retained and distributed profits was set at 25%; on the other hand, only 50% of the dividends paid to an individual shareholder were included in the personal tax base ("half-income" method). The combined burden of corporate and personal income tax was meant to be approximately the same as in the case of other income, such as income from a trade or business. This reform provided Germany with an attractive corporate tax rate (even taking into account the addition of trade tax) and removed possible conflicts with EU law since the "half-income" method was extended to dividends from nonresident companies. However, critics of the new system pointed out that tax neutrality between different legal forms for businesses (corporate structures, partnerships) had been sacrificed and neutrality of allocation (reinvestment or consumption) was adversely affected.

Due to the abolition of the imputation system and the introduction of a fixed tax rate for retained and distributed profits, the legislature had to find a way to provide relief for intercompany distributions. Therefore, the 2000 Business Tax Reform also introduced a participation exemption for corporate shareholders.[62] This exemption, which was chosen in order to provide for a single level of taxation on the income of a subsidiary, extends to dividends from German and nonresident corporations as well as to capital gains derived from the retention of (taxed) profits in a subsidiary. Only 5% of the respective dividends and capital gains are deemed to be nondeductible business expenses[63] and remain taxable.

Originally, the participation exemption did not contain a minimum shareholding requirement. However, this situation changed in 2013 in response to a 2011 CJEU judgment in which the Court considered the fact that the tax exemption did not apply to dividends on shares other than substantial shareholdings received by nondomestic holding companies to be an infringement of European primary law.[64] This judgment provoked a lively political debate about the future of the participation exemption. Finally, as a political compromise, the participation exemption for dividends was restricted to substantial shareholdings (10% or more), whereas capital gains remain tax-free even below this threshold. Since the new regime has significant cumulative tax effects, its conformity with the ability-to-pay principle is widely questioned.

Effective as of 2008, the 2007 Business Tax Reform reduced the tax rate for distributed and retained profits at the corporate level to 15%.[65] Another significant part of the reform concerns capital gains from financial assets. For these gains, a "dual" system was introduced which distinguishes between shares held as business assets and privately held shares. Dividends and capital gains from privately held shares are subject to a final withholding tax of 25%[66] but may be included in the taxpayer's personal income tax return and thus be subject to regular income taxation where the taxpayer's personal tax rate is lower than 25%.[67] There is no deduction for expenses with respect to these profits.[68] Where the shares are held as business assets, only 60% of the dividends and capital gains are included in the personal income tax base of the individual shareholder ("part-income" method).[69] Correspondingly, only 60% of expenses with respect to these profits are deductible.[70]

The 2007 Business Tax Reform also modified the deductibility of interest payments as business expenses, due mainly to concerns about the tax-planning

62. CITA, s. 8b.
63. CITA, s. 8b para. 5.
64. Judgment of November 20, 2011, C-284/09 (*Commission v. Germany*).
65. CITA, s. 23 para. 1.
66. ITA, s. 20 paras. 1, 2; ITA s. 32d para. 1.
67. ITA, s. 32d para. 6.
68. ITA, s. 20 para. 9 sentence 1.
69. ITA, s. 3 No. 40, s. 20 para. 8.
70. ITA, s. 3c para. 2.

potential of cross-border financial transactions between a parent and its subsidiary. An interest-limitation rule was introduced,[71] which allows the deduction of interest payments as business expenses only to a limited extent, on the basis of earnings before interest, taxes, depreciation, and amortization (EBITDA). There had been considerable debate about whether this provision is consistent with constitutional and EU law, which subsided after the adoption of the EU anti-tax avoidance directive (ATAD) in 2016 since the directive contains an interest-limitation rule which closely resembles the German model. In addition to the interest-limitation rule, a royalty-limitation rule was introduced in 2018, which also aims at combating aggressive international tax planning.[72]

Finally, in 2007, the legislature restricted the use of losses of a corporation with respect to substantial share deals (*Mantelkauf*).[73] The original provision limited the use of losses if 25%-50% of the shares were transferred to a particular person within a period of five years; it denied loss offsetting completely if more than half of the shares were acquired within that period. Although the provision was clearly aimed at fighting tax-avoidance transactions, it also covered many cases that could not reasonably be called aggressive tax planning. Over the years, some mitigating exceptions were introduced for failing companies, intragroup transactions, and losses covered by hidden reserves.

In 2016, the severity of the loss regime was alleviated by the introduction of a provision making it possible to preserve losses where a corporation continues its business without adding a different business after an acquisition of its shares.[74] In 2017, the Federal Constitutional Court declared the original 25%-50% shareholding requirement to be unconstitutional; as a result, it was abolished altogether, leaving the regime for acquisitions of more than 50% of the shares in force. At present, it is unclear whether this regime, complemented by the loss-preserving provision of 2016, will be upheld if it is subjected to a constitutional challenge.[75]

Finally, another prominent feature of German corporate taxation is "fiscal unity" (*Organschaft*), a tax consolidation regime for groups, requiring a profit-and-loss-absorption agreement.[76] Over the years, this regime has proven to be relatively unstable and has undergone various legislative adjustments.

5.3 Trade Tax

Besides individual income or corporate income tax, German businesses are subject to a second major tax, the *Gewerbesteuer* (trade tax).[77] For more than 100 years, trade tax has been one of the two pillars of tax autonomy at the municipal level (the other is real

71. ITA, s. 4h; CITA, s. 8a.
72. ITA, s. 4j.
73. CITA, s. 8c.
74. CITA, s. 8d.
75. An appeal against the original more than 50% regime without the complementary provision is still pending before the Federal Constitutional Court (2 BvL 19/17).
76. CITA, ss. 14-19.
77. Trade Tax Act (*Gewerbesteuergesetz*).

estate tax). Apart from agricultural and professional sectors, every trade or business carried on in Germany is subject to this tax. Foreign businesses are also subject to trade tax if they have a permanent establishment in Germany.[78]

Originally, trade tax was levied according to three factors—business income, business net value, and payroll—based on the idea that the tax should be a charge on the business itself and not on the income derived from it. However, in order to alleviate the tax burden, the business net value tax and payroll tax were abolished over time. As a result, trade tax has been transformed into an extra charge on business profits, with extremely volatile results for municipal revenue. A number of legislative efforts to protect the trade tax base from attempts by taxpayers to avoid the qualification of their profit as business income have led to various consequences for the structure of income taxation, in particular with regard to partnership taxation. Proposals are periodically made either to extend trade tax to professional services or replace it by a municipal surcharge on the income tax, but so far all have failed due to political resistance by the municipalities.

The tax base for trade tax is business profit as determined under the income tax rules,[79] subject to various adjustments, which (mostly) aim at eliminating the distorting effects of different financing structures of the enterprise.[80] Compared to the income tax base, these addbacks broaden the tax base.

The rate for trade tax on income is 3.5% (base tax rate),[81] multiplied by a municipal factor (*Hebesatz*), which is determined by each municipality.[82] In 2023, the average municipal factor was 403%, resulting in an average tax rate of 14%.[83] Among the municipalities, the trade tax rate varies between 7% and 21.6%.

The 2000 and 2007 German business tax reforms massively changed the character of the trade tax. For corporate taxpayers, trade tax now nearly equals the burden of corporate tax since the corporate tax rate of 15% is complemented by trade tax of roughly 14%. Since 2008, the trade tax burden is no longer deductible as a business expense for income and corporate tax purposes.[84] However, for unincorporated businesses, trade tax can largely be credited against the income tax (depending on the effect of the adjustments under trade tax, as described above).[85]

6 TAX LEGISLATION

6.1 Legislative Process

Legislation in income tax matters (both individual and corporate income taxes) is essentially framed by the fact that both the federal state and the *Länder* participate in

78. Trade Tax Act, s. 2.
79. Trade Tax Act, s. 7.
80. Trade Tax Act, ss. 8, 9.
81. Trade Tax Act, s. 11 para. 2.
82. Trade Tax Act, s. 16.
83. For 2023, *see* https://www.destatis.de/DE/Presse/Pressemitteilungen/2023/08/PD23_332_713.html.
84. ITA, s. 4 para. 5b.
85. ITA, s. 35.

the legislative process. Any change in income taxation requires the consent of both the *Bundestag* and the *Bundesrat*. This leads to (sometimes awkward) compromise-seeking. The tax legislative process usually begins with a government proposal, and simultaneously, a proposal by the majority faction in the *Bundestag*, which is discussed in the Finance Committees of both houses. There are public hearings of experts, and, of course, indirect influence by political pressure groups. Recently, there have been many justifiable complaints that draft laws are published with far too short consultation periods, so that a fruitful expert discussion is impossible before the laws come into force. On average, the legislative process takes about six to twelve months, until the new Act is published in the Federal Gazette (*Bundesgesetzblatt*).

Technical changes are initiated mainly by the tax administration. Since German political parties rarely have the power to enact major reforms, some of the most important substantive innovations in German income taxation are due to decisions by the Federal Constitutional Court.

6.2 Statutory Style

There is no single federal tax code in Germany, although there have been several attempts from academic circles to promote such a project. The major tax acts stem from the 1920s and 1930s and still bear their original structure; however, the increasing number of legislative changes has distorted their original inherent logic. There is a constant but rather unclear desire for "simplification" of tax law on the part of politicians, tax professionals, and citizens, but this desire for simplicity can clash with the German tradition, still strong, of achieving equity in each case (*Einzelfallgerechtigkeit*). Several factors contribute to the increasing complexity of tax legislation. For example, governments use the tax system to further specific economic or other (e.g., environmental) aims by granting tax incentives or disincentives. Moreover, members of the tax administration often demand specific changes to the technical provisions of the tax acts to prevent what they believe to be "abuses." It goes without saying that the necessity of finding a political compromise during the legislative process at the federal level (e.g., between *Bundestag* and *Bundesrat*) frequently leads to unsatisfactory solutions. Finally—as in most industrialized countries—the complexity of German tax law is also due to the growing complexity of domestic and international economic relations (a recent example is the taxation of financial instruments). Several reform proposals presented by academics in recent years have recommended a dramatic reduction in the size and complexity of tax legislation.

6.3 Statutory Interpretation

Although the starting point for the interpretation of statutory tax law is the wording of the statutory provisions (literal interpretation), the systemic context of the provision, its objective purpose, and legislative history must also be taken into account. These purposive, contextual, and historical approaches are particularly important where the wording of a statutory provision is ambiguous. In the past, the possibility of purposive interpretation in tax matters was sometimes contested with the argument that, in tax matters, there was no "purpose" besides the raising of revenue, but this criticism is no longer put forward.

In the 1920s and 1930s, a specific "economic approach" to tax law (*wirtschaftliche Betrachtungsweise*) was promoted by the tax courts and even enshrined in statutory law, allowing interpretation to extend beyond the limits of the wording of a statute. This idiosyncratic method of interpreting tax statutes is no longer accepted. Nevertheless, leading tax lawyers still support the "economic approach" as a tax-specific type of purposive interpretation, based on the idea that tax law aims at economic substance rather than legal form. The Federal Tax Court is split: there are chambers (*Senate*) which tend to a narrow and literal construction of statutory tax law, often strictly adhering to the private-law meaning of legal terms, while other judges are inclined to interpret tax law more broadly. This fundamental difference of attitude reappears in other contexts with respect to questions such as:

- whether tax law interpretation should adhere to the private-law meaning of the text or give way to an "autonomous" (and more flexible) interpretation;
- whether tax statutes may be extended by way of analogy or whether the "rule of law" prevents such an extension without express parliamentary consent; and
- whether "abuse of law" doctrines may be applied in order to re-qualify or recharacterize a situation irrespective of whether there is a valid business purpose behind the particular legal arrangement.

In 2023, the Federal Constitutional Court rendered a long-awaited decision on the limits of statutory interpretation. The Court made clear that the judiciary must not ignore or distort the obvious intention of the legislature; therefore, an analogy to a particular tax provision is inadmissible if a corresponding extension of the provision had already been proposed during the legislative process but was not adopted.[86]

7 COURTS DEALING WITH TAX MATTERS

7.1 Structure of the Courts

In Germany, tax disputes are not adjudicated by the general courts but are referred to a specific branch of the judiciary.[87] There are two levels of tax courts, the (lower) tax courts (*Finanzgerichte*, established by the *Länder*) and the Federal Tax Court (*Bundesfinanzhof*, the final appellate court in tax matters). The (lower) tax courts are responsible for both the investigation of the relevant facts of the underlying case and the proper application and interpretation of the law, while the Federal Tax Court decides only on questions of law. Where a court considers a statutory provision to be unconstitutional, the case must be referred to the Federal Constitutional Court, which

86. Federal Constitutional Court (*Bundesverfassungsgericht*), November 28, 2023, 2 BvL 8/13.
87. *See* Tax Court Act (*Finanzgerichtsordnung*).

alone is competent to decide on questions of constitutionality, and frequently does so. All domestic courts are entitled to refer matters of European law to the CJEU; the Federal Tax Court (the final court of appeal) is obliged to do so unless the *acte clair* doctrine applies.[88]

The lower tax courts sit with three professional judges and two laypersons, while the eleven chambers (*Senate*) of the Federal Tax Court in Munich each sit with five judges. An appeal against a judgment from a lower court may be filed with the Federal Tax Court only where a taxpayer can show that there are diverging judgments from lower courts or that the case is of fundamental importance.[89]

Any notice of assessment or any other formal act of the tax administration may be subject to judicial review. The taxpayer must file an appeal with the tax office responsible for the assessment. If this administrative appeal procedure fails (which happens only in one-third of cases), the taxpayer may then appeal to the courts.

In total, about 20% of cases are decided in favor of the taxpayer; this percentage would be higher if one leaves aside the large number of appeals that are rejected for formal reasons. Around 25,000-35,000 new cases come before the tax courts each year; numbers have been constantly decreasing in recent years. At the end of 2022, there were 30,768 cases pending before the lower tax courts and 1,883 cases before the Federal Tax Court. In 2022, a total of 29,551 cases were brought to the lower tax courts and 1,958 cases to the Federal Tax Court. The total number of cases resolved in 2022 was 33,872.[90]

7.2 Judicial Style

The Federal Constitutional Court has the power to review the compatibility of federal legislation with the German Constitution with *inter omnes* effect. Its decisions are binding for the other governmental bodies of the *Bund* and *Länder*.

The decisions of the Federal Tax Court (*Bundesfinanzhof*) are binding only for the parties in the specific case. Nevertheless, the decisions of the Court, which in most cases provide ample legal reasoning, carry great persuasive weight. If one chamber (*Senat*) wants to deviate from the *ratio decidendi* of another chamber, it must refer the case to the Great Chamber (*Großer Senat*) to find a solution that is binding for the whole court.

The publication of a particular decision in the Federal Tax Gazette (*Bundessteuerblatt*) or in the administrative tax regulations indicates that the tax authorities have agreed to extend the *ratio decidendi* of a specific decision of the Federal Tax Court to similar cases. On occasion, the tax authorities release a decree of nonapplication regarding a particular decision, which is sometimes to the advantage of taxpayers but more often to their disadvantage since it forces them to seek recourse to the courts

88. Article 267, Treaty on the Functioning of the European Union.
89. Tax Court Act, s. 115.
90. Source: Statistisches Bundesamt—Statistischer Bericht: Finanzgerichte, 2022, https://www.destatis.de/DE/Themen/Staat/Justiz-Rechtspflege/Publikationen/Downloads-Gerichte/statistischer-bericht-finanzgerichte-2100250227005.html.

again. In recent years, the official publication of some tax decisions has been deliberately delayed by the tax authorities, leaving taxpayers and tax officials in a state of uncertainty. Often, the tax authorities propose legislative changes in order to avoid the consequences of a court decision, frequently leading to a constitutional debate on retroactive legislation and issues of compatibility with the equality principle in German tax law.

8 TAX ADMINISTRATION

8.1 General

When the GG came into existence in 1949, the Western powers insisted that there be no centralized collection of taxes, but that taxes should be collected by the *Länder*. Conceptually, federal and state tax administrative functions are to be exercised by a separate hierarchy of federal and state authorities,[91] creating a remarkable divergence between legislative and administrative powers with respect to tax matters. Today, the collection of taxes remains decentralized but the *Länder* have adopted uniform collection practices.

The Federal authorities are, in particular, the Federal Ministry of Finance (*Bundesfinanzministerium*), the Federal Central Tax Office (*Bundeszentralamt für Steuern*), and the main customs offices (*Hauptzollämter*), which are the counterpart to the tax offices in customs and excise. The regional finance offices (*Oberfinanzdirektionen* (OFD)), which still exist in some *Länder*, are mixed entities, consisting of federal authorities in the customs field and state authorities in the tax field. The head of each regional finance office is both a federal and a state government official.

While the constitutional provisions on tax administration may indicate strong differences among the *Länder*, there is strong uniformity in practice. The general provisions on tax procedure and administrative procedural rules (the current General Fiscal Code (GFC) (*Abgabenordnung*) still follows its predecessor from 1919) are identical, as are the career and salary provisions for tax officials. The heads of the special tax divisions of the states meet regularly with their federal counterparts.

Every two or three years, the Federal Ministry of Finance publishes new regulations with respect to the most important taxes (income tax, corporate income tax, VAT, and trade tax), which provide guidance and help to ensure uniform application of tax laws throughout Germany.

Over the years, the *Bund* has expanded its own tax services in certain areas, particularly in the area of international taxation. The administrative arm of the *Bund* is the Federal Central Tax Office *(Bundeszentralamt für Steuern)*, which administers double taxation treaties, refunds of withholding taxes, refunds of VAT, exchange of information, attribution of ID numbers for EU purposes, etc.

German tax administration works in a quite bureaucratic and formalistic way, governed by strict adherence to the rule of law. More than 200 million tax assessments

91. Basic Law, Art. 108; *see also* the Tax Administration Act (*Finanzverwaltungesetz*).

are made every year, including separate assessments (e.g., for real estate valuation, partnership profits, and church tax). This practice of issuing separate assessments can result in some taxpayers receiving more than a dozen assessments for income tax for a particular year, taking into account subsequent adjustments and corrections.

8.2 Assessment and Audit

In principle, all taxpayers in Germany are obliged to file an annual income tax return[92] and report their income and expenses accurately. An exception exists for taxpayers whose income does not exceed the subsistence minimum of EUR 11,604 or who receive relatively low income from employment and no significant taxable income from other sources. However, such taxpayers will be assessed upon request. Labor income is subject to a withholding system[93] but is included in the annual assessment as well. Since the introduction of the final withholding tax for income from privately held financial assets, such income does not usually have to be reported in annual tax returns. In recent years, there has been a considerable shift to online tax returns, including the so-called *E-Bilanz* (electronic balance sheet), which became obligatory for business income in 2012.

Tax returns are checked by a medium-level tax inspector who scrutinizes the relevant facts and makes sure that the information is sufficient and correct. If any issues arise, more detailed information may be requested. The tax authorities have far-reaching powers to gather evidence.[94] Taxpayers that do not fulfill their obligations are not entitled to the "benefit of the doubt" and may be subject to disadvantageous estimates by the tax authorities.[95]

The desk audit is concerned mainly with plausibility (i.e., reviewing how the different categories of income of the taxpayer compare with earlier years, as well as with taxpayers in the same trade or profession). Following this preliminary examination, tax authorities are entitled to make their assessment subject to further review. In such cases—depending on the economic relevance of the case—desk audits are succeeded by field audits.[96] Field audits are highly developed in Germany, and most businesses or professional firms of significant size are typically subject to them. Smaller businesses are audited less frequently; their selection may depend on certain indicators. In 2016, the legislature enacted a reform of procedural tax law which explicitly permits the tax administration to employ electronic risk-management systems for targeting audits more efficiently. The practical execution of field audits has been criticized because the audit periods are seen as being too long, with audits often dealing with transactions which were completed six or more years in the past. Altogether, the German tax administration employs more than 10,000 field auditors.

92. ITA, s. 25 para. 3.
93. ITA, ss. 38-42g.
94. GFC, ss. 85 et seq.
95. GFC, s. 162.
96. GFC, ss. 193 et seq.

In order to exert effective control, in recent years tax legislation has significantly increased documentation obligations for taxpayers, regularly stretching back to ten years in the past. In 2020, mandatory disclosure rules for international tax arrangements were introduced based on an EU directive. In 2024, the federal government's attempt to extend this regime to national tax arrangements failed due to opposition from the *Länder*.

A taxpayer's request for judicial review does not affect the general rule that the amount of tax fixed by the assessment must be paid within the time given (usually one month). Only in rare situations will the execution of the assessment be suspended, either by the tax office or by the tax court, on the request of the taxpayer.[97]

8.3 Tax Compliance

The ability of the tax authorities to verify whether a tax return filed by a taxpayer is accurate varies significantly depending on the type of income.

Due to the extensive use of field audits with respect to business and professional income tax, compliance levels appear to be very high compared with those of other countries. The same holds true for labor income which, due to third-party reporting by employers, does not present many opportunities for tax avoidance. Frequent (usually every three or four years) field audits cover the withholding of income tax on wages by employers, and even smaller enterprises are audited for this withholding tax on a regular basis. The payment of social security contributions is field-audited separately by agents of the social security organizations.

In contrast, for a long time, tax compliance levels seemed to be very low with respect to income from capital investment. For many years, there was no serious effort to enforce the declaration of interest from bank accounts and bonds, no withholding tax on interest, and banks were not required to automatically provide information with respect to interest payments. In addition, the tax auditors of banks did not have the authority to copy lists of bank customers who received interest. Consequently, according to estimates from the 1990s, about 60% to 70% of domestic interest payments received by private investors was not reported. Due to this lack of enforcement, the Constitutional Court declared the system of taxation of interest to be unconstitutional because it violated the principle of equal treatment.[98]

As a consequence, a 30% withholding tax on interest received by residents (but not by nonresidents) was introduced in 1993. Since this withholding tax applied only to banks resident in Germany (i.e., not even to all debtors), there was a substantial outflow of capital, particularly to subsidiaries of German banks in Luxembourg and Switzerland. As a response to both international and domestic tax evasion, in 2009 a final 25% withholding tax for interest income became effective as part of capital income taxation, combined with a basic exemption for capital income of EUR 1,000 (in 2024).

97. GFC, s. 361; Tax Court Act, s. 69.
98. Federal Constitutional Court (*Bundesverfassungsgericht*), June 27, 1991, 2 BvR 1493/89 Reports (BVerfGE) 84, p. 239; March 9, 2004, 2 BvL 17/02 Reports (BVerfGE) 110, p. 94.

Exchange of information within Europe under an EU directive facilitates the taxation of cross-border interest payments. Driven by the Foreign Account Tax Compliance Act (FATCA) in the United States and various Organisation for Economic Co-operation and Development (OECD) and EU initiatives to combat tax evasion and tax avoidance, further disclosure duties and far-reaching tools for the exchange of information were implemented, and the traditional bank secrecy in tax matters was abolished.

Compared to other countries, Germany conducts an extremely high number of criminal tax investigations; it may even be argued that fear of a criminal investigation keeps the rather complicated tax system running. In recent years, prominent taxpayers, including executives of major companies, have been under investigation. In 2022, about 45,000 cases of criminal tax investigation were initiated, of which about 6,000 resulted in a conviction of tax fraud by a criminal court; such convictions are registered in the criminal record of the taxpayer.

The penalties adjudicated by the criminal courts are usually monetary, and prominent tax-evasion cases in the last few years have stimulated public debate about stricter penalties in criminal tax law. Under current jurisprudence of the criminal courts, imprisonment will result from tax fraud exceeding EUR 100,000, although prison terms are usually suspended unless the fraud exceeds EUR 1,000,000.[99] However, it is not unusual for those charged with serious tax fraud to be placed in preliminary detention in order to prevent them from disrupting the investigation or disappearing to a foreign country.

One of the ways in which tax fraud differs from other criminal offenses is that taxpayers have the right to avoid penalties by voluntarily disclosing earlier misstatements to the tax authorities. In order to increase the deterrent effect of the criminal law on tax fraud, the legal rules for avoiding penalties by voluntary disclosure were tightened considerably in 2011 and 2015.

8.4 Administrative Style

German tax officials are usually well trained and expected to strictly follow the rule of law. Thus, the power of discretion of an individual tax official is relatively small. Moreover, most actions by tax officials take place in a framework of numerous regulations, decrees, circular letters, etc., which tax officials (but not the courts) are bound to obey. Most internal circular letters are also published in order to inform taxpayers and their advisers about future treatment by the tax office. In a 2016 judgment, the Federal Fiscal Court made it clear that the scope for administrative discretion in tax law—even where exercised via regulations or circulars—is quite narrow: the legislature has sole prerogative to implement rules of general application.[100]

99. Federal Court of Justice (*Bundesgerichtshof*), February 7, 2012, 1 StR 525/11.
100. Federal Tax Court (*Bundesfinanzhof*), November 28, 2016, GrS 1/15.

In keeping with the rule of law, contracts or formal settlements between taxpayers and the tax administration with respect to the amount of tax due and the applicable tax law are not permitted. However, there are some deviations from this principle:

- Where the underlying facts of a particular case are difficult to investigate, a mutual agreement on the facts is possible; however, it is not binding if it leads to an obviously incorrect result.
- The tax administration is also entitled to issue rulings on questions of law under statutory provisions;[101] however, the tax office may refrain from issuing such rulings in cases of aggressive tax planning.

Corruption is rare among tax officials, at least in part because their salaries are thought to be competitive with those in the private sector, particularly if the more generous retirement plan is taken into account. Decisions on promotions are made according to merit and seniority.

8.5 Taxpayers' Style

It would seem very likely that, due to high tax rates and the complexity of statutory tax law in Germany, many taxpayers would try to reduce their tax liability. Nevertheless, in international comparisons, and especially when compared with Anglo-Saxon countries, the tendency to engage in aggressive tax planning seems to be relatively low in Germany. Recently, however, a series of tax-fraud cases—the so-called cum-ex-scandal—caused significant turmoil and resulted in a potential loss of revenue of several billion euros. Various fiscal and criminal proceedings were initiated, resulting in large payments to the tax authorities and several criminal convictions of tax advisers and bank consultants.

The opportunities for taxpayers to engage in aggressive tax planning vary significantly. On the one hand, taxpayers earning income exclusively from employment have very limited possibilities for reducing their tax burden because most available deductions are standard deductions and income is subject to third-party reporting and withholding. On the other hand, most multinational corporations are sensitive to tax issues and until recently many did not hesitate to engage in reasonably aggressive tax planning. Traditionally, the right of taxpayers to test the limits of "tax abuse" was accepted as long as the facts were fully and correctly disclosed to the tax authorities. However, in the last few years, public debate on multinationals not paying their "fair share" of taxes has resulted in a kind of "climate change," and it seems that there is a growing tendency to refrain from what might be perceived as clearly abusive arrangements. In addition, in 2024, following an EU directive of 2022, Germany introduced a global minimum tax of 15% for large multinationals.

101. GFC, ss. 204-207.

9 GENERAL PRINCIPLES

9.1 Relationship Between Tax and Commercial Accounting

German taxation of business income earned by both individual entrepreneurs and corporations has traditionally been marked by a strong connection between taxable income and accounting income. This "linkage" (*Maßgeblichkeit*) results from the principle that tax accounting is based on commercial accounting where there are no divergent, specific tax provisions.[102] In Germany, this linkage rule, in combination with the absence of express tax limitations, resulted in reserves and provisions being accepted as tax deductions more often than in other countries. In spite of high nominal tax rates, these reserves and provisions traditionally gave fast-growing domestic enterprises a temporary tax advantage compared to foreign enterprises.

However, in the last three decades, several developments have weakened this traditional "linkage." Tax legislation enacted in 1997 and 1999 substantially restricted the opportunities for including tax-free provisions in the tax base[103] and forced enterprises to claw back depreciation of shareholdings or real estate if the market value recovered during the years following the depreciation claim.[104] Moreover, German tax courts have consistently loosened the "linkage" between tax accounting and commercial accounting because commercial accounting is itself linked to European directives and tax courts tend to avoid referring matters of domestic taxation to the CJEU. Finally, in 2009, an accounting law reform was enacted which allows taxpayers to exercise tax accounting options independently from commercial accounting,[105] thus weakening the link between both types of accounting even further.

9.2 Respect for Legal Form

In Germany, the relationship between private law and tax law has changed dramatically over the decades. While the "economic approach" (*Wirtschaftliche Betrachtungsweise*) prevailed from the 1920s to the 1940s, tax courts in the 1950s and 1960s tried to find stability by recourse to civil law concepts. This tendency may be considered a countermovement to the almost boundless interpretation of statutory law during the Nazi regime. Currently, private law and tax law are largely regarded as separate fields of law, each subject to its own inherent logic, while constitutional law has taken over as the "leading" source of legal concepts. Nevertheless, there are still several connections between tax and private law. First, it is generally accepted that tax law must be applied to economic reality as formed by the rights and obligations of taxpayers under private law (the so-called precedence of private law). Moreover, because the wording of many tax provisions evidently refers to private law concepts, those provisions usually are applied in accordance with their private law meaning. It is highly disputed

102. ITA, s. 5 para. 1.
103. ITA, s. 5 paras. 2a-4b.
104. ITA, s. 6 para. 1 No. 1 sentence 4, No. 2 sentence 3.
105. ITA, s. 5 para. 1 sentence 1.

under what circumstances a court or a tax official may, under the rule of law, deviate from the private-law meaning of such terms where the purpose of a tax provision seems to require a broader interpretation.

9.3 Anti-avoidance Doctrines and Rules

German tax administration and, to a lesser extent, tax courts have always followed the principle of "substance over form" with varying intensity. There is a strong tendency in academic writing to apply this "substance-over-form" concept generally in the interpretation of tax statutes, thus returning to a predominantly "economic approach" to tax law. During the last few decades, the tax courts have seldom followed this approach openly, except in cases where the statutory law itself allows for it (e.g., by explicitly referring to the concept of beneficial ownership).[106]

Often, a type of "substance over form" approach is based on the German general anti-avoidance rule (GAAR).[107] The GAAR states that tax "cannot be circumvented" by abusive behavior, abuse being defined as the implementation of an inadequate arrangement producing a tax advantage not provided for by the tax code. Although the GAAR expressly excludes transactions where the arrangement serves a substantial business purpose, it is debatable whether subjective intent is relevant for its application. This debate goes back to a fundamental disagreement about whether it is possible to counteract tax avoidance simply by purposive interpretation and analogy or whether a GAAR is needed to give courts the necessary leeway; in general, proponents of the GAAR are of the opinion that it is precisely the subjective element (i.e., the intention to circumvent the law) which justifies departing from a strict interpretation of the statutory provisions and denying the tax advantage the taxpayer seeks.

There is also some debate over what types of tax advantages are "provided for by the tax code" for purposes of the GAAR. A thorough analysis of the case law makes one thing very clear: a tax advantage which lies within legislative intent may never be denied based on the GAAR, however tax-driven or contrived the particular arrangement may appear.[108]

Over the years, a large number of SAARs have been introduced in the German tax system. Major provisions include controlled foreign corporation (CFC) rules, the interest- and royalties-limitation rules, and restrictions on the future use of corporate tax losses in cases of sales of substantial shareholdings. In various instances, the Federal Tax Court has decided that the GAAR may not be applied in fields where the legislature has specifically defined abusiveness by the implementation of a SAAR.[109] In response, the legislature has twice tried to reverse this jurisprudence by amending the

106. GFC, s. 39 para. 2.
107. GFC, s. 42.
108. As an example, *see* Federal Tax Court (*Bundesfinanzhof*), June 26, 2006, I R 97/05 (on a "self-cancelling" scheme).
109. *See*, e.g., Federal Tax Court (*Bundesfinanzhof*), July 18, 2001, I R 48/97; August 11, 2021 I R 39/18.

GAAR but did not succeed because the reasoning of the Court is based on general legal methodology and not on the wording of any particular statutory provision.

10 TAX TREATY NETWORK

Germany has entered into ninety-six comprehensive double tax treaties and concluded over twenty-five tax information exchange agreements with tax havens. This remarkably tight network helps to maintain the competitiveness of the German economy and protect domestic tax revenue. In 2013, the German Ministry of Finance published a "model treaty" which serves as the basis for the negotiation of future tax treaties. As with all of Germany's existing tax treaties, the model treaty closely follows the OECD Model Convention, including the "authorized OECD approach" for the attribution of profits to permanent establishments. Major deviations from the OECD model are:

- the threshold for a substantial shareholding qualifying for the 5% rate of source taxation on dividends is set at 10% instead of 25%; the German model explicitly adopts a zero rate for dividends from substantial shareholdings;
- the source state has no right to tax interest, except interest derived from profit-participating loans or dormant partnerships;
- the capital gains article allows for an exit or departure tax on residents of Germany ceasing to be resident;
- the source state has the right to tax pensions, thus reflecting a shift to deferred taxation in national tax law;
- a switch-over from the exemption to the credit method applies where the other contracting state is entitled to tax certain items but does not actually do so (extended subject-to-tax clause).

Germany has signed the *Multilateral Convention on Mutual Assistance in Tax Matters* and the *Multilateral Convention to Implement Tax Treaty Related Measures to Prevent Base Erosion and Profit Shifting* (MLI), naming thirty-five double tax conventions as covered tax agreements. Reservations have been made, notably, with respect to Article 3 (transparent entities), Article 4 (dual-resident entities), Article 12 (artificial avoidance of permanent establishment status), and Article 14 (splitting up of contracts). However, Germany can approve the application of the MLI only after the modifications resulting from the MLI for an individual covered tax agreement (DTA) have been specified. At the end of 2023, this procedure was initialized by a draft bill which covers nine DTAs; two other DTAs have already been bilaterally adapted to the MLI.

Sometimes, particularly in cases of (perceived) danger of abusive behavior, the German legislature overrides a tax treaty provision through domestic legislation. The constitutional constraints of such a "treaty override" have long been subject to debate. In 2015, the Federal Constitutional Court finally decided that treaty-overriding rules do not violate constitutional law.[110]

110. Judgment of December 15, 2015, 2 BvL 1/12 Reports (BVerfGE) 141, p. 1.

11 SOURCES OF TAX LAW

Income tax cases are covered by the following sources of law, which are formally published in the Official Gazette (*Bundesgesetzblatt*) and/or the Official Tax Gazette (*Bundessteuerblatt)*:

- Federal Constitution (GG), especially the Basic Rights laid down in Articles 1-19 (https://www.gesetze-im-internet.de/gg/GG.pdf).
- ITA (*Einkommensteuergesetz*), which includes the bulk of material law regarding income taxation (www.gesetze-im-internet.de/bundesrecht/estg/gesamt.pdf).
- Income Tax Regulation (ITR) *(Einkommensteuer-Durchführungsverordnung)*; this regulation covers (mostly) procedural aspects and is released by the Federal Ministry of Finance (www.gesetze-im-internet.de/bundesrecht/estdv_1955/gesamt.pdf).
- Income Tax Guidelines 2012 (*Einkommensteuer-Richtlinien*); these guidelines are binding on members of the administration but not on the tax courts; a set of circular letters by the Federal and State Ministries of Finance periodically amends the Guidelines (https://esth.bundesfinanzministerium.de/esth/2022/home.html).

Other relevant cases are governed by:

- CITA (*Körperschaftsteuergesetz*) (www.gesetze-im-internet.de/bundesrecht/kstg_1977/gesamt.pdf).
- Reorganization Tax Act (RTA) (*Umwandlungssteuergesetz*) (www.gesetze-im-internet.de/bundesrecht/umwstg_1995/gesamt.pdf).
- Trade Tax Act (*Gewerbesteuergesetz*) (www.gesetze-im-internet.de/bundesrecht/gewstg/gesamt.pdf).

There are also regulations, guidelines, and circular letters with respect to these Acts.

In Germany, tax literature is largely found in commentaries and textbooks. The most relevant English-language publications are:

Florian Haase/Daniela Steierberg, *Tax Law in Germany*, 3rd edition (Munich: C.H. Beck, 2024).

Heike Jochum/Philipp J. Thiele, *Introduction to German Tax Law*, 2nd edition (Stuttgart: Richard Boorberg, 2018).

IBFD, *European Tax Handbook 2023*, country chapter Germany.

IBFD, *Global Individual Tax Handbook 2023*, country chapter Germany.

IBFD, *Global Corporate Tax Handbook 2023*, country chapter Germany.

India

D.P. Sengupta

1 HISTORY OF INCOME TAX

There has been income taxation in some form in India since ancient times. The *Arthashastra* of Kautilya, written in the latter half of the fourth century BCE, contains veritable gems about taxation.[1] However, it goes without saying that the structure of society and the economy have completely changed since those days, and the numerous discontinuities in Indian history make any comparison between older systems of taxation and the current system difficult.

Modern income tax was introduced in India for the first time in 1860, two years after the British Crown took over the administration of India from the East India Company. From an Indian point of view, the tax was most unfortunate since the proceeds from it were meant to pay for the costs of suppressing the 1857 "mutiny" rather than for the betterment of Indian society. Despite intense opposition at its first introduction,[2] the tax endured and, toward the end of colonial rule, was even described by some scholars as one of the happy legacies of British rule in India.[3]

The 1860 tax was imposed separately on income, which was classified into four schedules: income from landed property, professions and trades, securities, and salaries and pensions. The exemption limit for the general public was fixed at INR 200 per annum. Agricultural income was subject to tax at a rate of 2 % for incomes below INR 50 and 3 % for incomes above that amount. Those with income above INR 500 were charged an additional 1 % to pay for public works.[4]

1. For the origin of income tax in ancient India, *see* Balbir S. Sihag-Kautilya on Public Goods on Taxation, available at, https://sanjeev.sabhlokcity.com/Misc/sihag-public-goods-taxation.pdf (last accessed August 24, 2024).
2. https://www.biicl.org/files/6722_panel_two_harish_salve.pdf.
3. V.K.R.V. Rao, *Taxation of Income in India* (Calcutta: Longmans, Green and Co. Ltd., 1931).
4. *Ibid.*

After a brief hiatus, when the tax was reintroduced in 1886, agricultural income was excluded from its ambit and continues to remain so, with the result that almost 15% of national income is not subject to income taxation.[5]

The colonial-era income tax system lasted for almost eight decades and was marked by trial and error which shaped the development of the current income tax system in India.[6] While raising revenue for the war efforts of the British was the primary motivation for the tax, issues relating to the structure and nature of the tax, tax avoidance and evasion, and assessment and collection were also dealt with.

During the early years of the income tax, there were numerous princely states (nominally independent but subject to overall British suzerainty), some of which adopted their own income tax. The trade and commerce between these states and British India led to the development of nexus rules for taxation and a rich body of jurisprudence relating to "business connection." Double taxation and tax treaties were also important issues during these years.

Following independence in 1947, the colonial-era Income Tax Act (ITA) 1922 needed to be replaced. The structure of the Indian tax system was comprehensively considered by the Taxation Enquiry Commission, which reported in November 1954. In addition, Professor Nicholas Kaldor of the University of Cambridge reviewed the Indian tax system in light of the requirements of the Five Year Plans which had recently been introduced in India[7] and recommended a system comprising five taxes—income tax (with a maximum rate of 45%), capital gains tax,[8] wealth tax, personal expenditure tax, and a general gift tax—all to be assessed simultaneously, and on the basis of a single comprehensive return so that the five taxes would serve as checks against one another.[9]

In September 1958, the Law Commission submitted a proposal to make the provisions of the ITA more intelligible but without affecting the basic structure of the tax. A new Act was enacted in 1961, effective from April 1, 1962; it was largely based on the rules in the 1922 Act, with the changes in the new Act merely verbal and clarificatory in nature.[10]

---

5. https://economictimes.indiatimes.com/news/economy/agriculture/share-of-agriculture-in-indias-gdp-declined-to-15-in-fy23-govt/articleshow/106124466.cms?from=mdr. Under the British, agricultural income was already subject to land tax. Moreover, there was also a permanent agreement with the zamindars (aristocrats) in some parts of India, who considered this additional tax to be a breach of promise.
6. The 1886 Income Tax Act (ITA) was replaced by the ITA 1916, the ITA 1918, the ITA 1922, and the current ITA 1961, enacted seventeen years after independence.
7. "Indian Tax Reform," Report of a survey, Department of Economic Affairs.
8. Capital gains tax was introduced in India by the 1947 budget but was abandoned in 1949 on the alleged ground of its acting as a barrier to capital flows. It was reintroduced in 1956 following Prof. Kaldor's recommendation. For a detailed history of capital gains tax in India, *see* D.P. Sengupta, "India," in Michael Littlewood & Craig Elliffe (eds.), *Capital Gains Taxation: A Comparative Analysis of Key Issues* (Chelternham, UK: Elgar Publishing, 2017).
9. The government did not implement Prof. Kaldor's recommendation to reduce the maximum tax rate, nor was a comprehensive return for all direct taxes ever introduced.
10. As noticed by the division Bench of Bombay High Court in *D. Vakil v. CIT* [1946] 14 ITR 298.

Since 1962, the ITA has been subject to yearly amendments, principally through the annual Finance Acts, with the government using tax provisions to achieve social objectives through incentive provisions and to plug tax loopholes.

The evolution of the concept of residence in its historical context is an interesting and important aspect of the Indian tax system. Under the British, initially, "resident" and "nonresident" were not defined in the Act because income was taxable on the basis of origin, or on the basis of receipt where the income was received within three years of accrual. To counter the resulting avoidance and evasion, all income of residents became taxable on an accrual basis.[11] However, under a typical definition of "resident," those who did not habitually reside in India would have been liable to tax in India on their global income, thereby adversely affecting many British officials and traders. Therefore, the 1939 Act, in addition to defining residents and nonresidents, created a third category: "not ordinarily resident": "An individual is not ordinarily resident in British India in any year if they have not been resident in British India in nine out of ten years preceding that year or if they have not, during the seven years preceding that year, been in British India for a periods or periods amounting in all to more than two years."[12] Taxpayers in this category enjoyed a privileged status because, although they were resident, they paid tax only on income which accrued in India and foreign income brought into India. The use of a double negative in the definition could be read to mean either a person who can be treated as ordinarily resident in India or as "resident but not ordinarily resident."[13] Through an amendment in 2003, it has now been established that in order to be not ordinarily resident, one must be nonresident for nine of the ten previous years or be present in India for not more than 729 days in the previous seven years.

The haphazard system of yearly amendments to the ITA has led to growing complexity and difficulties in administering the tax law. The government initially proposed a direct taxes code (DTC) in 2009, with the object of simplifying the language and having a common code for direct taxes. A 2010 draft bill to adopt a DTC was rejected by the government of the time, so that the only direct tax left at the federal level is the Income Tax. In connection with the July 2024 budget, the Finance Minister announced a comprehensive review of the income tax to be completed in six months "to make the Act concise, lucid, easy to read and understand" and "reduce disputes and litigation, thereby providing tax certainty to the taxpayers."[14] The Minister also promised to expand the scope of safe harbor rules in order to reduce litigation, provide certainty in international taxation, and streamline the transfer pricing assessment procedure.

11. As a result of the report of the 1936 committee through the Income Tax (Amendment) Act, 1939.
12. ITA, 1922, s. 4B.
13. *See* AAR- P-5 of 1995, August 14, 1995.
14. Paragraph 137 of the Finance Minister's speech on the Budget 2024-25, July 23, 2024.

2 CONSTITUTIONAL ISSUES

The Constitution is the supreme law of India. All laws, including tax laws, are subject to the Constitution. The most important constitutional guarantee against arbitrary exercise of the taxing power of the State is contained in Article 265 of the Constitution: "No tax shall be levied or collected except by authority of law." In this context, it is also worth noting the provisions of Article 13(2) of the Constitution: "The State shall not make any law which takes away or abridges the right conferred by this Part [Part III-Fundamental Rights] and any law made in contravention of this clause shall, to the extent of the contravention, be void."

The Constitution guarantees several fundamental rights, one of the most important of which is provided in Article 14, which states that "the State shall not deny to any person equality before the law or the equal protection of the law within the territory of India." The use of the words "any person" implies that the protection of Article 14 is available to citizens and noncitizens alike and to both natural and legal persons. In addition, Article 19 of the Constitution guarantees certain freedoms to its citizens, including the freedom to "practice any profession, or to carry on any occupation, trade or business,"[15] although, of course, the State can impose reasonable restrictions. Another restriction on the State's taxing rights is contained in Article 27 of the Constitution, which states: "No person shall be compelled to pay any taxes, the proceeds of which are specifically appropriated in payment of expenses for the promotion or maintenance of any particular religion or religious denomination."

Since India is a federation, the power to make laws is allocated between the federal government and the states under Article 246 and the Seventh Schedule of the Constitution. Article 246 contains two lists, plus an additional "concurrent" list, which allocate taxing powers between the two levels of government. The Federal Government (Center) can make laws with respect to items in the Central List (List I), while States can make laws with respect to items in the State List (List II). Both of these lists also confer the power to make tax laws. The ITA was passed under Entry eighty-two of List I—"Taxes on income other than agricultural income." The Concurrent List sets out areas where both the Center and the States can legislate (List III), but that list does not confer any taxing power. The residual power to legislate rests with the federal government, including the power to levy a tax not mentioned in either the State or the Concurrent List.[16]

In 2016, as a result of the adoption of a Goods and Services Tax (GST), the allocation of these taxing powers was modified by the addition of Article 246A to the Constitution, which allows both levels of government to make laws with respect to GSTs.[17] However, the federal government has the exclusive power to legislate with respect to interstate trade and services.[18]

15. Article 19(1)(g) of the Constitution of India.
16. Article 248(2) of the Constitution of India, Entry 97 of List I in the Seventh Schedule.
17. Article 246A(1) of the Constitution of India.
18. Article 246A(2) of the Constitution of India.

The Constitution does not allocate any taxation powers to local governments, although the States on their own may assign any of the taxes in the State List to local government bodies; the taxes generally assigned to local governments are property taxes and taxes on vehicles.

Because most of the important taxing powers lie with the federal government, while State governments have responsibility for many areas requiring substantial expenditures, the Constitution also provides for transfers of resources to the States. Article 280 of the Constitution mandates a Finance Commission, to be appointed every five years, to determine how resources should be shared between the States and the federal government.

The constitutionality of taxing provisions has been challenged many times. However, there is a presumption in favor of the constitutionality of statutes, and therefore the burden of proof is on the person making the challenge. In tax cases, courts have occasionally used the doctrine of "reading down" a provision to save it from an attack on constitutional grounds.[19]

3 TAX RATES

3.1 General

Income tax is imposed on the total income of the "previous year" of every "person" at the tax rates set out in the Annual Finance Acts passed by Parliament, which are not part of the ITA.[20] Tax rates depend on the status of the person required to pay tax and includes "an individual, a Hindu Undivided Family (HUF), a company, a firm, an association of persons or body of individuals, whether incorporated or not, a local authority, and every other artificial legal person."

The HUF is a special category of taxpayer, being a separate taxable entity related to the "joint family" system of property ownership which was once widely prevalent in India. Although this family system is weakening, it still exists. However, since the HUF is a separate taxable entity with a separate threshold limit for taxation, it is now used mainly as a tax-planning tool.[21]

19. *See*, for example, *A. Sanyasi Rao v. Government of AP* (SC), February 13, 1996.
20. Tax rates are specified in Ch. XII of the ITA on certain items, such as capital gains, certain investment incomes of foreign institutional investors, lotteries, income of nonresident athletes, certain dividends received from foreign companies, and income from patents. Also notable is the fact that where the total income includes any unexplained credit, unexplained investment, etc., the tax rate is 60% plus surtax.
21. The Law Commission appointed in 2016 to develop a uniform civil code for India also studied the taxation aspects of the HUF and observed: "[T]he institution of HUF was a so-called gift by the British when they could not comprehend the complex socioeconomic structure of the Indian families. However, today, when it has been seventy-two years since independence, it is high time that it is understood that justifying this institution on the ground of deep-rooted sentiments at the cost of the country's revenues may not be judicious." Law Commission of India—Consultation Paper on Reform of Family Law, available at https://cdnbbsr.s3waas.gov.in/s3ca0daec69b5adc880fb464895726dbdf/uploads/2022/09/2022092674.pdf.

Effective for the fiscal year 2020, India has two tax regimes—the old tax regime (OTR) and the new tax regime (NTR)—applicable to the same taxpayers but with different brackets and rates. The new regime is apparently simpler to comply with and the tax rates are somewhat lower, but taxpayers forego numerous deductions and concessions, mainly pertaining to savings instruments, home loan repayments, etc. Initially, it was announced that taxpayers would have the option of choosing between the two regimes from year to year. For the filing of returns, the default regime was the old regime; those who wanted to adopt the new regime had to exercise an option by filing a particular form. However, by 2023, this arrangement has been reversed—the new regime is now the default regime and those who want to remain under the old regime have to exercise the option. There are exceptions for salaried persons with no business income, who can toggle between the two regimes from year to year, and for those with any business or professional income, although they can change regimes only once.

3.2 Individuals: Senior Citizens—OTR

The general tax rates for individuals and a HUF are usually the same. Senior citizens are entitled to special treatment by way of an increased threshold. Every resident subject to tax who at any time during the previous year had attained the age of 60 is entitled to the benefits. In 2012, a new category, popularly known as "very senior" or "super senior" citizens, was introduced for those above the age of 80, who are entitled to an even higher basic exemption limit.[22] These additional benefits for senior citizens are not available under the new regime.

3.3 Individuals and HUFs

In 2005, the government eliminated all tax rebates[23] and introduced deductions from gross income.[24] However, since the basic exemption limit was not linked to inflation, there were constant demands to increase the limit, especially during general election years. In response, in 2013 the government introduced a personal rebate for individuals which is currently equal to the lesser of the tax payable or INR 12,500; however, the rebate is available only for resident individuals having total income not exceeding INR

22. Finance Act 2012, First Schedule, Part III, para. A. There was also a special rate for women under 65 years of age, but this was withdrawn following the general increase in the exemption limit in the year 2005-2006.
23. Under the existing scheme of s. 80-C, a person gets tax relief at the highest marginal rate of tax applicable. Accordingly, the relief is more valuable to a person with a higher income compared to a person with a lower income. The scheme is, therefore, regressive.
24. Because of the resulting reduction in the tax base, the obligation to file a return of income was simultaneously changed to a gross income basis. Thus, if the gross income of a taxpayer before the usual deductions for savings, etc., exceeds the minimum threshold for a particular income, there is a filing obligation even if the net income after deduction is below the threshold (6th proviso to s. 139(1) introduced by the FA 2005).

500,000.[25] To make the NTR more attractive, effective from 2024, the amount of the rebate has been increased to the lesser of the tax payable or INR 700,000 for those opting for the new regime.[26] Therefore, despite the rate schedule below, resident taxpayers having income of INR 700,000 or less do not have to pay any income tax under the new regime.

25. ITA 1961, s. 87A.
26. ITA 1961, proviso to s. 87A introduced through Finance Act, 2023, read with s. 115BAC.

The most recent tax rates following the 2024 budget are as follows:

The Most Recent Tax Rates Are as Follows: Old Tax Regime (OTR)						*New Tax Regime (NTR)*	
		Individuals				*Taxable income (INR)*	*Tax Rate*
Ordinary (Resident and Nonresident)		*Resident Seniors*		*Resident Super Seniors*		Up to 30,0000	0
Taxable income (INR)	*Tax Rate*	*Taxable income (INR)*	*Tax Rate*	*Taxable income (INR)*	*Tax Rate*	300,000-700,000	5%
Up to 250,000	0	300,000	0	500,000	0	700,000-1,000,000	10%
250,000-500,000	5%	300,000-500,000	5%			1,000,000-1,200,000	15%
500,000-1,000,000	20%	500,000-1,000,000	20%	500,000-1,000,000	20%	1,200,000-1,500,000	20%
> 1,000,000	30%	> 1,000,000	30%	> 1,000,000	30%	> 1,500,000	30%

3.4 Surcharge and Cess (Surtax)

On the repeal of the wealth tax in 2015, the surcharge payable by those having total income above INR 10 million was increased from 10% to 12% and then to 15% in 2016. In 2017, a surcharge of 10% was introduced for those having total income between INR 5 million and INR 10 million and 15% for total income above INR 10 million. In 2019, a further surcharge on the superrich was adopted: 25% for total income between INR 20 million and INR 50 million and 37% for total income above INR 50 million.[27] Surcharge and cess apply both in the NTR and the OTR. However, in order to make the NTR more attractive, through the 2023 budget, the 37% surcharge on the superrich has been reduced to 25% if the taxpayer moves to the NTR. The highest surcharge on dividends and capital gains on shares is restricted to 15%. In addition, a surtax (the health and education cess) is imposed on both income tax and surcharge. Surcharge and cess do not form part of the divisible pool of central tax revenues to be shared with the states and are a source of friction between the federal government and some states.

3.5 Partnerships and Domestic Companies

Partnerships are currently taxed at a flat rate of 30% (plus surcharge and cess). The tax rate on domestic companies was lowered from 30% to 25% in 2017 for companies with income up to INR 2.5 billion. Currently, for domestic companies with income below INR 4 billion, the general tax rate is 25%, while the rate for others is 30%. However, for domestic manufacturing companies set up after March 2016 that do not have any other business and that exercise an option not to claim deductions available in a special economic zone or other specified incentives or deductions, the tax rate is 25% irrespective of the income limit.[28]

Effective April 1, 2020, two more optional regimes with even lower tax rates were introduced. If a domestic company forgoes specified exemptions, deductions, or incentives, it has an option to be taxed at 22%; however, once exercised, this option cannot be withdrawn.[29] Moreover, as part of the "made in India" initiative, a domestic company set up and registered on or after October 1, 2019 that commenced manufacturing before March 31, 2024 (again, at the option of the taxpayer) is taxed at 15%, subject to the company not claiming specified deductions and fulfilling other conditions.[30]

Until 2024, the statutory tax rate for foreign companies was 40%, although some foreign companies were able to set up operations in areas or zones where tax holidays or reduced rates were available. In the 2024 budget, the rate was reduced to 35%, apparently to attract foreign capital for the country's development needs.

27. There is a provision of marginal relief to ensure that the total amount payable as income tax and surcharge does not exceed the total amount payable as income tax on total income of INR 5,000,000 by more than the amount of income that exceeds INR 5,000,000.
28. ITA 1961, s. 115BA.
29. ITA 1961, s. 115BAA.
30. ITA 1961, s. 115BAB.

As with other taxpayers, both domestic and foreign companies are subject to surcharge and cess. However, for domestic companies having income between INR 10 million and 100 million, the rate of surcharge is 7% of the tax and 12% where income exceeds INR 100 million, while the corresponding rates for foreign companies are 2% and 5%, respectively. For domestic companies opting to be taxed in accordance with section 115BAA and 115BAB, the surcharge is 10%. As with other taxpayers, the cess is applied on top of the tax and surcharge.

4 COMPOSITION OF THE FISCAL SYSTEM

Since April 2016, the Central Board of Direct Taxes (CBDT) has released time series data, starting from fiscal year 2011, containing information on the number of taxpayers, number of tax returns filed, direct-tax-to-GDP ratio, etc., for wider use and analysis by the public.[31] Because more than 90% of tax returns are filed online, data collection has become relatively easy. Information on personal and corporate tax revenues for selected financial years is shown in the table below:

Financial Year	*Corporate Tax*	*Personal Income Tax*	*Other Direct taxes*	*Total*	*Corporate Tax as a Percentage of Total Direct Tax*	*Total Taxes*	*Direct Tax as a Percentage of Total Taxes*	*Direct Tax-GDP Ratio*
2000-2001	35,696	31,764	845	68,305	53%	188,119	36.31%	3.25
2016-2017	484,924	349,503	15,286	849,713	58%	1,711,228	49.65%	5.53
2022-2023*	825,834	833,307	4,545	1,663,686	49.63%	3,045,699	54.62%	6.11

*provisional.

Over the years, at the federal level, the share of direct taxes as a proportion of total tax revenues has increased from just over 36% in 2000-2001 to just over 49% in 2022-2023. Indirect taxes still account for about 46% of total federal tax revenues.

With respect to direct taxes (except for the 2022-2023 fiscal year), corporate taxes have accounted for a greater percentage of total direct taxes than personal income taxes, which include revenue from the Securities Transaction Tax (STT), as discussed below. Although the share of personal income tax as a proportion of total tax revenue has recently increased, it comes nowhere near the level seen in Organisation for Economic Co-operation and Development (OECD) member countries. The direct-tax-to-GDP ratio, although increasing and currently at roughly 6% (at the federal level), is still far below the OECD average.

31. Available at https://incometaxindia.gov.in/Documents/Direct%20Tax%20Data/Final-approved-Consolidated-Time-series-2022-23.pdf.

For a time, the government seemed intent on doing away with ordinary income taxes in certain areas and substituting transaction-based taxes instead. Thus, in 1997, the classical system for taxing dividends was eliminated and replaced by a dividend distribution tax (DDT). The DDT was easy to administer since responsibility for collecting the tax was shifted to companies distributing dividends, although at a fixed and somewhat lower rate; however, the DDT was abolished in 2020. In 2004, the STT was introduced to replace long-term capital gains tax on the transfer of listed securities and mutual fund units, thereby shifting responsibility to collect the tax (again at a fixed rate) to recognized stock exchanges and mutual funds. STT is also paid on short-term capital gains on shares, derivatives, and other securities, but at a lower rate. Although the rules for the taxation of long-term capital gains were changed again in 2018, the STT remains in place. Long-term gains made after July 23, 2024 from the transfer of equity shares in excess of INR 125,000 are taxable at a 12.5% rate plus surcharge and surtax. STT is also levied on futures and options trading, which has recently experienced a massive increase in retail trades. The budget 2024 has increased the STT rate on futures to 0.02% and on options to 0.1%.

The 2024 budget initiated a major reform of the taxation of capital gains, including holding periods for different class of assets, an increase in the tax rate for short-term gains with respect to financial assets from 15% to 20%, a rate of 12.5% for all long-term assets, and elimination of indexation. Only individuals and HUFs have an option to be taxed either at 20% with indexation or 12.5% without indexation for capital gains from the transfer of land or buildings acquired before July 23, 2024. These reforms are discussed in more detail in Parts II and III.

In 2008-2009, the government introduced a Commodities Transaction Tax (CTT) at 0.017% on futures and options, in line with the STT rate.[32] As a result of intense opposition, the CTT was diluted and then abolished. It was reintroduced in 2013 but applies only to nonagricultural commodity futures at a rate of 0.01%. In addition, a banking cash-transaction tax of 0.1% for withdrawals from banks of over INR 10,000 on a single day was adopted in 2005 but repealed in 2009. However, in the 2019 budget, deduction at source of 2% is required for cash withdrawals from banks aggregating more than INR 10 million in a year.[33] The threshold drops to INR 2 million if the person has not filed a return of income for three assessment years, and the rate increases to 5% if in such cases the total amount paid in cash exceeds INR 10 million.[34] The stated purpose of these provisions is to discourage cash transitions in the economy and to promote the digital economy.

32. Speech of the Finance Minister, para. 179, for the year 2008-2009.
33. ITA 1961, s. 194N introduced by FA 2019, substituted by FA 2020, amended again by Finance Act 2023.
34. ITA 1961, first proviso to s. 194N.

5 BASIC STRUCTURE OF THE INCOME TAX

5.1 Basic Principles

Section 4 of the ITA, the charging section, provides that the tax rate on the total income of every person for the previous year may be prescribed in any federal legislation (not necessarily the ITA) subject to and in accordance with the ITA. Section 5 defines the scope of total income, which varies according to the residence status of the taxpayer. For resident taxpayers, all income from "whatever source derived," whether actually received in India or deemed to be received in India, or accruing or arising or deemed to accrue or arise outside India in any previous year, is chargeable to tax in the assessment year. For nonresidents, the charge is imposed on all income received or deemed to be received in India or which accrues or arises or is deemed to accrue or arise in India. For taxpayers that are not ordinarily resident, the income which accrues or arises outside India is not taken into account unless it arises from a business controlled in India or a profession set up in India.[35]

The Indian income tax system is still schedular in nature. Under section 14 of the ITA, the categories or heads of income are salaries, income from house property, profits and gains of a business or profession, capital gains, and income from other sources.[36] Despite these classes of income, income tax is nevertheless one tax and is assessed as a single tax, not as multiple assessments of the different classes. As a result, even where the total income of a taxpayer under each schedule is below the threshold for taxation, tax may nevertheless be assessed. Where a particular item of income is properly classified under one schedule but cannot be charged under that particular schedule, it cannot be charged under any other schedule, including the residual category.[37] However, the character and nature of income must be determined according to common standards of reasonableness, since the ITA provides no guidance in this regard.[38]

Certain items of income (agricultural income is the most prominent item)[39] are not taxable at all as a result of tax policy or constitutional limits. These items are enumerated in Chapter III of the ITA and do not form part of total income.

Absent any specific provision to the contrary, courts in India often apply the "real-income" principle. As a result, a bad-debt deduction was allowed even when there was no specific provision for allowing it[40] and losses from embezzlement were

35. If a profession is set up in India and operates abroad, the income which accrues, even outside India to a taxpayer not ordinarily resident in India, is chargeable to tax.
36. There was a Schedule B—interest on securities—and many disputes arose as to whether income from securities held by banks could be taxed under this head or under the head of business, as well as to whether a loss could be claimed against business income. This head was eliminated by the FA, 1988. Where interest on securities is not taxable as business income, it is classified as income from other sources (ITA, s. 56(2)(id)).
37. *Nalinikant Ambalal Mody v. CIT* (SC), Civil Appeal Nos. 731-732, 1964, May 4, 1966.
38. *Ibid.*
39. Agricultural income is partially integrated in the sense that it is to be taken into account for the purpose of determining the rate of tax.
40. *Commissioner of Income Tax v. Sir S.M. Chitnavis*, April 26, 1932, Bombay HC.

allowed even where it did not occur in the course of a business.[41] Courts have also held that income from loans which might become nonperforming assets (so-called sticky loans) cannot be considered to have definitely accrued merely because the use of the accrual method of accounting was mandatory.[42] However, where the provisions of the ITA apply, the concept of real income cannot be read to defeat those provisions.[43] With respect to expenditures, there are also numerous provisions which derogate from the real-income principle.

An offshoot of the real-income principle is the concept of mutuality, which holds that persons cannot make a profit from themselves. Indian courts have held that the concept of mutuality postulates that all contributors to a common fund must be entitled to participate in the surplus of the fund and that all participants in the surplus must be contributors to the common fund.[44] This principle is generally applied in cases dealing with insurance companies, societies, clubs, associations, etc., and, on occasion, even multinational organizations have benefited from it.[45]

Section 2(24) of the ITA provides an inclusive definition of "income" with thirty-two clauses, most of which were added to overcome court decisions. Capital receipts are not taxable unless they are included in income. Winnings from lotteries, crossword puzzles, races, and card games, or from gambling or betting in any form, are deemed to be income.[46] Subsidies, grants, cash incentives, and duty drawbacks have all recently been deemed to be income.[47]

5.2 Treatment of Losses

Under India's schedular system of taxation, losses under a particular category are set off first against any income from the same category,[48] and any balance is then set off against income from other categories; any remaining unabsorbed loss can be carried forward, generally for eight years, to be set off against income from the same category.[49] Due to differences in the tax rates applicable to capital gains and other classes of income, as well as pervasive misuse (including, in some instances, the purchase of losses), the treatment of losses has been extensively modified. The current position is that short-term capital losses can be set off against both short-term and long-term capital gains of the same year; however, long-term capital losses can be set off only against long-term capital gains of the same year. Any loss from a speculative business or horse racing can be set off only against income from another similar

41. *Badridas Daga v. CIT*, Civil Appeal No. 149, 1956, April 25, 1958, 34 ITR 10 (SC).
42. Justice Tulzapurker's opinion in *State Bank of Travancore v. CIT*, January 8, 1986, civil appeal Nos. 1860-1862 (NT), 1973 (SC).
43. *Ibid.*
44. *Chelmsford Club v. Commissioner of Income Tax* (2000) 243 ITR 89 (SC), March 2, 2000.
45. KPMG India successfully claimed that its contribution to KPMG International, Switzerland, supposedly a nonprofit organization, was in the nature of a contribution to a mutual benefit society. *DCIT v. KPMG* (ITA 2493/Mum/2012), April 7, 2017.
46. ITA 1961, s. 2(24)(ix).
47. ITA 1961, s. 2(24)(xviii).
48. ITA 1961, s. 70.
49. ITA 1961, s. 71.

business and cannot be set off against regular business income.[50] With respect to the use of a loss from one schedule to offset income of another schedule, losses from business cannot be set off against salaries[51] and losses from the schedule "income from house property" can be set off against income from other heads only up to INR 0.2 million.[52] The carryback of losses is not allowed. No loss can be carried forward if the return of income is not filed in time. If pursuant to a search or survey (a less intrusive search of business premises), any undisclosed income is found, no set-off of loss or unabsorbed depreciation is allowed against such undisclosed income.[53]

5.3 Minimum Alternate Tax and Alternate Minimum Tax

In recent years, the government has expanded liberal depreciation deductions and increased investment allowances, along with other incentive measures for encouraging investment, exports, etc. At the same time, the need for additional revenue has also been increasing. As a result, so-called zero-tax companies—dividend-paying profitable companies which showed huge book profits but did not pay any income tax—became common. After earlier efforts to restrict deductions failed, in 1987 section 115J was introduced to deem such companies to have income equal to 30% of their book profits. This provision, known as the Minimum Alternate Tax (MAT), was repealed in 1990 but reintroduced in 1997.[54] Currently, where tax payable under the normal provisions of the ITA is less than 15% of the book profits (plus applicable surcharges and surtax), MAT is imposed at 15% of the book profits. The legislation is very complex and in effect an acknowledgement that, contrary to their stated intentions, successive governments have been unable to remove incentive provisions while reducing tax rates. For companies operating in the International Financial Services Centre (IFSC), discussed in section 5.6, the rate is 9%.[55] The MAT provisions do not apply to companies engaged in life insurance businesses or companies which opt to forego incentive provisions under section 115BAA or 115BAB.[56]

In addition, effective from 2013, there is an Alternate Minimum Tax (AMT) for taxpayers other than companies, at 18.5%, reduced to 15% in the case of cooperative societies and 9% in the case of IFSC participants. For individuals and others opting for the NTR, no AMT is payable. Moreover, no AMT is payable where a taxpayer (other than a firm) has adjusted total income not in excess of INR 2 million.[57]

50. ITA 1961, ss. 73(1) and 74A(3).
51. ITA 1961, s. 71(2A).
52. ITA 1961, s. 71(3A).
53. ITA 1961, s. 79A, with effect from April 1, 2022.
54. Originally, ITA 1961, s. 115JA, but now s. 115JB.
55. ITA 1961, s. 115JB(7).
56. ITA 1961, s. 115JB(5A).
57. ITA 1961, s. 115JC, read with s. 115JEE(2).

5.4 Business Taxation

Corporation tax is part of the ITA. Corporations are required to file income returns even where there is no income for the year or a loss has been incurred.[58] A company is resident in India if it is incorporated in India or its place of effective management (POEM) is in India. As in the case of individuals, the residence status of a company determines its liability to tax. According to case law, the status of an entity incorporated abroad as a corporation or other entity is determined according to the law of the country where the entity is incorporated or established.[59]

The taxable income of a business for purposes of the category of business taxation is based on the profit and loss account prepared by the business after making adjustments for business expenses which are not allowed by the ITA. There may also be certain types of expenses which are deductible only if certain conditions are met (e.g., VAT/GST liability or liability to pay bonuses or commissions) and are deductible only when paid.[60] Deductions for expenditures exceeding INR 10,000 on a day (singly or in the aggregate) are allowed only where payment for such expenses is made by crossed check/draft or through the use of electronic clearing through a bank account;[61] cash expenditures above this limit are no longer allowed. Moreover, payments made in a year in respect of an earlier year's liability are deemed to be income from business in the year in which the payment was made unless the payment was made using one of the methods described above.[62] To summarize, the general principle is that all noncapital and nonpersonal expenditures which are made wholly and exclusively for business purposes are deductible.[63] For businesses, there is an obligation to maintain books of account where income or turnover exceeds a certain limit[64] and an obligation to file a tax audit report, along with a return of income in a specified form where the turnover of the business/profession exceeds specified limits.[65]

Depreciation is allowed on a declining-balance basis with respect to groups of assets in accordance with rates prescribed in a separate schedule in the Income Tax Rules 1962.

5.5 Presumptive Taxation

Certain types of income derived by nonresidents and small business taxpayers are taxable on a presumptive basis. Nonresidents are taxed on a percentage of their gross

58. ITA 1961, s. 139(1)(a). The same filing requirements apply to partnerships. The central government can exempt certain classes of persons from the obligation to file.
59. *Technip SA v. Sms Holding (Pvt) Ltd*, May 11, 2005 (Civil Appeal Nos. 9258-9265, 2003) (SC).
60. ITA 1961, s. 43B.
61. ITA 1961, s. 40A(3).
62. ITA 1961, s. 40A (3A). The provision was tightened by the Finance Act, 2017 to counter moves to legitimize money following the demonetization in 2016.
63. ITA 1961, s. 37; certain other expenses, such as rent, repairs, interest, bad debts, etc., are separately dealt with in ITA 1961, ss. 30-36 and are subject to the conditions and limitations mentioned in those provisions.
64. ITA 1961, s. 44AA.
65. ITA 1961, s. 44AB.

receipts from the shipping of passengers or goods to ports in India at 7.5%, services rendered in connection with the extraction of mineral oils (including the rental of certain plant and machinery) at 10%, the operation of aircraft at 5%, the construction of power plants for turnkey power projects at 10%, and 20% for nonresident cruise ship operators.[66] Qualifying Indian companies (owning at least one qualifying ship) are allowed to pay an optional tonnage tax.[67]

Small taxpayers with business turnover of less than INR 20 million (or INR 30 million where cash receipts do not exceed 5% of the total turnover)[68] have the option to pay tax on income of 8% of turnover under section 44AD without the deduction of any expenses; to promote digitalization, the Finance Act 2017 reduced the percentage to 6% with respect to receipts through checks or digital means. For certain professions with receipts up to INR 5 million (INR 7.5 million if cash receipts do not exceed 5% of the total receipts), profit is presumed to be 50% of gross receipts.[69] Under section 44AE, for small transport operators engaged in the transport of goods (other than heavy goods), profit is presumed to be INR 7,500 per vehicle per month.[70]

5.6 International Financial Services Centre—GIFT City

The idea of an IFSC was first raised in 2007[71] in response to the growing pace of internationalization of the Indian economy and the significant growth of the banking, insurance, and financial services sector. It was originally planned to be established in Mumbai. However, in 2015, the government declared its intention to make the existing special economic zone (Gujarat International Financial Tec (GIFT) City) an IFSC to compete with Singapore, Dubai, etc. An important amendment to facilitate the relocation of Indian fund managers to India was the introduction of a measure providing that (subject to certain conditions), fund management activity carried out through an eligible fund manager would not constitute a business connection in India;[72] in the case of an IFSC, these conditions can be further relaxed through a notification.[73] In 2018, the government declared its intention to create a unified regulatory authority for the IFSC.[74] In 2019, further direct tax incentives were granted, such as a 100% profit-linked deduction under section 80-LA in any ten-year block within a fifteen-year period, exemption from DDT from current and accumulated

66. ITA 1961, s. 44BBC, introduced by Budget 2024. In terms of new s. 10(5B), lease rentals of ships operated by a foreign company are exempt up to March 31, 2030 if the non-resident payer and payee are part of the same corporate group.
67. New Ch. XII-G (containing s. 115V to 115VZC).
68. Introduced by the Finance Act 2023, effective April 1, 2024.
69. Section 44ADA introduced by the Finance Act 2016, effective April 1, 2017.
70. As modified by the Finance Act 2018. For heavy goods, the amount is INR 1,000 per tonne of gross vehicle weight.
71. https://prsindia.org/files/bills_acts/bills_parliament/2007/bill128_20070621128_Report_of_the_High_Powered_Expert_Committee_Percy_Mistry.pdf.
72. ITA 1961, s. 9A.
73. Notification is publication in the Official Gazette, the repository of all legal processes in India and through which the general public is made aware of important legal developments. Notification in the Official Gazette may be mandated by the law itself.
74. ITA 1961, s. 9A(8A).

income to companies and mutual funds,[75] exemptions on capital gains to Category-III AIF, and interest payments on loans from nonresidents. In 2021, the Finance Minister declared that the government is committed to making the IFSC in GIFT City a global financial hub, and announced: a tax holiday for capital gains for aircraft leasing companies, a tax exemption for aircraft lease rentals paid to foreign lessors, a tax incentive for relocating foreign funds in the IFSC, and a tax exemption for the investment divisions of foreign banks located in the IFSC. In 2022, subject to specified conditions, an exemption was announced for income of nonresidents from offshore derivative instruments or from over-the-counter derivatives issued by an offshore banking unit, as well as income from royalties and interest on account of ship leases and income received from portfolio management services in the IFSC.[76] In 2023, the distribution of income from such derivatives to nonresidents was also exempted. The 2024 budget provided that the interest-limitation provision of section 94B does not apply to finance companies located in the IFSC. In addition, surcharge is not payable on dividends and interest of specified funds set up in the IFSC

5.7 Taxation of Virtual Digital Assets (Crypto Taxation)

The Indian government has been grappling with the regulation of crypto currencies and other virtual digital assets for some time. Apparently, there have been about 40 crypto exchanges operating in India, with a turnover of around INR 1 trillion. Through the Finance Act 2022, the government introduced a provision for the taxation of income from the transfer of virtual digital assets[77] at 30% (plus the usual surtax and cess). No deductions are allowed except for the cost of acquisition. Losses, if any, are ignored.[78] To ensure compliance, tax must be deducted at source. The threshold for the taxation of digital assets in the case of payments made by individuals/HUF (who are not subject to audit) is INR 50,000 in a financial year and INR 10,000 in all other cases.[79]

5.8 Tax on Online Gaming Income

Considering the proliferation of online gaming platforms and the significant rise in the number of users, the government introduced a separate provision for the taxation of winnings from online games at 30% (plus surtax and surcharge) on net winnings at the end of the financial year.

75. DDT having been abolished, currently, dividends received by a nonresident from a unit in the IFSC are taxed at 10%, compared to the general rate of 20%.
76. The full range of taxation and other regulatory benefits for the IFSC are available at https://www.giftgujarat.in/downloads/Doing%20business%20at%20GIFT%20IFSC_booklet.pdf.
77. As defined in ITA, 1961, s. 2(47A).
78. ITA 1961, s. 115BBH.
79. ITA 1961, s. 194S.

6 TAX LEGISLATION

6.1 Tax Legislative Process

Taxation Bills must originate in the *Lok Sabha* (Lower House).[80] Since the days of the Raj, taxation proposals are normally made in the Annual Finance Bill, traditionally presented on the last day of February but moved to February 1 in 2017.

The Finance Bill is accompanied by a Memorandum explaining the provisions included in the bill. Because the Finance Bill is a Money Bill as defined in Article 110 of the Constitution, it requires the prior recommendation of the President under Article 117 of the Constitution (except in the case of the reduction or abolition of any tax).[81] There are three stages in the preparation of legislation: the formulation of the legislative policy, the creation of the legislative scheme, and the drafting of the legislation.[82] Initial drafts are prepared by the Finance Ministry and then submitted to the Ministry of Law, which is formally responsible for drafting. The Ministry of Law reviews the government's proposals, makes suitable linguistic changes to reflect the government's policy decisions, and ensures the constitutional validity of proposed legislation. The Finance Bill must be passed by Parliament within seventy-five days of its introduction.[83] During the time between the presentation of the Bill and its final passage, comments on the Bill are received and the final provisions may be modified accordingly. On occasion, a completely new provision may be introduced through government amendments. As a result, there are usually differences between the provisions of the Finance Bill and the Act as finally passed.

For historical reasons, the budget process is still secret. With respect to direct tax proposals, the Tax Policy and Legislation division of the CBDT, under the overall supervision of the Board, generally works on budget proposals in isolation, under severe time pressure.

6.2 Statutory Style

Referring to the ITA 1922, the Law Commission of India, which drafted the ITA 1961, observed:

> There is hardly any Act on the Indian Statute Book which is so complicated, so illogical in its arrangement, and in some respects so obscure as the Indian Income-tax Act, 1922. Courts and commentators have commented on the illogical

80. "A Money Bill shall not be introduced in the Council of States. After a Money Bill has been passed by the House of the People it shall be transmitted to the Council of States for its recommendations and the Council of States shall within a period of fourteen days from the date of its receipt of the Bill return the Bill to the House of the People with its recommendations and the House of the People may thereupon either accept or reject all or any of the recommendations of the Council of States." (Article 109 of the Constitution).
81. *See* Budget Manual, available at https://dea.gov.in/sites/default/files/Budget_Manual_1.pdf.
82. Dr. K.N. Chaturvedi, *Interpretation of Taxing Statutes* (New Delhi: Taxmann Allied Services (P.) Ltd., 2008), p. 42.
83. Provisional Collection of Taxes Act, 1931.

> arrangement of the provisions of the Act. It has been repeatedly pointed out that amendments made from time to time to the Act directed as they frequently are at stopping an exit through the net of taxation freshly disclosed, are too often framed without sufficient regard to the basic scheme upon which it originally rested. Provisions dealing with the same topic or subject matter are scattered through the various Chapters of the Act, and only a thorough knowledge of the whole Act would enable any one to find out all the provisions bearing on a certain point. Added to the illogicality of the arrangement are two other defects, inaccuracy in the use of language and a degree of obscurity which make it difficult to have a glimpse of the real intention of the legislature. (...)

The same comments and the same reasons apply equally to the ITA 1961, which now competes with the tax legislation of other jurisdictions in length. In addition, delegated legislation—the Income Tax Rules 1962, dealing with procedural requirements—has become equally voluminous. To ensure compliance with the law, the ITA and Rules must be read together. In defense of the drafters, it can be said that when too many objectives are sought to be achieved and various interests must be catered to and ring-fenced—and when trade and commerce itself are so complex—there is a limit on the extent to which the tax law can be simplified unless the old provisions are weeded out and a periodic rewriting of the tax legislation is undertaken.

Legislation is often made effective retrospectively from the date of the announcement of particular proposals.

6.3 Statutory Interpretation

The Supreme Court has observed that it is of paramount importance that the law declared by it should be certain, clear, and consistent. The Court added that the decisions of the courts are significant not merely because they resolve disputes between parties, but because in doing so they embody a declaration of law operating as binding principles in future cases.

Courts in India tend to follow the literal approach to statutory interpretation, although in certain situations purposive interpretation has also been used. Updated methods of statutory construction have also been adopted in some cases to allow the law to adapt to changing conditions. Certain broad principles can be discerned from various judgments relating to statutory interpretation, particularly in the area of taxation.

The Supreme Court has expressed its preference for the literal approach as follows:

> The literal rule of interpretation really means that there should be no interpretation. In other words, we should read the statute as it is, without distorting or twisting its language.
>
> (...) If we say that a certain object is a book, then we mean it is a book. If we say it is a book, but we mean it is a horse, table or an elephant, then we will not be able to communicate with each other. Life will become impossible. Hence, the meaning

of the literal rule of interpretation is simply that we mean what we say and we say what we mean.[84]

According to the Supreme Court, the long title, preamble, heading, marginal notes,[85] punctuation, illustrations, clauses, dictionary definitions, provisos to a section, explanations, examples, schedules to the Act, etc., are internal aids to construction, while parliamentary debates, legislative history, other relevant statutes, dictionaries, and thesauri are external aids.[86]

Courts have also held that reading words into a statute is unacceptable since doing so would be not to construe, but to amend the statute. Even where there is an error or omission in the statute, the defect can be remedied only by legislation and not by judicial interpretation.[87] Further, if the intention of the legislature is not found in the words, it cannot be found anywhere else.[88] However, where the plain literal interpretation produces a manifestly absurd or unjust result which could never have been intended by the legislature, the court may modify the language used by the legislature, or even do some violence to it, in order to achieve the obvious intention of the legislature and produce a rational construction.[89] The Supreme Court has also held that if one interpretation is more well settled than another, it is the preferred interpretation. Where the language of a statutory provision is ambiguous and capable of two constructions, the construction which gives meaning and effect to the other provisions of the enactment must be adopted.[90]

With respect to the conflict between strict and liberal interpretation, charging provisions are to be strictly interpreted, and where a competent legislature mandates taxing certain persons or objects in certain circumstances, it cannot be expanded or interpreted to include those which were not intended by the legislature.[91] Therefore, in interpreting the charging section of a taxation statute, the strict rule of interpretation is mandatory, and if there are two possible interpretations of a charging section, the one favorable to the taxpayer must be applied.[92] Courts have also adopted strict interpretation in the context of provisions relating to penalties,[93] limitations, etc.[94] In contrast, liberal construction is to be followed in respect of tax concessions aimed at encouraging industrial activity. However, liberal interpretation cannot be applied to advance the

84. *B.Premanand & Ors v. Mohan Koikal & Ors* (Civil Appeal No. 2684, 2007) March 16, 2011 (SC).
85. Marginal notes, although not controlling, may throw light on the legislative intent of a provision.
86. Courts in India often cite the English case, *Cape Brandy Syndicate v. IRC* (1921) 1 KB 64 (KB), which has also been approved by the Supreme Court: "In a taxing Act one has to look merely at what is clearly said. There is no room for any intendment. There is no equity about a tax. There is no presumption as to a tax. Nothing is to be read in, nothing implied. One can only look at the language used."
87. *Smt. Tarulata Shyam & ors v. Commissioner of Income Tax*, 108 ITR 345 (SC).
88. *Keshavji Ravji & Co v. Commissioner of Income Tax*, February 5, 1990 (SC).
89. *K.P. Varghese v. Income Tax Officer*, 1981 AIR 1922 (SC), September 4, 1981.
90. *Addl Commissioner of Income Tax v. Surat Art Silk Cloth Manufacturers' Association*, November 19, 1979 (SC).
91. *Commissioner of Customs (Import) Mumbai v. Dilip Kumar and Company and Others*, 2018(9) SCC 1, para. 24.
92. *CIT v. Podar Cement (P) Ltd.* [1997] 226 ITR 625 (SC).
93. *Commissioner of Income-tax v. National Taj Traders* (1980) 121 ITR 535 (SC).
94. *K.M. Sharma v. Income-tax Officer* (2002) 254 ITR 772 (SC).

purpose and object of beneficial provisions by disregarding the plain and simple language used in an enactment. It would not be reasonable or permissible for a court to rewrite a section or substitute words of its own for the actual words employed by the legislature in the name of giving effect to the court's view of the underlying object of the statute (except in cases of absurdity or unjust results, as noted above) because the underlying object of any provision must be determined on a reasonable interpretation of the language employed by the legislature.[95] A recent judgment of the Supreme Court in a nontax case overruled the prior jurisprudence and extended the same literal approach for interpreting charging provisions to incentive or exemption provisions:[96]

(1) Exemption notification should be interpreted strictly; the burden of proving applicability would be on the assessee to show that the case comes within the parameters of the exemption clause or exemption notification.
(2) When there is ambiguity in an exemption notification which is subject to strict interpretation, the benefit of such ambiguity cannot be claimed by the subject/assessee and it must be interpreted in favor of the revenue.

7 COURTS DEALING WITH TAX MATTERS

The first level for appeals against tax assessments and other actions of the tax authorities used to be the Commissioner of Income Tax (Appeals) (CITA), a senior-level officer of the Income Tax Department.[97] Given the increasing workload at this level, the government has empowered a lower-level officer, the joint CITA, to deal with certain classes of cases involving small amounts of disputed tax up to INR 1 million; hearings at this stage are conducted virtually under the e-Appeals Scheme 2023[98] and all communications are routed through the National Faceless Appeal Centre. For other cases, the CITA is the first appellate authority and even here, the proceedings are conducted virtually[99] (the CITA is required to follow the Faceless Appeal Scheme 2021). Appeals are assigned to a particular CITA by the National Centre.

An appeal from the first appellate authority and from orders of the Dispute Resolution Panel[100] can be made to the Income Tax Appellate Tribunal (ITAT). The ITAT is an independent body functioning under the Ministry of Law, whose judicial members are law practitioners and members of the Indian Legal Service, while accountant members are chartered accountants or members of the Indian Revenue Service (IRS). The bench hearing a case must have at least one judicial member and

95. *CIT v. N.C.Budharaja and co.* Civil Appeal Nos. 4238-4240, 1983, September 7, 1993 (SC).
96. *Commissioner of Customs v. Dilip Kumar*, July 30, 2018, Civil Appeal No. 3327, 2007 (SC).
97. ITA 1961, s. 246A.
98. CBDT Notification dated May 29, 2023 (S.O. 2352(E)).
99. The latest Notification is Notification No. S.O 5429E, dated December 28, 2021. https://thc.nic.in/Central%20Governmental%20Schemes/Faceless%20Appeal%20Scheme,2021.pdf.
100. The Dispute Resolution Panel consists of three commissioners to whom a taxpayer, including a foreign company, may object to the changes proposed by the assessing officer in transfer pricing cases. The directions of the Panel are binding on the assessing authority: ITA 1961 s. 144C.

one accountant member in order to bring different perspectives to the case. Under section 254 of the ITA, the ITAT is the ultimate fact-finding authority and its orders cannot be challenged unless they can be shown to be perverse.[101] The Finance Minister has promised to establish a National Faceless ITAT Centre where all communication between the Tribunal and the appellant will be electronic; where any personal hearing is required, it will be done through video-conferencing.[102]

On substantive questions of law, taxpayers and the tax administration may appeal to the High Courts, most of which have a tax bench.[103] However, High Court judges are not required to have tax expertise.

Under section 262 of the ITA, appeals to the Supreme Court are possible only where the High Court certifies that the issue is sufficiently important and in the public interest. Very few tax cases are heard by the Supreme Court through this process. However, under Article 136 of the Constitution, the Supreme Court can grant special leave to appeal from any order passed by any court or tribunal. This provision is liberally used by both taxpayers and the tax administration. The power of the Supreme Court to grant special leave to appeal is not subject to any serious restraints and is completely at the discretion of the Court. In general, the Supreme Court will not grant special leave unless exceptional and special circumstances exist, substantial and grave injustice has been done, or the case is sufficiently important to warrant review.[104] Although most appeals are dismissed by the Supreme Court, many important cases have been decided by the Court as a result of appeals by special leave.

Simultaneously with the opening up of the economy in the early 1990s, the Advance Authority for Rulings (AAR) was created to provide advance rulings to nonresident taxpayers on proposed transactions. AAR rulings were binding on the parties and, theoretically, did not have precedential value. Although the AAR functioned reasonably well for almost two decades, in the 2021 budget, it was abolished and replaced by a Board of Advance Ruling (BAR). The BAR consists solely of departmental officers and its rulings are not binding either on the taxpayer or on the department, but can be appealed to High Courts.[105]

The Supreme Court and the High Courts have the power of judicial review with respect to procedural aspects of decisions by the tax authorities and the lower courts.

The increasing amount of tax litigation has drawn widespread criticism. The number of tax cases pending in the courts at various levels for the three most recent years is as follows:[106]

101. ITA 1961, s. 252.
102. Budget Speech of the Finance Minister, 2021. The scheme has yet to come into force.
103. ITA 1961, s. 260A.
104. http://www.itatonline.org/articles_new/special-leave-petitions-the-complete-law/.
105. Handbook on Board of Advance Ruling at: https://incometaxindia.gov.in/pages/international-taxation/advance-ruling.aspx.
106. Constructed from the Annual Report of the Ministry of Finance for 2017-2018.

Fiscal Year	*CITA*	*ITAT*	*HC*	*SC*
2015-2016	258,989	91,971	32,138	5,399
2016-2017	290,227	92,388	34,481	6,357
2017-2018	260,617	94,481	38,864	5,876

The number of cases disposed of at each level is not made publicly available and cannot be estimated from the figures above since new cases are added during the year.

The number of tax disputes has increased exponentially. In order to reduce the number of disputes, the CBDT has established and increased monetary limits for appeals and has even begun to withdraw existing appeals to higher courts; by these means, it presumably hopes that the number of existing disputes will decrease by 41 %; currently, the government is set to lose approximately INR 100 billion.[107] In the 2024 budget, the Finance Minister announced a further increase in the monetary limits for filing appeals by the tax department,[108] besides announcing a scheme for the settlement of disputed taxes.[109]

Under the Constitution, the law as laid down by the Supreme Court is binding on all.[110] The doctrines of precedent and judicial discipline, as well as the constitutional guarantee of equality before the law, mean that case law is very important in the administration of tax in India. Only the holding in a particular case, and not every incidental observation, must be followed by lower courts. Case law decisions, particularly at the lower levels of the judiciary, tend to be lengthy and verbose, with representatives often citing innumerable cases for each of the points raised. In all cases, all the facts are stated, followed by the arguments advanced by the parties; cases are cited and analyzed and the final decision is given. Since only substantial questions of law are considered at the level of the High Court and above, the decisions of these courts tend to be more intelligible.

8 TAX ADMINISTRATION

Income tax is administered through a self-assessment system, along with a system of deduction of tax at source and advance payment of tax, complemented by third-party reporting obligations. Taxpayers must file annual tax returns and generally pay tax in four installments, subject to interest and penalties for failure to do so. Through increased use of computer technology, matching has become a viable tool for the tax authorities.

107. According to CBDT Circular No. 3/2018, subject to certain caveats, appeals should not be filed before a tribunal if the tax in dispute is less than INR 200,000, while the limits for filing appeals before the High Court and Supreme Court have been increased to INR 5 million and INR 10 million, respectively.
108. Limits of filing appeals to Tax Tribunals, High Courts, and Supreme Court have been increased to INR 6 million, INR 20 million, and INR 50 million, respectively.
109. In a nutshell, if eligible taxpayers pay the tax, no interest or penalty will be charged.
110. Article 141 of the Constitution.

The robust system of deduction of tax at source has been progressively expanded and now covers virtually every conceivable payment. Payers are subject to interest and penalties for failure to withhold properly and can even be prosecuted. Over the years, the burden of compliance has been shifted largely to taxpayers and third parties, and the bulk of tax is now collected through prepaid taxes (installments, withholding at source, and self-assessment). Approximately 85 % of total taxes were collected through these means for the financial year 2022-2023.[111]

The cost of collection for the government has been decreasing and now represents only .51 % of the total tax collected.[112] At the same time, however, the cost of compliance for taxpayers and third parties seems to have increased, although there are no verifiable statistics available (the only reliable study, completed in the 1990s, shows that compliance costs were quite high).[113] Nevertheless, compliance costs for both taxpayers and the tax authorities have been greatly minimized through extensive use of information technology. The 2002 report of the Kelkar Committee on Direct Taxes recommended that the tax department concentrate on its core functions, assessment and enforcement, and outsource its logistical functions (such as the allotment of permanent account numbers).[114] A Taxpayer Information Network was established to facilitate transactions and establish secure and seamless logistics of tax collection through the integration of primary information, record keeping, dissemination, and retrieval.[115] Tax payments can now be made online at any time, leading to increased accuracy and reduced transaction costs.

Other functions of the tax department have also been rapidly digitalized. Online filing of tax returns was first introduced as an optional measure; its use was made compulsory in stages and paper returns are now allowed only in very limited cases.[116]

Fewer than 1 % of returns filed are actually audited each year; the rest are merely processed for arithmetical accuracy, as discussed earlier. The selection of cases for audit is based mainly on a computer risk assessment tool (Computer Assisted System of Scrutiny).

The apex body for the administration of direct taxes is the CBDT. The CBDT consists of a Chair and six other members. The Chair reports to the Revenue Secretary, who is normally drawn from the generalists in the civil service and is supposed to coordinate the functions of the direct and indirect tax boards. The CBDT also has adjunct offices, known as Directorates, and field offices.

The CBDT is authorized to issue instructions to its officers for the smooth functioning of the ITA but cannot direct any assessing authority to frame a particular assessment in a particular way. The CBDT is also authorized to issue public circulars

111. Table 1.5 of the time series data released by the tax department.
112. Table 1.6 of the time series data.
113. "The Compliance Cost of the Personal Income Tax in India, 2000-01: Preliminary Estimates"—Arindam Das-Gupta, available at https://nipfp.org.in/media/medialibrary/2013/04/wp04_nipfp_009.pdf.
114. *Report of the Task Force on Direct Taxes* (Kelkar Committee report), available at https://the1991projest.com.pdf.
115. *Ibid.*, at 48.
116. ITA 1961, s. 139(1) read with Rule 12 of the IT Rules 1962.

and instructions clarifying its position on various issues, which are binding on tax officials but not binding on taxpayers or the courts. Taxpayers, however, frequently take advantage of circulars which support their positions.

Vestiges of the authoritarian tax administration of colonial times still remain. Many studies of the system over the years have commented on the arbitrariness of the tax administration, and there have been suggestions of corruption on the part of some officials. In the 2019 budget speech, the Finance Minister explicitly alluded to such corruption while introducing the so-called faceless assessment scheme in the law:

> The existing system of scrutiny assessments in the Income-tax Department involves a high level of personal interaction between the taxpayer and the Department, which leads to certain undesirable practices on the part of tax officials.

To eliminate such practices, a system of electronic assessment, involving no human interface, was launched and phased in. Cases selected for scrutiny are allocated to assessment units in a random manner and notices issued electronically by a Central Cell, without disclosing the name, designation or location of the Assessing Officer. The Central Cell is the single point of contact between the taxpayer and the Department.

In the 1970s, a Settlement Commission was set up to allow taxpayers a one-time-only opportunity to make voluntary disclosures of their unreported income; the Commission was authorized to give taxpayers immunity from penalty and prosecution and dealt mainly with search and seizure cases. In 2021, the government, without giving any reason, decided to abolish the Commission and instead established a dispute-resolution committee consisting of tax officers; they deal with disclosures in very limited circumstances (no search and seizure cases, etc.) where the returned income does not exceed INR 5 million and the addition to disclosed income does not exceed INR 1 million.[117]

Following a recommendation of the Kelkar Committee, a tax Ombudsman system staffed by retired tax officers was set up in major cities to deal with administrative grievances of taxpayers, such as delays in issuing refunds. In 2019, the government abolished the tax Ombudsman system on the alleged ground of ineffectiveness.

The attitude of taxpayers toward the tax authorities is generally one of suspicion and, at times, hostility. However, the growing formalization of the economy, coupled with digitalization and ease of compliance has forced taxpayers, particularly salaried employees, to become more accepting of their tax obligations. However, tax planning is rampant among all taxpayers who can afford it. Aggressive tax planning is common in international situations, and until recently was facilitated by the generally benign attitude of the courts toward tax avoidance.

117. ITA 1961, s. 245MA.

9 GENERAL PRINCIPLES

9.1 Relationship Between Tax and Financial Accounting

The relationship between financial accounting and tax was pithily stated in a 1997 case: "the income-tax law does not march step by step in the footprints of the accounting profession."[118] Nevertheless, books of accounts are the primary source for determining income. Business income for tax purposes is business profits, with specified adjustments. Consequently, disputes are common, particularly with respect to the accrual of income and expenses. Since each tax year is separate, income and expenses must be recognized in the appropriate year.

Companies must maintain their accounts on an accrual basis (referred to as a "mercantile" basis) under the Companies Act[119] and must also follow accounting standards. These standards generally require conservatism with respect to the accrual of income, whereas expenditures must be immediately expensed, which may conflict with tax rules.

The ITA itself contains specific derogations from accrual accounting. One of the most important, which may be peculiar to India, is the denial of deductions for certain statutory payments, such as excise duty and employers' contributions to provident funds. Under section 43B of the ITA, the deduction of such payments is allowed only in the year in which they are actually paid, irrespective of the year in which the liability to pay such amounts is incurred. This provision has been progressively expanded to include many additional items; for example, interest payable on bank loans is now allowed when paid.

Section 145 of the ITA requires business income to be determined in accordance with either the cash or accrual system of accounting regularly employed by the taxpayer (subject to the other provisions of the ITA). The government later developed tax accounting standards (TAS). Initially, only two such standards were formulated, which were roughly similar to the accounting standards issued by the Institute of Chartered Accountants of India. The courts have generally allowed changes in accounting methods in areas such as depreciation, construction expenditures, valuation of inventory and investments, and the treatment of goodwill where the changes are made in good faith. In light of the revenue implications of some of these decisions, the government appointed a committee to formulate TAS with respect to frequently disputed areas. In 2015, the government made it mandatory for income computation and disclosure standards (ICDS) to be followed by all classes of taxpayers with respect to all types of income. Subsequently, the CBDT issued the relevant notifications with respect to several areas, including inventory valuation, construction contracts, revenue recognition, foreign exchange fluctuations, government grants, and securities.[120] To

118. *Tuticorin Alkali Chemicals and Fertilizers Ltd v. CIT* (1997) 227 ITR 172 (SC).
119. Section 128 of the Companies Act, 2013.
120. *See* the notification of September 29, 2016 relating to the standards, available at https://incometaxindia.gov.in/Documents/Notification-86-87-88-2016.pdf.

avoid potential conflict with the case law,[121] the Finance Act 2018 incorporated the relevant provisions of the ICDS in the ITA itself.[122]

9.2 Respect for Civil or Private Law Form

Although the ITA is a self-contained statute and contains definitions of certain important terms, not all words, terms, or expressions used in the Act can be precisely defined. Other statutes, such as the Contracts Act, Sale of Goods Act, Partnerships Act, and Companies Act, may supplement the ITA, subject, of course, to any special provisions in the ITA. In addition, a General Clauses Act for interpreting certain terms commonly used in federal statutes may be resorted to, subject to the usual caveats.

Before 1971, under the ITA, "company" was defined to mean an Indian company or an association, whether incorporated or not, which was declared by the CBDT to be a company for purposes of the ITA. In order to be treated as a company, foreign companies had to apply to the CBDT for company status. This situation was changed through the 1971 Finance No. 2 Act, which redefined the term to include, along with any Indian company, any body corporate incorporated by or under the laws of any country outside India. Thus, at present, any foreign company may obtain the benefit of being treated as a company under the ITA.

A foreign partnership may obtain the same treatment as Indian partnerships where the provisions of the Partnership Act of the foreign jurisdiction are similar to those of the Indian Partnership Act 1932.[123] Otherwise, the foreign partnership is taxed as an association of persons.

In the context of tax avoidance, courts place much importance on legal form. The import of the much-debated decision of the Supreme Court in the *Vodafone* case is that a corporate structure, even where formed abroad, must be respected unless it is shown to be a sham or tax avoidance device.[124]

In addition, the provisions of the ITA relating to accounting principles requires that practices adopted by taxpayers should represent a true and fair view of the state of affairs of the business. One of the major considerations governing the selection and application of accounting principles is substance over form.[125]

The courts have consistently held that all agreements and documents must be read as a whole. It is settled law that the nomenclature of a document or deed is not conclusive of its nature; courts must consider all parts of a document in order to

121. *The Chamber of Tax Consultants v. Union of India*, November 8, 2017, W.P.(C) 5595/2017.
122. ITA 1961, s. 145A and 145B.
123. *See*, for example, *Canoro Resources Ltd v. DIT* (2009) AAR No. 779, 2008, where the partnership law of the Province of Alberta, Canada was found to be similar to the Indian Act.
124. *Vodafone International Holdings BV v. Union of India*, Civil Appeal No. 733, 2012, January 20, 2012 (SC).
125. Accounting standards notified u/s 145(2) [No. 9949 [F.N0.132/7/95-TPL], January 25, 1996], superseded by Notification No. 32/2015 [F.No. 134/48/2010-TPL]/SO 892(E), dated March 31, 2015.

determine its true effect.[126] The intentions of the parties entering into a contract must be ascertained only from the terms and conditions of the contract—neither the label attached to the document nor any particular activity undertaken by the parties is decisive.

9.3 Anti-avoidance Doctrines and Rules

9.3.1 General

Ever since the introduction of the income tax, there have been allegations of tax evasion and noncompliance with the tax legislation. In modern times, numerous studies have pointed out schemes for tax avoidance and evasion, and the response has often been to plug obvious loopholes as they became apparent over time. The Indian tax system contains many such special anti-avoidance rules.

India has also adopted several measures to counter tax evasion, which may also have an impact on tax avoidance. These measures include:

- the Black Money Act of 2015, which, in addition to criminal penalties, imposes a 30% flat-rate tax on any undisclosed (foreign) revenue or (foreign) assets of the previous year but allows a one-time voluntary disclosure, subject to payment of a 100% penalty;
- the Prohibition of Benami Property Transactions Act, which became effective in 2016, deals with nominee arrangements and makes the property held in such an arrangement subject to confiscation;
- the demonetization of INR 500 and INR 1,000 notes in 2016, which took almost 90% of cash out of circulation; and
- the Fugitive Economic Offenders Act, 2018, which seeks to confiscate properties of economic offenders who remain outside the jurisdiction of Indian courts.

The abolition of the gift tax in 1998 led to resourceful taxpayers acquiring large "gifts" free of tax from unrelated parties, often in jurisdictions lacking transparency. To counter this tax avoidance strategy, section 56(2)(vi) was added to the ITA in 2004, providing that, subject to certain exceptions such as gifts from relatives, gifts above INR 25,000 (currently INR 50,000) in value received from unrelated parties had to be included in the income of the recipients (individuals and HUF) as income from other sources. Although this provision began with modest goals, it has been transformed over the years into a tool for countering tax planning. The scope of the provision has been expanded to cover gifts of immovable property, and from 2017 to cover all persons.[127] Subsequently, in 2019 and 2023, in response to nonresidents and those not

126. Quoted in *Hammad Ahmed v. Abdul Majeed & Ors* (Civil Appeal Nos. 3382-3383, 2019), April 3, 2019 (SC).
127. ITA 1961, s. 56(2)(x); the threshold is INR 50,000; if the amount received exceeds INR 50,000, the entire amount becomes taxable and not merely the excess.

ordinarily resident declaring gifts from Indian residents, such gifts in excess of INR 50,000 in a year are deemed to accrue in India.[128]

In 2012, in the face of allegations of corruption, a new clause (viib) was added to section 56(2), providing that where in a fiscal year a privately held company received consideration from a resident for the issue of shares in excess of the face value of the shares, the excess must be taxed as income from other sources of the issuing company for that year. Although the scope of this provision was extended in 2023, it was very controversial and was repealed prospectively by the Finance (No. 2) Act, 2024.

9.3.2 Judicial Anti-avoidance Rules

Until recently, there was no General Anti-avoidance Rule (GAAR) in India. Courts grappling with tax avoidance cases tended to rely on the United Kingdom (UK) jurisprudence, and for a long time the UK *Duke of Westminster* principle (taxpayers have the right to order their affairs to minimize tax) was consistently followed.[129] As a result, tax avoidance was winked at unless the transaction involved was a total sham, although, in some exceptional cases, lifting of the corporate veil was permitted.[130] With the change in judicial attitude in the UK following the *Ramsay* decision in 1988 and subsequently in *Furniss v. Dawson*, the Indian Supreme Court followed suit in the *McDowell* case.[131] In that case, the Court held that tax planning may be legitimate provided that it is within the framework of law, that colorable devices cannot be part of tax planning, and that it is wrong to encourage or entertain the belief that it is honorable to avoid the payment of tax by resorting to dubious methods. One of the concurring judges in *McDowell* observed:

> It is neither fair nor desirable to expect the legislature to intervene and take care of every device and scheme to avoid taxation. It is up to the Court to take stock to determine the nature of the new and sophisticated legal devices to avoid tax and consider whether the situation created by the devices could be related to the existing legislation with the aid of "emerging" techniques of interpretation (as) was done in *Ramsay, Burmah* and *Dawson*, to expose the devices for what they really are and to refuse to give judicial benediction. (...)
>
> I have referred to the English cases at some length, only to show that in the very country of its birth, the principle of *Westminster* has been given a decent burial and in that very country where the phrase "tax avoidance" originated the judicial attitude towards tax avoidance has changed and the smile, cynical or even affectionate though it might have been at one time, has now frozen into a deep frown. The Courts are now concerning themselves not merely with the genuineness of a transaction, but with the intended effect of it for fiscal purposes. No one

128. ITA 1961, s. 9(1)(viii).
129. The *Duke of Westminster* principle has been followed by the Supreme Court in *CIT v. A Raman & Co* (Civil Appeal No. 768, 1966, July 18, 1967); *Union of India v. Azadi Bachao Andolan*, 263 ITR 706 (SC); and *Vodafone International* (*supra* note 124).
130. *Commissioner of Income Tax v. Sri Meenakshi Mills Ltd*, Civil Appeal Nos. 1084 to 1057, 1965, October 25, 1965 (SC).
131. *McDowell & Co v. Commercial Tax Officer*, April 17, 1985 (SC).

> can now get away with a tax avoidance project with the mere statement that there is nothing illegal about it.[132]

However, the opening up of the economy and the desire to attract foreign investment led the Supreme Court, in the *Azadi Bachao* case, to declare that the *Duke of Westminster* principle was alive and well in the land of its birth.[133] The Court went on to propound the astounding theory that permitting tax avoidance by multinationals through the use of treaty shopping was perhaps in the interest of developing countries. The next episode in the judicial anti-avoidance saga was the Supreme Court's decision in the famous *Vodafone* case dealing with the taxation of capital gains from the indirect transfer of shares. Again, prompted by concerns about discouraging foreign investment, the Supreme Court reiterated the *Azadi* position, citing jurisprudence from the UK.

To a large extent, it appears that the attitude of the judiciary toward tax avoidance depends on the personal predilections of the judges. While one bench of the Supreme Court gave its decision in *Vodafone*, another bench of the Court was considering a public-interest case dealing with actions taken by the government to counter tax evasion. The following observation of the Court is worth noting:

> [I]t would also appear that in this miasmic cultural environment in which greed is extolled, conspicuous consumption viewed as both necessary and socially valuable, and the wealthy viewed as demi-gods, the agents of the State may have also succumbed to the notions of the neo-liberal paradigm that the role of the State ought to only be an enabling one, and not exercise significant control. This attitude would have a significant impact on exercise of discretion, especially in the context of regulating economic activities, including keeping an account of the monies generated in various activities, both legal and illegal. Carried away by the ideology of neo-liberalism, it is entirely possible that the agents of the State entrusted with the task of supervising the economic and social activities may err more on the side of extreme caution, whereby signals of wrong doing may be ignored even when they are strong. (...). Ethical compromises, by the elite—those who wield the powers of the state, and those who fatten themselves in an ever more exploitative economic sphere—can be expected to thrive in an environment marked by such a permissive attitude, of weakened laws, and of weakened law enforcement machineries and attitudes.[134]

However, it appears that there has also been a change in the attitude of the judiciary, and more and more tax avoidance arrangements are being questioned. Courts seem to be more inclined to adopt a substance-over-form approach to deny tax benefits even in the absence of the GAAR. Agreements entered into by the parties are also being scrutinized more thoroughly for artificiality.[135]

---

132. *Ibid.*, para. 18.
133. *Azadi Bachao Andolan*, *supra* note 129.
134. *Ram Jethmalani v. Union of India*, (2011) 8 SCR 725, (2011) 8 SCC 1, para. 15.
135. *See*, for example, the Delhi High Court judgment in *CIT v. Abhinandan Investment Ltd.*, November 19, 2015, ITA 130/2001.

9.3.3 *General Anti-avoidance Rule*

The attitude of the government toward tax avoidance seems to have changed in response to the *Vodafone* case. In 2012, along with retrospective rules to nullify the Supreme Court's decision in that case, the government also introduced a GAAR in Chapter-X-A of the ITA (sections 95 to 102). The GAAR met with intense opposition and, in response, the government appointed a committee to review the rule. The committee recommended that the proposed GAAR be watered down in several ways. In 2017, the GAAR provisions as contained in Chapter X-A of the ITA finally became effective for transactions on or after April 1, 2017. In a departure from the normal Indian practice of treaty provisions overriding provisions of the domestic law, the GAAR applies notwithstanding anything contained in the ITA, implying that such provisions may override treaty provisions as well.[136]

Under the GAAR, an arrangement[137] entered into by a taxpayer may be deemed to be an "impermissible avoidance arrangement," which means an arrangement the main purpose of which is to obtain a tax benefit and which:

(1) creates rights, or obligations which are not ordinarily created between persons dealing at arm's length; or
(2) results, directly or indirectly, in the misuse or abuse of the provisions of the ITA; or
(3) lacks commercial substance or is deemed to lack commercial substance; or
(4) is entered into, or carried out, by means, or in a manner, not ordinarily employed for bona fide purposes.[138]

A "tax benefit" is defined to include a reduction, avoidance, or deferral of tax or other amount that would be payable under the ITA as a result of the application of a tax treaty.[139]

The burden of proving that the main purpose of a transaction was to obtain a tax benefit would perhaps have been impossible for the revenue authorities to discharge. However, there are two mitigating factors. First, the GAAR provides that an arrangement is deemed to lack commercial substance in certain circumstances.[140] Second, an arrangement is presumed to have been entered into for the main purpose of obtaining a tax benefit if the main purpose of a step in or part of the arrangement is to obtain a tax benefit, even where the main purpose of the whole arrangement is not to obtain the tax benefit. Of course, the taxpayer can rebut this presumption.[141]

Under the rules enacted subsequently to operationalize the GAAR, the GAAR does not apply where the aggregate tax benefits to all parties to an arrangement do not

136. ITA 1961, s. 95.
137. "Arrangement" is defined in s. 102(1).
138. ITA 1961, s. 102(1).
139. ITA 1961, s. 102(10)(c).
140. ITA 1961, s. 97(1).
141. ITA 1961, s. 96(2).

exceed INR 30 million in a year. The GAAR also does not apply to foreign institutional investors who have not taken advantage of any treaty benefits.[142]

The GAAR cannot be invoked by any assessing authority without approval of the highest administrative official, who is required to hear from the taxpayer before declaring an arrangement to be impermissible. Taxpayers can take their objections to a panel chaired by either a sitting or retired judge of a High Court and consisting of an officer of the IRS and an academic or scholar with specialized knowledge in the fields of direct taxation, business accounting, or international trade practices.[143]

9.3.4 Corporate Residence

The definition of a resident corporation, which was added to the ITA in 1939, provided that: "a company is resident in British India in any year (a) if the control and management of its affairs is situated wholly in British India in that year, or (b) if its income arising in British India in that year exceeds its income arising without British India in that year."[144] Although clause (b) and some other aspects of the 1922 Act relating to corporate residence were changed in the 1961 Act, this definition applied for sixty-six years, until 2015, when the government finally recognized that companies registered in tax-favored jurisdictions but controlled from India could avoid residence in India simply by holding one board meeting outside India. Under the amended definition, a company is considered to be resident in India (in any previous year) if it is registered in India or its POEM is in India at any time during the year. POEM means "a place where key management and commercial decisions that are necessary for the conduct of business of an entity as a whole are, in substance, made."[145] This definition has proved to be controversial and has generated intense lobbying. A first CBDT Circular laid down the conditions under which a foreign company would be considered to have a POEM in India.[146] A subsequent Circular clarified that a foreign company is not considered to have a POEM in India where the turnover or gross receipts of the company do not exceed INR 500 million.[147] This concession defeats the purpose of countering the mushrooming of paper companies formed abroad by Indian residents.

10 TAX TREATIES

In India, in order to be effective, tax treaties must be notified.[148] According to the latest information, India has 95 comprehensive tax treaties that have been notified. Tax

142. Rule 10U(1) of the IT Rules 1962. For a detailed discussion of the Indian GAAR, *see* R. Rawal, "GAAR Becomes Operational in India," 23 *Asia Pacific Tax Bulletin* 5 (2017), Journals IBFD https://doi.org/10.59403/2rsccne. *See also* Circular No. 7, 2017, January 27, 2017.
143. ITA 1961, s. 144BA(16).
144. ITA 1922, s. 4A(c).
145. Explanation to ITA 1961, s. 6(3).
146. CBDT Circular No. 6/2017, January 24, 2017.
147. CBDT Circular No. 8/2017, available at, https://www.incometaxindia.gov.in/news/circular-8-2017-clarification-on-place-of-effective-management.pdf.
148. ITA 1961, s. 90.

treaties exist with all important trading partners, including both developed and developing countries. In the past, some treaties were also entered into with jurisdictions such as Cyprus, Mauritius, Singapore, and the United Arab Emirates, which resulted in rampant treaty shopping. As a result, many of these treaties have been renegotiated, and recent treaties generally contain a limitation-on-benefits clause. The problem of misuse of tax treaties and round-tripping also highlighted the importance of having an appropriate exchange-of-information article in tax treaties, and many tax treaties have been renegotiated to incorporate the latest OECD standard in respect of Article 26. At present, India does not enter into comprehensive treaties with known tax havens. Instead, it has started to enter into separate tax information exchange agreements (TIEAs) with these jurisdictions. It currently has 18 such agreements, including with the British Virgin Islands, Cayman Islands, Isle of Man, Liechtenstein, and Seychelles. India also has limited (transportation) agreements with seven jurisdictions, the most notable ones being with Afghanistan and Pakistan. Independent India's first tax treaty was with Pakistan, in the aftermath of the partition of the country, but following the hostilities in the 1970s, the treaty has ceased to have effect.

As a net capital importer, India's tax treaties differ in many respects from the OECD Model and tend to follow the UN Model. The most common departures from the OECD Model are in relation to Article 5. In this regard, the main differences between the OECD Model and Indian treaty practices relate to Article 5(2), and in particular, the omission of the word "delivery," the inclusion of a provision with respect to services PEs and insurance PEs, and the minimum period for construction PEs. Indian treaties continue to use Article 14 dealing with independent personal services.

Moreover, India's tax treaties also include a provision with respect to fees for technical services, either as part of the royalties article or as a separate article, particularly in treaties with most developed countries. The definition of fees for technical services varies, however, and has been diluted to a large extent in the treaty with the United States by limiting it to "fees for included services" and by the stipulation that technology has to be "made available" before the Article applies. The existence of a most-favored-nation (MFN) clause in some tax treaties with Western nations means that the provisions of existing treaties were also automatically diluted.

With respect to passive income, India follows the UN Model rather than the OECD Model; in respect of capital gains, India also follows the UN Model, particularly in respect of Article 13(4) of the UN Model. Indian treaties also contain a provision relating to students, which is sometimes expanded to teachers and professors. In respect of the other income article, Indian treaties generally follow the UN Model.

India has signed the *Multilateral Convention on Mutual Administrative Assistance in Tax Matters*, which came into force for India on June 1, 2012. India also signed the *Multilateral Convention to Implement Tax Treaty Related Measures to Prevent BEPS* (MLI) on June 7, 2017. India listed all its 93 agreements (as of that date) as covered tax agreements. India has chosen the simplified limitation-on-benefits (LOB) option for the prevention of treaty abuse, which includes the principal purpose test (PPT). India has not made any reservation in respect of the PE provisions of the MLI but has not adopted Part VI relating to mandatory binding arbitration.

11 SOURCES OF TAX LAW

The Income Tax Department's website, www.incometaxindia.gov.in, contains all the tax provisions, rules, public circulars, and related acts.[149] The only drawback is that each section must be dealt with separately. Most practitioners use the annual publication of Taxmann in book format.

The annual Finance Acts are also available on the tax department's website. The website of the Ministry of Finance, www.indiabudget.gov.in, contains all the Finance Bills, Ministers' speeches, and Memorandums explaining the provisions of the budget (known as the Pink Book). The Finance Bills often differ from the Finance Act ultimately passed by Parliament, and the Finance Act is not available on this website. However, it can be accessed at either the website of the Income Tax Department or the Finance Ministry's website, https://www.india.gov.in/official-website-ministry-finance-0. All the Acts administered by the Ministry can be found there, although some of the items may not have been updated. Memorandums are supposed to explain the provisions of the Finance Bill in lay language. In some cases, courts have relied on the interpretations in the Memorandums. Memorandums are drafted by the Tax Policy Division and do not require parliamentary approval. Often, a Memorandum repeats the language of the statute and does not endorse any particular interpretation.

All Indian tax treaties are available on the Income Tax Department's website.

Decisions of the ITAT are also available on its website, https://www.itat.gov.in/judicial/tribunalorders, but the site is not user-friendly unless the name of the party or date of the order and the Bench that rendered the decision are known. Cases are also available on several fee-based websites: taxmann.in, taxindionline.in, taxindiainternational.in, taxsutra.in, and itr.in. There are other websites where these cases are freely available if the name of the case is known; the most prominent of these is indiakanoon.org. All decisions of the High Courts and Supreme Court are available on the websites of the respective courts (Supreme Court: https://main.sci.gov.in/judgments), but they require the case number. Another useful website where recent updates from all courts are available free is itatonline.org. There are numerous textbooks on particular subjects published by Lexis Nexis, Bharat, and Taxmann. For reference, tax practitioners generally refer to Arvind P. Datar, *Kanga and Palkhivala's The Law and Practice of Income Tax*, 11th ed. (LexisNexis, 2021) and *Chaturvedi & Pithisaria's Income Tax Law*, 8th ed. (LexisNexis, 2024).

149. https://www.incometaxindia.gov.in/Pages/acts/index.aspx.

Japan

Minoru Nakazato, Mark Ramseyer, Takeshi Fujitani & Yasutaka Nishikori

1 HISTORY

The income tax in Japan predated its first constitution, the Japanese Imperial Constitution of 1889. Although primitive, the income tax act (ITA) of 1887 reflected the then-transforming industrial structure of the country. Japanese industrialization began in the mid-1880s, taking off from the agricultural economy in which the two largest sources of tax revenue were land tax and liquor tax. This first ITA, modelled after the Prussian income tax, adopted a source-based, schedular system, with a mildly progressive tax rate structure.

In the late 1930s, the income tax had become the primary source of tax revenue, with steep progressivity and a broad tax base, mainly due to the dire need of financing the war. The 1940 tax reform laid the foundation for a Japanese tax system that continues to this day: the separation of the ITA and the Corporate Tax Act (CTA), and the massive reliance on pay-as-you-earn (PAYE)-type withholding income tax.

A series of post-World War II reforms brought two new elements that still characterize Japan's income tax system: a self-assessment system and a global system with some elements of a schedular system.[1] In particular, the 1950 tax reform, also known as the "Shoup Tax System,"[2] was a landmark in the history of Japanese taxation.[3] The Shoup Tax System was a product of idealistic tax reformers' proposals:[4]

1. Although, in principle, income is defined and taxed in a global manner, the calculation of income is first made in a schedular system and then aggregated to reach global (comprehensive) income. Nevertheless, certain types of income are still separately taxed, often at a flat rate.
2. General Headquarters of the Occupation Forces invited the mission for the much-needed tax reform in Japan. Columbia University economist Carl Shoup was the head of the mission, which included William Vickrey and Stanley S. Surrey, among others.
3. Hiroshi Kaneko, *Sozei ho* [Tax Law], 24th ed. (Tokyo: Kobundo, 2017).
4. After a rigorous study of the Japanese tax system and tax administration, the Shoup Mission compiled and submitted a report recommending fundamental tax reform. Under the authority of the General Headquarters, tax reform was achieved almost exactly as proposed.

it restructured the entire tax system around the ideal of a comprehensive income tax base as a basis for fair taxation; corporate tax was necessary solely because it complemented the ideal individual income tax.

During the era of Japan's rapid economic growth (from the mid-1950s to 1973), however, the Shoup Tax System was undermined by rampant tax preferences, some of which were enacted to promote economic growth, while others were simply a form of political largesse. As a result, income taxation moved increasingly further from the ideal of a comprehensive income tax base and much revenue was foregone. The forecasted demographic change (ageing) required a new tax base that was more stable than the income tax, which was not levied on most of the retired population. These problems led to another fundamental tax reform in the late 1980s: the progressive income tax was boldly flattened; the corporate tax rate was reduced; and a value-added tax (VAT) (i.e., Consumption Tax Act) was introduced along with the scrapping of miscellaneous indirect taxes.

Starting from the uniform tax rate of as low as 3%, it took almost three decades and a number of political battles for the consumption tax to finally reach the standard tax rate of 10% with a preferential rate of 8% for food and newspapers. Since 2020, the consumption tax has been the leading revenue-raiser, accounting for a third of national tax revenue, followed by individual income tax (raising 30% of national tax revenue) and corporate income tax (20%).

Recent reforms to the individual income tax seem to pursue two goals: first, to address widening economic disparity by adding to the tax burden of the wealthy and, second, to encourage the middle-income class to invest in financial assets so as to lessen the burden on the social security system. The 2022 reform enacted the NISA regime (i.e., *Nippon (Japan) Individual Savings Account*), modelled on the United Kingdom's ISAs (income from qualified investments is tax-free). The NISA regime marked a complete departure from the Shoup Tax System's ideal of a comprehensive income tax base.

2 CONSTITUTIONAL ISSUES

Because Japan is a unitary state, it does not confront the same constitutional issues regarding the allocation of taxing authority among the federal government and states or municipal entities as the United States (U.S.) or Germany. Although the Constitution mentions a guarantee of local public finance autonomy, it clearly prioritizes the national tax statutory law over the local tax ordonnance,[5] leaving the allocation of taxing rights to be dealt with by national legislative policy. The constitutional issues with regard to taxation law, including the income tax law, involve two principles: (1) the principle of statute-based taxation[6] and (2) the equality principle. The principle of

5. The Supreme Court of Japan, March 21, 2013, *Minshu* (Official Reporter of Supreme Court decisions) 67-3-438.
6. Hiroshi Kaneko, "The Principle of Statute-Based Taxation in Japan: Trends in Scholars' Opinions and Case Law," in Paul Kirchhof, Moris Lehner, Arndt Raupach, & Michael Rodi (eds.), *International Comparative Taxation: Essays in Honour of Klaus Vogel* (Kluwer, 2002).

statute-based taxation derives from Article 84 of the Constitution, which provides: "No new taxes shall be imposed, or existing ones modified except by law or under such conditions as law may prescribe" (Official translation: the term "law" here is the Japanese *horitsu*, which might better be translated as "statute"). This principle leads to the following conclusions:

(i) Nonlegislative regulations, such as cabinet orders and ministerial ordinances, may not impose tax unless a statute specifically delegates authority to do so; this principle is sometimes argued in the course of tax-related cases in which taxpayers challenge the constitutionality of tax laws and regulations on the basis of the overbroad delegation of tax requirements to nonlegislative regulations. However, such challenges seldom succeed before the courts.

(ii) Provisions of tax laws and regulations must be specific enough for courts to clearly construe the meaning as a matter of interpretation; this does not necessarily mean that provisions of tax laws cannot deal with abstract concepts. In fact, the Japanese income tax law often employs "standards" (in contrast to specific rules) such as "an arbitrarily expensive amount as executive compensation" without further defining the term "arbitrarily."[7]

(iii) No government guidelines or circulars can be a source of tax law, no matter how strong an effect they might have on tax practice. This principle also affects the administration of the tax system (*see* section 8 below).

The equality principle derives from Article 14 of the Constitution, which provides: "All of the people are equal under the law and there shall be no discrimination in political, economic, or social relations because of race, creed, sex, social status, or family origin" (Official translation). This principle is thought to require: (i) taxation according to ability to pay; (ii) equity in taxation; and (iii) neutrality. Although taxpayers often challenge the constitutionality of tax law provisions relying on this principle, courts typically leave the matter to the legislature, in particular with regard to the ability-to-pay principle. For instance, the Supreme Court upheld the constitutionality of the provisions of the ITA which distinguish between employment income and business income (a deduction for necessary expenses is allowed only for the former category, while a formula-based deduction applies to the latter); the Court indicated some sympathy for the taxpayer's argument that the ITA is unfairly biased against employment income earners, but eventually it emphasized a broad legislative discretion in the field of tax policy, and thus concluded that such a discrepancy did not amount to unconstitutional discrimination.[8]

In addition to these principles, tax laws and regulations are sometimes challenged for violating other constitutional rights, such as the right to property, the right to the pursuit of happiness, the freedom to choose an occupation, the right to maintain minimum standards of living, etc. The Supreme Court has never upheld these constitutional challenges. Tax legislation is usually based on Cabinet-proposed bills (*see* below 6.1), all of which are subject to the rigorous scrutiny by the Cabinet

7. Corporate Tax Law, s. 34(2).
8. *Oshima v. Sakyo zeimu shocho*, 39 Saihan Minshu 2-247 (Sup. Ct., March 27, 1985) (en banc).

Legislation Bureau (staffed with legal experts), so as to remove any concerns about unconstitutionality before the bill's submission to the National Diet. Therefore, it is very rare for tax legislation to involve an obvious violation of constitutional clauses. Moreover, as discussed in further detail below, the Japanese judiciary applies the least strict standard of judicial scrutiny to tax legislation, which, according to the Supreme Court, is inherently of a highly political nature. As a result, tax laws and regulations are rarely found to be unconstitutional by the courts.

3 TAX RATES

The individual income tax rates imposed at the national level since 2016 are:

Taxable Income (JPY 1,000)	*Marginal Rates*
1,950 or less	5%
over 1,950 to 3,300	10%
over 3,300 to 6,950	20%
over 6,950 to 9,000	23%
over 9,000 to 18,000	33%
over 18,000 to 40,000	40%
above 40,000	45%

From 2013 to 2037, a surtax of 2.1% on individual income tax amounts is also imposed. This special tax was introduced for the purpose of funding the necessary reconstruction budget after the 2011 Great East Japan Earthquake. Extension of this special tax is now being discussed by the Japanese government in order to finance an increase in defense expenditures in response to escalating global military tensions. In addition to this national tax, individuals are also subject to the local income tax (*Juminzei*) at a rate of 10%. Generally, investment income (e.g., capital gains on securities, dividends and interest on debt products) is subject to a separate income tax of 20%. The introduction of a minimum income tax for extremely wealthy individuals has been discussed by the Japanese government in light of the relatively low effective tax rate for these individuals, whose income tends to consist mainly of investment income. There are no formal rate bracket adjustments for inflation, but in the 1960s and 1970s the government reduced tax rates frequently, which had somewhat similar effects.

In the past decade, the individual income tax rate structure has been dramatically flattened. Prior to the 1987 reforms, the maximum income tax rate, which was applicable to income exceeding JPY 80 million, was 70% (or 86% including local income tax); since 2016, the maximum tax rate (excluding the surtax) has been 45% (or 55% including local income tax). This reduction reflects the view that a high maximum tax rate interferes with decisions to engage in risky enterprises or businesses in Japan. Until 2015, the maximum income tax rate was 40% (or 50% including local income tax). A slight rate increase of 5%, effective from 2016, was in response to the criticism of widening wealth differentials in Japan. Further, it is worthwhile noting that the effective national income tax rates are lower than those specified above because the income tax law permits various types of tax exemptions, such as the family-member exemption. As a result of such exemptions, as of 2023, an employee with a spouse and two children was totally exempt from income tax if the amount of gross income was approximately JPY 2.55 million or less.

The corporate income tax rate is 23.2%. A reduced tax rate (19% or 15%) is applicable to the first JPY 8 million of taxable income of companies with stated capital of JPY 100 million or less. This reduced tax rate is also applicable to nonprofit entities. It should be noted that companies are also subject to local income tax and enterprise tax; the effective tax rate including these taxes is approximately 30%. Despite recent reductions in the rates, Japanese corporate income tax rates are still higher than those of many other countries. In addition, as is apparent from the statistics below, Japan relies heavily on the corporate income tax compared to other developed countries. The corporate sector has long insisted that further reduction of corporate tax burdens is essential for Japanese companies to survive global competition. However, taking into account the current serious condition of the Japanese national budget and negative public reactions to an increase in the consumption tax, it seems unlikely that the corporate tax rate will be further reduced in the near future. On the contrary, the Japanese government has discussed imposing an additional tax in order to finance an increase in defense expenditures.

4 COMPOSITION OF THE FISCAL SYSTEM

According to the fiscal year (FY) 2023 budget estimate, the percentage contribution of each type of tax to national and local revenues in aggregate (excluding the proceeds of government debt) is shown in the table below. The national government and local governments can impose tax on the same tax base separately:

Type of Tax	*Percentage Contribution*
Taxes on Individual income	29.8%
Taxes on Corporate income	22.0%
Value Added Tax	25.3%
Municipal real estate tax	8.3%
Inheritance tax	2.3%
Other taxes (gasoline tax, liquor tax, and other miscellaneous taxes)	12.2%

For only national revenue for FY 2023, the percentage contribution of each type of tax is as follows:

Type of Tax	*Percentage Contribution*
Individual income tax	30.3%
Corporate income tax	21.0%

Type of Tax	*Percentage Contribution*
Consumption tax	33.7%
Inheritance tax	4.0%
Gasoline tax	2.9%
Liquor tax	1.7%
Tobacco tax	1.3%
Other miscellaneous national taxes	5.1%

The Japanese public finance system runs a structural deficit, relying routinely on massive government borrowing. Thus, the percentages noted above would be substantially lowered if calculated based on total national revenues.

The above two tables do not incorporate social security contributions (both national and local levels),[9] which amount to JPY 77.5 trillion in the FY 2023 budget estimates.[10] For FY 2023, tax revenue (national and local taxes aggregated) is JPY 118.4 trillion. Although social security contributions must be distinguished from taxes as a matter of Japanese constitutional law, economically speaking, they are no less a "tax" burden on citizens. If social security contributions are combined with national and local taxes, the nation's burden reaches as high as 46.8% of national income (as opposed to 28.1% when only taxes are considered). Indeed, for ordinary taxpayers, the heaviest burden is social insurance premiums, followed by local income tax; the national income tax is the lightest. Social security contributions are typically imposed on earned income (in some cases, capital income and wealth are also considered).

As for the breakdown of tax revenues alone, Japan is still heavily dependent on the corporate income tax compared to other Organisation for Economic Co-operation and Development (OECD) countries, even though the tax rates have gradually been reduced in line with Japan's trading partners. The VAT is expected to fill the revenue gap and raise further revenue to finance the ever-increasing social security expenditure and fiscal consolidation.

5 BASIC STRUCTURE OF THE INCOME TAX

5.1 Individuals

The Japanese individual income tax has two distinct features: it relies heavily on withholding tax and uses a schedular system.

In principle, Japan uses the self-assessment system for individual income tax purposes as well as for corporate income tax purposes. However, in fact, a substantial

9. Old-age pension systems are operated exclusively at the national level, while public health insurance coverage is provided by the national government, private employers, and local governments, depending on the status of individuals.
10. This massive revenue nonetheless falls short of the enormous social security expenditures, which annually amount to JPY 134.3 trillion. The balance is inevitably financed by the national government's general account.

portion of individual income tax is collected through the withholding system (according to the 2023 budget, the individual income tax revenue from self-assessment is estimated to be JPY 3.5 trillion, while the withholding income tax revenue amounts to JPY 17.5 trillion). For two primary reasons, this withholding system largely obviates the need for self-assessment and filing a tax return. First, wage earners generally send relevant information to their employers, who make appropriate adjustments (such as deductions for dependents and insurance premiums) on behalf of the taxpayers (wage earners) at the end of the year; in most cases, this adjustment alone eliminates the need for wage earners to file a return themselves.[11] Second, most investment income for small- or medium-sized investors, including dividends on equity securities and capital gains from listed equity securities or publicly-offered bonds, as well as interest on deposits and debt securities, is also subject to withholding; a substantial part of such income is taxed at a flat 20% rate regardless of the amount of gross income earned by the investor. Where this flat rate is applicable, there is no need for taxpayers (or the tax authority) to include these items in their declared income. However, since 2003, as a matter of principle, dividends on equity securities, interest on debt securities, and capital gains from securities fall into different categories of income under Japan's schedular system; these distinctions are disregarded once individual taxpayers choose to apply the withholding system.

While the majority of individuals are still exempt from filing a tax return, some individuals file a return, either pursuant to the statutory obligation (typically self-employed individuals, and certain wage earners whose revenue is above a certain threshold), or by an individual's choice in order to claim tax benefits and refunds. A joint return system has not been adopted in Japan.

Individual income tax still maintains a formally schedular system, in the sense that income is divided into ten categories and computed according to distinct rules of calculation. For example, only one half of retirement income (which essentially means retirement payments) is included in income, while employment income, which consists mainly of wages, is fully taxable, subject to certain special deductions.[12] The rationale for this schedular system is sometimes said to be that the "ability to pay" varies by category of income. However, this feature of the individual income tax definitely makes tax planning easier by means of changing the character of income from one category to another. For example, relatively favorable tax treatment is applicable to occasional income, especially compared to miscellaneous income, thus giving taxpayers an incentive to have their income treated as occasional income. Another indication of the schedular character of the Japanese system is the rule which limits the deductibility of losses in one category against income in other categories.

The categories of income under the Japanese schedular system cover almost all types of income. In addition, recent changes, as discussed above, have blurred the distinction among several categories of income in respect of financial products. It is fair to say that the schedular system has become, in substance, closer to a global regime.

11. ITA, s. 121. On the other hand, individuals need to file a return to claim certain types of deductions, such as the medical expenses deduction and charitable contributions deduction.
12. ITA, s. 30.

In order to avoid double taxation on corporate earnings at the individual and corporate levels, Japan has adopted the divided-received credit method. However, because of the limit on the creditable amount, double taxation is not completely eliminated. In addition, this dividend-received credit is not available to taxpayers who choose to be exempt from the annual obligation to file tax returns, as discussed above. Therefore, the dividend-received credit is effectively a tax credit for large equity investors who are subject to full-scale individual income tax on dividends.

5.2 Corporations

The features of the individual income tax discussed above are not applicable to the corporate income tax. The tax base of the Japanese corporate income tax is, in general, the amount of net profits earned in the whole business engaged in by a corporation and calculated on the basis of the accrual method. No distinctions are made on the basis of the nature of income. However, corporations as well as individuals are often subject to withholding tax according to the (Individual) ITA (*Shotokuzeiho*) because the withholding tax is imposed on the basis of the character of the payment (interest, dividends, etc.) and not the identity of the recipient of the payment. Of course, corporations are entitled to tax credits of the amount equal to the withholding tax; this feature is sometimes critical for financial institutions because one of the principal sources of their earnings is the time value of money. For this reason, financial institutions are often exempt from the withholding tax, subject to some procedural requirements to enable withholders (i.e., counterparties of transactions with financial institutions) to identify the financial institutions.

Since 2002, a consolidated corporate group consisting exclusively of wholly owned Japanese entities has been permitted to file consolidated tax returns. In 2022, the regime underwent conceptual changes, resulting in a system which allows income and loss adjustments among the members of a 100%-owned corporate group, but the functions and scope remain largely unchanged. Further details are set out in Part III.

In order to avoid double taxation, dividends received from other corporations in which a corporate taxpayer holds more than one-third of the outstanding shares are fully excluded from taxable income. In the past, this exclusion was more generous to corporations but has been limited as tax rates have recently decreased. As of 2023, the exclusion is permitted on a sliding scale of 20% to 100% depending on the shareholding percentage in the payer corporations.

6 TAX LEGISLATION

6.1 Legislative Process for Income Tax Measures

Japanese tax law, including income tax law (i.e., both the individual and corporate income taxes), is amended annually. The effective dates of such amendments are generally the first day of the taxable period. As a result, the ITA is usually amended as of January 1 and the CTA is usually amended as of April 1, since the taxable period for individuals is the calendar year and the taxable period for corporations is their FY (which, for many Japanese corporations, is from April 1 to March 31 of the following year).

Although the Constitution provides that tax must be imposed by statutory laws enacted by the National Diet, most tax legislation is initiated by the government rather than the Diet. The Japanese constitution grants the Cabinet the power to submit legislative bills (including tax bills) to the Diet because, realistically, technical expertise and resources are required to draft tax bills and such expertise is available solely in the relevant ministries (for national tax, the Ministry of Finance, and for local tax, the Ministry of Internal Affairs and Communications). The process normally follows these steps:

(1) The Tax Commission (*Zeiseichosakai*), an advisory committee of the Prime Minister, submits a report to the Minister regarding tax amendments.
(2) The government party (almost always the Liberal Democratic Party) and the Ministry of Finance announce the outline of tax amendments for the next taxable period, usually in December.
(3) Discussion in the Diet.
(4) Tax amendments pass the Japanese Diet.

Tax regulations corresponding to the amendments to tax laws are prepared under a similar time schedule by the Ministry of Finance but are published only after the passage of the related amendments.

Because the members of the Tax Commission include nongovernment persons and tax specialists, such as tax law professors, the views of the private sector are indirectly reflected in the first step. In addition, in the first and second steps, informal sounding of public opinion, especially from powerful pressure groups, takes place. Drafts of tax amendments are rarely subject to substantial modifications during the course of discussions in the Diet because most of the influential voices have already been incorporated into the bill in the second step.

In Japan, a process of public consultation similar to that applicable to draft U.S. Internal Revenue Service regulations is available, but only in very limited circumstances. Consequently, it is difficult for tax amendments to reflect the views of the private sector other than those of strong pressure groups. Even in the case of technical tax amendments, tax specialists other than the members of the Tax Commission do not have a substantial opportunity to participate in the amendment process. Moreover, the process of drafting the provisions for tax amendments in the Ministry of Finance has not been made public and, as a result, the general public often encounters difficulty in finding any meaningful legislative history of tax amendments.

6.2 Statutory Style

Compared to legislation in other areas of the law, the provisions of Japanese tax laws are quite detailed. This feature may be regarded as a reflection of the "statute-based taxation" principle under Article 84 of the Constitution, as discussed in section 2 above. However, it is notable that the statutes—detailed as they may be—still contain flexible terms, such as "extremely low price" or "appropriate amount." In addition, the tax laws delegate the details of tax rules to cabinet orders (*Seirei*) and ministerial ordinances (*Shorei*) issued by the Ministry of Finance. Although Article 84 of the Constitution prohibits absolute delegation of tax requirements to cabinet orders and ministerial ordinances, the volume of such orders and ordinances is much larger than that of tax laws, mainly because of their technical nature.

As a structural matter, there is no single Tax Code, but separate statutory laws for individual income tax (ITA) and corporate income tax (CTA). Further, there is an additional law for "special tax treatments," which contains provisions which could broadly be considered to be tax expenditures. Most procedural matters, as well as collection mechanisms, which are also applicable to ITA and CTA, are provided by the Act on General Rules for National Taxes and the National Tax Collection Act.[13] Because of this structure, corporations must refer to all of these laws in order to properly understand the tax effects of transactions. As discussed above, under the ITA, some types of withholding taxes are applicable to both individuals and corporations.

6.3 Statutory Interpretation[14]

Japanese courts are sometimes said to pay more attention to the actual text of the statute in tax law matters than in other fields (although this is obviously a difficult claim to validate), perhaps because of the existence of Article 84 of the Constitution.

As discussed further below, Japanese courts generally respect the legislative history of laws, including tax laws. Emphasis is placed on: (i) answers given by the Tax Commission in response to questions at the time of the promulgation of or amendments to the relevant tax law provisions; and (ii) interpretations (whether official or not) given by the staff of the National Tax Agency (*Kokuzei-cho*, the "NTA") or the Regional Tax Bureaus (*Kokuzei-kyoku*, the "Tax Bureaus") within the Ministry of Finance.

The actual legislative drafting of tax laws is done by young officials in the Ministry of Finance or NTA. As a result, it sometimes happens that the most valuable tax legislative materials exist only as internal documents within the Ministry of Finance or NTA. This internal information occasionally becomes public when an official of the Ministry of Finance or the NTA publishes a book or article in a "private" capacity.

Government interpretations of tax laws and regulations are officially announced by the NTA or other tax authorities in tax guidelines and circulars (*Tsutatsu*) and in tax rulings. In addition to these official interpretations, and similar to the case of legislative

13. Some parts of these laws are available in English at the Ministry of Justice website: http://www.japaneselawtranslation.go.jp/en.
14. For observations on this matter, *see* Yoshihiro Masui, "The Responsibility of Judges in Interpreting Tax Legislation: Japan's Experience" (2015) 52:2 *Osgoode Hall Law Journal* 491-512 https://doi.org/10.60082/2817-5069.2818 and Yoshihiro Masui, "Legal Interpretation of Tax Law: Japan," in Robert F. van Brederode & Richard Krever (eds.), Vol. 46 *Legal Interpretation of Tax Law*, Series on International Taxation (Kluwer Law International, 2014) 251-263; (2nd ed., 2017) 303-316.

history, interpretations by tax officials are often stated in books or articles written by them. Although these interpretations are unofficial, they are considered to be de facto tax rules in practice, because it can be reasonably expected that the tax authorities will follow such published interpretations.

7 COURTS DEALING WITH TAX MATTERS

7.1 Structure of the Courts

Taxpayers must first bring complaints against decisions by the tax authority (local tax office) to the National Tax Tribunal before bringing them to the courts. Although the Tribunal is a department of the NTA, it may make decisions on complaints independently of the NTA. This system has been adopted in order to efficiently use the sophisticated knowledge of tax laws and regulations held by tax officials. Although the Tribunal is independent of the NTA in the sense that the NTA does not control its decisions on tax disputes, the President of the Tribunal, who has the authority to make final decisions on all tax disputes at the stage of the Tribunal, is appointed by the Commissioner of the NTA. In addition, the members of the Tribunal, who manage tax disputes in practice, are tax officials as well as civil court judges and prosecutors. Although the President makes all final decisions on tax disputes at the Tribunal, the decisions are based on opinions submitted by the consultation panel, consisting of three members of the Tribunal. Where the Tribunal decides to reverse the tax authority's decision, it is considered to be the final word of the administrative branch—the NTA cannot challenge the Tribunal's decision. Needless to say, taxpayers can challenge the Tribunal's decision before a court.

Appeals against decisions by the Tribunal can be brought to a district court whose geographical jurisdiction covers the area where the taxpayer in question resides. In large-scale district courts, such as the Tokyo District Court, the same departments always deal with tax litigation; nevertheless, such departments are still general courts rather than special tax courts. Decisions of district courts can be appealed to the relevant high court and then to the Supreme Court.

In general, Japanese courts do not have specialized tax judges. Japanese judges are under the career system and are frequently transferred to different courts located all over Japan. While this feature has made it difficult for Japanese judges to specialize in a particular area of law, such as tax law, the potential lack of judges with expertise in tax matters is compensated for by counsel who specialize in tax law and can provide the courts with detailed tax arguments. In addition, career-system judges have been trained to adopt a neutral position between tax authorities and taxpayers. This may be one reason why Japanese judges do not simply follow the opinions of tax authorities, despite their potential lack of expertise in tax matters. Japanese judges tend to focus on the text of tax law provisions and their legislative history, and typically do not accept arguments unique to tax, such as substance-over-form arguments, without specific supporting provisions in tax laws.

The following table illustrates the number of tax disputes heard by the Tribunal and courts from April 2022 to March 2023 and the results of such tax disputes. The number of disputes decided in favor of taxpayers is small:

Level	*Number of Disputes Decided*	*Taxpayers' Win*	*Taxpayers' Partial Win*	*Taxpayers' Loss*	*Others*
Tribunal	2,873	73	153	2,263	385
District Court	86	2	3	78	3
High Court	52	3	1	48	0
Supreme Court	36	1	0	28	7

7.2 Judicial Style

Judicial opinions of Japanese courts, especially those of lower courts, are long and detailed with respect to the interpretation of the law as well as findings of fact. This feature of judicial opinions is called "minute judgment." Judicial opinions with respect to the interpretation of laws and regulations often refer to the legislative history. Although legislative history is not binding, a traditional approach for the interpretation of law by Japanese courts is that laws should be interpreted according to the intention of legislators. Therefore, especially when courts encounter controversial legal issues, they highly respect the relevant legislative history if it is sufficiently clear.

The general analysis described above is equally applicable to tax cases. In addition, with regard to tax cases, it appears that courts tend to respect the government's interpretation of tax laws and regulations as espoused by the NTA or other tax authorities even where such interpretations are legally nonbinding.

Following the continental influence on the Japanese legal system, judicial opinions are not formally a source of law, at least among equal levels in the judicial hierarchy—although, of course, judicial opinions by the Supreme Court have dominant authority in practice. This does not mean, however, that judicial opinions by district courts, the lowest level of courts in tax litigation, have no authority. Quite the contrary—they have enormous authority for Japanese tax practice. For example, if the tax office loses a case, even if the court is an obscure district court, the tax authority often changes its policies to conform to the court's decision. In general, if a court rejects a tax circular, the circular is usually amended.

Japanese courts tend to be conservative in the exercise of their powers to review the constitutionality of laws, and they defer broadly to the legislative branch. This tendency is particularly noticeable in fields such as tax law, where technical sophistication is at a premium. As the Supreme Court stated:

> Tax today involves more than its basic function of providing for the national fiscal needs. It also redistributes income, appropriately allocates resources, and adjusts economic performance. In deciding each citizen's tax burden, the determination of

> national fiscal, economic, and social policy on a comprehensive national scale becomes necessary. Because the prerequisites of tax liability must also be decided, however, the process requires specialized technical judgment as well. Accordingly, in the determination of tax law, it is necessary to defer to policy and technical judgment (based on accurate data regarding such issues as the national fiscal situation, the social economy, the national income, and the national living situation) of the legislative branch. At root, the courts have no choice but to respect the discretionary judgment of that branch.[15]

8 TAX ADMINISTRATION

The government agency in charge of the income tax administration is the NTA, an independent department of the Ministry of Finance. The NTA consists of the head office, eleven Regional Bureaus and, at the lowest level, more than 500 local tax offices engaged in the day-to-day management of tax affairs. The NTA's head office performs administrative functions and issues tax guidelines and circulars; tax collection is generally administered by the relevant local tax office or the Regional Bureau. These agencies have a budget of approximately JPY 640 billion and employ approximately 55,000 full-time officials. For the period between July 2016 and June 2022, the number of on-site audits for income tax was approximately 120,000. The number of on-site audits dramatically decreased during the COVID-19 pandemic. While the number has increased since 2022, it is still smaller when compared to the pre-COVID period.

Japanese tax law does not have a special provision for taxpayers' access to tax-related information. Although Japan has a general law regarding the disclosure of government information, in general, disclosure of specific tax-related information is very restricted. Tax officials are subject to a confidentiality obligation with respect to non-public information which they obtain in the course of their work.

In July 2002, a tax rulings system was introduced in Japan. In general, tax rulings are issued by the local tax office in the area where the applicant resides, although in some cases the Regional Bureau or the NTA issues tax rulings. Tax rulings are to be published within sixty days following the response by the tax authority to an application.

The government's administration of the tax system must be carried out in accordance with laws enacted by the Diet. This is a basic constitutional principle in Japan, and the notion is particularly important in tax matters because of Article 84 of the Constitution. Administrative interpretation is provided mostly in the form of guidelines or circulars issued by the NTA. Although these guidelines and circulars are not binding interpretations of law, they are always the result of careful consideration by a group of very knowledgeable and sophisticated specialists in the NTA. This feature seems to result in considerable judicial deference to these administrative positions.

The whole question of Japanese administrative style is a matter of some controversy. The conventional interpretation is that the system is characterized by a

15. *Oshima v. Sakyo zeimu shocho*, 39 Saihan Minshu 2-247 (Sup. Ct., March 27, 1985) (*en banc*).

strong bureaucracy using informal "administrative guidance" which is typically followed by the private sector. As applied to the tax area, this means that informal interpretations in the form of tax circulars or other administrative publications perform the same role as formally issued regulations in a more rule-oriented system. However, some commentators (including the authors of this chapter) have taken the position that the Japanese system is not unique in its use of informal regulations. Informal regulations are followed only if and to the extent that the parties believe the positions taken reflect formal rules. By governing informally, both the government and the private sectors save the costs associated with a more formal system.

The relatively small number of judicial cases with respect to tax matters in Japan might be viewed as an effect of this administrative style. Many decisions by local tax offices regarding the amount of tax payable are not challenged at judicial proceedings but are accepted by taxpayers, sometimes after some compromise by the local tax office.

At least according to conventional wisdom, Japanese taxpayers do not approach tax planning as aggressively as U.S. taxpayers.

In recent years, financial products developed for the purpose of acquiring tax benefits and other types of tax-planning schemes have become increasingly common in Japan. The NTA and other agencies are aware of this development and are making substantial efforts to identify illegal or questionable tax shelters. The NTA's stance against these tax-oriented products and tax-oriented behavior seems to have become firmer. In any event, the schedular system of the Japanese individual income tax, as well as the high tax rate of the corporate income tax and estate tax, give taxpayers strong motivation for tax planning. Struggles between the NTA and taxpayers have just begun and will likely take a long time to be settled.

Among taxpayer organizations, there are those which cooperate with the NTA (e.g., the Blue Return Organization), and those which are uncooperative (e.g., the Democratic Chamber of Commerce). The Democratic Chamber of Commerce has launched many legal challenges against the tax authority. Among the leftist tax adviser (*zeirishi*) groups, there is the Young Tax Advisers Association.

9 GENERAL PRINCIPLES

9.1 Relation Between Tax and Financial Accounting

The taxable income of a corporation is calculated on the basis of the profit and loss statement prepared in accordance with the Company Act,[16] with adjustments required by the CTA. The accounting provisions dictated by the Company Act, in turn, are based on generally accepted accounting principles (GAAP).[17] Therefore, for corporations, tax accounting is generally the same as financial accounting, although the tax law has special rules which differ in certain respects from Japanese GAAP. The rationale for

16. CTA, s. 74.
17. Company Act, s. 431.

this general reliance of the tax law on financial accounting is the need to simplify the tax law; but, at the same time, such reliance raises several problems. For example, suppose that the rules for financial accounting change. If tax accounting should be the same as financial accounting, the tax rules would automatically change as well, yet that seems to violate the general constitutional requirement of taxation according to law (*see* section 2 above). One recent example of this issue is whether the mark-to-market method for the valuation of certain assets, such as financial derivatives transactions, could be adopted without statutory changes for tax purposes if that method were adopted for financial accounting purposes. Although this issue was actually resolved by changing the tax law according to the changes in financial accounting principles, similar types of problems are possible. For example, in 2018, Japanese GAAP introduced specific rules for revenue accounting. This time, the NTA announced a package of new provisions in the tax guidelines instead of changing the text of tax laws.

For individuals, taxable income is calculated without regard to Japanese GAAP. Although the general method for the calculation of individual taxable income is the accrual method, under limited circumstances, the tax law permits individuals to use the cash method.

9.2 Respect for Legal (Civil Law) Form

In general, the Supreme Court's position has been that, where the tax law uses concepts which are commonly used in, or defined under, private law (such as the Civil and Commercial Codes), the concepts are interpreted in the same manner as in the Civil and Commercial Codes unless otherwise defined in the tax law.

According to most observers, courts respect contractual forms and do not impose tax based on the underlying economic substance, ignoring contractual forms. Because this judicial approach offers opportunities for tax avoidance, the tax authority sometimes asserts a substance-over-form argument; such attempts have not necessarily been successful. At least to some extent, recent tax revisions, especially those related to international taxation and estate tax, can be viewed as countermeasures to such unsuccessful attempts, in the sense that the Japanese tax authority tries to promulgate specific provisions addressing tax-oriented schemes rather than relying on the undocumented substance-over-form theory.

9.3 Anti-avoidance Doctrines and Legislation

Despite frequent discussions, Japanese tax law still does not have a general anti-avoidance provision authorizing courts to recharacterize tax-avoidance schemes. However, there are some provisions which negate tax-avoidance schemes in some specific circumstances. Historically, Japan has had an anti-avoidance provision applicable to the transactions of family corporations. According to this provision (with a variety of details omitted), if transactions among such corporations unreasonably reduce their tax liability, the courts can recharacterize the transactions and recompute their tax liability. In addition to such anti-avoidance provisions for family corporations, a similar provision was adopted at the time the consolidated tax system was introduced in 2002 for corporations which file consolidated tax returns. This provision is similarly applicable to the new system which succeeded the consolidated return system in 2022.[18] Further, a similar type of anti-avoidance provision has been introduced for corporate mergers and other corporate reorganization transactions.[19] Although there are a limited number of court precedents interpreting these anti-avoidance provisions, recent Supreme Court decisions seem to have adopted an approach to these anti-tax avoidance provisions which is similar to the approach it has taken to the anti-tax avoidance provision for family corporations.[20] Technically, the text of these anti-avoidance provisions authorizes the District Director of the relevant local Tax Office to recharacterize these transactions. However, functionally, "District Director" should be read as "courts," because courts can override decisions made by the District Director.

Although several court precedents have ruled to the contrary, the general scholarly view (and that of some other court precedents) is that the "tax according to law" principle under Article 84 of the Constitution prohibits courts from recharacterizing tax avoidance schemes without a specific provision authorizing such recharacterization. Currently, the tax authorities rarely insist on recharacterization without a specific provision but tend to try to achieve the same goals by narrowly interpreting tax provisions on which taxpayers rely in order to obtain tax benefits.

10 TAX TREATIES

Japan has comprehensive tax treaties with eighty jurisdictions (including a unique arrangement with Taiwan), as well as eleven Tax Information Exchange Agreements (TIEA) with low-tax jurisdictions, including Hong Kong. Although the Japanese government has become increasingly active in expanding its treaty network, and the number of countries in Central and South America with which Japan has entered into comprehensive tax treaties has increased over the past decade, it has only a small number of tax treaties with countries in Africa and Central and South America (e.g., it has entered into comprehensive tax treaties with only four countries in Africa). It appears that the Japanese government is selective in expanding its treaty networks, taking business needs into account.

As a member of the OECD, Japan's tax treaties follow the general pattern of the OECD Model Treaty, subject to several exceptions:

- Japan sometimes permits a source country to tax capital gains from assets located in the source country, even where the assets are not real estate; and
- Japan sometimes tries to specify that income from investment in Japan in the form of *tokumei-kumiai* (a type of investment agreement) is taxable by Japan

18. CTA, s. 132-3.
19. CTA, s. 132-2.
20. *Yahoo v. Azabu zeimu shocho*, 70 Saihan Minshu 2-242 (Sup. Ct., February 29, 2016).

(e.g., Japan-United States Tax Treaty, Protocol, Article 13(b); Japan-Netherlands Tax Treaty, Protocol, Article 9. For tax treaty purposes, *tokumei-kumiai* is known as a "sleeping partnership").

Japan has signed the *Multilateral Convention on Mutual Assistance in Tax Matters*. It has also signed the *Multilateral Convention to Implement Tax Treaty Related Measures to Prevent Base Erosion and Profit Shifting* (MLI) but has carved out several provisions from its application.

11 SOURCES OF TAX LAW

11.1 Sources of Tax Law

Sources of Japanese tax law include: (i) the Constitution; (ii) international treaties (or conventions); (iii) laws and statutes; and (iv) government regulations comprised of cabinet orders (*seiriei*) and ministerial ordinances (*shorei*; issued by the Ministry of Finance). Local ordinances (*jorei*; issued by municipalities) may also be sources of local tax law. As discussed above, as a civil law country, judicial opinions are not formally a source of law; however, they have practical authority, especially judicial opinions issued by the Supreme Court.

In theory, the tax guidelines or circulars (*tsutatsu*; issued by the NTA) are simply internal instructions from bureaucratic superiors to inferiors, and thus neither bind citizens nor constitute a source of tax law. However, in fact, as discussed above, courts almost always defer to these circulars and taxpayers seldom challenge their validity. The circulars should be understood as playing an important role in making tax administration predictable and thus providing certainty to taxpayers.

Similarly, tax rulings do not constitute a source of law, regardless of their importance in tax practice. Since the introduction of the rulings system in 2002, their number has steadily increased. Further, in 2008, the scope of tax rulings was expanded to include specific transactions as well as tax issues with general applicability.

Japanese tax law does not grant the Ministry of Finance or the NTA general authority to prescribe tax regulations (as discussed in section 2 above, such authorization, if made, would be disregarded as unconstitutional). Therefore, only cabinet orders and ministerial ordinances based on specific delegation by tax law constitute a source of law. The text of the current tax law, including cabinet orders and ministerial ordinances, can be found at http://elaws.e-gov.go.jp/search/elawsSearch/elaws_search/lsg0100 (only Japanese versions are available). In addition, the Japanese text of the tax guidelines and circulars is available at https://www.nta.go.jp/law/tsutatsu/menu.htm.

Partial translations of the ITA, CTA, and the Special Taxation Measures Act (STMA) applicable to nonresidents of Japan are available on the government website (http://www.japaneselawtranslation.go.jp). However, these translations have not been updated since 2009.

11.2 Available Materials

The NTA's website (http://www.nta.go.jp) contains not only the texts of the tax guidelines and circulars but also many other items, such as a summary of the tax revisions for recent years and tax rulings. With respect to certain items, including the annual report of the NTA (NTA Report), English translations are also available there. As for statistical data concerning tax administration, the *National Tax Agency Annual Statistics Report* is a useful source (https://www.nta.go.jp/publication/statistics/kokuzeicho/tokei.htm; as of December 2023, a part of the data for FY 2023 and the full package of the data for FY 2022 are available).

In addition to the NTA's website, Sozeishiryokan, a non-profit organization, offers an English translation of the CTA and the ITA (most current versions cover the CTA until 2023 and the ITA until 2022, respectively). The English translations of various other tax laws are also available in loose-leaf booklets issued by Eibun-Horei Sha.

H. Kaneko, *Sozei ho* [Tax Law], 24th ed. (2021) provides a comprehensive and insightful overview of the entire Japanese tax system. *Sozei ho kenkyu* [Studies in Tax Law], an annual journal, and *Nichi zei ken ronshu* [Essays in Japanese Tax Studies], a collection of essays, include various professional and scholarly essays on various topics, including international tax issues. The tax law commentaries issued by Daichi-Hoki-Shuppan and edited by S. Takeda are the most reliable commentaries for Japanese income tax law. These commentaries are authored by current and former NTA officials and accurately reflect the NTA's views.

Professor Yoshihiro Masui's website (http://www.masui.j.u-tokyo.ac.jp/english.html) provides a useful gateway to Japanese taxation for English-speaking readers, including selected materials.

Sweden

Peter Melz & Jérôme Monsenego

1 HISTORY

The Swedish income tax originated as a schedular income tax system. The first income tax law was enacted in 1810, influenced by English liberal thought. It was repealed in 1812 and replaced by a schedular system with eight income sources. During the nineteenth and the beginning of the twentieth century, the development toward a modern income tax system went on with important reforms in 1860, 1902, 1910, and 1928. At the same time, the income tax became more important as government revenue from duties and excises decreased.

As a result of successive reforms, schedular differences decreased and the concept of income was broadened by successive inclusions of capital gains. In 1985, the municipal income taxation of corporations was abolished. Since then, corporations pay national income tax only; as a result, there is no longer a need for national transfer pricing rules, leading to greater simplification. In 1991, a major tax reform was enacted. For individuals, the sources of income were reduced to three: income from employment, business income, and income from capital. For corporations, there is only one source: business income. In principle, however, the Swedish system is still a schedular system, which means that there is no general definition of income, although the definitions of income with respect to the different sources are broad.

Nonetheless, the source principle is still important since, if a specific income item cannot be included as income in any of the three sources, it is excluded from the income tax base. In general, it can be said that taxable income consists of all remuneration for performance of services, yield and gains on capital, and income from business. Since 1991, further important reforms have dealt with the taxation of proprietorships to equalize such taxation with the taxation of corporations, restructuring of businesses, and limitations on interest deductions for corporations.

2 CONSTITUTIONAL ISSUES

Sweden has a written constitution. There is not one law, but four different basic laws. Constitutional rules of importance for taxation are contained in *Regeringsformen* (the Instrument of Government).

Long before written constitutions, it was accepted as a basic rule that taxes should be levied only with the consent of the people. Accordingly, the Constitution states that taxes should be levied in accordance with law and tax rules should be enacted by Parliament (*Riksdagen*).[1] In accordance with this rule, it is not possible for Parliament to delegate legislative power to government or government authorities—delegated rules may prescribe only how to comply with the statutory rules, and no new rules may be implemented through them. In reality, regulations have great impact in some areas, especially with respect to the procedure to establish assessed values on real estate. This is such a technical field that the complete procedure cannot be prescribed in the statutory rules and parts of the procedure must therefore be prescribed in regulations.

Another constitutional rule with importance for taxation is that retroactive legislation is not allowed for penal law and tax law. This prohibition is relevant only for legislation which increases taxation, which, however, is normally the case. Anti-avoidance legislation often takes effect immediately after the intention to pass such legislation becomes public since the constitution allows legislation to take effect on the day the government informs Parliament that a bill will be sent to Parliament at a later time.

Constitutional control of legislation is limited. The Constitution states that courts should set statutory rules aside only where they are in contradiction of the Constitution.[2] For important proposals, a bill is preceded by a draft which is examined by three judges from the Supreme Court and the Supreme Administrative Court in the Law Council (*Lagrådet*), as part of a review of, among others, the constitutional questions.

Other rules in the Constitution which may act as safeguards for taxpayers are fairly vague. Apart from the prohibition against retroactive legislation, there is a prohibition on expropriation without compensation and a rule that legislation should be applied in a uniform way.

In recent years, it has become more common for taxpayers to appeal to the European Court of Human Rights (Strasbourg). The tax cases decided so far have dealt with questions of procedural remedies, etc., and not the substance of tax rules. The European Convention on Human Rights (ECHR) is incorporated as statutory law in Sweden.

Sweden has been a member of the European Union (EU) since 1995 and EU tax directives have been implemented in detail into Swedish statutory law.[3] The Court of Justice of the European Union (CJEU) (Luxembourg) has ruled in a number of cases that Swedish tax rules were in violation of the fundamental freedoms and Sweden has

1. The Instrument of Government (Ch. 8, s. 2).
2. The Instrument of Government (Ch. 11, s. 14).
3. *See* the Introduction for a brief discussion of European institutions and tax laws.

therefore amended these rules. Amendments have also been made in accordance with other decisions of the Court.

3 TAX RATES

The corporate tax rate is simply a flat rate of 20.6% of taxable income. There is a system of double taxation of corporate income, and dividends are, with a few exceptions, taxable to individuals, as discussed below.

A number of income taxes and social security contributions can be levied on the income of individuals. For income from capital, a flat rate of 30% is levied; this is a national tax only. For earned income (income from employment and business) taxation is progressive. After a basic allowance (*see* below in this section) local income taxes (county council/region and municipality) are levied on income. The rates are decided by the local governments and are on average 32.24%.[4]

For income above a certain prescribed amount, national income tax is also levied. For income (after the basic allowance) above SEK 598,500,[5] the national income tax is 20%. The rate bracket is normally adjusted for inflation; however, due to the current economic situation, there was no adjustment for 2024. In total, the tax rate on earned income starts with local income taxes at about 32% and rises to a maximum of about 52% for the top bracket (local and national income taxes). Social security contributions are paid by employers: 31.42% of income for employees and 28.97% for self-employed persons. The base for social security contributions is similar to the income tax base for earned income. To a large extent, payments of social security contributions do not result in social benefits[6] and these payments should therefore be considered to be taxes. The combined rate, including the part of social security contributions considered to be taxes, is about 63% for the top income tax bracket.[7]

Allowances in computing taxable income are calculated in a complex way,[8] with the basic allowance first increasing and then decreasing. For 2024, it begins with an amount equal to the taxable income and then increases to a maximum of SEK 44,200 at incomes between SEK 155,900 and 178,400. The allowance then decreases to a minimum of SEK 16,800 for incomes above SEK 451,500.

In 2007 a special in-work tax credit (*jobbskatteavdrag*) was introduced aimed at stimulating participation in the workforce.[9] It is calculated based on income from employment (salaries, etc., but not pensions). These calculations are very complicated. The maximum credit is SEK 35,395, increasing with income but decreasing at a certain

4. Rates, etc., are for 2023.
5. The exchange rate for 2023 was approximately 11.5 SEK per EUR and 10 SEK per USD.
6. On average, about 60% of the contributions can be regarded as taxes.
7. For an employee, the marginal rate can be calculated in the following way. An employer pays SEK 100 in salary to an employee and SEK 31 in resulting social security contributions. The employee pays SEK 52 in income taxes with respect to the salary. A total of SEK 83 of SEK 131 (63%) is paid in taxes and contributions to the government.
8. Income Tax Act (ITA), Ch. 63.
9. ITA, Ch. 65, s. 9 a-9 d.

level; this increases the marginal rate of income tax further. For retired persons with salaries, etc., the credit is somewhat higher.

4 COMPOSITION OF THE FISCAL SYSTEM

Taxes finance the central government and local governments (municipalities and county councils). In 2017, tax revenues for the general government sector amounted to about 44.4% of Gross Domestic Product (GDP). The Swedish tax-to-GDP ratio has decreased from 53% in 2002 to about 41.4% of GDP in 2023 but remains among the highest of developed countries. However, about 40% of government expenditures consist of transfers back to individuals and enterprises.

In the mid-1990s, the government ran large budget deficits (e.g., in 1993 net borrowing was 11.9% of GDP). In recent years, the budget has either been balanced or been in surplus. Parliament has implemented a budget expenditure ceiling which aims to run an average surplus of 2% of GDP for a business cycle. Government debt (Maastricht debt) was 30.7% of GDP in 2023.

The Swedish level of taxation is among the highest in the world. This is partially the result of the design of the Swedish tax system, which in some respects results in higher gross taxation than in other systems. For example, Sweden taxes transfers from government as taxable income, while in other countries transfers are often not taxed or are designed as tax deductions rather than open subsidies and grants. Individual social security charges outside the tax system are also more common in other countries than in Sweden. A government committee (*Swedish Government Official Report* (*Statens offentliga utredningar*, SOU) 2002:47) made recalculations for such factors (making adjustments for deficits and surpluses) based on a comparison with a number of other countries.

4.1 Types of Taxes

At the beginning of the twentieth century, indirect taxes on trade, consumption, etc., were the most important type of taxes. The trend since then has been the increasing importance of income taxation, although, in recent decades, compelled by the need to increase tax revenues, the relative importance of income taxes has declined and social security contributions have increased substantially. In the tax reform of 1991, the income tax was further decreased and instead the value-added tax (VAT) was increased through broadening of the tax base.

In Sweden, many different taxes are levied: local and national income tax on individuals; national income tax on corporations; VAT; taxes on alcohol, tobacco, and energy; sales (stamp duty) tax on real estate; and real estate tax. In 2022, total tax revenues[10] amounted to SEK 2,491 billion. Some of the components were: income taxes (1,085 billion), social security contributions (675 billion), and VAT (559 billion).

10. All social security contributions included.

The net wealth tax and the inheritance and gift tax were repealed as of 2006-2007. The national income tax forms a small part of national government revenues, but the combined income tax for national and local governments is still the largest source of tax revenue. Further, social security contributions function to a large extent as an income tax, since they are levied on the same base as the income tax and do not fully ensure individually earmarked future benefits.

Most taxes are constructed and levied only to pursue fiscal goals. However, at least officially, it is considered that the income tax should be used to a certain extent to redistribute income. Certain sales taxes, such as tobacco and alcohol taxes, as well as taxes on energy consumption, are intended to influence consumption behavior. In recent years, the tax system has been used for additional nonfiscal goals. In 2007 a tax credit for domestic costs was introduced; the credit is 50% of the costs, with a cap of SEK 50,000 per year. Domestic costs include washing, cleaning, gardening, childcare at home, etc. In 2008, a further tax credit was introduced for construction, maintenance, etc., in owner-occupied houses and flats. The credit is 30% of the costs, with a cap of SEK 50,000. The maximum sum for the two tax credits is SEK 50,000. The credits could be considered to be a deviation from strict neutrality in the income tax system, but the argument is that market imperfections exist which will be diminished by the credits.

5 BASIC STRUCTURE OF THE TAX SYSTEM

In Sweden, income taxes are paid by individuals to the national government and to two levels of local government (county councils and municipalities). Corporations pay income tax only to the national government. Taxable income for national and local purposes is calculated on the same base and according to the Income Tax Act (*Inkomstskattelagen*, ITA). All taxes are collected by the national tax agency and then distributed to the national and local governments.

5.1 Individuals

For individuals, income is calculated with respect to three sources: income from employment, business income, and income from capital. The first two sources consist principally of income derived from work, as an employee or self-employed person. The source of income from business comprises all forms of independent business (even, for example, agriculture and commercial real estate).

5.1.1 Earned Income

Income from employment and business (earned income) is combined; the combined income is subject to municipal and national income tax. Municipal tax rates vary according to locality and average around 32%. National income tax is levied only on income above a prescribed limit (*see* above, section 3).

Employment income is the major source of income and includes salaries, compensation for various dependent services, pensions, etc. To simplify tax administration, expenses, apart from the most essential categories, are deductible only for amounts exceeding SEK 5,000. The calculation of business income is more complicated. The same rules, with minor exceptions, apply for businesses carried out by both individuals and entities. Some of these rules are described below. Where the calculation of income from employment or business results in a loss, as a rule, the loss is not deductible from income from another source. However, such losses can be carried forward indefinitely and deducted against income from the same source in future years.

5.1.2 *Income from Capital*

With respect to income from capital, a national income tax is levied at a flat rate of 30% and no municipal tax is imposed. This means that there is often a major difference between the tax rate on capital income on the one hand and the tax rate on employment and business income on the other hand, which makes characterization an important issue. Thus, measures are necessary to prevent taxpayers from converting income from business or services into income from capital.

The lower tax rate on capital income is intended as a standardized compensation for the inflationary losses incurred in connection with capital income. In the preparatory works for the 1991 tax reform, the derivation of the tax rate is shown to be based on a rather simple calculation: a real interest rate of 3% and an inflation rate of 4% were anticipated. Thirty percent tax on a nominal interest rate of 7% means a tax of 2.1%, which is 70% of the real interest rate. This rate is roughly the same as (actually, some percentage points above) the rate for a high-income earner on earned income if social security contribution fees are included.

The inflation rate decreased after the tax reform and has been around 1-2 percentage points for the last decades, with the exception of 2023 and 2024, with the result that the real tax rate on capital was normally below what was expected; however, inflation is now considerably higher.

One reason for the choice of a flat tax is to counter tax planning. Moreover, because there is no basic allowance for income from capital and the tax rate is flat, there is no incentive to split income among family members. Further, for most types of assets, the full nominal amount of capital gains is taxable at realization, which reduces any incentive to transform capital income into capital gains.

Capital income includes current capital income—interest, dividends, etc.—and capital gains on realization of all types of assets and foreign debt (exchange gains). All types of capital income are taxable in full; as mentioned above, this is motivated by reasons of neutrality and equity and to decrease incentives for tax planning. However, some exceptions exist for personal property. For example, only around two-thirds of a capital gain from the sale of personal dwellings is taxable; for personal property, only capital gains above SEK 50,000 per year are taxable. Further, the taxation of capital gains on personal dwellings can be deferred if a new personal dwelling is bought.

In order to promote neutrality between persons who are able to invest out of equity capital and persons who need to borrow, interest costs are deductible for interest on loans for investments in equities, bonds, real estate (including owner-occupied dwellings), etc. Since 2024, interest on other types of loans (mainly loans for consumption) are deductible only to 50% and, from 2025, not at all. Income from capital is taxable at a flat rate of 30%. For losses from capital, 30% of the loss up to SEK 100,000, and 21% of the loss exceeding this amount is credited against national and local income tax due on earned income. The reduction of the tax credit to 21% for losses over SEK 100,000 was implemented to (somewhat) deter investments with front-loaded costs and deferred revenues.

The taxation of capital income also has a complicated relationship with the real estate tax, which is levied on most types of real estate. The Swedish income tax system has historically levied a tax on imputed income from owner-occupied dwellings, which was considered to be a tax on imputed capital income from these investments and could thus be said to form part of the system of capital income taxation. In the tax reform of 1991, the tax on imputed income was taken out of the income tax system and levied as a real estate tax; the tax rate was 1% of the assessed value, which should be 75% of the market value. In 2007, this tax was dramatically reduced to a municipal real estate fee capped at SEK 9,287 for 2023.[11] The rate of the fee is 0.75% on assessed values. Despite the considerable tax reduction, the deduction for interest cost was not changed.

5.2 Corporations

For corporations, all income is derived from one source, namely, income from business. A national income tax at a flat rate of 20.6% is levied on such income, although the effective tax rate is lower because up to 25% of the income can be set aside in a tax allocation reserve (*periodiseringsfond*) for six years. The intention is that, apart from that reserve, there should be no other special tax reserves, as had been the case under prior law, so that the tax is imposed on the effective income of corporations.

Special rules were introduced in 2008 to deny deductions for interest paid when such interest was created by advanced tax planning schemes. In 2018, general rules were introduced for a cap on deductions for interest. These rules are rather complicated; their design is in accordance with the EU Anti-tax Avoidance Directive (ATAD) (Directive (EU) 2016/1164). Interest deductions are limited to 30% of Earnings Before Interest, Taxes, Depreciation, and Amortization (EBITDA). The special rules are still in force, but in a somewhat less restrictive form. However, it is questionable whether these rules are in accordance with EU rules on freedom of capital movements, and presently the government is considering if they should be amended.

Income distributed from a corporation as dividends is taxed to individuals as income from capital at a tax rate of 30%. This means a combined tax rate of about 20.6% + (0.794 × 30%) = 44.42% on income earned by a corporation and distributed to its shareholders. In order to reduce the difference between the taxation of dividends and interest (30%), a lower tax rate applies to dividends distributed from

11. Municipal Real Estate Fee Act.

corporations whose shares are not quoted on an exchange. In such cases, the tax rate is 25 % and the combined tax on corporate and dividend income, calculated as shown above, is 40.45 %.

As stated above, the tax rate of income from employment and business for individuals is considerably higher than the tax rate of distributed income from corporations; this could create an incentive to transform earned income to capital income (dividends) by decreasing salaries from corporations in order to increase dividends, etc. When the dual system was introduced in the 1991 tax reform, some special provisions were introduced to counter this effect. The aim of these rules[12] is to ensure that income derived by shareholders from their corporations should be taxed at the rate applicable to earned income even where the income is distributed as dividends.

The rules apply to shares in closely held corporations, defined as corporations controlled by four or fewer persons (including close relatives), if owned by a person who is working to a considerable extent for the corporation. Where the rules apply, dividends above a certain threshold and capital gains are taxed as employment income for individuals. This results in roughly the same tax burden as for salaries paid by corporations (if dividends are paid, corporation tax is somewhat lower than social security contributions payable by corporations which pay salaries). The threshold is calculated as a normal yield on shareholders' investments. As a rule, the investment is calculated as the cost price for the shares; the yield rate is calculated as a long-term market interest rate plus nine percentage points. Further, the basis for calculating the threshold is increased, with an amount equal to 50 % of salaries paid to employees of the corporation. This can be a very large amount and thus, for many corporations, no dividends are in fact taxed as employment income. As an alternative to this calculation of the threshold, dividends up to SEK 195,250 can always be reported as income from capital. Dividends above this amount are taxed as employment income; dividends below this amount are considered to be the ordinary return on invested capital and are taxed as capital income, but at a special favorable tax rate of 20 %. The yield rate that establishes the amount of capital income is high. The overall result of this special regime is that many shareholders can avoid taxation of dividends as employment income. For most shareholders, taxation according to these special rules is more favorable than the normal taxation of shareholders, contrary to the original intent of the rules.

It is an important neutrality consideration that differences in the form of business should not result in differences in taxation. The rules for the taxation of individuals carrying on business have been expressly designed to be similar to the rules for the taxation of corporations (however, rules for the taxation of partnerships deviate in several aspects, mainly in order to prevent tax planning; these rules are not covered here). Income from business carried on directly by an individual is subject to social security contributions, local income tax, and (where the combined income for the individual is high enough) state income tax. The combined effect could result in a 63 % marginal tax rate for the highest income tax bracket (the tax burden on an individual

12. ITA, Chs. 56 and 57.

partner's share in a partnership's income is the same). According to the special rules described in the previous paragraph, the effective tax rate for distributions from closely held corporations is almost the same when dividends are taxed as earned income. Thus, the burden of taxation is almost the same in all three cases. However, as stated above, the rules for closely held corporations usually result in dividends seldom being taxed as income from employment, which to some extent results in non-neutral treatment.

The level of taxation for income retained in a corporation is 20.6%. Until 1995, income from businesses carried on by individuals was fully taxed irrespective of whether the income was retained in the business or used for private purposes. The present rules mitigate this hardship by allowing a deduction from income for the part of income retained in the business. The accumulated amount of such deductions may not exceed the net value (assets minus debts at cost) of the business, so that retained income is supposed to increase the net value of the business. A tax of 20.6% is paid on the deducted amount, which makes the tax equal to the tax on the undistributed income of corporations. A decrease in the net value of the business is considered to be a distribution of income, which triggers normal income taxation (less tax already paid of 20.6%). The accumulated amount of the deduction is referred to as the expansion reserve (*expansionsfond*).

6 TAX LEGISLATION

6.1 Legislative Process

Tax legislation is normally prepared by government committees or a sole government special investigator. A committee can be either parliamentary (where members of the committee are MPs) or an expert committee. Minor amendments or urgent legislation (e.g., anti-avoidance legislation) can be prepared directly by the Ministry of Finance.

SOUs are referred for consideration to central government agencies, special interest groups, courts, universities, or other bodies whose activities may be affected by the proposals. The government then presents a government bill (proposition) to Parliament (*Riksdagen*). For important proposals, the bill is preceded by a draft which is examined by three judges of the Supreme Court and the Supreme Administrative Court in the Law Council (*Lagrådet*). The bill is then scrutinized in Parliament by the Standing Committee for Taxation (*skatteutskottet*). Almost all tax legislation is included in the annual budget bill since that bill should include all legislation with major economic impact. As a result of this process, amendments in Parliament are rare. Government committees and investigations usually deal with rather comprehensive questions and can be active for years. The review process normally takes at least half a year and the remaining process in the Ministry and Parliament normally another half to a full year. Not all proposals result in immediate legislation. Some are aborted and others form the basis for further investigations in the Ministry by a new committee or a special investigator.

6.2 Statutory Style

Major changes in Swedish tax law are enacted through statutory rules. The statutes are written in a rather broad way, and therefore the courts have the possibility of creating law in some important cases. In recent years, especially since the tax reform of 1991, the tendency has been to codify case law into statutory rules.

The Swedish tax codes of the 1930s and following decades were written in a special way. There was first a fairly short principal statutory rule (paragraph); this rule was then explained in more detail in a regulation (which also was a statutory rule). In the beginning, the regulations were not intended to add any new content, but only to explain, and sometimes even contained arithmetical examples.

In 1999, the old municipal and national income tax laws were replaced with a new comprehensive tax law, the ITA. It has a modern structure in line with the standard for laws in Sweden and consists of sixty-six chapters. Each chapter is divided into several sections and subsections, with headings under which paragraphs are organized.

The statutory rules are quite detailed, although in the last few decades the aim has been to avoid complicated rules, and thereby complicated statutes. However, this is more a question of the structure of the system (avoiding different treatment of different types of income, etc.) than a question of statutory style. On the one hand, the general aim is to avoid enumerations and instead give a more abstract definition which is intended to give the courts the possibility of dealing with new developments (e.g., financial instruments) and place them in the proper categories. On the other hand, a lot of new mechanical rules have been introduced recently and, because of their mechanical character, the statutory rules regulating them are rather comprehensive. The need for greater clarity in statutes which impose tax has been emphasized in the past decade. This is partly a necessary reaction to a more literal interpretation of statutes by the courts and partly a result of increased respect for constitutional and other aspects. Increased predictability for taxpayers is also a goal, although it is not always easy to achieve. Thus, one can see an increasing tendency both to draft statutes more comprehensively and not to expect the courts to remedy shortcomings.

6.3 Statutory Interpretation

There is no uniform system of statutory interpretation in Sweden. In the Supreme Administrative Court (*Högsta förvaltningsdomstolen*), which handles tax cases and other administrative law matters, the method in general use is to give considerable value to opinions expressed in preparatory works to the legislation, primarily the government bill to Parliament. In some recent cases, however, a new tendency can be seen, with more willingness to ignore preparatory opinions when they are not clearly reflected in the statutes. There is also a tendency to use literal interpretation, or at least to give great weight to the literal meaning of statutes. Among academics, opinions vary regarding the degree of authority which should be given to preparatory works. In cases where the preparatory works and the statutory rule are clearly contradictory, there is a consensus that the statute cannot be set aside. Legislation based on EU directives lacks the traditional preparatory work and therefore also lacks that source of interpretation.

7 COURTS DEALING WITH TAX MATTERS

In the first instance, decisions by the tax authority may be reviewed by the authority itself. If the matter remains unresolved, the taxpayer may appeal to the administrative courts (*förvaltningsrätter*) and later to the administrative courts of appeal (*kammarrätter*). If the case is of importance to the interpretation of the law, the Supreme Administrative Court may grant leave to appeal and try the case. None of these courts are specialized tax courts; they deal with all types of administrative cases (cases where the national or local government is one of the parties). However, until the 1990s, tax cases were a clear majority of the cases heard by the courts; now, fewer cases are tax cases.

A special board (the Board for Advance Tax Rulings) gives advance rulings for important transactions. The board consists of two or three judges (active or former) and five or six laypersons (professors, tax officials, tax lawyers, etc.). Taxpayers can apply to the Board for a ruling with respect to planned transactions. The government, acting through the Tax Agency, may also apply for a ruling, but only for a pending case. Rulings can be appealed to the Supreme Administrative Court without the need for leave to be granted. Decisions of the Board are published on its website (www.skatterattsnamnden.se).

In principle, judgments take the same form in all courts. Facts and reasons forming the basis for the decision are presented. The court is normally presented with a proposal for judgment drafted by one of the judges or a special rapporteur. The Swedish tradition is not for judges to write individual decisions, but to adjust the proposal to arrive at a joint decision. Of course, dissenting opinions may be presented, and are attached to the judgment.

Judgments in the Supreme Administrative Court are more elaborate, due to better resources, access to the analysis in judgments by the lower courts, and their role as precedents. Cases decided by the Supreme Administrative Court are deemed to be binding on lower courts. There is no statutory rule to this effect, but, with rare exceptions, precedents are followed. The Supreme Administrative Court seldom changes a precedent, and when it does, the change must be made in a plenary session. Decisions of the Supreme Administrative Court are published on its website (Högsta förvaltningsdomstolen).

8 TAX ADMINISTRATION

The tax administration consists of the Tax Agency *(Skatteverket)* and its regional offices. In the past, there were different regional authorities, but they were merged into one single national tax authority. Tax officials are responsible for providing information to taxpayers, checking tax returns, etc. The Tax Agency issues nonbinding Tax Advice *(rättslig vägledning)* describing the state of law based on statutory rules, case law, and preparatory works. Tax Advice is published on the website of the Tax Agency (www.skatteverket.se).

For most taxpayers, the tax return is simplified, with statements of earnings, interest, etc., supplied by third parties (e.g., employers or banks) and prefilled tax returns. Tax returns are checked annually, although, in reality, many returns are not actively checked by the Tax Agency due to lack of resources.

In the last few decades, the number of tax field audits has been reduced considerably, partly because they now increasingly target larger corporations and more difficult cases. The Tax Agency also increasingly functions as a service administration instead of a control administration and, as a result, the Tax Agency is one of the most popular government agencies in Sweden.

The bulk of tax revenues is collected by withholding and prepayments. Taxes on income from business are pre-assessed in twelve installments per year; payments are registered in a special tax account for each taxpayer, and it is therefore possible to deviate from the predefined dates for installments. Where the final tax due exceeds the mandatory prepayments, further prepayments can be made to avoid interest charges.

In Sweden, it is a general principle that documents submitted to or from government agencies are accessible to the public. Exceptions to this rule are allowed only in accordance with the Official Secrets Act. The content of tax returns is secret, but the amount of total taxable income is made public. Similarly, proceedings and submissions in court cases dealing with taxation are secret but the judgments are public.

A surcharge is levied where a taxpayer has provided incorrect information in a tax return. The surcharge is normally 40% of the understated tax paid but is decreased to 20% in cases where the tax officials could have corrected the fault by using information from mandatory statements of earnings, previous years' tax returns, etc. The surcharge may not be levied in cases where the incorrect information is deemed to be excusable. These rules have, for the most part, been strictly applied by the courts and the surcharge is often considered to be disproportionately harsh. This led to widespread criticism. In a judgment concerning the Swedish surcharge, the European Court of Human Rights held that, although the system in general was not incompatible with the ECHR, certain rules were inappropriate and, as a result, new rules were enacted effective in 2004. The exemptions from the surcharge were widened and the possibility of partial exemption was introduced (the previous system gave courts only two alternatives, namely, full exemption or no exemption, which probably deterred them from giving exemptions). However, the courts have been rather reluctant to apply the partial surcharges.

Administrative surcharges are the most important penalties for misconduct. Criminal sanctions can be applied for more serious wrongdoing under the Tax Crime Code. The punishment for tax fraud is imprisonment for up to two years, and for serious tax fraud, up to six years. Judgments concerning administrative surcharges are normally delivered by the administrative courts, but judgments concerning the Tax Crime Code are delivered by the general courts. In accordance with case law from the European Court of Human Rights, this procedure has recently been amended so that in cases where both sanctions are applied, the judgment should be delivered by only one court, the general court (*ne bis in idem*).

9 GENERAL PRINCIPLES

9.1 Relation of Tax and Financial Accounting

Taxable business income is computed according to generally accepted accounting standards. Accounting profits form the basis for taxation. Corporations must follow the Annual Accounts Act of 1995 and the Book-Keeping Act of 1999 in preparing their financial statements. The Annual Accounts Act is based on the EU Fourth, Seventh, and Eleventh Directives. Credit institutions, brokers and dealers in securities, and insurance companies are covered by two special accounting acts. Accounting standards are established by the Swedish Accounting Standards Board *(Bokföringsnämnden, BFN)* and are published on the website of the Board (bfn.se). Larger corporations should instead follow International Financial Reporting Standards (IFRS).

In some instances, statutory tax rules, rather than accounting standards, specify how assets are to be valued and should then be applied. Annual depreciation of machinery and other equipment is allowed at 30% of the residual value or at 20% of the acquisition value. Buildings are depreciated by 2%-5% per year depending on their use. In the 1991 tax reform, the intention was that tax allowances should approximate commercial depreciation as closely as possible. This is the case for buildings, but tax depreciation for machinery may exceed commercial depreciation.

Where no statutory tax rule applies, accounting standards are applied. An important area where accounting standards apply on the cost side is the treatment of inventory; for example, research and development costs are normally deducted immediately instead of being included as part of inventory value.

The connection between tax accounting and accounting standards is broadly applicable, covering almost all revenues and some important costs. An advantage of this approach is a reduction in compliance costs and more neutral taxation where taxable income is closer to real (commercial) income. A disadvantage is the risk that accounting standards will be too conservative in order to avoid reporting results too early, although this risk is reduced because most accounting standards are based on International Accounting Standards. Another concern may be constitutional issues. Tax law should be enacted by Parliament, but to an important extent, it is now the result of decisions of private accounting boards. However, this could be seen as tax rules reflecting real life, with the possibility of Parliament changing the tax rules where accounting standards are considered to be inappropriate.

9.2 Respect for Legal Form

In general, words and concepts in tax laws which are similar to those in civil laws are interpreted in accordance with civil law. In many cases, the situation is not regulated in detail in civil law and has not been considered in Civil Court because the question of, for example, whether a contract should be considered a lease or a sale, has limited civil law consequences. In these circumstances, the tax courts must consider what the correct decision is based on civil law.

Legal form is respected as long as there is some economic substance behind the form. If a transaction is stated as, e.g., a lease in a contract, but is in substance a sale, it will be treated according to its real economic significance. However, for the most part, the courts are not willing to set the form aside when some substantial consequences of a contract are in accordance with the form. For instance, a sale and leaseback of real estate has been ruled to be treated as a sale, although it was most likely that the transaction in fact functioned as a loan with collateral. An important factor in this decision was that there existed some (however *ex ante* small) risk that the "lender" might be stuck with the real estate, with no right to repayment. Due to the vagueness of some civil law concepts, special tax aspects may be taken into consideration when interpreting the meaning of complicated transactions.

9.3 Anti-avoidance Doctrines and Rules

A special Tax Avoidance Act has been in force for several years. According to the Tax Avoidance Act *(Lagen om skatteflykt)*, transactions can be set aside if four conditions are fulfilled: (1) the transaction will result in a substantial tax reduction; (2) the taxpayer has directly or indirectly taken part in the transaction; (3) the main purpose of the transaction is the tax reduction; and (4) an assessment based on the form of the transaction contravenes the purpose of the relevant tax rules as interpreted from the relevant rules and the statutory tax rules in general. The law has seldom been used because it is hard to demonstrate that these conditions have been fulfilled.

The courts have been rather reluctant to use anti-avoidance doctrines other than the Tax Avoidance Act. As mentioned above, courts use only a restrictive form of the substance-over-form doctrine.

The application of the sham transactions doctrine is not controversial in principle, but it is sometimes hard to decide whether a transaction is a sham or not.

10 TAX TREATIES

Sweden has a large tax treaty network with over eighty-five comprehensive tax treaties, as well as over thirty-five agreements on the exchange of information. Sweden has treaties with its major trading partners and is a party to the Nordic multilateral convention. The Swedish treaty network largely follows the Organisation for Economic Co-operation and Development (OECD) Model treaty, with certain exceptions or deviations. The most important are:

- Article 5 largely follows the pre-Base Erosion and Profit Shifting (BEPS) Article 5, although a number of treaties, mostly concluded in the 1980s and 1990s, have a services PE provision.

- Article 7 largely follows the 2008 OECD Model, and sometimes the UN Model treaty, but, in principle, never follows the 2010 OECD version of Article 7 which implements the authorized OECD approach.
- Article 12 often deviates from the OECD Model, whether by allowing the state of source to levy royalties or by defining royalties in a broader manner than in the OECD Model.
- Article 13 often departs from the OECD Model with respect to the taxation of certain capital gains on the sale of shares. Sweden normally amends Article 13 in its tax treaties in order to safeguard a right to tax capital gains on shares in Swedish companies after a person becomes nonresident. The common practice is to shorten the duration of the taxing rights of Sweden from ten years in domestic law to a period of three to five years following the change of residence. Given Sweden's domestic law and treaty practice, Sweden has made a reservation on Article 13 of the OECD Model.
- Article 18 of the OECD Model is usually not preferred with respect to pensions since Sweden does not generally support the principle of exclusive taxation of pensions by the state of residence.
- Sweden has begun to adopt binding mandatory arbitration provisions in its treaties, largely inspired by Article 25(5) of the OECD Model. However, only a few treaties currently contain such a provision.
- Anti-avoidance provisions are increasingly included in Swedish treaties, albeit with varying wording.

Sweden is a dualist country, in which treaties must be implemented in domestic law through a separate act. The interpretation of tax treaties by Swedish courts often takes into account the Commentary on the OECD Model. However, the positions adopted in the Commentary are not considered to be binding, and the courts tend to follow a static approach whereby the Commentary which applied at the time of the conclusion of a treaty guides its interpretation. Later Commentaries may be taken into account where they do not differ materially from the contemporaneous Commentary.

Sweden has signed the *Multilateral Convention on Mutual Assistance in Tax Matters*. It has also signed the *Multilateral Convention to Implement Tax Treaty Related Measures to Prevent Base Erosion and Profit Shifting* (MLI), which has been ratified and entered into force on October 1, 2018. Over sixty treaties are listed as covered tax agreements. Sweden has made a reservation on all the provisions of the MLI (other than the minimum standards) but has adopted the optional part on arbitration.

11 SOURCES OF TAX LAW

Committee reports are published in the *SOUs* series and *Ministry publications* series *(Departementsserien, Ds)*. They are published on the website of the government: www.regeringen.se. Reports prior to 2000 are digitalized and published on the webpage sou.kb.se/.

Opinions expressed by the Law Council *(lagrådet)* are published on its webpage: www.lagradet.se.

Government bills are to be found on the webpage of the government: www.regeringen.se.

Statutes and amendments to statutes are published in the *Swedish Code of Statutes* (*Svensk Forfattningssamling*, SFS). The Swedish Parliament has a webpage with bills, committee reports, and statutes: www.riksdagen.se.

Case law is published in *The Annual Reporter of the Supreme Administrative Court (Högsta förvaltningsdomstolens årsbok)*. The Supreme Administrative Court also publishes recent cases on its webpage: Högsta förvaltningsdomstolen.se. Very few cases are translated to English. They can be found at www.domstol.se/en/supreme-administrative-court/rulings/.

Judgments from lower courts are not officially published. However, the Tax Agency publishes summaries of some judgments which it considers to be important. Advance rulings of the Board for Advance Rulings (*Skatterättsnämnden*) are published at www.skatterattsnamnden.se.

The Tax Agency publishes its general advice and information materials at www.skatteverket.se.

A large number of academic theses and monographs on tax issues are published. Two major tax journals (*Skattenytt* and *Svensk Skattetidning*) each publishes ten issues per year.

Accounting standards are published by the BFN: www.bfn.se.

Most of the web pages noted above contain pages in English, but with very limited content.

A comprehensive description of the development of the Swedish tax system is given in Henrekson and Stenkula (eds.), *Swedish Taxation: Developments since 1862* (Palgrave Macmillan, 2015).

A comprehensive textbook on Swedish income taxation is Melz, Silfverberg, Simon-Almendal and Persson Österman, *Inkomstskatt: en lärobok i skatterätt*, 20th edition (Studentlitteratur, 2024).

The Netherlands

Kees van Raad & Frank Pötgens

1 HISTORY OF THE NETHERLANDS INCOME TAX SYSTEM

An 1821 Act provided the first conceptual framework for the taxes existing at that time. Most of these taxes were excise taxes, except for the tax levied under the Patent Right Act of 1819, which was imposed on trades and businesses (operated under a license or "patent") according to their deemed income as apparent from external characteristics, such as the number of employees. The first true income taxes were introduced in 1892-1893. Income from capital was taxed under the Wealth Tax Act of 1892, under which income from capital was deemed to amount to 4% of the value of the capital. In addition, the Business Tax Act of 1893 imposed tax on income from business and employment activities.

The reason for taxing income under two separate acts was the intention to tax passive (unearned) income more heavily than active (earned) income. However, when the two acts were replaced by the (single) Income Tax Act (ITA) of 1914, in order to continue to subject wealthy individuals to a higher tax burden, an additional wealth tax was introduced in the same year. The 1914 income tax was levied, not on the income earned by taxpayers during the preceding year, but on the income that was assumed to be earned during the current year from income sources the taxpayer had at the beginning of that taxable year (May 1), and (i.e., the assumption) on the basis of the actual amount of income derived from such sources in the preceding year. As a result, disposing of income sources just before May 1 became a widespread tactic to avoid taxation on income from such sources. Although initially the 1914 ITA also covered the income of companies, in 1918 it was replaced for companies by a special tax on corporate distributions, while undistributed income remained tax-free.

Germany occupied The Netherlands in 1940. In 1941, the German occupier introduced an individual income tax and, in 1942, a company income tax, both based to a large extent on existing German taxes and both taxing real income (rather than deemed income, as was the case under the previous individual ITA). Although after the war both tax acts were substantially amended, it was not until the 1960s that they were replaced by the ITA of 1964 (for individuals) and by the Company Tax Act (CTA) of 1969. At the time they were enacted, these two statutes, which still reflected many of the concepts of the old tax codes introduced by Germany, were models of clear and concise tax legislation—as introduced, each of these acts was less than twenty print pages. However, as a consequence of a considerable decrease in tax morality in The Netherlands from the 1970s on and the subsequent (international) avoidance tactics resorted to by individual and corporate resident and nonresident taxpayers, the government was forced to add to both tax codes complex and detailed counteracting measures which often contained elements of overkill; this in turn led to further taxpayer reactions and, on the government side, to increases in both the size and detail of tax statutes and a corresponding reduction in their conciseness and clarity.

In the 1980s, The Netherlands joined the worldwide move toward rate reduction and base broadening of the income tax. In addition, it paid some lip service to tax simplification. Tax simplification, however, remained restricted mainly to the replacement of a detailed rate structure in the individual income tax by three tax brackets and an integration of individual income tax rates and general social security contributions. A government commission was appointed in the early 1990s to make recommendations for a true simplification of the individual income tax law, but its proposals received only lukewarm support from the government. In the late 1990s, however, an ambitious State Secretary of Finance developed blueprints for a partial return to the 1892 roots of the Dutch individual income tax system: the ITA 2001 provides for three schedules ("boxes") of income (income from "work and home," from "substantial interests," and from "capital"). The last box provides for taxation on a deemed-yield basis determined—as in 1892—as a percentage of the underlying assets which was initially fixed at 4%, with some later modifications. As a result, however, of a December 2021 Supreme Court decision that the application of deemed-yield rates much above the actual yields earned by the taxpayer violates human rights, the rules are now under a comprehensive review.

2 CONSTITUTIONAL ISSUES

2.1 In General

Under Article 104 of the Dutch Constitution, the State (i.e., the national government) is entitled to levy any taxes, provided that they are based on a statute. In addition to such national taxes, taxes may also be imposed by local public authorities (provinces, municipalities, and water authorities) but under Articles 132(6) and 133(2) of the Constitution, these local authorities are restricted to the taxes enumerated in the pertinent statutes (the 1992 Act on Provinces, the 1992 Act on Municipalities, and the 1991 Act on Water Authorities). While municipalities may impose an (annual) tax on the value of real property, provinces and water boards are generally restricted to levying user fees. The budgetary needs of provinces and municipalities, however, are met mostly through revenue-sharing with the national government.

2.2 Impact of Human Rights Conventions and EU Treaty Fundamental-Freedom Provisions

Under Dutch constitutional rules, statutory law (including tax law) cannot be challenged for a presumed violation of any Dutch constitutional provision. Therefore, individuals and companies cannot invoke the general non-discrimination clause laid down in Article 1 of the Dutch Constitution. For this reason, the non-discrimination provisions in the human rights conventions to which The Netherlands is a party are of greater importance in The Netherlands than in other countries as they provide the only basis for challenging discriminatory tax rules. In addition to the various human rights conventions, courts in The Netherlands frequently refer to the Charter of the Fundamental Rights of the European Union (EU) which, as part of primary EU law, contains rights similar to those of human rights conventions.[1]

In addition, the fundamental-freedom provisions of the Treaty on the Functioning of the European Union (TFEU), notably those on the freedom of workers (Article 45), the freedom of establishment (Article 49), and the freedom of capital (Articles 63-66), have been held by the Court of Justice of the European Union (CJEU) to prevent differential tax treatment of nonresident taxpayers. For example, in a 2008 decision,[2] the CJEU found that mortgage interest paid by a resident of Belgium on his Dutch dwelling was deductible from his Dutch salary income by virtue of Article 45 TFEU, despite the fact that under the Netherlands-Belgium tax treaty (positive and negative) income from immovable property situated in the taxpayer's residence state is taxable only in that state and income from employment exercised in The Netherlands is fully (without reduction by unrelated expenses such as mortgage interest) taxable in The Netherlands. Similarly, in a 2014 decision,[3] the CJEU found, based on Article 49, that a fiscal unity for corporate income tax purposes (group relief; *see* section 5.2 below) could be formed between two Dutch-resident subsidiaries (sisters) all the shares of which were held by a non-Dutch EU-resident parent company.

3 INCOME TAX RATES

In the current individual ITA 2001, separate rate structures apply to the three income schedules ("boxes"). In the first box (income from home and work) income is taxed at the following rates (2024)[4] applicable to both the income tax and the wages tax:

Taxable Income (EUR)	*Tax Rate (%)*
up to 75,518	36.97[5]
from 75,518	49.50

1. *See* the Introduction for a brief discussion of European institutions and tax laws.
2. CJEU, October 16, 2008, C-527/06 (*Renneberg*).
3. Joint Cases C-39/13, C-40/41, and C-41/1, June 12, 2014 (*SCA*, *X AG et al.*, and *MSA*).
4. The same rates apply to the wages tax.
5. Since 1990, the individual income tax rates have been combined with the contributions for general social security. Because social security contributions are due only in respect of an amount

The second box comprises ordinary income and capital gains (jointly: "gains") derived by an individual from a "substantial interest": a share interest of at least 5% in a company. From January 1, 2024, the rates applicable to Box 2 gains are 24.50% for the amount of gains up to EUR 67,000 and 33% for the excess amount.

Capital income is taxed in the third box. This income is determined on the basis of a deemed yield of capital assets and debts. The deemed-yield rates vary with the category of capital. The deemed-yield percentages for 2023[6] (to be applied to the deemed value of the capital assets on January 1, 2023) are:

- for balances of bank accounts: 0.01%;
- for investments and other assets: 6.17% (provisional).

The amount of the deemed (negative) "yield" from debts, which is computed at a (2023 provisional) deemed percentage of 2.46%, is deducted from the combined amount of the computed yields of these two categories of assets (bank accounts, investments and other assets) resulting in an overall "taxable net yield" amount (*belastbaar rendement* or "BR" amount). Next, the amount of "net capital" (*rendementsgrondslag* or "RG" amount) is computed by deducting the taxpayer's debts from the total amount of their assets. From this balance, the tax-free base amount is deducted, resulting in the amount of "taxable net capital" (*grondslag sparen en beleggen* or "GSB" amount). Finally, the fraction GSB/RG is computed and applied to the BR amount, resulting in the deemed amount of Box 3 income. To this amount the tax rate of 36% (in 2024) is applied.

Dividends are subject to a withholding tax of 15%, creditable against the income tax liability of residents and of nonresidents receiving dividends attributable to Dutch-source income for which they are subject to ordinary taxation. In addition, since 2021 interest and royalties (and, as of January 1, 2024, dividends) paid by a resident company to an associated company in a low- or no-tax country or paid in particular abuse cases are subject to a withholding tax at a rate equal to the higher rate of the (dual rate)[7] corporate income tax: 25.8% (in 2022, 2023 and 2024).

4 COMPOSITION OF THE FISCAL SYSTEM

	2024 Budget	*2023 Provisional Result*
	x EUR 1,000	*x EUR 1,000*
Taxes on consumption (indirect taxes)	122,903	115,299
import duties	4,964	4,711
turnover tax (Value-Added Tax (VAT))	80,383	78,148

of income of approximately EUR 40,000 and taxpayers past the general retirement age (as of January 1, 2024: 67 years) are exempt from individual contributions, the rate they pay on the income tranche up to approximately EUR 40,000 is 19.07%.

6. At the time this chapter was finalized, the percentages for 2024 were not yet available.
7. 19% on the first EUR 200,000 of company income and 25.8% on the excess amount.

	2024 Budget	*2023 Provisional Result*
	x EUR 1,000	*x EUR 1,000*
purchase tax on cars and motorcycles	1,495	1,466
excise taxes	13,915	11,712
tax on legal transactions	7,617	7,202
use tax on cars and motorcycles	4,910	4,572
environmental taxes	5,870	6,488
other	1,358	970
Taxes on income (direct taxes) & general social security levies	155,115	145,549
income tax (incl. gen. soc. sec. levies)	12,177	10,973
wages tax (incl. gen. soc. sec. levies)	79,484	75,530
dividend tax	6,497	6,365
company tax	48,685	46,475
gift & inheritance tax	2,958	2,932
other	1,455	1,424
Total taxes and general social security levies	278,382	261,209
Employee social security levies	91,785	85,353
Total taxes and social security levies	402,943	386,452

5 BASIC STRUCTURE OF THE INCOME TAX

5.1 Individuals

The income of individuals is subject to income tax under the ITA 2001. In addition to income tax, earnings from current or past employment and social security payments are subject to wage withholding tax (Wages Tax Act of 1964, or WTA—*Wet op de loonbelasting 1964*). Withheld wages tax is creditable against any income tax due. However, if the resulting amount of income tax exceeds a threshold amount (2024: EUR 51) no income tax is due and the amount of wages tax withheld is final.

Dividends distributed by a Netherlands-resident company are subject to a 15% tax (Dividend Tax Act, or DivTA), withheld by the company and creditable against the recipient's individual income tax liability (usually as "Box 3" capital income). In 2021, a withholding tax was introduced on interest and royalties (in 2024 extended to dividends) paid by a resident company to a related corporate recipient resident in a low- or no-tax jurisdiction.

With regard to income taxation of individuals, Dutch tax law employs the concept of "source of income": only income derived from a "source" is taxable. This term does not refer to the territorial source of the income, i.e., the source concept used by most countries to distinguish between domestic source and foreign source income. Rather, "source of income" refers to instances where taxpayers engage in economic activity with the intention of deriving a benefit, and where such a benefit can objectively be expected to materialize. Consequently, activities which are not expected to produce any positive amount of income (hobby farms, "inventing," etc.) are not considered to constitute a source of income, with the result that expenses incurred engaging in such activities cannot be used to offset other (taxable) income.

Nonbusiness capital gains realized by individuals are generally not subject to tax, with the exception of capital gains derived on the disposition of so-called substantial interest shares, i.e., a share interest of at least 5% in the capital of a company. Before the ITA 2001 came into effect, the absence of a general capital gains tax, combined with high tax rates on ordinary income, created a strong incentive for taxpayers to try to convert (taxable) ordinary income into a (tax-free) capital gain or a (lower-taxed) substantial-interest gain. One of the important aims of the introduction of ITA 2001 was to eliminate such avoidance tactics by taxing capital income on a deemed basis and by lowering the tax rate on ordinary income from substantial interest shares to the same tax rate as on capital gains realized on the disposition of those shares.

If an individual transfers property to a trust, fund, foundation, etc. which has been set up for the private benefit of, e.g., their family, the fund may be found to qualify as a "private wealth fund" ("APV" or *Afgezonderd Particulier Vermogen*), with the consequence that for tax purposes the assets remain attributed to the individual who established the fund (or to the heirs).[8]

5.2 Corporations

Companies are taxed on the basis of the Corporate Income Tax Act of 1969 (CITA, *Wet op de vennootschapsbelasting 1969*). All income earned by a company is deemed to be business income. For the general rules on the determination of business income, the CITA refers to the ITA. The CITA itself contains detailed rules on, *inter alia*:

- the participation exemption (Article 13-13k CITA). Dividends received from a qualifying shareholding ("participation") in a resident or nonresident subsidiary company are exempt from tax in the hands of the parent company. Similarly, capital gains realized on the disposition of shares of such subsidiary company are exempt;
- corporate reorganizations (exchange of assets for stock: Article 14 CITA; exchange of stock for stock: Article 13i; legal merger: Article 13k (in connection with Article 3.57 ITA 2001); legal division: Article 13j (in connection with Article 3.56 ITA 2001)). Gains realized in such reorganizations are granted tax deferral. The domestic deferral provisions have been extended to the cross-border reorganizations that are covered by the EU 1990 Merger Directive;

8. ITA, Art. 2.14a.

- the fiscal unity regime (Article 15-15a CITA). On the request of all group companies involved, the income of qualifying subsidiaries is taxed to the common parent company.

Further, in the last decade complex rules have been enacted to counter the erosion of the corporate tax base through the deduction of interest payments (particularly to nonresident recipients). As of January 1, 2019, these rules have been extended through the implementation of the EU Anti-tax Avoidance Directive 1 (ATAD 1), which provides for an earnings-stripping rule (Article 4).[9] This rule limits the deductibility of the "excess" net interest expense amount (i.e., interest costs in excess of interest income, including foreign exchange results on the loans). The excess amount, with an exception for the first EUR 1 million, is deductible for tax purposes only up to 20% of the adjusted Dutch taxable profit (Earnings Before Interest, Taxes, Depreciation, and Amortization (EBITDA)).

6 TAX LEGISLATION

6.1 Tax Legislative Process

While Parliament has a constitutional right of legislative initiative, virtually all bills are introduced in Parliament by the government, after the advice of the Council of State has been obtained. The bills are discussed in several rounds in the full Second Chamber of Parliament, which has the right of amendment (through a "motion" introduced by one or more members of this Chamber). The government, which also may amend a pending bill, has the right to withdraw a bill it has introduced. After a bill has been approved by the Second Chamber, it is introduced in the First Chamber of Parliament, which may approve or reject the bill but has no right of amendment.

6.2 Statutory Style

With the exception of the ITA 2001, the tax acts with respect to income taxation (CITA, WTA, and DTA) were drafted in the 1960s. At that time, their overall design was intended to provide a clear and lean framework of fundamental rules. The predecessor of the current (2001) ITA, the 1964 ITA (with provisions on taxable persons, categories of taxable income, personal deductions, loss compensation, tax rates, and special rules) comprised less than twenty pages in most text editions. The other acts were even briefer. Practical details and other specific matters (*inter alia*, amounts which may change frequently, lists, etc.) were typically relegated to implementing decrees. By 1996, the size of the 1964 ITA had grown to more than four times its original size. Its successor, ITA 2001, while still clearly structured, was on its introduction almost 50% longer than its predecessor and reflects the continuing tendency to counteract undesirable tax-planning techniques with detailed provisions.

9. CITA, Art. 15b.

The 1969 CITA has been greatly expanded over the last two decades. Very detailed rules have been added with respect to participation exemptions, fiscal unity, and anti-base-erosion measures. These additions have obfuscated the Act's original well-balanced structure. Largely as a result of the government's continued attempts to counter particular tax avoidance practices, highly detailed rules have been inserted, greatly adding to the size and affecting the accessibility of the statute (*see also* section 5.2 above).

The individual and company ITAs, along with the wages, dividend, and other direct tax acts and implementing decrees, currently comprise well over 750 pages in a typical print edition.

Interpretive decrees have been issued by the Minister of Finance with respect to many individual and company income tax provisions. If the position adopted in such a decree is more favorable to taxpayers than it would be under a strict application of the statute or an implementing decree, taxpayers are entitled to rely on that interpretation when preparing their tax returns. To the extent that a position taken by the Minister of Finance appears to be stricter than the law, taxpayers may challenge that interpretation in court.

Newly enacted tax legislation, like all law, is generally not retroactively effective. In a 1996 memorandum, however, the government took the position that the retroactive effect of newly enacted tax rules may be justified in three situations: countering abuse in cases that need to be addressed swiftly to prevent further budget loss, correcting an obvious legislative error as a result of which government tax claims may be lost, and the announcement of a new rule, as a result of which taxpayers will likely put plans into effect quickly before the new law stops such actions.

6.3 Statutory Interpretation

The Dutch Constitution includes a broad non-discrimination rule. It also provides that taxes may be levied only on the basis of a statute. The Constitution, however, further provides that courts may not test the constitutionality of statutes, including tax statutes. While this constitutional restriction is currently under discussion, as noted in section 2.2, courts may check the compatibility of possibly discriminatory statutory provisions with the non-discrimination provisions of the human rights conventions.

Because statutory tax provisions may not always be fully clear and thus require interpretation, a substantial body of case law has been developed over the years on the interpretation of statutory law in general and tax statutes in particular. In general, four methods are applied, without any clear hierarchy among them. The "grammatical" method stresses the literal meaning of statutory terms. The "historical" method emphasizes the importance of the official Explanatory Memoranda published by the government when introducing a bill in Parliament, and other parliamentary memoranda and records of debates. Further, there is the "systematic" method, which pays particular attention to the structure and cohesion of the relevant statute and, finally, the "teleological" method, under which the purpose and intent of the statute are decisive factors in its interpretation. Since courts are free to choose the means of interpretation in tax matters, there is no prevailing order for the use of these four methods.

7 COURTS DEALING WITH TAX MATTERS

If a tax dispute is not resolved on review within the tax administration, taxpayers may appeal to one of five District Courts (*Rechtbanken*) that have been designated to hear tax cases. The decisions of these courts can be appealed to one of the four regional Courts of Appeal (*Gerechtshoven*), and further appeal can be made to the Supreme Court (*Hoge Raad*). Each of these courts has one or more special chambers to hear tax cases. In important cases which are appealed to the Supreme Court, one of the "advocates general" (official advisers) to the Supreme Court issues an advisory opinion ("conclusion") to the court before it renders its judgment. Since January 1, 2016, for reasons of expediency, when dealing in a case with a general question of Dutch tax law, a lower court is permitted to request the Supreme Court to issue a preliminary ruling on the matter.[10] If the Supreme Court issues such a ruling (it may refuse if it considers the issue not to be sufficiently important), the lower court is bound to apply it.

Strictly speaking, court decisions are binding only for the particular case that is decided. In practice, however, they carry much greater weight, particularly when the court's considerations are broader than required by the case that is decided. Nevertheless, in instances where the government strongly disagrees with a particular decision of the Supreme Court, it may submit to the Court a similar case on the same issue. If the Court maintains its position, the government will often consider introducing in Parliament a statutory amendment that changes the law.

Decisions by Dutch courts do not include dissenting opinions. Consequently, court opinions may be quite brief since they are restricted to what the court members (for important cases: three at the District Courts and Courts of Appeal, and five at the Supreme Court) are able to agree on. Occasionally, the grounds given for a decision are phrased so tersely that the decision reads like an oracular statement from Delphi, giving ample room for divergent interpretations.

Tax proceedings are not public and published decisions are anonymous. Interestingly, the courts themselves select which cases to publish. While it appears that most cases that are not made public are of interest only to the litigating parties, in the past significant decisions have occasionally not been made public or were published much later. There is a growing sentiment to give an independent authority the power to select court decisions in tax matters for publication.

One final aspect concerns prospective overruling. In the 1990s, the Supreme Court issued a few decisions in which it overruled its earlier case law prospectively only—i.e., it protected the taxpayer concerned who had relied on the existing case law and ruled that it would not apply its new viewpoint to that case, but that it would apply it in the next suitable case.

10. General Taxes Act, Art. 27ga-27ge.

8 TAX ADMINISTRATION

8.1 In General

The Ministry of Finance is headed by the minister of Finance assisted by two state secretaries. The minister is primarily responsible for Budget and Treasury; one state secretary is responsible for the Revenue service and the central Directorate General for Tax Affairs, and the other state secretary for the central Directorates General for Customs and for Income Supplements.

Until the 1980s, the Revenue Service was highly decentralized, with local offices in some 100 cities and towns, many of these offices with separate divisions for the individual taxes administered (individual income tax, corporate income tax, turnover tax, inheritance tax, custom duties, etc.) As a result, in their dealings with the tax administration, companies typically would have to deal with different officials for each of the taxes to which it was subject (company tax, wages tax, turnover tax, and, occasionally, dividend tax and tax on legal transactions).

In the 1980s, the tax administration underwent a complete overhaul to change it from a government-oriented into a taxpayer-oriented organization. Departments and their divisions merged and, to the extent that they did not merge, each (corporate) taxpayer was assigned a coordinating official who generally acts as the single contact for the company for the various taxes of the company. To the extent questions arise that are outside the area of expertise of this official, such questions would be referred to an official in charge of the relevant tax. In addition, separate audits for company income tax, wages tax, and turnover tax were replaced by combined audits. A further step toward improving the relationship between the tax administration and taxpayers was the introduction in 2005 of "horizontal supervision," particularly for business taxpayers. The tax administration aims at concluding covenants with large and medium-size enterprises which replace audits by monitored agreements on the taxpayer's administrative processes. They also provide for mutual consultations and discussions of changes and developments in a company's business activities. The overall aim is, through transparency and partnership, to create greater certainty for taxpayers regarding their tax position and fewer conflicts regarding the tax consequences of events that have already taken place.

8.2 Taxpayer Bill of Rights: Ombudsman

Along with the reorganization of the tax administration, attempts were made to further improve the position of taxpayers vis-à-vis the Revenue Service. In 1991, the Ministry of Finance promulgated a "Taxpayers' Bill of Rights," after the example of the United States. In The Netherlands, however, the importance of this Bill is more psychological than real because the Bill is mainly restricted to restating taxpayers' statutory rights.

Of more substantive importance to taxpayers, however, has been the extension of the scope of the government's actions in respect of which the "Ombudsman" (an independent authority with which complaints against government may be lodged) is entitled to receive complaints from resident individuals and companies or to undertake investigations on the Ombudsman's own initiative. The Ombudsman is not permitted to investigate general government policy or individual cases where taxpayers have access to regular administrative or judicial remedies. Despite these restrictions, the Ombudsman is called on by taxpayers in a large number of cases, and in a substantial number of these cases has found that the government had been acting partly or wholly in an inappropriate manner. While the Ombudsman has no legal means to enforce any of its findings, its reports to the Revenue Service suggesting specific remedial action are usually effective in inducing the government to implement the recommendations.

8.3 Release of Government Information to Taxpayers

The 2022 Act on Open Government (*Wet open overheid* or WOO), replacing a 1991 statute, provides taxpayers and their advisers with an important instrument for obtaining insight into tax administration policy, both in general and in individual cases. Refusals by government bodies to make the requested information fully available can be appealed to the (administrative law chambers of) district courts and courts of appeal and, eventually, to the Council of State (*Raad van State*), The Netherlands' highest administrative court.

The requested information may range from audit reports on individual taxpayers (under current case law, the entire report must be made available to the taxpayer except for those parts containing information on sensitive issues such as audit strategies) to internal government studies, private rulings, etc.

8.4 Advance Rulings

Advance rulings are typically issued at a request submitted by Dutch and foreign companies engaged in international operations. They have been issued for many decades. In 2002, the procedures for obtaining a ruling were streamlined following inquiries by the EU and the Organisation for Economic Co-operation and Development (OECD) into unfair tax competition. Under the current rules, advance pricing agreements (APAs) are issued with regard to transfer pricing (establishing, e.g., the arm's length remuneration of Dutch-based entities providing intragroup services). In addition, advance tax rulings (ATRs) are available to deal with various aspects of international tax structures, such as:

- the application of the participation exemption to conduit companies in international structures and to top holding companies where none of the subsidiaries of the top holding company is conducting any business activity in The Netherlands;
- international structures involving hybrid finance and/or hybrid legal entities;
- whether or not a nonresident entity may be regarded as having a permanent establishment in The Netherlands; and

- the attribution to a permanent establishment in The Netherlands of shares in companies resident in The Netherlands.

APAs and ATRs are administered by a dedicated "APA/ATR team." As of January 1, 2014, this APA/ATR team was also given the mandate to decide on requests of nonresident taxpayers for tax treaty benefits within the framework of "safety-net rules" included in the anti-abuse provisions of Dutch tax treaties.[11]

For rulings issued on or after July 1, 2019, a new international ruling practice is applicable. Under this new ruling policy, a tax ruling is granted only: (i) where the taxpayer has a so-called economic nexus with The Netherlands, (ii) where saving Dutch or foreign tax is not the sole or decisive purpose for entering into the transaction for which a ruling is sought, or (iii) a tax avoidance structure is dismantled. A ruling will not be granted in situations where (i) the dismantling results in untaxed or low-taxed income elsewhere against which there is depreciation potential in The Netherlands, or (ii) in transactions with related parties established in countries listed in the Regulation on low-tax and non-cooperative jurisdictions. An additional feature of this new policy is the publication of anonymized summaries of rulings, including summaries of ruling applications which have been denied.

Under a 2015 EU Council Directive, many types of rulings issued by the Dutch Revenue Service are now automatically exchanged with the tax authorities of other EU Member States and are spontaneously exchanged with the tax authorities of other non-EU states.[12]

8.5 Assessment, Administrative Appeal, and Appeal to Courts

For individual income tax and corporate income tax, a tax inspector issues a tax assessment after having reviewed the tax return filed by the taxpayer and the taxpayer's answers to any questions which the inspector may have asked. In practice, the review of individual income tax returns is largely automated, with software selecting returns with unusual aspects that warrant individual review. Failure to provide adequate answers to any question from the tax inspector may result in the burden of proof shifting from the inspector, with whom it usually rests, to the taxpayer.

For business taxpayers, since 1990, the tax administration has undertaken efforts to have companies agree to "horizontal supervision" covenants (*see* section 8.1 above). Previously, an inspector would have a company audited every few years, with the 200 largest companies subject to a field audit every year. Through "horizontal supervision," the number of field audits has been reduced substantially, with a simultaneous lessening of the adversarial nature of relations between taxpayers and the revenue authorities.

The wages tax, value-added tax (VAT) and dividend tax are self-assessment taxes. Where a tax inspector disagrees with the self-assessed amount, a supplemental

11. Government Gazette 2013, No. 35978, December 31, 2013.
12. Council Directive 2015/2376/EU, December 8, 2015.

assessment (with or without a penalty) may be issued. This assessment is subject to administrative appeal by taxpayers.

The decision made by a tax inspector on an appeal lodged against an assessment may be appealed to the one of five District Courts (*Rechtbanken*). Taxpayers do not require representation by a lawyer for making such an appeal. Cases are heard in a District Court by one- or three-member panels of judges, who usually have a background in tax law and are recruited from the circles of senior government tax officials, senior tax advisers, and tax academics. In addition, prominent tax advisers and tax professors may serve as part-time deputy judges. A decision by a District Court may be appealed to one of the four Courts of Appeal, which review both the finding of the facts and the application of the law. A further appeal, but restricted to issues of law, can be made to the Supreme Court (*Hoge Raad*). In addition to a Civil Chamber and a Criminal Chamber, the Supreme Court has a Tax Chamber with two divisions each consisting of five justices (typically four of them with a tax background). The Supreme Court has no right to refuse to hear a case (no *certiorari*) but may decide to issue a summary judgment rejecting the appeal without giving reasons (other than that the case does not deserve review).

On complex issues presented to the Supreme Court, one of the five Advocates General of the Tax Chamber of the Court may issue in advance an Advisory Opinion to the Court. These opinions usually provide excellent analyses of the law at issue. The number of tax appeals, which has been rising over the last two decades, seems to have stabilized at an annual number of about 13,000 per year for appeals to any of the four Courts of Appeal, and at about 750 per year for further appeals to the Supreme Court.

9 GENERAL PRINCIPLES

9.1 Relationship Between Tax and Financial Accounting

In The Netherlands, the rules on tax accounting and commercial (financial) accounting diverge substantially. Whereas the aim of commercial accounting (including the International Financial Reporting Standards (IFRS) rules which, since 2005, have been compulsory in the EU for quoted companies) is to provide the information necessary to judge the financial policy and operations of a business undertaking, the purpose of tax accounting is to determine the income of a business operation as the basis for paying tax to the government. While the two goals partially overlap, there are important differences with respect to the degree of discretion in making accounting choices and the impact of inflation. With regard to inflation, tax accounting rules are generally "nominalist"—i.e., they require amounts to be taken into account at their nominal value without loss of value as a result of inflation being taken into account, whereas commercial accounting rules are "substantialist" and take into account the effects of inflation. Further, with regard to the valuation of assets and liabilities, tax rules are generally rather strict and conservative compared to commercial accounting rules. Finally, differences between tax and commercial accounting rules arise where tax legislation is employed to pursue economic, social, and cultural purposes.

9.2 Respect under Tax Law for the Civil (Private) Law Form of Contracts

Whereas Dutch tax law employs many terms and concepts that are based on civil (private) law, these terms and concepts do not necessarily have the same meaning for tax law purposes as they have under civil law. Under current doctrine, while civil law terms and concepts used in tax law are generally understood to have their civil law meaning, the aim and purpose of a particular tax law provision may justify giving to a particular term a meaning that differs from its general civil law meaning.

9.3 Anti-avoidance Doctrines and Rules

The application of tax law rules generally involves three steps. First, it must be ascertained whether what is presented as a fact is indeed a fact. Next, it must be determined whether the (truly existing) facts are to be recognized for tax purposes. Finally, the law must be applied to these ascertained and recognized facts. At either of the last two levels, the issue of substance over form may arise.

For tax law purposes, facts need not be accepted by the tax authorities as presented by the taxpayer—something presented as a fact may not be a fact. For example, if a hobby artist donates a painting to a local museum in order to obtain a charitable deduction, the "gift" may be found to be nonexistent if the painting is found to be worthless ("simulation": nonexistent facts are suggested to be true facts.) To the extent that facts—or legal situations—truly exist, the next step is to examine whether they should be recognized for tax purposes or whether, on the basis of their substance, they should be recharacterized. For example, while funds obtained through embezzlement are legally not income because the recipient may be under the legal obligation to return the funds to the owner, for tax purposes the amount may be recognized as income (with any later repayment constituting deductible negative income). Other examples include rental income in situations where a lessee is related to the lessor and pays an unrealistically low rent, and income from a void contract that nevertheless has been implemented.

After the facts have been accepted for tax purposes, the courts may apply the (case law based) *fraus legis* doctrine to attach to facts tax consequences different from the consequences which these facts normally entail. While taxpayers are generally free to organize their affairs in a manner which is most advantageous to them from a tax viewpoint, there are limits to this freedom. One such limit is reached when a taxpayer (alone, or in collaboration with other taxpayers) is able to reduce the amount of tax liability entirely at the taxpayer's own discretion (e.g., where a parent company pays tax-deductible interest to its subsidiary company on a loan obtained from the subsidiary, and the subsidiary subsequently returns the interest it received from the parent to the parent as a tax-free intercorporate dividend).

In applying the *fraus legis* doctrine, the following requirements must be met: (1) the nontax effects of the extraordinary (nontaxable) situation created by the taxpayer are identical or similar to those of the more ordinary (taxable) situation; (2) tax avoidance is the controlling ("primary") motive of the taxpayer; and (3) the tax effects of the situation created by the taxpayer conflict with the purpose and intent of the tax law.

While before 1970 *fraus legis* (and a related statutory substance-over-form rule) were rarely applied, since the 1980s the number of cases involving the application of this doctrine has substantially increased in both the lower courts and the Supreme Court. Many of these cases involve the erosion of the corporate tax base through interest payments and, with respect to individuals, the taxation of income derived from closely held companies (*see* section 5.2 above). So far, the courts have restricted the application of this doctrine to national law and have refused to extend it to tax treaties. Consequently, nonresident taxpayers (particularly former resident individuals of The Netherlands) have been successful in shielding their transactions from the application of *fraus legis*.

Effective January 1, 2019, the EU ATAD 1 was implemented by EU Member States, with the domestic implementing rules effective from that date. The General Anti-avoidance Rule (GAAR) in ATAD 1 has not been implemented by The Netherlands in a statutory rule since this rule is assumed to be covered by the court-developed *fraus legis* doctrine. An addition (ATAD 2) to the original ATAD Directive provides for measures against hybrid mismatches. As of January 1, 2020, the ATAD 2 was implemented in the Dutch CIT. The provisions of ATAD 2 combat hybrid mismatches by neutralizing the effects of differences in qualification between tax systems regarding financial instruments and entities. In addition, as of January 1, 2022, the tax liability measure for reverse hybrid entities became effective; it ensures that, under certain circumstances, the country of residence must follow the qualification of the country where the participants are located with respect to entities treated as transparent.

As of January 1, 2022, an additional transfer pricing rule entered into force. This rule limits a downward adjustment to the taxpayer's arm's length profit to the extent that the other party to the transaction does not make an upward adjustment to its tax base or makes a corresponding upward adjustment that is too low. The rule thus aims to neutralize transfer pricing differences and to avoid situations of double non-taxation (a deduction without an inclusion or a double deduction).

10 TAX TREATIES

As of October 2023, The Netherlands had ninety-six comprehensive income tax treaties, 7 inheritance tax treaties, and 31 Tax Information Exchange Agreements in force. It had also concluded treaty-like arrangements with its former Caribbean colonies Curaçao (2015),[13] Aruba (1964),[14] and St. Maarten (2015)[15] and, in addition, a special arrangement with the remaining three islands (Bonaire, St. Eustatius, and Saba), which until 2010 were individual countries of the Kingdom of The Netherlands but as of that year became special-status public bodies of The Netherlands.

13. Belastingregeling Nederland-Curaçao (the Netherlands-Curaçao Tax Arrangement).
14. Until 2015, the 1964 arrangement applicable to Aruba also applied to Curaçao and St. Maarten.
15. Belastingregeling Nederland-Sint Maarten (The Netherlands-Sint Maarten Tax Arrangement).

Except for Colombia and Costa Rica, The Netherlands has a tax treaty in force with all OECD member countries and with all Member States of the EU. Further, the Dutch tax treaty network includes treaties with four major transitional economies: Brazil, China, India, and Indonesia (the treaty with Russia was terminated as of January 1, 2022). Interestingly, The Netherlands has a "mini" tax treaty with Bermuda which applies only to individuals.[16]

The Netherlands is a member of the OECD (and before 1961, of the OEEC, its predecessor). In the first Memorandum on Dutch Tax Treaty Policy that the Dutch Ministry of Finance published (1987), it is expressly stated that "[i]n substance The Netherlands has taken the OECD Model as a starting point of its treaty policy in the past decades." This is confirmed in the 1996-1998, 2011 and 2020 Memorandums which were published—and discussed in Parliament—as updates to the 1987 Memorandum.

The 2020 Dutch Tax Treaty Policy Memorandum stresses that the Dutch tax treaty network is a core ingredient of the investment climate of The Netherlands, as tax treaties facilitate international trade and provide the necessary legal certainty for Dutch-resident companies engaged in international business. The Memorandum also discusses policy considerations for selecting the states with which The Netherlands will negotiate a new treaty or renegotiate an existing treaty, taking into account existing differences between the tax systems of the two countries, their economic relations, the relative competitiveness of Dutch business enterprises, and political or diplomatic considerations. Some of the core policy issues discussed in the 2020 Memorandum are:

- standard deviations from the OECD Model:
  - treaty residence: tax-exempt entities such as pension funds are nevertheless considered to be treaty residents and therefore entitled to treaty benefits on investment income (dividends, interest, royalties) and capital gains;
  - investment funds: The Netherlands' position is that tax-exempt investment entities are not entitled to (some) treaty benefits. In addition, with regard to investment companies that are subject to a zero CIT rate provided they distribute (virtually) all of their income, incoming and outgoing dividend payments should qualify for the 15% treaty rate;
  - offshore PEs: The Netherlands prefers to adopt a lower threshold PE provision for offshore activities;
  - gains from substantial share participations: preservation of exit taxation by the source state;
  - capital gains from shares in immovable property companies: The Netherlands applies the participation exemption to such gains and prefers that the other treaty state not be given the right to tax these capital gains;
  - sportspersons and entertainers: elimination of the special treaty rule (Article 17);

16. A "mini" tax treaty is designated as such because it applies only to individuals and certain income components which can be received only by individuals and not by corporate taxpayers (e.g., the treaty does not contain distributive rules on business profits, dividends, interest, and royalties).

  - pensions and social security payments: the source (past employment) state retains taxing rights.
- provisions of the UN Model that The Netherlands may accept: (higher) withholding tax rates on dividends, interest and royalties; source state taxation of (net) income from services, of income from international shipping, of (gross) income from technical services, of capital gains on the disposition of shares; technical assistance;
- special aspects of the Dutch treaties with neighboring countries Belgium and Germany;
- countering tax treaty abuse: a review of the choices The Netherlands has made in implementing Base Erosion and Profit Shifting (BEPS).

11 SOURCES OF TAX LAW

The official source of statutory tax law is the Official Gazette (*Staatsblad*) in which all acts and implementing decrees are published. It was available in print until 2009 and thereafter only online, along with the bulk of other government publications (*see officielebekendmakingen.nl* ("official announcements") and court decisions (available through *rechtspraak.nl*). Court decisions are also published (in print and online) by commercial publishers, often accompanied by expert commentary.

In the past, English-language publications (including translations of the Dutch tax codes) were important and necessary for foreigners to obtain access to Dutch tax law. The arrival of online translation tools has greatly reduced the need of such publications.

The Dutch Revenue Service has a variety of information relevant for foreigners and foreign companies available in English (search on "Belastingdienst English"). Online information in English regarding the Dutch Ministry of Finance can be found by searching on "Ministerie van Financiën in English."

The United Kingdom

Glen Loutzenhiser[*]

1 HISTORY: INCOME TAX

History is all-important in the United Kingdom (UK) tax system. Thus, since the UK tax system has been around since the Middle Ages, the tax year starts, not at some arbitrary date in mid-winter (such as January 1), but in the spring (April 6). However, as will be seen in the later sections, there are indications that some of the old pillars of the system are under review or even redesign, especially where companies are concerned.

The income tax was introduced in 1799 and, except for a gap between 1816 and 1842, has remained in force ever since. It is, in theory, a temporary tax in that Parliament has to decide each year that there is to be an income tax for that year. This doctrine of the annual tax is a relic from the days when Parliament wanted to make sure that the King would summon a Parliament each year; a perpetual source of income would make calling Parliament less necessary. This doctrine also applies to corporation tax, but not to capital gains tax (CGT) or inheritance tax.

The income tax was completely overhauled in 1803 by the introduction of the system of the taxation of income as such (as opposed to a person's total income), the abandonment of the general return of income, and the introduction of the schedular system backed up by an extensive system of withholding at source. These principles of deduction at source and a schedular definition of income have been extremely influential. Thanks to the Tax Rewrite Program, which ran from 1997 to 2010 (*see* sections 5 and 6 below), income tax is no longer expressed in a series of Schedules, lettered A to F. However, it remains a schedular system in substance: if income does not come within any particular part of the relevant Acts, then it is not chargeable to income tax. Each particular part has its own rules for dealing with, for example, how its particular income should be defined and taxed, and which deductions should be

* The author wishes to acknowledge the work originally done by Professor John Tiley in preparing this chapter for earlier editions of this book.

allowed, as well as rules about timing. A loss under one Schedule or Part cannot necessarily be set against income under another. Under the new system, one no longer talks of total income but of "net adjusted income."

The 1803 system included the taxation of imputed income arising from the occupation of property; this arose under the 1803 Schedule A, a system which remained in place until 1963.

The influence of this overall system is still with us. Thus, even today, the income tax consists of various heads of income, each with associated rules. However, today's new legislation finally spells out—in some detail—the different types of income and the different types of taxpayer liable to income tax. It also contains detailed but incomplete rules on how a person's income tax liability is calculated.

Another effect of the 1803 system was to make the introduction of graduation and differentiation a more difficult task; such a system demanded a personal return of total income and was inconsistent with the final character of the scheme of deduction at source. When introduced in 1907, differentiation originally took the form of a lower rate of tax on earned income, but this soon became a relief from income tax: only in 1973 was the tax rate expressed in terms of earned income and a new additional rate applied to investment income; this additional rate was itself repealed in 1984. In 1910, graduation took the form of a new tax, super tax, later remodeled and renamed surtax. Income tax was levied on income, surtax on the total income of an individual. Surtax being additional to income tax, a particular piece of an individual's income might be subject to income tax at 40% and surtax at 20%; it was thus an excess liability on those better able to pay. Only in 1973 were the two taxes merged, although this is often a matter of form rather than substance, as the continued existence of excess liability shows.

Probably the greatest legacy of history is a particular view of the scope of income and the distinction between income and capital. When income tax was first introduced in 1799, not only were there various existing forms of capital already subject to other taxes but there was also a substantial area of law, that of trusts, where a very sharp distinction between income and capital receipts had been drawn. Further, insofar as business was concerned, Adam Smith had already set out the distinction between circulating and fixed capital and between income profits and capital gains. The details of trading income had to be worked out at a time well before the first Companies Act when the business unit was relatively small and ownership and management were not completely distinct concepts. A tax on income introduced against such a legal and intellectual background would find little room for arguments based on a comprehensive income tax base. Moreover, since the tax was seen as temporary, the taxation of capital gains would have seemed unjust. A separate tax on capital gains (CGT) was eventually introduced in 1965. The distinction between capital and income remains central to the UK tax system despite a certain amount of convergence for the corporate sector, especially with regard to rates of tax. Convergence of rates in the personal sector was achieved in 1988 but was undone ten years later.

1.1 Corporation Tax

In the UK, the tax paid by companies on their profits is not "income tax" but "corporation tax"; the expression "profits" covers both income and capital gains. This tax was introduced in 1965, at the same time as CGT. Before 1965, companies paid tax on their profits but did so through a combination of the income tax (as opposed to surtax or supertax) and special taxes. Dividends were not subject to income tax but were grossed up to give a figure for surtax; this was done whether or not the company paid income tax on its profits.

The fact that a company was subject to income tax, but not surtax, meant that it was advantageous for a high-rate taxpayer to leave income behind the veil of a company, where it would be taxed at lower rates and so multiply more rapidly. Legislation was therefore introduced in 1922 to deal with what were then called one-man companies, in the form of a surtax direction which treated the income of the companies as if it were the income of their owners and therefore liable to surtax. This was the forerunner of the modern close company legislation. The reduction in tax rates over recent years enabled Parliament to repeal almost all of these attribution-of-income rules—although the extent of reduction of corporation tax rates as compared to individual tax rates might suggest these repeals were hasty. A special tax on profits, the National Defense Contribution, which in due course became profits tax, was introduced in 1937. This was an extra tax on the profits of a company but was not an income tax; it could be used to levy tax at differential rates on distributed and retained profits and was in fact used in this way between 1947 and 1958. Since one of the taxes in this two-tax system was income tax, the rate would be altered whenever the government thought it desirable to alter the rate in the personal sector. Profits under the two taxes were computed differently. Not only was profits tax levied on a current, as opposed to a preceding-year basis, but some items were deductible in computing profits for profits tax which were not deductible for income tax, necessitating two sets of calculations; thus, for example, until 1952 profits tax was deductible for income tax. Further, companies whose profits were less than GBP 2,000 were exempt from profits tax.

This untidy system was replaced in 1965 by a corporation tax based on the classical system, which was in turn replaced in 1973 by a partial imputation system. A number of imputation features were removed between 1997 and 1999; the current corporation tax is a classical system with dividends taxed at rates lower than the usual income tax rates and beginning with a zero-rate band.

The legislation on corporation tax was consolidated in the Income and Corporation Taxes Act 1988 and then rewritten into the Corporation Tax Acts (CTAs) 2009 and 2010 but, as seen above, certain rules dealing with capital gains are to be found in the Taxation of Chargeable Gains Act 1992. These Acts are supplemented by the Taxation of International and Other Provisions Act 2010 (TIOPA) and by (many) provisions in the annual Finance Acts. Although the new rewritten legislation contains several rules which are explicable only in terms of a schedular system, there are substantially fewer such rules in Corporation Tax than there are in Income Tax.

2 CONSTITUTIONAL ISSUES

It is notorious that the UK does not have a written constitution. However, it does have a long constitutional history and taxation has played a key part in that story. Thus, the Tudor monarchy, in particular, paid for its alliance with the middle classes by allowing Parliament (and especially the House of Commons) an increasing role in government and taxation. Charles I's attempt to govern—and tax—without Parliament led eventually to the English civil war and his execution. The Bill of Rights of 1688[1] provided that "no charge on the subject shall be levied by pretence of prerogative without the consent of Parliament." In the twentieth century, the attempt by the House of Lords to resist major taxation reforms led to the Parliament Act of 1911, which allowed the House of Commons to get certain legislation through despite the opposition of the House of Lords—and also removed any role for the House of Lords in relation to money bills (i.e., most tax laws).

The UK courts acknowledge the sovereignty of Parliament—that is, they recognize that they have no function of judicial review of primary legislation. For this reason, the courts for many years raised no objection to retrospective legislation. As a result, in 1978 an anti-avoidance measure was made to apply to events occurring after March 1976—a particularly effective form of anti-avoidance measure.

The courts do, however, have a review role in three important aspects. First, they have a full judicial review role in relation to secondary legislation, which includes statutory instruments which are becoming known, increasingly, as regulations. Second, post-Brexit, UK law contains a large amount of retained European Union (EU) law, which UK courts may be called upon to interpret.[2] Third, the UK has been a signatory to the European Convention on Human Rights since 1966 and so the UK courts give effect to the Convention—although not in an entirely straightforward way.

The human-rights dimension needs to be disentangled very carefully. The 1966 accession allowed UK complainants to take matters to the European Court of Human Rights (at that time, the Commission and the Court in Strasbourg). The Convention was not implemented in UK domestic law until the Human Rights Act of 1998, which came into force in 2000, and even then did so in a way which preserved the sovereignty of Parliament. UK courts must interpret legislation so as to give effect to Convention rights but, if this is impossible, they have no power to override the legislation; instead, they may declare it to be incompatible with the Convention. If Parliament decides that it does not want to amend the law, even by the fast-track process prescribed in the Act, there is nothing the litigant can do but follow the familiar path to Strasbourg (equally, there is nothing to stop the Westminster Parliament from repealing the Act itself or withdrawing from the Convention altogether).

Two other aspects of the Human Rights Act should be mentioned. First, section 6 of the Act makes it unlawful for a public authority, an expression covering a court or tribunal and a person whose functions are, even in part, of a public nature (e.g.,

1. 2 Will. and Mar. (c. 2), Art. 4.
2. European Union (Withdrawal) Act 2018; Retained EU Law (Revocation and Reform) Act 2023. *See also* the Introduction for a brief discussion of European institutions and tax laws.

revenue departments), to act in way which is incompatible with convention rights; judicial remedies are governed by section 8. The court or tribunal must "have regard to," but is not bound by, the jurisprudence of the "Strasbourg Organs." Second, new legislation presented to the House of Commons must carry a certificate from the relevant Minister asserting that the legislation proposed is (or is not) compatible with the Convention rights. Previous editions of this chapter took the view that Ministers trying to get a bill passed which they state is not compatible are unlikely to succeed. The previous UK Conservative government was less concerned with such matters when it came to immigration legislation—though not with tax law.

In addition to these matters, one may note that the Human Rights Convention has been of some influence in the development of other purely UK domestic administrative law rules.

Within the UK, the central government enjoys an almost unparalleled degree of power. There are local authorities in different parts of the country, but they are subject to tight control from the central government in a number of ways. First, a substantial part of their responsibilities is funded centrally rather than by their local taxes. Second, their revenue-raising powers have been made the subject of capping powers. Third, their ability to raise money from businesses has been reduced by the device of the business rate, a rate which applies to businesses but is fixed centrally and not locally. This leaves local authorities with little power to raise much money from local residents (the local tax is called the council tax). The level of the council tax is fixed by the local authority—subject to capping—and that rate is then applied to each house, the house being placed in one of a number of bands of value.

A local income tax has been considered from time to time in the UK but never implemented. Recent years have seen a dramatic shift toward devolution of some taxing powers from Westminster. Under the terms of the Scotland Act 2016, the Scottish Parliament has the power to set income tax rates and bands for Scottish taxpayers, to vary the basic rate of income tax by up to three pence in the pound, and to keep all the revenue raised in Scotland. From April 2019, under the terms of the Wales Act 2014, the Welsh Assembly has the power to set income tax rates payable by Welsh taxpayers and receives directly a portion of the income tax collected.

Treaties are made by the sovereign under his prerogative power and take effect under the normal rules for public international law. However, treaties (including tax treaties) have effects for individuals only if they are then ratified by the relevant parliamentary procedure. For tax treaties, this procedure is set out in TIOPA, sections 2-6, and reminds one that the treaty can be given effect only for the purposes set out therein.

Of all aspects of the UK tax system, the rates of income tax provide the most striking examples of the influence of history—and of politics. The record in this area does not justify the alleged reputation of the British for moderation. Rates of income tax in the last year of the Labour Administration (1978-1979) reached 83%; however, where the income was classified as investment income and exceeded a certain figure, a supplementary tax of 15% was due, making a marginal rate of 98%. This was fairly typical of the period after 1945 and demonstrated the great doctrinal belief in equity, in the sense of shared misery. It was highlighted by the very occasional (twice) surcharge on income, which, being expressed as percentage of tax normally due, could (and did) mean that the marginal rate of tax could exceed 100%. The ferocity of these rates emphasized the importance of the gap between income and capital gain (not generally taxed until 1965), and any gaps in the tax base, and the generally neutral attitude of the courts toward straightforward tax-avoidance schemes.

Since the election of the Conservative administration in 1979, led by Margaret Thatcher, the top rates have been reduced; in 1979, the general rate dropped from 83% to 60%; in 1984, the surcharge on investment income was abolished, and in 1988 the top rate was cut to 40%. In these ways, the doctrinal writings of the 1970s, with their emphasis on neutrality rather than equity, have come to hold sway with the same fervor as those of their predecessors arguing for equity. The New Labour administration, led by Tony Blair and Gordon Brown, which came to power in 1997, did not increase the low nominal rates of tax but did other things to increase revenue. The appalling state of the UK finances meant that this promise was abandoned in 2010 when the Labour government introduced a higher "additional rate" of 50% on income in excess of GBP 150,000. In 2013, the additional rate was reduced by the Conservative-Liberal Democrat coalition government to its present 45%. In 2023, the point at which the 45% rate kicks in was reduced to GBP 125,140, aligning with the amount of income at which the taxpayer will not be entitled to claim any personal allowance.

Indexation and inflation adjustments have been part of the UK tax system for many years. Income tax rate brackets are adjusted for inflation or other causes each year; the same is true of the personal reliefs. In part, this was attributable to the fact that the income tax was an annual tax and therefore subject to annual review. However, all adjustments depended on the needs of the Chancellor of the Exchequer (Minister of Finance) of the day. In recent years, adjustment of these values for inflation has been formalized in that they will be changed unless the annual Finance Bill directs otherwise. But the annual Finance Bill has directed otherwise more often than not, with smaller (or no) adjustments in years when the government needs money and larger adjustments when the government needs votes. More recently, and as inflation has re-emerged in the UK (and elsewhere), the government has frozen the key income tax bands, as well as the annual exemption for CGT and the nil rate bands for inheritance tax. The increased tax revenues from "fiscal drag" are expected to be substantial.

Adjustment for inflation has formed part of the capital gains system since 1982, but to a lesser extent in recent years and despite the relatively high levels of inflation experienced in the UK at the time of writing. The current position is that inflation adjustments are made to the base cost of an asset in determining a gain—but only for corporation tax, and even then, this indexation allowance cannot create a loss and has been frozen from January 2018 (*see* section 5 below). There are no inflation-based adjustments to the base cost used in determining the amount which may be claimed under the capital allowance system (depreciation).

3 RATE STRUCTURE AND RELIEFS: 2024-2025

The income tax rate structure in England begins with the rates of tax:

Taxable Income (Above the Personal Allowance)	*Tax Rate*
savings income (but *see* below) GBP 0-GBP 5,000	0% (starting, savings rate)
non-savings income GBP 0-GBP 37,700 and savings income GBP 5,000-GBP 37,700	20% (basic rate)
GBP 37,701-GBP 125,140	40% (higher rate)
over GBP 125,140	45% (additional rate)

As noted above, rate brackets and reliefs are meant to be index-linked, but the effects of indexing are more often than not overridden by express statutory provisions. Importantly, Finance Act 2023 froze the basic rate band limit and personal allowance for income tax until the end of tax year 2027-2028. Also, as noted above, different bands and rates for income tax apply to Scottish residents, with rates ranging from 19% to 48% for 2024-2025.

From October 30, 2024, CGT is levied at rates of 18% or 24% for gains on residential property and other assets, with the exception of a carried interest which is taxed at 18% or 28%. The rate of tax is determined by the taxpayer's income tax bracket and an annual exemption for individuals applies, which was formerly GBP 12,300 but was reduced to GBP 6,000 for 2023-2024 and to GBP 3,000 for 2024-2025 and subsequent tax years. If taxable income is above GBP 37,700, capital gains are taxable at the higher rates of 24% (or 28% on a carried interest). If taxable income is below GBP 37,700, the amount by which GBP 37,700 exceeds taxable income is the amount of taxable gains subject to the lower rate of 18%; any remaining gain is taxed at 24% (or 28% on a carried interest). Trustees pay the higher rate, with an annual exemption equal to one-half of the amount for individuals.

In addition, National Insurance Contributions (NICs) are imposed on both employers and employees; for 2024-2025, employees pay 8% of their weekly earnings between GBP 242 and GBP 967 and 2% above that figure. The maximum rate for employers is 13.8%. The self-employed pay 6% NICs on profits between GBP 12,570 and GBP 50,270, and 2% on profits over GBP 50,270. In recent years, these contributions have been raised, ostensibly to help fund the National Health Service. This is a weak example of the device known as hypothecation or the earmarking of a tax for a particular purpose; such hypothecation is very rare in the UK. Substantial increases in NICs during the Gordon Brown government (2007-2010) enabled the government to get more money from the public without touching the rate of income tax.

Savings income (other than dividends) is taxed as above, except that there is a 0% starting rate for savings income only, with a limit of GBP 5,000. If an individual's taxable non-savings income is above this limit, the starting rate for savings will not apply. From April 6, 2016, taxpayers have a tax-free Personal Savings Allowance of up to GBP 1,000 of savings income (e.g., interest earned on bank accounts) for basic-rate taxpayers and up to GBP 500 for higher-rate taxpayers. Additional-rate taxpayers are not eligible for the allowance. In addition, banks and building societies are no longer required to withhold tax at 20% on interest earned by account holders. Other tax-free allowances apply to individuals with relatively small incomes from trading or property, in both cases up to GBP 1,000.

The tax rates applicable to dividends above the tax-free "dividend allowance," which was originally GBP 5,000 but for 2023-2024 is GBP 1,000 and GBP 500 for 2024-2025 and subsequent tax years, are:

- 7.5% on dividend income within the basic rate band;
- 32.5% on dividend income within the higher rate band; and
- 38.1% on dividend income within the additional rate band.

The individual tax burden is then adjusted, first by reference to the personal allowance: all residents have a personal allowance of GBP 12,570 for 2024-2025; this amount is frozen until the end of the tax year 2027-2028. There is also a special blind persons' relief of GBP 3,070. As from April 6, 2010, the personal allowance is restricted for those with income over GBP 100,000; the allowance is reduced by GBP 1 for every GBP 2 of income above GBP 100,000 and disappears entirely when income reaches GBP 125,140. Non-taxpayers may transfer up to 10% of any unused personal allowance to their spouse where the spouse is a basic-rate taxpayer. Previously, people over 65 years of age were entitled to higher personal allowances, but these allowances and the standard allowance are now the same. A married couple's allowance worth between GBP 428 and GBP 1,108 per year is available for couples if at least one spouse was born before April 6, 1935.

A second group of reliefs are tax credits, which have their own separate statute, the Tax Credits Act 2002. These credits represented a major change, making the tax system a means to deliver what had previously been social security goals. The two primary credits are: (i) Child Tax Credit, which provides income-related support to the main caregiver; and (ii) Working Tax Credit, which provides income-related support to those in low-paid employment, with or without dependent children. A new Universal Credit is slowing being rolled out across the UK and eventually will replace the Child Tax Credit, Working Tax Credit, and other social benefits, including housing benefits and income-based jobseeker's allowance. Child Benefit, which was formerly a universal benefit, is now means-tested against the partner with the higher income. The benefit paid is clawed back on income greater than GBP 60,000 and entirely clawed back on income greater than GBP 80,000 by way of a separate tax—the high-income child benefit charge (HICBC).

The main rate of corporation tax for the financial year 2024 is 25%. A small profits rate of 19% applies for companies on profits up to GBP 50,000 with effect from April 1, 2023.

4 COMPOSITION OF THE FISCAL SYSTEM

The different taxes have different yields. The UK government projections for 2023-2024 put net taxes and social security contributions at GBP 951 billion, or around 43% of the

UK's Gross Domestic Product (GDP). That figure of GBP 951 billion breaks down into GBP 268 billion from taxes on personal income, GBP 82 billion from taxes on corporate income, GBP 172 billion from social security contributions taxes, and GBP 194 billion from value-added tax (VAT); CGT was expected to bring in GBP 17.8 billion.

5 BASIC STRUCTURE OF THE INCOME TAX

5.1 Individuals

The UK system of income tax is a schedular system. The tax unit is the individual, but (as noted above) there is a limited ability for spouses to transfer a portion of unused personal allowances from one to the other. UK-resident individuals are taxed on a worldwide basis, with residency determined in accordance with a statutory test. Nonresidents are liable to tax on UK-sourced income, including income and gains from UK real estate (subject to double tax treaties). A special regime is available to UK residents with a foreign domicile; very generally, such individuals can choose to be taxed on a remittance basis, in which case they are not subject to UK tax on income and gains earned outside the UK and not brought into the UK. Taxation under this special regime may require payment of an annual fee for longer-term residents. The remittance regime is not available to those deemed to be domiciled in the UK under legislation introduced in 2017, which includes individuals resident in the UK for at least fifteen of the past twenty years or UK residents born in the UK and with a UK domicile of origin. This special remittance regime is currently under review and is expected to be replaced by a temporary residence-based regime under which individuals will not pay tax in respect of foreign income and gains arising in their first 4 years of UK tax residence.

Today, as a result of the Tax Law Rewrite Program, the UK's legislation on income tax is stretched out over three principal—but not exhaustive—Acts: the Income Tax (Earnings and Pensions) Act 2003 (known as ITEPA), the Income Tax (Trading and Other Income) Act 2005 (ITTOIA), and the Income Tax Act 2007 (ITA 2007). The purpose of the rewrite was to use modern language to make legislation both more intelligible and more accessible.

While the UK income tax is indeed still a schedular system, it is no longer expressed in terms of Schedules A, B, C, etc., but in terms of a list of heads of charge. Unfortunately, the legislation contained in these three acts is not exhaustive of the various heads of charge; moreover, there is no comprehensive list of the heads of charge.

ITA 2007 begins by listing three charges to income tax under ITEPA—all previously under Schedule E:

- Part 2 (income from employment);
- Part 9 (pension income);
- Part 10 (social security income).

It then lists four heads under ITTOIA:

(1) Part 2 (trading income), the former Schedule D Cases I and II;
(2) Part 3 (property income), the former Schedule A;
(3) Part 4 (savings and investment income), the former Schedule D Case III and Schedule F; and
(4) Part 5 (miscellaneous income), including the former Schedule D Case VI.

ITA 2007 itself imposes the following charges:

- Part 10 (charitable trusts);
- Part 12 Chapter 2 (accrued income profits); and
- Part 13 (tax avoidance).

ITA 2007 also lists two other heads of charge, but expressly warns that the list is not comprehensive.

With the change in form, but not in substance, differences in the fiscal treatment of income from employment (ITEPA Part 2), income from business (ITTOIA Part 2), and income from property (ITTOIA Part 3) persist. The legislation contains many priority rules. ITTOIA section 2 lists many of these rules but then says, "but the rules in those sections need to be read with other rules of law (whether in this Act or otherwise) about the scope of particular provisions or the order of priority to be given to them."[3] Other major features of the UK income tax, such as the distinction between income and capital, have been mentioned in section 1 above.

5.1.1 Capital Gains Tax

The refusal of the courts and the legislature to widen the scope of income tax to cover capital gains is of great importance in the history of the UK tax system. Opportunities to convert income into capital were exploited by taxpayers and only occasionally stopped, and then on a piecemeal basis, by the legislature. Reform eventually came in 1965 with the introduction of the long-term CGT. A short-term gains provision had been introduced in 1962 which was designed to tax gains realized within six months of acquisition and to tax them as income. This was extended in 1965 to gains realized within twelve months and was preserved until 1971, despite the introduction of the long-term CGT in 1965, because of the difference in tax rates—CGT had a flat rate of 30% while income tax could exceed 90%. The rates of CGT and income tax were assimilated for companies (i.e., for corporation tax) in 1987. They were assimilated for individuals in 1988 but, as we shall see, this is no longer the case; lower rates of tax now apply to gains as compared to income.

CGT contains its own fundamental doctrines. It is restricted in that there must be a disposal (whether actual or deemed) and the disposal must be of an asset which is relevant to the tax system. Assets relevant to the system include shares and debts on a security, although there is a very important exception for qualifying corporate bonds; other debts are not generally relevant assets, although exceptions are made for debts on

3. Income Tax (Trading and Other Income Act) 2005 (ITTOIA), s. 2.

a security, for certain loans to traders, and for assignees of debts. A liability is not an asset so that a loss on a loan (e.g., due to the extra cost of paying off a foreign-currency loan when sterling has declined against that currency since the original borrowing) cannot give rise to any relief under CGT; conversely, there is no gain on a liability. This gap was the source of much frustration for many taxpayers and led to the introduction in 1995 of new rules for foreign exchange transactions and risk-management instruments as well as a comprehensive new regime for all loan instruments in 1996—but only for companies subject to corporation tax.

CGT has two other major restrictions. The first, introduced in 1988, is that it does not usually attempt to tax gains which accrued before March 31, 1982. The second is that individuals enjoy a separate exemption from tax on the first GBP 6,000 (2023-2024) of capital gains realized each year; this exemption decreased to GBP 3,000 for 2024-2025 and subsequent tax years.

In 1982, the UK introduced some relief for inflation. For CGT before 1998—and still for corporation tax but frozen from January 2018—this relief was delivered through the "indexation allowance." By 1998, the indexation relief could not be used to turn a gain into a loss, although this had been so in the past. In 1998, the UK replaced indexation relief for CGT—but not for corporation tax—with a tapering system. This system distinguished sharply between business assets (where the taper reduces the chargeable gain by 75% after just two years, thus reducing the effective tax rate from 40% to 10%) and non-business assets (where the taper extends over ten years and, at most, reduces the gain by only 40%, leaving 60% taxable, and so gives an effective rate of 24% for a top-rate taxpayer). Tapering did not reduce a gain to zero. In 2008, tapering relief itself was scrapped as part of a simplification package and replaced by a single rate of CGT of 18% for individuals, without indexation relief. The simplification package was found to produce losers as well as winners, and so a relief, formerly called "entrepreneurs' relief" and now known as "business asset disposal relief," was provided for certain business gains, which results in a tax rate of 10% on lifetime business gains of up to GBP 1 million for 2023-2024 and onward (previously GBP 10 million).

The simplified system was further complicated by the introduction in 2010 of a second, higher rate of tax of 28%, and then in 2016 of lower rates of 10% and 20%, which applied to gains on most assets other than residential property and carried interests. From October 30, 2024, most gains are taxed at either 18% or 24% (28% for carried interests). The relevant CGT rate is determined by reference to the taxpayer's income tax band (*see* section 2 above). Where an asset has a useful life of less than fifty years, it will be classified as a "wasting asset" and the costs written off over the life of the asset to avoid giving relief for the inevitable loss. If the wasting asset is a tangible asset, it will be exempt from CGT. Capital losses may be set only against capital gains of the same or any subsequent tax year, a rule which encourages a certain amount of tax planning and necessitates anti-avoidance legislation.

The CGT legislation was consolidated in the CGT Act 1979 and again in the Taxation of Chargeable Gains Act 1992. The reason for the change in title is that corporations do not pay CGT on their capital gains, but instead pay corporation tax.

The 1992 Act consolidates not only the rules for CGT but also a number of the corporation tax rules which had not been consolidated in the 1988 Act.

5.2 Corporations

In general, corporation tax is charged on the profits of companies which are resident in the UK and on nonresident companies carrying on business through a permanent establishment in the UK or with income/gains from UK real estate. Profits are determined as the sum of income, as defined under the income tax rules, and chargeable gains under the CGT rules. However, a number of rules apply only to corporation tax (e.g., those dealing with loan relationships, including foreign exchange matters, and derivatives). Other examples include the research and development tax credit, remediation relief, and the rules on intellectual property. As already noted, the rewrite program made the corporation tax legislation quite distinct from income tax.

6 TAX LEGISLATION

First, a general comment—although, as seen above, the tax law rewrite legislation is less than perfect, it does in several respects represent a major improvement on what had gone before. First, for years immediately before the rewrite, there was an Act known as the Income and Corporation Taxes Act 1988. This was not a complete code of provisions for income tax and corporation tax. Rather, it was the latest in a series of consolidations; these had occurred in 1918, 1952, 1970, and 1988. The 1988 Act could have been amended each year by the annual Finance Act; however, there was no need for the annual Act to do that, and so later Acts instead added their own provisions to the overall patchwork of legislation. One purpose behind the rewrite program was to prevent that situation from arising in the future; this aim has not been realized completely. It is expected that amendments to the provisions in the three ITAs will take effect as amendments to those provisions and will not be freestanding.

Second, it used to be that the combination of the consolidated or rewritten Acts and the subsequent Finance Acts contained all the relevant tax legislation. This is no longer true, and important provisions relating to tax are also to be found in freestanding tax statutes such as the Tax Credits Act 2002, and in more general enactments such as the Criminal Justice and Police Act 2001.

Because Parliament has to reenact the income tax each year, there is at least one major piece of tax legislation each tax year; this gives many opportunities for reform, although most of these are put forward by the government. Some will be anti-avoidance measures; others will be more wide-ranging reforms. Because of the nature of the UK political system, the government is almost certain to get its legislation passed—often unscathed. Opposition parties can propose amendments and sensible ones (such as technically helpful and zero-cost amendments) will often be adopted by the government, but only on the basis that it does the drafting.

Taxation bills originate in the House of Commons, the powers of the House of Lords being, as we have seen, very limited. Under the Budget timetable introduced in

2016, policy changes are meant to be announced at the Budget in the autumn and consulted on in winter and over the spring. Draft legislation should then be published in July for technical consultation ahead of the Finance Bill being introduced in the autumn and enacted the following spring. An annual Spring Statement from the Chancellor accompanies an updated economic and fiscal forecast from the Office for Budget Responsibility. The Chancellor is not expected to make significant tax or spending announcements at the Spring Statement unless the economic circumstances require it. However, those timetable plans have not been adhered to in recent years—Spring Budgets and Finance Acts enacted in Summer have once again become the norm. As a practical matter, the government can make a statement at any time and announce that legislation will be retrospective to the date of the announcement. Such retroactive legislation is generally regarded as normal and unobjectionable.

Major technical reforms, such as the loan-relationship legislation of 1996, are typically the subject of a very elaborate consultation process, with draft clauses and considerable Revenue explanations to accompany the draft and final legislation—the whole process taking well over a year. However, it has to be said that one effect of this consultation process has been a greater willingness to have very detailed legislation backed up by even more detailed subordinate legislation or statutory instruments, sometimes known as regulations. The power to make these statutory instruments sometimes includes the power to change the primary legislation itself. Although such powers are rare elsewhere in the tax system, they are needed to deal with complex technical areas and to enable the tax authorities to adapt the legislation as new instruments or arrangements come along. The 2002 rules on intellectual property followed a similar pattern, as did the more recent Base Erosion and Profit Shifting (BEPS)-inspired legislation restricting interest deductions and dealing with hybrids.

6.1 Statutory Style

The traditional UK tax statute was drafted in a very precise and very detailed way, a way entirely suited to, and perhaps a very appropriate response to, the tradition of literal interpretation. Until the last thirty years or so there was relatively little resort to delegated legislation (or statutory instruments).

The style of the rewrite program was very different. The new approach was meant to make tax statutes more intelligible, making the legislation clearer and easier to use but also, and inevitably, longer. The new system makes extensive use of "signpost" provisions. The extensive use of words which do not have any dispositive effect is something of a challenge for those accustomed to traditional legislation. The first great product of this process was the Capital Allowances Act 2001, an Act which applies to both corporation tax and income tax.

Although the courts are now taking a more purposive approach to the interpretation of statues and a "less blinkered" approach to the facts, it remains the case that the legislation itself is often very detailed. In recent years there has also been a tendency for highly prescriptive rules to be backed up by a purpose-based targeted anti-avoidance rule.

The UK transfer pricing legislation[4] is expressly based on the Organisation for Economic Co-operation and Development (OECD) guidelines[5] and refers to those in operation when the UK legislation was enacted in 1998 as well as any later principles adopted by the OECD, but only if approved for this purpose by statutory instrument.

6.2 Statutory Interpretation

The current mantra, which is particularly clearly stated in *Barclays Mercantile Business v. Mawson*[6] in 2005, is that courts approach tax statutes in the same way as any other statutes, by looking at the words to be interpreted in a purposive way, but in their context.

It is too much to expect that any exposition of the principles of statutory interpretation would remove all difficulties in their application because it is in the nature of questions of construction that there are borderline cases about which people will have different views. However, it is possible to achieve some clarity about basic principles. The modern approach to statutory construction, as Lord Steyn explained in *IRC v. McGuckian* in 1997,[7] is to have regard to the purpose of a particular provision and interpret its language, so far as possible, in a way which best gives effect to that purpose. The House of Lords traced its change in approach to the interpretation of statutes back from 1997 to the *Ramsay* case in 1981.[8] Before *Ramsay*, the approach of the courts was vitiated by formalism and, in particular, by insisting on treating every transaction which had an individual legal identity (such as a payment of money, transfer of property, and creation of a debt) as having its own separate tax consequences, whatever might be the terms of the statute. In combination, the literal interpretation of tax statutes and the formalistic insistence on separately examining steps in a composite scheme allowed tax-avoidance schemes to flourish. *Ramsay* liberated the construction of revenue statutes from being both literal and blinkered.

The question of the nature of the principle emerging from the *Ramsay* doctrine has been a matter of much discussion. Many saw it as a judicially created anti-avoidance doctrine. A few brave souls saw it more simply—as a much-needed new approach to the interpretation and application of tax statutes. In the *Barclays* case, the House of Lords decided that the few brave souls had been right.[9] The House cited with approval Ribeiro PJ's formulation of the *Ramsay* principle in the Hong Kong case *Arrowtown*, and this formulation is now regularly cited in UK cases:

4. Taxation (International and Other Provisions) Act 2010 (TIOPA) Parts 4 and 5, and *see* in particular s. 164, which provides that the UK rules are to be interpreted so as to secure consistency with the OECD Transfer Pricing Guidelines and the OECD Model Convention.
5. OECD, Transfer Pricing Guidelines (Paris: OECD, 2017).
6. [2004] UKHL 51, [2005] STC 1. For a recent Supreme Court decision following the *Barclays* approach, *see UBS AG v. Revenue and Customs Comrs; DB Group Services (UK) Ltd. v. Revenue and Customs Comrs* [2016] UKSC 13.
7. *IRC v. McGuckian* [1997] STC 908 at 915, [1997] 1 WLR 991 at 999.
8. *Ramsay (WT) Ltd. v. IRC* [1982] STC 174.
9. *See* further section 9.3 below.

> [t]he driving principle in the Ramsay line of cases continues to involve a general rule of statutory construction and an unblinkered approach to the analysis of the facts. The ultimate question is whether the relevant statutory provisions, construed purposively, were intended to apply to the transaction, viewed realistically.[10]

The extent to which the *Barclays* approach will produce results different from those obtained by using the older approach is gradually emerging. The change obviously affects the manner in which cases are argued, but judges have sometimes found that it is often very difficult to find a parliamentary purpose which is sufficiently specific to help them decide the particular case before them. The Tax Law Rewrite Program did not help in this regard because it was not meant to change the law and so was not set out in the form of principles.

A further problem is that when the structure of the Act is looked to, the policy assumptions underlying provisions may change. Thus, the rules about companies buying their own shares clearly assumed that qualifying companies would try to take advantage of the new rules allowing the transaction to be treated as one involving only capital gains legislation; later changes in the various rates of tax, including corporation tax, CGT, and income tax, made this assumption quite false, and as a result, companies might try to make their transactions fall outside the supposedly beneficial rules.

7 COURTS DEALING WITH TAX MATTERS

7.1 Structure of the Courts

A taxpayer who is dissatisfied with an assessment made by His Majesty's Revenue and Customs (HMRC) has a right of appeal. Since April 1, 2009, this appeal is made to a system of tribunals. The new rules apply right across the area of administrative tribunals; tax appeals are just one strand of the system.

The new system contains two tiers—a First Tier Tribunal and an Upper Tribunal. Appeal from the Upper Tribunal lies to the Court of Appeal and from there to the Supreme Court (which replaced the House of Lords Appellate Committee in 2009).

In the normal course of events, an appeal will be taken first to the First Tier Tribunal. There is then a right of appeal to the Upper Tribunal, but only on points of law (i.e., not facts). If the case started in the Upper Tribunal, the appeal is not confined to questions of law but requires the leave either of the Upper Tribunal or the relevant appellate body. The burden of proof lies on the taxpayer to disprove the assessment.

Before April 2009, appeals lay to a body known as "the Commissioners." This term is confusing, since the Members of the Board of HMRC are known as the Commissioners of HMRC. The appellate commissioners were either General or Special and their full title was General (or Special) Commissioners for the purposes of the Income Tax; despite the mention of income tax, their jurisdiction extended to other taxes, but not to VAT, which, until April 2009, had its own appeal tribunal. Among

10. *Collector of Stamp Revenue v. Arrowtown Assets Ltd.* [2004] UKPC 16; [2004] STC 1377 at para. 35; approved in *Barclays Mercantile Business Finance v. Mawson* [2004] UKHL 51 at para. 36.

many differences from the old system, two stand out. First, the new Upper Tribunal not only acts as an appellate body from the First Tier Tribunal but also has the power of judicial review. Second, both the First Tier Tribunal and the Upper Tribunal have a power to review their own decisions. Naturally, this is quite distinct from "judicial review" (*see* section 9.3 below).

Since appeals lie from the First Tier Tribunal (and, formerly, the Commissioners) only on questions of law and not of fact, the issue of the distinction between the two is important. Apart from errors of law in the most obvious sense, the courts have said that they will intervene in three situations which may well amount to the same thing: where there is no evidence to support the determination reached by the Commissioners, where the evidence contradicts that determination, and where the true and only reasonable conclusion contradicts that determination.[11] More recently, Lord Carnwath has advocated a more liberal approach to an expert appellate court's scope of review, which would include the Upper Tribunal reviewing a First Tier Tribunal tax decision.[12]

7.2 Judicial Review

As noted above, the distinction between appeal and judicial review became less important—in procedural terms—in 2009. Judicial review is one of the few ways in which an assessment may be disturbed. It has been used to challenge the Commissioners' decision at the hearing of an appeal or at some other procedural step (e.g., where a hearing is held to be unfair because the taxpayer was not given enough notice). However, judicial review may also be used to challenge decisions by HMRC prior to, and independent of, any appeal hearing. Consequently, it has been used to question the tax authorities' withdrawal of an informal clearance given by an inspector[13] and its decision not to treat a taxpayer as falling within an extra-statutory concession[14] or a statement of practice,[15] and not to assess another taxpayer,[16] as well as the lawfulness of settlement deals reached by HMRC with taxpayers.[17] Judicial review has to be distinguished from an appeal. On appeal, the court may uphold an assessment or vary it; in judicial review, the court either upholds the act complained of or quashes it and, if it quashes it, it sends the matter back to the original body to exercise its jurisdiction correctly—the court does not substitute its own decision for that of the body reviewed. If the Tribunals/Commissioners have conducted the hearing of an appeal in a way which breaches the rules of natural justice, they will have to hear the appeal again. If an assessment by an inspector is quashed, a new assessment must be made—although it may sometimes be too late for the tax authorities to make a new one. On appeal, the court goes into the merits of the decision; in judicial review, the court looks at the

11. *Edwards v. Bairstow and Harrison*, 36 TC 207 at 229.
12. *Jones v. First Tier Tribunal (Social Entitlement Chamber)* [2013] UKSC 19 and *HMRC v. Pendragon plc* [2015] UKSC 37.
13. *R v. IRC ex parte Matrix Securities Ltd.* [1994] STC 272 HL.
14. *R v. IRC ex parte Fulford-Dobson* [1987] STC 344.
15. *R v. IRC ex parte Kaye* [1992] STC 581.
16. *IRC v. National Federation of Self Employed and Small Business Ltd.* [1981] STC 260.
17. *R(oao) UK Uncut Legal Action v. HMRC* [2013] EWHC 1283.

procedures followed and ensures that the public body whose acts are being scrutinized had the power to do what it has done. In judicial review, the court does not interfere with the proper exercise of a power or jurisdiction.

7.3 Judicial Style

UK court judgments tend to be carefully and fully reasoned. The cases are fully argued (mostly orally) and the Tribunals and courts tend to give long and detailed judgments—out of a need to report what has been argued and then what is decided.

7.4 Legislative History

The court may look at the purpose and history of the relevant legislation and, to this end, reference may be made to the state of the law and the material facts and events with which Parliament was apparently dealing.[18] In *Pepper v. Hart*,[19] the House of Lords, reversing centuries of case law, held that the court could consult *Hansard* (as the official record of debates in the UK Parliament is known) in order to interpret the words of the legislation if: "(a) legislation is ambiguous or obscure, or leads to an absurdity; (b) the material relied on consists of one or more statements by a minister or other promoter of the Bill, together, if necessary, with such other Parliamentary material as is required to understand such statements and their effects; and (c) the statements relied on are clear."[20]

7.5 Precedent

As discussed above, in some circumstances, e.g., on appeal from the First Tier Tribunal to the Upper Tribunal or from the General Commissioners to the High Court, the higher court can overturn the decision appealed from only for errors of law—not for errors of fact. It follows that a court may dismiss an appeal even though the appellate judge might have decided the case differently from the original tribunal; such cases are of little value as precedents. Otherwise, judgments of superior courts bind inferior courts and judgments of the same level of court are usually binding.

8 TAX ADMINISTRATION

Since 2005, direct taxes, previously administered by the Inland Revenue, and indirect taxes, such as VAT, previously administered by Customs and Excise, have been administered by one combined department, HMRC. Both departments work closely with the Treasury but are not subordinate departments of the Treasury, even though they share common Ministers. One positive result of the merger has been a review of

18. Lord Macdermott in *IRC v. Rennell* [1964] AC 173, 198.
19. *Pepper v. Hart* [1992] STC 898.
20. *Supra* note 19, at 922.

the many powers each possessed, leading to harmonization and modernization. With respect to penalties, the new system has three degrees of culpability—"careless," "deliberate but not concealed," and "deliberate and concealed." The standard penalty is 30% of the lost tax for carelessness, 70% for deliberate but not concealed offenses, and 100% for deliberate and concealed offenses. The penalties may be reduced if voluntary disclosure is made.

After a long and honorable tradition of assessment to tax by the Revenue, the system changed to one of self-assessment as from 1996, but only for fewer than one-half of the UK's taxpayers. Self-assessment applies to corporation tax (and so to all companies) and to the relatively few individuals who have a substantial amount of income outside the system of collection at source. The vast majority of individual taxpayers do not file tax returns.

The corporation tax system requires companies to make a self-assessment and pay the tax due within nine months from the end of the company's accounting period. There is also a system of payment in advance by quarterly instalments beginning six months and thirteen days from the start of the accounting period. This system applies only to large companies which, in broad terms, means those with annual profits of GBP 1.5 million or more. However, where a company becomes large for the first time, the system applies only from the next accounting period unless its profits exceed GBP 10 million. For accounting periods beginning on or after April 1, 2019, companies with annual taxable profits exceeding GBP 20 million are required to make instalment payments earlier—in the third, six, ninth, and twelfth months of the period to which the liability relates. The risk of getting the instalment calculation wrong falls on the company. Since 2011, all corporation tax returns must be made electronically.

Income tax has very different rules. First, as just mentioned, only a minority of taxpayers are required to make a self-assessment. Those taxpayers subject to the self-assessment system who are willing to make their returns electronically must make a return of their income and calculate the tax due no later than January 31 following the end of their tax year (so by January 31, 2024 for the year April 6, 2022-April 5, 2023). Taxpayers wanting to make their returns other than electronically must file their return by the end of October. If a taxpayer has not calculated the tax due, the HMRC office will do so on the basis of the figures submitted (and will sometimes raise queries on the return). The bonus is that HMRC has to do the calculations and not the taxpayer. When the tax office calculates the tax due, it is on the basis of the figures submitted by the taxpayer and does not indicate that HMRC accepts them; HMRC may still come back later and make new calculations on some new basis if they are dissatisfied with the return.

Payment of the tax is due when the self-assessment return is made or the due date, whichever is earlier. Some tax will already have been paid by deduction at source under the Pay-As-You-Earn (PAYE) cumulative withholding system from employment income (*see* below in this section). In addition, there is a system of payment on account in two instalments (January 31 and July 31 preceding the date of the return). Continuing with the example of the tax for the year 2022-2023 which is finally due on January 31, 2024, there would have been payments on account on January 31 and July 31, 2023 so that only the balance is due on January 31, 2024 (along with the first payment on account for the next year). The payment on account system is meant to protect HMRC rather than victimize the taxpayer. The amount of the payment on account is related to the amount by which the taxpayer's payments on account fell short of the final bill for the previous year, and there is no obligation on the taxpayer to pay more than this even when the income of the current year is greater. Where the payment on account seems to the taxpayer to be excessive, there is a procedure for reducing it—but at the taxpayer's risk with regard to penalties and interest if the reduction proves to be incorrect.

HMRC may give notice that they are inquiring into a return and have a twelve-month period in which to do this; the subsequent investigation may take longer. The inquiry is ended by a "closure" notice. Once the inquiry period has passed or the closure notice has been given, HMRC have the power to seek unpaid tax if this situation was brought about carelessly or deliberately by the taxpayer and the officer could not have been reasonably expected, on the basis of the information then available, to be aware of the loss of tax.

The ordinary time limit for giving notice is four years after the date (January 31) on which the self-assessment return should have been made. This period is extended to twelve years for underpayment of income tax, inheritance tax, and CGT relating to an offshore matter. The ordinary four years is lengthened to six years if the loss of tax has been due to carelessness and twenty years if it has been deliberate.

Taxpayers outside the self-assessment system have their tax assessed by the HMRC. Perhaps the most important feature of the rules for taxpayers outside the self-assessment system was the introduction during World War II of the PAYE rules. This was a system of cumulative withholding at source on all income from employment. Under PAYE, the taxpayer would be given a code which would be based on the available deductions for that year; the deductions would then be allocated on a week-by-week cumulative basis. The rules allowed for an accurate deduction of tax even where the person's income level or employment changed during the year. A reduction in income level would bring not simply a reduced tax deduction for the rest of the year, but sometimes even a repayment. The purpose of this system was to establish the correct amount of income tax deducted at source by the end of the year so as to avoid additional paperwork. This imposed substantial extra cost on employers but the system appears to have worked reasonably well.

9 GENERAL PRINCIPLES

9.1 Relationship Between Tax and Financial Accounting

The traditional stance of UK tax law was to regard tax accounting and business accounting as distinct. Although the force of this distinction could be exaggerated, it was clear that in many areas the tax law rules were very different from the accounting rules (e.g., in relation to depreciation). Nonetheless, as a practical matter, both tax practitioners and HMRC started by looking at the business accounts and then made such changes as were needed for tax law.

The recent UK story has been one of continuous movement, usually gently, and mostly toward alignment. The UK tax legislation charges tax on the full amount of annual profits or gains arising or accruing from a trade, profession, or vocation.[21] By the early 1990s, the courts had come to recognize a significant role for business accounting.

A Court of Appeal decision[22] doubted whether any judge-made rule could override a generally accepted rule of commercial accountancy which: (i) applied to the situation in question; (ii) was not one of two or more rules applicable to that situation; and (iii) was not shown to be inconsistent with the true facts or otherwise inapt to determine the true profits or losses of the business. This decision was reinforced by subsequent legislation,[23] which required that profits be computed in accordance with generally accepted accounting principles (GAAP) "subject to any adjustments required or authorized by law" in computing profits for those purposes. Depending on the taxpayer, the GAAP are those recognized in the UK or the International Accounting Standards.[24]

In the latest pronouncement from the Supreme Court in *HMRC v. NCL Investments Ltd.*, the Court left the door open for a judge-made rule "which it is clear applies notwithstanding that the company's profits have been calculated in accordance with generally accepted accounting principles" but goes on to state that no such rule was cited to it and that "there is no general theoretical basis for the courts to calculate profits other than generally accepted accounting principles."[25] If different applications of an accounting standard are asserted, as may be the case, given that accounting standards involve judgments and are not the same as statutes, the court will see its role as being that of an adjudicator between those giving expert evidence.[26] If the accounting standards rely on legal concepts, judges will apply their own understanding of those legal concepts, unless the standards clearly apply a different standard.[27]

This is still some way from complete alignment, but there have also been substantial legislative changes which have made the two closer. Thus, the mid-1990s corporation tax rules on loan relationships, financial instruments, and foreign exchange (now merged with the loan-relationship rules) all use accounting rules for measuring and timing gains and losses; moreover, they usually override the distinction between capital and revenue. Likewise, the 2002 rules on intellectual property use accounting concepts both in their definition and their tax computation rules. One thing these provisions have in common is a willingness to abandon the old doctrines, such as the distinction between income and capital and the realization requirement. In place of the old doctrines is an accrual system of taxation covering both gains and losses and

21. CTA 2009, s. 35 for corporation tax on trading profits and ITTOIA, s. 5 for income tax on the profits of individuals engaged in a trade, profession, or vocation.
22. *Gallagher v. Jones* [1993] STC 537, especially 555-6, per Sir Thomas Bingham M.R. *See also HMRC v. William Grant & Sons Distillers Ltd.; Small (Inspector of Taxes) v. Mars UK Ltd.* [2007] UKHL 15.
23. CTA 2009, s. 46 for corporation tax and ITTOIA, s. 25 for income tax.
24. CTA 2010, s. 1127.
25. *HMRC v. NCL Investments Ltd. and Smith & Williamson Corporate Services Ltd.* [2022] UKSC 9.
26. *Heather v. PE Consulting Group* [1973] 1 All ER 843 (CA).
27. *The Union Castle Mail Steamship Company Limited v. HMRC* [2020] EWCA Civ 547.

allowing a choice of accounting systems. Finally, since 2013 smaller unincorporated businesses (with annual turnover less than GBP 150,000) have been able to elect to use the cash basis rather than GAAP in computing taxable profits.[28] From 2024-2025 onward, the cash basis is the default method for calculating business profits for self-employed traders and those in partnerships; businesses must opt in to use an accruals basis. In addition, former constraints, including the GBP 150,000 turnover limit as well as restrictions on claiming interest deductions and the use of losses for businesses using the cash basis, were abolished.

Some business people still want tax law to follow accounting treatment—usually because they believe that they can get more reliefs than are available at present and hope to save on accountants' bills for making tax returns. However, some accounting specialists want to be free to develop their accounting ideas, which are based on how to report profits to shareholders and other interested parties, without fear that their proposals will be rejected because of adverse tax implications. Some tax specialists want nothing to do with these ideas, believing that some of the answers produced by the accounting theorists are not only bad tax but also bad accounting.

This dispute reminds one of the words of Lord Hoffmann, who once wrote, "Like many rival tribes accountants and lawyers have opinions of each other which are largely based on ignorance. ... In fact both professions are deeply engaged in the intolerable wrestle with words and meanings, which give rise to philosophical problems having much in common with each other."[29]

9.2 Respect for Legal Form

The distinction between private law and public law has had little impact on UK substantive law—as opposed to procedural law—and it has been quite unnecessary to decide whether tax law is part of public law. The English genius for not categorizing things unless one must, combined with an instinctive wish to proceed on a purely pragmatic basis, is well illustrated by this issue, which is of such concern to lawyers brought up in the civil law tradition.

In answering the question of how far the UK tax law has respect for legal form, we have to divide the question into different issues and begin by recognizing that the rights and duties created by people in their personal or business dealings are part of the facts to which the tax law must apply its concepts; thus, the rights created by legal form are as much facts as the state of the weather or a person's age. As section 9.3 below shows, UK courts have wrestled hard with the question of how far they can go in recharacterizing the facts where tax-avoidance schemes are concerned. As the speech of Lord Hoffman in *MacNiven*, cited below in section 9.3, makes clear, there will be many contexts in which the courts give a strict legal meaning to a particular expression in the tax legislation. It would not occur to these judges that they are having "respect" for the legal form; they are simply interpreting the relevant (tax) legislation. Apart from the

28. ITTOIA 2005, ss. 31A et seq.
29. Foreword to Freedman and Power (eds.), *Law and Accountancy: Conflict and Cooperation in the 1990s* (P. Chapman Pub. Ltd., 1992).

avoidance context, there will be many occasions on which the tax legislation uses concepts which have familiar legal meanings. Thus, the question whether a person's income comes from employment or business turns on whether the relevant contract is one of service or for services, a distinction familiar to tort and labor lawyers. The question whether a business is being carried on by a company or by a partnership will have to be answered with the Partnership Act definition of a partnership very much in mind. Likewise, questions of status, such as whether a person is married, or whether Y is the child of X, will normally be answered by reference to family law rules. To take another example, the technicalities of property law will also be relevant in analyzing issues such as whether a person has an "interest" in property.

In response, the tax legislator may deliberately avoid the use of a word with existing technical overtones. This may be further encouraged by the fact that the tax legislation has to apply to Scotland as well as to England, and therefore the language should be able to accommodate two sets of concepts; this may be done by referring explicitly to English terms and then to Scottish terms—e.g., the definition of "settlement" for Inheritance Tax purposes[30] or by adopting broader terminology not confined to one system or the other. The UK tax system pays considerable respect to the legal form of a transaction. The issue, in all cases, is how far the legal form of the transaction determines the tax consequences, but that is a matter for the process of interpreting tax statutes.

9.3 Anti-avoidance Doctrines and Rules

The periodic shifts in the UK tax environment can also be seen in the willingness or unwillingness of the courts to control tax avoidance by judicial doctrine. As seen in section 6.2 above, the effect of the *Barclays* case is that the courts now try to look for the purpose behind the statute and to take a less blinkered approach to the facts. While *Barclays* does much to settle the intellectual basis for interpretation, it does little for certainty in the application of the rules. Despite the new judicial approach, tax legislation is still drafted in the traditional way with highly prescriptive rules, sometimes backed up by a purpose-based anti-avoidance rule. Some of these rules have proved difficult to interpret.

The UK tax system has a large number of anti-avoidance provisions, some broad, some narrow, and, since 2013, a general anti-abuse rule. The courts have shown a willingness to interpret in a broad way anti-avoidance provisions which are phrased in general language that deliberately eschews legal terms of art. The story is long and drawn-out and erratic, as the following quotation from fifty years ago shows:

> We seem to have traveled a long way from the general and salutary rule that the subject is not to be taxed except by plain words. But I must recognize that plain words are seldom adequate to anticipate and forestall the multiplicity of ingenious schemes which are constantly being devised to evade (*sic*) taxation. Parliament is very properly determined to prevent this kind of tax evasion (*sic*) and, if the courts

30. Inheritance Tax Act 1984 s. 43.

> find it impossible to give very wide meanings to general phrases, the only alternative may be for Parliament to do as some other countries have done, and introduce legislation of a more sweeping character which will put the ordinary well-intentioned person at much greater risk than is now created by a wide interpretation of such provisions as those which we are now considering.[31]

The House of Lords (now Supreme Court) has shown itself capable, on the one hand, of depriving a provision of any effect, and, on the other, of imposing double taxation.

Apart from the question of the strictness or otherwise with which statutes are construed, there is the closely related issue of the characterization of the facts, particularly where avoidance schemes are concerned. There has been no shortage of leading cases on the judicial approach to problems of tax avoidance, but one still begins with *IRC v. Duke of Westminster*.[32] This case lays down that, in applying the tax legislation to the facts, the courts must have respect for the legal rights which the parties have created, even if those rights were created for tax avoidance purposes. In this form, the decision is still good law, but it does not tell us what those legal rights are, and it is here that the new approach has made its impact.

As a result of some occasional odd drafting and a very aggressive tax avoidance industry, a number of avoidance schemes were peddled in the 1970s. These schemes frequently involved circular and ultimately self-canceling transactions carried through according to some timetable. A typical example was *WT Ramsay Ltd. v. IRC*,[33] where the House determined that it would be consistent with the *Westminster* doctrine to treat such circular and self-canceling transactions as one single transaction for tax purposes. Although the scheme in *Ramsay* failed not only at this abstract level but also on a narrow point of tax law, the decision was very important. If the scheme had succeeded, the tax (CGT) would have become voluntary—one would have paid either HMRC or the tax adviser. In assessing this apparently complacent attitude on the part of the judges, it should not be forgotten that Parliament passes a Finance Bill every year and loopholes could be filled by appropriate provisions. Moreover, the traditions of party discipline and of allowing clauses drafted by professional drafters meant that the government would usually get its way, and do so in a workable form.

In *Furniss v. Dawson*,[34] the *Ramsay* decision was extended to a linear transaction in a preordained series having no purpose (as opposed to effect) other than the avoidance of tax. This was perhaps the high-water mark of what became known as the New Approach or the *Ramsay* doctrine. The case itself involved the use of a share-for-share exchange to achieve a deferral of CGT on a corporate reorganization. The effect of that decision, exacerbated by some very wide statements by some members of the court, was to reduce much tax advice to a valueless exercise in guessing what the courts might do next. This period of uncertainty ended in 1988 when the court, in considering what was meant by a preordained series of transactions, concluded that

31. Lord Reid in *Greenberg v. IRC* [1972] AC 173 (HL) at 198.
32. *IRC v. Duke of Westminster* [1936] AC 1; 19 TC 490.
33. *WT Ramsay Ltd. v. IRC* [1981] STC 174; [1982] AC 300.
34. *Furniss v. Dawson* [1984] STC 153; [1984] AC 474.

such a series of transactions existed only when it was "practically certain" at the time of the first step that the second would follow.[35] This case also restricted the New Approach, so that the UK was left with a narrow step transaction doctrine which applied where there is no business purpose other than the avoidance of tax. However, the New Approach may well have had other effects, particularly in encouraging the courts to look more broadly at the facts even where there is no tax-avoidance motive. Meanwhile, the courts have stressed the need for tax to live in the "real world."[36]

The nature of the common law is such that the process of judicial development of doctrine is anything but smooth; much depends on the nature of the case before the court and the particular judges. Two further judicial decisions make this point. The first was *McGuckian v. IRC*[37] in which, as we have seen, the House of Lords enunciated the purposive approach to the interpretation of tax statutes, and two of the five members of the House of Lords sitting in that case were prepared to take a broad approach to an avoidance case without going through the step transaction doctrine at all. The other, and more dramatic, decision was the unanimous 2001 decision of the House of Lords in *MacNiven v. Westmoreland Investments Ltd.*,[38] in which the leading opinion was given by Lord Hoffmann. This case held that the step transaction doctrine did not have any role where the term in issue was "juristic" as opposed to commercial. The commercial/juristic distinction proved difficult to apply, and in the *Barclays* case it was downgraded to a useful insight. However, what mattered was that in *MacNiven* the House held that the question whether to apply the new approach was itself a question of construction. The courts have no power to strike down avoidance schemes; Parliament has not given them such power, and while they can develop purposive interpretations or a step transaction doctrine, the matter remains one of judicial attitude.

In the late 1990s, HMRC consulted on the possibility of introducing a statutory general anti-avoidance rule (GAAR). The result of the consultation was that the proposal was withdrawn—however, that was before the decisions in *MacNiven* and *Barclays*. In December 2010, the Exchequer Secretary asked Graham Aaronson, QC to lead a new study into a possible UK GAAR. In 2011, the Aaronson study group recommended that the UK adopt a narrowly focused general anti-abuse rule, rather than a sweeping anti-avoidance rule. Finance Act 2013, sections 206-215 and Schedule 43 introduced the new general anti-abuse rule. At the time of writing the GAAR has yet to be tested in the courts.

The GAAR applies to counteract tax advantages arising from abusive tax arrangements involving the income tax, corporation tax, CGT, inheritance tax, and many other taxes.[39] Arrangements constitute "tax arrangements" if it would be reasonable to conclude, having regard to all the circumstances, that their main purpose, or one of

35. *Craven v. White; Bayliss v. Gregory;* and *IRC v. Bowater* [1988] STC 476.
36. For example, *Ensign Tankers (Leasing) Ltd. v. Stokes* [1992] STC 226.
37. *Supra* note 7.
38. [2001] UK HL 6 [2001] STC 237.
39. Finance Act 2013 s. 206. By virtue of National Insurance Contributions Act 2014, s. 10(1), the GAAR also applies to NICs.

their main purposes, was obtaining a tax advantage.[40] Thus, the purpose is determined on an objective, not subjective, basis. A tax advantage includes tax reliefs, repayments, avoidance, and deferral. Whether a tax arrangement is "abusive" is determined under the crucial double-reasonableness test in Finance Act 2013, section 207(2)—arrangements are abusive where the entering or carrying out of the arrangements "cannot reasonably be regarded as a reasonable course of action" in relation to the relevant tax provisions, having regard to all the circumstances, and, in particular, to:

- the consistency of the substantive results of the arrangements with the principles and policy underlying the tax provisions;
- whether the means used in achieving those results involve the use of contrived or abnormal steps; and
- whether the arrangements are intended to exploit any shortcoming in the tax provisions.

An arrangement also might not be considered reasonable where it results in profits or losses which diverge from economic reality, and it is reasonable to assume that such a result was not the anticipated result when the relevant tax provisions were enacted.[41] In the event that the GAAR applies to the arrangement, the counteraction of the tax advantages under the GAAR is on a "just and reasonable" basis.[42]

Finance Act 2013, Schedule 43-43C sets out further procedural requirements, including those related to the creation and operation of the GAAR advisory panel. The panel is meant to act as a reality check on HMRC's view that the GAAR should be applied to a given arrangement. Significantly, section 211 contains a novel and unusually broad evidentiary rule which goes well beyond the normal *Pepper v. Hart* approach to extrinsic materials, including allowing evidence of HMRC guidance and established practice at the time. Moreover, the GAAR legislation provides that a court or tribunal "must take into account" the GAAR panel's opinion about the arrangements giving rise to the GAAR assessment.[43] However, the precise nature of the relationship between the GAAR advisory panel and the courts, and many other details, are still to be worked out. HMRC has issued guidance on the GAAR, which has been approved by the GAAR advisory panel and is available on the HMRC website. In addition, pursuant to Finance Act 2013, section 211(2)(a), a court or tribunal faced with a GAAR issue "must take into account" approved HMRC guidance. In 2016, the government attached a penalty of 60% of tax due to all cases successfully tackled by the GAAR.[44]

Meanwhile, the Court of Justice of the EU has developed its own approach to these issues. It has refused to give effect to transactions which "abuse" EU rules; this is closely related to a refusal to give effect to transactions which are wholly artificial.

40. Finance Act 2013, ss. 207 and 208.
41. Finance Act 2013, s. 207.
42. Finance Act 2013, s. 209.
43. Finance Act 2013, s. 211.
44. Finance Act 2013, s. 212A.

Post-Brexit, this doctrine is still relevant for the UK's VAT, which explains why the VAT is not one of the listed taxes to which the GAAR applies.

A wide range of other statutory provisions has been introduced in recent years which enhance HMRC's ability to target tax evasion and avoidance. In 2004, the Disclosure of Tax Avoidance Schemes (DOTAS) rules were introduced; they require promoters to provide HMRC with information about notifiable arrangements and proposals for notifiable arrangements within a specified time. These rules have been strengthened further over time. Finance Act 2009 introduced a requirement for senior accounting officers of large companies to take reasonable steps to establish and monitor accounting systems so that they are adequate for accurate tax reporting. Such officers also have to certify annually that the systems are adequate (or explain why not). In Finance Act 2014, HMRC was given statutory powers to target "high-risk" tax promoters, requiring disclosure of all information provided to prospective users of notifiable schemes. Finance Act 2014 also introduced "follower notice" powers, along with new "accelerated payment" powers. In particular, these powers are aimed at marketed tax-avoidance schemes and seek to reduce the economic advantages of entering into such schemes. They aim to encourage taxpayers who had used an avoidance scheme to settle their tax affairs once the scheme or a materially similar scheme has been defeated in the courts—or risk a penalty for failing to do so—and to require disputed tax in avoidance cases to be paid upfront rather than waiting until a final resolution of the matter (e.g., in the courts). Further measures introduced recently include requiring large businesses to publish their tax strategy, civil penalties for enablers of tax evasion and defeated tax avoidance, a strict liability criminal offense for failure to pay tax on offshore income, rules restricting tax reliefs for "serial avoiders," and a new offense of corporate failure to prevent tax evasion or the facilitation of tax evasion.

10 TAX TREATIES

The UK has one of the most extensive tax treaty networks in the world. It has comprehensive treaties with over 100 countries, as well as over 25 Tax Information Exchange Agreements, plus other treaties covering inheritance and gift taxes and social security. The UK's tax treaty network includes treaties with all of its major trading partners, most members of the Commonwealth, and all other OECD countries. As a member of the OECD, most of the UK's tax treaties follow the general pattern of the OECD Model Treaty, subject to several major exceptions:

- some treaties predate the OECD Model;
- treaty benefits can be limited in respect of income taxed on the remittance basis;
- the UK-United States treaty (2001) has more extensive limitation-on-benefits provisions; and
- over thirty treaties provide a fixed foreign tax-sparing credit.

The UK has signed the *Multilateral Convention on Mutual Assistance in Tax Matters*, the *Multilateral Competent Authority Agreement on the Exchange of Country-by-Country Reports*, and the *Multilateral Competent Authority Agreement on Automatic Exchange of Financial Account Information*.

The UK has signed the *Multilateral Convention to Implement Tax Treaty Related Measures to Prevent Base Erosion and Profit Shifting* (MLI), which entered into force on October 1, 2018, and began to have effect for UK tax treaties from January 1, 2019. The UK has expressed the wish that nearly all its treaties should be covered by the MLI. On treaty abuse, the UK has opted for the principal purpose test and has adopted the provision to treat dual-resident companies as resident in a contracting state only where there is an agreement between the competent authorities under the mutual agreement procedure. It has not adopted any of the changes offered with respect to BEPS Actions 2 (hybrids) and 7 (permanent establishment status), on the view that current legislation and treaty provisions are sufficient to address these issues. It has accepted the mandatory binding arbitration provisions in Part VI of the MLI.

In Finance Act 2020 the UK enacted a digital services tax (DST) of 2% levied on the UK revenues of very large digital businesses operating in the UK. In Finance (No. 2) Act 2023, the UK provided the legislative framework to introduce a multinational top-up tax and domestic top-up tax in order to implement the OECD's Inclusive Framework Pillar 2 proposals, with effect in relation to accounting periods commencing on or after December 31, 2023. This involves a new top-up tax on UK parent members within a multinational enterprise group in circumstances in which a subsidiary is located in a non-UK jurisdiction and the group's profits arising in that jurisdiction are taxed at less than the minimum rate of 15%. The UK has indicated it intends to transition away from the DST toward the OECD Inclusive Framework's Two-Pillar solution for reforming the international tax regime. The UK will keep the revenue raised from the DST until the Pillar One reforms become operational. Once Pillar One is in effect, companies will be able use the difference between what they have paid in DST from January 2022, and what they would have paid if Pillar One had been in effect instead, as a credit against their future corporation tax bill.

11 SOURCES OF TAX LAW

11.1 Legislation and Materials and Cases

A statute's legislative history can be traced not only in the legislation passed year-by-year together with the accompanying debates but also in the annual reports made to Parliament by HMRC. These are accompanied by many statistics. There is also useful information of a background nature in another government publication called *Social Trends*. Explanatory notes prepared by HMRC for Ministers when presenting bills to Parliament are now publicly available and can be traced through the HMRC website (https://www.gov.uk/government/organisations/hm-revenue-customs). Legislation produced under the Tax Law Rewrite Program can be traced through the various exposure drafts as well as the extensive explanatory notes which accompany the final legislation. These are available electronically via the HMRC website. The texts of the statutes are available through the normal commercial websites (e.g., LexisNexis and Westlaw). There are no official hard-copy versions of the complete tax statutes—everyone relies for hard copy on the annual versions produced by Tolley LexisNexis and CCH. Electronic versions of the statutes are available online, but they are not regularly updated and should be used with caution http://www.legislation.gov.uk/.

Parliamentary debates, reported in *Hansard*, are available online for the House of Commons and the House of Lords going back a number of years; a range of other publications, including committee reports, is also available (*see* https://www.parliament.uk/business/publications/).

UK judicial decisions are available online through websites such as Westlaw, the Bailii online database (http://www.bailii.org/databases.html), and the Tribunals/Courts own websites; for the Tribunals, High Court, and Court of Appeal *see* https://www.judiciary.uk/judgments/ and for the Supreme Court *see* https://www.supremecourt.uk/decided-cases/. The cases are also published weekly through series such as *Simons Tax Cases* (LexisNexis).

11.2 Official Practice and Rulings

HMRC (formerly Inland Revenue) for many years published extra-statutory concessions and statements of practice, both of which are now available electronically from the HMRC website. Statements of practice became more systematic in 1978. The scope of the legal basis for making these concessions has been the matter of much debate; recent legislation enables the Treasury to give legal effect to existing concessions by order. Since 1978, HMRC has published Revenue Interpretations and Decisions in their own magazine, *Tax Bulletin*.

Other sources include the publication of HMRC's manuals for the guidance of inspectors; some of these are particularly useful (e.g., those dealing with specialized matters such as banking and international transactions). Publication of the manuals is not complete—various passages, such as those on avoidance schemes, are omitted. Electronic versions of the manuals are available on the HMRC website.

Pre-transaction rulings have been a feature of some parts of the tax code but are not generalized. Informal advance clearances have long been available provided that full disclosure is made. The development of pre-transaction rulings is part of a recent HMRC process of improving its working relationship with large businesses. The process is intended to develop an "enhanced relationship" between the taxpaying company and HMRC, with better and quicker service and each company having its own Customer Compliance Manager at HMRC. This is all part of HMRC's wish to make the best use of its resources and to use a risk-based analysis for its compliance activities. HMRC also hope that this relationship may lead to less aggressive tax planning.

The question whether one can use concessions for tax-avoidance purposes was considered in *R v. IRC, ex parte Fulford-Dobson*.[45] The court held that since the official booklet published by the Inland Revenue setting out these concessions stated that the Revenue would not allow them to be used for avoidance purposes, the taxpayer could not reverse that refusal by judicial review. New extra-statutory concessions are much less common since the 2005 decision in *R v. IRC, ex parte Wilkinson*. In that case, Lord Hoffmann not only accepted that HMRC had a wide managerial discretion under the Taxes Management Act 1970 but also stated that the discretion was not so wide "as to enable the commissioners to concede, by extra-statutory concession, an allowance which Parliament could have granted but did not grant and on grounds not of pragmatism but of general equity...."[46] Following *Wilkinson*, the government has moved many longstanding extra-statutory concessions onto the statute books.

Where an application for judicial review is made on the basis of a ruling, in the case of an informal clearance, HMRC will be bound only if the taxpayer gave full details of the specific transaction in question, made it plain that a fully considered ruling was sought, indicated the use of any ruling given, and the ruling or statement made was clear, unambiguous, and devoid of qualification. A breach of a representation by HMRC will not amount to an abuse of power where the taxpayer knows that clearance at the local level is not to be treated as binding on HMRC or where the taxpayer has not fully disclosed all relevant material to the inspectors. There is not necessarily full disclosure merely because sufficient information has been disclosed to enable inferences to be drawn.

11.3 Secondary Sources

There are two leading practitioners' works. *Simons Taxes* (formerly *Simons Direct Tax Service*), recently completely revised and reissued, is available both electronically and in hard copy (ten volumes); it is published by Lexis Nexis. There is a similar service run by CCH. The best accounts for lawyers are to be found in the series of volumes published by Sweet and Maxwell and some stemming from the work of G.S.A. Wheatcroft in the 1960s, known collectively as the *British Tax Library*. For those with access to *Halsbury's Laws of England and Wales*, the taxation volumes 99 and 99A are updated annually by Loutzenhiser and may be a useful starting point.

The last Royal Commission on income tax reported in 1955. There have been various government documents or reports of committees on particular issues since then (e.g., the Keith Committee Report on the Powers of the Revenue Departments in 1983). As noted above, the House of Commons Parliamentary Papers is available on the internet.

There is much other writing on tax. Some of the most important are produced by the fiercely independent Institute for Fiscal Studies (IFS) (www.ifs.org.uk) and, of special interest to lawyers, its very influential Tax Law Review Committee (TLRC).

45. *R v. IRC, ex parte Fulford-Dobson* [1987] STC 344; 60 TC 168.
46. *R v. IRC, ex parte Wilkinson* [2005] UKHL 30, at paras. 20-23.

Publications from the IFS also include occasional commentaries, their famous green budgets, which are surveys of options for future government action and incisive comments on past choices, and the journal *Fiscal Studies*. The famous *Structure and Reform of Direct Taxation*, also known as the "Meade Report," was published by the IFS in 1978. A successor volume, *Tax by Design: the Mirrlees Review* was published by Oxford University Press in 2011, accompanied by a separate volume of commissioned papers published in 2010 as *Dimensions of Tax Design: the Mirrlees Review*. The Meade Report and both volumes of the *Mirrlees Review* are available online from the IFS website.

The main UK textbook is G. Loutzenhiser, ed., *Tiley's Revenue Law*, 10th ed. (Hart Publishing, 2022), with annual updates and other resources available on the publisher's website. The leading journal is the *British Tax Review*, founded in 1956 and available on Westlaw and indexed on HeinOnline. There are also some articles of interest in *The Tax Journal* and *Taxation* (both published by LexisNexis) and *Tax Adviser* https://www.taxadvisermagazine.com/, published by the Chartered Institute of Taxation. The Oxford University Centre for Business Taxation website is another good source of academic writing, principally but not exclusively by economists https://www.sbs.ox.ac.uk/research/centres-and-initiatives/oxford-university-centre-business-taxation.

Some relevant websites have been mentioned already but are repeated here. https://www.gov.uk/government/organisations/hm-revenue-customs is the website for HMRC. Those interested in policy matters and current legislation should also refer to the HM Treasury website—https://www.gov.uk/government/organisations/hm-treasury. The Office of Tax Simplification (OTS), formerly an independent office of HM Treasury charged with giving advice to the government on simplifying the UK tax system, produced regular reports (https://www.gov.uk/government/organisations/office-of-tax-simplification); however, the OTS was abolished by the government in Finance (No. 2) Act 2023.

The United States

James R. Repetti & Diane M. Ring

1 HISTORY OF FEDERAL INCOME TAX

The United States (U.S.) first adopted a tax on the income of individuals in 1864 to finance the Civil War. A taxpayer's income included their share of undistributed corporate income. The tax, which was repealed in 1872, affected only 1 % of potential taxpayers due to a generous exemption.

Over twenty years passed before Congress adopted a new act in 1895, which imposed a tax on the income of both individuals and corporations. The U.S. Supreme Court declared this act unconstitutional because Congress lacked authority to adopt an individual income tax without apportioning the tax among the states based on their relative populations. The final enactment of an individual income tax required the adoption of the 16th Amendment to the Constitution, which was ratified by the states in 1913.

The original 1913 income tax and subsequent changes through 1938 were enacted as self-contained Revenue Acts, with each new Revenue Act superseding the prior Revenue Act and containing all the income tax provisions. As a result, the process of referencing and amending the statutes was very complex and cumbersome. To remedy this problem, Congress codified all the revenue provisions in effect in 1939 into the Internal Revenue Code (IRC) of 1939. The change to a Code allowed subsequent statutory enactments to occur as amendments to the Code rather than as re-enactments of the entire Revenue Act.

Congress replaced the 1939 Code with the IRC of 1954. The 1954 Code revised the income tax treatment of partnerships, trusts and estates, annuities, and corporate distributions; it also introduced several new deductions and provided more accelerated depreciation rates. The most significant changes to the 1954 Code occurred in the 1980s. In 1981, Congress substantially reduced individual rates, decreasing the maximum statutory rate for individuals to 50 %, and adopted significant new tax incentives for savings and investments, including greatly accelerated depreciation rates. In 1986,

Congress adopted additional significant changes to the income tax structure. The Tax Reform Act of 1986 broadened the tax base, substantially eliminating many tax-incentive provisions and reducing individual rates still further, decreasing the maximum statutory individual tax rate to 28%. The deduction for personal interest was eliminated (except for home mortgage interest), as was the preference for capital gains. To mark the significance of the changes, Congress renamed the Code the IRC of 1986.

The period 1986 through 2000 witnessed several amendments to the Code which tended to increase the maximum statutory rates for individuals, reaching 39.6% in 1993. Concerns about budget deficits dominated legislation during that period, with little attention paid to the impact of the changes on the overall structure of the Code. Frequently, Congress hastily adopted amendments to the Code, with the result that still more "technical" amendments were necessary to correct the earlier changes. The focus on revenues, however, helped eliminate a budget deficit and, with the help of strong economic growth through 2000, created a surplus.

Beginning in 2001, a Republican President (George W. Bush) and a Republican majority in both houses of Congress existed for the first time in almost half a century. The result was a series of tax cuts. In 2001, Congress enacted a major tax cut intended to decrease revenues by USD 1.35 trillion dollars for the period 2001 through 2010. Because Senate Republicans lacked the votes needed to implement tax cuts beyond a ten-year period, the tax decreases were scheduled to end in 2010. These tax decreases generally applied to the individual income and estate taxes and were scheduled to be phased in over several years. In 2003, Congress accelerated the phase-in of the reduction in the maximum tax rate for individuals to 35% and reduced the maximum tax rate for individuals on capital gains and dividend income to 15%. Despite the fact that Republicans lost control of the House of Representatives in 2007, concerns about economic conditions prompted more generous depreciation and expensing provisions in 2008.

President Obama took office in 2009. After a lengthy debate, he and Congress agreed at the end of 2010 to extend the tax decreases adopted in 2001 and 2003 through 2012. Another protracted debate followed in 2012, and he and Congress agreed at the start of 2013 to make permanent many of the tax decreases adopted earlier. The maximum tax rate for high-income individuals, however, was increased to 39.6% for ordinary income and 20% for capital gains. In addition, the Patient Protection and Affordable Care Act (the "Affordable Care Act") in 2013 added a 3.8% Medicare surtax for higher-income individuals on most forms of investment income.

The election of President Trump and Republican control of both the House and Senate in 2017 set the stage for a significant tax decrease. Despite the fact that the economy was already expanding at a rapid pace, Congress enacted a significant tax decrease which was projected to reduce revenues by more than USD 1.7 trillion for the ten-year period between 2018 and 2027.[1] The tax decrease, known as the Tax Cuts and Jobs Act (TCJA), reduced corporate rates from a maximum rate of 35% to 21% and provided significant tax decreases for some individuals. TCJA also introduced a

1. Congressional Budget Office, The Budget and Economic Outlook, 2018-2028, p. 5 (April 2018).

complex new tax scheme, called Global Intangible Low-Taxed Income (GILTI), that imposes a significantly reduced—but current—tax on much of the income of controlled foreign corporations (CFCs) not captured by existing anti-deferral rules. The regime applies regardless of whether that income is distributed to the U.S. owner. However, when actually distributed to U.S. shareholders, income taxed under GILTI bears no additional U.S. tax.

President Biden, a Democrat, began his administration in January 2021 with a Democratic controlled Senate and a Republican controlled House of Representatives. The result was that most of his efforts at tax reform were stymied. Nevertheless, Congress did adopt a corporate alternative minimum tax (AMT) which imposes a minimum tax on U.S. corporations equal to 15% of their modified financial income. The scope is limited because only U.S. corporations with average annual modified financial income in excess of USD 1 billion are subject to the minimum tax. In addition, a new tax credit to encourage the manufacture of semiconductors was adopted in 2022.

2 CONSTITUTIONAL ISSUES

The general taxing power clause of the U.S. Constitution[2] grants Congress very broad powers to assess taxes. The clause states that Congress may "lay and collect Taxes, Duties, Imposts and Excises, to pay the Debts and provide for the common Defense and general Welfare of the United States." In 1913, the Sixteenth Amendment to the U.S. Constitution extended the scope of Congressional taxing powers to include an income tax in 1913. In 2012, the Supreme Court described the broad powers conferred by the taxing clause as follows:

> Put simply, Congress may tax and spend. This grant gives the Federal Government considerable influence even in areas where it cannot directly regulate. The Federal Government may enact a tax on an activity that it cannot authorize, forbid, or otherwise control. And in exercising its spending power, Congress may offer funds to the States, and may condition those offers on compliance with specified conditions. These offers may well induce the States to adopt policies that the Federal Government itself could not impose.[3]

Earlier cases which seemed to impose some restrictions on the ability of Congress to use tax statutes to accomplish objectives not related to raising revenue are now commonly disregarded. For example, it is now clear that Congress may use taxes to discourage certain activities without any consideration of whether the tax will in fact raise revenues.[4] Moreover, Congress may favor some groups with tax preferences without favoring all groups as long as the distinction among groups is not based on race, gender, national origin, or U.S. citizenship. For example, in *Regan v. Taxation With Representation of Washington*,[5] the Supreme Court ruled that the fact that Congress allows veterans' organizations to use tax-deductible contributions to engage

2. U.S. Constitution, Art. I, s. 8, cl. 1.
3. *National Federation of Independent Business (NFIB) v. Sebelius*, 567 US 519, 537 (2012).
4. *See*, e.g., *Sunshine Anthracite Coal Co. v. Adkins*, 310 US 381 (1947).
5. 461 US 540 (1983).

in political lobbying did not mean that Congress has to extend the same tax subsidy to other organizations. The Court explained that Congress has "broad latitude in creating classifications and distinctions in tax statutes."

Consistent with this "broad latitude" is the Supreme Court's treatment of tax statutes which apply retroactively. The Court has stated that the enactment or amendment of a tax statute which applies retroactively will be held unconstitutional under the due-process clause of the Fifth Amendment only where "the nature of the tax and the circumstances in which it is laid [are] so harsh and oppressive as to transgress the constitutional limitation."[6] Under this standard, the Supreme Court has permitted tax rates to increase for the calendar year in which legislation was adopted, even where the legislation is adopted late in the year.[7] Similarly, in *United States v. Carlton*,[8] the Court held that an amendment made in 1987 which applied retroactively to 1986 was not unconstitutional where Congress had acted promptly to correct a mistake in the statute adopted in 1986.

Another area illustrating the U.S. courts' view of the expansive nature of Congressional taxing power is the Supreme Court's decision in *NFIB v. Sebelius*,[9] which involved the constitutionality of the Affordable Care Act. The Affordable Care Act imposed a fine on U.S. residents who failed to acquire health insurance. On the one hand, if this fine were properly classified as a tax, it would likely be viewed as a valid exercise of Congress' broad taxing power. On the other hand, if it were classified as a penalty, and not a tax, it would be unconstitutional because it would exceed the less expansive powers granted to Congress by the Commerce Clause of the U.S. Constitution to regulate interstate commerce. While the Commerce Clause allows Congress to regulate interstate activity, it does not allow Congress to require residents to purchase a certain product, such as health insurance, by imposing a penalty on their failure to do so. The Supreme Court held that the fine was a tax and, therefore, did not exceed Congress' broad taxing powers.

After the Supreme Court characterized the fine as a tax in the *NFIB* case, as discussed above, opponents of the Affordable Care Act turned to the Origination Clause to challenge the fine. The Origination Clause (Article 1, section 7, clause 1 of the U.S. Constitution) states, "All Bills for raising Revenue shall originate in the House of Representatives; but the Senate may propose or concur with amendments as on other bills." In *Sissel v. United States Department of Health & Human Services*,[10] plaintiffs challenged the Affordable Care Act because it did not originate in the House of Representatives, as required by the Origination Clause. The Court of Appeals for the Federal Circuit held that the Origination Clause was not violated. It reasoned that, although the Supreme Court had characterized the Affordable Care Act's imposition of a fine for failure to purchase health insurance as a tax, the Origination Clause applies to "bills for raising *Revenue*" (emphasis added). The Court of Appeals determined that

6. *Welch v. Henry*, 305 US 134, 147 (1948).
7. *See*, e.g., *United States v. Darusmont*, 449 US 292, 297 (1981); *United States v. Hudson*, 299 US 495, 500-01 (1937).
8. 512 US 26 (1994).
9. 567 US 519 (2012).
10. 799 F.3d 1035 (D.C. Cir. 2015).

the fine which the Supreme Court had characterized in *NFIB* as a tax was not enacted to raise revenue and, therefore, the Origination Clause did not apply.

Several U.S. Courts of Appeal have also refused to apply the Origination Clause in somewhat different circumstances. In 1982, the House of Representatives adopted a tax bill consisting of three pages, which it then sent to the Senate. The Senate removed the provisions the House had adopted and substituted over 500 pages of new amendments to the Code. Both the House and Senate then adopted the "revised" bill, and it was signed by the President. All the U.S. Courts of Appeals that have addressed the validity of this process have held that the Senate's "revision" did not violate the Origination Clause.[11]

Recently, the issue whether the U.S. Constitution requires a "realization event" to occur before income may be taxed has emerged. The Supreme Court initially (in 1920) held that the 16th Amendment of the U.S. Constitution, which authorized Congress to enact an income tax, required a "realization" event, such as the sale of an asset or the receipt of property, to occur before income could be recognized.[12] Subsequent decisions, however, suggested that the requirement of a realization event was merely a matter of administrative convenience rather than a Constitutional requirement.[13] The current status of the realization requirement as a matter of administrative convenience has recently been opened to question due to the Supreme Court's decision in *Moore v. United States*.[14] The taxpayers in *Moore*, who were U.S. shareholders in a CFC, argued that the imposition of a tax by IRC, section 965 on the accumulated undistributed income of the CFC was unconstitutional because the shareholders had not realized such income. In finding for the government (and holding that the section 965 tax was constitutional), the majority determined that it was unnecessary to address whether realization is a constitutional requirement because the CFC had clearly realized the income that it had earned. Thus, the real issue, according to the majority, was whether such realized income could then be attributed to the shareholders. The majority concluded that attribution of income realized by an entity to its owners had always been permitted. However, four Justices, two in concurring opinions and two in dissenting opinions, took the view that realization was a constitutional requirement. It is likely, therefore, that the Supreme Court and lower courts will revisit this issue again in the future.

3 TAX RATES

The rates of the U.S. income tax have fluctuated widely depending on revenue needs and the economic objectives of Congress. Initially, in 1913, the maximum statutory tax

11. *See*, e.g., *Boday v. United States*, 759 F.2d 1472 (9th Cir. 1985); *House v. United States*, 593 F. Supp. 139 (W.D. Mich. 1984), aff'd mem. 787 F.2d 590 (6th Cir. 1986); *Liljenfeldt v. United States*, 588 F. Supp. 966 (W.D. Wis.), aff'd mem. 753 F.2d 1077 (7th Cir. 1984); *Rowe v. United States*, 583 F. Supp. 1516 (D. Del.), aff'd mem. 749 F.2d 27 (3d Cir. 1984); *Brasseur v. United States*, 765 F.2d 148 (9th Cir. 1985).
12. *Eisner v. Macomber*, 252 US 189 (1920).
13. *Helvering v. Horst*, 311 US 112, 116 (1940).
14. *Moore v. United States*, Slip Op. No. 22-800 (S.Ct. June 20, 2024).

rate was 6% for individuals and 1% for corporations. In subsequent years, the rate for individuals peaked at 91% and for corporations at 52% (excluding the excess profits tax, which during World War II subjected corporations to an overall maximum rate of 80%).

The IRC of 1986 significantly reduced both the level and progressivity of the rates, establishing the maximum statutory rate for individuals at 28% and the corporate rate at 34%. Since then, rates have varied depending on the political and fiscal climate. In 1993, Congress increased rates to 39.6% for individuals and 35% for corporations. In 2001, Congress adopted legislation which decreased rates for individuals during the five-year period through 2006. In 2003, Congress accelerated the decrease, with the result that the maximum individual rate was 35% through 2012. The maximum individual rate again rose to 39.6% in 2013 but was reduced to 37% beginning in 2018.

Different rate schedules are provided for different categories of individuals. The brackets for the lower rates are broader for married individuals filing joint returns and for heads of households as compared to the brackets for unmarried individuals. The brackets for rates which apply to all individuals are adjusted annually to reflect inflation. The rate schedules for the 2024 taxable year are as follows:

Unmarried Taxpayer	
Taxable Income (USD)	*Rate (%)*
0-11,600	10
11,600-47,150	12
47,150-100,525	22
100,525-191,950	24
191,950-243,725	32
243,725-609,350	35
Over 609,350	37

Married Taxpayers Filing Jointly	
Taxable Income (USD)	*Rate (%)*
0-23,200	10
23,200-94,300	12
94,300-201,050	22
201,050-383,900	24
383,900-487,450	32
487,450-731,200	35
Over 731,200	37

Taxpayer Who Is Head of Household	
Taxable Income (USD)	*Rate (%)*
0-16,550	10
16,550-63,100	12
63,100-100,500	22
100,500-191,950	24
191,950-243,700	32
243,700-609,350	35
Over 609,350	37

Beginning in 2018, the U.S. corporate tax rate is a flat 21%. Prior to 2018, corporate tax rates were graduated, ranging from 15% to 35%.[15]

4 COMPOSITION OF THE FISCAL SYSTEM

In addition to the income tax, the U.S. federal government also imposes a wealth transfer tax, social security taxes (funding both pension and medical benefits), and various excise taxes. There is no federal sales or value-added tax. Each state in the federal system is also allowed to impose taxes. The states in general impose some combination of income, property, wealth, sales, and excise taxes.

Social security taxes in the U.S. represent a significant tax which is imposed on net income from self-employment and wages from employment. For 2024, self-employed individuals pay social security taxes of 15.3% on net earnings of USD 168,600 or less. Income from self-employment in excess of USD 168,600 is taxed at 2.9%. Employees pay social security taxes of 7.65% on their wages of USD 168,600 or less and their employers also pay taxes of 7.65% on each employee's wages up to USD 168,600. The employee and employer each pay a tax of 1.45% on the employee's wages in excess of USD 168,600.

Federal receipts, as a percentage of gross domestic product (GDP), have been somewhat steady since 1960. During the period 1978 through 2022, federal receipts ranged from a low of 14.6% of GDP for the years 2009 and 2010, during a major recession, to a high of 20.0% of GDP for the year 2000.[16] Revenues in 2022 constituted 19.6% of GDP. The largest source of receipts for the U.S. government is the individual income tax. In 2022, 53.7% of federal receipts were from the individual income tax.[17] The next-largest category of receipts by the Internal Revenue Service (IRS) is social

15. The 2017 rate schedule actually peaked at a higher rate of 38% for income in the second-highest bracket in order to eliminate the benefit of the lower tax rates which applied to the lower brackets.
16. Office of Management and Budget, Historical Tables, Table 2.3 (2023) https://www.whitehouse.gov/omb/budget/historical-tables/.
17. *Ibid.*, at Table 2.2.

security taxes, which accounted for 30.3% of IRS receipts in 2022.[18] Taxes from corporations accounted for only 8.7% of receipts in 2022.[19]

It is interesting to note that the relative contributions of the corporate income tax and social security taxes have reversed over the past seventy years. In 1944, social security taxes accounted for 7.9% of federal receipts, while the corporate income tax accounted for 33.9% of receipts.[20] In contrast, in 2022, corporate income taxes accounted for only 8.7% of receipts, while social security taxes accounted for 30.3%.[21]

5 BASIC STRUCTURE OF THE INCOME TAX

5.1 Individuals

The U.S. individual income tax is global: it taxes the income of U.S. citizens and U.S. residents regardless of the geographic source or character of the income. The starting point for calculating the tax is gross income. The term "gross income" is defined broadly to include all accessions to wealth, with a few well-defined exclusions. Some significant exclusions are gifts, bequests, and proceeds from life insurance policies. Scholarships paid to degree-seeking students are also excludable from income if the scholarship is for tuition or book expenses and the student is not required to perform services. A broad range of fringe benefits is excluded from income, the most important ones being employer-provided health insurance and employer contributions to pension plans.

Income from the cancellation of debt is excluded from income only in certain narrow situations, such as when the taxpayer is insolvent or in a bankruptcy proceeding. Windfalls and gambling wins are clearly includable in income.

Although no statutory provision addresses the issue, imputed income is not taxed in the U.S. For example, taxpayers do not recognize income for the imputed rental value of their homes. Similarly, a taxpayer is not taxed with respect to the care provided by a spouse, parent, or child.

Gross income is recognized on the occurrence of a realization event. The scope of transactions which result in a realization event is fairly broad. For example, an exchange of one item of property for another qualifies as a realization event where the properties differ "materially in kind or in extent." Under this approach, the change in the yield of a debt instrument by more than twenty-five basis points will generally be treated as an exchange of an old debt instrument for a new instrument. In the corporate context, the distribution of appreciated property is normally a realization event to the distributing corporation, although it took Congress a surprisingly long time to reach this result.

The U.S. does not treat death as a realization event. Indeed, the appreciation inherent in property held by a taxpayer at death permanently escapes income taxation

18. *Ibid.*
19. *Ibid.*
20. *Ibid.*
21. *Ibid.*

because the tax basis of the property is stepped up (or down) to its fair market value at the time of death (or its fair market value at the time six months after death if the alternative valuation date is selected). However, property owned by wealthy taxpayers at death (taxpayers holding more than USD 13,610,000 in 2024) is subject to the U.S. estate tax, which is a wealth transfer tax.

An old Supreme Court decision, *Eisner v. Macomber*,[22] initially created doubt as to whether Congress had the authority to treat the mere appreciation of an asset as a realization event. However, the Court's statement in a subsequent decision,[23] which described the realization requirement as "founded on administrative convenience," reduced doubt about the authority of Congress to define a realization event in any way it wishes. Congress has elected to take a "mark-to-market" approach in narrow circumstances. For example, taxpayers in general are required to recognize any appreciation or diminution in value which has occurred during a tax year with respect to certain futures contracts and options. The Court's recent ruling in the *Moore* case, discussed above, however, has once again introduced some uncertainty about the scope of the realization requirement.

After calculating gross income, individual taxpayers may deduct expenditures that the statutes expressly provide are deductible. Taxpayers are permitted to deduct expenses they have incurred in producing income in a trade or business. Difficult judgments occur, however, where expenses incurred in the conduct of a trade or business also involve aspects of personal consumption. The U.S. tax system's treatment of such expenditures has been somewhat arbitrary. Some expenditures which involve mixed aspects of income production and personal consumption are always nondeductible in full regardless of whether the income-producing aspect dominates. For example, childcare expenses and the costs of commuting from a taxpayer's residence to a principal place of business are not deductible.[24] Other expenses, such as business-related meals, are partially deductible pursuant to a statute which arbitrarily allows a deduction for 50% of such expenditures.

The trade or business expenses which may be deducted currently are limited to expenses which do not have a significant benefit extending beyond the current taxable year. In general, expenses which have a significant benefit extending beyond the current year must be capitalized, although, until the issuance of regulations in 2013,[25] there had been substantial disagreement as to exactly how the test should be formulated. In general, the regulations require expenditures to be capitalized if they result in the "acquisition" or "improvement" of property. The regulations provide numerous examples which distinguish between expenditures for routine repairs, which do not have to be capitalized, and expenditures for "improvements," which do have to be capitalized.

22. 252 US 189 (1920).
23. *Helvering v. Horst*, 311 US 112, 115 (1940).
24. A special credit is allowed, however, for a portion of the expenses incurred in caring for children under age 18.
25. Treasury Regulation (Treas. Reg.) ss. 1-263(a)-1 et seq.

Expenses which are capitalized may be amortized or depreciated under various Code provisions. In general, the period for depreciation or amortization is determined by statute. Currently, the periods for real property correspond very roughly to their economic useful life. During the past two decades, Congress has allowed various capital expenditures involving tangible personal property to be expensed in order to encourage investment.

As discussed earlier, the TCJA reduced the maximum tax rate on individuals from 39.6% to 37% and the maximum tax rate on corporations from 35% to a flat 21%. The lower corporate tax rate reduced the combined statutory tax burden on income earned by a corporation and distributed to its stockholders as a taxable dividend from 48% to 36.8%. This reduction in the aggregate tax burden, in addition to the low 21% tax rate which applies to earnings accumulated by corporations, would have provided corporations with a significant tax advantage over flow-through entities (such as partnerships) held by individuals subject to the 37% rate, if the corporation were to accumulate its earnings over a period of years. In an attempt to retain some neutrality in the choice of entity for conducting a business, Congress adopted a complex new provision in 2017[26] which allows individuals to claim a deduction equal to 20% of the "qualified" trade or business[27] income derived from a flow-through entity or earned directly in a sole proprietorship. Proponents of the new deduction hoped that it would equalize taxation for individuals engaging in business through a corporation or a flow-through entity. However, in addition to being extremely complex, the new provision has not achieved this hoped-for parity.[28]

Trade or business expenses are generally deductible from gross income to obtain the statutorily defined amount of "adjusted gross income."[29] Most other deductions (the "itemized deductions") are then taken from adjusted gross income in order to determine taxable income. The calculation of adjusted gross income is significant because many of the itemized deductions are limited by reference to adjusted gross income. For example, the deduction for charitable contributions of appreciated property is, in general, limited to 30% of adjusted gross income; medical expenses are deductible only to the extent that they exceed 7.5% of adjusted gross income. Many of the itemized deductions represent tax expenditures.

Prior to the 2017 TCJA, individuals were allowed to deduct state and local taxes without limitation. A controversial provision in the TCJA limits the deduction to no more than USD 10,000 of state and local taxes for the years 2018 through 2025.[30] Residents of states which have higher income and property taxes have been particularly upset about this limitation.

Another controversial provision in the TCJA eliminates the deduction of a subset of itemized deductions called "miscellaneous itemized deductions" for the period 2018

26. IRC, s. 199A.
27. "Qualified" trades or business do not include most professional businesses such as accounting, medicine, law, and investment advising.
28. James R. Repetti, "The Impact of the 2017 Tax Act's Rate Changes on Choice of Entity" (2018) Vol. 22, No. 2 *Florida Tax Review* 687, https://doi.org/10.5744/ftr.2018.0011.
29. The 20% deduction under IRC, s. 199A, however, is deducted from adjusted gross income.
30. IRC, s. 164(b)(6).

through 2025.[31] "Miscellaneous itemized deductions" include expenses incurred in a profit-seeking activity which does not rise to the level of a trade or business and are not related to rent- or royalty-producing property. They also include expenses of an employee which have not been reimbursed by the employer. The temporary prohibition against deducting miscellaneous itemized deductions lacks any policy rationale other than to increase revenues and will likely intensify pressure on taxpayers to classify their profit-seeking activities as a trade or business.

In lieu of itemized deductions, individual taxpayers may deduct a so-called standard deduction. Usually, taxpayers will deduct the standard deduction if it exceeds the total amount of their itemized deductions which may be deducted. The main purpose of the standard deduction is to reduce the need for record-keeping for expenses; it also functions to exempt from tax a certain amount of income for those taxpayers, particularly in low brackets, who do not have such expenses. For 2024, the standard deduction for individuals will be USD 14,600 and for married couples filing jointly and for surviving spouses it will be USD 29,200.

After the various deductions, a tentative tax using the progressive tax rate is then calculated. Allowable tax credits, such as the childcare credit and earned income tax credit, are subtracted to determine tax liability. Most credits are not refundable. However, the earned income credit[32] and child tax credit (distinct from the childcare credit)[33] are examples of a few credits that are wholly or partially refundable and which in effect function as an income supplement system for low-income workers.

In calculating the tentative tax liability and actual tax liability, preferential tax rates apply to qualified dividends and capital gains. The maximum rate for both types of income is nominally 20%, but higher-income taxpayers also pay an additional Medicare surtax of 3.8% on most types of investment income, including qualified dividends and capital gains.[34] Qualified dividends are dividends paid by a U.S. corporation or a foreign corporation subject to a tax treaty with the U.S. which requires information sharing. In general, capital gains eligible for the preferential rate are gains attributable to capital assets which have been held for more than one year. A capital asset is defined generally in the Code as property which the taxpayer did not hold for sale to customers in the ordinary course of business and which was not depreciable property used in a trade or business. Special rules extend the preferential tax rate to gain from depreciable property used in a trade or business which is not held for sale to customers in the ordinary course of business. The portion of gain from depreciable personal property which is attributable to depreciation is recaptured as ordinary income. The portion of gain from depreciable real property which is attributable to depreciation is taxed at a rate of 25% (or 28.8% if the taxpayer is subject to the 3.8% Medicare surtax). Any excess gain from depreciable property (real or personal) is taxed at a rate not greater than 20% (or 23.8% if the taxpayer is subject to the 3.8% Medicare

31. IRC, s. 67(g). Prior to the 2017 TCJA, miscellaneous itemized deductions were deductible to the extent that they exceeded, in the aggregate, 2% of adjusted gross income.
32. IRC, s. 32.
33. IRC, s. 24(d)(1).
34. IRC, s. 1411.

surtax). Special rules also apply to gain from the sale of "collectibles" (e.g., stamp collections and rare coins) held for more than a year. Gain from such items is taxed at a maximum rate of 28% (or 31.8% if the taxpayer is subject to the 3.8% Medicare surtax).

In recent years, the U.S. tax system for individuals has tended toward a schedular system. Several categories of expenses are limited in their deductibility to similar categories of income. For example, losses from "passive activities" may be deducted only from income generated by passive activities. In general, a passive activity is a profit-seeking activity to which the taxpayer does not devote a significant amount of time. Similarly, investment interest expenses are deductible only from investment income. Where a personal residence is partly used for profit-seeking activities, expenses attributable to the personal residence (other than mortgage interest expenses) may in general be deducted only from income generated by the residence. Finally, the treatment of capital gains is schedular. Taxpayers may fully deduct capital losses from capital gains but can deduct only USD 3,000 of capital losses from ordinary income annually.

Another aspect of the individual income tax is the AMT. The AMT is, in effect, a "shadow" tax system which accompanies the regular U.S. tax system. Congress adopted the AMT "to ensure that no taxpayer with substantial economic income can avoid significant tax liability by using exclusions, deductions and credits."[35] The AMT provides an alternative calculation of a taxpayer's taxable income by limiting or eliminating many tax expenditure deductions and exclusions. Where the taxpayer's AMT liability exceeds the regular income tax liability, the taxpayer must pay the AMT liability. The AMT has historically been quite controversial. Although Congress sought to apply the AMT to a taxpayer's "economic income," the AMT frequently overestimates economic income because it denies a deduction for expenses incurred in a profit-seeking activity. Moreover, exemptions from the AMT were not fully adjusted to reflect inflation. Consequently, in a result not anticipated when the AMT was first enacted, many middle-class taxpayers living in areas with high local taxes, which are not deductible for AMT purposes, found themselves subject to the AMT. The increase in AMT exemption amounts in the TCJA, along with a requirement that the exemption amounts be adjusted for inflation, may mute some of the criticism of the AMT. The AMT exemption amount for single taxpayers in 2024 is USD 85,700 and begins phasing out at USD 609,350 (USD 133,300 for married couples filing jointly, phasing out beginning at USD 1,218,700).[36]

5.2 Corporations

The U.S. has a modified classical corporate tax system which taxes income at the corporate level at a flat rate of 21% and again taxes distributions at the shareholder

35. Staff of the Joint Committee on Taxation, *General Explanation of the Tax Reform Act of 1986* (1987), p. 432.
36. Rev. Proc. 2023-34, 2023-48 IRB 1287 (2023).

level, although at a reduced rate, of 20% (23.8% for higher-income taxpayers because of the additional Medicare surtax of 3.8%).

The income of a corporation is calculated in a manner similar to that with respect to individuals, but with several important variations. There is no adjusted gross income for a corporation since expenses and losses incurred by a corporation are generally assumed to be connected to a trade or business. Instead, deductions are subtracted directly from gross income to calculate taxable income.

Capital gains are not taxed at a preferential rate, as they are for individuals, and corporations are restricted to deducting their capital losses against capital gains. Unused capital losses may be carried back three years and forward five years.

Since corporations are treated as separate taxable entities, special rules are necessary to prevent the recognition of income on the formation of a corporation. In general, shareholders will not recognize income when they transfer appreciated property to a corporation in exchange for stock if they collectively own 80% of the corporation's stock after the transfer. The corporation itself never recognizes gain on the transfer of its own stock to a shareholder in exchange for property.

Because corporate income is taxable to a corporation when recognized and is taxable again when distributed to shareholders, special rules are necessary to prevent the "cascading" of corporate-level tax with respect to intercorporate distributions which qualify as dividends.[37] These rules allow a deduction for a percentage of the dividend a corporate shareholder receives. The amount of the deduction depends on the level of shareholding; the entire dividend can be deducted if the corporate shareholder owns 80% or more of the stock of the distributing corporation. Special rules apply to curtail the potential for tax arbitrage. For example, a provision prevents corporations from purchasing portfolio stock with borrowed funds in order to obtain the tax benefits of the interest deduction with respect to those funds and the dividends-received deduction with respect to amounts paid on the debt-financed portfolio stock. Similarly, Congress has sought to prevent corporations from obtaining capital loss deductions which are attributable to declines in the value of stock as the result of dividends paid to the corporations which were not taxed at all or only partially taxed.

Corporations are also allowed to acquire other corporations without triggering a corporate-or shareholder-level tax in certain transactions called "reorganizations." To qualify as a reorganization, several requirements must be satisfied. A business purpose for the transaction must exist, and a significant portion of the shareholders in the acquired corporation must receive stock in the acquiring corporation. In addition, the acquiring corporation must continue to conduct at least one of the target's historic businesses or use a significant amount of the target's assets. Finally, the structure of the transaction must correspond to one of the forms set out in the statute. There appears to be no substantive purpose for the transactional forms set forth in the statute and their intricacies are the product of historical accident. The rationale supporting nonrecognition that the shareholders have not significantly changed their relationship to the

37. Dividends are distributions to stockholders of the corporation's "earnings and profits," i.e., the corporation's taxable income with several adjustments.

target's business appears to be better addressed by the continuity of interest and business requirements.

Historically, dividend distributions to shareholders who are individuals were taxed at higher rates than on an individual's gain on the sale of the stock. The result was a substantial body of the corporate tax rules aimed at preventing shareholders from "bailing out" corporate earnings at capital gains tax rates. For example, special rules were formulated to determine whether a sale of stock to a corporation or a related corporation would be treated as a disguised dividend or a sale. In general, the form of the transaction as a sale would be respected where there had been a significant reduction in the shareholder's stock ownership of the company. Similarly, special rules were adopted to prevent shareholders from recognizing capital gains with respect to preferred stock which was distributed to them by the issuing corporation to the extent that the corporation had earnings and profits at the time the stock was issued. The importance of these rules has diminished as a result of the 2003 legislation, which causes dividends and capital gains both to be taxed at a maximum rate of 20% (23.8% if the taxpayer is subject to the Medicare surtax). However, individual taxpayers will still have an incentive to "bail out" corporate earnings as capital gains if their cost basis in the stock is high.

The corporate income tax had an AMT, which was repealed in the 2017 TCJA. A new form of the AMT was re-enacted effective for taxable years beginning in 2023.[38] In its current form, the AMT applies if the corporation's regular tax burden is less than 15% of the corporation's financial income with several adjustments.

6 TAX LEGISLATION

6.1 Legislative Process

As discussed in section 2, the Origination Clause (Article 1, section 7, clause 1) of the U.S. Constitution requires that all "bills for raising revenue" originate in the House of Representatives. The House Committee on Ways and Means commences the process by conducting a public hearing on proposed bills.

The proposer of the new legislation is normally the first witness to appear at the hearing. If the President is the proposer, which is usually the case, the first witness to appear will be the Assistant Secretary of the Treasury for Tax Policy, followed by other members of the executive branch, such as the Chair of the Council of Economic Advisors. Members of the public, including various special interest groups, then testify.

After the hearing, the House Ways and Means Committee members meet to consider the general outlines of the bill and the policies to be implemented. The Committee members do not draft the statutory language. Rather, attorneys at the Office of House Legislative Counsel compose statutory language implementing the policy objectives adopted by the Committee. The Office of House Legislative Council also drafts a report to accompany the bill. The Committee then reviews the statutory

38. IRC, s. 55.

language and report. Following approval of the language and report by the Committee, the entire House considers the bill.

The Senate normally starts to consider the bill at the same time as the House and follows the same process (the requirement that tax legislation originate in the House is satisfied by a sleight of hand: the number of the original House bill is assigned to the bill ultimately adopted by the House and Senate). The Senate Finance Committee conducts hearings. It then adopts statutory language and a committee report, which it submits to the entire Senate for its approval.

Differences between the House bill and Senate bill almost always exist. The differences are resolved at the Committee of Conference of the House and Senate (the "Conference Committee"), which consists of members of the House Ways and Means Committee and the Senate Finance Committee. The Conference Committee issues to the House and Senate a Conference Report setting out the revised bill with a brief explanation. The Senate and House cannot amend the Conference Report but must either approve or reject it. If approved, the bill is sent to the President, who can either sign the bill or veto it.

6.2 Statutory Style

The IRC is immense. What initially started as 16 pages in section II of the Tariff Act of 1913 has blossomed into a tome of approximately 6,000 pages.

Although there are many reasons for the current complexity of the Code, the use of tax expenditures accounts for much of the complexity, since the presence of tax expenditures requires additional provisions to prevent taxpayer abuse of the tax rules. For example, a preferential rate for capital gains necessitates many additional provisions to prevent taxpayers from converting ordinary income into capital gain. Tax expenditures also require courts to engage in difficult factual inquiries about whether taxpayers have satisfied the applicable statutory requirements. Moreover, the ability of taxpayers in the past to use tax expenditures to eliminate or significantly reduce their tax liabilities caused Congress to adopt the AMT, which is supposed to ensure that all taxpayers pay a minimal income tax where tax expenditures would otherwise eliminate or reduce tax liability.

Another source of complexity has been the willingness of Congress to disguise tax increases for political reasons. For example, rather than increasing revenue simply by raising the maximum statutory rate, Congress has adopted various provisions limiting itemized deductions for individuals.[39] Based on no overarching principles, limitations on deductions reduce or eliminate the "transparency" of the system for the ordinary taxpayer to whom they apply.

Complexity is also produced by the tendency of the Code to assign different meanings to the same word in different parts of the Code. For example, the term "property" often has a different definition for different Code sections. In addition, the use of different rates for different types of capital gains reduces transparency.

39. IRC, ss. 67, 68.

Finally, in recent years, Congress has tried to anticipate many of the ways taxpayers will attempt to abuse tax provisions and to address them in the statute. This practice is in contrast to earlier years when Congress would rely on the courts to police the boundaries of compliance. It is not clear that this more recent approach is productive. The failure of Congress to address all abuse situations may create an inference that Congress intended to permit the abuses not addressed in the statute.

6.3 Statutory Interpretation

In the U.S., as in all systems, there is a tension between a strict, literal approach to statutory interpretation and an approach which attempts to achieve the intent of the legislature. The Supreme Court has stated:

> There is, of course, no more persuasive evidence of a statute than the words by which the legislature undertook to give expression to its wishes. Often these words are sufficient in and of themselves to determine the purpose of the legislation. In such cases we have followed their plain meaning. When that meaning has led to absurd or futile results, however, this court has looked beyond the words to the purpose of the act. Frequently, however, even when the plain meaning did not produce absurd results but merely an unreasonable one "plainly at variance with the policy of the legislation as a whole" this Court has followed the purpose, rather than the literal words.[40]

As the foregoing statement clearly illustrates, U.S. courts have traditionally sought to determine the legislative purpose for a specific statute in order to determine whether the statute's plain meaning is unreasonable. In seeking to identify the legislative purpose for a particular Code section, the courts will normally examine reports from the House Ways and Means Committee, Senate Finance Committee, and Conference Committee. They may also examine an explanation of the statute drafted by the staff of the Joint Committee on Taxation, records of hearings, and analyses by commentators, although they will normally accord less weight to these sources.

Currently, however, there is disagreement among Justices on the Supreme Court about the extent to which the Court should consult legislative material, such as Committee reports, in interpreting statutes.[41] For example, the majority opinion in *Gitlitz v. Commissioner*[42] interpreted a tax statute without referring to the statute's legislative history, although a House Committee report suggested that Congress had intended an interpretation for the statute which was different from that adopted by the majority. Such a textualist approach, if continued, could have a significant effect in the tax field. For example, some have suggested that increased use of the textualist approach aids tax shelters,[43] since tax shelters often involve transactions which comply with the literal language, but not the legislative intent, of the statute. Moreover, a

40. *United States v. American Trucking Ass'n*, 310 US 534, 543 [1945].
41. *See*, e.g., Commentary: "At High Court, Fight over Textualism Lives On" *National Law Journal* (online) (February 22, 2018), http://bit.ly/3ud0mLO.
42. 531 US 206 (2001).
43. Noel B. Cunningham & James R. Repetti, "Textualism and Tax Shelters" (2004) Vol. 24, No. 1 *Virginia Tax Review* 1.

textualist approach may make it more difficult for a court to determine that the legislature did not intend the statute to be applied in the manner exploited by a tax shelter because it prevents the court from consulting the statute's legislative history.

Although the inclusion of the word "Code" in the name "IRC" implies a self-contained, systematic statutory treatment of the tax laws, the courts have developed many common-law principles which aid their efforts to apply tax provisions. In general, courts will narrowly interpret exclusions from gross income. That is, an item (other than imputed income) is generally excluded from gross income only where a statute expressly authorizes such exclusion. Similarly, the courts view deductions as a matter of legislative grace: they disallow a deduction unless it is permitted by statute and interpret the statute narrowly.

The courts have also created several requirements which are not in the statute. In order for a transaction to qualify for favorable tax treatment, the courts generally require that it must be entered into for nontax purposes. For example, the courts will ignore an entity's existence if it was not formed for a business purpose and has no business activity.[44] Moreover, courts will deny favorable tax treatment to a transaction which satisfies all the literal requirements of the governing statute if the transaction lacks a business purpose.[45] This judicially created approach, referred to as the "economic substance doctrine" was codified in 2010.[46] In order for a transaction to be respected for federal income tax purposes, the codified version requires that the transaction change "in a meaningful way (apart from federal income tax effects) the taxpayer's economic position" and that the taxpayer have "a substantial purpose (apart from federal income tax effects) for entering into" the transaction.[47] Taxpayers relying on the profit potential of a transaction to satisfy these requirements must show that the present value of the reasonably expected pretax profit is "substantial" in relation to the present value of the expected net tax benefits.[48]

In applying tax statutes to a transaction, courts will seek to identify the substance of the transaction rather than blindly follow the form cast by the taxpayer. For example, although a taxpayer may have drafted a financial instrument in the legal form of debt, the courts will treat it as equity if the taxpayer fails to respect the formalities of debt, such as prompt payment of interest and principal. Similarly, rather than accept the legal form of a transaction as a sale or a lease, the courts will analyze whether the burdens and benefits of ownership have shifted in order to identify the nature of the transaction for tax purposes. Finally, the courts may employ the "step transaction doctrine" to combine several steps into a single transaction where it appears that the taxpayer intended a single transaction. For example, suppose a taxpayer transfers stock in a target corporation for stock in the acquiring corporation in a tax-free acquisition. Under the "step transaction" approach, if the taxpayer sells the acquiring corporation's stock back to the acquiring corporation for cash shortly thereafter, the court may treat

44. *See*, e.g., *Moline Properties Inc. v. Commissioner*, 319 US 436, 438-439 (1943).
45. *Gregory v. Helvering*, 293 US 465 (1935).
46. IRC, s. 7701(o).
47. IRC, s. 7701(o)(1).
48. IRC, s. 7701(o)(2).

the taxpayer as having received cash rather than stock at the beginning of the transaction.

7 JUDICIAL STRUCTURE AND STYLE

The U.S. has no specialized system of courts which hears only tax cases. One court of first instance, the Tax Court, hears only tax matters and has jurisdiction where a taxpayer resists the payment of a tax asserted by the IRS. Alternatively, the taxpayer can pay the tax asserted and sue for a refund, either in the U.S. District Court, a court of general jurisdiction, or the U.S. Court of Federal Claims, a special court which handles claims against the government. The taxpayer may request that a jury be the finder of facts in the U.S. District Court but is limited to a judge as the fact finder in the Tax Court or U.S. Court of Federal Claims. Decisions from the U.S. District Court and Tax Courts may be appealed to the Court of Appeals for the Circuit in which the taxpayer resides. Decisions from the U.S. Court of Federal Claims may be appealed to the Court of Appeals for the Federal Circuit. Thus, taxpayers have a number of judicial options for contesting their tax liability and this structure creates a certain amount of "forum shopping."

All decisions may then be reviewed by the Supreme Court, although there is no right to review unless a constitutional issue is involved. In the event that the Courts of Appeal reach differing results on the same issue, the Supreme Court will usually agree to hear the case in order to resolve the issue.

Judicial decisions are issued in the form of full opinions which set forth the relevant facts and apply the law to those facts. Because cases are relied on by courts as precedents in deciding future cases, judges are usually careful to set out their reasoning in full.

Despite the extensive statutory material in the U.S. system, the courts have been responsible for a significant part of doctrinal development in the tax area. In some cases, case-law principles have subsequently been taken over in the statute. In others, the case law remains the primary source of law. For example, the definition of income is almost entirely based on case law. Similarly, the determination of the taxpayer to whom income should be attributed is based in many instances on case law. In addition, the case-law principles of statutory interpretation discussed above have had an important influence on the development of the law.

8 TAX ADMINISTRATION

8.1 Administrative Style

The U.S. tax system is a self-assessment system backed up with extensive information reporting and withholding requirements. For example, most employers who pay wages must file with the IRS the amounts paid to each of their employees and are also required to withhold income taxes on those amounts. The bulk of individual income taxes collected by the U.S. are through employer withholding. In 2022, for example, approximately 62.5% of individual income taxes were collected from withholding.[49] There are also reporting requirements for persons who use independent contractors in the course of their business, for persons receiving USD 10,000 or more in cash, and for most forms of capital income, including gains on the sale of investment assets.

The audit rate for individual taxpayers has been declining, although the recent increase in the IRS budget may result in an increase in future years. In 2020, the IRS audited 0.2% of individual tax returns,[50] compared to 1% in 2007[51] and 1.67% returns in 1995.[52] Not surprisingly, the probability of being audited increases with income. In 2020, 0.1% of taxpayers with adjusted gross income between USD 100,000 and USD 200,000 were audited compared with 2.4% of taxpayers with adjusted gross income over USD 10 million.[53]

In 2020, the IRS audited 0.5% of corporate tax returns[54] compared to 1.7% of all corporate tax returns in 2007[55] and 2.05% of all such returns in 1995.[56] The audit rate for corporations with assets between USD 10 million and USD 50 million in 2022 was 0.4%[57] compared with 15% in 2007.[58] For corporations with assets of USD 20 billion or more, the audit rate in 2020 was 17.7%[59] compared with 100% in 2007.[60]

To discourage taxpayers from playing the "audit lottery," the IRS charges interest on tax deficiencies at a rate equal to the federal short-term rate plus 3% and assesses penalties equal to 20% of the tax deficiency unless there was a reasonable cause for the deficiency. In addition, increasingly sophisticated use of computer checking of information returns reduces the audit-lottery odds.

Perhaps because of the self-assessing nature of the U.S. income tax, the IRS has tended in recent years to provide very detailed regulations. In addition, the Service publishes "public revenue rulings" similar to memoranda of law, which address various issues not resolved in the regulations. A taxpayer seeking additional advice may request the Service to issue a private ruling stating how the law will be applied in a situation which the taxpayer has presented to the Service. These private rulings are published in a redacted form to prevent discovery of the identity of the taxpayer.

The IRS is not permitted to disclose tax returns to the public.[61] However, it may disclose the returns to other federal agencies, state tax officials, and foreign officials

49. *See* Internal Revenue Service, *2022 Data Book*, Table 1 (2023) (noting that in 2022 USD 2.819 trillion was collected from the individual income tax and that USD 1.763 trillion of such receipts was withheld by employers).
50. *Ibid.*, at Table 17.
51. IRS, 2007 *Data Book*, Table 9 (2008); GAO, *Tax Administration: IRS should continue to expand reporting on its enforcement efforts* (January 2003), Table 6.
52. GAO, *Tax Administration: Audit Rates and Results for Individual Taxpayers* (April 26, 1996), Table 1.1.
53. IRS, *2022 Data Book*, Table 17 (2023).
54. *Ibid.*, at Table 17.
55. IRS, *2007 Data Book*, Table 1 (2008).
56. IRS, *1995 Data Book*, Table 11 (1996).
57. IRS, *2022 Data Book*, Table 17 (2023).
58. IRS, *2007 Data Book*, Table 9 (2008).
59. IRS, *2022 Data Book*, Table 17 (2023).
60. IRS, *2007 Data Book*, Table 9 (2008).
61. IRC, s. 6103.

(pursuant to tax treaties). In addition, the IRS is permitted to aggregate data from several returns, so that information cannot be traced to a particular taxpayer, and to publish that aggregate data.

8.2 Taxpayer Style

Given the low audit rates and the low level of legal authority needed to avoid penalties, taxpayers in the U.S. tend to be aggressive in interpreting the law. This likely contributed to the decline in corporate tax revenues even prior to the TCJA's reduction of the corporate tax rate to a flat 21%. For example, one study found that the cash effective corporate tax rates during the period, 1988-2012, declined by 5 to 10 percentage points.[62] Treasury has in part responded by requiring that legal opinions for tax shelters base their conclusions on reasonable factual and legal assumptions and not rely on representations, statements, or findings of the taxpayer or any other person "if reliance on them would be unreasonable."[63] However, taxpayers can often engage in aggressive tax planning without receiving legal opinions.

9 GENERAL PRINCIPLES

9.1 Relationship Between Tax and Financial Accounting

In most cases, tax accounting in the U.S. differs from financial accounting. The principle of conservatism in financial accounting creates a bias in favor of a rapid recognition of expenses and a delayed recognition of income. In contrast, tax accounting seeks, broadly speaking, exactly the opposite—that is, tax accounting seeks generally to recognize income as soon as it is reasonable to expect the taxpayer to pay tax but to recognize expenses only to the extent that they can be matched to the recognized income.

For example, tax accounting generally requires taxpayers who receive a cash payment before they have earned it by performing services or delivering property to include the payment in income regardless of whether they use the cash or accrual method of accounting. Moreover, even though an accrual-method taxpayer has a fixed liability which would normally justify a current deduction, the taxpayer may frequently not recognize the expense for tax purposes until it is actually paid. Similarly, while financial accounting principles require the establishment of reserves for estimated expenses which relate to current income, tax accounting does not generally permit such reserves.

Like financial accounting, tax accounting employs an annual accounting period which has been interpreted fairly strictly by the courts. Events which occur after the close of the year will not, in general, affect the tax treatment in the year. Nonetheless,

62. Scott D. Dyreng, Michelle Hanlon, Edward L. Maydew, and Jacob R. Thornock, "Changes in Effective Corporate Tax Rates over the Past 25 Years" (2017) Vol. 124 *J. Fin'l Econ.* 441, 442 https://doi.org/10.1016/j.jfineco.2017.04.001.
63. Treasury Department Circular No. 230 s. 10.37 (June 12, 2014).

taxpayers are allowed a deduction for items that they have included in income and are subsequently required to return. Moreover, in certain situations, the taxpayer may, in lieu of a deduction, be able to reduce current tax liability by the amount of taxes paid in the prior year attributable to the inclusion of the item in income. In the converse situation, taxpayers who have deducted an expenditure which is subsequently refunded must recognize income to the extent that the earlier deduction resulted in a tax saving. Expenses incurred in a trade or business which exceed business income may be carried forward to future years without limit but cannot eliminate more than 80% of the taxable income in the year to which they are carried forward.

Despite the differences between financial and tax accounting, corporations and partnerships that report assets on their balance sheets in excess of USD 10 million are required to file Schedule M-3, which reconciles their taxable income with their financial statement income. The reason for this disclosure is to help the IRS identify potentially aggressive tax positions.

In addition, recent changes in U.S. tax laws have linked the corporate income tax more closely to financial accounting. In 2017 Congress added a new provision that in general requires accrual-method taxpayers that prepare financial statements to recognize taxable income on their tax returns when they report corresponding amounts on their financial statements even though such taxable amounts have not yet accrued as income for tax purposes.[64] Also, beginning in 2023, the U.S. now imposes an AMT of 15% on the adjusted financial income of large corporations if such amounts exceed the corporations' regular tax liability.[65]

9.2 Respect for Legal Form

As discussed above in section 6.3, U.S. courts will look behind the form of a transaction to determine its substance. For example, a lease may be treated as a sale for federal income tax purposes, even though the governing instrument is a lease for state law purposes, if the lease effectively conveys all the burdens and benefits of ownership to the lessee.

In addition, the courts will refuse favorable tax treatment for a transaction if the only reason for the transaction was to save federal income taxes.[66] As discussed in section 6.3 above, this judicially created approach, referred to as the "economic substance doctrine," was codified in 2010.[67]

9.3 Anti-avoidance

As discussed earlier in section 6.3 on statutory interpretation, the courts have created several common-law doctrines to curtail tax avoidance activities. Although for decades there had been significant debate about whether a general anti-avoidance rule would

64. IRC, s. 451(b) and (c).
65. IRC, s. 55(b)(2).
66. *Gregory v. Helvering*, 293 US 465 (1935).
67. IRC, s. 7701(o).

be useful, Congress did not adopt such a provision until 2010. As discussed in sections 6.3 and 9.2 above, Congress codified the "economic substance" doctrine, which can be viewed as a general anti-avoidance rule, in 2010.

In other narrow contexts, Congress has either adopted anti-avoidance legislation or expressly authorized the IRS to adopt anti-avoidance regulations addressing specific abuses. In section 269, Congress sought to prevent a corporation which had acquired another corporation from deducting expenses or claiming credits with respect to the acquired corporation where "the principal purpose for which such acquisition is made is evasion or avoidance of federal income tax by securing the benefit of a deduction, credit or other allowance." In 1993, Congress also adopted section 7701(1), which authorizes the Secretary to "prescribe regulations recharacterizing any multiple-party financing transaction as a transaction directly among any two or more of such parties when the Secretary determines that such recharacterization is appropriate to present avoidance of any tax by this title." Pursuant to this statute, the IRS has promulgated regulations which allow it to treat an entity as a conduit if a principal purpose for using the entity in the transaction was to avoid U.S. income tax on income of foreign corporations which is not effectively connected with a U.S. trade or business.[68]

In the context of partnership taxation, the IRS has sought through regulations to require that a partnership's business purposes for entering into a transaction must be substantial in comparison to the transaction's tax savings.[69] In addition, the IRS has sought to require that courts interpreting partnership tax provisions expressly consider the legislative purpose of the provisions. Commentators disagree whether the IRS has the authority to impose such requirements without a directive from Congress.

10 TAX TREATIES

The U.S. maintains an extensive treaty network, with over 65 comprehensive bilateral tax treaties,[70] 13 Tax Information Exchange Agreements (TIEAs),[71] and 113 signed Intergovernmental Agreements (IGAs) under the Foreign Account Tax Compliance Act (FATCA).[72] The U.S. has released a series of Model Tax Conventions over the years; the most recent model was released in 2016. Although explanatory commentaries (i.e., Technical Explanations) accompanied two prior model treaties (the 1996 and 2006 models), no Technical Explanation was released for the 2016 Model. The U.S. relies on the U.S. Model as the starting point for the negotiation of income tax treaties with other

68. *See* Treas. Reg. s. 1.881-3(b)(1).
69. Treas. Reg. s. 1.704-2.
70. *See*, e.g., IRS.gov, *United States Tax Treaties A to Z* (November 27, 2018), at https://www.irs.gov/businesses/international-businesses/united-states-income-tax-treaties-a-to-z; IRS, Publication 901, U.S. Tax Treaties (September 2016), available at https://www.irs.gov/publications/p901.
71. Treasury.gov, TIEAs (visited December 5, 2023) at https://home.treasury.gov/policy-issues/tax-policy/tax-information-exchange-agreements-tieas.
72. Treasury.gov, FATCA (visited December 5, 2023), at https://www.treasury.gov/resource-center/tax-policy/treaties/Pages/FATCA.aspx.

countries, although it has been willing to depart from the Model, particularly with developing countries.

Over the years, the U.S. Model has closely tracked the Organisation for Economic Co-operation and Development (OECD) Model, but it incorporates distinctive provisions reflecting US treaty policy concerns.[73] In particular, the U.S. Model has long included a limitation-on-benefits (LOB) provision and a "saving" clause, which grants the U.S. the right to tax its own citizens and residents as if the treaty were not in effect. New features in the 2016 US Model included:[74]

- a denial of reduced withholding taxes on payments of highly mobile income where the payments are made to related persons that enjoy low or no taxation on income due to a preferential tax regime;
- a provision requiring the treaty partners to consult (with the expectation of amending the treaty as needed) when changes to domestic law after the treaty is entered into disturb the original balance of negotiated treaty benefits;
- a denial of reduced withholding taxes on US-source payments to related foreign persons made by companies which engage in inversions; and
- mandatory binding arbitration under a "last best offer" approach (similar to the arbitration provision in four U.S. tax treaties currently in force and three U.S. tax treaties awaiting the advice and consent of the Senate).

In the U.S., treaties are negotiated and signed by the executive branch of the government and then submitted to the Senate for "advice and consent."[75] Following Senate approval (requiring a two-thirds majority of senators present), the President exchanges signed ratification instruments with the treaty partner and the treaty is brought into force.[76] The U.S. did not ratify any new treaties from 2011 to July 2019 due to a strategic political block by one senator, resulting in a backlog of negotiated, signed tax treaties waiting for ratification. After this eight-year hiatus, on July 16 and 17, 2019, the U.S. Senate ratified several tax protocols and treaty amendments involving treaties with Japan, Luxembourg, Spain, and Switzerland. Further tax treaty ratifications are expected. For example, after more than a decade of delay, the U.S. Senate ratified the U.S.-Chile treaty in June 2023.

73. Although not the exclusive basis for interpreting U.S. tax treaties, OECD guidance has been relevant in interpreting U.S. tax treaties. U.S. courts have relied on the OECD Commentary to interpret U.S. tax treaties with language similar to the OECD Model. *See* e.g., *US v. A.L. Burbank* Co., 525 F.2d 9 (2d Cir. 1975 cert. denied 426 US 934 (1976)); *Air France v. Saks*, 470 US 392 (1985); *National Westminster Bank P.L.C. v. US*, 58 Fed. CI. 491 (2003). The IRS has sometimes relied on the OECD Commentary. *See* e.g., Rev. Rul. 86-145, 1986-2 C.B. 297; Private Letter Ruling 8131059 (May 11, 1981); PLR 200048011 (August 17, 2000).

74. Treasury.gov, *Treasury Announces Release of 2016 U.S. Model Income Tax Treaty* (February 17, 2016), at https://home.treasury.gov/news/press-releases/jl0356.

75. U.S. Constitution, Art. II, s. 2, cl. 2; *see also* Advice & Consent, U.S. Senate, http://www.senate.gov/general/Features/Treaties_display.htm.

76. U.S. Constitution, Art. II, s. 2, cl. 2; *see also* Advice & Consent, U.S. Senate, http://www.senate.gov/general/Features/Treaties_display.htm.

The U.S. has signed the *Multilateral Convention on Mutual Assistance in Tax Matters*,[77] but it has not signed the *Multilateral Convention to Implement Tax Treaty Related Measures to Prevent Base Erosion and Profit Shifting* (MLI) by modifying existing treaties, nor has it expressed an intention to do so.[78]

The U.S. is a monist jurisdiction. Thus, tax treaties are "self-executing," and no further legislation is required to implement a treaty.[79] In contrast to practices in many jurisdictions, U.S. domestic legislation can override treaties.[80] The 2017 U.S. tax reform includes several provisions which some observers consider to override existing US tax treaties, although that view has not yet been confirmed.

11 SOURCES OF TAX LAW

The primary source of tax law is the IRC. The Treasury Department issues regulations which interpret the Code. Prior to the Supreme Court's 2024 decision in *Loper Bright Enterprises v. Raimondo* (*Loper*),[81] the courts gave significant deference to regulations if the regulations addressed issues not addressed in the statute and were reasonable interpretations of the statute. This significant deference had been mandated by the Supreme Court's earlier decision in Che*vron U.S.A., Inc. v. Natural Resources Defense Council, Inc.*[82] However, the Court in *Loper* held that *Chevron* deference to a regulation was inappropriate because it delegated the role of the courts to interpret statutes to administrative agencies. The Court concluded, "Courts must exercise their independent judgment in deciding whether an agency has acted within its statutory authority … ."[83] The Court's opinion suggests that it has returned to the deference standard used prior to *Chevron*, the so-called *Skidmore* standard. That standard states that the degree of "weight" that a court should give to a regulation "should depend upon the thoroughness evident in its consideration, the validity of its reasoning, its consistency with earlier and later pronouncements, and all those factors which give it power to persuade, if lacking power to control."[84] Needless to say, this vague standard is likely

77. OECD, *Jurisdictions Participating in the Convention on Mutual Administrative Assistance in Tax Matters Status*—September 13, 2023, available at http://www.oecd.org/tax/exchange-of-tax-information/Status_of_convention.pdf.
78. OECD, *Signatories and Parties to the Multilateral Convention to Implement Tax Treaty Related Measures to Prevent Bose Erosion and Profit Shifting Status as of 11 January 2024*, available at http://www.oecd.org/tax/treaties/beps-mli-signatories-and-parties.pdf.
79. IRC, s. 894(a) states that the tax code shall be applied "with due regard to any treaty obligation of the United States." This section is interpreted as granting legislative effect to tax treaties.
80. Article VI, clause 2 of the U.S. Constitution provides that "[l]aws of the United States which shall be made in Pursuance thereof; and all Treaties made, or which shall be made, under the Authority of the United States, shall be the Supreme Law of the Land." The U.S. Supreme Court has interpreted this language to mean that statutes and treaties are of equal standing. *Reid v. Covert*, 354 U.S. 1 (1957). Further, the Supreme Court has held that where a treaty and domestic statute conflict, the "later-in-time rule" (the most recently enacted of the two sources) prevails.
81. Slip Op. No. 22-451 (S. Ct. June 28, 2024).
82. *Chevron U.S.A., Inc. v. Natural Resources Defense Council, Inc.*, 467 U.S. 837 (1984).
83. *Loper Bright Enterprises v. Raimondo*, Slip. Op. No. 22-451, at 35.
84. *Skidmore v. Swift & Co.*, 323 U. S. 134, 140 (1944).

to open the floodgates for litigation as taxpayers become more inclined to challenge the validity of tax regulations.

In addition to regulations, the Treasury Department, acting through the IRS, which is a division of the Treasury Department, issues several other forms of guidance. One form of administrative guidance, the Revenue Ruling, is similar to a memorandum of law. It states the issues to be addressed, the facts pertaining to the issues, and a legal analysis of the issues. Revenue Rulings may be relied on by all taxpayers unless the law on which the ruling is based has changed. The IRS has stated that its "general practice [is] ... to make ... revocation or modification prospective only."[85] Another form of guidance which may be relied on by all taxpayers is the Revenue Procedure, which is usually an explanation of a procedural issue. The IRS also issues private letter rulings to taxpayers who request guidance from the National Office of the IRS; only the taxpayer to whom the private letter ruling is addressed may rely on it. Technical advice memoranda and field service advice are similar to private letter rulings, except that the District Director of the IRS, not a taxpayer, requests that the National Office render advice pertaining to an issue which has arisen in the audit of a taxpayer. The taxpayer being audited is permitted to file a brief and request a hearing before the National Office renders a ruling. Although private letter rulings, technical advice memoranda, and field service advice have no precedential value for any taxpayers not directly involved, tax advisers study the rulings carefully to glean the IRS's perspective on the issues addressed. The rulings are published in redacted form to prevent disclosure of the identity of the taxpayer.

Finally, all the courts, described in section 7 above, render written opinions which are available to the public. The impact of the opinion depends on which court issued it. Supreme Court opinions are binding on all lower courts. Opinions of the Courts of Appeals for the various Circuits, in contrast, bind only the lower courts whose decisions are appealed to that particular Court of Appeals. The Tax Court and U.S. District Courts are bound by the decisions of the Court of Appeals for the Circuit in which the taxpayer resides. The Claims Court is bound by decisions of the Court of Appeals for the Federal Circuit.

Below are the websites for obtaining important court decisions and IRS rulings:
U.S. Supreme Court—www.supremecourtus.gov

Courts of Appeals

1st Circuit—www.ca1.uscourts.gov
2nd Circuit—www.ca2.uscourts.gov
3rd Circuit—www.ca3.uscourts.gov
4th Circuit—www.ca4.uscourts.gov
5th Circuit—www.ca5.uscourts.gov
6th Circuit—www.ca6.uscourts.gov
7th Circuit—www.ca7.uscourts.gov
8th Circuit—www.ca8.uscourts.gov

85. Rev. Proc. 89-14, 1989-1 C.B. 814.

9th Circuit—www.ca9.uscourts.gov
10th Circuit—www.ca10.uscourts.gov
11th Circuit—www.ca11.uscourts.gov

Federal Circuit—www.cafc.uscourts.gov
U.S. Court of Federal Claims—www.uscfc.uscourts.gov
U.S. Tax Court—www.ustaxcourt.gov.

IRS Administrative Rulings

Revenue Rulings, Revenue Procedures, Announcements, and Notices issued since January 1996 can be found on the IRS.gov website: http://www.irs.gov/irb/.

Private Letter Rulings and Technical Advice memoranda can be found at: https://www.irs.gov/privacy-disclosure/foia-library under the heading, "Non-precedential Rulings & Advice."

Part II Basic Income Taxation

SUBPART A

Global Versus Schedular Design of Income Tax

From a theoretical perspective, income tax is often said to be structured on either a global or a schedular basis. A pure global income tax involves tax applied to a person's total income, and income consists of all types of income. All amounts, whatever their nature or source, are included in income, and deductions are permitted without regard to the type of income in connection with which they were incurred. In short, income and deductions are combined to produce an overall taxable income amount to which the tax rate is applied.

In contrast, a pure schedular income tax involves separate taxes on different types or sources of income. For each category of income, amounts included in income and deductions allowed are determined separately. If an amount is not included in any schedule, it is not taxable, although there is usually a schedule that includes residual amounts (i.e., amounts not covered in other schedules). For certain income categories, such as investment income, the deduction of expenses may be limited or even prohibited. An overall loss in one category generally cannot be offset against income in other categories. The rate of tax applied to the income in the various categories often differs. Similarly, the assessment and collection measures often differ. The tax on some types of income may be collected by withholding, the tax on others by the assessment of tax returns.

A schedular income tax system presents difficulties which do not arise under a global system. First, to the extent that the tax rates of the various schedules differ, taxpayers will attempt to manipulate the character of amounts in order to minimize tax. The classification of different types of income can be quite difficult and take up considerable administrative resources. Second, a schedular income tax system makes it difficult to implement progressive taxation of individuals in accordance with the ability-to-pay principle. Tax is imposed separately on the income of each schedule rather than on the taxpayer's total income. As a result, for example, a taxpayer may be subject to significant taxation if the taxpayer has income in one schedule, even where the taxpayer has no overall income because of an offsetting loss in another schedule. In addition, personal exemptions, rebates, and other types of relief are difficult to implement under a schedular system.

The pure global and schedular systems described briefly above represent the ends of a spectrum. In between these extremes are income tax systems in which elements of both global and schedular systems are combined, although one type of system may be predominant. All the countries studied in this book have income tax systems that combine global and schedular elements to various degrees. Countries such as Australia, Canada, and the United States (U.S.), which take a global approach generally, have numerous provisions which reflect a schedular approach. For example, the deductibility of expenses or losses with respect to certain types of activities may be restricted to the gross revenue from those activities. In addition, some types of investment income (dividends and interest) are often subject to withholding tax, and capital gains are often subject to a lower rate of tax than other types of income. Similarly, some countries which have predominantly schedular income tax systems often have provisions which modify the effects of the schedular approach and introduce global elements. For example, some countries allow losses from one category to offset income from other categories.

Applying a global or schedular label to a country's income tax system does not adequately reflect the combined global and schedular elements in its system. However, an awareness of the basic structural principles on which the system is built is important for understanding a country's general approach. The effect of a country's general approach is pervasive. It affects the way in which the country determines which amounts are included in income and which expenses are deductible, which rules for computing income apply, how losses are treated, etc. Understanding whether a country's general approach to income tax is global or schedular can assist in explaining why particular aspects of its income tax system are the way they are.

SUBPART B

Inclusions in the Tax Base

The determination of the items to be included in the tax base is a central question in all income tax systems. As the materials in Part I have shown, the formal definitions of income in the countries under consideration here vary substantially. In general, each country's approach to the determination of amounts to be included in income is fundamentally affected by whether its income tax system reflects a global or schedular approach, as discussed above.

The *United States* has the most extensive statutory definition of income, essentially a tautological statement that income is income "from whatever source," followed by a nonexclusive list containing the most commonly occurring items.[1] Specific items which would otherwise fall within the broad definition are expressly excluded. The *Australian* system, as well, has a global income approach but, influenced by trust concepts, the judicially developed concept was not extended to capital gains, which required additional legislation. In the 1997 reenactment of the legislation, income was separated into two categories: ordinary income (what the judges have decided is income) and statutory income (what is made income by specific statutory provision), but the basic concept remains global.[2] The judges, in deciding what is ordinary income, have drawn from United Kingdom (UK) case law, which is to some degree an oddity given the very different nature of the UK system.

The *United Kingdom* definition is based on a number of categories of income.[3] As seen above in the UK chapter in Part I, until the Tax Law Rewrite Project, this definition was expressed in Schedules (sometimes subdivided into Cases); to be taxable, a particular item had to fall within one of the Schedules. The Schedules evolved historically and reflected the relative importance of the different sources of income

1. United States, Internal Revenue Code (IRC), s. 61.
2. Australia, Income Tax Assessment Act 1997 (ITAA), s. 6-5, 6-10.
3. United Kingdom, Income Tax Act 2007 (ITA), s. 3 referring, *inter alia*, to the Income Tax (Earnings and Pensions) Act 2003 (ITEPA), and the Income Tax (Trading and Other Income) Act 2005 (ITTOIA). As noted in the chapter on the United Kingdom in Part I, there is no definitive list of all the categories of income.

which existed at the time of the original legislation in 1802; as noted in the description of the UK system in Part I, the rewritten legislation adopts a different order. Some Schedules have broad coverage—for example, profits of a trade—and others are very narrow, such as income from foreign securities. The modern list of sources reflects all too well the absence of a general theory of income: the UK simply finds that a receipt is subject to income tax if it fits into a listed category and is not excluded by some other rule (e.g., as capital). Where income falls into a particular Part (formerly Schedule), the rules of that Part must be applied; this affects both the method of computation and the ability to offset losses in one category against income in another category.

The existence of the Schedules has also influenced other aspects of the system. Conceptually, each Schedule or Part is viewed as listing separate categories or "sources" of income; thus, trading income is distinct from employment income and each trade is a separate source. If a receipt has no taxable source, it cannot be included in income. The receipt of what would otherwise be income in a year in which the source no longer exists does not, in principle, give rise to tax—but this principle has been much eroded by specific legislation. In addition, the realization of a gain on the disposition of a "source" is not itself treated as an item of income, thus leading to the necessity of special rules to capture such receipts as capital gains.

The *Canadian* system, influenced historically by the UK and the U.S., has a global definition of income based on the source concept. Only amounts which have a source constitute income subject to tax. The principal sources of income—business, property, and employment—are specifically mentioned in the statutory definition of income.[4] As in the UK and Australia, special legislation was required to extend taxation to capital gains, but unlike the situation in the UK, losses from various sources can, in general, offset income from other sources. In addition, the statute has been amended to include in income most amounts which lack a source. Consequently, the source basis of taxation is of relatively minor significance.

The *Swedish* system, although growing out of a different tradition, also distinguishes between income from employment, business, and capital. The *Dutch* system likewise separates employment, business, and investment categories, with an additional category for periodic income.

As explained in The Netherlands chapter in Part I, since 2001 the Dutch system has employed a schedular ("box") system under which (1) income from (employed and self-employed) work and the rental value of an owner-occupied residence, (2) income and gains from substantial interest participations, and (3) income from capital, are taxed separately.

The *German* system provides for seven statutory income categories, with two basic methods of income calculation applicable to the various categories.[5] In theory, it follows from this basic structure that capital gains should be taxable only in the context of a business (agricultural, commercial, or professional), while capital gains from private investment assets remain tax-free. However, this clear distinction has been eroded over the years, in particular regarding capital gains on shares and other

4. Canada, Income Tax Act (ITA), s. 3.
5. Germany, Income Tax Act (ITA), s. 2 paras. 1 and 2.

securities, which today are fully subject to tax. Gains from the sale of real estate are tax-free only for owner-occupied houses and rental houses held for more than ten years.[6] Short-term gains from other assets are taxable if the asset is sold within one year after acquisition. A major move toward a more schedular approach occurred in 2009 when interest and dividend payments, as well as capital gains on shares and other securities realized outside a business, became subject to a final withholding tax of 25%.[7]

In *France*, income tax is a direct tax on the total income of individuals in a tax household, and on certain types of companies. "Income" is not defined in the French tax code but based on a legal-economic concept under which income is annual, global, net, and disposable. The system is not purely global, however, since there are eight categories of income, not all of which are taken into account in the same way: e.g., some items are taxed completely separately at a proportional rate, with an option for progressive taxation. Several factors contribute to the complexity of this system: each category contains a set of specific rules for calculating the income subject to tax; there is a lack of clarity as to whether progressive or proportional taxation applies to certain categories such as capital gains and dividends; and the distinction between different categories of taxpayer (individuals and companies) results in only certain entities (sole proprietorships and partnerships) being subject to the progressive income tax.

In *Japan*, the approach to the definition of income is a hybrid of the prewar European schedular tradition and the postwar American global view. The Income Tax Act (ITA) divides income into ten categories, such as interest, capital gains, business income, and employment income, in accordance with a schedular approach, but the "catch-all" category of "Miscellaneous" income gives the system a global character.[8] Some of the income categories (business, employment, miscellaneous, etc.) are aggregated and subject to progressive tax rates, while others (income derived from financial products, some types of capital gains, etc.) are separately calculated and often taxed at a flat rate. Even for those categories which are aggregated, only losses from business-related income categories are allowed to offset income from other categories. It is also interesting to note that, in spite of their fundamental nature, many of the structural aspects of the system are based on the Special Taxation Measures Act (STMA) as temporary modifications to the general rules of the ITA.

The *Chinese* Individual Income Tax (IIT) is schedular, whereas the Enterprise Income Tax (EIT) uses a global concept of income. In general, capital gains are treated the same as income from business but as investment income in the case of nonresidents. As explained in the chapter on *India* in Part I, the Indian tax system is still schedular in nature but has evolved over time to include global elements.

Despite these differences in starting point, however, there is more similarity in the results produced by the various systems studied here than the formal definitions of income would suggest. This subpart analyzes the treatment of the inclusion of a

6. Germany, ITA, s. 22 Nos. 2, 23 para. 1 No. 1.
7. Germany, ITA, s. 20 para. 2.
8. Japan, Income Tax Act (ITA), ss. 21-35.

number of specific items in the tax base in each country. Subpart C deals with deduction issues.

1 INCOME FROM EMPLOYMENT

1.1 General

The issue of the appropriate treatment of income from employment arises in a similar fashion in both schedular and global systems. In all the countries examined in this book, salaries and wages received by employees are subject to withholding by employers, and in most of the countries, deductions claimed by employees are restricted compared to those for self-employed individuals. Consequently, in order to distinguish between employees and independent businesspersons, it is necessary to characterize the relationship between the payer and the recipient. This distinction is discussed in section 1.2 below.

In addition, the inclusion in the tax base of fringe benefits from employment, which is necessary both in terms of horizontal equity and to prevent the erosion of tax on cash compensation received by employees, raises a number of structural issues. The question often arises whether an employee can be said to have obtained a personal or consumption benefit from the item in question or whether it is simply part of the "working conditions" of employment. Irrespective of whether some nonwork-related personal benefit is present, fringe benefits raise difficult issues of valuation. Often the employee does not have a choice whether or not to accept a benefit and, therefore, including the full market value in income may be inappropriate. From an administrative point of view, ensuring that an item is in fact included in the employee's tax base can be difficult, particularly in the case of small amounts or benefits which are shared among many employees. Similarly, where wage income is subject to withholding at source, the inclusion of in-kind fringe benefits can be a problem. Finally, some categories of fringe benefit, such as childcare, may be expressly excluded from the tax base for social policy reasons. Fringe benefits are discussed in section 1.3 below.

1.2 The Distinction Between Employees and Independent Contractors

The tax treatment of employees and independent workers differs significantly for all the countries studied here. For most countries, expenses deductible by employees are restricted compared to expenses deductible by independent workers. Also, salaries and wages paid to employees are subject to withholding at source by employers, whereas most payments to independent workers are not. For countries with schedular systems, employment income is included in a different schedule from business income derived by independent workers. Thus, all the countries require rules to distinguish between employees and independent workers, as discussed below in this section. In some countries, the distinction is based on the distinction in the country's labor law (either statutory or case law); in others, there is a special distinction for purposes of tax law. In some countries, the distinction is dependent on the facts and circumstances of each case, while in others it is based on a limited number of factors, such as the amount of control exercised by the payer on a worker.

In the *United Kingdom*, employees are subject to tax on their income from employment under the Income Tax (Earnings and Pensions) Act 2003 (ITEPA), whereas independent contractors are taxed on their professional or trading profits under the Income Tax (Trading and Other Income) Act 2005 (ITTOIA). The term "employment" is not exhaustively defined in ITEPA; it includes employment under a contract of service or of apprenticeship and employment in the service of the Crown.[9] The question whether someone is an employee or an independent contractor for tax purposes is ultimately left to the courts to decide.[10] The test for determining whether an employment exists is broadly the same as that used in other areas of UK law, including employment law. The distinction drawn is between a contract "of" service (employee) and a contract "for" service (independent contractor). Whether a contract is one of service is a question of law, but the balancing process of applying the relevant criteria is left to the courts as a question of fact.[11] The classic test for a contract "of" service is:[12]

(i) the "servant" agrees, in consideration of a wage or other remuneration, to provide work and skill in the performance of some service for the "master";
(ii) the servant agrees, explicitly or implicitly, to be subject to the payer's control in a sufficient degree to make the payer the servant's master; and
(iii) the other provisions of the contract are consistent with a contract of service.

The courts consider a number of factors in determining whether a contract of service exists:[13] (i) the degree of control by the engager; (ii) the prospect of profit or risk of loss; (iii) whether the individual is properly regarded as part and parcel of the engager's organization at the relevant time; (iv) whether the individual is carrying on business for the individual's own account or for that of the engager;[14] (v) who provides the capital? (vi) the incidence of tax and national insurance in respect of the contract; (vii) the parties' view of the relationship and their intention; (viii) the individual's profession and related arrangements; and (ix) the contractual terms. More recent cases have also considered the ability of the individual to provide a substitute worker, which is indicative of independent contractor status.[15] Another factor considered in some cases is mutuality of obligations: is the engager obliged to pay a wage or other remuneration and is the individual obliged to provide his or her own work or skill?

9. United Kingdom, ITEPA, s. 4.
10. HMRC offers a sophisticated online tool for "checking employment status for tax" (CEST); *see* https://www.gov.uk/guidance/check-employment-status-for-tax. The CEST determination can be relied on with respect to whether a worker should be paying tax as an employee through pay-as-you-earn (PAYE) and whether the anti-avoidance rules apply—but only if the information provided is accurate and not part of a contrived effort to game the software.
11. *O'Kelly v. Trusthouse Forte plc* [1983] 3 All ER 456, CA.
12. *Ready Mixed Concrete (South East) Ltd v. Minister of Pensions and National Insurance* [1968] 1 All ER 433, per MacKenna J.
13. This list is from *Addison v. London Philharmonic* [1981] ICR 261 at 271, per Waterhouse J.
14. This test is from *Market Investigations Ltd v. Minister for Social Security* [1969] 2 QB 173.
15. *Autoclenz Ltd v. Belcher* [2011] UKSC 41. The ability to provide a substitute must be real and not a sham.

However, His Majesty's Revenue and Customs (HMRC) takes a narrow view of the meaning of mutuality of obligations, essentially assuming that where work is provided for remuneration there is a contract for or of services, which is enough to satisfy this test.

The distinction between employees and independent contractors is an important one because the tax treatment of independent contractors under ITTOIA generally is more favorable than for employees under ITEPA. Although employment income and the profits of independent contractors are subject to the same rates of income tax, in practice, the rules for deducting expenses operate more leniently and with less scrutiny for independent contractors compared to employees; in addition, contractors have more opportunities for shifting income to lower-taxed family members by paying them salaries which are deductible in computing profits (within reasonable limits under the "wholly and exclusively" test in ITTOIA section 34). Most important, national insurance contributions (NICs) are levied on both employees and employers, but for independent contractors there is just a single, much lower charge; this provides a significant and longstanding tax incentive for carrying on economic activity as an independent contractor rather than as an employee, especially since the differences in NICs paid have little impact on contributory benefit entitlement.

Further, because NICs are not levied on company profits, dividends, or capital gains, there is often an even greater incentive to carry on economic activity through a company where possible, although the calculation is not straightforward and anti-avoidance rules may apply.[16] The calculation depends on several factors, including: a comparison of the low corporate tax with the personal tax on distributed profits; whether profits are retained in the company; how much profit is taken as employment income versus dividends or capital gains; and whether the arrangement is subject to anti-avoidance rules in ITEPA known as "IR35." The "IR35" legislation in ITEPA sections 48-61 was introduced in 2000 and applies in situations where:

(1) an individual worker personally performs services for the ultimate client;
(2) the worker has a material interest in the intermediary;
(3) the intermediary receives a payment for the services performed by the worker; and
(4) the worker would otherwise be regarded—absent the intermediary—as an employee of the ultimate client under the usual case law tests for contract of service.

If these conditions are satisfied, the worker is deemed by the legislation to receive from the intermediary a payment of an amount determined by reference to the payments received by the intermediary. This deemed payment to the worker is treated as employment income and is subject to PAYE and NICs; it is also deductible in computing the profits of the intermediary for corporation tax purposes. In 2007, the Government introduced supplemental managed-services companies rules in ITEPA

16. United Kingdom, ITEPA, ss. 48-61.

section 61A-61J, targeting in particular the problem of mass-marketed intermediaries. In 2017, important further steps were taken to strengthen IR35 by shifting the responsibility for determining whether IR35 applies in a particular situation from the service provider to engagers in the public sector from 2017 and to medium and large private-sector engagers beginning in April 2020.

In *France*, the same criterion applies in tax and labor law for purposes of defining an employer-employee relationship, i.e., the criterion of subordination.[17] Since 1996,[18] the social chamber of the *Cour de cassation* has defined subordination as "the performance of work under the authority of the employer, who has the power to give orders and instructions, to control their execution and to sanction the failings of his subordinate." There are certain exceptions, as statute law allows certain independent workers to opt for the employment category.[19] For a long time, taxpayers favored employment status, because it offered an automatic deduction of 20% of taxable income and a flat-rate deduction of 10% for professional expenses. Today, only the 10% flat-rate deduction remains, with an optional capped deduction of actual expenses if they exceed 10% of the amount of wages received. Other amounts are taxed as employment income if they replace or compensate for wages—for example, an indemnity paid on termination of the employment contract[20] or, under the influence of the UK and the U.S., sums from employee profit-sharing or incentive schemes, which, depending on the nature of the gain, may be taxed as wages or capital gains.

Under the *Canadian* system, income from "an office or employment" is subject to special rules compared to the rules applicable to business income. For example, employment income is taxed on a cash basis, whereas business income is generally taxed on an accrual basis; further, the deduction of expenses in computing employment income is restricted to amounts expressly authorized by statute, whereas business expenses incurred for the purposes of earning income are deductible unless expressly prohibited.

The Income Tax Act (ITA) defines an office and employment broadly, with both limited to individuals.[21] An office includes the position of a judge, member of a legislature, and director of a company. Employment means a position in the service of another person. Thus, as in the UK, a "contract of service" is employment but a "contract for service" is a business relationship. Because the Act does not provide a meaningful definition of employment, the courts have developed a facts-and-circumstances approach to distinguish between employees and independent contractors.[22] For this purpose, the level of control exercised by the payer (employer) over the work assigned to a worker and the manner in which the work is carried out are the most important factors but are not determinative. Other relevant factors include the financial risk assumed by a worker, the opportunity for a worker to profit, the level of

17. France, Code général des impôts (General Tax Code, CGI), s. 80.
18. Cour de cassation, Soc., November 13, 1996, n°94-13187 (*Société générale*).
19. France, CGI, s. 93.
20. France, CGI, s. 80 duodecies.
21. Canada, ITA, s. 248(1).
22. *Wiebe Door Services Ltd. v. MNR*, [1986] 3FC 553; *671122 Ontario Ltd. v. Sagaz Industries*, 2011 SCC 59.

investment and management provided by a worker, the equipment provided by a worker, and the intention of the parties as set out in their contract.

To prevent employees from using corporations to earn what would otherwise be employment income, the Act contains anti-avoidance rules which limit the deductions that a corporation carrying on a "personal services business" can deduct and deny the small business deduction for income from such businesses.[23]

The *United States* relies on a twenty-factor test, which is the product of years of case law development, to distinguish between independent contractors and employees.[24] These factors are generally based on the workplace reporting structure, the provision of training and guidance, the level of investment in equipment and materials, and client base. The tax test does not include any presumption in favor of either employee or independent contractor status (in contrast, for example, to some labor law worker-classification tests under state law). Despite the expectation that the test produces a neutral determination based on the totality of all twenty factors, in practice some factors are granted more weight than others.[25] Ultimately, for tax law purposes, a worker is usually classified as an independent contractor if the person for whom the work is performed controls only the results of the work and not the precise manner of its execution.

The major tax implications of worker status include: (1) the availability of the new section 199A deduction for qualifying income earned through pass-through entities (the deduction is available only to independent contractors; it is not available to employees); (2) who bears payroll and unemployment (Social Security and Medicare) taxes (the taxes are fully borne by independent contractors but are shared by

23. Canada, ITA, ss. 18(1)(p) and 125 (especially the definition of "personal services business" in s. 125(7)).

24. *See*, e.g., Rev. Rul. 87-41, 1987-1 C.B. 296. *See*, e.g., IRS, Independent Contractor Defined, https://www.irs.gov/businesses/small-businesses-self-employed/independent-contractor-self-employed-or-employee. The factors include: (1) whether the person for whom the services are performed has the right to require compliance with that person's instructions; (2) whether there is worker training; (3) whether the worker's services are integrated into business operations; (4) whether services must be personally rendered; (5) whether the person for whom the services are performed hires assistants; (6) whether there is a continuing relationship; (7) whether set hours are established; (8) whether full-time work is required; (9) whether the work must be done on the employer's premises; (10) whether the work must be performed in a particular sequence; (11) whether the worker must submit regular reports; (12) whether the worker is paid by the hour, week, or month; (13) whether the worker is reimbursed for travel or other business expenses; (14) whether the person for whom the services are performed "furnish[es] significant tools, materials or equipment"; (15) whether the worker invests in facilities used in performance of services that are not furnished by the employer (suggestive of independent contractor status); (16) whether the worker can realize profit or loss; (17) whether the worker works for more than one firm at the same time; (18) whether the worker makes his or her services available to the general public; (19) whether there is a right to discharge the worker; and (20) whether the worker can terminate the relationship at any time without incurring liability (indicating employee status). *See* S. Oei & D. Ring, "Tax Law's Workplace Shift," 100 *B.U. L. Rev*, 651, 683-85 (2020), available at https://papers.ssrn.com/sol3/papers.cfm?abstract_id=3285591; https://doi.org/10.2139/ssrn.3285591.

25. IRS, Independent Contractor Defined, https://www.irs.gov/businesses/small-businesses-self-employed/independent-contractor-self-employed-or-employee; *Schrantz v. Commissioner*, 102 TCM (CCH) 233 (2011); *Levine v. Commissioner*, TCM (RIA) 2005-86 (2005); Rev. Rul. 87-41, 1987-1 CB 296.

employers and employees);[26] (3) how wage withholding and/or information reporting is performed and whether estimated tax payments must be made;[27] (4) whether the worker is entitled to deductions for expenses incurred in the performance of the work (in general, only independent contractors can deduct business-related expenses);[28] and (5) the availability of tax-free fringe benefits (more benefits are available to employees, although some are also available to independent contractors).[29]

In addition, worker classification shapes the availability of health-care and retirement benefits that are delivered through the tax code. Although there may be some tax advantages for health-care benefits granted to employees, independent contractors traditionally have also secured tax advantages for their health-care payments. Despite this rough parity in health-care tax advantages across worker classifications, there is a commonly held view that health insurance is a distinctly valuable benefit of employee status. This view probably reflects the reality that employees are more likely to obtain better—and less expensive—health-care coverage through an employer than they could on their own in the market.

In *China*, limited official guidance is available with respect to the distinction between employment contracts, referred to as "labor contracts" in China, and independent contracts. Labor contracts are required by Labor Contract Law to contain detailed provisions governing the conditions of employment, such as the scope of and location of the work, hours of work, vacation time, compensation, and social insurance. In addition, the law requires hiring units to establish a labor management system and ensure that workers enjoy the right to work and are provided with the necessary conditions and tools. The existence of a labor contract is conclusive that the relationship between workers and the hiring unit is one of employment. A labor contract can be an oral or written agreement and can cover part-time work. Under all such contracts,

26. Federal Insurance Contribution Act (FICA) of 1935, 26 USC Ch. 21, ss. 3101 et seq.; Federal Unemployment Tax Act, 26 USC Ch. 23, ss. 3301 et seq. For 2024, federal tax law imposes a Social Security tax totaling 12.4% on worker wages up to USD 168,600, as well as a 2.9% Medicare tax with no salary cap, which applies to both employees and independent contractors. For employees, these taxes are collectively known as Federal Insurance Contributions Act taxes; the employer pays one-half of the tax and the employee the other half. For independent contractors, the taxes are known as Self-Employment Contributions Act taxes and are fully borne by the independent contractor.
27. *See* United States, IRC, ss. 3401, 3402, 3501 et seq., 6041, 6050W; *see also* IRS Pub. 15, at 24-29 (2024), available at https://www.irs.gov/pub/irs-pdf/p15.pdf (employer withholding obligations on employee wages).
28. The deductibility of business-related expenses changed notably with the 2017 tax reform. Prior to the 2017 reform, employees who incurred unreimbursed expenses in performing employment duties were able to deduct those employee expenses. But these expenses (together with others, known as "miscellaneous itemized deductions") were deductible only to the extent that they exceeded 2% of the taxpayer's adjusted gross income (IRC, ss. 62, 67). As a result, the deduction was realistically available only for taxpayers with high expenses relative to income. In contrast, prior to the 2017 tax reform, independent contractors were able to deduct fully their ordinary and necessary business expenses. The 2017 tax legislation suspended the deduction for miscellaneous itemized deductions (including the deduction for employee expenses) starting in 2018 and effective for taxable years beginning before January 1, 2026. This change is significant for employees with high business expenses. Independent contractors continue to be able to deduct their trade or business expenses in full.
29. United States, IRC, ss. 62, 67, 132.

workers are dependent on the hiring unit with respect to the type of work, location of work, and means of carrying out the work.

In contrast, independent contracts are used by freelancers or individuals in "independent occupations," which include professionals, skilled workers, artists, and brokers or agents. The relationship between an individual service provider and a "client" is not governed by a labor contract, but by a service contract. The amount of remuneration is not set by government regulations.

A salaried worker also can provide services under an independent contract. For example, performing artists who are employed by a performing arts company may give concerts in their own name, or teachers who are employed by a school may offer outside tutorial services in their spare time.

In *Sweden*, earned income of individuals can be taxed as income from employment or business. Salaries earned by employees and compensation earned by dependent contractors are taxed as income from employment. In contrast, income earned by independent contractors is taxed as income from business. Both types of income are taxed as earned income at rates according to the total sum of earned income. However, a number of differences exist between taxation of employment income and business income.

For income from employment, social security contributions are paid by the employer, whereas independent contractors pay these contributions themselves. For income from business, more favorable rules apply to the deduction of expenses and deferral of taxation. Services provided by an independent contractor are normally liable for value-added tax (VAT).

Services are categorized as independent services depending on a number of factors, such as the number of contracts with different customers, the use of employees, and inventories maintained for the purpose of providing the services; the number of contracts is the single most important criterion. In principle, it is a question of the opportunity for profit or risk of loss for the contractor.

According to Swedish case law, it is possible to incorporate most types of independent services into closely held corporations. The criteria for determining whether the services are independent are much the same as those for individuals described above. The tax treatment of closely held corporations and income from business derived by independent contractors is more favorable than the treatment of income from employment; *see* Part III for a description of the taxation of shareholders in closely held corporations.

Australian tax law has faced the problem, seen in most countries, of trying to distinguish between employees and independent contractors for tax purposes, as well as for industrial law and vicarious liability. The problem has become more pressing with government policies directed at increasing labor market flexibility (i.e., employers have greater flexibility in setting bespoke terms for the contracts under which they procure workers' labor) and the emerging "gig economy."

The tax authorities have been concerned to control four tax-related problems which arise from reorganizing from employee to contractor status: using companies and trusts to equalize income across all members of a family; labor income being taxed at the company tax rate and not at the progressive rates applied to individuals; the tendency for contractors to claim significantly higher amounts as tax deductions; and the absence of withholding on payments to contractors. There are also potential implications for the fringe benefits tax (FBT), compulsory contributions to pension funds, and State payroll taxes.

The problem is not new, and Australia has a wealth of case law, mostly won by the revenue authorities, examining attempts to recharacterize employment-like relationships as independent contracting. Australian courts have approached the problem in different ways: some have applied the general anti-avoidance rule as the instrument for defeating these arrangements; some have characterized arrangements as having the substance of employment (typically relying on labor-law notions), triggering the doctrine that the tax liability on wages cannot be shifted. These cases have tended to emphasize a variety of factors, such as the degree of control held by the "employer" over how the worker performs the work, whether the engagement is project-specific or indefinite, the ability of the worker to delegate responsibilities to others, who provides any necessary tools and equipment, in whose premises the work is performed, how the worker's remuneration is calculated, and so on.

In 1999, the government decided it would try to regularize the tax law in this area by enacting a dedicated regime to clarify the employee-contractor demarcation (while leaving the existing case law in place), and by expanding the withholding regime so that it could capture payments to contractors in more instances.

The statutory regime is constructed around the notion of "personal services income," which is defined to mean "income [that] is mainly a reward for [the] personal efforts or skills ..." of an individual. The regime limits the deductions which can be claimed in earning "personal services income" and purports to allocate the tax liability on this income to the individual rather than the company or trust through which the individual operates, unless that company or trust is operating a "personal services business." A company or trust is conducting a "personal services business" if it provides tools and equipment and is liable to its customers for the cost of rectifying defects in the work it performs. If that is not the case, and no more than 80% of the company or trust's income during the year came from a single customer, the company or trust is still considered to be conducting a "personal services business": if it made income during the year from work for at least two clients unrelated to the owners whom it attracted by advertising to the general public; if it engages unrelated people to perform at least 20% of its work during the year or has trainee staff; or if it owns or rents commercial premises throughout the year from which it conducts its business operations. These rules are undoubtedly clearer than the case law they supplement, but they have not proved to be a sound solution and have generated a large number of disputes. In addition, they also did not displace the previous rules, but operate in addition to them.

Under *German* tax law, the treatment of income from employment differs in several ways from the treatment of business income, the most important difference being that income from employment is taxed on a cash basis and is subject to third-party reporting and withholding by employers. For employees, a standard deduction of EUR 1,230 per year for income-related expenses applies unless the taxpayer provides evidence for higher expenses. In addition, only independent contractors can be subject to trade tax and VAT.

The underlying rationale for the distinction between employment and business income is tax-specific and differs from the rationale behind seemingly identical distinctions in other fields of law, in particular social security law, labor law, and general civil law. As a result, tax law does not necessarily follow classifications from these other fields, and there have even been cases where tax law has deviated systematically from them. For example, a corporate director is considered to derive income from employment for tax law purposes, but for labor law purposes does not qualify as an employee.

The Income Tax Act (ITA) provides no explicit definition of a contract of services or of employment, but an interpretative regulation issued by the government on the payroll tax specifies some basic criteria.[30] Under this regulation, whether a person owes their labor to the employer (which is the case where the employer controls the person's activity or the person is integrated into the employer's business organization) is determinative of employee status. This is a valid interpretation, but the criteria are not exhaustive for purposes of the ITA. The courts consider many factors to be relevant, and therefore various factors must be assessed and weighed in order to determine whether a person derives income from employment; however, it is sufficient if, all facts and circumstances considered, the overall picture corresponds to the concept of employment.

The essential criteria for income from employment are the level of control the employer has over the work, the integration into the business organization, and the lack of economic risk. Other factors may indicate the fulfillment of one of these essential criteria and are, in any case, taken into consideration when determining the overall picture. Such factors include whether salary and working times are fixed, whether the person is entitled to paid holidays or other social benefits, whether the person provides equipment, whether the person's income is influenced by the amount of work done, whether the work is performed on the employer's premises, whether the person must cooperate with other personnel of the employer, and whether the person works for various employers or just one employer.

In *Japan*, the distinction between employee and independent contractor is relevant with respect to the applicable category of income. Income earned by an independent contractor is most likely to be taxed as business income but could be categorized as employment income depending on the facts and circumstances.

Despite its significance, the statutory distinction between employment income and business income is highly abstract; detailed rules are found in the case law and administrative guidelines. According to the case law, multiple factors must be taken into account, but the most important factors indicative of employment income are: (a) subordination to the employer (i.e., control over the way in which the labor/personal service is rendered), (b) dependence on the employer (e.g., the location of the work is determined by the employer and equipment is provided by the employer), and (c) the

30. German Payroll Tax Regulation (*Lohnsteuer-Durchführungsverordnung*), s. 1 para. 2.

linking of remuneration to the services rendered, irrespective of the profit/loss made by the business activity for which the services are rendered. If the income earner bears the risk of business, the income is likely to be classified as business income. For example, although a university professor enjoys large discretion (and thus does not meet the "subordination" criterion), nevertheless the remuneration is classified as employment income because the facilities for work are mainly provided by the employer (the university) and compensation is linked to the services rendered, not the financial performance of the university. Importantly, the legal form of the relationship is irrelevant; even in the absence of an employment contract, the courts do not hesitate to find an "employment relation for tax purposes" where the above criteria are met. Thus, an independent contractor who renders personal services can be found to be earning employment income where the client controls the way in which the services are rendered, provides facilities/resources for the contractor, and pays remuneration based on the services.

As discussed in Subpart C below, employment income is computed by deducting a standard formula-based "employment-income deduction." This deduction is favorable to taxpayers in most cases, but it limits the deduction of expenses actually incurred to earn employment income to certain items expressly authorized by statute; in contrast, business expenses are deductible unless expressly prohibited. Yet another important tax consequence is that withholding applies to employment income, but not to business income. Perhaps peculiar to the Japanese system is that the amount to be withheld is computed, by way of complex rules, so as to approximate the employee's final taxable income as accurately as possible;[31] accordingly, where an employee earns employment income from one employer, the employee is exempt from the obligation to file a tax return. This method saves compliance costs to taxpayers and administrative costs to the tax authorities by shifting the expense to employers, who must collect information from employees and compute the correct amount of tax to be withheld. It is being seriously discussed whether this withholding-dependent system of tax collection is sustainable in the context of the gig economy, where an increasing number of taxpayers earn income from multiple sources, making it difficult for the tax authorities to collect, and impossible for the payers to withhold, the correct amount of tax.

In *The Netherlands*, employment status largely applies to persons who meet the definition of employment in the Civil Code, under which three elements are essential: an obligation on the employee to work; an obligation on the employer to pay a salary; and subordination, which is often the decisive factor. The extensive case law available for determining the meaning of subordination indicates that a situation of subordination exists where the employer is entitled to give the employee instructions about the task, the way of working, and the working hours. Subordination is also an important issue in the determination of whether a business exists. The jurisprudence of the Supreme Court indicates that a business is an organization of capital and labor on a continuous basis which participates in the economic process with the intention of making a profit.[32] Whether an individual's activities are characterized as a business

31. Japan, ITA, ss. 183-193.
32. *See*, for example, Dutch Supreme Court, November 14, 2014, BNB 2015/17.

depends on whether the individual bears economic and entrepreneurial risks,[33] is not dependent on one principal but instead has a number of principals,[34] and makes the appropriate and necessary investments and works under their own name, to which publicity is given.[35] Income from both employment and business is taxed as box 1 income at progressive rates. In addition to the deductibility of business expenses, entrepreneurs may be eligible to take into account certain business allowances (*ondernemersaftrek*; e.g., self-employed deduction and relief on termination of a business) and exemptions (*MKB-winstvrijstelling*) in determining profits.[36] These deductions and allowances may result in lower taxation of business income compared to employment income; however, since entrepreneurs are subject to lower overall social security contribution rules, the overall difference is less significant. The practical difficulty of applying the criteria to distinguish between the two categories of income led, in 2017, to a moratorium on the enforcement of these rules, which expired on January 1, 2025.

India has had its share of controversies relating to differences between salaried workers and independent professionals, both in the domestic and treaty context. Under domestic law, most professionals earning income up to INR 5 million (INR 7.5 million where cash receipts do not exceed 5% of gross receipts)[37] are taxable on a presumptive basis at a rate of 50% of their gross receipts without the need for audited books of accounts, whereas salaried employees are allowed only a meager standard deduction (INR 75,000 under the new regime, INR 50,000 under the old regime). In the international context, disputes often arise as to whether employees seconded to Indian subsidiaries are employees of the subsidiary or not. The Supreme Court has established some tests in a different context which would likely be applied for this purpose—the power to control the manner in which the work is done, integration in the employer's business, the power to select and dismiss, the deduction of insurance contributions, the supply of tools and materials, etc.[38] In the *Morgan Stanley* case, the Supreme Court held that employees of a foreign parent company did not become employees of an Indian subsidiary where they retained their status as employees of the parent company.[39]

1.3 The Taxation of Fringe Benefits

The systems considered here show a wide range of responses to the taxation of fringe benefits. These include the outright exclusion of some significant benefits, the use of arbitrary "standard" values for the inclusion of specific benefits, valuations which

33. Netherlands, Supreme Court, September 16, 1992, BNB 1992/370.
34. The Hague Court of Appeal, December 6, 1994, V-N 1994, p. 1305, and Dutch Supreme Court, October 14, 1992, BNB 1993/6.
35. Netherlands, Supreme Court, December 20, 2000, BNB 2001/88, and The Hague Court of Appeal, July 12, 1979, BNB 1980/307 and July 14, 1983, V-N 1984, p. 910.
36. Netherlands, Income Tax Act (ITA), Art. 3.74 through 3.79a.
37. India, Finance Act 2023, s. 44ADA, 1st proviso.
38. *Ram Singh v. Union Territory of Chandigarh*, 7/1/2003, 3166, 2002.
39. *DIT v. Morgan Stanley & Co Inc.*, July 9, 2007, CA No. 2914, 2007. More precisely, the Supreme Court stated that where the "deputationists maintain a lien" with the parent company, they do not become employees of the subsidiary.

clearly undervalue benefits, the denial or limitation of the employer's deduction for benefits which are not included by the employee, and finally, a separate employer-level fringe benefits tax (FBT) which, in effect, includes the value of the benefit in the employer's tax base in lieu of taxing the employee. To a certain extent, some exclusions apparently reflect differing societal views on what is appropriately viewed as a nontaxable working condition—for example, a free glass of beer in Germany and Australia[40] (provided the employer is a brewer and the beer is consumed on the employer's premises) and free coffee in Sweden. Several countries exclude certain benefits, such as gifts on special occasions which are provided to employees in their personal rather than their employee capacities. More generally, the countries' practices differ significantly in the extent to which a real attempt is made to tax the economic benefit accruing to employees. Several countries use unrealistic standardized amounts for certain types of commonly recurring fringe benefits such as automobiles and the like.

In the *United States* system, detailed statutory provisions deal with fringe benefits. The principal rules, enacted in 1984, supplanted administrative practices, which were increasingly unable to deal with the proliferation of fringe benefit programs.[41] The statutory pattern establishes a general rule that fringe benefits are taxable, but then creates a number of exceptions. Under the "working condition fringe" exception, an employer-provided benefit is not taxable if the expense would have been deductible if incurred directly by the employee. In addition, *de minimis* amounts of fringe benefits are excluded. In a concession to the transportation industry, services provided to employees at "no additional cost" to the employer are not taxed, thus allowing that form of compensation to be given to transportation employees on a tax-free basis. Employer discounts are also excluded, subject to some limitations. Exclusion is also available, usually subject to dollar limitations, for certain employer-provided transportation (but the employer is not entitled to deduct the cost of such transportation), day care programs, educational assistance, group life insurance, and meals and lodging in certain situations. From an economic point of view, one of the most important nontaxable fringe benefits is employer-funded medical care. Medical benefits provided directly or under insurance-financed plans are not taxable. The ability to obtain medical care on a before-tax basis has been identified as one of the factors affecting the escalation of medical care costs.

Where fringe benefits are taxable, in principle, they are taxed at fair market value; the employee's "subjective perception" of the value of the benefit is not relevant. Detailed regulations establish the values of employer-provided automobiles and aircraft, and a statutory provision requires the taxation of employer-provided parking to the extent that the value of the parking exceeds USD 315 per month.

In *Germany*, in principle, the employment income category includes all "benefits" received by employees to the extent that they can be determined to have a cash value.[42] The theoretical justification for the inclusion in income is based on the idea

40. Australia, Fringe Benefits Tax Assessment Act (FBTAA), s. 41.
41. United States, IRC, s. 132.
42. Germany, ITA, s. 19 para. 1 No. 1, s. 8 para. 1.

that such benefits result in an increased "ability to pay" because the employee has been saved an expense which would otherwise have been incurred. The fact that the benefit cannot be converted to cash is not relevant. There is a *de minimis* rule which excludes from income up to EUR 50 per month of otherwise taxable benefits.[43] Special employer discounts are taxable only if their net value exceeds EUR 1,080.[44]

There is a long statutory catalog of items which are not taxable for what are perceived to be social policy reasons, including employer-provided day care, employer-provided passes for public transportation between home and workplace,[45] and extra pay for overtime work on Sundays, holidays, or at night.[46] The private use of technical equipment in the workplace is tax-free because these benefits are hard to evaluate.[47]

There are also a number of case law exceptions which focus on the benefit to employers of a happy workforce (such as firm outings, "occasional" gifts, and free beer) but seem to ignore the parallel benefit to employees. The Federal Court has tended to reduce the scope of these exceptions and treat the statutory exemptions as exclusive.[48] In 2014, a novel statutory exemption of EUR 110 per employee for two "social events" (firm outings, Christmas parties) per year was enacted.[49]

In principle, benefits are valued at *retail* market value.[50] There are, however, standard-value tables for meals and lodging and other benefits, which apply unless there are unusual circumstances (e.g., a luxury apartment provided to an executive); these tables generally undervalue the benefits. In the case of employer-provided cars, employees may choose between a standard-value method or an "exact" method.[51] The standard-value method is based on the list price of the car and requires a percentage of that value to be included in income. Alternatively, employees can use the "exact" method based on actual costs and a driving record establishing private and business-related driving.

Special "lump-sum" rules apply at the employer level with respect to certain fringe benefits.[52] In effect, these rules make the employer-level tax the final tax on the benefit; it is not included in employees' assessable income. For policy reasons, the rules also provide a lower rate of tax on certain benefits.

In *Sweden*, in principle, all benefits which fall into the category of income from employment are taxable. However, no attempt is made to tax employee benefits such as free coffee, sports training facilities, and the like, largely because these rules would be difficult to administer. Where benefits are taxable, in principle, valuation should be done on the basis of fair market value. Standard values are used for meals and cars, the two most commonly provided fringe benefits. For employer-provided cars, a standardized amount is calculated based on the price of the car; this rule has been criticized

43. Germany, ITA, s. 8 para. 2 s. 11.
44. Germany, ITA, s. 8 para. 3 ITA.
45. Germany, ITA, s. 3 Nos. 32 and 33.
46. Germany, ITA, s. 3b ITA.
47. Germany, ITA, s. 3 No. 45.
48. Federal Tax Court (*Bundesfinanzhof*), June 22, 2006, VI R 21/05.
49. Germany, ITA, s. 19 para. 1a.
50. Germany, ITA, s. 8 para. 2 s. 1.
51. Germany, ITA, s. 8 para. 2 s. 2.
52. Germany, ITA, s. 40.

from an environmental point of view in that, in effect, it establishes a zero marginal cost for additional personal driving. However, the benefit of free charging of electric vehicles is tax exempt and the benefit of employer-provided bicycles is tax exempt up to SEK 3,000. These rules were recently introduced for environmental reasons.

Another special benefit is employer-provided health care. Sweden has an extensive public health-care system but with long waits for certain types of services. Where the employer pays the costs of private care, the amount is deductible by the employer and taxable to the employee.

In *The Netherlands*, most fringe benefits are included in income. Valuation is based on resale value or, if it is not possible or usual to sell the benefit received, the amount which the employee is assumed to have saved because of the employer benefit. In the case of employer-provided housing, a fair-market rental must be used as the standard for valuation. Special—and generally realistic—valuation rules apply to, *inter alia*, meals, low-interest loans, and transportation provided by the employer. Cars provided by the employer which are also used privately for over 500 km per year are taxed to the employee, usually at 16% or 22% of the car's list price, depending on its CO_2 emissions; for cars over 15 years old, the percentage is 35% of the fair market value of the car.[53]

Under the *French* system, all benefits in cash or kind granted in addition to salaries, wages, pensions, and annuities are taken into account.[54] The rules for valuing benefits in kind for income tax purposes are aligned with those for calculating social security contributions, namely, either on their actual value or on a lump-sum basis (for food, accommodation, vehicles, and IT or communication tools). Detailed valuation rules apply to various types of in-kind benefits, including gifts of modest value and employee discounts for products made or sold by the employer. Special rules apply to certain employees (apprentices, vacation camp instructors, nurses and educators, naval officers, and fishers) for employer-provided meals. To prevent abuse, reporting obligations have been introduced to enable the tax authorities to monitor these benefits. The amount of most cash and in-kind taxable benefits must be reported to the tax authorities, either in the annual social data declaration, in the nominative social declaration, or, if the employee is not covered by the general social security scheme, in the declaration of salaries and/or fees and/or employee shareholding. For their part, companies must also provide information attached to the accounts listing all the benefits allocated to each employee during the financial year.

Canada has a broad statutory provision which taxes "benefits of any kind whatever" received by an employee,[55] but a number of benefits are excluded by statute (e.g., health benefits, group term life insurance) or by administrative decision (e.g., merchandise discounts, subsidized meals where the employee pays cost, and recreational facilities).[56] Courts have held that reimbursement of moving expenses, of the

53. Netherlands, WTA, Art. 13 bis.
54. France, CGI, s. 82.
55. Canada, ITA, s. 6(1)(a).
56. Canada Revenue Agency, "Employers' Guide: Taxable Benefits and Allowances," T4130(E) Rev. 23.

loss on the sale of a house, and even of increased mortgage expenses arising in connection with a move, are not required to be included in income; however, the latter two results have been changed by statutory amendments.[57] Free parking spaces are generally considered to be a taxable benefit unless the employee does not have exclusive use of the space or is required to travel frequently in the course of employment. Complex rules attempt to value employer-provided automobiles. In general, it is difficult to find any consistent criteria in either the administrative practice or the jurisprudence on which to distinguish between taxable and nontaxable fringe benefits. The fair market value of taxable fringe benefits is generally required to be included in income, but the cost to the employer is included with respect to some benefits.

In *Japan*, due to the schedular character of the tax system, fringe benefits raise two questions: whether they are taxable at all, and if so, into which category they fall. In principle, all benefits constitute taxable income; however, as long as the character and value of fringe benefits are within the scope of social convention, such benefits are not taxed. The National Tax Agency normally disregards gifts for longtime employment, recreational trips for employees, and discount sales of employer goods and services, as well as meals and housing provided at below-market rates to employees. Business meals enjoyed by employees at the expense of employers could be of substantial value and taxable, but it is impractical to capture these benefits; rather, the law limits the amount deductible by corporate employers as entertainment expenses, which include the cost of business meals to some extent, instead of including their value in employees' taxable income.[58] Because there are few statutory provisions dealing with fringe benefits, administrative circulars serve as a de facto source of law; that is, despite its lack of the source-of-law status (*see* the Chapter on Japan in Part I), taxpayers normally follow the administrative positions in order to avoid uncertainty, and the courts often uphold the government's view unless it is unreasonable. Although some fringe benefits are only tangentially related to employment, in practice, most benefits are taxed as "employment income" if they are taxed at all.

The *United Kingdom* initially had difficulty taxing fringe benefits because of a court-developed principle that benefits could be taxed only to the extent that they could be converted to cash.[59] This led to a widespread use of fringe benefits which could not be resold or where real or nominal restrictions reduced or eliminated the resale value. In response, a special statutory regime was introduced in 1978 which was applicable to directors and employees with incomes over a certain level (GBP 8,500).[60] The income level was originally set to cover only higher-paid employees but was never increased, and by 2016, a full-time employee on minimum wage would be earning over GBP 14,000; in that year the threshold was finally abolished and the special regime extended to all employees. The rules apply to a wide range of benefits. However, the benefits are

57. Canada, ITA, s. 6(19)-(23).
58. Japan, The Special Taxation Measures Act (STMA), s. 61-4.
59. *Tennant v. Smith* [1892] 3 TC 158, now ITEPA, s. 62.
60. The rules, collectively referred to as the "Benefits Code," are gathered in United Kingdom, ITEPA, Part 3. On the relationship between the Benefits Code and ITEPA, s. 62, *see* s. 64.

generally valued at the marginal cost to the employer, which allows substantial value to be derived free from tax by employees. One particular aspect of these statutory rules has become important: the benefit is caught if it was provided "by reason of the employment." This condition is satisfied automatically where the benefit is provided by the employer and the employer is a company; in limited circumstances, it may be rebutted where the employer is not a company.[61] Thus, a payment by such an employer to an employee who is the victim of a terrorist attack is taxable income.

A standard-value approach is used for company cars and other common types of benefits. Free parking is expressly excluded from taxation. The court-developed principles technically remain applicable, along with the statutory regime, and continue to limit inclusion of such benefits to their cash conversion value (i.e., the resale price for employer-provided goods); however, this inclusion can then be topped up under the Benefits Code if those rules would result in a higher-income inclusion (i.e., the cost to the employer).

The *Chinese* IIT Law lists "wages and salaries" as the first item of taxable income. The term "wages and salaries" has a broad meaning, including bonuses, "labor dividends," subsidies, stipends, and any other income in respect of office or employment. Additional details are found in administrative rules regarding employee stock options, relocation payments, education, etc. Employer contributions to "basic" pension plans, basic medical insurance plans, and unemployment insurance plans pursuant to government regulation are not considered to be taxable income to employees.[62]

While the contours of the rules differ, most of the systems described above allow substantial amounts of employment income in the form of fringe benefits to escape tax because of the administrative and valuation problems involved in taxing such benefits. *Australia* has taken a different approach to the treatment of fringe benefits. In general terms, rather than attempting to value benefits and collect tax at the employee level, in 1986 Australia introduced a separate employer-level tax on fringe benefits while at the same time excluding such benefits from employees' income. The 1986 legislation also gave the government the opportunity to enact elaborate and more workable valuation rules.

Apart from the technical aspects referred to below, the decision to impose an FBT was very much a political one. The tax was introduced by a Labor (centrist-socialist) government whose constituency was to a large extent based on the trade union movement. Because of defects in the system for taxing fringe benefits at the employee level, untaxed or low-taxed fringe benefits had become widespread among all classes of employees and had been at least in part capitalized into wage rates. If the income tax on fringe benefits had been imposed on employees, there would have been an immediate reduction in after-tax wages, whereas the levy of the tax on employers meant that, in most cases, the initial incidence of the tax fell on employers. This resulted largely from the fact that, at that time, wage rates in Australia were set out in officially approved awards and could be changed only by elaborate procedures. After

61. United Kingdom, ITEPA, s. 201.
62. China, Caishui [2006] No. 10.

enactment, the burden of the tax has gradually been shifted to employees through the bargaining process.

From a technical viewpoint, the FBT was introduced primarily because of the perceived administrative difficulties of assessing and collecting tax on fringe benefits at the employee level. In addition, in principle, imposing the tax at the employer level allowed the tax to be collected without the need to allocate benefits to individual employees, which was one of the major administrative difficulties in the case of shared benefits.[63] The basic issue of the valuation of the total amount of the benefit, of course, remains, although the level of the inquiry has been shifted to the employer. The FBT legislation sets up a variety of valuation rules which roughly parallel the types of rules used in the income tax systems in other countries. However, since the FBT was completely new, more attention was given to details and the logical structure of the rules than is usually the case for gradually evolving rules for taxing fringe benefits to employees. Nevertheless, commonly recurring items such as employer-provided parking have continued to be a problem in the FBT system and complicated and arbitrary valuation rules have been required.

The use of a separate tax to deal with fringe benefits, while it has administrative advantages, raises its own problems. There are a number of issues involved in the interaction between the FBT and employers' income tax. If the FBT is nondeductible under the income tax and the employer is tax exempt or the employee's tax rate is less than the FBT rate, the FBT is not a perfect substitute for taxing employees on fringe benefits. This is because that part of the tax collected through the income tax (via nondeductibility of the FBT) varies as between employers taxed at the same income tax rate as the FBT rate, employers taxed at a different income tax rate from the FBT rate, and tax exempt (zero tax rate) employers. To equalize the treatment of the three categories of employers, it is necessary to make the FBT deductible in relation to the income tax on the employer and to gross up either the value of the fringe benefit (as Australia now does) or the FBT rate (as New Zealand does) by a factor of t/ (1-t) where t is the FBT tax rate. For example, if the FBT rate is 25%, the gross-up factor is 0.33. The original version of the Australian gross-up did not apply to all tax exempt employers and thus left a significant number of tax exempt bodies in an FBT-favored position. More recently, the government has capped the amount of benefit per employee of employers that still receive favored treatment at AUD 17,000 for hospital employees and AUD 30,000 for other favored bodies.[64]

In addition, if the rate of the FBT (as appropriately adjusted) is set at a rate below the maximum individual rate, an advantage will accrue to highly compensated employees, who would have been taxed at a higher rate under the income tax. In contrast, using the maximum individual rate indirectly overtaxes other employees. The problem of overtaxation of employees who are not subject to the maximum individual

63. In fact, the Australian system requires the allocation of benefits to employees in many situations—for example, in order to apply a fixed exemption level which is allowed for each employee. However, the possibility in principle of avoiding an allocation of benefits is present in the fringe benefit tax approach.
64. Australia, FBTAA, s. 5B(1E), Steps 2 and 3.

tax rate can be overcome by having employees "buy" the benefit from the employer, since this reduces the FBT base, and with it the tax rate, to the employee's actual rate (because the benefit is bought with after-tax dollars). Well-advised employees often negotiate to forego fringe benefits for extra cash, where it is possible to do so.

Another problem involves the treatment of fringe benefits which would have been deductible by the employee if the employee had purchased the benefits in the open market. Since taxation takes place at the employer level, there is no way to "wash" the employee inclusion and deduction, as would normally be the case with employee-level taxation. A notional deduction in the FBT, the "otherwise deductible" rule, was created to reduce the taxable value of fringe benefits which would have been deductible if paid for directly by the employee (e.g., in relation to payments of employee expenses by the employer).[65] In other cases, the issue is handled by the way the benefit is valued. Thus, for example, in the case of a company car which is used for both business and personal travel, the FBT valuation rules isolate the personal use and for this purpose, the business use can be established by a travel log or through a statutory formula which applies a percentage to the cost of the car depending on the number of kilometers driven.[66] While the "otherwise deductible" approach solved the "wash" problem, it reintroduced the question of allocation of benefits since, in order to determine whether the amount would be "otherwise deductible," it must be allocated to a particular employee (or class of employees) to determine whether an employee-level deduction would have been available.

A similar problem arises where fringe benefits are indirectly taxed in the employee's hands under the income tax, although not as wages. For example, the benefit of low interest on a loan which is used to buy an income-producing asset will be reflected in higher net income from the asset. Again, this discrepancy is handled by an "otherwise deductible" rule which reduces the employer's FBT and allows the subsidy to remain taxed in the employee's hands under the income tax.[67]

There are other difficulties with having two parallel systems, one for dealing with normal employee compensation in the income tax and another dealing with fringe benefits in a separate tax. There are borderline classification issues between normal compensation taxable to employees and fringe benefits taxed at the employer level which have complicated the administration of the system and provoked disputes between employer and employee over which is the taxpayer. Eliminating fringe benefits from employee taxation creates problems with means-tested benefits and other programs which are based on taxable income. This problem is now addressed by requiring that the value of fringe benefits (with some minor exceptions) be included in the employee's annual income statement received from the employer and basing other income-related benefits on the combined salary and fringe benefits figure.[68] As a result, allocation of virtually all benefits to employees is now required. Further, it is not a simple matter to adapt separate fringe benefit taxation on employers to international

65. Australia, FBTAA, s. 24.
66. Australia, FBTAA, ss. 9 and 10.
67. Australia, FBTAA, s. 19.
68. Australia, FBTAA, Part XIB.

tax and treaty relationships, which do not contemplate the possibility that the liability for tax on employee benefits would fall on employers.

On the whole, the introduction of the FBT in Australia has improved the tax treatment of such benefits but at significant cost in terms of compliance and complexity (leading to widespread evasion by all but the largest businesses and government agencies). Not surprisingly, some feel that, if some modest legislative and administrative effort had been put into improving the income tax treatment of fringe benefits (by enacting valuation rules and then enforcing the system), the overall results would have been even better. Various tax reform exercises since 1987 have recommended shifting the tax on fringe benefits back to employees, but these recommendations have been studiously ignored by successive governments.

In *India*, fringe benefits or perquisites have always been a fertile ground for tax planning. Free accommodation, the most common and perhaps the oldest form of such benefits for employees, became unequivocally taxable only in 1923.[69] Over the years, the scope of taxable fringe benefits has been gradually expanded; rules of valuation for the most common items are prescribed in Rule 3 of the IT Rules, 1962.

In 2000, the rules of valuation for fringe benefits were comprehensively revised and a "cost to the company" concept adopted.[70] In 2005, realizing that certain types of benefits which were in part personal and in part related to the employer's business could not be properly taxed, the government introduced a fringe benefit tax (FBT) to be collected from employers, similar to the Australian FBT. The FBT applied to a company, a firm, an association of persons or body of individuals, a local authority, and an artificial legal person[71] and was charged as a percentage between 5% and 50% of the expenses incurred by the employer. For individuals and other categories of employers (Hindu Undivided Family (HUF), trusts, etc.), the old rules for taxing employees were reintroduced in 2007, with the result that, in most cases, employers paid the FBT and employees were not taxed, although in some cases employees were taxable directly. In 2008, the government abolished the FBT and reverted to the classical system of taxing fringe benefits.

Although fringe benefits from employment are not exhaustively defined in the ITA, the following benefits are specifically mentioned:[72] (i) value of rent-free/concessional rent accommodation; (ii) any concession in the matter of rent; (iii) the value of any benefit or amenity provided to certain specified employees;[73] (iv) any sum paid by an employer in respect of an obligation actually payable by the taxpayer; (v) any sum payable by an employer, directly or through a fund, for life insurance or an annuity for employees; (vi) the value of any shares of the employer granted free or at a concessional rate to employees; (vii) any contribution in excess of INR 750,000 to

69. India, Income Tax Amendment Act, Act XV of 1923.
70. India, Notification SO 940(E).
71. India, Income Tax Act 1961 (ITA 1961), s. 115W.
72. India, ITA 1961, s. 17(2).
73. Broadly speaking, benefits can be divided into two parts—cash benefits and noncash benefits. Monetary benefits are taxable for all employees, while non-monetary benefits are taxable in the hands of certain specified employees.

the national pension scheme, superannuation fund, or recognized provident fund;[74] (viii) the value of any other prescribed fringe benefit.

With respect to accommodation, the benefit is valued as the fee determined by the respective government less any amount paid by employees. In cities, government accommodations are typically in prime locations and the fees are significantly below market rent and, as a result, government employees are somewhat advantaged.[75] For nongovernment employees, the value of the benefit is an amount equal to 10% of the salary in cities with a population greater than 4 million; 7.5% in cities with a population between 1 million and 4 million; and 5% for other areas (less any amount paid by the employees). If the accommodation is furnished, then a further sum of 10% per annum of the cost of furniture is taxable. Starting in fiscal year 2023-2024, if the accommodation is also occupied by employees in the private sector, the value of the benefit is adjusted for inflation and there is no automatic increase in the benefit solely due to an increase in the employee's salary.[76]

Employees of central and state governments who cannot be provided with housing, or those who choose not to take government housing, are given an allowance in addition to salary, the house rent allowance (HRA). Other employees are also often given a similar allowance. Such allowances should normally be taxable. However, under the Act and the rules, an exemption is available for the least of the following three amounts:[77] the HRA actually received by the employee; rent actually paid less 10% of salary (50% of salary in large cities),[78] and 40% of salary in other areas.[79] This deduction is no longer available for employees who choose to be governed by the new regime introduced in 2020.[80]

The benefit of the use of an automobile provided by an employer is taxable only for specified employees (directors, persons with a substantial interest in a corporate employer, and employees whose salary and allowances exceed INR 50,000) and the value depends on the use of the automobile. If the car is exclusively for the performance of the employee's official duties, the value is nil provided that certain prescribed records are maintained by the employer. Records are often falsified or not maintained. However, even in these cases, it does not necessarily follow that the benefit will be taxable with respect to the specified employees. If a car is used exclusively for personal

74. Finance Act 2020, s. 17(2)(vii).
75. The value is so great that government employees might not have any income left after paying tax on the benefit of the accommodation. The different valuation of accommodation for government and other employees has survived a constitutional challenge on the ground of equality; however, the Supreme Court has accepted that if private-sector employees could show that there was no concession in the amount of rent, the benefit would not be taxable. *See Arun Kumar and Others v. UOI*, September 15, 2006, Civil Appeal No. 3270 of 2003.
76. India, Income Tax Rules, 1962, 3rd proviso to Rule 3.
77. India, ITA 1961, s. 10(13A).
78. Delhi, Mumbai, Chennai, and Kolkata.
79. India, IT Rules 1962, Rule 2A; for this purpose, salary includes the inflation allowance if the terms of service so provide but excludes all other allowances and perquisites (per Rule 2(h) of Part A of the Fourth Schedule of ITA 1961).
80. India, ITA 1961, s. 115BAC. As explained in section 3.1 of the chapter on India in Part I, taxpayers opting for the old tax regime pay tax at a higher rate but are entitled to a broader range of deductions and concessions.

purposes, the value of the benefit is the actual expenditures incurred by the employer in operating and maintaining the car, along with the remuneration of any chauffeur, and normal depreciation less any amount paid by the employee. If a car is used partly for official purposes and partly for personal purposes and the expenses for the operation and maintenance are met or reimbursed by the employer, the value of the benefit depends on the engine capacity of the car (more than 1,600 cc—INR 2,400 per month; less than 1,600 cc—INR 1,800 per month). Where the expenses are fully paid by the employee, the benefit would be INR 900 per month or INR 600 per month, again depending on the engine capacity of the car.

The value of the benefit of education or training provided by employers for the children of employees is the amount of the expenditure incurred by the employer. If the educational institution is owned and maintained by the employer, the value is nil where the value of the benefit per child is below INR 1,000 per month or the reasonable cost of such education in a similar institution located nearby.[81]

With respect to free or reduced fares for travel provided to employees by an employer engaged in the carriage of passengers or goods, the value of the benefit is the amount at which the trip is offered to the general public less any amount paid by the employee. However, these provisions are not applicable to the employees of airlines or railways.[82]

For interest-free or concessional loans, the value of the taxable benefit is the excess of interest payable at the prescribed interest rate over any interest actually paid by employees or related persons.[83] However, loans up to INR 20,000 and loans for certain types of medical treatment[84] are exempt, provided that the expenses are not reimbursed under any medical insurance plan.[85]

Similarly, where free meals and nonalcoholic beverages are provided during working hours at business premises or through nontransferable vouchers, there is no benefit to the extent that the value does not exceed INR 50; free food provided in remote areas and offshore installations is also tax-free. Otherwise, the excess over INR 50 per meal is taxable.[86] This concession in respect of free food and nonalcoholic beverages is not available under the new regime introduced in 2020.

The taxable value of laptops and computers provided by employers is nil (perhaps in order to encourage the use of computers), while the taxable value for the use of other movable assets is 10% of the cost of the asset (if the asset is owned by the employer) or rent incurred by the employer (if the asset is leased) less any amount paid by the employee.[87] Where assets are sold to employees at discounted prices, the taxable

81. IT Rules, 1962, Rule 3(5).
82. IT Rules, 1962, Proviso to Rule 3(6). Attempts to tax these perks were vehemently resisted by the respective ministries.
83. The prescribed interest rate would be the rate charged by the State Bank of India on the first day of the relevant previous year in respect of loans of the same type and for the same purpose advanced by it to the general public; the benefit is calculated on the basis of the maximum outstanding monthly balance method.
84. As specified in IT Rules, 1962, Rule 3A.
85. IT Rules, 1962, Rule 3(7)(i) read with the Provisos.
86. IT Rules, 1962, Rule 3(7)(iii).
87. IT Rules, 1962, Rule 3(7)(vii).

benefit depends on the nature of the assets. Computers, laptops, and electronics items are valued at the actual cost less depreciation at 50% (using a declining-balance method) for each completed year of use by the employer less any amount paid by the employee; automobiles are valued at their actual cost less depreciation at 20% (using a declining-balance method) for each completed year of use by the employer less any amount paid by the employee; other movable assets are valued at the actual cost less depreciation at 10% (on a straight-line basis) for each completed year of usage by the employer less any amount paid by the employee.[88]

Expenses incurred by employers for the medical treatment of an employee or the employee's family (spouse, children, and dependent parents, brothers, and sisters) in any of the specified hospitals do not result in a taxable benefit to the employee.[89] Similarly, expenses for travel, accommodation, and attendants in connection with medical treatment do not result in taxable benefits, subject to monetary limits and conditions.[90]

Finally, since 2002, if employers choose to pay the tax relating to the fringe benefits of an employee, no amount is included in the employee's income[91] and the employer is not entitled to any deduction for that amount.[92]

2 IMPUTED INCOME FROM OWNER-OCCUPIED HOUSING

The in-kind return from the ownership of personal assets and self-provided services has long been recognized as an economic benefit, but only in the case of owner-occupied housing has there been a serious effort to include the benefit in the income tax base. The treatment of imputed income from owner-occupied housing is an important part of the overall treatment of housing for tax purposes. Failure to tax imputed income, when coupled, as it sometimes is, with a deduction for interest costs incurred in purchasing a personal residence and preferential treatment of gain on sale, may lead to a serious under-taxation of housing expenditures and a corresponding overinvestment in this sector as compared to rental housing. This has clearly been the case in the *United States*. Failure to tax imputed income from owner-occupied housing also creates equity problems in the relative treatment of renters and homeowners. However, real property taxes may to some extent operate as a surrogate for the taxation of imputed rental income. Thus, in *France*, for example, the taxation of owner-occupied housing was abandoned in 1966[93] but can be seen in the form of the occupancy tax (*taxe d'habitation*) for second homes and other furnished premises not used as a main

88. IT Rules, 1962, Rule 3(7)(viii).
89. A hospital maintained by the employer or by the government or local authority, any other hospital approved by government for the treatment of its employees, or any hospital approved by the Chief Commissioner (*see* ITA 1961, s. 17(2) Proviso).
90. India, ITA 1961, Proviso (vi) to s. 17(2)(viii).
91. India, ITA 1961, s. 10(10CC).
92. India, ITA 1961, s. 40(v).
93. Introduced in 1914, at the time of the creation of the income tax, it was originally intended to ensure equality between tenants, who were obliged to incur a substantial expense through the payment of rent in order to find accommodation, and owners, who saved the value of their rent.

residence applicable from January 1, 2023,[94] and the ownership tax (*taxe foncière*) on owners and occupants based on the estimated rental value. Until 2016, the imputed rental income of real estate owned by nonresidents was subject to tax in some situations, and France continues to tax the imputed rental income of lands located in France that are used for forestry activities.

In the systems considered here, the results with respect to the taxation of owner-occupied housing are varied. In *Canada*, *China*, and the U.S., although the matter has been discussed from time to time, no legislative proposals to tax income from owner-occupied housing have been seriously considered. In some other countries, the taxation of imputed housing income was attempted but then dropped because of difficulties in applying the tax on a realistic basis. For example, prior to 1987, *Germany* included in the category of rental income the income from owner-occupied housing. The rental value was based on either the assessed value of the real estate, which was seldom an accurate measure of the market value, or on comparable rentals, which also presented valuation problems. Since interest costs (as well as maintenance costs in the case of the comparable-rentals approach) were deductible, the result was often a loss which could be used against other income. After a transition period beginning in 1987, taxation of imputed income was eliminated. However, to a certain extent, tax rules for private pension contributions have reintroduced an imputed-income rule for owner-occupied housing.[95] Persons whose private pension contributions qualify for certain tax advantages can use these contributions to finance a house or condominium for their own living purposes; when they retire and occupy the home, there is deferred taxation of fictitious pension income associated with the housing.

For similar reasons, abolition of tax on imputed rent occurred earlier in *Australia* (1922) and later in *France* (1965),[96] with the aim of democratizing access to home ownership. In the *United Kingdom*, the tax was abandoned because of the perceived difficulty of obtaining accurate valuation of property for purposes of the tax at a time when rent controls meant there was no open market for real property.

In *India*, although, in principle, the annual value of a residential property is taxable, the value is deemed to be nil if the property is occupied by the owner throughout the year[97] or is unoccupied because it is too far away from the taxpayer's workplace.[98] In 2019, this generous treatment was extended to two residences. In addition, interest on borrowed funds used to acquire or construct a residential property is deductible within limits, although this deduction is not allowed under the optional new regime introduced in 2020.[99] The annual value—the amount for which the

94. From January 1, 2023, all taxpayers are no longer required to pay occupancy tax on their main residence. However, that tax continues to apply to second homes.
95. Germany, ITA, s. 92a, 92b.
96. Finance Law for 1965 n°64-1279 of December 23, 1964.
97. India, ITA 1961, s. 23(2)(a).
98. India, ITA 1961, s. 23(2)(b).
99. India, ITA 1961, s. 115BAC (2). Under the new regime, taxpayers are taxed at a lower rate but give up the right to claim certain deductions and concessions.

property could be rented—is included in income for more than two (more than one before 2019) residential properties.[100]

In *The Netherlands*, imputed housing income is, in principle, subject to tax. From a policy point of view, the taxation of imputed income from home ownership (main dwelling) is intended to help equalize the after-tax living costs of owners and renters but has also been an important stimulus to home ownership in a country where people historically have been renters rather than homeowners. This goal is accomplished by using a (modest) deemed semi-net rental amount from which any mortgage interest paid can be deducted, resulting for many taxpayers in a loss which offsets other income (within box 1: income from employment and business). The imputed income is based on a formula which is intended to reach results approximating the market rental value of similar occupied properties. The numbers used in the formula are reviewed periodically to take into account changes in market rents. For 2024, the required inclusion amounts to 0.35% of the standard tax value (WOZ) of the residence; a lower rate applies if the value is not more than EUR 75,000, and a higher rate if the value exceeds EUR 1,310,000.[101] Gain on the sale of the residence is not taxed, consistent with the general pattern of nontaxation of capital gains.

Imputed income from owner-occupied housing has historically been subject to income tax in *Sweden*. Originally, the fair market rental value was included as revenue in the tax base. The same rule was, and still is, applied to the use by the owner of property held in a business (e.g., personal use of an apartment in an apartment building). Valuation problems made the application of the system difficult in the case of owner-occupied private housing and was replaced with a system using standardized amounts. The imputed return was taken to be the interest rate on long-term government bonds, with no deductions for any expenses except interest. Thus, in effect, the return on the taxpayer's equity invested in the house was taxed.

During the tax reform of 1991, the basic principle of taxing imputed income was retained for equity reasons, but the structure of the tax was changed. A separate real estate tax was imposed at a rate of 1.5% (later decreased to 1%) of the assessed value of the property, which should, in principle, be equal to 75% of the market value. The rate was set with reference to the historical real yield on government securities. The combination of the tax rate and the calculation of the base was intended to tax the return at a rate equivalent to the rate for income from capital, after inflation adjustments are taken into account. A deduction is allowed for interest expenses where income from capital is computed at a tax rate of 30%. An important feature of the system is that the assessed values have been kept fairly accurately in line with market values, with assessments every third year. In areas with a rapid increase in market values, which was an almost unbroken trend from the mid-1990s until 2007, the effect was a considerable increase in tax payments. Many homeowners found they were unable to fund further tax increases, and, in response, some specialized reforms were carried out in order to mitigate these effects for persons with low incomes. The opposition (nonsocialist) parties promised to abolish the tax and, after forming the

100. India, ITA 1961, s. 23(4)(a) and 23(4)(b).
101. Netherlands, ITA, Art. 3.112.

government, they introduced a bold reform in 2007. The tax (renamed the municipal fee and paid to the local municipality) is now capped at SEK 8,847.[102] The rest of the system remains in place: a 0.75% fee on assessed value (with the cap) and unlimited interest deductions. Sweden appears to have moved from one extreme of taxing imputed income from owner-occupied housing to the other extreme: the Swedish taxation of owner-occupied housing has gone from being one of the highest to one of the lowest in Europe.

For cooperative apartment houses, a common legal arrangement in Sweden, the taxation model is the same as for owner-occupied houses. Overall taxation (fees) is lower for cooperative apartments than for owner-occupied houses, both before and after the reform.

Japan does not, in principle, tax the imputed value of privately held assets. However, there is a mechanism which effectively taxes some imputed income when a personal asset is sold. In general, a deduction for depreciation is not allowed with respect to personal assets. Nonetheless, taxpayers must adjust the basis of the personal asset as if depreciation had been taken. If the personal asset is later sold at a gain, the gain must be calculated from the adjusted basis.[103]

3 GIFTS

The proper taxation of gifts in a family context has been a matter of some discussion from a theoretical point of view in systems with a global approach to the definition of income. On the one hand, since the person who receives the gift (the donee) has the power to consume or save the proceeds, there is some logic to including the gift in income. On the other hand, since the donor has typically paid tax on the funds used to make the gift initially, taxing the donee represents a second tax on what is the same economic income. One response to this problem would be to give a deduction to the donor for the gift, but in systems with a progressive rate structure that approach would encourage income shifting to reduce taxes. The final possibility, which is the rule generally adopted, is not to tax the donee but also to give no deduction to the donor, thus ensuring that the initial income stream from which the gift is made is taxed only once (although, from one point of view, to the wrong person).

In schedular systems, the issue arises somewhat differently. In the case of private gifts, the issue of income inclusion generally does not arise, since typically the receipt does not fall within any taxable schedule. In some systems, the "other" category of income includes receipts from any source whatever if they arise on a periodic basis (e.g., a series of gifts over a period of time, reflecting an underlying notion of periodicity as an important characteristic of income). In all these situations, the existence of transfer taxes may also have an impact on the view of gifts from an income tax perspective.

---

102. Sweden, Municipal Real Estate Fee Act.
103. Japan, ITA, s. 38 para. 2.

A related problem involves gifts or bequests of appreciated or depreciated property. Some systems treat a gift or bequest as a realization event. Others postpone current taxation and preserve the potential taxation of the appreciation at the time of the gift by providing a carryover tax cost[104] in the property to the donee.

Some countries, in particular the U.S. and the UK, allow a fair-market-value tax cost in the hands of the transferee for transfers at death without treating the transfer as a realization event. These aspects are dealt with briefly here and discussed in more detail in the subsequent section dealing with realization in general.

Additional issues are raised by gifts in a business context, typically when the donor deducts the payment, and are considered following the discussion of nonbusiness gifts.

3.1 Gifts Outside a Business Setting ("Personal" Gifts)

The *United States* income tax system provides an example of the treatment of personal gifts in a global income setting. Gifts in a private context are not taxable to the donee and are not deductible by the donor.[105] In the case of appreciated property, a gift is not treated as a realization event and the donee's tax cost is the tax cost of the donor, thus preserving the possibility of tax on the appreciation in the hands of the donee.[106] A special rule prevents the shifting of loss in the case of depreciated property. Bequests are treated similarly with respect to deduction and inclusion, but the property receives a tax cost equal to fair market value in the hands of the transferee, thus allowing pre-death appreciation in the property to escape tax altogether.[107]

In *Germany*, gifts of privately held assets between private persons are neither taxable to the donee nor deductible by the donor. In the case of private investment assets (real estate, securities, etc.) the tax cost of appreciated assets carries over.[108] In *France*, the taxation of private donations and inheritances is complex. In principle, the donee or heir pays the gift or inheritance tax, depending on their relationship with the donor or deceased. This relationship determines the allowances and the applicable scale: the more distant the relationship, the higher the rate. The progressive rate scale ranges from 5% to 60%, depending on the tax base and the nature of the relationship between the beneficiary and the donor or deceased.[109]

As regards the deduction and inclusion of gifts, similar principles apply in the *United Kingdom*, *Canadian*, and *Australian* systems. Personal gifts are nontaxable, since they are not derived from a taxable "source" and similarly are not deductible by the donor. The Commonwealth systems differ, however, in their treatment of gifts and

104. The various systems use different terminology to express the notion of the taxpayer's capital investment in an asset for tax purposes. The United States term is "basis" or "tax basis." Other systems refer to "cost," "tax cost," "acquisition cost," "tax book cost," or some equivalent term. These materials will generally use the term "tax cost" to refer to this basic concept.
105. United States, IRC, s. 102.
106. United States, IRC, s. 1015.
107. United States, IRC, s. 1014.
108. Germany, Income Tax Regulation (ITR), s. 11d.
109. France, CGI, ss. 777 et seq.

bequests of appreciated property. In Canada, both *inter vivos* transfers and transfers at death of capital property are treated as realization events for the transferor, with the transferor being deemed to receive proceeds equal to the fair market value of the property and the transferee taking a fair-market-value tax cost;[110] however, an exception is made for interspousal gifts and bequests.[111] In Australia, *inter vivos* transfers are similarly realization events, while transfers at death result in a carryover of tax cost, thus postponing the possible taxation of pre-death appreciation until sale by the beneficiary, with the pre-death appreciation taxed at the beneficiary's rate.[112] The UK treats an *inter vivos* gift as a realization event for capital gains tax (CGT) purposes.[113] However, in the case of a transfer at death, as in the U.S., there is no realization and the transferee takes a fair-market-value tax cost. Unlike Australia and Canada, the UK still has an inheritance tax which applies to transfers on death and *inter vivos* transfers within seven years of death and transfers to trusts, but is subject to a threshold exemption, as well as several exemptions, including for transfers to spouses.

In *Japan*, both *inter vivos* gifts and transfers at death are neither taxable to the donee nor deductible by the donor, not because the gifts fall outside the definition of income, but because the donee is subject to gift tax on the value received and should not be taxed twice.[114] This rationale explains the different tax treatment of gifts made by corporations, where the Gift Tax (which is imposed as a backstop for the inheritance tax regime) is not applicable, as discussed below in section 3.2. Corporate gifts are taxable to donees as "occasional income" unless they are made in a business or employment context. This individual/corporate distinction also applies to the realization rule. A gift between individuals is not a realization event and the donor's tax cost is carried over to the donee; the same rule applies to the transfer of property at death,[115] unlike in the United States. On the contrary, when an individual makes a gift of appreciated property to a corporation, the donor is considered to realize a gain or loss.[116] When a corporation makes a gift to another person (either an individual or a corporation), it is also a realization event and triggers corporate tax liability to the donor corporation.[117]

Sweden reaches the same results with respect to deductions and income inclusions and generally provides a carryover of tax cost to the donee for use on the sale of the asset, which would otherwise be taxable.[118] The same is true for *The Netherlands*, except that where the gift concerns a substantial participation (5% or more) of the shares of a company (the only type of personal asset in respect of which capital gains are taxable), the gift is treated as a (deemed) disposal, giving rise to taxation of the

110. Canada, ITA, ss. 69(1), 73 and 70(5).
111. Canada, ITA, ss. 70(6) and 73.
112. Australia, ITAA 1997, ss. 112-20(1), 116-30(1), 128-10, 128-15.
113. United Kingdom, Taxation of Chargeable Gains Act 1992 (TCGA), s. 17.
114. Japan, ITA, s. 9 para. 1 No. 16. It is not necessary for the beneficiary to actually pay gift tax (or inheritance tax); there is a standard deduction to shield from taxation a certain amount of *inter vivos* gifts, as well as transfers at death.
115. Japan, ITA, s. 60.
116. Japan, ITA, s. 59, para. 1.
117. Japan, Corporate Tax Act (CTA), s. 22 para. 2.
118. Sweden, ITA, ss. 9 and 60.

donor and a step-up in cost basis for the donee unless particular statutory requirements are met, in which case the donor's basis is rolled over to the donee.[119]

The *Indian* treatment of gifts is quite different. In 1998, the gift tax was repealed. Since 2004, gifts in excess of INR 50,000 are generally included in the income of the donee and where gifts of property are made, the stamp duty value of the property must be included in income.[120] However, there are several important exemptions, including gifts received from relatives[121] and gifts on death and marriage.[122]

In *China*, there is a strong cultural tradition of gift-giving. The IIT is silent on *inter vivos* personal gifts. There is no tax on transfers at death. Difficulty in enforcing taxation of personal gifts may be one of the reasons for the current state of the law. For enterprises, the cost of making personal gifts is not deductible.

3.2 Gifts in a Business or Employment Context

Gifts in a business or employment context raise somewhat different issues. A donor who makes a gift for business reasons will typically deduct the amount of the gift as a cost of doing business so that where, as in the case of personal gifts, the gift is exempt in the hands of the donee, the entire amount would escape tax. The response to this problem is either to deny the deduction to the donor or require the gift to be taxable to the donee. Both approaches have been taken in the systems considered here.

In the *United States*, most gifts over a *de minimis* amount from an employer to an employee are taxable to the employee and deductible as a business expense by the employer.[123] Special rules apply to exclude from an employee's income tangible property awarded for length of service and other similar achievements (the "gold watch" exception). In the case of gifts in the business context to nonemployees, in principle, the donee may be able to exclude the gift as an expression of disinterested generosity by the donor (i.e., a true gift), but in that case the deduction by the donor is limited to USD 25, thus ensuring that most of the gift is not excluded from the tax base entirely.[124]

In the *Commonwealth* countries, business gifts are typically taxable to the recipient (or subject to the FBT in Australia in the case of employees) as arising from an employment or other business relationship. The gift can be excluded if the taxpayer shows that it arose out of personal regard, but the fact that the payer has deducted the payment may raise a presumption that it is taxable in some countries. In the *United Kingdom*, where the person providing the gift is the employer, it is deemed to arise by reason of employment and so is taxable; this presumption cannot be rebutted where the employer is a company, and otherwise only in limited circumstances. Certain trivial gifts (not exceeding GBP 50) and long-service awards (GBP 50 per year but only if total

119. Netherlands, ITA, Art. 4.17c.
120. India, ITA 1961, s. 56(2)(x).
121. India, ITA 1961, s. 56(2)(vii), Explanation (e).
122. The list of exclusions is found in the Proviso to s. 56(2)(x).
123. United States, IRC, s. 102(c).
124. United States, IRC, s. 274(b).

years exceed twenty) are exempt, as are certain gifts from third parties (GBP 250 a year). These statutory rules have no application in the business context, a vivid example of the schedular or Part system. In *Canada*, by administrative concession, certain gifts to employees (e.g., Christmas and wedding gifts), if limited to an annual *de minimis* amount (currently CAD 500), are not required to be included in income but are deductible by the employer. Similarly, in *India*, gifts to employees by an employer must be included in the employees' income if they exceed INR 5,000.

In *Germany*, business-related gifts are deductible by the donor up to a *de minimis* amount of EUR 50.[125] Such gifts are not taxable to the donee, but only if they are of a purely private nature. Where the purported "gift" is sufficiently related to a clearly identifiable category of income, the value of the asset must be included in the recipient's income. In these cases, for simplification purposes, the donor can pay a lump-sum tax on behalf of the donee (and it is debatable whether this additional tax burden must be included in the value of the gift).[126]

Gifts of business assets made for nonbusiness reasons (e.g., a business owner donating a used business car to a child) are subject to a complex set of rules emerging from general principles dealing with the withdrawal and contribution of business assets.[127] As a first step, the donation of an asset to a third party for nonbusiness reasons is treated as the withdrawal of the asset by the donor from the business. Therefore, the "fair value" of the asset must be included in the calculation of that year's profit so that all "hidden reserves" are taxed.[128] The tax treatment for the donee depends on what the gift is used for. If the gift is used for private purposes, there are no income tax consequences. If the donee uses the asset for business purposes (e.g., the child uses the car for the child's business), the asset must be included in the balance sheet as a "contribution" at fair market value at the time of transfer, but that amount is not included in income.[129]

The *Swedish* rules are similar, except that a transfer for business reasons results in realization and a corresponding fair-market-value acquisition cost for the transferee.

Gifts made by corporations or commercial law partnerships in *Japan* are, in principle, subject to income tax in the hands of the recipient. Depending on the causes and relationships involved, such gifts could be characterized as employment income or occasional income and may be deductible as business expenses, subject to a certain ceiling where the gifts are only partly related to business purposes.

In *The Netherlands*, gifts which occur in a business or employment context are treated as deductible by the payer and are generally taxable to the recipient, although exceptions are made for gifts received by employees on special occasions. In the case of appreciated property, the transfer is a realization event.[130]

125. Germany, ITA, s. 4 para. 5 No. 1.
126. Germany, ITA, s. 37b.
127. Germany, ITA, s. 4 para. 1 sent. 1.
128. Germany, ITA, s. 6 para. 1 No. 4 sent. 1.
129. Germany, ITA, s. 4 para. 1 s. 1, s. 6 para. 1 No. 5 s. 1.
130. Netherlands, CTA, Art. 16.

In *France*, business gifts offered to clients are considered to be expenses which are normally deductible in determining taxable income,[131] provided that they are part of the normal management of the company, are made in the company's interest, and are lawful. The value of gifts must not be excessive in relation to the size of the company, its sales, or professional practices. If the total amount of these gifts exceeds a EUR 3,000 threshold per year, the company must declare them in a detailed statement of overheads[132] under penalty of fine.[133] In principle, it is not possible to deduct VAT on business gifts, except for gifts of low value.[134] In addition, employers can offer gifts or vouchers to their employees. As far as social security exemptions are concerned, there is a discrepancy between the flexible position of the tax authorities, who accept a total exemption from contributions for gifts and low-value vouchers, subject to certain conditions, and the stricter position of the French Supreme Court, which refuses to accept these administrative exemptions.[135] With regard to tax exemptions, gifts in kind, gift vouchers, or vouchers for employees are not subject to tax declaration under certain conditions: low value of the gift, offered for a particular event, and with no direct link to the beneficiary's professional activity, seniority, or quality of services rendered. As with social security exemptions, to qualify for tax exemption, gifts received by an employee must not exceed 5% of the monthly social security ceiling (EUR 193 in 2024). However, for the 2024 Olympic Games and the 2023 Rugby World Cup, gifts by employers to employees benefited from an exemption scheme which raised the ceiling to 25% of the monthly social security ceiling per employee per calendar year (EUR 966 in 2024). The donation of a capital asset is a realization event for capital gains taxation purposes.

Although gift-giving is part of *Chinese* culture, the tax legislation makes no mention of gifts in either a business or an employment setting. Gifts to employees are taxable as wages and salaries and employers are legally liable for withholding the correct amount of tax. Gifts received by an individual (who is not an employee) from an enterprise where the enterprise sells goods or provides services to the individual are not taxable to the individual. However, gifts received by individuals from an enterprise as part of the enterprise's promotion or advertising campaigns are taxable as incidental income.[136] Enterprises which sell products as independent agents (such as car dealers) must include the value of any gifts (e.g., free trips) received from the manufacturer.

In *India*, business gifts are deductible if they are customary and satisfy the tests in section 37(1). However, in the case of pharmaceutical companies, the practice of giving free samples has been prohibited by the Indian Medical Council and, under the explanation to section 37(1), such samples are deemed not to be incurred for business

131. France, CGI, s. 39 5 e.
132. France, CGI, s. 54 quater.
133. France, CGI, s. 1763.
134. France, CGI, s. 257 II 1. 1° and Regulatory Schedule IV s. 23 N, which provides for VAT recovery if the price of the gift does not exceed the threshold of EUR 73, including VAT, per year and per beneficiary.
135. Cass. 2e civ., March 30, 2017, n°15-25.453 F-PB (*Urssaf Alsace*) and Cass. 2e civ., February 14, 2019, n°17-28.047 (*Urssaf d'Aquitaine*).
136. China, Caishui [2011] No. 50.

purposes. In addition, these samples may be taxable in the hands of the recipient medical practitioners.[137]

4 PRIZES AND AWARDS

As in the case of gifts, issues involving the treatment of prizes and awards arise somewhat differently in global and schedular systems. In a global system, the logic of the system clearly points toward taxation of the recipient unless extrafiscal considerations are thought to justify exclusion. In schedular systems, the question is whether the prize "fits" in a taxable category. In both systems, special rules sometimes apply to prizes or awards in the employment context.

In the *United States*, prizes and awards are in general fully taxable, regardless of the nature of the activity or accomplishment which is being recognized.[138] Thus, for example, the Nobel Prize is taxable, as are athletic awards. Special rules exempt certain prizes and awards in the form of tangible property for employee service or achievement and, since the amounts remain deductible by the employer, the entire amount escapes tax. Also, if a person who has been selected to receive an award based on personal achievement designates a charitable organization to receive the award, they are permitted to exclude the award from income even though the act of designating the recipient would otherwise cause them to be treated as constructively receiving it.[139]

In *Germany*, prizes and awards are taxable if they can be loosely related to one of the income categories.[140] In addition, they may be taxed as "other" income if they are awarded for a specific accomplishment. Awards to employees for suggestions, improvements, etc. are taxable. In contrast, prizes in recognition of a life's work (the Nobel Prize, Goethe Prize, etc.) are not taxable. Lottery prizes are exempt even if the lottery takes place in a business setting, as long as the chances of winning are low and all employees are entitled to participate, but prizes awarded to contestants in the context of a TV show can be taxable since they represent consideration for "occasional" services.[141]

Similarly, in *The Netherlands*, prizes and awards are taxable if they relate to the recipient's professional or business activities (e.g., a prize to a professional author, provided that the recipient could reasonably expect to receive it since there must be a "source" of income). However, a prize awarded to an artist for their entire oeuvre is not taxed. Prizes for "hobby" activities (e.g., awarded at an amateur dog show) are not taxable since there is no taxable source unless substantial effort is involved, resulting in a business or profession. Prizes won in a lottery are taxed at a rate of 30.5%.[142]

In *Japan*, prizes and awards received from corporations or commercial partnerships are taxed as occasional income if granted as part of corporate advertising and

137. India, Central Board of Direct Taxes (CBDT), Circular No. 5/2012.
138. United States, IRC, s. 74(a).
139. United States, IRC, s. 74(b).
140. Federal Tax Court (*Bundesfinanzhof*), April 23, 2009, VI R 39/08.
141. Federal Tax Court (*Bundesfinanzhof*), November 28, 2007, IX R 39/06.
142. Netherlands, Betting and Gaming Tax Act, Art. 5.

publicity campaigns. They might be taxed as employment income if awarded for work-related achievements. Certain listed prizes for scholarly and scientific achievements are exempt under explicit provisions.[143]

Under the *Swedish* schedular system, prizes and awards which cannot be characterized as "remuneration" for a "performance" are not taxable. Thus, lottery prizes where the winner is chosen by chance are not taxable, although they may be subject to a special lottery tax paid by the organizer.

Nevertheless, a court decision held that a prize for entering an advertising slogan in a contest was taxable. The court rejected the taxpayer's argument that there were so many entries that the jury could not have read all of them and that therefore the prize was in fact based on chance. It has also been held that it is not relevant that the amount of the prize might have no relation to the value of the performance. Prizes won on TV shows are taxable even if based on chance; the element of performance is supplied by the act of appearing on the program. In addition, lottery prizes won in a draw which is limited to employees are taxable as fringe benefits arising out of the employment relationship.

In Sweden (not surprisingly), the Nobel Prize has been held to be nontaxable, in part on the theory that the accomplishments on which the prize is based were not undertaken in order to obtain the prize (the case was decided before *The Double Helix* was written).

The *Australian* and *Canadian* rules reveal similar principles, with prizes arising in a field of endeavor regularly carried on by the taxpayer or paid on a periodic basis being taxable as income resulting from a taxable "source." The position in the *United Kingdom* is similar. A prize awarded to an author voluntarily (and not solicited by the author) was treated by the tax authorities as a windfall and therefore was not taxable. Some countries have an exemption for general public prizes such as the Nobel Prize, but the UK does not. In *Australia*, the High Court held that prizes, grants, bonuses, and sponsorships received by an Olympic-standard athlete were all taxable.[144] In Canada, although a publicly recognized prize awarded for meritorious achievement in the arts, sciences, or service to the public is exempt, sporting awards, including Olympic medals, are considered to be taxable.

In *France*, statutory law excludes the Nobel prize and a specific list of other equivalent international literary, scientific, and artistic prizes.[145] Other national or foreign prizes received by writers, artists, and scientists are not taken into account in determining taxable income if they are awarded by an independent jury for at least three years.[146] Until the 2010 Olympic Games, state grants paid to medal-winning athletes at the Olympic and Paralympic Games were exempt from income tax. However, since then, a system was introduced to spread the recognition of grants paid to medal-winning athletes. The amount of these grants and grants paid by the delegated sports federations to the management of these medal-winning athletes can

143. Japan, ITA, s. 9.
144. *Stone* [2005] HCA 21, 222 CLR 289.
145. France, CGI, s. 92 A.
146. France, BOI-BNC-BASE-20-20, para. 750.

be spread equally over the year of receipt and the following three years at the express and irrevocable request of their beneficiary.[147] In addition, since athletes are often in precarious professional situations, bonuses have been increased for the 2024 Olympic Games.

In *China*, prizes and awards are usually taxable under the IIT and are generally treated as fringe benefits to employees or service fees to independent contractors. Otherwise, prizes and awards fall into the category of "Incidental Income" and are taxable at 20%. However, prizes in science, education, technology, culture, health, sports, and environmental protection awarded by provincial governments, ministries or commissions of State Council or units of the People's Liberation Army, as well as foreign or international organizations, are exempt from tax.[148]

In *India*, any award in the public interest by the central government, any state government, or any other body approved by the central government is exempt from tax.[149] Moreover, any payment as a reward by the central or state government for certain approved purposes is also exempt. Other awards or prizes from any unapproved authority, such as game shows and entertainment programs, are taxable as income from other sources at the maximum marginal rate.[150]

5 SCHOLARSHIPS AND GRANTS

The tax treatment of scholarships is related both to the global or schedular structure of the tax system and to the overall system for the provision of educational services in the country. In countries which provide extensive no-fee or low-fee public education, scholarships involving tuition are generally not an issue and scholarship payments are usually in the form of support for living expenses. In a schedular system, one of the typical schedules of taxable income is periodic payments for living expenses; scholarships easily fit into this category. Similarly, in a global system which focuses on consumption as an important component of the tax base, payments for living expenses are clearly taxable.

In addition, where tuition is generally privately financed, the issue of scholarships covering tuition must be faced, with potentially different outcomes in global and schedular systems. Nonfiscal arguments about the importance of supporting education also play a role. Finally, even where, in principle, some scholarships are exempt, they may be taxable if they are sufficiently closely related to employment or some other taxable category of income. The systems considered here apply these principles in various ways.

In the *United States*, scholarships which cover tuition and related educational expenses are excluded from income.[151] Payments for other expenses, such as lodging or meals, do not qualify for the exclusion. The recipient must be a candidate for a

147. France, CGI, s. 163-0 A ter.
148. China, IIT Law, Art. 4.
149. India, ITA 1961, s. 10(17A).
150. India, ITA 1961, s. 56(2)(ib) read with s. 2(24)(ix).
151. United States, IRC, s. 117.

degree at a recognized educational institution and the exclusion is not available to the extent that the student is required to perform teaching, research, or other services as a condition of the grant. In that situation, the amount equal to the fair market value of the services performed is taxable and the remainder, if any, can be excluded as a scholarship. The reduction or remission of tuition fees for the children of employees of an educational institution is excluded from income as a qualified scholarship, as long as such reduction is available on a nondiscriminatory basis (i.e., not limited to professors).

In *Sweden*, despite the extensive low-cost public education system, a special statutory provision exempts scholarships. There were discussions during the 1991 tax reform on repealing the exemption, but it survived based on arguments about the necessity of supporting research. Payments in support of education which can be characterized as remuneration for services are taxable; for example, a "scholarship" paid by a publishing house to an author whose works were published by the publisher was held to be taxable. Grants for research, cultural activities, etc. are treated in the same way as scholarships.

In *Germany*, most scholarships are tax exempt by statute.[152] To qualify, payments must be made by government or charitable organizations and must not require any specific performance of services on the part of the recipient. The purpose of the payments must be to further research or education. The Federal Tax Court has extended this tax exemption to scholarships covering the cost of living, even for senior scholars.[153] Arguably, scholarships which do not meet these requirements and are not taxable as "employment income" (because the scholarship holder does not deliver any services to the grantor) do not fall under the existing categories of income. According to this position, the statutory exemptions are purely declaratory.

In contrast, in *The Netherlands*, while public "study grants" are exempt from tax, private scholarships and grants are taxable if they take the form of periodic payments (lump-sum payments are not taxed), which reflects the early role of periodicity in the definition of income.

In *Canada*, which also has extensive public education, scholarships, fellowships, and bursaries are excluded from income to the extent that they are received in connection with the recipient's enrolment in an elementary, secondary, or postsecondary school program.[154] Other scholarships, fellowships, bursaries, and prizes are included in income to the extent that they exceed CAD 500. Research grants must also be included in income, but only to the extent that the amount received exceeds the research expenses incurred.[155] Personal and living expenses other than research-related travel expenses may not be claimed as deductions against a research grant. In contrast, in *Australia*, while scholarships would normally be taxable as periodic payments covering living expenses, a specific statutory exclusion applies for full-time study at a school, college, or university unless receipt of the amount is conditional on

152. Germany, ITA, s. 3 Nos. 11, 44.
153. Federal Tax Court (*Bundesfinanzhof*), March 20, 2003, IV R 15/01.
154. Canada, ITA, s. 56(1)(n) and 56(3).
155. Canada, ITA, s. 56(1)(o).

providing services currently or in the future.[156] The *United Kingdom* similarly exempts scholarships, although amounts in support of study provided to children of employees by an employer are taxable to the employee under the fringe benefits legislation. The latter rule does not apply if the scholarships are provided under a trust scheme in which at least 75% of the relevant payments to beneficiaries are to those who are not relatives of employees.[157]

In *France*, state-provided educational assistance, which is awarded on the basis of social criteria, is not subject to tax but treated as social assistance. In addition, parents of middle school, high school, and university students receive a tax credit. Otherwise, scholarships and grants are taxable where there is some type of consideration on the part of the payee or some legal or contractual obligation on the part of the party funding such scholarships or grants.

In *Japan*, financial assistance for educational expenses is excluded from taxable income. Educational expenses must be directly related to educational activities and, therefore, financial assistance for meals is not excluded, but assistance for tuition is excluded from taxable income. In addition, the exclusion does not apply to financial assistance which can be considered to be consideration or compensation for services rendered. In this regard, employer-sponsored scholarships available to the children of employees are not generally excluded from the income of the employees.[158]

In *India*, scholarships (from foreign or Indian donors) granted to meet the costs of education are fully exempt from tax.[159] The term "education" and the costs of education have been interpreted very expansively by the tribunals; for example, the costs of education have been held to include not only tuition fees but all other incidental expenses incurred for education, a travel allowance given to a professional for attending seminars,[160] and a grant for research at a foreign university.[161]

In contrast, in *China* scholarships and grants are generally taxable as incidental income.

6 CANCELLATION OF INDEBTEDNESS

Where funds are borrowed, income is typically not realized under any of the systems dealt with here. The traditional explanation is that the increase in assets caused by a loan is offset by the corresponding liability to repay the loan so that, in balance-sheet terms, there is no increase in net worth at the time of the loan. Under this approach, all systems must deal with the situation where, contrary to expectations, a loan is not fully repaid. In principle, the failure to repay a loan in full results in taxable income to the borrower, because the loan proceeds were originally received on a tax-free basis on the expectation that they would be repaid in full. In many cases, however, where a debt is

156. Australia, ITAA 1997, s. 51-10, 51-35.
157. United Kingdom, exemption in ITTOIA, s. 377; further rules in ITEPA, ss. 211 et seq.
158. Japan, ITA, s. 9.
159. India, ITA 1961, s. 10(16).
160. *Dr J.C.N. Joshipura v. ACIT*, Mumbai, June 23, 1995.
161. *CIT v. VK Balchandran*, November 17, 1982, 147 ITR 4 (Mad).

forgiven in whole or in part, it is because the taxpayer is in financial difficulty, raising the practical issues of the desirability and feasibility of assessing and collecting tax under such circumstances.

The countries examined here have taken a wide variety of approaches to this problem. Most recognize in principle the taxability of forgiveness of indebtedness although, in the context of a schedular system, the debt must be related to a taxable category of income. However, all the systems make some concessions for financially troubled taxpayers. In some cases, no income is required to be recognized unless the taxpayer is made financially solvent after the forgiveness. However, some systems require the reduction of other tax attributes—for example, the tax cost of property or the availability of accrued operating losses—which, in effect, have been financed out of the loan proceeds.

The evolution of the rules in the *United States* shows some of the interplay among these principles. Income from cancellation of indebtedness is in principle included in income, although there are a number of exceptions.[162] In the private context, a cancellation may qualify for exclusion as a gift. Special rules allow taxpayers to exclude from income up to USD 750,000 of debt cancelled prior to January 1, 2026 if such debt was used to purchase or renovate their principal residences. In a business setting, specific statutory rules exclude cancellation of indebtedness from income where the taxpayer is in a bankruptcy proceeding or is insolvent both before and after the forgiveness; otherwise, cancellation in a business setting results in taxable income. Where exclusion is available, taxpayers are generally required to reduce certain tax attributes as a condition for the exclusion. First, net operating losses must be reduced, which means, in effect, the losses are treated as if funded by the forgiven loan. If those losses are not sufficient to absorb the forgiveness, the taxpayer must reduce the tax cost of other assets, thus increasing potential income in the future by reducing deductions or losses or increasing the amount of gain on the disposition of the assets.

Under an earlier statutory regime, all business taxpayers could elect to exclude cancellation income if tax attributes were correspondingly reduced. This rule was found to be too generous and was eliminated, thus limiting the exclusion to insolvency and bankruptcy situations.

In *Germany*, in principle, the tax treatment of cancellation of indebtedness depends on whether a debt was incurred in connection with a business. If the debt was incurred for private reasons or to finance the acquisition of privately held assets, no income results from its cancellation.[163]

Where debt was incurred in the context of a business, cancellation of the debt leads to a taxable increase in the net worth of the business, as with debt waivers by banks or suppliers who write off the value of the debt for tax purposes. Most of these measures are motivated by the intention of supporting the reorganization of a failing business. The search for an adequate treatment of cancellation of indebtedness can be described as a legislative zigzag course. In 1977, building on earlier jurisprudence, debt

162. United States, IRC, s. 108(a).

163. Federal Tax Court (*Bundesfinanzhof*), December 7, 2016, I R 76/14 (addressing the special case that the debt was cancelled several months after the discontinuation of the rental activities).

waivers in the context of the reorganization of a business in distress became exempt from tax under the ITA.[164] This beneficial provision was abolished in 1998, but mounting pressure by the business community convinced the Federal Ministry of Finance to establish similar rules under its administrative regulations in 2003. Against the background of this legislative history, the Grand Senate of the Federal Tax Court declared these regulations to be invalid given the clear intention of the legislature to abolish the earlier statutory tax exemption.[165] Moreover, it was unclear whether this beneficial treatment qualified as prohibited state aid under European Union (EU) law. In 2017, a new provision[166] was enacted which by and large reinstated the 1977 exemption and was cleared by the European Commission (EC).

A completely different set of rules applies where the forgiveness of debt is granted by an associated person due to a personal or corporate relationship with the debtor (e.g., a shareholder loan forgiven by the shareholder in order to secure the value of the underlying investment). Such forgiveness is regarded as a "contribution" of an asset for nonbusiness purposes and treated as tax-free to the debtor. However, the Federal Tax Court has decided that the tax-neutral effect of this contribution does not apply to the extent that the face value of the debt exceeds its market value, which might be substantially lower for companies in distress. The excess is fully taxed.[167]

In *Sweden*, cancellation of indebtedness is taxable if it takes place in a business context, unless the debtor is insolvent. Similarly, in *The Netherlands*, cancellation occurring in a business context is taxable unless it can be established that the debt could not have been repaid. Insolvency or bankruptcy is a factor in that determination but is not controlling. If the cancellation of a debt is not taxable, the amount of the forgiven debt must be used to offset any current losses or available loss carryforwards.[168]

In *Japan*, where the lender is a corporation, cancellation of indebtedness results in income to the debtor except in circumstances where the debtor is insolvent.[169] Where cancellation of indebtedness is taxable to the debtor, it is placed in one of the categories of income, such as employment income, business income, occasional income, etc., depending on the circumstances in which the debt is incurred and then cancelled. In contrast, where the lender is an individual (although this is relatively rare in Japan), it is a matter of gift tax, not of income tax (*see* the explanation in section 3.1 above); the gift tax liability applies in the same circumstances as the income tax.[170]

The treatment of forgiveness of indebtedness income in *Canada*, *Australia*, and the *United Kingdom* has been influenced by the capital gain/ordinary income distinction. Cancellation of debts arising in a business context, such as trade payables, has

164. Germany, ITA 1977, s. 3 No. 66.
165. Federal Tax Court (*Bundesfinanzhof*), November 28, 2016, GrS 1/15.
166. Germany, ITA, s. 3a.
167. Federal Tax Court (*Bundesfinanzhof*), June 9, 1997, GrS 1/94; May 31, 2005, I R 35/04; only the market value of the forgiven debt is regarded as a tax-neutral contribution, while the difference between the nominal value and the market value is ordinary taxable profit.
168. Netherlands, ITA, Art. 3.13(1)(a).
169. Japan, ITA, s. 44-2. This is a codification of long-established administrative practice.
170. Japan, Inheritance Tax Act, s. 8.

always been included as business income in Canada. When the taxation of capital gains was introduced, the possibility of treating the forgiveness of other types of liabilities as a taxable capital gain was considered but rejected. Instead, loss carryovers and the basis of certain property were required to be reduced to the extent possible by the amount of the forgiveness. If the amount forgiven exceeded the available tax attributes, there were no tax consequences with respect to the excess. Effective in 1994, the debt forgiveness rules were revised extensively.[171] The amount of the forgiveness is still applied to reduce loss carryovers and the tax cost of various assets; however, one-half of any remaining balance must be included in income unless it is transferred to a related taxpayer.

In *Australia*, there is no general legislative rule that cancellation of indebtedness results in income. If a company involved in a finance business buys back its long-term debt obligations at below face value, the corresponding profit is taxed as part of business income. However, if a commercial company completes the same transaction, no income results because the CGT, which would seem to be applicable to gains in this situation, deals explicitly with assets but not liabilities. Rules requiring the reduction of losses or tax cost similar to those in Canada were introduced in 1996.[172]

The *United Kingdom* continues to have very restrictive rules on cancellation of indebtedness income. In general, income arises only where the loan was employment-related, made to a shareholder of a closely held corporation, or involved a liability which had previously been deducted (e.g., in the business income context).[173]

In *France*, a distinction must be made between private and professional debt waivers. The cancellation of debt in a private context results in income unless the creditor can demonstrate that payment of the debt cannot be enforced. In a business context, a distinction must be made between two types of debt waiver, namely, commercial and financial debt waivers. A commercial debt waiver, granted to a partner to safeguard a business opportunity, is deductible.[174] In contrast, a financial waiver granted by a parent company to its subsidiary without any predominant commercial aspect, is in principle not deductible, except where the waiver is granted in the context of legal proceedings relating to companies in distress.[175] One of the major difficulties remains the characterization of the debt waived as commercial or financial; only waivers not motivated by a commercial purpose are considered to be financial waivers.

In *China*, although cancellation of indebtedness is not specifically mentioned in the IIT, it would likely be taxable as incidental income. For purposes of the EIT, forgiven debts are taxable as "monetary revenue derived by an enterprise."[176]

Before an *Indian* Supreme Court decision in 2018,[177] there were contradictory decisions about the treatment of the cancellation of debt (referred to in India as "waiver

171. Canada, ITA, s. 80.
172. Australia, ITAA 1997, Div. 245.
173. For example, for employment issues, *see* ITEPA, s. 188; for close companies, *see* CTA 2010, ss. 415 and 455 (CT); on released debt, *see* ITTOIA, s. 97 (income tax) and CTA 2009, s. 94 (CT).
174. Conseil d'Etat, November 27, 1981, n°16814.
175. France, CGI, s. 39 13.
176. China, EIT Regulations, Art. 12.
177. *Mahindra v. Com'r*, Civil Appeal, Nos. 6949-6950, 2004 (SC, April 24, 2018).

of loans"). However, the Supreme Court held that since the waiver of the debt in question resulted in a cash payment and the debt related to a capital asset rather than a trading liability, the statutory provisions requiring the inclusion in income of the cancellation of debt did not apply.[178] The Finance Act 2023 has reversed the Supreme Court's decision so that the value of any waiver of debt must be included in the debtor's business income.[179]

7 GAMBLING

The inclusion of gambling income is strongly influenced by the schedular or global nature of the tax system. In the global system in the *United States*, gambling winnings are, in principle, subject to tax whether they arise from occasional transactions or are received by a professional gambler. However, even in the case of professional gamblers, gambling losses for a year can be deducted only to the extent of gambling income.[180] This essentially schedular approach to gambling income may be influenced to some extent by the concern with artificial gambling "losses." In addition, the gambling losses may be viewed as consumption.

The restrictions in *Japan* are even stricter. Gambling income is taxable as occasional income and losses incurred in gambling are not deductible against other types of income. Moreover, because each gambling occasion is a separate event, gambling losses arising on one occasion cannot be deducted against gambling winnings derived on another occasion. These restrictions presumably reflect both the administrative difficulties of verifying losses and the possible characterization of the gambling losses as consumption.[181] A recent Supreme Court case held that gambling income could be viewed as Miscellaneous Income if it meets strict criteria relating to its systematic nature. Once categorized as Miscellaneous Income, gambling losses incurred during a fiscal year can be deducted from gambling gains for the same fiscal year.[182]

In many schedular systems, gambling income is taxable only if the gambler can be found to be in the business of gambling. For example, in *Germany*, case law holds that gambling income of a professional card player is taxable as business income.[183] Gambling winnings in TV shows are taxable "other" income to the extent that they are the result of a particular accomplishment.[184] Similarly, in *The Netherlands*, entrepreneurs who gamble with their business proceeds and incur gambling losses are not able to deduct such losses from their business income since no reasonable business person would engage in gambling with business money.

As discussed above, *Sweden* taxes gambling if the income can be considered to arise from the performance of a service, but not if it arises purely by chance. Winnings

178. India, ITA 1961, ss. 28(iv) and 41.
179. India, ITA 1961, s. 28(iv)(a) and (b).
180. United States, IRC, s. 165(d).
181. Japan, ITA, s. 34.
182. *Japan v. Katsumi Takayama*, 234 Keishu 69-2 (S. Ct., March 10, 2015).
183. Federal Tax Court (*Bundesfinanzhof*), March 22, 2023, X R 3/21.
184. Federal Tax Court (*Bundesfinanzhof*), November 28, 2007, IX R 39/06.

in the Swedish lottery and lotteries within the EU are expressly exempt; instead, there is a special Lottery Tax.[185]

In *Australia*, *Canada*, and the *United Kingdom*, income derived from gambling or lottery-type prizes is not taxable unless the activity amounts to a business. Otherwise, there is no taxable "source" and, accordingly, gains are not taxable and losses are not deductible. *France* reaches the same results as far as its progressive income tax is concerned,[186] but case law has recognized that such amounts are taxable where the player succeeds in mastering the risks of the game (e.g., as noncommercial profits, for professional gamblers).[187] In *China* and *India*, any income from gambling is taxable (in India, at the maximum marginal rate; gambling losses are not deductible even against gambling income).[188]

8 ILLEGAL INCOME

In all the systems considered here, in general, the fact that income is derived from illegal activities does not prevent its taxation (*pecunia non olet*). The common principle is that taxpayers cannot use the illegal nature of their activities as a defense against taxation.[189] This is the situation in *India*, where the courts have expressed concern that if illegal income is not taxed it might encourage illegal activities.[190] In a schedular system, the income must, of course, fall into a taxable category. Thus, for example, in *Germany*, illegal income often falls into the category of income from trade or business, or even miscellaneous income from the occasional performance of services (e.g., espionage).

Since illegal income typically involves a civil law obligation to repay the amounts taken, taxpayers have no legally recognized right to keep the income, and in some situations this has influenced the income-inclusion issue. For example, an *Australian* case held that earnings on embezzled funds were not taxable to an embezzler who was caught and had to return the funds with interest.[191] Some early *United States* cases reached a similar result on the ground that the taxpayer (an embezzler) had no "claim of right" to the income, although the result was later reversed.[192] A *Canadian* case held proceeds of embezzlement to be taxable and rejected the claim of right argument on the ground that the taxpayer had no intention of repaying the funds.[193] In *Japan*, illegal income is taxable as long as the funds are kept by the offender; once such proceeds are repaid in the due course of civil law, the income recognition is cancelled. Sometimes a line must be drawn between embezzlement and an informal loan (typically with an

185. Lag (1928:376) om skatt på lotterivinster.
186. Conseil d'Etat, March 21, 1980, n°11235.
187. Conseil d'Etat, June 21, 2018, n°412124, A.
188. India, ITA 1961, s. 115BB.
189. Germany, General Fiscal Code (*Abgabenordnung*), s. 40.
190. *CIT v. K. Thangamani* (T.C. (A) Nos. 391 & 392 of 2004, Madras, December 5, 2018).
191. *Zobory* [1995] FCA 1226, 64 FCR 86.
192. *James v. United States*, 366 U.S. 213 (1961).
193. *The Queen v. Poynton*, [1972] CTC 411 (Ont. CA).

intention to repay). The latter characterization requires the real or assumed acquiescence of the "lender." A related issue involves the deduction for the repayment of illegally obtained funds which are included in income.

In *Sweden*, there is in principle full taxation of illegal income which arises in a business. However, in most cases, illegal income is repayable and as such, deductible, so there is no net income. Illegal income which does not arise in a business is not taxable. It has also been established that illegal activity alone cannot constitute a business.

In *France*, according to the principle known as "tax law realism," income from illegal activities is taxed as lawful income in the appropriate income category. For example, income from activities such as prostitution[194] or procurer[195] is treated as noncommercial profit[196] unless it can be allocated to another category of profit or income. Similarly, in *The Netherlands*, income from illegal activities has always been recognized as taxable. Examples from case law include income from theft, trade in narcotics, bank fraud, and bribery. In the *United Kingdom*, case law holds that the profits of prostitution are taxable as business income—but whether as a trade or as a profession has not been decided.[197] Prostitution is not an illegal activity in the UK, whereas living off such earnings of another person is. In *China*, tax laws are silent on illegal income. Individuals who earn income through illegal means, such as accepting bribes or embezzlement, once caught, face severe criminal penalties, including the death penalty. Since the IIT relies on source withholding, it is difficult to imagine that anyone would withhold tax and reveal the illegal activity.

The treatment of expenses such as bribes and fines, which often arise in connection with illegal income, is discussed below in Subpart C.

9 WINDFALLS

The logic of a global system extends to the taxation of windfall gains such as found property, and this approach is followed in the *United States*. However, windfall gains may also be taxable in countries with schedular systems where the windfall is within one of the taxable categories. For example, *Japan* treats windfalls as taxable occasional income; in *China*, they are taxable as incidental income. In *Germany*, the treatment of windfalls depends on the situation. Normally, found property is not taxable, nor, for example, is the sale of a patent developed by a research student without the intention to earn income. However, where a windfall arises in a business setting (such as money found by businesspersons on their premises) it is included as part of business profits and therefore is taxable. Likewise, in *The Netherlands*, in general, windfalls are not taxable unless they fall within a taxable category (typically, business income). Compensation for personal injury damages is not taxable if the injury has permanently reduced the victim's capacity to earn but are taxable if the payment compensates for a

194. Conseil d'Etat, May 4, 1979, n°09337.
195. Conseil d'Etat, November 5, 1980, n°13222.
196. France, CGI, s. 92 1.
197. *IRC v. Aken* [1990] STC 497.

temporary loss of income. The same applies to awards for immaterial injury. In *Sweden*, windfalls have historically not been taxable, since they are not the result of efforts to earn income and are not periodic in nature. In the *Commonwealth* countries, because a windfall is not derived from a taxable "source" of income, it is not included in the income tax base.[198] The subsequent extension of taxation to capital gains typically did not affect this result.

Damages represent a special category of windfall gains. In general, in schedular systems, damages are taxable to the extent that they relate to assets or activities which are taxable. Awards for damage to property are typically treated as reducing the tax cost of the asset, with gain resulting if the total amount recovered exceeds the cost. In some cases, a gain can be deferred through the use of a reserve or rollover if the property is to be repaired or replaced. Damages for personal injuries are typically not taxable even if they are calculated with reference to lost earnings or earning capacity. In the *Commonwealth* systems, the introduction of a CGT expanded the taxation of damage awards, which previously had sometimes escaped tax, although the exclusion for damages to person or profession (e.g., defamation) was typically retained. In *India*, compensation received as a result of an automobile accident or a sexual harassment claim has been held not to be taxable.[199] Compensation from a government or local authority by an individual for disaster relief is exempt.[200] However, lottery income is fully taxable at the maximum marginal rate.

In *France*, exceptional income is defined as income which is unlikely to be collected annually and exceeds the average net income according to which the taxpayer was subject to income tax for the last three years (e.g., distribution of reserves by a company, fees received by an owner for granting a lease, and severance payments).[201] To mitigate the progressivity of income tax with respect to such income, taxpayers have the option of excluding the exceptional income from total income. In terms of income tax, personal injury damages are normally excluded from the tax base to the extent that they do not offset a loss of income.[202] In contrast, compensation for non-material loss awarded by a court is taxable as salary and wages to the extent that it exceeds EUR 1 million[203] and only a portion of certain life annuities acquired for consideration is taxable as income.[204]

Germany taxes damages which represent compensation for the lost opportunity to earn income.[205] Damages occurring in the personal sphere are not taxable income. The Federal Tax Court (*Bundesfinanzhof*) held that compensation for loss of maintenance paid by an insurance company to a widow resulting from malpractice which caused the death of her husband was not taxable.[206]

198. *Graham v. Green* [1925] 2 KB 37.
199. *Tamil Nadu State Transport Corporation v. Chinnaduari*, 2016 (CRP (PD)) No. 1343 of 2012 and *M.P. No. 1 of 2012 and Susmita Sen v. ACIT* (ITA No. 4351/Mum/2015), November 14, 2018.
200. India, ITA, 1961, s. 10(10BC).
201. France, CGI, s. 163-0 A.
202. France, CGI, s. 81 8 and 9 bis.
203. France, CGI, s. 80 4.
204. France, CGI, s. 158 6.
205. Germany, ITA, s. 24 No. 1 lit.a.
206. Federal Tax Court (*Bundesfinanzhof*), November 26, 2008, X R 31/07.

Personal injury damages are excluded from income in the *United States* only where the injury is physical in nature. Emotional distress does not qualify as a physical injury for this purpose.

10 SUBSIDIES

The treatment of government subsidies raises a number of structural issues. In the simplest case, where the payment is a form of payment for services (e.g., payments to private carriers for mail transport), it is typically taxable as business income. At the other extreme, some subsidies are so indirect or diffuse that, even with a global definition of income, they would not be included in the tax base. In still other cases, payments are not includable directly in income, but the tax cost of assets acquired or other tax attributes must be reduced accordingly so that the payments are indirectly included over the life of the asset. Public welfare payments are typically not taxed unless they are in the form of wage supplements such as unemployment compensation. In the *United States*, in general, the rules follow this pattern; government welfare payments are excluded,[207] but in general, government subsidies received in lieu of wages and subsidies to aid businesses are taxable.[208]

Similarly, in *Germany*, for business-related subsidies, capital contributions may, at the taxpayer's election, be treated either as current income or a reduction in the tax cost of assets produced or acquired with the funds.[209] In the latter case, income will result from the reduction of the depreciation base or a larger gain on disposal of the asset. If subsidies are not used to finance an asset, they are fully taxable. However, if they relate to conduct to be performed over a period of years (e.g., dairy operations not producing milk for five years), the payments may in effect be included over the period of the conduct as an accounting matter. Public welfare subsidies for individual taxpayers are not taxable but in some cases must be taken into account in determining the applicable tax rate on other income ("exemption with progression").[210]

In the same way, in *Sweden*, government subsidies are currently taxable where they are intended to subsidize current costs in a business. If they are in the nature of capital contributions, the cost basis of the appropriate assets is correspondingly reduced.[211] It is not clear whether these rules would apply to subsidies provided by private organizations such as research foundations. Such subsidies probably would not be taxable; instead, the tax authorities might attempt to deny the deduction of expenses financed by the tax exempt subsidies, which would produce the same result as if the subsidy had been included in income and the deduction of the expenses allowed.

In *The Netherlands*, subsidies granted in respect of the acquisition of assets are not currently taxable but result in a cost-basis reduction. Subsidies received in respect

207. *See*, e.g., Congressional Research Service, "The IRS's General Welfare Exclusion," (February 9, 2023), https://sgp.fas.org/crs/misc/IF12326.pdf.
208. During the Covid-19 pandemic, certain government subsidies to aid businesses were excluded from income.
209. Germany, Income Tax Regulations (*Einkommensteuer-Richtlinien*), R 6.5 para. 2.
210. Germany, ITA s. 32b para. 1 No. 1.
211. Sweden, ITA, Ch. 29.

of current expenses reduce the amount of any deduction for such expenses. The same approach applies in *Japan*, although corporations may elect for subsidies to be added to their current income.[212]

Under case law principles, in the *United Kingdom*, subsidies for current operations are included in income but payments to recoup a capital investment are exempt as nontaxable capital receipts;[213] the distinction between the two is not easy to draw. Subsidies are taken into account in calculating the tax cost of property under the capital gains or capital allowance legislation.[214] *Australia* follows the same pattern, although the interpretation of a long-existing statutory provision, the introduction of the CGT, and case law on general principles of income may have narrowed the scope of the exclusion for capital receipts.[215] There is an increasing tendency for the tax legislation to deal expressly with the tax status of newly introduced subsidies. In *India*, subsidies related to business activities of a revenue nature are included in income, while subsidies directly related to the cost of capital assets reduce the cost.[216] A 2015 amendment provides that income includes any government subsidy, grant, cash incentive, duty drawback, waiver, concession, or reimbursement (by whatever name called) in cash or in kind other than a subsidy which reduces the cost of an asset in accordance with the provisions of Explanation 10 to clause (1) of section 43 of the ITA.[217] In *Canada*, government subsidies (inducements or assistance in any form, including government subsidies and tax benefits) received in the course of earning income from business or property are expressly included in income to the extent that they have not otherwise reduced the cost of property or the amount of any deductible expenses incurred by the taxpayer and are received in the course of earning income from business or property.[218] Where a subsidy relates to depreciable, nondepreciable, or intangible property, taxpayers have an election to include the amount currently in income or reduce the tax cost of the property.

In *France*, balancing or operating subsidies received by a company from public or other sources constitute taxable income; however, special regimes allow the income to be spread over ten years (nondepreciable assets) or to be taken into account at the same time and rate as depreciation in respect of depreciable assets (applicable to capital grants awarded by the EU, the French State, or local authorities).[219] In *China*, government subsidies paid to individuals are exempt but may be treated as other income for enterprises.[220]

212. Japan, CTA, s. 42.
213. *Seaham Harbour Dock Co.* [1930] 16 TC.
214. For example, *see* United Kingdom, TCGA, s. 50 and Capital Allowances Act (CAA) 2001, ss. 209 et seq.
215. Australia, ITAA 1997, s. 15-10, as interpreted in *First Provincial Building Society Ltd* [1995] FCA 1101, 56 FCR 320; and *GP International Pipecoaters Pty Ltd* [1990] HCA 25, 170 CLR 124.
216. *CIT v. Chaphalkar Brothers*, Pune (Civil Appeal No. 6513-6514 of 2012), December 7, 2017. ITA 1961, Explanation 10 to s. 43(1).
217. India, ITA 1961, s. 2(24)(xviii) (welfare subsidies received by individuals are not included in income).
218. Canada, ITA, s. 12(1)(x).
219. France, CGI, s. 42 septies.
220. China, EIT Regulations, Art. 22.

11 PENSIONS

Pension benefits can be classified into three broad categories for analytical purposes: government-provided, employer-provided, and privately funded pensions. Government-provided plans can be financed from general revenues or special taxes imposed on employees and/or employers. In most countries, government pension arrangements are modest and inadequate to provide a reasonable standard of living during the extended periods of retirement that many people enjoy today. Thus, most people want to supplement their government pensions with other pension benefits and private savings. Many countries provide tax incentives for employers to establish pension plans for their employees, which are funded through contributions by both employers and employees. For individuals who are self-employed, several countries provide tax incentives to encourage them to save for retirement.

The tax treatment of pension benefits involves three major factors:

(1) whether contributions to pension plans are deductible;
(2) whether the investment income earned on contributions to the plan is subject to tax when earned; and
(3) whether withdrawals/distributions from the plan are taxable.

These three factors can be combined in various ways to provide different patterns for taxing pension plans which provide more or less generous support for retirement savings. At one extreme, the most generous tax incentives for retirement saving exist where no tax is imposed on contributions to the plan, earnings of the plan, and withdrawals from the plan. At the other extreme, no tax incentive for retirement saving is available where no deduction for contributions is allowed and the earnings of the plan are subject to tax (in this case, taxing withdrawals from the plan would result in inappropriate double taxation). One common pattern under which the primary benefit is deferral of tax is where contributions to a plan are deductible and earnings accumulated in the plan are exempt from tax, but withdrawals are taxable.

The various patterns for taxing pension plans are often described in short form by tax theorists using the letters "E" and "T" to refer to each of the three factors noted above. Thus, a pattern which involves a deduction for contributions to a pension plan, an exemption for income earned by the plan, and the inclusion in income of withdrawals from the plan would be described as exempt/exempt/taxable (EET). A lowercase "t" is used to designate a preferential rate of tax.

Where pension benefits are derived by employees from their employers, an additional consideration is whether employers' contributions to pension plans for employees are deductible by employers and taxed as fringe benefits to employees.

Numerous private and public pension plans exist in the *United States*. The U.S. has a mandatory pension plan known as Social Security,[221] which covers employees of

221. Social Security is often characterized as a form of social insurance because it provides not only retirement benefits but also disability and survivor benefits.

private employers[222] and self-employed individuals. In addition, it has adopted tax incentives to encourage employers and employees to participate in a wide variety of different types of private pension plans.[223]

The Social Security system, which is operated by the federal government, is funded by a tax of 12.4% on wages earned by employees or on trade or business income earned by self-employed individuals. In 2024, this tax applied to the first USD 168,600 earned by the individual. Employers and employees share the tax burden equally. The employer contributes an amount equal to 6.2% of the employee's salary, up to a maximum salary amount of USD 168,600. Similarly, the employee contributes 6.2% of the employee's salary up to the same maximum salary. The contribution by the employer is not included in the employee's income and the employee's contribution is not deductible.

Self-employed individuals pay the entire 12.4% Social Security tax on their income up to USD 168,600. They are allowed to deduct one-half of the tax so that, in effect, they obtain the same tax benefit as employees who are not taxable on the employer's contribution.

The Social Security benefits received on retirement depend on the amount of time worked, income earned, and age of retirement. The average Social Security retirement benefit was USD 1,866.44 per month in April 2024.[224] Single taxpayers in 2024 with income below USD 25,000 did not include their Social Security benefits in their taxable income; higher-income taxpayers include up to 85% of their benefits in taxable income.

In addition to Social Security, many employers sponsor pension plans—qualified defined contribution plans or qualified defined benefit plans—for their employees.[225] The tax treatment of both types of plan follows the EET pattern referred to above. Defined contribution plans, which are the most common type of plan in the U.S. today,[226] permit employers to make contributions to a trust for the benefit of employees. The contributions are not included in the income of the employee[227] but are

222. Certain state and municipal employees are excluded from Social Security and are covered by retirement plans established by the state and local governments.
223. Importantly, however, apart from Social Security, the retirement system in the United States is entirely voluntary. Employers are not required to provide other additional forms of retirement benefits to their employees.
224. Social Security Administration, Research, Statistics & Policy Analysis: Statistics Archive Monthly Statistical Snapshot Table 2 (April 2024) https://www.ssa.gov/policy/docs/quickfacts/stat_snapshot/.
225. However, despite the prevalence of employer-sponsored plans (beyond Social Security), only 73% of the U.S. civilian workforce had access to an employer-sponsored plan in 2023 (U.S. Bureau of Labor Statistics, The Economics Daily (September 29, 2023) https://www.bls.gov/opub/ted/2023/73-percent-of-civilian-workers-had-access-to-retirement-benefits-in-2023.htm.) Given the limited scope of retirement benefits under Social Security, this lack of access to employer-sponsored plans means that many Americans face retirement with inadequate savings.
226. Most private employers offer defined contribution plans. Only 15% of U.S. workers have access to defined benefit plans. U.S. Bureau of Labor Statistics, "Beyond the Numbers" (January 2022) https://www.bls.gov/opub/btn/volume-12/how-do-retirement-plans-for-private-industry-an

nevertheless deductible by the employer in the year they are made.[228] Some types of defined contribution plans also permit the employee to contribute portions of their salary to a pension trust which are excluded from taxable income.[229] The pension trust invests[230] the employer and employee contributions on behalf of employees; income earned from these investments is not subject to tax.[231] Strict rules govern the type of investments that pension trusts may make and prevent employers from discriminating in favor of highly paid employees. The amount of pension benefits received by employees at retirement is based on the amount of contributions and the investment income earned on the contributions. In the event of economic downturns, such benefits will be reduced as employees bear the burden of market performance. The retirement benefits paid to employees are included in their taxable income. Defined benefit plans, under which pension benefits are typically based on a percentage of an employee's wages and are not dependent on the investment performance of contributions made to the pension trust, are treated the same as defined contribution plans for tax purposes.

Congress has adopted several other types of tax-favored pension plans that individuals may use to save for retirement. In general, these plans fall into two broad categories. "Roth" plans permit taxpayers to make contributions to a pension trust from after-tax income. The benefit of these after-tax contributions is that they are never again subject to tax since neither the investment income earned nor the retirement benefits paid from contributions and investment income are subject to tax. Thus, Roth plans reflect a TEE pattern of taxation.

The other broad category of plans, non-Roth plans, which include Individual Retirement Accounts and Simplified Employee Plans, follows the EET pattern. In contrast to Roth plans (where contributions are made from taxable income and payouts to retirees are tax-free), contributions to non-Roth individual plans are effectively made before tax. The investment income earned by a non-Roth plan on the contributions is tax-free, but payouts to retirees are taxable. Non-Roth plans are designed to encourage savings and place various limitations on the amount of deductible contributions to a pension trust that individuals may make; whether these limitations apply depend on such factors as the individual's income level and whether the individual is participating in an employer pension plan.

In the *United Kingdom*, the primary pension legislation applies to both employer-provided schemes and personal pension arrangements.[232] There is also a state pension system paying up to GBP 204 per week (for 2023-2024) when an individual reaches the

---

d-state-and-local-government-workers-compare.htm. In contrast, state and local governments frequently offer defined benefit plans, although even here defined contribution plans are becoming more prevalent.

227. United States, IRC, s. 402(a).
228. United States, IRC, ss. 162(a), 404(a)(1), 404(a)(3).
229. *See*, e.g., United States, IRC, s. 401(k).
230. Employers often require that employees "self-direct" their contributions, pursuant to the Employment Retirement Income Security Act, s. 404(c) safe harbor.
231. United States, IRC, s. 501(a).
232. United Kingdom, Finance Act 2004, Part 4, which took effect on April 6, 2006 (known as "A-day").

state pension age (currently 65). The state pension is not means-tested and is funded from NICs, although the fund ultimately is backed up by general revenues.[233] NICs are paid by employees, employers, and the self-employed generally as a percentage of earnings above a threshold amount. Entitlement to a state pension requires a contribution record of at least ten years, and thirty-five years to receive the full amount. A contribution record can also be established by way of voluntary NIC payments. Importantly for the self-employed, there is no equivalent charge to the NICs paid by employers. At one time, lower NICs for the self-employed compared to the combination of employee and employer NICs could be justified by lower benefit entitlement, but currently the difference in contributory benefits between employees and the self-employed is insignificant.

The pension legislation permits various types of employer-provided and private pension schemes, including terminal salary (defined benefit) plans and money purchase (defined contribution) plans. From 2018, all employers in the UK must put their qualifying employees into a pension scheme and pay contributions; employees must also contribute. This is called "automatic enrolment," but employees can choose to opt out if they wish. Employer-provided pensions require that a fund be established under a trust, overseen by an administrator who is responsible for dealing with the tax authorities. Employee contributions are deductible from income (subject to limits) and are free of NICs. Employer contributions are deductible in computing taxable profit and are not treated as taxable income/benefits for employees. The tax reliefs for pension contributions to money purchase plans and for benefits accrued under defined benefit plans have been restricted in recent years. These formerly had a maximum value, called the lifetime allowance, but this was abolished in 2023; a maximum annual allowance of GBP 60,000 still applies, which is reduced by GBP 1 for each GBP 2 of income above GBP 260,000, to a minimum of GBP 10,000 (for 2023-2024). Income and capital gains from the funds held by pension plans are normally exempt from tax. Since 2014, individuals have a great deal of flexibility over how and when they withdraw their pension funds. From age 55, individuals can withdraw their pension, in whole or in part, as cash if they wish. Tax is levied at usual income tax rates on withdrawals above a 25% tax-free amount. This system can be described as EEt, the lowercase "t" reflecting the 25% tax-free amount.

The UK provides another tax-preferred general savings vehicle—the Individual Savings Account (ISA). An ISA is an investment account which may be used by a qualifying UK resident individual aged 16 or over. ISAs are not limited to savings for retirement benefits but are intended to promote savings for all purposes. ISAs are divided into two types: (1) stocks and shares ISAs (for individuals aged 18 and over) and (2) cash ISAs. The overall maximum ISA contribution level per tax year is GBP 20,000 (for 2023-2024); savers can invest this entire amount in cash ISAs, stocks and shares ISAs, or a combination of the two. From 2011, Junior ISAs are available for children aged under 18, with a maximum subscription limit of GBP 9,000 (for 2023-2024); they replaced an earlier investment product called Child Trust Funds.

233. United Kingdom, Social Security Contributions and Benefits Act 1992.

Junior ISAs remain tax-free until the child turns 18, at which point they are converted into normal ISAs. ISAs allow individuals to use tax-paid savings to invest free of income tax and CGT—and so follow the TEE tax pattern.

From April 2017, a Lifetime ISA allows individuals aged 18-40 to save up to GBP 4,000 per annum, plus receive a government bonus of 25% of the amount saved. The Lifetime ISA can be used to buy a first home or withdrawn after the age of 60; earlier withdrawals can be made, but with a penalty. Amounts saved in Lifetime ISAs count toward the GBP 20,000 annual ISA limit. Further, from April 6, 2016, basic-rate taxpayers do not pay tax on the first GBP 1,000 of non-ISA savings income, such as interest earned on bank current accounts. Higher-rate taxpayers can earn up to GBP 500 of non-ISA savings income tax free but additional-rate taxpayers have no tax-free allowance.

As with other countries, in *Japan*, there are three types of pensions: public pensions, employer-provided pension plans, and private pension plans. The public pension regime, administered by the central government, comprises two layers of pension benefits.. First, the national pension system ("basic pension") provides compulsory and universal coverage; second, the "employees' pension insurance system" is also compulsory, but coverage is limited to employees. All individuals who are resident in Japan and between the ages of 20 and 60 are automatically enrolled in the basic system unless they are already enrolled in the employees' pension system. Therefore (with some exemptions), self-employed individuals, certain (below-threshold) part-time employees, students, and jobless individuals are all enrolled in the basic system. They pay lump-sum contributions (JPY 16,980 per month for 2024); assuming that they make monthly contributions for the entire period of pension eligibility (40 years), they are entitled to the basic pension benefit of JPY 816,000 per year (for 2024) beginning at age 65. Individuals can elect an accelerated benefit as early as age 60, but in such cases, the pension amount is reduced; conversely, they can elect to postpone the benefit up to age 75, with an increased amount.

In addition to contributing to the basic pension system, employees must make contributions to the employees' pension system, to which employers must also make matching contributions. Although employees do not contribute directly to the basic system, the employees' pension system transfers funds to the basic system, thereby effectively achieving universal coverage. Contributions to the employees' pension system are based on a percentage (18.3%) of wages, with a wage cap (i.e., JPY 650,000 per month). This system is equivalent to an income tax on labor—indeed, public pension contributions are the most significant direct tax burden (even surpassing the burden of the income tax) for the majority of Japanese households. Pension benefits from the employees' pension system depend on the amount and the duration of contribution payments and can reach 50%-60% of an individual's final average wage.

For income tax purposes, the public pension regime follows an EEt pattern (the lower case "t" denotes "preferentially taxed"). Contributions by both employees and employers are deductible.[234] Employers' matching contributions are by their nature[235]

234. Japan, ITA s. 74.

excluded from employees' income. Public pension benefits are preferentially taxed because income from the public pension is calculated by applying the generous "public pension deduction" against gross pension receipts. The amount of this deduction is determined by a formula based on gross receipts. For instance, a retiree at age 65 receiving JPY 3.5 million annually of public pension benefits includes only JPY 2.35 million in taxable income; interestingly, pension beneficiaries below age 65 are less favorably treated, by applying a smaller deduction.[236]

"Employee pension plans" are private pension plans which meet the requirements under special legislation to provide workers with pension benefits in addition to the public pension. In accordance with this legislative goal, employee pension plans enjoy tax treatment that is almost as favorable as that of public pensions. Premiums are currently deductible by employers and are not included in employees' income.[237] Employee contributions are also deductible.[238] The investment income generated from contributions is subject to proxy taxation in the hands of the fund-managing corporation (such as insurance companies and trust banks) to eliminate the tax-deferral benefit, but this special corporate tax has been suspended since 1999 as a result of extremely low interest rates and the difficult economic environment for fund management.[239] At retirement, employees have the option of receiving the benefit either as a lump-sum payment or as periodic pension payments; where the lump sum is chosen, benefits are taxed as "Retirement Income," a special schedule that is very favorably taxed.[240] Where the pension payment option is chosen, the same preferential taxation as for public pension benefits is applicable.[241]

Private pension plans other than qualified employee pension plans are also available for individuals to prepare for their retirement. Where an individual pays the premiums to an insurance company, those premiums are deductible subject to certain limits.[242] In contrast to companies with employee pension plans, insurance companies offering private pension plans are subject to the normal corporate tax and therefore the concern about tax deferral is less acute. When the individual receives the pension benefits, those benefits less the premiums paid are included in income as "Miscellaneous Income."[243]

235. Unlike the superannuation system in Australia, employees do not have the right to an "individualized account" with respect to public pension plans, despite their contributions; the public pension legislation grants them the status of beneficiary (with the benefits dependent on the amount of their own contributions), which does not amount to a private-property right.
236. Japan, STMA, s. 41-15-3.
237. Japan, Order for Enforcement of CTA, s. 135; Order for Enforcement of Income Tax Act (OEITA), s. 64.
238. Japan, ITA, s. 75, para. 2, No. 1 and ITA, s. 76, para. 5.
239. Japan, STMA, s. 68-5.
240. Japan, OEITA, s. 72.
241. Japan, OEITA, s. 82-2.
242. Japan, ITA, s. 76, para. 3. The deductible amount (per year) is: (i) the entire amount (for the part not more than JPY 20,000); (ii) 50% of the amount that exceeds JPY 20,000 (up to JPY 40,000); (iii) 25% of the amount that exceeds JPY 40,000 (up to JPY 80,000). Accordingly, for individuals paying premiums of more than JPY 80,000, the deductible amount is capped at JPY 40,000.
243. Japan, ITA, s. 35, and OEITA, s. 183.

China also has three types of pension plans: basic or government plans, employer-sponsored pension plans, and individual retirement savings plans. The government pension program provides "basic pension benefits" and pays 1% of the indexed individual wage and provincial average earnings for each year of coverage, subject to a minimum of 15 years of contribution. It covers mostly urban workers.[244] Individuals can deduct contributions to the basic pension plan. Pensions for the disabled or for the family members of deceased taxpayers are exempt from tax under Article 4 of the IIT Law.

Since 1991, employers have been permitted to sponsor pension plans for their employees. At the end of 2017, about 80,400 employers (accounting for about 0.35% of total enterprises in China) had such plans, covering 23,310,000 individuals. Contributions to such plans are tax-deductible and investment earnings accumulated in the plans are tax exempt; however, benefits received from the plans are included in the recipients' income. Thus, employer pension plans follow an EET pattern. There are no tax subsidies for individual retirement savings.

Sweden has government, employer-provided, and privately funded pensions, which are taxed as income from employment. Private pension plans are taxable in accordance with an ETT pattern.

Government pensions are provided for all individuals resident in Sweden in proportion to their contributions, which are based on earned income. The calculated pension is based on a maximum amount of earned income (in 2024, SEK 571,500); contributions above this level are actually taxes. The amount of government pension depends on the age at which a person starts to receive payments. For a high-income earner who starts to receive a pension at the age of 67, the pension would be approximately SEK 28,000 per month. These persons almost always have additional employer-provided and private pensions. Although pensions are treated as income from employment, social security contributions are not levied on this income.

Eligible persons can choose to receive pension benefits starting at age 63. Employers and the self-employed pay statutory social security contributions to the government. The standard contributions for pensions are 10.21% of salary and 10.21% of business income for the self-employed. In addition, all individuals are charged a general pension fee of 7% of earned income; however, a credit for the same amount is provided, with the result that no tax is owing. The purpose of the general pension fee is apparently only to make taxpayers aware of the actual cost of pension funding.

There is a minimum government pension (in 2024, a maximum of SEK 11,640 per month for those who have been resident for at least forty years, reduced proportionately where the period of residence is shorter). Because they tend to have low incomes and fall short of the residency requirement for the full pension, many immigrants receive only the minimum pension.

244. *See* OECD, China: Pension System in 2022, https://www.oecd.org/els/public-pensions/PAG2023-country-profile-China.pdf. *See also* Haitong, Pension Funds Market and Products Research Report (5)—"Long Way to Go: China's Pension System" (2018).

For employees with salaries above the limit for government pension benefits, employers normally make contributions to a pension plan. Contributions are deductible up to the lower of 35% of salary or SEK 525,000. Employer contributions are not subject to social security contributions, but in order to decrease the difference between pension contributions and the payment of salaries, they are subject to a special wage tax of 24.26%. This rate roughly corresponds to the portion of social security contributions which functions as a tax (i.e., contributions on income over SEK 571,500, as explained above).

Contributions by individuals to private pension plans are not deductible, with exceptions for self-employed individuals and employees who have no employer-funded pension plan. Pension withdrawals from individual pension plans (mainly insurance) are taxable if contributions to the plan were deductible. Previously, the rules for deduction were more generous, so that large private pension funds still exist under which withdrawals are taxable as income from employment. Income from pension withdrawals is not subject to social security contributions.

Income earned on assets in pension funds has been taxable to the fund since the general tax reform of 1991; before 1991, such income was not taxable. The rationale for the change was to equalize the treatment of pension savings and private savings. However, complete tax neutrality has not been achieved, since earnings on pension funds are subject to a standardized tax, which is presumed to be approximately half of the tax on private savings. The standardized earnings on assets in a pension fund are calculated at the lesser of the government borrowing rate (2.48% in 2023) and 0.5%. On this yield, a tax rate of 15% is applied (the normal tax rate on private savings is 30%). In theory, full taxation of earnings in pension funds (an ETT pattern) would result in the same taxation as for private savings (a TTE pattern). Thus, standardized taxation results should normally result in a limited tax advantage for pension fund savings.

In *Canada*, the federal government provides two pension benefits. Under the Canada Pension Plan (CPP), employees and self-employed individuals must make contributions to the plan based on a percentage of their earnings; in addition, employers must make contributions for their employees equal to the employees' contributions. Benefits payable under the CPP, which begin at age 65 (or 60 if an individual elects) are dependent on the individuals' contributions; for 2024, the maximum monthly benefit is CAD 1,364. The Old Age Security Pension, which is funded entirely by the government, provides modest benefits to seniors (2024, a maximum of CAD 784 per month); the benefits are clawed back for taxpayers with higher incomes.

Employee pension plans must be registered with the tax authorities to qualify for tax benefits and registration is permitted only if various conditions are met. In addition, pension plans must meet several conditions imposed by provincial law. Legally, the plans are trusts. Registered plans must be either money purchase plans or defined benefit plans. There are limits on contributions by both employers and employees, which are related to the maximum pension benefit which can be received by an individual. In addition, the limits are integrated with the limits on contributions to private retirement savings plans.

Both employer and employee contributions to registered pension plans are tax-deductible within limits and employers' contributions are not taxable to employees. In addition, income earned by the plan is not taxable. There are restrictions on the investments that can be made by registered pension plans (e.g., no investments can be made in the employer or persons related to the employer). Amounts are taxable when withdrawn from the plan, except for certain rollovers to other registered plans.

The Canadian ITA also provides tax incentives for private pension plans called registered retirement savings plans (RRSPs). These plans are established by individuals and administered as trusts by financial institutions. Contributions to an RRSP are limited to 18% of the earned income for the previous year, subject to an annual maximum of CAD 31,560 for 2024 (which is indexed by reference to the average industrial wage). The funds accumulated in an RRSP can be invested by the individual owner, subject to certain limits on the types of qualifying investments; no tax is imposed on the income or gains realized by the plan. Withdrawals from an RRSP are included in the recipient's income. When the owner of an RRSP reaches the age of 71 years, the entire amount of the RRSP becomes taxable unless the owner converts the RRSP (tax-free) into an annuity (for life or until 90 years of age) or a registered retirement income fund (RRIF). Benefits payable under the annuity or the RRIF are taxable. An RRIF is a continuation of an RRSP in that the owner can continue to control the investment of funds in the RRIF and income derived by the RRIF is tax-free. However, the owner must make minimum annual withdrawals from an RRIF in accordance with a formula, and amounts withdrawn are included in income.

The primary benefit of the tax assistance for Canadian pension benefits is deferral—contributions are deductible, income earned on the contributions is not taxable, and amounts are taxable only when withdrawn. In effect, the statutory scheme uses an EET taxing pattern and provides deferral of tax for both private and employer-sponsored pension plans in order to encourage taxpayers to save for retirement.

The Canadian tax system also provides a special tax plan, the Tax-Free Savings Account (TFSA), which allows individuals to save on a tax-free basis. Contributions to a TFSA, which are subject to an annual limit of CAD 7,000 (indexed) are not deductible, but income earned from the investment of the contributions is tax free and withdrawals are also tax free (a TEE taxing pattern). TFSAs are not limited to savings for retirement benefits but are intended to promote savings for all purposes.

Australia has no national social security regime so government-funded pensions for the aged, people with disabilities, the unemployed, veterans, students, etc. are delivered out of current-year revenue—the current workforce pays taxes which are returned as pensions to the current generation of retired people. Many of these benefits are means-tested, meaning that the full entitlement is withdrawn where the recipient has other income or assets. For the most part, these government benefits are also treated as assessable income in the hands of the recipients, the theory being that to treat the benefits as tax exempt would make them more valuable to wealthy recipients than to the poor. But in some cases, the combination of withdrawal rate and the tax imposed on benefits can lead to very high marginal tax rates for people on quite low incomes. Successive governments have considered ways of resolving this "poverty trap" problem, but so far, the problem is acknowledged but remains unsolved.

For historical reasons, the only tax-preferred saving for retirement occurred through the workforce: sophisticated employers contributed to employer-specific pension funds for their executives and senior staff. While the wealthy could afford to save privately, there was no tax concession to encourage retirement saving, and because the system was an adjunct to the employed workforce, people who worked for small unsophisticated employers, lower-level employees, the self-employed, and people outside the paid workforce entirely or for long periods (such as spouses with childcare responsibilities) could not access any benefits under this system. This changed in 1992 with the introduction of compulsory employer contributions for almost all employees (currently, employers must contribute 11% of an employee's regular wages to a fund, rising to 12% in 2025), and the system has gradually expanded to allow contributions by people outside the paid workforce (a deduction of up to AUD 30,000 per year for people making personal contributions; contributions up to AUD 120,000 per year out of after-tax income are also allowed).

The government still plays no role in managing the pool of private retirement savings—the investment of contributions is handled mainly by investment managers associated with trade unions or large financial institutions, although some people maintain and operate their own self-managed funds. Except for funds operated for government employees, few funds offer guaranteed benefits on retirement. Instead, member benefits are based on the accumulated balance of their account at retirement, meaning employees bear the investment risk.

While the tax treatment of private retirement savings has varied over time, the system appears to have stabilized to a ttE pattern—a flat tax at 15% (rather than marginal rates) on deducted employer and member contributions, a flat tax at 15% on investment income earned by the fund, and no tax on benefits if taken after the age of 60. Even though some income tax is collected up-front, the concessions in the retirement income system remain one of the largest tax expenditures in the government budget, and much of the tinkering during the last thirty years has been directed at trying to reduce the cost of the concessions. The current system involves a combination of caps on the size of tax-preferred contributions which can be made each year, limits on the size of benefits that can be accumulated inside the fund for each member, and increases in tax rates on contributions effectively to 30% for high-income individuals.

In *France*, for the vast majority of employees, retirement benefits are derived exclusively from the compulsory social security system, resulting in a significantly simpler system than that of many other countries; employer pension plans are relatively uncommon and private pension funds do not really exist as such. In most cases, there is symmetry between the deduction of contributions and the taxation of retirement benefits.

Employers may deduct all contributions to mandatory basic and supplementary social security regimes, as well as those to supplementary pension plans created for their employees or a category of employees (e.g., managers) provided, for those created after 2009, that such plans are managed by independent funds or financial institutions. Employees are not taxable on the employer's contributions to pension plans and may deduct from the schedular wages category of income their own contributions to such regimes and plans, subject to certain limits for employer-created plans. Furthermore, contributions to a limited number of specific optional retirement savings plans, which have been growing steadily since 2019, are deductible from household global income, but within complex limits.[245] Similarly, self-employed individuals may deduct from their schedular category of income their contributions to mandatory basic and supplementary social security regimes as well as (within limits) to specific optional plans.

Investment returns on contributions by employers and employees are not taxable.

All retirement benefits actually received by employees or self-employed individuals are subject to the progressive income tax less a 10% allowance (capped for each tax household at EUR 4,123 in 2024).[246] Benefits derived from an optional plan in the form of a lump sum can also benefit from a 7.5% flat rate at the taxpayer's option. Withdrawals before retirement are allowed only in exceptional circumstances and do not qualify for any preferential treatment. The full amount of retirement benefits is liable to flat-rate social income taxes deducted from the gross pension amount: for the general social contribution (CSG) at a rate of 8.3 (normal), 6.6 (medium), or 3.8% (reduced); for the social debt reimbursement contribution (CRDS) at a rate of 0.5%; and the additional solidarity contribution for autonomy at a rate of 0.3% where the applicable CSG is at the standard or median rate (but not applicable to the reduced rate); however, such taxes are partially deductible from the base for the progressive income tax. In effect, the French system follows an EET pattern, although retirement benefits do qualify for preferential treatment.

In *Germany*, retirement benefits fall into four different categories:

(1) pensions for civil servants, which are paid out of the general budget of the state (or a subnational public entity);
(2) retirement annuities under a (largely mandatory) social security system established for employees and most self-employed persons (e.g., lawyers, tax advisers, and physicians); these annuities are paid out of a fund administered by a special agency and funded by beneficiaries' contributions; these schemes represent the most basic and widely used funding for retirement benefits in Germany;
(3) occupational pensions paid directly out of employers' funds or financed under an insurance scheme set up by the employer; and
(4) individual insurance policies taken out by taxpayers.

The tax treatment of retirement benefits received a shock in 2002 when the Constitutional Court declared the previous tax regime to be invalid because it discriminated against pensions derived by civil servants compared to pensions derived by private employees.[247] The Federal Constitutional Court made clear that the tax treatment of the different categories of pension must comply with the principle of equal

245. France, CGI, s. 163 quatervicies.
246. France, CGI, s. 158 5a.
247. Federal Constitutional Court (*Bundesverfassungsgericht*), March 6, 2002, 2 BvL 17/99.

treatment. As a result, the tax legislation was altered to ensure single taxation and equal treatment for the various types of retirement schemes:

- pensions for civil servants are fully taxable since the retirement benefits are funded out of the general budget of the state;[248]
- retirement annuities paid out of the general social security system are taxable, and contributions are deductible, subject to a limit of approximately EUR 26,500;[249]
- employer-provided pension plans are widespread, with nearly 48 % of all companies having more than fifty employees and 88 % of all companies having more than 1,000 employees providing such plans. More than one-half of the working population is covered by an employer plan. Under labor law, an employee can demand an occupational pension plan as long as the plan is financed by contributions from employees' wages (*Entgeltumwandlung*).

Plans can be structured under a direct commitment by the employer to pay the pension or through a third party as "pension insurance," via a "pension fund" or "direct insurance," or as a "benevolent fund." Large and medium-sized companies typically use the direct method, while smaller enterprises fund the pension obligation by purchasing insurance.

Direct pension commitments are funded through the creation of tax-deductible pension reserves.[250] For tax purposes, a reserve can first be established when an employee reaches the age of 27 and is based on actuarial calculations of the future pension obligation using a 6 % discount rate.[251] Subsequent adjustments to the reserve can be made. There is no restriction on employers' use of the funds in the reserve; however, employers are legally required to participate in a special guarantee fund. Although employees have a legal right to the future pension at the time the reserve is formed, they are not subject to tax until payments are received.

In contrast, where an employer finances retirement benefits through direct insurance, the premium is currently deductible by the employer[252] and taxable income for employees to the extent that the premium exceeds EUR 6,432.[253] When retirement payments are received, they are taxable to the extent of the tax exempt premiums. The part of the retirement payment that results from nondeductible and nonexempt contributions is partially taxed.[254]

248. Germany, ITA s. 19 para. 1 No. 2.
249. Germany, ITA, s. 10 para. 1 No. 2 lit.a and s. 22 No. 1 sent. 3 lit.a)aa. This system is subject to a long phase-in period and benefits will be fully taxable only in 2058.
250. Germany, ITA, s. 6a.
251. The compatibility of this 6 % discount rate with the ability-to-pay principle is currently being challenged in the Constitutional Court, as it has been hugely out of step for many years with a realistic assessment of the overall market interest rate and thus with the true value of the employer's debt (Tax Court Cologne, December 19, 2017, 10 K 977/17).
252. Germany, ITA, s. 4b.
253. Germany, ITA, s. 19 para. 1 No. 3 and s. 3 No. 63; the tax-free threshold was doubled as of fiscal year 2018.
254. Germany, ITA, s. 22 No. 5.

Where pension benefits are funded through a pension fund or pension insurance, the pattern of taxation is the same as for direct insurance; employers have a current deduction for the contributions[255] and employees have current income[256] which is partially tax exempt.[257] The fund itself is generally tax exempt and subject to substantial government oversight and regulation.[258] A similar method for funding involves so-called benevolent or relief funds. Benevolent funds are subject to less government supervision than formal pension funds, and correspondingly, there are substantial restrictions on employers' deductions.[259] The contributions of employers are not income for employees because they do not have a legal right to the future pension payment. The pension payments are taxed as wages.[260]

Individual taxpayers can increase their retirement benefits above the level provided by the mandatory social security system by taking out insurance policies on their own. As a general rule, life annuities paid out of private insurance policies are taxable only to the extent of the return on the paid-in capital. Contributions to these schemes are deductible up to an annual threshold (currently EUR 2,100).[261]

In *India*, before 2004, government employees received generous treatment through their participation in a provident fund.[262] These employees made a compulsory minimum contribution to this fund;[263] they received a lifelong defined benefit pension from the government,[264] a tax-free gratuity after a certain number of years of service,[265] and a lump-sum retirement benefit, all of which were tax-free.[266] From 2004, the central government adopted a new pension scheme (NPS) for all new employees, using an EET pattern.

Under the NPS, government employees (other than members of the Armed Forces, for whom the old rules still apply) must contribute 10% of salary to the NPS. There is a matching contribution by the government, which is included in the salary but is deductible.[267] The total deduction available to employees (exclusive of the matching contribution) in respect of contributions to the pension fund and all other savings instruments is currently limited to INR 150,000.[268] An additional deduction of INR 50,000 is available for deposit in the NPS but only if the employee continues to be

---

255. Germany, ITA, s. 4c.
256. Germany, ITA, s. 19 para. 1 No. 3.
257. Germany, ITA, s. 22 No. 5.
258. Germany, Corporate Income Tax Act (CITA), s. 5 No. 3.
259. Germany, ITA, s. 4d.
260. Germany, ITA, s. 19 para. 1 No. 2.
261. Germany, ITA, s. 10a.
262. Under The Provident Fund Act, 1925.
263. Contributions to the provident fund qualified for deduction from total income, subject to the overall limit (ITA 1961, s. 80C).
264. A part of the pension can be commuted in accordance with the relevant rules and is exempt under ITA 1961, s. 10(10A). The pension would be taxable as salary in the hands of employees during their lifetime. After their death, there was also a family pension for immediate family members, which is taxable as income from other sources.
265. Under the Gratuity Act, a gratuity is payable to employees upon retirement or at the end of employment, on the basis of fifteen days' average salary for each year of service.
266. India, ITA 1961, s. 10(10AA).
267. India, ITA 1961, ss. 17(1) (viii) and 80CCD (2).
268. India, ITA 1961, s. 80CCE.

taxed under the old regime.[269] On retirement, taxpayers must invest 40% of the balance in the account to purchase a lifetime annuity from a regulated life insurance company.[270] Withdrawals from the NPS are included in income, with the exception of the following amounts, which are tax-free:

- the amount used to purchase an annuity;[271]
- 40% of the total payable to the taxpayer at the time of closing or opting out of the scheme;
- 100% of any amount payable on the death of the taxpayer.[272]

Thus, only 20% of the balance in an NPS account is taxable on withdrawal. The EET pattern of the NPS was further diluted in December 2018 when the exemption for lump-sum withdrawals was increased to 60%, with the result that withdrawals are currently completely exempt. In addition, the government's contribution has been increased to 14%, while employees' minimum contribution remains at 10%.[273]

The government extended the benefits of the NPS to employees of state governments, with the matching contribution by the state government set initially at 10% but increased in 2022 to 14%. However, a growing number of states ruled by opposition parties have now reverted to the old pension scheme and the issue has become highly politicized.

The NPS was extended to private sector employees in 2007, with matching contributions by employers at 10% (increased to 14% in 2024 if the employee opts for the new regime).[274] It was subsequently extended to self-employed individuals; contributions by the taxpayer are deductible up to 20% of gross total income.[275] However, as a result of the new tax regime introduced in 2020, none of the tax benefits, except contributions by the employer, is currently available[276] unless the taxpayer opts for the old tax regime.

Although pension plans are not common for private-sector employees, employers sometimes establish superannuation funds in the form of trusts for the provision of

269. India, ITA 1961, s. 80CCD (1B). As explained in the chapter on India in Part I, under the new regime introduced in 2020, taxpayers are subject to a lower tax rate but give up entitlement to many deductions and concessions.
270. https://www.india.gov.in/spotlight/national-pension-system-retirement-plan-all; https://npscra.nsdl.co.in/download/FAQs%20on%20Final%20Exit,%20Annuity%20and%20Continuation_Deferment%20Process.pdf.
271. India, ITA 1961, s. 80CCD(5).
272. India, ITA 1961, s. 10(12A).
273. *See* https://www.business-standard.com/article/economy-policy/govt-contribution-to-national-pension-scheme-raised-to-14-of-basic-salary-118120601211_1.html.
274. ITA 1961, s. 36(1) (iva). Added by the Finance Act No. 2 2024 through a new proviso to s. 80CCD(2). The employer receives a deduction for this contribution as a business expenditure as long as the contribution does not exceed 10% (increased to 14% in 2024) of the employee's salary.
275. India, ITA 1961, s. 80CCD (1)(b).
276. India, ITA 1961, s. 115BAC (2).

pensions to certain employees. Employers' contributions to an approved superannuation fund[277] are deductible expenses,[278] but from 2021 contributions to such funds, provident funds, and pension funds, as well as income earned on those contributions in excess of INR 750,000, are treated as taxable benefits to employees.[279] Employees' contributions are deductible only if the employee opts for the old tax regime.[280]

Any gratuity for government employees on death or retirement is exempt from tax.[281] For other employees, such gratuities are also tax-free, within limits. All employers with more than ten employees must provide minimum gratuities.

Provident funds are an important component of Indian retirement benefits and take several forms. For central government employees, a minimum of 6% of salary (maximum 100%) must be contributed by employees. Withdrawals are permissible, subject to conditions. The government credits interest on the contributions at a rate which varies from time to time. Employees' contributions are deductible up to INR 150,000 for employees who opt for the old regime;[282] interest on the contributions is not taxable and withdrawals are exempt.[283] As noted above, this treatment is not available for new government employees after 2004.

For all other government employees, the minimum contribution is 10% of their remuneration (maximum 100%). Employers' contributions are prescribed by the government (currently 10%) and are credited to employees' accounts. A bonus is payable if the funds are not withdrawn before retirement.

For the vast majority of private-sector employees, the Employees' Provident Fund (EPF) provides the major retirement benefits. It is compulsory for every organization which has twenty or more employees and for employees earning a salary not in excess of INR 15,000 per month; it is voluntary for other employees. Employers and employees both contribute 12% of the employee's salary to the fund. Employers' contributions are deductible if the fund is recognized by the tax commissioner. Similarly, employees' contributions are deductible up to an overall limit of INR 150,000 where the employee opts for the old regime. If an employer contributes more than 12% of an employee's salary, the excess must be included in the employee's income. In addition, where interest credited by the employer on the contributions exceeds a specified amount (9.5% currently), the excess is included in the employee's income.[284] Of the employer's contribution of 12%, about 8.33% is earmarked for a pension scheme, resulting in a

277. Defined in ITA 1961, s. 2(6). Detailed conditions and rules are contained in Part B of the Fourth Schedule to the ITA 1961; however, there is no regulatory authority for such funds.
278. Subject to prescribed conditions in ITA 1961, s. 36(i)(iv).
279. India, ITA 1961, s. 17(2)(vii) as amended by the Finance Act 2020. While low-salaried employees are not able to allow the employer to contribute a large part of their salary to any of these three funds, high-salaried employees can design their salary package such that a large part of their salary is paid by the employer through contributions to these funds, which are not taxable because they are subject to the EEE regime. As a result, the absence of a combined upper cap would be inappropriate.
280. India, ITA 1961, s. 80C(2)(vii) and s. 115BAC.
281. India, ITA 1961, s. 10(10).
282. India, ITA 1961, s. 80C(2)(iv).
283. India, ITA 1961, s. 10(11).
284. India, ITA 1961, Rule 6 of Part A of the Fourth Schedule.

small pension. The pension is taxable but the accumulated balance is tax-free to the extent provided in Rule 8 of Part A of the Fourth Schedule.[285]

In 2021, the government changed the rules relating to interest on provident funds. Until 2022, interest on contributions to provident funds was not taxable and withdrawals were exempt.[286] Some employees took advantage of this treatment and contributed huge amounts to these funds, with the result that the entire interest accrued/received on such contributions was exempt from tax. To prevent this result, a threshold of INR 250,000 was established in respect of contributions to funds to which employers also contribute (INR 500,000 where employers do not contribute). Any interest accrued during a year in respect of contributions beyond these limits is taxable, effective from fiscal year 2022.[287] This limit also applies to the Public Provident Fund (PPF) where any Indian citizen can open an account in a Post Office or participating bank with a minimum contribution of INR 500 and maximum of INR 150,000; contributions are locked in for a period of 15 years. Contributions to the PPF are deductible up to the overall limit of INR 150,000 under the old regime but are not deductible under the new regime introduced in 2020.

12 REALIZATION AND RECOGNITION OF GAIN

In all the systems examined here, in general, income and capital gains must be "realized" before being taken into account for tax purposes. This realization principle is quite obvious with respect to the taxation of capital gains and losses. In general, a capital gain or loss is realized only when the property is sold, exchanged, or otherwise disposed of. Until such time, any change in the value of the property which results in an accrued gain or loss in respect of the property is not relevant. The realization principle also operates with respect to business income, although it functions somewhat differently in that context. Income from a business is usually computed on an "accrual" rather than a "cash receipts and disbursements" basis. In this setting, realization is not synonymous with a cash method of accounting. For example, under a system based on realization, business income from the performance of services is usually realized when the services are performed and billed, although the collection of the fees may take place only at a later time. Thus, in the business context, the realization principle means that income arises only when a transaction, such as the performance of services, occurs. In some settings, the realization requirement might be referred to as the transactional basis underlying the income tax. In other cases, a change in tax status—for example, ceasing to be a resident—is treated as a "deemed" realization with respect to certain assets held by the taxpayer.

The definition of realization events or the identification of transactions which give rise to income or gain is critical to all realization or transaction-based income tax systems. In all the countries examined here, some transactions, such as sales of property, are clearly realization events. However, some of the countries go much

285. India, ITA 1961, s. 10(12).
286. India, ITA 1961, s. 10(11) and s. 10(12).
287. India, ITA, 1961, Provisos to s. 10(11) and 10(12); Rule 9D of Income Tax Rules, 1962.

further and treat certain transactions as realization events even where no consideration is received by the transferor. Thus, for example, in several countries, gifts, transfers on death, and the withdrawal of property from a business for personal use are considered to be taxable dispositions.

While the concept of realization is firmly entrenched in all the systems, it seems that the realization requirement is increasingly being abandoned or narrowed in certain areas. For example, several countries have adopted some sort of accrual or "mark-to-market" method of taxation for financial instruments. This development began with the treatment of the implicit-interest element in bonds issued with an original discount and has been extended to other types of instruments. These matters are discussed in more detail in Subpart D since the approach has historically been tied to accounting rules. In addition, the realization principle has frequently been abandoned with respect to the taxation of foreign investment companies. For these companies, a mark-to-market approach is sometimes used, or an imputed income approach where the mark-to-market method proves difficult to apply. These matters are discussed in Part IV.

All the systems also contain rules which allow for the deferral ("rollover") of realized gain in some circumstances. These provisions typically involve property-for-property exchanges, reinvested proceeds (especially where the realization event was involuntary), and other similar situations. The rules vary substantially, in both their requirements and the techniques used to establish deferral. Various corporate exchanges which involve rollovers, usually in the context of corporate reorganizations, are discussed in Part III.

In the *United States* system, there is substantial case law on the doctrine of realization, which has been viewed as a matter of administrative convenience rather than as a constitutional requirement.[288] The current status of the realization requirement as a matter of administrative convenience has recently been cast into some doubt due to the Supreme Court's decision in *Moore v. United States*.[289] The taxpayers in *Moore*, who were U.S. shareholders in a controlled foreign corporation (CFC), argued that the imposition of a tax under Internal Revenue Code (IRC) section 965 on the accumulated undistributed income of the CFC was unconstitutional because the shareholders had not realized such income. The majority opinion avoided deciding the constitutional realization question by determining that the CFC had clearly realized the income it had earned and, therefore, the only question was whether that income could be attributed to the shareholders. The majority concluded that it was well established that income realized by an entity could be attributed to its owners. However, the question has not been laid to rest permanently because two concurring Justices and two dissenting Justices took the position that realization was a constitutional requirement.

Under current law, any exchange of properties in which there is a "material difference" will result in realization.[290] The gratuitous transfer of property *inter vivos* or

288. *Commissioner v. Glenshaw Glass*, 348 U.S. 426 (1955).
289. *Moore v. United States*, 36 F.4th 930 (9th Cir. 2022), *cert. granted*, 143 S. Ct. 2656 (2023).
290. *Cottage Savings Assoc. v. Commissioner*, 499 U.S. 554 (1991).

at death, however, is not treated as a realization event. In the case of gifts, a carryover of tax cost preserves the possibility of taxing accrued gains in the hands of the donee, but for transfers at death, the heir or transferee receives a fair market value tax cost, and appreciation to the date of death escapes tax altogether.

The placing of a mortgage on property, even where the mortgage is nonrecourse and involves no personal liability for the repayment of the funds, is not treated as a realization event. As a corollary of this rule, the transfer (or abandonment) of property subject to a mortgage is treated as involving an amount realized equal to the face amount of the mortgage.

A special statutory rule requires securities dealers to report gains and losses on securities on a "mark-to-market" basis as if the property had been sold on the last day of the taxable year.[291] In addition, taxpayers holding futures contracts which are traded on an exchange are also generally required to mark the contracts to market.

Realization of gain is also required where the nominal owner of stock, certain types of debt, or a partnership interest enters into a short sale, offsetting notional contract, or forward sale of such assets.

"Rollover" provisions allow realized gain to be deferred in certain situations, including the exchange of like-kind real estate held for investment or used in a trade or business and the reinvestment of proceeds from damage or condemnation of property involved in an "involuntary conversion."[292] A provision which allowed taxpayers to rollover the gain from the sale of their principal residences has been replaced with an exemption which allows taxpayers to exclude USD 250,000 (USD 500,000 for married individuals filing a joint return) of such gain from income.[293]

In *Germany*, gains on dispositions of property are fully taxable and losses are fully deductible if they occur in the context of a business or similar income category.[294] The taxation of the gain is subject to the accrual method of income determination; the overall profit of the business includes both operating profit and capital gains insofar as the value of the consideration received for an asset exceeds its book value. The mere increase in value does not lead to taxation as long as there is no disposal of the asset.[295] If, however, the increase "recaptures" former impairment losses, it must be taken into account for tax accounting purposes.[296]

Several rules provide for the taxation of "hidden reserves" where an asset is withdrawn from the business without consideration. Such withdrawals of an asset from a corporation, sole proprietorship, or partnership are added to the taxable profit according to the "fair value" of the asset.[297] The transfer of assets to a foreign permanent establishment (and all other cross-border transfers of assets, where the subsequent gain would not be subject to German tax) is also treated as a withdrawal

291. United States, IRC, s. 475.
292. United States, IRC, ss. 1031, 1033.
293. United States, IRC, s. 121.
294. Germany, ITA, s. 2 para. 2.
295. Germany, ITA, s. 5 para. 1 with reference to German Commercial Code, s. 252 para. 1 No. 4.
296. Germany, ITA, s. 6 para. 1 No. 1 sent. 4, No. 2 sent. 3.
297. Germany, ITA, s. 4 para. 1 sent. 1, s. 6 para. 1 No. 4.

and therefore taxed as an immediate realization event.[298] Where an asset is transferred to an EU Member State, taxpayers are allowed to take the gain into account over a period of five years unless there is an actual disposition of the asset by the foreign branch at an earlier stage.[299] Given a series of decisions rendered by the Court of Justice of the European Union (CJEU), it is widely accepted that these rules comply with the EC provisions on the Internal Market.[300]

A number of provisions in the German tax system allow the deferral or rollover of a realized gain. In the case of real estate held in a business context, current recognition can be avoided if the sales proceeds are reinvested in real estate.[301] Otherwise, taxpayers can avoid current recognition of gain by establishing a tax-deductible investment reserve which reduces current income. The reserve may be maintained for four to six years depending on the type of asset. Where the reserve is dissolved because no reinvestment is undertaken in the prescribed period, an annual interest charge of 6% is imposed on the amount of the reserve. Until 2015, this regime could not be invoked if the gains were reinvested outside Germany, a restriction held by the CJEU to infringe on the Internal Market.[302] Therefore, an option was enacted allowing taxpayers to extend realization of the profit over five years if the gain is reinvested in another Member State of the EU.[303]

Moreover, in the course of reorganizations of business entities, the transfer of assets to a partnership or corporation can lead to rollover treatment if the taxpayer becomes a partner or shareholder in the firm.[304] Additional consideration in kind or in cash is acceptable, but the fair value of this consideration must be the minimum value allocated to the contributed assets in the accounts of the firm.[305]

The Netherlands has the same basic pattern of rules, although the technical details differ somewhat. For example, reinvestment must be in similar property and the reserve may not be maintained for more than three years.[306]

In *Sweden*, in general, all property gains are taxed only on realization. One significant exception is gains on claims and debts denominated in foreign currency arising in a business, which are taxed on a mark-to-market basis, following accounting principles. Gain realized on an involuntary conversion of property can be deferred if the proceeds from insurance, damages, etc. are reinvested. Gain up to SEK 3,000,000 on the sale of a personal residence can likewise be deferred if the sales proceeds are reinvested.[307]

A simplified tax system was introduced in 2012 in the form of an investment savings account (ISK) for financial instruments such as shares and fund units. The simplification consists in the individual not being taxed on the actual income, gains,

298. Germany, ITA, s. 4 para. 1 sent. 3.
299. Germany, ITA, s. 4g.
300. CJEU, May 21, 2015, C-657/13 (*Verder Lab Tec*); January 23, 2014, C-164/12 (*DMC*).
301. Germany, ITA, s. 6b.
302. CJEU, April 16, 2015, C-591/13 (*Commission v. Germany*).
303. Germany, ITA, s. 6b para. 2a.
304. Germany, ITA, s. 6 para. 5 and s. 16 para. 3 sent. 2; RTA (Reorganization Tax Act), ss. 20, 24.
305. RTA, s. 20 para. 2 sent. 4 and para. 3 sent. 3.
306. Netherlands, ITA, Art. 3.54.
307. Sweden, ITA, Ch. 47.

and losses. Instead, a standard revenue is taxed. The standard revenue is calculated as the government borrowing rate plus one percentage point applied to the market value of the account's assets. A tax of 30 % (the standard tax rate for capital income) is levied on the standard revenue. For 2023, the standard revenue is 2.94 % and the tax thus 0.882 % of the capital base.

In *Japan*, the transfer of title to an asset is required for the realization of gain. Such transfers typically not only involve a sale or exchange but include contributions to capital by shareholders, involuntary transfers, such as the seizure and auction of collateral for a loan, and even the taking of property by eminent domain.[308] Gain on business assets may be deferred in a like-kind exchange.[309] Under prior law (influenced by the Shoup Commission and Stanley Surrey), a gift of appreciated property was treated as a realization event, but the system was very unpopular and was replaced with a carryover-basis mechanism (which extends to transfers at death).[310] Since 2000, the corporate income tax has used the mark-to-market method for financial derivative products and securities held for the purpose of trading.[311]

France requires realization, although in the business context, foreign currency gains on claims are taxed on a mark-to-market basis[312] and provisions are booked for impairment in the value of fixed non-depreciable assets such as land, goodwill, and investments.[313] Transfers of business property by gift or death are realization events, as are the withdrawal of assets from a proprietorship or the cessation of a taxpayer's business and a change in the tax regime applicable to a business (e.g., partnership to corporation) or the real activity of a business.[314] There are relatively few rollover provisions outside the context of corporate reorganizations. In principle, unrealized capital gains are not taxable. Prudent accounting practices prevent the recognition of such gains, whereas unrealized losses—indicating impairment of fixed assets—are accounted for as depreciation. As an exception to the historical cost principle, a company may freely revalue assets on its balance sheet, provided this revaluation applies to all tangible and financial fixed assets (excluding intangible assets and inventories). These revaluations, which discount the book value of assets, produce an increase in net assets, taxable under normal conditions.[315]

All the *Commonwealth* systems are based on the realization principle. The realization requirement was originally developed by the courts in the context of trading profits. With the subsequent introduction of capital gains taxation, broad statutory realization rules were enacted which, in general, treat any disposal or disposition (as compared to the "sale or exchange" language used in the U.S.) of an asset as a realization event. Thus, in *Canada*, for example, realization occurs if a taxpayer

308. Japan, ITA, s. 33.
309. Japan, ITA, s. 58.
310. Japan, ITA, s. 60.
311. Japan, CTA, s. 61-3 and 61-5.
312. France, CGI, s. 38-4.
313. France, CGI, Regulatory Schedule III, s. 38 sexies.
314. France, CGI, ss. 201 and 221, 221-2, 221 bis, 221-5 and 202 ter, respectively.
315. At the time of the Covid-19 crisis, to enable companies to strengthen their equity capital and facilitate refinancing, the Finance Act 2021 provided a tax neutralization mechanism limited to two years for revaluation differences.

disposes of most of the important incidents of ownership in an asset. In some cases, changes in the terms of debt or stock have been held by the courts to be a disposition of the debt or stock with tax consequences. In addition, as previously discussed, the disposition of property by gift or on death is generally treated as a realization event (although rollovers are available for interspousal and certain other transfers). In general, rollover relief is limited to capital gains and losses. However, recapture of capital cost allowance (depreciation) in respect of depreciable property may be deferred where the property is disposed of involuntarily and a replacement property is acquired.[316] Similarly, deferral is permitted with respect to dispositions of eligible capital property, which includes many types of intangible property, including goodwill, and dispositions of real or immovable property used in a business where the taxpayer acquires a replacement property within specified time limits.[317]

Special rules in Canada require financial institutions to account for gains and losses on certain debt and equity securities on a mark-to-market basis.[318] There are several other narrow exceptions to the realization requirement. For example, where property used in a business is converted to personal use or vice versa, the property is considered to be disposed of for its fair market value. Similarly, certain "transfers" of inventory, intangible property, and depreciable property by a Canadian resident to a foreign branch, or vice versa, are considered to take place at fair market value. Decreases in the value of inventory prior to the sale are recognized pursuant to the lower of cost or market accounting convention or pursuant to an optional rule which allows inventory to be valued at its fair market value.[319]

The *Australian* approach is similar, with statutory rules (principally in the CGT) dealing with what are called "CGT events." The Australian system contains special provisions dealing with the taxation of assets which could be viewed as "created" at the same time they are disposed of—for example, entering a covenant not to compete. A very broad rule treats as a CGT event any payment received with respect to an asset.[320] Australia has a comprehensive accrual system for the treatment of financial assets and liabilities. It uses a mixture of internal rate of return and mark-to-market principles for calculating income and expense on a broad range of financial instruments, which must be applied by large commercial and financial institutions; it is discussed in more detail in Subpart D.

Australia has a number of rollover provisions covering a wide range of circumstances, including involuntary dispositions, death, divorce, reinvestment, and certain like-for-like property exchanges. For historical reasons, the technical details differ depending on whether the property involved is inventory, depreciable business property, or capital property.

The *United Kingdom* system similarly focuses on "disposal" as the principal test of realization for its CGT; several of the various income schedules have their own

316. Canada, ITA, s. 13(4)-(4.3).
317. Canada, ITA, s. 44.
318. Canada, ITA, s. 142.5.
319. Canada, ITA, s. 10(1) and Regulation 1801.
320. Australia, ITAA 1997, s. 104-35, 104-155.

concepts of realization, using either a receipts basis or an earnings (accrual) basis. The term "disposal" is not defined for CGT purposes but has been held to cover any transfer of beneficial ownership. Where a disposal is other than at arm's length, it is deemed to be at fair market value. There are a number of "deemed" realization situations, including, for example, value shifting by changing rights attached to shares in a company.[321]

A case law principle treats the withdrawal of an inventory asset from business to personal use as, in effect, a deemed sale at fair market value resulting in the realization of income; it has now been turned into a statutory principle. Special legislative rules govern the interaction of this case law principle with the CGT regime.[322]

Rollover of realized capital gain is permitted in a variety of situations, including the replacement of business assets within three years of disposal. Express rollover provisions are not needed for reinvestment of sums realized from assets subject to capital allowances or giving rise to ordinary income.

Since 1996, the UK has introduced a number of statutory rules dealing with loan relationships, foreign exchange, and derivative contracts, all of which are based on accounting principles and disregard the distinction between income and capital. They apply only to corporation tax.[323]

In *China*, gains are recognized on the "transfer" of property (financial, tangible, and other property). The term "transfer" is not defined in the tax legislation but is understood to mean a change of ownership. A sale or exchange of an asset is a typical form of transfer. Gifts of property (especially immovable property or listed shares, the transfer of which must be registered) may result in a gain for the donor. However, gifts of personal property are not treated as realization events for IIT purposes.

In *India*, capital gains arise on a "transfer"[324] of a "capital asset."[325] A "capital asset" is broadly defined but specifically excludes stock-in-trade, consumables, stores or raw materials held for the purpose of business, personal effects, and nonurban agricultural land. A "transfer" includes a sale or exchange of a capital asset, extinguishment of any rights in capital assets, compulsory acquisition under any law, and conversion of a capital asset into stock-in-trade.[326] Even the act of giving possession of immovable property in part performance of a contract is regarded as a transfer. Since under the general law a firm is not considered to be a separate legal entity distinct from its partners,[327] it is specifically provided that the transfer of a capital asset by a partner to a firm is a transfer.[328] Similarly, a distribution of capital assets on the dissolution of

321. United Kingdom, TCGA, ss. 2 (general rule), 17 (gift) and 21 (disposal), 29 et seq. (value shifting). On bases for employment income, *see* ITEPA, ss. 16 et seq., and for trading income, *see* ITTOIA, ss. 25-27 (income tax) and CTA 2009, ss. 46-48.
322. The case law principle is *Sharkey v. Wernher* [1956] AC 36, TC 275 made statutory as ITTOIA, ss. 172A et seq. and CTA 2009, Part 3 Ch. 10. On the interaction with CGT, *see* TCGA, s. 161.
323. *See* United Kingdom, CTA 2009, Parts 5-9 ss. 292-931.
324. India, ITA 1961, s. 2(47).
325. India, ITA 1961, s. 2(14).
326. The fair market value on the date of conversion is taken as the full value of consideration.
327. Under the ITA 1961, a firm is a separate taxable entity.
328. India, ITA 1961, s. 45(3).

a firm is also considered to be a transfer.[329] However, the distribution of assets of a company in kind to the shareholders on a liquidation is not treated as a transfer.[330] Several other transactions are also excluded from the definition of a transfer, including, for example, a gift *inter vivos* or on death; a transfer to an irrevocable trust; a transfer of capital assets by a company to a subsidiary or by a subsidiary to its parent where certain conditions are fulfilled; a transfer of assets by a firm or a sole proprietorship on its conversion into a company; and a transfer in the context of a business reorganization, such as amalgamation or demerger, subject to the satisfaction of certain conditions.[331]

The courts held that the exclusion of gifts from the charge to capital gains applied to intercorporate gifts, although the tax department insisted that intercorporate gifts lacked the element of "natural love and affection" present in personal gifts.[332] In 2024, the legislation was amended to provide that only transfers of capital assets by an individual or a HUF, by way of gift, will, or irrevocable trust qualify as gifts for the purpose of CGT.[333] Consequently, intercorporate gifts are transfers which may give rise to capital gains.

The transfer of a work of art, archaeological, scientific, or art collection, book, manuscript, drawing, painting, photograph or print to the government, a university, the National Museum, National Art Gallery, or National Archives is also not considered to be a transfer.[334]

In certain situations, special relief is available in the form of deductions from long-term capital gains. Thus, relief is available to an individual or a HUF where the gains arise on the transfer of a residential house and a new residential house is acquired within a specified period.[335]

13 CAPITAL GAINS AND LOSSES

Although the term "capital gain" or its linguistic equivalent is frequently used in the tax systems examined here, the precise contours of the concept vary considerably from country to country. In addition, the concept plays a different role in different systems. In general terms, "capital gain" means a nonrecurring gain which is not part of the normal stream of income from a business or investment. The distinction between capital gain and income may rest on agricultural notions distinguishing between land and the yield from land, or the tree and its fruit. In Anglo-Saxon systems, the distinction has its origin to some extent in trust concepts, which distinguish between current

329. India, ITA 1961, s. 45(4).
330. India, ITA 1961, s. 46(1).
331. India, ITA 1961, s. 47.
332. For example, the Bombay HC decision in *Jay Trust v. Union of India*, March 8, 2024.
333. India, ITA 1961, s. 47(iii) as amended by the Finance Act, 2024.
334. *Ibid.*
335. India, ITA 1961, s. 54 1st Proviso. Effective April 1, 2020, taxpayers have the option to acquire or construct two residential houses in place of one where the amount of the capital gain does not exceed INR 20 million. This provision was intended to address the housing shortage but was abused by some individuals purchasing very expensive houses. As a result, in 2023 (ITA 1961, s. 54, 3rd Proviso) a limit of INR 100 million was adopted for the cost of new houses.

income and gains which are allocated to corpus for trust accounting purposes. Gains which are attributed to corpus are generally not available for distribution to income beneficiaries.

Regardless of how capital gain is defined, several basic patterns of capital gains taxation emerge. In some countries, typically Continental, all income which arises in a business is taxed in the same fashion: there is no distinction between income and capital gains. Thus, for example, gain on the disposition of an asset used in a business is treated the same as a gain from the sale of inventory. In contrast, gain on an asset which is not connected with a business or other taxable category of income often is not taxed at all, although sometimes there is an exception for short-term gains. Thus, gains realized by individuals on investment assets often are not taxed or are taxed only in special circumstances.

In systems influenced by the United Kingdom, the distinction between ordinary income and capital gain is applied both to business enterprises and private persons. Initially, capital gains were not subject to tax because such gains were not considered to be income from a source but rather gains from the disposal of the source itself. Subsequent legislation, typically in the form of a separate CGT regime, ultimately brought capital gains into the tax base, but often subject to a preferential rate of tax.

Finally, in countries with a global approach, capital gains were always included in the tax base, although here too taxation at a preferential rate was common. In most systems, capital losses are subject to limitations, reflecting either the special treatment of the gain or the fact that timing of the realization of the gains and losses is usually within the control of the taxpayer, especially in the case of investment assets.

These differing approaches can generate different structural issues in the various systems examined here. In many Continental systems, since all income derived by corporations is business income, there is no need to classify assets as capital or ordinary in that context. The situation is the same in *China* for all taxpayers. However, for assets held by individuals, the issue is whether the assets are held as business or private assets, leading either to full taxation or exemption, respectively. In a global system such as that of the U.S., the corresponding issue at the individual level is whether the assets qualify for preferential treatment or are subject to normal taxation. In systems which give a preferential rate for business-related capital gains on depreciable assets, some mechanism is necessary to "recapture" excess depreciation on the sale of an asset as ordinary income; in systems which tax all business income in the same fashion, this issue does not arise.

In all systems, the existence of a different treatment for a certain class of gains has led to statutory and jurisprudential complexity in attempting to delimit the classification of such gains. This problem is heightened by the lack of any consensus as to why gains from the disposition of certain types of assets should be given special tax treatment.

The taxation of capital gains in the *United States* has had a long and complicated history. Gain on the disposition of assets has traditionally been included in the tax base, whether or not arising in a business context. However, since 1922 certain gains for individuals have usually qualified for preferential treatment. Capital gains of corporations were also taxed at preferential rates from 1942 to 1987. The deduction of capital losses in general has been available only to the extent of the amount of capital gains, although individual taxpayers may claim a limited amount of capital losses against ordinary income. Unused capital losses can be carried forward.

At the present time, capital gains are taxed at a lower rate for individual taxpayers, who would otherwise be taxed at higher progressive rates, whereas corporate gains are taxed in full.[336] Both the treatment of capital gains and the definition of the class of gains entitled to such treatment have varied substantially over time. The result is a hodgepodge of technical rules which is impossible to rationalize.

In general terms, capital gain entitled to preferential treatment is gain realized on the sale or exchange of a capital asset which has been held for over one year. There is substantial statutory and case law material defining "capital asset," the central concept in the treatment of preferential gain. The definitional process is complicated by the fact that all gain is initially included in the capital gain category, with a number of exceptions then applying to treat the gain as ordinary income. Capital asset status is thus denied for inventory and other property held for sale to customers in the ordinary course of a business. The scope of this rule, especially in the context of real estate, has generated an enormous amount of litigation.[337]

Under complex provisions, gains on real estate and depreciable personal property used in a business are treated as capital gains if the disposition of all such property in the taxable period results in a net gain, but, inconsistently, a net loss can be deducted against ordinary income.[338] To the extent that a gain on depreciable assets is attributable to depreciation deductions which reduce the tax cost of the property, all or a portion of the gain is taxed at less-favorable preferential rates or as ordinary income, depending on the nature of the property.[339] In general, copyrights and other literary or artistic property cannot qualify as capital assets in the hands of the person who created the property;[340] an exception adopted in 2007, however, treats copyrights held by musical composers as capital assets. Patents, inventions, designs, and secret formulas are also excluded from capital asset status in the hands of the creator. However, under certain circumstances, patents held by inventors can qualify for capital asset treatment, even in circumstances where they would appear to be inventory.[341] Special rules also apply to gain from the sale of "collectibles" (e.g., stamp collections and rare coins) held for more than a year. Gain from such items is taxed at a maximum rate of 28%.

Gain from the disposition of personal assets is taxed but a deduction for losses is not allowed. Individuals may exclude USD 250,000 (USD 500,000 for married individuals filing a joint return) of the gain from the sale of a residence that was the seller's principal residence for at least two of the five years preceding the sale.[342]

The *German* system was typical of the schedular approach to capital gains taxation in Europe but has changed substantially over the years. The general rule

336. United States, IRC, s. 1(h).
337. United States, IRC, s. 1221.
338. United States, IRC, s. 1231.
339. United States, IRC, ss. 1245, 1250.
340. United States, IRC, s. 1221(a)(3).
341. United States, IRC, s. 1235.
342. United States, IRC, s. 121.

remains that private capital gains are not subject to tax and all gains realized in business are included in taxable business profits.[343] For all businesses (agricultural, commercial, and professional) run by sole proprietors and by partnerships, as well as for companies, there is no difference between business income and capital gains—both factor into the financial and fiscal accounts of the business entity. Correspondingly, capital losses realized in the course of a business are deductible in full and can be carried both forward and back. Outside the business context, gains from the disposal of real estate are taxable if the real estate is held for less than ten years,[344] and the disposal of other assets is taxable if held for less than one year.[345] Correspondingly, in general, private losses are not deductible, while losses realized in the course of a business are deductible in full.

Gains from the sale of a sole proprietorship, partnership interest, or all the shares in a wholly owned company are subject to special treatment;[346] the gain is subject to a reduced tax burden which is calculated on a notional basis. The tax authorities calculate the marginal tax rate applicable to one-fifth of the capital gain (on top of the ordinary income derived by the taxpayer in that year); the resulting tax burden on the capital gain is then multiplied by five (in order to flatten the erratic effects of higher tax brackets on the individual tax burden in a given year).[347] Capital losses from the disposal of these assets are fully deductible from profits and other income irrespective of their source.

Until December 31, 2008, gains resulting from the sale of corporate shares held for more than one year by private persons were taxable only if the participation exceeded a certain threshold.[348] The threshold was reduced from 25% to 10%, and then to 1% of a company's capital. Currently, 60% of capital gains from stock held as a business asset or which represents at least 1% of the company's share capital is taxed at the individual tax rate. Capital gains from shares held by a corporate shareholder are tax-free, except for 5% of the gain, which is intended to offset deductible expenditures related to the tax exempt gain and is effectively included in taxable income.

From 2009, all remaining capital gains from investment assets (e.g., from the sale of portfolio stock or other securities held as private assets) are subject to a final withholding tax of 25%;[349] however, taxpayers can choose to include capital gains in income if they are subject to a lower tax rate.[350] Capital losses can be set off only against capital gains of the same kind.[351]

The same basic pattern applies in *The Netherlands*,[352] except that the minimum level of shareholding for a taxable substantial participation is 5%. Capital gains and other income from a substantial participation are taxed as "box 2" income at a 33% rate

343. Germany, ITA, s. 2 para. 2.
344. Germany, ITA, s. 22 No. 2, s. 23 para. 1 No. 1.
345. Germany, ITA, s. 22 No. 1, s. 23 para. 1 No. 2.
346. Germany, ITA s. 16 paras. 1 and 3.
347. Germany, ITA, s. 34.
348. Germany, ITA, s. 17.
349. Germany, ITA, s. 20 para. 2, s. 32d para. 1, s. 43.
350. Germany, ITA, s. 32d para. 4.
351. Germany, ITA, s. 20 para. 6.
352. Netherlands, ITA, Art. 4.2.

(to the extent that the gain does not exceed EUR 67,000, the rate is 24.5%).[353] Losses from substantial participations can be carried over against gains from substantial participations; or, if the taxpayer no longer has a substantial participation, losses can generate a tax credit of 24.5% which can be used against the tax liability arising from income from business or employment (i.e., box 1 income) in the year in which the loss is incurred, and can be carried forward if there is no current tax liability.[354] In addition, there is no special tax on short-term gains, but such gains are taxed where they result from more-than-normal investment activities (e.g., restoring a building) or are based on special insider knowledge, so that a sale at a gain could be reasonably foreseen.[355]

In *Sweden*, capital gains realized by individuals outside a business context were initially taxed only if they were speculative and short-term. However, through successive reforms, taxation of capital gains has been extended; currently, all such gains are taxable as income from capital. The tax rate, 30%, is lower than the rate for business or employment income in order to partly reflect the impact of inflation. The principle set down in the tax reform of 1991 was that capital gains should be fully taxable but exceptions from the basic rules have proliferated since then. For example, capital gains for owner-occupied houses and flats in cooperative apartment houses are taxable at a 22% rate. The justification for this rule is in part based on a desire to reduce the lock-in effect, although a limited rollover is available for reinvested gains.

The basic principle for capital losses is that they are deductible up to 70% of the total loss. This limitation is intended to counter some extent taxpayers' ability to realize losses currently while deferring gains. Here, too, exceptions have proliferated, and there is no limitation for capital losses on stocks and bonds which are publicly traded. A loss on a personal residence is limited to 50% of the loss, paralleling the preferential treatment of the gain.

An overall deficit in the capital income category can be used against income in other categories after appropriate adjustment is made to reflect the fact that capital income is taxed at a preferential 30% rate. The deficit is converted into a 30% credit (for amounts above SEK 100,000, the credit is 21%), which reduces the tax on income in other categories.

As in some Continental systems, in general, *Japan* has no special rules dealing with capital gains realized by a corporation. Nor does it distinguish capital gains on business assets from gains on private assets, as is often the case with Continental systems. However, Japan has its own complex set of rules for the treatment of capital gains of individuals. In general, gains on assets held for not more than five years are fully taxable; only one-half of the gain is included in income for assets held for more than five years.[356] The tax treatment of capital gains on securities has changed frequently. Prior to 1989, gains on securities were not taxed. From 1989 to 2016, while, in general, capital gains on debt securities were not taxed, net gains on equity securities

353. Netherlands, ITA, Art. 2.12.
354. Netherlands, ITA, Art. 4.53 para. 2 jo. Art. 2.12.
355. These types of gains are taxed as income from miscellaneous activities against progressive rates (box 1); Netherlands, ITA, Art. 3.90.
356. Japan, ITA, s. 22.

were taxed at a special 20% rate (excluding local tax), although listed equity securities were entitled to a preferential tax rate. Further, since 2016, capital gains on securities are generally aggregated with other types of income derived from securities (i.e., interest on debt securities and dividends) and are taxed separately from other income. This feature has blurred the original distinction between types of income.

A separate set of rules applies to gains from real estate. In general, these rules apply higher-than-normal rates to certain real estate gains (e.g., short-term gains). They also provide for the classification of real estate gains as business income, capital gain, or occasional income, with differing consequences both to the calculation of the gain and the rate of tax. These rules reflect the special role that real estate gains have played in the Japanese domestic economy.

In *France*, the rules are complex because there is a distinction between private and professional capital gains. Business capital gains arise from the sale of fixed assets, as well as other events.[357] In 1965, a distinction was made between short-term and long-term capital gains, initially applicable to companies subject to income tax and corporate income tax. In 1997 this distinction was restricted to companies subject to income tax. For companies subject to corporate income tax, all capital gains are taxed as ordinary income at the standard rate of 25%. However, reduced rates, ranging from 10% to 19%, may apply depending on whether the sale concerns a small or medium-sized business, real estate, shares in a listed real-estate company, or a patent. Long-term gains from the sale of equity interests benefit from a reduced rate of 12%.[358] For companies subject to income tax, the treatment of capital gains or losses depends on the nature of the asset sold (depreciable or non-depreciable) and the length of time it has been on the balance sheet (more or less than two years), taking into account the distinction between short and long term. Short-term capital gains or losses are treated like any other income or loss, i.e., as ordinary income or expense, and taxed at the progressive income tax rate, with the possibility of spreading capital gains over three years.[359] Long-term capital gains or losses are treated as exceptional income or expenses, with a conditional compensation mechanism and a specific, separate tax rate of 30%.[360] Special rules exist for transfers of a company, sole proprietorship,[361] and the retirement of SME managers;[362] an annual allowance per year of ownership is intended to encourage the retention of business property.[363]

Private capital gains and losses have become subject to increased and more complicated taxes in recent years. Since 2004, the taxation of such gains has shifted from progressive taxation to proportional taxation at 19%, plus additional contributions (10.3% in 2004 and 17.2% in 2019), and the adjustment for inflation has been eliminated.[364] Since 2013, an additional tax has been levied on taxable capital gains in

357. France, CGI, s. 39 duodecies.
358. France, CGI, s. 219 I-a quinquies.
359. France, CGI, s. 39 quaterdecies.
360. France, CGI, s. 39 quindecies.
361. France, CGI, s. 41.
362. France, CGI, s. 151 septies A.
363. France, CGI, s. 151 septies B.
364. France, CGI, s. 150-U sq.

excess of EUR 50,000 at a rate from 2% to 6%, depending on the amount of the capital gain.[365] Similarly, the tax regime for capital gains and losses on securities has also changed considerably. For instance, capital gains realized by individuals on the sale of securities, corporate rights, and similar securities were taxed at 19% plus 15.5% for social security contributions, until 2013, when they began to be taxed on a progressive income tax scale. In 2018, these capital gains were again taxed proportionally; they are now taxed at a flat rate of 12.8% plus 17.2% for social security contributions,[366] although sales of movable and immovable property remain taxable at 19%, plus 17.2% for social security contributions.[367] The Finance Act for 2019 created a new category for the optional taxation of capital gains on digital assets either at a proportional rate of 30% or on the progressive scale.[368] These successive changes, the distinction between private and professional capital gains, and the existence of several special regimes make compliance difficult for taxpayers.

The development of capital gains taxation in the *United Kingdom*, *Canada*, and *Australia* has, in general, taken a somewhat different course. As indicated above, initially, gains on the disposition of assets outside the business context generally were not taxed. Within the business context, a distinction was drawn between inventory and current assets as compared to fixed and long-term assets. Only gains on inventory and current assets were subject to the income tax. In both the private and business settings, gains from the disposition of "capital assets" were not included in the tax base due to the "trust" concept of income (i.e., the income beneficiaries of a trust were not entitled to any appreciation in the value of the trust assets). Moreover, under the source concept of income, a capital gain could be considered to be derived from the disposition of the "source" itself rather than income from a source. Subsequently, all three systems (UK (1965), Canada (1972), and Australia (1985)) adopted separate systems for the taxation of capital gains which cover both private gains and gains on the disposition of capital assets used in a business. In addition, in the case of the UK and Australia, and to a lesser degree, Canada, the CGT legislation was used to mitigate certain defects and problems which had emerged in the operation of the traditional income tax system. Thus, the CGT system is, to some degree, a parallel taxing system which does substantially more than simply include gains from a certain class of assets in the tax base. With their somewhat parallel histories, the Commonwealth systems have a number of common features.

The *United Kingdom* adopted a short-term CGT as part of the income tax in 1962 and then enacted a separate tax on capital gains in 1965. The system has been modified several times since then, as discussed in the UK chapter in Part I. In formal structure, the CGT is a separate tax for individuals but a part of the corporation tax for capital gains realized by corporations. The outcomes are often, but not always, the same.[369] The basic structure of the tax is to impose a charge on gains from all dispositions of

365. France, CGI, s. 1609 nonies G.
366. France, CGI, s. 150 0-A.
367. France, CGI, s. 150 UA sq. and 200 B.
368. France, CGI, 150 VH bis.
369. United Kingdom, TCGA, s. 1; CTA 2009, ss. 2 and 4.

assets and then to exempt a number of types of gains from the tax. These include gains which are otherwise subject to the income tax—e.g., profit on the sale of inventory, gain from certain private assets (cars and personal residences), gain on certain government securities, and a number of other miscellaneous exceptions, including gain on the disposal of a decoration for valor acquired otherwise than for money or money's worth (!) A *de minimis* rule excludes gains and losses on personal assets which are disposed of for less than GBP 6,000. Relief for the effects of inflation was introduced in 1982;[370] this took the form of an adjustment to the tax cost of the asset. In its present form, the indexation system does not apply to create a loss on the disposition of a capital asset, although previously such treatment was possible. This indexation basis still applies for the corporate income tax but has been frozen from January 2018.

In 1998, indexation ceased to apply to taxpayers subject to CGT, principally individuals and trusts; from 1998 to 2008, these taxpayers had a "taper relief" instead. Taper relief was introduced in 1998 and applies only for years since then—so that an asset held since 1990 and disposed of in 2007 would have its early years dealt with under the indexation system and its later years under taper relief.[371] The taper relief was applied to the gain. The relief distinguished between business assets and nonbusiness assets, with business assets attracting a more generous taper. Business assets attracted a 75% reduction after just a two-year holding period, so that a gain otherwise taxable at 40% was taxed only at 10%; nonbusiness assets got a maximum reduction of 40%, and only after ten years, so that a gain taxed at 40% was taxed at 24%. The relief never resulted in a 0% rate. In 2008, as part of a simplification exercise, taper relief was abolished for those trusts and individuals subject to CGT. As part of the same simplification, the indexation relief which had been frozen since 1998 was abolished (i.e., for all disposals after April 5, 2008).[372]

The rate of tax on capital gains has varied, with a preferential rate applicable for certain periods. For companies, gains are added to the company's income to arrive at the profit subject to corporation tax. Individuals receive different treatment; they pay tax at either 10% or 20%, depending on the individual's income tax band, as explained in more detail in the UK chapter in Part I; the rates increase to 18% and 28% where the asset is a residential property or a carried interest. An annual exemption of GBP 6,000 applies in 2023-2024, which decreases to GBP 3,000 from April 1, 2024.[373] There is a special "business asset disposal relief," which, in effect, applies a 10% rate on business gains up to GBP 10 million (per lifetime).[374] Trustees pay tax on trust gains realized during administration at the trust rate, generally 20%, but 24% on residential property and 28% on carried interests; this may actually result in a higher rate than if the receipt had been treated as income. An annual exemption is available for trusts at a maximum of GBP 3,000 and a minimum of GBP 600 (for 2023-2024), depending on the number of

370. United Kingdom, TCGA, ss. 52A et seq.
371. For (repealed) taper relief *see* United Kingdom, TCGA, s. 2A and Sch. 7.
372. United Kingdom, TCGA, s. 4 as amended by Finance Act 2008, s. 8.
373. United Kingdom, TCGA, s. 3.
374. United Kingdom, Finance Act 2008, s. 9 inserting TCGA, ss. 169H et seq., etc.

settlements the settlor has made. If a trust is for a "vulnerable beneficiary," the trust is ignored and the gains are charged as if they had accrued to the beneficiary.[375]

Capital losses are, in general, deductible only against capital gains, although losses on securities in unlisted trading companies can be deducted in full. Individuals and trusts can sometimes apply trading losses against capital gains. There is a broader offset for trading losses against capital gains receipts in the corporate income tax.[376]

In *Canada*, initially, one-half of net capital gains was included in income; the includable portion was later increased to three-quarters and then reduced again to one-half in 2000.[377] In 2024, the inclusion rate for individuals was increased from one-half to two-thirds for capital gains exceeding CAD 250,000 in a given year; for corporations and trusts, the inclusion rate is now two-thirds for any amount of gains. A substantial lifetime exemption for individuals was introduced in 1988, but it was controversial and has been eliminated except with respect to family farms, family fishing operations, and shares of small business corporations.[378] The value of the lifetime exemption has been increased over time and represents a significant tax preference (in 2024 the maximum exemption is over CAD 1 million). Capital losses are in general deductible only against capital gains, although full deduction is allowed for certain losses incurred with respect to investments in small business corporations (referred to as "allowable business investment losses"). Losses can be carried back three years and forward indefinitely.

Special rules apply to "personal-use" property. Where the proceeds of disposition or adjusted cost base of the property are less than CAD 1,000, the proceeds or cost are deemed to be CAD 1,000. This provision is a type of *de minimis* rule which is intended to eliminate the need to keep records with respect to relatively small properties, although the amount has not been increased since 1972. In addition, losses are deductible only with respect to personal-use assets which have a potential investment character (e.g., coins, rare books, and artworks) and can be used only against gains with respect to the same type of property. Thus, a deduction for losses due to the decline in value of consumer durables is not allowed. In addition, gain on the disposition of a principal residence is exempt, without any limits.

In an attempt to reduce the amount of litigation concerning the distinction between ordinary income and capital gains, certain taxpayers are permitted to make a one-time irrevocable election to treat all gains in respect of all subsequent dispositions of "Canadian securities" to be on capital account. This election prevents taxpayers from claiming capital gains treatment in respect of gains and ordinary loss treatment in respect of losses from dispositions of Canadian securities. It is not available to traders in securities, financial institutions, or nonresidents.

Until 1999, the *Australian* system taxed capital gains at ordinary rates, with indexation of gains but not losses.[379] Indexation applied only if the asset was held for

375. On trusts in general, *see* United Kingdom, TCGA, Part 3 Ch. 2.
376. United Kingdom, TCGA, s. 2; on set-off of trading loss *see* TCGA, s. 261B, 261C and ITA, s. 71. On trading losses for CT, CTA 2010, ss. 37, 45-46 and *see also* TCGA, s. 8.
377. The capital gains rules are found mainly in ss. 38-55 of Canada, ITA.
378. Canada, ITA, s. 110.6.
379. The capital gains general rules are found in Australia, ITAA 1997, Part 3-1.

more than twelve months and applied only to the asset and not to associated liabilities. In 1999, the indexation regime was effectively replaced by a 50% discount on gains after offset of losses where an asset is held for twelve months. Companies are not entitled to the discount but were allowed to keep indexation up to the end of September 1999.

Capital losses are deductible against capital gains, but not against other income. Excess capital losses may be carried forward indefinitely to offset capital gains. Rules similar to those in Canada apply to gains and losses on personal assets and exempt gains on the disposition of a principal residence.

When Canada and the UK introduced the taxation of capital gains, assets were valued at the time of enactment for purposes of calculating gain or loss so that only capital gains or losses accruing after that time were taken into account. The UK rule was subsequently changed to a later valuation date in connection with the introduction of indexation.[380] Australia applied its CGT only to assets acquired after a certain date, thus necessitating complex rules preserving the "pre" and "post" character of gains (e.g., in the case of rollovers).

In *China*, capital gains are treated like investment income. Capital gains are computed by deducting the cost of acquiring the property from the proceeds of the transfer. Gains realized by resident individuals from the sale of publicly listed shares in China that are held for more than one month are taxed at preferential rates. Gains from selling a residence that has been owned and used for at least five years are tax exempt.

In *India*, capital gains are computed by deducting from the consideration received for the transfer the cost of acquisition of the asset, the expenditure incurred wholly and exclusively in connection with the transfer, and the cost of any improvements to the asset. Where the actual consideration cannot be determined or is not ascertainable, the fair market value of the asset is the consideration.[381] The determination of the cost of acquisition of financial assets, such as rights to acquire shares and bonus shares, has generated many disputes because the courts have held that the diminution of share value as a result of an issue of rights or bonus shares must be taken into account.[382] Currently, the ITA provides that in such cases, the cost to the shareholder is the actual amount paid and where nothing is paid, the cost is nil.[383] In special circumstances, the cost of the asset to the previous owner is taken as the cost of the asset to the transferee. This rollover treatment applies to gifts, bequests, partition of a HUF, the dissolution of a partnership, the liquidation of a company, and a transfer by an Indian subsidiary to its parent company or vice versa.

Indexation of the cost is allowed in the case of long-term capital gains, subject to certain conditions, as discussed below.[384] For assets other than equity shares or listed

380. For the original rule, *see* United Kingdom, Finance Act 1965; for 1982 rebasing, *see* TCGA, s. 35.
381. India, ITA 1961, s. 50D.
382. *Miss Dhun Dadabhoy Kapadia v. CIT*, 63 ITR 651 (SC); and *Escorts Farms (Ramgarh) Ltd v. CIT*, 222 ITR 509(SC).
383. India, ITA 1961, s. 55(2)(aa).
384. The cost inflation index is prescribed each year by the CBDT. For the cost inflation index for the financial year 2018-2019 *see* https://www.incometaxindia.gov.in/charts%20%20tables/cost-inflation-index.htm.

securities acquired before 2001, effective 2018-2019, taxpayers have the option to use the fair market value of the asset on April 1, 2001, as the cost of acquisition.[385] The distinction between long-term and short-term gains is based on the nature of the asset and the holding period. Listed assets, including shares, bonds, debentures, interests in trusts, zero coupon bonds, and units in equity mutual funds must be held for at least 12 months to qualify as long-term; for other assets, including unlisted shares, gold, and immovable property, the minimum holding period is 24 months.[386] Gains on unlisted bonds and debentures are taxed at the applicable rate irrespective of the holding period.[387] The tax rate is 12.5% on long-term gains and 20% on short-term gains; those rates apply to both residents and nonresidents. Inflation relief has been eliminated for immovable property, gold, and unlisted shares for transfers after July 23, 2024, except that the cost of such property acquired before April 2001 can be stepped up to its fair market value on that date at the taxpayer's option;[388] individuals and HUF can choose to pay tax at 12.5% on gains with respect to immovable property acquired before July 23, 2024 without any indexation relief or 20% with indexation relief.[389]

Since long-term capital gains are given preferential treatment, losses arising from the transfer of long-term capital assets can be set off only against long-term capital gains.[390] Excess losses can be carried forward for eight years.[391] Losses from the transfer of short-term capital assets can be set off against any other capital gains—both short-term and long-term[392]—and any excess can be carried forward for eight years.[393] Capital losses cannot be set off against any income under any other category of income.[394]

The following Table II-1 summarizes some of the inclusion rules discussed in Subpart B. To deal with the issues which arise in connection with schedular systems, the headings indicate the type of situation being considered. For example, in connection with Windfalls, the assumption is that the windfall does not occur in a business setting or in connection with profit-seeking activities. Similarly, with respect to Illegal Income, the assumption is that the income would otherwise fall into a taxable category if the factor of illegality were not involved.

385. India, ITA 1961, Explanation (b) to s. 55(2).
386. India, ITA 1961, s. 2(42A).
387. India, ITA, s. 50AA.
388. India, ITA 1961, s. 55(2)(b)(i).
389. The 2024 amendment states that where the tax calculated under the new regime at 12.5% without indexation relief exceeds the tax calculated at 20% with indexation, the excess shall be ignored. India, ITA 1961, s. 112(1)(a), second proviso.
390. India, ITA 1961, s. 70(3).
391. India, ITA 1961, s. 74(1)(b) and 74(2).
392. India, ITA 1961, s. 70(2).
393. India, ITA 1961, s. 74(1)(a) and 74(2).
394. India, ITA 1961, s. 71(3).

Table II-1 Some Aspects of the Tax Base: Inclusions

	Imputed Rental Income from Residence	*Personal Gifts*	*Business Gifts*	*Windfalls (Nonbusiness/ Profit-Seeking)*	*Illegal Income (Otherwise Taxable)*	*Public Subsidies (Business Context)*	*Debt Cancellation (Business Context)*
Australia	excluded	excluded	included	excluded	included	generally included	reduce tax cost or losses if capital; taxable if ordinary
Canada	excluded	excluded	included	excluded	included	included or tax cost reduction	reduce tax cost or losses if capital; taxable if ordinary
China	excluded	excluded	excluded generally	included	included	included for enterprises	included
France	excluded	excluded	included under certain conditions	generally excluded	included	generally included	included
Germany	mainly excluded	excluded	included under certain conditions	excluded	included	included or tax cost reduction	included

	Imputed Rental Income from Residence	*Personal Gifts*	*Business Gifts*	*Windfalls (Nonbusiness/ Profit-Seeking)*	*Illegal Income (Otherwise Taxable)*	*Public Subsidies (Business Context)*	*Debt Cancellation (Business Context)*
India	included in principle, but exempt for 2 residences	Included (if in excess of INR 50,000) unless received from a close relative or on death or marriage	included except for gifts to employees of less than INR 5,000	excluded, except lottery winnings included	included	included or tax cost reduction	generally included
Japan	excluded	excluded	included	included	included	included or tax-cost reduction	included
The Netherlands	included	excluded	included generally	excluded	included	generally not included	generally excluded (exception regarding prior losses)
Sweden	mainly excluded	excluded	included generally	excluded	included	included or tax-cost reduction	included if solvent; if not, excluded but loss reduction

United Kingdom	excluded	excluded	excluded (if not for business purposes)	excluded		included	included (unless specific)	generally excluded (unless business tax benefit from prior deduction)
United States	excluded	excluded	generally included (employee always includes)	included		included	included	included or tax cost/loss reduction

SUBPART C
Deductions

The basic notion that an income tax is, in general, imposed on net income—gross revenue reduced by deductions—and not on some broader category of receipts, is a fundamental premise of all the systems considered here. Although the implementation of this principle takes numerous forms, there are some common features. All the systems recognize that, in general, expenditures deductible in computing income must have some connection to taxable activities and that, at least in most cases, expenditures for personal consumption should not be deductible. The systems also distinguish between expenses which reduce income of the current period and capital expenditures which are taken into account through some sort of capital cost recovery system. In some systems, all income-related expenses are in principle deductible unless otherwise limited. In others, deduction is restricted to a more specific catalog of expenditures. In addition to a deduction for expenses necessary to properly determine net income, a number of systems allow deductions for certain personal expenses.

Beyond the definition of deductible expenses, all the systems display important schedular aspects in connection with deductions. Even where income is defined in a global fashion, various classes of deductions are often limited to reducing only certain categories of income.

Many systems have special rules dealing with deductions by employees. Some systems allow a standardized deduction from employment income but disallow specific employee deductions. In other situations, only a limited class of employee deductions is allowed, and then often only to the extent that the expenses exceed a certain floor. Limitations of this sort are based on the administrative difficulty of policing such deductions and the concern that, without limitations, substantial amounts of personal, living, and consumption costs would be deducted, whether deliberately or by mistake. These limitations are usually not applicable to an individual's business or professional income, although arguably the same problems exist there. Where employee deductions are restricted and not offset by some sort of lump-sum or standard deduction, but professional and business deductions are allowed without limitation, the general effect is to favor higher-income taxpayers.

Another recurring feature in the treatment of employees is an inconsistency between those costs which can be deducted if incurred directly and those which are excluded if reimbursed by an employer. The exclusion rules are usually more generous than the deduction rules. This may be explained in part by the assumption (perhaps mistaken in the case of small businesses) that the income-earning connection is more likely to be predominant if the employer is willing to bear the cost, at least in those cases where it is clear that the expense does not simply represent additional compensation. The exclusion thus serves as a netting of income and deduction for costs which are assumed to be income-earning because they are reimbursed.

Other limitations typically restrict losses arising from interest and capital-recovery deductions. These limitations frequently arise in response to perceived problems with "tax-shelter" investments. The various limitations on deductions are discussed after a consideration of the substantive deduction rules.

1 MIXED BUSINESS AND PERSONAL EXPENSES

All the systems analyzed here must deal with the basic problem of expenditures which have both an income-producing and a consumption dimension. The responses to the problem differ somewhat, in both general approach and specific rules. Following a description of the countries' general approaches to the problem, there is a discussion of selected expenses that usually have both personal and income-earning components. The same issue arises for both unreimbursed outlays incurred by individuals and outlays borne by an employer where the benefit is enjoyed by an individual (because the benefit is provided or paid for by the employer or the employee's expense is reimbursed by the employer), although the systems discussed below do not always equate the two situations.

Germany has a general statutory provision which disallows the deduction of any expense related to the economic or social position of the taxpayer even if it serves the taxpayer's profession or business.[395] Until 2009, the courts derived from this rule a general prohibition against the deduction of expenses of "mixed" character unless there was a specific statutory rule allowing such a deduction (e.g., business meals). In 2009, the Federal Tax Court overruled this line of judgments in a case dealing with the cost of a journey of mixed professional and private character.[396] Since then, a deduction is wholly denied only where business and private aspects are entangled in a way that makes it impossible to identify any reasonable criterion for allocating the expense; otherwise in general, an apportionment must be made.

In *Japan*, the "prohibition of division and deduction" appears to be based on the idea that, for reasons of tax equity, consumption should be included in the tax base, even if the consumption necessarily takes place in a business context.[397] Only in very limited circumstances, where the personal element is *de minimis* or the business and personal elements can be clearly separated, is any deduction allowed.

395. Germany, ITA, s. 12 No. 1.
396. Federal Tax Court (*Bundesfinanzhof*), September 21, 2009, GrS 1/06.
397. Japan, ITA, s. 45 para. 1 No. 1; OEITA, s. 96.

The *United Kingdom* reaches the same result using a somewhat different analysis, but attention must also be paid to the particular source of income. With respect to a trade or profession, deductions are allowed if they are incurred "wholly and exclusively" in connection with trade or professional activities; for business income, the test is based on the purpose behind the expenditure. However, the apparent breadth of this rule is offset by an absolute prohibition on the deduction of "dual-purpose" expenditures and by the refusal of the courts to apply the purpose test simply on the basis of what taxpayers say their purpose was.[398] In contrast, where a deduction relates to employment income, the general test requires that the expense be incurred wholly, exclusively, and necessarily in the performance of the duties of the office or employment. This language has been interpreted to mean that expenses of getting into a position to earn income, as opposed to the actual performance of the activities which generate the income, are not deductible, and has influenced the treatment of expenses involving commuting, moving, childcare, and the like.[399] The divergence between business and employment income deduction rules should not be exaggerated. In many of these instances, the expenditure would not be deductible against business income either, usually on the ground that it was incurred for mixed personal and business purposes.

The approach in *India* is somewhat similar. Under section 28 of Chapter IV of the ITA, profits or gains of any business or profession, as well as several other items (including interest, salary, bonus, commission, or remuneration received by a partner of a firm, noncompetition payments, and amounts received under a keyman insurance policy) must be included in income. Section 37 provides a general rule with respect to the deduction of expenses in computing business income, under which expenses (other than capital and personal expenses) are deductible only if "laid out or expended wholly and exclusively for the purpose of the business or profession." Apportionment of personal and business elements is possible and specifically recognized with respect to the deduction of rent of a building partly used for business.[400] The courts have interpreted section 37 liberally and not allowed the tax authorities to dictate how taxpayers should run their businesses. However, penalties and illegal payments, as well as certain social responsibility payments by companies, are not deductible.

In addition to this general rule, the courts have held that certain types of losses (e.g., from damage to or destruction of inventory, losses of amounts advanced in connection with a business, and embezzlement by employees) are deductible under section 28 itself, despite the fact that there is no specific provision in the ITA dealing with such losses.

There are also specific provisions in the ITA both allowing and disallowing the deduction of certain business expenditures. Sections 30-36 provide, subject to certain conditions, express deductions for certain specific expenses relating to business, including rent, taxes, repairs, and insurance with respect to buildings (other than capital expenditures), current repairs to plant, machinery, and furniture used for the

398. *Mallalieu v. Drummond* [1983] STC 665.
399. United Kingdom, ITTOIA, s. 34, CTA 2009, s. 54; ITEPA, s. 336.
400. India, ITA 1961, s. 38.

purpose of a business, depreciation, investments in certain depressed geographical areas, and scientific research. However, the deduction of certain expenditures is expressly disallowed. Such amounts include payments subject to withholding tax where the payer fails to withhold the tax,[401] payments of INR 10,000 or more in one day (INR 35,000 or more in one day for a business of transporting goods) otherwise than by check or bank draft or through the use of the electronic clearing system of a bank, statutory dues such as income and wealth taxes, and gratuities (subject to certain exceptions).

Certain deductions are allowed only when the amount is actually paid, even where the taxpayer uses the accrual method of accounting. Originally, this rule was limited to taxes, duties, and surtaxes; however, it has been expanded to a wide variety of expenses, including interest paid to banks and financial institutions, bonuses or commissions paid to employees, contributions to provident funds, and payments to small enterprises.

In *Canada*, the treatment of mixed business/personal expenses is a hodgepodge of statutory rules and administrative practice. In general, expenses must be categorized as either personal or business. They are deductible either in full or not at all, with the exception of business meals and entertainment, one-half of which is deductible. Where, however, an expense can be apportioned on some objective, verifiable basis, such as automobile expenses, the tax authorities allow the appropriate portion of the cost to be deductible. There is nothing in the statute to prohibit the apportionment of mixed business and personal expenses.

Even in countries like *Australia*, where apportionment of expenses as deductions is explicitly recognized,[402] the occasion and nature of the apportionment is still debated. For example, if a person flies to a foreign country for one week of business activities and one week of holiday, it is necessary to apportion the costs of accommodation, but it is not clear whether the airfare would be subject to apportionment or an all-or-nothing test.

In general, the *United States* seeks to apportion expenses between the personal nondeductible component and deductible business component. But in some cases, expenses may be treated as inherently personal and a deduction denied for the entire expense even though it could be viewed as having a business aspect. Thus, for example, commuting expenses are treated as inherently personal and a deduction is denied. In other instances, such as in the case of business meals, an arbitrary bright line is drawn and a deduction for the cost of 50% of the meal is permitted.[403] As a revenue-saving device (expired in 2025), the U.S. denies a deduction for most unreimbursed employee expenses,[404] in effect treating such expenses as inherently personal.

401. Since 2005, this rule also applies to domestic payments but currently only 30% of the amount payable is not deductible. If the tax is actually withheld or paid in a subsequent year, a deduction is allowed in that year. The denial of the deduction does not apply if the taxpayer can prove that the payee has paid tax on the payment.
402. Australia, ITAA 1997, s. 8-1.
403. United States, IRC, s. 274(n).
404. United States, IRC, s. 67(g).

In *Sweden*, the general approach is to attempt to identify the portion of the cost related to the business aspect of the expense. For example, costs for books and other reading material cannot be deducted, even if used in a business, if the material is such that it could reasonably be assumed that it would have been purchased for nonbusiness reasons. In contrast, an instrumentalist in an orchestra was allowed to deduct dental costs that were necessary for him to continue performing and which he would not otherwise have incurred. Deductible costs are, however, allowed only for amounts exceeding SEK 5,000.

The *French* approach is somewhat similar. No general principle prohibits the deduction of mixed expenses; the apportionment is made on a case-by-case basis and the taxpayer must make "a fair apportionment between deductible business expenses and non-deductible personal expenses."[405]

In *The Netherlands*, employees are not entitled to deduct from their employment income any employment-related expenses which they incur and pay themselves; the only exception is for commuting expenses, which are deductible at fixed amounts (*see* below section 1.1 below).

Since the introduction of the Work-Related Expense Scheme (*Werkkostenregeling* or WKR) in 2011, reimbursements made by an employer to an employee for employment-related expenses, along with the value of any employment-related goods and services provided by the employer to the employee, may or may not be received tax free by the employee, depending on the category to which they belong. The categories are:[406]

- zero-value provisions: not taxed to the employee and tax-deductible by the employer. In general, such benefits are limited to those consumed or used in the workplace, e.g., small bites, coffee, tea, office parties, housing (*see* further section 1.3 below), and clothing;
- exempt reimbursements and provisions: not taxed to the employee and tax-deductible by the employer. Examples include study costs, moving expenses, and commuting expenses (*see* section 1.1 below);
- other reimbursements and provisions by the employer to the employee to the extent that the employer treats them as WKR reimbursements and provisions: the amount can be deducted by the employer (for corporate income tax purposes) and is tax-free (no wage withholding tax and no individual income inclusion) to the employee to the extent of a tax-free allowance based on the total amount of taxable wages paid by the employer to the employee. Reimbursements and provisions in excess of the tax-free allowance are subject to a final withholding tax levy of 80% at the employer's expense; and
- other reimbursements and provisions by the employer to the employee which are not treated by the employer as covered by the WKR regime: the amounts can be deducted by the employer (for corporate income tax purposes) but is taxable to the employee.

405. France, Administrative doctrine, February 18, 2014, BOI-BIC-CHG-30-20 n°40.
406. Netherlands, Withholding Tax Act (WTA), Art. 31 and 31a.

In *China*, under the IIT, deductions are allowed only in computing income from business/productive activities. As a result, the issue of "mixed business and personal expenses" arises only in respect of this category of income. In practice, such individual business income earners are likely to be taxed on presumptive income. Under the EIT, reasonable expenses incurred for income-earning purposes are deductible. Although there are no specific rules on mixed business and personal expenses, apportionment is possible.

Whatever the general (typically case law-developed) rules, commonly recurring costs such as commuting, business entertainment, and moving are often dealt with in special statutory provisions setting forth the conditions for and limits on deductions. The rules are not always consistent with any general theory. One common approach is the allowance of a specified percentage of costs which typically have a significant consumption content, such as meals and entertainment. Strict substantiation requirements are also usually associated with such expenses. The following material examines some selected deductions which involve mixed business and personal components.

1.1 Commuting

Commuting expenses have a clear business connection in that, on the one hand, they are necessary to place the taxpayer in a position to begin income-producing activity; on the other hand, the level of commuting expense is tied up with the personal decision as to where to live in relation to the workplace and the means of transportation used. While several systems deny commuting deductions altogether, a number provide a limited deduction.

Thus, in the *United States*, the costs of commuting, defined as traveling from the taxpayer's personal residence to the principal place of work, are, in general, nondeductible. However, once a taxpayer is in "work status," traveling expenses between work sites are deductible so long as the taxpayer is not an employee.[407] A complex set of case law and administrative rules deals with the myriad issues which arise in applying this distinction. For example, the costs of occasional travel directly from the personal residence to a secondary work site are deductible; a taxpayer is not required to go first to the principal work site.

The commuting expenses of employees which qualify for deduction, like most other employee expenses, have historically been subject to a limit: such employee expenses were deductible only to the extent that they, together with other miscellaneous deductions, exceed 2% of income. However, even this limited deduction has been suspended until after 2025.[408]

Similarly, commuting expenses are not deductible in *Canada*, following earlier UK cases which reached the same result. Costs incurred to put the taxpayer in the position to earn income are not incurred in the course of work and are therefore viewed

407. United States, IRC, s. 67(g) prohibits the deduction of "miscellaneous itemized deductions." Unreimbursed employee expenses, including travel expenses, are a type of "miscellaneous itemized deduction."

408. *Ibid.*

as essentially personal. The costs are also related to the personal choice of where to live. As in the U.S., the expenses of traveling in the course of business are generally deductible. In some Canadian cases, taxpayers attempted to circumvent the rule by establishing home offices and claiming the home/business trip was in the course of business; substantial restrictions on the deductibility of home office expenses eliminated this tactic. In contrast, travel between two or more work sites away from home is allowed as a deduction. From 2007 to the end of 2017, a modest tax credit (15%) was available for the cost of public transit passes, but there was no requirement for the passes to be used for the purpose of commuting to work or school; this credit was eliminated from 2017.

In the *United Kingdom*, the deduction of commuting expenses was denied in the case of a barrister who worked at home. The barrister's office was his principal place of work and the cost of travel home in the evening was held to be personal, even though he also worked at home. Because the cost of travel was not "wholly and exclusively" business-related,[409] it was not deductible. In contrast, travel between two (exclusive) work sites is allowed as a deduction. The legislation on employment income (rewritten in 2003) allows a deduction for travel expenses which are "necessarily incurred" in the performance of the duties of the employment—words which usually mean that a taxpayer's claim to deduct the costs of travel from home to work will fail. A further rule allowing the costs of travel for "necessary attendance" is more generous for travel to temporary workplaces but contains an express exclusion for "ordinary commuting."[410]

Australian case law has followed the same pattern, also basing its analysis on UK cases. A decision in the High Court of Australia disturbed the common understanding that work-related travel was deductible when two separate income-earning activities were involved (in the particular case, one source was employment and the other was a business).[411] The government legislated to reinstate the common understanding.[412]

Similarly, in *India*, commuting expenses are not deductible. A statutory provision which previously granted an allowance for employees for such expenses was eliminated in 2018 when the standard deduction was increased.

In *Germany*, the deductibility of commuting expenses has been the subject of much political debate, legislative action, and a judgment of the Federal Constitutional Court. Until 2007, the statute provided a lump-sum deduction per kilometer. In 2007, this deduction was restricted to commuting in excess of 20 kilometers. The new rule was challenged in a constitutional review, and the Federal Constitutional Court held that a distinction based on distance violated the principle of equality since it lacked any reasonable rationale apart from fiscal considerations.[413] Consequently, in 2009, the previous legal framework was restored retroactively; it provides a deduction of EUR 0.30 per kilometer for the shortest route between the taxpayer's home and workplace

409. *Sargent v. Barnes* [1978] STC 322. *See also Samad Samadian v. HMRC* [2014] UKUT 13 (TCC).
410. United Kingdom, ITEPA, ss. 337 et seq.
411. *Payne* [2001] HCA 3, 202 CLR 93.
412. Australia, ITAA 1997, ss. 25-100.
413. Federal Constitutional Court (*Bundesverfassungsgericht*), December 9, 2008, 2 BvL 1/07 et seq.

regardless of the method of transportation, capped at EUR 4,500 per year.[414] In 2019, the deduction for travel in excess of 21 kilometers was increased for a transitional period until 2026; this provision is meant to alleviate the burden created by increased carbon pricing.

In *Sweden*, although in principle commuting expenses are viewed as personal, a special statutory provision allows the deduction of commuting expenses to the extent that they exceed SEK 11,000 per year. Only "reasonable" expenses are allowed, which in practice means the cost of public transportation. Taxpayers can deduct the costs of traveling by car only if it can be established that use of the car saves at least two hours per day in commuting time. The deduction is limited to a per-kilometer amount intended to cover the marginal costs of the car; in addition, the trip must be between the taxpayer's "residence" and workplace, which excludes costs of traveling from a summer house to work (a common occurrence in Sweden).

In *The Netherlands*, commuting costs were originally considered to be personal and nondeductible. Later, as housing shortages caused more people to live at a substantial distance from work, case law began allowing deductions in some situations. Beginning in 1964, legislation has allowed employees a limited fixed deduction for commuting expenses. Since 2001, the deduction has been restricted to expenses for commuting by public transportation;[415] it is intended to reflect both environmental and traffic considerations, as well as the mixed nature of the expenses. If an employer designates the reimbursement of commuting expenses as a final levy component for the WKR (as discussed above), the reimbursement is not taxable to the employee. The compensation for kilometers driven by car is EUR 0.23 per kilometer.[416]

The treatment of commuting expenses in *Japan* might be easier to understand as a dual regime for employees and self-employed individuals. For employees, the principles and practical issues are similar to those in other countries; a specific deduction for commuting expenses is allowed but strictly limited. Commuting costs for employees are usually paid by employers as a part of salary and are tax exempt for employees up to a certain ceiling.[417] Commuting expenses incurred by employees which are not covered by the employer are deductible at the election of the employee as a part of a "specific expenses deduction"[418] to the extent that the total of employment expenses eligible for the specific or itemized expenses deduction exceeds half of the amount of a standard "employment income deduction" (which varies with income but often amounts to 30% to 40% of an employee's salary, with a cap of JPY 1,950,000). While this standard deduction performs several functions, its main function is to alleviate the administrative burden of dealing with itemized deductions for employee expenses.[419] The itemized expenses deduction is intended to supplement the standard deduction and is permitted as an addition to, rather than a replacement for,

414. Germany, ITA, s. 9 para. 1 sent. 3 No. 4.
415. Netherlands, ITA, Art. 3.87.
416. This is the rate in 2024. Netherlands, WTA, Art. 13a.
417. Japan, ITA, s. 9 para. 1 No. 5.
418. Japan, ITA, s. 57-2.
419. In addition to the administrative burden, it has been suggested that the large standard deduction was related to the fact that salaries and wages were more likely to be reported than

the standard deduction. Only a very small number of taxpayers actually utilize the deduction for itemized expenses, despite the availability of the additional deduction, because of the generous standard deduction. However, this situation may change in the near future since the standard deduction has recently been reduced and the scope of specific deductions expanded.

In *France*, the general principle is that actual business travel expenses can be deducted, or employees can opt to deduct fuel expenses based on a per-kilometer rate,[420] provided that the distance between home and work is not "abnormal." "Normal" usually means a maximum of 40 kilometers unless the taxpayer can justify the extra distance on social or business grounds.[421] Most employees (95%) do not take itemized deductions for expenses such as commuting but instead elect a standard deduction of 10% of their compensation.[422] Under French industrial law, employers must cover 50% of the cost of public transport passes or public bicycle-rental services taken out by employees. These reimbursements are deductible to the employer and exempt in the hands of the employee.

1.2 Moving Expenses

Like commuting, moving expenses have both business and personal elements. Some moves may be entirely personally motivated while other moves may be required by the employer. Again, the countries' approaches vary. However, in many cases, employer-reimbursed expenses are not included in income, even though directly incurred expenses in the same situation are not deductible. This approach, in effect, uses the fact of employer reimbursement as a proxy for the establishment of a necessary income-earning connection for the move.

In the *United States*, case law originally held moving expenses to be nondeductible in the same manner as commuting expenses. However, administrative practice allowed the exclusion of certain employer-reimbursed expenses, creating a disparity both between directly incurred expenses and reimbursed expenses, and between different categories of reimbursed expenses. The statutory resolution was to allow a deduction for a limited category of moving expenses or, alternatively, to allow taxpayers to exclude from gross income reimbursement received for such expenses from the employer.[423] To be deductible or excludable, the move had to be in connection with the commencement of work at a new place of business and had to meet certain distance requirements. Unlike commuting expenses, moving expenses were not subject to a percentage-of-income limitation. However, the deduction for moving expenses

---

income in other categories, taxes were paid more promptly due to withholding and, more broadly, that it functioned as a surrogate for a deduction for "human capital."

420. France, CGI, s. 83 3° para. 8 and Regulatory Schedule IV, s. 6 B.
421. France, Administrative doctrine, August 30, 2016, BOI-BIC-CHG_40-20-40, n°60 (self-employed) and CGI, s. 83 3° para. 7 (employees).
422. France, CGI, s. 83 3° paras. 2 through 4.
423. United States, IRC, s. 217,132(a)(6).

and the exclusion for reimbursed expenses have, in general, been suspended until after 2025.[424]

In *Germany*, there are no special statutory rules dealing with moving costs. In some circumstances, they are deductible under case law principles interpreting the general deduction for income-producing expenses: the move must be exclusively or nearly exclusively for a business reason. The most frequent justification is a change of job location (which is itself assumed to be business-related). Without a change of job, a move can be business-related if it results in a saving of travel time to the job of at least one hour per day. Where the move is found to be business-related, a deduction is allowed for moving expenses incurred up to the amount which would have been paid as reimbursed expenses to a civil servant for a similar move, without proof of the actual costs. Higher costs can be deducted, but taxpayers must establish the business connection of all the costs. Any reimbursement of moving costs paid by a public employer to an employee is tax exempt.[425]

In the *Commonwealth* systems, as a matter of general principle, moving costs are considered to be personal in the same way as commuting expenses. However, a special statutory rule now allows moving expenses in limited circumstances in *Canada*.[426] Moving expenses are deductible if they arise in connection with the commencement of employment or business in a new location. The move must result in the new residence being at least forty kilometers closer to the new workplace than the old residence.

Originally, this distance requirement was interpreted by the tax authorities and the courts as measured in a straight line. As a result, a taxpayer was denied a deduction when he moved from the Quebec (east) side of the Ottawa River to the Ontario (west) side, even though the distance limitation was satisfied if measured in terms of normal driving distance.[427] This strict interpretation was reversed by the Federal Court of Appeal in favor of a more flexible interpretation which takes into account the normal means of transportation available.[428] However, the Canadian tax authorities did not give up easily. In a 2007 case, they argued that the distance requirement should be determined by using the shortest distance between two locations generated by a computer software program, despite the fact that in this case the route involved seventeen right turns, eighteen left turns, and went through several heavily populated areas. The Tax Court rejected this approach as the triumph of mechanical irrationality over common sense.[429]

The statutory deduction was added in part to remove discrimination between employees who received reimbursement of their moving expenses from their employers and employees who had to bear the costs of moving themselves. The court cases consistently held that such reimbursements were not included in income.

In the *United Kingdom*, moving expenses are not deductible. However, a special statutory provision exempts employer reimbursements of certain costs up to GBP 8,000

424. United States, IRC, s. 217(k).
425. Germany, ITA, s. 3 No. 13.
426. Canada, ITA, s. 62.
427. *Cameron v. The Queen*, [1993] 1 CTC 2745 (TCC).
428. *Giannakopoulos v. The Queen*, [1995] 2 CTC 316 (FCA).
429. *Nagy v. The Queen*, [2007] 5 CTC 2642 (TCC).

per move; the GBP 8,000 figure has not been reviewed for many years.[430] *Australia* reaches a similar result by not allowing an employee deduction for directly incurred expenses but exempting employer reimbursements from the FBT that would otherwise apply.[431]

In *Sweden*, in principle, moving expenses are not deductible, partly on the basis that they are personal costs and partly on the ground that they represent nondeductible capital costs incurred in acquiring a new source of income. A case law exception allows a deduction where the move is required by the employer.

Sweden has a statutory exclusion for employer-reimbursed moving expenses of certain kinds, even where those expenses would not be deductible if incurred directly. The somewhat unsatisfactory justification for the exclusion of employer-borne costs is to encourage labor mobility in a geographically large country. Size of country, however, does not seem to be a consistent factor in the treatment of moving expenses, given the restrictive rules in Australia and the UK and the more liberal provisions in Canada.

In *Japan*, moving expenses incurred due to a move at the request of the employer may be deducted in the same way as commuting expenses if the total of all eligible itemized expenses exceeds half of the standard employment income deduction.[432] In addition, similar to the treatment of commuting expenses, moving expenses of employees paid by employers are not included in the employees' income. As indicated above, *The Netherlands* generally does not permit the deduction of any expenses incurred by an employee in connection with employment. However, the employer may designate the reimbursement of moving expenses as a final levy component for the WKR (as discussed above), and therefore that amount is not taxable to the employee.

In *France*, while moving expenses are, in principle, deductible if the move is made in connection with a change in job, most employees choose the 10% standard deduction. Administrative doctrine has clarified that moving expenses incurred by employees required to change their place of residence due to a new job or a new geographical assignment in the job they hold are considered to be business expenses for tax purposes. In addition, where moving expenses are paid by the employer, for example in the form of a transfer allowance, the corresponding amounts must be deducted by the employees concerned from their taxable remuneration.[433]

In *India*, special allowances specifically granted for certain prescribed purposes are exempt to the extent that they are actually incurred for the performance of the duties of an office or employment. Any allowance granted for moving expenses, including any sum paid in connection with the transfer, packing, and transportation of personal effects, is exempt.[434]

430. United Kingdom, ITEPA, ss. 271 et seq.
431. Australia, FBTAA, s. 58AA-58F.
432. Japan, ITA, s. 57-2.
433. France, Administrative doctrine, February 24, 2017, BOI-RSA-BASE-30-50-30-20 n°270.
434. India, ITA 1961, s. 10(14), Rule 2BB(1)(a), and the Explanation.

1.3 Clothing

Clothing is a classic example of a mixed business and personal expense, and the results in all the systems are similar, involving an objective test as to the suitability of clothing for wear outside work, regardless of the lifestyle of the particular individual.

The traditional approach in the *United States* was to allow a deduction for clothing which is not adaptable to personal use, is not so worn, and is required as a condition of employment. Thus, costs of military uniforms which could be worn when off duty were not deductible, whereas the cost of required clothing such as fatigues, whose off-duty use was restricted, qualified for deduction. Expenses for employees' clothing are not deductible until after 2025 as a result of the general prohibition against the deduction of unreimbursed employee expenses.[435]

In *Germany*, expenses for professional clothing, such as uniforms for police, fire, military, and airline employees, which are necessary because of the nature of the business, are deductible even if they can be worn privately.[436] Special protective clothing, shoes, and the like are also deductible. The cost of "civilian" clothes which are not associated with a particular profession and can be worn in normal public settings are not generally deductible, even if as a practical matter they are necessary for the profession (e.g., dark suits for lawyers). However, cases have allowed the deduction of such expenses in limited circumstances (e.g., the cost of formal attire for a mortician or waiter (criticized in the literature), or the black suit of (Protestant) clergy).

The *French* rules are broadly similar, except that mixed costs can be apportioned. Employees' clothing expenses are deductible if they relate to clothing or outfits specific to or characteristic of the profession in which they work.[437]

In *Canada*, clothing is usually a nondeductible personal expense. Special employment-related clothing expenses are not deductible by employees in Canada since that is not one of the enumerated employee deductions. However, employer-provided special clothing and uniforms are not taxable as fringe benefits. Self-employed persons can deduct special clothing and uniform costs.

In the *United Kingdom*, administrative practice, which has been put into statutory form, provides special fixed allowances, varying from job to job, for tools and special clothing purchased by an employee.[438] For self-employed persons, in a leading UK case, a female barrister was not entitled to deduct the cost of cleaning ordinary clothing worn under court robes which she had purchased specifically to wear in court; the costs of cleaning the wig and gown and other court robes, however, were deductible.[439] The *Australian* rules are similar, although they have one special feature. In order to prevent employers from providing, on a tax-free basis, "uniforms" which are not noticeably different from ordinary clothing, such clothing must be registered in a

435. United States, IRC, s. 67(g).
436. Germany, ITA, s. 9 para. 1 sent. 3 No. 6.
437. France, CGI, s. 83 3.
438. United Kingdom, ITEPA, s. 367.
439. *Mallalieu v. Drummond, supra* note 398.

Register of Approved Occupational Clothing, which sets the standards for "borderline" clothing by specifying requirements (e.g., logos of a certain size) which must be met.[440]

In *The Netherlands*, the costs of "work clothing" incurred by employees are not deductible, in keeping with the general prohibition on the deduction of expenses by employees. Reimbursement of clothing expenses by the employer is generally taxable to the employee unless the employer designates the amount as a final levy component for the WKR (as discussed above). Wage tax is due by the employer only if, and insofar as, it exceeds the discretionary scope. "Work clothing" is defined as clothing that must be worn during work activity and which is exclusively or almost exclusively suited for such use. Uniforms, overalls, and professorial gowns are examples.

Sweden is more restrictive and approaches the issue from a somewhat different angle. No deduction is allowed for clothing costs even where the clothes are special items, such as uniforms. The theoretical justification is that expenses for business clothing are not in excess of the alternative "avoided" expenses for private clothing which would have been incurred in any event. Thus, there is no incremental cost attributable to the business connection. This reasoning is not applicable to outer clothing, such as overalls, which are required in addition to normal clothing, and the cost of such items can be deducted. Free clothing provided by employers which is not suitable for private wear is excluded from income (although costs incurred by employees for the same clothes would not be deductible).

In *Japan*, historically, clothing costs were not eligible for itemized deductions. However, since 2013 a deduction has been permitted for clothes certified by employers as directly necessary for work. In *India*, any allowance with respect to the purchase and maintenance of a uniform used during the performance of duties is exempt under the old regime but not under the new regime introduced in 2020.[441]

1.4 Business Travel

Deductions for costs incurred in business travel involve two separate issues. In those systems in which commuting expenses are either not deductible or deductible only within limits, one issue involves distinguishing between the cost of business travel and commuting expenses. The other issue is the extent to which the systems attempt to capture the potential consumption element in meals and lodging which are typically involved in business travel.

In the *United States*, travel expenses, including meals and lodging, incurred while "away from home" on business are in principle deductible for taxpayers who are not employees.[442] In order to prevent the deduction of commuting expenses, "home" in this context has been interpreted administratively (although not by all courts) to mean

440. Australia, ITAA 1997, Division 34.

441. India, IT Rules, 1962, Rule 2BB(1)(f). As explained in the chapter (section 3.1) on India in Part I, under the new regime, taxpayers are subject to tax at a lower rate but give up the right to claim certain deductions and concessions.

442. United States, IRC, s. 162(a)(2). Unreimbursed employee expenses, such as those for travel, are not deductible until after 2025. United States, IRC, s. 67(g).

the taxpayer's principal place of business. Similarly, to prevent the deduction of "normal" expenses for meals during the business day, "away" has been interpreted to mean a situation in which a stop for sleep or rest is necessary. Thus, generally speaking, the costs of overnight business travel are deductible. However, these principles have been applied to myriad factual situations, with results that are not easily reconcilable. If the taxpayer is away from home for more than one year, the taxpayer's "home" in the sense of principal place of business is, in effect, deemed to have been established in the new work location; thus, lodging and meal expenses are no longer deductible because the taxpayer is no longer "away" from home.

For domestic travel, transportation costs are fully deductible for non-employees if the "primary" purpose of the travel is business-related. The taxpayer may choose between substantiating actual expenses and claiming a geographically based per diem amount. More restrictive rules apply to foreign travel. Even if the primary purpose for foreign travel is business, a taxpayer is required to allocate expenses between business and nonbusiness aspects of the trip unless certain exceptions apply.[443] Meal expenses which would otherwise be deductible under these tests are limited to 50% of the costs incurred, as discussed in more detail below in connection with entertainment expenses.

In *Sweden*, travel expenses are, in principle, deductible to the extent that they exceed the personal costs which would have been incurred in any event. As a result, travel and lodging expenses are fully deductible. Meals are deductible only if a trip involves an overnight stay, in which case a standard amount is allowed as a deduction. This amount is intended to equal the additional cost compared to the cost of meals at home (a larger standardized amount can be excluded if the employer reimburses an employee for the meal expenses); employees can receive a larger deduction by showing that the increase in costs is, in fact, higher. For travel abroad, the amount of the deduction varies for each country.

In *Canada*, travel expenses incurred for the purpose of earning income from business are deductible. Such expenses are also deductible by employees, although subject to some restrictions. Only 50% of the cost of business meals, while traveling or not, is deductible. If a conference fee includes meals and beverages, CAD 50 per day of the fee is considered to be allocated to meals and is subject to the limitation, although no allocation is required for meals on airlines or trains.

Australia reaches roughly the same results through a combination of employee deductions and fringe benefits taxation in the case of reimbursed costs. With respect to deductions, there are detailed record-keeping requirements where the amounts claimed exceed the travel allowances given to public officials. Where the expense is incurred by the employer, the same rules effectively apply through the operation of the FBT.

The rules in the *United Kingdom* are more restrictive. Travel expenses must be incurred "wholly and exclusively" for the purposes of the business. In a leading case, a lawyer was denied the deduction for attending conferences where he admitted that

443. United States, IRC, s. 274(c).

there were social and holiday purposes associated with the trip. In another case, however, an accountant successfully argued that the social aspects of a similar trip were simply incidental to the business purpose and so was allowed a deduction. Thus, for example, doctors visiting patients in the South of France during the winter are able to deduct the travel costs if their sole purpose in incurring the expense is to look after their patients—and the pleasure of being there is simply an effect of the expenditure. In practice, apparently, some portion of the costs of "mixed" travel expenses is sometimes allowed.

In *Germany*, transportation expenses can be deducted on the basis of receipts for actual expenses incurred; a per-kilometer allowance can also be used.[444] Lodging expenses are deductible in full based on actual costs (although the portion of the amount attributable to breakfast must be treated as a meal expense).[445] For foreign travel, taxpayers can deduct either the actual costs or a per diem amount. For food costs, the deduction is limited to a fixed per diem amount depending on how long the taxpayer is away from the work site. For periods of twenty-four hours or more, a deductible per diem of EUR 28 is allowed. Special amounts are set for foreign travel. Taxpayers who stay for more than three months in one place are no longer considered to be in travel status; as a result, meals and lodging costs are no longer deductible and transportation costs are limited to commuting expenses.

The *French* rules on business travel are fairly relaxed, requiring only that the expenses be normal, incurred in the course of the business, and verified. Deductions for meal expenses of employees must be reduced by the deemed cost of a meal at home, the standard value of which is the same as that of an employer-provided meal (EUR 5.20 in 2023). The actual costs related to travel by private vehicles of employees (except for toll charges, parking fees, and interest) or an optional per-kilometer rate are deductible.[446]

In *The Netherlands*, travel expenses incurred by employees, like all expenses incurred in connection with employment, are not deductible. The reimbursement of business travel expenses by the employer is taxable to the employee as wage income. As of 2011, the employer may choose to bear the tax costs related to the reimbursement through the WKR (as discussed above); if the employer applies the WKR, the compensation is not considered to be part of the employee's wages. This option applies to all expenses for business travel, i.e., transportation, lodging, and meal expenses.[447] For self-employed persons and corporations, travel expenses are deductible to the extent that they are incurred in the course of business.

In *China* and *Japan*, for self-employed persons, travel expenses for business reasons are generally deductible. In Japan, with respect to employees, employers usually pay or reimburse travel expenses incurred by their employees. Such payment or reimbursement by employers is deductible by employers and is not income for

444. Germany, ITA, s. 9 para. 1 sent. 3 No. 4a.
445. Germany, ITA, s. 9 para. 1 sent. 3 No. 5a.
446. France, CGI, s. 83 3° para. 8 and Regulatory Schedule IV, s. 6 B.
447. Netherlands, WTA, Art. 31a(2)(a) and (b).

employees. Pursuant to recent tax revisions, travel expenses which are not reimbursed by employers are now eligible for itemized deductions.

In *India*, business travel expenses, in particular foreign travel, have given rise to many disputes. Prior to 1999, deductions for foreign travel expenses were limited to prescribed amounts (Rule 6D). Currently, where the purpose of foreign travel is predominantly commercial, the expenses are deductible as long as records of the expenses are kept and filed by the taxpayer.[448]

1.5 Business Entertainment

While business entertainment may bring somewhat less pleasure compared to freely chosen personal entertainment, the consumption element of entertainment activities is clear. Entertainment provided in a business context is particularly susceptible to abuse and, not unexpectedly, subject to special limitations in all the countries under consideration here. These limitations typically take the form of an overlay of additional requirements, especially substantiation, for any deduction at all, and a percentage limit on qualifying expenses. In view of the administrative difficulties, none of the systems attempts to tax the recipient of the entertainment directly. The denial or limitation on the deduction ensures that some amount is included in the tax base even though it is not taxed to the person enjoying the consumption.

In the *United States*, entertainment expenses historically were deductible if they met the normal tests of deductibility and, in addition, were either "directly related to" or "associated with" a taxpayer's trade or business. The rules were relaxed for meals and other recreational facilities provided on business premises or to employees, for meals in restaurants serving the general public, etc. Deductions for club dues were disallowed entirely. Special substantiation requirements applied, and only 50% of otherwise qualified expenditures could be deducted.[449] The 2017 tax reform created quite a stir in the business community by disallowing entertainment expenses entirely, even when they satisfied the requirements noted above. However, regulatory guidance states that the partial deduction of business meals, even in the context of entertainment, remains available.[450]

In *Germany*, the deduction of entertainment expenses is generally restricted in accordance with the "reasonableness" of the costs incurred.[451] Several items are not deductible at all (e.g., costs incurred for the maintenance of establishments for hunting, fishing, and yachting). In the case of meals provided to business partners, 70% of the "reasonable" amounts paid for food and beverages is deductible.[452] In order to assess the "reasonableness" of expenses, there must be an analysis of the situation from the point of view of a "diligent business manager" (a construct often used in

448. *DCIT v. Nokia India (P) Ltd.*, ITAT, Mumbai, ITA 2380/Del/2010, December 6, 2017. However, foreign travel expenses for doctors incurred by a pharmaceutical company are not deductible. *See Apex Laboratories Pvt Ltd. v. DCIT* (SC), 2022, SLP No. 23207 of 2019.
449. United States, IRC, s. 274.
450. United States, Treas. Reg. s. 1.274-12.
451. Germany, ITA, s. 4 para. 5 No. 7.
452. Germany, ITA, s. 4 para. 5 No. 2.

German tax law): the proportionality of the expenditure to the particular business transactions, the size and profitability of the business, and the amounts spent by comparable businesses in the particular field. The taxpayer must provide proof of the place, date, participants, and the reason for business meals through specific documentation requirements.

The pattern in *Sweden* is similar. In addition to meeting the normal deduction tests involving the relation of the expense to a business activity, entertainment expenses must, under special statutory provisions, have a "direct connection" with the business. Further, the expense must be incurred "solely" to establish or maintain a business relationship. This restriction would prevent, for example, the deduction of expenses of a yacht used to entertain customers, but also used personally. Assuming that the "direct connection" is present, the deduction is limited to a "reasonable" amount. In the case of business meals, no cost is deductible.[453]

The recipient is not required to include the value of entertainment in income. Thus, if an employee participates in a business lunch with a client which is paid for by the employer, neither the employee nor the client is required to include any amount in respect of the meal in income. Although the cost of the meal is not deductible by the employer, given the difference in corporate and individual rates, a lower total tax results than if the meal had been fully deductible and includable in the income of the employee (e.g., as a taxable fringe benefit).

In general, no deduction is allowed in the *United Kingdom* for entertainment expenses incurred by employees. If amounts are reimbursed, there is no employee inclusion, but the employer is denied a deduction. Otherwise, expenses must meet the "wholly and exclusively" test and then are still subject to substantial additional statutory limitations which bar any deduction except for the entertainment of staff. This rule also prohibits a deduction for the costs of providing many sorts of gifts, although a deduction for those costing less than GBP 50 is allowed if they contain a conspicuous advertisement for the business.[454] *Australia* also has a special statutory rule which in general denies a deduction for entertainment expenses, subject to a number of exceptions, such as restaurant meals of restaurant reviewers consumed as part of their jobs, business trips, and the like. In addition, there is an exception for in-house dining facilities for employees, which led some large legal and accounting firms to provide lavish private dining facilities for employees, especially those working after-hours. Club fees and the like paid by employers are generally not deductible.[455]

The overlay of the FBT in Australia makes the situation quite complex, since entertainment of employees and their associates is subject to the FBT, while entertainment of nonemployees is subject to the denial-of-deduction rule. To alleviate the potentially onerous record-keeping burden, two alternative elective methods for dealing with entertainment expenses apply, a straight 50/50 split and a split based on a typical twelve-week period.[456]

453. Sweden, ITA, Ch. 16 s. 2.
454. United Kingdom, ITEPA, ss. 356 et seq., ITTOIA, ss. 45 et seq.; CTA 2009, ss. 1298 et seq.
455. Australia, ITAA 1997, ss. 26-45 Division 32.
456. Australia, FBTAA, s. 37B-37CF.

In *Canada*, 50% of directly connected entertainment expenses involved in business activities are deductible.[457] No deduction is allowed for entertainment expenses incurred by employees, except salespersons in limited circumstances. Reimbursement of entertainment expenses by an employer does not result in an income inclusion for an employee. The Canadian rules expressly disallow any deduction for club dues and expenses for the use of yachts, camps, lodges, and golf courses (even for professional golfers).[458] *The Netherlands* allows businesses to deduct entertainment expenses only to the extent that they exceed EUR 5,600 on an annual basis (2024).[459] For employees, no deduction for entertainment expenses is allowed and reimbursement of these expenses by the employer constitutes wage income for the employee. However, as discussed above, the employer may opt for application of the WKR.

The *French* rules contain no particular standard on this issue, except that the deduction must not be abusive and must be in the company's interest. In addition, there is a special statutory provision which disallows a deduction for so-called extravagant spending (*dépenses somptuaires*) (i.e., costs incurred in connection with hunting, fishing, yachting, country houses, and real estate used for entertaining, except where incurred for a clear social objective or for all the employees of the business).[460]

In *Japan*, for self-employed persons, entertainment expenses may be deducted only where the greater part of the expenses are business-related and the business portion of the expense can clearly be identified. Special rules substantially restrict the deduction of entertainment expenses by corporations.[461] For employees, entertainment expenses incurred for customers, vendors, or other persons with whom they have a business relationship have been eligible for itemized deductions since 2013.[462]

In *China*, individuals engaged in earning business income are entitled to deduct entertainment expenses without any limit; however, enterprises are allowed to deduct only 60% of such expenses up to a maximum of 5% of revenue for the year. In *India*, entertainment expenses are deductible where they meet the conditions for the deduction of business expenses generally (i.e., they are genuine and serve some business purpose). Entertainment allowances provided to employees are taxable, except for government employees who are entitled to receive an entertainment allowance of INR 5,000 or 20% of their salary, whichever is less. This exemption is not available if the employee chooses to be taxable at the lower rate under the new regime introduced in 2020.[463]

The common technique of limiting the deduction for entertainment expenses as a substitute or surrogate for attempting to tax the beneficiary of the expenditure itself raises some problems. For example, it has no impact on tax exempt organizations. This aspect led Australia to include under its FBT a special rule to impose the tax on

457. Canada, ITA, s. 67.1.
458. Canada, ITA, s. 18(1)(l).
459. Netherlands, ITA, Art. 3.15.
460. France, CGI, s. 39 4.
461. Japan, STMA, s. 61-4.
462. Japan, ITA, s. 57-2, para. 2, No. 6.
463. *See* the chapter on India in Part I (section 3.1) for more details on the old and new regimes.

entertainment expenses of tax exempts.[464] As a more general matter, the Swedish situation shows that, where there is a difference in tax rates applicable to the payer and recipient, denial of the deduction can have quite different effects from the inclusion of the payment in the recipient's income, although it ensures that at least some amount is included in the tax base at some point.

1.6 Childcare

The treatment of childcare expenses has been controversial in many systems. Historically, the courts have treated the expenses as personal and nondeductible. However, as single-parent and two outside-worker families became more common, pressure to allow some tax relief for childcare expenses increased. The impact which nondeductible childcare expenses had on labor supply generally, and especially with regard to secondary workers, was an important factor in the policy debate. The response was typically to continue to treat the expenses as personal from an income-definition point of view but to provide some limited personal deduction or credit for the expenses. No country allows full deduction of childcare expenses as a business expense. However, a number of systems, while disallowing a deduction for directly incurred childcare expenses, allow an exclusion for employer-provided childcare.

The approach to childcare costs in the *United States* has varied considerably over the years. Although treated by the courts as personal expenses, early statutory provisions allowed a limited deduction for single parents and couples with low incomes. Subsequent legislation expanded the scope of the deduction but continued the dollar limitations. Currently, the expenses are not deductible but a limited childcare credit is provided for employment-related childcare expenses.[465] In addition, some forms of employer-paid childcare can be provided as a nontaxable fringe benefit.[466] In addition, a separate child tax credit helps reduce the financial burden for moderate-to-lower income families by providing a partially refundable credit based on the number of minor children, not the amount of childcare expenses.[467]

Canadian and *United Kingdom* courts have traditionally held childcare expenses to be nondeductible personal expenses. The UK continues to follow this approach, although there is a limited exclusion for employer-provided childcare. The tax credit scheme contains a substantial element for childcare, but only for expenses incurred with registered establishments; this preference for care outside the home is controversial.[468] In Canada, a special statutory provision allows a limited deduction for expenses incurred for a variety of childcare services, including day nurseries and boarding schools or camps.[469] The payments generally must be made to unrelated parties and taxpayers must provide the social security number of the recipient. The effect of the

464. Australia, FBTAA, s. 39.
465. United States, IRC, s. 21.
466. United States, IRC, s. 129.
467. United States, IRC, s. 24.
468. On the childcare exemption, *see* United Kingdom, ITEPA, ss. 318 et seq.; on credits, *see* Tax Credits Act 2002, s. 12.
469. Canada, ITA, s. 63.

deduction has had some positive effect on secondary workers entering the workforce, but the effect is limited by a rule requiring the lower-income parent to claim the deduction where there is more than one supporting person and by the fact that the deductible amount does not approximate actual childcare costs. Limited governmental subsidies are available for childcare facilities; these subsidies increased substantially in most provinces from 2023. Proposals for universal childcare surface from time to time but have not been adopted for budgetary reasons.

In 1994, the Supreme Court of Canada considered an important case involving childcare expenses.[470] The taxpayer, a partner in a large law firm, whose spouse also worked, tried to deduct the costs of a full-time nanny as ordinary business expenses, quite apart from the limited statutory deduction. She claimed that the limited deduction violated the Canadian Charter of Rights and Freedoms (Constitution) because it discriminated against women. In a seven-to-two decision, a majority of the court (all males) disallowed the deduction, holding that the statutory deduction for childcare expenses excluded the possibility of deducting the expenses as ordinary business expenses; moreover, the provision was held not to be discriminatory since there was no evidence showing that childcare expenses were paid disproportionately by women, although they were clearly borne disproportionately by women. Two dissenters (both women) would have allowed the deduction. They argued that there was no conflict between the full deduction of childcare expenses by business taxpayers and the limited statutory deduction (even though it applied explicitly to business taxpayers). The dissenting female justices also concluded that the statutory deduction for childcare expenses was discriminatory against women. The majority opinion intimated that, in the absence of the special statutory deduction, "the changing composition of the business class and changing social structure" might require the reclassification of childcare expenses as business expenses.

Case law in *Australia*, influenced by the UK, has also denied the deduction to employees for childcare expenses as business expenses, viewing them as not being incurred "in the course of" employment. In an effort to encourage employers to provide on-site childcare facilities, there is a limited exception from the FBT for employer-provided childcare, but the incentive has not proved especially enticing. As there is no generally provided governmental childcare, employees who purchase childcare do so mostly from private providers. Rather than use the tax system, government support for childcare is delivered by cash payments, made directly to the provider, but this approach has been criticized on the basis that the intended saving for parents has been offset by childcare providers increasing fees by the amount of the government payment.

In *Sweden*, childcare costs are not deductible. However, a taxpayer can apply for a tax credit for domestic costs, including childcare. The credit is 50% of the costs with a cap of SEK 50,000 per year.[471] This is a deviation from the principle that the income tax system should be neutral and not used for nonfiscal purposes. However, the tax credit can be justified on the basis that it is necessary to rectify market imperfections.

470. *Symes v. The Queen*, [1994] 1 CTC 40 (SCC).
471. *See* the chapter on Sweden in Part I for more details.

The personal choice to incur private expenses instead of using the available public facilities heightens the consumption element of the expenditure.

Germany has changed the treatment of childcare expenses substantially over the years. After the Federal Constitutional Court ruled in 1977 that childcare expenses are deemed to have a private character and are not business-related, there was no possibility of deducting the expenses.[472] Nevertheless, in 1984 the Federal Constitutional Court stated that single and disabled parents should be entitled to deduct a certain lump-sum amount in order to cope with childcare expenses—not as a "business-related-deduction," but as a special allowance for their personal hardship.[473] Later tax legislation introduced a general deduction for household services, which also included expenses for a nanny. In 1998, the Federal Constitutional Court changed the whole picture by holding that, while there should be a reasonable tax-free threshold for childcare, its applicability should not depend on whether parents themselves take care of their children or employ another person.[474] This decision was strongly criticized in the literature (because it probably would lead to the deduction of "opportunity costs") and the legislature did not follow the advice of the Court. Instead, from 2006 to 2011, it adopted a two-pronged approach: childcare was deductible as either a personal or a business expense depending on the relevant circumstances. Since 2012, childcare expenses have been subject to a uniform regime applicable to so-called special costs and their deductibility as business expenses is prohibited. Under this regime, two-thirds of childcare expenses are deductible, up to an annual limit of EUR 4,000.[475]

In *Japan*, childcare expenses are considered to be purely personal and are not deductible, although municipalities often provide some monetary assistance to parents which is usually excluded from taxable income. Employer-provided childcare is not taxed to employees as a fringe benefit. Japan allows a standard deduction of JPY 380,000 per child aged 16 years old or older (JPY 630,000 per child aged 19 to 23). This limited scope takes into account the financial burden on households due to tuition costs of high schools and colleges, which are typically paid by parents. For younger children, a moderate amount of child support is provided by the government to low- and middle-income families.

In *The Netherlands*, as of 2005, childcare expenses have been "de-fiscalized": they are no longer deductible but the government provides a (tax-free) subsidy.

France considers childcare to be a nondeductible personal cost but provides for taxpayers domiciled in France an annual tax credit equal to 50% of expenses actually incurred for the care of dependent children under the age of six, up to a maximum of EUR 3,500 per child, and half of this amount where the child is deemed equally dependent on both parents.[476] There is also a credit of 50% of the expenses actually

472. Federal Constitutional Court (*Bundesverfassungsgericht*), October 11, 1977, 1 BvR 343/73 et al., Reports (BVerfGE) 47, p. 1.
473. Federal Constitutional Court (*Bundesverfassungsgericht*), October 17, 1984, 1 BvR 527/80 et al., Reports (BVerfGE) 68, p. 143.
474. Federal Constitutional Court (*Bundesverfassungsgericht*), November 10, 1998, 2 BvR 1057/91 et al., Reports (BVerfGE) 99, p. 216.
475. Germany, ITA, s. 10 para. 1 No. 5.
476. France, CGI, s. 200 quater B.

incurred for the employment of a home-help employee, up to an annual ceiling which depends on the taxpayer's circumstances.[477] It is not necessary for both parents to work in order to qualify for these credits, which are refundable if they exceed the tax payable.

In contrast, *China* does not provide any deductions for childcare expenses but does allow deductions for senior care expenses. Similarly, in *India*, childcare expenses are not deductible; however, businesses can deduct the cost of childcare provided for employees and employees may be taxable on the benefit.

2 HOBBY LOSSES AND THE CRITERIA FOR DISTINGUISHING BUSINESS FROM PERSONAL ACTIVITIES

Activities which are ostensibly aimed at making a profit but which involve the potential for substantial personal consumption raise some of the same issues as mixed business and personal expenses, and are frequently dealt with by special rules. The questions arise somewhat differently in schedular systems and in systems which operate with a more global concept of income. In a schedular system, for either the profit to be taxable or the losses deductible, the activity in question must fit within one of the taxable categories. Thus, for an occasional activity (e.g., stamp collecting), which does not fall in any taxable category, neither income nor expenses typically would be taken into account for tax purposes. In a global system, the profit is taxable; the real issue is the deduction of the costs which arise in the activity (and which usually exceed the income).

The *United States* has had a series of statutory provisions dealing with the hobby-loss problem. Until 2018, if an activity carried on by an individual was found to be "not engaged in for profit," the deductions generated by the activity could be used only against the income from the activity.[478] However, deductions which would be available even in the absence of profit-seeking activity had to be "stacked" first against the income. The effect of the provision was thus typically to deny a portion of the deduction for maintenance and depreciation expenses of hobby activities against other income. The factors considered by the courts in determining whether a profit-seeking activity was present included the nature of the activity as potentially recreation (e.g., horse raising and car racing), whether the activity was carried on in a "businesslike" manner, the use of expert advisers, and the history of profits and losses from the activity and its potential for profit. The provision could be overly generous to taxpayers since, to some extent, it allowed what were consumption expenses to be offset against the otherwise taxable income generated by the activity.

The deduction for these hobby expenses was considered to be a miscellaneous itemized deduction, and therefore the actual deduction was subject to the rule allowing miscellaneous itemized deductions only to the extent that they exceeded 2% of

477. France, CGI, s. 199 sexdecies.
478. United States, IRC, s. 183.

income. However, in 2017 the deduction for miscellaneous itemized deductions, including the deduction for qualified hobby losses, was suspended through 2025.[479]

While originally aimed at limiting the deduction for the consumption element in what were essentially personal activities, the provision has been applied to tax-motivated transactions which were not likely to generate a profit apart from the tax benefits.

In *Canada*, the distinction between business and personal activities is closely related to the source concept of income discussed earlier. If an activity is clearly commercial in nature and there is no personal element, the activity qualifies as a source of income. However, if there is also a personal element, the taxpayer must establish by reference to objective "indicia of commerciality" or "badges of trade" that the predominant intention is to make a profit from the activity. In a 2002 case, the Supreme Court rejected any requirement for an activity to be carried on with a reasonable expectation of profit.[480] The Court even went so far as to indicate that the intention of eventually realizing a capital gain may support a finding that an activity is commercial in nature. Under the Supreme Court's approach, if a taxpayer's activities constitute a business, the revenues derived from the activities are included in computing income and the expenses incurred in connection with the activities are deductible. Conversely, if there is no business, any revenue derived from the activities is not taxable and any expenses are not deductible. This approach provides significant opportunities for tax planning by allowing taxpayers to argue that they have a business source of income if they have a net loss from their activities, or only a hobby (no source of income) if they have net profits.

A special rule applies to hobby farming, a common phenomenon in Canada.[481] Even if the activity is a business, where the hobby farmer's chief source of income is not farming or is a combination of farming and some other source, there is a dollar limit on the amount of losses which can be deducted against other income. Nondeductible farm losses can be carried forward and deducted against farm income in later years.

The *United Kingdom* approach has evolved somewhat differently. Under the basic case law tests, it was fairly easy to establish a "trading" activity which would, in principle, allow the deduction of costs. However, this rule is supplemented by a special provision which requires that a trade must be conducted on a commercial basis and with a view to a realization of profit. A further special rule applies to farming, which disallows losses after five consecutive years of loss unless it can be established that there would be a reasonable expectation of profit if the business were carried on by a competent person.[482] As seen elsewhere (*see* section 6.3), the UK has some restrictions on the ability to set a trading loss against income from other sources for that year ("sideways" relief) where the taxpayer is not actively involved in running the business. Under the UK system, it is usually not possible for a loss arising from employment expenses to exceed earnings—the employment income can be reduced to nil and no

479. United States, IRC, s. 67(g).
480. *Stewart v. The Queen,* [2002] SCC 46 (SCC).
481. Canada, ITA, s. 31.
482. United Kingdom, ITA ss. 66 et seq. and CTA 2010, ss. 44 et seq.

further. However, a loss can arise in other circumstances, e.g., where capital allowances exceed the earnings, on repayment of a taxed bonus from a previous year which exceeds current earnings, or because a contract of employment makes an employee liable for losses as well as entitled to profits.[483]

In *Germany*, there is extensive case law dealing with the issue whether a taxpayer's activities constitute a "business," self-employment, rentals, etc., or are private activities and therefore not taxable. The basic test is framed in terms of an intention to make a profit. While formally a subjective test, the courts have consistently based their decisions on the objective facts of each case as indicative of a taxpayer's intent. The cases deal with both "classical" hobby-loss situations and tax shelters. Activities with a "leisure element" (writing, art, sports) receive particular scrutiny by the tax authorities. For rental income, the courts apply a strong presumption that taxpayers have a profit-making intention, thus rendering the case-by-case test nearly obsolete.

For income to be taxable and losses deductible, in general, there must be proof of the intention to generate income based on objective evidence of the probability of a "total" profit—that is, that an activity will generate a net profit within a "reasonable" time after the activity has started. It is not sufficient for profits to be made in later years after a considerable period of large losses unless the subsequent profits are sufficient to offset earlier losses; the revenue must be sufficient to cover all costs of the operation and result in an overall profit. In determining the potential for profit, it is appropriate to take into account not only future operating income but possible increases in the value of the assets involved, as long as any gains on those assets would be taxable. With respect to rental activities which do not constitute a business, in general, the gain on sale of the property would not be taxed and thus cannot be taken into account in determining the potential for profit.

Although the case law allows an initial starting period of losses, a longer period of losses is seen as indicating a lack of intention to make a profit unless the taxpayer restructures the activity. However, it is accepted that taxpayers may start a loss-making activity which is meant to support another profitable activity (e.g., an art gallery combined with a restaurant) as long as overall profitability is envisaged.

In *Sweden*, income from the performance of services is taxable without regard to the existence of a profit motive. As a result, income from a hobby involving the performance of services is taxed in the "income from employment" category. Deductions are allowed only up to the amount of the income. Any excess loss cannot be deducted against other income, on the theory that the costs are personal.

In *The Netherlands*, there is substantial case law dealing with the definition of a "business" (enterprise) which draws a distinction between taxable business and nontaxable personal activities. For a business to be present, there must be: (1) a permanent organization of labor and capital; (2) participation in an economic interchange; and (3) a profit-making goal and reasonable expectation of success. These requirements, in effect, place most hobby activities on the personal side of the line,

483. United Kingdom, ITEPA 2003, s. 329 (for the general rule) and s. 11(3)(a), which provides for relief under ITA, s. 128.

with the result that no receipts are taxable and no expenses are deductible. In some cases, a hobby activity may be viewed as involving "income from other activities," but in practice, if there is a history of losses it is unlikely that deductions would be allowed.

Australia has no objective criterion of the likelihood of profit as the test for determining whether a taxpayer is engaged in a business, and as a result, there has been considerable litigation over the business/hobby borderline; for example, there have been some unsuccessful attempts to limit the deductibility of farming losses against other income. To deal with the problem, Australia introduced noncommercial loss rules in 2000.[484] Under these rules, losses on hobby-type businesses are not deductible currently but can be carried forward to future years for offset against income from the same type of activities. The rules do not apply where the revenue from the business is AUD 20,000 or more in a year, the business has made a profit in three of the last five years (including the current year), or the business utilizes real property worth AUD 500,000 or more or other property (excluding cars) worth AUD 100,000 or more. However, because the tests can be manipulated—for example, by buying a more expensive hobby farm or a bigger wine press—they do not make the losses deductible where a taxpayer's taxable income (with hobby losses added back) exceeds AUD 250,000 per annum. There is discretion to relax the operation of the rules in hardship cases (such as fire or flood in the case of farms). Australia also has a dedicated regime for quarantining losses arising from "boating activities that are not carried on as a business" (in other words, the losses suffered by the owners of luxury yachts who claim their yachts are available for occasional charter).[485]

Hobby-loss issues have not been extensively litigated or debated in *Japan*, although the deductibility of gambling losses from gambling gains is controversial, as discussed above in Subpart B, section 7. There is, however, some administrative guidance with regard to owners of racehorses. Where certain requirements as to the number of horses, the manner in which the operations are conducted, etc. are met, the income constitutes business income and any net loss can be used against other income in other taxable categories. Where these requirements are not met, the income is included in the Miscellaneous Income category and, while the expenses offset the racing income, any excess loss cannot be used against other income.

In *France*, hobby-related expenses cannot in principle be deducted, since hobby income is not taxable. Article 13 General Tax Code (Code général des impôts (CGI)) provides that only expenses necessary to earn and maintain taxable income can be deducted. There is no statutory definition of the hobby versus business boundary and the boundary is decided on a case-by-case basis. The main criterion for establishing the boundary is the existence of a profit-making purpose, which is inferred from examining the efforts made by the taxpayer to derive income from the activity. If sufficient efforts are made, the activity is considered to be a business; if not, it is considered to be a hobby.

484. Australia, ITAA 1997, Division 35.
485. Australia, ITAA 1997, ss. 26-47.

In *China*, hobby losses are not deductible but there are no legislative criteria for distinguishing between hobbies and business activities. Business activities are regulated by the government through permits or licenses. Article 6 of the IIT Regulations lists the following types of business activity:

- productive or business activities of "individual industrial and commercial households" and individual investors in "individual proprietorship enterprises" or an individual partner of a "partnership enterprise";
- lawful activities in education, health care, consulting, and other services rendered for compensation; and
- "any other type of business or productive activities."

Income from personal activities which do not qualify as business activities is taxed as incidental income at a flat rate of 20%, with no deductions.

In *India*, any income or losses from hobbies may be classified either as business income or income from other sources. The definition of "business" specifically includes an adventure in the nature of trade.[486]

3 CAPITAL COSTS AND RECOVERY METHODS

3.1 Determining Capital Costs

All the systems studied here recognize the distinction between currently deductible costs and capital costs. Capital costs are generally recovered under some sort of capital cost recovery system or on the disposal of the asset. While the details of the rules and the formulation of the distinction differ, in general, costs which create a benefit in future years must be capitalized where they represent relatively large, nonrecurring expenditures. In some systems, the treatment of capital gains for accounting purposes is an important element in determining the tax treatment of such costs. There is an unavoidable arbitrariness in the classifications in all the systems, although a surprising amount of similarity occurs in the results.

Taking the *United States* as an example, the formulation of the current/capital distinction in the case law has varied over time. At one point, the test was whether an expenditure could be said to have created a separate and distinct asset. Subsequently, the Supreme Court shifted the focus to the existence of a significant benefit from the expenditure which extends beyond the taxable year.[487] Regulations blend these concepts and require capitalization where an expenditure involves creating or acquiring a separate tangible or intangible asset or making a significant improvement to such an asset which will extend into future years.[488] Even here, however, the test is not

486. India, ITA 1961, s. 2(13).
487. *INDOPCO, Inc v. Commissioner*, 503 U.S. 79 (1992).
488. United States, Reg., s. 1.263-(a)-1(a).

applied consistently. For example, advertising expenses can generally be deducted currently despite, in many situations, the clear benefit in later periods.[489]

In the *German* system, there are specific statutory provisions requiring capitalization of any expenditure which has created an "asset," defined as a transferable object subject to separate valuation, the useful life of which will last for more than one tax period (one year).[490] However, in practice, the courts and fiscal authorities have allowed a current deduction for major outlays which have a recurring nature in the particular business involved. Similarly, current maintenance expenses are deductible, but modifications which substantially alter the condition or character of an asset must be treated as capital costs. Expenses such as those for painting, which would normally be maintenance, must be capitalized if incurred in connection with the original construction or a major renovation of the asset. The cost of assets not in excess of EUR 800 may be deducted immediately.[491]

In the *Commonwealth* systems, the basic distinction has historically been between currently deductible expenditures incurred in connection with the income-earning process and capital outlays. The latter are not deductible except as expressly provided by statute. Various court-developed tests have been applied in the *United Kingdom*, *Canada*, and *Australia* and, to a large extent, parallel the pattern in the U.S. The formulations have included whether the expenditure creates an enduring benefit for the business, whether it is a once-and-for-all expenditure, and whether it relates to a specific and identifiable asset of a capital nature.[492] In the case of expenses giving rise to intangible benefits, the courts have been relatively generous in allowing current deductions, since otherwise the result would often be that no recovery of the cost would be allowed at all due to the narrowness of the capital cost recovery systems.

In *Sweden*, a current deduction is allowed in calculating business income for the cost of assets whose useful life does not exceed three years and for *de minimis* costs of about SEK 28,000 (in 2024). Otherwise, costs must be capitalized.

When calculating employment income in Sweden, the deduction of capital costs is based on the cash receipts method of accounting. However, case law requires that the cost of assets which can be used for an extended period must be capitalized. In some cases, the rejection of a current deduction for capital costs is well founded; it may not be possible to determine in advance to what extent such an asset will be used to justify the current deduction of the full cost.

In the *French* system, the historical focus has been on the creation or acquisition of a distinct and legally identifiable asset or a substantial modification in the condition, character, or useful life of an existing asset. In practice, the accounting rules applicable for tax purposes since 2005 are used to make this determination.[493] Classifying an asset as a business asset in order to record it on the balance sheet is a simple presumption but can be challenged by the tax authorities. The cost of fixed assets is not deductible. A

489. United States, Reg., s. 1.162-20(a)(20).
490. Germany, ITA, s. 4 para. 1 sent. 1, s. 5 para. 1 sent. 1 with reference to Commercial Code, ss. 246 et seq.
491. Germany, ITA, s. 6 para. 2 sent 1.
492. For example, *Tucker v. Granada Motorway Services* [1979] STC 393.
493. France, General Accounting Plan, s. 211-1.

statutory exception exists for low-value goods not exceeding EUR 500, which can be expensed directly in the year of acquisition.[494] In addition, there are borderline difficulties for expenses incurred for the acquisition of goods, expenses relating to goods already capitalized, and expenses relating to contracts for the use of intangible fixed assets belonging to third parties. In this last case, the question has arisen whether royalties paid for the use of a patent should be treated as a deductible expense or as the cost of a contractual right akin to an intangible fixed asset. Case law has held that to consider contractual rights as fixed assets, three criteria must be met:

- the rights must constitute a regular source of profit (*economic* criterion);
- the rights granted must be sufficiently durable (criterion of *permanence*), and
- the rights must be transferable and have a market value (criterion of *patrimoniality*).[495]

However, in a case involving a wine brand, the existence of an autonomous intangible asset was recognized in the absence of the *patrimoniality* criterion.[496]

In *India*, there have been literally hundreds of cases involving the distinction between capital and revenue expenditures.[497] The decided cases have adopted various tests for distinguishing between capital and revenue expenditures but no test is paramount or conclusive.[498] Following UK jurisprudence, Indian courts have sometimes held that an expenditure which produces an enduring benefit for the business is a capital expenditure and have sometimes distinguished between fixed and circulating capital, with expenditures on fixed capital treated as capital expenditures.

In *Japan*, subject to some exceptions for *de minimis* amounts, a general rule in the income tax law requires capitalization of any expenditure whose benefits continue for more than one year. A detailed list of items which must be capitalized in accordance with this rule is set out in the guidelines issued by the tax authorities, and Japanese practice generally follows those guidelines.

In *The Netherlands*, historically a distinction has been made between currently deductible expenses and capital assets. This distinction has given rise to a sizeable body of case law dealing with, *inter alia*, research and development expenses, payments for goodwill, and advertising expenses. It is also necessary to distinguish between capital costs and capitalized expenses in order to determine whether certain tax incentives for capital investment apply, although this distinction has not resulted in much litigation.

3.2 Capital Cost Recovery Systems

Although there is a great deal of variation in the countries' systems of capital cost recovery, they all have three types of rules. First, there are attempts, however rough, to

494. France, General Accounting Plan, s. 212-6.
495. Conseil d'Etat, August 21, 1996, n°154488 (*SA Sife*).
496. Conseil d'Etat, December 28, 2007, n°284899 and 285506 (*SA Domaine Clarence Dillon*).
497. India, ITA 1961, s. 37(1).
498. *Empire Jute Co. Ltd v. Commissioner of Income Tax*, Supreme Court, May 9, 1980.

allow a deduction for capital costs over something like the actual useful life of wasting assets in order to properly reflect a taxpayer's income for each period. Second, in some situations completely arbitrary rules are used as a matter of administrative convenience. Third, certain types of capital costs are allowed to be written off immediately or over a short period of time in order to encourage investment in particular types of assets or to achieve other nonfiscal goals.

In the *United States*, depreciation rules have been modified a number of times; the development of the rules reflects both changes intended to simplify the administration of the system and changes in the attitude toward using accelerated depreciation allowances as an incentive for particular forms of investment. Historically, depreciation was mandatory and was based on the useful lives of assets to reflect actual experience with particular types of assets. The system was initially based on the experience of the particular taxpayer but then relaxed to provide for generally applicable classes of assets, which allowed taxpayers to vary the applicable lives somewhat. Straight-line methods were generally used, although accelerated methods were permitted to reflect the fact that certain assets depreciated more in early years and to provide investment incentives.

The system was changed substantially in 1981. Under the "Accelerated Cost Recovery System," (ACRS) class lives were established for all assets which generally had no relation to their actual useful lives, either in general or in the hands of the particular taxpayer.[499] For example, real estate was assigned a class life of fifteen years. Accelerated depreciation methods were applied to the class lives, which substantially increased the availability of early deductions. The year 1981 marked the high-water mark of noneconomic depreciation policies. Since then, while the class-life system has been retained, most class lives are now more realistic (although not entirely so) and straight-line depreciation is required for some assets. For example, the useful life of commercial real estate has been extended to thirty-nine years and straight-line depreciation is required. However, Congress has continued to adjust depreciation rates in light of changing economic conditions. In 2023, taxpayers were permitted to deduct 100% of the cost of newly acquired "qualified assets" (generally assets with a depreciable life less than 20 years).[500] The percentage of qualified asset cost that may be expensed is reduced by 20% each year. Thus, in 2024, taxpayers can deduct 80% of the cost of qualified assets purchased in 2024, but Congress is currently considering restoring the 100% deduction. The immediate expensing of assets has been controversial because of the significant revenue loss it creates and because of the lack of evidence that it contributes to economic growth.[501]

With respect to intangibles, traditionally, all assets which had a determinable useful life could be amortized over that life. Other assets (such as goodwill) were not amortizable. These rules put substantial pressure on the allocation of costs between arguably short-lived intangibles such as customer lists, favorable contracts, and

499. United States, IRC, s. 168.
500. United States, IRC, s. 168(k).
501. Steve Warmhoff & Richard Phillips, "The Failure of Expensing and Other Depreciation Tax Breaks," Institute on Taxation and Economic Policy Report (November 2018).

covenants not to compete, and nondepreciable goodwill. In response to the large amount of litigation over these issues, a statutory amendment in 1993 allowed all nonfinancial intangibles, including goodwill, obtained in the acquisition of all or part of a business, to be amortized over a fifteen-year period on a straight-line basis.[502] This simplifying rule allows a deduction for the amortization of goodwill but also requires that assets with actual useful lives of less than fifteen years be amortized over the uniform fifteen-year period.

A number of special rules have applied for certain types of assets and expenditures. Until 2022, research and experimentation costs could be deducted currently or amortized over a five-year period at the election of the taxpayer. Current rules eliminate the immediate deduction, but Congress is considering restoring it. Pollution-control facilities are subject to special rules, as are some costs related to natural resource exploitation. Subject to some limitations, up to USD 1,000,000 (USD 1,220,000, adjusted for inflation, in 2024) of costs for tangible property and computer software used by small businesses in a trade or business can be deducted currently.[503] Other special rules also limit deductions with respect to cars, computers, and other assets which would typically be used for both business and personal purposes.

Canada has a comprehensive system of capital cost recovery for all tangible and intangible capital assets.[504] Tangible assets and certain intangibles which have a limited useful life, such as patents and trademarks, are classified into different "classes" (currently, there are forty classes), and rates of depreciation are prescribed for each class based on rough estimates of their useful lives. In most situations, cost recovery deductions are determined on a declining-balance basis for all the assets in a class or pool. The cost of purchases of property of a particular class is added to the pool. In the case of a disposition, the lesser of the cost of the asset or the proceeds of disposition is subtracted from the pool. If there is a negative balance in the pool at the end of a year, that amount is included in income as recaptured depreciation. In contrast, if there is a positive balance in the pool at the end of the year and there are no assets left in the class, the unrecovered balance is deductible. Although the maximum amount of depreciation is determined for each pool or class on the basis of the prescribed rate of depreciation, taxpayers can choose on a year-to-year basis to deduct a smaller amount. Thus, a taxpayer without sufficient income to absorb the available depreciation deductions may postpone the depreciation deduction until later years rather than taking the deduction and creating an operating loss.

Land does not qualify for depreciation. Similarly, any asset which is not acquired for the purpose of earning income cannot qualify for depreciation. Certain types of property, such as pollution-control equipment, clean energy generation and energy conservation equipment, and certain manufacturing and processing assets, qualify for accelerated depreciation. From 2021 to 2024, an incentive measure allowed individuals and Canadian-controlled private corporations to deduct fully the cost of newly acquired property up to CAD 1.5 million annually.

502. United States, IRC, s. 197.
503. United States, IRC, s. 179.
504. Canada, ITA s. 20(1)(a), Reg. 1100, and Sch. B.

Prior to 1972, the cost of goodwill and other intangible capital property with no limited useful life could not be deducted and was not covered by the capital cost recovery system. The "eligible capital property" rules, in effect until the end of 2016, allowed 75 % of the costs of intangible capital property to be deducted on a declining-balance basis at 7 % annually.[505] On the sale of such property, 75 % of the proceeds were taken into account. The expenses and proceeds were accounted for on a pooled basis using the same techniques as those for the capital cost recovery system. Effective 2017, these rules were repealed and replaced with a new asset class in the capital cost allowance regulations.

The *Australian* system, like the Canadian, begins with a general prohibition on the current deductibility of capital costs. The next step is to decide whether the outlay is treated as a cost under a depreciation regime, under the so-called black hole regime, under the capital gain or loss provisions, or nowhere. If an outlay is recovered as cost under the capital gain tax provisions, recovery is delayed but the overall impact may still be concessional: one-half of the capital gain is exempt from tax on the sale of a business (including goodwill) with a net worth of less than AUD 6,000,000 or a turnover of less than AUD 2,000,000. (This exemption is in addition to the general 50 % discount in the case of individuals, so that in some cases 25 % of the total gain may be all that is taxed.)

Until 2001, discrete depreciation regimes were provided for plant and equipment, buildings, mines, a host of specific expenditures on tangible assets, and a limited class of intangibles such as copyrights and patents. In 2001, the capital cost recovery provisions were rewritten to bring them all within a single framework and to broaden the costs which could be recovered.[506] The coverage is still not comprehensive, especially in the area of intangibles. In general, there is no amortization for goodwill. Where depreciation is available, it is based on estimated useful lives and a choice of the straight-line ("prime cost") or declining-balance ("diminishing value") method. Prior to 1999, there were significant elements of acceleration in the system, but these were abolished for assets acquired after 1998. This change required revision of the tables of useful lives published by the fiscal authorities. These had not been reviewed for many years, and so some of the pain of the 1999 change was delayed for assets which, according to the tables, had lives for tax purposes which were shorter than their actual useful lives. As the revision proceeded, it became evident that there could be devastating effects in some industries, and in response, since 2002 the government has "capped" the lives of assets in the affected areas (mainly airlines, mining, energy production, and primary production) by prescribing a short effective life.

A further element of acceleration came back into the system in 2006 when the loading for the declining-balance method was increased from 150 % to 200 %. The tables of useful lives are not binding on taxpayers, who may determine shorter or longer economic lives. Taxpayers may also recalculate the useful life over time and must do so if expenditure amounting to 10 % more of cost is incurred on an asset in an income year. Small business entities are offered two concessions: the immediate

505. Canada, ITA ss. 14 and 20(1)(b) (before 2017).
506. Australia, ITAA 1997, Division 40.

expensing of assets costing less than AUD 20,000 and a pooling system for assets costing more. If immediate expensing is elected, the taxpayer deducts the cost of the asset in the year of purchase. If the pooling system applies, the cost is recovered at the rate of 30% per annum on a declining-balance basis. Depreciation for buildings is allowed under a separate regime on a straight-line basis at 2.5% or 4%, depending on the use of the building. Oddly, the deduction is recaptured on sale even though the purchaser must use the cost of the original person who incurred the expenditure in calculating depreciation deductions (i.e., the purchaser does not get a step-up in the cost of the property). The effect is that, in tax terms, a taxpayer is better off holding a building until it falls down or is replaced than selling it. Even though intellectual property is included under the unified capital allowances regime, it is also given a fixed statutory life and is written off on a straight-line basis.

Where an outlay is not deductible, not added to cost for calculating capital gain, and not recovered under a depreciation regime, the so-called black hole rules allow the outlay to be recovered evenly over five years. This regime is most commonly invoked for payments involving intangibles.

In *India*, depreciation is allowed with respect to the cost of capital assets (of a particular class or block) used in a business in accordance with a "written-down value" method, which is based on the actual cost of an asset (including all expenditures necessary to bring the asset into existence) other than amounts paid by another person and government subsidies.[507] Since 1998, depreciation is also allowed on intangible assets other than goodwill.[508] No depreciation is allowed for assets costing in excess of INR 10,000 unless the assets are acquired through a bank check/draft or through the electronic clearing system of a bank.[509]

In the *United Kingdom*, the class of assets subject to depreciation is much more limited than in other systems.[510] For example, depreciation has not been given for office buildings or retail stores; allowances formerly given for industrial buildings and agricultural buildings were phased out by 2011. However, a Structures and Buildings Allowance for new nonresidential structures and construction costs of buildings incurred on or after October 29, 2018 gives relief at an annual rate of 3% on a straight-line basis. The principal depreciable asset is machinery and equipment. The rate of depreciation has varied greatly, and neither the period of depreciation nor the rate has had any connection to the actual useful life of an asset. In the 1970s, an immediate write-off was allowed for machinery and equipment and 50% of the cost of an industrial building could be deducted immediately, with the remainder recoverable over twenty-five years on a straight-line basis. Later changes reduced the rates of recovery to straight-line depreciation over twenty-five years for buildings and a pooled basis for machinery with a 25% rate. The 25% rate was reduced to 20% in 2008 and to 18% in 2012, but at the same time an annual investment allowance of GBP 200,000 was adopted and later increased to GBP 1 million. In another boost to investment, from

507. India, ITA 1961, s. 43. *See Chellapalli Sugar Ltd v. CIT*, October 31, 1974 (98 ITR 167) (SC).
508. Depreciation is allowed based on groups of assets.
509. India, ITA 1961, 2nd proviso to s. 43(1), the Finance Act, 2017 effective from April 1, 2018.
510. United Kingdom, CAA 2001.

2023 expenditure on plant and machinery generally qualifies for full expensing. Taxpayers can elect not to claim the deduction in whole or in part in a particular year, thus deferring the deduction to a later period. The previous government introduced more generous reliefs for expenditure on certain assets; the list currently includes energy-saving and other environmentally friendly assets.[511]

In *Germany*, as a general rule, tax accounting follows commercial accounting. With respect to depreciation, however, tax law contains several specific provisions. Depreciation for wasting assets is based on useful lives, as determined in depreciation tables published by the Ministry of Finance. The tables are not binding on either the tax authorities or taxpayers, but are followed in the vast majority of cases, and deviations must be specifically justified. Until 2007, taxpayers could choose between the straight-line method and the declining-balance method. The justification for the declining-balance method was that the decline in market value in the early years of use is high and maintenance expenses low, while in later years the reverse is true. In 2008, the declining-balance method was abolished in order to generate tax revenue to offset reductions in the corporate tax rate. Since then, however, it has been reintroduced several times on a temporary basis as a means for promoting economic growth in difficult times. Currently, the declining-balance method may be used for movable assets acquired in 2020-2022 or between March 31, 2024 and January 1, 2025.[512] For other movable assets, taxpayers can use only the straight-line method based on the estimated useful life of the asset.[513] Special statutory rates of depreciation exist for buildings.[514] In 2024, in response to the housing shortage, the legislature introduced an option to use the declining-balance method for residential buildings.

Since 1986, business goodwill can be depreciated on a fifteen-year straight-line basis (different case law-based principles apply to professional goodwill). Depreciation can also be based on an asset's output, comparing its performance in one year with its total anticipated production.

There are a number of provisions allowing accelerated depreciation in order to encourage investment in particular assets (e.g., cultural heritage, ships, and small businesses).

While extraordinary depreciation can be taken for technical or economic obsolescence or heavy use, there is no general deduction for impairment losses available for all sources of income. However, in the calculation of business profits, special statutory rules allow all assets (including land and stock interests) to be written down to "going-concern value."[515] The basic idea is that business assets should be valued as if the entire business had to be disposed of to one potential buyer and the appropriate part of the purchase price was allocated to the asset in question. The going-concern value cannot be lower than the price for which the asset could be sold separately or higher than the replacement cost. The taxpayer has the burden of proof as to

511. United Kingdom, CAA, ss. 39 et seq.
512. Germany, ITA, s. 7 para. 2.
513. Germany, ITA, s. 7 para. 1 sent. 1.
514. Germany, ITA, s. 7 para. 4, para. 5.
515. Germany, ITA, s. 6 para. 1 No. 1 sent. 2, No. 2 sent. 2.

going-concern value. Although the going-concern principle introduces substantial uncertainty in the calculation of income, it is an accepted part of German rules on income determination. Any write-down to going-concern value must be recaptured in later years following a recovery of the original value.[516]

In *Japan*, taxpayers can elect between straight-line or declining-balance methods based on tables of useful life which are determined by the tax authorities, subject to some exceptions (e.g., only the straight-line method is available for buildings).[517] The tables are extremely detailed and are occasionally revised. Although it is difficult to generalize, the tables seem to reflect realistic estimates of actual lives. However, there have been some attempts to use artificial useful lives and accelerated depreciation in order to encourage particular investments. Assets which are not used for business purposes cannot be depreciated.

In *France*, companies are allowed a degree of flexibility in deducting depreciation, which depends on two factors: the nature of the asset and the method of depreciation. First, not all assets are depreciable. Only assets that are useful to the business can be depreciated. Depreciation can be technical (e.g., software which might have an indefinite life but is likely to soon be obsolete), or legal (e.g., a right, such as a patent, which is generally granted for a certain period). Tangible fixed assets are depreciable over time. With regard to intangible fixed assets, notably goodwill, case law permits amortization if the asset is identifiable, separable from the business, and subject to irreversible depreciation.[518] The question has arisen whether it is possible to depreciate what accounting law considers "goodwill" in the form of customer lists, brand names, trade names and, more broadly, market share. Under accounting law, goodwill may be amortized under certain conditions, over its useful life or over ten years if the useful life cannot be reliably determined.[519] These rules were enacted in response to a 2013 EU Directive on annual financial statements.[520] The Finance Act of 2022 allows companies to deduct from their taxable income the amortization recorded in the accounts for goodwill acquired between January 1, 2022 and December 31, 2025.[521] The end of this temporary connection between accounting and taxation may create a real competitive disadvantage for French businesses since most EU countries have adopted this treatment permanently. With respect to trademarks, the difficulty is that depreciation is linked to its foreseeable life, whereas in principle a brand has an unlimited life. The practical assessment is therefore tenuous and decided by the courts on a case-by-case basis.

The second factor is the method of depreciation. Depreciation is based on the actual useful life of the asset, as expected by the company, and is thus calculated by reference to the "practices" in force in the company's business sector. The tax

516. Germany, ITA, s. 6 para. 1 No. 1 sent. 4, No. 3 sent. 3.
517. Japan, ITA, s. 49 and CTA, s. 31.
518. Conseil d'Etat, October 1, 1999, n°177809 (*Foncia Particimo*).
519. France, Accounting Standards Authority, November 23, 2015, Regulation n°2015-06.
520. Directive 2013/34/EU of the European Parliament and of the Council of June 26, 2013 on the annual financial statements, consolidated financial statements, and related reports of certain types of undertakings; *Official Journal*, L 182, June 29, 2013, pp. 19-76.
521. France, CGI, s. 39, 1-2° al. 3.

authorities provide depreciation scales based on these practices,[522] and if the company deviates from these scales, it must explain why. There are three different methods: the straight-line method (*méthode linéaire*), the declining-balance method (*méthode dégressive*), and the exceptional or special depreciation method. In addition, there is an obligation to recognize minimum depreciation, preventing companies from refraining from depreciating assets during loss-making years and claiming unused depreciation when the company returns to profit.[523]

In *The Netherlands*, the rules regarding depreciation are quite flexible. All depreciation methods are allowed as long as they are used consistently and meet the standard of "good business practice" (*goed koopmansgebruik*).

Sweden allows depreciation deductions over standardized lives which are shorter than the actual useful lives for machinery and equipment. Depreciation rates are 20% on a straight-line basis or 30% on a declining-balance basis, at the taxpayer's choice. For buildings, the depreciation is on a straight-line basis over a period, depending on the type of building (e.g., residential houses are depreciated over a period of fifty years and normal factory buildings over a twenty-five-year period).[524] The rules on the deduction of maintenance costs are quite liberal; the combined deductions for real estate are also generous. Research and development costs are currently deductible in accordance with generally accepted accounting principles. Costs involved in inventory production are capitalized and deducted when the product is sold, in accordance with financial accounting rules.

The *Chinese* EIT law is not well developed with respect to the deduction of capital costs. In general, depreciation is allowed on a straight-line basis in accordance with an assumed useful life of the property. The period of depreciation is prescribed to be twenty years for buildings, ten years for machinery and equipment, and five years for electronic equipment and furniture. The cost of intangibles can be amortized over a period of not less than ten years.

4 EDUCATION COSTS

Education costs can involve personal consumption, business-related current expenses, or investment in "human capital," depending on the circumstances in which they arise. All the systems under consideration here take generally the same approach, disallowing expenses for basic education but allowing deductions where a taxpayer is improving or maintaining existing skills used to earn income. Thus, in the *United States*, expenses which maintain or improve a taxpayer's skills in an existing trade or business are generally deductible. However, if the expenses qualify the taxpayer for a new trade or business or are necessary to meet the minimum educational requirements of a trade or business, no deduction is allowed.[525] The test is an objective one; even if a taxpayer never intends to enter, and never does enter the new profession, the expenses are not

522. France, CGI, s. 39 II.
523. France, CGI, s. 39 B and Regulatory Schedule II, s. 25.
524. Sweden, ITA, Ch. 18.
525. United States, Reg., 1.162-5.

deductible. Thus, an accountant who attends law school cannot deduct the expenses even if the expenses are incurred only to further the accountancy career since in fact the accountant becomes qualified for a new trade or business. For nondeductible expenses, there is no provision for the amortization of the investment in "human capital."

In *Sweden*, in general, the same approach is taken. Educational expenses are usually not deductible, especially where they result in qualification for a new position. However, educational expenses to maintain an existing competence are deductible. The situation in *China* is the same, except that the education expenses of a taxpayer's children are expressly allowed as deductions.[526] Enterprises are allowed to deduct staff education expenses up to a maximum of 2.5% of total salaries and wages.

In *Canada*, education expenses are not deductible and are viewed as personal, capital, or a mixture of both. Continuing education or training expenses of a taxpayer already established in a business are deductible as ordinary business expenses. Education or training expenses incurred by employees are not deductible. A tax credit is available for certain postsecondary school and occupational training costs.

The *Australian* system operates along the same lines, with only educational costs related to an existing trade or profession being deductible. If an employer pays an employee's (deductible) education expenses, the otherwise deductible rules eliminate the FBT that would otherwise apply.

The *United Kingdom* followed similar principles until 1991, when a deduction for qualifying vocational training payments was introduced. However, the deduction was abandoned in 2001 owing to fraud. There are various exclusions from tax for training or retraining courses provided by employers, so that employees incur no tax liability in respect of these costs incurred by employers.[527] Business-related expenses, such as the cost of attending conferences, are usually deductible under general principles; there are no special rules for conference expenditures.

In *Germany*, originally, there was a distinction between basic education and further training for improving a taxpayer's professional skills, with only expenses for the latter deductible as business or professional expenses. However, starting in 2002, the courts changed their longstanding view, holding that basic education could also be closely connected to an income-earning activity and therefore the costs of basic education could also qualify as deductible expenses. This jurisprudence led to various amendments of the ITA to limit the deductibility of basic education costs. At present, basic education costs are classified as personal expenditures and are deductible only to a limited extent, under the provision for "special" personal costs (EUR 6,000 yearly in 2024);[528] statutory provisions explicitly deny the deduction, as business or professional expenses, of costs of the first professional education of a taxpayer.[529] In 2014, the Federal Tax Court referred the matter to the Federal Constitutional Court, arguing that

526. China, IIT, Art. 6. Employer-paid education costs of the children of nonresident individuals working in China are not treated as taxable benefits.
527. United Kingdom, ITEPA, ss. 250 et seq.
528. Germany, ITA, s. 10 para. 1 No. 7.
529. Germany, ITA, s. 4 para. 9, s. 9 para. 6.

the distinction between first professional education and any further education violated tax equality and the ability-to-pay principle.[530] In 2019, the Federal Constitutional Court upheld the current regime, arguing that the first professional education might be regarded as having a strong impact on the personality of the taxpayer and could therefore be deemed to belong more to his private (fiscally irrelevant) sphere than any additional education.[531]

In *The Netherlands*, education expenses incurred by employees to maintain current skills are treated as employment expenses and are not deductible. An employer, however, can designate the reimbursement of educational costs as a final levy component for the WKR (as discussed above), which means that the allowance is not regarded as taxable employment income for the employee.

The *French* system allows a deduction for educational costs to maintain or improve skills and, in the case of employees, to qualify for a new position. In addition, adult students (up to 25 years old) may either be included in the fiscal household of the parents or taxed separately. In the first case, although the student's taxable income must be added to the parents' taxable income, the result is often a decrease in the parents' income tax because a special tax credit is combined with the increase in the number of (family) shares generally (*see* Subpart E, section 1, below) or is combined with the grant of a standard deduction in the case of children who are married or members of a civil partnership and/or have family dependents.[532] Where adult children are taxed separately, payments made by the parents to the student can be deducted within certain limits.[533]

In *Japan*, for self-employed individuals, educational expenses are deductible if they have a direct relationship with the business. In contrast, for employees, only limited items specifically provided in the ITA are eligible for itemized deductions.[534] The eligible items were expanded in 2023 to include the cost of certain business seminars and payments made for obtaining business licenses, subject to specified certification requirements.

In *India*, expenditures for the training or education of employees are generally deductible by the employer. There have also been cases where foreign education expenses of a director's son have been allowed on the ground that it would benefit the business.[535] For individual taxpayers, tuition fees (for two children) (subject to an overall limit on most deductions of INR 150,000) paid to any school, college, or university are deductible in computing total income under the old regime.[536] Under the old regime, a deduction is also available for certain interest expenses on borrowed funds used for the education of the taxpayer, the taxpayer's spouse, and children; the

530. Federal Tax Court (*Bundesfinanzhof*), July 17, 2014, VI R 8/12.
531. Federal Constitutional Court (*Bundesverfassungsgericht*), November 19, 2019, 2 BvL 22/14.
532. France, CGI, ss. 6-3 and 196 B.
533. France, CGI, s. 156 II 2°.
534. Japan, ITA, s. 57-2, para. 2.
535. *Kostub Investments Ltd v. CIT* (Delhi High Court) February 25, 2014.
536. India, ITA 1961, s. 80C. *See* the chapter on India (section 3.1) in Part I for a description of the old regime and the new regime introduced in 2020, under which taxpayers are subject to a lower tax rate but give up the right to claim certain deductions and concessions.

deduction is available for eight years starting from the year in which repayment of the loan begins.[537] For employees, education allowances up to INR 100 per month, per child, for two children and accommodation allowances up to INR 300 per month for two children, are exempt.[538] None of these deductions is available under the new regime introduced in 2020.

5 DEDUCTION OF PERSONAL COSTS

As discussed in the Country Descriptions in Part I, a personal exemption or allowance, which in effect makes a certain minimum level of income tax-free, is arguably a way of reflecting some level of personal costs in the tax system. In addition, some systems allow a deduction for specific personal costs, such as medical costs or personal losses.

5.1 Interest

All the systems considered here allow a deduction in general for interest expenses incurred in connection with income-earning activities, and all countries other than the United Kingdom allow a deduction for such expenses in connection with personal investment activities. The deduction is sometimes limited to the amount of current investment income in order to prevent a current deduction for interest when the income is deferred. In addition, some systems require the capitalization of certain interest expense, typically interest incurred in connection with the production of long-lived assets such as buildings. The most striking difference in the systems is in the treatment of interest expense which does not have a connection with income-producing activities. From a theoretical point of view, whether personal interest, i.e., interest which is related to personal consumption, should be deductible has been the subject of considerable debate. There is general agreement that consumption should be included in the tax base. However, personal interest can also be viewed, not as additional consumption, but simply as the cost of a preference for current as opposed to deferred consumption. By borrowing to consume now, the cost of the consumption is increased by the amount of the interest expense but the absolute amount of the consumption, which is the appropriate measure of the tax base, has not changed. Thus, according to this view, a person who borrows to finance current consumption should be treated no differently from a tax perspective from a person who finances the consumption by "dissaving" and selling income-producing assets. If this analysis is accepted, a deduction for personal interest expense would be appropriate.

However, if the starting point of the analysis is that business-related expenses are the only type of expenses which should be deducted, personal interest would be disallowed. In addition, allowing a deduction for personal interest is often thought to encourage consumption rather than savings, which may not be desirable from an economic point of view. From a structural perspective, if a distinction is made between

537. India, ITA 1961, s. 80E.
538. India, ITA 1961, Rule 2BB, read with s. 10(14).

deductible and nondeductible interest, some mechanism must be provided for distinguishing between the two classes of interest expense. These varying considerations have played out differently in the systems examined here.

In the *United States*, prior to 1986, all interest expense was allowed as a deduction without any limitations on the deduction of personal interest. Limits on the deduction of personal interest were imposed in 1986, restricting the deduction for personal interest to interest on loans used to acquire a personal residence (within some dollar limitations). In addition, interest on up to USD 100,000 of loans secured by a personal residence has been allowed as a deduction, no matter to what use the proceeds are put.[539] However, effective for 2018 to 2025, this deduction for interest on home equity loans has been suspended. Complex tracing rules are applied to assign the interest expense to the appropriate category, based on the flow of funds, with some simplifying assumptions.

In *Germany*, in principle, interest on personal debt is not deductible, although, prior to 1974, such interest was fully deductible as a "special expense." Until 1994, a limited amount of interest on personal-residence mortgages was deductible. The current nondeductibility of personal interest makes the allocation of interest expense to personal or professional/business activities a major issue. In principle, taxpayers are allowed to decide freely on how to finance activities (e.g., borrowing for business activities and using savings for personal activities). However, in order to limit the tax planning potential arising from this freedom of choice, a specific statutory provision was introduced to limit the deduction of interest on business-related debt to the extent that there have been "excessive withdrawals" from the business. An "excessive withdrawal" is deemed to occur where the amount of the withdrawal exceeds both the business profit and the contributions made by the taxpayer to the business in the same period.[540]

The rules in *Canada* are similar. Under the statute, interest is deductible only if the borrowed funds are used for purposes of earning income from a business or property, and personal interest is thus not deductible. Strangely, the courts have consistently held that interest is a nondeductible capital expense; therefore, interest is deductible only if it meets the conditions of the statutory deduction.[541] Nondeductible personal interest involved in the purchase of personal assets is also not capitalized despite the fact that the capital gain on the sale of an asset is taxable, although at a preferential rate; the expense may be viewed as relating to the untaxed imputed return on the asset. A tracing-of-funds approach is the primary method used to establish whether the interest expense is incurred to earn income, although other methods, such as an ordering rule and apportionment, are occasionally used where tracing is impossible. It is accepted standard practice for taxpayers to use their savings or equity to finance consumption and to borrow for income-producing purposes. A Supreme Court case held that commingling of borrowed funds and savings did not preclude a

539. United States, IRC, s. 163(h).
540. Germany, ITA, s. 4 para. 4a.
541. Canada, ITA, s. 20(1)(c).

taxpayer from deducting interest.[542] Although the taxpayer could not trace the borrowed funds to an income-earning use, it was held to be sufficient for the taxpayer to show that an amount equal to the borrowed funds was being used for an income-earning purpose (a positive ordering approach).

Australia follows the same basic approach. The issue has attracted a great deal of interest in Australia. The High Court applied the general anti-avoidance rule to a so-called split loan, a product offered by financial institutions under which borrowings finance the purchase of a family home and an investment property. All repayments go to pay down the loan on the home, while the interest on the investment property is capitalized, so that the part of the loan relating to that property grows in proportion to the amount borrowed.[543] Further, the courts have denied deductions on loans classified as equity for banking regulatory purposes.[544] Conversely, the courts decided in favor of a taxpayer in relation to a capital-protected loan (i.e., the financier accepted recourse only to the asset in exchange for a higher interest rate), but legislation was passed to deny a deduction for the portion of the interest payment which related to capital protection.[545]

Japan has similar rules. Personal interest is neither deductible nor eligible for capitalization, while interest on borrowings which are used for business can be deducted from business income.

In the *United Kingdom*, a deduction for personal interest was originally allowed without restriction. However, since 1969 the deduction has been subject to substantial limitations.[546] If the interest is not connected to a taxable source of income, such as a trade or rental real estate, it must be related to a "qualifying purpose" to be deductible. The statutory list of accepted purposes is quite limited and includes investment in a closely held company or employee-controlled company, machinery and equipment used in employment or in a partnership (e.g., a car), and certain types of life annuity. At one time, the most important qualifying purpose was the purchase of a personal residence.

The deduction was restricted in that it applied only to interest on a loan up to GBP 30,000. Further legislation has reduced the value of this deduction by not allowing it to be set against the top tax rate otherwise payable and limiting it first to the basic rate of 25%, then to the lower rate of 20%, then to a notional rate of 15%, and then 10%. It was finally abolished in 2000. This exercise represents an interesting example of how to phase out a relief measure by progressively eroding its value. The UK has pursued a similar strategy with respect to mortgage-interest deductions for individual landlords, limiting them to the equivalent of a deduction against basic-rate tax from 2020-2021.

In *France*, personal interest is not deductible and more generally, no deduction is allowed for investment-related expenses even where the acquired asset is income-producing. Following the same logic applicable to the characterization of income (*see*

542. *The Queen v. Singleton*, [2002] 1 CTC 121 (SCC).
543. *Hart* [2004] HCA 26, 217 CLR 216.
544. *Macquarie Finance Ltd* [2005] FCA FC 205, 146 FCR 77 and *St George Bank Ltd* [2009] FCAFC 62.
545. *Firth* [2002] FCAFC 95, 120 FCR 450, overridden by Australia, ITAA 1997, Division 247.
546. *See* United Kingdom, ITA ss. 383 et seq.

section 2), personal interest on capital transactions cannot be considered as an expense incurred for the acquisition or preservation of income, and therefore cannot be deducted from the income received by the individual concerned. For example, interest on loans or advances on securities taken out by private individuals in the course of managing their private assets, for the acquisition of securities or for the preservation of their securities portfolio, as well as interest on a personal loan taken out by a director to subscribe to a capital increase in their company, are not deductible. However, owners of property subject to income tax can deduct from their property income (*revenu foncier*) the interest on loans incurred in connection with rental real estate taken out for "the conservation, acquisition, construction, repair or improvement of properties, including those of which the taxpayer is the bare owner and whose usufruct belongs to a low-income housing organization, a semi-public company or an approved organization."[547] An exception also applies to interest incurred in connection with the acquisition by employees or company directors of shares in the company for which they work if the company is engaged in an industrial, commercial, craft, agricultural, or liberal activity and the amount of interest is not disproportionate.[548] An income tax credit has also been introduced for interest on a loan used to purchase or construct a principal residence.[549]

In contrast, in *Sweden*, there are in principle no restrictions on the deductibility of interest by individuals. Interest connected with a business is deducted from the income in that category. All other interest, including personal interest, is deducted in computing income from capital. In general, a tracing rule is used to determine the treatment of interest expenses. Since business income is taxed at a higher rate than income from capital, a special rule prevents taxpayers from allocating excessive private interest expense from capital income to business income. If the amount of debt allocated to a business results in negative equity when compared to the tax cost of the business assets, interest is calculated on the "negative" equity using the government borrowing rate plus 1 percentage point. The interest amount is treated as additional income in the business category and as additional expense in the capital income category, thus, in effect, reallocating a portion of the excess interest expense to the more lightly taxed capital income.

In *The Netherlands*, personal interest is not deductible.

In *India*, under the general rule in section 37(1) of the ITA, interest paid on any debt incurred wholly and exclusively for the purpose of a business is deductible. In addition, any interest paid in respect of capital borrowed for the purpose of a business is specifically allowed as a deduction.[550] Interest on money borrowed for acquisition of a new asset (whether capitalized or not) is not deductible until the asset is put into use in the business.[551] Restrictions on the deduction of interest have recently been introduced where an Indian company or a permanent establishment of a foreign

547. France, CGI, s. 31 I 1°-d.
548. France, CGI, s. 83, 3° last paragraph.
549. France, CGI, s. 200 quaterdecies.
550. India, ITA 1961, s. 36(1)(iii).
551. India, ITA 1961, proviso to s. 36(1)(iii).

company borrows from an associated enterprise to the extent that it exceeds 30% of the earnings before interest, taxes, depreciation, and amortization (EBITDA) of the borrower.[552]

Personal interest is deductible in the case of residential property (referred to as "house property") up to INR 20,000 under the old regime, but otherwise is not deductible.[553]

5.2 Personal Losses

While losses incurred in connection with personal assets are generally not deductible, in some situations a deduction is allowed if the loss occurs in particular circumstances. Thus, in the *United States*, a loss due to damage to personal assets is deductible if the damage is attributable to a "casualty," which has been interpreted to mean a sudden and unexpected event.[554] There is a substantial amount of interpretive material around the issue of what constitutes a casualty, including an administrative rule that termite damage is not sufficiently sudden to qualify for a casualty loss. When a deduction is available, the amount of the loss is limited to the tax cost of the asset and is deductible only where the total of all losses exceeds a percentage of the taxpayer's income. However, effective 2018 through 2025, qualified personal casualty losses (exceeding casualty gains) are deductible only if attributable to a federally declared disaster.

In *Germany*, gains and losses on the disposition of private assets are generally not taken into account. The extension of taxability of private capital gains to real estate sold within ten years after acquisition and to other assets sold within one year after acquisition has led to the recognition of private losses either within the same period or under carryback and carryforward rules.[555] These losses can be set off only against gains from the same source. The same holds true for losses on privately held shares and other securities under the new rules on the "final withholding tax" (*Abgeltungsteuer*).[556] Under this new regime, losses arising from the alienation of privately held portfolio securities can be set off only against capital gains arising from the alienation of such securities. This rule extends to casualty losses. Even if a casualty loss has some business connection, no deduction is allowed (e.g., loss of jewelry on a business trip or a firm outing). However, as discussed in the chapter on Germany in Part I, the German tax system recognizes a general deduction for "extraordinary burdens." These expenditures must be unusually high when compared with those of similarly situated taxpayers and must be unavoidable. Casualty losses are covered by this provision. It is highly disputed whether the deduction applies only to uninsurable losses.

552. India, ITA 1961, s. 94B. The restrictions do not apply to banking or insurance companies, finance companies set up in the IFSC, or notified non-banking financial companies.
553. *Madhav Prasad Jatia v. CIT*, 118 ITR 200 (SC).
554. United States, IRC, s. 163(h).
555. Germany, ITA, s. 23 para. 3 ss. 7-9.
556. Germany, ITA, s. 20 para. 6.

In *Canada* and *Australia*, losses involving personal property are in general not deductible. However, with respect to "listed personal property" (referred to in Australia as "collectables"), i.e., stamps, coins, jewelry, and artworks, losses are deductible, but only against the gains from such property.[557] The loss is limited to the tax cost of the property. The *United Kingdom* restricts the deduction for losses on personal-use items which are tangible movable property by excluding any gain or loss where the assets are disposed of (including worthlessness) for less than GBP 6,000 and excluding any gain or loss where the asset is tangible movable property with a useful life of less than fifty years.[558] Australia uses a similar rule to eliminate small gains on nonlisted personal assets, but based on cost, so that records do not need to be kept where the cost is below the limit (AUD 10,000). A similar rule in Canada is limited to assets with a cost not in excess of CAD 1,000. These results all follow from the structure of the capital gains legislation in these jurisdictions.

In China, France, India, Japan, The Netherlands, and Sweden, gains and losses on private assets are not generally taken into account regardless of how those gains or losses arise. Thus, for example, in *The Netherlands*, neither the loss on an uninsured personal residence destroyed by fire nor the gain from insurance proceeds in excess of cost is relevant for tax purposes. In contrast, in *Sweden*, personal losses on personal dwellings are taken into account on the sale of the dwelling when computing a capital gain or loss. In *India*, personal effects,[559] excluding gold, jewelry etc., are not considered to be capital assets and no gain or loss arises from their disposal; however, in some circumstances, losses from owner-occupied properties, shares, and other securities can be taken into account. In *Japan*, catastrophic losses due to natural disaster, fire, or other catastrophic accidents, as well as a loss by theft of personal property, can be deducted from income in accordance with a certain formula. Further, insurance premiums for certain kinds of earthquake insurance are tax-deductible to a limited extent.[560] In *France*, only expenses listed in the CGI are deductible from overall income and only to the extent that they enable income to be conserved and preserved. For example, losses of property due to theft or damage are not deductible.

5.3 Medical Expenses

Medical expenses may be deducted or claimed as a tax credit in several of the systems, although they are viewed as personal expenses. In the *United States*, where there is no comprehensive public health-care system, a deduction is available for medical expenses which exceed a percentage of income.[561] What constitutes "medical" treatment has been interpreted quite broadly, although there is a statutory prohibition against the deduction of the costs of cosmetic surgery. Premiums for private health insurance are deductible but, because of the percentage-of-income threshold, persons who are

557. Canada, ITA, s. 41(2).
558. United Kingdom, TCGA, ss. 45 and 262.
559. India, ITA 1961, s. 2(14)(ii).
560. Japan, ITA, s. 77.
561. United States, IRC, s. 213.

insured typically do not benefit from the deduction. As discussed with respect to fringe benefits in Subpart B, section 1.2, employer-provided health care is not taxable.

Canada has a publicly funded health-care system, although not all costs are covered. A credit is available for 15% (the lowest rate of federal tax) of medical costs of an individual and their immediate family members over a threshold amount of the lesser of CAD 1,813 (indexed to inflation) or 3% of the individual's income.[562] The credit is available for a lengthy list of medical costs but if a cost is not listed, even a clearly legitimate one, no credit is available. (There is usually some time lag between the development of new medical technology and its addition to the list of qualifying costs for the medical-expense credit.) Canada also provides a similar credit for persons with severe and prolonged disabilities in recognition of the nonitemizable expenses that such persons incur. The *Australian* system provides a credit of 30% of the cost of private health insurance and imposes a tax rate surcharge on those without private health insurance (even though Australia has universal public health care).[563] Health expenses in connection with work-related injuries may be deducted under the general deduction provisions where such injuries are a clear occupational hazard.

Business-related medical expenses may also be deducted in the *United Kingdom*. There is no general deduction for medical costs, but a limited deduction was at one time available for medical insurance by persons over sixty; this was repealed by the government in 1997. Where medical expenses arise outside the UK and are thus not covered by the National Health Service system, special legislation allows an employee to avoid the income inclusion which would otherwise arise if the employer bears the cost of providing medical insurance or treatment.[564]

In *The Netherlands*, particular medical expenses qualify as a personal deduction to the extent that they exceed certain thresholds.[565] In *Japan*, medical costs exceeding JPY 100,000 per household are deductible.[566] In addition, in order to promote self-medication aimed at reducing medical expenditures borne by the public health insurance system, a special deduction is available for some specified types of medicines sold over the counter.[567]

In *Germany*, there is no specific deduction for private medical expenses. Medical costs which arise from a sickness incurred in the course of business (e.g., radiation sickness in the case of a radiologist, tuberculosis in the case of a pulmonary doctor) are deductible as business expenses. However, no deduction was allowed in the case of a heart attack suffered by a lawyer.

For personal medical expenses, the general deduction for "extraordinary expenses" above a certain minimum is available for some types of medical expenses.[568] These expenses must qualify as "direct" medical costs (e.g., doctors' costs, hospital costs, drugs) to meet the general requirement that extraordinary expenses may be

562. Canada, ITA, s. 118.2.
563. Australia, ITAA 1997, Subdivision 61-G.
564. United Kingdom, ITEPA, s. 325.
565. Netherlands, ITA, Art. 6.17.
566. Japan, ITA, s. 73.
567. Japan, STMA, s. 41-17-2.
568. Germany, ITA, s. 33.

deducted only if they are inevitable. "Indirect" costs, such as medical literature, are not deductible and there is considerable litigation over the "direct-indirect" distinction. No deduction is allowed for preventive medical costs.

Medical insurance premiums can be deducted to a large extent as "special" expenses. Since 2010, the cost of basic medical insurance is fully deductible; for additional insurance protection, deductibility is limited.[569] This regime was introduced following a decision of the Federal Constitutional Court in 2008 which required the legislature to extend the deductibility of insurance costs.[570]

Sweden has an extensive public health-care system which provides free or low-cost service. As a result, personal medical costs are not deductible.

In *France*, medical or pharmaceutical expenses and hospitalization costs incurred by a taxpayer are in principle not deductible. However, elderly taxpayers who incur expenses for accommodation in a long-stay establishment or medical facility are entitled to a tax credit equal to 25% of the expenses incurred for both dependency and accommodation. The annual amount of expenditure qualifying for the credit may not exceed EUR 10,000 per person.[571] Specific measures have also been introduced to allow a deduction, subject to certain conditions and limits, for contributions paid by the head of a farm or agricultural business to an optional supplementary old-age insurance scheme[572] and of social security contributions, in particular for the taxation of nonbusiness profits.[573]

In *India*, for taxpayers opting for the application of the old regime, a deduction is available with respect to medical expenses incurred for the taxpayer and dependents (including parents) up to INR 40,000 (INR 100,000 for dependents who are senior citizens);[574] health insurance premiums are also deductible with limits.[575] A special deduction is available to an individual (or HUF) for medical expenses of a disabled dependent of INR 75,000 (INR 125,000 in the case of a severe disability), subject to certain conditions.[576] These deductions are not available under the new regime introduced in 2020, under which taxpayers are subject to a lower tax rate but give up the right to claim certain deductions and concessions.[577]

5.4 Charitable Donations

Most of the systems allow a deduction or credit for contributions to organizations, private or public, which perform charitable, religious, cultural, or educational services. There are typically limits on the deductible amounts related in some way to the

569. Germany, ITA, s. 10 para. 1 No. 3 and No. 3a s. 10 para. 4.
570. Federal Constitutional Court (*Bundesverfassungsgericht*), February 13, 2008, 2 BvL 1/06.
571. France, CGI, s. 199 quindecies.
572. France, CGI, s. 154 bis-0 A.
573. France, CGI, s. 154 bis.
574. India, ITA 1961, s. 80DDB.
575. India, ITA 1961, s. 80D.
576. India, ITA 1961, s. 80 DD.
577. However, the taxpayer can elect to have the old regime continue to apply. *See* the chapter on India in Part I (section 3.1).

taxpayer's income. Thus, in the *United States*, gifts to qualifying organizations can, in general, be deducted up to 50% (60% for cash gifts in taxable years 2018-2025) of the taxpayer's income.[578] More restrictive limitations apply for gifts to "private" foundations, i.e., organizations which are not supported by the general public but by one or several large donors. Excess donations can be carried over and deducted in subsequent years to the extent that current deductions do not exceed the limitations. In the case of certain gifts of property, the fair market value of the property is deductible, thus giving a deduction for the appreciation in value of the property which has not been included in the tax base. No deduction is allowed for the contribution of services, although out-of-pocket costs in rendering services to charities may be deducted. Where a donor receives some benefit as a result of a contribution, the deductible amount is reduced to the extent of the value of the benefit. There are significant substantiation requirements.

In *Canada*, most individuals are entitled to a tax credit of 15% (the lowest rate of federal tax) for the first CAD 200 of contributions to registered charities and 29% (the second-highest rate of federal tax) for donations in excess of that amount.[579] Since 2016, individuals paying the highest federal tax rate (33%) can claim a 33% credit for donations in excess of the CAD 200 threshold. There are parallel provincial tax credits. Gifts must be evidenced by a written receipt which must be retained by taxpayers but is not filed with the tax return. Donations are limited to 75% of the taxpayer's income for a year, with a five-year carryforward. However, gifts of cultural property and ecologically sensitive land are not subject to this limitation. In the case of a donation of appreciated property, the taxpayer may elect to treat any amount between the cost basis of the property and its fair market value as the contribution. The amount elected is also treated as the amount realized on the disposition of the property for purposes of realizing gain.

The *Australian* system has few limitations on charitable deductions, although previously it had limits on gifts of appreciated property similar to those in Canada. In recent years, tax benefits for charitable gifts have been increased in a number of ways. Normally, a gift is a realization event at market value, but the gain is now exempt in some cases of charitable giving and a deduction is allowed for the fair market value of the property. Charitable deductions cannot give rise to a tax loss for a year, but the donor can elect to spread the deduction over five years in the percentages the donor elects. There are elaborate administrative procedures for an institution to qualify as charitable in order for deductions to be allowed; the administration of these procedures has been tightened in recent years, partly because of the more generous concessions now available. Most charitable giving involves donations made directly to large public charitable institutions, but a regime akin to the U.S. rules for private foundations allows wealthy benefactors to set up "private ancillary funds" as a tax-favored in-house vehicle for funding charitable activities. Under this regime, the charitable-donation

578. United States, IRC, s. 170.

579. Canada, ITA, s. 118.1. For five years from 2013 to 2018, there was an enhanced credit for first-time donors equal to an additional 25% of the amount of qualifying gifts.

deduction is triggered when the donor gives to the fund, rather than when the fund distributes the money to further its objects.[580]

In the *United Kingdom*, a deduction is generally allowed for payments of money to charity. There are also special rules for gifts of land, shares, and securities. Under the UK CGT rules, the transfer of an asset to a qualifying charity gives rise to no chargeable gain to the donor. From April 2024, these income tax, corporation tax, and CGT reliefs apply only where the charity is a UK charity. The receipt of various benefits from a charity may lead to the loss of the deduction.[581]

In the *Japanese* system, charitable contributions are deductible to the extent that they exceed an absolute floor of JPY 2,000 and do not exceed 40% of the taxpayer's income. The contribution must be made to a government agency or a limited number of government-approved public-interest organizations. For certain contributions, taxpayers can choose tax credits of 40% of the amount of the charitable contribution (in excess of JPY 2,000) instead of an income deduction.[582] The deduction for gifts of appreciated property is limited to the tax cost of the property.[583]

Charitable contributions are deductible in *The Netherlands* to the extent that their total amount exceeds both 1% of income and EUR 60. The deductible amount may not exceed 10% of income.[584] This restriction does not apply to annual gifts of up to EUR 250,000 where the donor is obliged by contract to make such gifts for at least five years.[585]

In *Germany*, charitable contributions are deductible as "special" personal expenses.[586] Contributions must be made to government agencies or private tax exempt nonprofit organizations. Following a 2009 judgment of the CJEU,[587] the tax deduction was extended to contributions to charities located in other EU Member States. However, deductibility still requires a certain link to Germany: the particular charity must either support German residents or contribute, via its activities, to Germany's reputation in the world. Moreover, the foreign charity must comply with the organizational requirements for tax exempt entities under German law.

The deduction is generally limited to 20% of a taxpayer's annual income. In the case of businesses, an alternative limitation of 0.4% of the payroll and turnover applies. Donations to publicly approved foundations can be deducted up to EUR 1,000,000 over ten years. If an individual gift subject to the 20% limitation exceeds that limit, the deduction can be carried forward and claimed in future years, subject to the statutory limits.

Normally, for contributions of property, the fair market value of the property is deductible. Since private capital gains are generally not taxed, the problem of

580. Australia, ITAA 1997, Division 30, s. 118-60.
581. United Kingdom, ITA ss. 413-446 and 518-564; for corporation tax, *see* CTA 2010, ss. 471 et seq.
582. Japan, SMTA, s. 41-18-3.
583. Japan, ITA, s. 78 and SMTA, s. 40.
584. Netherlands, ITA, Art. 6.39.
585. Netherlands, ITA, Art. 6.38.
586. Germany, ITA, s. 10b.
587. CJEU, January 27, 2009, C-318/07 (*Persche*).

appreciated property contributions does not arise. If assets are withdrawn from a business and given to a charity, the withdrawal is not a realization event.[588]

The deduction is denied if the donor receives consideration in return, since the transfer is no longer considered to be a "contribution." In addition, the nature and amount of the contribution must be documented.

In *France*, under certain conditions, donating companies are entitled to a tax credit equal to 60% of the amount of a charitable donation up to EUR 2,000,000 and 40% of any excess, capped at 0.5% of the company's sales. A carryover mechanism enables the unused tax credits to be carried forward for five years. Individuals are also entitled to a tax credit for charitable donations. These donations must be made to organizations of general interest or recognized as being of public utility, as listed by law. Individuals making a donation are also entitled to a tax credit equal to 66% of the donation, up to a limit of 20% of taxable income.[589] The credit is 75% of the amount paid, subject to a ceiling, where the purpose is to provide free meals to people in difficulty, to help improve their housing, or to provide medical care.[590]

In *China*, individuals are allowed to deduct charitable donations (up to 30% of reported taxable income) in computing taxable income. Donations to State Council-approved public-interest charities are fully deductible. Enterprises can deduct charitable donations up to 12% of the total profit in the year.[591]

In *Sweden*, although charitable contributions are viewed in principle as non-deductible personal expenses, a limited tax credit for charitable contributions is granted.[592] However, since gifts outside a business context are not treated as realization events, any appreciation in respect of the property given escapes tax.

In *India*, where the taxpayer opts for the old regime, charitable donations are deductible in full or to the extent of 50%; in some cases, they are subject to a limit of 10% of gross adjusted income, depending on the charitable institution to which the gift is made.[593] Charitable institutions must be designated by the government or approved by the Commissioner. In order to prevent fraud, cash donations are limited to INR 2,000. In-kind gifts are not deductible. None of these deductions is available under the new regime.[594]

6 LIMITATIONS ON DEDUCTIONS AND LOSSES

6.1 Illegal Payments, Fines, and Penalties

Where expenses are incurred which, under normal principles, would be deductible but are illegal, a number of the systems limit the deduction. This limitation is sometimes the result of a specific statutory provision (e.g., disallowing a deduction for bribes), and

588. Germany, ITA, s. 6 para. 1 No. 4.
589. France, CGI, s. 200.
590. France, CGI, s. 200 1 ter.
591. China, EIT Law, Art. 9.
592. Sweden, ITA, Ch. 67 paras. 20-26.
593. India, ITA 1961, s. 80G.
594. *See* the chapter on India in Part I (section 3.1) for a description of the old and new regimes.

sometimes follows from a general principle of denial of deductions which offend "*ordre public*" or public policy. Similarly, the deduction of business-related fines or penalties may also be limited.

In the *United States*, case law established the principle that illegal payments and fines were not deductible if the deduction would "frustrate sharply defined national or state policies."[595] Using this "public policy" principle, the cases disallowed deductions where the payment itself (e.g., a bribe) was illegal, or where the deductibility of a fine or penalty would reduce its effectiveness. Subsequent legislation narrowed the limitation of deductions on "public policy" grounds to several statutorily defined situations.[596] A special provision disallows all deductions for expenses (other than for cost of goods sold) incurred in connection with the illegal sale of drugs.[597] Another provision deals with the circumstances in which payments to foreign government officials can be deducted.

In *Canada*, until 1990, illegal payments were deductible subject to the ordinary restrictions on deductibility of expenses. This rule parallels the rule with respect to the inclusion in income of illegal amounts. In 1990, a statutory amendment denied the deductibility of bribes and similar payments.[598]

Until 2000, judicial or statutory fines and penalties were not generally deductible because any deduction would lessen the deterrent or regulatory impact of the fine. However, case law and administrative practice permitted a deduction for fines or penalties where the breach of law was relatively minor, the fine could be considered a normal risk of the business, and where the breach did not endanger public safety and was not deliberate or the result of negligence. For example, it was held that fines for overloaded trucks were deductible.[599] In 2000, the Supreme Court held that fines levied on an egg farmer for deliberately exceeding a production quota were deductible because they were incurred for the purpose of earning income.[600] According to the Court, public policy considerations are irrelevant to the question of the deductibility of fines and penalties. This result was overturned by statute in 2004.[601]

As a result of entering an international convention, in 1999 *Sweden* introduced statutory rules prohibiting the deduction of bribes.[602] The prior case law was not clear, but according to the general opinion—not shared by the Swedish contributors to this book—the cost of bribes was considered to be a deductible business cost, at least in practice. Fines are not deductible. Similarly, in *China*, the deduction of fines, penalties, and losses resulting from confiscation of property or late payment of interest charges on underpayment of tax is expressly prohibited.[603]

595. *Com'r v. Tellier*, 383 U.S. 687 (1966).
596. United States, IRC, s. 162(c), (f), and (g).
597. United States, IRC, s. 280E.
598. Canada, ITA, s. 67.5.
599. *Day and Ross v. The Queen*, [1976] CTC 707 (FCTD).
600. *65302 British Columbia Ltd. v. The Queen*, [2000] 1 CTC 57 (SCC).
601. Canada, ITA, s. 67.6.
602. Sweden, ITA, Ch. 9 para. 10.
603. China, EIT Law, Art. 10.

In *Japan*, there are no public policy limitations on the deduction of illegal payments as long as the payments can be established as "necessary" for the business, although the courts may scrutinize the alleged necessity carefully. In one case, the Supreme Court held that a corporation could not deduct the expenses incurred in pursuit of tax evasion since such expense is not consistent with the "fair and reasonable" accounting method (as explained below in Subpart D, section 1).[604] Specific statutory provisions have clarified that bribes, fines, and certain other administrative penalties (e.g., penalty charges under antitrust legislation) are not deductible.[605]

In *France*, for a long time, judges and tax authorities refused, as a matter of principle, to allow the deductibility of "bribes" on the ground that they were illegal. However, case law has gradually evolved to allow such sums to be deducted from taxable profits in the industrial and commercial profits category, provided that they are incurred in the company's interests, their deductibility is not expressly denied by law, and they are not criminal fines. In contrast, illegal expenses incurred by a member of a regulated profession are not deductible, since such expenses cannot be qualified as expenses necessary for the exercise of the profession. In addition, pecuniary penalties (surcharges, fines, confiscations, and penalty payments) and penalties (surcharges and interest for late payment) of all kinds are not deductible from taxable profit, regardless of whether the company is subject to income tax or corporation tax.[606] In line with the Organisation for Economic Co-operation and Development (OECD) recommendation, companies may not deduct sums paid or advantages granted directly or indirectly to a public official with a view to obtaining or retaining a contract or other undue advantage in international business transactions.[607]

In *The Netherlands*, fines and penalties imposed by a Dutch court are not deductible (and reimbursement by an employer of such amounts incurred by an employee is taxable to the employee). This includes amounts paid to avoid criminal prosecution, administrative fines (including tax penalties), and foreign fines imposed under criminal law, disciplinary law, or administrative law, as well as settlements concluded with foreign public bodies. For business income purposes, fines imposed by an institution of the EU are similarly nondeductible.[608] As with any other business expense, bribes are deductible if they are made for business purposes. The tax authorities generally assume a business purpose to exist if it is demonstrated by a taxpayer that, in view of the nature of the business, the amount paid does not deviate from what is commonly paid in similar circumstances. However, it may be difficult in practice to prove that a bribe has actually been paid.

In *Australia*, a specific statutory provision disallows a deduction for fines and penalties, a result which had already been reached in case law.[609] Illegal payments, however, seem to be allowed in principle under the general deduction rules—the Full

604. *S.V.C. Corporation v. The Government*, Keishu 48-6-357 (Sup.Ct. September 16, 1994).
605. Japan, ITA, s. 45; CTA, s. 55.
606. France, CGI, s. 39 2.
607. France, CGI, s. 39 2 bis.
608. Netherlands, ITA, Art. 3.14(1)(c) and WTA, Art. 31(4)(c).
609. Australia, ITAA 1997, s. 26-5.

Federal Court held that a drug dealer was entitled to a deduction when the proceeds of his drug dealing were stolen. Due to the public outrage caused by the decision, the government amended the law to prevent deductions in future to the extent that amounts are incurred directly in relation to an indictable criminal offense for which the taxpayer has been convicted.[610] In line with the OECD recommendation, Australia also amended its law to deny tax deductions for bribes to foreign public officials.[611] For appearances, a similar provision for bribes to local officials was also added.[612]

In the *United Kingdom*, particular rules forbid the deduction of any expenditure incurred in making a payment which constitutes the commission of a criminal offense (e.g., bribery) or, if made outside the UK, would have been a crime if it had taken place in the UK. A similar rule applies to payments made under a threat of blackmail or, in Scotland, extortion, but does not apply if the crime of blackmail or extortion is committed outside the UK. Under general principles based on public policy considerations, the payment of a fine is not deductible in computing business profits.[613]

Statutory provisions in *Germany* deal with the deduction of both fines and penalties and illegal payments. Fines and penalties as well as related expenses (e.g., lawyers' fees) are generally not deductible if imposed by a German, EU, or foreign court.[614] However, foreign fines and penalties may be deductible where they are based on considerations in the foreign jurisdiction which are inconsistent with the basic principles of the German legal system. Non-judicially imposed penalties which result from legal infractions are also not deductible unless the purpose of the penalty is simply to make restitution.

Bribes and similar payments are not deductible if they are punishable under the German penal code, irrespective of whether the payments are made to German or foreign recipients.[615]

In *India*, illegal payments and penalties, including foreign payments, are not deductible;[616] however, compensatory payments are deductible. Where a payment is in part a penalty and in part compensation, only the deduction of the penalty part is disallowed.

6.2 Expenses Associated with Tax Exempt Income

In a global system, the question of relating expenses to tax exempt income arises when certain categories of income are expressly exempted from tax (e.g., interest from state and local obligations in the U.S. context). For schedular systems, a similar problem arises in dealing with expenses related to items of income which are not formally exempt but which simply do not fall into any taxable category.

610. Australia, ITAA 1997, ss. 26-54, overriding *La Rosa* [2003] FCAFC 125, 129 FCR 494.
611. Australia, ITAA 1997, ss. 26-52.
612. Australia, ITAA 1997, ss. 26-53.
613. *McKnight v. Sheppard* [1999]; STC 669; *see also* ITTOIA, s. 55 and CTA 2009, s. 1304.
614. Germany, ITA, s. 4 para. 5 No. 8, s. 9 para. 5, s. 12 No. 4.
615. Germany, ITA, s. 4 para. 5 No. 10.
616. India, ITA 1961, Explanation 1 and 3 to s. 37(1).

In the *United States*, there is an express statutory rule that in general denies a deduction for expenses incurred in connection with tax exempt income.[617] Where an expense is directly related to an item of tax exempt income, the deduction is denied completely. Where expenses are related to several categories of income, an allocation is made based on the amounts of income or, in some cases, the value or cost of the assets generating the income. A special rule applies to interest expense incurred in connection with exempt interest income on state and municipal obligations. In this situation, the interest deduction is denied if the purpose of the borrowing is to purchase or "carry" tax exempt securities.[618] Thus, interest expense can be denied if a borrowing allowed a taxpayer to continue to hold tax exempt securities. In the case of financial institutions, interest expense must be allocated between tax exempt interest income and other taxable income based on the tax cost of the assets involved.[619]

The deduction of expenses associated with tax exempt income is also specifically prohibited in *Canada*.[620] However, deductions are allowed for expenses incurred to acquire dividend-paying shares, even though certain dividends are tax-free because dividends are expressly excluded from the definition of exempt income. A similar approach applies in *The Netherlands*. In general, in Canada, whether an expense is associated with exempt or taxable income is determined under a tracing method. Although capital gains are partially taxable, expenses incurred to generate such gains are not deductible (or capitalized).[621] Where the asset generates income (or is acquired for the purpose of generating such income) apart from the potential capital gain, the expenses are fully deductible. The *Australian* system reaches similar results since the general deduction rule requires that the deduction relate to assessable income. A specific exception is created for interest incurred to earn dividends from foreign subsidiaries; even though those dividends are exempt from Australian tax, the interest expense is allowed as a deduction, effectively reducing the tax on domestic income.[622] As in Canada, there is no deduction for the costs incurred in connection with capital gains, although in most cases the costs, including carrying costs, generally can be included in the cost basis of the assets.

In the *United Kingdom*, the schedular system is usually enough to protect the tax base. There is no general principle barring a deduction of expenses related to exempt income—it is all a matter of statutory interpretation for each category of income. As a result, the loan-relationship rules introduced in 1996 specifically deny a deduction for interest incurred for a trade which is carried on outside the scope of the UK corporation tax; this model has been used frequently since then.[623] The UK insists on distinguishing

617. United States, IRC, s. 265.
618. United States, IRC, s. 265(a)(1).
619. United States, IRC, s. 265(b)(2).
620. Canada, ITA, s. 18(1)(c).
621. Canada, ITA, s. 9(3).
622. Australia, ITAA 1997, ss. 25-90. The thin capitalization rules considered in Part IV operate in tandem with this rule to cap interest deductions at 30% of the payer's earnings before tax, interest and depreciation.
623. United Kingdom, CTA 2009, s. 327 (imported losses).

trading companies from companies with investment businesses but the same results are reached with respect to investment businesses.[624]

In *China* and *Sweden*, in general, expenses are deductible only where they are associated with a taxable income source. In Sweden, where income which would otherwise fall in a taxable category is explicitly exempt, the exemption has been interpreted to apply to the gross income and not the net income. Accordingly, the associated expenses were allowed as a deduction against other income in the category. Interest is deductible even where the debt to which it relates does not produce taxable income.

Japan has no explicit rule dealing with deductions relating to tax exempt income. The limitation flows from the basic rule that in order to be deductible, expenses must be related to a taxable category of income.

In *France*, early case law recognized that expenses relating to income exempt from income tax by virtue of a special provision cannot be deducted from other income earned by the taxpayer.[625] Thus, custodial fees for securities producing income exempt from income tax and expenses related to buildings used for the taxpayer's personal use are not deductible.

Germany has a specific statutory rule disallowing the deduction of expenses which have a "direct economic connection" with exempt income.[626] A limited deduction (60 %) is granted for expenditures in connection with dividend income from shares held by an individual or a partnership in a business context, which itself is taxed only up to 60 %.[627] For intercompany dividends, special rules apply, which are discussed in Part III.

In *India*, since 2001, any expenses incurred with respect to amounts "not includable" in total income are not deductible[628] even where the taxpayer does not earn any exempt income in a particular year.[629]

6.3 "Quarantining" and Other Limits or Restrictions on Certain Categories of Expenses

In an otherwise global system, sometimes activities or expenses are subject to special rules, and expenses and losses in those categories cannot be used to offset other items of income. In effect, there is a schedular overlay on the global system. In explicitly schedular systems, a similar result is achieved where an overall loss in a particular category cannot be used to offset or "compensate" income in other categories. Limitations have typically been applied in response to deductions generated in tax-shelter transactions or activities in which personal consumption is likely.

624. United Kingdom, CTA 2009, Part 16.
625. France, Conseil d'Etat, December 19, 1958, n°40509.
626. Germany, ITA, s. 3c para. 1.
627. Germany, ITA, s. 3c para. 2.
628. India, ITA 1961, s. 14A.
629. India, ITA, 1961, s. 14A, Explanation.

The *United States* has an extensive system of limitations on deductibility of losses, the most important of which are the so-called passive activity loss rules. Adopted in response to the widespread use of tax shelters in the 1970s and 1980s, the passive activity loss rules restrict the deductibility of losses which arise in any activity in which the taxpayer does not "materially participate."[630] This requirement has been administratively interpreted to require, in general, that a taxpayer spend at least 500 hours per year in the activity, although there are a number of other situations in which a material-participation requirement is satisfied. Special rules apply to real estate activities.

Losses incurred in passive activities can be used only to offset income from passive activities. In this context, "portfolio" income, typically investment income, is not passive activity income and cannot be reduced by passive activity losses. Unused losses are suspended and can be used in later years against passive activity income. When the passive activity is completely disposed of in a taxable transaction, suspended losses may be used against other income. While originally aimed at the "artificial" losses arising in tax-shelter activities, the rules can apply to real economic losses where a taxpayer does not meet the material-participation test.

The application of the rules on an activity-by-activity basis and the special treatment of portfolio income are extremely complex. In effect, taxpayers are required to categorize each activity into "normal" business activity, passive activity, and portfolio investments, making an allocation of income and deductions to each category. In addition, in order to determine whether an activity has been disposed of so that suspended losses may be used, the exact scope of each separate activity must be determined. In effect, the rules turn the otherwise global system of income definition into a schedular system in which each activity is potentially a separate income category.

There are some other, less extensive, limitations on the deductibility of certain expenses. The deduction of investment interest expense which is not incurred in a trade or business is limited to the amount of investment income, including, in some cases, realized capital gains.[631] Expenses incurred in connection with the business use of a residence (e.g., an office in the home or the rental of a summer house) are limited to the income which the activity generates.[632] As discussed previously, in general, capital losses can be deducted only against capital gains, although a limited deduction against ordinary income is allowed.

In the case of unreimbursed expenses of employees or expenses involved in profit-seeking activities which do not amount to a trade or business, these expenses could previously be deducted only to the extent that they exceeded 2% of income. Currently, such expenses cannot be deducted at all for the years 2018 through 2025 due to the suspension of miscellaneous itemized deductions for this period.[633] The effect of this limitation is to reduce substantially the availability of deductions for many

630. United States, IRC, s. 469.
631. United States, IRC, s. 163(d).
632. United States, IRC, s. 280A.
633. United States, IRC, s. 67(g).

taxpayers. Unlike in other countries, there is no specific lump-sum deduction granted to employees as a substitute for the deduction of these expenses.

In *Sweden*, losses in the category of business income cannot be used to reduce income in other taxable categories; however, the loss can be carried forward without limitation against business income in future years. The same rule applies to income from employment. There are, however, some exceptions. For example, losses from business as an artist can be offset against employment income; business losses during the initial five years of a business are deductible against employment income (up to SEK 100,000 per year); and a loss on the termination of a business can be deducted against income from capital.

A different technique is used for losses in the category of income from capital. The loss is converted into a credit at a 30% rate (the basic rate on income from capital) for up to SEK 100,000 and at a 21% rate for the excess. The credit can then be used to offset tax on income in the other categories. The restriction on excess losses is intended to limit the ability to use current losses (principally from interest deductions in highly leveraged investments) where the gain on the investment is deferred.

In *Japan*, losses are restricted as a result of the schedular system. Losses in the dividends, occasional, and miscellaneous categories cannot be used to offset other types of income. Income from forestry and retirement income are calculated separately. In addition, as discussed above, since 2016, capital gains or losses on securities are generally aggregated with other types of income (or loss) derived from securities (i.e., interest on debt securities and dividends on equity securities) and are taxed separately from other income. Japan also has a special rule restricting losses for the purpose of combating tax-oriented schemes in the form of civil law partnerships, where losses incurred by nonoperating partners in respect of the real estate category, which includes income or losses from aircraft or ships, are deemed to be nil. (Japan generally permits losses in the real estate category to offset business income.) This tax-oriented partnership scheme aims to utilize the accelerated depreciation available for aircraft and ships to create artificial losses for the partners.[634]

The *United Kingdom* distinguishes between relief carried forward to be set against income from the same source and "sideways" relief, where the loss is applied against other types of income. It is usually possible to carry losses forward indefinitely to be set against later income from the same source. It is sometimes possible to carry a loss backward.[635]

Thus, where income arises under ITTOIA Part 3 (Land), whether in the UK or abroad, and the taxpayer is subject to income tax, losses may be carried forward and set only against other income from the property business (which is taken to include all the various pieces of property in one trade). Sideways relief is also available, for the loss-making year and the following year, in calculating net income. It follows that the loss cannot be set against capital gains. A less restrictive rule applies to losses from property businesses for corporation tax; here the loss can be set off against any sort of (income) profits.

634. Japan, STMA, s. 41-4-2.
635. United Kingdom, ITA, Part 4.

Losses arising in a business can be used sideways and set against income in other categories for the same and the preceding year. Any unused loss can be carried forward and set off against income profits indefinitely, but only if these are income profits *of the same trade*.[636] Sideways relief was abused and so there is now a GBP 25,000 cap on sideways relief for trading losses if the taxpayer is not actively involved in the business. There is also a complete ban on tax-generated losses.[637] There are more generous loss-offset rules in the early years of a trade which allow a loss to be carried back and set off against general income of earlier years.[638] There are also more generous rules for terminal losses. In the case of wholly foreign trades, losses must be set against foreign profits.

For those subject to CGT, capital losses can be used only against capital gains, with an indefinite carryforward but (generally) no carryback of excess capital losses.[639] Trading losses can sometimes be set against capital gains, but capital losses cannot be set against ordinary income. If a trading loss is set off against capital gains, the GBP 25,000 cap for losses where the taxpayer is not active in the business applies. More relaxed rules apply for corporation tax but there is still a bar on the use of capital losses against income. Sometimes, for example, in the case of income from securities or dividends from shares accruing to taxpayers subject to income tax, no deductions at all are allowed and so no loss can arise in the first place. Trading losses arising after April 1, 2017 are handled more flexibly since these losses can be carried forward and set against the taxable profits of different activities within a company or surrendered to other group members. However, the amount of profit which can be relieved by these carried-forward losses is limited to 50% from April 1, 2017, subject to an allowance of GBP 5 million per group. For banks, the limit is 25% of profit.[640] For chargeable gains accruing to a company on or after April 1, 2020, the use of carried-forward allowable losses is similarly restricted to 50% of chargeable gains arising in an accounting period, subject to an allowance permitting unrestricted use of up to GBP 5 million of capital or income losses per year per group.[641]

Under the *Canadian* system, as a general rule, the net results from the various income sources are consolidated in computing total taxable income. However, there are some special rules which operate to limit certain types of losses. Capital cost recovery allowances with respect to rented depreciable property cannot be deducted in excess of the income that the particular property generates. In general, capital losses are deductible only against capital gains; capital losses on certain personal-use assets (coins, stamps, etc.) can be deducted only against gains on such assets. In addition, the lifetime exemption for capital gains in respect of farm property, fishing property, and shares of small business corporations is reduced by the taxpayer's cumulative net loss from investments—thus, in effect, restricting the deductibility of such losses. To the

636. United Kingdom, ITA, ss. 83 et seq.
637. United Kingdom, ITA, s. 74A-74D.
638. United Kingdom, ITA, ss. 72-74.
639. United Kingdom, TCGA, s. 2; note also s. 16A on restriction of relief for capital losses where avoidance is involved.
640. United Kingdom, CTA 2010, ss. 45A et seq.
641. United Kingdom, CTA 2010, s. 269ZBA.

extent that business losses cannot be deducted in the current year, they can be carried back for three years and forward for twenty years.[642] Capital losses can be carried back for three years and forward indefinitely but are deductible only against capital gains.

Australia has a similar treatment for capital losses. The hobby-loss rules and special regime for boating activities also add schedular elements to the system. For a brief period in the 1980s, there were rules capping interest deductions on real property investments at the amount of income which the property generated.

In *The Netherlands*, since the introduction in 2001 of the three boxes of income for individuals, a loss in income boxes 1 and 2 (i.e., not box 3 losses regarding capital income) can be carried back three years for box 1 and one year for box 2, and carried forward nine years for box 1 and six years for box 2 to offset income of the same box[643] (and, with a small exception, not the income of another box). Personal deductions, however, reduce income in boxes 1, 3, and 2 (in that order), with any excess carried forward to future years and applied to income in the boxes in the same order.

Traditionally, *Germany* allows losses in particular income categories to be offset against income in other categories. However, tax legislation has severely restricted these deductions over the years. Capital losses incurred by individuals can be set off only against gains from the same source (for assets other than financial instruments, depending on the length of the holding period, ten years for real estate and one year for other assets).[644] For business or professional taxpayers, losses from livestock farming, as well as from particular financial derivatives and certain shareholder loans, can be deducted only from profits from the same source of income.[645] A similar limitation applies to losses from loss-generating tax shelters.[646] Furthermore, a rather complex provision dealing with losses of limited partners limits the offset of their losses to the amount of their capital contribution and thus, the amount of loss actually suffered.[647]

All other losses can be offset against other profits in the relevant tax period. Where losses exceed profits for a period, the excess can be carried back to the preceding tax period up to EUR 1,000,000.[648] All remaining losses can be carried forward to future tax periods.[649] Again, there are limitations: a full deduction is allowed up to EUR 1,000,000 of income, while 70% of any excess income can be offset by former losses. Remaining losses can be carried forward to the next period. A case is currently pending in the Federal Constitutional Court on the question whether this type of "minimum tax" is compatible with the constitutional requirement of tax equity.[650]

No deduction is granted with respect to hobby or capital losses where the corresponding gain would not be taxable (i.e., because the holding-period requirement is not met). Special rules in connection with foreign losses are discussed in Part IV.

642. Canada, ITA, s. 111.
643. Netherlands, ITA, Arts. 3.150 and 4.49, respectively.
644. Germany, ITA, s. 20 para. 6, s. 23 para. 3 sent. 7-9.
645. Germany, ITA, s. 15 para. 4.
646. Germany, ITA, s. 15b.
647. Germany, ITA, s. 15a.
648. Germany, ITA, s. 10d para. 1.
649. Germany, ITA, s. 10d para. 2.
650. *See* Federal Tax Court (*Bundesfinanzhof*), February 26, 2014, I R 59/12.

In *France*, the rules are complicated by the distinction between industrial and commercial profits and noncommercial profits, which can be either professional or non-professional. This complexity arises from the numerous exceptions to the principle of offsetting profits and losses. In principle, losses in any category of income are deductible from total annual income and any excess loss is carried forward against future income for six years.[651] However, a special regime denies losses arising from industrial, commercial, or noncommercial activities carried out on a "non-professional" basis. Non-professional industrial and commercial losses can be offset only against "non-professional" profits of the same kind made in the same year or in the following six years.[652] "Non-professional" losses arise from activities which do not involve the taxpayer's personal, continuous, and direct participation. Property losses can be deducted from overall income up to a limit of EUR 10,700, with the excess deductible from property income over the following 10 years. Capital losses on securities are offset against capital gains of the same kind, with a 10-year limit on the carryforward of losses.[653] Long-term capital losses in business can be deducted only against long-term capital gains, with excess losses qualifying for a ten-year carryforward.[654] Finally, capital losses on real estate are not taken into account since it is feared that taxpayers may sell buildings at a loss for the sole purpose of minimizing their tax liability.[655]

In *China*, quarantining of losses occurs pursuant to the schedular system; thus, business losses cannot offset income in other categories and vice versa. Business losses can be carried forward for five years; losses in other categories can be carried forward to the following year. Similarly, in *India*, business losses cannot be set off against salary income and losses from a speculative business can be set off only against profits from other speculative businesses. In general, losses can be carried forward for eight years and unabsorbed depreciation can be carried forward indefinitely.[656]

The following Table II-2 summarizes some of the deduction rules discussed in Subpart C. The notation "limited deduction" indicates that either the class of costs deductible is restricted in some fashion or there is a limit on the amount deductible (e.g., a nondeductible floor or a ceiling on deductible amounts). In addition, the generality of the Table does not capture many of the refinements—for example, the distinction frequently made between domestic and foreign illegal payments.

651. France, CGI, s. 156 1 s. 1.
652. France, CGI, s. 156 I 1 bis.
653. France, CGI, s. 150-0 D 11.
654. France, CGI, s. 39 quindecies I-2.
655. France, CGI, s. 150 VD.
656. India, ITA 1961, s. 32(2).

Table II-2 Some Aspects of the Tax Base: Deductions

	Commuting Costs	*Entertainment Expenses*	*Illegal Payments*	*Childcare Costs*	*Personal Interest*	*Medical Expenses (Nonbusiness-Related)*	*Charitable Contributions*
Australia	no deduction	no deduction	deductions limited	no deduction	no deduction	limited credit	deduction with a generous limit
Canada	no deduction	percentage limitation (no deduction for most employees)	no general limitation (bribes and fines nondeductible)	limited deduction	no deduction	limited credit	limited credit
China	no deduction	60% deduction for enterprises	not deductible	no deduction	no deduction	deduction for major medical expenses	limited deduction
France	limited deduction	full deduction if related to business	no general limitation	no deduction; limited credit	no deduction	no deduction	limited credit
Germany	deduction	limited deduction	no deduction	limited deduction	no deduction	limited deduction	limited deduction
India	no deduction	full deduction for businesses	no deduction	no deduction	deductible only with respect to personal residence under pre-2024 rules	deductible including insurance under pre-2024 rules	limited deduction under pre-2024 rules

	Commuting Costs	*Entertainment Expenses*	*Illegal Payments*	*Childcare Costs*	*Personal Interest*	*Medical Expenses (Nonbusiness-Related)*	*Charitable Contributions*
Japan	limited deduction (eligible for itemized deduction)	full deduction for an individual; for business (limited deduction for employees); limited for a corporation	no general limitation (bribes and fines nondeductible)	no deduction	no deduction	limited deduction	limited deduction
The Netherlands	limited deduction	limited deduction	no general limitation	no deduction	no deduction	limited deduction	limited deduction
Sweden	no deduction	limited deduction	no deduction	no deduction	fully deductible	no deduction	limited deduction
United Kingdom	no deduction	no deduction unless own staff	no deduction	no deduction but tax credit system	limited deduction (e.g., interest in business)	no deduction (insurance premiums deductible)	limited deduction
United States	no deduction	qualified meals only	deductions limited	no deduction; limited credit	limited deduction (personal residence)	limited deduction	limited deduction

SUBPART D

Accounting

All tax systems must contain rules governing the assignment to taxable periods of the various income and expense items involved in the computation of taxable income. Since the same task must be performed for financial accounting purposes, a basic question in all systems is the extent to which the timing rules used in determining financial income also control questions of timing for tax purposes. While all the systems considered here use commercial accounting principles and concepts to some extent, they also generally recognize the need for special tax rules in many situations. The most obvious case where tax rules are needed is where the taxpayer, typically an individual employee or investor, does not normally keep commercial books and records. Thus, all systems recognize a simplified "cash" method of accounting for some taxpayers. In addition, and more fundamentally, in some cases, the goals and purposes of financial accounting are considered to be so different from the requirements of the tax system that the results produced by financial accounting rules are viewed as inappropriate for tax purposes. Here, there is a wide variation among the countries concerning the degree to which financial accounting principles are followed in the tax system. The differences rest in part on the extent to which there are legally binding accounting rules which are incorporated into the tax system, in contrast to accounting principles which are developed on the basis of professional standards. In the latter case, the flexibility allowed by accounting principles is often not accepted for tax purposes.

The following materials examine the basic tax accounting methods used and their relation to commercial accounting principles; they then consider some specific situations in which special tax rules have been developed.

1 BASIC ACCOUNTING METHODS

In the *German* system, the method of accounting is determined by the category of income which is involved.[657] Thus, for example, taxpayers may use one method for

657. Germany, ITA, s. 2 para. 2.

computing business income and another for computing income from employment. The "excess income" method, which is essentially a cash method of accounting,[658] is used to determine income from employment, capital, rents and royalties, miscellaneous income, and the income of small proprietorships and partnerships. Income is recognized when taxpayers receive money or other assets which are at their disposal. Checks are treated as cash and taxable on receipt as long as the check clears in the normal course. Expenses are recognized at the time the taxpayer pays the amount or disposes of the funds. A special statutory rule applies to items of income or expense which occur regularly and are paid "shortly before or shortly after" the period to which they relate, e.g., rent for December received in January. For tax purposes, such amounts are taken into account in the period to which they economically relate. Expenditures for depreciable assets are not deducted immediately but must be capitalized and recovered through depreciation deductions.[659]

One of the basic elements of this "excess income" approach is that the sale of assets in the course of a taxable activity does not constitute a taxable event. Thus, the sale of real estate employed to generate rental income or the sale of a car used in the course of employment has no tax effect. The general rule that private capital gains are not taxed (if the statutory holding period is met) prevails but, following the 2007 Business Tax Reform, does not cover capital gains from securities and other financial instruments.

For most taxpayers engaged in business, the use of an accrual method of income computation is required. In general terms, income or loss for a period is determined by comparing assets and liabilities at the end of the tax period with assets and liabilities at the end of the preceding period.[660] Thus, when performance of a contract is completed and income has been earned, an asset in the form of an account receivable is entered in the balance sheet and is reflected as income as a result of the balance-sheet comparison at the year-end. Similarly, a liability which is recognized for commercial accounting, and hence for tax purposes, functions as the accrual of a deduction item. A modified version of the accrual method (which contains some elements of the "excess income" method but does include capital gains) may be used by taxpayers deriving income from independent personal services or agriculture.[661]

The obligation to use the accrual method is tied to the commercial and corporate law requirements of maintaining certain books and records.[662] Correspondingly, there is a close connection between the financial balance sheet and the tax balance sheet used in the net-worth comparison. Under the traditional principle of "linkage" (*Maßgeblichkeit*), the tax balance sheet must be based on the commercial balance sheet and, unless a special tax rule provides otherwise, the recognition and valuation of assets and liabilities shown on the commercial balance sheet are relevant for tax purposes. This linkage has far-reaching implications for income determination because it incorporates

658. Germany, ITA, ss. 8-9a and 11.
659. Germany, ITA, s. 9 para. 1 No. 7 with reference to s. 7.
660. Germany, ITA, ss. 4-7i.
661. Germany, ITA, s. 4 para. 3.
662. Germany, ITA, s. 5 para. 1 sent. 1.

in the tax system the basic prudence concept, which is the basis for many generally accepted accounting principles under German law. Unrealized losses, which are recognized under the rules for financial accounting, are also effective for tax purposes. Similarly, provisions or reserves which are required for financial accounting reduce taxable income.

Beginning in 1997, German tax legislation gradually reduced the application of the prudence concept for tax purposes (i.e., by eliminating provisions for future losses or the introduction of a discount on liabilities and provisions),[663] thus eroding the original strong linkage between commercial and tax accounting under German tax law. Apart from reducing the application of the prudence concept, the tax code contains a number of special tax rules for the valuation of assets and liabilities.[664] For example, the principle of valuation according to "going-concern value," discussed above in connection with depreciation, is expressly allowed.

Until 2009, the linkage between commercial and tax accounting was further strengthened by the principle of "reverse" linkage *(umgekehrte Maßgeblichkeit)*. If the tax law provided advantageous treatment for an item and a taxpayer elected that treatment for tax purposes, it had to be reflected in the commercial statements in order to be effective. This meant, for example, that the decision to accelerate deductions for tax purposes necessarily reduced financial statement income and the ability of a corporation to pay dividends. This effect was widely criticized because of the distorting effects of tax law on commercial accounting. In 2009, the "reverse linkage" principle was eliminated altogether, making it possible to exercise tax options independently of financial statements.[665] The tax administration favors a broad interpretation of this provision, which weakens the traditional principle of linkage even further.

The *French* system is governed by roughly similar principles. The cash method is used for noncommercial income tax purposes, i.e., for private individuals, unless a professional has opted for the accrual method.[666] Accrual accounting applies to industrial and commercial profits (i.e., businesses) and to companies subject to corporate income tax.

For corporate income tax purposes, two definitions of net profit coexist. The first definition provides for a determination "based on the overall results of operations of all kinds carried out by the companies."[667] This is a global approach to the company's earnings, which compares the income and expenses recorded in the income statement.[668] The second definition complements the first since it refers to the theory of the balance sheet, allowing certain items not recorded in the accounting entries to be taken into account.[669] The text refers to "the difference between the net asset values at the end and beginning of the period whose results are to serve as the basis for taxation."

663. Germany, ITA, s. 5 paras. 2a-4b, s. 6 para. 1 Nos. 3, 3a.
664. Germany, ITA, s. 6 para. 1.
665. Germany, ITA, s. 5 para. 1 sent. 1 (end of sentence).
666. France, CGI, s. 93 A.
667. France, CGI, s. 38 s. 1.
668. With respect to noncommercial profits, Art. 93 of the CGI takes a similar approach, namely, the difference between revenue and expenses.
669. France, CGI, s. 38 s. 2.

Thus, the change in net assets is first determined by comparing the balance sheets of two successive years, and then adjusting the results by deducting external contributions and adding withdrawals made by the entrepreneur or partners. To determine the taxable profit, a link must be established between the accounting result and the tax result, which entails certain adjustments when tax law differs from accounting law.[670]

The linkage between book and taxable income is particularly close. Companies must comply with the definitions set out in the general chart of accounts, provided that they are not incompatible with the rules applicable to the tax base.[671] The annual financial statements must comply with the principle of accounting prudence,[672] which requires recording all events encountered by the company, with the exception of those not yet realized (an unrealized capital gain, for example). This means that probable decreases in value are taken into account, but not increases that have not yet been realized.

In *Sweden*, like Germany, the method of accounting is determined by the category of income. Income from capital and income from employment are accounted for on a cash basis. There is a principle of "constructive receipt" which taxes income prior to actual receipt where it is possible for the taxpayer to obtain payment earlier. Capital gains are subject to a special rule which, in effect, puts them on the accrual basis; this rule was introduced in 1991 to discourage deferred-payment sales of property.

Business taxpayers, including all corporations, must use the accrual method for tax purposes. Generally accepted accounting principles are controlling wherever there are no special tax rules. As a general matter, income items are usually determined under financial accounting rules, while there are a number of special tax rules for deductions. Under normal accounting rules, only the present value of potential future expenditures is deductible. Special tax rules limit the deduction for anticipated guarantee expenses. Because of the importance of accounting rules for tax purposes, tax considerations have sometimes influenced the development of financial accounting rules. This situation has been criticized as resulting in a distortion of the clear presentation of income for financial accounting purposes.

The relation between tax accounting and financial accounting is much different in the *United States* tax system. While in general taxpayers must report income for tax purposes using the same method of accounting as that used for commercial accounts, special tax rules substantially modify the accounting principles. For example, under the accrual method, the use of reserves for estimated future expenses is much more limited for tax purposes than the normally applicable rules for financial accounting. The courts have specifically recognized the "difference in objectives" between tax accounting and financial accounting in developing special tax rules.[673] In addition, the fiscal authorities can require modifications in accounting methods to "clearly reflect income" and, under this standard, a number of accounting practices have been rejected for tax purposes.[674]

670. In practice, there are different tax forms (*liasse fiscale*), which contain charts to facilitate the transition from one result to the other and to declare these elements to the tax authorities.
671. France, CGI, Regulatory Schedule III, s. 38 quater.
672. France, Commercial Code, L123-20.
673. United States, *Thor Power Tool Co. v. Commissioner*, 439 U.S. 522 (1979).
674. United States, IRC, s. 446(b).

Taxpayers can elect a method of accounting, and the statute specifically recognizes the cash method and the accrual method as well as "other methods" which meet the above standards.[675] For taxpayers using the cash method, typically individuals and small businesses, income is taxable on receipt or in situations where the taxpayer has "constructive receipt" of the income because of access to the income. A check is treated as cash if it clears in due course. Internal Revenue Service (IRS) regulations state that the receipt of a note in exchange for services is income to a cash-basis taxpayer to the extent of the note's fair market value, but several court decisions appear to create numerous inconsistent exceptions to this rule. Although the receipt of a note in exchange for property is also income, a statutory provision generally permits taxpayers to avoid recognizing income until payment on the note is received.

On the deduction side, deductions are taken into account when an expenditure has actually occurred (usually when an amount is paid). Where a taxpayer issues a note to make payment, the note does not constitute payment. Prepaid expenses are generally treated as capital expenditures. Special rules allow farmers using the cash basis, in effect, to deduct prepaid expenses, but those rules are limited to "real" farmers to prevent the use of prepayments in tax-shelter transactions.[676]

The accrual method is used by most business taxpayers. Where the business involves production, inventory accounting must be used and purchases and sales are required to be accounted for on the accrual method. On the income side, income must be recognized when the right to receive the income has been established and the amount can be determined. In general, any consistent method of accounting is accepted even where the right to the income has not technically accrued. The treatment of advance payments to taxpayers on the accrual basis is discussed below.

On the deduction side, deduction was historically allowed when "all events" had occurred which established the liability to make the payment. Although contingent or uncertain liabilities were not deductible, this rule allowed taxpayers to accrue fixed liabilities currently at their nominal amount even where the payment would not actually be made until sometime in the future. This approach overstates the true cost of the deduction because it does not take into account the time value of money between the period in which the deduction accrued and the time it is in fact paid. In extreme situations, taxpayers could actually be better off with the current accrual of the liability than if they had not incurred the liability at all. In response to this situation, the statute was amended to require that there be "economic performance" of the obligation before the "all events" test could be met.[677] This rule basically defers the deduction until payment is actually made or property or services are delivered or performed (e.g., in mining reclamation). For "recurring" items, that is, normally occurring business expenses, deduction is allowed currently if the amount is paid within eight and one-half months after the end of the tax year, the time that a tax return must be filed. This economic-performance approach makes the accrual of deductions for tax purposes much more restrictive in the U.S. than in the other jurisdictions.

---

675. United States, IRC, s. 446(a).
676. Rev. Rul. 79-229, 1979-2 CB 210.
677. United States, IRC, s. 461(h).

As a general rule, *Japan* requires the use of accrual accounting. However, small businesses have the option of using the cash method under strict conditions (electing the special "blue return" system).[678] Where the accrual method is used, it usually follows financial accounting principles which are generally accepted to be "fair and reasonable."[679] There are also more detailed tax accounting rules. Under the accrual system, liabilities are taken into account at face value and there are special provisions allowing reserves for mining restoration, oil spill cleanups, and similar occurrences. Paralleling the adoption in the financial accounting of the mark-to-market method with respect to some financial instruments, including derivative transactions, the Japanese corporate income tax law was amended to apply the mark-to-market method to such financial instruments.

Under the *Canadian* system, income from employment, farming, and fishing is calculated on a cash basis. Income from business and property, however, must be accounted for generally on the accrual basis. While the tax accounting rules are based on financial accounting principles, they have developed into an independent body of law.[680] The Supreme Court has consistently held that the computation of profits is a question of law for which the accounting treatment of an item of revenue or expense is merely evidence. In addition, there are a number of special tax rules which displace financial accounting rules. Moreover, courts have sometimes rejected financial accounting rules as inconsistent with more basic tax law principles. For example, last-in, first-out accounting for inventory costs has been held to be unacceptable for tax purposes despite its recognition in financial accounting. Liabilities are generally taken into account at face value in the year incurred as long as they are not contingent with respect to liability or amount.[681] In some cases, however, present-value accrual is at least acceptable and might be required.

In the *United Kingdom*, the appropriate accounting regime is determined by the particular part of the Act (e.g., schedule) applicable to the income. In some cases, the receipts or cash method is used, but for trading profits, the most important income category, an "earnings" basis, is generally required. According to a statutory amendment in 1998, the profits of a trade, profession, or vocation must be computed in accordance with generally accepted accounting practice, subject to any adjustment required or authorized by tax law in computing those profits.[682] Even before 1998, there were signs that the courts were moving closer to a financial accounting base in those cases where there was no specifically developed tax rule.

The mention in the 1998 amendment of adjustments required or authorized by law is of great importance. There are a number of specific statutory rules dealing with specific issues—for example, preventing a current deduction of interest where there is no corresponding income inclusion. There are also rules which displace depreciation in

678. Japan, ITA, s. 67.
679. Japan, CTA, s. 22.
680. *Canderel v. The Queen*, [1998] 2 CTC 35 (SCC).
681. Canada, ITA, s. 18(1)(e).
682. United Kingdom, ITTOIA, s. 25, CTA 2009, s. 46.

accordance with financial accounting; instead, the recovery of capital costs is governed by the elaborate rules in the capital allowance legislation.

In the early 2000s, the UK considered the even more radical move of adopting a financial accounting base for corporation tax. This would have meant following the financial accounting treatment for all things and so, for example, giving effect to a depreciation of capital costs. The proposals would also have included moving the taxation of capital gains from a realization basis to an accrual basis requiring the annual valuation of assets. The proposals even suggested the abolition of the schedular system by allowing losses of any type to be set off against profits of any type. The idea eventually fell away, but it still surfaces in nongovernmental tax reform proposals from time to time.

The situation in *Australia* is quite different. Tax accounting rules (at least until recently) have been developed through the interpretation of the statutory terms "derived" in relation to income and "incurred" in relation to deductions. While courts have sometimes looked to accounting principles, the tax rules have developed to a large extent independently. For example, whether an expense has been "incurred" depends in some sense on legal liabilities rather than on the commercial outcome and thus parallels the U.S. experience. In general, a cash method has been accepted for employees and small businesses and an accrual method for larger businesses. Under the accrual method, income is included when it is "earned" and there is case law establishing the contours of that concept. A special statutory regime is provided for inventory, which in general follows financial accounting principles, although it contains some important deviations. For example, the use of the lower of cost or market rule is optional and not mandatory.[683]

In contrast to the other Continental systems, in the *Dutch* system, tax accounting rules have developed relatively independently from financial accounting. Income from employment and a substantial participation in a company are accounted for on a cash basis. Amounts are included in income when received or available for collection even where they are not actually collected. Income from business activities is determined in accordance with "sound business practice" *(goed koopmansgebruik)* applied in a consistent manner. There is substantial case law developing this concept. The principles are different in many important aspects from financial accounting rules, and there is no necessary connection between financial treatment and tax treatment. However, in the interests of "prudence," the rules do allow the deduction of unrealized losses where there is a good chance the loss will be incurred and can be quantified. This tax rule is nonetheless stricter than the corresponding commercial accounting rule. In general, the tax rules emphasize the "realistic" possibility of a loss.

In *China*, income for purposes of the IIT is recognized on a cash basis, with the possible exception of business income. Even for business income, there is no requirement that individual business owners must use the accrual method of accounting and the Regulations allow the use of the presumptive method.[684] For purposes of the EIT, accrual accounting is required and the tax rules are generally consistent with financial

683. Australia, ITAA 1997, Division 70.
684. China, IIT Regulations, Art. 15.

accounting rules. For example, in the case of sales of goods, revenue is recognized where the following four conditions are met: (1) the contract for the sale has been concluded and the title to the goods and main risks and benefits of the goods have passed to the buyer; (2) the seller does not retain any continuous management rights or effective control over the goods; (3) the amount of revenue can be measured in a reliable way; and (4) the costs can be measured in a reliable way.[685] In the case of services, revenue is recognized when services are provided; where services are provided over a multiyear period, a percentage-of-completion method is used, as long as the amount of revenue can be measured in a reliable way.

In *India*, the ITA provides taxpayers with the option of computing business income in accordance with either the cash or accrual method of accounting "regularly employed" by the taxpayer.[686] Since under the Companies Act companies are required to use the accrual method, most companies also use the accrual method for tax purposes.[687] However, the ITA itself does not prohibit a company from using the cash basis.[688] Entities other than companies can follow either of the two methods. The Central government is authorized to issue tax accounting standards,[689] and has issued Income Computation and Disclosure Rules,[690] which apply for the purpose of computing business income (and income from other sources) but not for the purpose of maintaining books and records. In addition, in certain cases, the method of accounting (e.g., inventory valuation) is specifically provided in the Act.[691]

2 INCLUSION OF ADVANCE PAYMENTS

The treatment of advance payments is a classic example of the possible conflict between financial accounting principles and tax accounting. On the one hand, where amounts are prepaid prior to delivery of goods or the performance of services, from a financial accounting viewpoint, in general, income would not be taken into account because the unconditional right to the income has not yet been established; current inclusion of the income would prevent it from being accounted for in the period in which it is earned. On the other hand, from the perspective of the tax system, the fact that the taxpayer has received the cash and is in a position to pay the tax suggests the appropriateness of current inclusion of the income. In addition, the taxation of the advance payment to the seller can be seen as a surrogate for the failure to tax the implicit interest involved in the transaction to the purchaser. The systems examined here have resolved this conflict in a variety of ways.

685. China, STA, Guoshuihan [2008] No. 875.
686. India, ITA 1961, s. 145(1).
687. India, ITA 1961, s. 43B. However, certain business expenses are allowed based only on actual payments.
688. *DCIT v. Stup Consultants Pvt Ltd*, ITA No. 5671/Mum/2009.
689. India, ITA 1961, s. 145(2).
690. India, Notification September 29, 2016, available at https://incometaxindia.gov.in/Documents/Notification-86-87-88-2016.pdf.
691. India, ITA 1961, s. 145A and 145B.

In the *United States*, the treatment of prepaid income has generated a substantial amount of litigation, including three Supreme Court cases. In general, the courts have upheld the tax authorities' assertion that the inclusion of prepayments in income currently is necessary to "clearly reflect income."[692] The decisions rest primarily on the discretion of the tax authorities to determine what practices clearly reflect income. While litigation establishes that prepaid income must in principle be included currently, the rule has been relaxed somewhat by statute and regulations.[693] In the case of services, income recognition can be postponed until the taxable year after the year of receipt. For sales income, advance payments for inventory can be deferred to the following year. In addition, there are a number of specific statutory provisions which allow the deferral of advance payments. For example, deferral is allowed in the case of dues prepaid to an automobile club for road service, one of the situations in which the courts had required current inclusion.[694]

Canada deals with the problem through a specific statutory provision. Prepaid income must be included in taxable income in the year in which the payment is received, even where the amount is not properly accruable.[695] However, the taxpayer is allowed to deduct a reserve in the same amount, thus neutralizing the initial inclusion.[696] The reserve in turn must be included in income in the following year, but if the amount has still not yet been earned by the end of the year, another reserve may be claimed. The period of the reserve is thus, in effect, unlimited, except in the case of articles of food and drink and unredeemed transportation tickets, where a special rule limits the period to one year.

Despite the general absence of financial accounting principles in the *Australian* tax system, case law doctrine has adopted the financial accounting rule for prepayments. Such amounts are includable only when earned.[697] In the *United Kingdom*, there is also case law support for the position that prepayments may be deferred until the income has been earned, but only where the taxpayer can establish that this is indeed the appropriate financial accounting treatment.[698]

Similarly, in *The Netherlands*, case law interpreting "sound commercial practice" has allowed the deferral of prepaid income until the period in which it is earned. It is essential that consistent practice be followed. *Sweden* and *China* likewise follow general accounting principles which allow the deferral of the recognition of prepayments until they are earned.

Using the balance-sheet comparison approach to income determination, *Germany* treats advance payments as neutral from both a financial accounting and tax point of view. The transaction is treated as "pending" and its effects are thus suspended

692. *Schlude v. Commissioner*, 372 U.S. 128 (1963).
693. United States, IRC s. 451(c); Treas. Reg. s. 1.451-8 (2020).
694. United States, IRC s. 456.
695. Canada, ITA, s. 12(1)(a).
696. Canada, ITA, s. 20(1)(m).
697. *Arthur Murray (NSW) Pty Ltd* [1965] HCA 58, 114 CLR 314.
698. *Symons v. Weeks* [1983] STC 195.

until completion.[699] The increase in assets on the balance sheet caused by the payment is offset by the liability to deliver goods or perform services. Therefore, an advance payment generally has no tax results. *France* and *Japan* reach the same results, although the techniques are somewhat different.

In *India*, the treatment of income received in advance depends on the category of income. Employment income is taxable either on receipt or when it becomes due. Business profits and income from other sources are determined according to either the cash or accrual method of accounting regularly followed by the taxpayer. Therefore, for taxpayers using the accrual method, amounts received in advance can usually be deferred. Advances received with respect to the transfer of capital assets must be deducted from the cost of the asset.[700]

3 INCOME TREATMENT OF DEFERRED PAYMENTS

Where property is sold with the financing in effect being provided by the seller in the form of some sort of purchase-money security, accounting rules usually require the immediate recognition of the income from the transaction. This would be the normal result under accrual methods of accounting and could also be applicable under the cash method, depending on the nature of the buyer's obligation. The systems reviewed here have reacted in different ways to deferred payments. In some cases, a special rule allows the deferral of the recognition of the income until the payments are in fact received under the note. In other situations, a cash-basis taxpayer, who would normally be able to defer the recognition of gain until receipt, is in effect put on the accrual basis and required to take the gain into account when the property is delivered.

The *United States* system is an example of the first approach. Under the so-called installment sales provisions, the taxpayer reports the gain on the disposition of noninventory assets in the years in which the payments are received.[701] The payment is treated partly as a tax-free return of tax cost and partly as gain, depending on the overall ratio of gain to total purchase price. The installment obligation must bear a market rate of interest. There are a number of restrictions on the use of the installment method. It does not apply where the property sold or received is publicly traded. In addition, installment treatment is not available for any gain on the property which represents previously taken depreciation deductions. Even where deferral is allowed, if the amount of the outstanding indebtedness held by the taxpayer exceeds USD 5,000,000, interest is charged on the deferred tax.[702] The disposition of an installment obligation causes the recognition of all deferred gain, even for transactions in which nothing is received in return.

Chinese tax legislation does not provide any specific rules for deferred payments and accounting rules are likely applicable.

---

699. This is an unwritten rule derived from the prudence concept, which is codified in Germany, ITA, s. 5 para. 1 sent. 1 with reference to Commercial Code, s. 252 para. 1.
700. India, ITA 1961, s. 51.
701. United States, IRC, s. 453.
702. United States, IRC, s. 453A(c).

Under the *Dutch* system, the courts have allowed the deferral of income recognition in certain cases of deferred payment as an aspect of "sound business practice."

Sweden has taken a quite different approach to deferred-payment sales. Whether the taxpayer is on the cash basis or accrual basis, gain on the disposition of capital property must be included in the year the sale takes place. The purpose of the rule is to limit deferral of taxation of capital gains. The *Australian* system, in general, also requires profit on the sale of inventory and capital property to be taken into account in the year of sale, with subsequent adjustments where the promised payments are not received. The same result applies in *Japan* because, as a general rule, transactions must be accounted for on the accrual basis. The time when a taxpayer must take into account the amount realized from the sale or exchange of a capital asset is not affected by the time of receipt of the consideration. The specific provisions allowing deferral of recognition of earnings on installment sales were recently abolished.

Similarly, using the balance-sheet comparison method of income determination, in *Germany* the existence of the claim for the payment results in an increase in assets and hence in net worth. The claim is usually valued at its nominal amount, although it may be discounted if some sort of hidden interest is involved in the transaction. A judge-made modification applies in the case of the sale of a whole business; where the consideration is paid in installments, the taxpayer can elect to have the proceeds taxed at the time of sale (and receive beneficial capital gains treatment) or to spread the proceeds over the period during which the installments are paid.[703]

In *France*, under the accrual method, income is taxable when earned and an expense is deductible for tax purposes when the liability and its amount are certain, regardless of when it is due or payable. In principle, civil law determines the price and the date on which a claim arises from a contract.[704] A specific system applies to long-term construction contracts to ensure that taxation is not deferred until the end of the work: taxation takes place when the work is fully or partially accepted, even if acceptance may only be provisional or subject to reservations. It is possible to insert special terms into the contract enabling the taxable event to be modified by bringing it forward to the time of fulfilment of a condition. Because accrual accounting can cause cash-flow problems for companies due to late payments and persistent contractual non-performance, a company is able to set aside a deductible provision if it anticipates non-payment.[705]

Under the cash method, income is taxable when it becomes "available,"[706] usually meaning payment or entry in a current account. In the case of capital gains on securities, the taxable event is the date of transfer of ownership, or in the case of capital gains on real estate, the date of signature of the promise to sell.

The *Canadian* system takes an intermediate position. When business property is sold with deferred payments, the taxpayer is entitled to claim a deductible reserve for the portion of the profit from the sale which is not due until after the end of the taxable

703. Germany, Income Tax Regulations (*Einkommensteuer-Richtlinien*), s. 16 para. 11.
704. France, Civil Code, s. 1583.
705. France, CGI, s. 39 1 5.
706. France, CGI, s. 12.

year. However, the maximum period for which the reserve may be claimed is three years.[707] In the case of capital gain property, the same approach is taken. The maximum period for the reserve is five years, and at least one-fifth of the amount of the taxable capital gain must be included in income each year.[708]

The *United Kingdom* also makes a distinction between capital gain property and trading property. For capital gain property, gain must be recognized currently based on the value of the consideration received, with no discount for the fact that the payments take place over time. The actual payment of the tax, however, can be deferred where the consideration is payable for a period of over eighteen months. The situation with respect to business income is more complex. On the deduction side, statutory rules allow a write-off of debts which are bad, estimated to be bad, or released as part of a statutory insolvency arrangement; the corporation tax rules reflect accounting language and refer to debts which are "impaired."[709]

In *India*, although there is no specific provision in the ITA in relation to revenue recognition in installment sales, under the general accounting standard, the interest component related to the unpaid portion of the sale price can be deferred. Capital gains also become chargeable in the year of transfer even if part of the consideration is deferred, subject to some narrow exceptions (e.g., the conversion of capital assets to stock in trade, where the gain is recognized when the inventory is sold,[710] and the expropriation of property, where the gain is recognized when the compensation is first received).[711]

4 ORIGINAL ISSUE DISCOUNT OBLIGATIONS AND OTHER COMPLEX FINANCIAL INSTRUMENTS

Where obligations are issued at a discount from the stated amount payable at maturity, questions of both timing and character of income and expense arise for the borrower and the lender. From an economic perspective, the difference between the issue price and the amount due on redemption clearly represents interest expense for the borrower and interest income for the lender. However, it has taken some time for tax systems to reflect this economic reality in the tax rules. In some of the systems dealt with here, there is still no satisfactory resolution of the problem of original issue discount (OID), with the legal form of the transaction controlling its tax treatment in many situations.

Similarly, the emergence of complex financial "products," typically with hybrid or derivative characteristics, has also raised difficult timing and characterization issues. In general, there is an increasing tendency to abandon traditional realization and tax accounting approaches in this area and to tax such instruments on an internal

707. Canada, ITA, s. 20(1)(n) and 20(8)(b).
708. Canada, ITA, s. 40(1)(a)(iii).
709. United Kingdom, ITTOIA, s. 35 and CTA 2009, s. 55; on loan relationships, *see* CTA 2009, s. 476.
710. India, ITA 1961, s. 45(2).
711. India, ITA 1961, s. 45(5).

rate of return or mark-to-market basis. The exact scope of such rules, however, is uncertain, although many of the systems have adopted new approaches to these issues.

In the *United States*, prior to the enactment of explicit statutory provisions, the treatment of OID in the case law was uncertain, with some cases following the legal form of the transaction and treating the discount element as capital. Although the Supreme Court eventually determined that the discount element was properly characterized as ordinary income, Congress had, in the meantime, intervened with a specific statutory provision denying capital gain treatment for the discount realized at maturity. The next legislative response to OID was to require holders of OID bonds to include the original discount amount in income ratably over the life of the bond regardless of the normal accounting method. Subsequent provisions modified the method of inclusion to require the discount element to be treated on an "economic" or "constant interest" accrual basis (i.e., with less interest in early years and more in later years), reflecting the implicit reinvestment of the interest element.

Finally, in 1984, rules were introduced dealing with the calculation of OID where bonds are issued for property.[712] Except in the case of traded property, where bonds are issued for property, the value of the property is uncertain and hence the issue price of the bond and the resulting discount cannot be directly ascertained. To deal with this problem, the legislation, in general terms, provided for the determination of the issue price by discounting the payments to be made under the bond by a stipulated discount rate and treating that amount as the current value of the property, and hence the issue price of the bond. If the amounts to be received under the instrument exceed the hypothetical issue price, the excess is OID and is included and deducted in computing income currently under the usually applicable OID principles.

A number of special and complex rules deal with obligations providing for contingent payments or a variable interest rate. Proposals were made (although subsequently withdrawn) to apply the OID rules to "hybrid" obligations, such as convertible bonds, under a "bifurcation" approach, which would treat separately the option embedded in the convertible bond and the actual loan, applying OID principles to the loan portion of the transaction. Currently, the OID rules are applied to the entire convertible debt instrument. However, where a debt instrument is issued with a separate option that is not embedded, bifurcation is required.[713]

A different set of rules applies to so-called market discount, i.e., discount arising from a purchase of bonds in the market which has declined in value because of interest rate changes. No current accrual of the discount is required, but the gain is not entitled to capital gain treatment on disposition.[714] The realization rules are relaxed with respect to the disposition of market discount bonds so that a gift of the bond is a realization event.[715] In addition, there are limitations on the deduction of interest expense incurred in connection with market discount bonds. The taxpayer may elect to

712. United States, IRC, s. 1271-74.
713. United States, IRC, s. 1273(c).
714. United States, IRC, s. 1276(a)(1).
715. *Ibid.*

accrue market discount currently, in which case the interest expense is fully deductible.[716]

Beyond the treatment of discount bonds, the rules dealing with more complex financial instruments are still evolving. A mark-to-market approach is taken with respect to many types of commodities futures, foreign currency, and options contracts.[717] In addition, dealers in securities and derivatives are required to use a mark-to-market method for certain forward and option contracts and for notional principal contracts which are not covered by the general rule.[718] A broader accrual approach has been discussed in the academic literature.

In *Sweden*, under statutory provisions, OID on obligations held by private persons is treated as interest but not taxed until actually received, either on sale or on maturity of the bond. For corporations and individuals holding bonds as business assets, the general application of financial accounting principles for tax purposes requires the accrual of OID currently as interest income. Similarly, business issuers of OID obligations can accrue the interest expense currently.

Japan did not have general tax rules dealing with OID until 1998, although there was a movement to adopt a mark-to-market approach with respect to certain types of financial instruments such as derivative financial instruments. In 1996, the mark-to-market method was first adopted by banks and securities companies with respect to derivative financial instruments and marketable securities. This treatment has been generalized since 2000, and all companies in Japan are currently required to apply the mark-to-market method to their derivative instruments and marketable securities, except for some hedging transactions.[719] With respect to zero coupon bonds or similar types of bonds which do not fall within the category of marketable securities, the amount of OID attributable to a certain fiscal year must be included in the taxable income of holders. Such amounts must be calculated on a straight-line basis rather than on an implicit-interest basis.

In contrast to the tax treatment for corporate entities, for individuals, OID is not taxable until the maturity of the relevant obligations or their transfer. OID is now aggregated with capital gains from securities at maturity and is subject to the same tax treatment as those capital gains. Japan does not seem to be seriously concerned about the tax-deferral effect of this approach.

In *France*, OID has been subject to special rules since 1985. For individuals who do not hold the obligations in a business, the difference between the amount received on redemption (excluding annual interest actually received) and the sum paid on acquisition is treated as interest income in the year received. The same rule applies to obligations held in a business context but if the discount exceeds 10% of the acquisition price, the interest must be computed on a yield-to-maturity basis and included in income annually.[720] With respect to futures contracts, options, and

716. United States, IRC, s. 1278(b)(1).
717. United States, IRC, s. 1256.
718. United States, IRC, s. 475.
719. Japan, CTA, s. 61-3 and 61-5.
720. France, CGI, s. 238 septies A sq.

derivative instruments, statutory provisions require mark-to-market treatment where the instruments are traded on an organized market or have a value determined with respect to such markets.

The *German* rules have a similar pattern. If both the issuer and the holder of an obligation are required to use the accrual method of accounting generally—that is, they are business taxpayers—the OID is accounted for currently as interest expense and interest income, calculated on a yield-to-maturity basis. In addition, subsequent changes in interest rates which increase the value of the liability in the hands of the issuer are also taken into account currently, although the corresponding gain to the holder continues to be deferred. The OID is taxed only at redemption or on sale; it is treated as interest income and not as tax-free capital gain. For privately held obligations, the difference between the issue price and the amount received is treated as interest income or expense in full in the year of issue as long as the OID does not exceed the customary amount.

Some movement in the direction of an overall mark-to-market treatment of derivative financial instruments is discernible after years of the basic conservative approach of following accounting rules. Germany has reformed its financial accounting rules for derivative financial instruments held by financial institutions which are "available for sale," allowing a limited mark-to-market rule, which is also reflected in the tax law.[721]

The Netherlands has attempted to avoid timing and recognition issues involving bonds and complex financial instruments by adopting rules in 2001 for taxing capital income on a deemed-return basis (box 3). For business taxpayers, under case law (interpreting "sound business practice") the annual amount of interest accrued on discount bonds, etc., is taken into account for tax purposes currently.

With respect to the taxation of financial derivatives, tax inspectors generally apply the rules of "sound business practice" (a deduction can be taken where there is a more than negligible risk that a loss will be suffered; income not yet earned need not be reported) and taxpayers apparently have accepted this treatment.

The *Canadian* ITA does not contain comprehensive rules dealing with OID or sophisticated financial products, including derivatives. As a result, the tax consequences of these products must be determined by applying the basic provisions dealing with the character, source, and timing of income and deductions. Not surprisingly, financial products have been used by taxpayers to manipulate tax consequences. In certain cases, the government has responded with specific legislation on an ad hoc basis.

As a result of a misreading of old English cases, Canadian courts have traditionally considered interest to be a nondeductible capital expense. Accordingly, there is a special statutory deduction for interest expense incurred in respect of borrowed money, or the unpaid purchase price of property, where the money or property is used for the purpose of earning income.[722] The statutory requirement for borrowed money is an important limitation on the deduction. For example, interest in respect of unpaid

721. Germany, ITA, s. 6 para. 1 No. 2b.
722. Canada, ITA, s. 20(1)(c).

(compound) interest would not be deductible in the absence of a special provision since the unpaid interest is not borrowed money.[723] A special provision permits a deduction for compound interest only when it is actually paid.[724]

According to the express wording of the Act, interest is deductible where it is paid in the year or becomes payable in respect of the year. Nevertheless, by administrative practice, interest other than compound interest is deductible on an accrual basis. Interest is not defined in the Act, but the case law has established that interest is restricted to amounts which represent compensation for the use of money, which are computed in reference to a principal sum, and which accrue on a daily basis.

An OID, premium, or bonus is considered to be interest only where a loan does not provide for interest or provides for interest at less than a reasonable rate. If OID is not interest, it is deductible only when paid. In the case of a "shallow" discount (the issue price is not less than 97% of the principal, and its annual yield is not greater than 4/3 of the stipulated interest rate), the full amount of the discount is deductible.[725] For other "deep" discounts, only one-half of the amount of the discount is deductible when paid. The disallowance of 50% of the OID as a deduction reflects the fact that, in general, only 50% of the discount would be included in the income of the holder; in other words, the discount is treated as capital gain to the holder.[726]

Taxpayers could avoid the treatment of OID as capital by issuing zero coupon bonds. Because these bonds have no stated rate of interest, the discount is treated as interest for tax purposes. However, the Canada Revenue Agency takes the position that the interest must be bifurcated into simple interest and compound interest. The simple interest is deductible on an accrual basis, but the compound interest is deductible only when paid on the maturity of the obligation, as discussed earlier. This treatment effectively precluded Canadian corporations from using zero coupon bonds and OID as an effective means of borrowing.

In 1990, the government introduced detailed provisions with respect to certain long-term prepaid debt obligations.[727] These rules were intended to require the prepayment of interest to be treated as a reduction of the principal amount of the obligation. Inadvertently, the rules work in such a way that corporate borrowers can achieve exactly the same result as with a zero coupon bond simply by prepaying interest. In other words, under these rules, the amount of the prepayment is deductible on an actuarial basis over the term of the obligation. This result was clearly unintended.

Since the Canadian tax system does not contain comprehensive accrual rules dealing with financial products, the tax consequences of various products have been established largely by administrative practice and case law. Gains and losses in respect of futures and forward contracts are considered to be on income account where the transactions are connected with the taxpayer's business. Otherwise, the taxpayer may

723. Canada, ITA, s. 20(3).
724. Canada, ITA, s. 20(1)(d).
725. Canada, ITA, s. 20(1)(f).
726. The deductible portion of the discount increases from one-half to two-thirds in 2024, consistent with the increase in the capital gains inclusion rate.
727. Canada, ITA, s. 18(9.2)-(9.8).

report such gains and losses as ordinary income or loss or as capital gains or losses, but must do so consistently. Originally, the tax authorities applied a linkage approach to the treatment of foreign exchange gains and losses and swap transactions—in other words, the treatment of the gains and losses from the foreign currency fluctuations or the swap was dependent on the treatment of the underlying transaction. This type of approach leads to a mismatch where a capital asset or liability is hedged. Accordingly, the Canada Revenue Agency has taken the position that all interest-rate swaps should be treated on income account. However, in a 1999 case, the Supreme Court decided that a gain realized on a hedge of a long-term borrowing in a foreign currency was a capital gain.[728]

Financial institutions and investment dealers are required by legislation to use mark-to-market reporting for certain debt and equity securities. For other taxpayers, gains and losses are recognized only when realized. However, where the property constitutes inventory of a business, the lower of cost or market rule of inventory valuation requires the losses to be accrued.

Currently, the *Australian* system is a mixture of partial regimes dealing with various aspects of the issues considered in this section. The character and timing of OID was tested before the courts in the 1980s by capital indexed securities, stripped securities, etc. An accruals regime was introduced in 1984 for a wide range of debt securities issued at a discount or otherwise providing at issue for returns in forms other than periodic interest. Similarly, the character and timing of foreign exchange gains and losses was tested before the courts and then made subject to a special realization-based statutory regime.

A comprehensive regime for financial assets and liabilities was enacted in 2010.[729] It is a mixture of internal rate of return and realization systems based on whether the return on, or cost of, an instrument is "sufficiently certain," which has two elements: the gain or loss must be "effectively noncontingent" and the amount of the gain or loss must be "fixed or determinable with reasonable accuracy." There are several elective elements in the package which allow using financial accounts, marking to market, matching the timing and character for hedges, and foreign currency translation. The regime applies on a mandatory basis only to very large taxpayers; other taxpayers generally remain subject to the rules in the previous paragraph unless they elect into the new regime. The regime applies to most classes of "financial arrangement," a definition which proceeds from the idea of a "cash settlable legal or equitable right" to receive a financial benefit, or a "cash settlable legal or equitable obligation" to provide a financial benefit. No financial arrangement arises where either party has a right to receive, or an obligation to provide, something other than a financial benefit or something cash settlable, and where the value of that other item is not insignificant (i.e., only cash will flow under both legs of the transaction). Most debt, hybrid, equity, derivative, and foreign currency transactions potentially are within the scope of the rules. However, the rules have limited impact in certain situations (e.g., equity interests are largely unaffected unless the taxpayer makes

728. *Shell Canada Ltd. v. The Queen,* [1999] 4 CTC 313 (SCC).
729. Australia, ITAA 1997, Division 230.

certain elections). A separate regime already applies for tax exempt leasing of plant and equipment.[730] Leasing is not generally covered by the definition of financial arrangement because it does not involve cash flows on both sides.

The *United Kingdom*, like the U.S., began with a struggle to fit low-interest and zero coupon bonds into the tax framework. The taxability of profit arising from a discount has been part of the UK tax system since 1802, when such profits were listed as falling within Schedule D, Case III. However, in practice, while the holder was taxable on the discount, the income inclusion occurred only on redemption. This meant that the holder was not taxed on the profit made on a realization before redemption; conversely, however, at redemption, the holder was taxed on the entire profit arising from the discount. As a result of this rule, taxpayers who held such a bond had a strong incentive to sell it to a tax exempt body, such as a charity or a pension fund, so that no tax would be collected at all. A court decision in 1983 made it more likely that the holder of a bond would be taxed on an intermediate profit, but after the introduction of the 1984 rules, discussed below, this result was not explored further. Under administrative practice, a discount was not deductible by the issuing company until redemption, when it was deductible in full. Thus, the regime was at least symmetrical.

Statutory provisions dealing with this situation were introduced in 1984. For deep discount bonds, an income element was treated as arising, strictly in line with an algebraic formula, during the life of the bond; a discount was deep if it was greater than 15% or 1/2% per annum. The issuing company deducted the income element under the formula on a year-by-year basis. The holder, however, paid tax only on an actual (or deemed) disposal; there was no deemed disposal simply because a year had ended. When the holder disposed of the bond, the income element which had accrued up to that day was included in income; where the actual price difference was greater or less than that given by the formula, the balance was treated as capital gain or loss, or income gain or loss, under ordinary income/CGT rules. If the discount was not deep, or for some other reason the bonds fell outside the 1984 rules, the original administrative practice applied.

The deep discount rules apply only where the gain could be calculated at the start (e.g., where the redemption price was fixed). Some other instruments fell within subsequent rules created in 1989 for "deep gain" securities where the formulary approach was not possible, but with extensive exemptions (e.g., for convertible securities, qualifying indexed securities, and certain government bonds).

In 1996, the UK introduced new rules for the tax treatment of any "loan relationship" entered into by a company, thus covering discount bonds but having a much wider scope.[731] A loan relationship arises where the company is a debtor or creditor in respect of a money debt which arises from a contract for the lending of money; it follows that a simple trade debt does not give rise to a loan relationship. The 1996 rules apply for both income inclusion and deduction of expense. After further rule changes, the legislation now authorizes the application of any generally accepted

730. Australia, ITAA 1997, Division 250.
731. United Kingdom, CTA 2009, Parts 5 and 6.

accounting practice. Sometimes special rules apply—for example, where related parties are involved. The foreign exchange rules were merged into the loan-relationship rules in 2002; the rules for derivatives were also rewritten at that time.[732]

These loan-relationship rules apply only to corporate holders and issuers. For other taxpayers, a revised version of the 1984 and 1989 rules—or, in exceptional circumstances, the original administrative practices—continue to apply. The revised version of 1994 merges the two sets of rules and adopts the simple approach of repealing the algebraic formula and subjecting the holder to income tax only on the realized gain, but with equivalent relief for any loss. This 1994 legislation has been rewritten as part of ITTOIA 2005.[733]

China does not have any special rules for OID or complex financial instruments. Costs are recognized only when actually paid or payable; income is not recognized on a mark-to-market basis. Hybrid financial instruments which have both debt and equity attributes are classified as debt if they meet certain conditions.[734]

In *India*, the treatment of interest and capital gains arising from deep discount bonds was comprehensively reviewed by the Central Board of Direct Taxes (CBDT) in 2002,[735] and a circular was issued requiring taxpayers to use a mark-to-market method for such bonds. Under that method, the difference between the values at the beginning and end of the year is taxable as interest (where the bonds are held as investments) or trading income (where the bonds are held as trading assets). Where such a bond is transferred before maturity, the difference between the sale price and cost is taxable as a capital gain to an investor or as business income to a trader. Small investors (holding bonds of up to INR 100,000) have an option to treat the difference between the bid price and redemption price as interest income in the year of redemption. In 2005, new rules were adopted for zero coupon bonds issued after June 1, 2005, by certain authorized infrastructure or public-sector entities.[736] These bonds are treated as short-term only if they are held for less than a year.[737] For transfers before July 23, 2024, long-term gains are taxed at 10% where the taxpayer does not claim indexation relief, but at 12.5% for transfers after that date.[738] The interest accrual rules do not apply to zero coupon bonds.[739] For the issuer, the pro rata amount of discount is allowed as a deduction from profits.[740]

732. United Kingdom, CTA 2009, Part 7.
733. United Kingdom, ITTOIA, Part 4 Ch. 8.
734. China, STA Public Notice [2013] No. 41.
735. India, CBDT, Circular No. 2 of 2002 dated February 15, 2002.
736. India, ITA 1961, s. 2(48).
737. India, ITA 1961, s. 2(42A).
738. India, ITA, 1961, s. 112.
739. India, CBDT, Circular No. 3/2006.
740. India, ITA 1961, s. 36(i)(iiia) read with Rule 8C of the IT Rules, 1962.

Subpart E

Attribution of Income

A final element in the structure of an income tax is the attribution of the various elements of the tax base to a taxable person. Several different questions are involved. The most fundamental is the choice of taxable unit. Who is "the taxpayer" for purposes of applying the various substantive rules of a tax system? Once that question has been answered, a second, related issue involves taxpayer attempts to shift income among taxable units in order to reduce the overall tax burden of taxpayers who are, broadly speaking, related, but who constitute separate taxable persons. To what extent and under what conditions will those income transfers be respected? While the issue arises primarily in the context of progressive rate structures, where the splitting of income among several taxpayers can reduce the total tax burden, it can also arise in proportional rate systems if a related entity has available losses or can take advantage of various special deductions or allowances.

A related problem concerns the treatment of payments arising out of divorce and separation. Where a couple are in a domestic relationship (whether a marriage, civil union, or other recognized relationship) and are treated as a taxable unit, the question arises how payments which result from the dissolution of that relationship should be dealt with. Even in systems in which the individual is the taxable unit, there may be special rules for payments between divorced or separated parties, and for payments for the support of children.

The following material first examines the basic question of the taxable unit and then explores the related issues.

1 DEFINITION OF TAXABLE UNIT

The choice of the appropriate taxable unit involves complex issues of social and economic policy and has been the subject of much discussion in many countries. Any decision dealing with the taxable unit involves emphasizing some policy goals and social values at the expense of others. For example, a decision to treat the individual as the taxable unit may mean that couples with the same amount of income and who are otherwise similarly situated may pay a different amount of tax depending on how much income is earned by each partner. In contrast, a decision to treat a couple as the taxable unit may mean that such couples are treated differently from other couples whose economic and social arrangements are functionally similar. In addition, depending on the structure of the rate schedule, a decision to treat married couples as the taxable unit may result in a change in overall tax burden as a result of marriage (or divorce).

The resolution of these conflicting policy goals has taken several forms in the systems examined here. In some cases, each individual is treated as a taxable unit and there is no aggregation of income of family members. A variation of this approach is to treat the individual as the taxable unit for the purpose of taxing earned income but to have special rules dealing with unearned income. On the one hand, the taxation of each individual separately on earned income allows decisions about entry into the work-force to be made independently of consideration of the income earned by the other spouse. On the other hand, some type of aggregation of unearned income prevents the shifting of such income within the economic unit in order to reduce tax burdens.

Other systems either require or allow the couple to be treated as a taxable unit. This approach is sometimes accompanied by a rate structure which "splits" the income between the two partners equally—which means that, in the case of progressive rates, marriage does not increase the total tax burden on the couple. In contrast, a differentiated rate for couples raises the issue of the proper relationship in the rate schedules between the rates for couples and single persons.

Whatever approach is taken to the taxation of adults, the treatment of the income of dependent children raises a separate issue: should they be treated as separate taxpayers or taxed together with the adults who have responsibility for their care?

The development of the rules on the taxable unit in the *United States* illustrates the interaction of these various considerations. Prior to 1948, the individual was the only taxable unit. As a result, the tax burden on married couples varied depending on whether the income was earned by one spouse, both spouses equally, or something in between these two extremes. In addition, the Supreme Court had held that, in states which had adopted a civil law community-property system, each spouse was taxable on one-half of the income, regardless of who earned the income. As a result, under a progressive rate structure, married couples in community-property states could pay less tax on the same amount of combined income than couples in common law jurisdictions. In 1948, in response to this problem, couples were permitted to elect to file "joint" returns and to aggregate their income and compute their tax under a rate structure which had brackets twice as wide as the corresponding brackets used by unmarried persons. The election was available only to couples who were married for civil law purposes. While the couple could still file separate returns, it almost always worked in their favor to take advantage of the splitting of income which the joint return entailed.

The introduction of joint returns meant that a couple paid significantly less tax than an individual with the same amount of income filing separately. The perception that individuals were overtaxed in relation to couples under the rate structure introduced in connection with joint returns led in 1969 to the introduction of a new system of rate schedules. The new system retained the separate schedule for married couples but changed the relationships among the brackets to reduce the difference between married and single taxpayers. Under the new system, the bracket differences no longer represented a "splitting" of income between the spouses. The old rate schedules were retained for married couples who had elected to file separately in order to prevent them from taking advantage of the new, lower individual rates.

Moving away from a system of splitting, however, introduced a new problem. If two single persons with roughly equal income married, their tax burden was increased, since the aggregation of their income in the married rate structure would increase the impact of the progressive rates. This "marriage penalty" was partially addressed in 1981 with the introduction of a deduction for two-earner couples. The deduction was eliminated in 1986, following a substantial reduction in the progressivity of tax rates which had made the marriage penalty much less significant. However, since marginal tax rates have increased since that time, concern about the impact of marriage on tax burdens has reappeared.

There has been longstanding recognition in the U.S. that in a system of progressive rates it is impossible to provide equal treatment of married couples, a differential between the taxation of individuals and married couples which does not reflect income splitting, and no significant change in tax burdens as a result of marriage. Choices and compromises must be made, and the relative importance accorded these policy objectives has varied over time. Currently, attention is focused on the "marriage penalty" under existing law and the impact of aggregate taxation on entry into the workforce by secondary workers. The first five brackets for married couples of the 2024 rate schedule are double that of single filers, thereby eliminating the marriage penalty due to basic bracket structure (although other features of the tax law can create a marriage penalty or "marriage bonus").

In general, dependent children in the U.S. are treated as separate taxpayers. However, the unearned income of children under 19 years old (24 years old for full-time students) in excess of an inflation-adjusted threshold amount (USD 2,600 in 2024) is taxed at the parents' highest marginal rate.[741] This occurs even though the child's income is technically still treated as separate income and not aggregated with the parents' income.

Since 1957, the *German* system has also provided an election for joint taxation of married couples living together, which today covers same-sex as well as opposite-sex marriages. For electing couples, the total income of each partner is assessed and the sum of both amounts aggregated and divided by two in determining the statutory tax rate.[742] With respect to private expenditure, spouses are treated as one taxpayer but tax-free thresholds or maximum amounts for deductions are doubled. In contrast, children are treated as separate taxpayers for most purposes. In 1982, the Federal

741. United States, IRC, s. 1(g).
742. Germany, ITA, s. 26 para. 1.

Constitutional Court held that the current splitting regime for spouses reflects the specific protection afforded by the Constitution to marriage as an institution.[743]

With respect to wage taxation at source, the splitting system is combined with an option to combine low-tax deductions of the primary earner and high-tax deductions of the secondary earner, which is intended to roughly imitate the advantageous tax effect of the splitting system for couples with high income differences before the final assessment procedure. In practice, however, it entails a strong disincentive for women (as typical second earners) to re-enter the job market after childbirth beyond the limits allowed under a special tax regime for marginal employment. To alleviate this effect, the legislature introduced another optional regime in 2010, which is barely used and has largely failed to meet its objective. As a result, the regime remains subject to frequent political discussion, as are the effects of income splitting on the tax burden of high-income families in general, reflecting the divergent views of the role of traditional marriage in society. The ongoing debate as to whether income splitting for married couples should be replaced by income splitting for families with children irrespective of the legal status of the couple is at present unresolved.

The *Canadian* system takes a different approach. The individual has always been the taxable unit, although there has been periodic discussion to establish spouses or the family as the taxable unit. However, the income of both spouses (formally married or common law partner, which is defined to include same-sex partners) is aggregated for purposes of determining the entitlement to certain personal tax allowances and other payments. The *Australian* system is quite similar. The individual is treated as the taxable unit, although the income of one spouse can have an impact on the tax treatment of the other. Over the last decade, an increasing number of tax concessions and tax impositions use family income as the basis of measuring qualification. In both the Canadian and Australian systems, there are rules to prevent the shifting of income, as discussed below.

Historically, the *United Kingdom* in effect treated the married couple as a taxable unit by attributing all of the wife's income to the husband. Since the husband was the technical taxpayer, he was primarily responsible for the payment of the tax and for all dealings with the tax authorities. This approach was gradually liberalized, with the wife first given the authority to deal directly with the tax authorities, and subsequently the couple could elect to have the wife's earned income taxed separately. Given the rate structure and other secondary consequences of the election, separate taxation was most advantageous for higher-income taxpayers. In 1990, a system of separate taxation was introduced covering both earned and unearned income. In the case of income from property, where property is owned jointly, the income is divided evenly unless the parties can establish a different underlying ownership and elect to be taxed on that basis.[744] The reasoning behind the change included a need to recognize the changing role—and greater independence—of women in society and to provide them with privacy with regard to their income. Separate taxation applies for purposes of the CGT

743. Federal Constitutional Court (*Bundesverfassungsgericht*), November 3, 1982, 1 BvR 620/78 et al.
744. United Kingdom, ITA, ss. 836-837.

as well, with a separate annual exemption for both spouses. Children are also treated as separate taxpayers for both income and CGT purposes. There are rules to prevent the artificial splitting of income, but they do not apply where there is an outright gift between the spouses.[745] A nontaxpaying spouse can transfer up to 10% of their personal allowance to the other spouse, but only if the recipient spouse is a basic-rate payer (not a higher- or additional-rate taxpayer).

Since 1997, the UK has introduced a series of tax credits to assist families.[746] Since these credits are based to a large extent on the income of households rather than the income of individuals, the effect is to significantly reduce the number of households in which separate taxation is the rule. The tax credit system looks to the income position of the household, regardless of whether the parties are married or not. Unusually, Child Benefit is means-tested against the partner with the higher income rather than on the household's income. The benefit paid is clawed back on income greater than GBP 60,000 and entirely clawed back on income greater than GBP 80,000 by way of a separate tax—the high-income child benefit tax charge. This means that the person liable to repay Child Benefit via the tax may not be the person who received the Child Benefit in the first place. Parents can elect to stop receiving Child Benefit where it is clear that it will need to be repaid entirely.

The UK has a concept of civil partnership for couples of the same sex. The spouse rules apply equally to civil partners and spouses. The Marriage (Same Sex Couples) Act 2013 legalized same-sex marriage in England and Wales and the Marriage and Civil Partnership (Scotland) Act 2014 did the same there. In 2019, the Prime Minister indicated that civil partnerships would be made available to mixed-sex couples in England and Wales.

The *Japanese* system also adopts the individual as the taxable unit. At one time, there were rules which attempted to attribute investment income of family members to the principal wage-earner but they were dropped due to administrative problems. The eligibility criteria for a spousal allowance historically focused solely on the income of the lower-earning spouse. The allowance was phased out as the lower-earning spouse's income increased, while the income of the principal earner was irrelevant. The effect of this provision has been criticized as discouraging women from entering the workforce on a full-time basis. Under the system which took effect in 2018, the allowance depends both on the income earned by the lower-earning spouse (the floor for phase-out was raised, so as to address the criticisms noted above) and on the principal earner's income; the phase-out kicks in at income of JPY 9 million and the allowance is eliminated at income of JPY 10 million.[747]

The *Dutch* approach is based on the taxation of individuals, with some modifications. Regardless of whether an individual is part of a "couple" (*see* definition below), individuals are taxed on their own business income, employment income, income from certain annuity contracts and grants, and payments received to cover the costs of their own or their children's education. Other income items and all personal

745. United Kingdom, ITTOIA, s. 626; for interpretation, *see Jones v. Garnett* [2007] STC 1536.
746. *See* United Kingdom, Tax Credits Act 2002.
747. Japan, ITA, s. 83 and 83-2.

deductions of taxpayers who are part of a "couple" may be divided between the couple at their discretion (with the exception that mortgage interest can be taken into account only by the person to whom the rental value of the residence is taxed).[748] Minor children are taxed on their own business and employment income, but all their other income items are generally taxed in equal parts to each of the parents.[749]

For purposes of these income and deduction allocations, the term "couple" refers to taxpayers that (a) are married; (b) "registered partners": i.e., who have concluded a notarial civil partnership agreement (no affective relationship is required; siblings, a parent and an adult child living together, etc., can also enter into such an agreement) and are registered at the same address; or (c) share a home that is owned (i.e., not rented).[750]

Sweden currently also has a system of individual taxation. Since, currently, the rate on capital income is essentially proportional, there is no significant problem with income shifting and no need for rules attributing capital income to the higher-earning spouse.

The *French* system has taken a completely different approach[751] since it considers, through the concept of the tax household (*foyer fiscal*), that a group of individuals are legally a single taxable unit. Originally, it was the family unit, i.e., all the people living under the same roof, that formed the tax unit. For income tax purposes, a dependent may be attached to the household if they are the sole or main dependent of the taxpayer (such as minor children, infirm children of any age, adult children under certain conditions, and disabled persons or foster children) regardless of their relationship to the taxpayer.[752] As a result, the composition of the tax household varies according to the taxpayer's situation (single, separated, divorced, widowed, married, or civil union) and the number of dependents.

The family quotient mechanism was introduced after the Second World War to encourage the birth rate, by integrating family expenses directly into the tax scale, making it possible to neutralize the tax burden on couples taxed jointly and to reduce household taxation according to the number of dependents. To determine the tax payable, the incomes of all household members are aggregated and the total is then shared among the tax household, depending on its composition. The more people in a tax household, the higher the number of tax shares. The taxpayer and partner are each allocated a "share"; an additional half-share is granted for up to two other members of the household. A full additional share is granted for any further members of the household. Thus, a family consisting of two adults and two children constitutes three shares; a couple with three children constitutes four shares, and so on.

The same system applies to single persons (unmarried, widowed, or divorced persons) but, in order to decrease the tax burden on single persons living alone, and especially women with dependent children, they are granted an additional one-half

748. Netherlands, ITA, Art. 2.17.
749. Netherlands, ITA, Art. 2.15.
750. Netherlands, ITA, Art. 1.2 and GTA, Art. 5.
751. France, CGI, ss. 6 and 7, 156, 193 through 199.
752. France, CGI, s. 196A bis.

share if they actually support, solely or principally, at least one child. Conversely, whenever two single persons (e.g., divorced) share the cost of the upkeep of a child, each parent can benefit from only one-half of the half or full share for the child, as the case may be. Unmarried couples (except those joined by a *pacte civil de solidarité*) always constitute two distinct fiscal households. Married persons may, in exceptional circumstances, file separate tax returns, provided that they live separately and were married under the separate property regime (*régime de la séparation de biens*) rather than community property.

The total income of the family is divided into the relevant number of shares, the progressive income tax schedule is applied to one share (five brackets, from 0% to 45%), and the total tax payable by the fiscal household is determined by multiplying the tax on one share by the number of shares. However, a ceiling exists on the effects of the quotient. The tax advantage resulting from the application of the family quotient is capped for each half-unit (EUR 1,759 for 2023 income) that exceeds one unit (for single people or widows under certain conditions) and two units for married couples or couples linked by a *pacte civil de solidarité*.

The concept of a dependent child is also complex. A child who is 18 years or older is normally taxed as a single person but may elect to be attached to their parents' fiscal household provided they are less than 21 years of age, less than 25 if still in school or university, or any age if disabled or performing military service. Even married (or partners in a *pacte civil de solidarité*) children may, up to the above limits, elect to be part of the parents' household; however, this does not result in an increase in the number of shares, the only effect being the deduction of a set amount for each attached person, child, spouse, and grandchild, which varies from case to case. This complex system concerns solely the traditional progressive IIT. It was not retained by Parliament in the 1990s when the new flat-rate income taxes were created. Under the new taxes, the taxable unit is the individual and the family structure is not relevant.

In *India*, the individual is the taxable unit; there is no consolidation of family income (except in the case of a HUF, as explained in the chapter on India in Part I, and spouses resident in Goa whose income, other than salaries, is governed by a community of property regime).[753] Spouses and other members of a family are taxed separately. Given the progressive tax rates for individuals and the abolition of gift and estate taxes, there is a temptation to divide income among the members of a family. However, the ITA contains provisions in the Act to prevent some of the obvious tax-planning strategies.

2 ALIMONY AND CHILD SUPPORT

The treatment of payments which arise out of the dissolution of a marriage also raises issues of the attribution of income. Suppose, for example, that as the result of a divorce, one spouse is required to make monthly payments to the other spouse. There are several ways in which such payments could be viewed. One approach would be to treat

753. India, ITA 1961, s. 5A.

the payment as a kind of "splitting" of the income between the two former spouses. Under this view, the payment would in effect be deductible by the payer but taxed to the recipient, but could also be viewed as a personal expense to the payer, and therefore nondeductible. For the recipient, the payment could be taxable, on the view that it has increased the recipient's separate net worth and power to consume; alternatively, the payment could be treated in the same manner as interfamilial gifts, which generally do not result in taxable income to the recipient. The same issues arise with respect to payments of child support to the custodial parent by the noncustodial parent. The systems considered here have taken a variety of approaches to these questions.

The *United States* makes a basic distinction between alimony and child support. Historically, both alimony and child support were treated as personal expenses, nondeductible and not includable. Successive statutory enactments beginning in 1942 allowed a deduction and required a corresponding inclusion for alimony payments while continuing the nondeductible-excludable treatment for child-support payments. The distinction between the two types of payments, often turning on intricacies of state family law, led to substantial litigation. The law was simplified in 1984 by providing a federal definition of alimony that gave the parties substantial leeway in determining which payments are treated as alimony.[754] To qualify, the payments had to be made in connection with a divorce decree or written separation agreement, had to be made in cash, and the parties had to be living apart. The payments also had to end after the death of the payee and could not be linked to events which indicated that they were in the nature of child-support payments (e.g., changes made when a child reached a certain age). Special complex (and largely ineffective) rules sought to prevent "front-loading" of payments in what was essentially a property settlement rather than periodic alimony. However, for divorce or separation agreements entered into after 2018, the tax treatment flips: alimony is not deductible by the payer and not includible by the recipient—thus, the difference in tax treatment between alimony and other types of payments was eliminated. Historically, payments for child support and property settlements, which are essentially all payments which do not meet the statutory definition of alimony, have been (and continue to be) nondeductible and not includable. Property settlements in connection with a divorce continue to be covered by the rollover treatment usually applicable to transfers between spouses.

The *Swedish* system is essentially the same as the former system for alimony payments in the U.S. Periodic payments of alimony are deductible by the payer and taxable to the recipient. Alimony is viewed as an independent source of income for the recipient and is treated as income from services. Other periodic support payments, including those to children, are not deductible and not taxable.

Canada and *Australia* offer interesting contrasts. Under the Canadian system, until 1995, periodic payments of both alimony and child support were deductible by the payer spouse and taxable to the recipient spouse. Lump-sum payments and property settlements, in contrast, were neither deductible nor taxable. In determining

754. United States, IRC, ss. 71, 215.

of the level of alimony, child support, and property payments, it was common practice to take into account the relative tax brackets of the parties and utilize the form of payment which maximized the overall tax benefit. In a 1994 case, the Supreme Court of Canada rejected a constitutional challenge to the inclusion of child-support payments in the income of the recipient.[755] It was argued that the rule violated the equality provision of the Charter of Rights and Freedoms since only separated custodial parents were taxed on child support. Despite its victory in court, the government introduced sweeping changes to the treatment of child-support payments, including the elimination of the deduction for such payments and the taxation of the payments to the recipient. Alimony and spousal maintenance payments, however, remain subject to the deduction-inclusion system. Transfers of property between divorced or separated spouses qualify for rollover treatment.

The *Australian* system makes no distinction between alimony and child-support payments. Both are in effect taxed to the payer, since they are not deductible, and are exempt to the recipient.[756] Administratively, child-support payments are collected with the support of the tax administration. Where property has been set aside in trust to fund maintenance payments, the payments are taxable to the recipient and are in effect deductible by the payer, since the income is excluded from the payer's return. With respect to property settlements, there is an automatic rollover on property division between divorced or separated spouses.[757]

Similarly, the *United Kingdom* does not make any distinction between alimony and child support. Prior to 1988, both types of payments were deductible by the payer and taxable to the recipient. In 1988, a new system was introduced which eliminated the general deduction for such payments and also made them tax-free in the hands of the recipient. Initially, a limited deduction was allowed based on the married couple's allowance, which had survived the switch to separate taxation. That deduction was subsequently converted to a credit; it is now relevant only where one of the parties was born before April 6, 1935.[758]

The elimination of the deduction for support payments in 1988 took place at a time when there was a substantial reduction in tax rates, and it is unclear whether the change was simply part of a general base broadening or reflected a "family values" policy that was intended to make it more expensive to support separated families.

In *Germany*, alimony is historically treated as a personal expense and is therefore not deductible. This concept is based on the idea that alimony payments deal with the consumption of income, not the accrual of the income itself. Correspondingly, such payments are not taxable in the hands of the recipient. However, under a special statutory provision, up to EUR 13,805 of alimony payments may be deducted from the payer and correspondingly included in the income of the recipient if both parties so agree.[759] In addition, in some circumstances, alimony payments which do not qualify

755. *Thibaudeau v. The Queen,* [1995] 1 CTC 382 (SCC).
756. Australia, ITAA 1997, s. 51-50.
757. Australia, ITAA 1997, Subdivision 126-A.
758. United Kingdom, ITA, s. 454(3).
759. Germany, ITA, s. 10 para. 1a No. 1, s. 22 No. 1a.

for this special treatment can be considered to be an "extraordinary burden" and may be deducted subject to a limitation in the amount of the basic tax-free allowance (EUR 10,908 in 2023) per year.[760]

Traditionally, payments for child support (within or outside marriage) were also regarded as nondeductible consumption expenses. Over the years, the Federal Constitutional Court has consistently held that funds required for child support are not "at the disposition" of the taxpayer and therefore—according to the ability-to-pay principle—must be deductible for tax purposes. Currently, a tax-free threshold for child support of EUR 3,192 per parent (EUR 6,384 per couple) is set out in the statute, to which the "childcare threshold" (EUR 1,464 or EUR 2,928 per couple) must be added (*see* the discussion of childcare expenses above).[761] In practice, these tax expenditures are regularly "set off" against the payment of child subsidies by the government. Thus, the expenditures are recognized in the tax assessment (dual system) only to the extent of the tax advantage resulting from the excess of the tax-free threshold over the amount of child-support subsidies. Additional deductions for costs related to schooling, day care, etc., are also available.

In the *Dutch* system, periodic alimony payments, whether to a former spouse or a spouse from whom the taxpayer lives separately, are deductible as qualified personal expenses and included in the income of the recipient.[762] In addition, a lump-sum payment in lieu of periodic payments is deductible where made to a former spouse.

In *France*, amounts paid in compliance with the obligation imposed on family members by the Civil Code to support their children or parents are tax-deductible, provided that they are reasonable in relation to the wealth of the payer and the needs of the payee.[763] Where the child is a minor, the non-custodial parent can deduct the full amount. In the case of shared custody, no alimony is deductible, as the number of family quotient units is increased. If a child has reached the age of majority, the deduction may be available if the child makes a declaration and is destitute or unable to meet basic needs through work. In this case, there are two situations. Where the child does not live with their parents, the deduction cannot exceed EUR 6,674 for 2023, or double this amount if the child is married.[764] If an adult child lives in the same household as the family and does not have sufficient resources, a lump sum can be deducted per child without having to provide proof (EUR 3,968 for 2023 and double that if the child is married or in a civil partnership). In addition, payments made (*pension alimentaire*) to needy relatives under certain conditions are deductible and, again, the amount of the deduction depends on whether or not the person is a member of the tax household.

Alimony and most other court-ordered payments to an ex-spouse are also deductible, provided the parties are separated. Only sums paid as damages or as part of an amicable settlement are not deductible. Alimony payments and child support are

---

760. Germany, ITA, s. 33a para. 1.
761. Germany, ITA, s. 32 para. 6.
762. Netherlands, ITA, Art. 6.3.
763. France, CGI, 156 et seq.
764. France, CGI, s. 196 B.

taxable to recipients where they are deductible by the payer.[765] Compensatory allowances awarded following a divorce decree, which compensate for the ex-spouse's lower standard of living, may be paid in the form of a lump sum or an annuity. If the debtor of the compensatory allowance pays the obligation in capital within twelve months of the date of the judgment, they are entitled to an income tax reduction equal to 25% of the amount set by the judge, up to a limit of EUR 30,500.[766] The ex-spouse receiving the alimony is not taxed on the sums received. In other cases (annuities and lump sums paid after one year), the payments are taxed as alimony.

In *Japan*, payments of periodic alimony, other than for childcare, are not common and there are no special tax rules. Divorce settlements typically involve a lump-sum payment which is neither deductible nor taxable. Such payments are treated by analogy to tort damages for personal injury. Periodic child-support payments are also nondeductible and nontaxable, and are not taxable for gift tax purposes unless the amount is extraordinarily large. Similarly, in *China*, alimony and child-support payments are not deductible.

In *India*, there are no specific provisions dealing with the inclusion or deduction of alimony payments. As a result, only regular and periodic alimony payments are included in income, on the basis that they represent income from a source; lump-sum payments are nontaxable capital receipts.[767] Other alimony payments are neither deductible by the payer nor taxable to the recipient.[768]

3 LIMITATIONS ON ASSIGNMENT OF INCOME

In a system with progressive rates, taxpayers have an incentive to attempt to shift income to related taxpayers who are not treated as part of the same taxable unit but who are part of the same economic family unit. A similar incentive applies with respect to shifting income to or between related entities. The pressure for income shifting is a function of the definition of the taxable unit and is greatest where spouses are treated as separate taxpayers. Techniques to shift earned income typically involve contractual arrangements which create rights to income in related parties. With respect to income from property, the transaction often involves a transfer of the right to the income while the transferor retains the underlying property. In both situations, a basic question is the extent to which the tax system respects the underlying civil or commercial aspects of the transaction. The systems considered here have reached a variety of results in these situations.

In the *United States*, early case law established the proposition that earned income was taxable to the earner and the tax burden could not be shifted by contractual arrangements, even where those arrangements were not tax-motivated and were effective for civil law purposes.[769] With respect to income from property, the principles

765. France, CGI, s. 156 II 2°.
766. France, CGI, s. 199 octodecies.
767. *Princess Maheshwari Devi of Pratapgarh v. CIT* (1983) 147 ITR 258 (Bombay).
768. *Commissioner of Income Tax v. M.P. Ponchaj* 211 ITR 1005 (Bombay).
769. United States, *Lucas v. Earl*, 281 U.S. 111 (1930).

are more complex. Where the entire property is transferred, the tax on both the gain on the disposition of the property and the current income from the property is shifted to the donee. Where the right to the income is given away but the underlying property is retained, the transfer is generally not respected for tax purposes.[770] Where the only right the transferor has is the right to an income stream (e.g., a series of royalty payments), and the entire right is transferred, on the one hand, the transfer may be effective if the income stream is of long enough duration. On the other hand, the transfer of the right to one year's income while retaining the remaining stream would not be effective. Special rules deal with the transfer of property to trusts.[771] In general, the transferor must give up nearly all rights to the property (a *de minimis* reversionary interest is allowed) in order to shift the tax burden to the trust or trust beneficiaries. Under prior rules, if a ten-year income interest was transferred, the transfer was effective for tax purposes. This rule led to significant amounts of income shifting through trusts and was replaced by the present requirement of a complete transfer.

In business relations between related parties, in general, arm's length principles must be followed. A special statutory rule recognizes partnerships with family members as partners but requires that partners performing services must be reasonably compensated, thus preventing the indirect shifting of income to the partners (typically minors).[772]

In the case of interest-free or low-interest loans, either an arm's length interest rate is imputed or the income generated by the loan is taxed directly to the lender, depending on the circumstances of the loan.[773]

As might be expected, *Canada*, which has the most extensive system of individual taxation, also has the most restrictive rules on assignment of income. Where the taxpayer transfers property to a spouse or minor child, any income from the property, or any property substituted for it, is attributed to the transferor. A similar rule applies to capital gains, but only to property transferred to a spouse. The attribution rules also apply to interest-free or low-interest loans. Certain dividends and certain income derived through a trust or partnership by a minor are subject to a special "kiddie tax" at the top marginal rate (the scope of this tax was expanded in 2018, as discussed below).[774] Beyond the spouse or child situation, where a taxpayer assigns the right to income to a third party in a non-arm's length transaction, the income remains the income of the transferor. This rule prevents the assignment of salary income as well as income from property where the transferor retains the underlying property. A special statutory rule attributes the income generated on an interest-free or low-interest loan to a person related to the lender. However, spouses are entitled to elect to split pension income received by one spouse.[775]

In 2018, the government introduced rules to expand the kiddie tax to prevent the use of private corporations by owners to split income with adult family members.

770. United States, *Helvering v. Horst*, 311 U.S. 112 (1940).
771. United States, IRC, ss. 674-677.
772. United States, IRC, s. 704(e).
773. United States, IRC, s. 7872.
774. Canada, ITA, s. 120.4.
775. Canada, ITA, s. 60.03.

Where these rules apply, the relevant income is subject to tax at the highest marginal rate. In general, the rules apply to dividends and distributions from trusts and partnerships derived from businesses carried on by private corporations. In addition, the new tax also applies to capital gains other than those which qualify for the lifetime capital gains exemption (i.e., shares of small business corporations engaged exclusively or almost exclusively in active business and qualifying farm and fishing property).

The following bright-line exemptions from the new rules apply:

- income derived by the spouse of the owner of the private corporation if the owner is 65 years of age or older;
- family members who are 18 years of age or over and actively involved in the business of the corporation on a regular, continuous, and substantial basis (twenty weeks or more) in the year they receive amounts from the corporation or any five previous years;
- family members who are 25 years of age or older who own at least 10% or more of the shares of the private corporation, other than a professional corporation or a corporation which derives 90% or more of its income from services.

Where none of these exemptions applies, family members who are 25 years of age or older may avoid the application of the new rules where the amounts they receive from the corporation do not exceed a reasonable return. A reasonable return is determined on the basis of the facts and circumstances of each case and, in particular, on the family member's contributions (labor, capital, and risks assumed) to the business relative to other family members' contributions.

The rules in the *United Kingdom* are more liberal. An outright gift of property is effective to shift the burden of tax on the income to the transferee. If property is transferred in trust, the settlor remains taxable if the settlor retains any interest in the property. Special rules apply to trusts for the benefit of spouses, with the income of the trust remaining taxable to the grantor in most cases, even if the grantor does not retain any interest in the trust. The term "trust" is widely defined for these purposes and includes any transfer or arrangement. There are even wider rules treating income of unmarried minor children of the settlor as income of the settlor, but these rules do not apply to income which is accumulated and not distributed.[776] At one time, the UK CGT had its own rules under which gains accruing under a trust in which the settlor retained an interest were treated as gains of the settlor. With the 2008 changes in the rates of CGT, it would have been advantageous for taxpayers to bring themselves within this anti-avoidance rule; the rule was therefore repealed and was not reinstated when a second, higher rate of CGT was introduced in 2010.

In *Australia*, outright transfers of property between spouses are also effective to shift the incidence of tax on future income to the transferee (although the transferor is taxed on income and any capital appreciation up to the time of transfer). Further, under

776. United Kingdom, ITTOIA, ss. 619 et seq.

Australian commercial law, ownership of an asset can be retained, but the income generated by many types of assets can be assigned by the owner. Tax law respects this transaction subject to a special provision which insists that the income be assigned for at least seven years.[777] In addition, various income-splitting schemes involving a division of professional income through the leasing of assets and provision of services by a related trust have had varying degrees of success. Splitting of income with children has been prevented by a special statutory rule which taxes the unearned income of children (with limited exceptions, including the income from property received by will or transferred under a divorce settlement) at the highest marginal tax rate, regardless of the rates of the child or the parents.[778] In the 1998 tax reform, the government indicated that it would not be seeking to close down the income-splitting opportunities in current law (especially those involving trusts). A former conservative Prime Minister was a supporter of the family unit of taxation, and income splitting goes some way to achieving this end.

China and *Sweden* have no special statutory rules on assignment of income. In China, the general anti-avoidance rule might be applied to deal with the assignment of income in abusive cases. In Sweden, with respect to earned income, case law principles have required that income be taxed to the person who earned the income. The income source is performance of services, and therefore the income belongs to the person performing the services. Thus, income earned by an employee which, under contractual arrangements, is received directly by the employee's spouse, is taxed to the employee. The rules are more liberal with respect to income from property. Dividend income can be transferred effectively for tax purposes, although the transferor retains the underlying shares. In the case of an outright gift of property, the carryover basis results in the tax on the gain being shifted to the donee. No interest is imputed on interest-free loans, allowing the transfer of the income to the borrower.

The *German* rules on assignment of income are not set out in explicit statutory provisions but are to a large extent judge-made. Because there is no general assignment provision in the ITA, it is accepted that the issues are resolved by the definitions laid down in the provisions governing the particular source of income. The taxpayer is the person who "derives" income.[779] Therefore, income from a trade or business is assigned to the person who carries on that specific trade or business. Income from rent or royalty payments is attributed to the persons who are parties to the relevant contracts under civil law. Capital income is attributed to the person who is the (beneficial) owner of the underlying capital. Some scholars have expanded these ideas into a general theory allocating income on the basis of a person's "market presence."

In practice, these general rules lead to highly disputed questions of law. In the case of *Treuhand/fiducia* (which is similar to the "trust" concept of the common law), the prevailing opinion accepts the attribution of income to the "settlor" or the "beneficiary" only if they have control over the "trustee"; otherwise, the income is

777. Australia, ITAA 1936, Part III Division 6A.
778. Australia, ITAA 1936, Part III Division 6AA.
779. Germany, ITA, s. 2 para. 1.

attributed to the trustee.[780] With respect to partnerships and companies, there is an ongoing discussion whether the assignment of profit strictly follows the civil law treatment or whether there has to be some "adequate" relationship between the original contribution of a partner/shareholder and their stake in the profits.[781] In the case of married couples, in most cases, the "shift" of income to a spouse is not relevant because the couple is entitled to be taxed according to the "splitting" system, as described earlier. Abundant case law and literature exists with respect to the tax treatment of children participating in their parents' business. They may be recognized as limited or silent partners where actual legal and economic rights are transferred and exercised.

Much of the German case law dealing with the assignment of income involves the treatment of usufruct (*Niessbrauch*), a civil law institution roughly equivalent to an income interest or term of years in the common law tradition. A usufruct can be created in personal or real property but is most commonly a real property right; it can be either gratuitous or for consideration. In general terms, in the case of a gratuitous usufruct, the income is taxed to the transferee-usufructuary as a contractual obligation vis-à-vis third parties which generates income (e.g., rental income). In the case of a usufruct on a business, the transferee must manage the business in order to qualify as the relevant subject of the income from the business. The most problematic case concerns usufructs in shares and other securities. While the ITA recognizes the possibility of a usufructuary deriving income from investment assets,[782] it leaves open to what extent the usufructuary must be entitled to influence the course of events through voting or management rights in order to qualify for income attribution. The courts have tended to allocate dividend and interest income to the owner of the asset, given the similarity between the position of a usufructuary and a mere transferee of the dividend and interest claims.[783]

However, where the asset is a wasting one, no depreciation is allowed in the case of a gratuitous usufruct since the usufructuary does not bear the tax cost. Correspondingly, the transferor-owner is denied any depreciation deductions because they are not in receipt of any taxable income. Where the purpose is to shift income, the denial of the deductions makes the transaction unattractive from a tax point of view. However, if the owner of the asset transfers title to the transferee-usufructuary and retains the usufruct in order to derive income (e.g., rental income) from the asset, the previous owner remains entitled to depreciation allowances which reflect expenditure incurred before the transfer. The same holds true where the usufruct is transferred for consideration which qualifies as rental income to the owner.

Japan has no special rules on the assignment of income; under general rules, the attribution of income is determined by the legal entitlement.[784] The vagueness of the

780. Federal Tax Court (*Bundesfinanzhof*), July 12, 2016, IX R 21/15.
781. Federal Tax Court (*Bundesfinanzhof*), October 27, 2015, VIII R 47/12 (excessive profit allocation in a partnership held to be disguised consideration paid by the new partner to an outgoing partner).
782. Germany, ITA, s. 20 para. 5 sent. 3.
783. Tax Court (*Finanzgericht*) Münster, May 16, 2013, 2 K 577/11 E.
784. Japan, ITA, s. 12.

general rules has caused disputes in several different contexts. First, contractual arrangements between spouses[785] are rarely used in Japan; in any case, they cannot change the attribution of income for tax purposes, which follows the earner (in the case of earned income) and the legal owner (in the case of investment income). Therefore, if a sole-earner spouse shares half of their earned income with the other spouse by virtue of a contractual arrangement, the first spouse is taxed on the entire income and the second spouse is treated as the beneficiary of a gift, possibly subject to the gift tax. Second, for family businesses in which family members participate, the established administrative practice treats the head of the family business as the sole income earner, while other family members are treated as employees; hence, income splitting is allowed to a certain extent if the family complies with procedural requirements.[786] Attempts to shift property income have not been an issue since Japanese civil law does not recognize usufruct. Although trusts are recognized under Japanese civil law, there is a specific provision for tax purposes which deems the beneficiary, not the trustee, to be the owner of the trust property as well as any income from that property.[787] There still remains a significant level of uncertainty surrounding the tax treatment of family trusts.

In *France*, because of the aggregate household system of taxation, there are no special anti-assignment of income provisions. However, this concept is recognized in the French system and is frequently used to combat tax fraud and evasion. For example, the technique of temporary donation of usufruct can be used to transfer income, and the tax authorities keep a particularly close eye on such transactions for the benefit of descendants.

In *India*, where income is transferred without a transfer of the underlying assets generating the income[788] and where assets are transferred on a revocable basis,[789] the income continues to be taxed in the hands of the transferor. Any provision for the transfer of the income/asset back to the transferor or the right of the transferor to reassume control over the asset or income makes a transfer revocable.[790]

To prevent the most common form of diverting business income to a spouse, the ITA provides that all income arising directly or indirectly to the spouse of an individual by way of salary, commission, fees, or other form of remuneration from a business in which the individual has a substantial interest must be included in the income of the individual (so-called clubbing of income).[791] This provision also applies to transfers for inadequate consideration and reciprocal transfers between spouses[792] but does not apply where the transferee spouse has technical and professional qualifications and the income is solely attributable to such qualifications.[793] Income of a minor child (other

785. Japan, Civil Code, ss. 755, 756, and 758.
786. Japan, ITA, s. 57. If procedural requirements are not met, wages paid to family business members are not deductible to the head of business and not taxable to the other members.
787. Japan, ITA, s. 13.
788. India, ITA 1961, s. 60.
789. India, ITA 1961, ss. 61 and 62.
790. India, ITA 1961, s. 63.
791. India, ITA 1961, s. 64(1) and 64(1A).
792. India, ITA 1961, s. 64(1)(iv) and (v).
793. India, ITA 1961, Proviso to s. 64(1)(ii).

than a disabled child) is taxed to the parent with the higher income, except for income earned through manual labor or technical /professional skills.[794]

In *The Netherlands*, particular income elements and deductions can be assigned between couples at their discretion, as discussed above.

794. India, ITA 1961 s. 64(1A). The parent in whose hands the income of the minor is included will receive an exemption of up to INR 1,500 per month (ITA 1961, s. 10(32)).

PART III Taxation of Business Organizations

The taxation of business organizations generally falls into two basic patterns. "Corporate" taxation typically involves the imposition of tax on the income of certain types of commercial organizations, usually formed under special enabling legislation, as well as tax on profits distributed to the holders of ownership interests in those organizations, usually adjusting the taxation in the hands of the owners to reflect the fact that the income has been taxed to the organization. The other model, "partnership" or "flow-through" taxation, taxes the income derived by an organization in the hands of its owners, whether or not the income is distributed, and makes appropriate adjustments to reflect this fact when the income is actually distributed. The following Subpart A deals with corporate taxation, while Subpart B deals with partnership taxation.

These two models do not, of course, exhaust the possible patterns for the taxation of business organizations. In Australia, for example, substantial amounts of closely held commercial activity are carried on in the form of "trading trusts," and foundations or other types of organization are important in other jurisdictions. Nonetheless, most of the issues in the taxation of business organizations revolve around corporate and partnership patterns.

SUBPART A
Corporate-Shareholder Taxation

The corporate tax systems in the countries under consideration in this book have at various times ranged from traditional "classical" systems of full corporate taxation and individual-level taxation of distributed profits (*China*, *The Netherlands*, *Sweden*, the *United States* (U.S.)) to complete integration of corporate and individual tax on distributed profits (*Australia, France, Germany*). Presently, a wide variety of taxing patterns exists, with imputation systems falling out of favor (except in Australia) and being replaced with direct shareholder-level relief. *India* has a hybrid system.

This Subpart begins with a brief overview of the structure of the rules governing corporate taxation in each of the countries. It then examines a number of technical problems which are common to all the systems. A more detailed discussion follows of the relationship between corporate- and shareholder-level taxation—the extent to which the various systems deal with the "double taxation of dividends"—and the related topic of taxing capital gains on the disposition of shares in companies, particularly gains attributable to retained taxed profits.

1 OVERVIEW OF CORPORATE TAX SYSTEMS

Over the last fifty years, the two predominant corporate tax systems have been the classical system, which taxes a company on its income and then taxes shareholders separately on distributions received from the company, and the imputation system, which gives shareholders a credit for corporate tax paid, thus eliminating in whole or in part the double taxation of dividends. More recently, many countries have changed the basic structure of their corporate tax systems away from the classical and imputation systems to systems which give approximate or "rough-and-ready" relief from double taxation. Because of these changes, the descriptions which follow often include an indication of changes which have occurred in the last two decades or so. Much of the change has been driven by international considerations. These are dealt with in Part IV.

Currently, three classical systems (*China*, *India*, and *Sweden*) survive among the countries covered, but with some departures from the traditional classical system. Thus, *Sweden* has a classical system, although for a brief period in 1994 dividends were exempt from individual taxation. The basic corporate tax rate for 2021 is 20.6%,[1] gradually declining from 52% prior to 1991. For individuals, dividend income is usually taxed as income from capital at a flat 30% rate (compared to a top individual rate of 50% for noncapital income). Capital gains are also subject to 30% tax as income from capital. However, for unlisted shares in corporations, dividends and capital gains are taxed at a reduced rate of 25%; for closely held corporations, dividends deemed to be capital income are taxed at a rate of 20%, while other dividends are taxed as earned income, as discussed in section 5.3 below. Since 2012, individuals can invest in listed shares in a special account (*investeringssparkonto*) in which dividends and capital gains are not taxed; instead, tax is imposed at 30% on a deemed yield equal to the interest on long-term government bonds plus 1 percentage point. For 2023, the standard revenue is 2.94% and the tax is 0.882% of the capital base.[2] Almost all new investments in listed shares are now made using this account. Intercorporate dividends on unlisted shareholdings qualify for the participation exemption.

China has a pure classical system, with a separate corporate tax (Enterprise Income Tax (EIT)) and a further tax on dividends received by individuals (Individual Income Tax (IIT)). Thus, the corporate tax system is simpler than those of other countries studied in this book in that it does not deal with integration issues. The EIT is not used as an advance tax on shareholders and contains no anti-deferral rules (i.e., with respect to incorporated investment holdings or incorporated personal services) or anti-income-splitting rules. The EIT exists on its own and does not refer to the IIT system.[3] It serves the functions of raising revenue, taxing foreign investors, and acting as a regulatory tool by encouraging or discouraging certain activities.

The general rate of 25% was chosen in 2007 to be globally competitive; to date, there have been no serious discussions about lowering it. Intercorporate dividends between Chinese corporations are tax-exempt, subject to a twelve-month holding requirement, while dividends from foreign corporations are taxable with a direct and indirect foreign tax credit. Dividends paid to resident individuals are taxable under the IIT at the rate of 20%. The IIT has some features similar to those of the Swedish rules. For example, investment income (dividends, interest) and capital gains of individuals are taxed at a flat rate, while other kinds of income are taxed at progressive rates. The general 20% rate is reduced to nil on capital gains from the sale of shares traded on the Shanghai and Shenzhen stock exchanges. The rate is reduced to 10% or 5% on dividends paid on shares purchased on the stock exchanges, depending on the holding

1. Sweden, Income Tax Act (ITA), Ch. 65 para. 10.
2. Sweden, ITA, Ch. 42 paras. 35-37.
3. Individuals are mentioned in the corporate tax act (EIT) only in the context of anti-avoidance rules, such as defining control for purposes of the controlled foreign corporation (CFC) rules or relationships for purposes of the transfer pricing rules.

period (10% if the holding period is more than a month and 5% if the holding period is more than a year).[4]

Until 1997, *India* followed a classical system of corporate/shareholder taxation of dividends. The corporate tax rate on domestic companies differed depending on the structure of the company (i.e., a public,[5] industrial, or trading company, etc.). These differing rates were abandoned over time until all domestic companies were taxed at the same rate. However, following some gradual changes, the corporate tax rate on domestic companies once again varies depending on turnover, income, and sector.

For 2024, domestic companies with turnover up to INR 4 billion[6] are subject to a tax rate of 25%; companies with turnover above that amount pay at a rate of 30%. A surcharge is levied on these basic rates at 7% for companies with income up to INR 100 million and at 12% for companies with income above that amount; no surcharge is payable if the income of the company for the relevant year does not exceed INR 10 million. An additional health and education cess (surtax) of 4% is levied on the resulting tax and surcharge, making the final effective corporate tax rate for a particular year 26% for companies with turnover up to INR 4 billion and income up to INR 10 million, 27.82% for companies with turnover up to INR 4 billion and income up to INR 100 million, and 29.12% for companies with turnover up to INR 4 billion and income above INR 100 million. For companies with turnover over INR 4 billion and income up to INR 10 million, the effective tax rate is 31.20%, 33.38% for companies with income between INR 10 million and 100 million, and 34.94% for companies with income above INR 100 million.

As discussed in the chapter on India in Part I, where a taxpayer foregoes certain incentives and deductions, the tax rate is further reduced to 22% with a surcharge of 10% and cess of 4% for manufacturing companies that commenced production before March 31, 2024.

From 1997 to 2014 (with the exception of 2002), dividends received by individuals (which, before 1997, were taxable at the applicable progressive rate) were subject to an additional income tax, the dividend distribution tax (DDT), payable by the company distributing dividends at a rate of 15% plus surcharge and surtax; shareholders were exempt from tax on the dividends.[7]

The DDT, although administratively simple, generated considerable controversy. In 2020, the DDT was abolished and India returned to the classical system of taxing dividends separately in the hands of recipients at the applicable rates. Consequently,

---

4. *See*, for example, Ministry of Finance, State Taxation Administration and China Securities Regulatory Commission, "Notice on Differentiated Individual Income Tax on Dividends Received on Shares of Listed Companies," Caishui [2012] No. 85 [财政部 国家税务总局 证监会关于实施上市公司股息红利差别化个人所得税政策有关问题的通知》（财税〔2012〕85号)].
5. As defined in ITA 1961, s. 2(18).
6. In the earlier previous year (FY 22-23).
7. ITA 1961, s. 10(34). In 2014, a gross-up provision was introduced, further complicating the calculation of the DDT; shareholders (other than domestic companies and a few others) with dividend income above INR 1 million were required to pay tax at 10% on the excess. Thus, from 2014 to 2020 (the abolition of the DDT) both a company and its individual shareholders were subject to tax with respect to income earned by the company and dividends distributed to shareholders.

the exemption for dividends was withdrawn; companies distributing dividends to resident shareholders are now required to withhold tax of 10% on dividends in excess of INR 500 and 20%, or the applicable tax treaty rate, of dividends paid to nonresidents.

With the reversion to the classical system, the treaty rate on dividends has again become important. Some of India's tax treaties with non-OECD member countries provide a low 5% withholding rate. In one case, Dutch taxpayers claimed the 5% rate based on the most-favored-nation clause in the Protocol to the tax treaty. Although the taxpayers won at the lower level, the Supreme Court finally decided in favor of the tax department, holding that a separate notification was necessary to bring the provisions of the Protocol into effect.[8]

The system for taxing intercorporate dividends also changed with the Finance Act 2020. Such dividends are deductible from the gross total income of a domestic company, which includes in income any dividends from another domestic company (not necessarily a subsidiary) or a foreign company or business trust, to the extent of the dividend received, provided that such dividend received is distributed to shareholders on or before the due date (i.e., one month before the due date of filing tax returns).[9] In 2022, the special rate of tax on dividends from foreign companies was also withdrawn, with effect from 2023-2024.

During British rule and for some time after independence, income tax actually paid by companies was divided between distributed and undistributed profits, with the tax attributable to the distributable profits creditable in the hands of the shareholders (the gross-up mechanism). This practice ended in 1959-1960, and currently there is no provision for providing any underlying tax credit with respect to the corporate tax paid by a company distributing dividends. However, some of India's tax treaties contain provisions granting underlying tax credits with respect to dividends (e.g., treaties with Australia, Mauritius, Singapore, the United Kingdom (UK), and the U.S.). Only the treaties with Mauritius and Singapore provide for an underlying tax credit in respect of Indian companies investing abroad.

The corporate tax system in *The Netherlands* was a pure classical system until changes were made in 1997 and 2001. Since then, the system has been difficult to classify in traditional terms, although it may be regarded as a variant of the classical system. The Netherlands has a corporate rate of 25.8% (with a rate of 19% for corporate income up to EUR 200,000, in order to encourage small business).[10]

Before 2001, the progressive rates applicable to dividends received by individuals ranged from 37.7% to 60%. In addition, before 1997, capital gains on stock were not taxed to individuals unless the level of shareholding amounted to a "substantial interest," defined as at least a 33.3% interest held by the taxpayer, the taxpayer's spouse, or close relatives (and at least 7% held directly by the taxpayer or the taxpayer's spouse) at any time within five years of the disposition. Gains on the disposition of a substantial interest were taxed at 20%. This system led to individuals investing in growth funds, which in turn invested in companies and reinvested the

8. *Assessing Officer v. Nestle SA* (SC) Civil Appeal No. 1420 of 2023, October 19, 2023.
9. ITA, 1961, s. 80M(1) read with the Explanation.
10. Netherlands, Corporate Income Tax Act 1969 (CITA), Art. 22.

dividends received. The result was that individuals were not taxed on the reinvested dividends and were exempt on the capital gain.

Beginning in 2001, income from shares held by individuals which are not part of a substantial shareholding is taxed in the same way as all capital income, i.e., on the basis of a weighted deemed yield. As explained in more detail in section 3 of The Netherlands Chapter in Part I, this deemed yield increases with the individual's overall net wealth (from 0.01% to 6.04%). The deemed yield is subject to a fixed 36% tax rate, resulting in an effective (income) tax rate on the capital income, including dividends, ranging from 0.36% to 2.17% of the taxpayer's net wealth. This change was part of an overhaul of the taxation of income from capital.

Since 1997, dividends and capital gains from substantial shareholdings of individuals are subject to a flat tax, currently 24.5% (up to EUR 67,000) or 33% (from EUR 67,000). At the same time, the threshold for substantial shareholdings was lowered to 5% so as to be consistent with the participation exemption for corporations holding shares. In this way, individuals with substantial shareholdings are generally taxed at similar rates as those for individuals who operate businesses in noncorporate form, while portfolio investments in shares are covered by the "deemed yield" regime.

The *United States* has abandoned its classical system in recent times. Corporate profits are generally taxed at 21%, although certain offshore profits are taxed at a lower effective rate.[11] Since 2003, distributed profits are taxed to individual shareholders at preferential rates which currently do not exceed 20%. For individuals, the maximum tax rate on capital gains is also generally limited to 20%.[12] Previously, dividends were taxed at "normal" individual marginal tax rates. On the one hand, compared to the previous system, the preferential rates disproportionately benefit higher-income taxpayers whose dividend income and capital gains would otherwise be included in higher marginal brackets. On the other hand, the preferential rates reduce the element of double taxation of dividends and capital gains on shares. Capital losses can be used only to offset capital gains, although individuals can use USD 3,000 of capital losses annually against normal income. To avoid cascading tax effects for intercompany dividends from U.S. corporations, corporate shareholders are allowed to claim a deduction equal to 100%, 65%, or 50% of the dividend they receive from a U.S. corporation depending on the percentage of stock they own.[13] Moreover, U.S. corporations owning at least 10% of the stock of a foreign corporation may also claim a deduction for 100% of a dividend from a foreign corporation arising from its foreign earnings if several requirements are satisfied.[14]

The *Japanese* system has gradually reduced the degree of integration, partly as a result of the reduction in the corporate tax rate. The corporate tax rate is now 23.2% national tax and approximately 30% when municipal and local taxes are included (down from about 50% in 1997). The rate is still significant, but the decline has reduced the need for integration. In the past, Japan tried to eliminate double taxation

11. United States, Internal Revenue Code (IRC), ss. 11 and 250.
12. United States, IRC, s. 1(h).
13. United States, IRC, s. 243.
14. United States, IRC, s. 245A.

on dividends through a tax credit available to individual taxpayers. However, this dividend tax credit has been reduced and no longer eliminates double taxation in full. Currently, for individual taxpayers with income of JPY 10 million or less, a credit for 10% of the amount of a dividend is available, which can reduce both individual tax on the dividend and tax on income in other schedules. Where the income exceeds the threshold, the credit is limited to 5% of the dividend in excess of that amount and 10% on the remaining amount of the dividend.[15] The dividend tax credit is rarely used by individual taxpayers investing in listed companies since it does not eliminate double taxation and taxpayers may elect not to report dividends received from listed corporations at all in their tax returns. In this case, a withholding tax of 20.315% (including the 5% local income tax) is imposed on the dividends instead. Alternatively, taxpayers may choose to report dividends received from listed corporations in their tax returns separately from other kinds of income and can also offset the amount of dividends with capital losses from listed shares (in which case taxpayers cannot use the dividend tax credit). Under the separate-reporting system, the tax rate is the same as the withholding tax rate (i.e., 20.315%).[16] In many cases, both the nonreporting and separate-reporting systems can prove more advantageous than the dividend tax credit, and individual taxpayers often choose them for that reason.

Dividends received by corporations are excluded from tax if the recipient holds more than 33.3% of the shares of the payer; one-half of the dividends received are excluded where the shareholding is between 5% and 33.3%, and 20% of dividends are excluded where the shareholding is 5% or less.[17] Capital gains on shares realized by individuals are taxed at 20%, including municipal and local income tax, subject to certain exemptions available to small investors.[18] Capital gains on shares realized by corporations, including shares in subsidiaries, are generally taxable at ordinary rates.

In contrast to these systems, the *German* system for many years combined a split rate on distributed profits with an imputation credit in order to eliminate fully the impact of the corporate tax on profits distributed to resident individuals. In 2000, the system was radically changed: the imputation and split-rate system was abolished and replaced with a "shareholder-relief" system. This system is intended to achieve integration in a "semiclassical" setting by relying on partial integration in the form of relief at the shareholder level, combined with an overall reduction in the corporate tax rate. The starting point for the changes was a substantial reduction in the flat corporate income tax (CIT) rate from 40% (retained profits) and 30% (distributed profits) to a 25% rate irrespective of whether profits are retained. In 2008, the corporate tax rate was reduced to 15%.[19] Until 2008, in order to provide some "rough-and-ready" relief for the payment of tax at the corporate level, only 50% of cash dividends were taxed in the hands of individual shareholders. Since 2009, dividends from shares which are held as private assets are subject to a final withholding tax of 25%.[20] The tax is applied on

15. Japan, Income Tax Act (ITA), s. 92.
16. Japan, Special Taxation Measures Act (STMA), s. 8-4.
17. Japan, Corporate Tax Act (CTA), s. 23.
18. Japan, STMA, ss. 37-11 through 37-11-5.
19. Germany, Corporate Income Tax Act (CITA), s. 23 para. 1.
20. Germany, Income Tax Act (ITA), s. 32d para. 1 sent. 1.

a gross basis and, apart from a standard deduction of EUR 1,000 per person, no deductions are available. Where stock is held as a business asset, only 60% of the dividends are taxable in the hands of shareholders at the individual tax rate.[21] In order to avoid discrimination against foreign investment, both this final withholding tax regime and the "part-income method" mentioned above have been extended to dividends from foreign companies (the previous system did not take foreign corporate-level taxes into account).

To avoid cascading tax effects for intercompany dividends, there is a participation exemption which applies to shareholdings in German and foreign corporations.[22] Under this exemption, intercompany dividends are, in principle, tax-free except for 5% representing expenses allocable to the dividends.[23] In 2013, the participation exemption for dividends was restricted to substantial shareholdings over 10%.[24]

Unlike the former imputation system, the current corporate tax system also tries to align the treatment of dividends and capital gains. Capital gains from stock held as a private asset are subject to a 25% withholding tax.[25] The tax is withheld by the bank managing the custody account. Where an individual owns at least 1% of the capital stock or the shares are held as business assets, 60% of the capital gain is taxed at the individual tax rate.[26] Finally, under the participation exemption, 95% of the gain on the sale of shares held by a corporate shareholder is free of tax in order to parallel the treatment of intercompany dividends.[27] Unlike the participation exemption for dividends, this exemption also applies to nonsubstantial shareholdings of less than 10%.

The *United Kingdom* repealed its advance corporation tax system in 1999 and now has a system where dividends from resident corporations to resident individuals are taxed at reduced rates. The main rate of corporation tax is 25%. A lower rate of 19% applies to companies with small business profits, defined as GBP 50,000 or less. The benefit of this lower rate is effectively clawed back by imposing a tax rate of 26.5% for profits between GBP 50,000 and GBP 250,000.

Individuals are taxed at reduced progressive rates on receipt of dividends, and the first GBP 500 of dividends is tax-free. The 20% personal tax rate has been reduced to 8.75%, the 40% tax rate to 33.75%, and the 45% rate to 39.35%.[28] Currently, an individual deriving income through a corporation with small business profits is subject to a higher tax (by approximately 6 percentage points) than if the income were earned directly. For example, individuals on the 20% basic rate pay approximately 25% if they derive income through a corporation (19% corporate tax and 8.75% shareholder tax). Similarly, the 40% rate rises to a combined 46% and the 45% rate to 51%. If the full 25% corporate tax rate is imposed, these rates increase to 32%, 50%, and 55%,

21. Germany, ITA, s. 3 No. 40 and s. 20 para. 8.
22. Germany, CITA, s. 8b para. 1.
23. Germany, CITA, s. 8b para. 5.
24. Germany, CITA, s. 8b para. 4.
25. Germany, ITA, s. 20 para. 2.
26. Germany, ITA, s. 3 No. 40, s. 17 para. 1 s. 20 para. 8.
27. Germany, CITA, s. 8b para. 2.
28. United Kingdom, Income Tax Act 2007, s. 8.

respectively. These increases were a superficial response to a perceived overuse of the corporate form; reduction of the corporate rate to 17% reduces the differential.

For individuals, since 2008, capital gains are taxed at a general rate of 10% or 20% depending on their income tax bracket, increasing to 18% and 28% for gains on residential property and carried interests. An effective 10% rate applies for certain gains on the disposal of a business, to a cumulative lifetime maximum of GBP 1 million. A separate annual exemption for net capital gains continues (GBP 3,000 in 2024-2025).[29]

Intercorporate dividends received from resident corporations are largely exempt from tax.[30] However, capital gains on the disposal of shares by corporations are fully taxable with indexation relief. A substantial shareholder exemption was introduced in 2002 but is available only where the subsidiary is a trading company; the other conditions have recently been relaxed.[31]

France was one of the first European countries to adopt an imputation system. In 1965, France introduced a tax credit (*avoir fiscal*) attached to the distribution of dividends, accompanied by a levy on the company, known as the *précompte*, in cases where the CIT was insufficient. In practice, the withholding tax payable was equivalent to half of the net dividend paid, or one-third of the gross dividend, including the tax credit deducted from the company's profits or reserves. Initially, double taxation was only partially eliminated, but in time was completely eliminated. This system was removed for budgetary reasons and its inconsistency with European Union (EU) law, particularly with respect to the free movement of capital, due to the differences in tax treatment between domestic and foreign dividends.[32] The 2004 Finance Act abolished the *avoir fiscal* tax credit and replaced it with a 50% allowance for dividends received by individual shareholders.

Following the withdrawal of the *avoir fiscal* tax credit, the dividend tax system continued to evolve. Since 2018, dividends have been removed from the taxation of earned income and instead are taxed at the single flat-rate withholding tax of 30% (consisting of 12.8% income tax and 17.2% social security withholdings),[33] although taxpayers can opt for the progressive income tax scale, with rates as high as 45%, in which case 40% of the gross amount received is excluded.[34]

Where a shareholder is a company, dividends are subjected to CIT, or to a withholding tax if the shareholder is outside France. This double taxation is mitigated by a corporate tax rate that is lower than the progressive income tax rate and by tax regimes which reduce taxation at the shareholder level, such as the flat-tax mechanism and some specific regimes for groups of companies (*see* the chapter on France in Part 1, section 5.2).

The *Canadian* imputation system allows full imputation of the corporate tax in the case of Canadian-controlled private corporations (CCPCs) and, until 2007, allowed

29. United Kingdom, Taxation of Chargeable Gains Act 1992 (TCGA), ss. 3, 4 and 169H-169S.
30. United Kingdom, Corporation Tax Act 2009, s. 931B and 931D.
31. United Kingdom, TCGA, Sch. 7AC.
32. CJEU, June 6, 2000, C-35-98 (*Verkooijen*).
33. France, Code général des impôts (CGI), s. 200 A.
34. France, CGI, s. 158, 3 2.

partial imputation for publicly traded companies and other private corporations, with the degree of integration depending on the nature of the corporate activity.

In 2007, significant changes were made to the integration system in response to the elimination of the benefit of so-called income trusts. In the decade before 2007, many corporations, including large public corporations, were converting into income trust structures in order to eliminate the double taxation of income earned by Canadian corporations. In effect, the shareholders became unitholders in a trust, and the trust's income was reduced or eliminated through interest deductions. After allowing these income trust structures to flourish, and even promising that they would not be eliminated, the government was forced to act as a result of the loss of tax revenue. The legislative response was a tax on distributions by income trusts and a reduction in the tax on dividends paid by corporations so that there would no longer be any benefit for corporations to convert into income trusts. After 2011, when the changes were fully phased in, the result approximated full integration for dividends (called eligible dividends) received by Canadian-resident individuals from Canadian corporations (other than those paid by CCPCs out of active business income, which qualify for a reduced tax rate). More recently, increased top marginal tax rates on personal incomes, combined with insufficient dividend tax credits in some provinces, have weakened the integration of corporate and shareholder income for corporations other than CCPCs.

One of the most striking features of the Canadian system is that it provides the dividend credit regardless of whether the corporation distributing the dividend has actually paid any corporate-level tax. Thus, it goes beyond simply eliminating the double taxation of corporate profits and amounts to an incentive for Canadian-resident individuals to invest in Canadian corporations. Intercorporate dividends are entitled to a full dividend-received deduction. Capital gains on shares are subject to an exclusion of one-third of the gain (reduced from one-half in June 2024) for both individual and corporate shareholders.

Australia has the only remaining full imputation system among the eleven countries covered in this book. It gives full relief from corporate-level tax on distributions, but the technique used is somewhat different from the typical imputation systems formerly used by European countries. The basic corporate rate is currently 30% (25% for businesses with turnover under AUD 50 million), reduced from 49% in 1988. When fully taxed corporate profits are distributed, domestic individual shareholders receive a refundable credit for the full amount of the corporate tax.[35] The corporation distributing the dividend attaches or "franks" the dividend with a specified amount of corporate tax. The amount of corporate tax attached to the dividend is based on the amount of corporate tax and taxed dividends which the company estimates for the year. If over the course of the year a company attaches more corporate tax to dividends than it has paid, a compensatory tax is levied, which can be offset against future company tax liabilities but with penalties where over-franking exceeds 10%. The corporation must inform shareholders of the amount of credit attached to each dividend payment. "Anti-streaming" rules prevent some shareholders from receiving

35. Australia, Income Tax Assessment Act 1997 (ITAA 1997), Divs 67, 207.

dividends with tax credits attached while other shareholders receive "unfranked dividends."[36] Capital gains on shares acquired after the effective date of the capital gains legislation are taxed at ordinary rates, with individuals entitled to a 50% discount on the amount of taxable capital gain where the shares have been held for more than a year.[37]

Table III at the end of Subpart A summarizes these and other features of each of the systems.

2 DEFINING ENTITIES SUBJECT TO TAX

A basic structural decision in the design of a corporate tax is the determination of which entities or organizations should be subject to the tax. Depending on the state's commercial or business organization law, there may be a number of forms of business organization which would be possible subjects for corporate tax. In some systems, the determination is made on the basis of a statutory list or enumeration of organizations, which is exclusive. More typically, there is a nonexclusive list and a more general description of the characteristics which cause an organization to fall under the corporate taxing scheme. For organizations which are not subject to corporate tax, some pattern of single-level "pass-through" taxation is typically applicable and is discussed in Subpart B.

In the *United States* system, all entities which are formed under the general domestic corporate laws of the states are treated as corporations for federal tax purposes.[38] Thus, in principle, the tax applies to both one-person corporations and publicly traded corporations with thousands of shareholders. Other forms of business organization in the U.S., i.e., partnerships and limited liability companies with more than one member, which are not publicly traded, are taxable as flow-through entities unless they "check the box," i.e., elect to be taxable as corporations.[39] Publicly traded entities are usually taxable as corporations regardless of their form of organization.[40] Limited liability companies with only one member are disregarded ("tax nothings") unless they elect to be taxable as corporations.[41] The "check-the-box" rules replace earlier regulations which were a technical morass and created differences in classification based on relatively insignificant factors.

Some of the other systems have taken an approach to classification for tax purposes which follows more closely the commercial law classifications. Thus, in *Canada*, entities formed under federal or provincial corporation law are subject to corporate tax, while those formed under partnership provisions are treated under

36. Australia, ITAA 1977, Divs 201-205, Income Tax Assessment Act 1936 (ITAA 1936) s. 177EA.
37. Australia, ITAA 1977, Div 115.
38. United States, Treasury Regulations (Treas. Reg.), s. 301.7701-2(b)(1)-(7).
39. United States, Treas. Reg., s. 301.7701-3(b).
40. United States, IRC, s. 7704. Publicly traded entities which are organized as partnerships may be taxable as flow-through entities if at least 90% of their gross income is passive income for the current year and was passive for all prior taxable years beginning after 1987.
41. United States, Treas. Reg., s. 301.7701-3(b).

pass-through rules. There is no attempt to classify civil law partnerships as corporations.

Swedish rules follow the same pattern. There are no tax rules classifying entities for tax purposes and classification is based on private law characterizations. In general, all entities (except partnerships) which must be registered are treated as corporations for tax purposes.

The *German* Corporate Income Tax Act (CITA) lists specific organizational forms which are subject to CIT.[42] In general, these forms correspond to entities which are treated for civil law purposes as "legal entities." A special catch-all provision includes associations, institutions, foundations, and other "conglomerations of assets" to the extent that the participants are not subject to tax directly. The list is exclusive and only the enumerated forms are subject to corporate tax. Commercial general and limited partnerships, as well as civil law partnerships, are not subject to CIT; they are taxed, under the income tax, on a pass-through basis, with their income directly attributed to the partners. Because pass-through taxation may be advantageous for many businesses, in particular with regard to loss offsetting, a specific type of limited partnership has flourished in Germany: the *GmbH & Co. KG*, a limited partnership with a corporate general partner. Despite its economic resemblance to a corporation, this type of entity is not subject to CIT.

The Court of Justice of the European Union (CJEU) has required Germany to recognize the legal personality of foreign companies which have their "real seat" in Germany but their registered office in another Member State of the EU. In addition, the "Societas Europaea" has been introduced as a new supranational company form. As a result, the CITA now explicitly includes foreign and supranational corporate forms.

When the corporate tax rate was lowered to 15% in 2009, an election for partnerships to be taxed as corporations was rejected in favor of a reduced tax rate on reinvested partnership profits within the framework of the income tax.[43] However, in 2021, an election was introduced for German and foreign commercial or professional partnerships to opt for treatment as corporate taxpayers. In 2024, this election was extended to simple partnerships which are registered in the newly established company register. A tripartite system of partnership taxation has resulted: fully transparent taxation, taxation as a corporate entity, or taxation like a partnership with regard to distributed profits but with the corporate tax rate on reinvested profits. There is ongoing debate as to whether this regime is sustainable in the long run.

The subject-to-tax rules in *The Netherlands* are similar. The entities which are subject to corporate tax are defined in the CITA both in a "specific" manner, i.e., through enumeration (where Dutch entities are concerned, such as the NV and the BV), and in a "generic" manner, i.e., through listing of generic criteria (e.g., entities created under Dutch or foreign law whose capital is divided into shares).[44] As a result, all entities whose interests are freely transferable and whose income does not accrue

42. Germany, CITA, s. 1 para. 1.
43. Germany, ITA, s. 34a.
44. Netherlands, CITA, Art. 2.

directly to the participants, but require a decision as to distribution,[45] are subject to corporate tax. Certain other entities are also subject to the corporate tax if, and to the extent that, they carry on a business.[46]

A new regime applies from January 1, 2025 for the classification of foreign legal entities. This new regime codifies the "legal form comparison method" combined with the introduction of a "symmetrical" method and a "fixed" approach. The legal form comparison method compares legal entities incorporated or established under the law of another state with entities formed under Dutch law.[47] This remains the primary classification method. The "symmetrical" method and "fixed" approach have a catch-all function for foreign legal entities which do not have a comparable counterpart in the Netherlands. Examples include the Unlimited Company under Irish law, the Limited Liability Partnership (LLP) under UK law, and trusts. The fixed approach applies if, based on the circumstances, the foreign legal entity is deemed to be effectively located in The Netherlands; it is considered opaque, and therefore subject to Dutch corporate tax. The symmetrical approach is applicable if, based on the circumstances, the foreign legal entity is deemed to be effectively located outside The Netherlands; the tax classification follows that of the jurisdiction where the entity is located.

In *France*, there are two types of companies for tax purposes. First, capital companies (e.g., *société anonyme*, partnerships limited by shares—(*sociétés en commandite par actions*) and *sociétés par action simplifiée*)[48] are considered fiscally opaque and subject to corporate tax. Profits distributed to shareholders are taxed in their hands at the time of distribution. Second, sole proprietorships and partnerships (*sociétés de personnes*) are subject to income tax; however, in certain circumstances they can elect to be subject to CIT.[49] Conversely, some corporations can opt to be taxed under the income tax.[50] The rules are complicated further because some entities, depending on the nature of their partners (e.g., *sociétés en commandite simple*), are subject to a mixture of CIT and income tax.

In *Japan*, all organizations which constitute "juridical entities" under Japanese civil law concepts are, with some explicit statutory exceptions, subject to the corporate tax. Both general and limited partnerships formed under the Company Law are juridical entities and therefore are subject to the corporate tax. In contrast, unincorporated associations which are not juridical entities are not subject to corporate tax. This includes, for example, "undisclosed associations" which are structurally similar to "silent" or undisclosed partnerships under Continental civil law concepts. Although

45. The Dutch Supreme Court, in its decision of June 2, 2006, BNB 2006/288, set out the following criteria: the liability of the participants is limited to their (capital) contributions in the entity; the business is legally owned by the entity and is not effectively conducted on the account and at the risk of the participants in any other way. In its decision of September 23, 2011, BNB 2012/12, the Court further ruled that whether the liability of the participants is limited or not must generally be determined under the statutory and articles-of-incorporation rules which govern the relationship between the entity and its participants.
46. Netherlands, CITA, Art. 2(1)(e) with respect to associations and foundations.
47. Netherlands, CITA, Art. 1a(1) and (2).
48. France, CGI, s. 206.
49. France, CGI, s. 206-3.
50. France, CGI, s. 239 bis AB; *see* CGI, s. 239 bis AA.

these arrangements are functionally similar to a limited partnership, because they are not formed under the Company Law, and are not juridical entities for tax purposes they are not subject to the corporate tax.[51]

The classification of an entity as a "juridical entity," which is a Japanese civil law concept, generally controls the applicability of the corporate tax. The question of how to deal with organizations formed under the laws of other states is often a difficult one. In this respect, a Supreme Court decision held that similarity to the Japanese law concept of a "juridical entity," especially the capability of an entity to hold rights and obligations separately from its contributors or members, should be a key factor in determining whether a foreign organization is characterized as a "juridical entity."[52] While this Supreme Court judgment is important, the standards established in the case are very abstract.

In *Australia*, the statutory definition of a "company" for tax purposes is quite broad, including "a body corporate or any other unincorporated association or body of persons," with a specific exclusion for partnerships and unincorporated joint ventures.[53] A variety of special rules applies to associations, clubs, and the like which would formally fall under the definition but are not the usual subjects of corporate-shareholder taxation.[54] The *United Kingdom* similarly taxes all incorporated bodies and unincorporated associations other than partnerships.[55]

In *China*, owing to a legacy of the command economy from 1949 until the 1980s, many state-owned, collective, and privately owned enterprises do not take the form of corporations since corporations were associated with capitalism; they were permitted in law only after the launch of economic reforms in the late 1970s. When the current EIT was introduced to consolidate taxes imposed on domestic enterprises and enterprises with foreign investments, the name of the tax remained "enterprise income tax." An "enterprise" is an entity established under Chinese law and is a "legal person." A partnership is not a legal person and thus not a taxpayer under the EIT.

In *India*, all companies incorporated under the Companies Act are regarded as companies for tax purposes. Moreover, a body corporate incorporated under the laws of a country outside India is also regarded as a company. LLPs established in India are treated as partnerships, but an LLP incorporated abroad as a body corporate is treated as a foreign company for tax purposes. Any institution, association, or body, whether incorporated or not and whether Indian or not, can be declared by the Central Board of Direct Tax, by means of a general or special order, to be a company.[56] Partnerships are taxable entities and are not treated as transparent. By case law, foreign partnerships may be treated as partnerships for Indian tax purposes if the foreign laws are similar to

51. Japan, ITA, s. 5 and Japan, CTA, s. 4.
52. *Ikuta et al. v. Japan*, 1253 Minshu 69-5 (S. Ct. July 17, 2015).
53. Australia, ITAA 1997, s. 995-1(1) definition of a company.
54. Australia, ITAA 1997, s. 50-45 (exemption in relation to sports, culture, arts, and film). Australia inherited the doctrine of mutuality from the United Kingdom, under which persons cannot make a taxable profit out of themselves. This doctrine is applied to members' clubs: *The Bohemians Club* (1918) 24 CLR 334.
55. United Kingdom, Income Tax Act 2010, s. 1121 ("company") and Income Tax Act 2007, s. 992.
56. India, ITA 1961, s. 2(17).

the Indian Partnership Act, 1932; otherwise, they may be treated as associations of persons.

3 ISSUES IN CORPORATE FORMATION

Where a corporation is formed by the transfer of cash to the corporation in exchange for the issuance of its shares, the taxpayer typically has a tax cost or basis in the shares equal to that amount. From a corporate law viewpoint, the amount received is usually accounted for as paid-in capital or capital surplus. In some systems, the corporate law treatment of the capital contribution and its possible subsequent repayment affects the tax rules applicable to the shareholder and to the corporation. In other jurisdictions, the corporate law treatment is irrelevant for tax purposes.

Where appreciated or depreciated property is transferred in exchange for shares on formation, in principle, the transfer is an exchange causing gain or loss realization by the shareholder. Several systems take this approach and require current taxation of the transferor as the general rule in these circumstances. However, a number of systems allow a tax-deferred incorporation in certain situations. The clearest situation is where a sole proprietorship is continued in corporate form, the former owner receiving all the shares on incorporation. Arguably, the transferor has changed only the legal form of the investment, which, after the transfer, is represented by shares rather than direct ownership, and to require recognition of gain in those circumstances would be inappropriate. However, there are a number of possible variations. Suppose that the assets transferred do not constitute a business, or that the transfer is to an existing corporation and the transferor receives only a small share interest or receives shares and other consideration. The systems examined here have given quite different responses to these circumstances. In some cases, there are special rules dealing with corporate formations. In others, more general nonrecognition principles, which also apply to corporate reorganizations and restructuring, provide the possibility of tax-deferred corporate formation.

In the *United States* system, in general, neither gain nor loss is taken into account, regardless of the nature of property transferred, as long as persons transferring property in the formation transaction collectively have an 80% or greater stock interest in the corporation following the transaction.[57] The theoretical justification for this rule is that the incorporation merely represents a continuing investment by the shareholder in the underlying assets transferred and is not an appropriate time to require taxation of the gain or allow a deduction for the loss. In addition, if the transaction were taxable, it might discourage taxpayers from changing their form of investment through incorporation. Such treatment, however, allows several classes of taxpayers to engage in partial exchanges of their assets and thereby to avoid a current payment of tax on the gain. To prevent abuse, there are restrictions on the ability of taxpayers to pool passive investment assets on a tax-free basis.[58]

57. United States, IRC, s. 351(a).
58. United States, IRC, s. 351(e).

As is generally the case with respect to exchanges where no gain or loss is recognized currently, the tax cost or basis in the shares received by the transferor is the historical tax cost of the assets transferred.[59] This "substituted" basis thus potentially preserves the taxation of the deferred gain at the shareholder level on the sale of the stock. In addition, in the U.S. system, in general, the corporate transferee takes the historical cost of an asset in the hands of the shareholder as its tax cost for the asset.[60] Thus, following corporate formation, there is the possibility of two gains or losses for tax purposes for what is economically the same gain (or loss) which would have been taxed (or deducted) only once if it had been realized by the shareholder. However, where the aggregate basis of all the assets transferred to a corporation exceeds their aggregate fair market value, the corporation must reduce the cost basis of the assets with a built-in loss by the excess amount.[61]

If the transferor receives property other than shares of the transferee corporation (e.g., cash or a debt obligation), the appreciation in the transferred assets is taxed to that extent and the transferor is entitled to increase the tax cost of the shares by that amount.[62] Losses, however, cannot be recognized regardless of the consideration received.[63]

The above rules apply not only to the formation of a new corporation but also to transfers of assets by shareholders to an existing corporation where the 80% stock ownership requirements are met.

In other systems, the treatment of the shareholder on formation varies considerably and, in general, offers more explicit selectivity than does the U.S. system. Thus, in the *Canadian* system, in principle, the transfer of property in exchange for shares is a taxable disposition. However, the transferor and the corporation can elect the amount to be treated as the proceeds received for the property.[64] By electing to treat an amount equal to the tax cost of the property as the value received on the issue of the shares, the taxpayer can defer any gain. As a consequence, however, both the shareholder and the corporation keep the historical basis of the property for the assets they hold, thus creating the possibility of two gains in the future. There are some limitations on the elective treatment. The amount elected cannot be more than the fair market value of the transferred property, thus preventing the creation of a potential double loss. Similarly, the elected amount cannot, in general terms, be less than the tax cost of the property, thus preventing the creation of a current artificial loss.

The transferor may receive other property in addition to shares in the transferee corporation, and the elected amount is allocated first to that property to the extent of its fair market value. The remaining elected amount is allocated to the shares received. In this way, tax on appreciation in the transferred property is deferred through a reduced tax cost in the shares.

59. United States, IRC, s. 358.
60. United States, IRC, s. 362(a).
61. United States, IRC, s. 362(e). Alternatively, stockholders can elect to reduce their cost basis in their stock in lieu of the corporation reducing its basis in the transferred assets.
62. United States, IRC, s. 351(b).
63. United States, IRC, s. 351(b).
64. Canada, Income Tax Act (ITA), s. 85(1).

There is no requirement for the transferor to control the corporation or receive any minimum percentage of shares. However, there are some special anti-avoidance rules. If the transfer is to a corporation controlled by the transferor or related parties, no loss is recognized. A similar rule prevents the shifting of value to related-party shareholders. There are also restrictions on the type of property which can be transferred. For example, real property held as inventory and capital property owned by a nonresident are excluded.

The *Swedish* rules have a similar pattern. An individual shareholder can transfer assets to a corporation without taxation. Transfers of assets from a business are treated as realization events and taxed as if the assets had been sold for fair market value. However, tax can be avoided in a number of situations involving corporate formation, restructuring, and mergers of corporations in accordance with the EU Merger Directive. This result is functionally similar to the Canadian result, since the appreciation in the assets remains to be taxed both to the shareholder and the corporation, and the setting of the (non-arm's length) sales price amounts to an election by the taxpayer of the amount (if any) which will be subject to tax on a future transfer.

In *The Netherlands*, the transfer to a company of a business carried on as a sole proprietorship or partnership would normally be a taxable event. Under a set of administrative conditions, however, the transfer can be effected without current tax if the entire business (or share of the business in the case of a partnership) is transferred to a newly formed corporation in exchange for stock.[65] More technically, the tax-free transfer is conditional on a number of requirements, including: (a) at least 95% of the consideration must be shares of the transferee corporation (provided that the cash paid as "boot" does not exceed EUR 25,000); and (b) the shares must be held by the transferor for at least three years. If these (and other) conditions are met, the transferor is not taxed, but takes as the tax cost for the shares received the net amount of the book values of the assets and liabilities transferred, reduced by any boot received (prior to 2001, the transferor took fair market value as the tax cost, but this rule was changed to follow the pattern used in most other countries). Because the transferee corporation retains the historical cost basis of the assets, any appreciation in the transferred assets will be subject to tax later in the hands of both the transferring individual and transferee corporation.[66]

In *Germany*, in principle, the transfer of business assets in exchange for shares would be a realization event, with the transferor realizing gain or loss and taking as the tax cost in the shares the fair market value of the transferred assets.[67] The transfer of private assets would often not result in income recognition, since the disposition of such assets is, in many cases, not subject to tax. Despite the general rule of income recognition where business assets are concerned, the special rules dealing with tax-deferred corporate reorganizations may apply to the incorporation of a business

65. Netherlands, Income Tax Act 2001 (ITA 2001), Art. 3.65.
66. Details of the "standard conditions" are laid down in a Decree of June 30, 2010, nr. DGB2010/3599M.
67. Germany, ITA, s. 6 para. 6 sent. 1.

and are included in a specific act, the Reorganization Tax Act (RTA) (*Umwandlungssteuergesetz*). Basically, the tax treatment of the transfer of an existing business or independent division of a business in exchange for the newly issued shares of a corporation depends on the way the transaction is treated by the transferee. The transferee has the right to ascribe to the assets in its books any value between the old book value of the assets and their "going concern" value, and this amount is deemed to be the price paid for the assets transferred.[68] Thus, to the extent that the assets are written up in the books of the transferee, the transferor must recognize gain; if the assets are entered at book value, the transaction is tax-free. The acquisition cost of the shares in the hands of the transferor is the same amount. This treatment is available only for the transfer of an entire business or division of a business; the transfer of individual business assets would be a taxable event.

The *Australian* rules on formation distinguish between the types of property transferred and are not comprehensive. The rules relevant to the transfer of capital assets require that the transferor hold 100% of the issued shares of the transferee company after the transfer. In addition, the provisions do not apply to transfers by several persons unless they first form a partnership to become the formal transferor. However, the formation of a partnership has capital gains consequences, and so does not offer a route to overcome the narrowness of the rule. Where the rules apply, they provide for the carryover of the tax cost of the transferred assets in the hands of the company and a corresponding tax cost for the transferor of the shares received. The transferor may not receive cash for the transfer, although the transferor's liabilities may be assumed by the company as part of the transfer. Anti-avoidance rules seek to prevent value shifting by means of these rollover transactions.[69]

In the *United Kingdom*, a deferral of the otherwise applicable capital gains tax (CGT) is available where there is a transfer of an entire business by an individual in exchange for shares.[70] The business must be transferred as a going concern and all noncash assets transferred. Consideration other than shares may be received, but rollover relief applies only to the extent of the transfer for shares. If the transferor has unrelieved losses incurred in the business, these may be used against income in the form of dividends, interest, or employment income subsequently received from the corporation.[71] Effectively, the tax cost of the transferor's shares is the same as the cost of the assets transferred, while the corporation takes market value as the tax cost of the assets transferred (a step-up in tax cost).[72] Often an incorporator will not seek this rollover relief, since stamp duty is payable on the transfer of some types of assets, such as land. In this case, only some of the business assets may be transferred and a different form of rollover relief used. This relief is available for assets gifted to the corporation but does not result in a step-up in cost for the corporation.[73] An incorporator may not desire rollover treatment in any case because the reduced CGT rates and the annual

68. Germany, Reorganization Tax Act (RTA), s. 20 paras. 2, 3.
69. Australia, ITAA 1997, Div 122.
70. United Kingdom, TCGA, s. 162.
71. United Kingdom, Income Tax Act 2007, s. 86.
72. United Kingdom, TCGA, s. 17.
73. United Kingdom, TCGA, s. 165.

exemption (GBP 3,000 in 2024-2025) may mean that an incorporator's CGT liability is not great. A somewhat different set of rules applies to the transfer of a business from one corporation to another.[74]

In *Japan*, in general, the transfer of an asset to a corporation as consideration for the issue of new capital stock constitutes a taxable event, whether or not the transfer is made in the course of incorporation. However, a deferral regime applies to certain qualified corporate restructuring transactions, including the transfer of assets by one corporation to another in exchange for newly issued stock. The transfer is deemed to be made on the basis of the book value of the relevant assets for income tax purposes and no taxable income is deemed to be recognized by the transferor, with the transferee taking the transferor's tax basis. Further details are provided in section 7 below, but access to the regime is premised on continuity of control: as long as the transferred assets remain under the control of the transferor corporation (as a part of the corporate group), the transfer does not trigger the realization of gain. Access to the deferral regime requires the transfer of assets between companies with 100% common ownership, or the transfer of a business (not a specific asset) between companies with more than 50% common ownership where other conditions are met (e.g., approximately 80% or more of the employees who were engaged in the transferred business are assumed by the transferee), or the transfer of a business establishing a joint venture with a nonrelated entity which meets several other criteria. Where the conditions are met, the deferral is compulsory. These special rules apply only to corporate transferors; all transfers by individuals are fully taxable.[75]

In *France*, the transfer of assets to a new corporation on formation is generally a taxable event. However, a sole proprietor can elect, for nondepreciable assets, to defer the gain until the stock received is disposed of or the assets are disposed of by the corporation. For depreciable assets, tax on the gain may be spread over a five-year period (or fifteen years in the case of a building) and, with respect to inventory, it is possible to transfer inventory at book value, eliminating any gain for the transferor, provided the company takes book value as its cost.[76] A corporation establishing a subsidiary can transfer all the assets of a complete business to a newly formed corporation on a tax-deferred basis.

In *China*, companies must have registered capital. Contributions of capital may be in cash or in kind; there are no general tax-deferral rules in the legislation for shareholders who contribute capital in kind. However, exercising its "rule-making" powers, the State Tax Administration (STA) addressed the lack of deferral in a letter published in 2005,[77] stating: "When an individual contributes, as an investment and after appraisal, non-cash property to an enterprise and receives shares of the enterprise in exchange, the personal income tax shall temporarily not apply to the gain reflected

74. United Kingdom, TCGA, s. 171 and United Kingdom, Income and Corporation Tax Act 2010, Part 22.
75. Japan, CTA, s. 2, paras. 12-14 and s. 62-4.
76. France, CGI, s. 151 octies.
77. China, STA, "Reply Regarding the Temporary Exemption from the Personal Income Tax for Appraised Appreciation of Non-cash Property," Guoshuihan [2005] 319 (2005/4/13).

in any appraised appreciation. When the individual's investment is returned, transferred, or liquidated, the personal income tax shall apply to any income then received by the individual, using the pre-appraisal cost of the (contributed) property as the original cost of the investment." The Ministry of Finance and STA allow tax deferral for domestic intra-group restructuring.[78]

With respect to corporations transferring noncash assets to a corporation in return for an equity interest in the transferee, the Ministry of Finance and STA have issued a ruling stating that these transfers are to be treated as having two components: a sale at fair market value of the relevant noncash assets followed by the investment of the proceeds of the sale; any gain or loss from the transaction is therefore recognized.[79] If the transfer is part of a "special reorganization" (*see* section 7.1 below), the gain or loss is deferred.

In *India*, the Supreme Court has held that a transfer of capital assets to a company in exchange for shares is a "transfer" for purposes of CGT.[80] Until 2014, it was not possible to establish a one-person company in India. Although such companies are now allowed under the Companies Act, 2013, there is no special regime for them for tax purposes.

4 ISSUES INVOLVING CAPITAL STRUCTURE

Commercial and corporate law principles have traditionally recognized a sharp distinction between ownership interests in a corporation in the form of shares and creditor interests in the form of bonds or other debt obligations. For corporate tax purposes, regardless of the pattern of corporate taxation, important tax distinctions have also historically turned on the classification of an investment as "debt" or "equity." In "classical" systems, payments of interest on debt obligations are typically deductible by the corporation, unlike dividend distributions which bear full corporate-level tax. The importance of the debt/equity distinction is reduced somewhat in systems which have some degree of corporate-shareholder integration. However, even in such systems, the distinction between an interest payment on a debt obligation and a dividend payment on equity can be significant in some circumstances, particularly for cross-border payments, and is always an issue where the shareholder is not entitled to an imputation credit. Thus, all systems must deal with this classification issue for tax purposes. In addition, whatever the domestic rules, a number of countries have special debt-equity restrictions where the shareholders are nonresidents. These aspects are discussed in Part IV.

For the countries which are members of the EU, the 2016 EU Anti-Tax Avoidance Directive (ATAD) requires them to adopt restrictions on the deduction of the net interest expense of all domestic corporations irrespective of whether the interest is paid

78. China, Ministry of Finance and STA, Cai Shui [2014] No. 109, "Notice on Tax Treatment of Chinese Enterprises Undergoing Restructuring," Cai Shui [2014] No. 109 [财税[2014]109号 财政部 国家税务总局关于促进企业重组有关企业所得税处理问题的通知].
79. China, Cai Shui [1997] No. 77.
80. *CIT v. RR Ramakrishan Pillai*, [1967] 66 ITR 75 (SC).

to residents or nonresidents. Interest is deductible up to 30% of a company's earnings before interest, taxes, depreciation, and amortization (EBITDA). However, countries may adopt a threshold of up to EUR 3 million so that interest up to the threshold is deductible without any limit. In addition, a domestic company is entitled to deduct interest in excess of 30% of EBITDA where the company is part of a consolidated group for financial accounting purposes and it can demonstrate that the ratio of its equity to total assets is broadly equal to or higher than the equivalent group ratio. These earnings-stripping rules apply for 2019 and subsequent years.

In the *United States*, the debt-equity distinction was initially developed in the case law. In general, courts have not considered themselves bound by the civil or commercial law characterization of an investment.[81] Instead, the case law has examined the legal rights created by the instrument, the economic source of the funds for the payments required, the relation between creditor and shareholder interests, the ability of the corporation to obtain similar financing from third parties, the relation between the amount of equity and debt financing (i.e., whether the corporation is "thinly" capitalized), and other factors.[82] The results of the case law are difficult to reconcile in any principled manner and are very fact-specific.

Dissatisfaction with the case law approach led to an attempt to provide clearer administrative rules. Those rules focused more directly on the economic characteristics of the instrument in question and the relative importance of "debt" or "equity" features. The rules were ultimately rejected on the ground that they were too complex and as a result, the case law-based system of classification is still generally applicable.

Some special statutory rules have been enacted with respect to certain types of obligations. These rules often "bifurcate" an instrument with both debt and equity characteristics and treat each part of the obligation separately. The "normal" amount of interest is allowed as a deduction and the remainder is disallowed or deferred.[83] Thus, for example, where a bond issued at a discount bears excessive interest, the excessive amount is not deductible as interest.[84] Special rules on "earnings stripping" are important principally in the international context and are discussed in Part IV.[85]

Most of the systems considered here have traditionally given more weight than the U.S. to the civil or commercial law classification of an instrument in determining its tax classification. Thus, in *Canada*, there are no general statutory rules and the case law usually makes the distinction based on the legal form of the obligation.[86] Special rules apply in some circumstances with respect to certain preferred stock.[87] In general terms, the rules are intended to prevent corporations which are unable to use interest deductions from, in effect, transferring the advantage of the interest deduction to corporate investors who receive tax-free intercorporate dividends. While not formally

81. *See*, for example, *Slappey Drive Industrial Park v. United States*, 561 F.2d 572 (5th Cir. 1977).
82. *Ibid.*
83. United States, IRC, ss. 385, 163(e)(5), 279, 163(j) and 163(l).
84. United States, IRC, s. 163(e).
85. United States, IRC, ss. 163(j), 59A.
86. *See*, for example, *Barejo Holdings ULC v. The Queen*, 2015 TCC 274; additional reasons at 2018 TCC 200.
87. Canada, ITA, Parts IV.1 and VI.1.

debt-equity rules, the rules effectively impose limits on the ability to utilize the interest deduction. Where the rules limiting "after-tax financing" apply, they impose a tax on the distributing corporation which can then be offset against the corporation's mainstream income tax liability. This ensures that where the distribution is tax-free in the hands of the recipient, a single level of current tax will have been paid by the distributing corporation on the income out of which the distribution was made.

Like Canada, prior to 2001, *Australia* had no specific rules to distinguish debt and equity and the tax classification generally followed the legal form. In 2001, comprehensive debt-equity rules were introduced as part of the substantial business tax reform which had commenced in 1999. Under these rules, four types of interests which are used to finance a company are classified as "equity" (unless they also meet the "debt test"), namely: shares, interests whose return is at the discretion of the company or its associates, interests whose return is contingent on the company making profits, and interests convertible into one of the three preceding types of interests. A security satisfies the "debt test," and is thus not equity, where the company has a noncontingent obligation to ultimately return to the investor an amount which is substantially more likely than not to equal or exceed the amount received by the company from the investor. In measuring the values of the amount received and the amount returned, nominal values are used where the security has a life of ten years or less and present values where the security has a life of more than ten years.[88]

Returns on debt interests are generally treated as interest (deductible, and not included in the imputation system), while returns on equity interests are generally treated as dividends (nondeductible but potentially carrying a tax credit).[89] As a result of these rules, redeemable preference shares are now usually classified as debt interests, while returns on converting preference shares (shares which automatically convert into ordinary shares) are classified as equity interests. The classifications created by these rules do not apply for all purposes where shareholding is relevant; for example, the disallowance of losses where there is a 50% change in ownership still depends only on share ownership in the company law sense, not on equity interests in the tax sense. In addition to the debt-equity rules, in international situations, deductions for interest paid on debt obligations can be limited under thin capitalization provisions, which apply in addition to the debt/equity rules but do not lead to recharacterization as equity.

The *United Kingdom*, in general, has also followed commercial form in distinguishing debt and equity. However, there are a number of complex statutory provisions dealing with special situations. For example, where interest paid on a debt security is above a normal commercial rate, the excess is treated as a distribution. In addition, interest may be treated as a distribution where it is received in respect of convertible notes, certain securities linked to shares, or debentures where the return is dependent on the results of the company's business. Due to perceived abuses, the latter rules do not apply to interest paid between two resident corporations or to a UK

88. Australia, ITAA 1997, Div 974.
89. Australia, ITAA 1997 ss. 25-85, 26-26, 202-40, 202-45, ITAA 1936 s. 44(1).

permanent establishment of a nonresident corporation.[90] For individuals, the reclassification by statute is generally in one direction, from interest to equity distribution. So, for example, there is no attempt to reclassify dividends paid on redeemable preference shares as interest. For corporate shareholders, rules were enacted in 2005 (replaced in 2009) which treat certain shares as debt and so deny the intercorporate dividend exemption.[91] The types of shares covered are those that resemble interest-bearing debt, potentially including redeemable shares. The overall impact of the UK system is a series of discrete rules targeted at particular problems, with the result that the classification of an instrument as debt or equity for tax purposes may change depending on who holds it.

In *Sweden*, since 2019, there are general statutory rules dealing with the debt-equity distinction. Before the 2019 reform, there was only one specific provision with respect to the characterization of participating loans for closely held corporations.[92] Currently, there are some statutory rules with respect to the characterization of interest (e.g., the interest component of financial leasing) but most cases are decided by reference to the case law. In general, the civil law characterization is controlling: the court examines whether an instrument is in fact debt under civil law, and if so, it is treated as such for tax purposes. Where the amount of interest is determined by dividends paid or the profits realized by the corporation, the interest deduction is denied; however, the payment remains interest in the hands of the recipient. As a general rule, interest costs above 30% of EBITDA (subject to a threshold of SEK 5,000,000) are not deductible for corporations.

In *The Netherlands*, the civil law form of an instrument generally controls its treatment for tax purposes. There are important statutory exceptions with regard to interest on loans granted under conditions which, in effect, make the creditor a participant in the business ("participating loans")[93] and interest payments which are considered to erode The Netherlands tax base (e.g., interest paid by a parent to its loss-making subsidiary, interest paid in certain cases to a foreign-related company, and interest on convertible and/or profit-sharing bonds).[94]

As of January 1, 2019, pursuant to the EU ATAD, the deduction of net interest expenses is generally limited to 20% of EBITDA, subject to a threshold of EUR 1 million.[95]

Following several decisions by the Dutch Supreme Court, additional restrictions apply. First, debt is recharacterized as equity if the parties' real intention was not to make a loan (i.e., a sham) or, in the case of corporate shareholders, if the circumstances indicate that there is no expectation that the loan will be repaid ("bottomless-pit loan").[96] Further, if the loan is issued to a related party in a situation where an independent issuer would not have provided the loan (i.e., not at arm's length,

90. United Kingdom, Income Tax Act 2010, s. 1032.
91. United Kingdom, Corporation Tax Act 2009, Ch. 6A (ss. 522-535).
92. Sweden, ITA, Ch. 24 paras. 5-10.
93. Netherlands, CITA, Art. 10(1)d.
94. Netherlands, CITA, Art. 10a(1).
95. Netherlands, CITA, Art. 15b.
96. Netherlands, Supreme Court, January 11, 1988, BNB 1988/217.

"*onzakelijke lening*"), the issuer cannot (partially) write down the loan if the intention was to benefit the shareholder(s);[97] however, in such instances, the loan itself is not recharacterized as equity.[98] A 2003 decision by the CJEU (*Bosal*)[99] held that the statutory denial of an interest deduction for amounts a parent corporation pays on loans from a foreign subsidiary organized in the EU violates EC law where similar payments to a domestic subsidiary would be deductible. In reaction to this case, the statute now makes all such interest payments deductible.

There is little developed case law in *Japan* on the debt-equity distinction, and it is generally believed that the civil law form of instruments controls their tax treatment. As a result, dividends on most senior preferred shares are treated as dividends and are not tax-deductible. Most junior subordinated debts are treated as debt and the interest is tax-deductible. In line with the Base Erosion and Profit Shifting (BEPS) project, Japan has introduced earnings-stripping restrictions on the amount of deductible interest, which are discussed further in Part IV.[100]

France has no specific tax rules on the classification of financial instruments, although the tax authorities may reclassify some instruments for tax purposes. However, France has always had specific and complex rules limiting interest deductibility. First, the interest rate on loans between related parties is capped at the average annual effective rate charged by financial institutions for variable-rate business loans with a term of more than two years.[101] Second, the former thin capitalization regime has been replaced (where the interest expense exceeds EUR 3 million) by capping the interest deduction at 30% of EBITDA, with an unlimited carryforward of denied deductions. In addition, for companies belonging to a consolidated group, a partial deduction in excess of the threshold is provided under certain conditions[102] and a stricter cap has been introduced for thin capitalization situations.[103] Finally, the so-called *Charasse* amendment controls debt push-down structures and non-deductibility rules neutralize mismatch outcomes under hybrid financial instruments.

The situation in *Germany* provides two interesting examples of the evolution of debt-equity rules. Historically, court decisions followed the civil and commercial law characterization of obligations as debt or equity for tax purposes and consistently held that only company stock could generate corporate profits and dividends. Beginning in the 1920s, this case law resulted in the development of "hybrid" participations which did not grant a "share" in the company under civil law, but provided for an obligatory entitlement to a share of the profit of the company and a share of the assets distributed in the event of liquidation. As early as 1934, the Imperial Tax Court held that annual payments for these "jouissance rights" must be included in the taxable profit of the company, since there was no economic justification for distinguishing between profits distributed to shareholders and profits distributed to holders of "hybrid" participations.

97. Netherlands, Supreme Court, May 9, 2008, BNB 2008/191.
98. Netherlands, Supreme Court, November 25, 2011, V-N 2011/63.10.
99. CJEU, September 18, 2003, C-168-01 (*Bosal Holding*).
100. Japan, STMA, s. 66-5-2.
101. France, CGI, s. 39-1 3°.
102. France, CGI, s. 212 bis VI.
103. France, CGI, s. 212 bis VII, which lowers the thresholds to EUR 1 million and 10% of EBITDA.

This jurisprudence was subsequently incorporated in the statute. In contrast, payments to "silent partners" who also receive a share in the profit of a company's business are regarded as ordinary expenses, in the same manner as interest payments to common creditors.

The second example of the evolution of the debt-equity rules concerns thin capitalization.

Because the case law adhered to the tradition that interest payments are expenses even where the debt/equity ratio was "excessive" from a business perspective, in 1993 Germany adopted detailed statutory tax rules dealing with "excessive" debt capitalization. Since, in the domestic situation, taxation of dividends and interest in the hands of the shareholder or creditor did not have significantly different tax results, the rules applied only to foreign shareholders and domestic tax exempt organizations. In 2002, this provision was ruled by the CJEU to be in conflict with the fundamental freedoms of the EU Treaty.[104] Germany initially chose to extend its complex thin capitalization rules to domestic situations in order to comply with the requirement of nondiscrimination, but has since replaced the thin capitalization regime by interest-stripping rules in accordance with the EU ATAD.[105] The issue of compatibility of this "interest brake" with the constitutional principle of equal treatment of taxpayers in the light of ability to pay has been raised with the Constitutional Court and is still pending.

In *China*, the EIT system recognizes both debt and equity. Article 116 of the EIT Regulations defines "debt" for purposes of the thin capitalization rules in Article 46 of the EIT Law as "financing that is directly or indirectly obtained by an enterprise from its related parties, and that is to be repaid in principal and interest or to be compensated in ways similar in nature to paying interest." Related-party financing includes back-to-back financing arrangements, third-party debt guaranteed by a related party, and other financing arrangements that in substance result in financing from a related party. "Equity" is any investment received by an enterprise without the obligation to repay principal and interest and through which investors possess ownership rights in the net assets of the enterprise. Because the Chinese tax authorities can rely on the General Anti-avoidance Rule (GAAR) and the substance-over-form principle, they have the power to recharacterize financing transactions in some cases. Compared to other countries, however, taxpayers in China face more regulatory constraints on capitalization due to the monitoring and control by the People's Bank of China and State Administration of Foreign Exchanges on cross-border borrowing.

In *India*, in some transfer pricing cases, the tax authorities have attempted to treat preference shares as loans; however, the courts have rejected this treatment.[106] They have also tried to treat compulsory convertible debentures (CCDs) as equity and disallow the deduction of interest on such debentures. Again, the courts have held that until conversion actually takes place, the debentures retain the character of debt. Although CCDs are treated as equity for insolvency purposes,[107] that treatment may not

104. *Ibid.*
105. Germany, ITA, s. 4h.
106. *Cairn India Ltd v. ACIT* (ITAT), Delhi, ITA No. 1459/Del/2016 (October 24, 2018).
107. *IFCI Ltd v. Sutanu Sinha* (SC), Civil Appeal No. 4929 of 2023 (November 9, 2023).

be relevant for tax purposes. The tax authorities have also tried to treat certain hybrid instruments (perpetual bonds with a buyback feature) as equity in order to disallow the deduction of interest. In one such case, the tax authorities took the position that perpetual bonds were equity because of their equity features; however, the ITAT held in favor of the taxpayer and allowed a deduction of the interest.[108] Where a transaction is considered to be an impermissible avoidance arrangement under the GAAR, the tax department is empowered to treat equity as debt and vice versa.[109]

5 TAXATION OF CORPORATE DISTRIBUTIONS

5.1 Basic Structure of Distribution Rules

All systems must have rules which characterize for tax purposes payments to shareholders with respect to their stock and determine the consequences of that characterization. The payments can potentially be treated as a distribution of corporate profits, a distribution of the corporation's stated capital or capital surplus, or a return of the capital of the shareholder invested in the stock, all with differing tax results.

In the *United States* system, the tax treatment of distributions to shareholders depends on whether the source of the distribution is from "earnings and profits."[110] Earnings and profits are corporate taxable income, with several important modifications.[111] For example, tax preferences or deductions which have reduced corporate taxable income may nonetheless be included in earnings and profits. The composition of earnings and profits and its attendant complexities are historically rooted and have no particular current policy justification.

Distributions of earnings and profits are classified as "dividends" for tax purposes.[112] The corporate law characterization of the distribution as a formal dividend, a capital reduction, or even an illegal distribution which impairs capital is not relevant for tax purposes. Similarly, the treatment of the distribution on the books of the corporation has no effect on its tax characterization. Although dividends paid to individual shareholders were historically subject to normal income tax rates, such dividends currently are taxed at the same preferential rates as capital gains. Dividends paid to corporate shareholders are taxed as normal income but the dividends-received deduction, which provides various degrees of intercompany dividend relief based on the percentage of stock owned in a distributing U.S. corporation, usually reduces the attendant tax liability.[113]

108. *ICICI Bank Ltd v. ACIT*, ITAT Mumbai, August 22, 2022.
109. ITA 1961, s. 98(2).
110. United States, IRC, s. 316.
111. United States, Treas. Reg., s. 1.312-6 through 1.312-15.
112. United States, IRC, s. 316.
113. United States, IRC, s. 243. In addition, United States, IRC, s. 245A allows U.S. corporate shareholders to claim a 100% dividends-received deduction for dividends from foreign corporations to the extent the dividends arise from foreign source income. Some observers have suggested that in some industries where tangible assets are less significant, much of the income earned by a U.S. corporation through its controlled foreign subsidiaries will be subject

To the extent that a distribution exceeds earnings and profits, it is treated as a tax-free return of the shareholder's tax cost in the shares.[114] Where the distribution exceeds the stock investment, it is treated as gain on the disposition of the stock.[115] Since dividends and capital gains are taxed at the same preferential rates for individuals, the significant difference for individuals with respect to the source of the distribution is the opportunity to receive a tax-free return of their tax cost in their shares where the distribution exceeds the corporation's earnings and profits.

The patterns in other systems are generally quite different, in some ways more restrictive and in others more generous. Often corporate law and accounting treatment play an important role in tax characterization. Timing rules tend to relate the distributions to earnings of a particular year. However, the limitation of taxable dividends to distributions of corporate earnings is frequently not present. In *Canada*, for example, under case law principles, any distribution made by a corporation which is not in liquidation or pursuant to an authorized reduction of capital is taxed as a dividend regardless of the existence of profits at the corporate level.[116] In the *United Kingdom*, the concept of a "distribution" is central in determining the treatment of both the distributing corporation (nondeductible) and the shareholder (lower tax rate). To the extent that a "distribution" includes a dividend, the concept follows corporate law with respect to what is a dividend and what is a return of capital. To the extent that "distribution" includes items other than corporate law dividends, it is irrelevant whether the corporation in question has profits (although in some cases, the distribution must be out of the assets of the corporation).

Similarly, in *Sweden*, there is no connection between the earnings or income of the corporation and the taxation of corporate distributions. (In some situations, special rules may recharacterize a favorably taxed dividend as employment income.) In *The Netherlands*, any economic benefit received by the shareholder as such is taxable without regard to the financial results of the corporation. Thus, where a corporation with no earnings makes a lawful distribution from capital surplus in anticipation of profits in the future, the amount is taxed as a dividend despite the lack of corporate earnings.

The *Japanese* rules were substantially changed in 2006 with the introduction of the new Company Law. Although the Company Law imposes restrictions on the payment of dividends, it allows dividends to be paid out of capital surplus as well as retained earnings. With respect to dividends attributable to retained earnings, the amount is taxed as a dividend at the shareholder level. For dividends attributable to capital surplus, only a portion of such dividends is taxed as dividends, while the remaining portion is deemed to constitute the purchase price and may result in capital gains or losses.[117]

---

to current taxation in the United States through Subpart F and GILTI, leaving little CFC income to benefit from the new dividends-received deduction. United States, IRC, s. 951(a), 951A.

114. United States, IRC, s. 301(c).
115. *Ibid.*
116. *Northern Securities Co. v. The King*, [1935] 1 DTC 282 (Ex. Ct).
117. Japan, ITA, ss. 24 and 25, and Japan, CTA, ss. 23 and 24, 61-2 and Japan, STMA, s. 37-10.

In *Australia*, significant changes were made to corporate law rules on maintenance of capital in 1998, which had tax consequences as well. As a result of these changes, combined with the introduction of the new debt-equity rules discussed above, the taxation of distributions has become much more complex. A dividend for tax purposes must be "out of profits," which was traditionally determined by reference to company accounts or financial statements, although a public ruling and court case suggest that anything which is not debited to share capital is out of profits.[118] Corporate law amendments in 2010, which allowed "dividends" to be paid out of capital for corporate law purposes, further confused the position. In addition, the High Court of Australia held (in the view of many, incorrectly) that distributions which do not fit within the definition of dividend and the out-of-profits requirement can in any event be income under ordinary concepts, apart from the definition of dividend—which means they are assessable in full without any imputation credit. The case concerned a right which a company had issued to its shareholders to sell back 10% of their shares to the company at a premium to the market price.[119] In addition, even amounts debited to share capital can be taxed as unfranked dividends instead of as a return of capital, as explained below. Dividends on shares which are reclassified as interest on debt under the debt-equity rules are nonetheless taxable as dividends in the hands of the recipient, even though they are deductible at the corporate level and do not carry the imputation credit.[120] Distributions on an equity interest which is not legally a share under corporate law are taxable without regard to profits (because the company will be expensing these items in its accounts and not treating them as distributions of profits), but they are nondeductible at the corporate level. An indirect "out-of-profits" requirement applies before such distributions can be franked under the imputation system.[121] In the case of corporations which do not maintain adequate records, the tax authorities can reconstruct the accounts to establish the requisite profits.[122]

In *France*, shareholders of companies subject to CIT are taxed when they receive a distribution from the company. The notion of distribution is very broad, covering types of income which are not dividends in the strict sense of the term, such as sumptuary expenses, which are considered to be distributions in the hands of those who receive them, as well as distributions[123] linked to a change in capital (e.g., payments out of share premium), the distribution of liquidation surpluses, and all sums deemed to have been "disinvested by the company" (i.e., the value of the corporation's net assets has declined, to the benefit of a shareholder, even though the corporation does not have profits). The rules on distributions can apply to distributions to shareholders or associates and sums made available to third parties.

118. Australia, Income Tax Assessment Act 1936 (ITAA 1936), s. 6(1) definition of dividend, 44(1); *Sun Alliance Investments* (2005) 225 CLR 488; compare Ruling TR 2003/8, *Condell* [2007] FCAFC 44.
119. Australia, ITAA 1936 s. 44(1A), *McNeil* (2007) 229 CLR 656. The 2010 amendments affected both company and tax law and seem to be intended to abolish the "out-of-profits" requirement, but a ruling was issued which denied this outcome for tax purposes; Ruling TR 2012/5.
120. Australia, ITAA 1936, s. 44(1), ITAA 1997, ss. 25-85, 202-45(d).
121. Australia, ITAA 1936, s. 44(1), ITAA 1997, ss. 26-26, Div 215.
122. *MacFarlane* [1986] FCA 266.
123. France, CGI, ss. 108 through 117.

In *Germany*, all payments by the corporation to its shareholders are generally held to be taxable.[124]

In *China*, the EIT legislation adopts a broad concept of corporate distributions. Article 6 of the EIT Law includes "dividends, profit distributions and other returns on equity investments" in computing income. "Dividends, profit distributions and other returns on equity investments" are defined as "income derived by an enterprise from investees on account of equity investments."[125] Such income must be recognized "on the date on which the investee resolves to make a profit distribution" unless prescribed otherwise. In contrast, returns of capital are not income. The issue of corporate distributions is more important with respect to nonresident than to resident investors, since dividends paid to a resident enterprise are excluded from income (if the shares are held for at least twelve months).[126] The same exemption applies to nonresident enterprises only where the enterprise has a permanent establishment in China and the dividends are effectively connected with the permanent establishment.

In *India*, dividends are included in the category of "income from other sources." The term "dividend" is defined to have its ordinary meaning and also includes other distributions of profits or assets by a company to its shareholders, such as liquidating distributions, distributions on a reduction of capital, and loans to a substantial shareholder of a privately held company.[127]

5.2 Relating Distributions to Corporate Earnings

Where a distinction exists for tax purposes between types of distributions, ordering rules are necessary to determine the characterization of the distribution. Thus, in the *United States* system, because of the earnings-and-profits requirement, complex rules are provided which connect distributions and profits. In general terms, profits are deemed to be distributed first, regardless of the formal corporate characterization of the distribution. If the corporation has earnings for the year and an accumulated deficit, a distribution during the year is nonetheless taxable. Distributions are taxable to the shareholder receiving them even if they relate to earnings which were accumulated in years prior to the investment by the shareholder and thus, in an economic sense, represent a return of the shareholder's original investment in the shares.

For countries which generally tax distributions without regard to the existence of earnings at the corporate level, this type of rule is not necessary. Therefore, under the corporate tax rules applicable in *Germany*, specific "baskets," which categorize income according to its tax burden and which were used under the imputation system, are no longer necessary. However, reimbursement of the stated capital in the course of a liquidation or a capital reduction[128] and the repayment of other funds which have been

124. Germany, ITA, s. 20 para. 1 No. 1.
125. China, EIT Regulations, Art. 17.
126. China, EIT, Art. 26 and EIT Regulations, Art. 8.
127. India, ITA 1961, s. 2(22). *See Kantilal Manilal v. CIT*, 41 ITR 275 (SC).
128. Germany, ITA, s. 20 para. 1 No. 2.

contributed by the shareholders to the company funds are not taxable.[129] This exemption was extended to contributions made to companies resident in other EU Member States in 2006. Following a number of judgments by the Federal Fiscal Court, which urged the legislature to provide equal treatment, in 2023, this rule was extended to any foreign company irrespective of their seat.

France had complex rules for determining when a distribution was deemed to be from preferentially taxed earnings and thus subject to the compensatory tax (*précompte mobilier*), but this system was repealed in 2005.

For countries which allow the tax-free distribution of share premium or stated capital, rules are necessary to identify such distributions. Often the characterization for corporate law purposes is controlling. In the *Canadian* system, distributions of paid-up capital, which are determined under the applicable corporate law subject to certain adjustments required under income tax law, are deemed to be made before distributions of profits, with only the excess over the paid-up capital reduction taxable as a dividend. However, the recovery of capital before corporate profits is available only for certain transactions, such as liquidations, redemptions of shares, and authorized reductions of capital.[130]

The *Japanese* rules also generally follow the characterization under the Company Law between dividends attributable to retained earnings and those attributable to capital surplus. Distributing companies are required to inform their shareholders of the amount of dividends attributable to their capital surplus.

Similarly, the *United Kingdom* generally follows the characterization of returns of capital under corporate law. A return of capital is not subject to distribution treatment (although it may give rise to a capital gain). However, special anti-abuse rules apply to returns of capital before and after the capitalization of profits, e.g., through the issue of bonus shares.[131]

The changes to *Australian* company law in 1998 abolished the use of par-value shares and with it the need for a share premium account. Distributions which are treated for corporate law purposes as repayments of share capital are generally tax-free and reduce the tax cost of the stock, with any excess taxable as a capital gain. Where the distribution of share capital is part of a scheme involving the contribution of share capital by one shareholder and its distribution to another, an anti-avoidance rule may treat the distribution as a dividend. Those who benefit more from such distributions compared to dividends, mainly nonresident shareholders and shareholders with pre-CGT shares who are not subject to the CGT, are now subject to three different rules to prevent the manipulation of capital returns.[132]

In *Sweden*, as a general rule, distributions from corporations to shareholders are treated as dividends. However, an exception applies where shares are bought back by a corporation and where shareholders have contributed capital to a corporation in a

129. Germany, ITA, s. 20 para. 1 No. 1 s. 3 and No. 2 s. 1.
130. Canada, ITA, s. 84.
131. United Kingdom, Corporation Tax Act 2010, ss. 1022-1027A.
132. Australia, ITAA 1936, ss. 6(1) definition of dividend para. (d), 6(4), 44(1B), 45, 45A, 45B; ITAA 1997, ss. 104-135.

mixed loan/equity form called conditional capital contributions. Distributions on the liquidation of a corporation are taxed as if the shares had been sold.

In *India*, dividends are limited to amounts distributed out of a company's accumulated profits. In contrast, in *China*, distributions are not specifically related to corporate earnings. However, dividend distributions are linked to the circumstances under which the board of directors can declare dividends under corporate law and are thus implicitly linked to corporate earnings. In the case of shares with a fixed rate of dividends, payments of dividends where the corporate earnings are inadequate may not be taxed as dividends for purposes of the intercorporate dividends exemption.

5.3 Constructive Dividends

With the exception of China, all the systems studied here have either statutory or case law principles that tax as distributions benefits received by shareholders without the formal declaration of a dividend or profit distribution. In some situations, the payment is treated as a dividend for all purposes, although often, to discourage such payments, they do not carry the imputation credit or qualify for intercorporate dividend relief.

The *United States* system has case law rules which treat shareholder benefits as dividends. Under a special provision, unreasonable compensation may be disallowed as a deduction at the corporate level even where the payment is not formally recharacterized as a dividend to the shareholder, although the rule is normally applied only in the case of payments to shareholders.[133] Loans to shareholders may be treated as dividends.[134] Even where a loan is not recharacterized, if the loan does not bear a stipulated interest rate, under a special statutory rule, a dividend in the amount of the foregone interest is imputed to the shareholder, followed by a deemed transfer of that amount of interest to the corporation.[135] The deemed interest payment may be deductible by the shareholder, subject to the normal limitations, and is included in the income of the corporation.

In *France*, deemed distributions can arise in two situations. The first involves distributions in situations where the corporation did not receive an appropriate benefit for the payment. Such an "abnormal management decision" (*acte anormal de gestion*) results in a taxable distribution. A 2018 case[136] defines this act as one "by which a company decides to impoverish itself for purposes alien to its interest"—in other words, there must be an intention on the part of the company to impoverish itself and the company must actually be impoverished. Typical situations involve bargain sales or rentals of corporate assets, payment of personal expenses, and the like. Abnormal benefits granted to third parties who are not shareholders may also be treated as constructive dividends insofar as, after such benefits have been reinstated in the corporation's taxable income, the corporation realizes a taxable profit.[137] A second set

133. United States, IRC, s. 162(a)(1); Treas. Regs., 1.162-7(b)(1).
134. *See*, for example, *Crowley v. Commissioner*, 962 F.2d 1077 (1st Cir., 1992).
135. United States, IRC, s. 7872.
136. Conseil d'Etat, Assemblée plénière, December 21, 2018, n°402006 (*Croë Suisse*).
137. *See* France, CGI, s. 109, as construed by the Conseil d'Etat.

of rules dealing with irregular distributions deems sums made available to shareholders directly or through intermediaries as advances, loans, or down payments to be distributions until proven otherwise.[138] Deemed distributions can also arise from hidden distributions[139] and disguised distributions.[140] Hidden distributions include hidden remuneration for a service, function, or even a loan, granted to a third party outside the company's interests and not recorded in the accounts, as well as the concealment of receipts where it is not known how the receipt was used. Disguised distributions refer to a range of situations which have gradually emerged in case law, such as a debt forgiveness granted by a company to a shareholder, misappropriations by a shareholder, or the sale or lease of company assets to shareholders for less than their market value.

In *Canada*, any benefit conferred by a corporation on a shareholder must be included in the shareholder's taxable income.[141] Typical situations are bargain purchases and sales, rent-free use of property, and payment of personal expenses. A special rule, with some exceptions (such as loans to shareholders who are also employees for the purpose of acquiring a home, automobile, or shares of the corporation) treats as income loans by a corporation to an individual shareholder or related person if the loan is not repaid within one year.[142] These various shareholder benefits must be included in the shareholder's income but are not treated as dividends. As a result, they do not qualify for either the imputation credit or the intercorporate dividend deduction.

In *Australia*, specific legislation treats certain benefits provided to shareholders in closely held companies as non-deductible dividends—in particular, bargain sales of property, rent-free use of property, interest-free loans, forgiveness of shareholder debts, and excessive compensation or retirement benefits to shareholder-employees or associates.[143] Payment of personal expenses would typically be covered by the fringe benefits tax. As in Canada, the constructive dividend does not bring with it an imputation credit, except in hardship cases at the discretion of the tax administration.[144] The rules are highly complex and many attempts have been made to circumvent them. Australia's GAAR is likely to be applied to schemes which avoid the rules.

The *United Kingdom* also has special rules dealing with shareholder loans in the closely held context, which broaden the concept of "distribution" to cover benefits in kind provided by a closely held corporation to its shareholders.[145] In addition, a rule applicable to all corporations (but which is most frequently applied to closely held corporations) may treat a transfer of assets or liabilities to shareholders (or vice versa) for less than their value as a distribution.[146] This rule applies where value passes from

138. France, CGI, s. 111 a.
139. France, CGI, s. 111 c.
140. France, CGI, ss. 109 to 111.
141. Canada, ITA, s. 15(1).
142. Canada, ITA, s. 15(2).
143. Australia, ITAA 1936, s. 109-109F.
144. Australia, ITAA 1936, s. 109RB; ITAA 1997, s. 202-45(g).
145. United Kingdom, Corporation Tax Act 2010, ss. 455 and 1064.
146. United Kingdom, Corporation Tax Act 2010, s. 1020.

a corporation to a shareholder. By contrast, where in such a transaction value passes from a shareholder to a corporation, there is no reclassification of the transaction as a contribution to capital.

Dutch case law also deals with constructive dividends. Benefits to shareholders in their capacity as shareholders are generally taxable as dividends where both the corporation and the shareholder were aware (or should have been aware) of the advantage to the shareholder.[147]

In *Sweden*, prior to the 1990s, special statutory provisions dealt with constructive dividends in the case of closely held corporations, sometimes resulting in heavier taxation than would have applied to actual dividends. These rules were abandoned in order to provide more favorable treatment for small businesses and because the basic tax rules were considered sufficient to deal with constructive dividends. A special rule is still applicable to all types of corporate loans made to shareholders which are considered to be improper under company law. Such transactions are taxed in full as dividend distributions even where the loans are at arm's length. The rule was introduced in response to owners of closely held corporations refraining from taking dividends or salary from the corporation and instead using loans to receive funds from the corporation. For individual shareholders, these dividends are taxed as earned income;[148] for corporate shareholders, such loans are normally not taxable as dividends.[149]

Constructive dividends are most common with respect to closely held corporations. Where the distributing corporation does not receive appropriate consideration for the distribution, the distribution is taxed as a dividend. However, if the shareholder is also employed by the corporation, the distribution is normally taxed as earned income. In the case of publicly held corporations, constructive dividends arise occasionally, but minor benefits, such as rebates to shareholders for purchases in the corporation's stores, are not taxed since they have been found to be offered primarily for commercial reasons.

Germany has a statutory basis and highly developed case law for the treatment of constructive dividends.[150] Any transaction between a shareholder and corporation which is not undertaken at arm's length is a potential constructive dividend. To avoid constructive-dividend treatment, agreements between shareholder and corporation must meet the "prudent manager" test and must be shown to be in the interests of the corporation and not simply undertaken to benefit the shareholder. Agreements between the corporation and its controlling shareholder must be legally binding, formulated in clear terms, and concluded in advance. If the agreement deviates from the "standard," there is a danger that the courts will hold the whole transfer of assets (not just the "excessive" part) to be a constructive dividend. Moreover, even arm's length contracts may lead to constructive dividends if the courts find that they are aimed at "siphoning off" substantial parts of the company's profit. For large companies, dealings

147. Netherlands, Supreme Court, December 30, 1953, nr. 11.555, BNB 1954/61.
148. Sweden, ITA, Ch. 11 para. 45.
149. Sweden, ITA, Ch. 15 para. 3.
150. Germany, CITA, s. 8 para. 3 sent. 2.

between subsidiaries and group-wide transactions are constant sources of contention between taxpayers and the tax administration. For small- and medium-sized companies, the "adequacy" of salaries for executives who are also shareholders, including "reasonable" bonus payments and pension reserves, is the major point of disagreement. Before 2008, due to separate assessment procedures, a constructive dividend could be found at the shareholder level regardless of the treatment at the corporate level, and vice versa. This effect has been eliminated by provisions making shareholder relief provisions for the taxation of dividends dependent on a corresponding adjustment for the constructive dividend at the corporate level.[151]

Japan does not have a specific statutory rule focusing on constructive dividends. However, issues underlying constructive dividends are dealt with by the application of an anti-avoidance rule targeted at closely held corporations and denying deductions for excessive compensation for the management team of a company.

The *Chinese* tax legislation contains no specific rules to treat shareholder benefits as constructive dividends. As noted in section 5.1, in *India,* several types of distributions by companies are treated as dividends, including debentures, deposit certificates, and the consideration for a buyback of shares.[152]

5.4 Intercorporate Dividends and Capital Gains

All the systems analyzed here have special rules dealing with distributions by domestic corporations to domestic corporate shareholders (intercorporate dividends). (Special considerations apply with respect to distributions received from foreign corporations and are discussed in Part IV.) Although the basic purpose of the various provisions is to prevent the "cascading" of levels of corporate tax on distributions which move up a corporate chain to the ultimate individual shareholders, the structures of the provisions have significant differences, both in terms of the degree of relief granted and the techniques used. Because of the possibility of substituting intercorporate capital gains for dividends and vice versa (by paying dividends or retaining earnings and selling the shares), many countries have special rules in these areas. Further, a number of countries seek to achieve consistency in the taxation of intercorporate dividends and corporate capital gains on shareholdings.

In the *United States*, the mechanism for relief is a deduction for a certain percentage of the dividend received, the amount of which varies with the degree of share ownership. In the case of 80% to 100% share ownership, the full amount of the dividend is deductible, while for portfolio investment (below 20%) the amount is 50% of the dividend.[153] Where the stockholder owns at least 20%, but less than 80%, it deducts 65% of the dividend. Corporate capital gains are taxed at normal rates.

A series of special provisions restricts the ability of a corporate shareholder to combine the dividends-received deduction with other deductions. Where a portfolio investment is financed with debt, the dividends-received deduction is reduced in

151. Germany, ITA, s. 3 No. 40 lit. d sent. 2, 3; CITA, s. 8 para. 3 sent. 5.
152. India, ITA, s. 2(22)(b) and (f).
153. United States, IRC, s. 243.

proportion to the amount of the investment financed with debt, thus preventing a tax arbitrage between the fully deductible interest and the partially taxable intercorporate dividend.[154] Similar rules restrict the ability to claim a dividends-received deduction for a dividend and then claim a tax loss attributable to the stock's decline in value immediately after the dividend payment (sometimes referred to as "dividend stripping"). The rules generally require that the stock on which the dividend was received be held for a period of time before a loss on sale is allowed.[155] In the case of an "extraordinary dividend" (a dividend exceeding a certain percentage of the stockholder's tax cost in the stock), the stockholder is required to reduce its tax cost in the stock by the nontaxable portion of the dividend.[156]

Since intercorporate dividends are taxed at a reduced rate while a capital gain on the sale of stock is fully taxable, a corporate shareholder may attempt to withdraw dividends from the corporation prior to a sale in order to reduce the taxable capital gain. Case law principles have limited the use of this technique for "capital gain stripping," especially where the funds used to pay the dividend come indirectly from the buyer.[157] The purported dividend payment is treated as additional sale proceeds.

Canada also allows a deduction for intercorporate dividends but, unlike the situation in the U.S., the relief is complete:[158] 100 % of the dividend is deducted without regard to the degree of share ownership, subject to various exceptions. To prevent closely held corporations from being used as "incorporated pocketbooks" to hold portfolio investments of individuals, dividends received by these corporations are subject to a special refundable tax which is intended to replicate the tax that would have been due if the dividend had been received by an individual shareholder.[159] Other limitations apply to prevent the conversion of taxable capital gains into tax-free dividends. Under these rules, dividends received in some circumstances are deemed to be proceeds of sale of the shares and as such are taxable. The rules are, in effect, limited to gain which is not attributable to previously taxed corporate earnings.[160] Other specific rules deny the intercorporate dividend deduction for dividends received in respect of a "dividend rental arrangement" or "synthetic equity arrangement" and, effective in 2024, for dividends received by financial institutions in respect of shares held as portfolio investments.[161] In addition, no loss is allowed on the sale of stock preceded by a dividend distribution which is entitled to intercorporate dividend relief.[162]

In *Australia*, intercorporate dividend relief is given by means of a shareholder tax credit rather than a deduction. A dividend received by a company is taxable, and relief is given only to the extent that imputation credits are attached to the dividend.[163]

154. United States, IRC, s. 246A.
155. United States, IRC, s. 246(c).
156. United States, IRC, s. 1059.
157. *See*, for example, *Waterman Steamship Corp. v. United States*, 430 F.2d 1185 (5th Cir., 1970).
158. Canada, ITA, s. 112(1).
159. Canada, ITA, Part IV.
160. Canada, ITA, s. 55(2)-(5).
161. Canada, ITA, s. 112(2.01)-(2.9).
162. Canada, ITA, s. 112(3)-(7).
163. Australia, ITAA 1997, Divs 67, 207.

Therefore, if a company receives a dividend which is franked only as to half, it pays tax (typically at 30%) on the other half of the dividend. This change, combined with the introduction of a consolidation regime for corporate groups, has led to a change in the stacking rules for the carryforward of losses and current deductions. Companies now have the option not to claim losses carried forward if the loss would offset tax-free dividends, and current deductions which waste imputation credits are turned into a loss carryforward.[164]

Even with these changes, "dividend-stripping" schemes are still an issue. These schemes typically involve the sale by individuals of stock of closely held corporations which have substantial accumulated earnings. The sale transaction converts the potential dividend income into preferentially taxed (or tax-free) capital gain. The purchasing corporation (the "stripper") could extract the earnings from the purchased corporation on a tax-free basis and then dispose of the stock at a (deductible) loss. Several statutory provisions continue to deal with this technique. First, in some cases, under general anti-avoidance principles, the seller of the shares may be deemed to have received a taxable dividend rather than tax-preferred proceeds of sale.[165] In addition, more specific statutory rules deny the imputation credit to the purchaser.[166] Former problems of "capital gain stripping" transactions are now comprehensively dealt with by taxing the unfranked part of dividends and treating certain distributions of capital as unfranked dividends under several anti-avoidance rules.[167]

In the *United Kingdom*, distributions by a resident corporation to another corporation are generally exempt from corporation tax. In principle, this exemption is available irrespective of whether the profits from which the distribution is made have been subject to UK tax. Capital gains on shares held by corporations are generally taxable. If the corporation selling the shares holds 10% or more of the shares in another corporation which is a trading company, the capital gain is exempt.[168] If a corporation borrows to acquire shares in a resident corporation, the interest expense is deductible, although there are special restrictions on deductibility if the loan is not for the purposes of a trade of the corporation.[169] As in other countries, the UK has dividend-stripping rules which grant broad discretion to the tax administration and other rules which counteract the reduction in the value of shares through excessive intercorporate distributions ("depreciatory transactions" and value shifting).[170] The participation exemption for capital gains is also protected by anti-avoidance rules.

The situation in *Japan* is similar to that in the U.S. in the sense that intercorporate dividends are not fully exempt and capital gains are fully taxed. Intercorporate dividends may be excluded entirely where the share ownership exceeds 33.3%; 50% is

164. Australia, ITAA 1997, Div 36.
165. Australia, ITAA 1936, s. 177E.
166. Australia, ITAA 1997, s. 207-145(1)(d), 207-150(1)(e), 207-155.
167. Australia, ITAA 1936, s. 45, 45A, 45B.
168. United Kingdom, TCGA, Sch. 7AC.
169. *See* the loan-relationship rules in United Kingdom, Corporation Tax Act 2009, Part 5 and, in particular, s. 297.
170. United Kingdom, Income Tax Act 2007, ss. 682-705, Corporation Tax Act 2010, Part 15, and TCGA, ss. 29-31 and 176-177.

excludable in the case of ownership of more than 5% but no more than 33.3%; and only 20% is excludable in the case of ownership of 5% or less.[171] Corporate tax at ordinary rates applies to capital gains on shares held by companies.

France has a participation exemption regime (*regime mère-fille*) for companies which hold at least 5% of the issued capital of a French or foreign subsidiary and have held, or undertaken to hold, the shareholding for more than two years. When certain conditions are met,[172] the parent can elect for the dividend to be exempt, although an amount equal to 5% of the dividend, including tax credits, is non-deductible. In order to comply with European law,[173] the non-deductible amount is reduced to 1% in the case of dividends from members of the same tax consolidated group or dividends received by any nonintegrated French company from a European subsidiary, subject to certain conditions.[174] This regime is elective, but in practically all cases the treatment is more favorable than including the dividend in the tax base. The regime does not apply to dividends from certain subsidiaries engaged in real estate or finance businesses. Capital gains on equity investments held for two years are exempt unless the subsidiary is predominantly involved in a real estate or finance business. Only 12% of the capital gain is taxable, resulting in the exemption of 88% of the gain.[175]

In the *German* system, special rules for intercorporate dividends were introduced by the corporate tax reform in 2000. The legislation initially provided that all intercompany dividends were, in principle, tax-free, regardless of whether they were distributed by German or foreign corporations.[176] Until 2013, the participation exemption applied irrespective of the size of the shareholding in the payer corporation; since 2013, however, it has been restricted to substantial shareholdings of over 10%.[177] This amendment was made in response to a 2011 decision by the CJEU, which held that the German withholding tax on intercompany portfolio dividends distributed by a German corporation to foreign shareholders was an infringement of EU law.[178] Instead of granting foreign shareholders the same treatment afforded to German shareholders, the government decided to exclude from the participation exemption all dividends on nonsubstantial shareholdings.

To deal with gains on shares reflecting undistributed profits which would have been tax-free on distribution, the German legislation also provides for a participation exemption under which all gains on sales of shares by German companies are tax-free.[179] This rule applies to the entire gain, including increases in value which have no relation to retained profits. Unlike the participation exemption for dividends, the exemption for gains does not depend on a minimum shareholding requirement.

171. Japan, CTA, s. 23.
172. France, CGI, s. 145: relating to ownership, shareholding and voting rights, the time period the shares are held, and the subsidiaries held.
173. CJEU, September 2, 2015, C-386-14 (*Groupe Steria SCA*).
174. France, CGI, s. 216.
175. France, CGI, 219 I-a quinquies.
176. Germany, CITA, s. 8b para. 1.
177. Germany, CITA, s. 8b para. 4.
178. CJEU, October 20, 2011, C-284/09.
179. Germany, CITA, s. 8b para. 2.

Expenses (administrative and financial costs) which are related to tax-free dividends or capital gains may be deducted. To mitigate this asymmetry between nontaxable income and deductible expenses, 5% of the relevant income (tax-free dividends or capital gains) is deemed to be nondeductible and is therefore taxed. Thus, in effect, only 95% of intercompany dividends on substantial shareholdings and gains from the sale of shares by a corporation are tax-exempt.[180]

In *The Netherlands*, there is an exclusion for dividends received on "participations," defined generally as a 5% or greater stock interest in the distributing company.[181] The exemption for participations also extends to the gain (and any loss) on the sale of the stock.

Sweden likewise has an exclusion for intercorporate dividends.[182] Dividends from nonlisted corporations are in general exempt, with exceptions for special tax avoidance situations. Other dividends may also be exempt where the recipient corporation has a 10% or greater voting interest in the distributing corporation or there is a business relationship between the two corporations. For other "portfolio" investments, the dividend is taxable in full. In addition, in 2003, Sweden introduced a participation exemption for capital gains and losses. Where the conditions described above for dividends are met, an exemption applies for both capital gains and losses. The rules were intended to eliminate a "third" layer of corporate tax. Moreover, by making capital losses nondeductible, taxpayers are prevented from manipulating exempt foreign capital gains and deductible domestic capital losses.

The *Chinese* rules are relatively simple. Dividends received by a resident enterprise are exempt from EIT, unless the shares on which dividends are paid are listed shares held for less than 12 months. Capital gains do not qualify for exemption. The EIT legislation contains no rules to prevent the conversion of dividends into capital gains or vice versa, although the GAAR could apply to such transactions.

In *India*, intercorporate dividends are deductible from the income of the receiving domestic company.

5.5 Distributions of Appreciated or Depreciated Property

When appreciated or depreciated property is distributed, if the gain or loss is not recognized at the corporate level at the time of distribution, it will no longer be subject to the corporate taxing regime. While the logic of treating distributions as a taxable event seems clear, the *United States* initially did not take this approach: neither gain nor loss was recognized on distribution. However, in 1986 the rule was changed. The rules apply whether the shareholder is an individual or a corporation.

In the case of ongoing dividend distributions, gain is recognized on the distribution of appreciated property, but loss is not recognized.[183] The limitation with respect to property with an accrued loss reflects the fact that the timing of the distribution is

180. Germany, CITA, s. 8b paras. 3, 5.
181. Netherlands, CIT, Art. 13.
182. Sweden, ITA, Ch. 24.
183. United States, IRC, s. 311.

within the control of the taxpayer. However, as a result, the possibility of deducting the loss on the property is totally eliminated, since the shareholder takes the fair market value of the property as the tax cost. Where property is distributed in complete liquidation of the corporation, both gains and losses are recognized because the possibility of shareholder manipulation is not present.[184] However, there are restrictions on the deductibility of losses on property which has recently been contributed to the corporation. Distributions on the liquidation of an 80%-owned corporate subsidiary are not taxed; the parent corporation takes the historical cost of the assets as its tax cost.[185]

The other systems reviewed here typically require the recognition of gain or loss on property distributions. In *Canada*, the corporation is considered to have disposed of the property at its fair market value, while the shareholder includes the fair market value in income as a dividend and is considered to have acquired the property at a cost equal to that fair market value.[186] These rules are intended to ensure that the consequences of a dividend in kind are the same as those for a sale of the corporate assets followed by the distribution of the proceeds. In *Germany*, any distribution of an appreciated asset is a realization event, regardless of whether the distribution is treated as a dividend to the shareholder or as a return of capital. Similarly, in *The Netherlands*, the distribution is a taxable event, although there is the possibility, where certain conditions are met, of deferring the tax on the gain by the use of a reinvestment reserve if the property is going to be replaced (i.e., the amount reserved is intended to be reinvested in similar property).[187] In *Sweden*, the distribution is treated as the removal of the assets from the business, which is in principle a recognition event. *Australia*, as well, treats the distribution of an asset as subject to CGT at the corporate level. Where the transferor is a 100% subsidiary of the transferee, either a rollover is available on the transfer if the companies concerned cannot consolidate (e.g., if a nonresident company is involved), or the transaction is ignored in consolidation. Special rules restrict the ability to use such property distributions to shift value among shares. These rules were considerably strengthened in 2002.[188] The *United Kingdom* rules are similar to those in Australia, although the threshold for rollover on transfer between group corporations is 75%.[189]

The *Japanese* rules are similar to those in Canada. With respect to dividends in kind, shareholders are subject to income tax on the fair value of the distributed property as a dividend, and that fair value constitutes their cost basis. In turn, a distributing corporation must recognize gain or loss based on the fair value of the property.[190]

In *France*, there is no developed law on the distribution of appreciated or depreciated property as a normal dividend, although for accounting purposes it would

184. United States, IRC, s. 336.
185. United States, IRC, ss. 332 and 334(b).
186. Canada, ITA, s. 52(2).
187. Netherlands, ITA 2001, Art. 3.54.
188. Australia, ITAA 1997, Div 126-B, s. 701-1; for value shifting, *see* Divs 725, 727.
189. United Kingdom, TCGA, s. 171.
190. Japan, CTA, s. 22-2.

be treated as a recognition of gain, and this treatment is considered applicable for corporate tax purposes as well. In the case of liquidations, the rules are fully developed. The distributing corporation must realize all gains and losses on distributed assets, which are taxed as capital gain or ordinary income, as the case may be. In addition, any income items which have previously escaped tax as deferred income or tax-free provisions must also be included in the tax base.

The *Chinese* EIT legislation contains no specific rules on these types of distributions. Transfers would likely be treated as taking place at market value and might also be treated as dividends if the value of the transfer exceeds the contributed capital. In *India*, distributions of property in the form of dividends are taxable as dividends to the extent of the company's accumulated profits, but as a capital gain to the extent that the value of the property exceeds the accumulated profits.

5.6 Distributions Involving Changes in Corporate Capital Structure

5.6.1 General

Apart from formal or constructive dividends, many changes in corporate capital structure may involve distributions to shareholders. Typical examples are distributions in connection with a reduction in capital or a redemption of outstanding shares, or the capitalization of earnings through an increase in stated capital followed by a stock dividend. In all these situations, the distribution must be characterized for tax purposes. A recurring issue is the extent to which the corporate or commercial law characterization of the transaction is controlling for tax purposes. The systems show wide variation in this regard.

In the *United States*, as a general matter, the corporate law aspects of a change in the capitalization of a corporation are not relevant for tax purposes. Thus, if a corporation formally reduces its capital and repays that amount to its shareholders, the distribution is taxed as a dividend as long as the corporation has earnings for tax purposes; the fact that, from a corporate law point of view, the payment is a return of invested capital, is of no significance.[191] Similarly, if a corporation increases its stated capital by transferring undistributed earnings to the capital account, the corporate transfer has no effect on the "pool" of earnings for tax purposes which determines the taxability of later distributions.[192]

In the systems of most other countries, corporate law concepts play a more important role in determining the treatment of such distributions. In *Canada*, for example, amounts received by the shareholder from a reduction in the paid-in capital of a corporation, other than a public corporation, can be received tax-free.[193] However, where the amount received exceeds the portion of stated capital allocated to the shares, the excess is taxed as a dividend, regardless of the absence of accumulated profits. Similarly, where a reserve against earnings (corporate surplus) is transferred to capital,

191. United States, IRC, s. 316(a) and s. 312.
192. *Ibid.*
193. Canada, ITA, s. 84(4) and (4.1).

subject to some exceptions, the transfer is deemed to be a dividend since, after the earnings have been transferred to the capital account, they can be repaid free of tax.[194] In some circumstances, distributions of capital by publicly traded companies are fully taxable as dividends.

Australia has extensive rules to deal with problems of this kind, one of which has already been covered (streaming of capital distributions). In addition, if profits are converted to capital, the share capital account of the company becomes "tainted," with significant consequences: there is an immediate loss of an amount of available imputation credits, and all distributions out of share capital are thereafter treated as unfrankable dividends (so that they are taxed in full without imputation credits). The company can "untaint" the share capital account by utilizing a process operated through the imputation system, which effectively leads to a tax rate of 48% on the transferred profits.[195] In 2023, a further amendment was made to deny imputation credits where a franked dividend is substantially funded by a raising of capital.[196]

In the *United Kingdom*, payments effecting a reduction in capital are not treated as distributions. This rule extends to repayments of loan capital even where the interest payment itself is treated as a distribution. There is one exception: the repayment of capital on stock dividend shares (within certain periods of time, either before or after the issue of the shares) is treated as a distribution.[197]

In *France*, a capital reduction effected to eliminate balance sheet losses and not accompanied by a distribution to shareholders does not give rise to taxation. Other capital reductions result in taxable distributions to shareholders, although the tax consequences differ depending on the nature of the capital reduction. For example, where shares held by individual shareholders are cancelled, the sums allocated are considered to be a taxable distribution, except in the case of the repayment of capital contributions or share premiums.[198]

Germany also allows the repayment of stated capital or capital reserves on a tax-free basis.[199] In the case of capital reserves, they may be distributed only after all profits and profit reserves have been used up.[200] For corporations based in other EU countries, tax-free repayment is possible but depends on a formal request by the relevant corporation.[201] For corporations based in non-EU countries, the tax administration had refused to treat repayments of capital as tax-free, in spite of diverging recent judgments by the Federal Tax Court, but in 2023, the exemption was extended to repayments of capital irrespective of whether the seat of the corporation is inside or outside the EU.

If the shareholder holds the stock as a business asset or owns 1% or more of the stock, the distribution of the stated capital or capital reserves is deemed to be a

194. Canada, ITA, s. 84(1).
195. Australia, ITAA 1997, Div 197.
196. Australia, ITAA 1997, ss. 202-45(ea), 207-159.
197. United Kingdom, Corporation Tax Act 2010, ss. 1022-1027A.
198. France, CGI, s. 112.
199. Germany, ITA, s. 20 para. 1 No. 2.
200. Germany, CITA, s. 27 para. 1 sent. 3.
201. Germany, CITA, s. 27 para. 8.

disposal.[202] The distribution reduces the acquisition cost of the stock and can result in a taxable gain if it exceeds that amount.

In contrast, *Sweden* treats distributions of the amount of a reduction in the nominal value of stock as a dividend, without regard to the existence of corporate profits.

Japanese corporate law does not tie a change in the capitalization of a company to distributions to shareholders, and the tax rules follow this corporate law approach. Any change in the capitalization of a company, including a reduction or increase of statutory capital by way of a transfer from profits or capital reserve, has no impact on that company's income tax liability, and a distribution to shareholders on a reduction of capital is simply treated as a dividend payment to shareholders.

Since the *Chinese* EIT legislation contains no specific rules, the tax treatment of such distributions is determined on a case-by-case basis in accordance with the substance of the transaction. Where the substance is that of a distribution, it will likely be treated as a distribution.

In *India*, the Supreme Court has held that the amount distributed by a company on the reduction of its share capital has two components: distributions attributable to accumulated profits, which are treated as dividends,[203] and distributions attributable to capital (except capitalized profits), which are treated as a capital gain to the extent that they exceed the original cost of the acquisition of the shares.[204]

5.6.2 Stock Dividends

The distribution of dividends in the form of stock or "bonus" shares to existing shareholders typically involves a transfer for corporate law purposes of retained earnings into stated capital. It can be viewed as a deemed distribution of a cash dividend to the shareholders followed by a corresponding contribution to capital, or solely as an event at the corporate level which has no effect on the shareholders, whose economic interest in the corporation is unchanged by the receipt of additional shares. The countries examined here have taken varied approaches to the stock dividend problem. The particular treatment adopted is often a function of the rules dealing with distributions of stated capital.

The *United States* rules on the taxation of stock dividends are quite detailed. The basic rule is fairly straightforward: pro rata distributions of common stock of the same class as the stock on which the distribution is being made are not taxable.[205] The principal justification behind the rule is that there has not been a significant change of position of the shareholder as a result of the distribution, but the shareholder simply has more pieces of paper (share certificates) representing an unchanged underlying investment. Thus, the receipt of a pro rata common stock dividend should not be characterized as a distribution of the underlying corporate profits. This rule is possible

202. Germany, ITA, s. 17 para. 4.
203. India, ITA 1961, s. 2(22(e)).
204. *CIT v. G. Narasimhan* (SC 14/12/1998).
205. United States, IRC, s. 305(a).

in part because the U.S. system ignores the effects of the capitalization of earnings for corporate tax purposes which typically accompanies a stock dividend. As soon as one moves beyond the simple pro rata stock distribution, however, the situation becomes more complex. Where the shareholder has the right to choose between a cash dividend and a stock dividend, the stock dividend is taxable, even if all shareholders elect to receive stock and the distribution is thus pro rata.[206] The shareholder is in effect deemed to have received the equivalent of the cash dividend which the shareholder could have received.

Where the distribution is not pro rata, and thus results in an increase in the proportionate interest of the shareholders receiving the stock dividend, the distribution is generally taxable.[207] Technically, the distribution is taxable if it results in the increase in the proportionate interest of some shareholders and the receipt of a property distribution by others. Thus, for example, where a corporation has two classes of stock, one of which pays stock dividends and the other of which pays cash dividends, the stock dividends would be taxable. A series of stock redemptions which result in an increase in the proportionate interests of shareholders who do not have their stock redeemed may also be treated as a taxable stock dividend to the non-redeemed stockholders.[208]

The rules in other jurisdictions are simpler, and the results are varied. In *Sweden*, in principle, stock dividends are not subject to tax, being viewed as the equivalent of a split in the old stock. The tax cost of the old shares is allocated between the old shares and the new shares of the same type. If the stock is of a different class or type, it has a tax cost of zero. In *Japan*, stock dividends are no longer possible as a matter of corporate law, while stock splits are still possible but do not have any income tax implications.

In *The Netherlands*, stock dividends received by individuals are taxed as "box 3" income; i.e., they are not taxed as such but, as with all capital income, a deemed yield is taxed based on the value of the shares.[209] Where the stock dividend is received by an individual holder of a "substantial interest" (at least 5% of the shares), it is tax-free. Stock dividends are generally subject to dividend withholding tax on their nominal value,[210] but the tax withheld is credited or refunded to resident shareholders.[211] An exemption from the dividend withholding tax applies to qualifying corporate shareholders that reside within the EU or in a tax treaty jurisdiction and have a qualifying share interest of least 5% ("participation").[212]

In *Canada*, in general, a stock dividend is treated as a taxable dividend to the extent that the stated capital of the corporation is increased as a result of the payment

206. United States, IRC, s. 305(b)(1).
207. United States, IRC, s. 305(b)(2).
208. United States, IRC, s. 305(c). United States, Treas. Reg, s. 1.305-3(b)(3) (last sentence).
209. Netherlands, ITA 2001, Art. 5.2.
210. Netherlands, ITA, Art. 4.13.2.
211. Certain nonresident shareholders may also be entitled to a refund pursuant to the EU free movement of capital rules; compare Netherlands, Dividend Withholding Tax Act 1965 (DWTA), s. 10a.
212. Netherlands, DWTA, s. 4.

of the stock dividend.[213] Because the capitalized earnings can be distributed tax-free in certain circumstances, it is necessary to tax the earnings at the time they are capitalized.

Australia also taxes certain stock dividends which capitalize profits; the dividends carry with them the imputation credit, with the tax cost of the total shareholding increased by the amount of the dividend. This allows corporations wishing to retain after-tax income for commercial purposes to capitalize the income through the stock dividend, resulting, in effect, in full integration of corporate and individual tax on undistributed earnings. However, as a result of the tainting of share capital rules referred to above, this treatment is effectively available only for dividend reinvestment plans, under which a shareholder elects to receive shares instead of dividends.[214] Australia also permits stock splits, bonus issues which do not alter share capital or profit reserves (functionally equivalent to stock splits), and stock consolidations which do not result in any transfer of profit reserves to stated capital, on a tax-free basis. The tax cost of the original shares is spread over the cost of the new or consolidated shares.[215] Australia also permits so-called bonus plans for listed companies, under which shareholders can elect to receive bonus shares in place of dividends, but the shares are not treated as dividends and tax cost spreading applies.[216] The mechanism is different from that of dividend reinvestment plans, although the two are economically equivalent. Such plans are attractive to shareholders who are not subject to the CGT, but they run the risk of the application of the capital manipulation rules mentioned above. They also waste imputation credits by reducing the company tax available for franking future dividends (usually resulting in an implicit tax of 30% on the value of the bonus shares).

As a general rule, the *United Kingdom* does not tax the issue of stock dividends (called "bonus shares") and the cost of the original shares is spread over those shares and the bonus shares.[217] There are exceptions to this treatment. The amount paid up as share capital on the issue of bonus shares may be treated as a distribution where the issue is made within ten years of a share-capital reduction. Similarly, share capital repaid within ten years after a bonus issue may be treated as a distribution.[218] The other exception is similar to the treatment in the U.S. where the taxpayer has the choice of receiving dividends or bonus shares. In this case, an election in favor of shares gives rise to a distribution, usually in the amount of the cash dividend foregone, and a cost in the shares of an equal amount.[219]

French law distinguishes between stock dividends and other share mechanisms resulting in the capitalization of reserves or earnings. In the case of stock dividends, the

213. Canada, ITA, s. 248(1). "Dividend" is defined to include a stock dividend, and "amount" is defined to prescribe the amount of a stock dividend.
214. Australia, ITAA 1936, s. 6BA(5).The use of dividend reinvestment plans is curtailed by the changes referred to in section 5.6.1 to deny imputation credits where a franked dividend is substantially funded by a capital raising.
215. Australia, ITAA 1936, s. 6BA(3), ITAA 1997, ss. 112-25, 124-240, 130-20.
216. Australia, ITAA 1936, s. 6BA(6), ITAA 1997, s. 130-20.
217. United Kingdom, TCGA, s. 127.
218. United Kingdom, Corporation Tax Act 2010, ss. 1022-1027A.
219. United Kingdom, Corporation Tax Act 2010, s. 1049.

shareholder has a choice under corporate law. In principle, dividends are payable in cash, but they may also be paid in kind (*en nature*) for certain types of company (e.g., in the form of securities held in the company's portfolio). If a stock dividend is chosen, it is taxable in the same way as a cash dividend, similar to the situation in the UK and the U.S.

Germany represents another variation in approach. Generally, stock dividends are considered to be emoluments from capital and treated as taxable income.[220] The distributed shares are recognized at market value.[221] However, the allocation of new stock in the course of a formal increase in capital created from reserves is not subject to tax. The acquisition costs of the old shares are split between the old shares and the new shares of the same type. However, subsequent repayment of capital increases resulting from stock dividends leads to taxable dividends.

In *India*, the tax treatment of bonus shares depends on whether the shares are issued to equity shareholders or preference shareholders. In the case of equity shareholders, the cost of acquisition of the bonus shares is nil and the recognition of capital gain is postponed until the shares are alienated. In contrast, the issue of bonus shares to preference shareholders (to the extent that the company possesses accumulated profits) is treated as a dividend.[222]

5.6.3 Redemptions

The legal form of a redemption of shares by a corporation is a purchase by the corporation of its own stock from its existing shareholders. Where that characterization of a redemption is followed for tax purposes, the shareholder would have a gain or loss on the shares determined by the difference between the tax cost of the shares and the amount received. This gain or loss would be treated under the normal rules dealing with property dispositions. Thus, the gain might be fully taxable, taxed at a preferential rate, or exempt from tax depending on the structure of the capital gains regime. However, a redemption differs from a sale to a third party in that property is leaving the corporation and placed in the hands of the shareholder, which is similar in some respects to a dividend distribution or a repayment of stated capital. There is a wide variation in the manner in which the systems treat redemption transactions.

In the *United States*, specific statutory rules deal with redemptions.[223] A redemption is not treated as a distribution of profits if it is "not essentially equivalent to a dividend." There is substantial case law dealing with this standard, focusing on whether the taxpayer has had a "meaningful reduction" in the taxpayer's ownership interest in the distributing corporation. In addition to this general standard, there are several "safe haven" rules. If the distribution is "substantially disproportionate," exchange treatment is applicable. To meet this test, the shareholder must have a more than 20% reduction in the shareholder's ownership interest in the corporation and

220. Germany, ITA, s. 20 para. 1 No. 1.
221. Federal Tax Court, *Bundesfinanzhof*, April 11, 2018, I R 34/15.
222. India, ITA 1961, s. 2(22)(b).
223. United States, IRC, s. 302.

must own less than 50% of the corporation after the redemption. Thus, a redemption that reduces a shareholder's interest from 50% to 39% would qualify for sale treatment. A redemption which terminates a shareholder's interest is also treated as an exchange.

In applying these tests, stock owned by related persons and entities is attributed to the shareholder whose stock is being redeemed. Thus, in the above example, if the remaining stock in the corporation were owned by the taxpayer's spouse or child, the redemption would not qualify. The ownership rules based on family relationship are waived in some cases, such as where the shareholder being redeemed sells all the shares owned.

Any redemption which does not qualify as an exchange under the general test or the various safe havens is taxable as a dividend to an individual shareholder to the extent that it represents a distribution of earnings and profits.[224] For a corporate shareholder, a redemption which is not treated as an exchange would qualify for intercompany dividend relief. The tax cost of the redeemed shares is attributed to the remaining shares.

In the other systems, redemptions tend to take place less frequently, often because the reduction in stated capital with which a redemption is often accompanied is a complex procedure as a matter of corporate law. In addition, the corporate law accounting for the redemption may have an important influence on the tax treatment.

In *Japan*, the capital account of a corporation is divided for purposes of income tax into the profit reserve and capital (which consists of stated capital and capital surplus). The amounts of the profit reserve and capital are calculated in a different manner from similar concepts under the Company Law even though the profit reserve is, in many cases, equivalent to the accumulated earnings, and the capital is, in many cases, similar to the sum of the paid-in capital and the capital surplus under the Company Law. In the case of redemptions, any amount distributed to shareholders exceeding the proportionate amount of capital is taxed as a dividend. The difference between the remaining amount of the distribution (the proportionate amount of capital) and the book value of the shares is taxed as a capital gain (or recognized as a capital loss).[225]

In *Canada*, concepts are similar but the system is somewhat differently structured. In the case of redemptions, the shareholder is deemed to receive the paid-up capital of the redeemed shares first on a tax-free basis, regardless of whether the redemption changes the shareholder's proportionate interest in the corporation.[226] If the amount received on the redemption exceeds the paid-up capital of the shares redeemed, the excess is taxed as a dividend. The redemption transaction is also treated as a disposition for capital gains purposes. However, for this purpose, the proceeds of disposition are reduced by any amount deemed to be a dividend.[227] Accordingly, on the one hand, if the acquisition cost of the shares is more than their paid-up capital, a

224. United States, IRC, s. 301.
225. Japan, ITA, s. 25 and Japan, CTA, s. 24.
226. Canada, ITA, s. 84(3).
227. Canada, ITA, s. 53(2)(a)(iv) and s. 54 definition of "proceeds of disposition," para. (j).

capital loss results; on the other hand, if the acquisition cost is less than the paid-up capital, a capital gain results. As an exception to these rules, gains on shares acquired by a corporation in open-market transactions are taxed to the seller entirely as capital gains.[228]

Australia also treats buybacks involving traded stock as sale transactions for the shareholder where the purchase occurs in the ordinary course of trading on the stock exchange. In other situations, if the company is not a listed public company, the purchase price is treated as a dividend to the extent that it exceeds the amount charged to share capital in the buyback.[229] The dividend portion carries an imputation credit. Where the redemption involves traded stock but the transaction occurs off-market, the shareholder receives sale treatment; however, the transaction is still treated as a dividend from the company's perspective to the extent that it exceeds the amount charged to share capital, with the result that imputation credits are lost to the company (and not accessible by the shareholder).[230] There are limits on creating capital losses for company shareholders.

Off-market buybacks by listed companies had become an important capital-management tool for them because imputation credits were attached to the buyback price, but from 2024 the buyback payment is no longer treated as a dividend (although there is still a debit to the franking account).[231] It is also possible to achieve share redemptions by a reduction of capital which extinguishes the share. In this event, the entire amount received is treated as paid out of share capital unless any of the anti-avoidance rules referred to above are applied (such as those for capital manipulation).[232]

In *France*, recent statutory provisions have clarified and simplified the tax status of gains on redemptions. Since 2015, the sums attributed to shareholders are no longer considered to be distributed income; instead, they are taxed under the capital gains regime. Such gains are taxable according to the status and/or activity of the shareholder and are eligible for corresponding exemptions or standard deductions, provided that the required conditions are met.[233]

In *Germany*, there was serious discussion as to whether a redemption should be regarded as a "partial liquidation" of the company, which would have led to dividend-like treatment. Ultimately, however, the tax administration decided to treat redemptions like any other share transaction. This treatment remains unchanged even though the 2010 accounting law reform (*Bilanzrechtsmodernisierungsgesetz*) reignited the

228. Canada, ITA, s. 84(6).
229. Australia, ITAA 1936, Pt III Div 16K.
230. Australia, ITAA 1997, s. 205-30(1) Table Item 9.
231. Australia, *Treasury Laws Amendment (2023 Measures No. 1) Act 2023*, Schedule 4.
232. Australia, ITAA 1936, s. 6(1) definition of dividend para. (d), ITAA 1997, ss. 104-125. Under the legislation referred to in *infra* note 294, if there is a selective reduction of capital for some shareholders in a listed public company and not all the distribution is debited to the share capital account, the excess over the amount debited is not a frankable dividend, meaning that shareholders get no benefit from the imputation system in relation to the distribution but there is a debit to the company's franking account in a similar way as for share buybacks by listed companies.
233. France, CGI, s. 112 6°.

discussion because, for commercial accounting purposes, the new rules treat a redemption like a capital reduction, thus excluding its qualification as a regular acquisition by the corporation. In 2013, the tax administration clarified that, although tax law will follow commercial accounting law with regard to the characterization in the corporation's accounts, redemptions will still be taxed like regular share transactions with respect to the shareholder. As a result, the capital gain resulting from the redemption is subject to a mixed regime. Sixty percent of the capital gain is taxable in the hands of the taxpayer at the applicable individual tax rate if the participation amounts to at least 1% of the share capital (this is hardly ever the case for portfolio investments) or is held in a business context. Capital gains from a redemption of shares which are held as private assets are subject to a final withholding tax of 25%.

In *The Netherlands*, a redemption payment is considered to be income of the shareholder to the extent that the amount distributed on the redemption exceeds the allocated share of average paid-in capital. As "box 3" income, however, it is not taxed as such but rather, as with all capital income, a deemed yield is taxed based on the value of the shares.[234] In cases where the shareholder owns a "substantial interest" in the company that redeems the shares, the gain or loss realized by the shareholder on such redemption is treated like any capital gain or loss made in respect of shares which are part of the "substantial interest."

In *Sweden*, share redemptions are treated as a sale. In the *United Kingdom*, where the redeeming corporation is engaged in a trade and its shares are not quoted on an exchange, the redemption is treated as a capital transaction, with capital gains consequences.[235] Capital gain treatment is available, however, only if the company can establish a business purpose for the redemption and other anti-avoidance tests do not apply. Where the conditions for capital gain treatment are not met, the excess of the amount distributed over the amount paid up on the shares is treated as a distribution.[236] Such distributions are normally exempt in the hands of a corporate shareholder, but this does not extend to any corporation tax on capital gains.[237] Shareholders that have their shares bought back on the market receive capital gains treatment.

In *India*, until 2024, where a company acquired its own shares by way of the redemption of the shares, the shareholders were required to recognize capital gains. To avoid DDT on dividends, some privately held companies, instead of paying dividends, used accumulated profits to buy back shares. As a result, in 2013, a new 20% tax was imposed on the buyback of unlisted shares.[238] In 2019, the tax was extended to the buyback of shares of listed companies. In both cases, the tax is imposed on the company; the distributions are received tax-free by the shareholders.[239] Despite the elimination of the DDT as described in the overview in section 1, the buyback tax continued to apply and the distribution is tax-free in the hands of the shareholders. In the 2024 budget, the buyback tax was abolished and an acquisition by a company of its

234. Netherlands, ITA 2001, Art. 5.1.
235. United Kingdom, Corporation Tax Act 2010, ss. 1033-1048.
236. United Kingdom, Corporation Tax Act 2010, s. 1000(1)B.
237. United Kingdom, Corporation Tax Act 2009, s. 931RA.
238. India, ITA, s. 115QA.
239. India, ITA, s. 10(34A).

own shares is treated as a dividend for the shareholder;[240] in addition, the shareholder is allowed to claim a capital loss equal to the cost of the shares bought back by the company.

6 LIQUIDATIONS

The liquidation of a corporation is the last opportunity to tax at the shareholder level any undistributed corporate profits which have not yet borne shareholder tax. It is also an occasion to tax shareholders on the appreciation in value of their stock investments. The systems vary considerably in the extent to which they emphasize one or the other of these two aspects of liquidation.

In the *United States*, a liquidating distribution is treated entirely as an exchange transaction. The corporation has a gain or loss to the extent that appreciated or depreciated assets are involved, and the individual shareholder has a capital gain or loss determined by the difference between the tax cost of the shares and the fair market value of the distribution.[241] The property received on liquidation takes its fair market value as its tax cost.[242] No attempt is made to tax the undistributed corporate profits as a dividend; the assets which they represent are simply included in the calculation of capital gain or loss.

Where the liquidating corporation is a subsidiary (at least 80%-owned) of a corporate shareholder, the liquidation is tax-free to both the distributing corporation and the corporate shareholder.[243] The assets transferred to the corporate parent retain their tax cost in the hands of the subsidiary; the parent's tax cost in the stock simply disappears.[244]

This pattern of rules makes the form and timing of the liquidation important. If, for example, a corporation first makes a dividend distribution and then a liquidating distribution to an individual shareholder, the dividend is taxed in full, while the (reduced) amount received on liquidation is treated as a tax-free return of the shareholder's cost and as a capital gain to the extent that it exceeds such cost. If the entire amount were distributed in liquidation, only the return of the shareholder's cost is tax-free and capital gain treatment applies to any excess. In contrast, a dividend paid to a corporate shareholder would qualify for the dividends-received deduction, while a distribution on liquidation would be taxed in full as capital gain to the extent that the liquidating distribution exceeds the corporate shareholder's cost in the shares.

Many of the other systems use the occasion of a liquidation to tax the accumulated corporate profits as a dividend and to allow the repayment of the paid-up capital on a tax-free basis. In *Canada*, where a corporation makes a liquidating distribution, the rules are essentially the same as for a redemption of stock.[245] In general, the

240. India, ITA, s. 2(22)(f).
241. United States, IRC, ss. 331 and 336.
242. United States, IRC, s. 334(a).
243. United States, IRC, ss. 332 and 337.
244. United States, IRC, s. 334(b).
245. Canada, ITA, s. 84(2).

taxpayer's share of paid-up capital can be received on a tax-free basis; any additional amount received by the shareholder is taxed as a dividend. Further, a capital gain or loss results to the extent that the cost of the shares is more or less than the paid-up capital. Special rules allow the tax-free liquidation of 90%-owned domestic corporate subsidiaries.[246]

The pattern in *Japan* is very similar. The amount of liquidation proceeds which exceeds the amount of capital is taxed as a dividend. The difference between the remaining amount of the proceeds (i.e., the amount of capital) and the book value of the shares is taxed as a capital gain (or recognized as a capital loss). For the liquidating company, capital gains or losses with respect to any appreciation or depreciation on distributed assets are aggregated with other income of the liquidating company for its last fiscal year.[247]

In *France*, the liquidation of a company triggers tax for the company on any profits or capital gains, with the tax paid by the company (if subject to corporate tax) or by the members (if subject to income tax). For shareholders in capital companies, the recovery of their capital is not taxable, but any bonus on liquidation is treated as a taxable distribution.[248] For partners, the cessation of their professional activity on the liquidation of the company results in the taxation of a capital gain on the company's shares, which can be deferred under certain conditions.[249]

The *Australian* system treats liquidating distributions to the extent of after-tax taxable income (as opposed to after-tax profits, which are usually larger) as dividends,[250] which carry with them the imputation credit. As in Canada, for CGT purposes, the total amount of the liquidating distribution is treated as consideration for the disposal of the stock but the amount of the gain is reduced by the amount taxed as a dividend.[251] No loss is allowed unless the total amount received (whether characterized as a dividend or not) is less than the cost base of the shares. It is possible to overcome this problem by making interim distributions during liquidation which are treated as dividends because the mechanism for reducing the tax cost is not operative for such distributions and a loss can emerge on cancellation of the shares. With respect to the liquidation of a 100% subsidiary, in certain cases, there is a rollover of the tax cost of the subsidiary's assets outside the tax consolidation regime, although the transaction is still treated as a disposition of the parent company's shares, with the tax consequences outlined above adjusted to prevent double taxation.[252] There are no fixed ordering rules distinguishing between distributions of share capital and retained earnings and, in practice, the liquidator has considerable flexibility in obtaining the most favorable tax results on the liquidating distribution,[253] subject to the dividend and capital streaming and other anti-avoidance rules referred to above.

246. Canada, ITA, s. 88(1).
247. Japan, CTA, s. 62-5.
248. France, CGI, s. 112 3°.
249. France, CGI, s. 151 nonies IV.
250. Australia, ITAA 1936, s. 47.
251. Australia, ITAA 1997, s. 118-20.
252. Australia, ITAA 1997, s. 126-85.
253. *Archer Brothers Pty Ltd* (1953) 90 CLR 140.

In the *German* system, where a corporation is wound up and liquidated, it is generally taxed on the difference between the book value of the assets at the beginning of the winding-up period and the value of the assets which are distributed to the shareholders at the end of the period.[254] If appreciated assets are distributed in kind, the appreciation is subject to tax. In the hands of the shareholder, there is a two-step approach. First, the distribution is treated as a dividend to the extent that it exceeds the capital contribution attributed to the shareholder. As a result, the payment to a corporate shareholder is largely tax-free if the participation amounts to at least 10%, whereas the tax treatment of dividends to an individual shareholder depends on the nature of the holding. Dividends from shares held as private assets are subject to a 25% withholding tax. Where the shares have been held as business assets or amount to at least 1% of the capital of the corporation, 60% of the dividend is taxed at the shareholder level.

Second, with respect to the repayment of capital, the shareholder may realize a capital gain or capital loss if the historical acquisition cost is lower or higher than the shareholder's share in the company capital. This will be the case where the shareholder has acquired the shares after the formation of the company at a price not identical to the nominal share value. Where the shares are held as a business asset or amount to a participation of at least 1%, a gain would be taxable and a loss deductible. Where the shares are held as private assets and do not reach the 1% limit, the gain or loss is subject to the 25% withholding tax. Special rules apply where the business is not wound up but transferred to a partnership composed of the shareholders or is continued as a sole proprietorship. If the taxpayer wants the transaction to be tax-free, the book values of the transferred assets are continued. If the tax cost of the shares is lower than the book value of the assets, gain is recognized to that extent by the transferee.

In *The Netherlands*, for individual shareholders not holding their shares as a business asset, a liquidation distribution up to the amount of the average paid-in capital can be received on a tax-free basis.[255] Any excess is treated as a dividend. The shareholder's acquisition cost in the shares is not relevant (it should be remembered that private capital gains are generally not taxed). In cases where the shareholder owns a "substantial interest" in the company, for income tax purposes, the liquidation distribution is treated as a fictitious disposal of the shares and subject to "box 2" income taxation (at 24.5% or, from EUR 67,000, 33%).[256] Where the shareholder is a corporation whose holding does not amount to a participation or is an individual holding the shares in a business, the difference between the tax cost of the shares and the liquidation payment is subject to tax as a gain on sale. If the corporate shareholder qualifies for the participation exemption, the gain is not taxed and, correspondingly, losses are generally not deductible. However, under certain strict conditions, an exception to the nondeductibility of losses is available in the case of a liquidation of a

254. Germany, CITA, s. 11.
255. Netherlands, DWTA, Art. 3(1)(a).
256. Netherlands, ITA 2001, Art. 4.16(1)(c).

corporation which meets the requirements of a qualifying participation in the hands of its corporate shareholders.[257]

Sweden treats a liquidation entirely as a capital transaction, so that if a loss results, it is subject to the 70% deduction limitation discussed above in Part II, Subpart B, section 12. This result applies despite the fact that the realization of the loss is typically not a voluntary act by the shareholder and the 70% rule is generally aimed at taxpayers that intentionally realize losses while deferring gains. Where a subsidiary is, in effect, liquidated into its parent corporation in a merger, the transaction is tax-free to both parties with a carryover basis in the subsidiary's assets. The tax cost in the shares of the subsidiary disappears in the transaction.

The *United Kingdom* also treats liquidating payments as capital distributions, resulting in capital gains treatment both to the corporation and the shareholder.[258] There is no attempt to treat a portion of the payment as a dividend distribution, although an anti-abuse rule was enacted in 2016 to deal with so-called phoenix companies (companies whose assets are distributed in a liquidation and are then contributed to a new company which carries on the same business).[259]

In *China*, liquidation distributions to shareholders are treated as dividends to the extent that the liquidating company has accumulated retained earnings and earnings reserves.[260] As indicated above in the overview in section 2, in *India*, the tax on dividends applies to distributions of accumulated profits on liquidation, whether capitalized or not.[261] There are no capital gains consequences to the liquidating company.[262] However, where the shareholder receives any money or other assets from the company on liquidation in excess of the accumulated profits, the excess is subject to tax as a capital gain.[263]

7 CORPORATE REORGANIZATIONS AND RESTRUCTURING

7.1 General

Most of the systems analyzed here have special rules dealing with the tax treatment of corporate reorganizations.[264] Transactions covered include corporate mergers and acquisitions, divisions, changes in capital structure, and other similar rearrangements

257. Netherlands, CITA, Art. 13d.
258. United Kingdom, Corporation Tax Act 2010, s. 1030.
259. United Kingdom, Income Tax (Trading and Other Income) Act 2005 (ITTOIA), s. 396B.
260. China, Cai Shui [2009] No. 60, Art. 5.
261. India, ITA 1961, s. 2(22)(c).
262. India, ITA 1961, s. 46(1).
263. India, ITA 1961, s. 46(2).
264. For France, Germany, The Netherlands, and Sweden, the EU Merger Directive requires domestic legislation to allow mergers, share exchanges, and certain transfers of assets to take place on a tax-deferred basis where the participating companies and shareholders are organized or reside in different EU states. In modifying their legislation to meet the requirements of the Directive, several of the countries also modified the rules applicable to purely domestic transactions. Because, in general, an EU Directive has direct effect in Member States, the rules in the Directive should be applied even in the absence of domestic rules.

of corporate affairs. There are typically a number of structural issues of corporate taxation involved in such transactions. First, the exchanges and rearrangements of interests which take place in reorganization transactions are usually events which would cause a recognition of gain or loss under normal tax principles. Each system must determine the conditions and circumstances under which those rules are supplanted by special provisions which permit tax-preferred treatment. The factors taken into account might include the business or commercial reasons for the transaction; the corporate and commercial law aspects of the transaction; and the character of the assets involved and their role in the existing and emerging enterprises. In addition, the change in the extent and character of the ownership interests in the corporation is often an important factor in deciding whether the normal recognition rules should be displaced. While the form of the investment may change, that change may not be deemed to be a sufficient modification of the "continuity of ownership interest" to require a recognition of gain or allow a recognition of loss.

Where the judgment is made that the transaction should be only partially tax-free and some income or gain should be recognized, rules must be provided to characterize that income or gain. On the one hand, to the extent that an exchange is involved, capital gain or loss treatment may be appropriate. On the other hand, where property is withdrawn from the corporation, it may be treated similarly to a dividend distribution in connection with the otherwise tax-free reorganization. The effect of exchange treatment or dividend treatment may differ in some situations depending on the nature of the shareholder and the extent to which integration relief is available. Finally, rules must be provided for the continuance or carryover of various corporate tax attributes (tax cost, losses, carryovers, etc.) of the corporations involved.

Sometimes these issues are dealt with in detailed statutory rules, sometimes under broad general principles such as continuity of business or ownership interests, and sometimes with a combination of both approaches. The basic pattern of reorganization transactions and their effects is considered here. The next section deals with the carryover of corporate tax attributes in these situations and the limitations to which carryovers may be subject.

The *Chinese* rules for reorganizations are structured differently from the rules of other countries. The general rule is that an enterprise must recognize gains or losses from transfers of assets in the course of a reorganization, unless otherwise prescribed by the Ministry of Finance and/or STA.[265] The Ministry of Finance and the STA have issued several administrative rules with respect to reorganizations.[266] Under these rules, reorganizations are classified as either general or special. Transfers of assets as part of a general reorganization are taxable. However, special reorganizations of resident enterprises allow taxpayers to defer tax, in full or in part, where the taxpayers so elect and the reorganization meets the following conditions:

265. China, Art. 75 of the EIT Regulations.

266. China, Ministry of Finance and STA, Cai Shui [2009] No. 59; Cai Shui [2014] No. 109 and Cai Shui [2014] No. 116; STA Public Notice [2015] No. 33 and Public Notice [2015] No. 40 (Public Notice 40) to clarify the implementation rules in Circular 116 and Art. 3 of Circular 109, respectively.

- it must have a bona fide business purpose and its main purpose must not be the avoidance of tax;
- the business of the enterprise must continue for a prescribed period after the restructuring (currently twelve months);
- equity consideration must represent at least 85% of the total consideration for the transfer; and
- at least 75% of the total assets or equity of the enterprise must be transferred (50% of the assets for mergers (reduced from 100% in 2014)).[267]

In 2014, special reorganizations were expanded to include reorganizations involving 100%-owned enterprises (e.g., parent and wholly owned subsidiary and companies which are 100% owned by the same Chinese-resident parent company) where the transactions take place at net book value and no accounting gains/losses are recognized.[268]

In addition to these general conditions, each type of special reorganization must meet other conditions, as described in the following sections.

Additional conditions must also be met for cross-border restructurings (including those in Hong Kong, Macau, and Taiwan) to qualify as special reorganizations:

(a) where a nonresident enterprise transfers equity of a resident enterprise to another wholly owned nonresident enterprise, the amount of withholding tax on the income from the resulting equity transfer must not be reduced and the transferor must undertake, in writing, to the competent tax authority, not to transfer the equity of the transferee nonresident enterprise for a period of three years;
(b) where a nonresident enterprise transfers the equity of a resident enterprise to another resident enterprise, the transferee enterprise must be wholly owned;
(c) where a resident enterprise invests in a nonresident enterprise, it must be wholly owned; or
(d) other conditions as approved by the Ministry of Finance and the State Administration of Taxation.

Before 2015, special reorganizations had to be preapproved by the tax authority; this requirement was removed in 2015.[269]

7.2 Merger Transactions

In a typical merger transaction, an existing corporation disappears and its assets and liabilities are taken over by another corporation which continues the business activities of the disappearing corporation. The shareholders of the disappearing corporation may continue as shareholders of the continuing corporation or may receive cash, property,

267. China, Cai Shui [2014] No. 109.
268. *Ibid.*
269. China, STA announcement [2015] No. 48.

or creditor interests in the continuing corporation for all or a part of their shares in the disappearing corporation. As a formal matter, the merger may take place under special corporate law provisions or may be a "practical" merger, where there is an actual transfer of assets in exchange for stock or other property by the corporation ceasing business.

In the *United States*, the rules dealing with mergers have been developed both in the case law and in detailed statutory provisions which apply to all qualifying reorganizations, including mergers. Under the statutory scheme, a series of corporate rearrangements, including mergers, are defined as "reorganizations";[270] other rules then determine the consequences of the various transfers and exchanges involved in the reorganization.[271]

Beyond the statutory definition of reorganization, however, there are a number of judicial doctrines which have been adopted in modified form in regulations which limit the scope of reorganization treatment even where the formal statutory requirements are met.[272] First, the reorganization must have a business or commercial purpose. While this requirement is usually easily satisfied, it stands as a barrier to reorganization transactions which are focused exclusively on the tax benefits of reorganization treatment. In addition, the business of the acquired corporation must to some extent be continued, although substantial variation and changes are allowed. Most important, the shareholders of the disappearing corporation must have a significant continuing ownership interest in the acquiring corporation. This requirement of "continuity of ownership interest" is based on the idea that tax deferral is appropriate only where the shareholders have not changed the basic nature of their investments. However, the doctrine has developed to allow a substantial variation in the economic characteristics of an investment as long as it continues in the form of an ownership interest. Thus, for example, a merger transaction in which a target corporation wholly owned by a single shareholder is merged into a publicly traded corporation in which the former shareholder receives only a small percentage of the stock of the acquiring corporation would still qualify under the continuity-of-interest test. This would be true even if the stock interest had substantially different characteristics (e.g., limited voting rights).

While the exact degree of required continuing ownership is not clearly defined in the case law, something less than 50% is acceptable. That is, if the shareholders of the disappearing corporation, taken together, receive at least, say, 45% of the consideration for their shares in the form of stock in the acquiring corporation, the requirement would be met. Exactly where the lower limit is, however, is not clear. Regulations also require that the shareholders participating in the reorganization transaction not sell their shares to the acquiring corporation or a related person for a period of time after the transaction. Thus, a sale immediately after the reorganization to the acquiring corporation would defeat the required "post-reorganization" continuity requirement if it involves a sufficiently large number of shares.

270. United States, IRC, s. 368.
271. United States, IRC, ss. 354 through 362.
272. United States, Treas. Reg., s. 1.368-1.

Assuming that the merger transaction meets the various requirements, the statute provides special rules to determine the tax treatment of the participants.[273] If only stock in the acquiring corporation is used in the merger, neither the acquired corporation which transfers its assets in the merger nor the shareholders who exchange their shares for shares in the acquired corporation recognize gain or loss. The tax cost of the assets carries over to the acquiring corporation, and the shareholders take the historical cost in their old shares as their tax cost in the new shares. If other property (e.g., cash or a creditor interest in the acquiring corporation), is received, then gain, but not loss, must be recognized. If this receipt of nonstock property is functionally equivalent to a dividend distribution made in connection with the merger, dividend treatment results. Otherwise, gain is recognized on the disposition of the shares, which would ordinarily be a capital gain. The shareholders are allowed to increase their tax cost in the new shares by the amount of the recognized gain (or dividend) and the acquiring corporation is given a similar increase in the tax basis of the assets.

Some special provisions allow reorganization treatment where the stock consideration used is the stock of the parent corporation controlling the corporation that actually makes the acquisition. The extremely technical rules for these "triangular" forms of merger reorganizations have developed in a haphazard fashion and do not represent any consistent policies beyond the general notions of continuity of ownership interest and continuation of the business enterprise.

The *Canadian* treatment of the functional equivalent of a merger transaction is determined in part by the nature of the transaction for corporate law purposes. Federal and provincial laws allow two or more corporations to "amalgamate" and continue as a single corporation. The amalgamating corporations do not cease to exist for corporate law purposes; rather, they continue to exist in the form of the amalgamated corporation. As a result of this approach, no transfer of assets or discontinuation of business is considered to occur; in an analogy often used in the case law, it is as if two streams flow together to form a river.

The tax law accepts this characterization to some extent, and thus, at the corporate level, the amalgamation is not treated as resulting in dispositions for purposes of gain or loss recognition. As a result, no rollover is necessary for the assets of the predecessor corporations on an amalgamation. There are some special tax rules which do not follow the corporate concept. Thus, for some purposes, the resulting entity is treated as a new corporation and the statute provides detailed rules for the carryover of various corporate tax attributes from the predecessor corporations to the new corporation pursuant to the amalgamation.[274]

At the shareholder level, there is a disposition of the shares of the predecessor corporations. Where the shareholders of the "old" corporation receive only shares of the new corporation, the exchange is tax-free, with the tax cost of their new shares considered to be the tax cost of their old shares.[275] There is no requirement that the shares received be held for any particular period of time. Where there is a difference in

273. United States, IRC, ss. 354 through 362.
274. Canada, ITA, s. 87(2)-(2.3).
275. Canada, ITA, s. 87(4).

the values of the shares given up and the shares received and that benefit effectively accrues to a person related to the shareholder, gain is recognized to that extent. As a prophylactic measure, no increase in the cost basis of the shares is allowed for the gain recognized. Where the shareholders receive nonshare consideration in the amalgamation, the rollover does not apply and the shareholders are considered to have disposed of their shares in the amalgamating corporations for proceeds equal to the fair market value of the shares in the amalgamated corporation plus any nonshare consideration.

Apart from amalgamations under corporate law, the rules discussed in connection with corporate formation may apply to a transfer of property for shares which, at the corporate level, is similar to a merger. However, the distribution of the shares to the shareholders would be a taxable event under normal principles.

Under *Dutch* law, mergers can take place on a tax-deferred basis provided that the statutory conditions are met. In that case, the tax attributes of the disappearing company are transferred to the surviving company and the tax cost of the new shares to the shareholders of the resulting company is the same as their tax cost of the old shares.[276] Any consideration the taxpayer receives in cash (except for a small amount of "boot") is taxable up to the amount of the gain. The statutory conditions require, *inter alia*, that the merging companies be subject to the same tax regime.

Germany has a special statute dealing with reorganizations of both corporate and nonincorporated businesses, with differing requirements for the tax-free status of various types of reorganizations.[277] In the case of corporate mergers, a transaction may take the form of a downstream or upstream merger or a merger of two corporations into a newly established third corporation. The shareholders of a dissolved corporation receive shares in the surviving corporation. Where the merger does not include cash payments to the shareholders of the dissolved corporation and the book values of the assets are transferred to the surviving or newly established corporation in circumstances in which the potential gain remains subject to tax in Germany, no gain or loss is recognized by the transferring corporation.[278] However, it is up to the transferring corporation to decide whether the transfer is entered in the accounts at book value, fair market value, or a freely chosen intermediate value. The receiving corporation must enter the assets on its books at the value chosen by the transferring corporation. To the extent that the chosen value exceeds the book value, the transferring corporation must realize a gain. If the receiving corporation exchanges its shares for the assets of the transferring corporation at fair market value, there is no taxable gain at the level of the receiving corporation.[279] However, in the case of an upstream merger, 5% of the gain for the receiving corporation is taxable as an offset for deductible expenses.

With respect to the shareholders, the tax cost of the old shares can be rolled over to the new shares received in the course of the merger if the later taxation of the hidden reserves in the shares is not excluded or limited.[280] Otherwise, the shares of the

276. Netherlands, CITA, Art. 14b.
277. Germany, Reorganization Tax Act (RTA) (*Umwandlungssteuergesetz*).
278. Germany, RTA, s. 11.
279. Germany, RTA, s. 12 para. 2.
280. Germany, RTA, s. 13.

transferring corporation are deemed to be disposed at fair market value, leading to a realized gain for the shareholder. The fair market value of the old shares then becomes the tax cost for the new shares. Where, as a result of the merger, a former portfolio interest becomes a participation which would be subject to tax, the shares take a tax cost equal the fair market value of the former interest. In the converse situation, where a substantial participation becomes a portfolio interest, the tax cost of the shares is carried over and a subsequent disposition of the shares remains taxable. Cash payments may be received in some circumstances, although gains are taxable to that extent.

In *France*, reorganizations can take the form of a merger, a division, or a partial transfer of assets. In all cases, the aim is to transfer the assets and liabilities of one legal entity to one or more other entities. The merger regime applies to these operations, except where the legislation imposes special conditions on divisions and partial contributions of assets. The preferential merger regime was developed in France in the 1940s and applied on an optional basis.[281] Today it combines features of both EU law under the 2009 Merger Directive[282] and domestic commercial and tax law. However, French law has not fully incorporated the Directive and domestic tax definition of a partial contribution of assets adopted in 2018.[283]

With respect to accounting rules, companies must record transactions at net book value or real value, as the case may be. The accounting treatment depends on the direction of the merger (*à l'endroit ou à l'envers*) and whether or not the companies had joint control prior to the transaction.

With respect to tax rules, a distinction must be made between the consequences applicable to companies and other parties involved in the merger. With respect to direct taxes, restructuring is considered to be the continuation of the business by the merging companies in another form (provided that the acquiring company undertakes in the merger deed to comply with certain conditions) and should not have any tax consequences—the absorbed company continues its business activities in the absorbing company or companies. With respect to the absorbed company, capital gains or losses on the contribution are not taxed, and it is possible to request approval from the tax authorities to transfer losses from the absorbed company to the absorbing company.[284] The acquiring company is not subject to any immediate taxation. Instead, capital gains or losses on nondepreciable assets are taken into account only at the time of their disposal by the acquiring company, and capital gains on depreciable assets are taxed in installments over a period of five or fifteen years, depending on the facts. For the shareholders of the absorbed company, the bonus share issue resulting from the merger is not considered to be a distribution of income[285] and, as a result, is treated as

281. France, CGI, s. 210 A.
282. Council Directive 2009/133/EC of October 19, 2009 on the common system of taxation applicable to mergers, divisions, partial divisions, transfers of assets, and exchanges of shares concerning companies of different Member States and to the transfer of the registered office of an SE or SCE between Member States.
283. France, CGI, s. 210-0 A.
284. France, CGI, s. 209 II.
285. France, CGI, s. 115-1.

a capital gain. Tax on the capital gain or loss arising on the exchange of shares is deferred, whether the shareholder is an individual[286] or a company.[287] In all cases, the deferral regime does not apply where the amount paid to the shareholder of the absorbed company, known as the "balancing payment" (*soulte*), exceeds 10% of the par value of the units or shares allocated, or exceeds the capital gain realized.

United Kingdom corporate law does not provide for mergers proper, but similar results can be achieved for commercial law purposes through the transfer of a business owned by the target corporation and the issue of shares by the bidding corporation to the shareholders of the target. If the target is wound up as part of the arrangement (under the arrangement provisions of the corporate law),[288] there should be no distribution for tax purposes by the target to its shareholders (e.g., of the shares in the acquiring corporation). Rather, the shareholders of the target are treated as having received a capital distribution in respect of their shares in the target, which may result in a capital gain.[289] However, if the transactions qualify as a reorganization for tax purposes, no disposition is deemed to take place and the new holding is treated as a continuation of the old shares. One of the statutorily defined forms of reorganization is a reconstruction of a company or the amalgamation of two or more companies. To qualify, the reorganization must have a bona fide commercial purpose and the exchange must not be part of a scheme for tax avoidance.[290]

Prior to 2001, the *Japanese* rules on reorganizations were quite restrictive and far from consistent. Under the 2001 tax reforms, identical rules apply to all types of corporate restructuring transactions. The general principle is that any corporate restructuring transaction should be regarded as a taxable event triggering tax on any unrealized gains of the companies subject to the reorganization. Therefore, in the event of a merger, the disappearing corporation in the merger transaction is subject to corporate tax on any unrealized gains. In addition, the excess of the fair market value of the shares or other assets delivered to the shareholders of the disappearing corporation over the amount of the capital of that corporation is taxed as a dividend and the remaining amount of the delivered shares and assets is taxed as a capital gain.

However, the law also provides unified rules with respect to qualified corporate restructuring transactions which are not treated as taxable events; in such cases, income tax otherwise payable on unrealized gains accumulated in companies is deferred until further taxable events occur. These nontaxable merger transactions are:

(a) a merger between companies with a 100% equity relationship (i.e., cases where: (i) one company is a wholly owned subsidiary of the other or (ii) both companies are the wholly owned subsidiaries of a common parent);
(b) a merger between companies with more than a 50% equity relationship which also meets several criteria ensuring the continuity of the business (e.g.,

286. France, CGI, s. 150-0 B and s. 150-0 D 9.
287. France, CGI, s. 38-7 bis.
288. United Kingdom, Companies Act 2006, Parts 26 and 27.
289. United Kingdom, TCGA, s. 122.
290. United Kingdom, TCGA, Part IV Ch. II (ss. 126-140).

approximately 80% or more of the employees who were employed by the disappearing company must be assumed by the other corporation); or

(c) a merger for the purpose of establishing a joint venture between nonrelated entities which meets several other criteria.

Nontaxable mergers must be pure stock-for-stock transactions; no other consideration can be paid to the shareholders of the disappearing corporation. There is one exception to this rule: in a merger between a subsidiary and a parent holding two-thirds or more of the shares of the subsidiary, consideration can be paid to minority shareholders of the disappearing subsidiary in cash or other assets. In the case of a nontaxable merger, net operating losses of the surviving corporation and the disappearing corporation can be carried forward, subject to some additional requirements. As discussed in the chapter on Japan in Part I, while Japan has not introduced a GAAR, an anti-avoidance clause generally applicable to corporate restructuring transactions was enacted as a part of the 2001 reforms to prevent tax-motivated transactions. This clause has been applied to an intragroup merger transaction to deny a carryover of net operating losses.[291] Further, in the case of a nontaxable merger, the tax otherwise imposed on the shareholders of the disappearing corporation is deferred until the disposition of the shares of the surviving corporation.[292]

Sweden has special tax rules dealing with merger transactions based on the EU Merger Directive. These rules apply to transactions where a corporation is dissolved without liquidation and the business is transferred to another corporation. Under these rules, the business must be taxable in Sweden before and after the transfer. Corporations with different owners can be merged without taxation by combining several steps. For example, if a shareholder transfers shares to a corporation for newly issued shares, the exchange is tax-free but any cash payment received on the exchange is taxed as a gain. Thereafter, under the general merger provision, the acquired corporation can be merged into the acquiring corporation, thus providing the functional equivalent of a merger of the two companies, with the shareholders of the old company becoming shareholders of the acquiring company.

In *Australia*, corporate law does not generally provide specific procedures for mergers by transfer of assets, except with respect to the banking industry or by a procedure involving court approval. Accordingly, many mergers are effected by an acquisition of shares, either for cash or in share-for-share exchanges. Generally, mergers involving asset transfers give rise to tax consequences in the normal way, although there is a school of thought which holds that mergers in the banking sector achieved through universal succession are tax-free on the basis of general tax principles. In addition, effectively tax-free "contractual" mergers (referred to as dual-listed companies) have been used in international settings (mainly with respect to the UK), under which two listed companies agree to operate in concert in the future through common management and boards of directors, with dividend and other distributions by the companies being made at the same time and equal in amount. Mechanisms for

291. *Yahoo v. Japan*, 242 Minshu 70-2 (S. Ct. February 29, 2016).
292. Japan, CTA, s. 2, para. 12-8 and s. 62-2.

equalization payments between the companies are provided to deal with situations where one company cannot meet its payment obligations to its shareholders. Despite potential tax benefits from such transactions, the ongoing corporate governance complications and cost caused Australia's largest mining company, BHP, to exit its dual-listed structure in 2022, leaving only one such large mining company structure (Rio Tinto) in place.

In *China*, merging enterprises may elect to treat a merger as a special reorganization where it satisfies all the general requirements for a special reorganization described above in section 7.1; this election is also available where the equity consideration received by the shareholders of the merged enterprises represents 85% or more of the total consideration or where no consideration is paid because the merging enterprises were both controlled by the same enterprise. Although Chinese company law provides rules for mergers, the tax treatment of mergers does not seem to refer to the company law, presumably because many enterprises are not governed by company law.

In *India*, no CGT is charged in an amalgamation if the amalgamated company is an Indian company.[293] The transfer of shares of an amalgamating foreign company to the amalgamated foreign company is also not subject to CGT where at least 25% of the shareholders of the foreign amalgamating company continue to hold shares in the amalgamated foreign company and the transfer does not result in CGT in the country where the amalgamating company is incorporated.[294]

7.3 Share Exchanges

A second typical form of reorganization involves an exchange of shares entirely at the shareholder level. Unlike merger transactions, no transfers of assets are involved and the acquired corporation is unaffected at the corporate level. Normally, a share exchange would be a taxable event in all the systems described here, but special provisions allow such exchanges to be treated on a tax-deferred rollover basis where certain conditions are met.

In the *United States*, one form of statutorily recognized reorganization is the acquisition by one corporation of 80% ("control") of the stock of another corporation *solely* in exchange for the voting stock of the acquiring corporation.[295] The voting-stock requirement has been very strictly interpreted by the courts, and even a *de minimis* amount of nonqualifying consideration can prevent nonrecognition.[296]

The 80% control need not be acquired in one transaction as long as the final acquisition results in the 80% test being met. However, if some of the prior acquisitions have been made for consideration other than voting stock and are considered to be part of an integrated acquisition transaction, the entire exchange is taxable.[297] If the prior

293. India, ITA 1961, s. 47(vi).
294. India, ITA 1961, s. 47(via).
295. United States, IRC, s. 368(a)(1)(B).
296. *See*, for example, *Helvering v. Southwest Consolidated Corp.*, 315 U.S. 194 (1942).
297. *See*, for example, *Chapman v. Commissioner*, 618 F.2d 856 (1st Cir. 1980).

acquisitions were for voting stock, the subsequent acquisition of control can be effected on a tax-free basis. Where the transaction qualifies as a reorganization, the shareholder retains the tax cost of the old shares for the new shares.

The *Canadian* rules are quite different. Shares can be exchanged for shares in the acquiring corporation in any amount on a tax-free basis as long as, after the exchange, the selling shareholders and any non-arm's length persons do not have shares in the acquiring corporation representing more than 50 % of the value of all the shares or have control of the acquiring corporation.[298] In addition, the acquiring corporation and the selling shareholders must deal with each other at arm's length. Shares can also be acquired for other consideration in the same transaction as long as the vendor can clearly identify which shares were exchanged for cash and which were exchanged for shares. Similarly, the rollover applies to a fraction of the shares exchanged for other shares as long as the purchaser's offer indicates that the shares are exchanged for a specified fraction of the acquired shareholder's shares and cash or other consideration for the remaining fraction. The tax-deferred rollover treatment applies only to the shares or fraction of shares which are disposed of for shares. The shareholder keeps the tax cost in the old shares as the tax cost for the new shares and the acquiring corporation takes as its cost the lesser of fair market value or the paid-up capital allocated to the shares. The tax-free exchange applies only to exchanges of shares in Canadian corporations.

Australia introduced similar rules for "scrip-for-scrip" mergers in 1999.[299] The shareholders of the company being acquired in the merger can get rollover treatment for shares disposed of in the merger in exchange for shares, provided the acquiring company obtains 80 % of the voting shares in the acquired company. To the extent that the shareholders receive cash, they are considered to realize gain or loss in the ordinary way for the relevant proportion of shares. If the shareholders have shares that were acquired before the introduction of the CGT, that status is not maintained after the merger; instead, such shareholders get a market value tax cost for the new shares. As a result, the gain on the previous shares held up to that time is protected from tax, since the purpose of the rules is to remove immediate tax barriers to takeovers.

It is necessary that all shareholders can participate in the offer on substantially the same terms. The rules allow a subsidiary of the acquiring company to acquire the shares in exchange for shares issued by the acquiring company. In general, the acquiring company has a cost base in the acquired shares equal to the market value of the shares issued in the acquisition (in effect, the cost of the shares acquired is stepped up to their market value). However, a series of rules have been enacted to prevent this outcome. First, where there is a significant degree of continuity of control from the acquired company to the acquiring company, the original tax cost of the acquired interest is transferred to the acquiring company. This carryover of cost applies where a person (including associates) holds at least 30 % of the acquired company before and 30 % of the acquiring company after the merger, or a person holds 80 % or more of both companies before and after the merger. These rules are designed to prevent the rollover

298. Canada, ITA, s. 85.1.
299. Australia, ITAA 1997, Div 124-M.

being used to increase the tax cost of shares in anticipation of a sale of the shares to a third party; they have been strengthened over time to prevent tax avoidance. Second, a similar restriction insists on the carryover of cost to prevent the consolidation system from generating an increase in the depreciation deductions available. Third, the cost for the shares acquired is not increased to market value where a company without significant assets of its own acquires another company (so-called top hat restructures) in a scrip-for-scrip (i.e., stock-for-stock) transaction.[300]

The *Dutch* rules allow a tax-deferred exchange of shares if the acquiring corporation obtains over 50% of the voting stock (reduced from 90% in compliance with the EU Merger Directive and made applicable to domestic as well as EU-related transactions) of the acquired corporation.[301] Preexisting ownership of shares may be counted for purposes of the 50% test. Cash payments up to 10% of the nominal amount of the stock are allowed, although it is not clear whether these payments must be pro rata or could be made on a disproportionate basis in order to buy out a shareholder. There are special rules to ensure that the later disposition of the shares by a holder of a substantial participation remains taxable if, after the exchange, the shares no longer qualify as a substantial participation.

The *German* rules were changed in 1994 to comply with the EU Merger Directive, leading to an alignment of domestic and EU transactions. In 2007, a new set of statutory rules for the exchange of shares was enacted as part of the reform of the rules for business organizations.[302] An exchange of shares by which a shareholder contributes shares of a corporation (the acquired corporation) in the course of a capital increase of another corporation (the acquiring corporation) and the acquiring corporation thereby obtains a majority of the voting rights in the acquired corporation may lead to a tax-free rollover in the accounts of the exchanging shareholder. As in the case of formal mergers, the acquiring corporation has the option of entering the shares acquired at their book value, fair market value, or any value in between, provided that there is a "qualified exchange" of shares (i.e., the acquiring corporation must acquire a majority of voting rights). If an amount in excess of book value is chosen, the exchanging shareholder recognizes a gain to that extent, with the resulting tax treatment dependent on the status of the shareholder.[303] Until 2006, Germany also required this "doubling" of hidden reserves at both the shareholder and corporate level with respect to cross-border reorganizations, thus forcing foreign acquiring corporations to enter the German book value into their foreign accounts. This requirement was held by the CJEU in 2008 to be incompatible with the EU Merger Directive.[304]

Apart from the case where shares are used as a "contribution in kind" in the course of an acquisition, prior to 1999, case law allowed a tax-deferred exchange of shares where the shares received were identical in value, type, and function to the

300. Australia, ITAA 1997, ss. 124-784A-124-784C, 615-30, 615-65, 703-65-703-80, Div 715-W.
301. Where the shareholder is a company: Netherlands, CITA, Art. 13i(1) (shareholding company entitled to participation exemption) and CITA, Art. 13i(2) (not entitled to participation exemption). Where the shareholder is an individual, *see* ITA, Art. 3.55.
302. Germany, RTA, s. 21.
303. Germany, RTA, s. 21 para. 2.
304. CJEU, December 11, 2008, C-285/07 (*A.T. v. FA Stuttgart-Koerper-Shaften*).

transferred shares. This option has been explicitly repealed.[305] In the corporate context, a similar result can be achieved by using the "participation exemption" for share sales by corporate shareholders.

In general, in *France*, an exchange of shares is a taxable event, except where a reorganization takes place on a tax-deferred basis (*see* section 7.2 above). The legislation provides two mechanisms that allow tax to be deferred until the subsequent sale of the securities received in the exchange. An automatic mechanism applies to exchange transactions carried out as part of public exchange offers, various share conversion or exchange transactions, and bond-for-share redemptions,[306] and an optional mechanism applies to the exchange of corporate rights following a company merger or division.[307]

In the *United Kingdom*, several qualifying share exchanges are treated as reorganizations which do not result in a disposition for capital gains purposes.[308] Where the acquiring company already owns 25% of the stock of the acquired corporation or, as a result of the exchange, obtains voting control, the exchange may be made on a tax-deferred basis. Tax-deferred treatment is also available if the exchange is part of a general offer to obtain control. Finally, the exchange is tax-deferred if it in fact results in the acquisition of control of the acquired company. The reorganization must have a bona fide commercial purpose and the exchange must not be part of a scheme for tax avoidance. In the hands of the acquiring corporation, the shares in the target have a cost equal to the value of the shares given by the acquiring corporation (step-up in cost).

As mentioned above in connection with merger transactions, in *Sweden* shares may be transferred on a tax-deferred basis for newly issued shares of the transferee corporation. *Japan* does not have a rule enabling tax-free share acquisitions, although Japanese income tax law allows compulsory share swaps: creating a wholly owned subsidiary can occur tax-free where the transaction meets criteria similar to those for nontaxable mergers.[309]

In *China*, a share-for-share exchange can be elected by the parties as a special reorganization if it satisfies all the general requirements for a special reorganization described above in section 7.1, and at the same time: (a) the acquiring enterprise acquires 75% or more of the stock of the acquired enterprise and (b) the stock represents not less than 85% of the total consideration for the acquisition. Both of these conditions involve the acquisition of equity ownership, but not necessarily control.

In *India*, before 2021, certain restructurings ("slump sales")[310] involving sales for a lump-sum consideration could take place without any CGT. Since 2021, such slump sales are treated as transfers giving rise to capital gains.[311] All such transactions are

305. Germany, ITA, s. 6 para. 6 s. 1.
306. France, CGI, s. 38 7.
307. France, CGI, s. 38, 7 bis.
308. United Kingdom, TCGA, s. 135.
309. Japan, CTA, s. 2, paras. 12-16 and 12-17, and s. 62-9.
310. *CIT v. Bharat Bijlee Limited*, Bombay High Court (2014), 365 ITR 258.
311. India, ITA 1961, s. 2(42C).

subject to short-term capital gains if the period of holding of the undertaking transferred is less than three years.[312]

7.4 Nonmerger Asset Reorganizations

Some of the systems considered here have special reorganization provisions dealing with asset transfers or "enterprise" mergers which involve the transfer of assets in a transaction which does not formally constitute a merger for corporate law purposes. In the *United States*, this type of "practical" merger is possible if certain statutory requirements are met.[313] The corporation whose assets are being acquired must transfer "substantially all" of its assets to the acquiring corporation. At least 80% of the consideration received for the assets must be voting stock of the acquiring corporation (or a parent corporation in control of the acquiring corporation). In addition, liabilities of the acquired corporation can be assumed, subject to some special limitations. The corporation whose assets are acquired must be liquidated and must distribute the consideration received to its shareholders. If these requirements are met, no gain or loss is recognized by the acquired corporation with respect to the transferred assets and the acquiring corporation takes over the tax cost of the assets. At the shareholder level, the shares of the acquiring corporation can be received on a tax-free basis, with the tax cost of the old shares attaching to the new shares. Where nonstock consideration within the permissible limits is involved, that amount is taxable, either as gain on the share disposition or as a dividend, depending on the circumstances. The income inclusion increases the tax cost for the new shares. In addition, the acquiring corporation is allowed to increase its tax cost in the assets received by the amount of the income recognized at the shareholder level.

In the other systems, while there are frequently provisions which allow a tax-deferred transfer of assets to an existing corporation in exchange for shares, there is typically no mechanism which allows the shares received in exchange for the assets to be distributed tax-free to the shareholders unless the transaction meets the requirements of a tax-deferred division, discussed in the next section.

Thus, in *Japan*, although there are no rules similar to the U.S. "practical" merger rule, transfers of assets (including business transfers) to a corporation as consideration for the issuance of capital stock are treated as one type of corporate restructuring transaction. Thus, nontaxable business transfers are available with regard to transfers in exchange for stock, subject to criteria similar to those for nontaxable mergers.[314]

Similarly, in the *Canadian* system, there is no equivalent of the U.S. "practical" merger described above. The special rollover rules described above in connection with corporate formation allow the transfer of assets in exchange for stock to take place on a tax-deferred basis. However, there is no provision allowing the tax-deferred distribution of the stock of the acquiring corporation to the shareholders of the acquired corporation. The *United Kingdom* has no rollover rules under which one corporation

312. India, ITA 1961, s. 50B.
313. United States, IRC, s. 368(a)(1)(C).
314. Japan, CTA, s. 2, paras. 12-14 and s. 62-4.

transfers a business to another, unrelated, corporation in return for shares in the unrelated corporation. Further, the distribution by the transferor corporation to its individual shareholders of shares in the unrelated corporation would be a taxable distribution unless made in a winding-up. However, if the shares in the unrelated corporation are issued directly to the transferor corporation's shareholders, rollover relief is available, as described above in section 7.2.[315]

Sweden has comprehensive legislation dealing with tax-free reorganizations, which is discussed above in section 7.1. The basic method for a tax-free reorganization is a sale of business assets at a price equal to the cost basis of the assets. However, in principle, gain could nevertheless be taxed, since the statutory rules state that all sales of business assets should be treated as if sold for fair market value.[316] To prevent gain from being recognized in these circumstances, the reorganization rules provide that a sale at less than market value will be accepted and there will be no deemed constructive income as a result of the transaction if certain conditions are met.[317] For example, the transferee corporation cannot have losses from activity prior to the transfer, a gain cannot be transferred from a corporation qualifying under a special tax regime to a "normal" corporation outside the special regime, and any transferred gain must remain subject to Swedish tax. Under this method of tax-free transfer, the purchaser acquires the assets at the same tax base as the seller, and thus the gains will eventually be realized and subject to tax.

Another set of rules makes it possible to exchange assets for shares in the transferee corporation free of tax. A prerequisite is that all the assets and liabilities of one or more branches of the transferee corporation's business activity must be transferred. The cost basis of the assets is transferred to the shares. These rules are in accordance with the EU Merger Directive.

In *Australia*, the "scrip-for-scrip" rollover and the consolidation regime for corporate groups can be used to similar effect, although a recent amendment to the scrip-for-scrip rules, discussed above, prevents a tax cost increase through the insertion of a new holding company which is more or less entirely held by the same shareholders (in other words, in the absence of a real acquisition or merger involving two companies with their own businesses and different shareholders).

Broadly speaking, both *Germany* and *The Netherlands* allow the transfer of an independent business unit in exchange for shares on a tax-deferred basis. In Germany, a business unit transfer to a corporation for shares may take place at book value if the business unit is part of the corporate tax base of the acquiring corporation, the liabilities of the business unit do not exceed its assets, and the hidden reserves remain subject to German tax in the hands of the acquiring corporation. Further, any consideration in addition to shares must not exceed 25% of the book value of the transferred assets or an absolute value of EUR 500,000.[318] As with the merger and share-exchange situations described above, the tax treatment of the transaction on the

315. United Kingdom, TCGA, ss. 136 and 139.
316. Sweden, ITA, Ch. 22, paras. 3 and 7.
317. Sweden, ITA, Ch. 23.
318. Germany, RTA, s. 20 para. 1.

part of the transferor depends on the extent to which the transferee elects to write up the assets to an amount in excess of their book value. To that extent, the transferor will recognize gain and have a corresponding increase in the tax cost of the shares.

To prevent companies from shifting business units to subsidiaries on a tax-deferred basis in order to sell the subsidiary tax-free under the rules of the German participation exemption, a sale of shares in the subsidiary leads to a retroactive realization of capital gains with respect to the originally transferred business division. The potential capital gain subject to retroactive taxation is reduced by one-seventh for each year following the reorganization.[319]

In the *Dutch* system, the transferor corporation takes as its tax cost in the shares received the fair market value of the shares transferred, thus eliminating the theoretical ("theoretical" since the transferring company is almost always entitled to the participation exemption with regard to the shares received) corporate-level tax on the appreciation in the transferred assets. The transferee corporation acquires the assets at their historical tax cost and thus bears the burden of the tax on a subsequent disposition.[320] There is a requirement, however, that the stock be held for at least three years to prevent what is essentially a taxable cash sale from being converted into a tax-deferred exchange.

In *France*, asset reorganizations without mergers are available in the context of "partial asset contributions" (*apport partiel d'actifs*)[321] through the incorporation of the concept of "transfer of assets" (*apports d'actifs*) in Article 2(d) of the EU Merger Directive. In this situation, a company with several lines of business may contribute a "complete branch of activity" to a new or pre-existing separate entity in consideration for shares. In practice, it is often difficult to determine the requirements for a "complete branch of activity." Generally speaking, case law has shown a degree of flexibility by insisting that only the "essential" elements of the business must be transferred.[322] In one case, the contribution of a right to use a trademark was sufficient, even though the transferring company retained ownership of the trademark.[323]

The contribution of securities representing a business is treated in the same way as the contribution of a "complete branch of activity":[324] the contribution may be a majority interest (i.e., over 50% of the capital of the company whose securities are contributed) or a minority interest (i.e., over 30% of the voting rights of the company whose securities are contributed) where no other partner holds, directly or indirectly, a higher proportion of voting rights. However, the preferential merger regime is no longer especially attractive in this situation since capital gains on the sale of equity interests are exempt from tax (subject to the denial of the deduction of 12% of costs and expenses).

319. Germany, RTA, s. 22 para. 1.
320. Netherlands, CITA, Art. 14.
321. France, CGI, s. 210 B.
322. Conseil d'Etat, 8e et 3e s-s, n°259052, July 27, 2005 (*Sté BL*).
323. Conseil d'Etat, 10e et 9e s-s, n°346809, December 6, 2013 (*Promo Art*).
324. France, CGI, 115 2.

India allows tax-free transfers of capital assets between an Indian parent company and its 100% owned subsidiary.[325]

7.5 Corporate Divisions: "Demergers"

The division of the assets of an existing corporation can take a variety of forms, but all have in common the splitting of ownership at the shareholder level. In a typical "demerger" situation, shareholders of the original corporation emerge from the transaction with stock interests in two (or more) corporations.[326] The splitting of ownership at the shareholder level raises a number of tax issues. First, since property has left the original corporation, gain might be recognized by the distributing corporation under the normally applicable rules. Second, since the shareholder has received a property distribution, the usual rules for dividends or redemptions (if shares in the original corporation are exchanged for the distributed shares) may be applicable at the shareholder level. Finally, since the shareholder has two interests in place of the original single interest, it is possible to sell a part of the investment while retaining the remainder, thus involving the usual rules, including preferential treatment on the sale shares. From a policy viewpoint, the issue is whether and to what extent the results of the normally applicable rules should be modified where a transaction constitutes a corporate division.

The systems examined here have reacted quite differently to the tax issues which arise in corporate divisions. In some countries, special rules allow tax-free treatment and are crafted to limit the perceived tax avoidance possibilities of the transaction. In others, no attempt has been made to change the normally applicable rules to allow tax-free treatment. In contrast, in the U.S., detailed rules allow for a tax-deferred division of, broadly speaking, active businesses, but these rules also contain substantial restrictions intended to prevent the "bailing out" of corporate profits in a divisive transaction.[327] In Canada, there are no special rules on demergers, but divisive transactions are possible in some circumstances in accordance with general statutory provisions and administrative guidance.

Even among those jurisdictions which allow some form of tax-deferred division, there are substantial differences in the requirements which must be met. Almost all jurisdictions, however, recognize that some sort of "business" or commercial purpose must be established for the division and have rules preventing the division of business and investment assets.

The rules on corporate division are most developed in the *United States* and involve both case law principles, which have been codified in the regulations, and

325. India, ITA 1961, s. 47(iv) and (v).

326. In the terminology often used in connection with corporate divisions, the pro rata distribution of the stock of a subsidiary to the existing shareholders is referred to as a "spin-off." If the distribution is in exchange for the stock of the distributing corporation, the transaction is termed a "split-off." A split-off is often done on a non-pro rata basis and results in a change in the ownership of the distributing corporation. Finally, in a "split-up," the distributing corporation transfers assets to new or existing subsidiaries and then liquidates.

327. United States, IRC, s. 355.

statutory provisions. The rules apply to both the distribution of an existing subsidiary and the transfer of assets to a newly formed subsidiary followed by the distribution of the stock to the shareholders. As a basic requirement, the division must have a demonstrable business purpose to justify the transaction from a commercial perspective.[328] The purpose must be, in general, a "corporate" purpose, as opposed to a "shareholder" purpose, and must justify the division of ownership at the shareholder level. Thus, for example, on the one hand, a desire to isolate risky activities in a separate corporation is not a sufficient business purpose for the distribution of the stock of the corporation to shareholders; on the other hand, where a shareholder disagreement is affecting operations at the corporate level, a corporate division may be commercially justified.

Assuming that the division has a business purpose, there are several statutory requirements intended to prevent the division from being used to distribute corporate profits to shareholders.[329] First, both the corporation making the distribution and the distributed corporation must be engaged in the active conduct of a trade or business and must have been engaged in such business for at least five years prior to the division. This requirement prevents concentrating passive or investment-type assets in one corporation, which could then be disposed of at preferential capital gain rates after the division. In addition, the statute requires that the stock of a distributed subsidiary must not have been acquired in a taxable acquisition in the past five years. This prevents the distributing corporation from using its earnings and profits to purchase a corporation with an active business and then making a tax-free distribution of that corporation shortly thereafter. The statute further mandates that the division cannot be "used principally as a device for the distribution of [earnings]." Although the "device" and "active business" requirements overlap to some extent, the device requirement focuses in particular on the possibility of a post-division sale of one of the businesses and takes this as an important indication of a distribution "device."

If the above requirements are met, at the corporate level, both the transfer of the assets to a subsidiary corporation (where an existing subsidiary is not involved) and the distribution of the stock do not result in the recognition of gain or loss. The receipt of the stock by the shareholders is similarly tax-free, and the tax cost of the shares with respect to which the distribution is made is allocated to the shares of the distributed and distributing companies.

Canada allows divisive transactions—called "butterfly" reorganizations to reflect how the structures look when diagrammed—on a tax-deferred basis.[330] The most important structural requirement is that each transferee corporation must receive the same proportionate share of property of the corporation being divided, namely, business property, investment property, and cash. Thus, the transaction cannot be

328. United States, Treas. Reg., s. 1.355-2(b).
329. United States, IRC, s. 355(a)-(e).
330. Canada, ITA, s. 55(3)-(6). Somewhat strangely, the butterfly reorganization is an exception to an anti-avoidance rule which prevents capital gains stripping through tax-free intercorporate dividends.

used to "bail out" cash or liquid investment assets. The rules are complex and differ depending on whether the transactions involve related or unrelated parties.

Since 1980, the *United Kingdom* has had extensive statutory rules dealing with demergers. Basically, three situations are covered: (1) the distribution by the parent company of the shares of an existing subsidiary; (2) the transfer of a subsidiary by the parent company to another company in exchange for the other company's shares and a distribution of those shares by the transferor company; and (3) the transfer of a business of the parent company to a subsidiary in exchange for its shares and the distribution of those shares by the parent company.[331] There are a number of conditions, the most important of which are that the company must be a trading company or a member of a trading group and the demerger must benefit the trading activities. This latter test requires more than merely showing that there is some commercial purpose to the transaction. An advance ruling or clearance for the transaction can be obtained from the tax authorities. If the various requirements are met, the distribution of the shares is not treated as a distribution for tax purposes and is tax-free in the hands of the recipient; the cost of the original shares is spread over those shares and the new shares. In general, there are no capital gains consequences for the company in distributing shares or transferring assets or shares.[332]

The situation is similar in *Australia*. Prior to 2002, there were no special rules dealing with demergers, but various transactional forms of demerger were possible in the context of a corporate group. One approach involved the subsidiary to be distributed issuing stock rights to the shareholders of the parent company without the distribution being treated as a dividend or otherwise taxable.[333] The exercise of those rights was not taxable and resulted in the shareholders owning stock directly in the subsidiary. The tax cost of the stock was the exercise price of the option, and thus any transfer of value was taxed to the shareholders when the stock was sold. There were no restrictions on this form of transaction based on the business or commercial purpose of the transaction.

In 2002, demerger relief provisions were introduced in addition to the rules outlined above.[334] These rules allow the "head company" of a demerger group to distribute shares of a company in the group to shareholders in the head company tax-free (from both capital gains and dividend treatment) for both the demerger group and the shareholders. A number of conditions need to be satisfied. The head company must hold at least 20% of the demerged entity and must distribute at least 80% of its shares in that entity. The value of the shareholders' new and continuing interests must be the same proportion of the value of the demerger group after the merger as before and no cash or other benefit can be distributed to the shareholders as part of the transaction. Shareholders must be treated equally in the demerger. The shareholders' original tax cost and CGT status (shares acquired before the introduction of CGT are

331. United Kingdom, Corporation Tax Act 2010, ss. 1076 and 1077.
332. United Kingdom, TCGA, ss. 136, 139 and 192.
333. This was the generally accepted position at the time, but it was thrown into doubt by a subsequent court decision (*McNeil*), *supra* note 119, in relation to taxation of distributions.
334. Australia, ITAA 1936, ss. 44(3)-(6), 45B, ITAA 1997, Div 125.

excluded from the CGT) are allocated between the shareholders' continuing and new shares. There are anti-abuse rules to deal with value shifting at the corporate level in the demerger and to remove the dividend exclusion where the demerger is mainly of passive investment assets or where the capital and profit elements of the demerger do not reflect the circumstances of the demerger.

In *Sweden*, under special statutory rules for publicly traded corporations, a pro rata distribution of all shares of a subsidiary corporation is possible on a tax-free basis. This requirement indirectly prevents investment-asset bailouts. The tax cost of the shares of the distributing corporation is allocated between the distributing and distributed corporation based on fair market value. There is generally no tax at the level of the distributing corporation as long as the shares are investment assets and not current assets.

In accordance with the EU Merger Directive, rules for partial demergers were introduced in 2007.[335] These rules are basically the same as the German rules described below. Recent changes in corporate law have also made it possible to effect a complete demerger in accordance with the rules for tax-free reorganizations.[336] In practice, however, a demerger could also be accomplished tax-free at the level of both the distributing corporation and the recipient shareholder by using statutory rules for sales below market value (*see* above section 7.4).

Germany introduced tax-deferred demerger rules in 1994 when it changed its domestic laws in order to comply with the EU Merger Directive.[337] Under the German system, two forms of demerger are recognized: division and split-off. In a division, two or more potentially independent businesses are transferred to new or existing corporations. The shareholders of the transferring corporation acquire shares of the acquiring corporations and the transferring corporation is dissolved. In a split-off, one or more businesses are transferred to one or more new or existing corporations, with the transferring corporation continuing to operate at least one business. The transfer can be made without recognition of gain to the transferring corporation if the parties decide to retain the book values of the assets involved and the "hidden reserves" remain subject to corporate tax in Germany at the level of the acquiring corporation(s). The shares of the acquiring corporation(s) given to the shareholders of the transferring corporation are considered to be acquired at a cost equal to their book value, with the result that the capital gain realized on a subsequent disposal would be fully taxable in Germany.

In *France*, there a distinction between demergers and partial demergers. The definition of "demergers" (*scission*)[338] is in line with Article 2(b) of the EU Merger Directive and the concept of a "partial demerger" in Article 2(c) of the Merger Directive

335. Sweden, ITA, Ch. 38a.
336. Sweden, ITA, Ch. 37.
337. Germany, RTA, s. 15.
338. France, CGI, s. 210-0 A.

was recently incorporated into French law.[339] While the concept of a partial demerger now appears in the Commercial Code,[340] it does not appear in the General Tax Code (*Code Général des Impôts* (CGI)). Since partial demergers are not eligible for the preferential merger regime (although this is likely to change in the near future), the preferential regime currently applies only to demergers. With respect to mergers without any exchange of shares, the regime applies automatically to the demerged company if certain conditions are met,[341] or with prior approval if they are not met.[342] For the shareholders of the demerged company, the allocation of securities is not considered to be a distribution and any capital gain realized by these shareholders on the exchange of securities can benefit from a deferral of tax.

The *Japanese* system was substantially changed in 2001. Prior to 2001, while assets could be contributed on a tax-deferred basis to a newly formed subsidiary, there were no special rules allowing the tax-deferred distribution of the shares of a corporation; the distribution was treated as a taxable dividend or redemption. Under the 2001 legislation, corporate demergers are generally regarded as taxable events for both the dividing corporations and their shareholders. However, income tax is deferred at both the corporation and shareholder levels with respect to:

- a corporate demerger between companies with a 100% equity relationship (i.e., cases where: (i) the transferee company or the transferor company is a wholly owned subsidiary of the transferor company or the transferee company, as the case may be; or (ii) both companies are the wholly owned subsidiaries of a common parent);
- a corporate demerger between companies with more than a 50% equity relationship meeting several criteria which ensure the continuity of the business (e.g., the principal portion of a certain type of business must be transferred to the transferee company); and
- a corporate demerger for the purpose of establishing a joint venture between the transferor and the transferee which meets several other criteria.

Until 2017, because they did not meet the conditions for nontaxable demergers, spin-offs were taxable. Recent amendments have enabled spin-offs to take place on a nontaxable basis, subject to certain requirements which are intended to guarantee continued control of the spun-off business by the transferor company group.[343]

In *The Netherlands*, under a qualifying tax-deferred demerger, the new companies take the tax cost that the acquired assets and liabilities had in the hands of the demerging company.[344]

339. French law n°2023-171 of March 9, 2023, incorporating various provisions of EU law in the fields of economics, health, labor, transport, and agriculture; Order n°2023-393 of May 24, 2023; Implementing decree n°2023-430 of June 26, 2023.
340. France, Commercial Code, s. L 236-27.
341. France, CGI, s. 210 B 1.
342. France, CGI, s. 210 B 3.
343. Japan, CTA, s. 2, paras. 12-11 through 12-13 and ss. 62-2 and 62-3.
344. Netherlands, CITA, Art. 14a.

In *China*, a demerger can qualify as a special reorganization if it meets all the general requirements for a special reorganization described in section 7.1 above, and in addition: (a) all shareholders of the demerged enterprise receive stock of the spun-off enterprises in proportion to their original ownership in the demerged enterprise; (b) the demerged enterprise and the spun-off enterprises do not substantially change their respective business operations; and (c) the stock of the spun-off enterprises received by the shareholders of the demerged enterprise constitutes at least 85% of the total consideration.

India also allows demergers, as defined,[345] on a tax-deferred basis similar to the treatment of amalgamations discussed in section 7.2 above.[346]

8 TRANSFER AND LIMITATIONS ON TRANSFER OF CORPORATE TAX ATTRIBUTES

In many tax systems, when a corporation goes out of existence in connection with a merger or similar transaction, its tax attributes are transferred to the successor corporation. The tax attributes transferred typically include the tax cost of assets, various reserves and provisions, and most important, loss carryforwards. In connection with loss carryforwards, there are often restrictions on the ability of the successor corporation to use the losses against subsequently arising income. These limitations are intended to prevent the "selling" of losses to third parties by the corporation which incurred the losses. They are typically triggered by changes in the ownership of the loss corporation and/or changes in its business activities.

The *United States* has highly developed rules concerning both the carryover of attributes and limitations on those carryovers.[347] Basically, in situations which qualify as reorganizations under the various statutory definitions, the corporate attributes of the disappearing corporation are inherited by the surviving corporation. In situations involving divisions where there is more than one surviving corporation, some of the existing corporate tax attributes are divided among the surviving corporations. In addition, on the liquidation of a corporate subsidiary, the subsidiary's attributes are inherited by the parent.

There are substantial limits on the carryover of losses, credits, and other tax benefits in the situations in which those attributes are inherited.[348] In general, the limitations apply whenever there is a significant change in the share ownership of the loss corporation, even where the situation does not involve the transfer of tax attributes. In general, where there is a more than 50% change in share ownership, the losses of the corporation experiencing the change in ownership are limited. Thus, where a sale of over 50% of the stock of the loss corporation occurs, the carryovers are subject to the limitations. The limitations also apply where there is a change of over 50% of the ownership of the loss corporation due to its merger into a profitable

345. India, ITA 1961, s. 2(19AA).
346. India, ITA 1961, s. 47(vib) and (vic).
347. United States, IRC, ss. 381, 382, 383 and 384.
348. United States, IRC, s. 382.

corporation. The "50% ownership change" test is determined by looking back at changes in the prior three-year period. These rules apply only to ownership changes by shareholders who have at least 5% interests in the corporation, but there are complex rules aggregating less-than-5% shareholders for some purposes.

Where the limitations apply, the loss carryover can offset only income which is subsequently generated by the loss corporation's business. Rather than actually determining the amount of that income, an assumed rate of return is applied to the value of the loss corporation at the time the change in ownership takes place, and the loss is allowed to that extent. The basic theory behind this limitation is that the purchasers of the corporation should be able to make no greater use of the economic losses incurred by the selling shareholders than those shareholders would have enjoyed if there had been no change of ownership. Even this limited carryover is not allowed unless the corporation's business is continued or its assets used in another business. The loss limitations also apply to certain credit carryforwards.[349]

Similar limitations apply to losses which have accrued but have not yet been realized for tax purposes at the time of the change in ownership. The deduction of such "built-in" losses is limited if the losses are realized within five years after the ownership change.

In addition, there are some broad "purpose-based" anti-avoidance principles applicable to loss situations,[350] but they have been largely supplanted by more specific statutory provisions dealing with losses.

The *Canadian* rules are somewhat similar, although not as extensive. On the liquidation of a domestic 90%-owned subsidiary, corporate tax attributes are transferred to the subsidiary's domestic parent corporation. In addition, on the amalgamation of two or more corporations, the existing tax attributes are preserved in the amalgamated company. Where control of a corporation changes (technically, a "loss restriction event"), any existing capital loss carryforwards are restricted;[351] similarly, nonbusiness losses may not be carried forward after an ownership change.[352] With respect to operating loss carryforwards, the business of the loss corporation must be continued for profit or with a reasonable expectation of profit and the losses may be used only against the income from that business or a similar business. In addition, as a result of many statutory so-called stop-loss rules, any accrued but unrealized losses are deemed to be realized at the time of the change of control, thus subjecting them to the above limitations.

In *The Netherlands*, a reorganization in the form of a merger under corporate law results in the carryover of tax attributes (including losses) of the disappearing company at the taxpayer's request if certain conditions set out by the Ministry of Finance are fulfilled.[353] Under the general rules on loss carryovers, the use of losses is restricted in that situation, as well as in certain others, where there is a change of at least 30% in

349. United States, IRC, s. 383.
350. United States, IRC, s. 269.
351. Canada, ITA, s. 111(4).
352. Canada, ITA, s. 111(5).
353. Netherlands, CITA, Art. 14b and standard conditions pursuant to CITA, Art. 14b order of August 12, 2022, Stcrt. 2022, 22286.

share ownership involving those who were shareholders when the business activities ceased, unless the loss was incurred in a taxable year in which, for at least nine months, the company's passive investments did not represent over 50% of its total assets and the activities of the company in the course of the loss-making years did not shrink by more than 70%.[354]

The 2001 tax revisions changed the *Japanese* system with respect to the treatment of tax attributes. In general, in a nontaxable restructuring transaction, the tax attributes are transferred to a successor corporation. In addition, in a nontaxable merger, loss carryovers are permitted, subject to certain requirements. Otherwise, tax losses are not transferable from one corporation to another. As discussed above, the 2001 tax revisions introduced an anti-avoidance provision which is generally applicable to any type of corporate restructuring transaction.[355] This provision is intended to enable the tax authorities to challenge tax-motivated reorganization transactions.

In *Sweden*, corporate tax attributes, including loss carryforwards, are transferred in a merger transaction. However, where a change of ownership of a corporation with losses occurs, special limits apply to existing loss carryforwards.[356] As a rule, losses can be carried forward where the corporations could have made taxable "group contributions" between them before the merger. Group contributions allow a consolidation of profits and losses within a corporate group. In other situations, the carryforward of losses is normally subject to special restrictions.

In *France*, losses incurred by an acquiring company prior to a merger may in principle be carried forward in accordance with ordinary law. However, if the acquiring company changes its business activity at the time of the merger, the losses cannot be carried forward, since this change of activity is treated as a cessation of business. While the absorbed company loses the right to carry forward its losses as a result of ceasing to exist for tax purposes, it can transfer its net long-term capital losses. Similarly, loss carrybacks can be transferred to the acquiring company.[357] While, in principle, loss carryforwards are not transferable to the acquiring company, they may be transferred in their entirety, subject to approval by the tax authorities.[358] The same applies to non-deductible interest carried forward.[359] Under certain conditions, however, approval is not required (e.g., if the cumulative amount of losses is less than EUR 200,000).[360] In practice, the conditions under which approval is granted remain difficult to assess and the authorities have a certain latitude in assessing the facts. This situation explains why some companies prefer other alternatives, such as the tax-free revaluation of fixed assets (*réévaluation libre des actifs*) or reversing the direction of the merger.

With minor exceptions, *Australia* permits the transfer of tax attributes (tax cost, losses, imputation credits, and foreign tax credits) only when a 100%-related group of

354. Netherlands, CITA, Art. 20a.
355. Japan, CTA, s. 132-2.
356. Sweden, ITA, Ch. 37 paras. 21-26.
357. France, CGI, s. 220 quinquies.
358. France, CGI, s. 209 II, referring to s. 1649 nonies.
359. France, CGI, s. 212 bis CGI.
360. France, CGI, s. 209 II 2.

companies consolidates under the consolidation regime introduced in 2002.[361] In a merger, this will generally have the effect of transferring the tax attributes of an acquired company to the head company of a consolidated group, since the acquired company enters the consolidated group if 100% owned by the head company. There are elaborate provisions to prevent value shifting and the generation of multiple losses among related companies outside consolidation.[362] These rules limit certain tax attributes of a corporation whose stock ownership undergoes a 50% or greater change unless the corporation conducts a "similar business" and did not commence a new business or new kinds of transactions with the purpose of satisfying the test. Failure to satisfy the continuity of ownership and similar business tests results in the denial of carryforwards of operating losses, bad debts not yet written off for tax purposes, realized capital losses, and accrued losses.[363] The general limitations do not apply to imputation credits or foreign tax credits. Much more generous rules for testing continuity of ownership apply to the shares of a company listed on the stock exchange.

The pattern in the *United Kingdom* is basically the same. Where, within a five-year period after a change in ownership (an elaborately defined statutory concept), there is a major change in the nature and conduct of the business, the utilization of pre-change revenue losses is restricted.[364] Additional rules target capital allowances and deduction and profit transfers.[365] Historically, limitations did not apply to capital losses. However, due to perceived abuses, in 2006 rules were introduced which may restrict the use of capital losses following a change in ownership.[366] These rules are couched in anti-avoidance language and do not follow those applicable to revenue (operating) losses. The result is disjointed.

In *Germany*, the carryover of tax losses with respect to mergers and demergers has been dramatically restricted over the years. In a widely criticized move in 2007, the option to carry over tax loss positions from a merged corporation to the acquiring corporation and, in the case of a demerger, from the transferring to the acquiring corporation(s), was abolished.[367] This move was taken due to fears that, under emerging CJEU jurisprudence, Germany might be forced to recognize losses incurred by foreign companies merging with domestic companies. While it is debatable whether this fear was justified, the current law has created a substantial obstacle to business reorganizations in times of economic crisis.

With respect to the impact of changes in corporate control and in the activities of a corporation on loss carryforwards, German courts changed their attitude dramatically in the 1980s. Before that time, German case law had required a corporation to have some type of "economic identity" in order for losses to survive such changes. From

361. Australia, ITAA 1997, Divs 707, 709, 717-A.
362. Australia, ITAA 1997, Divs 165-CD, 170-D, 725, 727.
363. Australia, ITAA 1997, Divs 165-175.
364. United Kingdom, Corporation Tax Act 2010, s. 673.
365. United Kingdom, Capital Allowances Act 2001, s. 212A-212S and Corporation Tax Act 2010, s. 730A-730D.
366. United Kingdom, TCGA, ss. 16A and 184A-184I.
367. Germany, RTA, s. 12 para. 3 (mergers) and RTA, s. 15 para. 1 sent. 2 (demergers), with reference to RTA, s. 4 para. 2 sent. 2.

1986 on, courts began to allow losses where there was a change in share ownership or in the business carried on as long as the legal form of the corporation remained the same. A statutory provision enacted in 1988 changed this regime, requiring that the corporation utilizing the losses had to be not only "legally" but also "economically" identical with the corporation which suffered the losses. This provision expressly stated that a corporation would not be considered to be the same legal and economic entity where there was a transfer of more than 75% of its shares, it had recommenced business (in the same field or a different field), and the fair market value of any acquired assets exceeded the value of existing assets.

The 2007 Business Tax Reform amended the rule, providing that any "harmful acquisition of shares" triggered the restrictions on the use of losses at the corporate level irrespective of any change in the corporation's business or capital structure.[368] The provision limited the use of losses proportionally where 25% to 50% of the shares were transferred to a particular person or related parties within a period of five years; it excluded loss offsetting completely if more than half of the shares were transferred within that time. The provision was clearly aimed at fighting tax avoidance transactions; however, it also covered many cases of legitimate tax planning. Over the years, exceptions were introduced for the restructuring of failing companies, intragroup transactions, and losses covered by hidden reserves. The exception for restructurings was subject to challenge by the European Commission under EU law as prohibited state aid; however, in 2018 the CJEU declared the Commission decision null and void.[369]

In 2016, the strictness of the regime was modified by the introduction of a provision making it possible to preserve losses where a corporation continues its activity without adding a different business following a share deal. In 2017, the Federal Constitutional Court declared the original 25%-50% rule to be unconstitutional; as a result, it was abolished but the prohibition on losses where more than 50% of the shares are transferred was retained. At present, it remains to be seen whether this regime, complemented by the loss-preserving provision of 2016, will withstand a constitutional challenge.

In *China*, the tax legislation does not contain specific rules on the transfer of tax attributes. The EIT legislation does not impose any limitation on the use of losses on a change in control of a loss entity. In other words, a share transfer resulting in a change of the legal ownership of a Chinese company does not affect the carryover of the losses of that company. However, the GAAR may be applied where an equity transfer has no reasonable commercial purpose and the use of the losses of the target may be viewed as the primary purpose of the transaction.

In *India*, tax attributes may be transferred, subject to certain conditions, on amalgamations, demergers, the conversion of a partnership into a company, and certain other similar conversions.[370] Business losses may be carried forward for eight years after the amalgamation and unclaimed depreciation can be carried forward

368. Germany, CITA, s. 8c.
369. CJEU, June 28, 2018, C-219/16 P (*Lowell Financial Services*) and C-203/16 P (*Andres [Heitkamp BauHolding]*).
370. India, ITA 1961, s. 72A, including the disposal of public sector companies by the government.

indefinitely. The Finance Act 2021 extended the scope of these rules to any public sector company.

In cases of amalgamation, the amalgamating company must have owned an industrial undertaking, a ship, or a hotel, or must be a bank (to be amalgamated with specified banks), or a public-sector airline (to be merged with another public-sector company or an airline company). The definition of industrial undertaking has been artificially expanded and now comprises undertakings engaged in manufacturing and processing of goods, creation of software, provision of telecommunications services, mining, and construction of ships, aircraft, or rail systems.[371] In addition, the amalgamating company must have been in business for at least three years and must have continuously held at least 75% of the book value of the fixed assets during the two years prior to the amalgamation. The amalgamated company must continuously hold 75% of the assets of the amalgamating company and continue the business of the amalgamating company for a minimum period of five years; it must also satisfy other specified conditions (as laid down in Rule 9C) to ensure that the amalgamation was entered into for genuine business purposes.[372]

The ability to carry forward losses and depreciation claims applies to demergers. The accumulated loss and unabsorbed depreciation of the "demerged" company can be utilized by the "resulting" company as follows: where the loss or unabsorbed depreciation is directly related to the undertakings transferred to the resulting company, it may be carried forward and claimed by the resulting company; where they are not directly related to the undertakings transferred to the resulting company, they must be apportioned between the demerged company and the resulting company on the basis of the proportion of the assets retained by the demerged company and those transferred to the resulting company.[373] The central government is authorized to prescribe conditions to ensure that the demerger is for genuine business purposes.

Similarly, subject to several conditions, business losses and unabsorbed depreciation flow through to the successor on the conversion of a partnership or proprietorship into a company,[374] the reorganization of a private company or an unlisted public company into an LLP,[375] the amalgamation of banking institutions,[376] and the amalgamation and demerger of cooperative banks.[377] For public-sector companies, where the share-purchase agreement restricts disinvestment for a certain period, the benefit of the transfer of losses and other tax attributes is available if the amalgamation takes place within five years of the year in which the restriction expires.[378]

371. India, ITA 1961, s. 72A (7)(aa).
372. India, ITA 1961, s. 72A(2).
373. India, ITA 1961, s. 72A(4).
374. India, ITA 1961, ss. 72A(6) and 47(xiii) and (xiv).
375. India, ITA 1961, ss. 72A(6A) and 47(xiib).
376. India, ITA 1961, s. 72AA.
377. India, ITA 1961, s. 72AB.
378. Finance Acts 2021 and 2023, s. 72A and 72AA.

9 CONSOLIDATED CORPORATE TAXATION

While corporations are generally treated as separate taxpayers, most systems have special provisions under which affiliated corporations can be combined for tax purposes. These rules allow the overall economic results of the group to be taken into account despite the existence of formally separate corporate entities. The requirements for consolidation differ substantially, as do the techniques for treating the consolidated entity. In some cases, the separate corporate existence of the members of the group is ignored for most purposes and, in effect, each corporation is treated as a division of a single company. In contrast, some systems generally treat the corporations as separate taxpayers but have special rules which allow the separate profit or loss of group members to be transferred among members of the group. The differences in technique can have important consequences for the timing and character of the income of the group. In still other situations, there is no formal mechanism for consolidation, but the normal rules of income determination are relaxed in the context of related corporations.

The *United States* has a highly developed system of consolidated taxation. The rules are contained in a complex set of administrative regulations based on a broad statutory authorization.[379] To qualify for consolidated treatment, an "affiliated group" of corporations must have a domestic parent corporation which owns at least 80% of the stock of another domestic corporation. Lower-tier corporations may be included in the group if their higher-tier shareholder(s) in the group meet the 80%-ownership test with respect to those corporations. Under this definition, two brother-sister corporations owned by an individual or a foreign corporation are not entitled to consolidated treatment. Where the definitional requirements are met, the group can elect to file a consolidated tax return. Corporations subject to a special taxing regime (e.g., life insurance companies) may not be included in the group.

When consolidated filing is elected, "consolidated" income is calculated by combining the separate incomes of each of the members of the group. The income of each member of the group is determined under normal principles, with important modifications to reflect the consolidation. Intercompany transactions are accounted for on a "deferred" basis. In general, no gain or loss is recognized on intercompany sales transactions until the property is sold outside the group. At that time, the gain or loss that would have been involved in the intercompany sale is accounted for by the member who would have realized that amount in the original sale. Where depreciable property is used in the business of the buying member, an increased basis for depreciation purposes is allowed, but the selling member must include a corresponding amount in income as the depreciation deductions are taken. Deferred intercompany transactions also must be taken into account if for some reason the group stops filing a consolidated return. Intercorporate dividends are eliminated in the calculations of consolidated income. Consolidation allows losses of one member of the group to offset income of other members.

379. United States, Treas. Reg., s. 1.1502-1 through 1.1502-100.

The overall effects of the consolidation are reflected in the "investment account" with respect to the parent's stock in the subsidiaries in the group. In general terms, earnings in the subsidiary which are included in the consolidated income increase the parent's basis in the subsidiary stock, thus preventing double taxation of the same economic income if the stock of the subsidiary is sold. Correspondingly, actual dividend distributions reduce the basis in the stock, as do losses of the subsidiary which are used by other members of the group. Where the losses exceed the basis of the stock, a so-called excess loss account is established, a type of "negative" basis that, in effect, causes the loss to be recaptured if the stock is sold or the member leaves the group.

Prior to 2002, *Australia* had rules permitting the transfer of assets, losses, and foreign tax credits among members of a 100%-related group. These rules were replaced with a complete and complex consolidation regime which rivals that of the U.S. in complexity (over 600 pages of legislation).[380] In order to qualify for tax-free transfers of assets, loss grouping, and foreign tax credit pooling, it is now generally necessary to consolidate for income tax purposes; this is the main incentive for companies to enter the consolidation regime. The regime is elective for 100%-related resident companies, partnerships, and fixed trusts, but once elected, all entities with the necessary relationship must enter the consolidated group. The "head entity" of the group must be a company (or a trust or partnership taxed as a company), and most types of company may enter a group, including insurance companies, although some are excluded, such as credit unions.

When consolidation is elected, group income is calculated by the "single-entity rule" which treats all the subsidiary members of the group as divisions of the head company—that is, the members do not calculate taxable income separately for each member and then eliminate intragroup transactions. Pre-consolidation tax events are preserved by the "entry history rule," under which everything that happened to the subsidiaries before consolidation is deemed to have occurred to the head company. Hence, on entering consolidation, it is necessary to allocate all tax attributes of the members to the head company. In the case of assets, this allocation is generally achieved by pushing down the tax cost of shares and other interests in group members held by the head company and other group members (which disappear on consolidation) to the assets (other than shares, etc.). Liabilities are taken into account in this "push down" process, with intragroup liabilities eliminated. In the case of other tax attributes such as losses, imputation credits, and foreign tax credits, the process involves pushing them up to the head company. Losses are subject to numerous special rules but, in general, the "available fraction" approach applies, which is designed to ensure that the rate of using losses transferred from a particular member of the group remains approximately the same as it would have been if the losses had remained in that member (similar to the U.S. rules which apply to losses on mergers). Once these parameters are established for the head company, taxable income, etc., is calculated only at the level of the head company.

380. Australia, ITAA 1997, Pt 3-90 comprising Divs 700-721.

When a company leaves a consolidated group, the tax cost of the shares is reconstructed from the net assets of the leaving company. The head company calculates any gain or loss for the consideration received for the shares in the company accordingly. If the reconstructed tax cost is negative, the head company makes a capital gain equal to the deficiency and the tax cost is set at nil for calculating any gain to the head company on the departure of the subsidiary. Other tax attributes remain with the head company and are not allocated to the leaving company so that, for example, it will have no losses or imputation credits in its franking account immediately after departure from the group.

One of the main reasons for adopting consolidation in Australia was to prevent value shifting and multiple losses arising from the flexibility to manipulate the tax cost of shares and assets in a group. For related companies which remain outside consolidation (generally because of less than 100% ownership), there are revamped and comprehensive value-shifting provisions and rules on cost base adjustments in relation to the multiplication of losses referred to above.

The *Canadian* system takes a very different approach to the taxation of affiliated corporations. There are no formal provisions which allow the consolidation of profits and losses. While proposals for consolidation have been made, they have been opposed by the provinces, whose tax is usually a percentage of the federal tax. There was concern that a consolidation regime would allow an avoidance of provincial taxes through the shifting of profits and losses in the group. Nonetheless, informal consolidation has been recognized both administratively and legislatively. Most of the anti-avoidance and anti-loss-trading rules do not apply to transactions between related corporations; transactions which are structured to transfer profits and losses among the members of a group are generally effective, despite the fact that they are usually blatantly artificial.

Sweden also does not formally recognize consolidation among group members. However, a special tax rule provides a mechanism which allows for the consolidation of profits and losses.[381] It is possible for corporations connected with at least 90% ownership to a common parent corporation to make "group contributions" to other members of the group. The group contribution is deductible by the paying corporation and taxable to the recipient corporation. Thus, for example, a profitable parent corporation with a loss subsidiary could make a group contribution to the subsidiary which would reduce the parent's profit and allow the subsidiary to utilize its losses. Group contributions can also be made between subsidiaries of the same parent corporation. The rules are not, in general, applicable to corporations subject to special tax rules.

The *United Kingdom* similarly does not recognize group reporting of income. However, a number of special rules apply to the taxation of company groups. The most important of these rules deals with "group relief." If a parent company owns at least 75% of the stock of a domestic subsidiary company, then trading losses, capital allowances, and certain other tax attributes can be "surrendered" from one company to

381. Sweden, ITA, Ch. 35.

the other.[382] In this case, the whole amount of the loss, etc., can be surrendered even where there is less than 100% ownership. In addition, if a "consortium" of 5% or more corporate shareholders together owns 75% of the stock of a company, group relief is available; however, only a proportionate part of the loss, etc., can be "surrendered."[383] For example, group relief allows losses in one company to be surrendered and offset against income of the other company. Historically, only current-year losses could be surrendered. This rule was loosened in 2017 to allow the surrender of loss carryforwards; however, loss carryforwards above GBP 5 million can be used only to the extent of 50% of a company's total profits.[384]

Special rules apply for capital gains purposes which allow a tax-free transfer of assets within a 75%-owned group.[385] However, if the corporation receiving the asset on a tax-free basis leaves the group within six years, the transaction is retroactively taxable.[386] Capital gains and capital losses may be transferred between companies within the same 75%-owned group.[387] These rules differ from those applicable to revenue losses.

In contrast, *The Netherlands* has a complex system of consolidation. A parent corporation and some or all of its 95%-owned subsidiaries can make an application to the fiscal authorities to be treated as a so-called fiscal unity,[388] under which the corporations remain separate for corporate law purposes, but for tax purposes the activities, assets and liabilities, and income and losses are deemed to be those of the parent corporation. Generally, all the corporations must be organized under Dutch law, or, if organized under the law of an EU Member State or a tax treaty country, they must be similar to Dutch companies. Companies that are not residents of The Netherlands may join a fiscal unity only to the extent that they have a Dutch permanent establishment. Further, the companies must be subject to the same tax rules (i.e., an insurance corporation and a business corporation cannot form a fiscal unity). Finally, the companies must meet a series of further requirements, laid down in regulations issued under the statute (which may be supplemented with requirements geared to individual cases) to prevent, *inter alia*, the shifting of value to a subsidiary whose stock could be sold on a tax-free basis and to limit, *inter alia*, the use of pre-and post-unity losses. Pursuant to a CJEU judgment,[389] the rules regarding qualifying companies were relaxed as of December 2016. Since that time, a fiscal unity may also be formed: (a) between Dutch-resident subsidiaries of a parent company resident in another EU/EEA (European Economic Area) Member State (with the parent not forming part of the unity); and (b) between a Dutch-resident parent company and a Dutch-resident sub-subsidiary held through a subsidiary resident in another EU/EEA Member State.[390]

382. United Kingdom, Corporation Tax Act 2010, s. 99.
383. United Kingdom, Corporation Tax Act 2010, s. 143.
384. United Kingdom, Corporation Tax Act 2010, ss. 45A, 188AA-188FD and 269ZA-269ZZB.
385. United Kingdom, TCGA, s. 171.
386. United Kingdom, TCGA, s. 179.
387. United Kingdom, TCGA, s. 171A.
388. Netherlands, CITA, Art. 15 through 15b.
389. CJEU, June 12, 2014, Joined Cases C-39/13, 40/13, and 41/13 (*SCA Group Holding BV and others*).
390. Netherlands, CITA, Art. 15(2).

France has allowed optional consolidation (*intégration fiscale*) since 1988 (following a first draft in 1971).[391] The aim is to consolidate the results of group companies by offsetting profits and losses as well as capital gains and losses within the group, and by neutralizing certain intra-group transactions to avoid double taxation. The option to consolidate is valid for five years, renewable by tacit agreement, and can be terminated each year.[392] Some conditions must be met to create an integrated group:[393] the parent company must hold, directly or indirectly, at least 95% of the capital of the group companies; all group companies must be subject to CIT; all subsidiaries must give their consent individually, by means of a tax consolidation agreement; and all group members must open and close their fiscal year on the same date. Where all these conditions are fulfilled, the parent company becomes solely liable for the CIT of the group formed by it and its subsidiaries. The main consequence is the consolidation of the group's results,[394] which involves four stages: determining the individual results of each group member company; determining the group's overall results, taking into account deficits and profits; restating the overall results in order to determine the tax on the group's actual profits; and taxing the overall results. The tax is paid by the head company, although the principle of solidarity means that all the companies in the group are liable for the payment of the tax. In practice, the main difficulty is the requirement that all consolidated companies must be subject to CIT. This has been contested under EU law, which has gradually shaped French law. On the one hand, the recognition of vertical integration has meant that a French parent company can consolidate with a French sub-subsidiary held through a foreign company not subject to corporation tax in France but whose registered office is located in the EU.[395] On the other hand, the recognition of horizontal integration has led to changes in French law to allow the integration of French sister companies that are at least 95% owned by a parent company established in another EU Member State.[396]

An important outstanding issue is whether the territorial limitation on tax consolidation—in particular, whether restricting tax consolidation to French subsidiaries only—infringes the EU freedom of establishment. In a landmark case, the Conseil d'Etat[397] definitively condemned any possibility of setting off deficits made by 95% foreign subsidiaries against the overall result of a consolidated group regardless of the nature of the losses. Nevertheless, the lack of clarity in EU jurisprudence continues to give some French integrated groups hope that they can use the losses of their European subsidiaries. For the time being, while the domestic law response has been firm,[398] a few recent rulings have accepted the use of the losses of a qualifying foreign subsidiary.[399] A new decision from the Conseil d'Etat on this point is anticipated.

391. France, CGI s. 223 A through 223 U.
392. France, CGI, s. 223 1.
393. France, CGI, s. 223 A.
394. France, CGI, s. 223 B.
395. CJEU, November 27, 2008, C-418/07 (*Société Papillon*).
396. CJEU, June 12, 2014, C-39/13 (*SCA Group Holding BV*).
397. Conseil d'Etat, 9e/10e sous-sections réunies, April 15, 2015, No. 368135 (*Société Agapes*).
398. CAA Versailles, 3e ch., June 23, 2020, No. 19VE01012 (*Groupe Lucien Barrière*).
399. CAA Paris, December 15, 2023, n°21PA0300 (*Min. c/ Sté Compagnie Plastic Omnium SE*) and n°21PA01850 (*Société Générale*).

Germany has statutory provisions dealing with group taxation which are based on a complex and highly developed case law-based system of de facto consolidation (*Organschaft*).[400] Traditionally, consolidation was available only to domestic businesses (including German branches of foreign corporations and individual proprietorships). However, a "foreign" parent company can also qualify if it has a permanent establishment in Germany to which the profits and losses of the dependent corporation are attributed. Consolidation is possible only where a "dominant" entity has a majority of voting rights in the "dependent" entity. The former legislation, which also required economic and organizational integration, was repealed in 2000. However, an election for group taxation requires a valid profit-and-loss pooling agreement under corporate law between the parent and the subsidiary. Under this pooling agreement, which must last for at least five years, profits and losses of the dependent entities are calculated on a separate basis and then transferred to the dominant entity, which includes the amounts in its income calculations. The dominant entity is obliged to cover any loss suffered by the dependent entity and takes over its profits. This transfer of profit is not treated as a distribution. As a result of the transfer, the dependent entity experiences neither profit nor loss (under the agreement the loss is offset by the claim against the dominant entity for reimbursement). Losses arising prior to the *Organschaft* may not be used while the *Organschaft* arrangement is effective.

Despite the *Organschaft* arrangement, the participating companies are treated as independent entities for tax purposes. Thus, intercompany transactions generate income or loss which is taken into account currently. If transactions are not undertaken on an arm's length basis, a constructive dividend (treated as an advance transfer of profit) or constructive contribution to capital may result. Payments by the subsidiary to outside minority shareholders are treated as regular income of the subsidiary and as dividends in the hands of the shareholders.

Unlike the other systems, for a long time *Japan* did not allow any type of formal or informal consolidation: each corporation was treated as a separate taxpayer and transactions between related corporations had to be undertaken at arm's length, without exceptions. However, after strong pressure by Japanese companies, the 2002 tax revisions introduced a consolidated corporation tax system. Under this system, a consolidated group includes only direct or indirect wholly owned subsidiaries incorporated in Japan; a consolidated group filing a consolidated return must include all the qualified subsidiaries in the group.

In 2022, this consolidated return system was replaced with a system with a different concept, but with almost the same outcomes. Under the new system, a single consolidated return is no longer available. Instead, each company files its own tax return, but it can adjust the amount of its taxable income by taking into account the amount of taxable loss, including the loss carryforwards of other companies with a 100% capital relationship. Despite this considerable difference in the concept of the system, its practical outcomes remain mostly unchanged. For example, both systems apply only to a Japanese parent and its wholly owned Japanese subsidiaries, and no

400. Germany, CITA, ss. 14-19.

voluntary carve-out from a group is permitted. In addition, joint and several group liability has remained unchanged under the group adjustment system. Both systems are optional, not compulsory. However, among the few differences, the most important may be that under the new group adjustment system, no losses incurred prior to the adoption of a group adjustment may be used to offset the taxable income of other group companies; in contrast, under the consolidated return system, such losses of the parent company could be used to offset the taxable income in consolidated returns.

In addition to the consolidation or group adjustment rules, since 2010, profits or losses as a result of any transaction between Japanese companies with a 100% equity relationship (e.g., a parent and its wholly owned Japanese subsidiary) are generally deferred until such transactions are deemed no longer to be transactions between companies with a 100% equity relationship.[401] This rule, known as the "group company regime" is compulsory. Therefore, for any company groups with a 100% equity relationship, the group company regime applies first; they may then opt into the consolidation or the group adjustment regime described above in order to offset the gains and losses among member companies.

China and *India* do not have any provisions allowing the tax consolidation of a group of corporations.

10 SPECIAL TAX REGIMES FOR CLOSELY HELD CORPORATIONS

Regardless of the basic structure of their corporate tax system, some countries have special rules for the taxation of closely held corporations. These rules sometimes reflect the view that whatever the appropriate taxing pattern for widely held corporations, modifications should be made for closely held corporations that more closely resemble partnerships. Nonetheless, the technical details of the rules vary substantially. In some cases, they allow a single level of pass-through taxation following the partnership model. In other situations, the rules are intended to reinforce the normal pattern of taxation by dealing specifically with issues which typically arise in the closely held context or to prevent income from being shifted from one category to another through a closely held corporation.

In the *United States*, special rules provide for pass-through treatment for corporations which meet certain definitional requirements and elect to be treated on a pass-through basis.[402] The technical requirements for qualification have been strictly interpreted, and the rules are often criticized as being too complex for the relatively unsophisticated taxpayers to whom they are intended to apply. In general, the number of shareholders is limited to 100 individuals who must be residents of the U.S. Special rules apply to trusts, which allow them to be shareholders in certain situations. The corporation can have only a single class of stock which participates in dividends, although voting and nonvoting common stock is allowed. The corporation is permitted to have subsidiary corporations. If the corporation elects pass-through status, it may

401. Japan, CTA, ss. 61-13.
402. United States, IRC, ss. 1361 through 1378.

further elect to disregard its wholly owned subsidiaries as separate entities and be treated as though it owns the subsidiaries' assets and liabilities directly.

If the corporation elects pass-through status, each shareholder includes in income their share of the items of income and deduction that arise at the corporate level. Thus, the character of the items passes through and is retained (e.g., as a capital gain) at the shareholder level. The income is included in the shareholder's taxable year in which the corporation's year ends, whether or not it is distributed. If the share ownership changes during the year, income is generally prorated over the entire year and attributed to the shareholders accordingly. Income which is included increases the shareholder's tax cost in the shares as if the income had been distributed and then reinvested in the corporation. When an actual distribution is made, the tax cost of the shares is reduced accordingly; any excess over the tax cost is treated as a capital gain.

If the corporation operates at a loss, the loss similarly passes through to its shareholder and reduces the tax cost of the stock accordingly. The shareholder is allowed to take a current deduction for the corporate-level loss only to the extent of the shareholder's actual investment in the corporation, whether in the form of stock or debt. If the taxpayer's investment is insufficient to use the loss currently, the loss is suspended until the investment is increased (e.g., by additional capital contributions or by the recognition of corporate-level income which, in effect, increases the investment). Special "passive activity loss" rules limit otherwise deductible losses if the shareholder does not participate in the corporation's business.[403]

Special rules apply where the corporation electing pass-through treatment has previously carried on business as a "normal" corporation subject to the two-level tax system. The rules are intended to ensure that any previously earned but undistributed corporate income is subject to a second shareholder-level tax when distributed. Thus, complex "stacking" rules are provided which determine whether distributions are deemed to be from current or prior earnings. Similarly, appreciation which was accrued but unrecognized at the time that the corporation became subject to the pass-through regime may be subject to a double-level tax to approximate the pattern of taxation which would have applied if the appreciation had been realized and distributed while the corporation was subject to the two-level tax system.

While the corporate-level income and deduction items are subject to the special pass-through rules, the other normally applicable tax rules continue to apply to the corporation. Thus, for example, a reorganization is possible between a "normal" corporation and a pass-through corporation.

None of the other countries here under consideration has special pass-through treatment for formally organized corporations, although, in *Canada*, special rules apply to private corporations and CCPCs. Private corporations are corporations whose stock is not publicly traded on an exchange and are not controlled by a public corporation.[404] CCPCs qualify for full imputation relief in respect of their investment income and active business income up to CAD 500,000 annually. The latter income

403. United States, IRC, s. 469.
404. Canada, ITA, s. 89(1).

qualifies for a "small business deduction,"[405] which significantly reduces the rate of tax on the income. The small business deduction is not available for income from personal services businesses or investment businesses. The rules dealing with investment income, some of which apply only to CCPCs and some of which apply to all private corporations, are generally designed to prevent individuals from achieving a better result by holding investments in corporate form rather than directly.

In *Australia*, government-sponsored committees have twice recommended a pass-through regime similar to the American rules, but no action was taken. In practice, pass-through treatment for taxable profits (but not tax losses), along with the benefit of limited liability, is achieved by operating most closely held businesses in the form of trading trusts rather than companies.

Many countries have more restrictive rules dealing with closely held companies. In *Sweden*, there are rules to prevent income from employment from being converted to (more lightly taxed) income from capital.[406] In particular, the rules are meant to deal with situations in which dividends from closely held corporations are received by shareholders who also work on behalf of the corporation. A yield on the shareholder capital invested in the corporation is calculated based on the government borrowing rate plus 9%. Further, the basis for calculating the threshold is increased by an amount equal to 50% of salaries paid to employees of the corporation. Dividends up to this threshold are taxed as income from capital. Dividends above this amount are treated as income from employment in the hands of the shareholder. At the corporate level, the dividends are neither deductible nor subject to social security tax. Given the levels of corporate and social security tax, the result is that the total tax burden on actual salary distributions and "deemed" salary in the form of excess dividends is roughly the same. This form of taxation also applies to capital gains when shares in such corporations are sold. In recent years, the threshold for taxation of dividends as employment income has been raised considerably for most corporations, since the basis for the calculation now includes not only capital invested but also employee salaries. Thus, for many corporations, no dividends are in fact taxed as employment income.

Other countries have similar rules to prevent closely held corporations from taking advantage of possible tax differentials between individual- and corporate-level taxation. In *Japan*, "specified family corporations," defined as corporations in which one shareholder together with its affiliates holds the majority of voting interests, are subject to additional corporate tax of 10% to 20% on their undistributed profits. This additional corporate tax aims to negate or reduce the advantage of the lower rate of corporate tax compared to the IIT.[407] In addition, although Japan does not have a GAAR, it has an anti-avoidance clause that is broadly applicable to "family corporations," defined as corporations in which three shareholders, together with their affiliates, hold the majority of voting interests.[408]

405. Canada, ITA, s. 125.
406. Sweden, ITA, Ch. 57. For a more detailed explanation, *see* the chapter on Sweden in Part I.
407. Japan, CTA, s. 67. For a more detailed explanation *see* the chapter on Japan in Part I.
408. Japan, CTA, s. 132.

Similarly, in the *United States*, the fact that the 21% corporate tax rate is significantly lower than the 37% maximum individual rate creates a significant incentive for stockholders of a closely held corporation to arrange for income from their performance of personal services or from their investments to be taxable to and subsequently accumulated in the closely held corporation. A special penalty tax is imposed on the corporation's accumulations of such income.[409]

In 2017, the *Canadian* government proposed complex and draconian rules to prevent the use of private corporations to split income among family members and defer the individual shareholder level tax on investment income. The proposals generated widespread public opposition, and the government abandoned some of the proposals and watered down others. The final changes, which apply for 2018 and subsequent taxation years, prevent income splitting among family members who are shareholders of private corporations. They apply where a family-member shareholder is not actively involved in the business carried on by the corporation. Certain family members may be excluded from the rules through the application of bright-line tests based on age, the labor contributed to the business, and the nature of the business. Individuals over 25 years of age are subject to tax at the highest marginal rate on amounts received from the corporation in excess of a "reasonable return," determined on a factual basis with reference to certain listed factors (work performed for, capital contributed to, and risks assumed with respect to the business).[410]

As previously mentioned, in *Germany*, additional restrictions apply to arrangements between a controlling shareholder (as defined) and the corporation. In addition to the normal arm's length rule, the agreement must be legally valid, clearly expressed, and concluded in advance of the transaction in question. However, there is no specific regime for closely held companies since the corporate tax law treats public and private corporations in essentially the same way.

In *Australia*, in the context of private companies, various concessions have been made in defining the tax base and a lower corporate rate may be available. With respect to distributions, loans to shareholders and similar benefits (such as payments of shareholder's expenses, forgiveness of shareholder debts, or private use of corporate assets) can be treated as dividends, which are not usually entitled to the imputation credit. A similar restriction applies to excess employee benefits. Australia generally adopts a 75/20 rule for determining widely held and closely held status—that is, whether 75% of the company is held by twenty or fewer persons.[411]

The *United Kingdom* also has restrictive rules which apply to closely held companies, defined as companies where five or fewer "participators" have control of

409. United States, IRC, ss. 541-545. Another provision allows the IRS to disallow tax benefits for a "personal service corporation" where its employee-owners provide personal services to a single other entity and the principal purpose for the personal service corporation is to obtain tax benefits for the employee-owners which are not otherwise available. United States, IRC, s. 269A. For example, the shareholder's status as an employee of the personal service corporation might provide tax-favored fringe benefits available to employees that would not have been available if the shareholder were self-employed.
410. Canada, ITA, s. 120.4.
411. Australia, ITAA 1936, Pt III Divs 7, 7A.

the company. Special rules apply to directors and creditors who can qualify as participators. Where a company which meets the definition of "close" makes a loan to a participator, the company is liable to make a payment to the tax authorities equal to 33.75% of the loan (the dividend upper rate), as if the amount due "were an amount of corporation tax."[412] The amount paid is refunded if and when the loan is repaid. The definition of "distribution" is also broader in the case of close companies and covers most in-kind benefits.[413] Further, where an individual provides personal services through a company where, if the services were provided directly, the individual would be regarded as an employee, the individual may be allocated income received by the company for those services.[414]

In *India*, although listed companies and privately held companies were subject to different tax rates for many years, since 1993-1994 both types of company are subject to the same tax rates. However, the distinction between listed and private companies is still relevant; in particular, special anti-avoidance measures apply to private companies. For example, restrictions apply to the carryforward of losses by a private company following a change of control. In addition, where a privately held company receives any consideration in excess of the face value of its shares, the aggregate consideration received for such shares in excess of the fair market value was considered to be income of the company from other sources.[415] However, under pressure from start-ups, the 2024 budget repealed this treatment effective April 1, 2025. Also, to prevent the use of disguised share capital, there is a rebuttable presumption that such transactions by privately held companies are not genuine (unless the capital is recorded in the name of a venture capital fund or company or funds regulated under a special economic zone).[416]

11 INTEGRATION OF CORPORATE AND SHAREHOLDER TAXES

11.1 General

It is often stated that the policy goal for the taxation of entities is that income should end up being taxed to the same extent whether it is derived directly by an individual or indirectly through an entity. It is possible, as we have just seen, to achieve this goal reasonably well in the case of closely held corporations, although not every country does so. Partnership taxation, dealt with in Subpart B below, is another situation where most countries provide equal treatment for income earned directly or through a partnership.

It is not really feasible to achieve the goal of equal treatment in the case of widely held (especially publicly traded) corporations, for a number of reasons. One reason is

412. United Kingdom, Corporation Tax Act 2010, s. 455.
413. United Kingdom, Corporation Tax Act 2010, s. 1064.
414. United Kingdom, Income Tax (Earnings and Pensions) Act 2003, ss. 50 and 51.
415. India, ITA 1961, s. 56(2)(viib) (exceptions apply to amounts received by venture capital enterprises and amounts received from certain start-up businesses).
416. India, ITA 1961, proviso 1 to s. 68, as amended by the FA 2022.

that listed corporations typically do not distribute all their income, which causes two problems. First, it is not possible to determine currently which shareholders, if any, will ultimately benefit from the income, and second, if a shareholder sells shares before the income is distributed, any benefit of the retained income enjoyed by the shareholder can be captured only by the CGT, and then not easily. Further, most countries have a variety of special tax rules for institutional investment vehicles (pension plans, mutual funds, life insurers, etc.) and in most countries, these vehicles are major investors in listed corporations. It is not easy to put the corporate-shareholder tax regime and these special regimes together to achieve the goal of taxing corporate income as if it were derived directly by the individual members of such investment vehicles. Finally, the international tax system also complicates the achievement of the goal, as discussed in Part IV.

During the period 1960-2000, many countries, including some of those covered here (Australia, Canada, France, Germany, and the UK), abandoned the classical system and adopted an imputation system as the preferred way of moving toward a single level of taxation at individual rates on distributed corporate income. Under this system, in general, the shareholder grosses up dividends by reference to the underlying corporate tax attributable to the dividends and then is taxed at normal marginal tax rates on the grossed-up amount, with a tax credit equal to the gross-up, thus integrating the corporate-level tax paid with the individual-level tax. However, from the mid-1990s, there has been a worldwide move away from imputation so that of the countries examined here, only Australia retains that system. This change in approach is attributable to a number of factors. First, imputation systems must deal with a number of complex structural issues which are not present, or not present to the same degree, in classical systems. The following are the principal structural issues which have been dealt with in different ways in the imputation systems which grew up in the 1960-2000 period:

(1) Should tax preferences at the corporate level "pass-through" to the individual shareholders when distributed?
(2) If the answer to question 1 is no, should distributed preferences be taxed only at the shareholder level or should they be subject to some kind of "compensatory" tax when distributed so that all dividends carry with them the imputation credit?
(3) If the shareholder's tax liability is less than the attributed corporate tax, should the excess be refunded to the individual shareholder?
(4) How should income which passes through several tiers of corporations before reaching an individual investor be treated?
(5) How should retained earnings, which would have carried the credit with them when distributed, be treated if the shareholder sells the shares prior to distribution?
(6) How should shareholders with different "tax characteristics" (e.g., pension funds, investment companies, etc.) be treated?

The imputation systems in the countries considered here dealt with these issues in different ways, often in increasingly complex fashion, as taxpayers probed the systems for weakness and governments responded with ever more detailed anti-abuse rules.

Second, beyond the complexities of operating the imputation system domestically, the introduction of imputation systems raised important international issues, because, in general, they favored domestic investment over foreign investment and domestic shareholders over foreign shareholders. These issues are discussed in more detail in Part IV. As a result of domestic complexity and international discrimination (and in the case of EU countries, the requirements of the CJEU), imputation systems have fallen out of favor and have been increasingly replaced with some sort of "rough-and-ready" integration relief, typically taking the form of shareholder relief for dividend distributions or some other adjustments in the overall rate applicable to distributed profits.

At the same time, countries which historically had used the classical system began to move to some form of shareholder-level relief for distributed profits, either through a special rate of tax for dividends or, more generally, in the context of a "dual" tax system, through a special lower rate for capital income generally.

Thus, for individuals at the top marginal tax rate, the half-inclusion system in France and the modified part-inclusion system in Germany have been designed to produce roughly the same overall tax burden on distributed profits and income earned directly. In 2004, France introduced a system of progressive taxation based on the German model, with a rate of 50% of the dividend received, raised to 60% in 2006. The 2008 Finance Act introduced the option of a proportional withholding tax on the entire dividend; this system became mandatory in 2013, once again subjecting dividends to the progressive tax scale with respect to 60% of their gross amount. The 2018 Finance Act added a flat tax of 30% (12.8% flat withholding tax plus 17.2% for social security contributions) on dividends.[417]

In Canada, approximately the same result is achieved for small privately held companies, and, after 2011, for public corporations as well. Similarly, the reduction of the corporate tax rate in the U.S. to 21% in 2018, coupled with the 20% rate on dividends (23.8% for higher-income taxpayers subject to the 3.8% Medicare surtax), means that, in some situations, the tax burden on distributed profits and income earned directly are almost equal. In the UK, in most cases, the total tax on distributed corporate income for taxpayers subject to the maximum individual tax rate is higher than if they had derived the income directly. In the UK, the tax is 6 to 12 percentage points higher, depending on the particular facts.

The following table describes some basic features of the "old" imputation and classical systems and the systems that replaced them. The international issues which arise in connection with imputation systems are examined in more detail in Part IV.

417. France, CGI, s. 200 A.

	Dividends	
Country	*Individual Shareholder*	*Company Shareholder*
Australia	full imputation tax credit at variable rates from 1987, surplus credits refundable since 2000	imputation system applies since 2002 (previously usually not taxed via separate tax credit)
Canada	imputation tax credit produces approximately full dividend relief for small companies and for large companies after 2011; nonrefundable	full dividend-received deduction
China	taxable at 20% flat rate (lower rate for dividends on listed shares held for more than one month or more than one year)	exempt if shares held for 12 months; otherwise, taxable at 25% flat rate
France	flat tax of 30% since 2018 or progressive scale with a 40% deduction of the gross amount received	25% for single companies; exemption for groups of companies, except for the denial of the deduction of expenses and charges of 1% or 5%, depending on the case.
Germany	25% withholding tax for dividends from shares that are private assets; for business assets, 60% of dividend income taxable at individual progressive rates	95% exempt if participation ≥ 10%
India	Taxable in the hands of the recipient at applicable rates; withholding tax at 10% in respect of dividends in excess of INR 5,000	For domestic companies, withholding tax at 10% and 20% (the treaty rate for foreign companies); rate is doubled in cases of recipients not providing Permanent Account Number; credit available for dividends from a domestic or foreign company or a business trust
Japan	10% tax credit (without gross-up); 5% for dividends > JPY 10m; from 2003, taxpayers may opt not to report or to separately report dividends with respect to listed shares; in such cases, the rate is 20.315% (including 5% local income tax) on dividends	exempt if participation > 33.3%; 50% taxed if < 33.3% but > 5%; 80% taxed if < 5%

	Dividends	
Country	*Individual Shareholder*	*Company Shareholder*
The Netherlands	deemed yield of 0.01%-6.04% (depending on value of total amount of net assets) of the value of shares at the start of year taxed at 36% rate, for an effective tax rate of 0.36%-2.17% of the value of the shares; flat rate of 24.5 or 33% for share interests of over 5%	exempt if generally > 5% participation; otherwise taxable
Sweden	30% tax under dual income tax system for income from capital, no relief for company tax; 25% for dividends from unlisted corporations; 20% for dividends taxed as capital income from closely held companies	exempt if shares are unlisted or > 10% participation; otherwise taxable
United Kingdom	lower tax rates for dividends 8.75%, 33.75%, and 39.35%, corresponding to 20%, 40%, and 45% general rates; in addition, a GBP 500 exemption	generally exempt
United States	tax up to 20% maximum since 2003, plus the additional 3.8% Medicare surtax for higher-income individuals since 2013	dividends-received deduction 50%-100% depending on holding
	Capital Gains on Shares	
Australia	50% exclusion if held > 1 year	taxable
Canada	50% exclusion (66.6% after June 25, 2024 in excess of 250,000 annually)	50% exclusion (66.6% after June 25, 2024); private companies can pay exempt part of the capital gain tax-free to shareholders
China	taxable at 20% flat rate and exemption for gains on listed shares	taxable at 25% flat rate
France	flat tax of 30% since 2018 or progressive scale with the possibility of holding period allowances for shares acquired before January 1, 2018	taxed at standard CIT rate (25% or 15% depending on the size of the company); or at a reduced rate e.g.: equity investments held for > 2 years (12% of gross gain); real estate company (19%): mutual fund securities held for > 5 years (15%); assignment of a patent (10%)

	Dividends	
Country	*Individual Shareholder*	*Company Shareholder*
Germany	60% of capital gain taxed at individual tax rate if there is a substantial participation (≥ 1% of stock) or business property; for portfolio investments, 25% withholding tax if shares are private assets	95% exempt
India	equity shares if held > 1 year, and STT has been paid at the time of acquisition or transfer, on capital gains > 125,000 at 12.5% (plus surcharge and surtax); if held < 1 year and STT paid, tax at 20%; unlisted shares if held for > 2 years, tax at 12.5%; in other cases, tax at applicable rate	equity shares if held > 1 year, and STT has been paid at time of acquisition or transfer, on capital gains > 125,000 at 12.5% (plus surcharge and surtax); if held < 1 year and STT paid, tax at 20%; unlisted shares if held > 2 years, tax at 12.5%; in other cases, tax at applicable rate
Japan	20.315% (including 5% local income tax) tax; for listed shares, taxpayers can choose capital losses to offset dividends and interest on securities	taxable; additional tax at 10%-20% on specified family corporations for certain undistributed profits
The Netherlands	no special tax in addition to tax on deemed income from shares	exempt if participation exemption applies; otherwise taxable
Sweden	tax at 30% under dual income tax system for income from capital; 25% for unlisted shares	exempt if participation > 10% since 2003; otherwise taxable
United Kingdom	tax at 10%-20% with exemption for first GBP 3,000 (approx.)	exempt if participation in trading companies > 10% and held for > 1 year; otherwise taxable
United States	taxable capped at 20% plus 3.8% Medicare surtax for higher income individuals if held for > 1 year	taxable

11.2 Treatment of Capital Gains on Shares

As the table above indicates, an issue which has been the subject of considerable detailed analysis in various corporate tax reform proposals is the treatment of capital gains on the sale of shares and its relation to corporate-shareholder taxation in general. Imputation and dividend relief systems do not operate where the income of a corporation is earned and retained, and in the case of the classical system, there is no immediate double taxation. It is effectively left to the CGT on sales of shares to deal with double taxation issues in relation to retained earnings. On the one hand, it is sometimes argued that there is double taxation of retentions where CGT applies to shares unless an adjustment is made to the gain to reflect the retained income or the tax on it. On the other hand, it has been argued that full CGT on sales of shares by individuals, combined with a full imputation system, results in corporate income being taxed at the marginal tax rates of the individual shareholders who held the shares when the income was derived, whether or not the shareholder receives a distribution of the income or sells the shares. One consequence of this argument, if full CGT applies on the sale of shares by an individual, is that tax preferences enjoyed at the corporate level are likely to be eliminated for retained income, which is a reason to have the same result where the income is distributed.[418]

These arguments depend, critically, on the extent to which the market price of shares reflects both retained earnings and the tax attributes of the corporation and shareholder. There is no general agreement about the effects of retained earnings and tax attributes on share prices, and hence it is difficult to properly evaluate arguments about the double taxation of retained earnings.

With respect to particular countries, there has been a trend to consider the issue more systematically than in the past and to try to align the capital gains treatment with the treatment of dividends. Thus, in *Germany*, the modified shareholder-relief system applies to those capital gains which are taxed to individuals as well as to dividends,[419] and in *Japan* and the *United States*, the same reduced rate of tax is applied to dividends and capital gains on shares realized by individuals. Japan also permits capital losses to offset dividends in respect of listed shares. In *France*, similar flat-rate taxes are imposed on dividends and certain capital gains at the taxpayer's option. In *The Netherlands*, the deemed yield on shares is meant to include dividends as well as capital gains, while in *Sweden* the same flat rate of tax for income from capital is applied to both.

In contrast, in *Australia, Canada, China,* and the *United Kingdom*, the special treatment of capital gains on shares for individuals is not linked in any systematic way to the tax treatment of dividends but instead flows from the general treatment of capital gains. Some of the countries which do have consistent treatment for dividends and capital gains on shares also apply the same treatment to capital gains generally (Sweden and the U.S.), but it is clear that there is an intended linkage between dividends and capital gains on shares in these countries.

With respect to capital gains realized by corporations on shares, a similar trend of aligning their treatment with dividends is evident in The Netherlands, Sweden, and France (both exempt in all cases), to some extent in Germany (both exempt if the participation exemption applies, otherwise dividends but not capital gains are taxable in full), and the UK (dividends generally exempt and capital gains exempt for participations in trading corporations). In the other countries, dividends are either exempt or subject to reduced taxation, while capital gains are taxable in full. Hence, in these countries, there is unlikely to be consistency in the extent of integration between dividends and capital gains on shares.

---

418. *See* generally, Richard J. Vann, General Report, "Trends in Company/Shareholder Taxation: Single or Double Taxation?" in International Fiscal Association (IFA), *Cahiers de droit fiscal international*, vol. 88a (2003), pp. 35-43.
419. Germany, ITA, s. 3 No. 40 and s. 20 para. 1 No. 1, para. 2, s. 32d para. 1.

As between individuals and corporations, the result can be complementary tax positions. For example, in *Australia*, individuals are taxable on dividends to a greater extent than on capital gains, and corporations are taxable on capital gains to a greater extent than on dividends. This naturally gives rise to tax planning designed to have dividends received by corporations and capital gains by individuals (dividend stripping), which in turn leads to complex anti-avoidance legislation. Other countries also demonstrate similar complementary positions, although to a lesser degree. Again, tax planning undermines the policy intent of the rules, and as a result, it is difficult to make judgments about the level of corporate-shareholder tax integration.

In *India*, arguments have been raised about the double taxation of dividend income. However, the treatment of capital gains on shares is not considered to be linked to the tax treatment of dividend income. When dividends on which DDT was paid were completely tax-free to shareholders, taxpayers created artificial losses by buying shares at a higher price shortly before dividend payment dates and selling the shares after receiving the dividend at a loss, which could then be set off against other income. The Supreme Court held that such transactions were acceptable.[420] Amendments were introduced to deny such losses where the shares are held for less than a specified period of time[421] and since its introduction, the GAAR has been applied to this type of transaction.[422]

The following *Table III* summarizes some of the features of the corporate tax systems discussed in Subpart A. The notations "Partial Imputation" or "Full Imputation" refer to the degree to which tax imposed at the corporate level is relieved in the hands of the shareholder on distribution. The amount of unrelieved corporate tax on distributed profits is shown in the column headed "Residual Corporate Tax."

420. *CIT v. Walfort Share & Stock Brokers P. Ltd.* (SC, July 6, 2010).

421. ITA 1961, s. 94(7). Similar stop-loss provisions apply to bonus stripping with respect to mutual funds units (s. 94(8)).

422. *Ayodhya Rami Reddy Alla v. Principal Commissioner of Income Tax, Central* (WP 46510/2022), June 7, 2022, Telangana High Court.

Table III Some Basic Aspects of Corporate Taxation

	Basic Approach	*Corporate Rate on Retentions*	*Residual Corporate Tax on Distributed Profits*	*Total Tax Burden (Corp. Tax + Max. Shareholder Tax) on Dividend Distribution*	*Profits Requirement for Taxable Distributions*	*Intercorp. Dividend Relief*	*Corp. Level Tax on Distribution of Apprec. Property*	*Consolidated Taxation Possible*
Australia	full imputation	30% (or lower rate if turnover < AUD 50m)	0%	45%	yes	yes via imputation system	yes	yes
Canada	partial imputation for public corps. and other non-CCPCs; approximately full imputation for CCPCs	23%-31% (depending on province and type of income); lower for CCPCs	23%-31% (depending on province and type of income); 0% in some cases for CCPCs	47.3-62.3% depending on province; lower for CCPCs	no	yes (100% relief)	yes	no (some equiv. techniques)
China	classical	25%	25%	40%	no, but distributions must be made in accordance with company law	yes (100% relief) if shares are held for 12 months	yes	no

France	individual shareholder-relief system (40% allowance and 17.2% flat-rate taxes) or 30% flat-rate taxes; full imputation before 2005	33.33% in 2018 with a gradual reduction to 25% in 2022	33.33% in 2018 with progressive decrease to 25% in 2022 (partial or full imputation before 2005)	For individuals, up to 62.2%; for corporations, up to 25%	no	yes (100% relief) but recapture of related expenses up to 5% of dividend	yes	yes
Germany	shareholder-relief system (partial-income method and final withholding tax)	15% (plus 12%-14% trade tax)	15% (plus ca. 12%-14% trade tax)	48%-49%	no	yes (95% relief) for shareholdings ≥ 10%	yes	yes
India	modified classical	15%-30% (plus surcharge and surtax)	applicable tax rate (plus surcharge and surtax)	maximum corporate tax rate -30% plus surcharge and surtax; maximum individual tax rate 30% plus surcharge and surtax.	yes, out of profit in accordance with the Companies Act	yes, limited to one level	yes	no
Japan	very limited imputation (10% credit)	23.2% (approximately 30%, including the local tax)	20%	57%	generally no	limited (20%-100%)	yes	yes

	Basic Approach	*Corporate Rate on Retentions*	*Residual Corporate Tax on Distributed Profits*	*Total Tax Burden (Corp. Tax + Max. Shareholder Tax) on Dividend Distribution*	*Profits Requirement for Taxable Distributions*	*Intercorp. Dividend Relief*	*Corp. Level Tax on Distribution of Apprec. Property*	*Consolidated Taxation Possible*
The Netherlands	classical	19% (profits < EUR 200,000), 25.8% (profits > EUR 200,000)	19% (profits < EUR 200,000), 25.8% (profits > EUR 200,000)	19% or 25.8% CIT plus (max.) 1.76% of value of shares; for substantial participations: 19% or 25.8% CIT plus 24.5%/33% on dividend (of 81 or 74.2) = 38.85/45.73% or 43. 99/50.29%	no	yes (5% > shareholding)	yes	yes
Sweden	classical	20.6%	20.6%	44.4%	no	yes (10% + shareholding for unlisted corporations)	yes	no (some equivalent techniques)
United Kingdom	lower dividend rate	25%	25%	55%	no	yes	yes	no (some equivalent techniques)

United States	classical	21%	21%	36.8% (if 3.8% Medicare surtax does not apply)	yes	limited (50%-65% -100%)	yes	yes

SUBPART B
Partnership Taxation

All the systems considered in this book have rules for the taxation of business activities carried on through certain types of commercial organization which allow the income and losses of those organizations to be passed directly through to the participants. These organizations are typically formed as partnerships for commercial law purposes, and often the commercial law classification is determinative of the tax regime. In this Subpart, the reference to "partnership" is to an organization, typically but not necessarily organized as a commercial law partnership, to which pass-through principles of taxation generally apply. Similarly, the reference to "partner" is to the participant to whom the income and losses are attributed.

The taxing patterns examined here are all based on the principle that the income of a partnership should be taxed directly to the individual partners in much the same way as if they had earned it directly. Within that framework, however, the techniques and mechanisms used to achieve pass-through treatment, and the actual results, vary considerably, as does the sophistication of the systems.

In some cases (in *Japan*, for example), there are no specific rules dealing with the taxation of partnerships and little administrative guidance. The same is true, to some extent, in *France*, where case law developed principles are important but still leave a number of questions open. In the *United Kingdom*, there are limited statutory provisions dealing with partnerships.[423] In other systems, partnerships have been used frequently, often in connection with tax-shelter investments, and the principles are correspondingly more highly developed. *Sweden*, for instance, has introduced a number of special rules to counter the use of partnerships in tax planning schemes. As usual, the *United States* seems to have the most highly articulated set of rules.

Although all the systems generally use a pass-through model, they recognize the partnership and the partner as separate tax subjects for some purposes. Thus, a consistent theme in all the systems is the tension between "aggregate" pass-through treatment in some situations and "entity" treatment in other situations. For example, in

423. For example, United Kingdom, ITTOIA, Part 9 and Corporation Tax Act 2009, Part 17.

some systems, loans made by a partner to the partnership are treated in the same fashion as loans by third parties; interest payments are taxed to the partner making the loan, and the interest deduction which arises at the partnership level is deducted by the appropriate partners. To the extent that interest income is treated differently from business profits, the characterization of the income as interest controls. In other systems, the partnership-partner loan is disregarded and the "interest" payments are treated as a distribution of partnership income, with corresponding tax results. The following materials first examine the basic methods of implementing a pass-through taxation system and then look at several situations in which aggregate-entity issues arise.

The worldwide trend toward lower corporate tax rates causes serious problems for countries where partnerships play a major role in the economy as a whole. This is true in *Germany*, where commercial partnerships not only represent a substantial portion of small- and medium-sized enterprises but also represent a major part of large enterprises which are not listed on the stock market (large family businesses). In order to avoid disadvantageous treatment for these taxpayers, the Business Tax Reform of 2007 introduced a low tax rate for profits derived by a nonincorporated enterprise which are not withdrawn but reinvested in the business;[424] any further withdrawal of such low-taxed reserves is subject to a further layer of income tax resembling a final withholding tax on dividends and interest payments.

1 QUALIFICATION FOR PASS-THROUGH TAXATION

In most of the systems reviewed here, entities are treated as partnerships for tax purposes and taxed on a pass-through basis if they are formally organized under commercial partnership statutes. In addition, more informal arrangements for pooling assets and labor in a business activity may also be found to be partnerships for tax purposes. Thus, in the *United States*, any cooperative activity aimed at a profit which goes beyond simple co-ownership of property is treated as a partnership for tax purposes (assuming that it is not classified as a corporation).[425] The *Canadian* rules are similar. There is no definition of partnership for tax purposes, but the typically very broad (provincial) commercial law definition of a partnership, as a business carried on jointly with a view to a profit, covers most arrangements which extend beyond co-ownership. This characterization is controlling for tax purposes. The Supreme Court of Canada has held that even an ancillary intention to make a profit is sufficient to support the existence of a partnership.[426]

In *Sweden*, according to civil law, only organizations registered as partnerships are treated as legal persons. Tax rules for partnerships apply to civil law partnerships. Similarly, in *China*, only businesses carried on through partnerships established under Chinese law are entitled to flow-through treatment for tax purposes.[427]

424. Germany, ITA, s. 34a.
425. United States, IRC, s. 761(a).
426. *Spire Freezers Ltd. v. The Queen*, [2001] 2 CTC 40 (SCC).
427. China, Art. 1, Cai Shui [2008] No. 159.

In *France*, there is no general definition of a partnership for tax purposes. Tax status as a partnership is based on a specific enumeration of types of entities listed in the French tax code.[428] These entities are subject to income tax and include different forms of structure, with a few exceptions related to the form of the company or the nature of the activity. Partnerships have their own legal personality and are based on the concept of unlimited liability for the partners. For tax purposes, they are considered to be semi-transparent, i.e., both the partnership and the partners are taken into account: the partnership's results are used to calculate the taxable base, but the partners have to pay the tax on their share of the partnership's results. An optional system allows some limited companies under certain general[429] or specific conditions (e.g., family limited companies—*SARL de famille*)[430] to opt for the partnership tax regime. The reverse is also possible, as some partnerships subject to income tax (e.g., *sociétés en participation* or *sociétés en nom collectif*) can opt for CIT.[431]

The definitional rules in *Australia* go so far as to treat jointly owned property which generates income as a partnership, although the possibility of unincorporated joint ventures which are not classified as partnerships allows certain operations (typically in the natural resource field) to be treated, in effect, as separate enterprises of each participant.[432] In practice, partnerships arising from joint ownership of property are not generally required to file partnership tax returns. Limited partnerships are excluded from pass-through treatment, with the exception of venture capital activities and foreign hybrids.[433] In the *United Kingdom*, there is no formal definition of partnership as such. The partnership rules apply to joint undertakings which, unlike clubs or associations, are organized to do business. However, income from jointly owned property is not treated as partnership income.

In *The Netherlands*, there are no specific provisions defining the forms of organization which are subject to pass-through taxation. Instead, all associations which are not covered by the generic definitions of taxable entities in the corporate tax law are transparent for tax purposes and the income is taxed directly to the participants. A special rule, split into two parts, applied up to January 1, 2025 to limited partnerships with transferable shares. To the extent that the income was allocable to the limited interests, the partnership was subject to corporate tax and distributions were again taxed to the limited partners when distributed. To the extent that income was allocated to the general partners, the partnership was transparent and the income was directly taxable to them. As of January 1, 2025, all partnerships are considered to be transparent.

428. France, CGI, ss. 8, 8 bis, 8 ter, 8 quater, 8 quinquies, 238 bis L, 238 bis LA, 239 ter, 239 quater, 239 quater A to D, 239 quinquies.
429. France, CGI, s. 239 bis AB.
430. France, CGI, s. 239 bis AA.
431. France, CGI, s. 239 1.
432. Australia, ITAA 1997, s. 995-1(1) definitions of "partnership" and "limited partnership"; *see also* the definitions of "company" and "non-entity joint venture."
433. Australia, ITAA 1936, Pt III Div 5A.

In the *German* system, characterization of an organization as a partnership for civil law purposes is a necessary precondition for partnership tax treatment.[434] For a taxpayer to qualify as a "partner," there are some additional tax requirements.[435] In particular, the partner must participate in any appreciation in the value of the assets, at least on the liquidation of the partnership, and must also play an active part in the conduct of the business. In 2021, the German legislature introduced an "option" for commercial partnerships to be taxed as corporations, which in 2024 was extended to registered civil partnerships.

Partnerships organized under the Company Law in *Japan* are taxed as corporations. Although it is possible to organize partnerships under the Civil Code, there are no statutory rules for their taxation, except for limited provisions with regard to withholding tax for nonresidents.[436] The government guidelines permit corporate partners of Civil Code partnerships to choose, on a consistent basis, any of the following treatments:

(i) full-scale pass-through treatment, where a partner is deemed to hold proportionate interests in assets and liabilities of the partnership as well as in its revenues and costs;
(ii) income pass-through treatment, where a partner is deemed to proportionately enjoy the revenues and costs earned and incurred by the partnership but assets and liabilities are deemed to belong to the partnership, or
(iii) net pass-through treatment, where a partner is taxed on a proportionate basis on the income or loss calculated by the partnership.

According to the guidelines, under the second option, a partner can claim exemptions for dividends and income tax credits, but cannot claim benefits related to allowances and tax-deductible reserves. Disproportionate treatment of partners may be deemed to be a gift from one partner to another, which is taxable as corporate income in cases where the recipient is a corporation (with regard to tax treatments for individuals, *see* Part II). Under the third option, a partner cannot enjoy any benefits attributable to specific assets or liabilities of the partnership, including the exemptions for dividends and income tax credits. With respect to the contractual relation set up as an "undisclosed association" or *tokumei-kumiai*, the third option is applied to any undisclosed participants. Because these rules are so abstract, taxpayers face considerable uncertainty in the use of the partnership form. Taxpayers reasonably try to avoid such uncertainty and, as a result, partnerships are not widely used in the Japanese business context, except for certain types of transactions where plain-vanilla partnerships with tax certainty are used. This situation accounts for the scarcity of case law and statutory provisions with respect to partnerships.

434. Germany, ITA, s. 15 para. 1 sent. 1 No. 2.
435. Compare Germany, ITA, s. 15 para. 1 sent. 1 No. 2 and ITA, s. 20 para. 1 No. 4.
436. Japan, ITA, s. 212 para. 5. Japan's tax treaty policy is to negotiate with its treaty partners to accept this tax treatment. *See*, for example, Japan-UK Tax Treaty, Art. 20, Japan-The Netherlands Tax Treaty, protocol 9.

In *India*, partnerships are not transparent and the concept of pass-through treatment does not apply. However, pass-through taxation is allowed under the Income Tax Act (ITA) for certain investments in and by venture capital funds, as well as by certain business trusts and investment funds.[437]

The Indian Partnership Act, 1932 governs the definition of partnership and partners. A partnership is taxable as a "firm" (defined in the ITA as having the meaning under the Partnership Act) only if it satisfies the conditions laid down in section 184 of the ITA, which requires an agreement in writing, the individual shares of the partners to be specified, and a copy of the agreement to be filed with the tax department for the firm's first year (and subsequently if there is any change in the constitution of the firm). Since 1992, partnerships are taxed as firms or as associations of persons. Currently, a firm is taxed at 30% (plus surcharge and surtax). Although a partner's share of the income of a firm is exempt from tax,[438] any interest (up to a maximum of 12% simple interest per annum), salary, bonus, commission, or any other remuneration, provided by the firm to a partner is taxable as business income.[439] The payment of remuneration, which is subject to certain limits, can be made only to working partners, who are restricted to individuals. Although under the partnership law a firm is not considered to be a separate legal entity distinct from its partners, it is specifically provided in the ITA that transfers of capital assets by a partner to a firm and distributions of capital assets on the dissolution of a firm are taxable transactions.[440]

In 2021, the rules were completely overhauled.[441] Where a partner receives stock in trade or a capital asset in connection with the dissolution or reconstitution of a firm, the firm is deemed to transfer the property to the partners at its fair market value and, depending on the nature of the assets, the firm realizes either business income or capital gains. The new rules apply to changes in the profit-sharing ratio on the admission of a partner or on the dissolution or reconstitution of a firm. Also, where a partner receives any money or capital asset from a firm in excess of the balance in their capital account, the excess is taxed as a capital gain in the hands of the firm. The balance in the capital account is to be calculated without considering any increase on account of revaluation or due to self-generated goodwill or any other self-generated asset. The capital gains are attributed to the remaining assets of the firm in a prescribed manner.[442]

The limit on the remuneration of working partner was increased in 2024 and all payments of salary, interest, etc. paid by a firm to the partners are subject to deduction of tax at source.

Since 2008, the government has allowed the formation of LLPs, which are considered to be firms for tax purposes and taxable at a rate of 30%. However, LLPs registered outside India are considered to be foreign companies and taxed at a rate of

437. India, ITA 1961, ss. 10(23FB), 115U, 115UA and 115UB.
438. India, ITA 1961, s. 10(2A).
439. India, ITA 1961, s. 2(24)(ve).
440. India, ITA 1961, s. 45(3) and (4).
441. India, ITA 1961, s. 9B and CBDT Circular No. 14, July 2, 2021.
442. India, ITA, 1961, s. 48(iii) read with rule 8AB of the Income Tax Rules, 1962.

35%. Most domestic companies are currently taxed at a lower rate than the 30% rate applicable to firms, including LLPs.

2 BASIC STRUCTURE OF PASS-THROUGH TAXATION

In the *United States*, income and deductions arising at the partnership level are either aggregated at the partnership level or are passed through directly to the individual partners to the extent that special computations may be necessary at the partner level.[443] For example, capital gains and losses are stated separately so that they may be aggregated with the individual partner's gains and losses. Most elections (e.g., method of depreciation) are made at the partnership level and are binding on the partners.[444] The partnership income is included in the tax year of the partner in which the partnership's tax year ends, irrespective of whether it is distributed.[445] There are restrictions to prevent manipulation of the tax years to achieve tax deferral.

A partner's tax cost of a partnership interest is increased by the amount of income attributed to the partner and decreased by distributions and losses.[446] Distributions are taxable only to the extent that they exceed the partner's tax cost of the interest in the partnership.[447] Tax-exempt income increases the tax cost of the interest and thus avoids an indirect tax on the income on a sale of the interest. Losses incurred at the partnership level can be deducted currently only to the extent of the partner's tax cost in the partnership interest.[448] Special "passive activity loss rules" may limit the ability of partners who are individuals to deduct otherwise-deductible partnership expenses. If individual partners do not materially participate in the partnership's business, they may deduct partnership losses only to the extent of income generated by the partnership or other flow-through activities in which they do not materially participate.[449] In addition, in general, individual partners may not deduct partnership expenses which are financed by nonrecourse debt, which is debt secured only by the property in question and for which no partner is personally liable. An important exception exists for a partnership's investment in real estate using nonrecourse debt where the nonrecourse debt satisfies several requirements intended to curb abuses.[450] Another rule limits the ability of individual partners to deduct expenses from the partnership's trade or business against the individual's other income which is not derived from a trade or business.[451]

As part of the 2017 tax reform, individual partners (and sole proprietors) are entitled to a new deduction equal to 20% of their share of a partnership's "qualified" trade or business income. The deduction was designed to provide a rate reduction for

443. United States, IRC, s. 702.
444. United States, IRC, s. 703(b).
445. United States, IRC, s. 706(a).
446. United States, IRC, s. 705(a).
447. United States, IRC, s. 731.
448. United States, IRC, s. 704(d).
449. United States, IRC, s. 469.
450. United States, IRC, s. 465.
451. United States, IRC, ss. 465 and 461(l).

individuals conducting business through a flow-through entity comparable to the rate reduction enacted for corporations (from 35% to 21%).[452] This provision, in addition to being extremely complex, has not achieved parity in the tax treatment of the various types of entities available for conducting business.

Complex rules deal with the allocation of income and deductions among the partners.[453] In general terms, special allocations of items of income and deductions (i.e., allocations which differ from the normal profit- and loss-sharing arrangements) are respected for tax purposes only where they have "substantial economic effect." In other words, the allocation for tax purposes must actually affect the economic situation of the partners apart from the tax consequences of the allocation. The economic effect of the allocation is generally determined by the partners' "capital accounts," which reflect the actual economic relations among the partners. Normally, allocation for tax purposes must be reflected in the capital accounts, and those accounts must control the amounts which the partners are entitled to receive on the liquidation of the partnership. If a partner has a negative capital account, for example, as a result of receiving a larger share of partnership losses, that amount typically must be required to be made up on the liquidation of the partnership in order for the special allocation of the losses to be recognized. Since nonrecourse debt, by definition, does not have to be repaid by the partners, additional restrictions apply to deductions based on nonrecourse debt.

The special allocation rules are enormously complex and have been criticized as unworkable for unsophisticated partnerships.[454]

In general, the *Canadian* system is quite similar, although it is substantially simpler. Partnerships are not taxable entities. Each partner's share of the partnership's income is included in the partner's income in the taxable year in which the partnership's taxable year ends.[455] Where a partnership interest is disposed of, the new partner's share of the income is the amount that the new partner would have received if it had been a partner for the entire year, and the former partner is not taxable on its share of the partnership's income for the year. The source and character of the income earned by the partnership flows through to the partners. Distributions are not taxable, regardless of whether they are characterized as income or capital distributions. In general, the partnership agreement controls the allocation of income and deductions among the partners. Rather than limiting special allocations by detailed regulatory rules, the allocation is subject to an anti-avoidance rule which allows the allocation to be ignored if the "principal reason" for the disproportionate allocation is the reduction or postponement of tax.[456] A similar rule applies where the partners do not deal at arm's length.

---

452. United States, IRC, s. 199A.
453. United States, IRC, s. 704(b); Treas. Reg., s. 1.704-1 through 1.704-4.
454. James Repetti, William H. Lyons & Charlene Luke, *Partnership Income Taxation*, 7th ed. (Foundation Press, 2023), p. 77.
455. Canada, ITA, s. 96.
456. Canada, ITA, s. 103.

The partner's cost basis in the partnership interest is increased by the partner's share of undistributed income and decreased by distributions and losses.[457] Adjustments are made to ensure that income or losses which are subject to special treatment are appropriately reflected in determining the cost base of the partnership interest. Thus, for example, because only part of capital gains are included in income, the full amount of the gain increases the partner's basis to ensure that the gain is not, in effect, taxed when the interest is disposed of. Unlike the situation in the U.S., for active partners, the cost in the partnership interest can become "negative" if losses or distributions in excess of the investment are passed through to the partner. The "negative" basis increases the gain on the disposition of the partnership interest; however, for limited and passive partners, a negative basis is deemed to be a capital gain.[458]

The partnership rules in *Sweden* follow the same general pattern. Income is computed at the partnership level and then attributed to the individual partners. The income is normally taxed as business income. The use of losses was substantially restricted following an explosion of tax-shelter activities in the 1980s. For individual partners, losses from a partnership can be used only against income from the same partnership; perhaps as a result of this limitation, the rules on special allocations are not well developed. A partner's cost basis in the partnership interest is increased by capital contributions and retained taxable earnings and reduced by withdrawals and tax-deductible losses.

In the *United Kingdom*, income is calculated at the partnership level according to the schedular system and then the partners pay tax with reference to their shares.[459] For this purpose, allocations of profit and loss in the partnership agreement are generally respected. For CGT purposes, however, the partnership assets are deemed to be owned and disposed of by the individual partners.[460]

In *The Netherlands*, the system is somewhat different. The character of income is basically determined at the individual level. Thus, for example, income of a limited partner is income from capital in general, since the activities of a limited partner do not constitute a business. In contrast, where the limited partnership interest is held in a (separate) business, the income is business income. Each general partner is treated with respect to its share in the partnership's business as being involved in its own business undertaking. Consequently, where options such as rates of depreciation, formation of reserves, etc., are available, each partner may make its own individual choice. In general, contractual allocations are respected, but limited partners may deduct losses only to the extent of their actual contributions.

The *Australian* rules on the computation of income are a mix of partnership and partner-level calculations.[461] In general, gains or losses from the disposition of inventory and business activities are determined at the partnership level and passed through

457. Canada, ITA, s. 53(1)(c) and 53(2)(c).
458. Canada, ITA, s. 40(3.1)-(3.19).
459. United Kingdom, ITTOIA, ss. 849-851 and Corporation Tax Act 2009, ss. 1258-1262.
460. United Kingdom, TCGA, s. 59.
461. Australia, ITAA 1936, Pt III Div 5. There are many specific rules for various cases in other parts of the tax legislation, which generally reinforce flow-through treatment.

to the individual partners. Partnership agreement allocations are generally respected and based on the accounts at the end of the taxable year. While there is some potential for tax planning through manipulation of the timing of partnership accounts, this has not proved to be a problem (there is a provision intended to prevent income splitting through family partnerships, although it is no longer of much relevance in light of the income attribution rules as discussed in Part II). Various tax attributes (foreign tax credit, imputation credit, etc.) also flow through. However, capital gains are taxed at the partner level as if each partner had disposed of its share of the partnership capital assets.[462] This treatment applies whether there is a sale of a partnership asset or partnership interest, admission of a new partner, or a change in the relations of existing partners.

Under the *German* system, the characterization of income for purposes of schedular classification takes place at the partnership level. However, where the only general partner in a limited partnership is a corporation, all the income derived by the partnership is treated as business income. Where a partnership carries on a business or trade, all other income received by the partnership is deemed to be business income as well.[463] Elections must be made at the partnership level, and income and deductions are also determined at that level. In general, no special allocation of income or losses is allowed, and either the general ratio set out in the statute or the partnership's articles for the sharing of profits and losses controls. Thus, for example, in a cross-border partnership among lawyers, it is not possible to allocate foreign income only to the foreign partners. Payments received by partners from the partnership on a contractual basis (salaries, rents, interest, and royalties) are included in the business income of the partnership in order to ensure that the trade tax on partnership profits is appropriately applied.[464] Complex rules also restrict the ability of limited partners to deduct losses in excess of their capital contributions.[465] Basically, the losses attributable to a partner may not exceed that partner's share of the assets of the partnership less the partnership-level liabilities (i.e., the partner's net equity in the partnership).

In *France*, the semi-transparent tax regime takes into account both the partnership and the partners. On the one hand, the partnership generates profits and must assess and declare income for tax purposes.[466] The nature of the partnership's activity determines the tax character of the income.[467] Depending on the nature of the activity, profits may be classified as commercial, noncommercial, or agricultural. However, where the partners of the partnership are legal entities or where the partner is a company subject to income tax (including a sole proprietorship), the share of the profits accruing to the legal-entity partner or sole proprietor is taxed according to the rules applicable to that partner and that partner's status. The realization of income by the company is determinative, irrespective of any actual distribution to the partner. On the other hand, the partners pay the tax, even if the profits are not actually distributed.

462. Australia, ITAA 1997, s. 106-5.
463. Germany, ITA, s. 15 para. 3 No. 1.
464. Germany, ITA, s. 15 para. 1 sent. 1 No. 2.
465. Germany, ITA, s. 15a.
466. France, CGI, s. 60.
467. France, CGI, s. 238 bis K.

This direct attribution of income to the partners is particularly interesting where losses are incurred. The loss is passed on directly to the partners, to be deducted from taxable income, making this type of company attractive for groups of companies or for use in patrimonial schemes. With respect to the taxation of capital gains on the sale of partnership interests, under certain conditions, tax law classifies partnership interests as business assets.[468] This characterization means that capital gains realized on the sale of these interests are taxed as "professional" capital gains and interest on loans taken out to acquire these shares is deductible from the partner's taxable income. In the case of capital gains, case law has allowed the avoidance of double taxation on securities by artificially increasing the acquisition price by the amount of reserves and adding to the cost price for tax purposes[469] the amount of undistributed reserves that have already been taxed.[470]

In *China*, taxable income or loss is determined at the partnership level. Because the IIT and EIT are separate systems, this determination is presumably governed by the IIT rules where all partners are individuals, or the EIT rules in other cases. The IIT and EIT provide rules for computing the taxable income or loss of partnerships, which consist mainly of limitations on deductions, but the rules are not comprehensive.[471] In the case of dividends, pass-through treatment applies to individual partners and the dividends are taxed as dividends (not as a share of the business income of the partnership) at a flat rate of 20%. In the case of corporate partners, however, there is no pass-through of the tax-free treatment of dividends. Under the EIT system, dividends are subject to special rules (i.e., an exemption for dividends between resident corporations and a foreign tax credit for dividends from foreign corporations). The STA's position seems to be that because the exemption applies only to "direct" investments with a minimum holding period of twelve months, an equity investment in a corporation through a partnership is considered to be an "indirect" investment and therefore is not eligible for the exemption. There is no specific guidance on passing through foreign tax credits.

3 LIABILITIES, TAX COST, AND LOSSES

Two basic patterns emerge in the treatment of liabilities at the partnership level and their effect on the tax cost or basis of a partner's interest in a partnership and the corresponding ability to claim current loss deductions. Under the *United States* system, liabilities incurred at the partnership level are reflected in the partner's tax cost in the partnership interest.[472] The liability is allocated to those partners who would ultimately have to pay the debt if the partnership assets were insufficient to pay the debt in the

468. France, CGI, s. 151 nonies.
469. The cost price for tax purposes equals the acquisition value of shares, plus the share of the corporate profits taxed in the hands of the associate, plus any losses made up by the associate less any losses deducted (except for special tax advantages), and less any profits distributed.
470. Conseil d'Etat, 8ᵉ et 3ᵉ s-s, 16.2.2000, n°133296 (*SA éts Quémener*).
471. China, Cai Shui [2008] No. 159.
472. United States, IRC, s. 752.

case of liquidation. This means that, in general, in a limited partnership, partnership-level debt is allocated to the general partners and increases their tax cost; limited partners, who are not liable beyond their capital contributions, are not allocated any portion of the debt and, accordingly, cannot share in losses financed out of the liabilities. A special rule applies to "nonrecourse" debt, that is, debt which is secured only by the property in question and for which no partner is personally liable. In general, such debt is allocated in accordance with the partners' share of partnership profits. Since no partner is personally responsible for the debt, it will be repaid, if at all, out of partnership profits and is so allocated for tax cost purposes.

Essentially, the *Dutch* system follows the general principle that liabilities incurred at the partnership level are treated at the level of the partners as if they had been incurred directly. However, it does not have a complex set of allocation rules similar to those of the U.S. tax system.

In contrast, in *Canada*, liabilities incurred at the partnership level do not affect the cost basis of the partner in the partnership interest. However, there is no restriction on the ability of a general partner to deduct its share of losses at the partnership level in excess of the actual investment (capital plus retained earnings) in the partnership. Excess losses are accounted for by allowing a "negative" basis in the partnership interest, which increases the potential gain on the disposition of the interest. Losses allocated to a limited partner are restricted to the amount of the partner's capital investment in the partnership (the "at-risk amount") by specific statutory rules.[473]

The *German* system is similar. Liabilities incurred at the partnership level do not affect the partner's basis in its partnership interest. Where limited partners are involved, the existence of the liability is taken into account in calculating that partner's equity in the partnership and deductions are correspondingly limited. Liabilities incurred by partners in their personal capacity (i.e., liabilities incurred in order to acquire their interests in the partnership) are also treated as liabilities in the context of the assessment of the partnership but are directly allocated to the partner at a second stage.

In *France*, a distinction must be made between two cases. First, if the company makes a loss, the shareholders (partners) can deduct their share of the loss directly from their overall income. If the shareholder (partner) is an individual, this share must be declared in the relevant income category in order to be deducted. If the shareholder (partner) is an entity (*groupement*) subject to income tax, the share of the loss is treated as an expense under the relevant income category. If the shareholder (partner) is subject to CIT, the share of the loss is treated as an expense deductible from the company's income. Second, where the partner makes up a company deficit, it cannot be deducted as a loss for tax purposes. In all cases, the partner's spouse is put at risk because the debt is contracted by the partner at the level of the tax household and not at the level of the partnership. Spouses and partners in a civil solidarity pact are jointly

473. Canada, ITA, s. 96(2.1)-(2.7).

liable for income tax when taxed jointly.[474] In this respect, case law has established that the taxpayer's household is liable for the tax, not the company.[475]

In the *United Kingdom*, revenue losses sustained by the partnership are claimed by the partners separately in accordance with the allocation under the partnership agreement. If the allocation of losses results in losses for some partners and profits for others, the losses are reduced to the net amount of partnership loss.[476] Generally speaking, limited partners can deduct losses only to the extent of their contribution to the partnership.[477]

In *Australia*, for partnerships that are treated as such under the general partnership law, losses and profits can be distributed freely as the partners agree, but it is not possible to have some partners with a profit and other partners with a loss for tax purposes.[478] For "tax law partnerships" arising from joint ownership of property, profits and losses must be strictly distributed in accordance with the interests in the property.[479] Given that limited partnerships have been given pass-through treatment with respect to venture capital and foreign hybrid entities, rules have been introduced to limit the use of losses to the amount of the partner's contribution less any amounts repaid to the partner, losses allowed to the partner in previous years, and any debt owed by the partner which is secured by the interest in the partnership.[480]

In general, *Japan* has only the conceptual rules set out in the administrative guidelines referred to in section 1 above, with the exception of a special provision negating the tax losses incurred by nonactive partners with respect to certain types of investments in the form of a partnership. This special provision is intended to combat tax-motivated investments in aircraft, ships, or other assets which may constitute real estate income under the schedular system applicable to individual taxpayers.

In *China*, losses of a partnership cannot be passed through to the partners. Partnership losses for a particular year can be carried forward to offset production and business income for five years. Where a partner has interests in two or more partnerships, the losses of each partnership must be kept separate and cannot be used to offset the income of other partnership interests.[481] The tax cost of a partner's interest in a partnership is not spelled out in STA circulars.

4 TRANSACTIONS BETWEEN PARTNERS AND PARTNERSHIP

The systems vary considerably in the extent to which transactions between a partner and the partnership are given independent significance for tax purposes. Under *United*

474. France, CGI, s. 1691 bis.
475. Conseil d'Etat, March 27, 2009, n°293871 and n°293872 (*Dalamel de Bournet*).
476. United Kingdom, ITTOIA, s. 850A, Corporation Tax Act 2009, s. 1263, and Income Tax Act 2007, s. 62.
477. United Kingdom, Income Tax Act 2007, s. 104.
478. Australia, ITAA 1936, s. 92.
479. *McDonald* (1987), 18 ATR 957.
480. Australia, ITAA 1997, Div 830-C in relation to foreign hybrids, ITAA 1936, s. 92(2AA) for venture capital partnerships.
481. China, Cai Shui [2008] No. 159, Art. 5.

States rules, if a partner engages in a transaction with the partnership "other than in his capacity as a partner," the form of the transaction is generally respected.[482] Thus, a partner can receive compensation for services rendered to the partnership or for money loaned to the partnership with a corresponding deduction or capital expense at the partnership level. In addition, the statute recognizes a special form of partner-partnership relationship where the partner is guaranteed a payment regardless of partnership profits.[483] In some respects, such payments are treated as payments to third parties for purposes of determining taxation of the recipient partner and the deductibility of the payment at the partnership level.

The rules in *Canada* and *China* are generally similar. The partnership is usually treated as a separate entity for purposes of transactions with partners. A partner can lend funds to the partnership or perform services for it. The latter principle is also followed in *The Netherlands*, although its application in the international context is unclear.

In the *United Kingdom*, for income tax purposes a partner can have dealings with the partnership as a third party (other than as an employee); for example, a lease of property to the partnership results in rental income to the partner and a corresponding deduction to the partnership.[484] The rules are more complex for CGT purposes since each partner is deemed to own directly a share of the capital assets.[485] Thus, a disposal of an asset by a partner to the partnership is treated as only a partial disposal since the partner retains an interest in the asset.

In *Sweden*, most transactions between partner and partnership are ignored. This can be important because the treatment of income as income from services, capital, or business may result in different tax treatment at the partner level. Payments by the partnership for partner services or capital are not deductible by the partnership or includable in the income of the partner. The increased partnership income is simply allocated to the partners under normal principles and retains the character it had in the hands of the partnership.

The *Australian* rules are somewhat similar to the Swedish rules, although they rest on a different principle. Under private law principles, a partner cannot be an employee of the partnership and any purported "wages" paid to the partner are treated as partnership distributions. This characterization is followed for tax purposes.[486] Similarly, loans by partners which bear interest but are accounted for as interest-bearing capital or retained profits do not generate interest income or corresponding deductions.[487] However, other partner loans and transactions are respected, although it is unclear to what extent this is based on an entity or aggregate basis.[488] Disposals of

482. United States, IRC, s. 707(a).
483. United States, IRC, s. 707(c).
484. For example, *see Heastie v. Veitch & Co Ltd*, [1933] 18 TC 305 (CA). There are special rules for "salaried members" of LLPs: United Kingdom, ITTOIA, s. 863A-863G.
485. United Kingdom, TCGA, s. 59.
486. Ruling TR 2005/7.
487. *Beville* (1953), 5 AITR 458.
488. In practice, most taxpayers use the entity approach to self-dealing between a partner and the partnership (full deduction for the partnership, full inclusion in the income of the partner), but the case law is divided: *Grollo Nominees* (1997) 36 ATR 424, 482-483, 97 ATC 4585, 4635-4637

inventory or depreciable assets by a partner to a partnership may, by election, be subject to a rollover so that the partner's tax cost carries over to the partnership.[489] Other disposals of assets by partners to the partnership are taxable on the basis that the partner has disposed of fractional interests in the assets to the other partners.[490]

Similarly, in *France*, since all the participants are considered to be co-owners of the operation, in general, no employment relation can exist between the partnership and a partner, and everything a partner receives from the partnership is deemed to be part of the allocation of profits which the parties have agreed on. However, certain tax consequences arise from the fact that the partnership is considered to be an entity distinct from its partners due to its legal personality, which gives it legal capacity. Therefore, the partnership and its partners can enter into contracts (e.g., loan or lease agreements). From a tax viewpoint, the rules remain varied. Rentals of property between partner and partnership are respected; the rental payments are deductible by the partnership and treated as rental income or commercial profits in the hands of the partner, depending on the circumstances. In addition, interest on partner current-account loans is deductible by the partnership, subject to the limitation that the rate must not exceed the average bank lending rate. To the extent that the interest is deductible, it is treated as capital income to the partner; any nondeductible interest is treated as partnership income allocated to the partner. Conversely, certain rules deny the existence of the partnership as a distinct entity in order to prevent artificial tax arrangements. For example, remuneration paid by the partnership for functions performed by the partners within the partnership is not deductible; such amounts are considered to be part of the income which is allocated to the partners for tax purposes. The same treatment applies to benefits granted by the partnership to one of its partners who is a shareholder in a company subject to corporation tax, and that company is itself a partner in the partnership. Moreover, the "abnormal management decision" (*acte anormal de gestion*) principle developed in the case law (e.g., in the case of excessive bargain sales) can apply to the relationship between a partnership and a partner where both have a business activity.

Germany reaches somewhat similar results with different techniques.[491] Payments for services, interest on loans, or rental payments for leased property received by a partner from a partnership reduce the profit at the entity level but are accounted for in a separate "special" balance sheet for the individual partner; they are, in effect, included in the income of the partnership, which is then allocated to the individual partners. The basic policy considerations behind this rule are not directed principally at the income tax, but are trade tax related: partners should not be able to reduce the trade tax basis by turning regular profit participations into contractual payments.

(deduction and income do not arise to the extent of the self-dealing); *Poole & Dight* (1970) 122 CLR 427, 440-443 (entity approach).

489. Australia, ITAA 1997, ss. 40-295(2), 40-340, 70-100.
490. Australia, ITAA 1997, s. 106-5.
491. Germany, ITA, s. 15 para. 1 sent. 1 No. 2.

5 DISPOSITION OF A PARTNERSHIP INTEREST

While, in general, most of the systems reviewed here treat the disposition of a partnership interest as the disposition of a separate asset, in accordance with an entity approach, some require fragmentation. In the *United States*, a partnership interest is treated as a capital asset and gain or loss is treated accordingly.[492] However, where the partnership holds certain assets the sale of which would generate ordinary income (in particular, appreciated inventory and property subject to depreciation recapture), the sale of the partnership interest generates ordinary income to that extent.[493] *Sweden* also treats a partnership interest in the same way as shares in a company.[494] Thus, a partnership interest is treated as a separate asset; the gain or loss on the disposition is treated as income from capital (capital gain) and the participation exemption may apply. In special situations, the gain can be taxed as income from business, which is the case where business income of a partnership which is earned prior to the sale of an interest in the partnership is transferred to the purchaser. Partnership interests held by corporations are normally treated the same way as shares (participating exemption). In general, *Canada* and *China* treat the gain or loss on the disposition of a partnership interest as capital gain.

In contrast, in *The Netherlands*, the tax treatment of the gain on disposition depends on the character of the partnership's operating income. Where that income is treated as business income in the hands of the individual partner (general partner), the gain or loss is similarly treated as business income. However, where the income is treated as income from capital (limited partner), the gain on the disposition is not subject to tax since private capital gains of individuals are not generally taxed. Where the partner is a corporation, the gain is subject to full CIT. The underlying theory for this treatment is that the partnership, viewed from an aggregate point of view, is simply the sum of the activities of the individual partners. As indicated above, this principle extends to allowing, for example, different depreciation methods for different partners for the same asset.

Germany follows the same pattern.[495] The nature of the partnership activities (trade or business, agriculture, etc.) determines the treatment of the gain or loss on the partnership interest. The distinction between a share in the operating profits and a gain from the disposition essentially relates to the applicability of a reduced tax rate.[496]

The *Australian* approach operates on the theory that there is generally no partnership interest separate from the assets of the partnership. A number of questions have been raised concerning the operation of the capital gains rules in the partnership context; as a practical matter, these issues have been resolved by a mix of changes to the law, the Australian Taxation Office's flexible interpretation of the law, and the way in which partnerships (especially large partnerships) are structured. It is common for

492. United States, IRC, s. 741.
493. United States, IRC, s. 751(a).
494. Sweden, ITA, Ch. 25a para. 3.
495. Germany, ITA, s. 16 para. 1 No. 2.
496. Germany, ITA, s. 34 para. 1, para. 2 No. 1 and para. 3.

large professional partnerships to have no tangible assets. All such assets are held in a separate unit trust owned effectively by the partners and made available to the partnership. The partners generally agree that there is no goodwill so that an incoming partner does not pay to enter the partnership, and conversely, a departing partner does not receive anything on departure (apart from adjustments in relation to work in progress). Payments for work in progress were previously taxable to the departing partner but not deductible by the partnership, but this problem has now been overcome by legislation.[497]

The *United Kingdom* treats any change in ownership interests in a partnership as a disposal of partnership assets. The extent to which and manner in which tax law recognizes the allocation of specific assets to specific partners under a partnership agreement is an open question.

Several of the systems allow the "inside" basis of partnership assets to be adjusted when there is a sale of a partnership interest. In *Germany*, such an adjustment is mandatory. As a result, the "inside" and "outside" bases of partnership assets and partnership interests are always the same. The increased tax cost at the partnership level is related only to the purchasing partner's tax calculation and is accounted for in a special "complementary" balance sheet. For purposes of determining the deductibility of losses by a limited partner, the assets shown on the complementary balance sheet are considered to be part of the partner's equity in the partnership.

The *United States* has similar rules with respect to the sale of a partnership interest.[498] The tax basis of partnership property must be reduced with respect to the buying partner if the value of such property is significantly below its tax basis at the time of the sale. In contrast, if the partnership property has increased in value, the partnership may (but is not required to) elect to increase the property's tax basis with respect to the purchasing partner.

The *French* system is different from the others in several respects. During partnership operations, no adjustment to the cost basis in the partnership interest is made for distributions, retained earnings taxed to the partner, or losses which have been passed through and deducted. Instead, adjustments are, in effect, postponed until the interest is sold. Thus, under case law principles, the acquisition cost is increased by earnings taxed to the partner and losses effectively borne by the partner and reduced by deducted losses and distributed earnings. With respect to the gain or loss on the disposition, the treatment depends on a complex set of rules involving in part the status of the partner and in part the nature and extent of activities of the partnership. For example, regardless of the partnership activities, for corporate partners and individual proprietorships holding a partnership interest, a gain or loss is treated as a business capital gain or loss subject to a preferential rate, or to the usual loss limitations if it is a long-term gain or loss. The same result applies where the partnership is involved in a trade or business or professional activity and the interest is disposed of by an individual partner who is involved in the business. Where the partnership is engaged

497. Australia, ITAA 1997, ss. 15-50, 25-95.
498. United States, IRC, s. 743.

in real estate or securities investments, the gain is treated as falling within the category of private capital gains unless realized by a corporate or sole-proprietorship partner.

6 LIQUIDATION OF A PARTNERSHIP

Where a partnership is liquidated, potential gain or loss may be present at both the partnership level and the partner level, depending on the relation between the fair market value of the partnership assets, their tax cost in the hands of the partnership, and the tax cost of the partnership interest in the hands of the partners. The systems differ substantially in their treatment of the potential gain or loss involved.

The *United States* system provides the most extensive deferral of gain or loss recognition. As a general rule, if property other than cash is distributed, there is no recognition of gain or loss at either the partnership or partner level, and the partner's tax cost in the partnership interest becomes the tax cost for the property received.[499] If cash is received, it first reduces the tax cost of the partner's interest and may result in gain to the extent that it exceeds that amount. Any additional property received would correspondingly take a zero-tax cost. A loss may be recognized if only cash or certain ordinary income assets are distributed.

The situation is more complex where the assets are not distributed pro rata and the partnership holds certain assets the sale of which would have generated ordinary income.[500] In effect, the partners are treated as having made a taxable exchange of the assets to the extent that they receive non-pro rata amounts.

Other systems provide more extensive recognition of gains and losses on a liquidation. In *Sweden*, the distribution of the property is viewed as a removal of the property from business use and the withdrawal results in the recognition of gain under normal principles. In addition, if the value of the property exceeds the partner's basis in the partnership interest (increased for the gain recognized on the withdrawal), the partner may recognize additional gain since the liquidation is treated as a taxable disposition of the partnership interest. Until 2008, it was possible to distribute assets in and out of partnerships and businesses without taxation as long as the transactions took place between businesses at prices equal to the tax basis of the assets. These rules could be manipulated in complex tax avoidance schemes, which created large artificial tax losses at the price of minimum income recognition, and were subsequently abolished.

The *Canadian* rules have the same basic structure but also provide other possibilities for rollover relief. Where the partners receive undivided interests in the partnership property, there is no current recognition,[501] and where a single partner continues the business, no gain or loss is recognized by that partner.[502] Similarly, in the *United Kingdom*, if the partners receive their fractional share of partnership assets, there is no current recognition of gain for capital gains purposes, which is deferred

499. United States, IRC, ss. 731 and 732(b).
500. United States, IRC, s. 751(b).
501. Canada, ITA, s. 98(3).
502. Canada, ITA, s. 98(5).

through an adjustment to the tax cost of the assets received. If the distributions are non-pro rata, gains are recognized currently to that extent. As with Australia (below), rollover relief is often available where inventory or assets for which capital allowances are granted are transferred from a partnership to a partner.[503] By contrast, in *Australia*, which generally disregards the interest in the partnership for tax purposes, each partner is treated as having disposed of the fractional interest held in the partnership's capital assets, either to the other partners or to third parties, if the liquidation is effected by a sale of assets and distribution of the proceeds. Rollover relief is often available for inventory and depreciable assets which are transferred from the partnership to one or more partners.

In *Germany*, the distribution of a partnership's property is viewed as a withdrawal of the property from the business resulting in the recognition of gain,[504] although the gain qualifies for a preferential tax rate.[505] In addition, if independent business units or particular business assets are transferred to different partners, the distribution is regarded as a mere separation of assets and the tax consequences are deferred.[506]

In France, the dissolution of a partnership is treated as a cessation of business, regardless of the legal form and nature of the company's activity. Dissolution entails immediate taxation of any untaxed operating profits made since the end of the last taxable year as well as deferred profits and capital gains on fixed assets realized or recognized at the time of sale or winding-up, subject to statutory exemptions.

In *The Netherlands*, the same approach is taken as on the disposition of a partnership interest: the transaction is a taxable event, and the character of the gain or loss depends on the character of the partnership interest as business or investment in the hands of the partner.

503. United Kingdom, ITTOIA, ss. 177 and 179 and Capital Allowances Act 2001, ss. 266 and 267.
504. Germany, ITA, s. 16 para. 3.
505. Germany, ITA, s. 34.
506. Germany, ITA, s. 16 para. 3 ss. 2 et seq.

PART IV International Taxation

The patterns of international taxation adopted by the countries examined in this book show a high degree of similarity in their structure, despite significant differences in technical detail. This broad consensus stems in large part from early efforts in international cooperation and, in particular, the tax work of the League of Nations in the 1920s and 1930s. Those efforts produced the conceptual framework for allocating taxing rights in an international context, which became the basis for the fundamental aspects of most countries' systems.

Generally speaking, countries assert their right to tax based on the personal connections of a taxpayer to the country. Individuals and legal persons with the requisite connections to a country are customarily referred to as residents. Typically, the taxation of residents extends to all their income, generally referred to as worldwide income, regardless of the geographical source of the income (although some countries do not assert taxing jurisdiction over foreign business income of resident corporations and there is a trend in favor of exempting the dividends received from certain foreign corporations). In addition, virtually all countries claim the right to tax income that has its "source" in the country, regardless of the personal status of the recipient. To summarize, all the countries studied in this book, and most other countries, tax residents of the country on their worldwide income (with the exception of foreign business income for some countries) and nonresidents on their income from sources in the country.

Since most countries tax their residents on their worldwide income and nonresidents on their domestic source income, many items of income are subject to double taxation: once by the country in which the income is derived or has its source and again by the country in which the taxpayer is resident. This problem of overlapping tax claims, arising from the parallel assertion by different states of residence and source jurisdiction to tax the same item of income, is resolved in one of three ways. First, the residence country may cede the primary jurisdiction to tax to the state in which the income arises (often referred to as the source country). In this situation, the primacy of the source country's right to tax is recognized by the residence country through the mechanism of a foreign tax credit (FTC) for the taxes levied by the source country. Second, the residence country may exempt the income arising outside the residence country from tax, so that the income is taxed exclusively in the source country. Third, in a few situations, the source country gives up its right to tax despite the fact that the income arises in its jurisdiction, with the result that the income is taxed exclusively by the residence country. These methods for relieving international double taxation are usually implemented in both domestic legislation and bilateral treaty practices.

The Organisation for Economic Co-operation and Development (OECD), the successor to the League of Nations in the tax area, continued the League's work on the development of international tax principles through the OECD Model Treaty, modifying and refining the various provisions of the draft Model Tax Convention of the League of Nations. The OECD Model Treaty then became the basis for most bilateral treaties. More important, in the past two decades the OECD's work has evolved from refining the OECD Model Treaty to attempting to establish international tax norms for several aspects of domestic tax legislation. In 1995, it published its Transfer Pricing Guidelines, which had a significant impact on domestic transfer pricing legislation for both OECD member countries and nonmember countries. In 1998, the OECD produced its *Report on Harmful Tax Competition*, which recommended restrictions on some methods used by countries to attract certain types of foreign investment (such as "ring-fenced" preferential regimes, which were limited to foreign investors). In addition, based on the analysis in the Report, the OECD set up the Forum on Harmful Tax Practices (FHTP). The FHTP was tasked with establishing procedures for peer review of the preferential regimes established in member countries in order to determine the extent to which domestic law provisions complied with the requirements of the Report. In addition, the Global Forum on Transparency and Exchange of Information (GFTE) was established, which, beginning in 2009, was expanded beyond OECD member countries. The GFTE sets out procedures to monitor the extent to which countries' domestic law provisions comply with OECD-established norms on the exchange of information (e.g., the elimination of bank secrecy). As of January 2024, 171 countries were members of the GFTE.

One of the most important extensions of the OECD's role in establishing international tax principles was the 2012 Base Erosion and Profit Shifting (BEPS) Project and its 2015 Reports on the fifteen action items of the BEPS Project. In response to highly publicized reports of aggressive tax planning and tax avoidance by multinational enterprises, and increasing revenue needs, the Group of 20 (G20) mandated the OECD to develop new approaches to deal with base-erosion and profit-shifting activities. The OECD opened up work on the BEPS project to non-OECD countries and, ultimately, forty-four countries participated in one form or another in the work, culminating in the fifteen BEPS action items. The analytical framework for the BEPS action items was driven by the need to identify situations where uncoordinated domestic tax rules facilitated tax avoidance and to better align taxing rights with economic activity. The BEPS action items cover a wide range of topics, from changes in the Transfer Pricing Guidelines to limits on the deductibility of interest and the treatment of hybrid payments. The impact of the various BEPS action items on the structure of domestic tax rules is described in the Country Reports in Part I and throughout Part IV, especially in the material dealing with treaties and in Subpart C, section 7, discussing the tax aspects of the digitalization of the economy.

The BEPS project has also had an impact on the institutional structure for cooperation on international tax matters. In response to the G20's call for broad and consistent implementation of the BEPS package, the OECD/G20 Inclusive Framework on BEPS was established in June 2016 and as of May 2024 had 147 member countries, representing 95% of the global economy. Countries other than G20 and OECD member countries, referred to as BEPS Associates, participate on an equal footing with G20 and OECD member countries in the ongoing standard-setting activities of the BEPS project, as well as the review and monitoring of the implementation of the BEPS package in domestic legislation. As a condition for joining the Inclusive Framework, Associates must agree to implement the BEPS action items which are classified as "minimum standards" (e.g., measures dealing with treaty abuse and improvements to the mutual agreement procedure).

The original BEPS Report stated explicitly that its solutions for problems of BEPS were not intended to "change the existing standards on the allocation of taxing rights on cross-border income." Nonetheless, many of the BEPS recommendations clearly raised basic questions with respect to the allocation of taxing rights among jurisdictions. The expanded country participation in the BEPS project, especially by Brazil, Russia, India, China, and South Africa (the BRICS), and other developing countries, has clearly had an impact on some BEPS policies. Moreover, recent BEPS work on the taxation of the digital economy, discussed in Subpart C, section 7, has focused on fundamental changes to international taxing rules; it is being carried out by the Inclusive Framework through a Steering Group, the Task Force on the Digital Economy, and several OECD Working Parties, as well as the OECD secretariat.

In 2020, the Inclusive Framework announced its intention to work on a two-pillar solution to the challenges which the digitalization of the economy poses for the international tax system. These two pillars are: Pillar One—new nexus and profit-attribution rules for the world's largest and most profitable multinationals, and Pillar Two—a 15% global minimum top-up tax on the foreign source income of multinationals with consolidated revenue in excess of EUR 750 million. The two pillars are discussed in Subpart C, sections 7 and section 9.

With its mandate from the G20, the OECD has clearly been the leader in formulating approaches to international taxation, but other international organizations have also played a role. The adoption of Article 12A and Article 12B of the United Nations Model Convention, which provide for the source country taxation of fees for technical services and income from automated digital services where there is no physical presence in the country, presages some of the work of the Task Force on the Digital Economy. In addition, as indicated in the Country Reports in Part I, the domestic laws of European Union (EU) member countries have been impacted by European Commission Directives and decisions of the Court of Justice of the European Union (CJEU) (formerly known as the European Court of Justice (ECJ)). Thus, the relatively stable pattern of international taxation principles originally established in the 1920s under the auspices of the League of Nations has been substantially influenced by subsequent developments; it remains to be seen what the final results of this process will be. The most recent indication that the existing structure of international taxation is under serious pressure to change is a United Nations initiative, which began in late 2023, to develop a multilateral Framework Convention dealing with international cooperation in tax matters, which would allow all countries to participate equally and effectively in norm setting and decision-making with respect to international tax issues.

The following Subpart A examines the issues which arise in the assertion of personal taxing jurisdiction (residence taxation) and the mechanisms for the relief of double taxation. Subpart B considers the structure of source-based taxation, and Subpart C examines some selected additional international issues.

SUBPART A
Residence Taxation

1 BASES FOR THE ASSERTION OF PERSONAL TAXING JURISDICTION

1.1 Individuals

Personal taxing jurisdiction over individuals is typically asserted on the basis of "residence" and is often referred to as residence jurisdiction. The determination of residence often rests on a facts-and-circumstances test which looks at the various social and economic connections taxpayers have to the taxing jurisdiction, as well as taxpayers' intent with regard to their stay and their connections to other jurisdictions. This general test is frequently supplemented with a mechanical test based on the number of days of presence in the jurisdiction. Residence for tax purposes may or may not be connected with residence in terms of immigration status.

The *United States* approach combines objective and facts-and-circumstances tests. Individuals are resident for tax purposes if they possess the right to permanent entry to the United States under the immigration laws (a so-called green card) or if they are physically present in the jurisdiction for 183 days or more during the taxable year. In addition, they may be treated as a resident if they are present in the jurisdiction for thirty-one days or more and meet a cumulative-presence test, which looks to the days present in the current year and in the past two years. If the total days in the present year and the weighted days for the past two years are 183 or more, an individual is a resident for tax purposes unless they can establish that their "tax home," usually their principal place of business, is in another country and that they have a "closer connection" to that country than to the United States. The factors in establishing the "closer connection" are those which are typically used in a determination of residence. Special rules apply for students and diplomats, which allow them to be present in the country without triggering the mechanical physical-presence tests.[1]

Unlike other jurisdictions, the United States also asserts personal jurisdiction based on citizenship. In principle, United States citizens are taxable on their worldwide income regardless of where they are resident. This basis for personal jurisdiction increases the possibility of overlapping claims for worldwide taxation, an issue which is frequently dealt with in U.S. tax treaties.[2]

In *Canada*, in general, residence is determined on a case-by-case basis, applying a case law-developed set of factors, including the availability of a dwelling in Canada, the residence of family members, physical presence, and social and economic ties. The most important factors are the presence of a dwelling in Canada (which is available for the taxpayer's use) and the presence of immediate family members in Canada. Where a resident taxpayer leaves Canada, the intention to return to Canada is relevant in determining whether the taxpayer remains a resident. In addition, a specific statutory provision deems a person to be a resident of Canada if the person "sojourns" in Canada for 183 days or more during the taxable period.[3] The meaning of the term "sojourn" is not entirely clear, but it is not synonymous with physical presence; for example, if a person is resident in Canada (based on the case law) for part of the year, they are not "sojourning" in Canada. Certain individuals who are frequently absent from Canada, such as diplomats and members of the armed forces, are deemed to be residents of Canada.[4]

Australia also applies a facts-and-circumstances test. In addition, there is deemed residence where a taxpayer is "domiciled" in Australia and has no "permanent place of abode" outside the country, or where a taxpayer has physical presence for more than one-half of the tax year and cannot establish that their usual place of abode is abroad and they do not intend to take up residence in Australia. A special rule treats as residents certain government employees who would not normally be taxed under the usual residence rules and typically would be exempt from tax in the foreign jurisdiction to which they are posted.[5] The law is currently under review, with the goal of providing more certainty and robustness to the rules—certainty in the former case by adopting an approach similar to that now applied in the United Kingdom, and robustness, in the latter case, by making it harder for a taxpayer to lose Australian-resident status.[6]

In 2013, the *United Kingdom* introduced a comprehensive statutory residence test for individuals which replaced the previous facts-and-circumstances approach.[7] This statutory residence test is mechanical in operation, involving asking whether the individual fails to meet any of the automatic overseas tests and meets one of the automatic UK tests or the sufficient-ties test. It remains the case that a person who

1. United States, Internal Revenue Code (IRC), s. 7701(b) sets forth the various tests.
2. United States, IRC, s. 7701(a)(30)(A).
3. Canada, Income Tax Act (ITA), s. 250(1)(a).
4. Canada, ITA, s. 250(1)(b)-(g).
5. Australia, Income Tax Assessment Act 1936 (ITAA 1936), s. 6(1) definition of "resident" para. (a), Ruling TR 2023/1.
6. Australia, Treasury, Modernising individual tax residency: Consultation paper (2023).
7. United Kingdom, Finance Act 2013, s. 218 and Sch. 45.

spends 183 days in the United Kingdom in a tax year is resident in the United Kingdom. Otherwise, the automatic overseas tests involve a mixture of testing residence in prior years, determining the number of days spent in the United Kingdom in the current year and, in the case of workers, establishing that they work full-time overseas. The UK tests focus on the individual having a home in the United Kingdom, presence in the United Kingdom, not having an overseas home, and having full-time UK work. There are additional rules for split-year treatment.

In *The Netherlands*, the statute requires residence to be determined "according to the circumstances"[8] and case law has focused on "durable ties of a personal nature" to The Netherlands.[9] The principal focus is on the existence of a home in The Netherlands and the abode of the family. However, all relevant circumstances are to be taken into account to assess the "sustainable ties of a personal nature,"[10] and individuals may be found to have such ties with both The Netherlands and another state.[11] Dutch diplomats stationed abroad and similar persons are deemed to be resident in The Netherlands if they are Dutch citizens.[12] In addition, individuals who give up their Dutch residence but return within twelve months without having become resident in another country are deemed not to have given up their Dutch residence unless the other country is an EU Member State or a treaty country where they have been subject to tax as residents on income from sources similar to those for which Dutch residents are subject to Dutch tax.[13]

In *Sweden*, individuals are regarded as resident if they have a "real dwelling and home" in Sweden or Sweden is their "habitual abode." This latter test has been interpreted as being met if the taxpayer is continuously present in Sweden for six months; however, even shorter periods of presence, if they occur frequently, might suffice to create a "habitual abode."[14] As discussed below, Sweden also has a complex set of rules the purpose of which is to continue to tax residents who have left the country but retain substantial connections to Sweden.

Germany treats individuals as resident for tax purposes only if they have either their residence or habitual place of abode in Germany.[15] Foreign nationals who receive more than 90% of their income from sources in Germany have the option to be treated as a resident when that could be beneficial for tax purposes.[16] Residence is based on the availability to the taxpayer of a home (house, apartment, etc.) which they intend to

8. Netherlands, General Act on Taxation (GAT), Art. 4(1).
9. *See* for example *Hof Amsterdam*, October 27, 1993, m. 92/3106, V-N 1994, p. 785 (married employee who was working and living in different locations abroad while his family remained in The Netherlands was found to have tax residence in The Netherlands).
10. Netherlands, Supreme Court, January 21, 2011, No. 10/00563, BNB 2011/127 and Netherlands Supreme Court, December 21, 2018, No. 18/02981, V-N 2019/7.10.
11. Netherlands, Supreme Court, April 12, 2013, No. 12/02980, BNB 2013/123.
12. Netherlands, Income Tax Act (ITA), Art. 2.2(2).
13. Netherlands, ITA, Art. 2.2(1).
14. Sweden, *Högsta Förvaltningsdomstolen*, No. 6034-17, May 30, 2018, where a regular stay of five months per year was considered to create a "habitual abode."
15. Germany, Income Tax Act (ITA), s. 1 para. 1.
16. Germany, ITA, s. 1 para. 3.

retain and use.[17] There is a highly developed case law applying this facts-and-circumstances test. Some of the factors considered are the period of time during which the home is used and the regularity and frequency of the use. "Habitual abode" is established by presence in Germany indicating an intention to stay more than temporarily.[18] In practice, a continuous stay of six months (even where it spans two calendar years) constitutes a habitual abode, although there are nuances in the rules.

The *French* system has an extensive statutory definition of residence.[19] Individuals are resident for tax purposes if they have their permanent home in France, or, if their permanent home cannot be determined, they are physically present in the jurisdiction for over 183 days or for a substantially longer time than in any other country. In addition, professional or employment activity in France leads to resident treatment unless the taxpayer can establish that the activity is secondary to activities performed elsewhere. The Finance Act 2020 added a presumption that the directors of companies headquartered in France with annual sales in excess of EUR 250 million are residents of France unless proven otherwise. Finally, taxpayers having their "center of economic interest" in France are treated as residents regardless of the nature of the activity.

The focus in the *Japanese* statute is both on domicile, defined as the base of personal operations, and more than a year of residence, defined as the place of day-to-day living.[20] An administrative regulation provides that where a person is engaged in a business which ordinarily requires living in the country for one year, they are treated, unless otherwise provided, as domiciled in Japan for tax purposes when they arrive in the country. However, if personal connections to Japan are significant, domicile in Japan exists even where business activities are conducted outside Japan for significant periods. In this regard, the tax law provisions are interpreted in light of civil law concepts of domicile and, as a result, the administrative rule is not the exclusive test for domicile.

Japan also distinguishes between ordinary residents and "short-term" residents. A short-term resident is one who meets the normal residence test but is not a Japanese national and has not maintained a residence for five years during a ten-year period.[21] Short-term residents are taxed only on domestic source income and foreign source income which is remitted to Japan.[22]

In *China*, an individual is resident for Individual Income Tax (IIT) purposes where the individual is "domiciled in China" or not domiciled in China but has stayed in China in the aggregate for 183 days or more in a tax year.[23] The "domicile test" and the "183-day test" are further elaborated in the IIT Regulations and administrative circulars. Article 2 of the Regulations provides that "domiciled in China" means habitually residing in China due to household registration or "family or economic ties,"

17. Germany, General Fiscal Code (GFC) (*Abgabenordnung*), s. 8.
18. Germany, GFC, s. 9.
19. France, Code général des impôts (CGI), s. 4B.
20. Japan, Income Tax Act (ITA), s. 1 para. 1 subpara. 3.
21. Japan, ITA, s. 1 para. 1 subpara. 4.
22. Japan, ITA, s. 7.
23. China, Individual Income Tax (IIT), Art 1.

but leaves the meaning of "habitually residing" and factors giving rise to "family or economic ties" undefined. The State Tax Administration (STA) interprets "habitually residing" broadly; it does not require presence in China for any particular period of time, and temporary absences from China to study or work do not mean that an individual is not habitually residing in China.[24] Household registration, which was introduced in the early 1950s as part of China's population-control system, represents the "legitimate or lawful" status of a natural person, and is the basis for claiming government services and benefits. Once an individual is registered, deregistration requires the approval of the public security office. Therefore, any Chinese individual with household registration in China is generally considered to habitually reside in China.

The tax residence of an individual who is not a Chinese citizen is established by the 183-day test. Temporary absences from China of not more than thirty days and total absences of not more than ninety days are not taken into account. Absences of less than one day are not counted at all.[25]

In *India*, residence is determined primarily on the basis of the number of days that a person stays in India. An individual is resident in India if, during the previous year, the individual is present in India for at least 182 days or, during the previous four years, is present in India for more than 365 days and during the current year for at least sixty days. For members of the crew of an Indian ship and Indians employed abroad, the only condition for residence in India is presence of 182 days or more in the previous year. Indian citizens and persons of Indian origin visiting India are also considered to be resident if they are in India during the year for 182 days or more. However, where such persons have income sourced in India exceeding INR 1.5 million, they are considered to be resident in India if their total stay in India during the year exceeds 120 days. They are also treated as resident but not ordinarily resident (NOR) if their stay in India exceeds 120 days but does not exceed 182 days.[26] Moreover, effective April 1, 2021, Indian citizens who are not resident by reason of their presence in India but who have Indian income in excess of INR 1.5 million during the tax year and are not "liable to tax"[27] anywhere else by reason of domicile or other similar criteria are deemed to be residents of India,[28] but NOR.[29]

In addition, there is a class of taxpayers who are treated as NOR where they remain nonresident for nine of ten previous years or where during the preceding seven years they have been in India for 729 days or less. Taxpayers who are NOR in India are not taxable on their foreign source income unless it arises from a business controlled in India or a profession set up in India.

24. China, State Tax Administration (STA) Guoshuifa [1994] No. 89.
25. China, Ministry of Finance (MOF)/STA circular [2019] No. 34.
26. India, Income Tax Act 1961 (ITA 1961), s. 6(6)(c).
27. India, ITA 1961, s. 2(29A).
28. India, ITA 1961, s. 6(IA).
29. India, ITA 1961, s. 6(6)(d).

Indian diplomats posted abroad are not deemed to be residents in India, but their salary income is always deemed to accrue in India;[30] however, their allowances and perquisites are specifically exempt from tax.[31]

1.2 Corporations

Two basic approaches are used in establishing a jurisdictional connection for corporations. One is to focus on some formal legal connection to the jurisdiction such as incorporation or registry in the commercial register. The other is to select some economic or commercial connection such as the place of management, principal business location, or, less frequently, the residence of shareholders. Many jurisdictions combine these approaches, treating a corporation as resident if either test is satisfied. In some cases, the test of place of management becomes, in effect, a formal test by focusing on easily controlled events such as the place at which the board of directors meets, rather than the situs of day-to-day management decisions.

The *United States* is an example of a jurisdiction which relies on a purely formal test. All corporations organized under the laws of the United States or one of the federal states are treated as "domestic," (i.e., resident) corporations, regardless of any other connection to the jurisdiction.[32] Conversely, all other corporations are "foreign," (i.e., nonresident) corporations, even if all of their commercial and economic activities are linked to the United States.[33] *Japan* also has a formal test, although the technical structure of the rule is somewhat different. Under the statutory definition of resident corporation, a corporation is resident if its "headquarters" or "principal office" is located in Japan.[34] These terms are derived from civil law and commercial law, under which all corporations incorporated in Japan must have either a registered headquarters or registered principal office in Japan—thus, in effect, turning the test into one of incorporation in the case of domestically organized corporations. In contrast, where a corporation organized in a foreign country has a registered principal office or headquarters in Japan (if that is possible under the laws of the incorporating jurisdiction), it is also treated by Japan as a resident corporation.

Sweden also has a formal test which turns on formation and registration under Swedish corporate law; alternatively, corporations which are not registered in Sweden are deemed to be resident there if the place of meetings of the board of directors (or "another similar circumstance") is located in Sweden.[35]

The *Commonwealth* countries, which have traditionally focused on the place of central management and control to determine corporate residence, combine that test with a test based on formal incorporation. Thus, in the *United Kingdom* prior to 1988, the only test was the factual one of central management and control of the company's

30. India, ITA 1961, s. 9(1)(iii).
31. India, ITA 1961, s. 10(7).
32. United States, IRC, s. 7701(a)(4).
33. United States, IRC, s. 7701(a)(5).
34. Japan, ITA, s. 1 para. 1 subpara. 6.
35. Sweden, Income Tax Act (ITA), Ch. 6 s. 3.

business, which was generally, although not conclusively, considered to be located where the board of directors met.[36] In 1988, this test was supplemented by an incorporation rule which made companies incorporated in the United Kingdom resident there, but left companies incorporated elsewhere liable to UK-resident status under the old rule.[37]

The *Canadian* rules follow the UK pattern. Either incorporation[38] or central management and control in Canada results in resident treatment. The case law has focused primarily on the place of the meeting of the board of directors (assuming that the board exercises control of the affairs of the corporation), thus giving the test a formal character, although in some situations the courts have examined the question of actual day-to-day control.

Australia has adopted a similar approach. Formal incorporation under Australian law will cause a corporation to be treated as resident. In addition, where a corporation is doing business in Australia and has its place of central management and control in Australia, it is likewise resident, although a recent case is regarded by the tax administration as reading the "carrying on business" test out of the definition.[39] The Australian rules also take into consideration the residence of shareholders. Where a corporation is doing business in Australia and a majority of voting power is held by Australian residents, the corporation is considered to be resident.[40] However, the shareholder test is applied without attributing share ownership through interposed companies or trusts, and it can therefore be avoided by interposing a nonresident entity between the corporation and the ultimate Australian shareholders.

China, *Germany*, and *The Netherlands* combine incorporation and management tests. In China, corporations are residents of China if they are created in China or have their place of effective management there. In Germany, a corporation is resident if it has its "statutory seat" in Germany.[41] Since all corporations formed under German corporate law are required to designate a statutory seat in Germany, they are automatically treated as resident. In addition, where a corporation organized under foreign law has its place of management in Germany, it is treated as a resident taxpayer[42] (the focus being on the activities of day-to-day management and not the supervisory activities of the legal structure roughly equivalent to the (outside) board of directors).

Similarly, *The Netherlands* uses both formal incorporation[43] and, as with individuals, a determination "according to the circumstances."[44] Case law gives great

36. For example, *see De Beers Consolidated Mines v. Howe* [1906] AC 455 (HL) at 458.
37. United Kingdom, Corporation Tax Act 2009, ss. 14 and 15.
38. Canada, ITA, s. 250(4).
39. *Bywater Investments* [2016] HCA 45, Ruling TR 2018/5. In 2020, the previous Australian government announced a change to ensure that the carrying on business test retained an independent operation in the test; the current government has not yet indicated whether this measure will proceed.
40. Australia, ITAA 1936, s. 6(1) definition of "resident," para. (b).
41. Germany, Corporate Income Tax Act (CITA), s. 1 para. 1.
42. Germany, CITA, s. 1 para. 1 s. 2.
43. Netherlands, Company Income Tax Act 1969 (CITA), Art. 2.
44. Netherlands, GAT, Art. 4(1).

weight to the place of effective management, i.e., the place where the key strategic management decisions in respect of the core business of the entity are taken; the place where the day-to-day management takes place is irrelevant.[45] Factors to be taken into account to establish the place of effective management include the place where board meetings are held (provided that the directors of the board prepare and take the strategic decisions at that place), the place of residence of the board members, and the location of the main office. Where it is not possible to determine an entity's residence based on the place of effective management, additional factors are taken into account, such as the place where the entity has been entered in the commercial register, its statutory seat, its main place of business, the location of the shareholders' meetings, and the place where the entity's accounts are held and its financial statements prepared.

In *France*, a corporation formed under French law and having its registered office in France is treated as a resident. However, since France applies the territorial system to corporations, the law on corporate residence is not highly developed with respect to, for example, the extent to which a corporation must have its place of actual management in France in connection with its registered office. The legislation does not specify the criteria for the seat of effective management, nor the factors to be taken into account with respect to the seat of management and registered office tests. It is therefore up to case law to determine the set of indicators to be taken into consideration in determining the residence of legal entities.

A company is resident in *India* if it is either an Indian company (i.e., formed under the Companies Act or established under any Central or State government Act) or its place of effective management is in India in the relevant year. The place of effective management is the place where key management and commercial decisions necessary for the conduct of the business are, in substance, made.[46] The Central Board of Direct Taxes (CBDT) has prescribed guidelines for this purpose[47] and also has the power to declare any institution, association, or body to be a company.

2 CHANGE OF STATUS

2.1 Change of Status of Individuals

Changing factual circumstances may cause an individual to establish or terminate residence status in a particular jurisdiction. A number of technical issues arise in connection with a change in personal taxing jurisdiction. From the perspective of the

45. *See* the decisions of the Dutch Supreme Court, July 2, 2021, No. 20/01212, BNB 2021/156; January 19, 2019, No. 16/03321, BNB 2018/68; February 3, 2012, No. 10/05383, BNB 2012/26; and September 23, 1992, No. 27 293, BNB 1993/193. For an overview, *see* the Opinion of Advocate-General Overgaauw for Supreme Court decision December 1, 2004, No. 37.719, BNB 2005/105.
46. India, ITA 1961, s. 6(3).
47. Central Board of Direct Taxes (CBDT), Circular No. 6, 2017. A January 24, 2017, press release clarified that these guidelines do not apply to companies with turnover of less than INR 500 million.

receiving country, the principal question is how to establish the "tax history" of the new tax subject. Here, there are basically two approaches. One is, in effect, to reconstruct past events as if they had taken place while the taxpayer was subject to the tax system of the receiving jurisdiction and then use these historical factors in determining the taxpayer's current tax liability. Thus, for example, the historical cost of an asset, adjusted for notional depreciation, could be used to determine the gain on the disposition of the asset in the new jurisdiction. Alternatively, a "fresh-start" approach could be taken, focusing on market values at the time residence was established.

From the perspective of the departing jurisdiction, the issue is what, if any, attempts should be made to enforce taxing claims on income or gains which arose or accrued while the taxpayer was a resident. One approach (so-called exit or departure taxes) is to treat the departure as a realization event for any income which would otherwise cease to be subject to tax in the hands of the departed (nonresident) taxpayer. Alternatively, modifications may be made to the normal taxing pattern for nonresidents to allow the continued taxation of former residents on certain types of income (so-called trailing taxes).

In principle, for new residents, the *United States* uses the historical cost of assets, although the rules are not well developed. The United States treats termination of residence as a realization event for taxpayers who had an average income of more than USD 201,000 (in 2024, adjusted for inflation annually) during the prior five years or who have a net worth of more than USD 2 million. Such taxpayers are treated as selling their assets at fair market value on the day prior to expatriation and must recognize gains in excess of USD 866,000 (in 2024, adjusted for inflation annually) which accrued while the taxpayer was a U.S. citizen or permanent resident.[48] *Canada* deals with these issues by giving a new resident a tax cost for property equal to its fair market value at the time the individual becomes a resident.[49] Thus, only appreciation or depreciation which takes place during the period of Canadian residence is taken into account for Canadian tax purposes. Correspondingly, when an individual ceases to be a resident, the individual is deemed to have disposed of the property for its fair market value, generating a current gain or loss. This departure or exit tax also applies to corporations and trusts. An exception is made for certain types of property, such as real estate located in Canada and property of a business carried on in Canada through a permanent establishment (PE). The excepted property ("taxable Canadian property") is property over which Canada retains source-based taxing rights. Taxpayers can elect to have such property deemed to be disposed of for fair market value; they can also postpone payment of the departure or exit tax until the property is actually sold if adequate security is provided to the tax authorities. In addition, relieving provisions deal with post-emigration losses and foreign taxes on predeparture gains in order to reduce problems of double taxation.

In some circumstances, Canada extends its taxing right to former residents.[50] Where a former resident receives employment income from a Canadian resident, the

48. United States, IRC, s. 877A.
49. The rules governing immigration and emigration are found in ITA, s. 128.1.
50. Canada, ITA, s. 115(2).

income remains taxable in Canada unless the taxpayer can establish that the services were rendered abroad and the income was subject to foreign tax. Canada also insists on retaining the right in its tax treaties to tax its former residents on their taxable capital gains for a period of five or ten years.

The *Australian* system is similar, although only for capital gains tax purposes. When nonresidents become resident in Australia, they are deemed to have acquired assets at their then market value. When residence is terminated, gain is deemed to be realized on all assets over which Australia does not retain source-based taxation rights, thus ensuring that all (and only) appreciation which took place during the period of Australian residence is subject to tax. It is also possible for individuals to elect to defer the tax until the asset is actually disposed of, although in this case all appreciation is subject to tax.[51] In the 2001 Protocol to the treaty with the United States, problems which arise from the interaction of the U.S. and Australian systems were dealt with by giving individual taxpayers a market-value tax basis in the United States when moving from Australia to the United States, and giving up Australian taxing rights altogether where taxpayers elect to defer tax on moving to the United States. The 2003 treaty with the United Kingdom contains the latter, but not the former, provision and vice versa with respect to the 2006 treaty with France. Australia's most recent treaties do not consistently include such provisions, so it is unclear to what extent they will be a feature of Australia's future treaty policy.

In contrast, as a general rule, the *United Kingdom* does not treat change of status as a taxable event and has no special rules for deemed acquisitions when residence status is established. However, a special rule does apply to individuals who cease to be resident but then resume UK residence within five years. In such cases, a capital gain realized while the individual was nonresident may be treated as accruing after residence is resumed.[52] Similarly, *China* did not have any rules for departing residents until 2018, when the IIT was amended to require departing residents who revoke their household registration to "clear their tax payments," although it is not clear what this means. It would not be surprising if an exit tax is introduced in the future.

Sweden uses historical cost as the basis for taxing capital gains of incoming residents. For business income, the basis can be increased from cost to a higher value if the transfer of assets has been taxed by the state of former residence.[53] With respect to departing residents, there is a special rule which, in effect, extends the residence concept. Where taxpayers have been resident under the basic statutory definition but cease to be resident, they continue to be taxed as residents if they maintain an "essential connection" to Sweden.[54] There is a statutory catalog of factors which are considered in determining whether an essential connection is present: Swedish citizenship, the period of former residence in Sweden, the existence of permanent residence abroad, the reason for being abroad, access to a dwelling in Sweden, family and/or business connections in Sweden, and other comparable factors. Determining

51. Australia, Income Tax Assessment Act 1997 (ITAA 1997), ss. 104-160, 104-165, 855-845.
52. United Kingdom, Taxation of Chargeable Gains Act 1992 (TCGA), s. 1M.
53. Sweden, ITA, Ch. 20 a.
54. Sweden, ITA, Ch. 3 s. 7.

whether an "essential connection" to Sweden exists is made by considering all the relevant factors taken together. There are numerous cases providing illustrations of circumstances which do (or do not) trigger an "essential connection" to Sweden.[55] A special evidentiary rule applies where a taxpayer is a Swedish citizen or was a resident of Sweden under the normal rules for at least ten years. For the first five years after departure, the taxpayer is deemed to have an essential connection and has the burden of proof of negating enough of the factors to establish that no essential connection to Sweden is present. Thereafter, the tax authorities have the burden of establishing the essential connection with respect to the same factors.

Sweden also retains the right to tax gains on the disposition of shares and other financial assets in Swedish corporations for ten years after the departure of an individual.[56] In response to a tax-planning scheme, this rule was extended in 2007 to shares in foreign corporations. (The scheme involved a tax-free transfer of shares in a Swedish corporation to a foreign corporation followed by the sale of the shares of the foreign corporation.) In its double tax treaty negotiations, Sweden attempts to preserve these taxing rights; in a number of its tax treaties, it has retained the right to tax gains on Swedish shares (but not gains on foreign shares) for periods extending from three to seven years.

Germany likewise uses historical cost in determining the tax consequences of transactions undertaken after an individual establishes residence. However, according to recent legislation, the sale of a "substantial participation" does not give rise to the taxation of capital gains which accrued before the individual became a resident of Germany if the other country taxed this accrued gain at the time of the sale.[57]

The termination of residence is generally not considered to be a realization event. However, in the case of "substantial participations" in companies which would have been taxable on disposition, termination of residence is a realization event for gain (but not loss) purposes, where an individual has been a tax resident of Germany for at least seven years within the last twelve years.[58] After the European Commission deemed this provision to be a violation of the fundamental freedoms under the Treaty on the Functioning of the EU (TFEU), the legislation was amended to provide an unconditional deferral of payment until the disposal of the shares where the taxpayer is an EU national and moves to an EU Member State. However, in 2021 the German legislature ordered that the deferred tax would not be suspended but had to be paid in seven annual installments following the change of residence.[59] Given that the free movement of persons is also protected under a specific agreement between the EU and Switzerland, the CJEU has recently decided that migration to Switzerland must not result in

55. For example, keeping a permanent dwelling has been considered to trigger an "essential connection" to Sweden (*Högsta Förvaltningsdomstolen*, No. 6314-11, May 21, 2012). In contrast, the circumstance of a 17-year-old child studying at a boarding school in Sweden did not result in the parents having an "essential connection" to Sweden (*Högsta Förvaltningsdomstolen*, No. 905-12, September 21, 2012).
56. Sweden, ITA, Ch. 3 s. 19.
57. Germany, ITA, s. 17 para. 2 s. 3.
58. Germany, Foreign Transactions Tax Act (*Aussensteuergesetz*), s. 6.
59. Germany, Foreign Transactions Tax Act (*Aussensteuergesetz*), s. 6 para. 4.

immediate taxation of hidden reserves and that payment must be suspended until the latent gains are finally realized.[60] In their final judgment in this matter, the judges of the Federal Tax Court followed the reasoning of the CJEU;[61] it is widely assumed that the Federal Tax Court will hold the new legislation—which does not allow for a suspension of the tax until the shares are sold—to be incompatible with the fundamental freedoms.

In addition, special rules apply to German citizens who have been resident in Germany for an extended period and then transfer their residence to a low-tax jurisdiction (or to no jurisdiction) if they maintain "substantial connections" to Germany. Where the provisions apply, the former resident is taxed at the usually applicable domestic rates on income from German sources. The extended tax liability lasts for ten years after the termination of German residence.[62]

The Netherlands has a highly developed system for dealing with the taxation of newly arrived resident companies (i.e., foreign-incorporated companies whose effective management has moved to The Netherlands) and individuals engaged in business who move their residence to The Netherlands. Business assets which were not previously subject to Dutch tax are considered to have a cost equal to their fair market value. Existing Dutch business assets keep their historical cost.

Where residence is transferred abroad, there is a deemed disposition (and recognition of any resulting capital gain) of business assets at the time of the change of residence (for purposes of this deemed disposition rule, the term "business" includes other gainful activities).[63] For substantial participations, the deemed disposition takes place at fair market value. With respect to the emigration of individuals, in general, termination of residence does not result in taxation, although The Netherlands retains taxing rights over substantial participations in resident companies[64] and certain annuities (pensions)[65] and insurance policies[66] where premiums have been deducted in The Netherlands.

The Dutch Supreme Court has repeatedly ruled that the application of exit taxes levied at the time of emigration, on the assumption that the emigrating taxpayer's assets are disposed of at that time, violates the good faith that The Netherlands should observe in interpreting and applying the rules of the treaty with the country to which

60. Case C-581/17, February 26, 2019 (*Wächtler*): this does not constrain the right of the home state to demand collateral for future tax payments on a current basis.
61. Federal Tax Court (*Bundesfinanzhof*), September 23, 2023, I R 35/20.
62. Foreign Transactions Tax Act (*Außensteuergesetz*), ss. 2-5.
63. A draft bill is currently pending that would introduce an exit tax into the Dividend Withholding Tax Act (DWTA) in the event that profit reserves are transferred to a qualifying state as a result of certain cross-border reorganizations (e.g., transfer of the place of effective management). This concerns Netherlands-based parent corporations of (international) groups. There is no qualifying state in the case of an EU/EEA Member State. Otherwise, a qualifying state is (i) a state which does not impose source taxation on dividends comparable to the Dutch dividend withholding tax, or (ii) a state that designates the profit reserves as paid-in capital on entry ("step-up states"). The exit tax is designed as a deemed distribution of the profit reserves.
64. Netherlands, ITA, Art. 4.16(1)(h).
65. Netherlands, ITA, Art. 3.83(1) in connection with Art. 3.136(3).
66. Netherlands, ITA, Art. 3.136 (1) and (2).

the taxpayer emigrates.[67] These decisions of the Supreme Court resulted in an amendment of the exit taxes for pensions and annuities of individuals who emigrate to a treaty country. Where the treaty with the new residence state provides (in conformity with the OECD Model) for exclusive taxation of particular gains by the residence country, the exit tax is restricted to a recapture of the previously deducted premiums rather than taxing the full fair market value of the accrued claims at the time of emigration.[68]

In *France*, newly arrived so-called *impatriates* (i.e., employees and corporate officers who come and work in France) are exempt (for a maximum period of eight years, starting from the date they assume their position) from IIT on the compensation supplement directly related to their expatriation to France and on 50% of various types of passive foreign source income (in particular, on gains on the disposition of stocks and securities calculated on the basis of their historical cost).[69]

Departing taxpayers are normally taxed on their worldwide income (subject to tax treaties) received or accrued before departure and not yet taxed.[70] In addition, from 1999, some taxpayers leaving France were liable for an exit tax on various unrealized or tax-deferred gains on shares; these provisions were deleted from the Code in 2005, since they were ruled to be incompatible with the EU freedom of establishment.[71] A new exit tax was enacted in 2011.[72] Unrealized gains (actual value less acquisition cost or value) on stocks or securities the value of which exceeds certain fixed ceilings, as well as realized but tax-deferred gains on such assets held at the time of the transfer of residence, are immediately taxable and the corresponding tax immediately assessed. However, in most cases (i.e., transfers to EU member countries or jurisdictions which have treaties with France on exchange of information and assistance in the collection of taxes), an automatic suspension of payment is granted. Where stocks and securities are disposed of by the then nonresident taxpayer within a period of two to five years (fifteen years before 2019), the tax becomes due or is recalculated, as the case may be, according to the actual amount of the gain (with an anti-double taxation mechanism). Otherwise, an automatic relief or refund is awarded. Finally, the 2024 Finance Act amended the penalties applicable to failure to file the exit tax declaration, and extended the social contributions relief available to taxpayers on unrealized capital gains on rights or securities held for a certain number of years.

Japan introduced a new system in 2015, whereby a change in status from a Japanese resident to a nonresident is deemed to constitute a realization event for

67. *See*, for example, The Netherlands, the Supreme Court in its decisions of February 20, 2009: No. 42701, BNB 2009/260 (emigration to Belgium), No. 43760, BNB 2009/261 (emigration to the United States), and No. 07/12314, BNB 2009/262 (emigration to the United Kingdom); and June 19, 2009, No. 43978, BNB 2009/263 (emigration to France), No. 07/13267, BNB 2009/265 (emigration to Korea), No. 08/02288, BNB 2009/266 (emigration to the Philippines), and No. 44050, BNB 2009/264 (concerning the former 1970 Belgium-Netherlands tax treaty).
68. In its decision of November 24, 2017, No. 17/00515, BNB 2018/74, the Supreme Court agreed that the new statutory rules are in agreement with the treaty rules.
69. France, CGI, s. 155 B; *see* section 2.4 below.
70. France, CGI, s. 167.
71. CJEU, March 11, 2004, C-9/02 (*de Lasteyrie du Saillant*).
72. France, CGI, s. 167 bis.

securities and some types of financial transactions, such as derivative transactions, if the present value of such financial assets held by the individual exceeds JPY 1 billion at the time of departure. Therefore, certain unrealized capital gains are taxed at the time of departure from Japan. This tax on deemed capital gains is not imposed (or, more precisely, is deferred) in the event of a temporary move abroad by a Japanese resident, so that employees of multinationals are not taxed when they work abroad for a definite term.[73] A gift of these financial assets by a Japanese resident to a nonresident is also deemed to be a realization event.[74] Japan has also introduced a step-up basis for assets held by a new resident who was subject to a similar type of exit tax abroad.[75]

India does not have an exit tax. Where an individual resident in India ceases to be resident during a year, the individual is taxable in India on their global income for that year, subject to any treaty provisions. An individual who becomes resident in India during a year is considered to be NOR in India for two years. However, a tax clearance certificate is required in certain exceptional circumstances for Indian-domiciled taxpayers wanting to leave India.[76]

2.2 Change of Status of Corporations

The personal taxing jurisdiction over a corporation can change if the corporation is formally reincorporated or "continued" into another jurisdiction. In addition, for those countries using a management-and-control test of corporate residence, residence can change if the requisite management activities are shifted to another country. There are several models for the treatment of changes in corporate residence. One approach is to treat the original domestic corporation as if it had been liquidated, with the attendant consequences to the corporation and shareholders. The assets received by the shareholder would then be treated as if they had been contributed to the nonresident corporation, with the usual tax results for an outbound transfer in those circumstances. Alternatively, the domestic corporation could be viewed as transferring its assets to the nonresident corporation for its shares, followed by a liquidating distribution of those shares to shareholders, again with the tax consequences which those transactions would have under normally applicable rules. Only a few of the countries considered here have fully developed rules dealing with this situation. For example, *China* does not have explicit rules for corporations ceasing to be resident, although deregistration requires a tax clearance.

In the *United States*, a transaction in which a domestic corporation is reincorporated as a foreign corporation is treated as a transaction involving an outbound transfer. The normal nonrecognition treatment given to reorganization exchanges is not available and the transaction is usually fully taxable unless conditions exist which allow the U.S. to eventually tax the deferred gain. Consequently, both the deemed

73. Japan, ITA, s. 60-2.
74. Japan, ITA, s. 60-3.
75. Japan, ITA, s. 60-4.
76. India, ITA 1961, s. 230(1A), read with CBDT Instruction No. 1/2004, February 5, 2004 and CBDT clarification, Press Information Bureau release dated August 20, 2024.

transfer of the assets by the domestic corporation and the deemed share exchange by the shareholders are often taxable events.[77] In contrast, the "continuation" of a foreign corporation as a U.S. domestic corporation would, in general, be treated as a qualifying tax-free reorganization as long as the corporation's foreign earnings are eventually subject to U.S. tax in the hands of U.S. shareholders. As a result, the new resident corporation would continue the tax cost of the assets received, and shareholders would similarly transfer the tax cost of their old shares to the shares of the continued corporation.[78]

In *Canada*, the same principles are applied to corporations as are applied to individuals.[79] For a corporation which becomes resident in Canada, there is a "fresh-start" fair market value for its assets other than taxable Canadian property and property of a business carried on in Canada. A new taxation year is deemed to commence at the time that the corporation becomes a resident of Canada. Loss carryovers are permitted only to the extent that they relate to businesses carried on in Canada.

In the case of a Canadian corporation which becomes nonresident by reincorporation or continuation into another jurisdiction and which is no longer managed or controlled in Canada, the "expatriation" is a realization event with respect to most property other than real property in Canada and assets of a business carried on through a PE in Canada. The corporation's taxation year is deemed to have ended immediately before the emigration and the corporation is deemed to have disposed of all its assets for their fair market value immediately before that time. This deemed realization gives rise to capital gains and other tax consequences. In addition, a special departure tax of 25% is imposed on the excess of the fair market value of the corporation's property over the aggregate of its paid-up capital and liabilities. This special tax is intended to prevent corporations from avoiding the withholding tax on dividends by shifting their residence to another country. The 25% rate is reduced where the corporation emigrates to a country with which Canada has a tax treaty which provides a reduced rate of withholding on dividends.

The *United Kingdom* also has explicit rules dealing with a change of corporate residence. At one time, it was a criminal offense for a company to cease to be resident in the United Kingdom without the permission of the Treasury, but this rule was repealed in 1990. In the case of a change of residence, in general, there is a deemed disposal of all assets over which the United Kingdom no longer has a source-based taxing claim.[80] The possibility of postponing this charge was repealed in 2019. At the same time, the UK introduced a step-up in the cost base of assets to market value for corporations becoming resident in the UK, if they are subject to an EU exit tax.[81]

As a matter of company law, *Australia* does not allow the continuation of an Australian corporation into a foreign jurisdiction, and outbound changes in place of

77. United States, IRC, s. 367(a). The section is implemented by extensive regulations.
78. United States, IRC, s. 367(b). The section is implemented by extensive regulations.
79. Canada, ITA, s. 128.1.
80. United Kingdom, TCGA, s. 185.
81. United Kingdom, TCGA, s. 184J.

incorporation are probably treated as liquidations. Foreign corporations can be continued into Australia under special procedures but the tax consequences are generally unclear. When a nonresident corporation becomes resident in Australia, it is deemed to have acquired its assets at their fair market value at that time for capital gains tax purposes. Conversely, when an Australian-resident corporation ceases to be resident in Australia, it is deemed to have disposed of its assets at fair market value.[82] Reincorporation in Australia means that a company becomes an Australian resident under the place of incorporation rule if it is not already. For companies not incorporated in Australia, it is possible to move residence to and from Australia by shifting central management and control or the residence of shareholders. In these cases, the normal change-of-residence rules apply. The provisions in the U.S. and UK treaties referred to above in section 2.1, with respect to the change of residence of individuals, are not available to corporations.

In *Sweden*, under corporate law, a Swedish corporation cannot change its status to become incorporated in a foreign state. Where a corporation liquidates in order to reincorporate as a foreign corporation, the transaction is taxable under the normal rules. Where a Swedish corporation has its management abroad and, under the applicable tax treaty, the corporation is deemed to be a resident only of the other country (*see* section 2.3), with the result that Sweden cannot tax the corporation's foreign source income, the transfer of management is treated as a deemed realization. However, this tax was considered by the Swedish Supreme Administrative Court to contravene EU law, and the rule has been amended to provide the possibility of deferring the tax until the assets are sold.

In *Germany*, the tax treatment of corporate mobility has changed substantially within the last 20 years.[83] Until 2006, where a corporation transferred its seat or place of effective management to a country outside Germany, terminating its residence and therefore its unlimited tax liability in Germany, the transfer was generally considered to be a liquidation of the corporation and the normal rules with respect to liquidation, which require recognition of gain on transferred assets, were applicable.[84] In 2006, the introduction of the European Company as a new supranational legal form, which entitles a company to transfer its statutory seat and place of management abroad, led to a substantive rewriting of the rules for corporate taxpayers in general.[85] Under these rules, whenever a corporation transfers its seat or place of effective management to a country outside the EU, terminating its residence and therefore its unlimited tax liability in Germany, the transfer is generally considered to be a liquidation of the corporation and the normal rules with respect to liquidation, which require recognition of gain on transferred assets, are applicable.[86] However, where the statutory seat or place of effective management is transferred to another EU Member State (or a Member State of the European Economic Area (EEA)), hidden reserves are taxed only if

82. Australia, ITAA 1997, ss. 104-160, 855-845.
83. Germany, ITA, s. 4 para. 1 s. 3 and CITA, s. 12.
84. Germany, CITA, s. 12 para. 3 s. 1.
85. Germany, CITA, s. 12.
86. Germany, CITA, s. 12 para. 3 s. 1.

Germany does not otherwise maintain jurisdiction to tax the assets at the time of their later disposal.[87] In 2021, this beneficial treatment was expanded to any transfer of corporate residence to jurisdictions outside the EU and applies not only to transfers of the place of effective management (this is of particular importance for intangibles) but also to transfers of assets to a foreign branch. As of 2020, the EU Anti-Tax Avoidance Directive (ATAD) requires all Member States of the EU to introduce and enforce exit taxation for corporate taxpayers unless assets remain under their respective tax jurisdictions. The exit tax can be deferred for five years and paid in annual installments.[88]

The transfer of the head office of a corporation from *France* to another country results in the immediate taxation of all income not yet subject to tax and is a realization event as far as capital gains are concerned, unless there is a treaty between France and the host country which provides for the continuation of the legal personality of the moving corporation. No such treaty has yet been concluded. But, as a major exception to this rule, the transfer of a French company to another EU country (or to Ireland or Norway), with or without loss of legal personality, is now tax-free in order to comply with EU law (i.e., with respect to freedom of establishment, the legal status of the European Company, and the tax directive on mergers). When the transfer of the registered office is accompanied by a transfer of assets, the company can choose between immediate taxation of unrealized capital gains or taxation over five years.[89] Finally, company law has recently introduced the concept of a "cross-border transformation,"[90] based on the incorporation of EU directives into French law.[91] As a result, the conditions for transferring the registered office of an LLC have been relaxed: the requirement for a unanimous shareholder agreement has been dropped in favor of majority agreement, and only the transfer of the registered office from one Member State to another is required, which does not automatically imply relocating the registered office or transferring its assets or business.

In *The Netherlands*, the transfer by a Dutch-incorporated corporation of management abroad does not affect Dutch taxing rights because corporate residence is still deemed to be in The Netherlands by virtue of domestic incorporation. However, if under a treaty tiebreaker rule the other country has the exclusive right to treat the corporation as a resident, realization is required with respect to all assets over which The Netherlands no longer has taxing rights.[92] Further, in a much-contested decision,

87. Germany, CITA, s. 12 para. 1.
88. Council Directive (EU) 2016/1164 of July 12, 2016, setting out rules against tax avoidance practices which directly affect the functioning of the internal market: OJ EU L 193/1 of July 19, 2016, Art. 5.
89. France, CGI, s. 221-2 and 3. This seems to be compatible with EU law: *see* CJEU May 21, 2015, C-657/13 (*Verder LabTec GmbH amp Co. KG*).
90. Order n°2023-393 of May 24, 2023 and implementing decree n°2023-430 of June 2, 2023, creating Art. L 236-50 of the French Commercial Code.
91. Directive (EU) 2019/2121 of the European Parliament and of the Council of November 27, 2019, amending Directive (EU) 2017/1132 with respect to cross-border conversions, mergers and divisions and French law n°2023-171 of March 9, 2023, incorporating various provisions of EU law in the fields of economics, health, labor, transport, and agriculture.
92. Netherlands, CITA, Art. 15c and 15d.

the Supreme Court ruled that such companies no longer qualify as resident companies for purposes of treaties with third countries.[93] The exit tax is deferred for five years where certain conditions are met.[94]

Japan does not have a special concept of "reincorporation," and in the event that a Japanese corporation liquidates and transfers its business to a newly incorporated foreign corporation, the transaction is taxed under normal rules unless the transaction qualifies as a tax-free corporate restructuring, as discussed in Part III. In this situation, a triangular merger (or similar corporate restructuring), in which the capital shares of a corporation located in a low-tax jurisdiction are to be distributed, cannot qualify as a tax-free corporate restructuring.[95] Where such transactions do not qualify as a tax-free corporate restructuring, the shareholders of the corporations involved in the triangular merger must recognize capital gains on the shares they hold.[96]

In *India*, there are no special rules with respect to changes of residence of Indian companies. A company incorporated in India remains an Indian resident even if its place of effective management is shifted outside India. The CBDT has issued guidelines to deal with situations where a foreign company becomes resident in India as a result of shifting its place of effective management.[97] It is curious that the rate of tax applicable to foreign companies continues to apply in such cases.

2.3 Dual Residence

Problems of dual residence are often dealt with by treaty rules establishing a single residence jurisdiction for treaty purposes, which in turn limits the taxing rights of the other country. Apart from treaty rules, some jurisdictions have special domestic legislation preventing taxpayers from utilizing corporations which are treated as residents of two (or more) jurisdictions (so-called dual-resident corporations) to deduct losses in both jurisdictions. For example, on the one hand, in the *United States*, special rules restrict the use of losses in the United States by a dual-resident company where the losses, generally speaking, can also be used in a foreign consolidated group. On the other hand, in general, the rules do not prevent a corporation from using the losses to reduce its own income in both jurisdictions (e.g., through the mechanism of a loss carryover). Since the income is potentially taxable in both jurisdictions, allowing the loss in these circumstances is not viewed as inappropriate. The perceived problem arises only where the income which is being offset against the loss in the foreign consolidated group is not subject to the taxing claim of the United States.[98]

93. Netherlands, Supreme Court, February 28, 2001, No. 35.557, BNB 2001/295. This result is consistent with the position in the OECD Commentary on Art. 4, which was added as part of the 2008 update.
94. Netherlands, Collection of Taxes Act 1990, Art. 25b. As a result of the implementation of ATAD 1, the maximum period of deferral was reduced from ten to five years.
95. Japan, Special Taxation Measures Act (STMA), s. 68-2-3.
96. Japan, STMA, s. 68-3.
97. CBDT, notification No. 29/2018, available at https://incometaxindia.gov.in/communications/notification/notification29_2018.pdf.
98. United States, IRC, s. 1503(d).

The United States also has developed a complex set of rules which are intended to prevent taxpayers from using "hybrid" entities (entities taxable as corporations in one nation and as partnerships in another) to avoid paying tax in any jurisdiction. Legislation introduced in 2017 further curbs the use of hybrid entities.[99]

In *Canada*, a dual-resident person that is considered to be resident in another country pursuant to the provisions of a tax treaty is deemed not to be a resident of Canada for all purposes.[100] This provision applies to corporations, individuals, and other persons and has been reasonably effective in removing most of the tax-planning advantages of dual residence. Dual-resident companies can still be utilized with respect to nontreaty countries.

The *United Kingdom* similarly has rules which restrict the use of losses and other reliefs by dual-resident investment companies.[101] The UK has a rule similar to the Canadian rule, under which a corporation which is considered to be resident in the other country pursuant to the tiebreaker rule in a treaty is considered to be nonresident for all purposes.[102]

Australia has also experienced problems with deductions, principally interest, being claimed by dual-resident companies. The problem first arose in 1984 when the right to transfer losses among 100%-related companies was introduced. The response was to deny the right to transfer losses by dual-resident investment companies: the definition of dual-resident investment company[103] effectively eliminated many of the dual-resident financing structures. Like the Canadian system, the controlled foreign corporation (CFC) provisions also have a rule which treats an otherwise dual-resident corporation whose residence the treaty allocates to the other country as a foreign company for CFC purposes.[104] In 1997, for dual-resident companies, this approach was extended to certain tax benefits available to residents, such as capital gains tax rollovers and transfers of losses within 100%-related groups;[105] in addition, the consolidation regime introduced in 2002 does not permit such companies to be members of a consolidated group.[106] The 2003 review of international taxation recommended that Australia drop these specific rules and, along the lines of Canada and the United Kingdom, adopt a general qualification to the company residence rules for dual residents, but this has not occurred.

China, France, India, Japan, and *The Netherlands* do not have any special statutory rules dealing with dual residence. Japan and China have left the issue of dual residence to be dealt with solely by tax treaties. In recent times, the Indian tax authorities have used tax treaty principles to resolve dual residence issues.[107]

99. United States, IRC, s. 267A. *See* Subpart C, section 8 for a discussion of anti-hybrid rules.
100. Canada, ITA, s. 250(5).
101. United Kingdom, Corporation Tax Act 2010, s. 109.
102. United Kingdom, Corporation Tax Act 2009, s. 18.
103. Australia, ITAA 1936, s. 6F.
104. Australia, ITAA 1936, s. 317 definition of "Part X Australian resident."
105. Australia, ITAA 1936, s. 6(1) definition of "prescribed dual resident," which also covers cases of dual central management and control.
106. Australia, ITAA 1997, s. 703-15(2) Table Column 3.
107. *DCIT v. Shri Kumar Sanjeev Ranjan*, ITAT, Bangalore, March 15, 2019.

In *Germany*, tax issues involving dual-resident companies were previously not relevant due to the "real seat" theory which, under company law, did not recognize the legal existence of a corporation which had its central management and its registered office in different jurisdictions. Because the CJEU forced Germany to accept the legal personality of a foreign company which has, in accordance with its "home state" law,[108] transferred its place of management to Germany without changing its legal form, more "dual-resident" companies exist today. Consequently, German legislation in the area of corporate law has opened the door for companies registered and having their statutory seat in Germany while having their place of management abroad.

Companies established under foreign law are characterized as corporate taxpayers where they are (as regards their legal structure) comparable to corporate taxpayers under German law.[109] This has led to particular difficulties in the case of U.S.-based Limited Liability Companies (LLCs), whose structures range from commercial partnerships to corporations.[110] These companies are deemed to be resident in Germany if either the statutory seat or the "real seat" is located within Germany. Nevertheless, until 2013, the beneficial provisions on "fiscal unity" were applicable only to subsidiary corporations having both their statutory seat and their effective place of management in Germany. Today, both EU/EEA corporations and domestic corporations can use this regime, provided that the place of management is located in Germany.[111] There are however, specific "dual consolidated loss rules" which prevent the multiple use of losses within cross-border corporate groups where the parent company or the subsidiary company is a dual resident.[112]

2.4 Temporary Residents

Although some countries, such as the *United Kingdom*, have long recognized different categories of residence, in more recent times other countries have begun to enact special regimes for expatriate individual employees who are seconded by their employer for a limited period (say, two to four years) to another country but plan to return. Which country should be regarded as the one with which these employees have the closer social and economic connections, and so is their real country of residence? On the one hand, such employees usually become residents of the country of secondment under both the domestic tax law of that country and an applicable tax treaty; for example, they may qualify for free health care in that country, which may suggest that they should be taxed there on a residence basis. On the other hand, they usually retain very close links with their country of origin, such as membership in a pension plan there; this may suggest, at least for such longer-term issues, that they should be regarded as residents of the country of origin. For these types of reasons,

108. CJEU, November 5, 2002, C-208/00 (*Überseering*).
109. Germany, CITA, s. 1 para. 1 No. 1.
110. Federal Tax Court (*Bundesfinanzhof*), August 20, 2008, I R 34/08; Federal Tax Court (*Bundesfinanzhof*), May 18, 2021, I B 76/20.
111. Germany, CITA, s. 14 para. 1 s. 1.
112. Germany, CITA, s. 15 para. 1 No. 5.

some countries try to soften the hard line between the tax treatment of resident and nonresident individuals with special tax regimes for temporary residents.

In *Australia*, rules were introduced in 2006 for more limited taxation of temporary residents, who are defined by reference to their visa and social security status in a way designed to target short-stay expatriate employees (four years generally being the limit). Temporary residents are generally exempt from tax on their non-Australian source income (other than services income, including share options); they are not subject to the CFC regime and are not required to pay interest withholding tax on payments of interest to nonresidents (which is mainly, but not only, a problem in cases where an expatriate maintains a home in the other country subject to a mortgage to a bank resident in that country and makes payments to the bank on the mortgage, including an element of interest).[113]

Canada formerly provided special exemptions from the nonresident trust rules and foreign investment fund (FIF) rules for new residents of Canada for a temporary period of five years (removing so-called immigration trusts from the ambit of the rules). Those exemptions were repealed in 2014.[114] There is, however, an exception for first-year residents from the requirement to file returns concerning certain foreign information.[115]

Since 2004, *France* has granted special tax benefits to its so-called *impatriates* (employees and corporate managers who have become French residents insofar as they did not have such status for the preceding five years).[116] Their annual so-called impatriation bonus and the remuneration of their work abroad, if any, are granted wide-ranging tax exemptions from income tax, property wealth tax, and payroll taxes. Payments to foreign social security schemes are tax-deductible.[117] Only 50% of passive foreign source income (i.e., dividends, interest, royalties, and gains from the sale of stocks or securities) is taxed when received by individuals who meet the conditions for income tax exemption (taking up employment and tax residence in France). Their foreign assets are also exempt from the French wealth tax for a five-year period.[118]

The concept of short-term resident in *Japan* is similar in the sense that a short-term resident is taxed only on domestic source income and foreign source income which is remitted to Japan. However, its historical background is unique. The predecessor of the current system was first introduced in 1950 as a substitute for the absolute exclusion of non-yen-denominated income from taxable income (this exclusion was one of the measures taken by the General Headquarters after World War II). In 1957, this system was changed to the short-term resident system, where short-term residents are taxed only on domestic source income and foreign source income which is remitted to Japan. Until 2006, a short-term resident was defined as a resident of Japan who did not intend to remain permanently in Japan and had not maintained a residence for five years. The 2006 tax revisions replaced the first requirement with

113. Australia, ITAA 1997, Subdiv. 768-R.
114. Canada, ITA, s. 94(1) definition of "resident contributor" and s. 94(3).
115. Canada, ITA, s. 233.7.
116. France, CGI, s. 81 B and, for those having become resident after January 1, 2008, s. 155 B.
117. France, CGI, s. 83 1° 0 bis and 2° 0 ter.
118. France, CGI, s. 964.

foreign nationality and the second requirement with five-year residence in Japan during the most recent ten years. The purpose of this revision was to deny benefits of short-term residency to Japanese nationals and to combat some abusive practices of foreign nationals who had tried to remain short-term residents by returning to their home countries shortly before the expiration of the five-year period.

The primary relief for temporary residents in the *United Kingdom* is the traditional preferential taxation of residents who are not domiciled in the United Kingdom. While the rules vary depending on the type of income, broadly, "nondoms" are taxable on foreign source income only when (and if) the income is remitted to the United Kingdom. This rule was tightened in 2008 so that, after a residence of seven years, the special treatment applied only if a nondom paid a flat tax of GBP 30,000 per annum.[119] From 2017, this charge rises depending on the number of years of residence in the United Kingdom; the remittance basis is removed once a nondom is resident for fifteen of twenty years.

In *China*, temporary residents (individuals not domiciled in China) are exempt from tax on income derived from foreign sources if their stay in China is less than five years.[120] In *India*, as noted above in section 2.1, temporary residents are considered to be NOR in India for two years after their arrival in India. After the first two years, the global income of such persons becomes taxable in India; however, relief may be available under the tiebreaker rule of an applicable tax treaty.

3 MECHANISMS FOR RELIEF OF DOUBLE TAXATION

All the countries considered here have some domestic law mechanism for the relief of the double taxation which results when residence-based and source-based taxing claims are asserted on the same item of income derived by the same taxpayer. The residence country generally eliminates double taxation, either by exempting the item of income from its tax base or giving a credit against domestic tax liability for the foreign tax.

Under the FTC mechanism, foreign income is included in the tax base and the prior right of the source country to tax is recognized by giving a credit for the foreign tax liability which displaces or reduces the normally applicable domestic liability. To the extent that the residence country rate is higher than the foreign rate, a residual domestic tax is collected, but international double taxation is eliminated. Where the foreign rate is higher than the domestic rate, all domestic tax is eliminated, and again, double taxation is avoided.

Beyond resolving the perceived inequity of subjecting the same taxpayer to conflicting taxing claims on the same income, from an economic point of view, the FTC system is generally viewed as consistent with an overall policy of capital export neutrality—that is, from the perspective of the residence country investor, the credit system tends to ensure that the choice between domestic or foreign investment is not

119. United Kingdom, ITA 2007, Part 14 Ch. A1.
120. China, IIT Regulations, Art. 4.

influenced by tax considerations. In practical operation, credit systems fall far short of this goal, in particular where the tax rate in a foreign jurisdiction is higher than the domestic rate. In addition, in practice, the interaction of the various provisions dealing with international income often makes it difficult to determine whether a particular rule furthers capital export neutrality. Nonetheless, especially in the context of portfolio investments, capital export neutrality has historically been an important factor in the decision to adopt or maintain a credit system.

International double taxation can also be avoided by exempting from domestic tax certain classes of foreign source income, thus ceding exclusive taxing jurisdiction to the country of source. If the foreign income is simply exempt and does not affect the taxation of other foreign or domestic source income which is subject to tax, the result is essentially the same as it would be by not asserting jurisdiction to tax the income at all. More typically, the exempt income is taken into account in determining the tax treatment of other income—for example, in determining the applicable rate of tax in a progressive rate structure ("exemption with progression").

While the exemption approach is often contrasted with the credit approach, the actual operation of the two methods for relieving double taxation often yields similar results. In the systems considered here, exemption is usually limited to specific categories of foreign income—most typically, active business or employment income—which are likely to be subject to a level of foreign tax comparable to that which would have been applicable in the residence country. In a credit system, where foreign and domestic rates are roughly comparable, the residence country does not collect much, if any, additional tax on the foreign source income; this result is functionally equivalent to exempting the income. Ancillary differences are reduced still further if an "exemption with progression" technique is used.

Nonetheless, there may be some important differences in the effects of the two techniques in particular situations. While foreign and domestic rates may be roughly similar in general terms, there may be important variations across industries and with respect to different companies, and the choice of exemption can lead to residual domestic tax not being collected in some significant cases. In addition, great pressure is put on the source rules. For example, where the source rules of the two jurisdictions are not completely congruent, the decision that a particular item of income is foreign source income may mean that it is not taxed anywhere. Similarly, transfer pricing differences have different implications in an exemption system.

Beyond its role as a mechanism for relieving potential double taxation, from a policy point of view, an exemption method is consistent with a policy of capital import or competitive neutrality. It ensures that income from foreign activities is not subjected to a higher rate of tax than the rate faced by local competitors. It also ensures that foreign tax holidays or preferences are not "washed out" by additional residence country tax. These effects have been a factor in the decision of some countries to utilize the exemption method and is important from the perspective of developing countries.

Another aspect of the exemption method which is often stressed is its relative simplicity. Since the foreign income is simply exempt, there is no need to establish in detail the foreign tax burden on particular items of income. However, this asserted advantage over the credit system can be overstated, especially in the context of business taxation. As discussed below, while the exemption system eliminates some technical issues, it raises others. The level of simplicity or complexity seems less a question of the basic approach than the degree to which rough and simple solutions are accepted for administrative or compliance reasons.

Finally, some countries have recently adopted exemption systems in order to achieve "conduit" tax treatment—that is, where an entity is resident in a country but the owners of the entity are resident elsewhere and the income earned by the entity is sourced outside its country of residence. Given the tax at source and the tax by the country in which the owners are resident, the claim of the entity's country of residence to tax the income is not considered to be strong and the tax is given up through the use of the exemption system. As a result, the exemption is usually limited to legal entities (and typically limited to corporations).

Whatever their relative advantages and disadvantages, in practice, no country uses a "pure" exemption or "pure" credit approach for all income or all taxpayers. All the countries examined here use both methods, exempting certain classes of income and giving credit for foreign taxes imposed on others. However, the relative "mix" between exemption and credit varies substantially. *China* relies on the credit method almost exclusively under its domestic law. The *United States* historically has made general use of the credit approach,[121] while *Australia*, the *Continental* systems, and the *United Kingdom* rely more on exemption features. *Canada* falls somewhere in the middle. Although in the past *Japan* generally relied on the credit approach, it introduced exemptions for dividends from foreign affiliates in 2009.

With respect to the specific systems, the *United States* employs a FTC for most foreign income,[122] although there is a limited exemption for foreign-earned income of individuals.[123] After the 2017 tax reform, U.S. corporate shareholders owning 10% or more of a foreign corporation receive a 100% dividends-received deduction on the residual income[124] of that foreign corporation when the dividends are distributed to the U.S. corporate shareholder.[125] To the extent that this dividends-received deduction (akin to a dividend exemption) applies, the 2017 tax reform introduced a limited territorial approach into the U.S. tax system. However, tax reform also added the new Global Intangible Low-Taxed Income (GILTI) regime (a U.S. version of a minimum tax on foreign source income of U.S.-owned foreign entities), which notably expanded the worldwide reach of the U.S. tax system. Under the GILTI regime, U.S. shareholders (corporate and individual) of CFCs are subject to current U.S. taxation on their share of CFC income which is not Subpart F income and which exceeds a statutory 10% return on tangible business assets.[126] To the extent that CFCs have limited tangible business

121. In 2017, tax reform introduced a 100% dividends-received deduction for the *residual* income of a foreign corporation distributed as a dividend to a 10% or more U.S. corporate shareholder. United States, IRC, s. 245A.
122. United States, IRC, s. 901(a).
123. United States, IRC, s. 911.
124. That is, income not already taxed to the U.S. corporate shareholder under the Subpart F or GILTI regimes. United States, IRC s. 245A.
125. United States, IRC, s. 245A.
126. United States, IRC, s. 951A.

assets, the new GILTI regime results in much of the CFC income being currently taxed to the U.S. shareholders.

Taxpayers have the choice between crediting and deducting foreign taxes. The credit is restricted to foreign income taxes which are comparable to U.S. income taxes and are imposed on income from foreign sources. The credit cannot exceed the U.S. tax on the foreign income. However, rather than tracing particular taxes to particular items or segments of income, the limitation is expressed in terms of a formula which allows high and low foreign taxes in each of four (as of 2018) classes or "baskets" of foreign income (passive income, nonpassive income, foreign branch income, and GILTI) to be averaged.[127] In the case of current inclusions of Subpart F and GILTI income by a U.S. corporation owning at least 10% of the votes or value of a foreign corporation, the credit available includes an indirect credit for income taxes paid by the foreign corporation.[128]

The FTC system is also used in *Japan*, and taxpayers have the choice between crediting and deducting foreign taxes, while the indirect tax credit system has been replaced with the exemption system for dividends paid by affiliates. Credit is given for all foreign income taxes, as well as excess profits taxes and taxes on distributed earnings. The credit cannot exceed the Japanese tax on the foreign source income. In general, an overall limitation is used which allows averaging of high- and low-taxed foreign income. However, there are certain limitations on averaging; for example, untaxed foreign source income must be totally eliminated in calculating the credit.[129] Ninety-five percent of dividends paid by a foreign company in which a Japanese company holds 25% or more of the shares is excluded from the taxable income of the Japanese company.[130] This 25% threshold is reduced to 15% or 10% in some tax treaties.

The *United Kingdom* historically used the credit system. The credit is limited to the foreign tax on each particular source of income, thus preventing averaging of foreign rates on directly received income. An indirect credit is still available by election with respect to dividends received by resident corporate shareholders who own at least 10% of the voting power of the payer foreign corporation.[131] In 2009, in response to difficulties with EU Law, the United Kingdom introduced a very broad exemption for foreign dividends received by UK corporations, which also applies to domestic intercorporate dividends.[132] The exemption is available for most, although not all,

127. United States, IRC, s. 904(a), 904(d)(2).
128. United States, IRC, s. 960(a), (d). Although a 100% credit is available for foreign taxes paid on Subpart F income, the credit for foreign taxes paid on GILTI income is capped at 80% of the foreign taxes. The indirect credit has the effect of eliminating multiple levels of corporate taxation on income earned through a corporate chain. Any income of a foreign corporation not required to be currently included in the U.S. corporate shareholder's income as Subpart F or GILTI income will receive a 100% dividends-received deduction on distribution (which also has the effect of eliminating multiple levels of corporate tax). United States, IRC, s. 245A. Prior to the adoption of s. 245A, an indirect FTC was available for all taxable distributions by foreign corporations to 10% U.S. corporate shareholders.
129. Japan, ITA, s. 95 and Japan, Corporate Tax Act (CTA), s. 69.
130. Japan, CTA, s. 23-2.
131. *See* generally UK Taxation (International and Other Provisions) Act 2010, Part 2.
132. United Kingdom, Corporation Tax Act 2009, Part 9A.

types of payments which are treated as distributions for tax purposes. In principle, the exemption is available for all dividends, irrespective of the level of shareholding, of a UK company in the distributing foreign corporation. Interest on associated debt financing of the foreign shares continues to be deductible, subject to restrictions (discussed below).[133] Similarly, in 2010, an exemption for profits of foreign PEs of resident corporations was introduced.[134] As with the dividend exemption, the PE exemption is elective. No similar exemptions are available for individuals, although for individual shareholders the lower tax rate for domestic dividends is also available for foreign dividends (plus the direct FTC).

Canada uses both the FTC method and an exemption system for certain income. Credit is given for "income or profits" taxes paid by a resident taxpayer[135] and is limited to the Canadian tax on foreign source income from sources in the particular country (a so-called per-country limitation). Separate limitations are provided for business and other income. Taxpayers have the option of deducting nonbusiness foreign tax in computing their income.[136] A form of indirect credit is also available for taxes paid by foreign corporations in which there is a direct or indirect 10% share ownership by a Canadian corporation.[137] The credit takes the form of a grossed-up deduction, which in effect limits the credit to the Canadian tax that would have been payable on the foreign income. In addition to the indirect credit, there is an exemption for dividends paid out of active business income of foreign affiliates resident in countries with which Canada has a tax treaty or, since 2008, a tax information exchange agreement.[138] Because the Canadian treaty network of over ninety countries includes most countries in which Canadian corporations have substantial foreign direct investment, almost all dividends repatriated to Canadian corporations by their foreign affiliates qualify for the exemption. Dividends which would qualify for the indirect credit are rarely paid because, until 2011, the funds could be repatriated in the form of interest-free loans and since 2011, the funds can be held and invested offshore.

A similar combination of credit and exemption method is used in *Germany*. The basic statutory system provides for worldwide taxation with a FTC for foreign income taxes on income which is determined to be foreign source income under German source rules.[139] The credit is limited to the amount of German tax paid and the limitation applies on a per-country basis. The taxpayer can also choose to deduct foreign taxes as business expenditures where the foreign income is taxable. There is no carryforward or carryback for excess credits. A special rule allows taxation of foreign source income at a reduced flat rate in certain circumstances (with the approval of the tax authorities). In addition, foreign losses arising from, broadly speaking, foreign activities which do not amount to an active trade or business cannot be deducted against other categories of income.

133. *Ibid.*
134. United Kingdom, Corporation Tax Act 2009, s. 18A to 18S.
135. Canada, ITA, s. 126.
136. Canada, ITA, s. 20(12).
137. Canada, ITA, s. 113(1)(b).
138. Canada, ITA, s. 113(1)(a).
139. Germany, ITA, s. 1 para. 1 and s. 34c; CITA, ss. 1 and 26.

Under its treaty policy, as documented in the Federal Ministry of Finance's (MOF's) "Basis for negotiation" released in 2013,[140] Germany exempts income from immovable property, income from employment and, in particular, business income generated in the context of a foreign PE (as well as dividends from subsidiaries). In light of Germany's extensive treaty network, it is effectively an exemption country as far as business income is concerned. For investment income, pensions, directors' fees, and income derived by sportspersons and artists, the credit method applies.[141]

Under domestic legislation, Germany has introduced a policy establishing "catch-all" clauses dealing with "white income." Income from employment is exempt only where the taxpayer proves that the treaty partner has de facto exercised its taxing right.[142] Moreover, all income which is generally exempt under a treaty is taxable in Germany if the source state does not exercise its taxing right due to a different interpretation of the treaty or special rules for foreign residents.[143] Some revenue items (but not entire categories) are also taxable in Germany if they are not taxed by the treaty partner in line with the treaty's allocation rules.[144] In addition, qualification conflicts regarding contractual payments by commercial partnerships to their partners underlie a similar regime ensuring one-time taxation.[145]

In light of Germany's strong historical commitment to exemption, this sweeping extension of German taxation has been heavily criticized by academics and business representatives alike. Nevertheless, the extension seems to be a deliberate policy shift on a broad scale, given that the "Basis for negotiation" released by the MOF in 2013 contains similar subject-to-tax and "switchover" clauses which are intended to be introduced in treaty negotiations.[146] Moreover, according to the "Basis for negotiation," business income is not exempt unless the underlying activity meets the criteria of a genuine commercial entity as set out in the model treaty.[147]

Sweden allows either a deduction[148] or a credit[149] for foreign income taxes. The amount of the credit is limited to the Swedish taxes due on all foreign income—an overall or general limitation. The general rule is that qualifying dividends from foreign corporations are exempt from tax. There is also an exemption for foreign employment income where the resident is present outside Sweden for more than six months.

With respect to active income (profits arising in a foreign PE and income from foreign employment) and income from foreign real estate, *The Netherlands* provides for double tax relief in domestic law, primarily by using the exemption method, effected

140. Germany, "Basis for negotiation for agreements for the avoidance of double taxation and the prevention of fiscal evasion with respect to taxes on income and on capital" ("Basis for negotiation") (2013), s. 22 para. 1.
141. Germany, Basis for negotiation, s. 22 para. 3; technically speaking, a tax credit under a treaty is different from a tax credit under Germany's unilateral scheme (Germany, ITA, s. 34c para. 6); in fact, it works along the same lines.
142. Germany, ITA, s. 50d para. 8.
143. Germany, ITA, s. 50d para. 9.
144. Germany, ITA, s. 50d para. 9 s. 4.
145. Germany, ITA, s. 50d para. 10.
146. Germany, Basis for negotiation, s. 22 para. 5.
147. Germany, Basis for negotiation, s. 22 para. 4.
148. Sweden, ITA, Ch. 16 ss. 18 and 19.
149. Sweden, Foreign Tax Credit Act.

through a (proportional) reduction of the tax computed on the basis of the worldwide income[150] rather than by eliminating the foreign income from the taxable base. This system was changed to an income exemption effective January 1, 2012.[151] In addition, a FTC is applied with respect to investment income received from certain developing countries and with respect to income earned by sportspersons and artists abroad.[152] Where foreign finance profits are taxed abroad at a low rate, a FTC applies rather than exemption.[153] A credit also applies where, under the Dutch CFC rules, a PE qualifies as a low- or no-taxed PE (e.g., where the PE is located in a jurisdiction which is blacklisted by the EU).[154] In general, the application of the CFC rules is accompanied by the credit method.[155] Dividends received from a foreign company qualify for the participation exemption on essentially the same terms as dividends from domestic companies, with the additional requirement that the foreign company must not be subject to tax at a rate of less than 10% of the corporate income as determined under Dutch rules.[156] The taxpayer may also elect to deduct the foreign tax.

The form of double tax relief in *Australia* depends on the type of income. Passive investment-type income is dealt with by a credit system which provides a credit for the foreign (usually withholding) tax.[157] Profits of a resident company arising from direct activities abroad through a PE (other than income which would be caught by the CFC regime if the foreign branch were instead a subsidiary), and foreign equity distributions paid by foreign corporations to 10% or more resident corporate shareholders, are exempt from Australian tax. A sliding-scale participation exemption, based on the level of active business assets of the subsidiary, was introduced in 2004 for capital gains on shares in 10%-owned foreign subsidiaries of Australian parent companies. This change was part of an international tax reform which also considerably broadened the existing exemption regimes for resident companies. As a consequence, the previous indirect FTC for dividends which did not qualify for exemption was removed.[158] Until 2009, foreign employment income was exempt with progression if the taxpayer was abroad for at least ninety-one days and was subject to tax in the foreign jurisdiction. In 2009, this exemption was limited essentially to employees working on foreign aid and similar projects. In most circumstances, a FTC is allowed for foreign taxes on foreign employment income, although in very limited cases an exemption is available (*see* section 3.2.2 below).

150. Netherlands, Decree Avoidance of Double Taxation 2001 (DADT), Art. 10. This has important consequences for the offsetting of foreign losses and the preservation of the full effect of a progressive tax rate.
151. Netherlands, CITA, Art. 15e. It is not an "income exemption" because, as a result of a CJEU decision, the exchange results on profits or losses attributable to the PE remain part of the taxable income (CJEU, February 28, 2008, C-293/06 (*Deutsche Shell*)).
152. Netherlands, DADT, Arts. 25 and 36-38 (investment income), Arts. 13 and 14 (sportspersons, etc.).
153. Netherlands, CITA, Art. 15h in connection with Art. 23d.
154. Netherlands, CITA, Art. 13ab(4).
155. Netherlands, CITA, Art. 15e(11) in connection with Art. 23e.
156. Netherlands, CITA, Art. 13(11).
157. Australia, ITAA 1997, Div. 770.
158. Australia, ITAA 1936, s. 23AH, 23AJ, ITAA 1997, Subdivs. 768-A, 768-G.

The *French* system is unique in that, apart from treaties, it does not normally grant relief for double taxation and foreign taxes are simply deductible from the tax base. However, there are some important exceptions. The principle of territoriality exempts from corporate tax profits arising from a trade or business carried on abroad;[159] dividends from qualifying foreign subsidiaries are likewise exempt.[160] Wages and/or bonuses for working abroad may be exempt in certain circumstances,[161] and a tax credit is granted to French corporations to which the CFC rules apply.[162] In addition, before September 2011, French corporations could obtain special permission to file a consolidated tax return including the operations of both domestic and foreign branches and subsidiaries, in which case foreign taxes were creditable and foreign losses deductible. However, few companies took advantage of the election, so this special but increasingly less attractive worldwide consolidation regime was finally repealed. The law also provides for the elimination of double taxation of gift duties by allowing the deduction of foreign tax paid on movable and immovable property located outside France from the tax payable in France.[163]

In *India*, where India has a comprehensive tax treaty with another country, the FTC is governed by the provisions of the treaty. However, where there is no tax treaty, a unilateral tax credit is provided in the Income Tax Act (ITA), which is limited to the lesser of the foreign tax paid and Indian tax on the foreign source income.[164] The person claiming the credit must be a resident of India, and the relevant income must not be deemed to accrue or arise in India.

3.1 Issues in the Structure of a Foreign Tax Credit System

3.1.1 Creditable Taxes

All systems which give a credit for foreign taxes paid against domestic income tax liability must determine which foreign levies are eligible for the credit. Several approaches are possible. One is to list specific foreign taxes which qualify for the credit. Another is to credit foreign taxes which bear a general resemblance to the domestic income tax without too much concern for the technical details of the foreign tax law. Another approach is to define the specific characteristics which a foreign tax must have in order to be creditable as an income tax. In addition, it is common practice in treaties to specify which taxes qualify for the credit.

Most countries focus on a general resemblance between foreign and domestic taxes. Only the *United States* has detailed regulatory rules setting out the criteria which a foreign income tax must meet. The regulatory structure is based in part on some case law principles developing the concept of an income tax for tax credit purposes. Under

159. France, CGI, s. 209 I.
160. France, CGI, ss. 145 and 216.
161. France, CGI, s. 81 A.
162. France, CGI, s. 209 B; *see* section 4.2 below.
163. France, CGI, s. 784 A.
164. India, ITA 1961, s. 91.

the regulatory scheme,[165] the foreign "levy" must be a tax and not a payment for some type of economic benefit and must be likely to reach net gain in normal circumstances. Taxes imposed by national and subnational political subdivisions can both qualify for credit.

In determining whether a tax is an income tax, the tax must meet the "net gain" requirement, which itself requires satisfying four tests: realization, gross receipts, cost recovery, and attribution. (Alternatively, a foreign tax can meet the "net gain" requirement by meeting the definition of a "surtax.") Realization requires that the tax be imposed on one of several events mirroring realization under U.S. tax law, although some taxes imposed pre-realization qualify. The tax also must use gross receipts in the computation of taxable income. Thus, taxes imposed on the basis of artificially "posted" prices would not qualify; however, a tax based on a likely estimate of gross receipts (e.g., costs plus a reasonable profit markup) would qualify. To satisfy the cost recovery requirement, the tax base must be reduced by reasonable allowances for significant expenses (including capital outlays). A gross-based tax would qualify in circumstances where there are no significant expenses. A foreign tax with an alternative cost-recovery mechanism can satisfy this requirement only if it allows recovery in excess of, but not less than, the actual significant costs. Finally, the fourth (and new) requirement, attribution, requires that the creditable tax rely on one of three jurisdictional nexus rules consistent with and not greater than the reach of U.S. jurisdictional rules: income attributable to activities in the jurisdiction, income based on source in the jurisdiction, and situs of the property in the jurisdiction. Effectively, this new attribution rule precludes a tax based on a jurisdictional factor such as customer location from satisfying the "net gain" requirement.

Social-security-type taxes used to fund retirement benefits are generally creditable as long as the payment is not based on age, life expectancy, or other similar characteristics. The payments are not viewed as a charge for a specific economic benefit. Neither a credit nor a deduction is permitted for such social-security type taxes paid to a country with which the United States has a social security agreement.

Taxes "in lieu of" an income tax are also creditable. A gross-based tax, such as the withholding tax typically imposed on investment income of nonresidents, is treated as a creditable tax as long as it meets a multi-pronged "substitution" requirement. No credit is allowed for so-called soak-up taxes—taxes which are imposed only in situations in which they would qualify for the credit in the residence country.

Treaties may expand the category of creditable taxes to cover taxes which would not meet the regulatory definition.

Canada restricts the FTC to "income or profits" taxes, but there is no statutory or regulatory definition and little case law on the question. Certain payments to foreign governments pursuant to oil and gas production-sharing agreements are deemed to be income or profits taxes.[166] U.S. social security taxes have been held to be creditable

165. United States, Regs., s. 1.901-2. In 2021 and 2022, Treasury significantly rewrote the regulations detailing what constitutes a creditable tax—a move widely viewed as limiting the scope of creditable taxes. The regulations continue to be highly controversial.
166. Canada, ITA, s. 126(5).

despite the limited tax base and the fact that the payments are loosely tied to specific benefits. Income taxes paid to political subdivisions are also creditable. Soak-up taxes are not creditable, and there are anti-avoidance rules to prevent the creation of FTCs inappropriately.[167]

Sweden similarly limits the credit to "income taxes" paid to all levels of government. Normally, no tax credit is available for foreign social security contributions, unless such contributions are explicitly included in the scope of a tax treaty. In addition, credit is allowed for real estate taxes that are similar to the tax which Sweden levies on real estate used in business and the "fee" levied on personal dwellings. *China* also limits the FTC to income taxes which are similar to Chinese income tax and includes taxes covered by a tax treaty. A creditable foreign tax also includes foreign income tax paid by qualified CFCs. Administrative guidelines indicate certain types of payments which do not qualify for credit, including tax paid by mistake, tax which is later refunded, interest and penalties, taxes paid on income exempt from Chinese tax, and taxes which are deductible in computing Chinese income.

The *Australian* rules, which were rewritten with effect from 2008, are somewhat more complex. The statutory definition covers any foreign tax on income, profits, or gains. (Taxes covered by tax treaties are mentioned specifically as being covered.) Under an administrative ruling in relation to the pre-2008 system, which would seem to continue to be applicable, creditable taxes must be imposed on a basis "substantially equivalent" to the Australian legislation, which includes a net-basis tax on income or gains and a final gross-basis withholding tax on passive income. The ruling contains somewhat outdated lists of taxes which do or do not meet these criteria. Social security taxes generally are not creditable, but credit is given for subnational income taxes and, since 2008, for supranational taxes such as EU taxes on EU employees. Special rules exclude credit for unitary taxes (targeted at the taxes of some American states) to the extent that they are not applied on a "water's-edge" basis. In addition, no credit is allowed for "soak-up" taxes, defined as taxes which would not have been imposed if the taxpayer had not been entitled to credit in Australia.[168]

The *United Kingdom* allows a credit for any tax which "corresponds" to UK income tax or corporation tax.[169] This limitation has been liberally interpreted, and a tax on 90% of gross receipts has been held by the courts to be creditable.[170] The administrative position is to allow credit for taxes which serve the same function in relation to business profits as an income tax, thus excluding turnover taxes but not necessarily taxes on gross receipts. Taxes paid to subnational governments are creditable. Social security payments do not qualify.

Germany similarly limits the FTC to taxes which are comparable to the German income or corporate tax. The tax authorities have published a detailed list of creditable taxes. Following the lowering of the corporate tax rate to 15%, more excess tax credits are available for Germany-based multinational enterprises. Since these corporations

167. Canada, ITA, s. 126(4)-(4.2).
168. Australia, ITAA 1997, s. 770-10, 770-15.
169. United Kingdom, Taxation (International and Other Provisions) Act 2010, s. 9.
170. *Yates v. GCA International Ltd* [1991] STC 157.

must pay trade tax to domestic municipalities (average rate: 14%), the problem of crediting foreign income tax against domestic trade tax has become more acute. So far, German legislation does not allow cross-crediting between different tax categories, which leads to significant "tax overhangs." However, the Tax Court of Hessen held in 2020 that the tax treaty requires a tax credit for foreign withholding taxes with respect to the German trade tax.[171]

The *Japanese* system has a broad regulatory definition which covers individual and corporate income taxes (CITs) as well as excess profits taxes, revenue taxes, and distributed-earnings taxes, while certain kinds of taxes, such as those whose tax rates can be chosen by taxpayers, are excluded from creditable taxes. While local income taxes are generally creditable, social security taxes are treated as non-creditable.

Since *The Netherlands* primarily uses the exemption method, the issue of creditable taxes is not as significant as it is for other countries. Under Dutch domestic law, a foreign tax must be an income tax in order to be creditable but the notion of a creditable income tax has been interpreted quite liberally. The situation is the same in *France*, where the territorial principle controls the taxation of foreign corporate income. Most credits are granted by treaty, which specify the taxes in question.

In *India*, with respect to treaties, creditable taxes are usually the foreign taxes mentioned in the treaty and are usually restricted to the taxes levied at the federal level. However, the courts have held state income taxes paid by the taxpayer to be creditable under section 90(2) on the basis that the explanation to section 91 clarifies that tax charged by the government or any part of the government of a country is covered.[172] Like India, *China* generally recognizes foreign taxes described in tax treaties as creditable. Chinese domestic legislation is silent on what taxes are creditable foreign income taxes.

3.1.2 Limitations on the Credit

All the systems reviewed here have limitations on the extent to which foreign tax paid can displace domestic tax liability. While, from a theoretical point of view, an unlimited FTC is sometimes urged as the structure most consistent with complete capital export neutrality, practical revenue constraints make such a policy unattractive. In addition, to the extent that the principal function of the credit is to relieve double taxation on foreign source income, there is no reason to allow the credit to reduce domestic taxes on domestic source income. Within these broad constraints, however, there is a wide variety in the actual form a limitation might take. At one extreme, the foreign tax could be traced to a particular item of foreign income and the credit limited to the domestic tax on that item. At the other extreme, all foreign income and foreign taxes could be aggregated and the credit limited to the corresponding domestic tax. This approach allows an "averaging" of high-taxed and low-taxed foreign income and allows the credit in full to the extent that the amount of domestic tax is not exceeded.

171. Tax Court Hessen (*Finanzgericht Hessen*), August 26, 2020, 8 K 1860/16.
172. *WIPRO Ltd v. Dy CIT*, Karnataka High Court, March 25, 2015.

Any number of intermediate structures are also possible. The credit could be limited to the foreign tax on particular categories of income, such as income from a particular country (a "per-country" limitation) or a particular class or type of income (a "basket" limitation), or some other similar combination of the two.

All the systems fall somewhere between a per-item and an unlimited overall limitation. In most cases, there are restrictions on the ability to average foreign taxes on active business income and passive income, and, in particular, on interest income. For those systems which exempt certain forms of income, possibilities for averaging are also limited since the exempt income and corresponding foreign tax do not enter into the calculations of the limitation. To some extent, the scope of the limitation is related to the breadth of the definition of creditable taxes.

The *United States*, in part because of its historical role as a capital-exporting country, has the most complex and developed set of rules limiting the FTC. However, since, in general terms, the system allows averaging with respect to such income regardless of the tax rate or source, it may in fact be less restrictive than some of the other systems. Prior to 2007, the United States applied limitations to nine baskets of different types of income as part of its system of worldwide taxation.[173] Subsequently, it implemented a mechanism for limiting the credit using only two baskets of income—the passive category and the general category.[174] The 2017 tax reform added two additional baskets, the foreign branch basket and the GILTI basket.[175] All foreign source income[176] received directly or reported by a U.S. taxpayer is assigned to one of the four baskets. Most active business income historically fell into the "general category" basket, and Subpart F income reported by U.S. shareholders fell into the passive or general basket (based on certain look-through rules).[177] Similarly, such shareholders could have placed portions of dividend income they received from a CFC in the active basket using the "look-through rule" (allowing U.S. shareholders to look through the receipt of the dividend to the underlying income of the CFC in order to classify the dividend for FTC basket purposes).[178]

The addition of the GILTI basket in 2018 further complicates the basket system for U.S. shareholders. The basket treatment of Subpart F inclusions remains the same. However, the possibility that non-Subpart F income earned by a CFC might be currently included in a U.S. shareholder's income as GILTI income—with its own FTC basket—means that little dividend income from the CFC might remain to be included in the active basket via the look-through rule. Averaging is allowed across businesses

173. United States, IRC, s. 904(d) (prior to amendment).
174. United States, IRC, s. 904(d)(2).
175. United States, IRC, s. 904(d)(1)(A), (B).
176. Thus, foreign source income includes income received through foreign activities, operations, or investments, from Subpart F income inclusions, from GILTI income inclusions, and from dividends from foreign corporations.
177. United States, IRC, s. 904.
178. United States, IRC, s. 904(d)(3). Similarly, for purposes of the U.S. shareholder's own determination of its FTC baskets, where a foreign corporation is controlled by U.S. persons, rentals, royalties, and interest payments received from it are deemed to be out of the relevant baskets of income determined at the level of the foreign corporation. United States, IRC, s. 904(d)(3)(c).

and geographical sources within a given basket. Passive income is placed in a separate basket. Where passive income is itself subject to a foreign tax rate comparable to the U.S. rate, it is moved to the general basket, thus ensuring that low-taxed passive income cannot be averaged with comparably taxed passive income and will bear some residual U.S. tax. Where a foreign corporation is controlled by U.S. persons, rentals, royalties, and interest payments received from it are deemed to be paid out of the relevant baskets of income determined at the level of the foreign corporation. In addition, dividends received by non-corporate and corporate U.S. shareholders holding 10% or more of the shares in a CFC are also deemed to have been paid out of the relevant baskets of income determined at the foreign corporation level on a pro rata basis.[179] This look-through rule is irrelevant for a 10% or greater U.S. corporate shareholder receiving a dividend, because such dividend is eligible for the 100% dividend-received deduction and, therefore, not eligible for the FTC.[180] In sum, where applicable, look-through rules enable the character of the foreign corporation's income to "pass through" to the U.S. shareholder.

In *Japan*, the limitation on the FTC is calculated by multiplying the domestic tax liability by a fraction in which the numerator is the total amount of foreign source income subject to tax and the denominator is total global taxable income. However, two special restrictions apply to counteract what was perceived as excess averaging of foreign taxes. First, foreign source income which is not subject to foreign tax is excluded from the numerator of the fraction. Second, the foreign source income included in the numerator cannot exceed 90% of the total income.[181] Source rules are generally identical to those applied with respect to the taxation of foreign taxpayers. Therefore, income from export sales of inventory is treated as foreign source income only if it is attributable to a foreign fixed place of business or other forms of PE.

In *Canada*, a per-country limit is used as the basic limitation on business income which is not exempt. In addition, there is a "basket" limitation for nonbusiness income which is also applied on a per-country basis. For individuals, the credit in respect of income from property other than real property is subject to an absolute per-country limitation of 15% of the amount of income sourced in the country. The excess tax can be deducted.[182] The 15% limitation does not apply to real property rental income. The nonbusiness basket is important primarily for purposes of provincial taxation but does have the effect of limiting averaging for federal purposes. While source rules are important to the operation of the Canadian system, they are relatively undeveloped and largely administrative. Foreign taxes are generally attributed to foreign income on a tracing basis.

Germany similarly has a per-country limitation.[183] This creates a tax wedge between taxpayers spreading their investment across several countries and taxpayers investing only in one (foreign) country. Nevertheless, the Federal Tax Court has held

179. United States, IRC, s. 904(d)(3).
180. United States, IRC, s. 245A(d).
181. Japan, ITA, s. 95 and Japan, CTA, s. 69.
182. Canada, ITA, s. 20(11).
183. Germany, ITA, s. 34c para. 1 s. 1; CITA, s. 26 para. 1.

that this result does not call into question the compatibility of the per-country limitation with the fundamental freedoms under European law.[184]

Limitations on FTCs have become more and more detailed over time. Since 2003, statutory provisions prevent the averaging of taxable and tax-free income within a particular foreign country.[185] In 2009, a special rule for portfolio investment income was introduced. Under this provision, foreign withholding taxes on interest and dividend payments are creditable against the 25% flat tax on a per-item basis.[186]

While *The Netherlands'* tax treaties provide for a per-country limitation, taxpayers have the right to opt for an overall limitation which applies where relief is granted in the absence of a tax treaty. In *China*, the limitation on the FTC is calculated on a per-country or regional basis.

The limitation in *Sweden* is a function of the schedular system of taxation. For individuals, business income and employment income are treated together; in the initial computation of the limitation, capital income is included in a separate category. Under the limitation, the tax on each category of income is limited to the Swedish tax on the same category. However, if the foreign tax exceeds the limit in one category because the amount of Swedish tax is lower than the foreign tax, excess Swedish taxes in the other category can be used to absorb the excess from the first category. The foreign source character of the income is determined by its treatment under foreign law. Because corporations have only one source of income, the limitation operates on an overall basis. According to the case law, a loss in one country is not deducted from positive foreign income in other countries.

Australia has a worldwide limitation. It was previously based on four baskets, but these were eliminated in 2008; in addition, the application of the limit was removed where the taxpayer's total foreign tax is AUD 1,000 or less (i.e., such foreign tax is creditable in full).[187]

Previously, the credit applied only if the income was considered to be foreign source income under Australian tax law. From 2008, "foreign source" in this sense is no longer relevant for income which has been subject to foreign tax on a basis other than residence. Foreign source is now important only where the calculation of the credit limit includes income which has not been subject to any foreign tax. Australia has few explicit legislative source rules dealing with resident taxpayers, although the courts have developed some jurisprudence based on a facts-and-circumstances approach. Some rules are fairly clear. For example, interest is sourced where the funds are made available, which may be the place where the contract is executed or the funds advanced. With respect to treaties, until 2019 Australia generally included a source rule in its treaties based on whether a country has a taxing right over the income on a basis other than residence. Treaties usually provide that the source rule also applied for the purposes of Australian domestic tax law and so can change the source which otherwise would arise under domestic tax law. For the Australia-Israel treaty signed in 2019 and

184. Federal Tax Court (*Bundesfinanzhof*), December 18, 2013, I R 71/10.
185. Germany, ITA, s. 34c para. 1 s. 3.
186. Germany, ITA, s. 32d para. 5.
187. Australia, ITAA 1997, s. 770-75.

future treaties, this source rule is no longer included in treaties; instead, a provision to similar effect has been inserted in Australian domestic tax law, where it always should have been.[188] The limitation on the FTC was previously calculated using the average rate of Australian tax on the taxpayer's income. Now the foreign income is effectively treated as the top slice of income in determining the amount of Australian tax on the income; this treatment is more generous for individuals who are subject to a progressive income tax rate scale.

As a predominantly capital importing country, in the past, *India* did not pay much attention to the detailed aspects of the FTC. But with a significant increase in foreign investment by Indian companies, a comprehensive set of tax credit rules was issued in 2016 (effective from April 1, 2017). These rules apply for both the FTC under domestic law and the credit granted under tax treaties. The credit is limited to the lesser of the tax payable under the ITA (including surcharge, surtax and alternative minimum tax, but not interest or penalties) on the foreign income and the foreign tax paid on such income, and is computed separately for each source of income from a particular country. Any foreign tax paid in excess of the domestic tax is not creditable.[189]

The *United Kingdom* limitation is, in principle, quite restrictive. Direct credit relief is given on a source-by-source basis and unused credits cannot be used against the UK tax on other income or carried forward, although in some cases excess credits can be deducted.

3.1.3 Allocation of Expenses to Foreign Source Income

A crucial element in the determination of the credit limitation is the foreign source *taxable* income of the taxpayer in the various categories to which the limitations apply. To determine this amount, deductions must be allocated to the appropriate types of positive income (or a negative amount established in a particular category). Despite the centrality of this issue in applying limitations on the FTC, only the United States has any fully developed rules in this area. In other countries, the rules are quite general and leave much to taxpayer choice. To some extent, the rules are influenced by financial accounting practice and generally accepted accounting principles.

Since 1977, the *United States* has had detailed administrative rules dealing with the allocation of expenses between foreign source and domestic source income.[190] Under the regulations, deductions are first allocated to general classes of income based on the "factual relationship" between the income and the expense. Deductions allocated to a particular class may exceed the positive income in the class in a given year. Deductions which are not definitely related to a class of income are ratably allocated to all gross income, but the specificity of the rules leaves little scope for such allocations. Once allocated to a class of gross income, deductions are then apportioned to the relevant categories of income, in this case foreign source and domestic source. The regulations deal with the factors to be considered in the apportionment and include

188. Australia, ITAA 1997, Div 764.
189. India, IT Rules 1962, Rule 128.
190. United States, Regs., s. 1.861-8.

units sold, gross receipts, cost of goods sold, and the like. Special rules are applied to interest and research and development costs.

In the case of interest, the interest cost is apportioned on an asset method based on the tax cost of assets generating foreign source and domestic source income.[191] The tax basis of stock in foreign corporations is adjusted to reflect retained earnings or deficits in earnings, thus, in effect, accounting for the current operations of the foreign corporations.

This method is based on a "fungibility" approach and assumes that borrowing costs relate to all productive assets. However, a special rule requires the allocation of interest expense directly to foreign source income if there is "excess" borrowing in the United States which has been loaned to foreign subsidiaries. A portion of the domestic interest expense is in effect treated as if it had been incurred abroad in a related subsidiary and was thus directly allocable to foreign source income.[192]

In the case of a domestic consolidated group of companies, interest expense and associated income must be computed on a consolidated basis. Prior to a statutory change, it was common practice to isolate interest expense in members of a consolidated group which did not have significant foreign source income.[193]

The approach to research and development costs has constantly changed since the introduction of the 1977 regulations. Under the original regulations, research costs were first allocated to the appropriate product categories in broad classifications. Amounts within those categories were then apportioned to different sources of income based, in part, on where the research was performed and in part on the relative amounts of sales or gross income (with appropriate adjustments in royalties and other similar payments), in order to arrive at amounts comparable to sales figures. Legislative changes suspended the application of the rules for several years and replaced them with a provision which allocated all research expenses incurred in the United States to U.S. source income.

Regulations enacted in 1995 adopt the same general approach as the 1977 regulations but were more generous in reducing the amount of research expense apportioned to foreign source income. New regulations were issued in 2020 to reflect the view that successful research expenses "result in the creation of intangible property that will be used to generate income."[194] Accordingly, research expenses are considered definitely related to "gross intangible income [GII] ... reasonably related" to the relevant product category.[195] After this allocation, research expenses are apportioned 50% to U.S. source GII if at least 50% of the expenditures occurred in the United States. If more than 50% occurred outside the United States, then 50% of the expenses is apportioned to foreign source income in the GII of the product category. After this

191. United States, Regs., s. 1.861-9T-13T.
192. United States, Regs., s. 1.861-10T. An elective method of allocation which takes into account interest expense of foreign affiliates is available for taxable years after December 31, 2020. United States, IRC, s. 864(f)(1).
193. United States, IRC, s. 864(e)(1).
194. United States, Regs., s. 1.861-17.
195. *Ibid.*

allocation step, the remaining research expenses are allocated based on gross receipts.[196]

In *Canada*, interest and other expenses are ordinarily allocated to foreign source income on a factual tracing basis. This approach allows taxpayers to plan their affairs to "stream" their borrowings to Canadian assets or Canadian income in order to maximize FTCs. If tracing is impossible, the Canada Revenue Agency (CRA) permits expenses to be allocated in accordance with a reasonable formula based on asset values or gross income. There are no specific statutory rules or case law dealing with the allocation of expenses to foreign source income. Even the CRA's administrative positions do not provide much detail.

In *Australia*, expenses must be allocated in a manner which is reasonable, although there is little guidance in the published material. Since 2001, interest expense receives special treatment due to a thin capitalization regime, which is outlined below in Subpart B, section 1.3 in relation to source taxation. Bizarrely, the Australian foreign hybrid mismatch rules, which are effective from January 1, 2019, seem to have undermined the credit by denying Australian deductions relating to foreign income even where both countries are taxing the same income to the same taxpayer on a net basis.[197]

After the 2014 tax revisions, *Japan* applies the same cost allocation rules to the calculation of the income attributable to a PE abroad as those applicable to a PE in Japan of a foreign corporation. Therefore, where indirect costs or expenses are related to both the foreign and domestic business activities, a formulary approach is used, subject to documentation requirements, whereby such costs and expenses are allocated on the basis of revenues, assets, number of employees, etc., depending on the nature of the expense. For other types of foreign source income, expenses are allocated on a "rational" basis, with substantial taxpayer choice. The regulations give examples of allocation based on revenues, assets, and number of employees.

In *Sweden*, there are no statutory rules dealing with expense allocation, although it is clear that the FTC limitations must be applied on a net basis. Some principles developed in the context of allocation of income between domestic and foreign branches may have some application but, in general, the area is undeveloped. Similarly, in *China*, common expenses are expected to be reasonably allocated between Chinese source income and foreign source income on a jurisdiction-by-jurisdiction basis.

Historically, the *United Kingdom* had few rules in this area. The domestic law simply referred to the "relevant foreign income," and this was viewed largely as a reference to the domestic schedular system. This view proved to be problematic with respect to trading income: the tax administration lost a case in which an insurance company successfully argued that the limitation on the FTC was calculated by reference to its whole trading profits (including UK profits) and not just that part of the

196. *Ibid.*
197. G.S. Cooper, "The Curious Reform of Foreign Source Income" (2018) 22 *Tax Specialist* 2.

profits pertaining to the foreign income.[198] As a result, in 2005 the concept of "relevant income" was narrowed for the purposes of calculating the limitation on the credit where foreign income is earned as part of a trade.[199] For the purpose of calculating the limitation, the relevant income is income "arising out of the transaction, arrangement or asset in connection with which the credit arises." That income must be reduced by any deductible expenses directly relating to it and by indirect expenses (e.g., general overheads) "reasonably attributable" to the income.

In *Germany*, case law principles require that "directly or indirectly connected" expenses be attributed to foreign source income under a tracing approach. There is no allocation of general expenses. As of 2003, for some items of foreign income attributable to a domestic business, the amount of income relevant for determining the German tax burden is calculated on a net basis, involving the deductibility of "indirect" business expenditures which are economically related to the foreign income (e.g., financing costs for foreign investment income).[200] In 2014, following a judgment by the CJEU,[201] German legislation clarified that deductible personal expenditures (e.g., family deductions) must be spread across both domestic and foreign income in order not to overly reduce the amount of foreign income subject to German taxation.[202]

In *The Netherlands*, the FTC limitation under tax treaties is computed on the basis of a full allocation of expenses (i.e., both directly attributable expenses and a proportional share of general expenses). The same rules apply in the absence of a treaty.

With respect to foreign tax-free dividends, *France* has for a long time applied the rule in the EU Parent-Subsidiary Directive, according to which 5% (2.5% before 2000) of dividends (plus FTC, if any) are deemed to be taxable in order to offset deductible expenses.[203] In addition, since the CJEU *Steria* case in 2015, dividends paid in the context of tax consolidation are treated the same way as those paid by nonintegrated European subsidiaries that are more than 95% owned. A rate of 1% currently applies to dividends in the context of tax consolidation and 5% in other cases. According to case law, the allocation of costs and expenses has a hybrid nature since it aims both to (1) neutralize the deduction of costs relating to equity investments by reinstating the costs actually incurred in the taxable result, and (2) parallel taxation of the difference between the amount of the actual reinstated costs and the lump-sum amount of the share, thus allowing the parent company to set off FTCs against the corporate tax on the taxed portion of the dividend.

198. *Legal & General Assurance Society Ltd v. Revenue and Customs Commissioners* [2006] EWHC 1770.
199. United Kingdom, Taxation (International and Other Provisions) Act 2010, s. 44.
200. Germany, ITA, s. 34c para. 1 s. 4; where those costs can be traced back to both domestic and foreign items of income, deductibility depends on either the principal factor causing the expenditure or the costs, being partially allocated to both the foreign and the domestic income (Federal Tax Court (*Bundesfinanzhof*), April 6, 2016, I R 61/14).
201. CJEU, C-168/11, February 28, 2013 (*Beker and Beker*).
202. Germany, ITA, s. 34c para. 1 s. 2.
203. France, CGI, s. 216.

3.1.4 *Treatment of Losses in the Credit Computation*

Where the expenses in a particular credit category exceed the income, the resulting loss may have an impact on the remaining credit calculations. Several situations must be distinguished. First, where expenses allocated to a given category of foreign income exceed the income, the excess could be: (a) allocated to domestic income, thus not affecting the other credit calculations; (b) allocated on some basis only to the other foreign income baskets, potentially reducing the amount of credit available in those baskets; or (c) allocated pro rata to foreign as well as domestic income, having a more limited effect on the credit calculation. Second, assuming that some allocation rule has been established, an ancillary principle must determine what, if any, effect a later positive amount has in a basket in which a loss was previously allocated to other baskets (or to domestic source income). Finally, where the overall results are negative, so there is an overall net operating loss which may be carried forward, rules must be provided to deal with the effect of the carryover on the credit computation in later years. The systems considered here have taken a variety of approaches. Where active business income is exempt when subject to significant foreign taxation, the issues are generally not of great significance, since the credit will be applied in respect of categories of foreign income in which losses are unlikely to occur.

Again, the *United States* has the most complex rules for dealing with losses.[204] The complexity is traceable to the prior extensive use of the basket system and the policy decision that foreign losses in a particular basket should not be allowed to reduce domestic source income in any situation where there is positive foreign source income in another basket. Thus, foreign losses in one basket must first reduce proportionally the foreign income in the other baskets, with any excess reducing U.S. source income. When foreign income is subsequently generated in the basket which initially incurred the loss, that income is recharacterized for basket purposes in the same fashion that the loss was used. However, any foreign taxes imposed on the income are not reattributed to the other basket. Where the foreign loss exceeds foreign source income and reduces U.S. income, so that the taxpayer experiences an "overall" foreign loss, subsequently arising foreign source income is recharacterized as U.S. source income for credit-limitation purposes. Similarly, in the reverse situation, where domestic losses reduce foreign income, subsequently arising domestic source income is recharacterized as foreign source income.

Until 2008, the *Australian* rule for losses was the strictest of the systems examined here. Where the deductions allocated to foreign source income exceeded the income, the loss could not be used against domestic source income in the current year but was carried forward indefinitely for use against future foreign income. In 2008, this limitation was abolished and foreign losses can now offset domestic source income. *China's* rules are also very strict. Because of the per-country limitation, losses for branch operations in one country cannot offset income from another country or from China and, therefore, have no effect on the FTC.

204. United States, IRC, s. 904(f).

In *Canada*, the limitation is calculated on a country-by-country basis, and, in general, losses in one foreign jurisdiction do not affect the credit calculation for other jurisdictions but do reduce domestic source income. There is no recharacterization of domestic income arising subsequently as foreign income for credit purposes. Where domestic losses exceed domestic income and reduce foreign source income, the credit is limited to the amount of Canadian tax payable. An overall net operating loss for a year does not have any impact on the FTC calculations for subsequent years, except to the extent that the amount of foreign or Canadian tax payable in those subsequent years is reduced as a result of the loss carryforward.

In principle, the *United Kingdom* source approach does not take losses from other sources into account. However, where foreign activities are part of a domestic trade, the "source" is the whole trade, with the result that a loss on the foreign activities reduces profits of the trade and so indirectly reduces any profits from the domestic activities.[205] FTCs are calculated on income "arising" in a foreign country from the trade.[206] Where the foreign activities create an overall loss for the trade, that loss may be used in the same manner as any other loss from a UK trade—i.e., against profits from any other source for the current year (with a one-year carryback) and carried forward against future profits but subject to the restrictions discussed in Part III.[207] Because in this common situation the FTC limitation is calculated separately from the charge on the profits of the trade, the use of any loss has no impact on the future calculation of FTCs. However, where the losses are attributable to a foreign PE and the taxpayer has elected to use the exemption system, the losses are disallowed.[208]

In applying its per-country limitation, *Germany* does not reduce the positive income from one country by losses incurred in another country. In contrast, where several different sources of income (e.g., several PEs) or types of income are attributable to the same country, gains and losses are offset unless items of income are fully tax-exempt in the source country (although portfolio investment income is subject to a strict per-item treatment).[209]

Moreover, as far as worldwide income taxation applies, in principle, foreign losses reduce domestic or other income in the final calculation of a taxpayer's income. In order to limit the deductibility of certain foreign losses (arising principally in passive activities which are likely to create tax shelters), these losses can be deducted only from income from the same source in the same country.[210] For source countries located within the EU/EEA, specific tax legislation waives this limitation on loss relief following a CJEU judgment on foreign participations.[211] Those losses do not affect the credit calculation with respect to other income arising in the same country. An overall foreign loss which reduces domestic source income has no effect on the calculation of the credit in subsequent years.

205. United Kingdom, Corporation Tax Act 2009, s. 35.
206. United Kingdom, Taxation (International and Other Provisions) Act 2010, s. 9.
207. United Kingdom, Corporation Tax Act 2010, ss. 37, 45, and 45A.
208. United Kingdom, Corporation Tax Act 2009, s. 18A.
209. Germany, ITA, s. 34c para. 1 s. 1, 2nd limb.
210. Germany, ITA, s. 2a.
211. CJEU, March 29, 2007, C-347/07 (*Rewe Zentralfinanz*).

In *China*, the losses of a branch in a foreign jurisdiction cannot offset income derived from China or another jurisdiction; such losses can be used to offset income from the same jurisdiction in the current year and subsequent five years.

In *India*, where a taxpayer had a loss from its branch business in one country but profit from a branch in another country, the tax department set off the loss against the profit before allowing a FTC; however, on appeal, the court held that the credit had to be given on a per-country basis.[212]

The question of losses in the *Japanese* system is of relatively minor significance since the overall limitation is used and there is no problem with respect to the allocation of losses among income baskets. Where foreign losses reduce domestic income, there is no provision for later recharacterization of foreign income as domestic income.

3.1.5 Carryover of Excess Credits or Limitations

Where limitations on the credit are applicable and excess FTCs are generated, all systems must deal with the structural question of how such excess credits should be treated. Strict adherence to annual accounting principles would require each computation to be made on an annual basis and if credits could not be used in the years in which the foreign taxes were incurred, they would be lost. The most appealing case for some kind of relief from strict annual accounting is where the inclusion of the foreign income in the domestic system differs from its inclusion in the foreign system due to differences in accounting rules. Here, the timing rules can cause the foreign tax and the corresponding domestic tax on the same income to fall in different accounting periods. Other timing differences can arise because of differences in the principles governing the allowance of deductions and the recognition of income. Beyond timing issues, a broader policy question is the extent to which temporal averaging between high- and low-taxed foreign source income should be allowed as a general matter.

Assuming that some type of temporal averaging is desirable, the question with respect to technical structure is whether the excess taxes themselves should be carried over to other periods in which there is an "excess limitation" or whether the excess limitation should be allowed in the year the taxes were incurred. Most of the systems use the tax-carryover method and allow varying degrees of temporal averaging. The structure of the rules is generally the same, although the (essentially arbitrary) periods of carryover differ. The carryover periods may sometimes relate to statute-of-limitations periods.

In the *United States*, excess credits generally can be carried back one year and forward ten years, subject to the availability of excess limitation in the appropriate basket.[213] However, FTCs in the new GILTI basket cannot be carried back or forward, thus increasing the likelihood of unused FTCs.[214]

---

212. *CIT v. Bombay Burmah Trading Corporation Ltd*, Bombay High Court, November 22, 2002.
213. United States, IRC, s. 904(c).
214. *Ibid.*

In *Canada*, excess foreign business taxes can be carried back three years and forward ten years.[215] No carryforward is allowed for excess taxes arising in connection with nonbusiness income but the excess can be deducted in the year incurred.

In the context of the overall limitation system in *Japan*, excess credits can be carried forward three years. In addition, any excess limitation from the preceding three years can be carried forward and excess credits can be absorbed in the current year to that extent.[216] Any remaining excess credit is then carried forward.

China and *Sweden* similarly allow a five-year and four-year carryforward, respectively, but no carryback.

Australia previously allowed a five-year carryforward of excess credits, but this was abolished in the simplification of the regime in 2008 as a counterbalance to the removal of the previous four baskets, with transitional relief for excess FTCs of the previous five years. Under the current worldwide limitation, no carryover of excess credits is permitted. Timing differences are dealt with by moving the foreign tax for credit purposes to the year Australia taxed the equivalent income, even if the foreign tax is paid in a different (earlier or later) year.[217] The permitted period for amendment of the credit calculation is four years from the date of payment of the foreign tax, rather than from the year for which the credit is claimed, so that foreign tax paid later can be credited even if the payment is made many years later.

In *The Netherlands*, an unlimited carryforward applies. In contrast, no carryover at all is allowed under the *Indian* and the *United Kingdom* direct FTC system. However, since 2001, excess credits attributable to a foreign PE of a UK-resident company may be carried back three years and forward indefinitely.[218] Of course, this carryover is irrelevant where the payer has elected for exemption of the profits of a foreign PE. *Germany* also has a restrictive system which does not allow any carryforward or carryback for excess credits. As a partial response to the problem, taxpayers can elect (on a country-by-country basis) to deduct rather than credit the foreign taxes.

3.1.6 Indirect Credit for Foreign Taxes Paid by Foreign Subsidiaries

In all the systems, there is some mechanism for eliminating or reducing multiple burdens of corporate-level tax when corporate profits are distributed by domestic corporations to domestic corporate shareholders. Similarly, all the systems have some form of relief where the distributing corporation is a foreign corporation. This relief can be seen as performing two functions. First, in the domestic context, it avoids a cascading of corporate-level taxes. Second, at the same time, it relieves the potential international double taxation which would result from the taxation of profits in the state where they are earned as well as in the state of residence of the shareholder. This second effect also makes more comparable the treatment of foreign operations carried out through foreign branches and foreign subsidiaries.

215. Canada, ITA, s. 126(2).
216. Japan, ITA, s. 95, para. 2 and Japan, CTA, s. 69, para. 2.
217. Australia, ITAA 1997, s. 770-10, Note 1.
218. United Kingdom, Taxation (International and Other Provisions) Act 2010, s. 73.

Several countries considered here deal with the problem of multiple corporate taxation in general by exempting most intercorporate dividends from the tax base. *Canada, China, France,* and *Sweden* use or have used an indirect credit system in some situations, but the exemption of foreign corporate dividends is much more common in practice. In *Germany*, the full abolition of taxes on dividends from domestic or foreign shareholdings (unless the share amounts to less than 10% of the company's capital)[219] has rendered the previous application of an indirect tax credit superfluous. A related issue comes up under the German CFC rules, which require an indirect tax credit to be granted for a foreign subsidiary's income imputed to the domestic shareholder.[220]

Similarly, when *Australia* and *Japan* adopted an exemption system for dividends received by a resident company, the indirect credit was eliminated. When the *United Kingdom* did so, it provided an option for taxpayers to continue to apply the indirect FTC. *The Netherlands* uses an exemption method exclusively. The issues which the exemption system raises are considered below.

3.1.6.1 Share-Ownership Requirements

As is usually the case with respect to relief from domestic multiple taxation, all the systems require some minimum level of shareholding before an "indirect" FTC is given for foreign taxes paid by the distributing corporation. The requirements are based in part on considerations of administrative simplicity and in part on the more basic notion that the function of the credit is to relieve international double taxation on "direct" foreign investment rather than on portfolio investment.

The basic requirement in the *United States* is that the U.S. corporate shareholder must own directly a 10% or greater interest by vote or value in stock of the foreign corporation. From 2018 onward, the use of an indirect credit as a method of relief from multiple levels of corporate taxation is applicable only to U.S. corporate shareholders with Subpart F and GILTI income.[221] Any residual income received from their foreign corporations brings a 100% dividends-received deduction.[222] To the extent that the *United Kingdom* continues to apply an indirect FTC system (from 2009, most dividends from foreign subsidiaries are exempt), it also has a 10% voting-stock threshold.[223] The *Canadian* test is more liberal, allowing the credit where a 10% or greater interest in any class of shares is present and held directly or indirectly. Moreover, the ownership threshold is determined merely by reference to the number of shares of the class owned by the Canadian corporation, not by reference to votes or value. *Japan* had required 25% ownership of an equity interest in the foreign corporation to be eligible for the indirect tax credit, subject to the reduced threshold of 15% or 10% in some tax treaties; this 25% requirement, together with the reduced threshold under those treaties, has been maintained for the new exemption system. The ownership threshold for the

219. Germany, CITA, s. 8b, para. 4.
220. Germany, Foreign Transactions Tax Act (*Außensteuergsetz*), s. 12, para. 1.
221. United States, IRC, s. 951(a), 951A.
222. United States, IRC, s. 245A.
223. United Kingdom, Taxation (International and Other Provisions) Act 2010, s. 14.

Chinese indirect FTC is 20% of the equity interests in the foreign corporation, reduced to 10% in several tax treaties.

3.1.6.2 *Tier Limitations*

The problem of multiple layers of corporate tax also exists where the first-tier foreign corporation itself receives distributions from lower-tier corporations. *Canada* allows the credit without restriction as to the corporate tier at which the tax was paid, as long as the ultimate domestic shareholder owns, directly or indirectly, the requisite 10% stock interest. Similarly, under the *United Kingdom* system, indirect credit is available with no limits on the number of tiers.[224]

China allows the indirect credit for five tiers (before 2017, only three tiers were allowed).

3.1.6.3 *Computation of the Indirect Credit*

The computation of the indirect credit involves several structural issues. The profit distributions (or in the case of the United States, income inclusions under Subpart F or GILTI by a corporate shareholder) must be related to particular profits of the foreign corporation and foreign taxes must be attributed to those profits. In addition, since the actual dividend (or, in the case of the United States, income inclusion) brings with it the indirect credit, the amount of the dividend (or inclusion under Subpart F or GILTI) should in principle be "grossed up" so that the foreign tax itself is included in the domestic tax base.

In the *United States*, profits and associated taxes were initially computed on an annual, last-in, first-out basis. That approach encouraged tax planning to artificially increase taxes from which distributions were made and also created technical difficulties where years with deficits in earnings occurred. In 1986, the system was replaced with a "cumulative pooling" approach, which pools all earnings and foreign taxes (on a prospective basis) and treats all distributions as bringing back the appropriate portion of the total pool.[225] However, the 2017 tax reform introduced the 100% dividends-received deduction for U.S. corporate shareholders on their foreign dividends, thus ending the use of the indirect credit on dividends received by U.S. corporate shareholders of foreign corporations. Nevertheless, the need for an indirect credit remains for those U.S. corporate shareholders that are required to include income under Subpart F or GILTI. In those cases, the indirect credit is determined on a current year, not a pooling basis.[226] Indirect credits are "grossed up" in the computation of the domestic parent's income.[227]

The *Canadian* system is complicated by the fact that distributions from "taxable surplus" and "hybrid surplus" (limited to certain capital gains) bring with them the

224. United Kingdom, Taxation (International and Other Provisions) Act 2010, ss. 63-65.
225. United States, IRC, s. 904(c).
226. United States, IRC, s. 960.
227. United States, IRC, s. 78.

functional equivalent of a credit, and distributions from "exempt surplus" are exempt. In general, foreign taxes are allocated among the three categories on a "reasonable in the circumstances" basis. Distributions are deemed to be first out of the "pool" of exempt surplus, then out of hybrid surplus and thereafter out of taxable surplus, where the calculation of the credit-equivalent deduction is made.

In *China*, foreign tax paid and attributable to the dividends received by a Chinese resident is computed from the lowest tier of creditable foreign subsidiary. With the approval of the in-charge tax authority, a taxpayer may adopt a simplified method to claim tax of 12.5% of taxable dividends received from a foreign country where the following conditions are met: the taxpayer can produce evidence issued by the foreign tax authority for the payment of tax, but cannot determine the true and accurate amount of foreign tax due to uncontrollable (objective) reasons; and the effective tax rate (ETR) in the foreign country is not less than 12.5% (i.e., 50% of the Chinese Enterprise Income Tax (EIT) rate).

3.1.7 Interaction Between Indirect Credit and Limitation System

Where the ability to average is limited by some kind of basket system, that limitation must be coordinated with the indirect credit. "Passing through" the various basket limitations is necessarily complex and is a function of the underlying complexity of the basket system itself. It involves the treatment of distributions in the form of both dividends and deductible payments, such as interest and royalties, which can be viewed as being paid "out of" the various basket categories.

The problem is most acute in the *United States* because of the extensive use of the complex basket structure in its limitation rules. In general, Subpart F income in respect of a foreign corporation is deemed to be in the passive basket for FTC purposes to the extent that the amount is attributable to passive income.[228] GILTI income included from a CFC is placed in its own GILTI FTC basket.[229]

In *Canada*, while a distinction is made between distributions out of exempt surplus, hybrid surplus, and taxable surplus, no attempt is made to pass through the normal per-country limitation in the case of taxable dividends which qualify for the indirect credit. Thus, it is possible for high and low foreign taxes to be averaged. However, the effective credit is limited on an overall basis with respect to the foreign affiliate paying the dividend to the amount of Canadian tax on the dividend.

3.2 Issues in the Structure of an Exemption for Foreign Income

3.2.1 Structure of the Exemption

Where foreign income of a resident taxpayer is exempt from tax, the structure of the exemption can take several forms. The most extensive is to exclude the income from

228. United States, IRC, s. 904(d)(4).
229. United States, IRC, s. 904(d)(1)(A).

the coverage of the tax system altogether simply by not asserting jurisdiction to tax the income. Thus, for example, in *France*, in the case of business income, the tax base for resident corporations is limited to income arising in France; in principle, business income attributable to a foreign trade or business is not subject to tax. The same holds true in *Germany* with regard to trade tax which, under the domestic tax regime, requires a business to be carried on in a specific municipality. Alternatively, as in *Canada*, the foreign income can be included for certain purposes, although ultimately relieved from tax liability. One approach ("exemption with progression") is to calculate the tax liability which would have resulted if the income had been included and then apply the resulting rate of tax only to the included income. This is the approach taken, for example, in Germany, where foreign income of a resident individual is exempt under a tax treaty. But under domestic tax law, the German legislature has waived the right to apply exemption with progression with regard to income derived from EU/EEA countries in order to avoid the necessity to grant "negative progression" in case of foreign losses.[230] Another approach is to "stack" the excluded income in the lower progressive rates in calculating the rates applicable to the taxable income. This approach has been used in the past in *Australia* and the *United States* in connection with the exemption for foreign-earned income.

3.2.2 Classes of Exempt Income

As indicated above, none of the systems exempts all foreign source income of resident taxpayers. Thus, rules must be provided to classify exempt foreign income and includable income, with a credit for foreign taxes typically given for foreign taxes on includable income. The distinction is usually between active income such as business income, either earned directly in a foreign branch or as a dividend from a qualifying foreign subsidiary, and portfolio income in the form of interest, royalties, and other passive income. Sometimes there is a requirement that the exempt income, either actually or in principle, must be subject to tax in the foreign jurisdiction. In other cases, the exemption is restricted to income from certain countries (e.g., those with which the country has a tax treaty).

Thus, in *Canada*, which generally uses a FTC system, exemption is provided for dividends received out of the "exempt surplus" of foreign subsidiaries ("foreign affiliates") in which the Canadian corporate shareholder holds a 10% or greater stock interest.[231] Exempt surplus is defined as active business income earned in countries with which Canada has a tax treaty or tax information exchange agreement, as well as certain capital gains. The definition of active business income is quite complex and excludes income from certain real estate rental, licensing, financing, and investment businesses.[232] Pass-through rules apply which treat certain interest, royalties, and other deductible payments made out of the active business of one foreign affiliate to

230. Germany, ITA, s. 32b para. 1, s. 2.
231. Canada, ITA, s. 113(1)(a).
232. Canada, ITA, s. 95(1). The same definitions which apply for purposes of the CFC rules also apply for purposes of the dividend exemption.

another as active business income to the recipient. In addition, dividends received by one foreign affiliate from another are added to exempt surplus, hybrid surplus, or taxable surplus, depending on the surplus account of the payer from which the dividend is paid. An exemption is also provided for a limited amount of foreign employment income earned in qualifying activities.[233]

The *French* system exempts all income derived by French corporations from a trade or business carried on abroad, including passive income effectively connected to the trade or business. The level of activities qualifying as a trade or business is roughly equivalent to that of the treaty concept of PE.[234] In addition, an exclusion is granted for intercorporate dividends received from foreign subsidiary corporations under the same conditions as for investments in the domestic context, that is, in general, if there is a 5% or greater stock interest.[235] In both cases, the exemption is available whether or not any foreign tax is paid abroad.

As for individuals, bonuses and special payments for working abroad are generally exempt (with progression). In general, wages for working abroad are granted the same exemption if they bear a foreign income tax equal to two-thirds of the French tax otherwise due or if earned by workers involved in foreign construction, extraction, or commercial canvassing activities.[236]

In contrast, *Sweden* limits its exemption to dividends received from foreign corporations which are similar to Swedish limited corporations or cooperative associations in circumstances where the dividend would have been exempt under the domestic intercorporate dividends regime. An exception to this rule applies where the payment, considered in Sweden to be a dividend, is deducted for income tax purposes in the country of the payer.[237]

An exemption is also given to foreign source employment income where the Swedish resident is abroad for six months and the income is subject to tax in the foreign country or where the Swedish resident is abroad in the same country for at least a year, irrespective of the taxation of the income overseas.

Australia also exempts foreign business income of corporations. The exemption extends to profits and capital gains earned directly in branch form (unless the income would be taxed under the CFC regime if the foreign branch were a CFC) or foreign equity distributions (determined under the Australian debt-equity rules discussed in Part III) received by Australian corporate shareholders holding 10% or greater voting or dividend interests in foreign subsidiaries.[238] In the case of foreign companies, as opposed to branches, the CFC regime can apply if its threshold tests are satisfied, thus subjecting the income to current taxation in the hands of shareholders, whereas for branches such income is taxed directly to the company on a similar basis. Where

233. Canada, ITA, s. 122.3. Certain income derived by offshore banking centers was also exempt (s. 33.1), but this exemption, which was clearly a harmful tax practice, was repealed effective March 2013.
234. France, CGI, s. 209 I.
235. France, CGI, ss. 145 and 216.
236. France, CGI, s. 81 A.
237. Sweden, ITA, s. 24:39.
238. Australia, ITAA 1936, s. 23AH, 23AJ, ITAA 1997, Subdivs. 768-A, 768-G.

income is taxed under the CFC regime, it qualifies for a different exemption when distributed as dividends whether or not it would meet the requirements of the foreign equity distribution exemption. The main difference is that any withholding tax on such dividends is creditable under the FTC, which is not the case for dividend withholding tax on foreign equity distributions which qualify for the general exemption.[239] The theory underlying this different treatment is that the purpose of exemption for dividends out of previously taxed CFC income is to remove double counting of the income; through a combination of the CFC regime and special dividend exemption, effectively all the income is taxed, with credit for both corporate and dividend withholding tax.

Up to 2009, foreign employment income also qualified for exemption where the Australian resident was abroad for at least three months and the income was subject to tax (with some exceptions) in the foreign jurisdiction. An "exemption with progression" feature affects the taxation of other income based on average rates. From 2009, this exemption is limited to employees working on foreign aid and similar projects.[240]

The *Dutch* system is structured somewhat differently and is not formally an exemption system (except with respect to the exemption of the profits of a foreign PE), although in operation it has that result. Rather than technically exempting foreign income (an "income exemption"), initially, all income, both taxable and exempt, is included in the tax base and the tax calculated. The tax is then reduced by the percentage which the income qualifying for exemption is of the total income (referred to as a "tax exemption").

The exemption under domestic law applies to foreign income which is derived directly as business income from a foreign PE, income from foreign real property, or income from employment abroad where the income is "subject to tax" under an income tax in a foreign jurisdiction.[241] This requirement has been interpreted as requiring only that the income be "objectively" subject to tax; whether the particular taxpayer effectively pays tax on the income is not relevant.[242] In the case of employment income, the requirement is deemed to be met if the taxpayer is employed by a Dutch company or a company resident in an EU Member State and is employed abroad for a period of at least three months,[243] while in respect of employment abroad for less than thirty consecutive days, a stricter requirement applies: the income must have been taxed effectively in the foreign country.[244] Under tax treaties, no "subject-to-tax" requirement applies.

The most important aspect of the Dutch exemption system for dividends received by corporate shareholders is the extension of the domestic participation exemption to investments in foreign corporations. Dividends received by a 5% or greater domestic corporate shareholder from a foreign corporation are exempt from tax (completely and not proportionately) if the shares are not held as a "low-taxed portfolio" investment.

239. Australia, ITAA 1936, s. 23AI, ITAA 1997, s. 770-10(2).
240. Australia, ITAA 1936, s. 23AG.
241. Netherlands, DADT, Art. 9(1).
242. Netherlands, *see* e.g., *Hof's-Gravenhage*, November 13, 1995, No. 94/0888, V-N 1996, p. 2876.
243. Netherlands, GAT, Art. 38(2).
244. Netherlands, DADT, Art. 9(4).

Shares of a foreign corporation are not considered to be low-taxed portfolio investments where:

- the assets of the foreign corporation do not consist mainly, directly or indirectly, of "free investments";[245]
- the foreign corporation is not subject to foreign tax of less than 10% of the taxable profit calculated under Dutch rules;[246] and
- the foreign corporation is not a real estate investment company.[247]

Where the Dutch CFC rules apply, the participation exemption does not apply.[248]

Because foreign participation dividends are exempt, no credit as such is given for foreign withholding taxes imposed on foreign dividends. However, if certain conditions are met, a portion of the withholding tax on the "inbound" dividend is allowed to reduce the tax which the Dutch company must remit on the payment of "outbound" dividends.

Under *German* tax law, full unilateral exemptions apply only to dividends from foreign shareholdings where a corporate taxpayer holds 10% or more of the capital of the subsidiary.[249] An earlier version, which was even more liberal and provided for full exemption for all intercompany dividends, was abandoned after the CJEU required the German legislature to provide equal treatment of domestic and foreign corporate taxpayers receiving dividends.[250] Individual taxpayers can benefit from either a partial exemption (where shares are held in a business context in a wider sense)[251] or a reduced final withholding tax.[252] However, it should be kept in mind that these full and partial exemptions are not specific reliefs granted for foreign income. They developed out of the German shareholder relief system established for domestic dividends and aim at the equal treatment of domestic and foreign investment under the principles of free movement of capital and freedom of establishment set out in the TFEU. Moreover, these exemptions depend on the nondeductibility of the underlying payments at the level of the distributing company.[253]

With respect to treaty policy, in 2013, the German tax authorities explicitly set out their overarching policy in the "Basis for negotiation" mentioned above.[254] According to this document, most categories of income (immovable assets, employment, business carried on in a foreign PE) are subject to the exemption method, while investment

245. "Free investments" are investments other than those reasonably required for the business activities of the entity holding the investments. Free investments include assets which are used for direct or indirect financing of related entities or are made available to such entities for their use (e.g., through leasing), unless it is clear that these financing and leasing activities amount to "active" activities as defined in a ministerial decree. CITA, Art. 13(12).
246. Netherlands, CITA, Art. 13(13).
247. Netherlands, CITA, Art. 13.
248. Netherlands, CITA, Art. 13ab.
249. Germany, CITA, s. 8b paras. 1 and 4.
250. Case C-284/09, November 20, 2011 (*Commission v. Germany*).
251. Germany, ITA, s. 3 Nos. 40 and 32d para. 2 No. 3.
252. Germany, ITA, s. 32d para. 1.
253. Germany, CITA, s. 8 para. 1 s. 2; ITA, s. 3 No. 40 lit. d s. 2.
254. *See* below Subpart C, section 4.5 for a discussion of the German "model treaty."

income (dividends and interest) and other categories, such as directors' fees, income derived by artists and sportspersons, and pensions, are subject to the credit method.

The circumstances in which exemption is available vary substantially, with earlier treaties being less restrictive and newer ones typically restricting exemption to income from an active business or income which is subject to tax in the foreign jurisdiction. Foreign dividends are tax-free by virtue of a domestic statute. The only case in which income from foreign subsidiaries is subject to tax is where the CFC rules apply. As mentioned above, a recently enacted provision of the ITA functions as a "catch-all" switchover clause for exempted income which is not taxed in the other country, either due to a conflict in characterization or special rules in the source country.

The *United States* provides a limited exemption for foreign-earned income where the recipient is a foreign resident or is abroad for a substantial portion of the tax year.[255] The exemption is limited to USD 80,000, adjusted for inflation after 2004 (USD 126,500 in 2024) and does not involve "exemption with progression"; the exempt income reduces the applicable tax rate on the other items of taxable income. Beginning in 2018, U.S. corporate shareholders owning 10% or more of a foreign corporation receive a 100% dividends-received deduction on the receipt of a dividend distribution, effectively exempting the income.[256]

In addition, the 2017 tax reform introduced a new deduction (Foreign Derived Intangible Income (FDII)) for U.S. corporations, which, in effect, may serve as an export subsidy and may counter the potential incentive in the GILTI regime for U.S. corporations to move certain operations out of U.S. corporations and into foreign subsidiaries. Under GILTI, returns earned by a CFC in excess of the statutory 10% return on tangible assets is taxed currently to its U.S. shareholders (the elimination of deferral) but at a lower effective rate (10.5%) given the new deduction equal to 50% of GILTI income.[257] One concern is that after the introduction of GILTI, domestic corporations earning comparable foreign source income directly, but taxed currently at the statutory rate of 21%, would be at a disadvantage compared to U.S. multinationals earning that income through a CFC and taxed at the effective 10.5% GILTI rate (up to 13.125% with the reduction in FTCs on GILTI inclusions). This disadvantage could entice domestic corporations to shift the production of foreign income from domestic corporations to CFCs. The new FDII regime could counter this incentive by allowing a deduction equal to 37.5% of FDII. The deduction would produce a de facto rate reduction to 13.125% for the foreign source income generated by a U.S. corporation from specified activities to the extent that the returns exceed a statutory return on tangible assets.[258]

The *United Kingdom* predominantly uses the FTC system. However, as noted above, from 2009 there is a broad exemption for UK corporations receiving dividends from foreign corporations. This exemption extends to all dividends; it is not restricted

255. United States, IRC, s. 911.
256. United States, IRC, s. 245A.
257. United States, IRC, ss. 951A, 250.
258. United States, IRC, s. 250.

to nonportfolio dividends, as in most of the other countries.[259] From 2010, the United Kingdom also provides an election for exemption of foreign PE profits.

As discussed above, in 2009 *Japan*, which until then had relied solely on a tax credit system, introduced an exemption system for certain foreign dividends, replacing the indirect credit system. The exemption applies to dividends from a foreign company in which a Japanese company holds 25% or more of the equity ownership.[260] Other foreign-earned income remains subject to a FTC system. In general, *India* does not exempt foreign source income derived by residents of India except in very limited circumstances.

3.2.3 Allocation of Deductions to Tax Exempt Income

Where an exemption system is used to relieve international double taxation, in principle, the exemption should extend only to net foreign income. Accordingly, deductions related to exempt foreign source income should not be deductible against taxable domestic or foreign source income. The issue of allocation of deductions to exempt income is functionally the same as the allocation of deductions to foreign source income for limitation purposes in a credit system. Until recently, many of the countries reviewed here ignored this issue or restricted the deduction of interest on a tracing basis, making it relatively easy to avoid the allocation of interest expense to exempt income. Recently, however, some countries have become very concerned about the issue, especially with respect to the deduction of interest expense to earn exempt foreign income such as dividends.

In *Canada*, although expenses incurred to earn exempt income are not deductible as a general principle, there are no specific rules for allocation of deductions to exempt income and, in general, a factual tracing approach is used. The deduction of interest expense by Canadian companies in relation to exempt dividends received from foreign affiliates is not prohibited because dividends are expressly excluded from the definition of exempt income. The deduction of such interest expense is recognized as a problem by critics of the present system but is justified as important with respect to the international competitiveness of Canadian companies. A 2008 Advisory Panel recommended that Canada should not adopt any restrictions on the deduction of interest, even though at the same time it recommended that the exemption for foreign dividends be broadened. However, as noted below, in 2023 Canada introduced earnings-stripping rules based on the OECD BEPS Action 4 Report to limit the deduction of interest by resident and nonresident multinationals.

While *Sweden* has a relatively sophisticated mechanism for allocating interest expense of individuals between business and capital income, the rules in the international area have long been quite rudimentary. However, limitations on the deduction of interest expense have been introduced and can be said to exceed the requirements set

259. For example, *see* United Kingdom, Corporation Tax Act 2009, s. 931D.
260. Japan, CTA, s. 23-2.

by the EU ATAD,[261] although a reform is expected due partly to compatibility issues with EU law. *The Netherlands*, too, has no specific rules on the general allocation of deductions to exempt branch or participation income, although under the case law some sort of tracing approach is taken. For participation income, however, there is a specific rule with respect to interest paid on acquisition debt. The interest expense is not deductible unless bona fide commercial reasons apply or the parent is effectively taxed (i.e., tax is not reduced by existing or foreseeable loss carryovers, FTCs, etc.) at a rate of 10% (unless the tax authorities can demonstrate that the debt or underlying commercial transaction was not predominantly entered into for valid business reasons).

Australia uses allocation rules for exempt income similar to those used in the context of the FTC limitation discussed above in section 3.1.3. Expenses allocable exclusively to exempt foreign income are nondeductible in their entirety. Under case law, expenses allocable to both foreign and domestic income may be allocated in a manner which is reasonable. Deductions which cannot be allocated to particular income, such as charitable donations, are not prorated. Interest expense used to be allocated on a tracing basis generally, and this is still the case for the exempt income of a foreign branch of an Australian-resident company. From 2001, interest is deductible even where it relates to income from exempt foreign equity distributions on a tracing basis as long as the interest does not contravene the outbound thin capitalization regime, outlined below, in relation to source taxation.[262]

In *Germany*, deductions related to foreign source income, which qualifies for exemption, are disallowed under the general statutory provision dealing with expenses and tax-exempt income in general. Since this disallowance involves the nondeductibility of expenditures related to foreign businesses, it has major consequences for foreign PEs under the exemption method. In a recent judgment, the Federal Tax Court extended nondeductibility to costs incurred in a failed attempt to set up a foreign branch even though the foreign jurisdiction had never exercised taxing rights on a source basis.[263]

Moreover, additional limitations may arise out of the newly introduced general rules on deductibility of interest payments in the context of the BEPS Action 4 Report.[264] In the case of foreign dividends paid to domestic shareholders and exempt from tax under the Parent-Subsidiary Directive or a tax treaty, German tax law basically accepts the deductibility of income-related expenditure. Nevertheless, following the model set by the Parent-Subsidiary Directive, 5% of dividends are deemed to constitute nondeductible expenses, which effectively reduces the exemption to 95%.[265] While this sounds insignificant, it can have dramatic “cascading” effects in a chain of share investments in corporations.

261. *See* the discussion of the Swedish restrictions on the deduction of interest below in section 4, “Limitations on Base-Eroding Payments to Nonresidents.”
262. Australia, ITAA 1997, ss. 25-90.
263. Federal Tax Court (*Bundesfinanzhof*), July 9, 2014, I R 56/12.
264. *See* below section 4, “Limitations on Base-Eroding Payments to Nonresidents.”
265. Germany, CITA, s. 8b para. 5.

France has numerous rules limiting the deductibility of expenses, which have been modified and/or strengthened since the implementation of the ATAD I and ATAD II directives. There are two general mechanisms for limiting the rate of interest on loans[266] and the amount of such interest, depending on whether or not the company is a member of a group of companies.[267] Special mechanisms have also been introduced for hybrid arrangements.[268] In addition, and as discussed above with regard to foreign tax-free dividends, France considers that 1% or 5% (depending on the situation) are deemed to correspond to nondeductible expenses. Finally, a distinction is made between commercial and financial write-offs (*abandon de créances*). Indeed, commercial aid granted to a subsidiary or sister company is deductible, while financial aid is not.[269] This prohibition was introduced in 2012. As a result, there is now an outright ban on deductions for financial debt waivers granted for financial years ending on or after July 4, 2012 (except in cases where the recipient is in financial difficulty and subject to insolvency proceedings).

In the *United Kingdom*, expenses continue to be deductible for corporations even where, after 2009, they receive exempt foreign dividends.[270] The only substantial limitation is a general one: the deductibility of interest incurred by a UK corporation is subject to the interest restriction referred to in Part III (earnings-stripping rules) and in addition to the total amount of interest incurred by the corporation's worldwide group on borrowings from nonrelated parties.[271]

In *Japan*, 95% of dividends paid by a foreign company in which a Japanese company holds 25% or more of the shares is exempt from the taxable income of the Japanese company. The remaining 5%, which is included in the amount of taxable income, is intended to offset the deductibility of the expenses related to such exempt dividends, following the German approach.

3.2.4 *Treatment of Foreign Losses*

The treatment of foreign losses, that is, the excess of deductions allocated to foreign income over gross foreign income, also raises some special problems. In principle, the overall foreign loss arising in a situation which would be entitled to exemption should not reduce otherwise taxable domestic or foreign source income; the exemption is for the net foreign income and the existence of a foreign loss simply indicates that there is no net income to exempt. In systems which use an "exemption with progression" approach, however, a foreign loss may affect the rate of tax on domestic income ("negative" progression). Nonetheless, several of the jurisdictions have special rules for foreign losses which allow current deductions.

266. France, CGI, s. 39-1 3° CGI.
267. France, CGI, s. 212 bis (for non-group companies) and CGI s. 212 (for group companies).
268. France, CGI, s. 205 B to 205 D.
269. France, CGI, s. 39-13.
270. In the context of resident companies with investment business, such as holding shares in other companies, *see* United Kingdom, Corporation Tax Act 2009, s. 1222.
271. United Kingdom, Taxation (International and Other Provisions) Act, s. 400.

In *The Netherlands*, where a resident company derives business profits which are attributable to a foreign PE, these profits qualify for exemption, with the consequence that foreign losses attributable to the PE are not deductible.[272] Other foreign losses are deductible against domestic income on a per-country basis, i.e., even if other foreign income is positive. There is a recapture of the deducted loss in later years when the operations in the country which generated the loss become positive.[273] The per-country limitation was introduced in 1995. Prior to that time, foreign income and losses from nontreaty countries and under pre-1980 treaties were combined, and the resulting loss reduced domestic source income, with subsequent recharacterization as taxable income when any foreign source income was realized.

Where *Germany* exempts income under a treaty, in principle, foreign losses have no impact on German income. In a line of judgments, the Federal Tax Court emphasized the underlying "symmetry" of profits and losses.[274] In a landmark decision, the CJEU accepted the compatibility of this principle with the freedom of establishment for PEs located in other EU Member States.[275] Nevertheless, until recently, the CJEU required deductibility of "final" foreign losses in the residence state in order to avoid disproportionate disadvantages for cross-border investment.[276] Following a line of contradictory statements,[277] the CJEU finally stated in 2022 that foreign and domestic income are not "comparable" in the light of the fundamental freedoms, thus declaring that the full denial of the deduction of foreign losses under German tax law is in line with the Internal Market.[278]

The Federal Tax Court has also ruled that the "subject-to-tax" clauses established under German tax law for the exemption of foreign income (e.g., where the foreign tax authority does not recognize the existence of a PE on its territory) apply to foreign losses—thus forcing the German tax authorities to grant loss relief.[279] In contrast, the denial of loss offset applies if the foreign loss is "effectively" taken into account by the foreign jurisdiction, e.g., by including it in the local tax base.[280]

In *France*, the principle of territoriality applies for purposes of the corporate tax, the main consequence of which is that foreign losses incurred by a company cannot be taken into account. Moreover, France has recently been applying this principle more and more strictly, ending all the exceptions that existed in the past through various provisions such as the global and consolidated profit regimes (1965-2011), the provisions relating to establishments abroad (1972-2003), and the provisions relating to

272. Netherlands, CITA, Art. 15e.
273. Netherlands, DADT, Art. 12.
274. Federal Tax Court (*Bundesfinanzhof*), June 9, 2010, I R 107/09; February 5, 2014, I R 48/11.
275. CJEU, May 15, 2008, C-414/06 (*Lidl Belgium*).
276. Case C-414/06, *supra*.
277. Case C-388/14, December 17, 2015 (*Timac Agro*) (stating that domestic and foreign business income are not comparable in exemption cases); Case C-650/1, June 12, 2018 (*Bevola*) (reconfirming the earlier line of cases on final losses); Federal Tax Court (*Bundesfinanzhof*), February 22, 2017, I R 2/15.
278. Case C-538/20, September 22, 2022 (*W-AG*); the Federal Tax Court followed this route in its final judgment in this matter (*Bundesfinanzhof*), February 22, 2023, I R 32/18.
279. Federal Tax Court (*Bundesfinanzhof*), July 11, 2018, I R 52/16.
280. Federal Tax Court (Bundesfinanzhof), April 12, 2023, I R 44/22.

establishments abroad for small businesses (2009-2014). However, the CJEU's *Marks & Spencer* ruling raised the hopes of French cross-border groups which had benefited from the tax consolidation regime and thought they would be able to deduct "definitive" (final) losses incurred by a nonresident subsidiary from the overall income of the group consolidated in France. For the time being, French case law maintains a strict interpretation of the concept of definitive losses and does not allow the deduction of definitive losses incurred by a European subsidiary. Indeed, in the *Lucien Barrière* case,[281] the Conseil d'Etat refused to allow the appeal (despite the support of the public rapporteur), which might have made it possible to put a preliminary question to the CJEU on the application of the *Marks & Spencer* case law to the French system, as well as on the interpretation to be given to the notion of "definitive losses by virtue of a foreign tax law limiting the use of disposal losses." The issue has again been raised by two recent rulings of the French Administrative Court of Appeal, which recognized the possibility of setting off in France definitive losses incurred in another EU country against the results of the tax consolidation.[282] The decision of the Conseil d'Etat with respect to this strict French application of the concept of definitive loss is eagerly awaited.

Sweden introduced rules on the deduction of certain final foreign losses after its domestic group-contribution rules were found to be in breach of EU law. The new rules (*koncernavdrag*) define and compute strictly the final foreign losses which may be deducted in Sweden.[283]

Australia generally does not allow losses where foreign income is exempt, but this rule was modified in the thin capitalization regime to allow interest deductions relating to foreign equity distributions which are exempt. As discussed above, the *United Kingdom* now adopts a similar approach with respect to expenses incurred by UK corporations in deriving exempt foreign dividends.

In *India*, there are no special provisions in domestic law dealing with foreign losses.

4 LIMITATIONS ON EXEMPTION OR DEFERRAL OF INCOME OF FOREIGN CORPORATIONS

Under the basic jurisdictional principles discussed above, the foreign source income of a foreign corporation is not taxed to domestic shareholders when earned by the foreign corporation. Taxation occurs, if at all, when the income is distributed, and in the case of countries which use the exemption system to relieve international double taxation, even distributed income may not be subject to tax. In the systems under consideration here, the deferral of or exemption from tax for distributed income usually arose without much consideration of the tax policy implications of that result. Deferral seemed to be the natural consequence of the recognition of the separate existence of the foreign

281. *See* CAA Versailles, June 23, 2020, n° 19VE01012 (*Groupe Lucien Barrière*).
282. *See* CAA Paris, December 15, 2023, n° 21PA03001 (*Société Compagnie Plastic Omnium*) and CAA Paris, December 15, 2023, n° 21PA01850 (*Société Générale*).
283. Sweden, ITA, Ch. 35a.

corporation and the exemption of the distributed income when received by domestic shareholders was often consistent with the treatment of dividends received from domestic corporations.

All the systems, however, have recognized that the mechanical application of the basic rules can lead to tax results which are inappropriate in light of other aspects of the country's tax system. Thus, for example, if, as a general rule, dividends from a substantial participation in a foreign subsidiary are exempt from domestic tax but passive foreign income earned directly is taxed currently, it is questionable whether passive income earned by a foreign corporation and distributed to a domestic shareholder as a dividend should fall under the basic rule that foreign dividend income is exempt. Similarly, even if deferred taxation is taken as a basic principle, the avoidance of current domestic taxation on portfolio investment income by lodging investment assets in a foreign corporation formed in a tax haven jurisdiction would cause concern.

More generally, all the countries examined here have been forced, in varying degrees and at varying times, to reexamine the economic and commercial consequences which flow from the application of the historically accepted principles of residence taxation and methods of double tax relief. This process has produced a more explicit consideration of when (and whether) deferral or exemption is appropriate and has led to the introduction of special tax regimes which limit the tax advantages flowing from the normally applicable rules. Although the results of these changes differ in many respects, some basic themes recur and there has been much "borrowing" between systems, in terms of both concepts and technical rules.

All the systems considered here make some distinction between types or classes of income earned by foreign corporations with domestic shareholders. Active foreign business income is more likely to be entitled to deferral or exemption than passive portfolio or investment income. This distinction is sometimes based on considerations of capital import (or competitive) neutrality. Foreign business activities carried on in a foreign subsidiary must compete with local businesses, which face only the local tax rate; competitive considerations, it is argued, require exemption from, or at least deferral of, any additional domestic tax. These considerations are not present in the case of passive income. The distinction can also be seen as necessary to protect the domestic tax base in the case of "mobile" types of business income.

Most of the systems are also concerned with the level of foreign tax which the income arising in the foreign corporation bears. This may be tested by an explicit comparison of foreign and domestic rates on income earned, by some sort of minimum rate benchmark, or by the mere fact that the corporation is organized in a particular jurisdiction with a high or low tax rate.

Finally, many systems apply the limitations on deferral or exemption only in the case of a significant level of share ownership by domestic shareholders. In some cases, the foreign corporation must be controlled by domestic shareholders, while in others a significant but noncontrolling interest is sufficient. Where a significant level of domestic ownership is not present, other mechanisms are often employed to discourage domestic portfolio investors from transferring funds offshore to foreign-owned investment companies.

In the elaboration of these basic concepts, there is a wide variation in the lines drawn and the structure of the tax rules in each country. These differences result in part from different policy judgments and in part because of the choice of different techniques to implement similar policy decisions. In some countries, the issue of limitations on exemption and deferral arose only when exchange controls were eliminated, which made foreign investment possible, while in others they have been present in the system for a considerable period of time. Thus, some rules have grown "organically" while others have been enacted relatively quickly. The following material first examines limitations used by exemption countries and deferral countries where there is a significant level of domestic share ownership. The subsequent sections consider the response to domestic portfolio investment in foreign investment companies.

4.1 Limitations on Exemption or Deferral for Foreign Source Income Earned by Foreign Corporations with Significant Domestic Share Ownership

From a structural point of view, limitations on the exemption of foreign source income have arisen in several ways. First, as discussed above, the definition of the situations in which exemption is permitted itself typically restricts exemption to certain classes or categories of income. In addition, the general exemption rules are often limited by special provisions, typically enacted after the more general rules, which eliminate exemption in certain circumstances (e.g., where operations in tax havens are involved or the foreign income is of a certain type). The two approaches can obviously reach the same functional results, and it is partly a matter of historical accident which features appear as part of the "general" exemption definition and which take the form of special limitations.

In addition, all the countries which exempt dividends from foreign corporations have adopted CFC rules, under which certain income of certain foreign corporations controlled by residents, or in which residents have a substantial interest, is subject to domestic tax currently as the income is earned by the foreign corporation. CFC rules are discussed in the next section. There is obviously a close relationship between an exemption for dividends from foreign companies and CFC rules. CFC rules operate in part to protect the domestic tax base from the diversion of domestic income to a CFC. Where dividends from foreign companies are exempt, such income can be distributed by the CFC back to its residence country shareholders and received by them exempt from residence country tax. CFC rules restrict this result by taxing certain income of the CFC (primarily passive income which is easily shifted) to the resident shareholders currently. Notably, however, in most countries, the CFC rules and the exemption for dividends from foreign companies are not coextensive. Often the dividends or participation exemption applies to nonportfolio dividends (defined as dividends received by resident corporations owning a minimum percentage of the shares of the foreign corporation), whereas the CFC rules typically apply only to foreign corporations controlled (usually defined as the ownership of more than 50% of the voting shares) by residents.

Originally, in both *Australia* and *Canada*, the exemption for dividends from foreign corporations was limited to distributions out of active business income earned in countries where it was likely that the income would have borne significant foreign tax. In structural terms, this result was reached by the definition of income which qualified for exemption and the residence of the foreign corporation earning the income, rather than as a limitation on a broader class of exempt income. The Canadian approach causes enormous compliance and administrative problems because it requires foreign corporations to keep detailed surplus accounts in respect of the various types of income earned in accordance with Canadian tax rules. The Canadian exemption system was expanded in 2008 such that the foreign corporation can be resident in any country with which Canada has a tax treaty or a tax information exchange agreement, but the requirement to track surplus accounts remains. In Australia, the limit on the exemption was removed in 2004.

In contrast, in the *United Kingdom*, the system is much simpler: all dividends received by UK corporations from foreign corporations are exempt, and the CFC rules apply only to foreign corporations controlled by UK residents.

In *France*, intercorporate dividends distributed by foreign subsidiaries qualify for the intercorporate dividends exemption in the same way as domestic dividends and, under the territoriality principle, as a general matter, profits and losses arising in a foreign trade or business are not taken into account in determining the base for the French CIT. However, this treatment is limited where the corporate taxpayer is subject to the CFC rules in section 209B of the tax code. These rules, which were enacted in 1980, were modified in 2005 in order to comply with CJEU case law relating to the compatibility of domestic anti-avoidance provisions with the freedom-of-establishment principle.

4.2 Controlled Foreign Corporation Rules

Under CFC rules, the resident shareholders of a CFC are subject to residence country tax on their share of certain income of the CFC as it is earned without waiting for the shareholders to receive dividends. These rules are used both by countries which exempt dividends from foreign companies and countries which tax such dividends subject to direct and indirect FTCs, such as China. In the case of countries using the exemption method, CFC rules provide protection for the domestic tax base by effectively nullifying the exemption for foreign dividends. In the case of countries using the credit method, CFC rules limit the benefit of the deferral of residence country tax for income earned through a CFC, because otherwise there would be no residence country tax until the resident shareholders received dividends from the CFC or disposed of their shares in the CFC.

The BEPS Action 3 Final Report on CFC rules established best practices for countries to follow in designing CFC rules but did not recommend that all countries should adopt such rules. In 2016 the EU issued its ATAD I requiring all EU member countries to adopt CFC rules, although the minimum standards for those rules are not rigorous. Of the five EU member countries analyzed in this book, *The Netherlands* was the last to adopt CFC rules. The Dutch CFC rules, which became effective after 2018, apply to certain passive income items of CFCs and foreign PEs. An entity is a CFC of a Dutch entity where the Dutch entity has either a direct or indirect interest of more than 50% in the entity and the entity is subject to a foreign (statutory) tax rate of less than 9%, or is resident in a country which is included in the EU blacklist. Where the CFC rules apply, certain passive income of the CFC (such as dividends, interest, royalties, leasing income, and capital gains from the sale of shares) are taxed to the Dutch parent company at the standard CIT rate. The CFC rules do not apply where the passive income and capital gains of the CFC make up less than 30% of its total income, or where the CFC carries on substantial economic activities in its country of residence.

The *United States* has very extensive (and complex) rules limiting exemption of income earned through CFCs. Historically, limits on deferral for portfolio income of individuals were imposed in 1937 in the foreign personal holding company provisions. Those rules, which were repealed in 2004, restricted deferral for closely held, individually owned foreign corporations which had predominantly investment-type income.

In 1962, a comprehensive set of rules restricting deferral was enacted and became the predecessor of similar legislation in several other countries. The "Subpart F" rules, as they came to be known internationally, were the outcome of a complex legislative compromise between those favoring the complete elimination of deferral for the income of CFCs in all circumstances and those who argued for a more limited approach.

Broadly speaking, those supporting the elimination of deferral were arguing in terms of capital export neutrality and the need to eliminate the incentive which deferral gave for foreign investment. The justifications for continuing deferral were based on the asserted need to preserve the competitive position of U.S. enterprises in foreign markets. The resulting compromise eliminated deferral for passive income, about which there could be no argument based on competitive considerations, and so-called base company income resulting from transactions between related parties, where income can be said to have been diverted through a related company. In those situations, the undistributed income of the foreign corporation must be included currently by the U.S. shareholder. More technically, exemption is eliminated for the "Subpart F income"[284] earned by a "CFC."[285]

While the definition of Subpart F income is extremely complex, two basic strands run through the provisions. One is the attempt to distinguish between passive investment-type income and business income. Thus, for example, rents and royalties are normally included in Subpart F income but are excluded if they are derived in the active conduct of a trade or business.[286] Similarly, income from dealings in commodity transactions is generally covered but is excluded if it arises from a hedging transaction carried out in the normal course of the business of a producer or processor. Second, the

284. United States, IRC, s. 952.
285. United States, IRC, s. 957(a).
286. United States, IRC, s. 954(c)(2).

provisions attempt to define those situations where the foreign corporation is being used as a "base company." This second strand of the definition of Subpart F income is aimed at transactions with related parties which have no significant economic connection with the "base" country jurisdiction. On the one hand, a typical situation covered by the provisions is the purchase of goods manufactured by a related party and the subsequent sale of the goods outside the country of incorporation of the selling "base" company. On the other hand, where the goods are sold in the country of incorporation or manufactured there and are sold to related parties in other jurisdictions, no Subpart F income arises.[287]

These basic rules are hedged with a number of exceedingly complex refinements. For example, transactions carried out through branches rather than separately incorporated corporations can generate base company income if the overall result has the same economic effect as a related-company transaction.[288] An overall relief provision excludes from the definition of base company income any item of income which bears a rate of tax equal to 90% of the maximum U.S. corporate rate, and a *de minimis* rule exempts the lesser of 5% of the foreign corporation's gross income or USD 1,000,000.

In addition to covering passive and base company income, the Subpart F provisions deal with a number of other situations where, for various reasons, the legislative decision was made that deferral, and now exemption, is inappropriate. Thus, exemption is denied for income arising in connection with an international boycott, for certain bribes or illegal payments, and for income attributable to countries which the United States does not recognize diplomatically.

The overall impact of the Subpart F rules was substantially weakened in 2006 with the introduction of a new provision which made it possible, in effect, to transfer profits between CFCs without incurring current U.S. tax. Deductible payments such as interest, rents, and royalties can be made between related parties without the receipt of the payments being treated as Subpart F income in the hands of the recipient CFC. As a result, payments can be channeled from one operating company through a tax haven to another operating company without running afoul of Subpart F.[289]

The 2017 tax reform, however, significantly moved the U.S. tax system further in the direction of worldwide taxation. Under the GILTI rules, U.S.-resident corporations are subject to a minimum tax (equal to 10.5%, i.e., 50% of the regular U.S. tax rate of 21%) on their share of all the income of their CFCs (other than their Subpart F income) in excess of a 10% return on the CFCs' tangible assets. Only 80% of the foreign tax paid by a CFC on its GILTI is creditable against the U.S. minimum tax. The U.S. GILTI rules appear to be the initial basis for the proposal of the Inclusive Framework for the adoption of a global minimum tax on CFCs (Pillar Two) (*see* the discussion of the Inclusive Framework's proposals below in Subpart C, section 9).

The inclusion of the new GILTI regime, as a complement to the existing Subpart F regime, expands the current taxation of CFC profits. To the extent that much CFC income is now taxed immediately to U.S. shareholders, the separate accounting for

287. United States, IRC, s. 954(d).
288. United States, IRC, s. 954(d)(2).
289. United States, IRC, s. 954(c)(6).

shareholders and subsidiaries reflected in the deferral compromise in 1962 has been undone and U.S. tax reform has expanded immediate worldwide taxation. But any effort to easily characterize the policy shift in international tax represented by the 2017 tax reform was forestalled by the simultaneous enactment of the 100% dividends-received deductions (comparable to a participation exemption) for U.S. corporate shareholders of CFCs.[290] If much of a CFC's income is captured by neither Subpart F nor GILTI, then the dividends-received deduction available on distributions to U.S. corporate shareholders marks a shift toward an exemption system.

Currently, there is discussion in the United States as to the net effect of the GILTI and Subpart F regimes on various businesses. Some observers have suggested that, at least in some industries where tangible assets are less significant, much of the income earned by a U.S. corporation through its foreign subsidiary will be subject to current taxation in the United States through Subpart F and GILTI, leaving little CFC income to benefit from the dividends-received deduction. In contrast, for CFCs engaged in tangible-asset-intensive activities, such as manufacturing, a much smaller portion of CFC income might be covered by Subpart F and GILTI. Most of such a CFC's income could be distributed to U.S. corporate shareholders with no U.S. taxation due to the dividends-received deduction, thereby ensuring permanent exemption from U.S. tax. To summarize, the 2017 tax reform expanded worldwide taxation with the new GILTI regime while simultaneously introducing new important exemption opportunities through the new dividends-received deduction. The net effect for the U.S. tax system overall will ultimately depend on which regime proves more dominant in practice.

Under either Subpart F or the GILTI regime, current taxation of undistributed income occurs only where the income is earned by a CFC. CFC status, in turn, requires that over 50% of the stock (in terms of either voting power or value) is owned by "United States shareholders"—that is, U.S. persons who own, either directly or by attribution through foreign entities, at least 10% of the votes or value of the foreign corporation. Thus, the focus is on control lodged in concentrated U.S. ownership.[291] For example, CFC status is avoided if eleven unrelated persons own ratably 100% of the voting stock of a foreign corporation or exactly 50% of the voting stock is owned by one U.S. person, with the remainder held by foreign persons.

In general, the rules limiting exemption or deferral in other jurisdictions are more restricted in scope. Their focus is primarily on passive income and income which could be said to have been diverted from domestic taxation without any "real" activity by the foreign corporation in a "real" foreign jurisdiction.

Thus, in *Canadian* legislation, exemption is eliminated only for passive income (foreign accrual property income (FAPI)), which is currently taxable to the Canadian shareholders of a CFC regardless of the level of foreign tax imposed on the income.[292] There is a limited concept of base company income, and the use of tax haven subsidiaries for most sales and services transactions is accepted as necessary to support the international competitiveness of Canadian corporations. Thus, the scope of the

290. United States, IRC, s. 245A.
291. United States, IRC, s. 957(a).
292. The Canadian CFC rules are found for the most part in ITA, ss. 91-95.

Canadian rules is limited to passive income and business income derived from transactions with Canada which directly erode the Canadian tax base. The basic pattern of taxation, however, is quite similar to that found in Subpart F.

The Canadian CFC rules apply only to the FAPI of a "controlled foreign affiliate," defined as a foreign corporation which is controlled directly or indirectly by five or fewer Canadian residents. Unlike in the United States, there is no minimum shareholding requirement for determining control. FAPI (in excess of an insignificant *de minimis* amount of CAD 5,000 for each foreign affiliate) is included directly in the income of 10% or greater shareholders (individuals or corporations). FAPI of lower-tier corporations is attributed directly to the Canadian shareholders. A credit is allowed for the Canadian shareholders' portion of the foreign taxes imposed on the FAPI of the controlled foreign affiliate. The basis of the shares is increased by the amount of the income inclusion. Subsequent distributions of the income as dividends are tax-free, and a credit is allowed for withholding tax on the dividend if the distribution is made within five years of the inclusion in income of the FAPI.

The *Japanese* CFC regime has become much more complicated and effective over the years. Introduced in 1978 as a crude countermeasure against tax avoidance practices taking advantage of tax havens and low-tax jurisdictions, the regime was intended to capture the entire undistributed profits of CFCs located in certain blacklisted jurisdictions. The drafters considered the income approach in U.S. Subpart F to be overly complex and compromised with entity/jurisdiction-based rules. The blacklist method was replaced with a "low tax rate" regime in 1992; any CFCs whose ETR fell below 25% were captured, unless certain exemption conditions (e.g., active CFC business operations) were met. The low rate was reduced to 20% in 2010, following the global trend of lower CIT rates. In response to the introduction of the exemption system for certain foreign affiliate dividends in 2009, the 2010 amendment was a significant step toward an income-based approach. After the 2010 amendment: (i) it was no longer the undistributed or "retained" profits of CFCs, but all the after-tax profits of CFCs, which became subject to current taxation in the hands of their Japanese shareholders; and (ii) certain types of passive income of CFCs became taxable in the hands of their shareholders, even if such CFCs met the exemption criteria from the entity-based current taxation of CFC income.

The 2017 amendment further complicated the Japanese CFC regime. All technicalities aside, this 2017 regime (the current rules) divides CFCs into three categories; (a) CFCs meeting all the substantive economic activity tests: engaging in active business, with actual operations and management in the same jurisdiction, or alternatively, dealing with unrelated parties, etc., (b) CFCs that do not meet any of these economic activity tests, and (c) certain "suspicious category" CFCs (e.g., shell companies, cash-box subsidiaries, etc.).[293] CFCs falling in category (a) are subject to "partial" taxation on certain types of passive income, unless the ETR applicable to such CFCs is 20% or higher; those in category (b) are subject to "entity-based" taxation on their entire after-tax profits, unless the ETR applicable to such CFCs is 20% or higher; and

293. Japan, STMA, ss. 40-4 and 66-6.

finally, those in category (c) are automatically subject to CFC taxation. Ultimately, the Japanese CFC rules have become a complex hybrid of rules taxing both certain types of passive income (as many jurisdictions do) and the entire profits of certain "suspicious" CFCs located in low-tax jurisdictions.

The CFC rules apply to an "affiliated foreign corporation," (the term for a CFC in Japan.) which is defined to be a corporation in which Japanese residents (individuals and corporations) hold the majority of the capital shares. There is no minimum shareholding requirement for testing this requirement in respect of direct shareholding, but only majority owners are counted for indirect shareholdings. Only those shareholders who own 5% or more of the shares of an affiliated foreign corporation, or who are part of an affiliated corporate group which owns 5% or more of the shares, are subject to current taxation on the profits of CFCs.

The CFC rules distinguish between CFCs that have good economic reasons for being located in low-tax jurisdictions and "suspicious" CFCs that do not. For this purpose, a CFC is considered to have good economic reasons for being in a jurisdiction if it engages in active business, has fixed assets in the jurisdiction, carries out local managerial activities, and operates its principal business in that location or deals mostly with unrelated parties. If a CFC fails to meet any of these tests, its Japanese shareholders are potentially subject to current taxation on its entire profits. Financial and transportation businesses have difficulty meeting these economic activity tests and are subject to an alternate test of generating more than 50% of their gross income from dealings with unrelated parties. If a CFC falls within the "suspicious category," such as shell companies, cash boxes, and those located in certain listed non-cooperative jurisdictions for tax purposes, it is subject to entity-level taxation on all its CFC profits.

Certain income and entities are exempt from CFC taxation. As outlined above, category (a) CFCs are exempt from taxation on certain types of passive income, category (b) CFCs are exempt from taxation on all their profits if their ETR is no less than 20%, and "suspicious" category (c) CFCs are still exempt if the applicable ETR is no less than 27% (reduced from 30% since April 2024). These applicable ETRs are computed on an entity basis, i.e., the ETR in the jurisdiction in which the CFC is established. In order to reduce taxpayer compliance costs, where the ETRs are clearly above the threshold, taxpayers are exempt from the substantive economic activity tests.

Sweden takes yet another approach. Prior to 1990, there were no restrictions on the deferral of foreign income earned in foreign corporations, which was not regarded as a problem at the time because exchange controls effectively prevented the use of foreign corporations for portfolio investments and deferral was deemed to be appropriate for ordinary corporate activities. When exchange controls were eliminated, restrictions were imposed on deferral through the use of CFC rules.[294] This legislation was substantially amended in 2003 and 2007, and then again in 2018, in order to implement the provisions of the EU ATAD. Under the Swedish legislation, a Swedish shareholder with a 25% or greater interest (votes or value) directly or indirectly in a

294. Sweden, ITA, Ch. 39 a.

foreign corporation is taxed currently on the income of the foreign corporation where the corporation tax paid abroad is less than 55% of the Swedish rate (11.33%). In addition, the legislation is accompanied by a "white list" of countries to which the CFC rules do not apply if the foreign corporation is subject to "normal" taxation there. For countries not on the "white list," which includes uncooperative tax havens under the OECD Harmful Tax Competition project and special regimes, the CFC rules tax the income directly to the Swedish shareholder with a corresponding credit for any foreign tax paid. Under the 2007 amendments, which were enacted to adapt the CFC rules to the decision of the CJEU in *Cadbury Schweppes*,[295] income of foreign corporations within the EEA is exempt from the Swedish CFC rules if the foreign corporation is "genuinely established" in the foreign state. The rules mention a number of factors for deciding whether there is a genuine establishment. The rule has been criticized for being more restrictive than required by the CJEU's decision.

Where income is subject to current tax, there is intentionally no basis adjustment in the shares so that the same income could be taxed again on the sale of the shares. Subsequent dividends, however, are exempt from tax and the capital gain can be avoided by timely distributions.

The *United Kingdom* CFC legislation is focused on corporations resident outside the United Kingdom and controlled by UK residents.[296] Control is defined as a more than 50% interest in the shares, voting power, profits, or assets of a company (but the level can be as low as 40% where no other person has a 55% interest); no minimum shareholding level is used in making this determination; however, only UK-resident companies with at least a 25% interest in the foreign company are attributed the undistributed profits.[297]

Since 2012, the UK CFC rules attribute only income which passes one of the "gateway" tests ("chargeable profits"), a tainted-income approach.[298] There are essentially five separate gateways—profits attributable to UK "significant people functions"; nontrading finance profits; trading finance profits; profits of captive insurance businesses; and profits of certain bank subsidiaries. The gateways incorporate various exemptions. These include: an exemption for companies resident in certain listed countries; a *de minimis* exemption of GBP 50,000 profits; an exemption for companies with substantial expenses; and an exemption where tax paid by the CFC is 75% or more of the tax that would have been paid if the CFC were resident in the United Kingdom.[299]

In addition to the above regime, there is a provision attributing the capital gains of a nonresident company to its "members" where the company would have been classified as "closely held" had it been a UK resident.[300] Following a challenge before the CJEU, this provision was amended to exclude gains on assets used for "a foreign trade or other economically significant foreign activities."

295. CJEU, C-196/04 September 12, 2006 (*Cadbury Schweppes*).
296. United Kingdom, Taxation (International and Other Provisions) Act 2010, Part 9A.
297. United Kingdom, Taxation (International and Other Provisions) Act 2010, s. 371BC and 371BD.
298. United Kingdom, Taxation (International and Other Provisions) Act 2010, Part 9A, Chs. 3 to 8.
299. United Kingdom, Taxation (International and Other Provisions) Act 2010, Part 9A, Chs. 11 to 14.
300. United Kingdom, TCGA, s. 3.

The *German* provisions,[301] which originally followed the U.S. model, were introduced in 1972. They are focused on "tainted" income realized by German CFCs in low-tax jurisdictions. While the institutional design of CFC legislation has remained rather stable over the last several decades, the underlying rationale, as well as many details, have changed dramatically over the years. A wide-reaching tax exemption for intercompany dividends was introduced in 2001, along with the application of the "modified part-income method" for shareholders who are individual taxpayers; with these measures, it became clear that the future purpose of CFC rules would go beyond taxing "deemed dividends," aiming instead at ensuring an overall minimum level of taxation on the profits of foreign subsidiaries. In 2021, the German CFC regime underwent another major reconfiguration.

In recent years, the impact of EU law has become overwhelming, but with somewhat countervailing effects. On the one hand, the compatibility of German CFC rules with EU law was highly disputed. Following the CJEU decision in *Cadbury Schweppes*,[302] the German rules were restricted to CFCs lacking economic substance, although borderline cases are still highly debated;[303] this requirement might also cover some subsidiaries outside the EU with respect to the "free movement of capital."[304] On the other hand, Article 7 of the 2016 EU ATAD[305] establishes a mandatory minimum standard for CFC legislation as applied by Member States. Against this background, the German coalition government implemented a major reform of CFC legislation in 2021.

Under the current rules, where income is attributed to German shareholders, it is characterized as capital income.[306] The attribution of income takes place even where treaty rules provide for a "participation exemption" for dividends. This aspect of the revised CFC legislation has been subject to criticism as an implicit "treaty override."

With respect to the requirements for the application of the German CFC rules, "tainted" income is defined indirectly by excluding from the definition most active business income, including income from manufacturing, agriculture, banking and insurance, local distribution, and processing.[307] Income from trading and services is generally active income where a foreign corporation conducts its business operations without assistance from the German shareholder and deals with the public, even if the goods are purchased from related parties. Thus, many situations which would be treated as base company sales or services income under the United States Subpart F rules would not be covered by the German provisions.

As of 2023, a foreign corporation is subject to low tax if it pays tax on a residence basis at a rate of less than 15%.[308]

301. *See* Germany, Foreign Transactions Tax Act (*Aussensteuergesetz*), ss. 7-14.
302. *Supra* note 295.
303. Germany, Foreign Transactions Tax Act (*Aussensteuergesetz*), s. 8 paras. 2-4.
304. CJEU, (C-135/17), February 26, 2019 (*X GmbH*).
305. EU, ATAD I (EU), 2016/1164.
306. Germany, Foreign Transactions Tax Act (*Aussensteuergesetz*) s. 10 para. 2.
307. Germany, Foreign Transactions Tax Act (*Aussensteuergesetz*), s. 8.
308. Germany, Foreign Transactions Tax Act (*Aussensteuergesetz*), s. 8 para. 5; this threshold was introduced in 2023 in the context of the implementation of the EU Minimum Tax Directive (between 1972 and 2022 the threshold was 25%).

Germany used to apply a broad notion of "control." Control was defined as more than 50% of the votes or number of shares held by German residents with the attribution of ownership of shares through other corporations or partnerships;[309] the rules also included former German residents who had moved to low-tax jurisdictions. This situation changed with the 2021 tax reform. Under those rules, CFC treatment applies only where the domestic taxpayer—alone or in concert with related persons—holds (directly or indirectly) more than 50% of the voting rights or share capital in the foreign company or is entitled to receive more than 50% of the profits or liquidating distribution of the foreign company.[310] Only for foreign companies deriving substantial income from portfolio capital (more than 10% of the company's income or more than EUR 80,000) is there no minimum ownership requirement. In addition, where the foreign company is listed on a regulated stock market and the shareholding of the domestic investor is below 1%, the CFC rules do not apply. Finally, the German CFC legislation applies to both individual and corporate shareholders.

Where income is attributed, foreign taxes can be credited;[311] subsequent distributions are not tax-exempt per se but receive beneficial treatment. Partial or full tax exemptions applicable to regular dividends apply and the amount that was previously taxed under the CFC rules is deducted from the cost base of the shares at the level of the shareholder on distribution.[312]

The *Australian* approach to restrictions on deferral and exemption has undergone significant change over the past thirty years. It has come almost full circle, from a full "subject-to-tax" exemption regime for all taxpayers, to, in effect, a full FTC regime with deferral only for active income of companies, to a full exemption regime for companies. Along the way, a broad CFC regime was introduced in 1990, expanded in 1997, and cut back considerably in 2004, with a further proposed narrowing cut short by the OECD BEPS project, while a very broad FIF regime was enacted in 1992 and abolished in 2010. These changes were driven in the first instance by the abolition of exchange controls in 1983, which opened up the possibility for Australians to shelter passive income offshore and led to a desire for increased taxation of foreign source income. More recently, Australia has experienced significant growth in outbound real direct investment and outbound portfolio collective investment, leading to a policy of more balanced taxation of foreign source income.

Australia's CFC regime[313] applies to passive and related-party (tainted) income of CFCs from countries other than seven listed countries (Canada, France, Germany, Japan, New Zealand, the United Kingdom, and the United States), for which only a very narrow range of income is caught. The control test is a 50%-or-more rule rather than the more common more-than-50% rule. The tainted-income rules are very similar to the U.S. rules. In addition, there is an active income test which prevents attribution of tainted income where less than 5% of the CFC's gross income is passive.

309. Germany, Foreign Transactions Tax Act (*Aussensteuergesetz*), s. 7 para. 1.
310. Germany, Foreign Transactions Tax Act (*Aussensteuergesetz*), s. 7 para. 2.
311. Germany, Foreign Transactions Tax Act (*Aussensteuergesetz*), s. 12 para. 1.
312. Germany, Foreign Transactions Tax Act (*Aussensteuergesetz*), s. 11.
313. Australia, ITAA 1936, Pt X.

As noted above, a broad participation exemption regime for Australian-resident companies sits alongside the CFC regime, with the result that tax at the corporate level on foreign source income in Australia is limited to tainted income from countries other than those with which Australia has had strong investment ties, and only where the company does not pass the active income test. Australia's imputation system has influenced this policy stance since all profits which have not borne Australian company tax are subject to tax at the resident shareholder level through either the capital gains tax on the sale of shares or the distribution of unfranked dividends. Imputation means that it is unnecessary to levy tax on foreign source active income from nonportfolio outbound investment at the company level since Australian companies with Australian shareholders have a considerable incentive to pay Australian company tax rather than foreign company tax.

The *French* CFC rules are contained in Article 209B of the *General Tax Code (Code général des impôts* (CGI)), which was enacted in 1980 and modified in 2005 in order to comply with EU case law relating to the compatibility of domestic anti-avoidance provisions with the freedom-of-establishment principle. In general terms, Article 209B is aimed principally at passive investment-type income earned through branches or subsidiaries in tax haven jurisdictions. More technically, a French corporation is subject to tax currently on foreign income which arises in a foreign branch operation or with respect to a more than 50% (or 5% if more than 50% is held through controlled or non-arm's length entities) investment directly or indirectly held in the share capital, voting rights, or financial rights in any foreign entity where the foreign branch or entity is not subject locally to an income tax or is subject to an effective rate of less than 50% (40% as of 2020) of the French rate.

For purposes of such taxation, the tax results of the foreign branch or entity are recalculated under French tax rules. The profits are deemed to be realized by (in the case of a branch) or distributed to (in the case of an entity) the French corporate taxpayer on the first day of the month following the end of the foreign branch's or entity's tax year. Conversely, losses of the foreign branch or entity are not taken into account in determining the tax on domestic income. Article 209B seems to be compatible with most French tax treaties because of the characterization of the profits of a CFC as distributed income; however, the treaty article dealing with business profits seems to forbid the application of Article 209B to branches,[314] at least where it provides that business income is taxable in the state of the branch only, or where no provision of the treaty explicitly or implicitly authorizes France to apply section 209B of the Code. In the case of litigation, the burden of proof as to the low-tax status of the foreign branch or entity lies on the government.

Tax paid locally is creditable against the corresponding French separate CIT, provided that the foreign tax is comparable to French income taxes. Withholding taxes on actual distributed dividends also entitle taxpayers to a credit against such separate tax where the subsidiary is based in a tax treaty country. This credit applies only if the distributions exceed the profits of the same entity which were previously taxed in

314. *See Conseil d'Etat*, June 28, 2002, No. 232276, *Société Schneider Electric.*

accordance with Article 209B and which were actually taxed (i.e., did not qualify for the intercorporate dividend exemption). A credit is also granted for that part of the profits taxed in France which corresponds to dividends, interest, and royalties subject to withholding tax in third countries where the branch or entity is based in a country with a tax treaty which includes an OECD-type exchange-of-information clause.

Most important, Article 209B is not applicable where a branch or entity is established in another EU Member State and its operation or the holding of an interest in it cannot be considered to be an "artificial arrangement"[315] intended to escape the French tax normally payable. With respect to other countries, current taxation can be avoided where the French corporate taxpayer can establish, for example, that the principal purpose and effect of a foreign branch or entity is not to localize profits in a low-tax jurisdiction where it is engaged in actual industrial or commercial activities.

The *Chinese* CFC rules apply to a foreign corporation controlled by a Chinese resident (enterprise or individual) or jointly by a resident enterprise and a resident individual. The meaning of "control" is defined to include de jure control through shareholding and de facto or effective control in terms of financing, business operations, purchases, and sales. De jure control refers to situations where a resident shareholder, directly or indirectly: (a) holds at least 10% of the voting shares; and (b) jointly (together with other Chinese residents) owns more than 50% of all the shares of the foreign company. In determining indirect shareholding, a Chinese resident's ownership is computed by multiplying the shareholding percentage of each tier of foreign companies. If an intermediary shareholder owns more than 50% of the shares of the lower-tier company, that shareholder is deemed to own all the shares. The CFC rules apply only where a CFC is resident in a country/region and is subject to an ETR of less than half the Chinese tax rate (i.e., 25%).

The STA has stated that the CFC rules do not apply to a CFC: (a) located in white-listed jurisdictions (e.g., Australia, Canada, France, Germany, India, Italy, Japan, New Zealand, Norway, South Africa, the United Kingdom, and the United States); (b) where the CFC's income is generated mainly from active business operations; or (c) where the annual profits of the CFC are less than CNY 5 million. Several audit cases dealing with the CFC rules have been reported. In one case audited by the Suzhou tax bureau, the effective-tax-rate test was applied to the income of a Hong Kong CFC which had paid no tax in Hong Kong on income derived from third jurisdictions (effectively ignoring the nominal rate of 16.5% in Hong Kong).[316]

India does not have CFC rules, although the adoption of such rules has been seriously considered in the past.

315. Within the meaning of the term "wholly artificial arrangement" as used by the CJEU in its *ICI* (July 16, 1998, C-264/96) and *Cadbury Schweppes* (September 12, 2006, C-196/04) decisions.
316. For further discussion, *see* Cui Xiaojing and Zhang Han, "Chinese Controlled Foreign Company Rules in the Post-BEPS Era: New Developments" (2018) vol. 24 No. 2 *Asia-Pacific Tax Bulletin*, Journals IBFD.

4.3 Special Provisions Dealing with Domestic Portfolio Investment in Foreign Investment Companies

Initially, limitations on exemption or deferral were typically focused on situations in which there was a significant level of domestic investment in a foreign corporation and were often restricted to cases in which there was actual control of the foreign corporation by domestic shareholders. However, as intermediated investment in foreign corporations became more common, the failure to impose current tax on undistributed earnings of portfolio investment in FIFs began to be recognized as a significant problem. Where the level of domestic investment was not substantial, there was some reluctance to require direct inclusion of foreign earnings because domestic shareholders were unlikely to have access to information or to have any influence on the distribution policies of foreign corporations. As a result, a number of surrogate taxing techniques were employed, ranging from taxation on a mark-to-market basis to the taxation of an assumed notional return on investments.

In the *United States*, when the Subpart F provisions were introduced in 1962, a provision was included which denied preferential capital gains treatment to gains realized by domestic investors on portfolio investments in the stock of foreign investment companies. The provision was intended to reduce the incentive for U.S. investors to invest in foreign mutual funds where the undistributed earnings would not be subject to current U.S. taxation and would not be reached by the foreign personal holding company rules or the Subpart F rules because of the absence of concentrated U.S. ownership. However, the temporary elimination of the capital gains preference in 1986 made this provision ineffective in discouraging U.S. investment in foreign investment companies. The legislative response was a rule aimed more directly at the deferral of U.S. tax on passive income earned abroad.

Under the passive foreign investment company (PFIC) rules enacted in 1986,[317] an interest charge is imposed on foreign earnings which are accumulated and then subsequently distributed to U.S. shareholders. The distribution is treated as having been received ratably over the period the U.S. shareholder has held the stock, and an interest charge is imposed on the taxes (calculated at the highest marginal rate for the year in question) which would have been due on the hypothetical distributions. Similarly, where the stock is disposed of at a gain, the gain is attributed ratably to the period that the stock has been held and an interest charge calculated accordingly. The interest-charge mechanism was chosen because of perceived disadvantages in requiring current taxation where U.S. interests were not substantial. In some circumstances, it is possible for U.S. shareholders to avoid the interest-charge regime by electing to include in income currently the undistributed income of the foreign corporation. Two alternative mechanisms to the interest-charge approach for U.S. holders of PFIC stock are available, but only in limited circumstances.[318]

While the PFIC rules are aimed primarily at investment in foreign investment companies, their definitional scope is substantially broader. A foreign corporation is

317. United States, IRC, s. 1291.
318. United States, IRC, ss. 1293, 1296.

classified as a PFIC if (1) 75% or more of its income is passive or (2) 50% or more of the fair market value or adjusted cost basis of its assets generates passive income. Unlike Subpart F, there is no minimum shareholding requirement and no required overall level of U.S. investment.[319]

Similarly, in *Canada*, in addition to the FAPI rules applicable to CFCs, a special provision was enacted in 1984 aimed at foreign investment vehicles. Where a resident taxpayer invested in "offshore investment fund property," defined broadly as an interest which derives its value primarily from investments in "portfolio" investments, the investment was deemed to generate a notional return which was currently taxable. However, the rule applied only if one of the main reasons for the investment was a tax advantage compared with a direct holding of the investment.[320]

This rule was found to be crude and ineffective, and in 1999, the government proposed to replace it with detailed "foreign investment entity" (FIE) rules for taxation years beginning after 2002. These proposed rules went through various iterations and were subject to intense criticism from taxpayers and tax practitioners. As a result, the government finally withdrew the proposed rules in 2010 and reverted to the former rules (with generous transitional rules for taxpayers who had relied on the proposed rules in the intervening years).

In *The Netherlands*, as a result of the taxation of individuals on their passive investment income on a deemed-return basis (return deemed to be a weighted percentage of the fair market value of the investment assets less liabilities), there is no need for special provisions in respect of foreign investment income. In these cases, the tax paid by a foreign corporation is irrelevant and the deemed-return treatment is not restricted to tax haven operations. Where an individual's investment is a substantial interest (an interest of at least 5%), the general deemed-return rules apply only to shares in a foreign investment company (FIC).[321] For corporate shareholders who hold 25% or more of the shares of a FIC, the investment is taxed on a mark-to-market basis unless the participation in the FIC qualifies for the participation exemption.[322]

In *Australia*, a separate FIF regime applied to non-CFCs with primarily passive income but, as noted above, it has been repealed and accordingly is not described here. Plans to replace the regime in a narrower form have been abandoned.

Germany has detailed rules on foreign-based investment funds and investment companies, which were subjected to major change in 2016 in order to comply with CJEU decisions mandating equal treatment of domestic investment funds and FIFs[323] and in response to pressure for lower compliance costs in order not to deter FIFs from entering the German market.[324] According to the 2016 amendments, investments in

319. United States, IRC, s. 1297.
320. In *Gerbro Holdings Company v. The Queen*, 2018 FCA 197, the Federal Court of Appeal affirmed the decision of the Tax Court (2016 TCC 173) that none of the taxpayer's main reasons for investing in foreign hedge funds was to minimize Canadian tax.
321. Netherlands, ITA, Art. 4.14.
322. Netherlands, CITA, Art. 13a.
323. CJEU, Joined Cases C-338/11 and C-339/11-C-347/11, May 10, 2012 (*Santander*) and Case C-190/12, April 10, 2014 (*Emerging Markets*).
324. CJEU, C-326/12, October 9, 2014 (*van Caster und van Caster*).

domestic or foreign investment companies are no longer subject to a fully "transparent" tax regime. Today, both domestic investment funds and FIFs are subject to a 15% tax rate on domestic dividends, domestic real estate income, and other domestic income.[325] Appreciation in the value of a fund's assets (including nondistributed dividends) is taxed by "deeming" that the fund's value at the beginning of the fiscal year is increased by a risk-free base rate (reflecting interest on long-term bonds issued by the federal government) unless the taxpayer can show that the real increase in value is lower.[326] Distributions by FIFs are subject to full or partial exemptions available for dividend payments under a tax treaty only where the FIF is subject to "general income taxation," meaning a 10% (or higher) rate in the fund's country of residence.[327]

Under German law, treatment of Collective Investment Vehicles (CIVs) must be distinguished from treatment under CFC legislation. The tax regime applicable to CIVs prevails in cases of conflict,[328] but it must first be established whether a foreign entity falls under the (rather complicated) definition of a CIV under German investment fund legislation.

In *France*, since 1999, an "anti-abuse" mechanism is applicable to income from holdings in foreign financial entities subject to a privileged tax regime. The idea behind this provision was to combat a widespread technique whereby shares in a listed company were invested in a foreign company benefiting from a preferential tax regime in order to receive the dividends paid out by that company on a tax-free basis. Under this provision,[329] French-resident individuals are subject to tax on undistributed foreign income which arises with respect to a 10% or greater direct or indirect interest held in any foreign entity the assets of which principally consist of stocks and securities, deposits, or current accounts, and which is not subject locally to an income tax or is subject to an effective rate of tax of less than 50% (40% as of 2020) of the French rate. The Finance Act 2022 created a new deemed 10% ownership interest with respect to the settlor or the beneficiary deemed to be the settlor of a trust. For purposes of such taxation, the income of the foreign entity is recalculated under French tax rules and the profits are deemed to be distributed to the French taxpayer on the first day of the month following the end of the foreign entity's tax year. Tax paid locally is deductible. Where no exchange-of-information clause exists between France and the entity's country, the taxable income cannot be lower than a notional return equal to the average bank business lending rate applied to loans to businesses. Earnings actually distributed are exempt as long as they do not exceed the undistributed profits previously taxed in the hands of the taxpayer. This provision seems to be compatible with most French tax treaties because of the characterization of the entity's income as distributed income. As is the case with the French CFC rules, the provision is not applicable where an entity is established in another EU Member State (or a jurisdiction having a treaty with France providing for exchange of information to counter tax

325. Germany, Investment Tax Act (*Investmentsteuergesetz*), s. 6 para. 2.
326. Germany, Investment Tax Act (*Investmentsteuergesetz*), s. 18.
327. Germany, Investment Tax Act (*Investmentsteuergesetz*), s. 16 para. 4.
328. Germany, Foreign Transactions Tax Act (*Aussensteuergesetz*), s. 7 para. 5.
329. France, CGI, s. 123 bis.

avoidance or evasion and assistance in the collection of taxes) and its operation or the holding of an interest in it cannot be considered to be an "artificial arrangement"[330] intended to escape the French tax normally payable. With respect to other countries, current taxation can be avoided where a French taxpayer can establish that the principal purpose and effect of the foreign entity is not to localize profits in a low-tax jurisdiction. Case law relating to this provision is developing, in particular to determine how the notion of a "privileged" tax regime should be understood.

The *United Kingdom* has no provisions which seek to tax nonportfolio investors in FIFs or companies on a current (whether actual or deemed) basis. However, under anti-abuse rules, where a resident individual transfers assets out of the United Kingdom such that income from the assets would otherwise arise to a nonresident, the individual may be treated as having derived the income directly.[331] The attribution occurs only where the individual can enjoy the income or is entitled to receive a capital sum connected with the transfer and the taxpayer cannot demonstrate the lack of a tax avoidance purpose. Under different rules, where a person disposes of an interest in an offshore investment fund which does not distribute a substantial portion of its income, the person may be subject to income tax treatment on any gain rather than preferential capital gains treatment.[332]

Indian residents are now allowed to invest in foreign funds, subject to the conditions in the Liberalised Remittance Scheme (LRS), which permits foreign investments up to USD 250,000 per financial year.[333] The Finance Act 2020 as modified by the Finance Act 2023 imposes a 20% tax to be collected at source by any authorized dealer of foreign exchange where the amount invested in a financial year (along with other permissible remittances) exceeds INR 700,000.[334] In addition, the investments have to be reported in the return of income as part of the schedule of foreign assets (Schedule FA). The reporting is required even if there is no income from such investments during the year.[335] Such reporting is also required under the Black Money (Undisclosed Foreign Income and Assets) and Imposition of Tax Act, 2015 and in case of failure, a penalty of INR 1 million may be imposed.[336] In a recent case, where the taxpayer had invested in a foreign fund through LRS but failed to report the investment in her return, the ITAT confirmed the application of the penalty even though the source of investment was explained.[337]

China, *Japan*, and *Sweden* do not have any rules to deal with residents investing in FIFs. However, Swedish residents investing in foreign and Swedish investment

330. Within the meaning of the term "wholly artificial arrangement" as used by CJEU in its *ICI* (July 16, 1998, C-264/96) and *Cadbury Schweppes* (September 12, 2006, C-196/04) decisions.
331. United Kingdom, Income Tax Act 2007, Part 13 Ch. 2 (ss. 714-751).
332. United Kingdom, The Offshore Funds (Tax) Regulations 2009 (SI 2009/3001).
333. https://files.caclub.in/wp-content/uploads/mof-goi-notification-dt-22-08-2022-foreign-exchange-management-overseas-investment-rules-2022.pdf.
334. India, ITA 1961, s. 206C(1G).
335. India, ITA 1961, 4th proviso to s. 139(1).
336. India, Black Money (Undisclosed Foreign Income and Assets) and Imposition of Tax Act, 2015, s. 43.
337. *Ms Shobha Harish Thawani v. JCIT*, BMA 01-03/Mum/2023, August 9, 2023, ITAT Mumbai.

funds are taxed on a deemed-return basis, which eliminates any advantage for investments in foreign funds.

5 OUTBOUND TRANSFERS TO FOREIGN BRANCHES OR SUBSIDIARIES

Transfers of assets outside a taxing jurisdiction raise issues in both credit systems and exemption systems. From the perspective of an exemption system, any appreciation in the value of an asset which is transferred to a foreign business operation whose income qualifies for exemption will not be taxed by the country of residence of the transferor. Similarly, income from assets transferred to a foreign corporation will not be subject to tax where the dividends from the direct investment are exempt. Several of the systems reviewed here have provisions which ensure that tax is collected in these situations, either by accelerating the recognition of income to the time of the transfer or retaining a tax claim on the income when it is later realized.

From the perspective of a credit system, the transfer of an asset to a foreign branch does not terminate the claim of the taxing jurisdiction. However, the existence of the credit gives the primary tax claim to the country of source and, where the rates are similar, has the same effect as an exemption system from the government's point of view. Transfers to foreign corporations raise the same issues where the indirect credit is available and involve the benefit of deferral since whatever domestic tax may be due is deferred until repatriation. A number of special rules respond to these problems.

Several countries treat the transfer of an appreciated asset to a foreign branch as a realization event. Thus, in *Sweden*, a transfer of assets is deemed to be a withdrawal of the assets from domestic business operations and is a realization event where the asset is transferred to a foreign branch in a country and Sweden has given up its right to tax in the tax treaty with that country. In the case of a transfer to a foreign subsidiary, the transfer is normally treated as a realization event.

Germany completely revamped its rules on cross-border transfers of assets after the European Company was introduced Europe-wide. Under this law, which entered into force in 2007, in principle, the transfer of an asset from the head office to a foreign branch is treated as a realization event. Although the Federal Tax Court ruled in 2008 that the transfer of assets between different jurisdictions does not constitute a realization event at all,[338] this ruling referred only to the pre-2007 legislation. Following the EU ATAD, which requires all Member States of the EU to introduce exit taxes on transfers of corporate assets, the German legislature amended its legislation again in 2021.

Taxpayers may elect deferred taxation of the gain (through the use of a reserve) over a period of five years where an asset is transferred to a branch within the EU/EEA.[339] It is assumed that this rule is in line with recent jurisprudence of the CJEU

338. Federal Tax Court (*Bundesfinanzhof*), July 17, 2008, I R 77/06.
339. Germany, ITA, s. 4 para. 1 s. 3, ITA, ss. 4g, 36 para. 5; CITA, s. 12 para. 1.

on free movement within the EU[340] and that it is also covered by Article 5 of the ATAD. The taxpayer must dissolve the reserve immediately in the case of a disposal or a transfer of an asset to a third country. Until 2021, this privilege was not granted if the taxpayer ceased to be subject to unlimited tax liability in Germany in the course of the reorganization. However, since Article 5 of the ATAD does not support this additional requirement for deferral, the German legislature deleted it. Where depreciable assets (which are not likely to be sold) are involved, the deferred income must be taken into account over the remaining useful life of the asset. The taxpayer can, at its option, treat the original transfer as a realization event.

The *Dutch* rules are somewhat more complex. In principle, the transfer of an asset to a foreign branch is not a realization event. However, in calculating foreign exempt income, case law requires that the fair market value of the asset be considered as the cost basis for computing depreciation of the asset in the foreign branch. Historical cost, however, is used in computing worldwide income. Thus, over the life of the asset, the appreciation is included in the tax base, in effect, by reducing the amount of foreign source income which qualifies for exemption. Similar rules apply to inventory. These rules continue to apply to the "income exemption" for foreign PEs of Dutch-resident corporate income taxpayers.[341]

France treats a transfer to a foreign branch or subsidiary as a realization event, although a tax-free transfer of assets to a foreign subsidiary can be made under certain conditions. Prior to 2017, contributions made to foreign legal entities by French legal entities could benefit from the preferential merger regime only with administrative approval. Since the CJEU *Euro Park Services* ruling in 2017,[342] the legislature has reformed the regime applicable to international transactions by abolishing the prior-approval procedure and introducing an *a posteriori* rule based on the absence of abuse. Any merger, demerger, or partial asset contribution carried out for the benefit of a foreign legal entity must be the subject of a special declaration by the transferring company, making it possible for the tax authorities to assess the reasons for and consequences of the transaction.[343] In addition, the preferential regime applies to restructuring operations carried out for the benefit of foreign legal entities by French legal entities only where the contributed assets are effectively attached to a PE of the foreign legal entity located in France.[344] Finally, under 2015 case law,[345] transfer pricing provisions[346] are applicable to all companies taxable in France, including a French branch of a company headquartered abroad, despite the fact that a branch has no legal personality. Thus, a transfer of intangible assets from a French branch to its foreign head office may constitute an indirect transfer of profits within the meaning of

340. CJEU, C-657/13, May 21, 2015 (*Verder Lab Tec*); Case C-162/12, January 23, 2014 (*DMC*).
341. Netherlands, CITA, Art. 15e.
342. The prior requirement for administrative approval was held by the CJEU to be contrary both to the freedom-of-establishment principle and to the merger directive: Case C-14/16, March 8, 2017 (*Euro Park Services*).
343. France, CGI, s. 210-0 A IV.
344. France, CGI, s. 210 C.
345. Conseil d'Etat, 9-11-2015 n°370974 (*Sté Sodirep Textiles SA-NV*).
346. France, CGI, s. 57.

the transfer pricing rules. However, the existence of a customer base attached to the branch must be proven.[347] Finally, driven by European law, France has introduced the concept of cross-border mergers into company law,[348] which applies only where a French company leaves France and takes the form of a company governed by foreign law; however, the legislature has yet to take any action.

In the *United States* transfers to a foreign branch are, in general, not taxable. The Internal Revenue Service recently has promulgated regulations, however, which impose tax on the appreciation in assets transferred to a foreign partnership which operates a branch.[349] The concern is that the income may not be subject to later U.S. tax if it can be allocated to a foreign partner.

Transfers to a foreign branch are, in general, not taxable. The Internal Revenue Service tightened its rules on tax-free outbound transfers of property in 2017. Transfers from a U.S. taxpayer to a foreign corporation of assets used in a trade or business which would previously have escaped taxation[350] are generally subject to tax. With respect to transferred intangibles, a U.S. taxpayer is required to include in income deemed-royalty payments (treated as U.S. source income) from the transferee foreign corporation over the life of the intangible which reflects the amounts commensurate with the income generated by the intangible. The deemed-royalty rule is aimed at preventing the deduction of research costs in the United States and then transferring the resulting income stream from the intangible abroad, but it has a much broader scope. In addition, where branch operations have been operating at a loss and are then transferred to a foreign corporation, gain must be recognized to the extent of the loss up to the amount of appreciation in the assets transferred. There are also extensive restrictions on transfers of stock or securities, in light of the ease of resale, although tax-deferred transfers are available in some circumstances where the taxpayer enters into an agreement to pay tax if the stock is in fact later sold or disposed of by the transferee corporation.

In 2016, *Japan* adopted a new regime which treats cross-border transfers of assets between the head office and branches as realization events;[351] prior to the 2014 tax reform, the transfer of assets between a head office and branch was not taxable because it was considered to be an internal dealing within a single legal person. Currently, such transfers are not only taxable, but are also subject to the transfer pricing rules as transactions between related parties. The *Canadian* rules treat transfers of assets, both to foreign branches and to foreign corporations, as realization events. However, a tax-deferred rollover is allowed for transfers of shares of a foreign affiliate (a foreign company in which the Canadian corporation owns at least 10% of the shares of any class) to another foreign affiliate of the taxpayer in exchange for its shares.[352] This

347. Conseil d'Etat, 9e-10e ch. 21-12-2022 n°450796 (*Sté Bupa Insurance Ltd*).
348. France, Commercial Code, s. L. 236-50.
349. Regulations under United States, IRC, s. 721.
350. United States, IRC, s. 367 ((old), allowing nonrecognition in connection with exchanges under IRC, ss. 332, 351, 354, 356 and 361).
351. Japan, CTA, s. 138(1), No. 1, s. 69(4), No. 1.
352. Canada, ITA, s. 85.1(3).

rollover is denied if the transfer is part of a series of transactions whereby the shares are transferred to an arm's length party.[353]

The tax law of *Australia* generally takes a strict view (except with respect to foreign banks) that there can be no income realization or deductions in transactions between a head office and branch, whether outbound or inbound.[354] Instead, the realization event is the disposal of the asset by the taxpayer to a third party. For inventory property, income and deductions are then allocated among the countries and taxed or exempted on the basis of source-of-income and apportionment-of-deductions rules (with arm's length transfer pricing principles used to allocate income and deductions where the books are not in conformity with this principle). Thus, in the case of inventory manufactured in Australia and shipped to an overseas branch which sells it, the sale price is allocated partly to Australia and partly to the country of the branch (with the part allocated to the foreign branch generally exempt, as discussed above, where the income would not be attributable (i.e., not subject to the CFC rules) if the foreign branch were a CFC). The expenses allocated to the Australian income are deductible but those allocated to the branch, including interest, are not deductible.

In practice, the tax administration accepts the treatment of an outbound transfer of inventory as a current realization event on the basis that it is a suitable proxy for the sourcing of income ultimately realized on sale even if the sale occurs in a later tax year.[355] A similar approach is also accepted for intra-entity loans and derivatives of Australian-resident banks.[356] For capital gains, no recognition occurs for an outbound transfer but the exemption for foreign branches of Australian-resident companies applies if the asset is used "wholly or mainly" for producing income of the foreign branch, other than for taxable Australian property (*see* the next paragraph) and assets which would be taxed under the CFC rules if the branch were a CFC.[357] More complex rules apply to depreciable assets.

In the case of the transfer of assets to foreign subsidiaries, the transfer is a realization event and gives rise to income or capital gain. For most capital assets, a rollover is available where the subsidiary is 100% owned and the asset transferred is a taxable Australian asset in the hands of the transferor and the transferee. Since in this case the rollover is limited to taxable Australian assets, there is no escape from the capital gains net because the subsidiary is subject to capital gains tax on disposal. The rollover is limited to land in Australia, nonportfolio interests in land-rich entities, and assets held at some stage by a PE in Australia.

In the *United Kingdom*, surprisingly, transfers to a foreign branch have no tax consequences. As a general matter, the transfer of assets outside the United Kingdom by a resident company to a related foreign company would be a disposition triggering capital gains taxation and the recapture of previously deducted capital allowances in excess of market value of the asset at the time of transfer. However, current taxation

353. Canada, ITA, s. 85.1(4).
354. Australia, ITAA 1997, Subdiv. 815-C; foreign banks with branches in Australia are dealt with in ITAA 1936, Pt IIIB.
355. Taxation Ruling TR 2001/11 paras. 5.5-5.16.
356. Taxation Ruling TR 2005/11, Practical Compliance Guideline (PCG) 2017/8.
357. Australia, ITAA 1936, s. 23AH.

can be avoided if the business is first transferred to a foreign branch, the business is then exchanged solely for shares in a nonresident company, and the resulting interest amounts to at least 25%.[358]

China does not have any rules for outbound transfers but exchange controls limit potential problems.

The following *Table IV-1* summarizes the rules dealing with residence-based taxation of foreign source income. The column "CFC Legislation" refers to provisions aimed at foreign corporations with concentrated domestic ownership, while the column "Foreign Investment Company Legislation" is focused on portfolio investment in foreign entities with predominantly passive income.

358. United Kingdom, TCGA, s. 140.

Table IV-1 Taxation of Foreign Source Income of Resident Taxpayers

	Double Tax Relief: Business Income	*Double Tax Relief: Subsidiary Dividends*	*Double tax Relief: Portfolio Income*	*Controlled Foreign Corporation (CFC) Legislation*	*CFC Basic Approach*	*Foreign Investment Company (FIC) Legislation*	*FIC Basic Approach*
Australia	mainly exemption; otherwise credit	exemption	FTC	yes	jurisdictional and transactional	1992-2010; plans to replace repealed regime have been abandoned	simplified actual calculation; mark-to-market; deemed return
Canada	FTC	exemption and deemed FTC	FTC and deduction	yes	transactional	yes	deemed return
China	FTC	FTC	FTC	yes	jurisdictional	no	n/a
France	exemption (territorial system)	exemption	no domestic relief (only in treaty)	yes	jurisdictional and transactional	yes	actual income and deemed return
Germany	exemption for active PE income (treaty)	exemption	FTC and modified half-income method and final withholding tax for dividends	yes	jurisdictional and transactional	yes—self-standing set of rules	taxability of FIF, distributions and tax on deemed appreciation of shares in foreign funds

	Double Tax Relief: Business Income	*Double Tax Relief: Subsidiary Dividends*	*Double tax Relief: Portfolio Income*	*Controlled Foreign Corporation (CFC) Legislation*	*CFC Basic Approach*	*Foreign Investment Company (FIC) Legislation*	*FIC Basic Approach*
India	FTC	FTC	no special rules; normal FTC rules apply	no	n/a	no	n/a
Japan	FTC	deemed FTC until March 2009; exemption from April 2009	FTC	yes	jurisdictional and transactional	no	n/a
The Netherlands	exemption	exemption	FTC	yes	jurisdictional and transactional	yes	deemed return
Sweden	FTC	exemption	FTC	yes	jurisdictional	no	n/a
United Kingdom	exemption for foreign PE, otherwise FTC	exemption	FTC/exemption for dividends received by UK companies	yes	jurisdictional and transactional	yes	ordinary income on disposal

United States	FTC, some exemption	exemption for dividends, although in some industries it is possible that much CFC income will be taxed on current basis (Subpart F and GILTI) with indirect credit for corporate shareholders	exemption for 10% or greater shareholders	yes	principally transactional, but note important addition of GILTI regime	yes	interest charge on deferred distribution or gain on sale

SUBPART B

Source Taxation

Regardless of their approach to residence-based taxation, all the countries under consideration in this book assert the right to tax income which, broadly speaking, can be said to arise or have its source in the country. This source-based, or in rem, jurisdiction focuses on the connection of the particular item of income to the taxing jurisdiction. The pattern of taxation applied to such income is similar in all the countries. A distinction is generally made between business-type income which is taxed on a net basis with the allowance of deductions, and investment-type income which is taxed on a gross basis, often collected through the mechanism of a withholding tax. Withholding tax often applies regardless of the status of the recipient of the income, but in the case of taxpayers without a residence connection, it represents a final tax; in other words, taxpayers do not have an opportunity to file a return and compute tax payable on a net basis. The following materials first analyze the structural issues of net-basis taxation of business and employment income and then consider the treatment of investment income. In this area in particular, the normally applicable domestic rules are often modified by tax treaties limiting the scope of source-based taxation, and the domestic rules should be viewed with these qualifications in mind. The special problems raised by the digital economy are discussed below in Subpart C, section 7.

1 ISSUES IN THE STRUCTURE OF NET-BASIS TAXATION OF BUSINESS INCOME

1.1 Threshold of Activity

Income from business operations is typically taxed only if the activities which take place in the country reach a certain level, although in some countries that level is very low. This approach is based in part on practical and administrative considerations. Where the activities are not significant, it may often be difficult to collect the tax, since it is usually not possible to use withholding techniques and the tax must be directly assessed. In addition, if the local activities are not substantial, the compliance burden imposed on taxpayers to file returns and keep appropriate records may discourage nonresidents from carrying on limited temporary income-earning activities in a country.

The degree of commercial penetration required varies, as does the formulation of the applicable test. Some jurisdictions impose net-basis taxation where a taxpayer carries on any business activities within the jurisdiction, although the contours of what constitutes a "business" can differ. Other jurisdictions impose tax only where a nonresident taxpayer has a PE in the jurisdiction, which represents a more extensive presence in a country than simply carrying on business activities there. The PE concept is often similar to, but not identical to, the same concept used in tax treaties. It involves either the presence of some sort of fixed business location, such as a store or an office, within the country, or the presence of agents in the country with certain types of legal authority.

In the *United States*, the basic threshold for net-basis taxation is engaging in a trade or business in the United States. The concept has been developed by case law, which in general focuses on the continuous and regular nature of the activities, although results of the cases and rulings are hard to rationalize.[359] In addition, there are some specific statutory rules. For example, in most circumstances, the performance of personal services in the United States constitutes a trade or business. There are some specific statutory exclusions for certain financial activities, such as trading in stock or securities with a resident broker for the foreign taxpayer's own account.[360] An election is permitted with respect to real estate activities which allow the taxpayer to be taxed on a net basis even where the level of actual activities does not constitute a trade or business.[361] A 2023 Tax Court case has raised questions about the circumstances in which an offshore lender (including specialized funds and hedge funds) could be considered to be engaged in a U.S. trade or business if it is sufficiently engaged in the underlying commercial activities of their borrowers or portfolio companies.[362]

Canada also uses a business-activities test. There is no statutory definition of what constitutes carrying on a business in Canada. Instead, the case law focuses on where contracts are entered into and where activities "essential" to the making of the business profits are performed. Under a special statutory rule, soliciting orders or offering goods for sale in Canada is deemed to be carrying on business in Canada, as does any processing, construction, or manufacturing activity in Canada.[363] Nonresidents who engage Canadian residents to provide investment management services are not considered to be carrying on business in Canada by reason of those activities alone if certain conditions are met.[364] In addition, capital gains from the disposition of

359. United States, *see, e.g., Chang Hsiao Ling v. CIR*, 23 TC 1040 (1955).
360. United States, IRC, s. 864(b)(2).
361. United States, IRC, s. 871(d).
362. *YA Global Investments LP v. Commissioner*, 161 TC No. 11 (November 15, 2023).
363. Canada, ITA, s. 253. The mere holding of a limited partnership interest is not sufficient to consider the partner to be carrying on business in Canada (s. 253.1).
364. Canada, ITA, s. 115.2.

"taxable Canadian property," such as real property or natural resource property by a nonresident, is subject to Canadian tax.[365] Special rules impose net-basis taxation on income from employment activities performed in Canada.[366]

In the *United Kingdom*, income derived by nonresidents is categorized into the same schedules or cases as those applicable to domestic taxpayers. With respect to business income, the jurisdictional question is whether a business is being carried on *in* (as opposed to *with*) the United Kingdom, and the question is determined on a facts-and-circumstances basis. In this connection, the place where contracts are entered into is an important factor.[367] From 2003, the test for the taxation of nonresident corporations is based on the existence of a PE (defined in a manner similar to the definition in the OECD Model Convention) in the United Kingdom.[368]

In general, *Japan* uses a PE test as the threshold for net-basis taxation.[369] The domestic law concept follows the treaty definition of PE, although, of course, there are differences in detail since each treaty definition may be different. Japan is a party to the *Multilateral Convention to Implement Tax Treaty Related Measures to Prevent Base Erosion and Profit Shifting* (MLI) and chose to generally apply the PE modifications, excluding those regarding the splitting up of contracts. Therefore, the Japanese definition of PE is generally subject to the revisions contemplated in the MLI (excluding those regarding the splitting up of contracts), to the extent that the counterparty jurisdictions have also agreed to them. Some categories of income are taxed on a net basis even in the absence of a PE. These include income from the sale of domestic real estate, income from the "use or holding" of certain assets in Japan, and gain on certain stock sales.

Although capital gains on stock sales are generally untaxed in the absence of a PE, such gains are taxed on a net basis where a nonresident together with its affiliates holds 25% or more of the total number of outstanding shares and sells 5% or more of the shares in a tax year.[370] However, in most tax treaties with developed countries, Japan waives its taxing rights under this provision.[371] Capital gains on stock sales of a "real estate company" are also taxed on a net basis irrespective of the absence of a PE. A real estate company is a company the majority of whose assets consists of real estate in Japan.

The Netherlands in general, also uses a permanent-establishment approach. The statutory provision imposing tax liability on nonresidents includes a definition of a PE[372] which follows the definition contained in the applicable tax treaty.[373] In non-treaty situations, a statutory definition corresponding to Article 5 of the 2017 OECD

365. Canada, ITA, s. 2(3).
366. Canada, ITA, s. 115(1) and (2).
367. For a famous case in this regard, *see Grainger & Son v. Gough*, [1896] AC 325 (HL).
368. United Kingdom, Corporation Tax Act 2009, s. 19.
369. Japan, ITA, s. 164 and Japan, CTA, s. 141.
370. Japan, ITA, s. 161(1), No. 3, Order for Enforcement of Income Tax Act, s. 281(1), No. 4 and (6).
371. One of the few exceptions is the Japan-France Income Tax Treaty, Art. 13(2)(a).
372. Netherlands, ITA, Art. 1.10 (referring to the CITA definition), CITA, Art. 3(4). This definition applies to the whole of both the ITA and the CITA. As far as the CITA is concerned, the same definition applies to the income exemption under the CITA (CITA, Art. 15e).
373. Netherlands, CITA, Art. 3(4)(a).

Model applies.[374] In addition, there is a statutory rule which treats real property held as a business asset as a PE.[375]

Sweden likewise bases business taxation on the presence of a PE in Sweden. The domestic law concept of PE is interpreted in the light of Swedish treaty practice, which in general follows the OECD Model Convention with respect to the definition of a PE as it read before the 2017 amendments.

Under the *Chinese* EIT, the threshold for the taxation of nonresidents is an "establishment" or "place of business" (or "site") in China through which production and business activities are conducted and includes management offices, business organizations, and offices; factories, farms, and premises where exploration for natural resources is carried out; premises where labor services are provided; premises where construction, installation, assembly, repair, and survey projects, etc., are carried out; and any other premises where production and business activities are carried out. Business agents also give rise to an establishment or place of business in China. There is no similar threshold under the IIT.

Under *German* domestic law, business income derived by nonresidents is subject to tax only where it arises in a PE in Germany or from the presence of a permanent representative in Germany.[376] Both terms are defined in some detail in the legislation[377] and are broader than the corresponding treaty concepts. Thus, a PE is present if a stock of goods is available, and a permanent representative is not required to have authority to conclude contracts on behalf of the principal. Over the years, German law has expanded the taxation of commercial income beyond the PE concept: income from cultural, sporting, etc., events can be taxed even in the absence of a PE,[378] as well as income and capital gains from real estate or brokering services of sportspersons.[379] Gain on the disposition of an interest representing at least 1 % of the share capital in a German corporation is subject to tax without further connection to the jurisdiction.[380] However, in the context of the implementation of the BEPS Action Plan, Germany has chosen not to introduce additional concepts for commissionaire arrangements and the splitting up of contracts. Germany has agreed to expand the treaty definition of a PE in accordance with Article 13 of the MLI, but only for cases of artificial avoidance of PE status through the specific-activity exemptions.

Foreign self-employed taxpayers deriving income from professional services are taxed under German domestic law if they have a fixed place of business in Germany or render or "utilize" those services in Germany.[381] Although under German tax treaties source country taxation is largely limited to taxpayers maintaining a fixed place in the source country, some (in particular, older) treaties provide for source taxation exclusively or alternatively under a test of presence.

374. Netherlands, CITA, Art. 3(4)(b) in connection with Art. 3(5)-(12).
375. Netherlands, CITA, Art. 17a.(a); ITA, Art. 7.2(6).
376. Germany, ITA, s. 1 para. 4; ITA, s. 49 para. 1 No. 2 lit.a.
377. Germany, GFC, ss. 12 and 13.
378. Germany, ITA, s. 49 para. 1 No. 2 lit.d.
379. Germany, ITA, s. 49 para. 1 No. 2 lit.d, f. and g.
380. Germany, ITA, s. 49 para. 1 No. 2 lit.e.
381. Germany, ITA, s. 49 para. 1 No. 3.

The *Australian* regime revolves around source rules rather than an explicit threshold test, with source generally determined as "a practical, hard matter of fact" and developed through case law; for business income, source is usually where the income-earning activity is carried on.[382]

Foreign corporations are taxed in *France* on the business income they realize through "a trade or business carried on in France" (*entreprise exploitée en France*).[383] As construed in the case law, this concept is very close to the PE concept in the OECD Model Treaty. It is, however, somewhat broader because there is no exclusion for activities of a preparatory or auxiliary nature and because, in addition to fixed places of business and dependent agents, it includes the performance in France of a "complete commercial cycle" on a customary basis (e.g., several purchases followed by sales, or even large one-shot purchase and sale transactions).

Under *India's* domestic tax law, the nexus for taxing nonresidents on business income is a "business connection" in India, a legacy from colonial days which continued to apply after independence. The term "business connection" was not defined and originally applied only to agency arrangements. Courts took the position that it was impossible to precisely define the term.[384]

To remedy the vagueness and uncertainty of the business-connection concept, the ITA has been amended to specify the situations in which income is deemed to accrue or arise in India in respect of business, real estate, capital gains, salaries, interest, royalties, and fees for technical services. Section 9(1)(i) of the ITA provides that "all income accruing or arising, whether directly or indirectly, through or from any business connection in India" is deemed to arise or accrue in India. Explanation 1 indicates that where a business is partly carried out in India (other than a business connection through a significant economic presence), only the part of the income reasonably attributable to the operations carried out in India is considered to arise or accrue in India. However, income derived by a nonresident from the mere purchase of goods in India for export is not taxable. Section 9(1)(i) provides specific exemptions to nonresidents for income from running a news agency, income from shooting a film in India and, most recently, income of foreign companies from activities limited to the display of uncut diamonds in specified special economic zones.[385] In addition, certain activities in the International Financial Centre (special economic zone, as discussed in the country chapter on India in Part I) are considered not to result in a business connection in India.[386]

There is no requirement for a fixed place of business or a minimum time period in establishing a business connection in India. Importantly, where a business

382. Australia, ITAA 1997, ss. 6-5(3), 6-10(5); for a recent example, *see Resource Capital Fund IV LP* [2019] FCAFC 51, paras. 51-66.
383. France, CGI, s. 209 I.
384. HC [High Court] Allahabad, January 3, 1945, *Hira Mills Ltd v. Income Tax Officer*, 1946 14 ITR 417 All.
385. India, Finance Act, 2018 adding s. 9(1)(e).
386. India, ITA, 1961, s. 9A.

connection does not exist, the existence of a PE under a tax treaty is irrelevant.[387] However, the concept of a business connection is generally considered to be broader than the concept of a PE in tax treaties, with the result that where there is a PE in India, it may safely be presumed that there is also a business connection in India.[388] Similarly, a business connection is irrelevant if there is no PE in India under an applicable treaty.[389] The scope of a business connection has been further enlarged in the context of the digital economy through the addition of the concept of significant economic presence, discussed in Subpart C, section 7.

1.2 Attribution of Business Income for Net-Basis Taxation

Whatever the threshold for net-basis taxation, rules are necessary to determine which items of income are sufficiently associated with the domestic branch[390] to be subject to tax. The approaches used by the countries considered here differ substantially. One approach focuses on the actual economic connection between a particular item of income and the branch: all income with such a connection is subject to net-basis taxation, and all other income is either not subject to tax or subject to the withholding regime. This type of approach typically does not use independent source rules with respect to business income.

Another approach treats all income with a domestic source as attributable to the branch, and thus subject to net-basis taxation even where there is no actual economic connection between the item of income and the branch. This "force-of-attraction" approach usually involves an independent set of source rules, since whether an item of income is subject to net-basis taxation depends on whether it has a domestic source. A number of variations in this approach are possible. Under a "limited" force-of-attraction approach, only certain types of income are subject to net-basis taxation without regard to their actual economic connection to the branch. In other cases, income which technically has a foreign source may be subject to net-basis taxation if it has an economic connection with the domestic activities.

These "direct" methods attempt to allocate a particular item of *gross* income to the branch operations. A conceptually distinct "indirect" approach is used to determine the *net* income of the entire enterprise and then allocate that profit to the various geographic locations on some basis. The allocation may be made on the basis of turnover, assets, payroll, or other similar factors. This approach is often used in special industries such as banking, insurance, and transportation, while the direct approach is used for sales and manufacturing operations. The results of the two approaches can be

387. This is because courts in India have interpreted s. 90(2) of the ITA to mean that a taxpayer has the option of choosing between the provisions of the domestic law or the provisions of a tax treaty, whichever is more beneficial to the taxpayer.
388. *Formula One World Championship Ltd v. CIT*, April 24, 2017, Civil Appeal No. 3849 2017. For a brief summary of the case decision and the full text of the decision, *see also Formula One World Championship Ltd. v. CIT*, Tax Treaty Case Law IBFD.
389. *CIT v. Mitsubishi Corporation India P. Ltd*, February 16, 2024, ITA 180/2014 (Delhi HC).
390. In the subsequent material, the term "branch" is used to refer to the applicable domestic threshold for taxation, i.e., business activity, "trade or business," PE, etc.

quite different. For example, a branch operation can show a profit on the direct method but have no allocable net income on the indirect method if the overall operations resulted in a loss.

While the general outlines of the various approaches are fairly clear, in practice, the details tend to be relatively undeveloped. This result is attributable partly to the fact that, in general, cross-border operations tend to be conducted through subsidiaries, except in the case of special industries such as banking, real estate, and natural resources.

In addition, special problems arise in determining the income attributable to transactions which involve dealings between the domestic branch and the foreign head office or other foreign branches. These issues arise in connection with both income attribution and the determination of appropriate deductions for the branch and are discussed in the following section.

The *United States* combines a "limited" force-of-attraction approach with a focus on the economic connection of the income with the domestic activities. The rules for establishing the tax base are related to the complex set of rules for establishing the source of income which applies to both resident and nonresident taxpayers. With respect to investment-type income such as dividends and interest from U.S. sources, the income is subject to net-basis taxation if it is "effectively connected" with the U.S. business activities. The focus is on the function which the asset generating the income plays in the business and the business activities with respect to the asset. The same rules apply to determine whether capital gains from the disposition of assets are effectively connected with the U.S. business and are thus subject to net-basis taxation. (Income in these categories which is not effectively connected to the U.S. business is either taxed on a gross basis or not taxed at all.)[391]

Other items of income from U.S. sources are treated as effectively connected even if there is no factual connection between the item of income and the U.S. business activities. Thus, for example, sales of inventory property in the United States which are made directly from the foreign head office, with no involvement of the U.S. branch, would nonetheless be treated as effectively connected income.[392]

In *Australia*, as noted above, the regime for taxing nonresidents starts with the basic assumption that all Australian source income is assessable and taxed on a net basis, including business income. The tax administration has the power to determine the source of income for branches when making an adjustment under transfer pricing rules. Australian tax law does not generally recognize "deemed" transactions and payments in the case of branches, except for foreign banks, and so brings to account only the actual income derived, but achieves similar results by using notional transfer prices to allocate income between different parts (branches) of a taxpayer.[393] For certain types of business income, there are a few special regimes which mix assessment and withholding elements and may be regarded as examples of the indirect approach.

391. United States, IRC, s. 864(c).
392. United States, IRC, s. 864 (c)(3).
393. Australia, ITAA 1936, Part IIIB (foreign banks), ITAA 1997, Subdiv. 815-C (taxation of branches).

For example, in the case of nonresident insurers and overseas ships, a certain percentage of receipts is deemed to be Australian source taxable income and an assessment, which effectively operates as a kind of withholding mechanism, is raised against a convenient local deemed agent (master of a ship, insurer's agent).[394] In practice, tax treaties govern most of the business income derived in Australia by nonresidents (although the domestic insurance and shipping rules are generally preserved in whole or in part) and the source rules for business income (profits attributable to a PE) effectively govern, since Australia's tax treaties (until recently) and now domestic law provide that the source rule in the treaty applies for all purposes of Australian tax law.

In general, *Canada* does not use the force-of-attraction principle, although certain items of Canadian source income become subject to tax where the taxpayer is otherwise subject to net-basis taxation. There are no detailed statutory source rules specifying the geographic source of income. In the case of a nonresident's Canadian branch operations, income which may be allocated in a "reasonable manner" to the Canadian branch is treated as domestic source income and taxed on a net basis to the nonresident. A nonresident's Canadian branch income must be computed on the assumption that the nonresident's only income is from carrying on business in Canada.[395] Moreover, the nonresident is entitled only to those deductions which are reasonably attributable to the Canadian business. If inventory, intangible property, or depreciable property is transferred to, or withdrawn from, a Canadian branch by a nonresident, the branch is considered to have acquired the property at a cost equal to its fair market value at that time or to have disposed of the property for proceeds equal to its fair market value at that time.[396] Although there are no further statutory rules or administrative guidance with respect to the allocation of profits to a Canadian branch, the matter is likely to be governed by the provisions of a tax treaty because of Canada's broad treaty network.

The *Dutch* rules likewise do not apply a force-of-attraction approach and are similarly open-ended. Income which is "realized" by a Dutch branch is treated as domestic source income and subject to net-basis taxation. Income and expenses, as well as assets and liabilities, are attributed to a branch if they are functionally related to the branch activities. For this purpose, the Dutch tax administration generally applies the "authorized OECD approach" (AOA) included in Article 7 of the 2010 OECD Model and Commentary with respect to treaties entered into after 2010.[397] With respect to Dutch treaties concluded before 2010, taxpayers are permitted to apply the 2010 OECD rules if they prefer,[398] subject to the condition that the profit allocation based on

394. Australia, ITAA 1936, Pt III Divs. 12, 15.
395. Canada, ITA, s. 4.
396. Canada, ITA, ss. 10(12) and (13), 13(9), 14(14) and 14(15).
397. Netherlands, Decree of June 14, 2022, No. 2022-0000143421, V-N 2022/36.3.
398. *Ibid.* However, in its decision of June 3, 2016, No. 14/05100, BNB 2016/171 the Supreme Court ruled that with respect to the 1971 Spain-Netherlands tax treaty (based on the 1963 OECD Model), no account was taken of internal royalties between a Dutch-resident company and its PE located in Spain (at least for the years at issue: 2002-2006). Internal royalties may be taken into consideration under the AOA included in the 2010 version of Art. 7.

the AOA is also applied consistently in the other contracting state.[399] In case law, a payment attributable to branch activities but received after the branch activities had ceased was still considered to be attributable to the branch.[400] Investment-type income such as dividends and interest are taxed to the branch only if the assets which generate the income are part of the business assets of the branch. The manner in which the assets are carried on the books of the branch may provide evidence as to the business character of the assets, but is not controlling.

In *Germany*, income is generally attributed to a PE in accordance with a "direct" method focusing on the activities in Germany; the force-of-attraction principle is not used. Following the AOA, German domestic law was amended in 2013 to allow for the treatment of PEs as separate entities;[401] the details were set out in a regulation issued by the MOF.[402] Moreover, Germany has introduced the AOA approach into its "Basis for negotiation" and uses it as a model in treaty negotiations.[403]

Sweden attributes income based on a "true and fair" calculation of the economic results of business operations in Sweden, based to some extent on the accounting

399. Netherlands, Decree of June 14, 2022, No. 2022-0000143421, V-N 2022/36.3, para. 1.3. The possibility of opting for the AOA with respect to tax treaties based on the pre-2010 version of the OECD Model was confirmed by the District Court of North-Holland in its decision of October 24, 2018, No. 16/3231, V-N 2019/13.2.2. The Court referred to the option provided for in the Decree of January 15, 2011, No. IFZ2010/457M, BNB 2011/91 (old), i.e., the predecessor of the Decree of June 14, 2022, which allows an allocation based on the AOA in relation to Art. 7 of the 1973 France-Netherlands Tax Treaty (which is based on the 1963 OECD Model). However, on appeal the Amsterdam Court of Appeal in its decision of December 22, 2020, No. 18/00688, V-N 2021/14.1.2 was unwilling to recognize the possibility of opting for the AOA. Instead, the Court of Appeal examined whether the 2010-2017 Commentary could be applied because it took the view that the differences in the wording between Art. 7 of the tax treaty in question (based on the 1963 OECD Model) and Art. 7 of the 2010-2017 OECD Model (incorporating the AOA) did not permit the OECD Commentaries to be applied dynamically. However, the limited dynamic application of the 2010-2017 OECD Commentaries followed by the Court did not allow the AOA to be applied in this case because it went beyond a mere clarification. Advocate-General Wattel, in an Advisory Opinion of August 26, 2021, No. 21/00415, V-N 2021/52.8, considered the application of the AOA, but concluded that the issuance costs in question (in relation to shares and convertible obligations (*Obligations Remboursale en Actions*)) were not really covered by the OECD Commentaries on Art. 7 (nor by those of 2010-2017). The District Court of Zeeland-West-Brabant, in its decision of November 11, 2019, No. 17/4994, V-N 2020/8.10 and on appeal the 's-Hertogenbosch Court of Appeal, in its decision of April 13, 2022, No. 19/00771, V-N 2022/31.1.3, allowed reliance on the AOA. *See also* the decision of the Court of Appeal of The Hague of October 27, 2021, 19/00754, V-N 2022/7.7, in which the former 2011 Decree and the AOA were considered. In this respect, the taxpayer's reliance on this Decree based on the principle of legitimate expectations may be a relevant feature.

400. Netherlands, Supreme Court, February 25, 1976, No. 17804, BNB 1976/110, Supreme Court, March 22, 2013, No. 11/05599, BNB 2013/114, and Supreme Court, April 6, 2018, No. 16/01934, BNB 2018/115. For a similar approach for income from dependent personal services (cf. former Art. 14 of the OECD Model), *see* Netherlands, Supreme Court, December 6, 2013, No. 12/00252, BNB 2014/38.

401. Germany, Foreign Transactions Tax Act (*Aussensteuergesetz*), s. 1 para. 5.

402. Germany, Foreign Transactions Tax Act (*Aussensteuergesetz*), s. 1 para. 6; PE Profit. Allocation Regulation (*Betriebsstättengewinnaufteilungsverordnung*) of October 13, 2014.
Official Gazette 2014, Part I, p. 1603, latest amendment of December 20, 2022, Official Gazette 2022, Part I, p. 2730.

403. Germany, Basis for negotiation, Art. 7 para. 2.

principles used to allocate income among the divisions of a single company. However, Swedish courts tend to follow the recommendations of the OECD in applying the transfer pricing guidelines by analogy.

The *United Kingdom* does not have any form of force-of-attraction rule. Income is attributed to the UK business activity on a factual-connection basis: if the income can be said to "arise" in the business, it is subject to net-basis taxation. In addition, income from rights or property used or held in the business is subject to tax, as is gain on the disposition of business assets.[404] In the case of nonresident corporations, these types of income are calculated under a provision which is broadly consistent with Article 7 of the OECD Model Convention.

Since, in principle, a branch is assimilated to an independent enterprise, *France* does not follow the force-of-attraction approach and the indirect or unitary method is used only in exceptional circumstances. Emphasis is generally placed on the branch's books; the branch is taxed only on the active income attributable to it and to passive income effectively connected with it. There are no special source rules with respect to business income since the existence of a "trade or business carried on in France" is the criterion for both taxability and source.

Historically, *Japan* had a system combining source rules, income classes, and types of activity in respect of the determination of income taxable to Japanese branch activities. Under these old rules, an extensive force-of-attraction principle was applied to branches and other fixed places of business which would constitute a PE under general international rules. The 2014 tax revisions, which have been officially stated by the Japanese tax agency to be adjustments to the AOA, have changed this basic approach to some extent. In general, net-basis tax has been limited to the business income attributable to a PE (such as branch offices).[405] Technically, the new rules have introduced the concept of business income attributable to a PE[406] as one of the types of income with a source in Japan. More specifically, this concept is defined as income attributable to a PE as if the PE were a separate and independent enterprise, taking into account the functions performed and assets used by the PE, as well as intracompany transactions.[407] However, the practical effects of these revisions may not be very substantial because, even prior to the 2014 tax revisions, Japan followed the OECD Model Convention in many of its tax treaties, and therefore the application of the force-of-attraction principles was effectively limited.

In *China*, attribution of income for net-basis taxation includes income derived from an establishment or place of business ("establishment") as well as from foreign income which is effectively connected with the establishment. Effectively connected foreign source income typically includes interest, rent, royalties, and dividends.[408]

404. United Kingdom, Corporation Tax Act 2009, s. 19.
405. It is to be noted that some categories of income (e.g., gains from the sale of domestic real estate, profits from dealing in Japanese government bonds, and remuneration for personal services rendered in Japan) are subject to net-basis tax even in the absence of a PE.
406. Japan, ITA, s. 161(1), CTA, s. 138(1).
407. Japan, ITA, ss. 161 and 164, and Japan, CTA, ss. 138 and 141.
408. China, EIT Regulations, Art. 8.

Where profits cannot be determined on the basis of the financial accounts of an establishment, presumptive or deemed methods are used.[409] Under these methods, a deemed profit rate is applied to actual revenue, actual cost, or gross income, depending on the availability of evidence. The deemed profit rates are as follows:

- project construction, design, and consulting: 15%-30%;
- management services: 30%-50%; and
- other services or activities: not less than 15%.

Some of *India's* tax treaties contain the limited force-of-attraction rule in the UN Model Treaty, although the rule differs significantly from treaty to treaty. In some treaties, the principle is restricted to sales of goods and merchandise of the same or similar character (omitting the reference to similar activities). In many treaties, the outcome of a force-of-attraction rule is achieved by providing that the source country may tax all profits directly or indirectly attributable to a PE. In some treaties (e.g., India-China,) the enterprise may rebut the force-of-attraction rule by proving that the PE could not have undertaken the activities or that the activities are unrelated to the PE. In the treaty with Germany, the force-of-attraction rule applies only where the PE was involved in a tax avoidance transaction.

1.3 Determination of Deductions in the Net-Basis Taxation of Business Income

The rules for determining the deductions attributable to business income arising in a branch generally focus on the factual or "causal" connection between the expenditure and the income. Following treaty practices, some of the domestic rules give considerable weight to the manner in which the expense is accounted for in the books of the branch or head office. Some expenses are allocated on a formulary basis which takes into account factors such as the ratio of the branch assets to total assets of the enterprise or relative sales volume.

Also following treaty practices, in general, none of the countries analyzed in this book recognize in their domestic rules "self-charged" expenses for payments or transfers made between branches and head office. Thus, internal "interest" or "royalty" charges do not affect the income of the branch or head office. Only expenses which are actually paid or accrued to third parties support deductions, determined on either a "direct" or formulary basis. It remains to be seen whether the new Article 7 of the OECD Model, which allows the deduction of notional expenses in some circumstances, will have an impact on domestic law. In the case of individuals, deductions for personal allowances and other personal costs are generally quite limited or not allowed at all.

In the *United States*, the same allocation of deduction rules which are applicable to domestic taxpayers for purposes of the FTC limitation are used to determine the net

409. China, STA, Guo Shui Fa [2010] No. 19.

income of foreign business operations.[410] No deduction is allowed for self-charged expenses and no income results from transactions between the head office and the branch operations. The focus is on expenses which are "definitely related" to the income generated by the U.S. business activities. In addition, a formulary approach is allowed for certain expenses; for example, general and administrative expenses can be allocated on a sales or gross-income basis between U.S. and foreign source income.

A special rule applies to the allocation of interest expense to U.S. business operations.[411] The basic approach is to look to the overall capital structure of the foreign taxpayer and the relation of that structure to the assets used in the United States. It combines what is, in effect, a tracing rule with a residual allocation rule. In determining the relation between U.S. assets and related liabilities, taxpayers may use either the actual ratio of assets to liabilities or a fixed arbitrary percentage. Actual and "allocated" interest expenses deducted by the branch may be subject to gross-basis taxation. The special allocation rules are principally important to foreign banks which, for regulatory reasons, typically operate in the United States in branch form.

In *Canada*, expenses are generally allocated on a factual tracing basis, although a formulary apportionment of interest and overhead expense is allowed in certain circumstances where tracing is impossible. However, the deductible interest expense of a Canadian branch of an authorized foreign bank is determined by a formula which makes allowance for notional interest on funds advanced to the branch by the bank.[412] Where all or substantially all of a nonresident's income is earned in Canada, the nonresident is, in effect, assimilated to a resident and other deductions are available to the extent that they can be considered applicable to the income earned in Canada.[413]

The *Japanese* approach also combines elements of direct and indirect allocation of costs, focusing on whether certain costs are attributable to business activities engaged in by a PE in Japan. Costs and expenses directly attributable to a PE in Japan (e.g., for depreciation of fixed assets used solely for the business activities of the PE) are generally deductible in accordance with the same tax accounting rules applicable to domestic corporations.[414] For indirect costs or expenses related to both the business activities of the PE and other parts of the enterprise, a formulary approach is used, subject to documentation requirements, where such costs and expenses are allocated on the basis of revenues, assets, number of employees, etc., depending on the nature of the expense. Interest expense may be deducted directly where it can be traced to domestic activities; otherwise, it is allocated on a formulary basis. The deductibility of interest expense is subject to a limitation, which is calculated based on the amount of capital that should be allocated to the PE. Japan introduced detailed rules with respect to this limitation in the 2014 tax revisions.[415] Non-Japanese enterprises with a PE in Japan must retain sufficient documents and records regarding transactions attributable

410. United States, Regs., s. 881-6.
411. United States, Regs., s. 882-5.
412. Canada, ITA, s. 20.2.
413. Canada, ITA, s. 115(1)(f).
414. Japan, CTA, s. 142.
415. Japan, CTA, s. 142-4 and 142-5.

to the PE, including intracompany transactions. With respect to intracompany transactions, contractual documents are also required, as if the PE were a separate and independent entity.[416]

The *Swedish* rules on allocation of deductions are quite undeveloped. For clearly identifiable costs incurred in a branch, such as salaries of local employees, the expenses are directly deductible. In other situations, a formulary approach based on gross sales, a standardized head office charge, etc., may be used. Generally, the approach must be consistent with the principles of the Swedish ITA and the provisions of Article 7 of the OECD Model Treaty on the attribution of profits to PEs. In the *United Kingdom*, the deduction of expenses of a branch is a factual determination. For nonresident corporations, this determination is expressly required to be performed according to provisions consistent with Article 7 of the OECD Model Treaty. In particular, expenses are allowable if "incurred for the purposes of the permanent establishment." "Royalties" paid by a PE to the nonresident company are expressly not deductible. However, interest paid by a PE to the nonresident company may be deducted where incurred in the ordinary course of a financial business.[417]

In *Germany*, the situation has become more complicated as a result of the introduction of the AOA into domestic law and (new) tax treaties. In general, domestic legislation focuses on the economic connection between the expense and the German activities under a tracing approach,[418] although there is no requirement that the expense be incurred in Germany. This test applies to both direct and indirect costs and, again, there is no requirement that the expense be incurred in Germany. There is no deduction for "internal" costs since contractual arrangements between the branch and the head office are generally not recognized. Debt is allocated in light of the allocation of assets and risks to the respective business units of the enterprise.

It is debatable whether this approach has been effectively replaced by the AOA since its introduction into German law in 2013. The Federal MOF regards the AOA as applicable solely in the context of profit adjustments and only to the extent that it favors the German tax authorities.[419] Taking this position seriously entails the application of a double standard: allocating profits and losses to PEs under the traditional "tracing approach" and adjusting profits and losses (but only to the detriment of the taxpayer) under the AOA approach. Moreover, the full application of the AOA will occur only after Germany has renegotiated its existing treaty network, which currently uses a limited separate-entity approach. This conundrum has been criticized heavily by both academics and practitioners.

In *The Netherlands*, the same "functional" approach taken with respect to income attribution applies to deductions. There are no statutory rules or court decisions concerning the deduction of "internal" expenses. In a 2016 decision, the Dutch Supreme Court held that internal royalties should be disregarded when determining the

416. Japan, CTA, s. 146-2.
417. United Kingdom, Corporation Tax Act 2009, ss. 21-32.
418. *See* in general Germany, ITA, s. 4, para. 4 (not limited to international allocation).
419. Federal Ministry of Finance, Circular of December 22, 2016, Federal Tax Gazette 2017 Part I, p. 182 para. 10.

profits of the branch where a treaty is based on a pre-2010 version of the OECD Model.[420]

All expenses effectively connected with and borne by the *French* branch of a foreign corporation, whether incurred by it or on behalf of it and wherever incurred, are deductible from taxable income. An expense incurred for the purposes of several branches must be allocated among them according to appropriate criteria. The general administrative expenses of the head office are usually allocable based on the ratio that the branch's turnover bears to that of the corporation as a whole. According to the French tax authorities, no allowance is normally made for payments by the branch to the head office in return for money loaned or patent rights conceded by the head office to the branch, where they do not constitute the reimbursement of expenses paid or accrued to third parties; however, case law seems to have diverged from this position.[421] Subject to exceptions, nonresident individuals are denied the personal deductions from global net income and tax credits to which residents are entitled unless these are expressly permitted by statute.[422]

In *Australia*, the normal allocation rules for deductions apply in this area as they do in others—expenses are deductible if they relate to income which is assessable. The special regimes which apply to overseas ships and nonresident insurers deem a certain percentage of freight charges (5%) or premiums (10%) to be taxable income to which the normal tax rates are applied, and thus amount to formulary measures allowing deductions for expenses of 95% and 90% of income, respectively. In some cases, the local agent of the taxpayer can elect out of the special regime in favor of net-basis taxation.

When it became possible for foreign banks to operate branches in Australia, a special regime was enacted for the calculation of their income. By way of exception to the single-entity approach in Australian law, branches of foreign banks are treated as separate entities for certain purposes of Australian tax law. Most important, only 6% of the branch's liabilities are treated as equity; the rest, multiplied by the LIBOR interest rate, is deductible and subject to interest withholding tax at 5% (which often does not apply due to the application of withholding tax exemptions for global capital markets). A branch of a foreign bank may elect to be taxed under tax treaty rules where a more generous treaty is applicable, ensuring that the statutory regime is not in breach of treaty obligations.

In determining the profits of an establishment in *China*, actual expenses incurred by the establishment and apportioned overhead expenses are deductible. Nonresident taxpayers must provide information pertaining to the nature and amount of expenses and the methods of apportionment in order to demonstrate that the expenses are reasonable and related to the activities of the establishment. However, rental and royalties paid by a Chinese establishment to its foreign head office are not deductible.

420. Supreme Court, June 3, 2016, No. 14/05100, BNB 2016/171, relating to the 1971 Spain-Netherlands tax treaty, which is based on the 1963 OECD Model.
421. *See* Conseil d'Etat, November 9, 2015, No. 370974 (*Société Sodirep*), in the opposite situation (interest received in consideration for a loan to the foreign head office). *See* Art. 7(2) of the 2017 OECD Model Convention.
422. France, CGI, s. 164 A.

Interest paid by a Chinese establishment to another establishment of the same enterprise is not deductible, unless the enterprise is a bank. Service and management fees paid by a Chinese establishment or site to its head office in the course of production and business operations are deductible, but only if they are at arm's length and the payments can be substantiated. However, management fees paid by a Chinese-resident enterprise to a nonresident enterprise are not deductible.[423]

In *India*, the normal rules for the computation of business income apply to branches. However, special limits apply to the deduction of head office expenses because of the difficulties involved in verifying the accounts, especially where the books and records for the branch are maintained abroad.[424] The allowable amount of "head office expenditure" attributable to a business in India is limited to 5% of the "adjusted total income."[425] The courts have reduced the rigors of the provision to some extent by holding that any expenditures incurred exclusively for the purposes of a branch are deductible. Where a taxpayer does not have any business overseas and the entire operations are carried out in India, the question of allocating a part of the expenditure in question to the business carried on in India cannot arise.[426] Notional expenses with respect to transactions between the head office and a branch are not deductible, except in the case of banks under tax treaties.[427]

1.4 Taxation of Income from Services, Including Employment

Most jurisdictions examined here tax income from services earned by nonresidents on a net basis, typically with an exemption where the contacts with the jurisdiction are not extensive. Two basic approaches are used in determining the source of income from services. One focuses on the place where the services are performed, taking into account the days of physical presence of the service provider in the country or the availability of a fixed place of business. The other is based on the place where the services are used or consumed, that is, the locus of the benefit from the services. In general, expenses incurred in earning domestic source services income are deductible (except in the case of fees for technical services in India), but personal allowances or preferential rate schedules either are not available or are limited.

In many of the countries, the rules differ depending on whether the nonresident service provider is an employee or an independent contractor, since nonresident independent contractors are taxable under the provisions of an applicable treaty only

423. China, EIT Law, Art. 49.
424. India, ITA 1961, s. 44C.
425. "Head office expenditure" is defined to mean executive and general administration expenditure incurred outside India, including rent, taxes, insurance, salary, wages, traveling expenses, etc., of employees involved in managing offices outside India.
426. *Rupenjuli Tea Co Ltd v. CIT*, August 25, 1989, Calcutta High Court. Traveling expenses by employees of a foreign company to visit a branch in India are deductible on the ground that they are incurred exclusively for the branch. *CIT v. Emirates Commercial Bank Ltd*, April 30, 2003, Bombay High Court. Section 44C contemplates allocation of expenses among various entities.
427. *Sumitomo Mitsui Banking Corporation v. DDIT*, ITA No. 6496 of 2006, November 22, 2012, ITAT, Mumbai.

where they have a fixed place of business or PE in the source country, whereas nonresident employees of resident employers (or nonresident employers with a PE in the source country) are taxable on any income derived from employment services provided in the source country. In addition, in some countries, the deductions available to both resident and nonresident employees are strictly limited, whereas in general, nonresident independent contractors are entitled to deduct all expenses incurred in earning their income. *See* Part II, Subpart A, section 1.2 for a discussion of the distinction between employees and independent contractors.

The *United States* considers services income to have its source where the services are performed. The provision of personal services is treated as a trade or business, thus satisfying the threshold for net-basis taxation. A *de minimis* rule exempts the income where both the presence in the jurisdiction and the amount of income are minimal and the payer is a foreign person.[428]

In *Japan*, income from personal services likewise has a domestic source where the services are performed in Japan, and there is no further requirement for the income to be subject to net-basis taxation. In the case of employees, domestic law allows only very limited deductions. A special rule treats directors' fees paid by a domestic corporation as Japanese source income regardless of where the services are performed, thus assimilating such payments to corporate distributions.[429]

The *Canadian* rules also focus on employment or independent services performed in Canada. Income from such employment is taxed on a net basis, although the deductions in respect of such income are limited for both resident and nonresident employees.[430] Under a special provision, where a nonresident was formerly a resident of Canada, their entire employment income received from a Canadian payer is subject to Canadian tax except to the extent that the amount received for employment outside Canada is subject to tax in a foreign jurisdiction.[431] Income from independent services performed in Canada is taxable on a net basis where the nonresident is carrying on business in Canada.

In general, *The Netherlands* does not allow the deduction of employment-related expenses and personal allowances are available to nonresidents employed in The Netherlands only under very strict conditions (including an income threshold and a requirement that the employee be a resident of a qualifying state).[432] As a general rule, nonresidents are subject to tax on income from employment where the employment activities are carried out in The Netherlands (i.e., the employee is physically present in The Netherlands to render the services).[433] In addition to this general rule, in particular cases employment activities exercised abroad may be deemed to be exercised in The

428. United States, IRC, s. 861(a)(3).
429. Japan, ITA, s. 161 para. 8.
430. Canada, ITA, s. 8(2).
431. Canada, ITA, s. 115(2).
432. Netherlands, ITA, Art. 7.8, i.e., a qualifying nonresident taxpayer.
433. Netherlands, ITA, Art. 7.2(2)(b).

Netherlands.[434] Directors' fees paid by domestic corporations to nonresident directors are taxed even where the services are performed abroad.[435]

In *Australia*, the source rule for employment income under case law is a mixture of place of performance, place of contract, and place of payment, although place of performance is regarded as the most important.[436] The normal collection rules (deduction, assessment, and withholding) apply to nonresident employees, although a different rate scale is used for nonresidents taxed by assessment.[437] The international jurisdictional rules for the fringe benefits tax levied on employers effectively track those used for employment income.[438] In a number of its more recent tax treaties, Australia has dealt with the fringe benefits tax by giving the exclusive right to tax fringe benefits to the country which has the primary right to tax the salary of the employee (the source country if the conditions in the equivalent of paragraph 2 of Article 15 in the OECD Model Convention are not satisfied, otherwise the residence country).

The *United Kingdom* taxes all compensation for services performed within the United Kingdom. Where duties are performed partly within and partly outside the United Kingdom, the income is generally apportioned on a time basis. Taxation is levied on a net basis but certain personal deductions are not available.[439]

Sweden taxes employment income of nonresidents primarily on a gross basis with a flat tax amounting to 25% of the gross remuneration.[440] However, nonresidents can opt for taxation on a net basis, with higher progressive tax rates.

Germany taxes employment income where the services are carried out in Germany or "utilized" by employees (e.g., by exploiting IP rights resulting from their work).[441] Taxation is levied on a net basis, but in the case of employment income some deductions are limited (subject to constraints under EU law). Special rules, mostly laid down in bilateral agreements, apply to cross-border workers.

France levies a complex progressive (0%, 12%, and 20%) withholding tax (which does not apply to French residents), on employment income of nonresident individuals performing their activities in France.[442] The rates of 12% and 20% are reduced to 8% and 14.4% where the activities take place in the French overseas departments. The tax is assessed on a net basis in that the salary is reduced by the standard 10% professional expense deduction, but the election to deduct actual expenses, open to residents, is not available to nonresidents. The 12% tax is final but

434. Netherlands, ITA, Art. 7.2(7); where an employee of a Netherlands-resident employer (wage tax withholding agent) performs employment activities partly in The Netherlands and partly outside, the employee is deemed to have carried out the employment fully in The Netherlands. An exception applies where the employment activities are exercised in a treaty state and the income may be taxed in that state or where the activities are exercised in a nontreaty state which effectively taxes the income from the employment exercised in that state.
435. Netherlands, ITA, Art. 7.2(17)(b).
436. *French* (1957) 98 CLR 398; exceptions include a number of cases involving sailors, a movie star (*Mitchum*) (1965) 113 CLR 401, and an academic on sabbatical leave (*Evans*), 81 ATC 4512.
437. Australia, Income Tax Rates Act 1986, Sch. 7.
438. Taxation Determination TD 2011/1.
439. United Kingdom, Income Tax (Earnings and Pensions) Act 2003, ss. 9, 11, and 27.
440. *See* below in this Subpart B, section 2.
441. Germany, ITA, s. 49 para. 4.
442. France, CGI, s. 182 A.

income taxed in the upper bracket is included in global annual income and therefore is subject to progressive IIT according to the same rules which apply to wages earned by French residents; the 20% withholding tax is then creditable against such income tax. A refund of the excess of both the 12% and 20% withholding taxes is possible under certain conditions. From 2010 onward, the same rules apply to nonresidents and residents. A withholding tax, the rate of which depends on the income tax paid in the preceding year, is levied on employment income before deduction of any professional expenses. It is then creditable against the progressive income tax calculated on the nonresident's global income taxable in France, including employment income after the deduction of professional expenses (10% standard deduction or actual expenses). In addition, any excess over the portion of this income tax attributable to such employment income is refundable. Special rules continue to apply to sportspersons (15% withholding tax on gross income)[443] and artists (15% on net income, creditable and refundable); these rates are raised to 75% when the payment is made to persons domiciled or established in an uncooperative state or territory, unless the debtor provides proof that these sums correspond to actual transactions which have a purpose and effect other than enabling them to be located in an uncooperative state or territory.[444]

In *China*, under the IIT, like residents, individual nonresidents who derive employment income or income from labor services are taxed at progressive rates and tax is deducted at source. Nonresident individuals may be exempt from tax if they are present in China for no more than 90 days. In computing the amount of taxable income, a nonresident individual can deduct CNY 5,000 (approximately USD 710) each month from employment income or 20% of the fees for providing labor services. Actual expenses are not deductible.

In *India*, section 9(1)(ii) of the ITA declares that salaries earned in India are deemed to accrue in India. The explanation to the section provides that payment for services rendered in India (including payments for weekends, holidays, and periods of leave), which are preceded and succeeded by services rendered in India as part of the service contract of employment, constitute income earned in India. The provisions of most of India's tax treaties dealing with employment income and income from services follow the provisions of the UN Model Treaty. In particular, most Indian treaties contain an article on fees for technical services. Disputes often arise where a nonresident company sends employees to render services in India for the company or for its Indian subsidiary.[445]

443. France, CGI, s. 182 B.
444. France, CGI, s. 182 A bis (same rules as those for sportspersons before 2009).
445. *Centrica India Offshore Pvt Ltd Offshore.*, WPC No. 6807/2012, April 25, 2014, Delhi HC, and *CIT v. Karl Storz Endoscopy India Ltd*, ITA 13, 2008, September 13, 2010 (Delhi HC). *See also Flipkart Internet Private Limited v. DCIT*, W.P. No. 3619/2021, June 24, 2022 Karnataka High Court.

1.5 Other Situations Involving Net-Basis Taxation

A number of other types of income are often taxed on a net basis, although there is considerable variation in approach. Most often, the income has substantial associated deductions or deduction levels which vary from situation to situation so that gross taxation, even at a low level, might yield inappropriate results. Often, net-basis treatment is available for real estate income, where depreciation and interest deductions can be substantial. Gains from the disposition of substantial investments in domestic corporations are also often taxed on a net basis, with the underlying domestic business activity of the corporation, in effect, attributed to nonresident shareholders for purposes of taxing the gain.

The *United States* allows an election for net-basis taxation with respect to real estate. Where the real estate activities constitute a trade or business, the income would be subject to net-basis taxation even without a special rule; however, in other cases, rental income would be subject to gross withholding tax. A special election allows taxpayers to elect to have all real estate income taxed on a net basis.[446] In addition, gain on the sale of domestic real estate is also taxed on a net basis, and that treatment is extended to gain on the shares of domestic corporations which have substantial domestic real estate holdings.[447]

Canada similarly has an election to have real estate rental income, timber royalties, pension and related benefits, and income from acting services taxed on a net basis.[448] In the absence of an election, these types of income are subject to gross-basis withholding tax at 25%, or 23% in the case of acting services. In addition, gains from the disposition of "taxable Canadian property" by nonresidents are subject to Canadian tax on a net basis. Taxable Canadian property includes unlisted shares of a Canadian-resident corporation, unlisted shares of nonresident corporations and interests in partnerships or nonresident trusts which derive their value principally from real property and resource property situated in Canada, and listed shares of a corporation where nonresidents and non-arm's length persons own 25% or more of the shares.[449]

Most other jurisdictions tax real estate income on a net basis regardless of the level of activity or whether the real estate activities would otherwise qualify as a business. This is the case in *Germany*, where rental income is subject to source taxation if the underlying immovable assets are located in Germany.[450] Special legislation was necessary in the case of foreign corporations: because income derived by corporate taxpayers is deemed to be business income and source taxation of business income generally requires the existence of a PE, foreign real estate entities had claimed to be exempt from tax in Germany. A special provision ensures that these entities can be taxed even in the absence of a PE.[451] The same is generally true for *The Netherlands*.

446. United States, IRC, ss. 871(d); 881(d).
447. United States, IRC, s. 897(a).
448. Canada, ITA, ss. 216, 216.1 and 217.
449. Canada, ITA, s. 248(1).
450. Germany, ITA, s. 49 para. 1 No. 6.
451. Germany, ITA, s. 49 para. 1 No. 2 lit. f.

In *Australia*, a hybrid system applies where rent is derived through a CIV (property trust) by a nonresident; a gross final withholding tax is applied to the rent component of the distribution, although normal deductions for property investment are available at the level of the CIV in calculating the amount of rental income subject to the withholding tax.[452]

Results are more varied with respect to gains from the disposal by nonresidents of substantial shareholdings in domestic corporations. In general, *Australia*, *Sweden*, the *United Kingdom*, and the *United States* do not impose tax on this category of income. In contrast, *Canada*, *Germany*, *Japan*, and *The Netherlands* (under varying conditions), include such gains in domestic source income and impose a net-basis tax. Thus, in Germany, for example, nonresidents are subject to tax on gains from the disposition of a greater than 1% interest in a German corporation but do not pay taxes on capital gains from shares under the 1% threshold.[453] Under Dutch tax law, dividend and interest payments received on shares in a domestic company and capital gains realized on the disposal of such shares[454] are subject to tax on a net basis where the nonresident person owns at least 5% of the shares and those shares are not an active business asset of the nonresident person.[455] Under tax treaties, however, The Netherlands typically cannot apply this domestic taxing rule except with respect to dividends.

Other miscellaneous types of income are often subject to tax on a net basis independent of the general classification of the activity generating the income as a business or PE. For example, *Australia* levies a withholding tax on natural resource payments to nonresidents, but the rate is negotiated with the tax administration and is meant to reflect expenses; taxpayers can file returns for refunds or be assessed on a net basis if it turns out that the estimated expenses are incorrect.[456] *Japan* subjects income from the "use or holding" of domestic assets to net-basis taxation, regardless of the absence of a PE, but only where such income is not covered by other provisions requiring gross-basis taxation of Japanese source income.[457] In short, major income items sourced in Japan are taxed either on a net basis (in the presence of a PE) or gross-basis withholding (in the absence of a PE), while some miscellaneous income (such as profit from dealing in Japanese government bonds and interest from nonbusiness loans to residents) is subject to net-basis taxation regardless of the existence of a PE.[458]

In *China*, gains realized by a nonresident individual or enterprise from transfers of property in China are taxable through withholding tax at a flat rate of 20% on the net amount of the gain.

In *India*, certain types of income, such as royalties and fees for technical services, are taxed on a gross basis. Income in the other income categories is taxed taking into

452. Australia, ITAA 1997, Div. 840-M, Income Tax (Managed Investment Trust Withholding Tax) Act 2008, Taxation Administration Act 1953, Sch. 1 Div. 12-H.
453. Germany, ITA, s. 49, para. 1 No. 2 lit.e.
454. This may include reverse hybrid entities. *See* Netherlands, ITA, Art. 7.2(19).
455. Netherlands, ITA, Art. 7.2(2)(c) in connection with Art. 7.2(3) and Art. 7.5(1).
456. Australia, ITAA 1936, s. 6CA, Taxation Administration Act 1953, Sch. 1 Div. 12-G.
457. Japan, ITA, s. 161(1), No. 2, and CTA, s. 138(1), No. 2.
458. Japan, ITA, s. 161 para. 1 and CTA, s. 138 para. 1.

account certain expenditures.[459] As discussed in the chapter on India in Part I, some types of income, such as income from shipping, are taxed on a presumptive basis.

2 ISSUES IN THE STRUCTURE OF GROSS-BASIS TAXATION

All the systems studied here impose a gross-basis withholding tax on certain categories of income. Sometimes the withholding tax is part of the domestic system and is applied to residents and nonresidents alike, although for nonresidents it represents a final tax. In other cases, the withholding tax is aimed only at foreign persons. The income subject to withholding is typically investment-type income which is not connected with a business activity and is deemed to have a domestic source. Thus, the structural rules involve issues of classification of the income by type as well as by source. In some cases, the source rules are the same as those used in determining the income entitled to domestic double tax relief (usually a FTC); in some cases, there are special source rules for income accruing to foreign persons.

The *United States* rules imposing gross-basis taxation on foreign persons apply to "fixed or determinable annual or periodic" income from domestic sources.[460] The taxable category has been broadly interpreted and applies essentially to all income which does not involve the sale of property. The rate of tax is 30% regardless of the type of income. However, there are statutory exceptions which exempt interest on domestic bank deposits and most interest paid by U.S. corporations or the U.S. government on publicly traded debt.[461]

Detailed statutory source rules deal with commonly recurring types of income such as dividends, interest, royalties, etc.[462] In general, the same source rules which apply to domestic persons apply to foreign persons. The source rules focus in part on economic connections and in part on formal legal relations. For example, royalties are sourced where the property is used while interest, in general, is sourced where the payer is resident. Special rules apply to interest paid by a U.S. trade or business. The interest is treated as if paid by a U.S. corporation and, as such, is subject to tax in the hands of the foreign recipient. In addition, if, under the rules allocating interest expense to a U.S. branch, more interest has been deducted than was paid directly, the branch is subject to the usually applicable gross-basis tax on that excess.[463]

Domestic source income is subject to withholding by the payer and the withheld amount functions as a final tax. No withholding is required where the income is part of the business income of the foreign taxpayer. If, for some reason, the appropriate tax is not withheld, the foreign person as well as the domestic withholding agent are both liable for the tax. Special withholding rules also apply to partnerships with nonresident partners and to dispositions of U.S. real estate.[464]

459. India, ITA 1961, s. 57(iii).
460. United States, IRC, ss. 871(a), 881(a).
461. United States, IRC, s. 871(h).
462. United States, IRC, s. 871(a).
463. United States, IRC, s. 884(f).
464. United States, IRC, s. 1441-45.

Japan takes a somewhat similar approach. Source rules deal with rentals, interest, dividends, royalties, prizes, annuities, income from certain financial instruments, and "silent partnership" income. All such income is subject to withholding even where it arises in connection with a business which is taxed on a net basis.[465] (Nonresident individuals and corporations with a PE can apply for an exemption from withholding.)[466] The withheld tax is credited against the net-basis tax liability. The source rules are generally the same for both inbound and outbound transactions.

The *Swedish*[467] system does not have extensive source rules and simply defines certain categories of income which are subject to withholding as a final tax. Unlike other systems, Sweden taxes employment income from services performed in Sweden on a gross basis. Withholding is imposed on the following types of income at the given rates: employment income, directors' fees, pensions (25%); dividends (30%); artists and entertainers (15%). No withholding tax is levied on outbound payments of interest. The rates of withholding were set at a level which tries in a rough way to take into account the costs associated with the income. The Swedish "special income tax" (*Särskild Inkomstskatt*) is a 25% tax on gross income earned by nonresidents; it applies mainly to income from employment by a Swedish employer (or by a foreign employer if the employee stays for more than 183 days per year in Sweden) and to pensions paid by the Swedish government or in respect of private employment carried out in Sweden. Following criticism from the CJEU that the 25% tax on gross income could result in harsher taxation than taxation according to normal rules, an election for taxation under normal rules was introduced (thus making it possible for taxation on a net basis, albeit at higher tax rates),[468] but the election is available only for persons whose employment income is earned wholly or almost wholly in Sweden.

Canada imposes a 25% withholding tax on a statutory catalog of income amounts paid by Canadian residents to nonresidents.[469] The statute is not structured in terms of source rules but in practice the provisions function in that manner. Thus, in general, listed amounts paid by a Canadian resident to a non-arm's length nonresident are subject to the withholding tax. This is functionally the same result as in the United States, which relies on explicit source rules.

Withholding is required on some types of interest, including participating interest and interest paid to non-arm's length persons, but exceptions are made for interest paid to arm's length nonresidents, interest on governmental obligations, and mortgage interest on real property located outside Canada.[470] Estate and trust income is generally subject to withholding when paid to nonresidents. Amounts paid by a resident for the use of, or the right to use, property in Canada, including intangibles, are subject to tax, with the charging provision in effect functioning as a source rule. Dividends paid by Canadian corporations, including constructive dividends, are subject to tax, as are

465. Japan, ITA, s. 212.
466. Japan, ITA, ss. 180, 214.
467. Sweden, Act on special income tax for foreign residents.
468. *See* CJEU, July 1, 2004, C-169/03 (*Wallentin*).
469. Canada, ITA, Part XIII.
470. Canada, ITA, s. 212(1)(b) and (3).

management fees, alimony, pensions and other deferred compensation, the interest element in annuities, and a wide variety of other payments.

The scope of the withholding regime is extended substantially by rules deeming certain payers to be Canadian residents (and thus subject to withholding obligations) and by parallel rules deeming recipients to be nonresidents, again triggering a withholding tax liability.[471] Thus, payments by a nonresident which are deductible in computing Canadian business or real estate profits are deemed to be made by a Canadian resident and thus subject to withholding when paid to a nonresident. Specific rules apply to partnerships to treat them as residents with respect to amounts paid to nonresidents which are deductible in Canada, and as nonresidents with respect to amounts received from Canadian-resident payers.[472]

A special regime applies to nonresident actors and their companies. Such nonresidents are subject to a flat-rate final withholding tax of 23% of the income from acting services performed in Canada.[473] As noted above, nonresident actors have the option of filing a tax return and paying tax on their net income.[474]

The *United Kingdom* requires withholding at the basic rate of 20% on a wide range of investment income.[475] In the case of rent from land, withholding applies only to payments to nonresidents. The withholding is not a final tax and is credited against any tax liability declared by the nonresident. In contrast, interest is subject to withholding but there are many exceptions; in particular, withholding does not apply to payments of interest to a resident company. Annuities and certain other annual payments (including royalties) are subject to withholding at the basic rate of 20%. Dividends are not subject to any withholding tax. Where any of these types of payment (other than rent from land) is received by a nonresident that has no UK representative, UK tax is limited to any withholding tax.

In *Germany*, withholding taxes are imposed on some categories of income regardless of the status of the recipient and are also imposed specifically on certain income paid to nonresidents. With respect to capital income (dividends, certain types of interest, income of silent partners), the withholding tax, imposed at a 25% rate, represents a final tax for nonresidents.[476] In addition, a final 15% withholding tax is imposed on income from artistic, sporting, or cultural activities, royalties for the use of intangibles, and rentals for personal property.[477]

In 2020, a "special rule" which had been dormant in the German ITAs since 1925[478] was finally "discovered" and created a major upheaval for international business. Under this rule, royalty payments for the use of IP rights "registered" in Germany are subject to source taxation irrespective of whether these IP rights are

471. Canada, ITA, s. 212(13) and (13.2).
472. Canada, ITA, s. 212(13.1).
473. Canada, ITA, ss. 212(5.1) and 215(1).
474. Canada, ITA, s. 216.1.
475. Generally, *see* United Kingdom, Income Tax Act 2007, Part 15 and regulations made under that Part.
476. Germany, ITA, ss. 43-45e, s. 50 para. 2b.
477. Germany, ITA, s. 50a paras. 1 and 2.
478. Germany, ITA, s. 49 para. 1 No. 2 lit.f and No. 6.

"utilized" in a traditional sense in Germany. As a result, royalty payments between two foreign taxpayers that can be traced to a patent or trademark registered in Germany are taxable in Germany. Practical cases concern the production of pharmaceuticals or consumer goods which are manufactured outside Germany under a license granted by a related or unrelated IP owner and then delivered to German customers. Since this provision is not in line with international tax practice and threatens to undermine the principle that source taxation is not applied on the basis of mere sales, the German tax legislature reduced its scope in 2022 to intragroup transactions not protected under tax treaties.

In 2003, the CJEU declared the concept of "gross basis" taxation to be an infringement of the EU freedom of services.[479] In response, Germany has broadened the deductions for direct costs available to nonresident EU/EEA taxpayers[480]—the downside being that taxation on a net basis requires the application of twice the tax rate for individual taxpayers.[481]

Under a case law principle which was later incorporated into the statute, the usual rule that all the income of a corporation is treated as business income is not applied in the case of nonresident corporations.[482] Thus, they can be taxed on, for example, royalty or dividend income from German sources even in the absence of a PE.

In *Australia*, final withholding tax on dividends, interest, and royalties paid to nonresidents is levied at rates of 30%, 10%, and 30%, respectively.[483] The interest withholding tax has an important exemption for widely held offshore fundraisings which extends to all cases where the loan is open to public bidding, even where one lender takes the whole loan, and, under treaties since 2001, to foreign financial institutions. Foreign pension funds which are tax exempt in their home country are generally exempt from withholding tax on dividends and interest.

The basic source rule in each case is payment by a resident to a nonresident. However, the interest and royalty withholding rules also reflect the emphasis on the concept of a PE in tax treaties, in the sense that the tax applies to payments of interest *by* nonresidents with Australian PEs and payments *to* Australian residents with offshore PEs. The basic criterion is the use of the funds or property in an Australian business. In the case of payments to an offshore PE of a resident, the income is included in assessable income (unlike all other payments subject to the nonresident withholding tax) unless the exemption for an Australian branch of an Australian-resident company applies. But no credit is given for the tax withheld, which in this case operates as a surrogate tax on interest payments made by the offshore PE to third parties. Consistent with the approach in tax treaties, in general, under domestic law, tax by assessment

479. CJEU, June 12, 2003, C-234/01 (*Gerritse*); *see also* CJEU, November 13, 2019, C-641/17 (*College Pension Plan of British Columbia*) for the application of a net basis on corporate portfolio income.
480. Germany, ITA, s. 50a para. 3.
481. Germany, ITA, s. 50a para. 3 s. 4.
482. Germany, ITA, s. 49 para. 2.
483. Australia, ITAA 1936, Pt III Div. 11A, Income Tax (Dividends, Interest and Royalties, Withholding Tax) Act 1974, Taxation Administration Act 1953, Sch. 1 Div. 12-F.

rather than final gross withholding applies to dividends, interest, and royalties received by a nonresident through a PE in Australia.[484]

Dividends are in a special position because of Australia's imputation system. The franked part of dividends is not subject to withholding tax when paid to nonresidents. Where the dividend is attributable to an Australian PE, the nonresident is entitled to the imputation credit, contrary to the normal rule that the imputation credit is not extended to nonresidents; but, unlike the case of certain residents, the credit is nonrefundable.[485] Where an Australian-resident company receives foreign income, it may be exempt or assessable depending on the kind of income, as discussed above. When the company pays out such income, it will be an unfranked dividend to the extent that no Australian company tax was paid on the income as a result of the foreign income exemption or FTC systems. The company may track such "conduit foreign income" and match it with dividends paid, which are not subject to nonresident dividend withholding tax to that extent.[486] Although in theory this benefit is available to Australian multinational companies with nonresident subsidiaries and nonresident shareholders, strict rules to prevent streaming of dividends under the imputation and conduit foreign income systems mean that the benefit generally has the greatest relevance to headquarters companies. In relation to capital gains, the government introduced a participation exemption for capital gains on nonportfolio interests in foreign subsidiaries in 2004 and removed the tax on sales by nonresidents of nonportfolio interests in Australian-resident companies in 2006 (apart from land-rich companies) so that Australia now effectively has a full conduit regime for capital gains as well as dividends.[487]

The *French* tax code contains a list of French-source income; foreign source income is defined as anything else. Source is determined, according to the categories, on the basis of economic connections or formal legal relations, or a combination of both. Some categories of income are subject to withholding taxes. Two withholding taxes are levied on gross income, one final[488] and the other creditable against income tax.[489] Those levied on a net basis[490] are final taxes for individual taxpayers only. Those creditable are also refundable when levied on gains or on income realized mainly by European taxpayers, in order to comply with CJEU case law. The withholding tax on employment income is complex in that it is assessed partly on a net basis and partly on a gross basis, as well as partially creditable against income tax and, in that case, partially refundable.[491]

---

484. In the case of royalties, this position applies only where the recipient is a resident of a country with which Australia has a tax treaty; International Tax Agreements Act 1953, s. 17A(4).
485. Australia, ITAA 1936, s. 44(1), ITAA 1997, s. 67-25(1DA).
486. Australia, ITAA 1997, Div. 802-A.
487. Australia, ITAA 1997, Divs. 768-G, 855.
488. France, CGI, ss. 119 bis 2 and 187 (distributed income).
489. France, CGI, s. 182 B (income from independent personal services, copyrights, industrial property rights, remuneration for services of any kind supplied or used in France, and remuneration of artists and athletes).
490. France, CGI, s. 244 bis and 244 bis A (real property gains) and 244 bis B (gains on more than 25% holdings).
491. France, CGI, s. 182 A. *See* section 1.4 above.

Of all the jurisdictions considered here, *The Netherlands* has the least extensive gross-basis source taxation. Historically, this appears to reflect a conscious policy—relinquished at the end of the last century as a result of EU and OECD pressure—to encourage the use of The Netherlands as a location for holding and intermediate companies often engaged in treaty-shopping activities. Currently, the sole withholding tax on capital income is a tax (15%) on dividends (including profit-related interest)[492] paid by Dutch-resident companies. For nonresidents, this tax is a final tax unless the dividends are attributable to a PE, in which case the tax is credited against the net-basis tax liability. In addition, an exemption applies to nonresident corporate shareholders with a participation (5% or more of the nominal paid-in capital) in the payer company, provided that: (i) the corporate shareholder is resident in the EU or the EEA or in a jurisdiction with which The Netherlands has concluded a tax treaty which includes a dividend provision comparable to Article 10 of the OECD Model Treaty[493] and (ii) certain anti-abuse requirements are met.[494] In general, other interest, royalties, and similar payments are not subject to any tax when paid to nonresidents. However, a conditional withholding tax[495] is levied on interest,[496] royalties,[497] and dividends[498] payable by a Netherlands-resident withholding agent[499] to an affiliated recipient entity[500] established in a low-tax jurisdiction,[501] as well as in situations involving abuse.

Under the *Chinese* EIT Law and Regulations, a 20% withholding tax is imposed on various types of payments made to nonresidents. The list of payments subject to withholding is somewhat open-ended and includes gains from transfers of property, dividends, interest, rent, royalties, and other income to be determined by the MOF or STA.[502] The MOF and STA have the authority to deem fees for engineering services to be subject to withholding tax.[503] The amount of income subject to withholding tax is

492. Netherlands, Dividend Withholding Tax Act 1965, Art. 4(1)(a).
493. Netherlands, DivTA, Art. 4(2).
494. Netherlands, DivTA, Art. 4(3) and (4).
495. Netherlands, Withholding Tax Act 2021 (WTA 2021).
496. Netherlands, WTA 2021, Art. 3.1(a) in connection with Art. 3.3.
497. Netherlands, WTA 2021, Art. 3.1(b) in connection with Art. 3.4.
498. Netherlands, WTA 2021, Art. 3.1(c) in connection with Art. 3.4a (applicable from January 1, 2024).
499. Netherlands, WTA 2021, Art. 1.3(1) provides a deeming provision according to which a withholding agent incorporated according to Netherlands law is deemed to be resident in The Netherlands for the purposes of this legislation. Withholding tax is also due if the affiliated withholding agent is not established in The Netherlands, but the interest or royalties (or dividends, *see* below) are attributable to a PE in The Netherlands (Netherlands, WTA 2021, Art. 3.3 and 3.4).
500. The withholding agents affiliated with the beneficiary are defined in Netherlands, WTA 2021, Art. 1.2(1)(c).
501. A low-tax jurisdiction is defined in Netherlands, WTA 2021, Art. 1.2(1)(e) as a jurisdiction that (i) has a generally applicable statutory rate of less than 9% or (ii) is included in the "EU blacklist." In this respect, the same ministerial regulations apply as in the case of the CFC legislation (Netherlands, CITA, Art. 13ab(3)(d) and (e)).
502. China, STA, Guo Shui Fa [2009] No. 3 and other circulars provide further details.
503. China, EIT Law, Art. 38.

the gross amount of the payment.[504] There is no election in respect of rental income to pay tax on a net basis.

Under the IIT, dividends, rent, royalties, service fees, capital gains, and incidental income paid by residents to nonresidents are also subject to a 20% withholding tax. The withholding agent is entitled to a 2% commission.[505]

In 2017, perhaps in response to the U.S. tax reform, China introduced measures to boost inbound and outbound investment. One of the most important measures waives dividend withholding tax on after-tax profits which are reinvested in China.

Several structural issues which affect Chinese withholding tax are: (a) characterization, especially the scope of "royalties" in mixed transactions (e.g., transfer of proprietary information along with the provision of services or sale of equipment) and a substance-over-form approach to characterizing service fees as royalties; (b) determination of Chinese source with respect to offshore indirect transfers through the General Anti-avoidance Rule (GAAR); and (c) lack of a mechanism for recognizing expenses in certain cases (such as rent).

In *India*, withholding, known as deduction of tax at source (TDS), is an important part of the effort to broaden the tax base. The provisions dealing with TDS are contained in chapter XVII-A relating to collection and recovery of tax. Responsibility for deducting tax at different rates is placed on the payer and includes individuals (including Hindu Undivided Families), corporate entities, residents, and even nonresidents, and applies to a wide range of payments to both residents and nonresidents. With the abolition of the dividend distribution tax (DDT) and reversion to the classical system of taxation of dividends, tax must be deducted at source from dividends. The most-favored-nation clause in Protocols to tax treaties with some OECD Member Countries was invoked by some taxpayers to demand the lower rate of withholding granted to countries that were not members of the OECD when those treaties were entered into. Although the taxpayers won in lower courts, the Supreme Court finally ruled against such claims.[506]

Under section 195, TDS applies at the "rates in force"—the rates fixed by the Act or the reduced rates under an applicable tax treaty—to any payment to a nonresident subject to tax (other than salary). Under section 192, TDS on salaries is required at an average rate. TDS is also required with respect to capital gains, except capital gains of foreign institutional investors. The rate of TDS on income derived by nonresident sportspersons is 20%. Payments by nonresidents to nonresidents are subject to TDS as long as the payments are subject to Indian tax, irrespective of whether the nonresident has a residence, place of business, or a business connection in India or any other presence in any manner in India.[507]

504. China, EIT Law, Art. 19.
505. China, IIT Law, Art. 17.
506. *Assessing Officer (International Taxation) v. Nestle SA*, Civil Appeal No. 1420 of 2023, October 19, 2023 (SC).
507. India, ITA 1961, s. 195, explanation 2.

Where a payment to a nonresident is not subject to Indian tax under the provisions of the ITA or a treaty, there is no obligation to withhold.[508] However, payers must be very sure about the chargeability of the payments involved, since the payments may not be deductible where the payer fails to withhold. Alternatively, nonresidents can request the tax authorities for a determination of the appropriate rate of TDS. In certain circumstances, the payee may also obtain a certificate to allow a lower rate of TDS.[509]

In general, withholding in India is not final. The taxpayer concerned can always file a return and claim a refund. Final withholding applies in cases of presumptive taxation and taxable passive income. With respect to foreign withholding taxes, some court decisions held that only amounts received net of taxes withheld could be charged to tax in India[510] In 2024, the provision was amended to deem such taxes to be received in India.[511]

3 BRANCH PROFITS TAX

Absent special rules, the remittance of profits from a branch activity would not be subject to any further source-based taxation. In contrast, dividends paid by a domestic corporation would typically be subject to a withholding tax. This difference in treatment of alternative investment structures caused some countries to impose a second "level" of tax on branch income of foreign corporations. Although the technical rules differ in many respects, the basic impact of the tax is to subject the net after-tax profits of a branch to tax roughly equivalent to the tax which would have been applicable to a distribution of profits by a domestic subsidiary.

Until 1986, the *United States* attempted to impose a second "level" of tax where a foreign corporation with U.S. branch activities made a dividend distribution to its shareholders. The tax was very difficult to enforce and was resented by other countries as an attempt at "extraterritorial" taxation, involving as it did the taxation of a distribution by a foreign corporation to a foreign shareholder. In 1986, this second-level withholding tax was replaced in most situations by a branch profits tax imposed on the net after-tax income of the branch.[512] After-tax profits which are not reinvested in a U.S. business are subject to the same 30% tax that a dividend distribution by a U.S. corporation would attract. If the tax is avoided currently by reinvesting profits, subsequent decreases in investment trigger a "recapture" of the tax. If branch activities are terminated, there is no recapture of the tax previously not paid through reinvestment. If the assets are transferred to a U.S. corporation, the taxpayer can defer current tax by agreeing that a subsequent sale of the stock will result in recognition of the deferred branch tax. The treatment is based on the model of a liquidating distribution

508. *GE India Technology Centre Private Ltd v. CIT*, Civil Appeal No. 7541-7542 of 2010, September 9, 2010 (SC).
509. India, ITA 1961, s. 197.
510. *Shri Sushil Shinde v. ACIT*, 2017, ITAT, Bangalore, following *CIT v. Yawar Rashid* 1996, Madhya Pradesh HC.
511. India, ITA, 1961, s. 198.
512. United States, IRC, s. 884.

by a domestic subsidiary which, similarly, would not be subject to a dividend withholding tax. As discussed above, a somewhat similar "branch interest" tax is imposed on interest expense which has been allocated to U.S. branch activities. Where tax rates on dividends on direct investments and interest are reduced or eliminated by treaties, the treaty rate applies for purposes of the branch profits tax.

Canada has a similar branch profits tax which antedated the U.S. tax. It is imposed at a 25% rate, the normal withholding rate on dividends, on the after-tax profits of a Canadian business operated by a foreign corporation which are not reinvested in the Canadian operations.[513] The statutory rate of branch tax is typically reduced in Canadian tax treaties to the rate applicable to dividends. Any amount claimed by a nonresident corporation as reinvested profits in computing the branch tax payable for a particular year must be included in computing the base for the branch tax for the succeeding year. Accordingly, as in the U.S. system, if a nonresident corporation decreases its branch investment in subsequent years, the prior reduction of the branch tax is recaptured. A similar result occurs where a branch operation is terminated. However, where a nonresident corporation forms a Canadian corporation and transfers to that corporation the assets of the Canadian branch, the recapture is effectively deferred. In effect, a nonresident corporation may transfer the assets of a branch operation to a wholly owned Canadian subsidiary on a rollover basis.

An authorized foreign bank operating through a branch in Canada is required to pay a special 25% tax on its "taxable interest expense," which is defined to be 15% of the amount of notional interest which is deductible in computing the Canadian branch profits.[514] This tax does not apply to banks resident in a country with which Canada has a tax treaty if that country does not impose a tax similar to the Canadian tax on Canadian banks operating in the country. Even if this exemption does not apply, the rate of the tax may be reduced where there is an applicable tax treaty which provides a lower rate on interest payments to related residents of that country.

Under the *French* territoriality system, any company operating in France and any PE located in France is subject to CIT. In addition to CIT, there is a specific tax, commonly known as "branch tax,"[515] which is in fact a withholding tax, the rate of which has been aligned with the CIT rate since 2020 (currently 25%). Branch tax applies to the presumed transfer of after-tax profits by a foreign company to its shareholders since profits made in France by foreign companies are deemed to be distributed to nonresident shareholders. The basis of these deemed distributed profits is the total amount of after-tax profits earned in France by the foreign company, whether taxable or exempt. Branch tax can be reduced or eliminated where: (i) the foreign company can prove that, in the year following the realization of the income, it has not distributed any dividends or that all its shareholders are French residents; (ii) the company can show that the deemed distributed profits are less than its income in France and/or in proportion to the percentage of French residents among its shareholders; (iii) an international tax treaty applies; or (iv) the foreign company has its

513. Canada, ITA, s. 219.
514. Canada, ITA, s. 218.2.
515. France, CGI, s. 115 quinquies.

effective headquarters in a Member State of the EU or other EEA state and is subject to CIT in that state.

Australia previously had a branch profits tax, but it was eliminated when, in connection with the introduction of the imputation system, the corporate and maximum individual tax rates were aligned and the nonresident dividend withholding tax on the franked part of dividends was abolished. Although the corporate rate is now significantly below the maximum individual rate, which would provide some justification for both a nonresident dividend withholding tax and a branch profits tax, neither has been reintroduced (perhaps originally to forestall efforts by the United States to obtain imputation benefits by treaty). Australia has progressively lowered its company tax rate to 30% on the grounds of international competitiveness, and, as discussed above, is now reciprocally eliminating dividend withholding tax by treaty on holdings of 80% or more in Australian subsidiaries. In that case, there is no need for a branch profits tax, which is the position achieved in the Protocol to the treaty with the United States in respect of the U.S. branch profits tax.

China, Germany, India, Japan, Sweden, The Netherlands, and the *United Kingdom* do not have a branch profits tax.

4 LIMITATIONS ON BASE-ERODING PAYMENTS TO NONRESIDENTS

Where, as is usually the case, tax rates on business income taxed on a net basis are higher than rates on deductible gross-basis taxed payments, taxpayers have an incentive to reduce the net-basis tax base as much as possible. This is particularly true where treaties reduce or even eliminate the gross-basis taxation. In response, several countries have imposed restrictions on the deductibility of such base-eroding payments. The focus here is on restrictions which are exclusively or primarily aimed at nonresident-owned domestic operations.[516] The most common problem is debt financing of domestic subsidiaries by nonresidents, with the attendant interest deduction reducing the income of the domestic subsidiary. To deal with this issue, special debt-equity rules (thin capitalization rules) are sometimes applied to nonresident-owned domestic corporations. Other provisions limit the extent of the interest deduction where interest payments are deemed to be excessive in relation to the domestic income. These "earnings-stripping" rules are also typically focused on payments to nonresidents.

In 2015, the OECD BEPS Action 4 Final Report, *Limiting Base Erosion Involving Interest Deductions and Other Financial Payments,* recommended best practices for countries to adopt to limit the deduction of net interest and other financing expenses in excess of 10% to 30% of earnings before interest, taxes, depreciation and amortization (EBITDA) by both resident and nonresident entities carrying on business in a country.

516. The limitations are sometimes applied to all "tax exempt" recipients, thus covering domestic tax-exempt organizations as well as foreign taxpayers; but the main impact of the rules usually is, and is intended to be, on foreigners, with the extension to tax-exempt organizations aimed at avoiding treaty-based complaints of discrimination.

The Report rejected a limitation based on a fixed debt:equity ratio, such as that typically used for thin capitalization rules, although the Report indicated that countries could have both earnings-stripping and thin capitalization rules.

At a minimum, the recommended rules would apply to domestic members of a multinational group but could be extended to domestic groups and standalone domestic entities. The rules would not apply to banking and insurance enterprises, or to financing expenses under a *de minimis* threshold or related to public benefit projects. Interest and other financing expenses would be defined broadly based on economic substance.

The rules would deny the deduction of an entity's net financing expenses (in excess of its financing revenue) in excess of a percentage of its EBITDA. Any nondeductible expenses for a year could be carried over to past and future years and, where an entity did not use all its deductibility room, the unused room could be carried forward and used in future years or transferred to other domestic group entities. In addition, a domestic entity would be allowed to deduct financing expenses in excess of the adopted percentage of EBITDA (based on the group's consolidated financial statements prepared in accordance with GAAP) where the worldwide net interest to EBITDA ratio of the multinational group of which it is a member exceeds the basic percentage of EBITDA plus an additional 10%. For example, if the basic rule is set at 30% of EBITDA and a multinational group has a net interest expense to EBITDA ratio of 38%, a group member in a particular country would be allowed to deduct its net interest expenses up to 38% of its EBITDA.

This section examines the extent to which the countries examined here have adopted thin capitalization rules, earnings-stripping rules, or other limitations on the deduction of base-eroding payments. With respect to earnings-stripping rules, the following material identifies the countries which have adopted earnings-stripping rules along the lines of the recommendations in BEPS Action 4 Report and the extent to which their rules deviate from those recommendations.

The *United States* has long had earnings-stripping rules. Under the current rules, which were significantly expanded in 2017, deductions for business interest expense for a year generally cannot exceed the sum of the taxpayer's business interest income for the year plus 30% of the taxpayer's "adjusted taxable income" for the year.[517] An entirely new regime was also added in 2017, the base erosion and anti-abuse tax (BEAT).[518] The BEAT regime imposes a 10% minimum tax to target deductible payments made by a U.S. corporation (other than regulated investment companies, real estate investment trusts, or Subchapter S corporations) to foreign related parties that are not subject to the U.S. 30% withholding tax. The BEAT is triggered if such deductible payments exceed 3% of a base equal to allowable deductions plus certain addbacks which reflect the base-erosion benefit. The BEAT is generally applicable only to entities with gross receipts of at least USD 500 million; the minimum tax rate increased to 12.5% for tax years beginning after 2025.

517. United States, IRC, s. 163(j).
518. United States, IRC, s. 59A.

Canada has statutory thin capitalization rules which apply to loans by nonresident shareholders to Canadian corporations. These rules apply only to foreign shareholders of a Canadian corporation who own at least 25%, by votes or value, of the shares of a Canadian corporation (referred to as "specified shareholders") and nonresidents who do not deal at arm's length with such shareholders. Constructive ownership rules apply for this purpose. A 1.5:1 debt-equity ratio is required and is calculated on the basis of the average of the greatest amount of debt outstanding at any time in each month to the specified shareholders and persons not dealing at arm's length with them. The equity of the corporation is defined as the aggregate of its retained earnings, any surplus contributed by the specified nonresident shareholders, and the average of the monthly paid-up capital of the shares owned by such shareholders. Equity is computed on a nonconsolidated basis. In 2013, the thin capitalization rules were extended to partnerships, trusts, and branches. The rules, first introduced in 1972 with a 3:1 debt:equity ratio, were revised in 2000 to reduce the ratio to 2:1, and then revised again in 2013 to reduce the ratio to the current 1.5:1.

Special anti-avoidance rules prevent the circumvention of the thin capitalization rules and withholding taxes through the use of back-to-back arrangements. These back-to-back rules were broadened in 2016 to deal with arrangements involving multiple intermediaries and to prevent the use of equity and royalty arrangements to avoid the rules. Thus, where a nonresident uses equity or a royalty arrangement to provide funds to an intermediary which then makes a loan to a Canadian-resident corporation, the back-to-back rules apply where there is a sufficient connection between the two or more legs of the back-to-back arrangement.

Canada has also introduced earnings-stripping rules known as the "excessive interest and financing expenses limitation" (EIFEL) regime, effective from October 2023.[519] These provisions are generally consistent with the recommendations in BEPS Action 4. In particular, they restrict the deduction of net interest and financing expenses by corporations and trusts (both resident and nonresident) where those expenses exceed 30% of the entity's "adjusted taxable income"—essentially its EBITDA computed according to tax rules. A member of a multinational group may elect to use a threshold higher than 30% where the group net interest expense as a percentage of group EBITDA justifies the higher ratio. There are exceptions designed primarily for domestic corporate groups, wholly domestic financing transactions, and public-private infrastructure projects. Any nondeductible interest paid to nonresidents is deemed to be a dividend for withholding tax purposes and may be carried forward indefinitely. Rules are also provided for an entity to transfer its unused deductibility room to related entities.

Australia has thin capitalization/earnings-stripping rules which deal with base-eroding payments with respect to both inbound and outbound investment. Just as it is possible for a nonresident to erode the source country tax base by interest deductions, so a resident can erode the residence country tax base by keeping its interest deductions onshore (especially where an exemption regime applies to most foreign

519. Canada, ITA, s. 18.2 and 18.21.

business income, as in Australia). As noted previously, the United States has rules in its FTC system to deal with the latter possibility, but these are quite distinct from the U.S. rules just described dealing with nonresidents. Until mid-2023, Australia dealt with both inbound and outbound investment with rules which, in effect, isolated the debt which finances the Australian operations of residents and nonresidents alike and then applied limitations to interest deductions on that debt.[520]

From mid-2023, Australia adopted the fixed ratio rule based on 30% of tax EBITDA for inbound and outbound investors. Net interest expense disallowed under the fixed ratio rule can be carried forward for up to 15 years. Surplus capacity for net interest deductions among Australian entities within a 50% controlled group is made available to other entities in the group based on the level of relationship but is lost if not immediately utilized.

Australia also replaced an alternative group ratio rule based on group debt to group assets for inbound and outbound investors with a group ratio rule based on group net interest divided by group EBITDA. Neither of these changes applies to banks and other financial institutions, which remain under the existing rules.[521] For inbound and outbound investors other than banks, the former alternative (an arm's length debt test) was replaced by a third-party debt test which allows net interest deductions in excess of the fixed ratio limit to be deducted if they can be traced under very restrictive rules to third-party debt of the taxpayer or its group.[522]

In addition, under the same legislation but effective from mid-2024, Australia introduced a debt-creation regime, which applies in priority to the rules described above. The rules disallow certain interest deductions generated by debt created for acquiring an asset or meeting a legal obligation (such as borrowing to pay a dividend) involving an associated entity unless the third-party debt test has been elected by the taxpayer.[523] These last two changes, which were not best practices recommended in BEPS Action 4, are proving very controversial and have been amended to overcome technical defects.

For many years, the primary approach of the *United Kingdom* in denying a deduction for excessive interest was to rely on transfer pricing rules, which are broadly consistent with the approach under the OECD Model Convention and so incorporate the arm's length principle.[524] These rules apply both domestically and internationally. A deduction for interest may be denied where the interest paid by a resident company to a related nonresident company is not an arm's length amount. Further, a deduction is denied for interest paid on any part of a loan that could not have been borrowed under arm's length conditions. The interest is classified as a distribution only where it represents more than a reasonable return on the amount borrowed.[525]

From 2017, these rules were supplemented with earnings-stripping rules which are broadly consistent with BEPS Action 4 (but are much more intractable and

520. Australia, ITAA 1997, Div. 820.
521. Australia, ITAA 1997, Subdiv 820-AA.
522. Australia, ITAA 1997, Div 820-EAB.
523. Australia, ITAA 1997, Div 820-EAA.
524. United Kingdom, Taxation (International and Other Provisions) Act 2010, Part 4.
525. United Kingdom, Corporation Tax Act 2010, s. 1000(1)E.

complex).[526] The UK rules apply on a group basis to deny a deduction for interest in excess of an allowance. For this purpose, a "group" is defined by reference to accounting standards. The allowance is calculated as the higher of 30% of the group's taxable EBITDA or a group ratio calculated as worldwide external debt of the group to the group's worldwide EBITDA. The disallowed amount is then allocated to group companies with UK profits, with some taxpayer flexibility. There is a *de minimis* exemption of GBP 2 million.[527] Denied interest can be carried forward indefinitely and excess EBITDA capacity may be carried forward for 5 years.[528] There is no recharacterization of the denied interest, which remains taxable to the recipient as interest. Intragroup debt is recognized in calculating EBITDA and a group's EBITDA.

Japan has both thin capitalization rules and earnings-stripping rules. The thin capitalization rules, which restrict the deduction of interest paid by domestic corporations to foreign shareholders under certain conditions, have a longer history than the earnings-stripping rules. The thin capitalization legislation, enacted in 1992, provides that the interest deduction on loans to Japanese corporations by controlling foreign shareholders is limited where the debt-equity ratio of both related-party and overall borrowing exceeds 3:1. If the taxpayer can establish that comparable Japanese companies have higher ratios, those ratios are used. Where this provision applies, it disallows a deduction for interest on that portion of the debt which exceeds the relevant ratio. There is no carryover of disallowed deduction under the thin capitalization rules, in contrast to the earnings-stripping rules mentioned below. The thin capitalization rules also apply to branch operations.[529]

In addition, in 2013 Japan introduced earnings-stripping rules limiting the deductibility of excessive interest without waiting for the BEPS Action 4 Final Report. The original Japanese rules differed in various respects from those recommended in the Final Report. The original rules focused only on net interest payments to affiliated entities that were not taxed in the hands of recipients, and the benchmark rate was 50%. The 2019 revisions to these rules, effective from April 2020, were viewed as an effort to harmonize the Japanese rules with the best practices recommended in the BEPS Report, but the current rules still retain some unique features. Under the current rules, the excessive amount of interest is calculated by subtracting 20% of the adjusted amount of taxable income from the applicable interest amount. While the concept of the adjusted amount of taxable income can be viewed as similar to the concept of EBITDA in the sense that, in calculating the adjusted amount, the amount of interest expenses, as well as the amount of depreciation and amortization, is added back to the amount of taxable income, Japan still allows the amount of interest which constitutes taxable income in the hands of the recipient to be reduced in calculating the excessive amount of interest. These earnings-stripping rules apply to all corporate entities,

526. United Kingdom, Taxation (International and Other Provisions) Act 2010, Part 10.
527. United Kingdom, Taxation (International and Other Provisions) Act 2010, s. 392.
528. United Kingdom, Taxation (International and Other Provisions) Act 2010, ss. 378 and 395, respectively.
529. Japan, STMA, s. 66-5.

including financial institutions, and apply both to domestic and international transactions. Japan does not allow a step-up of the benchmark rate of 20% for domestic entities where their multinational group's worldwide interest expense ratio exceeds that benchmark.

The *German* thin capitalization rules, which previously applied both to nonresident and resident corporations, have been replaced by an interest-stripping rule ("interest barrier") which also applies to nonresident shareholders.[530] The provision displays a strange mixture of traditional thin capitalization legislation and a broad-based limitation on the deductibility of interest payments. This "interest barrier" concept has spread across the world, having been taken up both by the OECD under BEPS Action 4 and by the EU, since the ATAD obliges all Member States to establish earnings-stripping rules under their domestic law.[531] Nevertheless, it has been challenged in the Constitutional Court.

Under general income tax law, all owners of a "business" (incorporated or not) are subject to a disallowance of the deduction of interest payments exceeding 30% of EBITDA. This general rule does not apply to interest of less than EUR 3,000,000 or to single enterprises not belonging to a "group" of companies. In the case of a group company, the interest limitation applies unless the taxpayer can show that its leverage does not exceed the overall leverage of the group. Apparently, the "true aim" of the new provision is to combat the strategic allocation of interest expenditure within corporate groups. Nevertheless, the exceptions (for single enterprises and uniformly leveraged groups) do not apply where more than 10% of the overall interest expenditure flows to a shareholder owning more than 25% of the company's shares.[532] In this case, not only the interest on the shareholder loan, but the interest on all loans falls under the harsh 30% rule described above.

In the wake of the BEPS Project, Germany has introduced additional restrictions on the deductibility of outbound payments. Under a provision introduced in 2017, business expenditures are disqualified where they are also deductible in another jurisdiction.[533] In particular, such "double dipping" used to occur where foreign partners in German partnerships were able to deduct in both countries financing expenses related to the acquisition of their partnership interests (due to the attribution of the underlying debt to the partnership's business under German tax law). The broad language of the statute aims at implementing the BEPS recommendations on "hybrid mismatches" (BEPS Action 2) as well as the ATAD.[534]

An even more important provision is the "royalty barrier" introduced in 2018,[535] which renders royalty payments flowing to affiliate entities resident in a low-tax jurisdiction (or subject to a preferential regime) nondeductible unless the favorable treatment is in line with the "nexus principle" established under BEPS Action 5. In 2020, this list of nondeductible items was complemented by the denial of the deduction

530. Germany, ITA, s. 4h.
531. ATAD (EU), 2016/1164, Art. 4 (Interest-limitation rule).
532. Germany, CITA, s. 8a.
533. Germany, ITA, s. 4i.
534. ATAD (EU), 2016/1164, Art. 9 para. 1.
535. Germany, ITA, s. 4j.

of expenditures in the context of the use or the alienation of investment assets (shares, bonds etc.) if there is no "congruent" taxation of the resulting income on the part of a foreign-based transaction party.[536] In addition, following EU policy, payments to residents of listed tax havens are not deductible.[537]

In *The Netherlands*, there have been case law restrictions on the deduction of interest paid on hybrid loans since the late 1980s. In addition, in the late 1990s and the first decade of this century, the government introduced anti-base-erosion rules to consolidate and restrict earlier case law with respect to interest paid on related-party debt. Under the statutory rules, interest is not deductible on tax-driven loans between group companies unless the taxpayer demonstrates that the transactions were effected primarily for valid business purposes or the interest has been effectively taxed (i.e., not reduced by existing or foreseeable loss carryovers and FTCs) at a rate of at least 10% in the hands of the recipient.[538] Further, as a result of the implementation of the EU ATAD, a generic interest-limitation rule has been introduced, which is stricter than either the EU or BEPS Action 4 Report limitations. Under this rule, taxpayers can deduct interest only up to 20% of their total EBITDA,[539] subject to a reduced threshold exemption of only EUR 1 million of net interest expenses instead of EUR 3 million. Nevertheless, in general, the Dutch rules are in alignment with BEPS Action 4.

For many years, *Sweden* had no special provisions dealing with base-eroding payments to nonresidents. However, in 2008 a special limitation on the deduction of interest payments was introduced in reaction to a tax-planning scheme which had taken advantage of the lack of Swedish thin capitalization rules and withholding tax on interest payments. The rules basically covered interest on debt created by intergroup sales of shares where the interest is not taxed to the recipient at a rate of at least 10%. The rules were amended in 2013 and again in 2018, mainly to implement the EU ATAD and the changes to the Parent-Subsidiary Directive. Two main types of limitation exist. First, the deduction of all net interest expenses (the difference between interest income and interest expenses) is limited to 30% of a company's EBITDA.[540] This rule applies to all interest expenses, whether loans are taken from related or independent companies, and whether paid to Swedish or foreign recipients. Second, interest expenses on intercompany debts are deductible only if the beneficial owner is resident in the EEA, is resident in a country with which Sweden has a comprehensive tax treaty, or is taxed on the interest income at a minimum rate of 10%; however, in any case, net interest expenses are not deductible where the underlying debt is wholly or almost wholly intended to give a group of companies a significant tax advantage.[541] Due to compatibility issues with EU law and the intention of improving the functioning of the rules, a proposal for reform was presented in 2024 and it is expected that Sweden will keep a combination of general and specific interest-limitation rules targeting intercompany

536. Germany, ITA, s. 4k.
537. Germany, Tax Haven Defence Act (*Steueroasenabwehrgesetz*), s. 8, Federal Gazette 2021, p. 2056.
538. Netherlands, CITA, Art. 10a.
539. Netherlands, CITA, Art. 15b.
540. Sweden, ITA, Ch. 24 s. 24.
541. Sweden, ITA, Ch. 24 s. 18.

debts. Other limitations, such as those to prevent the effects of hybrid mismatches, are also expected to apply.

France has specific rules which, although they do not recharacterize debt as equity, limit the deductibility of interest. From January 2007, these rules were modified in order to comply with EU case law[542] and make them operate more efficiently. France then progressively developed a very complex set of measures limiting the deductibility of interest. The Finance Acts for 2019 and 2020, which respectively implemented the ATAD I and II directives, have considerably strengthened the provisions limiting the deductibility of financing expenses in order to limit abusive deductions. Before 2019, France had two general mechanisms for limiting the rate of interest on loans[543] and the amount of such interest, depending on whether or not the company was a member of a group of companies.[544] Since 2019, the general limitation on the rate of interest on loans has been retained but the general limitation on the amount of interest has been modified. Concerning group companies, thin capitalization rules have been simplified (previously, three ratios were used to determine the notion of undercapitalization: debt, interest cover, and interest paid by affiliated companies). Currently, undercapitalization occurs only where group debt is more than 1.5 times the company's equity. However, undercapitalized companies can deduct more interest by proving that their consolidated group's debt-to-equity ratio is greater than or equal to their own debt-to-equity ratio for the year. In addition, for fiscal years beginning on or after January 1, 2019, as required by the EU ATAD, "exceeding borrowing costs" (interest expense less interest revenue) is deductible only up to 30% of a taxpayer's EBITDA (or 10% for undercapitalized companies) or EUR 3,000,000 (or EUR 1,000,000 for undercapitalized companies), whichever is greater.[545] Safeguard clauses have also been introduced. Consolidated groups can go beyond the deduction ceiling (75% of excess expenses) where the ratio between shareholders' equity and total assets is greater than or equal to the same ratio for the consolidated group. Taking into account the option offered by the ATAD Directives, France has chosen to offer companies not belonging to a consolidated group the possibility of deducting an additional 75% of excess expenses under certain conditions. For fiscally integrated groups,[546] the same rules apply to the overall results of the integrated group. Since 2019, France has removed specific rules limiting interest deductions with respect to the acquisition of equity interests (*amendement Carrez*)[547] but kept such rules dealing with intragroup transactions in integrated groups of companies (*amendement Charasse*).

In *China*, the EIT law (Article 49) specifically limits the deduction of intercompany management fees. More general limitations on base-eroding payments to non-residents are found in the thin capitalization rules, transfer pricing rules, and the GAAR. The thin capitalization rules set the debt/equity ratio at 5:1 for financial

542. CJEU, December 12, 2002, C-324/00 (*Lankhorst-Hohorst GmbH*) and Conseil d'Etat, December 30, 2003, No. 249047 (*min.c/ Sarl Coréal Gestion*).
543. France, CGI, s. 39-1 3° CGI.
544. France, CGI, s. 212 bis (for non-group companies) and CGI s. 212 (for group companies).
545. France, CGI, s. 212 bis.
546. France, CGI, s. 223 B bis.
547. France, CGI, s. 209 IX.

companies and 2:1 for non-financial companies. Interest on debts in excess of these ratios is not deductible. Loans between arm's length parties are not subject to the thin capitalization rules. Under the transfer pricing rules, service fees paid to related nonresidents may be challenged under the transfer pricing rules where the benefits to the Chinese payer are questionable. Under the concept of "location-specific advantage" (i.e., market premium and location savings), the STA may also deny a deduction for outbound royalties for the use of brand names where the value of the name is "monetized" in China. A famous example dealt with the "Head & Shoulders" brand of shampoo products. Because the Chinese translation of this brand is "Flying Hair in Ocean Breeze" (Hai Fei Si), the STA took the position that royalties paid to the offshore legal owner of the "Head & Shoulders" brand were excessive. Thus, the substance-over-form approach taken by the STA in applying these rules sometimes functions as an anti-abuse measure.

Until 2017, *India* did not have any thin capitalization rules and the efforts of the tax authorities to limit interest deductions, even in cases involving absurd debt-to-equity ratios, were not allowed by the courts.[548] Section 94B of the ITA currently restricts the deduction of interest by an Indian company or a PE in India where the interest payable to a nonresident related party exceeds 30% of EBIDTA. The restriction applies only where a taxpayer's deductible interest exceeds INR 10 million, and does not apply to a banking or designated financial company or a finance company located in the International Financial Services Centre.

5 RESTRICTIONS ON SOURCE-BASED TAXATION OF NONRESIDENTS WITHIN THE EU

The differential treatment of residents and nonresidents reflected in source-based taxation has raised some important issues in the EU. As discussed in the General Description of the EU in the Introduction, the provisions on freedom of movement of employees and businesses, goods, services, and capital which are now enshrined in the TFEU date back to 1957, when the EEC Treaty was concluded. In addition, the 1992 Maastricht Treaty expanded the scope of the European treaties beyond cross-border movements of an economic nature.

It was not until 1986, however, that the CJEU ruled that these provisions were applicable to differential direct taxation by Member States of resident taxpayers of other Member States. To the extent that taxes have not been harmonized, the Court has ruled that the application of domestic tax laws must not interfere with intra-Union movements of individuals and businesses. While these freedom-of-movement provisions forbid EU Member States from discriminating on the basis of nationality, the CJEU has ruled that since nonresidents typically have a foreign nationality, discrimination in the treatment of nonresident taxpayers as compared to resident taxpayers is also forbidden by these rules unless domestic and foreign residents are—from the perspective of the tax provision in question—not in comparable situations.

548. *Besix Kier Dabhol S.A v. DDIT* (ITAT No. 4249/mum/07, November 10, 2010).

A substantial jurisprudence has developed significant limitations on source country taxation of nonresidents, and the CJEU has decided several cases dealing with various aspects of the problem. With respect to direct taxation of individuals, the CJEU has declared the following types of differential taxation to be in violation of the EU Treaty:

- discriminatory IIT rates (the *Asscher* case[549] dealing with The Netherlands 25% tax rate in the first bracket for nonresidents, in contrast to 6.5% for resident taxpayers);
- discriminatory definitions of the income tax base (the *Hollmann* case[550] dealing with Portuguese tax law applying a reduced tax base (50%) on capital gains from sales of real estate only for resident taxpayers);
- the denial of the right of a nonresident taxpayer to file for a refund (the *Biehl*[551] and *Schumacker*[552] decisions);
- the taxation of services income of self-employed nonresidents on a gross basis compared to the taxation of residents on a net basis (*Gerritse*);[553] in contrast, expenditure only indirectly related to the domestic source of income may not be deductible (*Centro Equestre,*[554] *Commission v. Germany,*[555] and *Miljoen*[556]);
- the denial of the right of a nonresident taxpayer to deduct tax advisory costs related to domestic income (*Conijn*[557]);
- the denial of the right to personal deductions (e.g., medical expenses and alimony) and income splitting (*Schumacker*)—but only if the nonresident taxpayer derives virtually all of their income from the source state; this has been confirmed for income splitting (*Gschwind*[558] and *Zurstrassen*[559]); if there is no income in the residence state, but income from two source states, there is a right to personal deductions in both source states on a pro rata basis (*X*);[560]
- the denial of the right of nonresident individuals (workers and self-employed persons) to deduct losses from owner-occupied housing and similar situations if they derive (nearly) all their income from domestic sources (*Ritter-Coulais,*[561] *Lakebrink,*[562] *Renneberg,*[563] *Busley-Cibrian,*[564] and *K*[565]).

549. CJEU, June 27, 1996, C-279/93.
550. CJEU, October 11, 2007, C-443/06.
551. CJEU, May 8, 1990, C-175/88 and October 26, 1995, C-151/94.
552. CJEU, February 14, 1995, C-279/93.
553. CJEU, June 12, 2003, C-234/01.
554. CJEU, February 15, 2007, C-345/04.
555. CJEU, November 22, 2012, C-600/10.
556. CJEU, September 17, 2015, joined Cases C-10/14, C-14/14, and C-17/14.
557. CJEU, July 6, 2005, C-346/04.
558. CJEU, September 14, 1999, C-391/97.
559. CJEU, May 16, 2000, C-87/99.
560. CJEU, February 9, 2017, C-283/15.
561. CJEU, February 21, 2006, C-152/03.
562. CJEU, July 18, 2007, C-182/06.
563. CJEU, October 16, 2008, C-527/06.
564. CJEU, October 15, 2009, C-35/08.
565. CJEU, November 7, 2013, C-322/11.

With respect to direct taxation of businesses, the CJEU has declared the following types of differential taxation to be in violation of the EU Treaty:

- the imposition of a higher rate of tax on the profits of a branch of a corporation with its seat in another EU Member State than the rate on domestic companies (*Royal Bank of Scotland*[566]);
- the denial of benefits arising under a tax treaty with a third country to a local PE maintained by a corporate taxpayer resident in another Member State (*Saint Gobain*[567]);
- the right to the imputation credit ((*Com'r v. French Republic*) (*avoir fiscal*)[568]) (where shares of a French company were held by a French branch of a nonresident taxpayer);
- thin capitalization rules distinguishing between local and foreign affiliates which go beyond provisions targeting merely artificial arrangements (*Lankhorst-Hohorst*,[569] *Test Claimants in the Thin Cap Group Litigation*,[570] and *NV Lammers & Van Cleef*[571]);
- the denial of loss compensation between affiliated domestic companies due to the fact that the common parent company is resident in another Member State (*Felixstowe Dock and Railway Company*[572]);
- the denial of loss compensation in the context of withholding taxation of dividends paid to nonresident shareholders as opposed to the granting of loss compensation in the context of mainstream income taxation of resident shareholders (*Sofina*[573]); in contrast, losses incurred abroad by the nonresident parent company cannot be deducted at the level of a local PE (*Futura Singer*[574]);
- the denial of a tax exemption for outbound intercompany dividends where domestic intercompany dividends benefit from a participation exemption (*Denkavit Internationaal*[575] and *Amurta*[576]). In recent years, this line of reasoning has been extended to FIFs insisting on equal treatment with tax-exempt domestic investment funds (*Santander Asset Management*,[577] *Emerging Markets*,[578] *Commission v. Belgium*,[579] *Fidelity Funds*,[580] *Köln-Aktienfonds Deka*[581]).

566. CJEU, April 29, 1999, C-311/97.
567. CJEU, September 21, 1999, C-307/97.
568. CJEU, January 28, 1986, C-270/83.
569. CJEU, December 12, 2002, C-324/00.
570. CJEU, March 13, 2007, C-524/04.
571. CJEU, January 17, 2008, C-105/07.
572. CJEU, April 1, 2014, C-80/12.
573. CJEU, November 22, 2018, C-575/17.
574. CJEU, May 15, 1997, C-250/95.
575. CJEU, December 14, 2006, C-170/05.
576. CJEU, November 8, 2007, C-379/05.
577. CJEU, May 10, 2012, Joined Cases C-338/11-C-347/11.
578. CJEU, April 10, 2014, C-190/12.
579. CJEU, October 29, 2015, C-589/14.
580. CJEU, June 21, 2018, C-480/16.
581. CJEU, January 30, 2020, C-156/17.

In developing restrictions on the taxation of nonresidents, the CJEU does not always seem to be fully aware of the extensive impact of its decisions in the highly technical area of international taxation. Apparently animated by a desire to do away with all potentially discriminatory national restrictions, in whatever form they take, the CJEU has increasingly limited the right of source countries to apply traditionally accepted methods of taxing nonresidents. The governments of the Member States have become more and more aware of the vast number of longstanding rules which may not withstand the CJEU's scrutiny. So far, this development has not triggered extensive voluntary harmonization of the taxation of nonresidents by the Member States.

The following *Table IV-2* summarizes the rules dealing with the taxation of various types of domestic source income received by nonresident taxpayers. The typically applicable treaty rates are indicated, although there can be substantial variations in individual treaties. The column "Sale of Stock of Domestic Corporation" deals with source-based tax on gains derived from the sale of stock in a domestic corporation by a foreign shareholder who has no other contact with the source country.

Table IV-2 Taxation of Domestic Source Income of Nonresident Taxpayers

	Dividends	*Interest*	*Royalties*	*Business Income Threshold*	*Services Income Threshold*	*Sale of Stock of Domestic Corporation*
Australia	0% if corp. tax paid; 30% gross withholding if not; treaty 0%-15%	10% gross withholding (publicly offered debt, foreign pension funds exempt); treaty 10% except bank interest	30% gross; treaty 5%-10%	any Australian source income	Australian source (place of performance in general)	10% + interest in land-rich companies
Canada	25% gross withholding; treaty 5%-15%	25% gross withholding (government and arm's length debt exempt); treaty 0%-10%	25% gross withholding; treaty 10%, 0% for technology royalties	carrying on business in Canada	any employment or carrying on business in Canada	any private company shares, 25% of public company or real estate in Canada taxable
China	20% for individuals/10% for enterprises; treaty 10%	20% for individuals/10% for enterprises; treaty 10%	20% for individuals/10% for enterprises; treaty 10%	establishment in China	establishment or 90 days or more in China	20% for individuals/10% for enterprises; treaty 10%

France	12.8% (individuals); 25% (corporate) gross final withholding; treaty 0%-25%	0%	corporate tax rate (25% since 2022), 15% (athletes) gross creditable and refundable withholding; treaty 0%-25%	PE (some differences from treaty rule)	any services performed in France	0%-12.8% (individuals) and corporate tax rate on > 25% holdings—19% (individuals + EEA companies) or corporate tax rate, on interest in real estate companies
Germany	25% gross withholding tax; treaty usually 15%	0% (unless profit-participating loans or dormant partnerships)	15% withholding tax; treaty 0%-15%	PE/permanent representative	services rendered or utilized in Germany	25% withholding tax
India	general rate 20% (plus surcharge and surtax) treaty rate generally 10%, 5% in some treaties with non-OECD countries; treaty rate generally 10%	general withholding 20% (plus surcharge and surtax); in some cases, 5% (e.g., long-term foreign currency borrowing); 4%, if such bonds are listed on IFSC	currently 20% (plus surcharge and surtax) under domestic law and generally 10% under treaties	business connection	services performed in India	taxable subject to treaty provisions
Japan	20% gross withholding; treaty 10%-15%	15% gross withholding; treaty 10%	20% gross withholding; treaty 10%	PE	any services performed in Japan over de minimis	25% shareholding + sale of 5% taxable (all interests in real estate companies)

	Dividends	*Interest*	*Royalties*	*Business Income Threshold*	*Services Income Threshold*	*Sale of Stock of Domestic Corporation*
The Netherlands	15% gross withholding or 25.8% when the WTA 2021 applies; treaty 0-5-15%	15% gross withholding or 25.8% when the WTA 2021 applies; treaty 0-5-15%	exempt but 25.8% if the WTA 2021 applies; limited to treaties with low- and no-tax jurisdictions 0-5%[582]	PE/permanent representative	any services performed in NL	substantial interest (5% +) taxable
Sweden	30% gross withholding; treaty 5%-15%	generally exempt	taxed as business income; treaty exempt	PE	services performed in Sweden	generally exempt
United Kingdom	effectively exempt	20% withholding; treaty 0%-15%	20% withholding; treaty 0%-15%	PE	any services performed in UK	exempt but taxation of land-rich companies
United States	30% gross withholding; treaty 5%-15%	30% gross withholding (portfolio exempt); treaty 0%	30% gross withholding; treaty 0%	trade or business	any services performed in U.S. over de minimis	generally exempt; interest in domestic real estate corporation taxed

582. As of January 1, 2024, the tax treaties with Bahrain (2009), Barbados (2007) and Panama (2011). Under Art. 1.2(2) of the Withholding Tax Act 2021 (WTA 2021), the conditional withholding tax does not apply in respect of these treaty states until three calendar years after the state is first designated as a low-tax jurisdiction under the applicable ministerial regulations. During these three calendar years, consideration must be given to whether and how the relevant treaty should be amended (Art. 1.2(4) WTA 2021).

SUBPART C

Additional International Topics

1 SPECIAL INTERNATIONAL AVOIDANCE RULES

The general approach to tax avoidance by the jurisdictions examined in this book is discussed in the country descriptions in Part I. Beyond the generally applicable principles and rules, several countries have enacted provisions aimed specifically at certain types of international transactions. In some cases, the same results might have been reached under normally applicable principles and the international rule only clarifies the situation. In others, the rules are unique to the international area.

In the *United States*, general substance-over-form and "step-transactions" principles have allowed interrelated financing arrangements to be recharacterized where the particular structure was tax-motivated. However, questions about the extent to which the rules would be applied and their limits left room for substantial aggressive tax planning in the international area. Congress responded by authorizing regulations to recharacterize "multiple-party financing transactions" as occurring directly between participants, ignoring intermediate parties.[583] Regulations issued under this provision deal with international "back-to-back" arrangements designed to take advantage of reduced treaty rates available to intermediate entities. Interest paid to the intermediary is treated as paid directly to the ultimate source of the financing and taxed as such. Recharacterization occurs only where the financing transaction is part of a "tax avoidance plan," one of the principal purposes of which is the avoidance of U.S. tax. The regulations list a number of factors to be taken into account in making this determination.[584]

For many years, the United States has had rules to limit corporate inversions—transactions whereby U.S. corporations reincorporate abroad by merging with an (often smaller) foreign corporation in order to obtain certain benefits available

583. United States, IRC, s. 7701(l).
584. United States, Regs., s. 1.881-3.

to foreign corporations controlling U.S. corporations which are not available to U.S.-based multinationals.[585] To supplement these rules, the 2017 tax reform included rules to tax the accumulated offshore profits of U.S. multinationals which had previously inverted at the full pre-2018 rate of 35% rather than the reduced 8% and 15.5% rates applicable to other U.S. multinationals.[586] In addition, dividends received by U.S. individuals from newly inverted corporations are taxable at ordinary rates rather than the reduced 15% or 20% rate generally applicable to dividends.[587]

The *Canadian* GAAR applies to abusive international transactions and to treaty abuses, although the government has been unsuccessful in the two treaty-shopping cases to date.[588] Special Canadian anti-avoidance rules are aimed at the use of nonresident trusts[589] and attempts by nonresidents to strip the surplus of Canadian corporations through a transfer of the shares to another non-arm's length Canadian corporation in exchange for shares of the purchaser.[590] Such transfers would have the effect of increasing the paid-up capital of the purchaser corporation, which could then be distributed as a tax-free return of capital to the nonresident shareholder. The sales amount is recharacterized as a dividend (or results in a reduction in the paid-up capital of the transferred corporation), which defeats the benefit which would otherwise be available. There are also rules targeting weak-currency borrowings,[591] upstream loans,[592] debt push-down arrangements,[593] and investments in passive offshore entities.[594] In 2007, rules were introduced attacking certain double-dip financing arrangements.[595] These rules were not slated to become effective until 2012 and were repealed in 2009 before ever becoming effective. Broad anti-avoidance rules to deal with back-to-back arrangements used to avoid the thin capitalization rules and withholding taxes on interest, rent, royalties, and other similar payments were enacted in 2016. These rules apply not only to arrangements involving multiple intermediaries but also to payments of different character (e.g., dividends, rent, or royalties to an intermediary and then a loan to the Canadian taxpayer).[596]

In *Germany*, there is a general anti-avoidance provision under domestic law,[597] but it was controversial whether general concepts of tax avoidance could be invoked by the authorities in treaty cases. In response, in its "Basis for negotiation" released in 2013, the MOF introduced an amended preamble to (future) German tax treaties explicitly referring to the avoidance of "nontaxation" as a main goal of treaty policy and

585. United States, IRC, s. 7874.
586. United States, IRC, s. 965(l).
587. United States, IRC, s. 1(h)(11)(C)(iii).
588. *MIL (Investments) Ltd. v. The Queen*, 2007 FCA 236 and *Alta Energy Luxembourg v. The Queen*, 2021 SCC 49.
589. Canada, ITA, s. 94.
590. Canada, ITA, s. 212.1.
591. Canada, ITA, s. 20.3.
592. Canada, ITA, s. 90(6)-(15).
593. Canada, ITA, s. 212.3.
594. Canada, ITA, s. 94.1.
595. Canada, ITA, s. 18.2.
596. Canada, ITA, s. 18(6) and (6.1) with respect to the thin capitalization rules and s. 212(3.1)-(3.94) with respect to withholding taxes.
597. Germany, GFC, s. 42.

interpretation. Under both BEPS Action 6 and the EU ATAD,[598] Germany is obliged to establish a "principal purpose test" (PPT) as a constraint on the availability of treaty benefits. While Germany intends to amend its treaties in this respect, it does not see any need to introduce additional domestic legislation, given the existence of the broadly designed GAAR under the General Fiscal Code (GFC).

There are also some special unilateral rules which aim at eliminating tax advantages for abusive cross-border structures involving tax treaties. The most important provision[599] aims at "treaty shopping" (and "directive shopping")[600] in cases where intermediate companies lacking economic substance have been set up by shareholders resident outside the treaty partner's jurisdiction. In recent years, the CJEU has consistently reduced the discretion of Member States' tax authorities to define the threshold of genuine business activities in the context of EU directives.[601] In 2021, the relevant provision[602] was amended to fulfill the requirements established by the CJEU but it is highly controversial whether the outcome is fully in line with the constraints formulated by the CJEU.

Irrespective of the general anti-avoidance provision mentioned above,[603] a switchover to worldwide taxation was enacted to cover situations of "white income" (i.e., income which is exempt under a treaty) where the treaty exemption does not correspond with effective taxation by the source state due to a different characterization of the income or the absence of tax liability in the source country.[604]

The *French* anti-avoidance theories of abuse of law (*abus de droit*) and abnormal management decision (*acte anormal de gestion*) apply both to international and domestic tax matters; their international counterparts are treaty abuse and transfer pricing. In addition, some statutory provisions specifically embody these theories in order to combat certain types of international tax avoidance more effectively, especially by placing the burden of proof on the taxpayer. New anti-abuse measures have been developed as a result of the implementation of the ATAD I Directive. Thus, a new general anti-abuse rule applicable specifically to CIT was enacted and the concept of abuse of rights has been extended to include a principal "purpose," similar to the PPT clause in tax treaties.[605] Another provision, outside CIT, is the "mini abuse of rights" (*mini abus de droit*), where the concept of abuse of rights has been extended to include a primarily fiscal "motive."[606] As a result, France now has an extensive anti-abuse arsenal.

598. ATAD (EU), 2016/1164, Art. 6.
599. Germany, ITA, s. 50d para. 3.
600. In cases where fiscal benefits are granted under an EU directive (e.g., withholding tax reductions under the Parent-Subsidiary Directive or under the Interest Royalty Directive).
601. CJEU, December 20, 2017 Joined Cases C-504/16 and C-613/16 (*Deister Holding*); February 26, 2019, Joined Cases C-116/16 and C-117/16 (*Skatteministeriet v. T Denmark and Y Denmark APS*); February 26, 2019, Joined Cases C-115/16 et al. (*N Luxemburg 1 and others v. Skatteministeriet*).
602. For further details *see* above Subpart C, section 4.3.
603. Germany, GFC, s. 42.
604. Germany, ITA, s. 50d para. 9.
605. France, CGI, s. 205 A.
606. France, Book of Tax Procedures (*Livre des procédures fiscales*) (LPF), s. L 64 A.

Under the "rent-a-star company" provision, sums received by a natural or legal person domiciled or established outside France (interposed person), as remuneration for services rendered by one or more natural or legal persons domiciled or established in France (actual provider), are taxable in France where: (i) the actual provider directly or indirectly controls the interposed person; (ii) the actual provider does not establish that the interposed person is predominantly engaged in an industrial or commercial activity other than the provision of services; or (iii) the interposed person is domiciled or established in a country with preferential tax treatment. These provisions also apply to individuals or legal entities domiciled outside France for services rendered in France.[607] The Finance Act 2024 extended the scope of this provision from sums received as remuneration for services to include all sums received as "consideration for services or the commercial exploitation of rights attached to the image, name or voice of one or more persons, the use of copyright or related rights, or industrial or commercial property or similar rights, rendered or granted." These clarifications counter the restrictive interpretation which judges have given to remuneration for services rendered. In addition, a provision has been introduced to eliminate the double taxation of remuneration in order to take into account a reservation of interpretation made by the Constitutional Council.[608] Thus, when a person domiciled or established abroad pays to a person domiciled in France all or part of the sums falling within the scope of this provision, the tax corresponding to this income is deemed to have already been paid.

Similarly, interest, royalties, and remuneration for services paid to individuals or legal entities residing or established in a low-tax jurisdiction, and payments of any kind to an account in a financial institution established in such a jurisdiction, are not deductible unless the French taxpayer can prove that the transaction is bona fide and the amount paid is not excessive.[609] Finally, a French corporation is taxed on income arising from assets previously transferred, directly or indirectly, to a foreign person or trust without any immediate consideration in order for the transferee to manage such assets or pay interest and capital on a debt on behalf of the transferor.[610]

The *United Kingdom's* GAAR applies to abusive international transactions and treaty abuses. Special "settlement" rules may attribute income to certain persons, typically the transferor.[611] These rules are broad and potentially apply to "any disposition, trust, covenant, agreement, arrangement or transfer of assets" where there is an element of gift or value shifting. The rules are primarily targeted at sheltering income from tax in various types of entities (especially companies), income splitting (e.g., between family members), and income assignment. These rules apply only for income tax, not corporation tax, purposes, and so affect only individuals and trusts. In this context, the rules impose substantial limitations on tax planning with respect to

607. France, CGI, s. 155 A.
608. Constitutional Council, Décision n°2010-70 QPC of November 26, 2010, M. Pierre-Yves M, section 4.
609. France, CGI, s. 238 A.
610. France, CGI, s. 238 bis-0 1.
611. United Kingdom, Income Tax (Trading and Other Income) Act 2005 (ITTOIA), Part 5, Ch. 5 (ss. 619-648).

international transactions. Other special anti-abuse rules are more narrowly targeted, including those aimed at arrangements to avoid royalty withholding tax and intellectual property held in low-tax jurisdictions.[612] Other rules are targeted at noncompliance, including a strict liability criminal offense for those who have not paid the tax due on offshore income, civil penalties for enablers of offshore tax evasion or noncompliance, and penalties in respect of requirements to correct certain offshore tax noncompliance.[613]

From its introduction, *Australia's* GAAR has clearly applied to tax benefits generated by tax treaties, although it has not yet been argued by the ATO in a tax treaty case. It has broad rules for transferor trusts used to move foreign source income into foreign trusts.[614] It also has rules in its corporate tax system which are designed to eliminate dividend and capital streaming, which are particularly relevant for nonresidents.[615] In 2024, the government announced that from July 1, 2026 a new penalty applies to taxpayers who are part of a group which exceeds the country-by-country reporting threshold that are found to have mischaracterized or undervalued royalty payments to which royalty withholding would otherwise apply.[616]

India introduced a GAAR effective from April 1, 2017, which potentially applies to abusive international transactions. The GAAR overrides any contrary provisions of India's tax treaties.

Under case law in *The Netherlands*, in international cases, anti-avoidance rules do not apply where a tax treaty applies. Therefore, in 2001, statutory rules were introduced to stop dividend stripping and other transactions where, as a result of a share transaction (such as stocklending or usufruct), the amount of the dividend would effectively be received tax-free by the (resident or nonresident) shareholder.[617] As of January 1, 2024, these rules have been strengthened as regards the burden of proof: persons claiming an allowance (refund or credit) must demonstrate that they are the beneficial owner (previously, the burden of proof was on the tax authorities.) However, in the recent *Morgan Stanley* decision, the Supreme Court significantly refined the anti-dividend stripping rules.[618] The Supreme Court adhered to its decision in *Marketmaker*[619] with respect to the concept of beneficial owner, a consequence of which is that the purchaser of dividend certificates could credit the dividend withholding tax. In *Morgan Stanley,* the Supreme Court held that a person is the beneficial owner of the dividends if they can freely dispose of the distributions received and are not acting as an agent or nominee. Thus, the Court has adopted an interpretation of the concept of beneficial owner which is broader than the meaning in the anti-dividend stripping rules as enacted. If the legislature wants to change the Supreme Court's

612. United Kingdom, Income Tax Act 2007, s. 917A and ITTOIA, Part 5, Ch. 2A, respectively.
613. United Kingdom, Taxes Management Act 1970, s. 106B-106H, and Finance Act 2016, s. 162 and Sch. 20, and Finance (No. 2) Act 2017, s. 67 and Sch. 18.
614. Australia, ITAA 1936, Pt III, Div. 6AAA.
615. Australia, ITAA 1936, ss. 45, 45A, 45B, 177EA, ITAA 1997, Div. 204.
616. Australia, 2024 Budget Paper No. 2, p. 11, amendment to existing measures.
617. Netherlands, Dividend Tax Act (DivTA), Art. 4(7).
618. Netherlands, Supreme Court, January 19, 2024, No. 20/01884, V-N 2024/5.8 (*Morgan Stanley*).
619. Netherlands, Supreme Court, April 6, 1994, No. 28 638, BNB 1994/217.

interpretation of a particular term, it must insert an express provision to that effect. A further amendment to the law is therefore necessary.[620]

In addition, under the Dutch rules introduced to implement the anti-avoidance rule in the EU Parent-Subsidiary Directive, the dividend tax exemption is denied where two conditions are met: (i) the shares are held with the main purpose (or one of the main purposes) of avoiding Dutch dividend tax; and (ii) the structure is considered to be artificial (i.e., it is not set up for sound business reasons which reflect economic reality).[621]

A similar anti-abuse provision applies to dividends and capital gains earned by nonresident companies.[622] Further, to avoid the transfer of wealth to a private wealth fund (generically called *afgezonderd particulier vermogen* (APV)) set up to manage private assets (e.g., trusts), a special provision attributes this wealth to the individual (or the individual's heirs) who set up the fund.[623]

In *Sweden*, the GAAR has been found by the Supreme Administrative Court to be applicable to situations covered by a tax treaty.[624]

As part of the 2014 tax revisions, *Japan* introduced an anti-tax avoidance clause in respect of the income attributable to a PE, intended to combat artificial behavior aimed at reducing a PE's attributable income. The tax authorities have continuously, but unsuccessfully, pressed for the enactment of more GAARs. So far, the Japanese legislature has addressed tax avoidance issues by way of specific anti-avoidance rules. One such example is a provision to disallow the FTC for foreign taxes artificially incurred using back-to-back loans in which a foreign PE of a Japanese corporation intentionally takes part.[625]

The *Chinese* anti-avoidance rules in both the IIT and EIT legislation target international scenarios, mainly those involving foreign-based multinationals or individuals investing in China. In contrast, outbound tax avoidance arrangements have not been a serious concern; for example, the CFC rules have rarely been invoked until recently.

Without amending the law or regulations, the STA has issued circulars to expand the scope of transfer pricing rules (including using the "location-specific advantages" concept) and the GAAR in the case of offshore indirect transfers and treaty shopping. The BEPS Project has emboldened the STA's anti-abuse efforts and, to some extent, has been understood as affirming China's views on certain issues, such as transfer pricing.

620. In a letter of February 12, 2024, No. 2024-0000161213, V-N 2024/9.8, the Undersecretary of Finance indicated that the *Morgan Stanley* decision is being further studied and will be part of further amendments to the relevant domestic legislation on dividend stripping.
621. Netherlands, DivTA, Art. 4(2) provides an exemption for dividends paid to nonresident companies holding a participation (5% or more of the nominal paid-in capital) in a Dutch-resident company, provided that the recipient is a resident of the EU/EEA or a jurisdiction that has a tax treaty with The Netherlands which includes a dividends provision similar to Art. 10 of the OECD Model.
622. Netherlands, CITA, Art. 17(3)(b).
623. Netherlands, ITA, Art. 2.14a.
624. Sweden, *Högsta Förvaltningsdomstolen*, No. 1335-11, March 26, 2012.
625. Japan, CTA, s. 69(1), Order for Enforcement of Corporate Tax Act, s. 142-2(5).

2 SELECTED INTERCOMPANY PRICING ISSUES

All the systems examined here recognize, as a general principle, that dealings between related parties must be undertaken at arm's length, although the specific approach takes different forms: for example, some countries have detailed administrative rules, while others take a more "facts-and-circumstances" approach. The arm's length principle is usually applied on a transactional basis and formulary rules are not used. The terminology and methodology of comparable uncontrolled price (CUP), resale price, cost-plus, and "other" methods are thus present in most of the systems. Profit-based methodologies, such as the profit-split and transactional net margin methods (TNMMs), are becoming increasingly acceptable. The general framework for analyzing intercompany pricing issues in the OECD Transfer Pricing Guidelines[626] seems to be widely followed, except in China and India. The Guidelines were revised to reflect the recommendations of BEPS Actions 8-10 which, in general, were intended to ensure that "transfer pricing outcomes are aligned with value creation." The revisions to the Guidelines are extensive and include, in particular, guidance on hard-to-value intangibles, contractual allocation of risks, routine intragroup services, the recharacterization of transactions which are not commercially rational, cash-box group companies, and cost contribution arrangements. In addition, BEPS Action 13 required countries to adopt country-by-country reporting rules under which large multinationals must provide a wide variety of information to the tax authorities of all the countries in which they operate. Although this information is not broken down on an entity-by-entity basis, it is nevertheless useful to the tax authorities in targeting their transfer pricing and other enforcement activities on taxpayers that pose the greatest risks of tax avoidance. Although, in principle, many of the countries examined here follow the OECD Guidelines, it remains to be seen what impact the most recent revisions to the Guidelines, which are not binding, will have on the countries' transfer pricing practices described below.

The following discussion is limited to the general approach taken by the countries and any special or distinguishing features of interest.

The *United States* has historically been a leader in the development of transfer pricing rules and its system is still the most highly developed. Rather than establishing an order of preference for a particular transfer pricing technique, the transfer pricing regulations instruct taxpayers to use the "best method," that is, the method which provides the most reliable measure of an arm's length price under the circumstances.[627] Taxpayers may use transactions which involve "inexact" comparables if adjustments can be made to improve the reliability of the comparison between the controlled and uncontrolled transactions. The factors involved in determining comparability include the functions performed by each party, the contractual terms involved, and the allocation of risks. The focus is on arriving at a range of possible arm's length prices using statistical techniques to establish the limits of the appropriate range.

626. OECD, *Transfer Pricing Guidelines for Multinational Enterprises and Tax Administrations* (Paris: OECD, 1995) (looseleaf) as amended.
627. United States, Regs., s. 1.482-1(c)(1).

The Regulations provide various methods which can be used in the absence of reliable data for establishing comparability. They permit a profit-split method, in which the aggregate profit is allocated between the controlled parties in the light of the functions performed, risks assumed, and resources provided by each party.[628]

The Regulations also allow the "comparable profits method" (CPM) of price determination.[629] Under the CPM approach, the determination of an arm's length price is based on comparable profit-level indicators which measure the relationship between profits and costs involved and resources employed. The price charged to the controlled taxpayer with respect to particular transactions must result in appropriate profit levels from those transactions, as determined by the profit-level indicators of comparable but unrelated parties. Unlike previous proposed regulations, which stressed the importance of a profit-based methodology as a check on other methods, the final regulations state that the CPM is simply another possible method and subject to the "best method" principle. Thus, where better information can be obtained by using some of the traditional methods, those methods are to be used. CPM will be the method of choice only where the information used to establish the appropriate profit margins is more reliable than the information for the other methods.

Beyond the substantive rules, important procedural requirements must be followed to avoid significant penalties in the event of a subsequent transfer price adjustment. The penalties can be avoided only if the taxpayer has followed one of the prescribed methods of price determination and has contemporaneous documentation establishing how the price was determined. Thus, the new regulations offer a substantial degree of flexibility in the choice of method, but taxpayers must be prepared to demonstrate in detail how prices were in fact arrived at.[630]

In addition, the United States has encouraged the use of Advance Pricing Agreements (APAs), through which taxpayers can obtain a binding commitment in advance from the fiscal authorities as to the appropriateness of the methodology to be used in establishing the transfer price. In many cases, these agreements involve both the United States and the other countries impacted by the business activities in question.

The application of the "arm's length" principle has two foundations under *German* law. First, the general rule that a "constructive dividend" arises where a company provides value to a shareholder without adequate consideration[631] also applies to cross-border situations. Second, the Foreign Transactions Tax Act provides that all economic or financial relationships between related parties must be scrutinized according to the arm's length standard.[632] This is especially important where there is a hidden shift of profits from the shareholder (parent company) to the company (subsidiary), which is not covered by the rules on constructive dividends. The CJEU has, in principle, approved these regimes insofar as they are meant to address "wholly

628. United States, Regs., s. 1.482-6(a).
629. United States, Regs., s. 1.482-5.
630. United States, IRC, s. 6662(e).
631. Germany, CITA, s. 8, para. 3 s. 2.
632. Foreign Transactions Tax Act (*Aussensteuergesetz*), s. 1.

artificial arrangements" aimed at shifting profits out of Germany to another Member State of the EU.[633] Nevertheless, non-arm's length dealings must be recognized where taxpayers can demonstrate that contractual conditions for intra-firm dealings which deviate from third-party arrangements nevertheless have a genuine business purpose (e.g., saving a failing subsidiary from bankruptcy).[634]

With respect to the basis for transfer pricing adjustments in Article 9(1) of the OECD Model Treaty, the Federal Tax Court has clarified that while the tax authorities can rely on this provision only if there is a legal basis under German law (as set out above), taxpayers can rely directly on the inherent limitations of the provision. Against this background, the Federal Tax Court declared judge-made formal requirements for the recognition of dealings between a company and its dominant shareholders to be inapplicable in treaty situations.[635]

In recent years, there has been an avalanche of contradictory judgments by the Federal Tax Court with respect to the possibility of disregarding intragroup loans as such. According to current jurisprudence, a full disregard is possible only if it can be shown that no third party would have extended a loan to the borrower in question (in particular, because of a lack of collateral that cannot be compensated for by a higher interest rate)[636] and the agreed interest rate can be adjusted to account for "implicit support" by the group.[637] Moreover, the Constitutional Court required the Federal Tax Court to refer cases to the CJEU whenever it was in doubt whether adjustments of cross-border loans within corporate groups could be justified in the light of the fundamental freedoms.[638]

In 2007, in a widely discussed move, Germany introduced a provision on "business restructurings" which tries to emulate the outcome of a third-party transaction at arm's length where a function is relocated within a multinational group.[639] This has been heavily criticized as overreaching since it seems to tax the mere shift of "profit potential" to other countries by including location benefits of the other country in the transfer price and by providing for retrospective adjustments in cases of unexpectedly high profits following relocation.

The tax administration has issued administrative principles to provide taxpayers with guidance on transfer pricing issues. While not binding on taxpayers, they are followed in practice. They are based in part on the OECD Guidelines (which have only limited authority) and in part on prior German judicial and administrative practices. With respect to the implementation of the BEPS Action Plan, the German tax authorities support the application of Action Items 8-10 under the existing statute.

In 2003, the law was changed to formally authorize the tax administration to require extensive documentation of cross-border relationships with related parties.

633. CJEU, January 21, 2010, Case C-311/08 (*SGI*).
634. CJEU, May 31, 2018, Case C-283/16 (*Hornbach*).
635. Federal Tax Court (*Bundesfinanzhof*), October 11, 2012, I R 75/11.
636. Federal Tax Court (*Bundesfinanzhof*), January 31, 2022, I R 15/12.
637. Federal Tax Court (*Bundesfinanzhof*), May 18, 2021, I R 4/17.
638. Constitutional Court (*Bundesverfassungsgericht*), order of November 8, 2023, 2 BvR 1079/20.
639. Germany, Foreign Transactions Tax Act (*Aussensteuergesetz*), s. 1 para. 3.

Following the BEPS Project, Germany introduced additional country-by-country reporting requirements[640] in order to meet the requirements of an EU Directive implementing a common regime throughout the EU.[641]

In 1986, *Japan* adopted legislation dealing with transfer pricing. The rules apply to transactions between affiliated corporations where one party is Japanese (or a foreign corporation subject to corporate tax in Japan) and the other is foreign. Under the 2014 tax revisions, the transfer pricing rules also apply to intracompany transactions between a branch and its headquarters. As a matter of basic structure, the Japanese transfer pricing provision allows the tax authorities to make an assessment based on arm's length prices. Until 2011, Japan prioritized the traditional transaction methods, namely, the CUP method, the resale price method, and the cost-plus method, over alternative methods (the TNMM and the profit-split method). The 2011 tax revisions abolished the priority of the traditional transaction methods and instead adopted the most-appropriate-method rule, in line with the current OECD position. Although at present the tax authorities seem to prefer the TNMM, in general, Japan follows OECD practice. For example, the 2019 tax revisions introduced the OECD's suggested approach regarding hard-to-value intangibles[642] and the courts have also respected OECD positions, including the OECD Transfer Pricing Guidelines.[643] APAs have been available since shortly after the legislation was enacted.[644]

In *Canada*, statutory provisions require that transactions between resident and nonresident related parties occur at prices which would have applied in similar transactions between arm's length parties.[645] While there are no detailed regulations for interpreting the statute, the tax authorities have issued various publications setting forth their approach to transfer pricing.[646] The positions taken are clearly based on, and consistent with, the approach of the OECD Transfer Pricing Guidelines. Serious penalties apply if transfer prices are adjusted unless the taxpayer has made reasonable efforts to determine the arm's length price and has contemporaneous documentation to prove those efforts. The tax administration has significantly increased its resources devoted to transfer pricing over the past several years. Transfer pricing issues are often raised on audit but are usually resolved by negotiation, without the need for litigation. There is a special procedure for APAs, both unilateral and bilateral, and several of these APAs are concluded every year.[647]

There is little case law. The Supreme Court of Canada has decided only one transfer pricing case, and it involved the former statutory provision, which simply

640. Germany, GFC (*Abgabenordnung*) s. 138a.
641. Council Directive (EU) 2016/881 of May 25, 2016, amending Directive 2011/16/EU with respect to mandatory automatic exchange of information in the field of taxation, O.J. L 146/8 of June 3, 2016.
642. Japan, STMA, s. 66-4.
643. *Honda v. Japan*, 76 Zeimusoshoshiryo 265 (Tokyo High Ct., May 13, 2015).
644. Japan, STMA, s. 66-4.
645. Canada, ITA, s. 247.
646. CRA, Information Circular 87-2R and the Transfer Pricing Memoranda series 94-4R (advance pricing arrangements) and 06-1 (transfer pricing and customs valuation).
647. CRA, Information Circular 94-2R and Transfer Pricing Memorandum TPM-02.

required prices to be reasonable in the circumstances.[648] In the cases involving the current transfer pricing provisions, which were enacted in response to the 1995 OECD Guidelines, the courts have generally decided in accordance with the OECD Guidelines but have also decided that those Guidelines are not equivalent to statutory provisions and are not binding on the courts.[649]

A specific statutory rule allows the tax authorities (the CRA) to recharacterize transactions or series of transactions if they would not have been entered into by arm's length persons and were entered into primarily to obtain a tax benefit.[650] This provision is intended to allow the CRA to apply the part of the OECD Guidelines dealing with the circumstances in which transactions between non-arm's length persons may be recharacterized where arm's length parties would not have entered into the transaction. Canadian courts have interpreted this provision narrowly, holding that it cannot apply where the arrangements, viewed in their totality, could have been adopted by independent enterprises acting in a commercially rational manner.[651] Any CRA assessments issued under this provision must be approved by a special Transfer Pricing Review Committee.[652]

The CRA has indicated in the past that, in principle, it would not follow a comparable profit method and would not make corresponding adjustments based on that approach. However, it accepts the profit-based approaches in the OECD Guidelines and rules to implement the recommendations of BEPS Actions 8-10 have been enacted.

In *Australia*, doubts about the efficacy of the 1982 transfer pricing rules, particularly in relation to "profit methods" and replacement of other features of transactions apart from price, led to a new regime in 2013. This new regime tied domestic law very closely to OECD positions by reflecting the treaty wording of transfer pricing rules in domestic law and explicitly requiring that OECD guidance be taken into account (the 2008 version of the Commentaries on Article 7 for PEs and the 2022 Transfer Pricing Guidelines for separate enterprises and PEs).[653]

The operation of the rules is confined to cross-border cases where there is detriment to Australian revenue, but the rules cannot be used to undermine the safe harbors in Australia's thin capitalization regime, outlined above. (In the case of banks and other financial enterprises, in a reversal of the previous position, the 2023 thin capitalization/earnings-stripping changes are applied after the transfer pricing rules for other inbound and outbound investors.) There is no requirement that the parties to the transaction be related. The rules for separate enterprises have an extensive reconstruction power, which recent case law suggests may not have been necessary.[654] The rules

648. *Canada v. GlaxoSmithKline Inc.*, [2012] 2 SCR 3.
649. *See*, for example, *McKesson Canada Corporation v. The Queen*, 2013 TCC 404; *Marzen Artistic Aluminum Ltd. v. Canada*, 2016 FCA 34; and *Cameco Corporation v. Canada*, 2020 FCA 112.
650. Canada, ITA, s. 247(2)(b).
651. *Cameco Corporation v. Canada*, 2020 FCA 112.
652. CRA, Transfer Pricing Memorandum TPM-13.
653. Australia, ITAA 1997, Subdivs 815-B-815-D, Taxation Administration Act 1953, Sch. 1, Subdiv. 284-E; the reference to the Guidelines is in the process of being updated to the 2022 version, Exposure Draft, Treasury Laws Amendment Bill 2024: 3 Miscellaneous and technical 4 amendments—Autumn 2024.
654. *Chevron Australia Holdings* [2017] FCAFC 62.

for branches continue to use Australia's single-entity approach and adjustment of the source of actual income and deduction of related expenses; Australia has not accepted the application of the functionally separate-entity "AOA" to branches, which is why it uses the 2008 Commentaries for guidance on this issue. The rules introduce a time limit of seven years for transfer pricing adjustments, whereas previously there was no time limit; however, they deny the reduction of administrative penalties based on a reasonably arguable position if transfer pricing documentation is not created by the due date for filing the tax return. As a result of the BEPS Project, the transfer pricing rules were further amended to meet the new OECD documentation requirements, including country-by-country reporting for groups with more than AUD 1 billion revenue[655] and, more generally, to increase penalties for such taxpayers (called "significant global entities").[656] In addition, the tax administration shifted emphasis from its former reliance on rulings on transfer pricing to also utilizing a risk framework to identify features which will attract its attention (even if the identified features are hard to fit within the law on transfer pricing).[657] Australia entered into the first bilateral APA in the world with the United States in 1990 in relation to Apple and has been active in issuing unilateral, bilateral, and multilateral APAs since then, although there was a lull during the BEPS project.[658]

The *United Kingdom* replaced its transfer pricing rules in 1998 so that they apply automatically (previously the rules required action by the tax administration). This was necessary as part of the move to a self-assessment system. The new rules are consistent with Article 9 of the OECD Model Convention and the law expressly provides for the rules to be construed in accordance with OECD principles, including its Transfer Pricing Guidelines. The rules apply only where there is a potential advantage in relation to UK taxation.[659] The UK tax administration has the statutory power to enter into APAs; this power is quite broad and extends to cover the issue of whether income arises outside the United Kingdom.[660]

While *Sweden* has a statutory provision which requires arm's length dealings where an "economic community" exists between the parties,[661] there are limited administrative regulations interpreting the provision[662] and the case law is also quite

655. Australia, ITAA 1997, Subdiv. 815-E.
656. Australia, ITAA 1997, Subdivs. 815-E, 960-U, Taxation Administration Act 1953, Sch. 1, ss. 284-90(1A)-(1B), (4), 284-155(3), 286-80(4A)-(4B). Australia has proposed to introduce public country-by-country reporting similar to that adopted in the EU. Australia, Treasury, Public country-by-country reporting—February 2024, available at https://treasury.gov.au/consultation/c2024-488354.
657. PCG 2017/1 (transfer pricing issues related to centralized operating models involving procurement, marketing, and sales and distribution functions), PCG 2017/4 (related-party financing), which are progressively being expanded by the addition of new schedules.
658. Australian Taxation Office, Advance Pricing Arrangements, available at https://www.ato.gov.au/businesses-and-organisations/international-tax-for-business/in-detail/pricing/advance-pricing-arrangements/advance-pricing-arrangement-apa-program.
659. United Kingdom, Taxation (International and Other Provisions) Act 2010, s. 147.
660. United Kingdom, Taxation (International and Other Provisions) Act 2010, Part 5.
661. Sweden, ITA, Ch. 14 s. 19.
662. For an exception with respect to market contributions, *see* the administrative guidance *Avdragsrätten för marknadsföringsbidrag och korrigeringsregeln*, January 15, 2019.

sparse. The Supreme Administrative Court considers that the principles set out in the OECD Transfer Pricing Guidelines can be considered to be "guidelines" in establishing an arm's length price.[663] The Court has also stressed that the commercial situation should be judged as it was at the time that the intercompany agreements were entered into, and seems to consider that price adjustments required under the U.S. "commensurate-with-income" standard might not be accepted.

It has also been established that the arm's length standard requires not only that transfer prices be set at market levels but also that the behavior of the parties (including whether or not they should enter into a given transaction) must correspond to the way independent parties would act.[664] From a procedural point of view, the burden of proof is initially on the government to show that a deviation from an arm's length price has taken place which has resulted in lower taxable income in Sweden. The Supreme Administrative Court has clarified that the tax authority has the burden of proof that non-arm's length prices have been applied.[665] In 2006, rules were introduced with respect to requirements for documentation based on the OECD Transfer Pricing Guidelines. The rules were amended in 2017 to implement the recommendations of the BEPS Action 13 Final Report. An APA program was launched on January 1, 2010.[666]

In *France*, the requirement to deal at arm's length to determine transfer prices results from the abnormal-management-decision theory (i.e., *acte anormal de gestion*) a decision which is not in the interests of the enterprise) which, since 1933, has been embodied in section 57 of the tax code as far as international matters are concerned. There are few formal administrative guidelines and the approach has always been a facts-and-circumstances one; however, the French tax authorities do apply the OECD Transfer Pricing Guidelines. After several years without any real change in French transfer pricing policy, the Finance Act for 2024 modifies it in line with the Plan to combat tax, social, and customs fraud (*Plan de lutte contre la fraude fiscale, sociale et douanière*) published in May 2023 by the Ministry of the Economy. Four main measures have been taken. First, the threshold for companies to provide documentary evidence to support their transfer prices was reduced to EUR 150 million. Second, the enforceability of transfer pricing documentation was strengthened, with the addition of a simple presumption of indirect transfer of profits abroad where the transfer pricing method deviates from that in the documentation provided to the tax authorities. This presumption reverses the burden of proof and places it on the taxpayer. Third, the minimum fine for failure to submit documentation was raised to EUR 50,000 for each year audited, increasing the former amount by a factor of five. Fourth, a provision[667] was introduced to tighten controls on transfers of intangible assets and rights that are difficult to value, with the adoption of the OECD guidelines on "hard-to-value intangibles."

663. Sweden, *Högsta Förvaltningsdomstolen*, No. 6664-14, June 7, 2016, which confirmed the position of the 1991 *Shell* case.
664. Sweden, *Högsta förvaltningsdomstolen*, No. 6664-6666-14, June 7, 2016.
665. Sweden, *Högsta förvaltningsdomstolen*, No. 1913-18, June 19, 2019.
666. Sweden, APA Act (*Lag (2009:1289) om prissättningsbesked vid internationella transaktioner*).
667. France, CGI, s. 238 bis-0 I ter.

The tax authorities must show that a deviation from an arm's length price has taken place and, except where the foreign person is resident in or established in a low-tax jurisdiction, that the parties to the transaction are related to each other. Such transferred income is then added back to the tax base and is treated as a deemed distribution of income to the foreign resident. It is subject to withholding tax unless the taxpayer can prove that the price was normal; or that failure to charge an arm's length price is justified according to the particular economic circumstances; or that the price has, or could have, resulted in an equivalent increase in French-source income (e.g., because of subsequent sales); or, since 2015, unless the sums at stake are repatriated. Case law is quite liberal in these matters.

Appropriate correlative adjustments are now available through the 1990 EU arbitration mechanism,[668] which may apply after the mutual agreement procedure has failed to arrive at a satisfactory solution. The first decision arising from this procedure was issued in 2003 and involved two subsidiaries (French and Italian) of a Swedish parent.

A bilateral APA procedure was introduced in 1999; since 2005, a unilateral procedure has also been available where no bilateral APA procedure exists in the other country or the transactions involve many countries, a small business, or a very specific issue.[669] The powers of tax auditors to make requests for clarification about the relationships of French businesses with foreign persons and for documentation substantiating transfer prices were increased in 1996. When, in the course of an audit, the authorities have gathered information which leads them to believe that there has been an indirect transfer of profits to an associated foreign enterprise, they may require the French enterprise to produce appropriate documents and information specifying the nature of the transactions and the methods used in determining the intercompany pricing for those transactions. Failure to comply is subject to a fine and entitles the tax authorities to assess the income on the basis of the available data.[670] In addition, the statute of limitations is extended when French tax authorities request international administrative assistance in connection with transfer pricing issues.[671] Beginning in 2010, major French corporations have had to comply with a set of increasingly strict rules relating to transfer pricing documentation (general to the group and specific to each corporation), which are now in line with the OECD standards; rulings from foreign tax authorities have had to be reported since 2014.[672] Moreover, since 2016, OECD-type country-by-country reporting has been required from the largest groups.[673]

Since 2002, *The Netherlands* has had a specific statutory provision along the lines of Article 9 of the OECD Model Treaty, requiring arm's length pricing between related parties.[674] However, the principle that profits can be "adjusted" in transactions

668. 90/436/EEC: Convention on the elimination of double taxation in connection with the adjustment of profits of associated enterprises.
669. France, LPF, s. L 80 B-7°.
670. France, LPF, s. L 13 B.
671. France, LPF, s. L 188 A.
672. France, LPF, s. L 13 AA and CGI, s. 243 quinquies B.
673. France, CGI, s. 223 quinquies C.
674. Netherlands, CITA, Art. 8b.

between a corporation and its shareholders was already firmly established in the case law pursuant to the statutory rule that business profits comprise "all benefits, under whatever name and in whatever form, derived from business." On the basis of this provision, the OECD Transfer Pricing Guidelines were considered to be generally applicable.[675] From 2001, the revenue authorities have issued a series of decrees outlining instances where the taxpayer may obtain an APA or an Advance Tax Ruling (ATR). An amending decree effective as of July 1, 2019, provides that a ruling can be obtained only if there is a sufficient economic nexus with The Netherlands.[676]

The *Chinese* transfer pricing rules in the EIT Law and Regulations and STA administrative rules are the most detailed and sophisticated in the entire Chinese tax system, indicating the importance of transfer pricing to the Chinese tax administration. The STA has made no secret about its misgivings with respect to the OECD Transfer Pricing Guidelines, which are not considered to be binding, the use of comparables, and the weight given to "legal arrangements." Chinese domestic rules emphasize "results" (taxable income in China) and "substance." The STA seems to be moving increasingly toward the use of the profit-split method and assigning value to intangibles based on development, enhancement, maintenance, protection, and exploitation. The STA has used the notion of location-specific advantages in its circulars and in practice (including during negotiations for APAs). It has not published specific guidance for identifying and quantifying these advantages, although STA circulars mention value creation and valuation of intangibles.

The STA has a fairly well-established APA program and publishes annual reports. Currently, most APAs are unilateral. The mutual agreement procedure has been increasingly used in China, in part owing to the increase in outbound investment by Chinese companies and the increasing number of tax assessments of Chinese companies doing business in other countries (especially with "belt and road initiative" countries).

The STA has developed software programs using big data to take advantage of information from country-by-country reporting during transfer pricing audits, part of a drive by the STA to "modernize" tax administration in general through the use of information technology. However, China generally considers the arm's length principle and the transactional, comparative analysis approach difficult in practice and favors a more "holistic" and substance-over-form approach based on economic realities.[677]

675. The Decree of June 14, 2022, No. 2022-0000139020, V-N 2022/36.2, paragraph 1.5 no longer adopts the direct effect of the Transfer Pricing Guidelines, but merely states that these Guidelines provide an internationally accepted interpretation of the arm's length principle and, in this sense, can be considered as an appropriate clarification and explanation of the arm's length principle.

676. Most recently amended by the Decree of December 19, 2023, No. 2023-0000020007, V-N 2024/5.10.

677. *See* United Nations, *Practical Manual on Transfer Pricing for Developing Countries 2021*, Part D, Country Practices, China.

India first adopted transfer pricing provisions and the arm's length standard in 2001.[678] When introduced, the rules applied only to international transactions involving associated enterprises; however, in 2012, they were extended to "specified domestic transactions."[679] The terms "international transactions," "associated enterprises," and "arm's length price" are defined in the Act. The taxpayer is responsible for reporting international transactions with associated enterprises and has the burden of proof with respect to arm's length prices. The taxpayer is also required to maintain contemporaneous documents to support its arm's length prices. No transfer pricing adjustment is made where it results in a reduction of income; further, there is no provision for corresponding adjustments under domestic law. Since the main purpose of the provisions is to prevent tax avoidance, some taxpayers have argued that the provisions cannot be applied except where there is an avoidance of tax or a transfer of profit outside India; however, the courts have rejected this argument.[680]

The Act and the Rules provide six methods for determining an arm's length price: the CUP method; the resale price method; the cost-plus method; the profit-split method; the TNMM; and any other prescribed method. The CBDT has prescribed any method which takes into account the price which has been charged or paid, or would have been charged or paid, in the same or similar uncontrolled transactions between nonassociated enterprises under similar circumstances and considering all the relevant facts.[681] There is no hierarchy in the selection of a method; the method which is best suited to the facts and circumstances of the case should be adopted. In practice, TNMM is the method most frequently used by both taxpayers and tax authorities.

Although the transfer pricing legislation originally provided that, where more than one arm's length price is determined in accordance with the rules, the arithmetic mean of those prices had to be used as the price, since April 1, 2014 any price within a range is acceptable except where the profit-split method or the prescribed method is used.[682] However, the range of prices requires at least six comparables; otherwise, the arithmetic mean continues to apply.[683]

In 2012, legislation was introduced authorizing unilateral, bilateral, and multilateral APAs.[684] APAs are valid for a maximum of five years. An APA can be applied to the four preceding years as well as the current year.[685] The taxpayer is required to prepare an annual compliance report for each year of the APA containing information relating to the actual results for the year and to demonstrate compliance with the terms of the APA. Since 2017, the CBDT has published an annual APA report. The APA program is an apparent success in India's otherwise dispute-ridden world of taxation. In fact, since April 2020, the program has also been extended to the attribution of

678. India, ITA 1961, s. 92.1 provides: "Any income arising from an international transaction shall be computed having regard to the arm's length price."
679. India, ITA 1961, s. 92BA.
680. *Aztec Software & Technology Service Ltd* [2007-TII-01-ITAT-BANG-SB-TP].
681. CBDT, Notification No. 18/2012, May 23, 2012.
682. India, ITA 1961, s. 92C.
683. Rule 10CA.
684. India, ITA 1961, s. 92CC and Rules 10F to 10T.
685. Rule 10MA and 10RA.

income to a business connection.[686] The latest report (2023) shows that since the beginning of the program in 2012-2013, India has entered into 516 APAs, with 315 applications disposed of due to other reasons; the total number of applications for APAs has also increased substantially (1,659 as of 2023).[687]

3 CORPORATE-SHAREHOLDER TAXATION IN THE INTERNATIONAL CONTEXT

3.1 General

In the case of cross-border investment by corporations, relieving double taxation has two aspects: the taxation of the earnings of a corporation by more than one country and the taxation of the earnings of a corporation at both the corporate and shareholder levels. Corporate tax integration issues in a domestic context are discussed in Part III, where it is noted that international considerations have been one of the driving forces in the abandonment of imputation systems for relieving the double taxation of dividends.

Most imputation systems operated by giving a tax credit only to *resident* shareholders in *resident* companies in respect of *domestic* corporate tax (not foreign corporate tax). As a result, where any one of these elements was lacking, imputation did not apply: foreign companies, foreign shareholders, and foreign taxes did not benefit from the imputation system. These aspects of imputation systems resulted in discrimination in an economic sense against cross-border investment through corporations, and also in a legal sense within the EU because they violated the four freedoms of the EU Treaty. Several decisions of the CJEU dealing with imputation systems are generally regarded as having decided implicitly that such systems were not consistent with EU law and were the main immediate reason for the abandonment of imputation by EU Member States. At the end of 2004, it was finally directly affirmed by the CJEU that the standard imputation system was indeed contrary to EU law.[688]

Within the EU before the abandonment of imputation and outside the EU currently, countries have grappled with the economic side of the issue. Both *France* and the *United Kingdom* regularly extended imputation benefits to foreign shareholders of resident companies, typically through treaties, although the shareholders benefiting from the relief and the mechanisms and extent of the relief varied. *Australia* maintains an imputation system limited to resident shareholders in resident companies in respect of domestic tax paid (which is extended to dividends received by PEs of nonresidents in Australia).

In *Canada*, the tax system has always dealt with part of the international bias of the imputation system by not requiring that imputation credits be supported by domestic tax payments and so, in effect, grants imputation relief in respect of foreign

686. India, ITA s. 92CC(1)(b).
687. APA Annual report 2022-23, available at: https://incometaxindia.gov.in/Lists/Latest%20News/Attachments/601/APA-Report-Final-2023.pdf.
688. CJEU, October 23, 2004, C-319/02 (*Manninen*), p. 4.

income and foreign tax. For a period, the *United Kingdom* gave separate nonrefundable tax credits for dividends received by resident shareholders from resident corporations out of foreign income in respect of foreign tax on that income. As noted earlier, the United Kingdom now applies lower rates of tax on the dividend income of individuals. The result is a much simplified (but arbitrary) system.

As far as foreign corporations are concerned, *Australia* and New Zealand have enacted complementary legislation to pass through imputation credits.[689] Australian shareholders in New Zealand corporations receive imputation benefits for Australian tax paid directly or indirectly by the corporation, and vice versa. Both countries have very similar imputation systems, which makes this system feasible.

The dividend tax relief systems introduced in the last two decades in several countries are better able to deal with corporate tax integration issues in an international setting and are thus more neutral with respect to foreign and domestic investment. In particular, the French (from 2005), German (from 2001), UK, and U.S. systems give the same treatment to most dividends from foreign corporations received by resident individual shareholders as they do to dividends received from domestic corporations. Thus, dividends received by *German* individual shareholders from foreign corporations are partially (60%) included in income.[690] If the shares are held as private assets, the foreign dividend income can also qualify for the 25% final withholding tax.[691] Under certain circumstances, shareholders who are simultaneously managers of the corporation enjoy an election as to which of the two regimes shall apply (given that the application of the final withholding tax excludes any deductions of income-related expenditures).[692]

A similar result applies for *French* individual shareholders whose dividends are, in principle, subject to the 30% single-rate withholding tax (*prélèvement forfaitaire unique*, composed of 12.8% income tax plus 17.2% flat-rate social taxes), but there is an option to be subject to the progressive income tax scale, in which case only 60% of the dividend paid is actually taxed. If that option is chosen, all the taxpayer's capital income is included in the taxable base.[693] Dividends from foreign sources benefit from the 40% allowance applicable to dividends from French sources, subject to a number of conditions: (i) the distribution is made by a company resident in the EU or by a state linked to France by an agreement containing an administrative clause; (ii) the foreign company is liable for a tax equivalent to corporation tax; and (iii) the distribution is made by virtue of a lawful decision by the competent bodies of the company concerned. Dividends received by a resident corporate shareholder are taxed, in principle, like the company's other profits at the applicable CIT rate. Dividends distributed to nonresident shareholders are subject to a specific withholding tax, the rate of which varies according to the status of the beneficiary, subject to the provisions of tax treaties. The rate applicable to individuals is set at 12.8%; for legal entities, the

689. Australia, ITAA 1997, Div. 220.
690. Germany, ITA, s. 3 No. 40A.
691. Germany, ITA, s. 32d para. 1.
692. Germany, ITA, s. 32d para. 1 No. 3.
693. France, CGI, ss. 158 3-2° and 200 A.

rate is 15% for dividends paid to certain non-profit organizations based in an EEA country (EU, Iceland, Liechtenstein, and Norway), and 25% for other distributed income (which is in fact the standard corporate tax rate).[694] All these rules are subject to the application of tax treaties and the group tax regime.

For *United States* individual shareholders, such dividends are subject to a maximum tax of 20% if received from a corporation resident in a country with which the United States has a tax treaty providing for adequate exchange of information or from a corporation whose shares are traded on a U.S. stock exchange.[695] A dividend from a foreign corporation does not qualify for this treatment in the United States if it is a FIC or a PFIC because in these cases, it is unlikely that the foreign corporation will have paid a significant level of foreign tax. In the *United Kingdom*, individuals are entitled to the reduced rate when receiving foreign dividends.[696]

With respect to international double taxation and dividends, it is often said that the standard tax treaty arrangements are premised on a classical system. Two typical cases of cross-border corporate investment can be used to explain why this is the case. If an individual shareholder resident in country A invests in a corporation resident in country B, country B will levy its corporate tax on the corporation and (as usually limited by treaty) a 15% dividend withholding tax on dividends paid to shareholders resident in country A. Country A will then tax the dividend in full and give a FTC for the country B tax on the dividend. Hence, there is both corporate and individual tax on the income without any integration relief (i.e., no relief for the economic double taxation of profits earned by a corporation resident in one country that are distributed to its shareholders resident in another country). *Australia*, *Canada*, *China*, *Japan*, *The Netherlands*, and *Sweden* follow this pattern. As noted above, *France*, *Germany*, *the United Kingdom*, and the *United States* have departed from this pattern and give relief for dividends from foreign corporations. All the countries except Australia (in respect of franked dividends) and the United Kingdom also follow this pattern when they are the source country and collect withholding tax on the dividends.

In the case of intercompany dividends, *Germany* followed a generous path after 2001, applying full exemption for domestic and foreign dividends received by a corporate shareholder (except a 5% amount deemed to represent nondeductible expenditures). After the CJEU found this treatment to be discriminatory because it did not apply to foreign corporate taxpayers holding shares in domestic corporations, Germany eliminated the exemption regime for portfolio shareholders. Since 2013, intercompany dividends (irrespective of whether they are cross-border or domestic) are subject to the full corporate tax rate of 15% where the size of the shareholding does not amount to 10% or more of the distributing company's capital.[697]

Alternatively, and more commonly, an individual shareholder may invest in a resident parent corporation in country A, which then invests in a subsidiary in country B. In this case, country B will collect corporate tax from the subsidiary but little or no

694. France, CGI, ss. 119 bis 2 and 187.
695. United States, IRC, s. 1(h)(11)(C)(i)(II).
696. United Kingdom, Income Tax Act 2007, s. 13.
697. Germany, CITA, s. 8b paras. 1 and 4 (*see also* section 3.2.2 above).

withholding tax on dividends paid to the parent company. As a result of the Parent-Subsidiary Directive within the EU and recent treaties entered into by *Australia*, *Japan*, and the *United States*, there is no source withholding tax on direct-investment dividends. Under most other treaties which follow the OECD Model Treaty, the tax rate on the dividends is limited to 5%. As noted above, all countries, except Australia (with respect to franked dividends) and the *United Kingdom*, collect this withholding tax as permitted by the treaty. The elimination or reduction of the withholding tax effectively does away with a potential source of double taxation of corporate income in an international setting.

In addition, country A will give the country A parent corporation either an exemption for the dividends received or an underlying FTC so that there is little or no tax on the parent in country A (thus reducing or eliminating double corporate-level taxation on the corporate income). This relief may arise under domestic law (typically in *Australia*, *Canada*, *Japan*, and *the United Kingdom*), under treaty or domestic law reinforced by treaty (typically in *France*, *The Netherlands*, and *Sweden*) and in countries following the Parent-Subsidiary Directive, which gives the parent company's residence country the choice of applying an exemption or an indirect tax credit. Country A will then tax dividends received by an individual shareholder from the parent company. Such dividends are taxable in full, with neither international nor domestic integration double tax relief in *Australia*, *China*, *France*, *Germany*, *The Netherlands*, *Sweden*, and the *United States*. The foreign corporate-level tax is not taken into account in the domestic shareholder tax system and thus, there are effectively two levels of full taxation (typical of the classical system), one on the corporation in country B and one on the individual shareholder in country A. One of the major changes in the last two decades has been to give integration relief in such cases so that the general type of integration relief available in a country now applies in *Canada*, *France*, *Germany*, the *United Kingdom*, and the *United States*. Therefore, as these developments show, the "classical" double tax model for international corporate investment is increasingly being replaced by a variety of integration models which provide more neutral treatment of foreign and domestic investment than proved to be possible under most imputation systems.

In contrast, *Japan* has never provided integration relief for foreign corporate tax in assessing tax on dividends received by Japanese individual shareholders. Similarly, *India* does not provide any underlying tax credit with respect to dividends from foreign companies, except for Indian-resident companies holding a substantial share interest pursuant to the provisions of the treaties with Mauritius (10% ownership requirement) and Singapore (25% ownership requirement).

3.2 International Aspects of Capital Gains

The discussion of corporate tax integration in Part III also considers the treatment of capital gains. Again, similar issues arise internationally as well as domestically with respect to the effect of capital gains tax on the retained income of corporations. Putting aside the case of companies holding substantial real estate investments, most countries generally accept the international treaty norm that capital gains on shares are taxable only in the residence country of the shareholder. In their treaties, *Canada, China, France, India, Japan,* and *The Netherlands* continue to seek to preserve their capital gains tax in respect of certain shares in domestic corporations.

In relation to direct investment in foreign companies (parent/subsidiary cases), in most countries the effect is that there is no tax at source on the sale of shares in a foreign subsidiary and thus no tax on retained income of those companies. Where the residence country of the parent grants a participation exemption in such cases (*Australia, France, Germany,*[698] *The Netherlands, Sweden,* and the *United Kingdom*), there is no double taxation at the level of the parent. Where capital gains tax is levied on the sale of the shares of the subsidiary by the country of the parent, similar issues of corporate tax integration are raised, as in the purely domestic case discussed in Part III. All the countries except Australia treat the domestic and international cases of parents selling shares of subsidiaries in the same way so that neutrality between the domestic and international situations is achieved, with the one exception. As far as individual shareholders in the parent corporation are concerned, the domestic capital gains tax rules apply and, consequently, the discussion of the issue in Part III is relevant.

Where an individual shareholder makes a portfolio investment in a foreign corporation, no country seeks to tax the capital gain at source. In this case, all countries apply the same capital gains tax rules as apply to a resident individual selling shares in a purely domestic context (apart from FIF regimes). Hence, there is neutrality between domestic and international investment. Consequently, the degree of corporate tax integration achieved for retained earnings is the same as in the domestic case. As noted in Part III, only *Germany,*[699] *Sweden,* and the *United States* provide consistent treatment of dividends and capital gains in the context of corporate tax integration. In the international setting, the noticeable difference between dividends and capital gains received by individual portfolio shareholders is the levy of a significant withholding tax at source on dividends (15% under the usual treaty limits) but not on capital gains. It is not clear what the continuing justification for this difference is. As already noted, neither the *United Kingdom* nor *Australia* (on franked dividends) levies the tax at source. The appropriate treatment of capital gains and its relation to the taxation of dividends is thus still evolving.

Indian tax treaties generally follow Article 13(5) and (6) of the UN Model Treaty. Thus, India tries to retain taxing rights with respect to capital gains arising from the transfer of shares in companies and other entities which derive their value from immovable property located in India and from the transfer of substantial shareholdings in Indian companies. Although, in the past, Indian treaties with Cyprus, Mauritius, Singapore, and the United Arab Emirates gave taxing rights with respect to capital gains

698. Apart from a corporate tax of 15% on 5% of the capital gain, which is deemed to represent nondeductible expenses.
699. However, the additional minimum shareholding requirement introduced in Germany in 2013 for the tax exemption of intercompany dividends has not been extended to intercompany capital gains.

to the country in which the alienator was resident (which resulted in treaty shopping), these treaties have since been renegotiated.

4 SELECTED TREATY ISSUES

All the countries reviewed here, except China and India, have treaties which are broadly based on the OECD Model Convention, although Canada and Australia generally insist on greater recognition of source-based taxation than the other countries. China and India generally follow the UN Model Convention in their treaties. The following materials consider several topics which have been important in tax treaty policy discussions.

All the countries, with the exception of the United States, have signed the MLI. The United States has not signed the MLI because it considers that its existing tax treaties satisfy the BEPS minimum standards.

The MLI was initially signed by seventy-six countries in June 2017, entered into force on July 1, 2018, and as of June 2024 had 103 signatories. The MLI resulted from Action 15 of the BEPS Project, which developed a multilateral treaty to modify the provisions of existing bilateral tax treaties in an efficient manner so as to reflect the tax treaty measures adopted in the BEPS Final Reports. In the absence of the MLI, it would have taken decades for countries to renegotiate their existing bilateral tax treaties individually (especially for countries with large treaty networks, which is the case with all the countries examined here).

The provisions of the MLI allow countries to choose which of their tax treaties are covered by the MLI and, by making reservations on the optional provisions of the MLI, not to apply those provisions; however, reservations are not allowed with respect to those provisions which constitute minimum standards (i.e., the provisions dealing with treaty abuse and improvements to the mutual agreement procedure). Once a reservation has been made, it can be replaced only by a more limited reservation. A tax treaty is modified by the MLI only where both contracting states agree to have the treaty covered by the MLI and agree to the same modification.

The optional provisions of the MLI, all of which have been added to the 2017 OECD and UN Model Treaties, deal with:

- the entitlement of hybrid entities to treaty benefits;
- a revised tiebreaker rule for dual-resident entities;
- a switchover clause for eliminating double taxation;
- a 365-day holding period for access to the benefit of the lower rate of tax on direct dividends;
- a 365-day testing period for determining whether gains from the disposal of the shares of land-rich companies are taxable;
- an anti-abuse rule for PEs in third countries;
- a saving clause to ensure that tax treaties do not prevent a country from taxing its own residents except as expressly provided; and
- anti-abuse rules to prevent the avoidance of PE status.

The countries examined here have taken significantly different approaches to the optional provisions in the MLI. Some countries have embraced all or almost all of them, while other countries have entered reservations on all or most of them. Each country's positions with respect to the optional provisions of the MLI are dealt with in the country chapters in Part I.

4.1 Relation Between Domestic Law and Treaties: Treaty Override

Under constitutional principles in the *United States*, statutory law and treaties are of equal status.[700] As a consequence, in the case of a conflict between domestic legislation and treaty provisions, the provision which is later in time prevails. Thus, although in principle treaty obligations can be overridden by later, inconsistent domestic legislation, the courts have required that the legislative intent to override a treaty obligation must be "clearly expressed"; historically, there have been relatively few examples of treaty overrides, although the introduction of the taxation of foreign-owned real estate in 1980 is an important exception. In addition, Congress enacted several technical provisions in connection with the extensive tax reform in 1986 which did explicitly override treaty obligations, and the Internal Revenue Code (IRC) was amended to make explicit that treaties have no "preferential status" in relation to domestic law.[701] More recently, there was some debate in the United States as to whether certain new provisions in the 2017 tax reform constituted treaty overrides.

In *Canada*, treaties are put into force by an implementing act which typically provides that the treaty prevails over domestic law in the case of a conflict. In principle, treaties can be overridden by subsequent legislation. However, treaty overrides occur infrequently, are often simply clarifying in nature, and are intended to bring Canadian treaty practice into conformity with that of its treaty partners (e.g., domestic legislation overrules the position taken by the Supreme Court with respect to the static interpretation of a treaty). In addition, a number of terms, such as "annuity," "Canada," "immovable property," "real property," and "periodic pension payment" have been defined by statute for purposes of Canada's tax treaties despite the absence of any definition in the treaties. Moreover, the Canadian GAAR applies notwithstanding any provisions of a tax treaty to the contrary. The treaty "overrides" are all found in one statute: the Income Tax Conventions Interpretation Act.[702]

In general, *Sweden* does not allow subsequent legislation to increase the tax liability that would have been established using treaty rules. In a 2008 case, the Swedish Supreme Administrative Court decided that subsequent legislation took precedence over treaty rules:[703] the Swedish CFC rules, which were enacted after the Swiss-Swedish double taxation treaty was concluded, were found to be applicable irrespective of whether they contravened the treaty. This decision was strongly

700. United States, Constitution, Art. VI, s. 2.
701. United States, IRC, s. 7852(d)(1).
702. RSC 1985, c. I-4 as amended.
703. Sweden, *Högsta förvaltningsdomstolen*, No. 2697-05, April 5, 2008.

criticized by academics and practitioners, and the Supreme Administrative Court soon overturned it.[704]

In one situation, legislation was passed which was intended to clarify that a certain tax holiday regime was not covered by a treaty; in a sense, this legislation could be viewed as a treaty override. However, the position taken in the legislation is also a plausible reading of the treaty without the legislative gloss.

It is now clear in *French* case law that, according to the Constitution, duly ratified and published treaties take precedence over prior or subsequent conflicting domestic law. The French situation is special in that, as far as the legislature is concerned, any income which France is given the right to tax by treaty is taxable, even where it would not be subject to tax under the provisions of the tax code defining the territorial scope of French taxes.[705] The courts are split on this issue. The administrative court has recognized, on the basis of the jurisprudential principle of treaty subsidiarity, that a tax treaty can be applied only after it has been established that the item of income at stake is taxable according to French domestic tax law, whereas the judicial court rejects the application of this principle.[706]

Similarly, *Japan* does not allow domestic legislation to override treaty obligations. A Japanese constitutional article states that treaty obligations should be "faithfully observed."[707] This article has been interpreted as establishing the superiority of international rules over domestic rules, even where the domestic rules are later in time. Thus, under this approach, treaty overrides through domestic law are not possible. Treaty rules can be displaced only if the treaty itself contains a "saving" clause which, within the context of the treaty, preserves the application of domestic legislation.

Some Japanese treaties provide specific source rules for certain categories of income, often giving a domestic source to income which would have had a foreign source under domestic law rules. Japan accepts the result that a change in source rules can result in income being subject to Japanese taxation in the hands of a foreign taxpayer even where the income would not have been taxed under the normally applicable domestic source principles.

Australia gives effect to treaties by enacting them into domestic law through the normal parliamentary process under the International Tax Agreements Act 1953. The Act states that its provisions have effect notwithstanding anything inconsistent in the basic domestic tax law, with the conspicuous exception of the GAAR. Under normal rules of interpretation, the Act could be overridden by later inconsistent legislation but, in general, Australia avoids treaty overrides and courts would be reluctant to reach such a conclusion. However, some provisions in the Agreements Act have been enacted as interpretive measures, which could be viewed as treaty overrides. For example, a court decision which held that land-rich company provisions in the capital gains article of Australia's treaties did not extend beyond one tier was overruled in

704. Sweden, *Högsta förvaltningsdomstolen*, No. 283-10, December 14, 2010.
705. France, CGI, ss. 4 bis and 165 bis (IIT) and 209 I (CIT).
706. *See* Conseil d'Etat, June 28, 2002, No. 232276 (*Société Schneider Electric*). Compare with Cour de cassation, Ass. plén., October 2, 2015, n°14-14.256 (*Mme Eshagh et al.*).
707. Japan, Constitution, Art. 98.

legislation providing for the look-through of multiple tiers of companies.[708] Whether the exclusion of the GAAR from the general rule that treaties prevail over domestic law constitutes an override is unlikely to raise treaty issues in future now that the PPT is being widely adopted into treaties under the MLI. The source rule commonly found in Australian treaties which explicitly operates for domestic tax law purposes can make income taxable which would not otherwise be taxable under domestic law.[709]

In the *United Kingdom*, treaties come into effect through a special legislative mechanism and it is that version of the treaty relief, and not the treaty itself, which is controlling. As a result, what is, in effect, a treaty override would be possible but has happened only very rarely in practice. In one case, a legislative grant of authority to the tax authorities to deny tax credits in connection with jurisdictions which use unitary taxation would have amounted to a treaty override. On a number of occasions, the United Kingdom has been found to be in breach of a treaty but not liable to refund tax to the taxpayer because the relevant treaty was not fully implemented into domestic law (sometimes referred to as a treaty underride).[710] To the extent that the diverted profits tax (DPT) (introduced in 2015) or the digital services tax (introduced in 2020) might be considered to fall within the scope of tax treaties, the United Kingdom intends treaty underride.

Under the *Dutch* constitution, the application of domestic law is restricted by directly applicable treaty provisions. This may lead occasionally to an increase in the amount of tax to be paid. For example, if a dual-resident business taxpayer is a treaty resident only of the other state, The Netherlands is restricted to taxing only the income attributable to a PE. However, if the taxpayer were taxed as a resident, the (domestic) business income might be offset by losses from foreign business activities.

German constitutional law distinguishes clearly between tax treaties binding on the state according to the rules of international public law and internal legislation under which enactments of tax treaty rules enjoy a preference[711] (although they can easily be overridden by subsequent legislation). In a landmark judgment, the German Constitutional Court decided that even an outright "treaty override" does not conflict with the German Constitution and fundamental principles of international law.[712] In a number of cases involving Germany, the CJEU also declined to interfere, holding that possible breaches of an international treaty would not necessarily involve an infringement of EU law.[713]

In *China*, tax treaties prevail over domestic law and treaty overrides are not allowed. In practice, the STA's substance-over-form and pragmatic (sometimes at the

708. *Lamesa Holdings BV* (1997) 35 ATR 239, International Tax Agreements Act 1953 s. 3A.
709. *Tech Mahindra* [2015] FCA 1082 and *Satyam Computer Services* [2018] FCAFC 172. As noted above in section 3.1.2, for tax treaties signed from 2019, the same result is achieved directly by domestic tax law.
710. For example, *R v. IRC ex parte Commerzbank* (1993) 68 TC 252 (HC), *Boake Allen Ltd & Ors v. Revenue & Customs Commissioners* [2007] UKHL 25 (HL), and *Sun Life Assurance Co of Canada v. Pearson* [1984] 59 TC 250 (CA) involved tax treaty underride.
711. Germany, General Fiscal Code, s. 2.
712. German Constitutional Court (*Bundesverfassungsgericht*) Order of December 15, 2015, 1 BvL 1/12.
713. CJEU, June 6, 2007, C-298/05 (*Columbus Container*); February 12, 2009, C-67/08 (*Block*).

risk of the end justifying the means) approach to treaty interpretation, which has been deferred to by the courts in several cases (including *PanAmSAT* and *Dongwa*), may have the effect of denying treaty benefits which are arguably legitimate (especially where the other country is an OECD member country and largely follows the OECD Commentaries).[714] The Chinese GAAR has been invoked to deny treaty benefits, especially with respect to indirect transfers and treaty shopping.

In *India*, section 90(2) of the ITA provides that a taxpayer has an option to choose either the treaty or the domestic law provision, whichever is more beneficial. Therefore, normally, treaties override the provisions of domestic law in the event of a conflict. However, the Indian GAAR expressly overrides tax treaties even where the provisions of a treaty are more beneficial to the taxpayer.[715] In addition, Explanation 1 to section 90, which provides that taxing a foreign company at a higher rate than the rate applied to a domestic company shall not be regarded as less favorable, seems to be a case of treaty override. There have also been a few cases where courts have questioned the firm belief that treaties always override domestic law.[716]

4.2 Approach to Treaty Interpretation

The *United States* has signed, but not ratified, the Vienna Convention, and there is no consensus whether or to what extent the positions in the Convention reflect customary international law. On the one hand, the interpretive methods used by U.S. courts are often consistent with the Vienna Convention approach, although there is generally a tendency to look beyond the "ordinary meaning" of the treaty language to the purposes and objects of the treaty in general and the treaty article in particular. "Context" is thus given a broader interpretation than the Vienna Convention would seem to allow. On the other hand, recent cases have shown more of a tendency to reject the use of unilateral material such as the Treasury's Technical Explanation of the treaty or the legislative history of the treaty's consideration by the Senate.[717]

Canada has ratified the Vienna Convention and its courts frequently refer to its provisions in cases involving the interpretation of tax treaties. Commentaries on the various articles of the OECD Model Convention are also often relied on (the Supreme Court has said that the Commentary is "of high persuasive value"),[718] although how such material is relevant, given the Vienna Convention's restrictions on the use of extrinsic material, is not entirely clear. Canada has a specific statute dealing with tax treaty interpretation (the Income Tax Conventions Interpretation Act). The legislation makes clear that treaty references to domestic law concepts are to be interpreted in an "ambulatory" fashion, reflecting changes in domestic law which occur subsequent to the ratification of the treaty. However, the courts have refused to use provisions of the

---

714. *See* Jinyan Li, *International Taxation in China: A Contextualized Analysis* (IBFD, 2016) 112-131 for a brief discussion of the *PanAmSAT* and *Dongwa* cases.
715. India, ITA 1961, s. 90(2A).
716. *T. Rajakumar v. Union of India* 17241-17243 (Madras High Court) and *Vodafone South Limited v. Dy Director* (WP No. 13210-14/2012 (Karnataka)).
717. United States, *Xerox Corp. v. United States*, 41 F.3rd 647 (Fed. Cir. 1994).
718. *The Queen v. Crown Forest Industries Ltd.*, [1995] 2 CTC 64 (SCC).

OECD Commentary made after the conclusion of a treaty in interpreting the treaty unless the subsequent version of the Commentary merely clarifies the prior version and does not amount to a revision of the meaning.[719] In general, Canadian courts purport to interpret treaties more liberally than domestic legislation, although this result is difficult to see in practice. Typically, the courts consider a wide range of extrinsic materials, such as other treaties, foreign cases, and scholarly writings, when interpreting a treaty.

Sweden has also ratified the Vienna Convention and tax treaties are interpreted in accordance with its principles. Following the reference in Article 31(3) of the Vienna Convention to the subsequent administrative practices of the parties, an important case held that a treaty term should be interpreted in the light of those practices rather than using the domestic law concept.[720] While the Swedish text is the starting point for interpretation, the English version is also given special weight when, as is often the case, the treaty was negotiated in English. The Commentary on the OECD Model Convention is given special consideration, although it is not binding and does not apply retroactively.[721]

Although *Japan* has signed the Vienna Convention, it seems to have had little impact on treaty interpretation practice in Japanese courts. Courts have not referred to the Convention in connection with tax treaties and the topic is not dealt with extensively in academic writing, although the actual decisions in what sparse case law exists can be said to be consistent with the result that would have occurred under the OECD Model Treaty.

In *The Netherlands*, treaty interpretation and the role of the OECD Model Convention and Commentary are the subject of lively discussions among commentators. The Dutch Supreme Court has clarified how to deal with the OECD Commentary when interpreting and applying tax treaties.[722] According to the Supreme Court, later OECD Commentary (i.e., the Commentary as it read after the conclusion of the relevant treaty) has only limited importance as a supplementary means of interpretation in accordance with Article 32 of the Vienna Convention. Thus, in the Court's view, later OECD Commentary is relevant if the text of the treaty provision to be interpreted is similar to the OECD Model and the later Commentary constitutes a specification or clarification of (i) the relevant provision of the OECD Model or (ii) earlier OECD Commentary to which great significance is attached. The Supreme Court stated that earlier Commentary is of great significance if the text of a provision of a tax treaty is also closely aligned with the comparable provision of the OECD Model, but that later Commentary has no importance if it goes beyond a clarification or specification, even as a supplementary means of interpretation within the meaning of Article 32 of the Vienna Convention. The Supreme Court has occasionally referred to the Vienna Convention and over the past decades has increasingly shown an awareness of treaty

719. *Prévost Car v. The Queen*, 2009 FCA 57; *Canada v. Alta Energy Luxembourg S.A.R.L.*, 2021 SCC 49.
720. Sweden, *Högsta Förvaltningsdomstolen*, No. 1169-1987, October 27, 1987.
721. Sweden, *Högsta Förvaltningsdomstolen*, No. 3960-14, June 20, 2016.
722. October 14, 2022, No. 21/00747, BNB 2023/33.

interpretation issues. At the same time, the Court seems to have moved away from a strict grammatical interpretation of tax treaties and appears more inclined to arrive at a reasonable result through broad references to the (assumed) object and purpose of tax treaties.

Australia is a party to the Vienna Convention, and in an important 1990 case, the highest court used it to interpret a tax treaty in accordance with the OECD Commentaries.[723] In this case, the court's approach to the Vienna Convention was more in the spirit of international law, which regards the interpretive provisions of the Convention as a codification of a fairly diffuse tradition, rather than as detailed provisions of a tax statute. Nonetheless, especially for treaty provisions which do not follow OECD standards, Australian courts tend to take a literal approach to the treaty text in a growing body of case law.

The *United Kingdom* is also a party to the Vienna Convention. Its courts have referred to OECD Commentaries for interpretive assistance and approached treaty interpretation in a different manner from statutory interpretation, with more focus on purpose and intent.[724] This approach was reinforced in the *Ben Nevis* case in the Court of Appeal in 2013.[725] The Court confirmed its view that the Vienna Convention incorporates rules of customary international law; it also found that a memorandum of understanding between tax authorities was an admissible aid to interpretation falling within Article 31(2) or (3) of the Convention. In 2020 the Supreme Court accepted the potential "persuasive force" of subsequent Commentaries.[726]

Since 1990, when the *French* Administrative Supreme Court reversed its prior policy of referring to the Ministry of Foreign Affairs for the interpretation to be given to ambiguous treaty wording, French tax judges have been fully competent in the field of treaty interpretation. Courts rarely explicitly specify the construction methods and rules they apply, but there is an increasing amount of academic writing on the subject. For a long time, the practice of the courts seemed to be based mainly on a narrow principle of literal construction—and only when strictly necessary, on examining the context in its narrowest sense, with no reference to the interpretation given in the other contracting state, with very few references to the OECD Commentary (which was not seen as binding), and with wide recourse to the meaning of corresponding terms in domestic tax law. Today the OECD Commentaries are referred to more often, especially where they were published before the treaty was signed, and the courts now seem more inclined to make reference to the object and purpose of tax treaties. Although France is not a party to the Vienna Convention, its principles are taken into account in practice, since they are considered to be a codification of preexisting customary rules or sometimes even as principles of international public law.

In *Germany*, which is a signatory to the Vienna Convention, the courts tend to follow an "autonomous" interpretation, focusing on the wording of the treaty and the

723. *Thiel* (1990) 171 CLR 338.
724. For a classic statement, *see R v. IRC ex parte Commerzbank* (1993) 68 TC 252 (HC) at 297-298. More recently, *see Bayfine UK v. RCC*, [2011] EWCA Civ 304 at para. 17, where the Court of Appeal noted the importance of a tax treaty's purpose for interpretation.
725. *Ben Nevis (Holdings) Ltd v. HMRC*, [2013] EWCA Civ 578, particularly at para. 16.
726. *Fowler v. RCC*, [2020] UKSC 22 at para. 18.

treaty context. The courts have stressed the need for both parties to come to a uniform interpretation, which is facilitated by an "objective" approach. The Vienna Convention has had some impact on German interpretive practice, moving it in this "objective" direction.

There is still a tendency in German tax jurisprudence to interpret the language of treaties in line with similar concepts under domestic law, relying on the equivalent to Article 3(2) of the OECD Model Convention. The Federal Tax Court does not regard OECD materials as having authoritative status; instead, it cites the OECD Commentaries and the OECD Transfer Pricing Guidelines as nonbinding statements issued by a group of tax authorities. Moreover, the Court explicitly rejects any "ambulatory" interpretation of tax treaties to reflect changes to the OECD Model's Commentaries after the conclusion of a treaty.[727] Finally, the outcomes of consultations between competent authorities are not binding on individual taxpayers or the courts.[728] However, in a circular published in 2023, the MOF declared ambulatory treaty interpretation to be the proper approach to treaty interpretation in Germany;[729] the circular met fierce resistance from tax scholars and will probably not survive judicial scrutiny.

Under the *Chinese* Constitution, the courts have no power to interpret domestic law or tax treaties. In practice, however, in order to adjudicate tax disputes, Chinese courts must attempt to interpret disputed treaty provisions. In both the *PanAmSAT* and *Dongwa* cases,[730] the courts found the tax authority's interpretation to be correct. Although the small number of court decisions to date makes it difficult to determine whether Chinese courts have a particular approach to treaty interpretation, the STA has published several circulars on treaty interpretation which have the status of administrative rules.[731] The STA's interpretation of treaty provisions is, in general, consistent with the positions taken in the OECD Commentaries, but deviates in some areas to protect source taxation and the STA's substance-over-form approach. For example, in the *PanAmSat* case, the American corporate taxpayer provided services to transmit television programming of a Chinese company through its satellites; it did not carry on business through a PE in China and characterized the payments received from the Chinese client as service fees. The Chinese courts found, however, that the service fees were rental payments for the use of the "effective," although not "actual," use of the transponder in the satellite and that such rental payments were "royalties" for purposes

727. Federal Tax Court (*Bundesfinanzhof*) July 11, 2018, I R 44/16.
728. Federal Tax Court (*Bundesfinanzhof*) June 10, 2015, I R 79/13; May 30, 2018, I R 62/16.
729. Federal Ministry of Finance (*Bundesfinanzministerium*), Circular of 19.4.2023—IV B 2—S 1301/22/10002.
730. *See* Jinyan Li, *International Taxation in China: A Contextualized Analysis*, *supra* note 714, at 112-131 for a brief discussion of these cases.
731. The most influential of these circulars is STA, Guo Shuifa [2010] No. 75, an article-by-article commentary on the China-Singapore treaty which has been applied to the interpretation of other treaties. *See also* the most recent STA, Gong Gao [2018] No. 11, with respect to treaty provisions for partnerships (the China-France treaty may be the only treaty which deals with partnerships), PEs, international transportation, and entertainers; and STA, Gong Gao [2018] No. 9, on beneficial ownership.

of the China-U.S. tax treaty. The courts did not follow the OECD Commentary, which regards such service fees as "business profits."

Although *India* has not signed the Vienna Convention, the courts, including the Supreme Court, have referred to the Vienna Convention as customary international law in a number of cases.[732] The courts have also applied some of the principles in the Vienna Convention without specifically referring to them.[733] In the *Azadi Bachao* case, the Supreme Court dealt extensively with the principles of treaty interpretation and suggested that, since tax treaties are drafted in broad general language, they should be interpreted in accordance with the ordinary meaning of the text—the meaning of a diplomat rather than a lawyer.[734]

4.3 Anti-treaty Shopping Policy

Until recently, the countries analyzed here, with the exception of the United States, did not appear to be concerned about treaty shopping or treaty abuse more generally; instead, tax treaties seemed to have been viewed as tools to attract foreign investment and eliminate double taxation. This attitude changed gradually in the early 2000s, as can be seen in the changes in the Commentary on Article 1 of the OECD Model Treaty from 2003 on, and countries began to focus increasingly on double nontaxation. BEPS Action 6 recommended the addition of a preamble to the OECD Model Treaty explicitly indicating that tax treaties were not intended to facilitate treaty shopping, as well as a treaty general anti-abuse rule (the PPT) or limitation-on-benefits provision. These recommendations were agreed to be minimum standards which all countries participating in the BEPS Project and the Inclusive Framework must implement. They were also incorporated in the 2017 updates of the OECD and UN Model Treaties. Moreover, they were included in the MLI and, since all the countries considered here (other than the United States) have signed the MLI, most of their tax treaties have been modified to incorporate the BEPS anti-treaty shopping minimum standards.

For the last twenty years, *United States* treaty policy has been to insist on a limitation-on-benefits, or anti-treaty shopping, article in its treaties and all treaties approved by the Senate since 1981 have contained such an article. While the details of the articles differ, they have in common a focus on the lack of economic connection between the corporation claiming treaty benefits and the foreign jurisdiction. While the provisions originated in connection with jurisdictions with relatively low effective tax burdens, they are now present even in treaties involving high-tax jurisdictions. Thus, the treaty with Germany, a traditionally high-tax country, contains a complex limitation-on-benefits article.[735] Companies which are otherwise resident for treaty

732. *See*, for example *Ram Jethmalani v. Union of India*, Civil writ petition No. 176 of 2009 (SC) July 4, 2011; and, more recently, *Assessing Officer (International Taxation) v. Nestle SA*, Civil Appeal No. 1420 of 2023, October 19, 2023 (SC).
733. *See*, for example, *CIT v. Vishakhapatnam Port Trust* (Andhra Pradesh HC) June 17, 1983, 144 ITR 146.
734. *Union of India v. Azadi Bachao Andolan*, October 7, 2003, Civil Appeal No. 8161-81634 of 2003 (SC).
735. United States-Germany tax treaty, Art. 28.

purposes are entitled to treaty benefits only where they meet certain share-ownership and base-erosion tests, are engaged in the active conduct of a trade or business, are publicly traded, or can obtain the agreement of the competent authorities to permit treaty benefits.

Other countries have seemed less concerned with insisting in all cases on detailed treaty-shopping rules. The reasons for this difference in attitude are varied. In the case of *Canada*, until recently treaty shopping was not viewed as a serious problem since Canada had a fairly uniform policy concerning the level to which it would agree to reduce its source-based taxation. As a result, there was typically no advantage for a third-country resident to enter Canada from a particular jurisdiction. Only in the case of residents from countries which have no treaty at all with Canada could treaty shopping be a problem and, in that case, Canada's extensive treaty network made these situations fairly uncommon.

Although Canada has agreed to include the general anti-abuse rule (the so-called PPT) in its treaties through the MLI, it has indicated that, on a long-term basis, it may accept a limitation-on-benefits provision instead. This difference in approach was reflected in the Third Protocol to the United States-Canada treaty. There, the anti-treaty shopping article applied only where the United States was applying the treaty to investments from Canada; Canada did not feel it needed an anti-treaty shopping provision to deal with third-country investment into Canada from the United States. However, the protocol explicitly stated that either state could deny benefits under the treaty where the granting of such benefits would result in an "abuse" of the treaty. This clarified that Canada could apply its domestic anti-abuse provisions in appropriate cases of inward investment from the United States, which was apparently all the protection Canada thought it needed.

Several treaties already include a limited anti-avoidance rule dealing with treaty shopping with respect to dividends, interest, and royalties. These provisions are similar to the anti-abuse rule included in many UK treaties. Further, several (thirty-five) recent treaties contain a provision denying treaty benefits to a resident entity that is beneficially owned or controlled by the residents of a third country where the tax on the entity is substantially lower than it would have been if the entity were beneficially owned or controlled by residents of the same country in which the entity is resident. A similar provision is included in the Commentary on Article 1 of the OECD Model Convention as an alternative provision which countries may choose to include in their treaties.

Canada's attitude to treaty shopping seems to have changed in the last two decades. In the 2007 Fifth Protocol to the United States-Canada treaty, the limitation-on-benefits article became applicable bilaterally. The CRA has aggressively (although unsuccessfully) attacked treaty-shopping arrangements on the basis of the beneficial-ownership requirement and domestic anti-avoidance rules.[736] In 2013, the government issued a consultation paper proposing various options to deal with treaty shopping and

736. *The Queen v. MIL (Investments) SA*, [2007] 4 CTC 235 (FCA); *Prévost Car Inc. v. The Queen*, 2008 TCC 231, aff'd 2009 FCA 57; *Velcro Canada Inc. v. The Queen*, 2012 TCC 57; *Alta Energy Luxembourg S.A.R.L. v. The Queen*, 2021 SCC 49; and *Husky Energy v. The King*, 2023 TCC 167.

subsequently proposed detailed anti-treaty shopping rules which would have overridden tax treaties. These proposed legislative rules were subject to criticism; the government withdrew them and indicated that it would rely instead on the changes proposed by BEPS Action 6 (the statement in the new preamble to the OECD Model to the effect that tax treaties are not intended to facilitate treaty shopping, and the PPT). Since the PPT is similar to the Canadian GAAR, it is questionable whether it will be more effective than the GAAR in preventing treaty shopping.

Until 2001, *Australia* was in a similar position to Canada. Its treaties reflected a very strict adherence to withholding rates of 15%, 10%, and 10% for dividends, interest, and royalties, respectively, and so the major scope for treaty shopping related to the use of treaties by residents of nontreaty countries. Since the 2001 Protocol to the Australia-United States treaty, Australia has reduced the royalty withholding rate to 5%, removed equipment leasing from the royalty article, removed withholding tax on interest on bank loans, and reduced withholding tax on dividends, in some cases to zero. Hence, post-2000 treaties provide significant opportunities for treaty shopping. Correspondingly, protocols and treaties since 2000 have included more detailed provisions on treaty shopping and, in particular, a purpose test applying to the dividends, interest, and royalties articles (or to treaties generally), which are now becoming much more common under the MLI. Australia is prepared to use its GAAR against treaty shopping since this rule is not overridden by tax treaties, but to date there have been no court cases in which the GAAR has been applied to treaty shopping.[737] It is also adopting the PPT test more generally in domestic law in relation to international tax rules apart from treaty issues such as in its DPT.

The Netherlands, until recently, did not pursue an anti-treaty shopping policy and has historically been a base for treaty-shopping activities. Under pressure from the United States and some of its other treaty partners, as well as OECD and EU policies on harmful tax competition, it has on occasion agreed to a limitation-on-benefits article and other treaty provisions against abuse of its tax treaties. Further, by statute, treaty benefits can no longer be claimed with respect to payments received from abroad which merely pass through a Dutch corporation. However, the Dutch Supreme Court has been very reluctant to apply the Dutch general abuse of law doctrine (*fraus legis*) to tax treaties unless both states have expressly agreed that this doctrine is applicable in the context of the tax treaty. Pursuant to the OECD's BEPS Project, The Netherlands has opted to apply the PPT to counter tax treaty abuse by denying tax treaty benefits where one of the main purposes of a transaction is to obtain these benefits. The positions taken by The Netherlands on both the mandatory and non-mandatory elements of the MLI are the official tax treaty policy of The Netherlands. As a result, The Netherlands has adopted the BEPS Action 6 Final Report, which contains various measures to combat tax treaty abuse.

737. *See* taxation ruling TD 2010/20, which arose out of a notorious case where the tax administration sought to prevent the profit on a sale by a private equity firm of shares in a company owning a chain of department stores from being repatriated from Australia but was too late in taking action, so that the issue whether the anti-avoidance rule was applicable was never tested.

Swedish treaty policy has been guided substantially by the OECD Model Convention. In general, Swedish treaties have not contained anti-treaty shopping articles unless such articles were insisted on by the treaty partner. Even after the changes to the OECD Commentary in 1992 and 1994, recognizing the problem of treaty shopping and the possibility of requiring shareholders to be residents of the contracting states, Sweden's policy has remained unchanged. With respect to the relationship between the Swedish CFC rules and treaties, prior to 1992, the white list of countries for purposes of the CFC rules included all treaty countries. However, Sweden has altered its practice and, occasionally, treaty countries are now excluded from the CFC white list. Sweden has very few limitation-on-benefits provisions in its treaties (even after the entry into force of the MLI), but several treaties now include provisions inspired by the PPT, with different wording.

Until recently, *Japan* had taken no serious measures to deal with treaty shopping. However, Japan has opted to apply the PPT and has included the PPT in recent tax treaties. In addition, Japan is also trying to include or add a limitation-on-benefits article to its tax treaties; it has recently included such an article in its tax treaties with a few developed countries and, to a more limited extent, with some developing countries.

French tax treaties rarely contain anti-treaty shopping clauses other than those in the OECD Model Convention, despite the fact that France has an extensive treaty network (about 130 treaties in 2023, including treaties with Eastern European, African, and South American countries) which third-country residents would perhaps like to utilize. Besides the limitation-on-benefits clause in the 1994 French-United States convention, some specific exclusions are found in treaties with countries whose tax law could provide some incentive for tax avoidance (e.g., Switzerland). Moreover, French courts apply the domestic anti-abuse-of-law provisions in the tax treaty context[738] and France is inserting the PPT anti-abuse rule of the MLI in its treaties.

In *Germany*, the "Basis for negotiation" drafted in 2013 by the MOF accepted the necessity of fighting treaty shopping. Germany signed the MLI in 2017 and chose the PPT over the option to introduce extensive limitation-on-benefits clauses. In current revisions of existing treaties, Germany insists on the insertion of the PPT, although this depends on the scope of the treaty in general.

Under its domestic law, Germany applies an exception from withholding tax reductions for intermediate companies to the extent that their shareholders would not be entitled to the same withholding tax reductions and the source of income (e.g., shares, IP) has no "significant connection" with real economic activity of the intermediate company unless it is shown that none of the main purposes of the intermediate company is to obtain a tax advantage. Publicly traded companies are excluded.[739]

Historically, the *United Kingdom* has not included broad anti-treaty shopping articles in its tax treaties (other than with the United States). However, this approach

738. The traditional exclusive purpose test in LPF, s. L 64 and the new (2019 Finance Act) PPT in LPF, s. L 64 A.

739. Germany, ITA, s. 50d para. 3; for the details and prevailing EU law, *see* above Subpart C, section 1.

has changed and the UK now adopts an article based on the PPT, which is consistent with its approach for the MLI.

Over the past decade, the *Chinese* STA has been aggressive in attacking treaty shopping, mainly by interpreting the "beneficial owner" requirement so as to look through holding entities. However, the STA's position seems recently to have become more nuanced, providing, for example, safe harbors and a more "pragmatic" approach to multitier holdings.[740] In addition, China's recent treaties contain anti-abuse provisions. For example, the China-France treaty (renegotiated in 2013) contains a PPT and an anti-abuse rule in the dividends, interest, royalties, and other income articles. Post-2014 treaties tend to have similar provisions. Further, the China-France treaty also contains an anti-abuse rule in Article 13 (capital gains) allowing China or France to tax gains from indirect transfers of immovable property. Anti-abuse rules dealing with PEs have been included in several recent treaties. The MLI entered into force for China on September 1, 2022. China has implemented the BEPS minimum standards through the preamble and the PPT.

In *India*, in the *Azadi Bachao* case,[741] the Supreme Court approved treaty-shopping arrangements by taxpayers, equating them with deficit financing. Since then, the government has renegotiated many of the problematic tax treaties and insisted on the incorporation of some type of limitation-on-benefits clause. India has opted for the simplified limitation-on-benefits clause in the MLI. However, since most of India's treaty partners have opted for the PPT, that test is likely to be incorporated into the treaties covered by the MLI.

4.4 Nondiscrimination

While most of the countries considered here usually have nondiscrimination articles in their treaties, there are some important exceptions and restrictions. Most striking is the case of *Australia*, which until 2008 reserved its position on the nondiscrimination article in the OECD Model. Since 2003, Australia has included a nondiscrimination article in nearly all its treaties but adds exceptions to protect specific features of Australian tax law, such as the imputation system, research and development deductions, limitations on rollover relief designed to prevent assets being transferred tax-free outside Australia's jurisdictional net, and rules directed at tax avoidance or evasion (among which are thin capitalization, CFC, and grantor trust regimes, although the list has been reduced over time). The first case under the article came before the courts recently and Australia's highest court held that a special backpacker income tax, which applies to certain foreign nationals present in Australia under a special visa category, breached the nationality nondiscrimination treaty rule because the tax applied whether the backpacker was resident or nonresident. The reaction was swift: in the following treaties signed by Australia, the backpacker tax was excluded from the nondiscrimination article, and more recently, Australia has introduced legislation to override a

740. China, Gong Gao [2018] No. 9.
741. *See infra* note 734.

number of Australia's treaties and reduce the coverage of the article to taxes covered by the treaty even where the article itself was expressed to apply (as in the OECD Model) to all taxes.[742]

Canada's approach to nondiscrimination articles also contrasts with that of the other countries. While the scope of nondiscrimination clauses in Canadian treaties varies slightly, they typically do not grant to nonresidents the usual protections against nondiscrimination found in the OECD Model Treaty. Thus, Canadian treaties do not contain an article guaranteeing national treatment of domestic corporations owned by nonresident shareholders; instead, such investments are entitled only to a type of "most-favored-nation" treatment, according to which they will not be treated less favorably than comparable investments held by residents of other countries with which Canada has treaties. In addition, the provision ensuring nonresident enterprises the right to deduct expenses on the same terms as residents is usually not included and, as a result, Canada takes the position that it is entitled to apply its thin capitalization rules to interest paid by Canadian corporations to nonresidents. As is the case in Australia, in Canada, the desire to implement certain domestic tax policies which might be viewed as contravening traditional concepts of nondiscrimination has led to a much more limited acceptance of treaty limitations on domestic action. Canada has reserved its position on the nondiscrimination article in the OECD Model Convention.

In contrast, *China* (except for the provision dealing with stateless persons) and *Sweden* have followed the nondiscrimination article in the OECD Model in their tax treaties. Swedish courts have given the article a fairly broad interpretation. Thus, a domestic provision allowing the deduction of an intragroup contribution only where the members of the group were all domestic corporations was found to be discriminatory when applied to two Swedish subsidiaries owned by a parent company resident in a treaty country. Similarly, where a foreign company with Swedish branch operations was merged into another foreign company, losses accruing in the branch operations were held to carry over to the merged company in the same way they would have if the merger had been between two Swedish companies.

French courts have liberally applied treaty nondiscrimination clauses, under which they have, for instance, granted French PEs of treaty-country corporations the exemption from withholding tax on French-source dividends and the intercorporate dividends exemption. In 2003, the *Conseil d'État* ruled that a limitation on the deductibility of interest paid to a parent company in the other contracting state was discriminatory because interest paid to a French parent would have been deductible.[743]

French treaty practice generally follows the OECD pattern, but with respect to the nondiscrimination article, France has entered two reservations which it tries to incorporate in its bilateral tax conventions.[744] First, France is willing to apply the general nondiscrimination provision contained in Article 24(1) of the OECD Model

742. *Addy* [2021] HCA 34; for example, Australia-Iceland tax treaty (2022) Art. 22(5); Treasury Laws Amendment (Foreign Investment) Bill 2024, the particular concern being state and federal tax laws imposing various kinds of non-income taxes on residential property owned by foreign nationals.

743. *Conseil d'Etat*, December 30, 2003, No. 233894 (*SA Andritz*).

744. OECD Model Tax Convention, Commentary on Art. 24, Nos. 88 and 91.

Treaty solely to individuals, given that French case law equates the nationality of corporations with their residence.[745] The second reservation, which relates to a limitation on the deduction of interest paid by a French company to a related company, should have been deleted since it has become irrelevant under the revised thin capitalization rules.

The other jurisdictions generally follow the pattern in the OECD Model Convention, with some differences in detail. In *The Netherlands*, there has been a rapid increase in the number of cases where taxpayers have invoked the nondiscrimination articles of a tax treaty (along with the nondiscrimination provisions in the EC Treaty), and in many important cases the courts have decided in favor of the taxpayer. In the *United Kingdom*, the nondiscrimination article reached the House of Lords in the *Boake Allen* case in 2007.[746] While adopting a broad approach to the necessary comparator, the House of Lords interpreted the article in a fashion not wholly consistent with the 2008 OECD amendments to the Commentary. In the later *FCE Bank* case, in determining the comparator, the Court of Appeal took account of the relationship between a parent and subsidiary, although in doing so it did not refer to the Commentary.[747]

Germany follows the OECD pattern. In recent years, several judgments by the Federal Tax Court have increased the relevance of the nondiscrimination article for tax practice. Earlier versions of the German provisions on thin capitalization have been regarded as nonapplicable in the light of a treaty's nondiscrimination clause.[748] In a hugely debated judgment, the Federal Tax Court allowed the cross-border application of German rules on "fiscal unity" with respect to the trade tax, which might have resulted in a major loss of revenue, but those rules have not been applied by the German tax authorities beyond the case at hand.[749] In a widely discussed judgment, the Federal Fiscal Court held that a non-EU citizen resident in another EU country cannot rely on the benefits awarded to nonresident EU citizens under the fundamental freedoms.[750]

Most *Indian* tax treaties follow the nondiscrimination article in the OECD Model Treaty. There have been many cases involving this article, and taxpayers have often benefited where the comparable treatment of domestic companies was more beneficial.[751]

4.5 "Model" Tax Treaties

A number of countries have published, formally or informally, "model" tax treaties which set forth the basic positions that their treaty negotiators take in the opening round of treaty discussions.

745. *Conseil d'Etat*, July 5, 2010, No. 309693, *Pinacothèque d'Athènes*.
746. *Boake Allen Ltd v. IRC*, [2007] UKHL 25 (HL).
747. *RCC v. FCE Bank Plc*, [2012] EWCA Civ 1290.
748. Federal Tax Court (*Bundesfinanzhof*), January 16, 2014, I R 30/12.
749. Federal Tax Court (*Bundesfinanzhof*), February 9, 2011, I R 54, 55/10.
750. Federal Tax Court (*Bundesfinanzhof*), September 3, 2020, I R 80/16.
751. *CIT v. Herbalife International India*, May 13, 2016, ITA 7/2007 (Delhi High Court).

The *United States* Model Convention, first published in draft form in 1977, was modified in 1981, 1996, 2006, and 2016. The 2016 Model Convention provides for a 15% withholding rate for portfolio dividends and a 5% rate for dividends paid to 10% or greater stockholders. The Model Convention also includes a provision for determining the residence of fiscally transparent entities and denies treaty benefits to partnerships and other pass-through entities unless their partners or members are subject to tax as residents. Thus, for treaty benefits to apply, income must be taxable either to the entity or to the entity's owners in the treaty country. The 2016 Model introduced mandatory binding arbitration and also expanded the various anti-abuse provisions by: (1) denying treaty benefits for deductible payments to related parties of mobile income bearing little tax due to a preferential regime; (2) inclusion of anti-inversion rules; and (3) adding a triangular PE rule (already seen in some U.S. treaties over the past twenty years). The U.S. Model is intended to apply only to treaties with developed countries. In treaties with developing countries, in the past, the U.S. has been willing to accept substantially more source-based taxation than is contemplated in its Model Treaty.

Canada does not have a public model treaty and Canada's treaty policy differs from the OECD Model in several respects. For example, Canada insists on the right to impose a 10% withholding tax on certain royalties, a branch tax, and a tax on other income arising in Canada. In addition, as noted above, Canada does not follow the nondiscrimination article in the OECD Model. In the 2007 Protocol to the treaty with the United States, Canada agreed to zero withholding on interest paid by a Canadian resident to a related U.S. resident. This position has not been extended to treaties with other countries.

Sweden has a model treaty which is accessible to the public, although it has not been officially published; nevertheless, some of its negotiating positions are well known. For example, it favors the lowest withholding taxes possible on dividends, interest, and royalties with respect to direct investment. Because a large number of Swedes retire to countries with warmer climates, Sweden also attempts to establish the principle of source-based taxation of pension income with a credit in the residence country for the source tax. The PE provision generally follows the pre-2017 OECD Model Convention.

China and *Japan* have not published model treaties. In general, Japan's treaties follow the OECD Model. China's earlier treaties usually followed the UN Model Convention. More recent Chinese treaties tend to be closer to the OECD Model, reflecting China's position as a capital exporter.

In 1987, *The Netherlands* published a "standard" treaty which, in general, followed the OECD Model. This standard treaty is accompanied by a detailed explanation, which has been supplemented and updated a few times; however, no further updates of the standard treaty will be published, since no single text is used in negotiating tax treaties. The 2011 Memorandum on International Tax Treaty Policy states that The Netherlands generally follows the OECD Model (and not the 1987 standard treaty) when negotiating tax treaties with other countries. The 2020 Memorandum on Tax Treaty Policy contains various positions adopted by The Netherlands with regard to the MLI, including the hybrid entity provision (Article 3 MLI), the preamble (Article 6 of the MLI), the PPT (Article 7(1) of the MLI), the MAP tie-breaker rule (Article 4(1) of the MLI), effective dispute resolution (Articles 16-17 of the MLI), the PE-related measures (Articles 12-15 of the MLI),[752] and the switch-over clause option provided in Article 5(2) of the MLI.

Since dividends on direct investments are exempt from Dutch tax and, consequently, no credit is available for foreign withholding tax in such cases, The Netherlands tries to reduce dividend withholding tax to zero. Under Dutch treaty policy, there is also no source taxation on interest payments.[753] As noted above, there is an exception for withholding taxes under the Withholding Tax Act (WTA) 2021, although the scope is rather limited in terms of its tax treaty implications. Under Dutch tax treaty policy, this levy (rate 25.8%) has full effect under the relevant tax treaties.[754]

Germany released a model treaty in 2013 under the rather unambitious title of a "Basis for negotiation."[755] The treaty is largely aligned with the OECD Model Treaty and includes a number of elements which are meant to address the risk of "double non-taxation." An extended preamble is meant to enlarge the purpose of the treaty to include the avoidance of "non-taxation"; a number of provisions (e.g., subject-to-tax clauses) are meant to ensure that "white income" will not be affected by the wide-reaching application of the exemption method. Withholding taxes on interest and royalties are eliminated completely, while withholding tax on portfolio dividends is set at 15%. However, this "Basis for negotiation" is currently awaiting a new edition as it has not yet incorporated the outcomes of the BEPS Project, including the MLI, update of the 2017 OECD Model, and other recent developments.

The *United Kingdom* has no published model treaty and generally follows the OECD Model Convention. Likewise, *France* has not published an official model and its treaties generally follow the OECD pattern. Modern French treaty practice is, however, characterized by the following specific features: a wide definition of dividends encompassing all types of deemed distributions under French law; a 10% minimum shareholding as a prerequisite for the reduced rate of withholding tax on intercorporate dividends; exemption of interest from withholding tax; the right of source countries to tax income and gains from shares in real property companies and from the sale of large shareholdings in domestic corporations; a definition of treaty-country residents including French partnerships; provisions expressly enabling France to use its domestic anti-avoidance provisions in the treaty context; certain exceptions to the nondiscrimination article (*see* section 4.4 above); a special type of tax credit (always equal to the

752. The Netherlands initially opted for Art. 12 of the MLI/Art. 5(5) and (6) of the OECD Model (2017) to prevent commissionaire and similar strategies from being used as a means to avoid activities being classified as a (dependent) agency PE. Following the amendment tabled by two Members of Parliament, The Netherlands made a temporary reservation regarding the provisions of Art. 12 of the MLI; this will be withdrawn in the event of effective dispute-resolution arrangements and sufficient clarity on attributing profits to an agency PE. Effective dispute-resolution arrangements are seen (primarily) as meaning mandatory binding arbitration (Part VI of the MLI and Art. 25(5) of the OECD Model (2017)).

753. The 2020 Memorandum on Tax Treaty Policy, para. 4.5.

754. The 2020 Memorandum on Tax Treaty Policy, para. 5.3.

755. Germany, *Basis for negotiation for agreements for the avoidance of double taxation and the prevention of fiscal evasion with respect to taxes on income and on capital* (2013).

corresponding French tax) in its post-1989 treaties, replacing the exemption-with-progression provision in its old treaties; and special clauses (although less and less the case) favoring developing countries.[756]

In order to preserve flexibility in its treaty policy and negotiations, *Australia* made a decision not to publish the Australian model treaty in 2003, and this remains its position. On substantive matters, until recently, Australia gave greater emphasis to source taxation than does the OECD Model Convention because it was a substantial net capital importer and possesses considerable natural resources. That policy direction changed in the period 1999-2006, in recognition of the substantial amount of outbound investment by Australian multinationals, and moved closer to the OECD position, although Australia continues to closely guard its taxing rights over natural resources. Thus, the 10% minimum tax rate on royalties has been reduced to 5% and source taxation of capital gains has been brought more closely into line with the OECD Model. As well, the changes to the articles with respect to interest and dividends outlined above may be considered to go further than the OECD Model. However, Australia continues to adopt an expansive definition of a PE and real property in order to protect its taxing rights over natural resources.

Despite the reintroduction in 1990 of an exemption system for most direct investment overseas by Australian companies, which was turned into a full participation exemption in 2004, Australia continues to rely exclusively on a credit provision in its tax treaties, on the theory that there is no double taxation to relieve in cases where a domestic exemption provision applies.

India has an internal model treaty which it follows in negotiating tax treaties and exchanges with other countries. Although this model has not been made public, recent Indian tax treaties indicate that the Indian model is a combination of the OECD and UN Model Conventions, with some peculiarities of its own.

4.6 Tax Sparing by Treaty

Tax sparing, or the crediting of taxes not actually paid, has been an important issue in treaty relations between developed and developing countries. Where a developed country uses the FTC method to relieve double taxation, any tax reductions or exemptions enacted by developing countries usually benefit the treasury of the developed country rather than the investor. The issue comes up with respect to both net-basis taxes on business profits and withholding taxes on investment income.

The *United States* has historically rejected tax sparing as a matter of treaty policy, viewing tax treaties as an inappropriate vehicle to administer what is, in effect, a program of assistance for foreign investment. Other countries, however, have included tax-sparing credits in their treaties with developing countries, for both foregone business taxes and reduced withholding taxes.

756. Since the abolition of the imputation credit in 2005, the only effect of such clauses has been to grant nonresident individual shareholders a residual credit (50% of the dividend capped at EUR 115 or EUR 230 for married persons or civil partners).

For example, *The Netherlands* uses an exemption method for foreign business profits but uses a credit method for payments of dividends, interest, and royalties. It has granted tax-sparing credits with respect to such payments in ten treaties. In more recent treaties, the credits are typically limited to payments of dividends, interest, and royalties made within ten or fifteen years from the entry into effect of the treaty. Since 2011, Dutch tax treaty policy is not to include tax-sparing provisions in any new or renegotiated tax treaties.[757]

Canada does not generally give tax-sparing credits for investment income but does accept such credits for business income. Canada gives credits for spared taxes on business income for a limited period, usually ten years. A few older treaties also provide for tax sparing in respect of certain dividends, interest, and royalties. Where a Canadian corporation receives dividends out of the exempt surplus of a foreign corporation, the dividends are not taxable in Canada and, as a result, tax-sparing credits are irrelevant. Therefore, the only dividends which give rise to tax-sparing credits are dividends which are taxable in Canada (i.e., dividends received out of the hybrid and taxable surplus of foreign affiliates and dividends received from foreign corporations which are not foreign affiliates).

Japan gives tax-sparing credits for both business income and withholding taxes, as do *Sweden* and *Germany*, although in 2003 the Japanese government announced its policy to reduce tax-sparing credits and, under its recent treaties with developing countries, *Germany* has decided to set time limits for these benefits.

The *United Kingdom* has granted tax-sparing credits in a limited number of treaties, typically those with former colonies. The use of such credits has been heavily criticized, primarily on the ground that it is inconsistent with the neutrality of treatment between domestic and foreign investment which underlies the granting of the basic FTC. Recent treaties have not included tax sparing, which may be a reflection of the move to the exemption system of foreign tax relief.

Australia was happy to grant tax sparing for both tax holidays and withholding tax reliefs in developing countries and included such provisions in many of its treaties, especially those with Asian countries. A change of policy was announced in 1997, in line with an OECD review of the issue,[758] to the effect that in future Australia would not grant tax-sparing relief by treaty and existing provisions would not be extended. Since 2004, Australia has used a comprehensive participation exemption in domestic tax law for dividends from foreign subsidiaries, and so the change in policy has had little impact, except in relation to withholding taxes.

In *France*, traditional tax treaty policy used tax-sparing credits and a wide definition of the concept of PE as a way of supporting the tax revenues of developing countries. Many treaties with Asian, South American, and African countries provide for tax-sparing credits for passive income (dividends, interest, royalties). A special technique (*la décote africaine*) grants French investors tax credits which are inversely proportional to local withholding taxes on dividends distributed by corporations based in French-speaking Africa or deemed to have been distributed from the profits of PEs

757. Netherlands, 2011 Memorandum on International Tax Treaty Policy, p. 63.
758. OECD, *Tax Sparing: A Reconsideration* (Paris: OECD, 1997).

(extraterritorial taxation) in those countries. These special clauses have become rare in recent treaties and have been removed from some conventions. However, in a recent case, the French Conseil d'Etat recognized that the information on a declaration form or leaflet (listing Togo as one of the countries eligible for the *décote africaine*) may, in certain circumstances, constitute a formal position enforceable against the authorities on the basis of these provisions.[759] Tax-sparing mechanisms are of less interest today because the rate of withholding taxes in developing countries has often greatly increased and many statutory incentives to local investment have been eliminated, thus eliminating the need for tax-sparing credits.

China is in an interesting position with respect to tax sparing. As an emerging economy, China received tax sparing in a number of its earlier treaties with developed countries; however, these tax-sparing provisions are being eliminated and are not included in new treaties. There is a tax-sparing clause in some of China's treaties with developing countries (e.g., Bulgaria, Cyprus, Ethiopia, India, Jamaica, Malaysia, Pakistan, Portugal, Sri Lanka, Syria, Thailand, Tunisia and Vietnam).

Until the 1990s, almost all the treaties concluded by *India* contained a provision for a tax-sparing credit. India's insistence on a tax-sparing provision and the U.S. refusal to agree to tax sparing explains why the two countries were unable to conclude a treaty for many years. Most of the tax-sparing provisions in India's treaties with developed countries were unilateral; however, some of the treaties (e.g., those with Bangladesh and China) are reciprocal. Similarly, under the treaty with Oman, India is obliged to grant a credit in respect of the tax that would have been payable but for the tax incentives granted for promoting the economic development of Oman. An Indian taxpayer operating a fertilizer plant in Oman under a joint venture received dividends that were not taxed in Oman but claimed a credit under the sparing clause. India's Supreme Court held that the tax payable in Oman for the purpose of tax credit would include tax incentives granted for promoting the economic development of Oman.[760] India's recent tax treaties do not generally contain a tax-sparing provision.

5 PATENT BOXES

Before the BEPS Project began in 2012-2013, several European countries had adopted special preferential tax regimes for income derived from the licensing and sale of patented products which were developed from research and development activities in the country. These so-called patent-box regimes were obviously intended to attract foreign investment in research and development (R&D) and quickly initiated a race to the bottom.

The 2015 BEPS Action 5 Report, *Countering Harmful Tax Practices More Effectively Taking into Account Transparency and Substance*, recommended that all preferential regimes, including intellectual property regimes or patent boxes, should be viewed as harmful tax practices unless they have a substantial-activity requirement.

759. CE 9e-10e ch. 20-6-2023 n° 462501.
760. *P.CIT v. Krishak Bharti Cooperative Ltd.* (Civil Appeal No. 836 of 2018), September 15, 2023 (SC).

This so-called nexus approach is intended to ensure that taxpayers benefiting from a preferential regime actually engage in the R&D activities and actually incur the R&D expenditures. It limits tax benefits for intellectual property income to income derived from R&D activities conducted by the taxpayer, and only to the extent that the taxpayer incurs qualifying expenses; thus, the nexus approach uses expenditures as a proxy for substantial activity. In addition, the tax benefit must be limited to the proportion of the income from an intellectual property asset that the qualifying expenses with respect to the asset are of the total expenses with respect to the asset. Qualifying expenses are limited to expenses which are directly connected to an intellectual property asset.

Of the eleven countries analyzed in this book, only three—France, The Netherlands, and the United Kingdom—have adopted patent-box regimes. The original patent-box regimes of all three counties were found by the BEPS Action 5 Report not to comply with the nexus requirement. As discussed below, all three countries have since revised their regimes to comply with the nexus approach.

Four of the other eight countries—Canada, Germany, Sweden, and the United States—do not have patent-box regimes and have not shown much, if any, interest in adopting such regimes. The U.S. FDII regime,[761] which provides a tax-rate reduction for foreign source income earned by U.S. corporations but does not require any substantial activities, has sometimes been criticized as a patent-box regime. Australia announced a patent-box regime under the former government but the proposal has been abandoned. China and India have preferential regimes for intellectual property, but those regimes satisfy the BEPS Action 5 nexus requirement. In the 2024 tax revisions, Japan introduced moderately preferential tax treatment, satisfying the nexus requirement, for patents and AI-oriented copyrights.

China provides numerous tax incentives for taxpayers involved in intellectual property activities, including a lower tax rate (15%) for small enterprises and strategically supported enterprises engaged in advanced and new technology which meet several conditions,[762] a "super" tax deduction for investment in start-up technology firms by venture capital firms,[763] a "super" tax deduction for R&D,[764] and a lower tax rate for income from transfers of technology.[765] According to the peer review conducted by the FHTP, these tax incentives are not contrary to the BEPS nexus approach.

According to circulars issued by the MOF and STA, enterprises qualifying as "integrated circuits manufacturing enterprises" or "integrated circuits design or software enterprises" are eligible for tax holidays (two to five years) and super tax reductions (120% or 220% of the actual expenses).[766]

761. United States, IRC, s. 250.
762. China, EIT Law, Art. 28. The conditions are similar to the conditions for the BEPS nexus requirement.
763. China, EIT Law, Art. 31.
764. China, EIT Law, Art. 30.
765. China, EIT Regulations, Art. 90. The first CNY 5 million each year is exempt from tax and qualifying income exceeding CNY 5 million is taxed at half the normal rate (i.e., 12.5%).
766. China, Cai Shui [2018] No. 27; Cai Shui [2015] No. 6; Cai Shui [2012] No. 27; Announcement of the MOF, National Development and Reform Commission and the Ministry of Industry and Information [2023] No. 44.

In 2018, the *French* preferential regime for intellectual property, which dates back to 1965 and applied to royalties and gains realized on the disposal of patents and similar intellectual property rights, was found to be a harmful tax practice under the OECD principles because there was no requirement for the R&D activities to take place in France. The 2019 Finance Act introduced a "nexus approach," whereby the benefit of the tax advantage relating to such income is linked to the research expenditures incurred by the company, in order to make the regime compliant with BEPS Action 5.[767]

This IP Box system is an optional preferential regime, which allows net income from the sale, license or sub-license of intangible property products to be taxed at the reduced rate of 10% for the fraction of its amount resulting from the application of the "nexus" ratio. For each intangible asset or category of intangible assets involved in the production of goods or services or a group of goods or services, a taxpayer must make a formal election in its annual tax return. Qualifying income from net licensing, sublicensing, or sales income is determined as the difference between the income generated from an eligible asset (or group of assets) during the financial year and the R&D expenses related to the asset and incurred, directly or indirectly, by the company during that year. After the election is made, for the first year in which an item of income becomes eligible for the special regime (i.e., the year it begins to generate income), a recapture mechanism takes into account the eligible expenses incurred in the prior tax years. The net income is then calculated annually based on the following nexus ratio (which can never exceed 100%):

- numerator: 130% of R&D expenses (including those recaptured) directly related to the creation or development of the intangible asset and directly incurred by the taxpayer or by unrelated companies;
- denominator: all R&D or acquisition expenses (including those recaptured) directly related to the intangible asset and directly or indirectly incurred by the taxpayer or by related or unrelated companies.

For groups of companies, the eligible income and nexus ratio must be determined at the group level.[768] In this regard, the French provision seems to go further than the OECD recommendations. Indeed, in the case of tax consolidation, certain specific revaluations lead to the inclusion in the denominator of the nexus ratio of the actual value of the assets held by a company joining a tax group. This approach adversely affects the calculation of the liability ratio where entities holding intellectual property rights have recently joined the group. To limit this unfavorable effect, the tax authorities have specified that these provisions do not apply where a company joined the tax group before January 1, 2019. In some respects, despite the fact that the new regime is more favorable to taxpayers than the previous one, the IP Box system remains marginal and is perceived as too complex in practice compared with the research tax credit system.

767. France, CGI, s. 238.
768. France, CGI, s. 223 H.

The *United Kingdom* introduced a patent-box regime in 2012.[769] The regime applies a special corporate tax rate of 10% to a portion of the profits derived from the sale or licensing of patent rights or from the sale of patented inventions or products incorporating the patented invention. The qualifying rights are UK or European patents, and the holder must satisfy certain development conditions in relation to the rights. The rules for identifying "relevant IP profits" are complex, but there is a simplified treatment for small claims. Following the development of BEPS Action 5, in 2016, the United Kingdom modified the regime to comply with the nexus approach.[770]

In *India*, deductions are allowed for both capital (other than land) and current expenditures incurred for scientific research.[771] In addition, 150% of expenditures are deductible in respect of in-house R&D expenditures incurred by taxpayers engaged in biotechnology and the manufacturing or production of goods other than certain excluded articles, such as alcohol and tobacco products. Qualifying projects must be approved by the Department of Science and Technology and the deduction is subject to certain conditions. The deduction was limited to 100% starting in 2021.

In 2016, the government introduced a special tax regime for patent income (effective April 1, 2017)[772] to encourage R&D activities in India, with the overall aim of making India a global R&D hub. The rules provide that where the total income of the eligible taxpayer includes any royalty income in respect of a patent developed and registered in India, the royalty is taxable at the rate of 10% (plus applicable surcharge and cess) on the gross amount of the royalty. However, no expenditure or allowance in respect of such royalty income is allowed under the Act. This concessional tax regime in respect of royalties from patents is available only to a person resident in India who is the true and first inventor of the invention and whose name is entered on the patent register as the patentee in accordance with the Patents Act, 1970.

The preferential regime is optional, since, under the ITA, intangibles are depreciable assets subject to 25% depreciation on the written-down value. Therefore, taxpayers must determine which option is more beneficial. Having exercised the option to be assessed under the preferential regime, taxpayers that later opt out are not eligible to claim the benefits of the preferential tax rate for the next five years.

The Indian patent box regime differs from the OECD regime in certain ways. Whereas the OECD allows PEs of foreign companies in a country as well as PEs of domestic companies outside the country to benefit from the regime, Indian law restricts the regime solely to Indian residents. In addition, the true-and-first-inventor restriction is not mentioned in the OECD regime. Moreover, the concessional rate is applicable only to the royalty income from patents; unlike BEPS Action 5, the Indian regime does not include capital gains which may arise from the alienation of patent rights. The Indian regime also restricts its operations to patents registered in India under the

769. United Kingdom, Corporation Tax Act 2010, Part 8A.
770. The most recent statistics on the uptake of the patent box are available at https://www.gov.uk/government/statistics/patent-box-reliefs-statistics/patent-box-relief-statistics-september-2023.
771. India, ITA 1961, s. 35 and 35(2AB)(1), Proviso.
772. India, ITA 1961, s. 115BBF.

Patents Act; further, its operation is limited to inventions which are capable of being used in any type of industry.

Under the OECD regime, there must be a nexus between expenditures on research and the preferential rate of tax. Under the Indian scheme, no direct linkage between expenditures and the patent box regime is required. However, the Indian regime is restricted to patents "registered and developed" in India. The term "developed" means that at least 75% of the expenditure must be incurred in India by the eligible taxpayer for any invention in respect of which a patent is granted under the Patents Act, 1970. According to the OECD/G20 Harmful Tax Practices 2018 Progress Report on Preferential Regimes, the Indian regime has been considered not to be harmful in that "substance requirements (nexus approach) [are] in place."[773]

Japan introduced preferential tax treatment for patents and certain copyrights related to artificial intelligence (AI), effective from April 2024. The Japanese regime does not offer a direct reduction of the income tax rate but allows for a certain percentage of the revenue derived from transfers of qualified intellectual property (i.e., patents and AI-related copyrights), including royalties from licensing such property, to be excluded from taxable income. The percentage is the portion of 30% that the amount of qualified R&D expenses is of the amount of the total R&D expenses related to qualified IP, subject to a maximum of 30% of the qualifying revenue. Qualified R&D expenses are defined as R&D expenses incurred in Japan so that this new IP-oriented tax treatment satisfies the BEPS Action 5 nexus requirement. Taking into account the approximately 30% effective income tax rate in Japan, this regime would, in effect, reduce the income tax rate in respect of income from qualified IP by a maximum of approximately 9%. Judging from its moderate features as a tax expenditure regime (the ETR of qualified IP income would be at least 21%), this new regime seems to be intended to prevent outbound shifts or movements of R&D activities of domestic enterprises rather than to invite R&D functions from abroad.

6 INDIRECT TRANSFERS

The term "indirect transfers" refers to situations in which a resident of one country disposes of an interest in an entity which owns property in another country.[774] The classic example of an indirect transfer is a sale by a resident of one country of shares in a company which owns immovable property in another country. The country in which the immovable property is located would usually impose tax on any gain realized on the direct sale of such immovable property by a nonresident. If, however, it does not tax the gain on the sale of interests in a resident or nonresident entity which owns immovable property located in the country, taxpayers will use such an indirect holding structure to avoid source country tax.

773. https://www.oecd-ilibrary.org/docserver/9789264311480-en.pdf?expires=1556592565&id=id&accname=guest&checksum=AA4FCA13D590C7B2BF97A2F1E34EA07D (p. 21).

774. *See* generally The Platform for Collaboration on Tax, *Discussion Draft: The Taxation of Offshore Indirect Transfers—A Toolkit* (August 2017) and Draft version 2 (July 16, 2018) available at www.oecd.org.

The taxation of gains from indirect transfers raises the fundamental issue whether the residence or source country should be entitled to tax gains from indirect transfers. Further, if, as appears to be the case, source countries are taxing such gains, the issue arises whether they should extend their taxing rights to property other than immovable property located in their countries—for example, to government licenses with respect to the extractive and telecommunications industries. Currently, Article 13 of the OECD and UN Model Conventions limits a country's right to tax gains from indirect transfers of interests in entities deriving their value principally from immovable property in the country.

There are two major ways for source countries to impose tax on indirect transfers. First, a country can tax the entity owning the immovable (or other) property located in the country by deeming a disposition of the immovable property to occur where there is a change of control of the entity. Second, a country can tax the nonresident owner of the interests in the entity by deeming the gain to arise in the source country. Some countries, such as *China*, use their GAAR to deal with indirect transfers.

In *India*, the taxation of indirect transfers became a controversial issue as a result of the well-known *Vodafone* case, in which a Dutch subsidiary of the UK multinational Vodafone acquired the Indian telecom business of a Hong Kong company through the transfer of shares of a Cayman Islands company. The Indian revenue authorities took the view, shared by a lower court, that the Hong Kong company was subject to tax under Indian domestic law and Vodafone, as purchaser, was required to withhold tax from the proceeds of sale. Reversing the decision of the lower court, the Supreme Court held in favor of the taxpayer[775] on the basis that a company and its shareholders are separate entities and lifting the corporate veil is permitted only in abusive situations. Under section 9(1) of the Indian ITA, income is subject to tax in India if it accrues or arises "directly or indirectly through or from any business connection in India, or through or from any property in India, or through or from any asset or source of income in India or *through* the transfer of a capital asset situate in India." [emphasis added] The Supreme Court held that the existing domestic law was not sufficient to tax the capital gains arising from an indirect transfer of assets. The government responded by making retroactive changes to section 9, which the government claimed were simply clarifications of the existing law.[776]

In response to the critical reaction of foreign institutional investors, the government appointed an advisory committee, which recommended that the amendment not apply retroactively. Although the government rejected the committee's recommendation, it nevertheless announced that in future the provision should be used sparingly

775. *Vodafone International Holdings v. Union of India* (SC, Civil Appeal No. 733 of 2012), January 20, 2012.

776. India, Explanations 4 and 5 were added to s. 9 as follows: "For the removal of doubts, it is hereby clarified that the expression 'through' shall mean and include and shall be deemed to have always meant and included 'by means of,' 'in consequence of' or 'by reason of'." (Explanation 4). "For the removal of doubts, it is hereby clarified that an asset or a capital asset being any share or interest in a company or entity registered or incorporated outside India shall be deemed to be and shall always be deemed to have been situated in India, if the share or interest derives, directly or indirectly, its value substantially from the assets located in India." (Explanation 5).

and only with the approval of a special committee. Then, in its 2015 budget, the government clarified that the Indian tax on indirect transfers would apply only where, on a specified date, the value of assets located in India exceeds INR 100 million and represents at least 50% of the value of all the assets owned by the company.[777] The value of the assets must be determined in a prescribed manner. The rules do not apply to small investors that have no right of management or control of such companies and that hold less than 5% of the total voting power or share capital of the company which directly or indirectly owns the assets in India, or to interests in regulated and widely held FIFs.[778] In addition, an Indian company whose shares are substantially held, directly or indirectly, by a company or entity registered or incorporated outside India has an obligation to report with respect to certain disposals of its shares.[779] Thereafter, the government introduced a mechanism to allow foreign companies subject to an obligation to withhold tax with respect to indirect transfers to avoid penalties and prosecution by paying the tax before disputing it. Vodafone did not opt to pay the tax in advance and filed for arbitration under the India-Netherlands Bilateral Investment Protection Agreement. On September 25, 2020, the Permanent Court of Arbitration issued its final award in favor of Vodafone, holding that the asserted liability to tax despite the Supreme Court judgment was in breach of the guarantee of fair and equitable treatment as laid down in Article 4(1) of the Agreement, as was the imposition of interest and penalties for the non-payment.[780]

Subsequently, in 2021, the government, noting that the retrospective amendment was damaging India's reputation and was a sore point for potential investors, decided to nullify the retrospectivity of the provisions and refund the taxes collected without interest. Necessary changes in the section were incorporated through the Taxation Laws Amendment Act, 2021; as a result, taxpayers must give some undertakings, and a procedure has been laid down for that purpose.[781]

The taxation of offshore indirect transfers is not addressed explicitly in the *Chinese* IIT or EIT law or regulations. Transfers of shares of an offshore holding company are not subject to Chinese tax because the source of capital gains from the transfer of shares is determined by the residence of the company whose shares are transferred.[782] However, the STA has relied on the GAAR and Circular [2009] 698 to tax gains from offshore indirect transfers where the value of the shares is derived from a Chinese-resident company or Chinese immovable property and the transfer has no reasonable business purpose.[783] A transfer fails the reasonable business purpose test

777. Rule 11UB.
778. India, s. 9, Explanation 7. In addition, the Central Board of Direct Taxation has clarified that the indirect transfer provisions would not apply to income of a nonresident from the redemption or buyback of certain shares or interests held indirectly in the specified funds where such income accrues or arises from or in consequence of the transfer of shares or securities held in India by the specified funds and such income is chargeable to tax in India.
779. India, ITA 1961, s. 285A.
780. Only the operative part of the award has been released and the balance withheld, apparently for confidentiality reasons.
781. Rules 11UE and 11UF. The Undertaking is in Appendix IV of the Income Tax Rules, 1962.
782. China, EIT Regulations, Art. 7.
783. China, STA, Gong Gao [2015] No. 7.

where: (1) at least 75% of the value of the shares of a nonresident intermediary is derived from Chinese taxable property (a PE in China, immovable property, or an equity investment in a resident company); (2) a nonresident intermediary does not undertake substantive functions and risks; or (3) the tax consequences of an indirect transfer in the foreign country are less onerous than the Chinese tax that would have been payable if the transfer had been a direct transfer.

An indirect transfer is deemed to lack a reasonable business purpose if more than 75% of the value and more than 90% of the income or assets of the offshore intermediary company are derived from or attributable to China. There is also a "safe-harbor rule" which deems a transaction to have a reasonable business purpose where the shares of the intermediary are sold on the public market, where the gain would be treaty-protected if the property in China were disposed of directly, or where the transaction involves an intragroup reorganization.

The buyer or transferee is required to withhold 10% of the gain from an indirect transfer and failure to withhold tax is subject to penalties; however, the buyer can avoid such penalties by making a timely reporting of the transaction to the Chinese tax authorities.

In a famous Supreme People's Court decision in 2016 on indirect transfers,[784] the taxpayer, a Cayman Islands company, realized a large gain on the sale of 26.32% of the shares of another Cayman company, which indirectly owned a 95% equity interest in a Chinese-foreign joint venture company. The STA took the position that the GAAR applied because the transfer lacked a reasonable business purpose. The Supreme Court upheld the SAT's assessment that the indirect transfer had no reasonable business purpose, on the grounds that the taxpayer and the intermediaries were located in low-tax jurisdictions, were not engaged in production, sales or management, or other substantive business activities, and the purchaser's real purpose was to acquire the equity interest in the China joint venture enterprise. The Supreme Court cited the GAAR Circular [2009] 698 as authorizing the tax assessment.

In *France*, distinctions must be made between legal and natural persons and also between occasional or regular capital gains. In principle, non-professional capital gains realized by individuals on the sale of real estate or rights relating to such property are subject to income tax at a rate of 19% plus social security contributions (17.2% or 7.5% for those subject to the social security system of an EEA state or Switzerland); as well, where applicable, capital gains in excess of EUR 50,000 are taxed on a progressive scale.[785] Professional (business) capital gains from the sale of fixed assets are in principle subject to different tax regimes, depending on whether the company is subject to corporation tax (standard rate of 25%) or income tax (distinction between short-term and long-term gains). Subject to international conventions, occasional capital gains realized on the sale of shares in French property companies by legal entities or individuals not domiciled in France are subject to a specific withholding tax

784. *The Children's Investment Master Fund v. Xihu District of Hangzhou City State Tax Bureau of the People's Republic of China* (2016) Zui Gao Fa Xing Shen No. 1867.
785. France, CGI, s. 1609 nonies G.

at a rate of 19% or 25% depending on the case.[786] This specific levy for occasional capital gains is charged on: profits from the sale for valuable consideration of built or unbuilt property located in France, excluding property used for professional (business) purposes in France, and rights over such property; shares in real estate investment funds or equivalent foreign funds; shares in listed real estate investment companies, shares in open-ended real estate investment companies, shares in equivalent foreign structures or shares in real estate companies listed on a French or foreign stock exchange, where the seller directly or indirectly holds at least 10% of the capital of the company whose shares are sold; and shares or other rights in unlisted real estate investment companies other than those mentioned above. Regular real estate profits made by individuals or legal entities, whatever their form, not domiciled or established in France, are in principle subject to a levy of 25%.[787] France tries to include in its treaties a clause which is at least equivalent to Article 13(4) of the OECD Model in order to allow it to impose its capital gains tax.

Historically, the *United Kingdom* largely did not tax nonresidents on capital gains from immovable property located in the United Kingdom. This situation began to change in 2013 with the introduction of a charge on gains of certain high-value UK residential property held through nonresident corporations. The approach was steadily broadened (and complicated) until the government announced in the 2017 Autumn Budget that it would tax all gains made by nonresidents on the disposal of UK land. The revised tax, which took effect from 2019, applies to gains on the disposal of assets (such as shares) deriving at least 75% of their value from UK land where the nonresident has a "substantial indirect interest in that land."[788] In the case of shares of a company, "substantial" means a 25% or greater investment.

Japan has never had a tax system that captures indirect transfers, except those related to real estate. As discussed in section 1.1 of Subpart B, capital gains on stock sales of a "real estate company" are taxed on a net basis even in the absence of a PE. A real estate company, which is defined as a company the majority of whose assets consist of real estate in Japan, includes foreign as well as domestic companies.

Canada imposes tax on nonresidents realizing capital gains from the disposition of "taxable Canadian property," which includes immovable property located in Canada, resource properties located in Canada, shares of both Canadian and nonresident corporations (other than listed shares and shares of mutual funds) and interests in partnerships and trusts which derive their value principally from taxable Canadian property.[789] The definition of taxable Canadian property also includes shares of mutual funds and shares of companies listed on a designated stock exchange, but only where the taxpayer and non-arm's length persons own 25% or more of the shares and the shares derive their value principally from taxable Canadian property. One-half (two-thirds in some cases after mid-June 2024) of any such gains is taxable on a net basis at

786. France, CGI, s. 244 bis A.
787. France, CGI, s. 244 bis and 244 quater A.
788. Taxation of Chargeable Gains Act 1992, s. 1A(3).
789. Canada, ITA, s. 248(1).

the regular individual or corporate tax rates.[790] Taxable Canadian property does not include "treaty-protected property" (property which, if disposed of at a gain, would not be subject to Canadian tax).[791]

Nonresidents who realize gains from listed Canadian mutual fund shares deriving their value principally from taxable Canadian property, but who own less than 25% of the shares, are subject to Canadian tax on the gain at a 15% rate.[792]

Australia is concerned about indirect transfers of real property because of large foreign investment in its natural resource sector, but its policy in relation to other areas where companies have a potential monopoly or superprofits is less clear. Australian domestic law taxes capital gains on 10% or more interests in companies and other legal entities, wherever resident, if real property in Australia directly or indirectly constitutes more than 50% by market value of the assets of the company or other entity. A 15% non-final withholding tax applies to the proceeds of sale of land, including in such indirect sale cases.[793] Income (as opposed to capital gains) from the alienation of shares in any company is taxable in Australia on the basis of source, although the withholding tax applies as if the income were capital gains. Since 2006, Australian treaties generally follow the OECD Model with respect to capital gains or income realized on the sale of shares and apply a similar treaty test to the capital gains rule in domestic law. However, the drafting of the law and tax treaties has varied over the years, and foreign sellers of shares in mining companies have argued in favor of treaty protection against Australian tax, with some success.[794] However, the more recent case law suggests that the courts will generally favor the levy of tax in such cases.[795] Australia has adopted the modifications to Article 13 of the OECD Model through its ratification of the MLI. From 2025, Australia proposes to strengthen the operation of the capital gains tax on foreigners in relation to land, mainly affecting indirect transfers, by including in domestic law the MLI 365-day testing period for indirect transfers of land, expanding the meaning of real property, and requiring foreign investors to give advance notice of indirect transfers exceeding AUD 20 million in value.[796]

In relation to other areas where monopoly or superprofits may be present, in three cases where taxpayers without a PE in Australia sold significant interests in Australian companies, the courts granted treaty protection to the taxpayers (companies in the technology, airline, and insurance industries).[797] No arguments were made in the cases about the significance of economic rents in justifying taxing rights. Australia has specifically sought to preserve its taxing rights over the telephone spectrum, which

790. Canada, ITA, s. 115(1).
791. Canada, ITA, s. 248(1).
792. Canada, ITA, s. 118.3(2).
793. Australia, Taxation Administration Act 1953, Sch. 1 Div 14-D.
794. In *Lamesa Holdings BV* (1997) 35 ATR 239, the trial judge and the Full Federal Court on appeal both held in favor of the taxpayer; the result was reversed by legislation; *see* section 4.1 above. In the two cases referred to in *infra* note 797 below, both trial judges found for the taxpayer but were reversed on appeal.
795. *Resource Capital Fund III LP*, [2014] FCAFC 37, *Resource Capital Fund IV LP*, [2019] FCAFC 51.
796. Australia, 2024 Budget Paper No. 2, pp. 17-18, "Strengthening the foreign resident capital gains tax regime."
797. *Thiel* (1990) 171 CLR 338, *Virgin Holdings SA*, [2008] 1503, *Undershaft*, [2009] FCA 41.

may be a source of economic rent. It amended the domestic tax law definition of royalties to include payments in relation to such spectrum licenses, and, through regulation of the industry, also ensures that any holder of such a license is an Australian resident or has a PE in Australia.[798] Treaties are negotiated to preserve this taxing right, but, surprisingly, no corresponding domestic law or treaty rule protects the tax base against indirect transfers of such licenses.[799]

Before 1980, the *United States* did not impose tax on a nonresident's gain from the sale of real property located in the United States unless that property was used in a U.S. trade or business or the nonresident was an individual present in the United States for at least 183 days. However, in 1980, Congress adopted the Foreign Investment in Real Property Tax Act (FIRPTA) after it became concerned about the increased level of foreign investment in U.S. real estate and agricultural operations. Under FIRPTA, gain or loss from the sale of U.S. real estate is treated as effectively connected income[800] and the transferee is obligated to withhold 15% of the purchase price paid to the transferor.[801] The withheld amount is not the transferor's ultimate tax liability. Rather, it serves to ensure the transferor's compliance with the obligation to pay tax on the net gain, which is treated as effectively connected income.

FIRPTA contains look-through features for partnerships and corporations. Foreign partners are taxed when they sell an interest in a partnership (U.S. or foreign) which has assets 50% (or more) of which consist of "U.S. real property interests" (generally, U.S. real property or entities holding significant amounts of U.S. real property).[802] The gain or loss subject to tax is the portion attributable to the U.S. real property interests and is treated as effectively connected income.[803] A somewhat similar rule applies to the sale of stock in U.S. corporations whose assets consist of 50% or more of U.S. real property interests.[804] However, an important distinction from the treatment of partnerships is that *all* the gain or loss on the sale of stock in such a corporation is treated as effectively connected income, not just the portion attributable to the corporation's real property interests.

Another tax on indirect transfers was adopted in the Tax Cut and Jobs Act (TCJA) of 2017[805] and applies to transfers on or after November 27, 2017. This provision extends FIRPTA's look-through provision for partnerships beyond real estate assets to all trade or business assets held by a partnership. The IRS had previously attempted to impose such a look-through rule for all partnership trade or business assets in Rev. Rul.

798. Australia, ITAA 1936, s. 6(1) definition of "royalty," para. (dc), *Radiocommunications Act* 1992, s. 69A.
799. Sometimes by including spectrum licenses in the definition of royalty, and sometimes by ensuring that the business profits article applies, and, if all else fails, by a deeming provision in the *International Tax Agreements Act* 1953, s. 3(11A), that the holder is considered for the purposes of the business profits article of a treaty to have a PE in Australia to which the profits are attributable. The tax administration may be inclined to apply the GAAR to indirect transfer cases.
800. United States, IRC, s. 897(a).
801. United States, IRC, s. 1445(a).
802. United States, IRC, s. 897(g); Treas. Reg., s. 1.897-7T(a).
803. United States, Treas. Reg., s. 1.897-7T(a).
804. United States, IRC, s. 897(c)(1)(a).
805. United States, IRC, s. 864(c)(8).

91-32, but the Tax Court invalidated Rev. Rul. 91-32 on the basis that there was insufficient statutory authority for such a broad look-through provision.[806] The provision treats gain or loss from the sale or exchange of a partnership interest as effectively connected with a U.S. trade or business to the extent that the partnership would have allocated to the selling partner effectively connected gain or loss on a deemed sale of all its assets. TCJA also imposes an obligation on the transferee to withhold 10% of the amount realized by the selling partner.[807] If the transferee fails to withhold the required amount, the partnership is required to withhold that amount from distributions to the transferee.[808]

In 2018, *Germany* adopted new rules effective January 1, 2019, to impose tax on the sale of shares in a foreign company by a foreign resident where the following conditions are met:

- the shares represent at least 1% of the capital of the company at any time during the last 5 years;
- at least 50% of the book value of the company's assets consists or consisted of direct or indirect holdings of immovable property in Germany at any time in the 365 days before the sale; and
- the shareholder was the economic owner of the shares when the second requirement was met.[809]

7 MEASURES TO DEAL WITH THE DIGITAL ECONOMY

The taxation of income from digital activities raises fundamental issues about base erosion and the allocation of taxing rights on business profits between source and residence countries. Under the traditional international norm for the allocation of taxing rights, source countries are allowed to tax business profits of a nonresident only where the nonresident has a PE in the source country and only to the extent of the profits attributable to the PE. However, enterprises engaged in digital activities can earn substantial amounts of revenue from a source country without any physical presence or PE in the source country.

The initial proposals of the BEPS Project recognized the base-erosion possibilities of digital activities but did not reconsider the fundamental allocation of taxing rights between source and residence countries. In 2015, the G20/OECD issued its BEPS Action 1 Final Report on the digital economy, without any firm recommendations but with a promise to continue working on a multilateral solution. The Report identified several measures which countries could take on an interim basis. As described below, several countries adopted a variety of these unilateral measures—a substantial economic presence test, withholding taxes on payments for online services, and an excise

806. *Grecian Magnesite Mining, Industrial & Shipping Co., SA v. Commissioner*, 149 TC No. 3 (July 13, 2017) (Revenue Ruling 91-32).
807. United States, IRC, s. 1446(f)(1).
808. United States, IRC, s. 1446(f)(4).
809. Germany, ITA, s. 49(1) No. 2 lit. e) cc).

tax on certain online revenues—to deal with what they considered to be a pressing problem.

In March 2018, the Inclusive Framework[810] delivered its interim report on BEPS Action 1: *Tax Challenges Arising from Digitalisation: Interim Report 2018*. The report indicated that the implementation of the BEPS recommendations was already having an impact on base erosion: MNEs had altered their transfer pricing practices, repatriated intangibles, and created a taxable presence in market countries through the establishment of distribution subsidiaries. However, the interim report also acknowledged that MNEs engaged in both highly digitalized and traditional businesses could still shift profits to low-tax countries. The report also expressed skepticism that consensus could be reached on a new allocation of taxing rights with respect to digital businesses which rely heavily on intangible assets, data, and user participation. The Report indicated that some countries thought the existing international tax rules were sufficient, some countries thought the international tax rules required fundamental changes with respect to all businesses, and some countries thought fundamental changes were necessary only for highly digitalized businesses.

Since releasing its interim report, the Inclusive Framework, through a subgroup, the Task Force on the Digital Economy, continued studying fundamental changes to the existing allocation of taxing rights (Pillar One). In February 2019, the Inclusive Framework issued a Consultation Document proposing a multilateral solution to the challenges posed by the digital economy, involving new nexus and profit allocation rules for the world's largest and most profitable multinational digital companies. Detailed rules (Blueprints) for both Pillar One and Two (a global minimum tax) were issued in October 2020 and were subject to intense criticism because of their complexity. In July 2021, the Inclusive Framework reached agreement on revised proposals applicable to all large companies, not just those engaged in digital businesses. Model Rules for Pillar One were issued in December 2021. Further work on Pillar One culminated in October 2023 with the publication of the Multilateral Convention to Implement Amount A of Pillar One to govern the allocation of taxing rights over the residual profits of large multinationals to market jurisdictions. The Convention has not yet been opened for signature. In February 2024, the Inclusive Framework released a report on Amount B of Pillar One, providing optional simplified and streamlined transfer pricing rules for determining the profits of group entities performing baseline marketing and distribution activities.

Amount A of Pillar One will apply to multinationals with global turnover in excess of EUR 20 billion and a profit ratio of 10% or more, which is estimated to include approximately 100 of the world's largest and most profitable companies. The rules are intended to apply to all multinationals meeting the threshold, except for those in the extractive industries and regulated financial services businesses. Participating countries will obtain the right to tax a share of the residual profits of multinationals within the scope of Amount A only where a multinational meets a domestic revenue threshold of EUR 1 million (less for certain developing countries). A multinational's residual

810. The Inclusive Framework is the body formed to implement the BEPS recommendations. *See* the Introduction to Part IV for further discussion of the Inclusive Framework.

profits are defined to be 25% of its consolidated global profits in excess of 10% of its revenue (called Amount A). Amount A will be allocated among the countries meeting the domestic revenue threshold based on the proportionate sales revenue from each country (where the goods and services sold by the multinational are used or consumed).

The countries in which multinationals subject to tax under Pillar One are resident will be under an obligation to provide relief from double taxation of Amount A by exempting the residual profits or by granting a FTC for any source country tax on those profits. All issues with respect to Amount A will be subject to a mandatory dispute-prevention and dispute-resolution mechanism (called "tax certainty processes").

The countries examined in this book have taken a variety of different approaches to the problems of the digital economy. Some countries, such as *China, Japan, Sweden, and the United States,* appear to consider the existing international rules to be adequate and have not taken any special measures to deal with the digital economy. Presumably, some of these countries may be waiting for the results of the work on the digital economy carried on by the Inclusive Framework. China has several prominent digital companies operating in other countries and currently, Google and Facebook are prohibited from operating in China; thus, it would appear that China has less interest than many other countries in taxing nonresident enterprises on income from digital activities in China. China has not indicated whether it will sign the new multilateral convention on Pillar One when it is ready for signature. China has not proposed any new digital services tax, although the proposed amendments to the Value-Added Tax (VAT) legislation call for imposing VAT compliance obligations on nonresident providers of digital services.[811] In contrast, some countries, such as Australia, India, France, and the United Kingdom consider the existing international rules to be outdated and inadequate and have taken unilateral measures to deal with the digital economy.

Germany has no intention to enact specific provisions governing the cross-border taxation of the digital economy but is willing to sign up to Pillar One in due course.

India has taken three specific measures to deal with some of the issues arising out of the digital economy but has indicated that it will not endorse Pillar One until its concerns about dispute resolution and withholding tax are addressed. First, in 2016, India adopted a 6% Equalization Levy on "specified services," initially limited to digital advertising services performed by nonresidents for an Indian resident or a nonresident with a PE in India.[812] The levy is restricted to payments for business purposes in excess of INR 100,000 in a year; payments for personal consumption are not subject to the

811. The proposed VAT Law has not yet been promulgated. Under this law, which will replace existing VAT measures introduced by the State Council, digital services "consumed" in China are subject to tax and nonresident providers of digital services are legally required to withhold VAT and remit it to the Chinese tax authorities. For the Chinese text of the proposed law, *see* https://baike.baidu.com/item/%E4%B8%AD%E5%8D%8E%E4%BA%BA%E6%B0%91%E5%85%B1%E5%92%8C%E5%9B%BD%E5%A2%9E%E5%80%BC%E7%A8%8E%E6%B3%95/18298785.

812. India, ss. 164 and 165 of the FA, 2016. The Equalization Levy is not part of the income tax legislation.

levy. Specified services provided through a PE in India are subject to income tax rather than the Equalization Levy[813] and any income from services subject to the levy are exempt from income taxation.[814] Under the Equalization Levy, Indian residents and nonresidents with a PE in India are required to deduct 6% of the gross amount paid to the nonresident service provider.[815] In 2020, the scope of the levy was extended to e-commerce operators or suppliers and providers of services to Indian residents, nonresidents having a PE in India, and buyers of such goods or services from an internet protocol address located in India.[816] The rate of the levy is only 2% of the consideration. There is a safe harbor of INR 20 million. Again, the income, if any, of the e-commerce operator is exempt under the ITA.[817] It has been clarified that such exempt income of the nonresident does not include and was never intended to include any income chargeable as royalty or fees for technical services under the Act read with any tax treaty.[818] To ensure compliance, failure to withhold the levy or remit it to the government is subject to interest and penalties.[819] Under pressure from the United States, a compromise (effective until June 30, 2024) was reached under which the 2% levy was to be applied against Amount A of Pillar One. In a surprise move, the 2% levy was eliminated in the 2024 budget effective for services provided after August 1, 2024.

Second, in 2018, India adopted the concept of "significant economic presence" as a threshold for taxing nonresidents on business income earned in India. This concept represents an extension of the traditional "business connection" threshold, which, although broader than the treaty concept of a PE, does not cover digital services performed remotely. A significant economic presence means: (i) transactions in respect of goods, services, or property carried on by a nonresident in India, including the download of data or software in India, where the aggregate payments in respect of such transactions exceed a prescribed amount; or (ii) systematic and continuous soliciting of business activities or engaging with a prescribed number of users in India through digital means.[820] Only income which is attributable to such transactions or activities is taxable in India.

The definition of significant economic presence involves two thresholds: one based on local revenue and the other on the number of users. The first threshold applies to both physical and digital goods and services; the second threshold applies only to digital transactions. The prescribed amounts for the two thresholds were not established until 2020, in the hope of an agreed solution on Pillar One.[821] However, in the absence of a multinational solution, the CBDT operationalized the substantial economic presence concept through a notification of the Rule.[822] The prescribed

813. India, FA, 2016, s. 165(2)(a).
814. India, ITA 1961, s. 10(50).
815. India, FA, 2016, s. 166.
816. India, FA 2016, s. 165A, inserted by the FA 2020.
817. India, ITA 1961, s. 10(50), as amended by the FA 2020 and FA 2021.
818. Explanation 1 to s. 10(50) of the ITA, inserted by the FA 2020.
819. India, FA, 2016, s. 166(2).
820. India, ITA 1961, s. 9(1)(i), Explanation 2A.
821. Memorandum explaining the provisions of the Finance Bill, 2020.
822. Notification No. 41 of 2021, Rule 11UD of the IT Rules, 1962.

thresholds are: INR 20 million during a year for specified transactions of the nonresident with a person in India; and the systematic and continuous soliciting of business activities or interactions with 3,000,000 or more users in India. As for attribution, the CBDT has issued a discussion draft with respect to the attribution of profits to a PE which includes a section on the attribution of profits to a significant economic presence PE.[823]

The significant economic presence threshold does not affect residents of countries that have treaties with India since those treaties generally limit India to taxing nonresidents on business profits only if they have a PE in India. However, since the Equalization Levy is not considered to be an income tax, it is not affected by India's tax treaties.

Another important change relates to the deemed accrual of income. Effective April 1, 2021, income attributable to operations carried out in India includes income from (i) advertisements targeting customers resident in India or customers who access advertisements through an internet protocol address located in India; (ii) sale of data collected from persons resident in India or from persons using an internet protocol address located in India; and (iii) sale of goods or services using data collected from persons resident in India or from persons using an internet protocol address located in India.[824]

In the context of the digital economy, India has also put in place a withholding mechanism under which, effective October 1, 2020, an e-commerce operator must withhold tax at .01% of the consideration for the sale of goods or provision of services by the operator to an Indian resident where such consideration exceeds INR 0.5 million.[825] CBDT is authorized to issue guidelines to remove any difficulty in giving effect to the provision.[826]

France introduced a tax on digital services in 2019,[827] pending the entry into force of Pillar One. France undertakes to abolish its digital services tax as soon as the agreement comes into force. Although referred to as a sales tax, it is in fact legally a tax on gross corporate income. Companies, wherever they are based, are taxable if two cumulative annual sales thresholds are met: EUR 750 million for services provided worldwide assessed on a consolidated basis, and EUR 25 million for services provided nationally. A rate of 3% applies to annual sales generated by intermediary services provided via a digital interface and to targeted advertising services. The scope of the tax was modified by the Finance Act for 2023 to take into account a decision issued by the French Supreme Court,[828] which overturned several interpretations made by tax doctrine. As a result, the law was amended to specify that (i) only the provision of a

823. CBDT, F. No. 500/33/2017-FTD.1, April 18, 2019. The Discussion Draft proposes that, depending on the level of user intensity in the digital business, user contributions should be given some weight in the allocation of profits.
824. Explanation 3A to s. 9(1), introduced through the FA 2020.
825. India, ITA 1961, s. 194-O.
826. For Guidelines, *see* CBDT circular No. 20/2021, November 25, 2021 and circular No. 20 of 2023, December 28, 2023.
827. Originally codified in Arts. 299 et seq. of the General Tax Code (2019-2022), this tax is now contained in Art. L 453-45 to L 453-83 in the Code on Taxes on Goods and Services (since 2022).
828. *Conseil d'Etat*, 3° et 8° ch.-r., March 31, 2022, n° 461058 (*Sté Amazon Online France*).

digital interface for which interactions between users are incidental within the meaning of Article 257 ter of the CGI shall be excluded from the scope of taxable services; (ii) the exclusion of certain digital content supply services, assessed in the light of the characteristics of the interface which makes this content available, is a different issue from that of the taxability of the digital content itself, where it enables interactions between users independently of the supply service (e.g., the exclusion of a software supply service has no impact on the liability with respect to each software product supplied); and (iii) the exclusion of services supplied between companies belonging to the same group applies only to services provided exclusively to those companies.[829] Revenues from this tax continue to rise every year. In 2023, it raised EUR 700 million (EUR 621 million in 2022), with projected revenue of EUR 800 million by 2024.

The *United Kingdom* introduced a Digital Services Tax, effective from April 2020, which applies until an acceptable global solution is reached.[830] The tax is 2 % of the UK revenues of digital businesses which are considered to derive significant value from the participation of their users. The tax is applied to business activities involving the provision of a social media platform, search engine, or online marketplace and is linked to revenues from participation of the UK user base. The tax applies to businesses generating more than GBP 500 million in global profits with at least GBP 25 million of related UK revenues. The tax is deductible against corporation tax. The UK is one of the countries that has agreed with the United States to credit the tax against amounts that will become due if a Pillar One agreement is reached.

Once the BEPS project commenced, *Australia* moved relatively quickly to deal with the taxation of large multinationals involved in the digital economy. The Australian tax administration began closely auditing the companies and a Senate committee was established, which ran for over three years and monitored the situation, putting the companies on the defensive.[831] Two additions were made to the Australian GAAR, based on the UK DPT, to form a powerful alternative to traditional PEs and transfer pricing rules.[832] By 2017, companies were testifying before the Committee that they were booking more revenue in Australia, settling their disputes with the tax administration, and paying more Australian tax than in the past, partly as a result of the legislation, although still making deductible payments offshore.

In its 2018 budget, the government announced that it would release a discussion paper to explore options for taxing digital businesses in Australia. By the time the discussion paper was released later in the year, the work of the Inclusive Framework on BEPS in relation to the digital economy had gained momentum; early in 2019, after

829. *See* BOI-TCA-TSN-10-10-10 and BOI-TCA-TSN-10-10-20, June 21, 2023.
830. United Kingdom, Finance Act 2020, Part 2.
831. Parliament of Australia, Senate Economics References Committee, "Corporate Tax Avoidance" (October 2, 2014-May 30, 2018). The reports, testimony, and submissions are available at https://www.aph.gov.au/Parliamentary_Business/Committees/Senate/Economics/Corporat etax45th. The inquiry was not limited to the digital economy, and Australia's preoccupation with the taxation of natural resources was also prominent in the proceedings.
832. Australia, ITAA 1936, s. 177DA (multinational anti-avoidance law directed at PEs used to avoid tax), 177H-177R (DPT directed at noninclusion of income or deductions which produced income taxed at low rates overseas); special procedural rules similar to the UK DPT apply to the latter, Taxation Administration Act 1953, Sch. 1, Div. 145.

considering the submissions on the discussion paper, the government announced that it would not take unilateral action for the time being, pending the outcome of the international work. However, Australia's political parties continue to compete in the rhetoric of being "tough on multinationals."[833]

Canada was relatively slow to respond to the BEPS proposals regarding taxation of the digital economy. In 2020 the Canadian government announced that it intended to enact a DST in the absence of a multilateral solution. Draft legislation to implement the DST was published in 2021, revised in 2023, and enacted in June 2024, with the first payment due June 30, 2025. The DST applies at a rate of 3% to Canadian in-scope revenues, namely, revenues from online marketplace services, online advertising services, social media services, and Canadian user data, to the extent that those revenues exceed CAD 20 million annually.

The Netherlands has not enacted a DST and will not unilaterally do so, but instead will adhere to an EU solution in this respect. The Netherlands intends to become a party to the Multilateral Convention to Implement Amount A of Pillar One. The Netherlands also agrees with the determination of Amount B, which has been included in the Transfer Pricing Guidelines.

Japan has not yet officially decided to follow any aspect of Pillar One. However, it is almost certain that Japan will fully follow the OECD/Inclusive Framework and will probably not introduce any type of DST, at least in the near future, even if the United States and some other countries that are important from the viewpoint of the tax allocation targeted by Pillar One do not join the Pillar One arrangements.

8 ANTI-HYBRID MISMATCH RULES

The OECD BEPS Action 2 Final Report on hybrid mismatch arrangements (2015) provided recommended best practices for countries to adopt to deal with hybrid entities and hybrid financial instruments. In general, the Report, which is long and complex, provides countermeasures with respect to three types of hybrid mismatches:

- Deduction/no inclusion mismatches: a payment is deductible by the payer resident in one country and is not included in the income of the recipient resident in the other country; for example, a payment on a financial instrument is treated as deductible interest in one country but as an exempt dividend in the other country.
- Double deduction mismatches: a payment is deductible in two countries; for example, a payment by an entity that is treated as transparent by one country, resulting in the deduction of the payment by the members of the entity, and is

833. Australia, Treasurer (former government), Media Release Government response to digital economy consultation, available at https://ministers.treasury.gov.au/ministers/josh-frydenberg-2018/media-releases/government-response-digital-economy-consultation;Treasurer(current government), Media Release Strengthening multinational tax integrity, available at https://ministers.treasury.gov.au/ministers/jim-chalmers-2022/media-releases/strengthening-multinational-tax-integrity.

treated as a company (a separate entity) by the other country, resulting in the deduction of the payment by that company as well.
- Imported mismatch arrangements: the effect of a hybrid mismatch is shifted to a third country; for example, a deduction/no inclusion mismatch can be moved to a third country by having the payer under the deduction/no inclusion mismatch receive a payment from a related entity in a third country which is deductible in that country and included in the income of the recipient.

The anti-hybrid rules In BEPS Action 2 apply both to inbound and outbound hybrid arrangements. Two alternative rules are recommended to neutralize a hybrid mismatch. In the case of a deduction/no inclusion mismatch, the country in which the recipient of the relevant payment is resident should deny the exemption for the payment, and if it fails to do so, the other country is expected to deny the deduction of the payment. In the case of a double deduction mismatch, the country in which the parent entity is resident should deny the deduction, and if it fails to do so, the other country should deny the deduction. In the case of an imported mismatch arrangement, the third country is expected to deny the deduction of the payment unless one of the other countries takes action to neutralize the mismatch.

In general terms, the anti-hybrid rules apply to payments on financial instruments, broadly defined, where the payer and recipient are related or connected through direct or indirect ownership of at least 25% and where the mismatch in the treatment of the relevant payment by the countries in which the payer and recipient are resident is attributable to the hybrid nature of the relevant instrument or entity (referred to as "hybridity").

In *France*, the Finance Act 2020 introduced anti-hybrid measures,[834] in particular to combat hybrid financial products. For example, the measures deny the deduction of interest paid by a company established in France to another company in the same group where the other company is not sufficiently taxed on the interest received. This mechanism enables France to neutralize the asymmetrical effect of hybrid financial instruments where the debtor or creditor is resident in France.

Since 2009, the *United Kingdom* has denied the intercorporate dividend exemption for deductible payments.[835] In 2017, the UK replaced its existing anti-hybrid mismatch rules with a full suite of rules which largely follows the OECD BEPS Action 2 recommendations.[836] As a result, the rules are targeted at related-party (which can be as low as a 25% investment) and structured arrangements and include rules for imported mismatch arrangements. Unlike the earlier rules, there is no exception for hybrid mismatches which lack a tax avoidance purpose. During the legislative process, the government resisted many suggestions to modify the rules, on the basis that modification would be inconsistent with the OECD approach.

Australia adopted hybrid mismatch rules in 2018, following the OECD recommendations closely. Because Australia's regime for taxing PEs is a mixture of AOA and

834. France, CGI, s. 205B to 205D.
835. United Kingdom, Corporation Tax Act 2009, s. 931B(c) and 931D(c).
836. United Kingdom, Taxation (International and Other Provisions) Act 2010, Part 6A.

non-AOA elements, some elements of the branch mismatch rules have not been adopted. In addition, Australia added an anti-avoidance rule to the regime not found in the OECD best practices, applying a PPT test to treat rates of tax of 10% or less as not counting as tax paid for the purposes of the rules.[837]

In response to concerns regarding hybrid mismatches, *Japan* limits the exemption for dividends from foreign subsidiaries to those not deductible by the payer in the relevant source countries. However, Japan does not have other rules directly addressing hybrid financial instruments.

The Netherlands has adopted the OECD hybrid mismatch recommendations through the incorporation of the similar provisions of the EU ATAD I into the Corporate Income Tax Act (CITA)[838] together with ATAD II, which covers hybrid mismatches involving non-EU jurisdictions (third countries).

Canada has introduced hybrid mismatch rules, which are effective from July 2022.[839] These provisions are generally consistent with the recommendations in BEPS Action 2 regarding "deduction/no inclusion" mismatches. In particular, the rules target three kinds of "hybrid mismatch arrangement": hybrid financial instrument arrangements, hybrid transfer arrangements, and substitute payment arrangements. Where a payment arises under a hybrid mismatch arrangement, one of three rules may apply. The primary rule denies the deduction of a payment made by a Canadian taxpayer to the extent of any "hybrid mismatch amount" where the otherwise deductible payment is not included in computing the income of the nonresident recipient. The secondary rule requires a Canadian recipient to include an amount in income to the extent of any hybrid mismatch amount; this rule does not apply where the nonresident payer is already subject to a comparable deduction limitation in the foreign jurisdiction. The third rule can restrict the ability of a Canadian taxpayer to claim a foreign affiliate dividend deduction where the foreign affiliate is able to claim a foreign tax deduction in respect of the dividend. The Canadian rules also contain a special provision (not part of the OECD recommendations) which deals with foreign deductions for notional interest even where the mismatch is not attributable to hybridity.

Similar to the approach that Canada has taken with its proposed global minimum tax, the hybrid mismatch legislation provides that the rules must be interpreted in an ambulatory manner which is consistent with BEPS Action 2, unless the context otherwise requires.

India and *China* have not enacted any specific rules to deal with hybrid mismatches.

9 PILLAR TWO: GLOBAL MINIMUM TAX

In early 2019, the OECD published a Policy Note and a Public Consultation Document, releasing for public scrutiny several proposals under discussion by the Inclusive Framework on BEPS. The document noted that several members of the Inclusive

837. Australia ITAA 1997, Div 832.
838. Articles 9-9b ATAD I have been incorporated mainly in CITA Art. 12aa-12ag.
839. Canada, ITA, ss. 12.7, 18.4, and 113(5).

Framework considered that the measures in the 2015 BEPS package did not deliver "a comprehensive solution to the risks that continue to arise from structures that shift profit to entities subject to no or very low taxation." The document outlined proposals for a comprehensive solution comprising two elements: a 15% global minimum tax and a subject to tax rule (STTR) for tax treaties.

The minimum tax (referred to as the "GloBE rules") applies to large multinational groups (annual turnover in excess of EUR 750 million in two of the preceding four years) and consists of two top-up taxes: the IIR (often mistakenly referred to as the "income inclusion rule") top-up tax and the UTPR (often mistakenly referred to as the "undertaxed payments rule") top-up tax to supplement the IIR tax. In general terms, the IIR top-up tax is imposed on the ultimate parent entity of a multinational group where the ETR of all the group's "constituent entities" (its subsidiaries and PEs) in a foreign jurisdiction is below 15% of their "net GloBE income," as determined in the group's consolidated financial accounts. Where the jurisdiction in which the ultimate parent entity of a group is resident does not impose the IIR tax, the countries in which lower-tier parent entities (referred to as "intermediate parent entities") are resident are entitled to apply the tax. The IIR top-up tax is imposed on the "excess profit" of the constituent entities in each country where the group operates; the excess profit is the group's net GloBE income earned by its constituent entities in a country less its "substance based income exclusion" (SBIE) for that country, which is 10% of the net book value of the tangible assets of the constituent entities and 8% of their payroll costs (both declining to 5% over 10 years). In effect, the SBIE is a rough proxy for nonmobile business income earned by the group entities in a country; such income is not considered to pose serious base-erosion risks.

The UTPR top-up tax is computed in the same way as the IIR top-up tax and is designed to apply where the jurisdiction of the ultimate or a lower-tier parent entity does not apply the IIR top-up tax or where group entities, including the parent, in the parent's jurisdiction are subject to an ETR of less than 15%. In short, the UTPR top-up tax is intended to supplement the IIR top-up tax and applies only where the IIR top-up tax does not apply; where the IIR top-up tax is imposed, no UTPR top-up tax is payable. The UTPR top-up tax is allocated among the countries in which group entities are resident in accordance with a formula based on the number of employees and the net book value of tangible assets in a jurisdiction (with both factors equally weighted). The UTPR top-up tax allocated to a country can be imposed in any manner (e.g., as a separate tax or the denial of deductions) which results in a cash tax expense for the group entities in the country.

As noted above, the IIR top-up tax is imposed at a rate equal to the difference between 15% and a jurisdiction's ETR on the excess profits earned by the group entities in the jurisdiction. The resulting amount is reduced by the amount of a "qualified domestic minimum top-up tax" (QDMTT) imposed by the jurisdiction. Unlike the ETR, which is based on net GloBE income, a QDMTT is based on the excess profits earned by group entities in a country. In effect, a QDMTT operates as a substitute for the IIR top-up tax, with the important exception that the QDMTT is collected by the source country (i.e., the country in which the constituent entities earn their income), whereas any IIR top-up tax is collected by the residence country (i.e., the country in which the parent entity or entities are resident). A QDMTT is a defensive measure that countries can adopt in order to prevent other countries from collecting IIR or UTPR top-up taxes. A QDMTT must meet three conditions: it must be imposed on "domestic excess profit"; it must increase domestic tax liability on excess profit to 15%; and it must be implemented and administered to be consistent with the outcomes under the GloBE rules and not provide any "offsetting benefits." A domestic minimum tax which does not qualify as a QDMTT will be taken into account in computing the country's ETR but will not reduce the IIR top-up tax directly, as a QDMTT does.

In December 2022, the Council of the EU adopted a Council Directive (Council Directive on ensuring a global minimum level of taxation for multinational enterprise groups and large-scale domestic groups in the EU) mirroring the Inclusive Framework's GloBE proposal. The EU Council Directive also included an option for Member States to implement a QDMTT. Many countries, including many low-tax jurisdictions, have announced their intention to enact a QDMTT, often effective from January 1, 2024. Many countries have enacted GloBE rules into domestic law, with the IIR often effective from January 1, 2024 and the UTPR to start from January 1, 2025.

Pillar Two also includes a STTR, implemented through a multilateral tax treaty. Under the STTR, defined developing countries are entitled to request the revision of their tax treaties with developed countries that are members of the Inclusive Framework to allow the imposition of a top-up tax on certain intercompany payments. The tax applies only where the country in which the recipient of a covered payment is resident imposes corporate tax on the payment at a rate (adjusted for permanent tax preferences) of less than 9%. The covered payments include interest, royalties, guarantee and other financing fees, insurance premiums, distribution rights, rent for industrial, commercial, or scientific equipment, and payments for services. The Multilateral Convention to Facilitate the Implementation of the Pillar Two STTR was signed by only ten countries in September 2024. The application of the STTR is subject to many conditions which make it largely irrelevant for the countries examined in this book.

Of the eleven countries examined here, eight have either implemented or proposed implementing Pillar Two. *China* and *India* have not yet indicated whether they will adopt Pillar Two or enact a domestic minimum tax. It is conceivable that China might introduce a QDMTT to pre-empt the imposition of the IIR or UTPR in other countries where the Chinese ETR is below 15%.

The *United States* does not appear to be interested in adopting the Pillar Two GloBE rules given the GILTI regime enacted in 2017, which provided some impetus for the development of the Pillar Two rules. However, there has been some discussion about modifying the GILTI rules to more closely align them with the Pillar Two rules. The U.S. situation raises the important question for other countries adopting Pillar Two whether the U.S. GILTI rules should be treated as equivalent to the mandated Pillar Two rules. If the GILTI rules are not considered to be compliant with Pillar Two, the possibility exists that countries will impose the IIR top-up tax on U.S. source income earned by subsidiaries and PEs of their resident multinationals where that income is not subject to U.S. tax at an ETR of at least 15%. Some countries (e.g., Canada), have enacted special rules as part of the Pillar Two implementation package to recognize the U.S. GILTI as effectively compliant with Pillar Two.

Australia,[840] *Canada,*[841] *Germany, The Netherlands,* and the *United Kingdom* have all enacted the IIR top-up tax and a QDMTT (or have issued draft legislation), with effect for tax years beginning after January 1, 2024. *Japan* has enacted the IIR tax for tax years beginning after April 1, 2024 but has not yet enacted the UTPR tax or a QDMTT, although it seems likely that it will do so. For all of these countries, the UTPR was delayed until January 1, 2025 at the earliest. For Canada, Germany,[842] the Netherlands[843] and the United Kingdom,[844] the Pillar Two rules have been enacted as a separate statute rather than as part of the basic income tax or corporate tax law. In contrast, the Japanese rules have been incorporated into the normal international tax rules of the Corporate Tax Act (CTA).

840. Australia, Taxation (Multinational–Global and Domestic Tax) Act 2024 and Taxation (Multinational–Global and Domestic Tax) Rules 2024.

841. Canada, Global Minimum Tax Act, available at https://fin.canada.ca. The Act provides that some parts of the rules (including the IIR and UTPR) must be interpreted in an ambulatory manner consistent with the OECD GloBE Model Rules, Commentary, and administrative guidance, unless the context otherwise requires.

842. Germany, Minimum Tax Act, incorporating the EU Pillar Two Directive and the Pillar Two GloBE Rules into German law. Important consequential changes have been made to the CFC rules and the royalty barrier discussed in Subpart B, section 4 (reduction of the threshold rate to 15%) as a result of the enactment of Pillar Two.

843. The Netherlands, Minimum Tax Act 2024 (*Wet minimumbelasting 2024*).

844. United Kingdom, Finance (No. 2) Act 2023, Parts 3 and 4, respectively. The provisions of the Act are to be interpreted in accordance with the Pillar Two GloBE Model Rules, Commentary, and other related documents, as well as the EU Pillar Two Directive.

Index

C

F

G

V

W

www.ingramcontent.com/pod-product-compliance
Lightning Source LLC
LaVergne TN
LVHW020650300926
849161LV00004B/875